THE UNIVERSITY OF NOTRE DAME

THE
UNIVERSITY OF
NOTRE
DAME

A History

THOMAS E. BLANTZ, C.S.C.

University of Notre Dame Press

Notre Dame, Indiana

Published by the University of Notre Dame Press
Notre Dame, Indiana 46556
undpress.nd.edu

This book is made possible in part by support from the Institute for Scholarship in the Liberal Arts, College of Arts and Letters, University of Notre Dame.

Library of Congress Control Number: 2020940873

ISBN: 978-0-268-10821-2 (Hardback)
ISBN: 978-0-268-10824-3 (WebPDF)
ISBN: 978-0-268-10823-6 (Epub)

To

generations of Notre Dame students

who

have taught me much

CONTENTS

A gallery of images can be found between pages 326 and 327.

CONTENTS

PREFACE

A few years ago, when speaking with a group of his former students, the author mentioned that, at age eighty, he had decided to write a history of the university. One suggested, facetiously, that he did have the advantage of having lived through most of it. The author was not quite that old, of course, but he did have other advantages. He is a member of the Congregation of Holy Cross, the religious community that founded the university in 1842 and has governed or staffed it ever since. He has resided at the university as student, professor, or administrator for more than sixty years. He served as university archivist throughout the 1970s and gained wide acquaintance with the records housed there. And for a number of years, he offered an undergraduate seminar on the history of the university, learning much from the students' original research.

The author has acquired many obligations in this research. He profited immensely from—and at times relied heavily on—the work of others, especially James E. Armstrong's *Onward to Victory: A Chronicle of the Alumni of the University of Notre Dame du Lac, 1842–1973*; David Joseph Arthur's "The University of Notre Dame, 1919–1933: An Administrative History"; Robert E. Burns's *Being Catholic, Being American*; Philip Gleason's *Contending with Modernity: Catholic Higher Education in the Twentieth Century*; Arthur J. Hope, C.S.C.'s *Notre Dame: One Hundred Years*; Anna Rose Kearney's "James A. Burns, C.S.C., Educator"; George Klawitter's *After Holy Cross, Only Notre Dame: The Life of Brother Gatian (Urbain Monsimer)*; Thomas Timothy McAvoy's *Father O'Hara of Notre Dame: The Cardinal-Archbishop of Philadelphia*; Philip S. Moore's *Academic Development, University of Notre Dame: Past, Present, and Future*; Michael O'Brien's *Hesburgh:*

A Biography; Marvin R. O'Connell's *Edward Sorin*; Thomas J. Schlereth's *The University of Notre Dame: A Portrait of its History and Campus*; James M. Schmidt's *Notre Dame and the Civil War: Marching Onward to Victory*; John Theodore Wack's "The University of Notre Dame du Lac: Foundation, 1842–1857"; and Ralph Edward Weber's *Notre Dame's John Zahm: American Catholic Apologist and Educator*.

Most of the research was conducted in the University of Notre Dame Archives, and the author is deeply grateful to archivists Wendy Schlereth, Angela Fritz, Kevin Cawley, Elizabeth Hogan, Angela Kindig, Charles Lamb, Peter Lysy, Joseph Smith, and Sharon Sumpter. Most record groups of the recent seventy years are not open for research but the archives hold an excellent collection of student and administration publications, and these proved most beneficial.

The staffs of other archives were invariably accommodating also: Christopher Kuhn and Deborah Buzzard at the United States Province of Priests and Brothers Provincial Archives; Sister Kathryn Callahan at the Sisters of the Holy Cross Archives; Lawrence Stewart at the Midwest Brothers' Archives; Suzanne Isaacs at the National Archives in Washington, DC; and Leo L. Belleville, III, at the National Archives at Chicago. The author is grateful to the University of Notre Dame Archives, the United States Province of Priests and Brothers of the Congregation of Holy Cross, and Professor Thomas Schlereth for providing the photographs used in the gallery. James Blantz, Mary Kay Blantz, John Conley, John Deak, Carl Ebey, and Thomas Kselman read all or parts of the manuscript and made valuable suggestions. It was a pleasure to work closely with the professional staff at the University of Notre Dame Press: managing editor Matthew Dowd, Stephanie Hoffman, Wendy McMillen, Kathryn Pitts, Michelle Sybert, and especially manuscript editor Elizabeth Sain. The comments and recommendations of the outside readers improved the manuscript immensely. All errors that remain, of course, are the author's own.

With a generous discretionary fund from the University of Notre Dame's College of Arts and Letters, the author was able to hire several undergraduate assistants over the semesters who did valuable research and put the handwritten manuscript into computer form: Moira Griffith, Evelyn Heck, Elliot Marie Kane, Lindsey Mathew, Tara Hunt McMullen, Hope Moon, Sara Quasni, and Elizabeth Weicher. Madelyn Lugli efficiently and professionally prepared the long and at times poorly organized manuscript for the publisher. Notre Dame students have been a significant and beneficial part of the author's life for more than fifty years, and this book is gratefully dedicated to them.

CHAPTER 1

Background in France, 1789–1841

Father Edward Sorin, C.S.C., an immigrant from France and, with seven companion religious brothers, founder of the University of Notre Dame in 1842, confided to his religious colleagues years later: "I bless God that I was not baptized under a French saint's name. What makes my English St. Edward's Feast so pleasant to us all is the total absence of every vestige of nationality."[1] His comment was sincere—and accurate. From the first day he stepped ashore, he wanted to be an American, not an émigré Frenchman, and he remained an American the rest of his life. He wrote in his *Chronicles* that, on arriving, "one of his first acts on this soil so much desired was to fall prostrate and embrace it as a sign of adoption."[2] He opened Notre Dame's first end-of-year celebration in 1845—not a graduation since no one had yet qualified to graduate—with a formal reading of the Declaration of Independence. He became an American citizen in 1850 and was soon appointed local postmaster and superintendent of the roads, both government positions. He named one of the early buildings he constructed, Washington Hall, not for a Catholic saint but in honor of the first American president. During the tragic Civil War of the 1860s, he permitted seven priests and approximately eighty sisters to volunteer as chaplains and nurses, although their absences caused serious hardships at Notre Dame, Saint Mary's, and other Holy Cross ministries. He was sufficiently respected in the American Church to be invited to the Provincial Council of Cincinnati in 1882 and the Plenary Council of Baltimore in 1884, and Archbishop John Ireland of Saint Paul paid high tribute to him on the fiftieth anniversary of his priestly ordination:[3]

> I will be permitted, before I conclude, to note in Father Sorin's life a characteristic that proves his high-mindedness and contributed in no small degree to his success. It is his sincere and thorough Americanism. From the moment he landed on our shores he ceased to be a foreigner. At once he was an American, heart and soul, as one to the manor born. The Republic of the United States never protected a more loyal and devoted citizen. He understood and appreciated our liberal institutions; there was in his heart no lingering fondness for old regimes, or worn-out legalisms. . . . Father Sorin, I thank you for your American patriotism, your love of American institutions.

Proudly and thoroughly American though he was, he had still been shaped and influenced in his early years by his native France. French politics, culture, and society had been turned upside down in the French Revolution in the late eighteenth century, and the French Church had been so devastated that for decades after the Revolution it was challenged to find means to resurrect and revitalize long-neglected or damaged local parish churches and long abandoned parochial schools. Two French priests of the early nineteenth century devoted their lives to the reopening of the closed schools and churches, and together they founded a new religious community with this in mind. Father Sorin and other young men joined that community and eventually sailed west as missionaries to the United States. Thus it is not inaccurate to say that without the French Revolution of the 1790s, there would be no University of Notre Dame in the 1840s. The history of Notre Dame then must begin with a study of the generation before Father Sorin and the founding brothers, the generation of Father Jacques Dujarié and Father Basil Anthony Moreau who founded that religious congregation, and the French Revolution that caused those schools and churches to close.

The causes of that Revolution were multiple, and the abuses giving rise to it had been festering for years. The poor had long been discontented. Unfavorable weather conditions had made for sluggish harvests, and widespread hunger and malnutrition had resulted. The urban poor often could not afford even necessary firewood. The government insisted that it could do little since it was already deeply in debt, chiefly as a result of its recent wars with England, including the War of Austrian Succession (1740–1748), the Seven Years' War (1756–1763), and the War of American Independence (1775–1783). Soldiers felt they were underpaid, and the emerging free market economy cut into the profits of local merchants. The philosophy of the Enlightenment awakened in many the desire for wider representative and popular government, and the king himself seemed isolated and remote from his subjects. Queen Marie Antoinette was criticized for squandering large sums on luxuries and even for possibly spying for her native, but now hostile, Austria.[4]

The Church itself was not spared blame. More than 90 percent of the population was Catholic, although regular churchgoing could vary by region and even family by family. The clergy numbered approximately one hundred thirty thousand, almost equally divided between diocesan priests and religious (those with vows), and women in vows numbered close to sixty thousand. Almost all of the bishops of the 135 dioceses were of noble families, and they were nominated for their positions by the king before being confirmed by Rome. The Church was also the nation's largest landed proprietor, owning between 6 and 10 percent of the land, and still it was exempt from taxation and even received significant tithes from the state. But the Church did provide essential public services. Hospitals and orphanages, the care of the sick and the impoverished, were chiefly the Church's responsibility, and most children were educated, if at all, in the twenty-five thousand parish schools. Although there are indications of the beginning of a decline in religious fervor and practice during the second half of the eighteenth century—a decline in vocations to the priesthood and religious life, fewer requests for Masses for the deceased, etc.—the faith of millions continued strong and vibrant.[5]

In the late spring of 1789, the Estates General, a representative body consisting of clergy, aristocrats, and ordinary subjects of the king, met to consider reforms for these abuses and sought to check the absolute power of the monarch through a written constitution. When Louis XVI tried to shut down the assembly, the discontented lower classes mobilized and stormed the Bastille in search of arms to defend the National Assembly, a battle that led to the freeing of the prisoners. The king belatedly recognized a new National or Constitutional Assembly, and that body in the fall issued a Declaration of the Rights of Man and Citizen, guaranteeing the rights of liberty and property, freedom of speech and religion, and also abolished the tithes that the Church had been receiving (eighty or ninety million livres a year) and confiscated Church property, putting it at the disposal of the nation.[6] It was gradually sold off, chiefly to lawyers, bankers, and others in the middle class, to relieve the government's indebtedness and to provide some assistance for the hospitals, orphanages, and schools that until then had been the responsibility of the Church. Because the majority was still Catholic, parishes had to be maintained, and the local curés were guaranteed an annual salary from the state, leaving them almost wholly dependent on the government in power and subject to its wishes. In a further attack on the Church, the taking of religious vows by men was forbidden, contemplative orders were abolished as contributing nothing to public life, and, by law, all religious were free to leave their monasteries if they wished.[7]

In the summer of 1790, the National Assembly passed the Civil Constitution of the Clergy. All 135 dioceses were abolished and a new diocese established in each of the eighty-three civic departments or provinces. Six thousand members could make up a parish, and current parishes were merged or suppressed until that figure was reached. Bishops and parish priests were to be elected by the department or district assemblies, bishops were to seek confirmation by the local metropolitan, not Rome, and the title and position of archbishop was abolished. The pope was simply notified of a bishop's selection. Finally, all bishops and priests were obliged to take an oath to "be faithful to the nation, the law, and the King, and to maintain with all their power the Constitution decreed by the National Assembly and accepted by the King."[8]

Fewer than eight of the 135 bishops took the oath (among them Bishop Tallyrand of Autun, later French foreign minister) and less than half of the lower clergy. Most of the laity preferred the non-jurors, clergy not taking the oath, but the state favored the jurors and began withholding salaries from the others. Those refusing the oath could also be imprisoned. But with the government in continued turmoil and with more serious problems to face, many of the stipulations of the Civil Constitution were not enforced. Numerous non-jurors remained in their posts without salaries, sustained by the charity of the faithful parishioners, and the laity in many parishes rejected the services of those taking the oath. Within a year, the Vatican condemned the Civil Constitution, annulling all ecclesiastical elections under it and ordering all who took the oath to retract, under pain of excommunication.[9]

The break between the Church and the government in France was then complete, fueling tensions that drove the Revolution in a more violent direction. Churches were broken into and sacred vessels desecrated. In Lyon, a donkey, dressed in episcopal robes with a miter on its head and Bible and missal tied to its tail, was paraded through the town. In the September Massacres of 1792, more than a hundred non-juring priests were among the one thousand killed in Paris, scores more were bound and drowned in the Loire near Nantes, and thousands were deported or sought exile voluntarily. Many were accused of favoring the enemy as France fell deeper into the war that began in April 1792. One of the young seminarians leaving France at the time was Stephen Badin, who in two years would be the first priest ever ordained in the recently independent United States. Father Badin was ordained by the newly consecrated Bishop John Carroll.[10] Tumult within the Church continued when a law was passed in late 1792 permitting priests to marry, and many did, some to keep their positions and livelihoods. With the new civil calendar of "decades," Sundays were no longer recognized, feast days were abolished, wholly secular liturgies were introduced, and the goddess of reason, an opera dancer, was enthroned on the altar of Notre Dame Cathedral in Paris. The king was executed in January 1793 and a Reign of Terror continued until Maximilien Robespierre was deposed in July 1794. By the end of the century, close to three thousand priests had been killed, another thirty thousand had gone into exile, most by force, Church property had been confiscated, schools were closed, parishes were without priests, and seminaries held little promise for the future.[11]

General Napoleon Bonaparte was summoned to restore order in 1799, and this he did, but his relationship with the Church was uneasy at best and almost schizophrenic at worst. He realized that religion (Catholicism) was a unifying bond among the population and that its teachings, including respect for authority and obedience to law, were good for civic order, but he also intended to be unquestioned ruler of France and would brook no opposition to his policies. His major accomplishment in his relations with the Church was the Concordat signed in 1801. Catholicism was not yet recognized as the official state religion, but the agreement did note that Catholicism was the religion of the majority and was to be exercised freely. Bishops would be obliged to take an oath of loyalty to the government, and bishops and priests would both be guaranteed a suitable income from the state. Rome would not attempt to reacquire Church property that had been confiscated and sold, and married priests would be permitted to return to communion with the Church. The Concordat clearly did not restore the Church to the position it had enjoyed under the monarchy—that was gone forever—but it did gain some of its earlier rights and freedoms.[12]

After the fall of Napoleon in the blistering cold of Moscow in 1812, his abdication in 1814, and his defeat at Waterloo, the Church enjoyed government support under kings Louis XVIII and Charles X, and less support under Louis

Philippe after the Revolution of 1830. Benefits were occasionally bestowed and occasionally removed: clergy could again own property, congregations of women religious were recognized, profanation of Church vessels was criminalized, but respect for the pope declined and the union of Church and state was strengthened, leaving Rome with even less influence. Historian Adrien Dansette describes the state of French Catholicism at the time:[13]

> When Louis Veuillot was still a skeptic and he was starting his journalistic career in Périgueux, not a single one of his acquaintances, he tells us, fulfilled his religious duties. He never once heard a mother speak to her children of God, of the Church, or of anything relating to religion. The Revolution had devastated the Church and deprived it of any influence in education. It had been followed by a regime that contemptuously reduced the role of the priest to one of maintaining order. . . . The rectors of the various *académies*, or sections into which the university was divided, granted certification of aptitude to teachers, and the bishops then gave them permission to teach. Members of the authorized religious congregations, however, were not required to hold such certificates. But in elementary education even more than in the secondary field, the Church had a manpower problem. There were from 27,000 to 28,000 schools and less than two hundred Brothers of the Christian Schools. Most of the teachers were ignorant, ill-nourished men whom the four teachers' colleges were insufficient to train.

Such was the state of France in which young Fathers Jacques Dujarié and Basil Anthony Moreau began their lives as priests.

Jacques Dujarié was born in Rennes-en-Grenouilles in northwestern France on November 9, 1767, the first of seven children. His parents, through inheritance, owned between 125 and 150 acres of land, scattered in small holdings throughout the region, and his father was later elected mayor of the small town of Sainte-Marie-du-Bois where the family then resided. The Dujarié family was quite religious, being active in local parish services and apparently numbering one or more priests among their extended family.[14]

Of young Jacques's early life, little is known, but his education seemed at least haphazard. With no school nearby, he probably received his early education from the local pastor, as did other young boys of the district, and the pastor may have noticed qualities in him that could lead to the priesthood and encouraged his study of Latin. In 1778, at age eleven, he entered the *collège* of Lassay, a combination middle and high school about three miles from the Dujarié residence. The school numbered perhaps a hundred day and boarding students, taught by a faculty of only two, and Jacques was probably a day student, returning home each evening. After three years at Lassay, he transferred to the minor seminary of Saint-Ouen-des-Fossés in Le Mans where he could receive an even better education. The seminary had a faculty of ten and could house up to two hundred students. It was situated about sixty miles from the Dujarié home and thus young Jacques must have boarded there, with the expenses shared by his parents and the local pastor. For some reason, Jacques remained at Saint-Ouen for only a short time and then finished his humanities studies with two additional years at the college in Ernée. Then it was another transfer, this time to the seminary at Domfront-en-Passais for two years, an excellent school conducted by the Congregation of Jesus and Mary (Eudist Fathers) where Jacques developed a special devotion to the Sacred Heart of Jesus, a favorite devotion of that congregation and a devotion Jacques would retain for the rest of his life. It is difficult to know how good a student Jacques was, but with all these transfers his schooling must have suffered. All records agree that he was pious, and fellow students for a time called him "the little saint," but a notice in one archive also mentions his "quite mediocre talents." Still, he was sufficiently respected to be admitted to tonsure and sent on for further priestly studies in 1787 at the highly esteemed major seminary at Angers.[15]

Jacques must have entered into this final phase of his priestly training with high hopes and enthusiasm, but the years would end in grave disappointment. The Angers seminary offered a five-year academic program, two years of philosophy and three of theology, with some courses being offered at the much larger University of Angers. There were lectures, discussion seminars, examinations, and practical exercises in public speaking and the teaching of catechism. The seminarians were certainly aware of the problems, financial and other, that the nation was facing in the 1780s, and may have agreed with the majority of the local clergy in welcoming the calling of the Estates General in early 1789 to address them. But their hopes soon faded. As radicals gained control in the National Assembly, the law was passed permitting the confiscation of Church property, including seminary property, for disposition by the nation, although life remained normal in the Angers seminary for several months. The following year, however, the Civil Constitution of the Clergy was passed and all priests on the seminary staff, and the bishop and all priests of the diocese except one, refused to take the required oath.

On March 18, 1791, the day before a newly consecrated (and oath-taking) bishop was to assume his position as bishop of Angers, the seminary rector, in defiance, closed the seminary and requested all seminarians to leave.[16]

The next few years of Jacques's life were clouded in uncertainty. Most bishops refusing the oath and remaining loyal to the Holy See had fled the country, and the newly consecrated "Constitutional" bishops were generally spurned and even ridiculed by the laity. Each diocese now had two sets of priests, juring and non-juring. The pastor in Jacques's hometown of Sainte-Marie-du-Bois had first taken a very modified oath, then a few months later, perhaps under threats, he took the more radical oath required by the Civil Constitution, and then still later he retracted, only to be imprisoned and exiled. He probably had little to fear from exclusively local authorities because by this time, 1791–1792, the mayor was Jacques Dujarié's father. An oath-taking priest was assigned to the parish but shortly thereafter left both the priesthood and the Catholic faith, but one of the non-juring priests in hiding continued to provide the sacraments in secret.[17]

Young Dujarié was not personally affected by the Constitutional oath since he was not yet a priest and thus he was not required to take it. He was free to travel about since he possessed a certificate of patriotism, probably issued by his father, and he assisted loyal underground priests whenever he could, although he also went into hiding at times. He apparently learned the trade of weaving while living with one of his sisters and possibly earned some livelihood as a weaver for a time, he may have dressed as a shepherd and herded sheep, and he may have even sold lemonade or soft drinks on the streets of Paris, although this has been disputed.[18] But he was clearly determined to continue as a seminarian toward the priesthood. Of his work with underground priests at the time, he later recalled:[19]

> The touching piety of the faithful who feared no trouble, got up at night to come from afar, in terrible weather and along worse paths, to assist at the Holy Mysteries and to prepare to be fed the Bread of the Strong, in fear of no danger. For they were well aware that, if they were discovered, death was the penalty of their generosity in hiding the minister of Jesus Christ.

Opposition to the Church moderated for a time after the Reign of Terror in 1794 but intensified off and on the following year. It might have been during one of those periods of relaxation that Jacques was advised to go to Ruillé-sur-Loir and live with the pastor Abbé Jacquet de la Haye. He assisted the abbé in visiting other parishes in the district, thirty-five in all, and in assisting oath-taking priests to retract and return to communion with the Holy See. In the evenings, the abbé tutored Dujarié in the seminary studies he missed because of the closing of the seminary. The abbé also oversaw the necessary pre-ordination paperwork and in December 1795, he and Dujarié made the trip to Paris incognito. There Bishop de Maillé de la Tour-Landry, hiding out at times as a laundryman and at others as a sentry in the National Guard, ordained the young man subdeacon and deacon. On December 26, the feast of Saint Stephen, the first martyr, the bishop ordained him to the priesthood, probably secretly in the home of a trusted Catholic.[20]

Shortly after his ordination, Father Dujarié returned to Ruillé to begin his priestly ministry, a ministry that would center in that town for the rest of his life. At that time, of course, his ministry had to remain secret, as government persecution could flare up at almost any time, and he offered his first Mass there on January 1, 1796, among only a few friends and neighbors in the hidden cellar of a local farmhouse. He and Abbé de la Haye felt responsibility not only for the Catholics of Ruillé but for those in the surrounding communes as well. A neighbor reported: "Together they led a rough and austere life, making long trips at night in frightful weather and along terrible roads to console the sick, bringing to them the help of religion and administering the Sacraments, and also baptizing children."[21] Another recalled of Father Dujarié: "He sometimes slept in stables, sometimes in barns, attics, and cellars."[22] For several years the young priest had admired and worked with underground priests, and now he was one of them.

One of his most important, and most dangerous, ministries was assisting priests who wanted to retract the government oath they had taken. Between 1795 and 1799, new oaths were decreed, one promising fidelity to the laws of the Republic and another professing "hatred of royalty and anarchy."[23] It seems certain that Father Dujarié never took any of the oaths, but other priests did, either the earlier Constitutional oath or one of the later ones. Abbé de la Haye and Father Dujarié both assisted priests in retracting. Sometimes this was done in public, and sometimes more secretly, in the presence of only a few witnesses. Sometimes the priests could be returned to active priestly ministry and sometimes, especially if they had married, simply to the lay state. It was an anxious time for Father Dujarié. He was at risk of being arrested for declining the required oaths and even more so for aiding and abetting those who wished to retract them. Much of his priesthood was exercised in secret and on the run.[24]

With the signing of the Concordat between Napoleon and the Vatican in 1801, however, Father Dujarié could begin exercising his priestly ministry in public. Abbé de la Haye, his pastor, friend, and mentor, was transferred to another parish in 1803 and Father Dujarié, after some confusion, was named pastor of Ruillé, which meant he was pastor of more than one thousand parishioners over an area of twelve square miles.[25] In his first sermon as pastor, he promised "to be the consolation of the widow, the father of the orphan, the support of the poor, and the friend of those who suffer."[26] He apparently began carrying out this mission immediately because the village council set his state salary, mandated by the 1801 Concordat, at 1,200 francs per year, noting that, besides needing a horse to reach his far-flung flock, "M. Dujarié, in addition to the religious functions which he provides regularly, is devoting himself zealously and carefully to teaching school to young boys and helping them free of charge to learn how to read and write, which is an advantage for this commune" and "M. Dujarié goes to help the unfortunate as much as his means will allow, and there is every reason to believe that he will make good use of whatever provision is made for him."[27] With catechetical instruction and almost all systematic schooling having been neglected over the past fifteen years, Father Dujarié, after finding ways to repair and refurbish the parish church to allow for dignified worship, turned his attention, as the village council noted, to the young.[28]

Father Dujarié had been instructing the children of his parish in reading, writing, and the catechism since his ordination in 1795, but now as pastor he could do it more openly. He was long convinced that such a basic education was necessary to prepare the children not only for heaven but also for responsible citizenship on earth. All 321 schools in the district of La Mayenne had been closed and he was also concerned about the youngsters of his parish living four or five miles from the commune, in a district called the Heights of Ruillé. Twice a week he arranged to meet with thirty or forty of them there, in a shed or barn or whatever he could find. He soon rented a small shelter to serve as his school there and in 1806, on property donated by a Count Beaumont, he built his own structure, which he called La Petite Providence. He had already asked his parishioners for assistance and a small group of young women had volunteered. Father Dujarié hoped they would not only teach the children but also visit the sick in the area, and he sent seven of them to spend a few months in the novitiate of the Daughters of the Sacred Heart of Mary in Baugé, to advance their schooling further and to receive some training also in medicine and care of the sick. Although they did not take vows, when they returned to La Petite Providence they adopted a religious habit and began calling themselves the Sisters of Providence. As other schools in the area began to reopen over time and religious teachers were needed, Father Dujarié sent them to assist, and other young women, admiring their life and ministry, requested to join, and the Sisters of Providence grew into an international teaching and ministering religious congregation. Within a hundred years, they were serving in Belgium, England, the Netherlands, Peru, Taiwan, and the United States. Their first foundation in the United States was in Terre Haute, Indiana.[29]

With the founding of the Sisters of Providence, Father Dujarié had made at least a start in providing education for the girls in his and surrounding parishes, but he realized that he had to do something similar for boys also, and he realized that he could not do it alone. At first he thought of organizing a society of missionary priests who might travel from parish to parish with both the sacraments and catechetical instruction, but this did not seem feasible at the time. There were institutes of religious brothers in France that might serve as models but they generally preferred to live in community, thus often in urban areas where service in two or more schools might be available, and Father Dujarié envisioned young men who could be sent out even singly to assist pastors, often in poorer, country parishes, in their work as sacristans, choirmasters, and schoolteachers. In 1820 he began recruiting such young men, and six answered his call that first year. He tried to provide them with a basic education in arithmetic, penmanship, reading, plain chant, and catechism, but daily life was hard as an early chronicle indicates:[30]

> The meals of these new Brothers were indeed frugal. They had a piece of dry bread for breakfast: at noon and in the evening they had soup and vegetables, sometimes meat, and usually fruit. Their beverage was a weak sour wine made from the last pressing of the grapes. Their refectory was used for devotions, study, and recreation. It was a large room in the presbytery, having formerly been used as a parish classroom. It had but one small window near a glass door, and as a consequence it was naturally dark and poorly ventilated. An attic and another small room served as dormitories. Rats roamed at will through the dormitory, troubling the sleep of the occupants and carrying away their combs and brushes. As there were no bedsteads, the straw mattresses and bedding were laid on the floor.

Additional young men arrived, although others also left, and the program continued. A distinctive religious habit was devised for them in order that they be recognized as a single community although spread out among different schools and parishes. As workers they were dedicated to Saint Joseph, a carpenter, and these "Brothers of Saint Joseph" bound themselves with only one vow at first, that an annual vow of obedience to their superior, at that time Father Dujarié. A year of novitiate was established for all candidates, a year of prayer and religious study and reading, and all the brothers were to come together annually for retreat. Each brother was to say the following prayer daily:[31]

> O Jesus, who have said: "Let the little children come unto Me," and have inspired me with the desire to bring them to You, deign to bless my vocation, to assist me in my work and to clothe me with the spirit of strength, charity, and humility, in order that nothing may turn me aside from Your service and that, fulfilling zealously the duties to which I have devoted myself, I may be of the number of those to whom You have promised salvation because they have persevered to the end. Amen.

After years of uncertainly and even opposition, a royal decree in 1816 permitted legally recognized religious communities to supply teachers to any municipality requesting them and such communities could be provided financial assistance from the government. In 1823, Father Dujarié applied for and received official legal approbation of his small community, although its teaching would still be under the jurisdiction of the Royal University, and the following year received his first subsidy of 4,000 francs.[32] In August 1825, records indicate that there were seventy-three brothers serving in thirty-two schools, but this number probably includes aspirants also. Father Dujarié attempted to visit each school and see for himself the brothers' living conditions and teaching progress but he soon had to delegate this to one of his closest collaborators, Brother André Mottais. He urged Brother André to be sure that the brothers "teach the children to be virtuous and religious, that they teach them to love Jesus Christ, that they establish confraternities of Saint Aloysius in the larger schools, that they invite the pastors to visit the schools once a week and examine the progress of the students, and that they should be generous with prizes as a means of causing emulation among the students."[33]

The academic side of their work was not to be neglected, and the brothers were reminded that at the time of the annual retreat they would all be examined in grammar, writing, arithmetic, and religion. Father Dujarié urged them to be patient, understanding, and generous:[34]

> The faults and weaknesses of your children should not discourage you. All of your beloved fellow-religious have the same difficulties to put up

with; by putting up with them in charity you will acquire greater merit. The more your children are uncouth, dishonest, scatter-brained, and anything else you want that is bad, the more also are they worthy of your compassion. To love them in this way, it is sufficient to know that Jesus Christ has loved them. The one among them who seems the lowliest is perhaps the most pleasing in His eyes.

An increasingly serious problem the brothers were facing was that the community was bound together primarily by the personality and leadership of its founder, Father Dujarié, and his health declined. His early years in hiding and being on the run, with irregular meals and interrupted sleep, had undoubtedly taken a toll. He had also developed gout and travel, even short distances, was painful, and, at age sixty, his mental faculties seemed to be failing. The recruiting and training of his brothers may not always have been as stringent as needed. Added to these, the superior always had financial worries since many parishes could not contribute the agreed-upon assessment and he had worries over public educational policies as government ministries changed. This latter concern was especially serious because the government of Louis Phillipe, brought in with the Revolution of 1830, seemed less friendly. Father Dujarié in 1834 had given up his governance of the Sisters of Providence and in 1835 realized it was time to relinquish the brothers also. He consulted the bishop and they both agreed that the best person to whom to entrust his community was Father Basil Moreau, a seminary professor in Le Mans who had often preached the annual retreat for the brothers. On August 31, 1835, at the close of the annual retreat that year, Father Dujarié, with tears in his eyes, formally asked the bishop to accept his resignation as Superior of the Brothers of Saint Joseph and entrust them to Father Moreau. The resignation was accepted and, at the request of the bishop, Father Moreau agreed to assume leadership of Father Dujarié's brothers.[35]

Father Moreau had been spared most of the political turmoil and persecution that Father Dujarié had experienced as a young man, but his devotion to the Church and his zeal for souls were no less. He had been born the ninth of fourteen children on February 11, 1799, in Laigné-en-Belin, a few miles southeast of Le Mans and only a little further from Ruillé-sur-Loir. His father was both a farmer and wine merchant but was probably illiterate and eventually blind. Both parents were deeply religious, although infant Basil's baptism was delayed during those days of the Constitutional priests until a non-juring priest was available. As did Jacques Dujarié before him, he received his early education in reading, writing, arithmetic, and catechism from his parish priest who had also ministered from hiding during the first years of the Revolution and the Reign of Terror and had emerged to public service only with the Concordat of 1801. The pastor also saw signs of a possible priestly vocation in young Basil. He helped around the sacristy, enjoyed serving Mass, and even trained his schoolmates to serve. The pastor eventually approached Basil's parents and suggested that he be sent to the seminary to further discern his vocation. His parents at first hesitated, perhaps because they were not convinced themselves, and perhaps they were concerned about the finances. The pastor promised to meet any expenses himself that the family could not afford, and young Basil entered the seminary of Château-Gontier in 1814 at age fifteen.[36]

Seminary studies were not difficult for Basil. He was at or near the top of his class at Château-Gontier, being appointed a student-prefect and even asked to teach one of the lower-level classes since the faculty was shorthanded due to the upheaval of the Revolution. After two years at Château-Gontier, young Moreau was transferred to the major seminary, Saint Vincent's, in Le Mans. The major seminary had been forced to close during the Revolution, had reopened in a hotel in 1810, and only in 1816 had it been moved to Saint Vincent's Abbey, with Basil Moreau in its first student class. French theological education was in a state of confusion in these immediate post-Revolutionary years: some professors had simply not received adequate preparation, some were ultramontanist and would adhere carefully to Vatican directives, some were Gallicanist and would adapt more to French life and culture, some were Jansenist and were overly strict in their interpretation of morality, and some were probably all or none of the above. Basil Moreau was undoubtedly a fine student but his seminary training overall must have been confusing and weak.[37]

On August 12, 1821, Basil Moreau was ordained to the priesthood, with a special dispensation from the bishop since he was eighteen months short of the canonical age required. The dispensation indicates the respect in which he was held by his ecclesiastical superiors. The young priest had hoped to be selected for a foreign mission assignment but his bishop had other plans. As a top student in all of his classes, the bishop wanted to prepare him for a position on the seminary faculty. His first assignment was to the Seminary of Saint-Sulpice in Paris for a year, enrolling in additional courses in theology, sacred scripture, and Hebrew, and he learned firsthand of the goals and programs of the Order of Saint Sulpice for the training of seminarians. The following year he spent at the Sulpician Solitude at Issy, a house of quiet retreat on the outskirts of Paris. This was to be a year of prayer, religious reading, reflection, and spiritual growth to prepare him better to guide seminary students in their paths of prayer and piety. It was at Issy that he met the saintly Sulpician priest Gabriel Étienne Joseph Mollevaut who would remain his spiritual director and close confidant for the next thirty years.[38]

At the end of his time in Paris, Father Moreau returned to Le Mans and for two years taught philosophy at the minor seminary of Tessé. In 1825 he was transferred to Saint Vincent's major seminary where he began teaching theology. His theological opinions eventually came in conflict with the more Gallican views of the seminary rector and in 1830 he was transferred to the chair of sacred scripture. He was named vice rector of the seminary from 1834 to 1836, and throughout all these years he continued to serve as spiritual director for the seminarians and preached parish missions and retreats throughout the diocese. In 1833 he was also appointed ecclesiastical superior and confessor for the Sisters of the Good Shepherd, an assignment he held for twenty-five years.[39]

From his experience in preaching parish missions and retreats, Father Moreau saw the advantage of a group of auxiliary or missionary priests who could be available to temporarily assist parishes in need. This idea was not new, nor did it originate with him. Father Dujarié had had the idea as far back as 1823, and had actually asked Father Moreau to join, but Father Moreau at the time was already committed to teach at Tessé. Because of his continued work as pastor at Ruillé-sur-Loir and his responsibilities to his growing community of Brothers of Saint Joseph—and perhaps because of his declining health—Father Dujarié did not carry his plan further. In 1832, however, Brother André Mottais, encouraged by his confessor, Father Moreau, presented a plan to the bishop for a new society uniting the Brothers of Saint Joseph, a band of auxiliary priests dedicated to the Sacred Heart, and an association of lay teachers called the Sons of Mary for service in the diocese. Unfortunately, the bishop of Le Mans died the following year and no action was taken. During the discussions of possibly taking over direction of the Brothers of Saint Joseph, in early 1835 Father Moreau asked the bishop's approval to found a group of diocesan missionary priests who might also care for infirm and retired priests as needed. The new bishop, the former seminary rector, simply answered "Yes." Four young men—two priests (Fathers Cottereau and Nourry) and two seminarians (Misters Veron and Moriceau)—very quickly asked to join.[40]

Thus in the summer of 1835 Father Moreau unexpectedly found himself superior of two diverse religious groups. One of the first steps he took was to transfer the brothers' novitiate and motherhouse to a seven-acre plot of land in the Le Mans suburb of Sainte-Croix that he had been given in 1832. He wanted them close so he could offer them guidance and direction. He designed a different religious habit for the brothers, in part to symbolize that this was a new beginning for them. He made plans to transfer their school in Ruillé to Sainte-Croix and open a secondary school (*collège*) there also. The challenge was to unite the two diverse groups—priests and brothers—into one harmonious society, although the brothers had professed religious vows and the auxiliary priests had not, presenting a major complication to union. But in the midst of these discussions, in October 1836, Father Moreau was relieved of his position as professor of sacred scripture and vice rector at Saint Vincent's Seminary, and he could devote himself more fully to his priests and brothers. In March 1837, he drafted the Fundamental Pact, agreed to by all fifty-one brothers and ten auxiliary priests, a judicial document uniting the two groups, establishing common property, and preparing the way for a formal constitution.[41]

Father Moreau drafted a preliminary constitution the following year. He had spent the year getting to know the brothers better and visiting their schools, and he sent this first draft of a constitution to them for their comments and advice. The congregation was to be headed by a priest, assisted by a council of at least twenty, who would eventually be elected by the members. Some brothers would dedicate their lives to teaching, and regulations were set for the opening of schools, and other brothers would be devoted to manual labor, building maintenance, and the kitchen. All were encouraged to practice the virtues of humility, charity, and religious poverty, and to be faithful to spiritual direction and the annual retreat. With this preliminary constitution in place, there was one final obstacle to union and, on August 15, 1840, after a retreat of eight days, Father Moreau and four auxiliary priests—Fathers Pierre Chappé, Paul Celier, Augustin Sauvier, and Edward Sorin—made profession of the three religious vows of poverty, chastity, and obedience.[42]

With the priests and brothers that well established, Father Moreau, certainly influenced by the visions of Father Dujarié and Brother André, sought to complete his congregation with a third group. In the schools where the brothers taught and in the parishes where the priests served, there were frequently young women who assisted by preparing meals, cleaning, laundry, and caring for the ill. As time went on, some of these desired a greater religious unity and permanence. Earlier Father Moreau had attempted to attract a community of nuns to assist him in this work but all declined. He thus decided to form his own. He provided these few young women with a distinct religious garb and, although they took no vows at first, they were usually addressed as "Sister." In April 1841 four of them were sent to the cloister of the Good Shepherd Monastery (of which Father Moreau was still the ecclesiastical superior) for religious training. That September, even before any constitution had been drafted for them, Father Moreau wrote in a Circular Letter:[43]

> Here we have a striking representation of the hierarchy of the heavenly spirits, wherein all the different choirs of angels are arranged in three Orders which are mutually subordinated one to another. Our Association is also a visible imitation of the Holy Family wherein Jesus, Mary, and Joseph, notwithstanding their differences in dignity, were one at heart by their unity of thought and uniformity of conduct. . . . From all this it follows that, just as in the Adorable Trinity, of which the house of Notre-Dame de Sainte-Croix is still another image, there is no difference of interests and no opposition of aims or wills, so among the priests, Brothers, and Sisters there should be such conformity of sentiments, interests, and wills as to make all of us one in somewhat the same manner as the Father, Son, and Holy Ghost are one. . . . Furthermore, in order the better to cement this union and this imitation of the Holy Family, I have consecrated and do hereby consecrate anew, as far as lies in my power, the Auxiliary Priests to the Sacred Heart of Jesus, the Shepherd of souls; the Brothers to the Heart of St. Joseph, their Patron; and the Sisters to the Heart of Mary pierced with the sword of sorrow.

As this small community of Father Moreau continued to grow, requests for assistance began to arrive from dioceses throughout France and even beyond, especially requests for brothers to staff recently opened schools. Father Moreau tried to respond as generously as his numbers permitted. In his early priesthood, he had hoped to be a foreign missionary himself and, in 1840, he was pleased to answer the request of the newly consecrated bishop of Algiers and sent two priests and four brothers to assist. Over time a few other priests and brothers followed but the mission was not to be permanent. Misunderstandings with the bishop over assignments, lack of financial support on-site, frequent disease, and very difficult living conditions eventually doomed the mission, and the last brothers were recalled to France in 1853.[44]

As Father Moreau sent the priests and brothers of his young community to minister in schools and parishes in western France, and even abroad, he shared with them his views of teaching and education, an education of both mind and heart. "We shall always place education side by side with instruction," he wrote in 1849, "the mind will not be cultivated at the expense of the heart."[45]

> We can state in a word the kind of teaching we hope to impart. We recognize no genuine philosophical system save that which is based on Catholic Faith. . . . Even though we base our philosophy course on the data of faith, no one need fear that we shall confine our teaching within narrow and unscientific boundaries. No; we wish to accept science without prejudice, and in a manner adapted to the needs of the times. We do not want our students to be ignorant of anything they should know. To this end, we shall shrink from no sacrifice. But we shall never forget that virtue, as Bacon puts it, is the spice which preserves science. . . . While we prepare useful citizens for society, we shall likewise do our utmost to prepare citizens for Heaven.

But he also insisted upon competence:[46]

> If, as Saint Paul says, "knowledge without reverence makes one proud" and thus becomes dangerous, it is likewise true that reverence without knowledge makes a teacher useless and compromises the honor of the mission of a teacher. That is why Daniel, speaking of the reward prepared for those who teach others does not assume that they are merely "just" and hence reverent, but also "learned and knowledgeable." Without knowledgeable teachers, what can be said to families who want to have their children acquire all the learning needed to earn a good position in life? "You cannot give what you do not already have." This axiom applies to teaching as well—it would be useless for a person to try to teach who did not possess the knowledge sufficient for the goals of instruction. Teachers should definitely have enough knowledge and instruction themselves to be able to deal with the subjects which they are presenting and to be able to make lessons more interesting and more complete. In order to succeed in acquiring a superior degree of knowledge, teachers must have a constant desire for self-improvement and lose no opportunity to satisfy this ambition when it is not detrimental to their other duties. To teach with success, teachers must know good methods, be skillful in applying these methods, have clear ideas, be able to define exactly, possess

language which is easily understood and correct; all these are acquired and perfected only through study. I think we must assume that good teachers are not content simply with obtaining a degree or credential to show their capabilities, but will try to increase their knowledge even further by studying as much as they can.

If Father Moreau's first overseas venture, to Algeria, ultimately proved a failure, his second would be the congregation's greatest success. In 1834, the diocese of Vincennes in Indiana had been established by Rome to care for the growing number of Catholics in Indiana and eastern Illinois. Indiana had become a state in 1816 and Illinois in 1818. Simon Bruté de Rémur, a native of France but a longtime seminary professor in the United States, was named first bishop, and in 1836 he returned to France to seek priests and brothers to help staff his new diocese. He visited Saint Vincent's seminary in Le Mans, and one of the seminarians enrolled there who heard his appeal was young Edward Sorin. The bishop, worn out from his labors in the new world, died in 1839 but his successor, Bishop Célestin de la Hailandière, renewed the request that same year, and Father Moreau agreed to send assistance. Because of other requests, financial concerns, and the mission to Algeria, however, the promise to America was not fulfilled until 1841. On August 5 of that year, the feast of Our Lady of Snows, Father Sorin, as superior and necessary sacramental minister, and six brothers left Le Mans for Le Havre, to board the American ship *Iowa* to begin their mission in the United States.[47]

CHAPTER 2

The Founding,
1841–1844

Father Moreau had apparently selected each member of that first group with a purpose. The leader and superior was Father Edward Sorin, one of the first four priests pronouncing religious vows with Father Moreau the year before. Born on February 6, 1814, in Ahuillé, about seven miles southwest of Laval, the seventh of nine children, his parents were well-to-do thanks to an inheritance, on an economic level with physicians and lawyers and living in an impressive three-story manor home on several acres of land. Deeply religious, they had sheltered two non-juring priests during the final years of the Revolution, enabling them to continue their ministry. Young Edward's early education was carried on for a short time in the village school (from which he abruptly withdrew after what he considered unfair treatment by the teacher) and then in the local parish with a few other young boys, instructed by the pastor. Sorin excelled, as a classmate later recalled: "Among all of us, Edward Sorin was always first. He knew how to succeed by commanding others. He was born for that."[1]

After two or three years of this parish tutoring, Sorin enrolled in the School of the Sacred Hearts of Jesus and Mary in Laval to pursue further study, but he remained only one year. He had decided to be a priest, his parents gave their full support, and he transferred to the diocesan minor (high school) seminary at

Précigné, not far from Solesmes. There he completed his humanities course in 1834 and continued on to the major seminary in Le Mans to study theology. A fellow-seminarian, Guillaume Meignan, later archbishop of Tours, remembered him well: "He was amiable and pious and a friend of all. He always edified us, his fellow-students."[2] Two important events occurred during his years in Le Mans that would impact the rest of his life. In 1836 he was one of those seminarians who heard Bishop Simon Bruté of Vincennes, Indiana, plead for missionaries to his diocese, and he became interested. In Le Mans also he made the acquaintance of the vice rector and professor of sacred scripture, Father Basil Moreau, and each was deeply and favorably impressed with the other. Ordained a priest on May 27, 1838, Sorin was immediately assigned as curate in the parish of Parcé-sur-Sarthe, about thirty miles from Le Mans. He remained there for fourteen months, serving effectively, but in his heart he wanted something more. Father Moreau had recently organized his auxiliary priests, he had united them with Father Dujarié's Brothers of Saint Joseph, and, with the bishop's permission, young Father Sorin accepted Father Moreau's invitation to join. After a brief period of novitiate, he pronounced his vows of religion with three others on August 15, 1840, and one year later was asked to lead the mission to America. The choice was excellent. He was young enough to adapt well to a new culture and a new language, he had outstanding leadership abilities, and he was highly motivated to work in this foreign mission.[3]

The oldest of the brothers was Brother Vincent (John Pieau), born in 1797. He had entered Father Dujarié's young community in 1822, taught at different parish schools, was one of the first to pronounce religious vows, and was a valued counselor to Father Dujarié in those early years. A deeply religious man, he could serve as counselor to Father Sorin, be a mentor and guide to younger brothers, bake, do outdoor labor, and especially serve as community steward or school principal. He proved to be a steady pillar for the young community.[4]

Next in age was Brother Joachim (William Michael André), born in 1809. He was a tailor by profession, as was his father before him, and, although that was a valuable trade to have in the new mission, he could also cook, an even more valuable trade. He had joined the young Holy Cross community in July 1841, less than a month before leaving for America. He soon contracted tuberculosis, however, it continued to advance, and he would die in April 1844, the first member of the community to be buried in America.[5]

Brother Lawrence (John Menage) was a farmer before entering religious life and remained one for the rest of his life. Born in 1816, he made his religious profession in 1841, perhaps with Brother Joachim. His farming experience would serve to feed the young community (and its ministries) in America, and his business acumen would try to keep the budget balanced and creditors from pounding too loudly at the door.[6]

Brother Francis Xavier (René Patois) was next in age. Born in 1820, he made his religious profession in 1841 also, possibly with Brothers Joachim and Lawrence. He had originally taken the name of Brother Marie (in France, Marie was a common name for men, as in Jean-Marie, Jacques-Marie, etc.) but changed it to Francis Xavier in America. He was a carpenter by trade, another valuable skill to have on the new mission. He would also serve as the coffin-maker and, from that, would double as undertaker for both the religious community and the local citizenry. In good health himself, he would outlive—and bury—all the others, dying in 1896.[7]

Brother Anselm (Pierre Caillot), born in 1825, was the second youngest of the group, sailing to America at age fifteen or sixteen. His youth was an advantage since he could learn the new language quickly. A man of great promise, his life proved short. Although an excellent swimmer, he apparently got caught in a strong current and steep drop-off in the Ohio River in July 1845, a companion on shore was not able to reach him, and he was pulled under and drowned.[8]

The youngest of the brothers was Brother Gatian (Urbain Mosimer), born in 1826. Bright and talented, he learned English well, taught mathematics and bookkeeping, and served as secretary of the local council. He was meticulous, even a perfectionist, and could be outspoken in his criticisms of others, especially of those in authority. Unhappy, he eventually left the community and returned to France, dying on the family farm in 1860.[9]

With appropriate ceremony and prayers, this small band departed Le Mans for Le Havre on August 5, the feast of Our Lady of Snows. When they arrived at Le Havre, they discovered that their passports were not in order. This complication was eventually remedied—and new ship accommodations were arranged since the cabins allotted to them were much more expensive than they could afford—and the American packet boat *Iowa* lifted anchor on August 8. For the mid-nineteenth century, this five-week voyage was probably little better or worse than others, although many passengers took sick whenever the ship rolled through heavy storms. The ship's captain, an Episcopalian, allowed Father Sorin and the brothers to use the deck for fresh air and exercise, an area normally reserved for cabin passengers. When the seas permitted, arrangements could be made for Mass for the brothers and five Sisters of the Sacred Heart who were also on board. A two-year-old daughter of German Protestant parents became gravely ill and the sisters received permission from the parents to have her baptized, with Brother Vincent and the superior of the sisters serving as godparents. The child died shortly thereafter, and the captain asked Father Sorin to provide a burial service. Four sailors served as pallbearers, Father Sorin recited appropriate prayers, and the young body was allowed gently to slip into the sea. Confident that she went straight to heaven, the brothers often prayed to "little Mary" the rest of their lives.[10]

The *Iowa* docked in New York in the late afternoon of September 13. Since it was too late in the day to unload, the passengers were requested to remain on board until the following morning, although Father Sorin and a few others were allowed to disembark that evening. One of Father Sorin's first acts on American soil was to kneel down and kiss the ground "as a sign of adoption and at the same time of profound gratitude to God for the blessing of a prosperous voyage." He was able to offer Mass the following morning, his first in America, on the feast of the Exaltation of the Holy Cross (September 14), a major feast of the young community.[11]

Bishop de la Hailandière had arranged for them to be met by Mr. Samuel Byerley, a recent convert to Catholicism. His father had been a partner of Josiah Wedgewood, the inventor of Wedgewood china, but had died early, leaving Samuel an orphan at thirteen. He wandered about Europe for a time, learned French, Spanish, German, and Italian, married, and immigrated to America in 1832. He rose quickly in the shipping and mercantile company of Howland and Aspinwall and became quite wealthy. Father Sorin and the brothers spent three days in New York with all their needs provided for by the Byerleys, and they also had a long visit with New York's bishop, John Dubois.[12]

The party left New York on September 16, steaming up the Hudson River to Albany by paddleboat. From there they made a seven-day trip to Buffalo through the recently completed (1825) Erie Canal. The canal was forty-five feet wide and each barge was pulled along by horses trudging on paths along the shore. Father Sorin and Brother Vincent left the boat before Buffalo and made a short detour to view Niagara Falls. Before leaving France, Father Sorin's father had asked the elderly Brother Vincent to watch over his young priest-son and, on this occasion, Brother Vincent apparently had to hold on tight to Father Sorin's cassock as he leaned over a ledge as far as he could to get a full view of the spectacular falls.[13] From Buffalo on Lake Erie, the group made a three-day trip by steamship to Toledo, then they travelled by a second steamship down the Maumee River to Maumee, and finally on to Napoleon, Ohio, where—disappointingly for them—Father Sorin noted that no one spoke French despite the town's French-sounding name. By boat and carriage, at times over terribly rough roads, they slowly made their way to Defiance, Ohio, then on to Fort Wayne, then to Logansport, Lafayette, Terre Haute, and finally, by the Wabash River, to Vincennes, arriving on October 10 after a twenty-four-day trip from New York and sixty-six days from Le Mans. Between Napoleon and Defiance, their two guides or drivers apparently tried to rob them, but two of the Americans traveling with them carried guns and the would-be robbers backed off. When the party reached Logansport, however, Father Sorin did take the time to purchase a gun.[14]

The young community remained in the Vincennes area only a year and a half. The bishop received them graciously and first offered them property and ministry in Francesville, a small collection of homes across the border in Illinois, about four miles from Vincennes but still in the Vincennes diocese. After a brief visit, Father Sorin declined, writing simply to Father Moreau: "I decided that this first proposed location was not a suitable place for us, though I cannot exactly tell you why."[15] The next day, Father Sorin visited a second location, St. Peter's Mission at Black Oak Ridge, twenty-seven miles east of Vincennes. Father Sorin described it two days later:[16]

> There is a farm here of about 160 acres, of which only 60 are under cultivation. Its location seems to me sufficiently agreeable. The air, I am told, is very healthy. The buildings are large enough, but they are a little old. There is even a small but pretty chapel built of wood, but I can see already that repairs will be necessary in many places. All in all, I am pleased with the place. . . . Oh yes, we are happy. We have our good Lord close by us. This very evening we have hung up in our little chapel our beautiful [sanctuary] lamp, only the second to be found in this vast diocese. It burns now before our modest altar, and I cannot speak of it without shedding tears of happiness. . . . If you could experience as we do, good Father, our little chapel. We gather there as though lost in the middle of an immense forest; when across the woods we see the lamp that lights up the mean dwelling where our good Master resides, we know full well that we are not alone. Jesus Christ dwells in our midst, and so we take courage.

There were already the makings of a primitive school there—perhaps what remained of an earlier school begun by the Sisters of Nazareth—with a few young boys being taught by a thirty-three-year-old German immigrant named Charles

Rother. Having earlier expressed to the bishop an interest in becoming a religious, Rother became the first to enter the Holy Cross community in the United States, and he took the name Brother Joseph. Others followed and twelve were received into the community during the community's fifteen months there, although almost half eventually departed. Father Sorin's views of local vocations are interesting:[17]

> They are mostly Irish and German that present themselves. The former are by nature full of faith, respect, religious inclinations, and sensible and devoted; but a great defect often paralyzes in them all their other good qualities: the lack of stability. They change more readily than any other nation. The latter are ordinarily less obedient, prouder, more singular in their tastes and less endowed with the qualities of heart; but they are more persevering.
>
> As to the genuine Americans, there is no hope of finding subjects amongst them for a religious house of this kind. . . . The spirit of liberty as it is understood in the United States is too directly opposed to the spirit of obedience and submission of a community to leave any hope for a long time to come of any addition of subjects in a country in which the nature of the men appears to offer so few dispositions towards the religious life. Hence it comes to pass that the young men who spend some time amongst Americans soon imbibe their spirit and manners and become in reality all the more unfitted for the religious life the more years they have passed in the new world.

The community set to work immediately. The brothers and newly arrived recruits began clearing about eighty acres of land and planted corn. They were not fully successful at first. They employed French farming methods, including steps not to exhaust the land since land was scarce in France, but local residents at Black Oak convinced them that land was plentiful here, and the brothers soon adopted American methods. There were perhaps thirty-five Catholic families in the area and Father Sorin offered Mass for them regularly in Latin. He began learning English and preached each Sunday—partly in English but mostly in French—to the Catholics and Protestants who attended. A makeshift novitiate was opened to receive and train the new recruits, and two of the original brothers taught in the school Mr. Rother was conducting. Brother Vincent, at the bishop's request, remained in Vincennes and taught in a French school there, and Brother Gatian was soon sent off to found a second school for about thirty-five young boys and girls in the area.[18]

Despite this initial progress, problems soon developed. There were serious disagreements over finances, especially when Father Sorin asked the bishop for 3,000 francs to cover their expenses so far and to purchase needed supplies. The bishop admitted that he had promised Father Moreau funding when he requested the missionaries in 1839, but when they did not arrive he had to use the money elsewhere. Despite this, he was willing to accept some financial responsibility for the community if it were he rather than Father Moreau who had final jurisdiction over them. He would not fund them if they were not under his and the diocese's control and if Father Moreau could remove them at any time. Father Sorin, of course, insisted that the young community had to remain ultimately under Father Moreau and the motherhouse in France. The crisis was partially averted when a priest, Father Julian Delaune, volunteered to travel to the East Coast and French Canada to solicit funds for the new mission. He collected approximately 15,000 francs ($3,000), which was divided between the Black Oak mission and the bishop's other needs in the diocese.[19]

A second disagreement emerged when the bishop discovered that Father Sorin also intended to start a *collège* (high school–college), hoping perhaps that it might even make a profit and ease the financial burden. In fact, Father Sorin had already begun collecting supplies and arranging for construction. The bishop objected. The Eudist Fathers were staffing a college, St. Gabriel's, begun by Bishop Bruté in Vincennes a few years earlier, and the bishop insisted that there was no need for another that close. He had also promised the Eudist Fathers that they would have no competition for students and funds. The conflict was resolved when the bishop mentioned that he had a piece of property further north in Indiana that Father Sorin and the brothers could have for a college if they were interested. After a brief consultation with the brothers, and without notifying France, Father Sorin accepted. [20]

The land the bishop offered had an important history of its own. The earliest known inhabitants may have been Algonkin tribes, chiefly the Potawatomi, probably driven from their earlier dwelling in the East and North by encroaching Iroquois, and gradually migrating into the area around the southern tip of Lake Michigan. As the French began to explore the area in the 1670s and 1680s, Jesuit missionaries Jacques Marquette, Louis Hennepin, Claude Allouez, and their successors brought the Christian faith into the area, but the "Black Robes" departed in the 1760s with the British victory in the French and Indian War (1763) and the suppression of the Jesuits by the king of France in 1764. The Potawatomi retained their faith as best they could and one of their chiefs, Leopold Pokagon, travelled to Detroit in 1830 to ask that a priest be sent among them again.[21]

It happened that Father Stephen Badin, the first priest ever ordained in the United States, was visiting his brother in Detroit at the time and he was asked to accept the mission. He had been a seminarian in France when the Revolution broke out in 1789 and had fled to the United States. He completed his seminary studies in Baltimore and was ordained by Bishop John Carroll in 1793, the bishop's first priestly ordination. Badin served among the French- and English-speaking Catholics in the Ohio Valley in the early nineteenth century and then accepted the mission to the Potawatomi in 1830.[22]

Within weeks of his arrival, he described his work:[23]

> I am consecrating the little strength left to me to spread the seeds of the Faith among the good Potawatomi savages. I have the name of twenty-four of them who came to be instructed and baptized. . . . I am too old to learn their language and I am obliged to use an interpreter. . . . Consequently, there is need of patience and the grace of the Holy Spirit above all. Ask it for me in your fervent prayers.

Badin set out immediately to establish a school and an orphanage. He tried unsuccessfully to attract some sisters in Kentucky to staff them, and both eventually failed. By 1832 he had purchased 524 acres of land, half from the government and half from two private landowners. He later gave the land to the bishop on condition that a school and an orphanage be built there, and he constructed a log cabin on it to serve as both a chapel and his residence. He encouraged the Potawatomi in the cultivation of wheat and corn and, since in Potawatomi culture chiefly women tilled the soil while the men did the hunting, Badin cultivated his own garden to give an example that farming was for men also. He travelled widely, usually on horseback, from Fort Wayne to Chicago to Kentucky and once mentioned that he had spent $1,000 of his own money on his Indian ministry.[24]

In 1836, Badin, sixty-nine years old and worn out from his missionary travels, decided to leave his Indian mission, but only because he had a worthy successor. Father Louis Deseille, a thirty-eight-year-old Flemish priest, ordained twelve years, had immigrated to Detroit in 1832 to work among the Indians and was immediately sent to assist the tiring Badin. He seems to have made his home at Chief Pokagon's village just north of the Indiana-Michigan border, but he travelled frequently to Badin's mission at the two lakes on his 524 acres and to the Potawatomi settlements along the Yellow River twenty-five miles to the south. At each location the ministry was the same—days filled with religious instructions, baptisms, Mass, marriages, care of the sick, and burials—and he shared Badin's interests in chapels, schools, and agriculture.[25]

On May 28, 1830, at the urging of President Andrew Jackson and after heated debate, Congress had passed the Indian Removal Act. This act gave the president the authority to buy lands presently owned by Indians east of the Mississippi River, including the Potawatomi Indians in northwest Indiana, transfer the Indians to federal lands west of the Mississippi, and support them financially for one year until they could get settled and support themselves. Five hundred thousand dollars were appropriated for this. Government agents throughout the 1830s negotiated with the Indians, urging them to sign treaties and leave their lands voluntarily. Some did sign treaties willingly, others only under threat, and others only when the chiefs had been made drunk on the white man's whiskey.[26]

There were four Indian settlements along the Yellow River to the south of Badin's property at this time, and three of the four Potawatomi chiefs may have signed land sale treaties. The fourth, Chief Menominee, earlier baptized by Father Deseille, had not, and he thus insisted that his settlement did not have to move:[27]

> The President does not know the truth. He, like me, has been deceived.
> He does not know that your treaty is a lie and that I have never signed it.
> He does not know that you made my chiefs drunk, got their consent, and
> pretended to get mine. He does not know that I have refused to sell my
> lands and still refuse. He would not by force drive me from my home,
> the graves of my tribe and children, who have gone to the Great Spirit. . . .
> I have not signed any treaty, and I shall not sign any. I am not going to
> leave my land. I do not want to hear anything more about it.

Father Deseille supported him in this and also continued to favor chapels, schools, and agricultural pursuits, all suggesting Indian permanence and stability. His patience exhausted, the local Indian agent ordered Father Deseille to leave the public property or be arrested for disturbing the peace and alienating the Indians from the government. Deseille, acknowledging that he was not an American citizen (and thus might be deported), obediently left the reserve, returning to Pokagon's village for a brief period, then, seriously ill, came to Badin's mission by the two lakes. There was no other priest in the vicinity, although Indian runners set off to Chicago, Logansport, and New Albany to find one. Father Deseille asked his Indians to help him into the chapel, gave himself Viaticum, and died there in the arms of his Indians, a scene commemorated in the mural in the Log Chapel on campus today.[28]

With Father Deseille now gone and a crisis developing over removal, Bishop Bruté ordained young Benjamin Petit and sent him north from Vincennes to replace Father Deseille. After three months, he wrote of his Indians to his family back in France:[29]

> Ah, I love them tenderly! If you saw, when I enter a cabin, the little children who surround me and climb on my knees, the father and mother and elder children who gather together, piously make the sign of the cross, and then with a trusting smile come to press my hand—you could not help loving them as I do. . . . I am beginning to speak their language a little—to appreciate something of what they say to me. . . . I am truly happy. Do not wish anything better for me but that God protects us! This mission is menaced by approaching destruction—the government wants to transport the Indians to the other side of the Mississippi. I live between fear and hope, but I entrust my hope and fear to the hands of the Lord.

Although still only twenty-six years old, Father Petit had graduated both college and law school in France, he had practiced as an attorney for three years before entering the seminary, and he now assisted the Indians in drafting an appeal to Washington. The government eventually insisted, however, that the land sale treaties had been validly signed. During the delay, white settlers began to move into the disputed territory and the military was called in to preserve order. On September 4, 1838, the long-feared removal began under the watchful eye of the military. A few days later, the bishop gave Father Petit permission to accompany them, on condition that he return as soon as the march reached its destination. He gathered his few belongings and caught up with the march at Danville, Illinois.[30]

This Trail of Death covered 660 miles and lasted exactly two months, ending at Potawatomi Reserve, Kansas, in November. Approximately 800 began the march in September, some escaped along the way, at least 40 died, and Father Petit estimated that there were only 650 left at the end. He himself had been sick on several occasions, at one time remaining behind for nineteen days with fever. The daily journal he kept records deaths and burials, Masses when possible, occasional baptisms, shortages of food, heavy rains and changing temperatures, and impure drinking water. Leaving the Indians in the care of Jesuit Father Christian Hoecken at the Catholic Mission in Kansas, Father Petit began his return trip to Indiana on horseback. The long march and various sicknesses had weakened him terribly, and he could go no further than Saint Louis. The Jesuits there received him generously and gave him what medical attention they could, but nothing could be done. He died there peacefully on February 10, 1839.[31] It is appropriate that he, along with his predecessor missionaries Stephen Badin and Louis Deseille, lies buried in the Log Chapel on the Notre Dame campus, a replica of the one Father Badin himself had constructed in the early 1830s as the center of the Potawatomi ministry.

In 1840, this land in northern Indiana had first been offered to the Fathers of Mercy in the hope that they would be able to carry out Father Badin's stipulation that a college be established there. Father of Mercy Ferdinand Bach surveyed the situation but decided that it was not a project he and his community could undertake. He did purchase an additional 375 acres of land and then he returned everything back to the bishop. In 1841 Bishop de la Hailandière offered Father Sorin only Father Badin's original 524 acres, although he would later offer the second parcel also.[32]

Father Sorin and seven of the brothers left Saint Peter's on November 16 in one of Indiana's harshest winters. Two of the brothers, Francis Xavier and Gatian, were of the original group that had arrived from France, and the other five, only novices, had joined the community during the past few months at Saint Peter's. Of these five, four had been born in Ireland—Brother Patrick (Michael Connelly), Brother William (John O'Sullivan), Brother Basil (Timothy O'Neil), and Brother Peter (James Tully)—and one in Alsace, Brother Francis (Michael Disser). The latter four all departed from the community within ten years and only Brother Patrick, a butcher and candlemaker, remained longer, dying in the community in 1867. Brothers Vincent and Anselm remained in Vincennes, and Lawrence and Joachim and eight novices at Saint Peter's.[33]

With horses, a wagon, and an ox-drawn cart, the 250-mile trip north, over roads sometimes frozen, sometimes muddy, was slow and arduous. The group left Saint Peter's and went first to Vincennes where Bishop de la Hailandière blessed their undertaking and gave them $310 and a letter of credit to Mr. Alexis Coquillard in South Bend in the amount of $231.12½. They followed the Wabash River north to Terre Haute, where they felt they could not delay to visit a school recently founded there by Father Dujarié's Sisters of Providence, and then on to Lafayette. Somewhere along the trip Father Sorin decided to divide the group, with himself, four brothers, the horses, and the wagon going ahead, and three brothers with the slower ox-cart trailing at a more leisurely pace. The first group arrived in South Bend probably on the afternoon of November 26, were welcomed by Mr. Coquillard, and then made a quick two-mile trip to visit the property itself before retiring to South Bend to spend that first night with the Coquillards. They returned to the property in full light the next day, eager to see more precisely what they had been given.[34] Father Sorin wrote to Father Moreau a few days later:[35]

> Our arrival had been expected and much desired. . . . A few hours afterward we came to Notre Dame, where I write you these lines. Everything was frozen, yet it all appeared so beautiful. The lake particularly, with its mantle of snow, resplendent in its whiteness, was to us a symbol of the stainless purity of Our August Lady, whose name it bears. . . . Yes, like little children, in spite of the cold, we went from one extremity to the other, perfectly enchanted with the marvelous beauties of our new abode. . . . [A]s the weather was becoming colder, we made all haste back to the first lodgings that had been prepared for us in the village.

The property they surveyed was situated close to the Saint Joseph River, flowing southwesterly from its sources near Detroit and then making an almost right-angle turn to the north to empty into Lake Michigan, the river's abrupt turn to the north giving the then village of South Bend its unusual name. In his *Chronicles* Father Sorin notes that only 10 of the 524 acres had been cleared and prepared for cultivation, but that the soil was "suitable for raising wheat, corn, potatoes, cloves, buckwheat and all kinds of edible roots."[36] There were three buildings on the property at that time: Father Badin's forty-foot by twenty-four-foot log construction that had served as a chapel and priest's residence; a small two-story clapboard structure that served as a residence for an Indian interpreter, Charon, and his family; and a small eight-foot by six-foot storage shed. There were two lakes on the property—one of twenty-five acres and the other of seventeen—but because the marshy land connecting them was covered by that heavy November snow, Father Sorin thought it was one large lake and called the mission Notre Dame du Lac, Our Lady of the Lake.[37]

Father Sorin and the brothers could see that the most immediate need was for additional living accommodations. Residence space in Father Badin's chapel might be adequate for a single person, Father Badin or Father Deseille, but not for Father Sorin and seven brothers. Furthermore, snow and bitterly cold winds that winter easily found cracks between the roughly hewn logs around the windows, and spring rains would cause similar inconveniences. It was, in fact, so cold that Father Sorin could later write: "Even at Holy Mass, before taking the Precious Blood, I had to clasp the Sacred Cup in my hands, in order to melt the frozen Sacred Species." Brother Vincent, Brother Lawrence, Brother Joachim, Brother Anselm, and eight recruits were still at Saint Peter's or in Vincennes, eager to come north, but they could not be summoned until new lodgings were provided.[38]

Father Sorin decided to build a second log structure, a little to the east of Father Badin's chapel and about the same size, and, having no money to pay workmen, he appealed to the people of South Bend that December to donate either funds or their labor. Men did arrive and, despite the cold, felled enough trees to construct a building that was forty-six feet by twenty feet. The walls were put in place and then most of the men departed, leaving Father Sorin and the brothers to finish the project and add the roof. The building was completed and dedicated on the feast of Saint Joseph, March 19, 1843. The new accommodations were badly needed because Brother Vincent, Brother Lawrence, Brother Joachim, and the eight novices had arrived the month before, during the bitterly cold northern Indiana winter. One of the novices wrote that when they were hungry, Brother Vincent "would take a loaf, place it on the trunk of a fallen tree, and with an axe give it three or four heavy blows before he succeeded in cutting a piece."[39]

But Father Sorin's purpose in moving north was to begin a college, and this was his next project. In fact, the bishop had provided the land on condition that a college and an orphanage be established within two years. Father Sorin had discussed plans for a college building with an architect in Vincennes, a Mr. Marsile, and had arranged for him to begin construction that summer. The architect, however, did not arrive, and Father Sorin decided to construct at least a temporary college building to meet the bishop's deadline. He and the brothers constructed a two-story brick building near the shore of St. Mary's Lake that summer to provide a bakery, dormitory, and classroom space. That building, Old College, still stands today and, with two additional floors in front added, serves as a residence for college students studying for the priesthood. The building was ready for occupancy by the fall of 1843 and, with a small band of students—and even smaller curriculum—the college officially opened.[40]

In August of that year, the architect from Vincennes finally arrived with two workmen. Any funds that Father Sorin had were now depleted, but Mr. Byerley, who had recently moved from New York to South Bend, extended a loan of $500 and a line of credit for $2,000 in his store. While in Vincennes, Father Sorin and the architect had agreed on a building eighty feet long, thirty-six feet wide, and four-and-a-half stories high, and this was constructed on a rise a little further from the lake, approximately where the present Main Building stands. The ground floor was for the refectory, kitchen, recreation rooms, and washrooms. Classrooms, study halls, an art gallery, and the residence and office of the president were on the second floor. The third floor held private residences for priests, brothers, and lay faculty and student dormitories, and additional dormitories, a museum, and an armory were on the fourth floor. Hired workers could sleep in the garret. The building opened in the fall of 1844 and, with two wings added in 1853 giving it the appearance of an "H" or a double hammer, it was the complete college until the second Main Building was constructed in 1865.[41]

The additional accommodations were needed. Father Sorin and the first four brothers had arrived on November 26, 1842, and the three other brothers with the oxcart of supplies arrived a few days later. Brother Vincent, Brother Lawrence, Brother Joachim, and the eight novices followed in February, leaving only young Brother Anselm to teach in Father Delaune's parish school in Madison, Indiana, across the state from Vincennes. Later that summer, a second group arrived from France: Fathers Francis Cointet and Theophile Marivault; Brother Eloi (Jean-Marie Leray); Sisters Mary of the Heart of Jesus (Marie Savary), Mary of Bethlehem (Marie Desneux), Mary of Calvary (Marie Robineau), and Mary of Nazareth (Marie Chauvin); and seminarian François Gouesse. With these welcomed arrivals, Father Badin's chapel was converted into a carpenter's shop on the first floor and a residence for the brothers on the second, and Father Sorin's log structure served as a chapel on the first floor and the sisters' residence on the second. Finally, additional young men had arrived, as they had at St. Peter's, and asked to be accepted as brothers. In the fall of 1843, Father Sorin had made a retreat in a makeshift structure on the rise of land between the two lakes, called "The Island" at that time, and he decided that would be an attractive spot for a brothers' novitiate. A larger structure was put up and the novitiate opened in 1844 with Brother Vincent as novice master, but two years later, at the insistence of the bishop, the novitiate was moved to Indianapolis.[42]

Fortunately, the expanded facilities were needed not only for the expanding Holy Cross community but to accommodate the desired student population also. Five students arrived in the fall of 1843 to begin the new school year, and apparently seven others drifted in during the next few months. They lived, studied, and attended class in the newly constructed Old College building. By the close of the 1844–1845 school year, early records indicate that a total of forty students had been in attendance, although some perhaps for only a few or several weeks before returning home to assist with the farming or other family chores. Twenty or twenty-five might be the more accurate number.[43]

Father Sorin had hoped to organize his school on the model of the French *collège*, the only model he and the brothers knew, a six-year program combining two years of high school and four years of college, although few if any students who had enrolled qualified for the upper levels. As the bishop had required, Father Sorin also began accepting orphans from the beginning. These may have attended a class or two each day (reading, writing, arithmetic, catechism) but most of the day was spent working and learning a trade from the brothers—farming, carpentering, blacksmithing, tailoring, and so on, qualifying them for satisfactory employment on leaving the university.[44]

If the student population was a haphazard lot, the early curriculum may have been even more so. An early record described the offerings:[45]

> The Council of Professors assembled in F. Superior's room appointed F. Cointet to teach Latin and Greek; Bro. Paul for Writing and Mathematics; Mr. Riley for Oratory, Grammar, Orthography and Reading; Bro. Vincent for Mensuration; Bro. Augustine for Geography; Bro. Gatian for ancient and Modern History; Bro. Gatian was also appointed Professor of the French Language and Bro. Augustine to teach Botany and Zoology.

This seems a rather impressive list of offerings for a one-year-old wilderness school with no more than twenty-five students, and the daily schedule about that same time might give a more realistic picture of the academic levels:[46]

5:30 A.M.: All students rise (5:00 A.M. from May to August)
5:50 A.M.: "Vocal and Mental Prayer" in the study room, followed by Mass, and then a short study period.
7:30 A.M.: Breakfast, followed by recreation until:
8:00 A.M.: Study period.
8:30 A.M.: Class period: Grammar.
10:00 A.M.: Recreation.
10:30 A.M.: Class period: Writing.
11:30 A.M.: Class period: Reading.
12 noon: Dinner, followed by recreation.
1:30 P.M.: Class period: Orthography or Dictation.
2:00 P.M.: Recreation, two and one-half hours.

4:30 P.M.:   Class period: History and Geography (alternating days). Some students also took Bookkeeping at this time.

6:00 P.M.:   A spiritual conference to end the school day.

An advertisement in the *South Bend Free Press* announced the terms. Board, room, and tuition for regular, full-time students was $100 per year, day students paid $20 per year, and those boarding for only half a year $40. Students at the advanced classical level (with Latin and Greek, etc.) paid an additional $20, those taking other foreign languages (French, German, Spanish, Italian) paid $8 for each, and students paid $20 to take drawing or instrumental music.[47]

Most of the day-to-day work of the college was done by the brothers. When a Council of Professors was established in January 1844 to oversee almost all of college life, Father Cointet was named president and was the only priest appointed. He was joined by Brothers Vincent, Gatian, Augustine, and Paul, and one layman, a Mr. Riley.[48] The council met weekly and determined who would teach which classes and to what grade or level each student should belong, depending on previous educational background. The council also established the order of the day, the order in which the ranks of students should enter the chapel or refectory, and what penalties desultory or misbehaving students might receive. The attending students in those early years qualified for only the three lowest of the five or six levels, and a brother was assigned to oversee or supervise each one. The brothers also did most of the teaching, of course (Brothers Paul, Augustine, Vincent, and Gatian). The only priest-teacher was Father Cointet, offering Greek and Latin.[49] It seems, however, that all twenty-five students (if there were that many at any one time), whatever their ages, may have been taking many of the same basic courses—reading, writing, grammar, spelling, history, geography—with a few other options for more advanced students, and it also seems that botany, zoology, and mensuration, noted in the Council of Professors minutes, were not offered at first since no students qualified for them.

The brothers were doing most of the nonacademic work also. Only 10 of the 524 acres had been cleared when the first band arrived, but they set out immediately and cleared another 50 acres that first year and a further 50 acres or more the second year. The brothers working the land under Brother Lawrence could get fifteen to eighteen bushels of wheat per acre, twenty-five to thirty bushels of corn, and sixty to seventy-five bushels of potatoes. By that second year they were caring for 140 pigs, 85 sheep, 17 cows, 17 calves, 10 horses, and more than a dozen oxen. In addition, 200 fruit trees were planted near the lake, and necessary barns and storage sheds were constructed. Other farmhands needed to be hired but, as Father Sorin noted of the brothers: "This year [1844] they did almost all of the work themselves and thus they saved a considerable amount." The farm helped feed both the community and the students, and the produce left over was sold. Despite the early expenses, the brothers' farm was soon making a profit.[50]

The contributions of the Holy Cross sisters were similarly crucial for any success the mission would have. The first four sisters, ages 45, 25, 21, and 19, arrived in the summer of 1843, and for two years they lived on the upper floor of Father Sorin's Log Chapel, together with various creepy varmints occasionally seeking shelter from the winter snows or spring rains. The sisters immediately took charge of the linens, clothing, and laundry. The work was a challenge as one sister remarked that the brothers' clothing was so worn that there was no area left strong enough to sew on a patch. One of the sisters also found time to take care of the cows and chickens, another stepped in as infirmarian, and at least one of them washed the faces and combed the hair of the very young.[51]

Soon three young women arrived and asked to be received into the community. Father Sorin immediately notified Bishop de la Hailandière of his intention to establish a novitiate for them, but once again the bishop demurred. Father Dujarié's Sisters of Providence had established their novitiate in Terre Haute, also in the Vincennes diocese, and the bishop did not think there would be sufficient vocations for both. What to do? The Michigan state line was only five miles north of the Notre Dame mission, Bishop Peter Paul Lefevre of Detroit had met with Father Cointet and his companions on their trip from New York to South Bend, and Father Sorin asked the bishop if he could establish the sisters' novitiate in his diocese. The bishop was happy to have the additional religious, and agreed. When Bishop de la Hailandière heard of this, he immediately protested, and Bishop Lefevre notified Father Sorin that he was withdrawing his permission. Father Sorin left immediately for Detroit to plead his cause further and, fortunately, Bishop John Purcell of Cincinnati was visiting in Detroit at the time and he sided with Father Sorin. Bishop Lefevre granted his permission. Father Sorin acquired a suitable house from a Joseph Bertrand just across the state line, in a village Bertrand had founded (and named for himself), and the novitiate was established there. The laundry was sent from Notre Dame to Bertrand and the novices washed it in the adjacent Saint Joseph River, borrowing from a friendly neighbor a large boiler in which to heat water over an open fire. The sisters preferred the flowing river for laundering since it was clearer than the rather muddy Saint Mary's Lake. Food and other supplies were sent to the sisters in Bertrand from the farms at Notre Dame.[52]

A Mr. and Mrs. Louis Beaubien of Detroit also donated a piece of land for the sisters on condition that they care for two young orphans, and the sisters immediately began a school for them and others. Chief Pokagon's village was nearby and the sisters began to minister to the Potawatomi. Another ministry they undertook was to visit and comfort the sick and the aged in the area. On at least one occasion—and probably on several—a horse and wagon were not available and a couple of the sisters had to walk the five miles to and from Notre Dame for the food, supplies, or laundry. Father Cointet decided that this should not happen and gave the sisters five dollars (a large sum at that time, one-fourth of a year's tuition) to have for any emergencies. By the end of 1844, there were eleven sisters in the United States, six at Notre Dame and five in Bertrand, and the house remained in Bertrand until 1855 when a change in bishops made it possible to return the novitiate to Indiana.[53]

While the brothers and sisters handled most of the teaching and other chores at the school and on the farm, the priests were equally busy at Notre Dame and elsewhere. As president and religious superior, Father Sorin oversaw the religious life and ministries of all the Holy Cross priests, brothers, and sisters in the United States. He presided at the weekly meetings of the minor chapter, his board of advisors, and he was the liaison with Father Moreau and the motherhouse in France. It was apparently he who admitted or dismissed students and who decided what room, board, and tuition would be in terms of preferred land or livestock. He bought and sold land frequently and travelled widely throughout the Midwest to inspect acreage that was offered or was available. He oversaw the construction of new buildings and shops, down to the location of the necessary privies, and he found time in emergencies to substitute for teachers in the classroom, chiefly in Latin or writing. He and Father Cointet also provided the sacramental ministry—Mass, Confession, and spiritual conferences—for the sisters, brothers, and students. In addition to teaching Greek and Latin (and French in South Bend), Father Cointet regularly visited Catholic families in the surrounding areas, probably served as principal confessor for the sisters both at Notre Dame and Bertrand, and spent time with the Potawatomi Indians at Pokagon's village. Father Marivault also served for a time among the Potawatomi, assisting Brother Joseph (Rother) who was assigned there in 1843 and the Bertrand sisters who were caring for both the young and the aged at Pokagon's village.[54]

Although the small Holy Cross community had reason to be pleased with the progress it was making in only two years at Notre Dame, they faced challenges and difficulties. One of these was the ever-present danger of fire. The first of several fires broke out in December 1843 while the first college building was still under construction. A large furnace had been installed in the sand under the building and, during the night, a partition on the first floor somehow caught fire and, with scattered timber and construction discards strewn about, it could have spread rapidly. It was discovered in time, however, the brothers and hired workmen put it out, and no serious damage was done. Two other fires would occur within the next two years but Father Sorin refused to install even a lightning rod ("Fr. Sorin and his council preferred to trust in the guardianship of the Blessed Virgin"), although he did eventually take out a $3,000 insurance policy.[55]

An even greater concern of the small community was, to be expected, finances. Father Sorin and the brothers had about $380 in cash when they arrived at Notre Dame ($310 from the bishop from Father Delaune's collection and $70 from Mr. Byerley) and a bill of credit from the bishop for $230.[56] Even living as frugally as they could, purchasing bricks for Old College and the construction of the first Main Building left them deeply in debt. Father Marivault donated his family inheritance of a little more than $1,000 but it took time for this to clear the French legal system.[57] A Father Narcisse Hupier in France gave them $740, and Father Moreau sent what he could. The true savior of the mission was the Society for the Propagation of the Faith in Lyon and Paris because it sent approximately $2,500 a year to help spread the faith in the new mission. The school occasionally received land in lieu of tuition dollars (for example, the Beaubien grant to assist the sisters in Bertrand) and this could be sold also. The college's museum had been purchased from a Doctor Louis Cavalli of Detroit with money Father Sorin received from the sale of land there. On one occasion, Father Sorin was forced to borrow $2,000 from a Miami Indian chief trading furs near Fort Wayne. The balance of the cash on hand dropped to as low as $39.60 in November 1843, and by the beginning of 1844 the mission was approximately $4,000 in debt.[58]

The happy climax of these first two years came in early 1844 when the Indiana state legislature granted the struggling young school a full university charter. The local state senator, John Dougherty Defrees, South Bend lawyer and Methodist, had approached Father Sorin with the suggestion and Father Sorin immediately agreed. The charter of January 15, 1844, stated:[59]

> Be it enacted by the General Assembly of the State of Indiana, that Edward Frederick Sorin, Francis Louis Cointet, Theophilus Jerome Marivault, Francis Gouesse, and their associates and successors in office be, and are hereby constituted and declared to be, a body corporate and politic, by the name and style of the "University of Notre Dame du Lac"

and by that name shall have perpetual succession with full power and authority to confer and grant, or cause to be conferred and granted, such degrees and diplomas in the liberal arts and sciences, in law and medicine as are usually conferred and granted in other universities of the United States, provided, however, that no degrees shall be conferred and diplomas granted except to students who have acquired the same proficiency in the liberal arts and sciences, and in law and medicine as is customary in other universities in the United States.

It was indeed an impressive document for an institution numbering perhaps twenty-five students, mostly in their teens, and a faculty of eight, some of whose English might still carry an accent, and whose first college building, having survived a small fire the previous month, was still not completed and ready for occupancy. The charter was unrealistic for the present, but it opened outstanding possibilities for the future.

CHAPTER 3

Toward an American Institution,
1845–1854

On December 5, 1842, only ten days after arriving at Notre Dame from Vincennes, Father Sorin sent a long letter to Father Moreau, explaining in part:[1]

> While on this subject [the trip from Vincennes], you will permit me, dear Father, to express a feeling which leaves me no rest. It is simply this: Notre Dame du Lac has been given to us by the Bishop only on condition that we build here a college. As there is no other within five hundred miles, this undertaking cannot fail of success, provided it receive assistance from our good friends in France. Soon it will be greatly developed, being evidently the most favorably located in the United States. This college will be one of the most powerful means of doing good in this country, and, at the same time, will offer every year a most useful resource to the Brothers' Novitiate; and once the Sisters come—whose presence is so much desired here—they must be prepared, not merely for domestic work, but also for teaching; and perhaps, too, the establishment of an academy. And who knows but God has prepared for them here, like at St. Peter's, some good and devoted Novices? Finally, dear Father,

you may well believe that this branch of your family is destined to grow and extend itself under the protection of Our Lady of the Lake and of St. Joseph. At least such is my firm conviction; time will tell whether I am deceived or not.

Despite this confident prediction of success and great accomplishments for his school, not yet begun, in the following paragraph he surprisingly asks that someone else be appointed to direct the work:[2]

But the more I feel penetrated with gratitude for so many blessings from Heaven upon our work, the more do I realize my own incapacity to long direct the undertaking. . . . But, it may be asked, am I then tired of the work of the Brothers, and do I want to be recalled to France? No, Father, neither the one nor the other. I love the work of the Brothers as much, I think, as one can love it, and less than ever do I think of a return. But to declare everything without reserve, I love, too, the Indians of M. Deseille and of M. Petit. I thank Heaven that I am now among them. No, I cannot believe that it was without some special design that, for many years, God inspired me with so great a desire to labor for them; I cannot suppose that, without any premeditation on my part, He has brought me among them from so far, simply to see them without being of any service to them. Do not be afraid, dear Father, to wound my self-love by changing my first obedience. I shall be glorious, for I see nothing in the world to be preferred to the condition of a missionary among the Indians. . . . I am still young, I shall learn their language in a short time; in a year I hope to be able to understand them. . . . Let me then hasten to my dear Indians. Yes, it is settled—you grant my request—you permit me to look upon this flock, now without a shepherd, as my own portion. Thank you, Father; please write me as soon as possible, that I may see your permission with my own eyes. Tomorrow, or rather, this very day, I shall commence to study the language. When your letter comes, I may be able to return you my thanks in Indian.

What to make of this? Was it just a moment of discouragement when he suddenly realized how great the challenge was to begin a college in such a wilderness? Was he emphasizing the Indian ministry now in order to plead for increased funding in the future? Was he sincere, recognizing the tremendous need for priestly ministry among the natives and realizing that someone else could ably direct such a wilderness school? Whatever his motivation, Father Moreau apparently never responded to the request, and Father Sorin never renewed it.

The Indians, however, were not forgotten. In a letter to Father Pierre Chappé that same December, Father Sorin acknowledged that "I have not yet seen my poor Indians; they have gone hunting, not being aware of our arrival. . . . Their return is fixed for the 6th of January, and then I shall undertake to give them a retreat with the aid of an interpreter."[3] Once the hunters returned and the weather improved, he made an extended visit to them. "I stayed for three weeks at Pokagon with our dear Indians," he wrote that spring to Father Moreau. "I saw their savage tents, I ate and slept with them. I said the holy mass two times in the midst of these good savages."[4] In addition to catechizing and administering the sacraments on this visit, Father Sorin also tried to unravel a land dispute between the Indians and the diocese. A priest-successor of Father Petit may have tricked Potawatomi Chief Pokagon into selling 674 acres of his property to the diocese. Father Sorin here sided with the Indians against the diocese, encouraging the bishop "to renounce, purely and simply, all his rights to the land," and later the circuit court, in fact, invalidated the sale.[5] Within a year Brother Joseph was assigned to assist at Pokagon's village, two sisters opened a school in Bertrand, and in 1845 Father Marivault was delegated to work with the Indians also. Father Louis Baroux replaced Father Marivault in 1847 and served, off and on, until 1852 when he was succeeded by Father Almire Fourmont (Fourmond). However, in part because of a serious internal dispute between Father Sorin and Father Moreau, the bishop of Detroit no longer welcomed Father Sorin's religious to active ministry in his diocese. Father Fourmont decided to leave the Congregation of Holy Cross and join the diocese of Detroit, continuing his work at Pokagon's village, and the religious ministry of the Holy Cross to the Potawatomi in Michigan came to an end.[6] Father Sorin himself, however, did not forget them. In his Last Will and Testament, written in 1892, he provided:[7]

> Fourth. Moreover, apprehending that I may possibly, although unintentionally, have done wrong or caused injury to anyone, I hereby, as an act of reparation more specially directed, give and bequeath unto Saint Joseph's Orphan Asylum, at Lafayette, in this State, the sum of five hundred dollars ($500), the same to be used or distributed as may seem meet for the benefit of orphans of the Indian race, whom may God in his bounty pity and protect.

Whatever Father Sorin's interest was in the local Potawatomi Indians in these early months at Notre Dame, his primary concern was now to found a college. That was the principal reason for leaving St. Peter's in southern Indiana and that was one condition the bishop imposed when offering the property in northern Indiana.

For a newly arrived French Catholic community, however, to found such a public institution could be a questionable undertaking amid a growing anti-Catholic and anti-immigrant animosity pervading much of the United States at the time. The anti-Catholic newspapers *The Protestant* and *The American Protestant Vindicator* were founded in the 1830s, and Samuel F. B. Morse published his *Foreign Conspiracy against the Liberties of the United States* in 1835. An Ursuline convent in Charlestown, Massachusetts, was torched in 1834, Catholic churches were burned in Philadelphia in 1844, and Catholic Saint Louis University was threatened by a mob.[8] In May 1842, a recently immigrated Catholic priest in southern Indiana was falsely accused of assaulting a young woman after hearing her confession, he was convicted in a celebrated public trial and sentenced to five years in prison, and was eventually released by the governor and restored to active ministry through the intervention in 1844 of the wife of President-Elect James Knox Polk.[9] Father Sorin himself was concerned, as his *Chronicle* indicated:[10]

> All the surroundings were strongly Protestant, that is to say enemies more or less embittered against the Catholics. . . . Moreover, it was added that the Pope of Rome had already sent Fr. Sorin ninety thousand dollars and that he would send another ten thousand to make the even number. A little later, when the walls of the college began to appear, people seemed to take delight in saying that we might go ahead with our college but as soon as it was completed they would burn it down.

Notre Dame's neighbors never did burn down his college, of course, but Father Sorin was determined to demonstrate over time that his college and his community were in no way foreign and had nothing to hide. For that first end-of-year celebration in 1845, he sent out formal invitations to some of the leading families, Catholic and Protestant, of South Bend, Mishawaka, and Bertrand. The invitation read:[11]

> The Revd E. Sorin presents his respects to Mr. Miller and would be pleased to receive him and his family at Notre Dame du Lac on Friday

July 4th at ½ past 7 o'clock P.M. to participate in the celebration of the Anniversary of American Independence.

It was an "open house" evening: guests were encouraged to wander the grounds, and tours were arranged of the dormitories, dining areas, and the few surrounding buildings. The most popular attraction proved to be the museum, recently purchased from a doctor in Detroit and described by a contemporary as "a splendid collection of beasts, birds, fishes, reptiles, antiques, etc., from the various parts of the globe."[12] The formal program began that evening in the college music room with a solemn reading of the Declaration of Independence by one of the lay professors, followed by an academic address probably delivered by Father Michael Shawe, recently arrived from England and a professor of history and literature. The evening concluded with a short theatrical presentation by the students in full costume. The applause was loud and prolonged, Father Sorin judged the evening a great success, and the guests were invited to return the next month for the awarding of student prizes.[13]

The visitors had reason to be impressed. Although Notre Dame was in no sense a university—rather a rural boarding grade, middle, and high school—the landscape had certainly changed over three years. At the center of the campus was the new college building, eighty feet in length and thirty-six in width (about twice the length and width of the present Log Chapel), four stories in height, plus an attic. The ground floor contained the dining room and kitchen on one side, and a study hall and furnace room on the other. The main entrance was to the second floor, and to the right was the parlor and Father Sorin's room, and to the left the museum and the exhibition hall. The third floor held rooms for the professors, a library, and, for a time, the infirmary. The fourth floor contained the student dormitories, rows of wooden beds separated by curtains. The attic held sleeping quarters for the brothers, and the building was mounted by an eighteen-foot tower and cross.[14]

A half-acre of mostly cleared land, but with a few impressive oak trees, lay in front of the college building surrounded by a fence and with two small cottages on either side of a central gate, one for a layman operating a small store for student needs and the other for Brother Cyprian, the school porter and community shoe-maker. Southwest of the college building and closer to the lake stood Father Sorin's log cabin and the Old College building, both now in transition. The log cabin still served as the main church for the students and the few Catholics in the surrounding area, and, with the students and professors moving into the new college building, the sisters moved from the log cabin into the vacated Old College structure and continued their work of cooking and laundry and caring for the youngest of the students. The area further to the south of the lake was farmland, with the necessary rough barns and storage sheds. Behind the college building and to the north were the shops of the brothers who provided maintenance work for the institution and mentored the apprentices in the various trades. On the so-called "island" between the two lakes stood the brothers' novitiate, also a place of quiet retreat for Father Sorin and other religious seeking relief from the hectic pace of the growing institution.[15]

Construction continued at a moderate rate over the next ten years. Sister Mary of Providence had arrived at Notre Dame in November 1843 and was soon named infirmarian. If she had an office at all, it was probably at first in the brick Old College building, and then moved to the third floor of the new college building when it was completed in late 1844. As enrollment, and perhaps illnesses, increased, additional space was needed and a new structure was completed the following year, behind and to the east of the college building. It was sixty by twenty feet, two stories high, with the printing and probably other apprentices' shops on the ground floor and a few rooms on the second floor comprising the infirmary.[16] Sickness, of course, had plagued the university from the beginning. Brother Joachim had died in April 1844, Brother Paul one month later, and a sufficient number of students could be feeling ill at any one time that a sister-infirmarian could be a full-time position and a separate infirmary building, apart from the regular living quarters, seemed advisable.[17]

With the student population increasing, Father Sorin's Log Chapel was becoming too small for religious exercises of students and religious together, and the walk from the college was certainly inconvenient in bad weather. There was no money in 1847 to build a larger church, but that August Father Sorin decided to begin anyway. The construction took two years, chiefly because it had to be halted occasionally until the necessary funding could be found. The final structure was ninety feet in length, thirty-eight in width, and twenty in height, with twin spires in front, and it stood only a few feet to the west and south of the college. The stained glass windows were made by the Carmelite Sisters in Le Mans, some of its statuary was donated by King Louis Philippe of France, and the chancel organ held 1527 pipes. The church, dedicated to the Sacred Heart of Jesus, was solemnly consecrated by Bishop Maurice de Saint Palais of Vincennes in November 1849.[18] A few years later, Father Sorin, on a visit to France, purchased a magnificent carillon to enhance religious worship and call the community together for prayer, but the spires proved too weak to bear the carillon's weight and a two-story bell tower was built in front of the church in 1852.[19] As the number of regular students increased year by year, so did the number of apprentices. Many of these were orphans, sent by relatives or by local clergy, and none were admitted under the age of twelve. They were assigned to separate dormitories in the college building, but there were always rivalries and even hostilities between them and the regular academic students.[20] With different schedules, there were advantages in housing the apprentices in a separate building, so in 1848 a Manual Labor School building was constructed behind (a little to the north and west of) the college, approximately where Brownson Hall later stood.[21]

The building was large enough to include (besides the dormitories and some shops for the apprentices) a bakery, sacristy supplies, and other storage rooms, but, unfortunately, it caught fire during the night of November 18 the following year. Despite the efforts of the brothers, other workmen, and students, almost nothing was saved. No one was injured but all the clothes and bed linens of the apprentices and the sacristy supplies were destroyed. Father Sorin estimated the loss at 16,000 francs, or about $3,200.[22] Fundraising efforts were begun immediately: two local women solicited donations in South Bend, Niles, Detroit, and Cincinnati, Father Baroux was on a fundraising trip to France, and the Society for the Propagation of the Faith contributed over $1,000. Eventually almost $4,000 was collected.[23] Construction was begun immediately, but this time in front of the college, approximately where Walsh Hall now stands and closer to the farm fields and sheds. It was completed in September 1850, was seventy-seven feet in length, and included (in addition to the Manual Labor School) a bakery, a refectory, an infirmary, and private sleeping quarters.[24]

In 1853 the college building itself was becoming too small and a wing was added at each end. Each wing was forty feet in width but sixty feet in depth, giving the building then the shape of an "H" or barbell. The wings were chiefly divided into dormitories, the former dormitories were converted into classrooms, and the total capacity was increased to 250, although less than one hundred students were then enrolled.[25]

At the same time, a new residence was provided for the increasing number of sisters. The new and enlarged Manual Labor School building in front of the college now housed the infirmary and apprentice shops, and the former infirmary, to the northeast of the college building, may have been converted into a residence for the sisters, or perhaps a new residence was constructed nearby. The sisters were then closer to the college building and the students they served than when living in the Old College building on the shore of the lake.[26]

Early records of the university indicate that the students on special occasions put on theatrical exhibitions and musical performances, and lessons in vocal and instrumental music were available almost from the beginning. A band was organized early on also. It seems probable that there was no college band as early as 1845 since, at the end-of-year ceremonies on July 4 that year, a band from South Bend arrived and provided the music. In 1846, instrumental music was taught by seminarian François Gouesse. He requested space in the Main Building where his students could practice, and premiums (awards) were given to the most accomplished musicians at the end-of-year ceremonies. The Council of Professors' minutes note that, during those ceremonies, "Our pupils will play a few pieces at the distribution (of premiums)," suggesting a band may have been formed. There is also a reference to a cornet band being organized that year: on one occasion it attempted a concert from a raft on the lake, the raft overturned, the musicians got soaked, and some of the instruments may still lie on the bottom. The band was clearly functioning the following year, a separate Music (or Exhibition) Hall was constructed about this time to the east of the Main Building, and several persons taught in the area of music: Francois Gouesse, Brother Basil, Professor Maximilian Girac, and two or three others.[27]

The academic curriculum of the young institution grew as slowly, and as haphazardly, as the physical plant. In theory it was divided into two tracks: a preparatory course for those seeking a basic general education and a Latin course for those desiring to pursue a teaching career or an advanced degree. There were five grades or levels in each track, as distinct from six in the French system. An entry in the register of the Council of Professors for September 2, 1844, lists the courses for each level of the preparatory course—appropriate levels of reading, writing, spelling, religion, history, French, mathematics, and geography—and notes that no student at the time qualified for the highest two levels. No curriculum was given for the Latin course, probably indicating that no student was qualified for, or interested in, that program either.[28] The only textbooks mentioned were "Mr. Emerson's Arithmetic, Mr. Mitchell's large Geography and Mr. Hales History of the U.S.," and it appears that Father Sorin in some ways did want to Americanize the French boarding school he was founding. Classes were small, with close student-teacher contact, students were called on regularly for class recitation and were given written assignments ("duties" or "tasks" they were then called), and awards and prizes were announced periodically.[29]

The program remained about the same for the next two years, with the school years beginning in early October and closing in late July. The classes taught, and examined, in the spring of 1846 were reading, grammar, poetry, history, geography, arithmetic, Greek, Latin, French, religion, and bookkeeping. There was also a class in linear drawing, and music lessons were available. The fact that examinations were scheduled for both Greek and Latin indicates that some students had enrolled in the Latin track by that date. Two brothers, Moses and Louis Letourneau, were among the first.[30]

By the start of the 1846–1847 academic year, the faculty realized that changes needed to be made. An entry in the register of the Council of Professors stated boldly: "Whereas our plan cannot be followed to advantage in America, as it is directly opposed to American virtues, Mr. Shawe shall be requested to write to Georgetown, St. Louis and St. Mary's Emmitsburg, to have their plans of studies that we may compare them with ours and form a plan for ourselves."[31] The Jesuits at St. Louis, and maybe others, responded. The curriculum at Saint Louis was based on the late sixteenth-century *Ratio Studiorum* (Plan of Studies) of the Society of Jesus, adapted throughout the years to different times and places. If the program was succeeding in Saint Louis, it would probably succeed also at Notre Dame, and it was at least worth the attempt. The issue was discussed throughout the 1848–1849 academic year and put into operation with the beginning of classes in the fall of 1849.[32]

The curriculum was confirmed as a six-year program, with two years of preparatory studies (the Junior Department) and four of college studies (the Senior Department). In the first year of the Junior Department, the student took reading and writing, English, Latin, and Greek grammar, and Greek, sacred, and United States history. In the second year, the student continued in most of these, substituted ancient and modern history for Greek and sacred history, and added arithmetic and bookkeeping.[33]

Each year of the Senior Department was given a title: "Humanities," "Poetry," "Rhetoric," and "Philosophy." In the first or "Humanities" year, the student translated the Latin of Caesar, Sallust, Virgil, and Cicero, the Greek of Xenophon and Lucian, had writing exercises in three languages, and studied algebra and geometry. In the "Poetry" year, the student translated Livy's *History*, Virgil's *Aeneid*, Cicero's *Orations*, and Horace's poetry in Latin, Homer's *Illiad* in Greek, and enrolled in advanced prose writing, surveying, trigonometry, and analytical geometry. In the third or "Rhetoric" year, the student translated Tacitus and Quintillian in Latin, more Homer and Demosthenes in Greek, and took composition in Latin and English, rhetorical analysis, and "debates on grave subjects." In the final, "Philosophy," year, the student was enrolled in logic, ethics, metaphysics, moral and natural philosophy, chemistry, and anatomy. In most years, lessons in music, drawing, French, German, Spanish, and Italian were available for an additional cost. A bachelor of arts degree was awarded on the completion of the six-year program, and a master of arts degree after one or two additional years of study, or after admission into one of the learned professions.[34]

This was the program Notre Dame announced over the next several years, a program similar to those at Georgetown and Holy Cross, and one not out of step with the influential *Yale Report of 1828* that favored retention of Greek and Latin, but there were clearly no students qualified to enter those last few grades, and no faculty to teach them.[35] This was a vision into the future at best. But Notre Dame had been chartered as a *university*, this was a program a *university* might offer, and Father Sorin was probably bold enough to believe that, if and when qualified students arrived, he would somehow have begged, borrowed, or stolen a faculty qualified to teach them.

An earlier historian of Indiana could ridicule such classical education: "One cannot be serious even yet," he wrote in 1923, "thinking of half a score of brawny youths with huge bare feet and one suspender each, crooning over Greek paradigms, while all people of the state fought the equal battle with the primitive forest, swamps, and wild varmints."[36] If he was including Notre Dame in this criticism, it was at least an exaggeration. Not all students were country bumpkins. Young William Corby of Detroit was, according to one historian, the son "of one of the wealthiest landed proprietors in the country," Patrick Dillon had been schooled in both his native Ireland and in Chicago, Eugene O'Callaghan had studied English and mathematics in Ireland, Neal Gillespie attended school in Brownsville, Pennsylvania, Edmund Kilroy in New York, and Peter Cooney in Michigan.[37] It is uncertain how solid their pre–Notre Dame education was but, obviously, not all students had "huge bare feet and only one suspender," some came from well-to-do families, and three of the above—Corby, Dillon, and Kilroy—eventually became college presidents. The academic program was sufficiently respected that the diocese of Milwaukee in 1849 sent four of its seminarians to study at Notre Dame, at a cost of sixty dollars each.[38]

Of course, many students did not want such a classical education, and many fathers did not desire it for their sons. A priest from Fort Wayne wrote to Father Sorin in 1848:[39]

> The children of Mr. Wolke have written to their father to know what he wanted them to study. Mr. Wolke does not intend his children to follow any of the learned professions, but wants for them a business instruction.

English language, its grammar, composition, etc., Arithmetic, Elements of Algebra and Geometry, Modern Geography and as extensive religious instruction as practicable, is all he expects from them. Next year he may allow them to take an instrument of music, but for the present he thinks they have enough to learn.

For these Father Sorin set up a so-called "commercial track," a shorter course that eliminated the advanced classical language courses and substituted additional English, mathematics, bookkeeping, and similar courses. Father Sorin was in favor of giving students the choice. "This new plan presents a great advantage in the United States where everyone wants to be free to study what he likes. It pleases everybody."[40]

Student discipline, if not a major problem, was at least an ever-present concern. Boys will be boys and despite the fact that a priest, brother, or seminarian seemed to be present as prefect or overseer whenever the students assembled, normal boarding school frictions, pranks, and antagonisms occurred. Corporal punishment was discouraged, and more common punishments seemed to be depriving the delinquent of tea or a second piece of bread, or the deduction of merit points toward premiums of honor.[41] By 1846–1847, however, the situation had become alarming to some.[42] The minutes of the Council of Professors offer the clearest evidence but it must be noted that these were taken by the council secretary, Brother Gatian, who (along with Father Gouesse) often strongly disagreed with Father Sorin's administration. On January 14, 1847: "All the rules being violated with impunity and every possible disorder being allowed by the Superior, F. Gouesse asked a dispensation from his conference for three weeks as it would be absurd to go and speak to the pupils about unimportant rules, when the most essential were laughed at"; and "Bro. Gatian said that there were insufferable disorders in the college, but that there was no possibility of correcting them, as long as Superiors adhered to their temporizing plan."[43] A special meeting of the council took place four days later, and the problems did not seem so severe:[44]

The Council assembled on this extraordinary occasion to devise some means of correcting the general insubordination now existing among the pupils—the principal disorders to be corrected were stated as follows: disobedience, going to town without leave or companion, pushing, touching (except in very regular games), holding their hands in their pantaloons, talking and hissing in the ranks, talking in the chapel; also staying in bed on Sunday morning and on other days.

Three students did pose special problems. One was Louis Lafontaine, son of a Miami Indian chief in nearby Huntington, Indiana, apparently in Brother Gatian's class primarily, and he appeared frequently in the council's minutes: "Bro. Gatian said that he could do nothing with Mr. Lafontaine; that impunity had spoiled him and that he should be either exemplarily punished by F. Cointet or the Superior, or dismissed without delay."[45] "Bro. Gatian said he could not keep Mr. Lafontaine in his classes any longer because the latter demanded privileges which could not be consistently conceded."[46] "Bro. Gatian spoke of Mr. Lafontaine . . . [he] is almost irretrievably spoiled; his desires have been too indiscriminately gratified and if he intends staying any longer should return without delay to his class."[47] Father Cointet agreed, reporting that "his duties are seldom complete" and that he "grins, laughs, and plays during class . . . [is] always talkative and turbulent . . . refractory and disobedient."[48] When Father Sorin declined to discipline the student, either because he did not want to forfeit the tuition or because he did not want to antagonize the boy's father from whom he had recently borrowed $2,000, Brother Gatian referred to Father Sorin sarcastically in the minutes as "the Rev. mild-measure-taking Superior."[49] Discipline problems seem to have run in the family. When his brother enrolled in Notre Dame two years later, the council minutes repeat earlier criticisms—of both an unruly student and a less-than-cooperative president: "When Mr. Thos. Lafontaine's turn came and Bro. Gatian asked for his dismission [sic] for having three times attempted to strike Bro. Stephen and having made use of horrible oaths and cursed his professors and overseers, the President, in direct violation of the rules, declared himself absolute, by the very fact of his not only refusing to dismiss him, but even to consult the Counsellors, according to the laws of custom, in order to ascertain what should be done with him."[50]

The third student of concern was a local boy, whose mother was a friend and benefactor of Father Sorin, and once again Brother Gatian was a prosecutor. "Brother Gatian asked how long Mrs. Coquillard would be allowed to dictate Rules to Notre Dame du Lac University, whereupon the Council answered that [her son] should be treated as any other boy and that he should not be allowed to see his mother except for good conduct."[51] "Bro. Bernard said that Mr. Coquillard was ungovernable. But nothing was done to remedy this evil."[52] "If order must be established next year, Mr. Coquillard ought not to be readmitted."[53] "The 7th article of the last Council was modified as follows: either Mr. Coquillard shall not be received or his parents shall leave us perfectly free to treat him as we see fit."[54] "Mr. Coquillard was received in spite of all the remonstrances of every professor and overseer, becoming worse every day, the Counsellors again asked that he should be dismissed and F. Superior promised to see his parents that they might not send him to school any longer."[55]

The minutes clearly expose the differences between the president and some of his faculty, especially Brother Gatian and Father Gouesse. Father Sorin certainly did not want to lose essential tuition money by expelling students, and money was almost certainly a major concern in the cases of these particular students. The fathers of both of these boys had loaned Father Sorin large sums, possibly unknown to the other councilors, and he did not have the wherewithal to repay the loans had they been recalled.[56]

But Father Sorin also seemed to be veering slowly away from the stricter discipline of a traditional French boarding school, which Brother Gatian and others may have preferred, and toward a more tolerant American policy. Joseph Lyons, a former student and later professor has written:[57]

> It was natural that the whole system of French college discipline should at first be introduced, or at least that an attempt should be made. Yet in those early days the Founder of Notre Dame quickly seized the peculiarities of Young America as distinguished from Young France. We well remember the transition from the stringent measures required by the lively and giddy French boys to the broader liberty given to comparatively more sober and sedate Americans. Like a judicious man, who, instead of transplanting a tree to a strange soil and thereby running the risk of losing it, takes its most thriving branches and engrafts them on a strong and thrifty tree of native growth, thus bettering both grafts and tree, especially the tree, Father Sorin did not impose the European system of discipline, but merely grafted on the system of the country those regulations which perfected it, and made it bring forth good fruit instead of the bitter Dead Sea fruit that the unmodified American system too frequently produces.

Discipline was only one part of a student's training at Notre Dame; religion was another. The university's *Catalogue* at the time stated:[58]

> The religion professed in the institution is Catholic, but in reception of pupils no distinction of creed is made, and there is no interference with the principles of non-Catholics. Good order, however, requires that all should conform with decorum to the usages of public worship. Catholic

parents may rest assured that the most zealous care will be exercised over their children, in respect to frequent and regular compliance with their religious duties, and that no effort will be spared to instruct them fully in the principles and obligations of their holy religion.

The "most zealous care" was indeed exercised. Rising each day was at 5:30, followed by a period of vocal and mental prayer and then Mass. There were prayers before (and probably after) each meal, an examination of conscience, and a spiritual conference and night prayer each day. There seems to have been a second (High) Mass each Sunday, and afternoon Vespers and Benediction. Students went to confession each month, periodic daylong retreats were scheduled, and there were special devotions to the Blessed Virgin during May. All Catholic students had classes in religion.[59]

There were apparently two voluntary religious associations that the students might join. The first was the Archconfraternity of the Sacred and Immaculate Heart of Mary, canonically erected at Notre Dame by Bishop de la Hailandière on January 1, 1845. The archconfraternity was open only to Catholic students in the Senior Department and its goal was to pray, through the intercession of the Blessed Virgin, for the conversion of sinners throughout the world. A second association was the Society of Holy Angels. This was a society open to members of the Junior Department and younger pupils, and its goal was to ask the holy angels to assist them in remaining pure and holy and in fulfilling their religious duties, one of which was serving at Mass and other liturgical ceremonies.[60]

The spiritual director of the archconfraternity, and the organizer of a weekly Nocturnal Adoration Society, was Father Alexis Granger.[61] He had been born in Daon, France, in 1817, and, after early studies at home, entered the College of Château-Gontier at the age of fifteen, the same college where Father Moreau had studied twenty years earlier. He then transferred to the major Seminary of Saint Vincent in Le Mans (where he undoubtedly made the acquaintance of Father Moreau) and he was ordained a priest in 1840. After two years as a parish priest in the diocese of Le Mans, he requested admission into Father Moreau's small band of auxiliary priests, made a year of novitiate in 1843–1844, and was then sent to the United States to serve with Father Sorin, his seminary companion at Saint Vincent's from 1836 to 1838.[62] Although he would hold several high administrative offices during his years at Notre Dame—vice president, director of novices, pastor of the parish, assistant provincial, and provincial superior—he apparently never overcame his natural shyness nor lost his French accent. He was a man of prayer and deep spirituality, a very popular confessor, and a guide to several generations of Notre Dame students on their journey of faith. An early student on his graduation thanked Father Granger for his assistance:[63]

> I am again about to leave home and embark once more upon the world. I feel grateful to God and his Blessed Mother, for having guided me this far through its perils. I rejoice at having been a member of the Adoration Society and of the Arch Confraternity [*sic*]; and feel that I am now reaping the fruits of the sweet hours I spent at the feet of Jesus and Mary in that dear chapel of St. Aloysius. . . . I feel under great obligation to you, dear father, for your untiring zeal and care in watching over me, yours has been truly, like a father's ———[*illegible*].

The brothers' novitiate had been constructed on the "island" between the two lakes in 1844 and the chapel was dedicated to Our Lady of the Angels. Father Sorin (and others) used to repair there for periods of retreat, prayer, and quiet. Father Granger's archconfraternity and the Society of Holy Angels held their religious exercises there, and it was also the chapel of the weekly nocturnal adoration.[64]

Despite the solid progress being made in the fledgling school in the wilderness of northwest Indiana, problems had developed, perhaps serious ones, and Father Moreau sent his associate, Father Victor Douelle, to Notre Dame to see for himself and make a firsthand report. Father Moreau had hoped to make the visit in person but the outbreak of the revolution in February 1848 made that unfeasible. The major issues involved some combination of personnel, finances, and religious autonomy.

Father Augustin Saunier was at the center of one such controversy. St. Mary's College, about fifty miles southeast of Louisville in Kentucky, had been founded in 1821 and had been staffed by the Jesuit fathers since 1833. In early 1846, the Jesuits decided to leave the college and take over one in New York (now Fordham University), and the auxiliary bishop of Bardstown asked Father Sorin to replace them in Kentucky.[65] Father Sorin was on the verge of departing for France but replied that he was willing to accept the four-hundred-acre plot and establish an English school. He would present the proposal to Father Moreau on his visit, confident of his approval. He also asked Father Julian Delaune, in nearby Madison, Indiana, to take a careful look at the property and send him a full report in France. Father Delaune did even more and signed an obligation to purchase the

Jesuits' furniture and supplies for approximately $2,000. That amount, approximately 10,000 francs, was requested by the bishop from the Society for the Propagation of the Faith but, after a delay of four months and through a clerical error, only 2,000 francs were appropriated, about $400. Father Delaune went ahead and reopened the school with approximately fifty students, more than at Notre Dame at the time. Father Moreau and his assistants, becoming concerned, asked Father Sorin to remain at Notre Dame and sent Father Saunier to Kentucky as their representative instead. On his arrival in Kentucky, Father Saunier, a seminary classmate of Father Sorin, began to countermand most of the decisions Father Delaune had made and may have hoped to establish a college to rival Notre Dame, with himself as president. With more delays, and with some confusion over who was actually in charge—Sorin, Delaune, or Saunier—Bishop Martin Spalding of Louisville, running out of patience, decided to reclaim the college for the diocese, the Jesuits agreed again to staff it, and Father Saunier eventually departed from the Congregation of Holy Cross.[66]

Father François Gouesse was also a source of difficulty. He had been sent to America as a seminarian in 1843, together with Fathers Cointet and Marivault; he began to offer classes in music, and he was also named prefect of discipline. As noted earlier, he generally sided with Brother Gatian in opposing Father Sorin's more tolerant exercise of discipline. After his ordination to the priesthood in 1847, he served for a time at the college in Kentucky and in an orphanage that the Congregation had opened in New Orleans. Father Gouesse apparently had a serious drinking problem, which was possibly why Father Sorin did not want him at Notre Dame, but Father Moreau may not have known this and had appointed him religious superior in both Kentucky and Louisiana. Father Sorin strongly opposed both appointments. Father Gouesse was eventually recalled to France, and he was later dismissed from the Congregation.[67]

A third thorn in Father Sorin's side was, of course, Brother Gatian. Only fifteen when he was assigned to accompany Father Sorin and the others to America, he was undoubtedly talented. An early historian called him "a genius, an incomprehensible Frenchman. He was capable of doing anything and everything. He was at that early day the intellectual soul of the institution." He mastered English quickly, began teaching mathematics, French, and bookkeeping almost immediately, and was a frequent critic of Father Sorin's leadership. But he also had serious personal problems, could be a disruptive force among the students, and Father Sorin made several attempts to assign him away from Notre Dame. He eventually left the Congregation and, seriously ill, managed to return to his father's farm in France, where he died at the age of thirty-four.[68]

There were frequent disputes between Notre Dame and the motherhouse in Sainte-Croix over finances, and this was probably to be expected. With members increasing and schools spreading out across both France and the United States, Father Moreau needed to know that revenues were balancing expenditures, and bookkeeping at Notre Dame could be quite haphazard. Father Sorin simply never took the time to keep meticulous books, and perhaps he could not anyway. He needed students and if their families offered to pay in livestock or crops or acreage, even at distances as far as Chicago or Detroit, he accepted. As one historian has noted, good bookkeeping "was all very well for France, where business was conducted in legal tender, but in Northern Indiana transactions were often conducted according to the barter system, and there was no place on the French ledger to show a balance of seven pigs and a barrel of molasses."[69] Land and livestock prices could wobble up and down with the seasons and the weather, and Father Sorin sold when prices were high or when he simply needed to pay debts. He took risks with his spending—buying Doctor Louis Cavelli's museum in 1845 and later putting a massive golden dome on his college building—and at times he had to spend in emergency, such as after the fire of 1849, but overall, all his collecting of tuition (in money or in kind), his buying and selling of land, and his begging from the Society for the Propagation of the Faith kept the university solvent. A ledger entry for June 1847 shows receipts of $39,965 over the preceding six years (including Saint Peter's) and expenditures of $39,391, showing a balance of $574. The entry also notes outstanding current debts in the amount of $3,979, but debts owed the institution and property available for sale amounting to $8,436.[70] The figures are probably close to accurate, with allowance for estimated values of "pigs and molasses," and the fiscal balance was possible only because the priests, brothers, and sisters received no salaries.

Closely allied to the questions of finances and risk-taking was the matter of religious obedience. Father Sorin had pronounced his religious vows of poverty, chastity, and obedience before Father Moreau that August 1840, and in his religious life he was to be guided by the will of Father Moreau. Distances at times, however, made it wholly impractical to seek that will. When Bishop de la Hailandière offered him a choice of the Saint Francis settlement in eastern Illinois or Saint Peter's in Indiana that October 1841, he obviously could not delay the decision the three or four months it would take to hear from France. He transferred from Saint Peter's to Notre Dame du Lac without seeking any permission. He had to rebuild the Manual Labor School and the apprentices' sleeping quarters after the fire of 1849 without delay also. With a twelve- to sixteen-week delay in getting messages to and from France, Father Sorin simply made decisions and acted independently as situations in far-off northern Indiana developed, and superiors in France became increasingly concerned. Father Sorin did at times ask the advice of the minor chapter that Father Moreau had established, but he also ignored their advice when he wished.[71]

Father Drouelle, accompanied by five brothers and three sisters, left Le Mans on May 28, 1848, and spent several weeks visiting the Holy Cross institutions in Canada.[72] He arrived at Notre Dame on September 1 and began his official visit. He was deeply impressed with the physical progress. He remarked that where a heavy forest had covered the land only seven years before, now 327 of the 617 acres were under cultivation. The farm included twelve English thoroughbreds, twenty-five heifers, twenty cows, and two hundred pigs. It was already considered one of the finest farms in the area and he knew Father Moreau would be pleased to learn of such progress. He had praise for the program of studies that Father Sorin had borrowed from the Jesuits in Saint Louis but he did not think highly of the students, considering them "of an extremely independent character, proud to the point of haughtiness, and so cold as to make one forget they are children."[73] He seemed satisfied with the religious life the community was striving to live amid the uncertainties of such a young foundation, and was especially impressed with the quiet retreat of the brothers' novitiate on the "island" between the lakes: "A few feet further on, we find the Brothers' novitiate. In the choice of the location and the arrangement of this dwelling place of true peace, we have a wonderful expression of the pious sentiments which caused them to rise here in the midst of savage nature."[74] He had words of praise for Fathers Cointet and Granger, and especially for Father Sorin:[75]

> At the end of this room which serves as a recreation room, reception room, and music hall for these gentlemen, we find a sort of little workroom, where Father Sorin maps out his pious projects, writes his heartstirring appeals to the charity of his numerous friends, and draws up plans with his fellow workers, as with people who form only one heart and soul with him, regarding the good to be done and the sacrifices to be imposed upon themselves. There he listens to the respectful suggestions of some and the disrespectful outbursts of others; there he is obliged to pass out to others consolations which he does not himself have and to give them the encouragement which is refused to him.

He also took time to visit Pokagon's village and saw the work of Father Baroux and the sisters:[76]

The inhabitants were scattered along a very irregular line around the lake, in poor huts with no other opening than the door and the chimney, without provisions and without furniture. When I saw our Lord in the barn, the priest in the cabin, and the Sisters in the stable, and when I saw the savages in their rags, I was on the point of giving way to sadness. . . . But before long the dignity and the poverty of the sanctuary, the joy and the courage of the religious, along with the simplicity and evident satisfaction of the natives, made me look at things in an altogether different light. . . . I had never had before me any more perfect picture or more heart-touching representation of the apostolic life of the early missions.

Father Sorin had to be pleased, and relieved, with the report he knew Father Drouelle would carry back to France.[77]

It was fortunate for Father Sorin that the visit occurred when it did because the report would have been much less favorable two or four years later. Financial problems had haunted the university from the beginning but they were accentuated after the fire of 1849. The new plan of study was in place, student enrollment was increasing, and Father Drouelle's favorable report eased relations with France, but continued progress depended on further funding. Reports were circulating about the discovery of gold in California and the opportunities it offered for instant wealth. It was a risk, of course, but Father Sorin was never one to shy away from one of those. The minor chapter minutes of September 28, 1849, note:[78]

Whereas our debts, and of course, their interest, are constantly increasing; whereas we do not see any ordinary means to be able for a long while to pay so many debts, we have unanimously resolved to make use of a means, which, though it will appear strange and extraordinary to some, is in no way unjust or unlawful. That is, three Brothers will be sent to California to dig gold. . . . None of these will go but by his own accord.

Eventually four brothers and three laymen were selected for the trip. The leader was Captain George Woodworth, aged forty-five and a former naval officer recently moved from New York to South Bend. The other two laymen were Gregory Campau and Michael Dowling, both former Notre Dame students and both apparently still affiliated with Notre Dame in some capacity. Brother Lawrence, farmer, businessman, and one of the original brothers coming to America with Father Sorin, was named second-in-command. Brother Justin was the oldest of the group at fifty, he came from France as a shoemaker and taught that trade to the apprentices. Brother Placidus was a baker and apparently had no formal education since he did not sign his name but only marked with an "X." Brother Gatian was the fourth but why send this "intellectual soul of the institution" on such a trip? Father Sorin boldly suggests a reason in his *Chronicles*: "Brother Gatian was going to leave the Society to marry, and to settle down near the college. He consented to depart for those distant regions." He was also struggling with a strong attraction to one of his students, and Father Sorin apparently decided it was better for him to be absent from the college at least until he could reconcile his sexuality with his religious vocation.[79]

Father Sorin invested $1,500 in the venture, and it set out on February 28, 1850, with eight horses pulling two wagons, and perhaps a spare horse or two. Their supplies included 100 pounds of ham, 50 pounds of sausage, 75 pounds of sugar, 100 pounds of salted codfish, and a few gallons of whiskey and brandy each. The trip west took four and a half months along rivers and grasslands, in rain and mud, through snow and desert, to Independence, Fort Laramie, around the Great Salt Lake, and into Placerville (Hangtown), California. There were delays along the way as they had to wait at times until the vegetation had grown high enough to feed the horses—and their own nutrition was spotty, as Brother Gatian noted on May 19: "Mr. G. Campau mixed beans, pepper sauce, pork, molasses, tea and bread. I tasted the mixture and found it excellent. Capt. Woodworth tasted it and puked."[80]

The expedition was a failure—and worse. Only a few flakes of gold were discovered, horses were sold to purchase food and supplies, Brother Justin brought in some money making and repairing boots and shoes, others hired themselves out for odd jobs as needed, all took sick at one time or another, Brother Placidus died there—without the ministry of a priest—and Brother Gatian finally decided to withdraw from the Congregation. Brothers Lawrence and Justin returned to Notre Dame empty-handed in early July 1851. Father Sorin had taken the risk, he had not asked permission of Father Moreau, Holy Cross had lost two members, and, due to expenses, it was poorer rather than wealthier. The whole project had been a major blunder, and Father Moreau was understandably and rightfully critical when he learned of it.[81]

Bad as it was, the expedition to California was not Father Sorin's biggest blunder. That would occur two years later. Father Moreau had founded his small community in 1837 with the permission and approval of the bishop of Le Mans but by 1850, with nearly four hundred total members in several countries, he was seeking the official approbation of Rome. On November 15, 1851, while this approval was under discussion, a high-ranking cardinal in Rome wrote to Father Moreau and asked if he might be willing to send some of his missionaries to serve in East Bengal, India, hinting that official approval of his Congregation might come more quickly if he assented. The mission would be centered in Dacca, and the priest-superior would presumably be named its first bishop in time. Father Moreau and his counsellors, after long and serious consideration and with some assurance that the Society for the Propagation of the Faith would fund the necessary travel and first-year living expenses, agreed to the mission in the summer of 1852.[82]

But who should lead the mission to East Bengal and become its first bishop? The person, first of all, should have some missionary experience and be able to adjust to a radically different culture and explain Catholicism to peoples perhaps wholly unfamiliar with it. Second, the person should know English since India was still a British colony. One possibility was Father Granger, but, for all his fine qualities and even deep spirituality, he was not a strong, or even effective, administrator. The faculty complained that the good order of the college declined when Father Sorin was absent and left Father Granger in charge.[83] Another option was Father Cointet but he had recently been appointed superior of the Holy Cross community in New Orleans and had contracted a serious fever there. That left, of course, Father Sorin, and he seemed to have all the qualifications desired— command of English, missionary experience, administrative abilities, and even episcopal potential. On September 13, 1852, Father Sorin was notified that he was Father Moreau's choice for India.[84]

Father Sorin objected strongly, and replied on October 6: "I need to declare to you in my own person that after mature reflection before God, I believe it my duty to refuse unequivocally the charge you wish to impose on me, unless the pope himself should order me to accept it. I have absolutely neither the knowledge nor the virtues required to make a good bishop." The Holy Cross community in the United States supported Father Sorin, insisting that, if he were reassigned, the outstanding ministry that he had established would almost certainly fall into ruin. His strong leadership would be missing and worried creditors would demand their loans. The archbishop of Cincinnati and the bishop of Chicago both wrote to echo these sentiments.[85]

The controversy dragged on, in part because of the time lag getting letters to and from France, and because Father Sorin was also embroiled in a dispute over the leadership of the community in New Orleans. Father Cointet was to be reassigned to Notre Dame to replace Father Sorin, and Father Gouesse was to be the new superior in New Orleans. By this time, Father Sorin had lost all confidence in Father Gouesse, and even the archbishop of New Orleans had noted: "It is a great calamity that he should be a priest; but it is ridiculous that he should be a religious." Father Sorin spent several weeks in New Orleans in an effort to resolve the issue and returned to Notre Dame in early 1853 to readdress the Bengal question. He sought advice of a canon lawyer friend in France, spoke with the new bishop of Vincennes, Maurice de Saint Palais, and took the difficult decision to separate for five years the United States Province of Holy Cross, of which he was provincial superior, from the rest of the Congregation.[86]

Father Moreau then decided to send another visitor to the United States, Father Pierre Chappé, who had pronounced his religious vows the same day as Father Sorin. After a few weeks in Canada, Father Chappé arrived at Notre Dame on September 7 where Father Sorin received him as a personal friend but not as an official visitor since he now considered himself separated from Father Moreau's jurisdiction. Father Sorin remained adamant throughout the discussions and Father Chappé was discouraged. Then, on September 20, as Father Chappé was preparing to leave Notre Dame for New Orleans, Father Sorin asked to see him and agreed to withdraw the separation and accept the assignment to Bengal. Father Moreau relented also, appointed Father Michel Voisin to Bengal, allowed Father Sorin to remain as superior at Notre Dame, but removed him as provincial superior and named Canadian Joseph-Pierre Rézé as provincial superior of both Canada and the United States.[87]

In the midst of these serious personal blunders and embarrassments, and in the face of increasing anti-Catholic feeling across the nation, manifested in the rise of the American or "Know-Nothing" Party in the early 1850s, Father Sorin continued his efforts to demonstrate his, and his institution's, loyalty and patriotism. On January 4, 1850, he became a United States citizen, and that same year he apparently petitioned the federal government to establish a post office at Notre Dame. This was turned down, but after much prayer—"The Blessed Virgin and St. Joseph were alternately importuned by all the house," the *Chronicles* state—a post office was commissioned the following year through the sponsorship of Senator Henry Clay of Kentucky. Father Sorin himself was appointed postmaster. It may not have been a major financial benefit to the university but it certainly was a convenience. The regular stage from Logansport to Niles, Michigan, would now stop at Notre Dame with mail three times a week, conveniently picking up and dropping off passengers right at the entrance to the campus. As a post road, the access would always be cleared also. This latter benefit was enhanced when Father Sorin was named inspector of public roads at about that same time, and it became part of his responsibility to see that the roads were passable. At that time, everyone was taxed for road maintenance but one could be exempted by volunteering time to work on the roads oneself, and Father Sorin occasionally assigned apprentices to road work to relieve the university of this tax burden.[88]

Father Sorin was demonstrating his Americanism by his public service, and he was not averse to suggesting the political influence he might wield in local elections if he chose to do so. He admitted this openly in his *Chronicles*:[89]

> It may not be out of place to remark that it is important for an Institution like Notre Dame du Lac, generally looked upon by Americans with all the prejudice of the public against convents, to come into close contact with neighbors and to take an interest in all that concerns the general good of the area, to show zeal in those matters and to convince everyone that we are citizens in heart as well as in name. . . .
>
> For these reasons, Father Sorin recently judged it advisable to present himself with some Brothers at the elections for the offices of the area. He has done it only once, but the results only make him regret that he did not begin to do it sooner. From this time, even the most insignificant offices brought him some candidates, honest men who are always disposed to act fairly toward the Institution and toward Catholics in general.
>
> Perhaps there is no people that nourishes a greater desire for offices. Hence, it is easy to guess what consideration an Institution will have in their eyes which can decide two-thirds of all the local elections. The Presbyterians in particular are galled at seeing their power with all its consequences in the hands of a Catholic priest. In fact, if it is only used prudently, it is a precious resource both for the House and for the locality because of the good choice that can be made of public officers.

Father Sorin was not only an American but a political power broker.

CHAPTER 4

The End of An Era (?),
1855–1865

Sickness is always a problem at boarding schools. Sore throats, runny noses, upset stomachs, and slight fevers are common, and living in such close quarters only enables the illnesses to spread. As early as 1843, one in the first group of sisters was assigned as infirmarian, and a separate infirmary building was begun the following year. But the situation at Notre Dame did not seem normal, and the sicknesses seemed much more serious. The land along the lakes was considered unhealthy even before the community arrived from Saint Peter's, and two brothers took sick and died in early 1844: Brother Joachim in April and Brother Paul in May. In the fall of 1846 Brother John the Baptist and Brother Anthony both died, as did Joseph Garnier, a postulant for the Holy Cross community. The following year Sister Mary of Carmel died, and also William Richardville, who was an orphan, the son of a local Miami Indian chief, and the first regular student to die. Father Sorin and Brother Gatian were both sick that summer, and reports of illnesses on campus may account for the limited enrollment that fall.[1]

A much more serious outbreak occurred in the summer of 1854. In July two young persons died, a postulant for the Holy Cross sisters and an apprentice, but neither of these deaths seem related to the epidemic that followed. That epidemic, some combination of fever, typhus, and dysentery, struck first in Bertrand where Sister Mary of St. Aloysius Gonzaga and Sister Mary of St. Anastasia were taken that August, and two sister novices and one postulant also died. It then struck Notre Dame and one professed brother, Dominic, and four brother novices— Clement, Joseph, Cesaire, and Daniel—passed quickly. In September, Father John Curley, ordained only one year, died, to be followed shortly by a student and then Father Cointet, Father Sorin's trusted assistant. Of Father Cointet's death, Father Sorin wrote: "I was in no way prepared for it. The day I saw that Father Cointet was going to die my mind almost failed me. I still cannot get it into my head that he is really gone. . . . The void he has left behind grows more frightening every day." In all, twenty members of the small community must have succumbed to the disease that summer, one-fifth of the total number. When the students returned in the fall, hurried arrangements had to be made for the classes of teachers now gone, and even most of those available to teach had been seriously weakened by the disease. Neither the students nor the people of South Bend learned of the seriousness of the affliction since most burials were carried out at night and other excuses could be made for absences, and only a few students contracted the illness, with perhaps two dying. "We are reduced to burying our dead secretly," Father Sorin wrote. "Every day for the past week we have been going in silent procession to the cemetery."[2]

There were two additional deaths the following spring, Brother John of the Cross and young Mr. Louis Devos, a novice for the priests and also a teacher at the college, and questions were once again raised about the healthiness of the location. Deaths had occurred in the summer, fall, winter, and spring, and thus weather did not seem to be a factor. Some wondered if at least a few of the fish in the lakes might be poisonous, or one of the local herbs. Others worried that it might be the well water, although Father Sorin insisted that "it was just as cool and agreeable to drink as possible." The most common opinion centered on the marshy land between the two lakes. In times of heavy rain and flooding, the area might come in contact with campus sewage, other germs might grow there, and it was an ideal breeding ground for flies and mosquitoes to spread the germs abroad. A stream from the spring-fed lakes to the nearby Saint Joseph River passed through the property of a Mr. Rush, and he had built a dam to prevent the lakes' run-off. In 1847 and 1848, Father Sorin had attempted to get the dam lowered through legal action but was unsuccessful. He then proposed buying and demolishing the dam but Mr. Rush refused. Stymied on that front, Father Sorin and the brothers first sought to dig a ditch themselves and drain the marsh or to fill in the marsh with dirt, but both efforts failed.[3]

The deaths of 1854–1855 made action all the more urgent and Father Sorin was, if nothing else, a man of action. The resolution actually began well. On the same day that Brother John of the Cross was buried, Mr. Rush called on Father Sorin and offered to sell his property between Notre Dame and the river for $8,000, $1,000 less than he had offered previously, to be paid over the next four years. Discussions continued for four days, an agreement was reached, and the final papers were signed, but Mr. Rush then suddenly left town before the deed and down payment could be exchanged and the contract filed. Had it all been a ruse and did Mr. Rush never intend to complete the sale and lose his property? Did he learn the details of the serious illnesses and deaths and decide that Father Sorin would pay even more? That is not clear. It was now Holy Thursday and Father Sorin ordered five or six of the workers, possibly brothers, to march over to the dam and tear it down, regardless of any opposition they might meet. One historian says that he then went off to offer Mass. The bold action took Mr. Rush by surprise. He was not a well-liked citizen and most of South Bend apparently sided with Father Sorin in the dispute, and Mr. Rush eventually agreed to finalize the exchange of necessary documents.[4]

Closing the deal came at a most opportune time because Saint Mary's Academy in Bertrand, operated by the Holy Cross sisters, needed to be relocated. As early as December 1842, Father Sorin had written to Father Moreau: "Once the sisters come—whose presence is so much desired here—they must be prepared, not merely for domestic work, but also for teaching; and perhaps, too, the establishment of an academy."[5] This the sisters did. With funding from the Society for the Propagation of the Faith, and on the seventy-seven acres donated by the Beaubien family of Detroit, a two-story building with a one-story annex was constructed in 1846, and a nearby log cabin was connected at one end to serve as a chapel. A few novices were sent to Notre Dame for lessons to prepare them better for teaching, and one or two others to Kentucky to study music and art.[6] Fifty students were enrolled in 1850, and an early prospectus paints an attractive picture:[7]

ST. MARY'S ACADEMY, BERTRAND MICHIGAN
Under the direction of the Sisters of Holy Cross

This institution is beautifully situated in a healthy and pleasant location on the bank of the St. Joseph River, four miles from Niles and six from South Bend. A daily line of stages running from the former town to the latter, and passing through Bertrand, forms the connection between the

Michigan Central and Southern Railroads, and renders access to the academy easy from all parts of the country. . . . At all times the sisters guard with maternal vigilance the pupils entrusted to their charge, regarding them as a precious deposit, for which they will be responsible to their parents and to God. . . . The institution possesses fine philosophical and chemical apparatus, globes, and a planetarium. . . . Pupils of all denominations [are] received and [there is] no interference with their religious opinions, but discipline requires that all should conform with decorum to the public worship of the Catholic Faith. . . . In case of sickness, due notice is given to parents who, should they prefer leaving their children at the academy, may rest assured that they will receive excellent medical attendance and careful nursing. A skilled physician connected with the College of Notre Dame visits the institution weekly, or oftener if necessary.

The basic cost seemed to be fifty dollars per semester, with an additional six to ten dollars for each course in art, music, or languages. The prospectus ends with the notice: "At St. Mary's the Sisters of the Holy Cross have also opened a school for deaf-mutes. Terms $100.00 per annum."[8]

Although the school made good progress under the direction of Mother Marie du Sauveur, imported from Canada for this purpose, problems began to appear. The village itself was not growing and businesses were not attracted to the area. The five-mile distance from Notre Dame was also a disadvantage, especially in winter weather. Finally, relations with the bishop of Detroit had become strained. With the resignation of Bishop de la Hailandière and his return to France in 1847, Father Sorin had relocated the sisters' novitiate back to Notre Dame. Bishop Lefevre had not approved. He forbade any communication between the sisters still in Bertrand and those at Notre Dame, and he even forbade Father Sorin to hear the confessions of the Bertrand sisters. By 1855, it was time to close the school at Bertrand and re-establish it on the property recently acquired from Mr. Rush.[9]

One of the more fortunate events in the history of Notre Dame and St. Mary's, and even of the Church in America, was the arrival of an extraordinarily talented young woman to assume the directorship of the relocated St. Mary's Academy. Eliza Gillespie had been born in Washington County, Pennsylvania, in 1824, had reportedly learned to read at the age of three, attended an elementary school operated by the Dominican Sisters in Somerset, Ohio, and later graduated from the Visitation convent school in Georgetown, DC. Her younger brother, Neal, is often considered Notre Dame's first graduate because he and James Shortis received their degrees in 1849, the university's first commencement, and since the degrees were probably awarded alphabetically, Neal may have been the first. Eliza's aunt, Maria Louise, had married Ephraim Blaine, and thus her son, James G. Blaine, later a prominent statesman and presidential candidate, and Eliza were first cousins. Eliza's sister, Mary Rebecca, married Philemon Ewing, whose sister, Ellen, became the wife of General William Tecumseh Sherman. Eliza taught for a brief period at St. Mary's Seminary for girls in Maryland, and then she decided that God was calling her to the religious life.[10]

In the spring of 1853, Eliza and her mother set out for Chicago where Eliza intended to enter the Sisters of Mercy, with a stop along the way to visit Neal who had recently decided to enter the Congregation of Holy Cross at Notre Dame. As their carriage approached the main entrance of the university, they happened to meet Father Sorin who, now the postmaster, was on his way to carry mail from the Notre Dame post office to the train in South Bend. They spoke very briefly, and then Father Sorin boldly announced: "Miss Gillespie, you are the one I have been praying for to direct our Sisters." Eliza did not need to reply because Father Sorin had to return to his mail delivery, but the following morning he renewed his request: "Say no more, please, about going to Chicago to be a Sister of Mercy. God has called you here to be a Sister of Holy Cross."[11]

Eliza was twenty-nine years old, mature and thoughtful. A priest who knew her well once told her mother: "Eliza should never marry; I do not know a man who is her mental superior." She was not one to make snap decisions but would certainly consider all options. She and Neal drove to Bertrand to visit the sisters there, she saw the meager resources they had, and she visited the classroom where the sisters, some still struggling with English, were doing their best to teach the children. She told Neal and her mother that she wanted to spend another three days there in prayer and quiet retreat to consider her decision fully. On the third day her mother came with a carriage, and Father Sorin came with her. When Eliza saw Father Sorin she is reported to have knelt before him and said: "Give me your blessing, Father. I have come to be a daughter in your House."[12]

On April 17, 1853, Eliza received the religious habit of Holy Cross and the name Sister Mary of Saint Angela. She was then sent to France to make her novitiate with the Sisters of the Good Shepherd at Caen and to study how best to teach deaf-mutes. She pronounced her perpetual vows before Father Moreau in Le Mans on December 24, 1853, and Father Sorin was in France for the occasion.

On their return to the United States, Father Sorin appointed her directress of the academy in Bertrand, and thus she was the first directress of St. Mary's Academy when it relocated back to Indiana.[13] The relationship between the two would grow through the years, an almost father-eldest daughter relationship. She was ever caring and concerned, obedient when necessary, but always a talented, highly respected, and almost equal partner in numerous joint ventures.

Relocating St. Mary's from Bertrand back to Indiana was the most important of many concerns Father Sorin had during his years as United States provincial superior or provincial vicar (1855–1866), but there were many others as well. By 1855, parishes had been opened in Mishawaka, Lowell, St. John's, LaPorte, and Michigan City; the brothers were staffing schools in Cincinnati, Louisville, Toledo, Hamilton (Ohio), and Milwaukee; the sisters were serving in schools in LaPorte, Lowell, Michigan City, Mishawaka, and St. John's; and the Congregation had apostolates in New Orleans and New York.[14] Over the next ten years, schools were opened in Baltimore, Philadelphia, Columbus, Zanesville, Fort Wayne, Madison (Indiana), Alton (Illinois), and South Bend. In Chicago, the Congregation staffed a college and four parish schools with two priests, ten brothers, and nineteen sisters, but a serious misunderstanding with a newly appointed bishop led them all to be withdrawn after only three years.[15] Much of Father Sorin's energy, administrative talent, and travel time was absorbed in opening, maintaining, and sometimes closing such far-flung establishments, and he did not delegate well to others. Notre Dame, and its growth and progress, was never his only concern.

But growth and progress did continue. Student enrollment increased from approximately 150 in 1857 to 203 in 1860 to 540 in 1864.[16] By that latter date the students were clearly divided into four groups—apprentices in the Manual Labor School, the Minim Department, the Junior Department, and the Senior Department—although the numbers in each group are not always certain.

The Manual Labor School grew out of the orphan program Father Sorin had promised Bishop de la Hailandière he would establish, and for which he received a charter in 1844, the same year in which Notre Dame was chartered as a university. The prospectus for the Manual Labor School in 1855 read:[17]

> In this Department, conducted by the "Brothers of St. Joseph," boys are taught several useful Trades, and receive, at the same time, a good, common education. They are constantly under the vigilant and paternal care of the Brothers. Their moral and religious training are the special objects of an association of men who devote their lives and energies to the noble

task of preparing the children of the poor to become good Christians and useful members of society.

The number of apprentices that year was forty-five, not all, of course, orphans. They had to be at least twelve years old when they entered, and they stayed until twenty-one. They were required to pay a fee of fifty dollars on entering, have sufficient clothing for one year, and they would receive clothing valued at fifty dollars when leaving. The trades taught were farming, carpentering, tailoring, shoemaking, bookbinding, and blacksmithing; the apprentices' work clearly benefitted the college; and they were paid a small wage for their work starting at age eighteen. In 1864, the entrance fee had risen to one hundred dollars, and the prospectus that year spoke of "children of the laboring class" rather than "children of the poor."[18]

Boys younger than twelve may have been admitted into Notre Dame almost from the beginning, and by the mid-1850s a stable and regularized program had been established for them. The university *Catalogue* stated: "In this course are admitted the very young Students of the Minim Department, who are carefully taught by highly competent female teachers, Spelling, Reading, Writing, and the elements of English Grammar, Geography, History and Arithmetic, so as to fit them, after a lapse of time more or less extended, for the higher branches of study."[19]

These youngsters, aged six to thirteen, were under the supervision of Holy Cross sisters and brothers, they had their own eating and sleeping areas in the college building until their separate residence, St. Edward's Hall, was built in the 1880s, and they had their own separate recreation field. For the very young, the sisters combed their hair, tied neckties, put out their clothes each morning, and helped them wash. Prizes were awarded periodically for politeness, good behavior, and success in their various studies. They were the special favorites of Father Sorin, and he called them his "princes;" they always had a part to play in festivities for his feast day; and he almost invariably brought them special treats after his trips, often a bushel of fruit. The minims, eventually reaching numbers as high as 150, would be part of the Notre Dame community until 1929.[20]

The Junior or Preparatory Department was a two-year program intended primarily to prepare students for standard college courses. Each student who applied to Notre Dame was given an examination by the prefect of studies and was placed in the class for which he seemed most prepared and qualified. In the first decade of its existence, almost all Notre Dame students were taking a majority of preparatory classes, but by the mid-1850s there was a clearer distinction between the Junior and Senior Departments. In the Junior Department, most of the teaching was apparently done by the brothers; classes in English, Latin, history, mathematics, writing, geography, and catechism predominated; and much personal attention was given to each student. Students were called upon to read publicly in class, to recite lessons learned, and to work out problems on the blackboard before the class. The university *Catalogue* noted that each student "is encouraged and incited in every possible manner to study, and should he make unusual progress, he is not allowed to be retarded by his classmates, but he is promoted to a higher class." Although the Junior Department was intended to be a preparation for college courses, many students entered the program simply to receive a basic (high school) education with no intention of continuing on to college. Throughout the whole of the nineteenth and early twentieth centuries, students in the minim, manual labor, and preparatory programs always outnumbered those in the strictly college program.[21]

The Senior Department, or Collegiate Course proper, was by the 1860s being referred to also as the Classical Course, and it led to the bachelor of arts degree (see table 4.1).[22] Opportunities to study French, German, Spanish, Italian, Hebrew, painting, drawing, and music were available. Since the number of students in the Senior Department was still not large—not more than five graduated with the bachelor of arts degree in any year before 1883—the faculty of twenty could conveniently cover all these classes as needed, and apparently almost all were needed. In 1860–1861, prizes were given to students for high academic success in the Senior Department for Latin (four years), Greek (two years), Christian doctrine, English grammar, rhetoric, orthography, bookkeeping, mathematics, French, German, elocution, and instrumental music; in the Junior Department for Christian doctrine, English grammar, algebra, arithmetic, geography, United States history, scriptural history, orthography, and elocution; and in the Minim Department for catechism, arithmetic, geography, grammar, orthography, reading, composition, letter writing, and penmanship.[23]

For those who did not desire the classical education, or who did not have the money or the four years to devote to it, a Commercial Course was provided in the mid-1850s (see table 4.2):[24]

> Students who propose to apply themselves to Mercantile pursuits, will find in this Institution all possible advantages to attain their aim. The course is conducted by Professors thoroughly acquainted with whatever appertains to business or commercial transactions.

Table 4.1. Classes in the Classical Course (1860s)

First Year
Latin (Grammar, Sallust, Virgil)
Greek (Grammar, Xenophon)
English
Mathematics (Algebra)
Modern History

Second Year
Latin (Grammar, Cicero, Horace)
Greek (Grammar, Xenophon, Homer)
English
Mathematics (Geometry)
Ancient History

Third Year
Latin (Cicero, Horace, Christian Lyrics)
Greek (Demosthenes, Euripides)
English (Debate)
Mathematics (Advanced Geometry)
Physics (Natural Philosophy, Chemistry)

Fourth Year
Latin (Tacitus, Perseus)
Greek (Plato, Herodotus)
Natural History (Botany)
Logic

Latin (Grammar, Sallust, Virgil)
Greek (Grammar, Xenophon)
English
Mathematics (Algebra)
Modern History

Latin (Grammar, Livy, Horace)
Greek (Grammar, Homer)
English
Mathematics (Trigonometry)
Ancient History

Latin (Tacitus, Juvenal)
Greek (Sophocles, Thucydides)
English (Debate)
Mathematics (Calculus)
Physics (Natural Philosophy, Chemistry)

Latin (Quintillian, Plautus)
Greek (Aristotle)
Natural History (Geology)
Metaphysics and Ethics

Source: *Catalogue*, 1863–1864, p. 14.

Table 4.2. Classes in the Commercial Course (mid-1850s)

First Year	Second Year
Arithmetic	Algebra
English	English
Book-Keeping	Book-Keeping
German	German
Geography	Geography
History	Commercial Law
Writing Lessons	Elocution

Source: *Catalogue*, 1863–1864, p. 15.

The course extends over two years; but candidates for admission into it must have already acquired a fair knowledge of Grammar and Arithmetic.

The program proved most successful. Four students received final diplomas in the Commercial Department in 1860, five in 1861, and seventeen in 1864.[25]

By the mid-1860s, there were also optional academic societies to assist students in learning and advancing outside of class. The first of these was the St. Aloysius Literary and Historical Society. According to the *Catalogue*, the "object of this Society, organized in 1851, is the cultivation of Eloquence, and the acquisition of an accurate knowledge of History. Being essentially a Debating Society, its members cannot fail to acquire a certain facility in writing, and fluency in debate. Its ordinary meetings are held every week."[26] The university offered a Thespian Society to encourage "the cultivation of Dramatic Art and the Study of Elocution" and a Philharmonic Society "to afford its members the opportunity of perfecting themselves in the theory and in the practice of Sacred and Secular Music, and to give dignity and spirit, by their performance, to the celebration of our Religious, National, and Literary Festivals."[27] For the Junior Department exclusively, the university in 1860 established the Philopatrian Society "to accustom its members, by means of oral discussion, to speak with ease and fluency on useful and interesting subjects."[28]

Student discipline did not seem to be as major a concern as it appeared earlier to Brother Gatian and Father Gouesse. The Council of the Faculty still met weekly, and most of the matters discussed were routine—who could fill in and teach linear drawing, should an algebra class be divided into two, and what students merited premiums or deserved to sit at the table of honor in the refectory—and disciplinary problems surfaced only sporadically. Non-Catholic students who refused to kneel for prayers before and after class were given the choice of conforming or leaving, students occasionally visited faculty or staff members in their private rooms in violation of the rules, three students were expelled for having "a bad book" in their possession, and the smoking regulations were not always obeyed. Punishments could vary from a breakfast of only bread and water to expulsion, and any corporal punishment, apparently quite rare, could still be administered only by an officer of the university.[29]

By the charter of 1844, Notre Dame was empowered to grant "such degrees and diplomas in the liberal arts and sciences, and in law and medicine, as are usually conferred and granted in other universities of the United States," and this included graduate degrees. Ten years later, the *Catalogue* (1854–1855) announced:[30]

A candidate for the degree of Master of Arts must have pursued the usual classical course and have undergone an examination in Moral and Natural Philosophy and in Chemistry; and if he can give satisfactory proof of having pursued the study of Philosophy and Literature for three years after leaving College or should he be admitted to any of the learned professions, he may receive the degree of Master of Arts.

This does raise a question. The student who spends three years in the study of philosophy and literature after the bachelor of arts degree may deserve an earned master of arts degree, but if one is simply admitted into "any of the learned professions" at that time, without additional study, should that master of arts degree be considered not earned but honorary, an honor for that professional acceptance? The university did not always make a distinction between earned and honorary degrees in its official publications. The first master of arts degrees were awarded in 1859 to Rev. E. B. Kilroy and Rev. Eugene O'Callaghan, with no indication whether they were earned or honorary, but in 1864, three were awarded: earned degrees to Joseph Lyons and Timothy Howard and an honorary degree to J. B. Runnion. The number of master's degrees increased steadily in succeeding years.

Campus life was rather quiet for a time after the terrible blunders of the California venture and the temporary withdrawal from Holy Cross in 1853, but misfortune struck again in 1856. This time it was another fire, the constant worry and bane of the university. Fire had broken out in the first college building in December 1843, the following year a student meddling with a stove had caused another small fire, a third fire had started in one of the college building chimneys in 1846, and the Manual Labor School had burned in 1849.[31] The fire in 1856 began on the bitterly cold night of December 17 in one of the barns close to the lake and the Old College building. The cause was uncertain but candles were being made in a room next to the stables and the fire may have started there. It was not discovered immediately and when it was finally extinguished, two or three horses had been killed, large quantities of corn, oats, salt, and meat had been lost, and farm implements had been destroyed. Arson was suspected by some, as a local paper noted: "For such we believe it to be from the fact that valuable horses were in the stable attached to the College buildings during the Conflagration of Sunday Night last, and only the remains of three were discovered, proving conclusively that the other valuable horse was taken by the incendiary and that he set fire to the building so as to mislead the proprietors of the College as to the real intention of his villainy." But the wind fortunately was not strong enough to blow the flames, at times fifty feet high, as far as the church and the college building, and these were saved. The damage was estimated at $3,000, and once again with no insurance on nonresidential buildings.[32]

The following year two happy events occurred for the Congregation of Holy Cross in the United States, although they did not affect the day-to-day operations of the university. The first was the formal approval of the Constitutions of the Congregation of Holy Cross by Rome, giving the Congregation added standing and prestige and exemption from some control by local bishops. Father Moreau had been seeking such approval for years, but delays and complications always erupted. Although Father Moreau had patterned his community of priests, brothers, and sisters after the Holy Family of Jesus, Joseph, and Mary, Rome preferred that the sisters be independent and not under a male superior general.[33] Some cardinals in Rome were concerned about whether even the priests and brothers should be united in the same community.[34] In May 1856, Rome issued a "Decree of Praise," the preliminary step to final approval, and one year later official approval of the Congregation of priests and brothers was given:[35]

> The Rules and Constitutions of the Institute or Congregation of Holy Cross erected in the city of Le Mans, having been submitted upon presentation by the Reverend Mary Basil Moreau, Superior General of said Congregation, a first and a second time to a serious examination in a general session of the Sacred Congregation of the Propaganda, to the end that the Apostolic See might deign to approve and confirm them, the Most Eminent Fathers, who had already, with the consent of our Most Holy Lord, Pope Pius IX, sanctioned the approbation of the above-mentioned Institute on June 18, 1855, have likewise decreed the approbation and ratification of its Rules.

Although there was much joy throughout the Congregation over this approval from Rome, there was major concern over the status of the sisters, especially in the United States. The priests, brothers, and sisters at Notre Dame ministered together as one community—priests may have been more numerous in teaching in the Senior Department, the brothers in the Junior Department, the sisters in the Minim Department; priests served as confessors for the sisters; the sisters provided the cooking, laundry, and health care at Notre Dame; the brothers' farm supplied food for St. Mary's Academy; and so on—and would this essential cooperation continue? A sister superior general was named in France, new Constitutions were eventually written for the sisters and approved, but the local communities of Holy Cross sisters in the United States were allowed to govern themselves, as before, without significant intervention from France, and cooperation among the three societies continued almost without change at Notre Dame, at least for a time.[36]

A second important event in Holy Cross life in 1857 was Father Moreau's only visit to his Congregation in North America. He had long desired to accomplish this but other events had always intervened—political unrest in France in 1848, two trips to Rome in 1850 and 1856, and negotiations with Rome over the mission to Bengal that Father Sorin had earlier declined—and he had been forced to send representatives instead, Father Drouelle in 1848 and Father Chappé in 1853. But nothing was detaining him in France in the summer of 1857 and he wanted to assist with the separation of the temporalities of the sisters from those of the priests and brothers since the societies had now been separated, and to settle some growing jurisdictional conflicts in the foundations in New York and New Orleans.[37]

He left Le Havre on July 28 on the steamer SS *Fulton*, accompanied by Father Louis Letourneau to serve as translator, and, after a rather rough voyage, reached New York on August 11. He met briefly with the Archbishop of New York, John Hughes, and then boarded the train for Montreal to visit first the community in Canada. He and Father Letourneau apparently left Canada on August 24 and arrived at Notre Dame on August 26, one day earlier than expected. When their carriage arrived at the entrance to Notre Dame, the first person they met was a brother in the post office busy sorting mail. Father Sorin was due to return later that day from preaching a retreat to the sisters in Chicago. Word soon spread of the visitor's arrival, the twenty-three-bell carillon rang out, and Father Sorin hurried back from La Porte. The eighteen-day visit was crowded but fruitful. Father Moreau addressed the assembled community at Notre Dame on several occasions, met individually with each religious, and did the same at St. Mary's. At this stage there seemed to be no major complications in separating the finances and properties of the (now) two societies, although that separation was the source of some discontent and criticism. The priests and brothers opposed the separation because the work of the sisters was so essential in the day-to-day life of Notre Dame, and the United States sisters themselves did not want to be placed under direct governance of the sisters in France who might not be familiar with the culture and needs of America. But there were no major flare-ups. Father Sorin was reappointed superior at Notre Dame and vicar of the province of Indiana, and Mother Angela was named directress of St. Mary's Academy and provincial superior of the Holy Cross sisters in the United States. Mother Angela was also charged with translating into English the new Constitutions, Directory of Prayers, and part of Father Moreau's treatise on teaching. After a brief visit to Chicago with Father Sorin accompanying him, Father Moreau departed from Notre Dame on September 14 for Philadelphia, New York, and Le Mans.[38]

In a Circular Letter of September 25, drafted while still on board the *Arago* returning to France, Father Moreau expressed his favorable impression of his American visit:[39]

> Since I cannot record here the many houses and names which are all dear to me, I beg them all to receive this expression of my satisfaction and of my thanks for their touching welcome. Thanks to their docility, the closest union exists among all the members of each house, as also among all the houses I have just visited. I owe a tribute of gratitude to all those who have accompanied me with their good wishes and prayers during the dangerous and long journey which has brought me so many consolations.
>
> Thus always inspired by the thought which makes me see in the Salvatorists, Josephites, and Marianites of Holy Cross members of one same family united under one same authority, with common sentiments and interests—at least in spiritual things, if not in temporal—I felt the need and regarded it as a duty, to share with you all my joys, for your edification and your example.

The correspondence between Father Moreau and Father Sorin through the years often shows differences between the two, and even criticisms of Father Sorin for his expansionist undertakings and large expenditures without the permission of France. However, it is interesting to note that when the two met together, there seemed to be general agreement, even in 1853 after Father Sorin had temporarily withdrawn from the community. When the two met on that occasion, Father Moreau reversed his decision to assign Father Sorin to Bengal, reappointed him superior of Notre Dame, and only replaced him temporarily as provincial superior of all Holy Cross in the United States. One wonders if some of the advisors around Father Moreau in France were less patient with Father Sorin's expansionist tendencies and influenced Father Moreau against him, but whenever the two met face to face, they generally reached agreement.[40]

One constant source of concern had been the financial stability of Notre Dame and the liability the motherhouse might assume for any debt default, but

Father Moreau must have been relieved to see how close to self-supporting the university could be. Donations, especially from the Society for the Propagation of the Faith in France, were certainly a major part of this; tuition payments, both in money and in kind, were still a regular source of income; the brothers' farm supplied food for both Notre Dame and St. Mary's and produce for sale; and brickmaking was also becoming an important financial benefit.

Soon after their arrival in northern Indiana, Father Sorin and the brothers had noticed the extensive deposits of marl along the banks of St. Mary's Lake. When describing the advantages of Notre Dame's location that year, Father Sorin noted in the *Chronicles*: "Moreover, the two lakes were a source of enjoyment and of profit to the community and to the college by their fish and their beds of marl, from which lime could be made and bartered."[41] A kiln was built, $90 invested, and in 1844 fifteen hundred bushels of lime were produced, selling for approximately $300. A few years later, the minor chapter discussed the possibility of buying the property, later purchased from Mr. Rush, between St. Mary's Lake and the river:[42]

> It was calculated that it would be a great benefit for the Institution, this giving the chance 1st to lower the water of the lake; 2nd to sell marl for two hundred dollars a year; 3rd to have the monopoly of the lime; and to make, instead of three or four kilns of it, every year, as it is done now, a dozen of kilns on which there might be a benefit of nine hundred dollars.

The industry gradually branched out and the brothers and hired laborers began mixing sand with marl and making bricks. The first bricks were used in building the brothers' novitiate in 1845 and the larger church in 1848. Two of the first buildings of the relocated St. Mary's Academy were built of Notre Dame brick, at significant savings. On his visit to America, Father Moreau had decided that brickmaking was too difficult for the brothers in the hot Indiana summer and that only hired laborers should be employed but the brothers managed to continue working until 1868. It was a major benefit. It not only cut the cost of any new building at Notre Dame and St. Mary's but also provided bricks for sale to local builders. By 1858 the kilns were producing half a million bricks a year, and as many as eight hundred thousand by 1866, with bricks never selling for less than three dollars per thousand.[43]

The truly cataclysmic event of the 1860s, the Civil War, had a major impact on the university and on the Congregation of Holy Cross. "Contrary to all the anticipations of thinking men," Father Sorin wrote in his *Chronicles* of 1861, "war broke out at the beginning of spring by the attack on Fort Sumter near Charleston, and before the end of the year more than a million men had taken up arms, each in defense of his rights."[44] Notre Dame faced no major disruptions that first year, as he noted further: "The hard times this year, which caused half the colleges of the country to close, has thus far had no such effect on this institution."[45] Schools closest to the actual fighting suffered the most, but as the war dragged on, with no early end in sight, the economy began to weaken. A report sent to Father Moreau, probably in late 1863, noted the threat this held for Notre Dame:[46]

> A panic has seized upon the banks and the houses of commerce. The war preoccupies everybody and Notre Dame du Lac must look with trepidation to her finances. Fortunately, she just successfully received from Father Sorin who is again absent 50,000 francs which would free him from his most pressing debts. But regarding the floating debt of more than $60,000, almost each creditor had full confidence in him until now. They press him to pay them back and if Providence were not watching over her in such a particular way, it would be the end of the institution.

Confronted by such a danger, the local council adopted the bold step of undertaking new construction, in the words of the report, "to shock the country by the construction of a new Academy at St. Mary's." The bold stroke worked. Presuming that the institution must be solvent, the banks did not call in their loans, suppliers sold construction goods to Notre Dame at favorable prices, and workers were happy to find employment.[47]

Another reason for Notre Dame's success in weathering the storm of the Civil War was the steady increase in student enrollment. Father Sorin was concerned that a large number of students might withdraw but apparently this did not occur. The minutes of the Council of the Faculty in April 1861 noted: "Rev. Father Superior said that in consequence of the Civil War many of the students were uneasy in mind and wished to go home. It should be the aim of all the professors and officers of the house to make their stay as pleasant as possible till the end of the school year."[48] The student listings in the annual *Catalogues* suggest the following enrollment figures:[49]

1860–1861	200
1861–1862	217

1862–1863	268
1863–1864	366
1864–1865	460
1865–1866	524

University rosters did not make distinctions among minims, apprentices, Junior Department students, and Senior Department students, and thus these figures include all four. As Father Sorin noted in 1863: "The pupils came the first days in such number that soon every spot was occupied, and beds had to be placed wherever they could be crowded in."[50] Beds were installed even in the student exhibition and theatre hall.

Why this surprising increase? It took the first eighteen years for the enrollment to reach two hundred, and that figure nearly tripled during the five years of war. Location certainly played a part. Safely situated in remote northwest Indiana, Notre Dame was far from any fighting and a safe haven where concerned parents might entrust their sons. Some of this wartime increase came from the South. The only southern students at Notre Dame in 1861–1862 were three from Louisiana. Students from Louisiana were not surprising since that state had a considerable Catholic population and Holy Cross priests and sisters were ministering in New Orleans. The number of students from the Confederacy steadily increased each year after, and in 1864–1865 there were six students from Louisiana, twenty-nine from Tennessee, and one from Mississippi. The number from Tennessee jumped to thirty-two the following year. Students from the border states of Kentucky and Missouri increased from two to fifty-two during the war years. But most of the increase did come from the Midwest: Indiana, Illinois, Michigan, Ohio, and Iowa supplied 179 students in 1861–1862 and 371 in 1864–1865.[51]

Daily life at the university did not seem to change that much. Several of the faculty left to join the war, both priests and laymen, and brothers (and perhaps seminarians) were called upon to replace them in the classrooms. On one occasion, Father Sorin noted that "laborers became so scarce that it was hard to find men to cut wood in the country. The council of Notre Dame suddenly found itself face to face with the almost impossible task of obtaining the amount of wood necessary for the winter, which had already set in. After the most serious deliberation, it was resolved to introduce steam heating as an escape out of the difficulty, as had been done at St. Mary's." Steam heat was installed by Christmas 1863.[52]

The order of the day remained much as it had been since the university's founding, at least according to the recollections of student James McCormack.[53]

Life started every morning at half past five during my four years, but since then I have forgotten all about the rising sun. We went to Mass on Wednesday morning—that was the only required church attendance during the week. The real work of the day started with a study hour at six o'clock, breakfast at seven, dinner at twelve and supper at six p.m. We returned to the study hall at seven and at eight we retired after a very short day that began at five thirty a.m. So far as living was concerned, the boys never had reason to complain. The food was plain, but bountifully served. We had the usual supply of turkey and mince pie on holidays—in fact, I can still taste the delicious pies and bread made by the good Sisters of the Holy Cross.

He noted also that "cotton mattresses were introduced to take the place of ticking stuffed with straw or corn shucks. From then on the boys snored louder and longer."[54] The schedule could be altered on special occasions, of course. On March 4, 1861, one student began his letter home: "We are having 'recreation' here this afternoon in honor of 'Old Abe's' inauguration."[55]

Despite this celebration of "Old Abe's" inauguration, Father Sorin tried to keep national political debate from disturbing student life. He was not fully successful. With the American victory in the Mexican War of 1848 fresh in memory, and the exploits of Generals Zachary Taylor, Winfield Scott, and even Andrew Jackson still honored, the students of the Senior Department had organized a military company in the 1850s, the Notre Dame Continental Cadets. The student magazine later described the uniform:[56]

The coat was of blue, with buff facing and braiding, and buttons of brass; the vest was buff and the necktie was white. The breeches were of blue cloth and came down to the knee, where they were fastened with brass buttons. The stockings of white reached to the knee, while the tops of the boots were ornamented with buff. The hat was three-cornered, ornamented with a red and white cockade.

Not to be outdone, the younger students formed their own company, called the Washington Cadets. Father Sorin at least tolerated the programs for the "excellent physical training and gentlemanly bearing and manner which they were calculated to impact the young men."[57]

It is uncertain how many Notre Dame students actually joined the military. Historian Timothy Howard thought that most of the Continental Cadets did, perhaps two or three dozen, although Father Sorin insisted that no one under twenty-one could enlist without parental permission.[58] Most joined the Union Army, of course. Orville Chamberlain received the Medal of Honor, William Lynch and Robert Healy rose to Brigadier General, James Taylor became a well-respected war illustrator, and William and Robert Pinkerton, though not enlisting in the military, assisted their father in his wartime secret service operation for the Union. A few students and graduates lost their lives in the war, and many were wounded. William Lynch did not have full confidence in the medical personnel's decisions. "When they put me on the table," he recalled later, "I gave my revolver to my orderly, and told him to shoot the surgeon if he tried to take off the leg." At least two students, one from Virginia and one from Louisiana, joined the Confederacy.[59]

With feelings running high on both sides and with an increasing number of students arriving from the South, it is not surprising that conflicts broke out among the students who remained. In one incident, John Walker, a "stout, handsome youth, aggressive and foremost in expressing his loathing for Southerners," got into a serious confrontation and, in retaliation, his opponent hit him on the head with a brick. Sometime later, a student from Indiana and a student from Mississippi had a dispute over a swing in the recreation yard, and one eventually picked up a club and fractured the other's skull. The club-wielder was immediately expelled.[60]

If anyone was still questioning the loyalty and patriotism of this young French-founded community of Holy Cross in America, its service in the Civil War should have removed all doubts. Seven Holy Cross priests volunteered and served as chaplains (although in one regiment a third of the soldiers protested that "they could find their way to hell without the assistance of the clergy").[61] Three of the seven ruined their health and served only briefly. Father Zepherin Lévêque, born in Canada, served with the New York State Militia for only a few months and died in February 1862. Father Julian Bourget arrived from France in early 1862, cared for the wounded and dying in a military hospital in Illinois, contracted malaria, and died that June. Father James Dillon joined the 63rd New York Volunteer Infantry in 1861, successfully established a temperance society among the soldiers, rallied the troops at the Battle of Malvern Hill when the regular officers were incapacitated, and was honorably discharged after one year for deteriorating health.[62]

Father Paul Gillen was the first priest to volunteer, and he served the longest. Born in Ireland, he immigrated to the United States possibly in his teens, worked for the *Boston Pilot* for a time, was ordained a Holy Cross priest, and joined the troops around Washington, DC, in July 1861. He did not enroll in a particular regiment but obtained a horse, harness, and buggy that served as his altar and sleeping quarters, and he travelled from regiment to regiment as need arose. One officer called his conveyance "a combination of Plimpton bedstead, a Cathedral, and a restaurant all combined." For a time, Father Gillen's reputation was marred by allegations of occasional heavy drinking and misuse of soldiers' money, but these accusations were eventually proven false. He was courageous in exposing himself to danger on the battlefield, joined the 170th New York Infantry when General Grant forbade all civilian (which he was at that time) vehicles within army lines, and remained in the military until the end of the war, in the words of one officer, "one of the d——dest venturesome old clergymen I ever saw."[63]

Much is known about Father Peter Cooney's military career because he wrote frequent letters home, especially to his brother, and these have been published. Father Cooney was also born in Ireland, came to the United States with his family at age five, worked on his family's farm in Michigan until entering Notre Dame in his late twenties, taught school, was ordained a priest in 1859, and was appointed chaplain to the 35th Indiana Volunteer Infantry in late 1861. He saw action in Kentucky and Tennessee, especially the bitter battles of Stone's River, Chickamauga, Chattanooga, and Kennesaw Mountain, he celebrated Mass for Catholic General William Rosecrans, converted and baptized Major General D. S. Stanley, and retired at the end of the war, extolled by his regiment:[64]

> Of Father Cooney chaplain of the thirty-fifth regiment, I commend him as an example of the army chaplain; meek, pious, and brave as a lion, he worked with his brave regiment in the valley of death, affording the ministrations of his holy religion to the wounded and dying and giving words of encouragement to his fellow soldiers.

Father Joseph Carrier was born in France, was educated early by a private tutor, studied mathematics and science at the College of Belley, and taught physics at a small college in Switzerland before coming to America in 1855. He was ordained a priest in 1861, taught Greek and Latin at Notre Dame, and served as pastor of a local South Bend parish. He joined the 6th Missouri Infantry Regiment in 1863 and was with General Grant's army at the Battle of Vicksburg. Well acquainted with Generals Grant and Sherman in the western war, he was occasionally tapped by Father Sorin as his emissary to President Lincoln and Secretary of War Edwin Stanton. Leaving military service before the end of the war, he returned to Notre Dame, helped establish its Science Department, and in 1866

returned to France to collect scientific laboratory equipment and biological specimens for the university's museum.[65]

The best remembered of the Holy Cross chaplains who served in the Civil
War was Father William Corby. He had been born in Detroit, and like Father
Cooney was of a fairly well-to-do family. He attended Notre Dame as a student,
was ordained a priest in 1860, and the next year was sent as a chaplain to General
Thomas Francis Meagher's "Irish Brigade" of the Army of the Potomac. He served
in the Chickahominy swamps and at the battles of Fair Oaks, Antietam, Fred-
ericksburg, Chancellorsville, Gettysburg, the Wilderness, and Spotsylvania. He
is most remembered for his action at Gettysburg on July 2, 1863, a description of
which, written by Major General St. Clair Mulholland, he included in his later
Memoirs:[66]

> Father Corby stood on a large rock in front of the brigade. Addressing
> the men, he explained what he was about to do, saying that each could
> receive the benefit of absolution by making a sincere Act of Contrition
> and firmly resolving to embrace the first opportunity of confessing his
> sins, urging them to do their duty, and reminding them of the high and
> sacred nature of their trust as soldiers and the noble object for which they
> fought. . . . The brigade was standing at "Order Arms!" As he closed his
> address, every man, Catholic, and non-Catholic, fell on his knees with
> his head bowed. Then, stretching his right hand toward the brigade, Fa-
> ther Corby pronounced the words of absolution. . . . The scene was more
> than impressive; it was awe-inspiring. . . . I do not think there was a man
> in the brigade who did not offer up a heart-felt prayer. For some, it was
> their last; they knelt there in their grave clothes. In less than half an hour
> many of them were numbered with the dead of July 2.

In 1910, a commemorative statue of Father Corby, with his hand raised in
absolution, was erected at the Gettysburg battlefield on the very spot where the
absolution had been given, and the following year a replica of the statue was
placed on the Notre Dame campus, in front of the residence hall that bears
his name.[67]

With their greater numbers, the Holy Cross sisters were even more generous in their service in the war. In October 1861, Governor Oliver Morton of Indiana issued an appeal for nurses to assist the Union Army. Father Sorin brought
the request over to the sisters at St. Mary's, and several immediately volunteered.
The sisters, of course, had been trained and dedicated to teaching children and

young women and performing domestic service, but they were willing to try their hand at caring for the war wounded and dying also. Mother Angela and five others packed their few belongings, arranged for substitutes for their present teaching and other responsibilities, and arrived in Cairo, Illinois, on October 24.[68]

General Grant first asked the sisters to take charge of the hospital in Mound City, Illinois. As more sisters arrived from St. Mary's and Notre Dame, they staffed hospitals in Louisville and Paducah, Kentucky, Saint Louis, Memphis, and Washington, and they served on the first hospital ship in the United States, the *Red Rover*, a converted side-wheel commercial steamer that cared for the wounded along the Mississippi battlefields. The medical facilities were often primitive. The "hospital" at Mound City was a large unfinished warehouse, dirty, bare, and with wide cracks in the floor. One sister later recalled:[69]

> A fearful sight met our gaze. Every room on the first floor was strewn with human legs and arms. . . . Some of the wards resembled a slaughter-house, the walls were so splattered with blood. . . . Sister Isadore and I cried with horror. Sr. Augusta looked pityingly at us, but said—"Now stop; you are here and must put your heart and soul into the work. Pin up your habits; we will get three buckets of water and three brooms and begin by washing the walls and then the floors."

An experience of Mother Angela's demonstrated the crude conditions of the makeshift hospitals:[70]

> [On a] February day in 1862, soon after the battle of Fort Donelson, . . . Mother Angela was assisting the Chief Surgeon on the lower floor. He was performing a difficult operation, the exact accuracy of which would determine the life of the soldier. His head and that of Mother Angela were bent over the poor boy. Suddenly from the ceiling a heavy red drop fell upon the white coif of Mother Angela, who . . . did not move. Another, and still another, drop after drop came till a little stream was flowing. At last, the final stitch had been taken, and the two heads rose simultaneously. Not till then did the doctor know that a stream of blood, trickling through the open chinks of the upper floor, had fallen steadily upon the devoted head of Mother Angela, who now stood before the Surgeon with her head and face and shoulders bathed in the blood of some unknown soldier.

In all, approximately eighty Holy Cross sisters served during the war, out of a total of approximately two hundred in the United States, and at least two died of illnesses they contracted. Their service was similar at each hospital: setting up a satisfactory kitchen, petitioning better food for the suffering patients, assisting doctors with surgery, bandaging wounds, and comforting those near death. At times the sisters gave up their own beds in the crowded hospitals and slept on the floor. They cared for the Confederate wounded whenever they were brought to the hospital, on one occasion at the risk of their lives from angry Union soldiers in Memphis. Their spiritual ministry was not neglected, as Father Sorin noted in his *Chronicles* for 1862: "During the course of this year the Sisters of Holy Cross baptized with their own hands more than seven hundred soldiers, often having duly prepared them and made them desirous of belonging to the Religion of their good nurses."[71] They met with prejudice at times but it was usually soon overcome, and their dedication and service were praised by soldiers and officers alike. Early in the war, the wife of General Lew Wallace wrote: "Mother Angela of St. Mary's Academy has come with thirty nurses—a flock of white doves—to nurse in the hospitals, where the stillness is like the silence of death. . . . When [laywomen] get tired, they go home, but the Sisters of the Holy Cross live among the patients without thought of avoiding contagion by flight."[72]

With these priests and sisters absent for war service, the brothers were called on to play even larger roles at the university, and they were soon the center of a political controversy. The conscription law of 1863 exempted priests from the draft because they were ordained clergy, but the brothers, not ordained, were not exempt. Nonexempt persons might hire a substitute for a few hundred to a thousand dollars, and Indiana law allowed one to pay a $200 commutation fee and be exempt, but the community had no such sums available. On September 28, 1863, Father Sorin, with Father Carrier, addressed a letter to President Lincoln, noting that Holy Cross priests and sisters had both volunteered to serve as chaplains and nurses, that community members, with vows of poverty, did not have money to provide substitutes, and that the brothers were now essential to carry on the work of the Congregation's educational establishments. Father Carrier obtained written endorsements from General Grant and General Sherman, and went to Washington and hand delivered the letter to Secretary of War Stanton. The exemption was granted.[73]

The congressman from the South Bend district at the time was Republican Schuyler Colfax, recently also elected speaker of the house (and later to be vice president in the President Grant administration). He feared that he was facing a close reelection contest in 1864 and asked Father Sorin to be sure that the Holy Cross community at Notre Dame voted for him heavily. It was not an unexpected request since, in that thinly populated district, the votes of the priests and brothers might determine the outcome. In fact, a few years before, Father Sorin had acknowledged this possible political influence, as a visitor recalled:[74]

> He even told me, with a curiously quiet consciousness of power in his tone and manner, how he had put down some bigotry in the neighborhood, which had at one time threatened them, by exercising the political influence given him by the vote of his community. "It is not necessary for us to vote," said he; "we have not that trouble; but the fact that we can do so whenever we choose, and defeat either party, is quite enough to make both treat us with a respectful consideration."

Congressman Colfax was easily re-elected in 1864 but when the election figures were released, it was clear that the votes from Notre Dame had favored his opponent. Father Sorin had certainly tried. The local chapter had passed a resolution that "no other ticket than the Republican or Union ticket shall be voted by the Members of the Congregation on tomorrow," but the person charged with notifying the community had failed to do so, the Irish members of the community perhaps felt that the Republicans, some of whom were former Know-Nothings, were hostile to Catholicism, and three-fourths of the members had voted for Colfax's opponent.[75]

Speaker Colfax was understandably angry and, in retaliation, threatened to have the brothers' exemption repealed and perhaps even the post office removed. Father Sorin urged each member of the community to say one thousand Hail Marys that no changes be made and he sent Father Carrier back to Washington to plead the cause. He also asked Mrs. Sherman, the general's wife, in South Bend to be close to a daughter and son enrolled in Saint Mary's and Notre Dame and, ironically, living in Representative Colfax's now-available home, to add letters to President Lincoln and Secretary Stanton. This she did, and it appears that her letters arrived in Washington late that December at the same time that word was received there of her husband's successful march through Georgia and the capture of Savannah. The Shermans were in high favor in Washington as a consequence, and the brothers' exemption, and the post office, remained.[76]

The Sherman family's relationship with Notre Dame was touched with sadness at this time also. On June 11, 1864, while the general was marching from

Chattanooga toward Atlanta, his wife gave birth to a baby boy, Charley. Mrs. Sherman took sick a few days later, ran a high fever, and was unable to nurse the baby, but young Charley seemed to be progressing well. She soon recovered and felt well enough to make two short family visits to Cincinnati, but on her return from the second visit she noticed that the baby was experiencing some difficulty breathing. There was a strain of asthma in the family and the doctor thought that might be the problem. The child then developed pneumonia and, despite the best care of its mother and Mother Angela, the child died on December 4, a child the general had never seen. Father Sorin celebrated the funeral Mass in the college church, and the baby was buried in the campus cemetery, later named Cedar Grove.[77]

On June 7 the following year, with the war ended, the general visited the campus to see where his son Willie had lived and studied as a minim. Father Sorin and the students prevailed on him to say a few words, and this he did, concluding with the following:[78]

> So I call upon the young men here to be ready at all times to perform bravely the battle of life. We might never have to go to war anymore on this continent but then again we might. War is possible and we must be ready for the contingency. But more than this I want to say that there is a kind of war which is inevitable to all—it is the war of life. A young man should always stand in his armor, with his sword in hand and his buckler on. Life is only another kind of battle and it requires as good a generalship to conduct it to a successful end as it did to conquer a city, or to march through Georgia.
>
> I assure you young men and your parents that I will always regard you and your pursuits with interest and will note your careers if circumstances permit. I know that each of you will try to make your careers honorable as well as successful. You must not forget the instructions which you have received in this College from your preceptors. I heartily wish you Godspeed. This may be the last time you will hear my voice for I intend to leave these parts tomorrow, so let me bid you good-bye.

Whether he also visited Charley's grave on that occasion is not clear, but he wrote to Father Sorin two years later to say that he had recently purchased a family plot in Calvary Cemetery in Saint Louis and now wanted to have Charley disinterred and reburied there. Father Sorin was most willing, the grave was reopened, the coffin was removed and transported to Saint Louis, and Father Sorin would accept no payment.[79]

After the serious dispute Father Sorin had with Father Moreau over the appointment to Bengal in 1853, when Father Sorin went so far as to withdraw from the Congregation temporarily, Father Moreau eventually reconsidered and reassigned him to Notre Dame but replaced him as provincial superior of Holy Cross religious in the United States with Father Joseph Reze, the provincial superior in Canada. The arrangement was not a good one and, in 1855, Father Sorin was renamed provincial superior (or vicar) of all of the United States except New Orleans, which was established as a separate vicariate. Year by year the office of provincial was demanding more and more attention, with new schools opening almost every year, with parishes not always able to cover the agreed-upon salaries, and financial problems exacerbated by the Panic of 1857 and the uncertainties of the Civil War. As his responsibilities increased, Father Sorin decided to retain his position as provincial superior but leave the presidency of Notre Dame in May 1865, appointing the vice president, Father Patrick Dillon, as his successor.[80]

Father Dillon had been born in County Galway, Ireland, in 1832. He began seminary studies in Ireland, came to America as a boy with his family, continued his studies in Chicago for a time, and enrolled at Notre Dame in 1856. He was soon so well respected that Father Moreau, on his visit to Notre Dame in 1857, appointed him steward (business manager or treasurer) of the university, although he was still a student-seminarian, and it was he who presented the university's financial report to Father Moreau toward the close of his visit. He was ordained a priest in 1858, and was first sent to be president of St. Mary's College in Chicago, which Holy Cross was still operating despite differences with the bishop. He was then recalled to Notre Dame to be head of the Commercial Department, and in 1863 was named vice president of the university. A student later recalled that "Father Patrick Dillon, while Vice President, also taught book-keeping and practiced it himself, as he was a very successful businessman." New buildings were constructed at both Notre Dame and St. Mary's Academy, and the day-to-day supervision of the construction was apparently often left to Vice President Father Dillon.[81]

One of the first major projects may have been a permanent building at St. Mary's. When the academy was transferred from Bertrand to the former Rush property on the banks of the Saint Joseph River, a few frame buildings had been transported from Bertrand, Mishawaka, and perhaps from one other location to comprise the new academy. But as student enrollment and the number of sisters increased, larger facilities were needed. A permanent structure was begun, apparently in 1861, constructed chiefly from bricks made from the marl along the stream from Saint Mary's Lake to the river. The building, which was completed within a few years and was eventually named Bertrand Hall, is still part of the current Saint Mary's campus.[82]

A second building project, an unusual one, was one that Father Sorin had had in mind for quite some time—a home for retired missionaries and perhaps wayward priests. Some priests, because of excessive drinking or other failures, were no longer able to continue in active ministry, individual dioceses often had no facilities to care for them or for their elderly or disabled priests, and Father Sorin thought this community might help. He had hoped to build such a home as far back as 1852 but funding had not been available. The situation had changed by 1861; he received the approval of the local bishop, discussed his project with officials in Rome on a trip to Europe that spring, and solicited funds on his return through France. A few bishops sent assistance and Father Dillon did some fund-raising in Pennsylvania, but in 1865 the Holy Cross provincial chapter finally had to appropriate the money to complete the project. The building was completed that year. It was three stories, 136 feet by 75 feet with forty-eight private rooms, and situated on the north side of Saint Joseph's Lake, a short ten-minute walk from the campus. Few priests ever arrived, so the building was then converted into a novitiate for Holy Cross priests and remained a novitiate until 1934.[83]

The major construction of Father Dillon's vice presidency and brief presidency was a new Main Building. The first Main Building had been constructed in 1844, a four-and-a-half story structure approximately 80 feet by 36 feet, and two wings were added to the building in 1853. But with the further increases in student population during the Civil War, an even-larger building was needed, and a second Main Building was constructed in the summer of 1865. The roof of the standing Main Building was removed, a fifth and sixth story were added, and the building was topped with a dome and eventually a statue of the Blessed Mother. The interior of the building was reconfigured also. The kitchen, two refectories, and the washrooms comprised the ground floor; the floor above held three study halls (for the minims, the prep students, and the collegians); the third floor offered classrooms and private rooms for priests; and the top three floors were mostly dormitories. In the center of the sixth floor was a chapel with a stained glass window. The statue of the Blessed Mother was not added until the following spring, and the building was blessed "in the presence of the largest concourse of people ever gathered at Notre Dame" on May 31, 1866, by Archbishop Martin J. Spalding of Baltimore.[84]

Father Dillon was president for only one year, from May 1865 to August 1866. During that year the Commercial Course, which he personally directed while also vice president, was strengthened with new classes and was elevated to department level—the Mercantile Department. A new Scientific Program was introduced as well, but that may have owed more to the efforts of Father Carrier, recently returned from the Civil War. Professor Joseph Lyons was a member of the faculty that year and noted that Father Dillon was also able to renovate many of the buildings on campus. With increased enrollment and reduced faculty during the war, there was increased student discontent. Father Dillon addressed it and sought to remedy it, perhaps liberalizing discipline at times. "He was . . . extremely popular with all classes," a student later recalled. "He gave me his picture that I still retain in my album as one of my treasured possessions."[85]

In August 1866, Father Dillon resigned the presidency and accompanied Father Sorin to France to attend the general chapter of the Congregation. Father Moreau, amid bitter disputes with leading officials of the Congregation, had resigned as superior general, Bishop Pierre Dufal of Bengal was elected his successor, and Father Dillon was named one of his assistants. While in France, Father Dillon's brother, a businessman in Chicago who had been providing for their mother and grandmother, suffered a business failure and could no longer offer them his support. In early 1868, Father Dillon returned from France and, at his request and with his provincial superior's permission (Father Sorin), he and his brother, Father James, moved to Chicago, were appointed pastors there, and helped support their mother and grandmother with their salaries. Father Dillon died later that year and was buried in the Holy Cross community cemetery at Notre Dame.[86]

Historian and Notre Dame faculty member Timothy Howard later wrote of Father Dillon as vice president and president:[87]

> Much of the prosperity of the time was also undoubtedly due to the presence there at Notre Dame of a man of uncommon ability and force of character. . . . During the period while Father Patrick . . . was vice president, and during the year or more thereafter, when he was himself president, great work was done at Notre Dame. Father Patrick was a man of the greatest executive ability and of most excellent judgment. . . . He was one of the great men of Notre Dame.

Father Sorin's resignation as president should have marked the end of an era, but it probably did not. Father Dillon had been a close collaborator and continued his predecessor's policies, so closely in fact that it is often not clear to whom credit belongs. On one occasion their views did diverge. With the decline of enrollment at the end of the Civil War, Father Dillon reduced tuition by fifty dollars to attract more students. Father Sorin disapproved of the measure, ordered the earlier tuition restored, and the following year restored it was.[88] Five other priests were to hold the office of president over the next quarter century, but as provincial superior and then superior general Father Sorin always considered it *his* school, and often still his to direct.

CHAPTER 5

Father Corby to Father Corby, 1866–1881

When Father Sorin, accompanied by Father Dillon, sailed for France to attend the Congregation's general chapter in the fall of 1866, he could feel proud that he was handing on a successful and well-established educational institution. Twenty-four years before, the bishop had offered him a spread of 524 acres of wilderness, only 10 of which were cleared of forest, and close to twenty buildings dotted the area now. The Log Chapel had burned in the fire of 1856 but the first brick building, Old College, had survived, serving now as the bakery and the residence of the brothers working the nearby farm. The second Main Building had been completed only a few months before and housed most of the university's day-to-day activities—teaching, studying, eating, and sleeping. Behind the main college building and to the west was the beginning of the so-called French Quarter, later Brownson Hall, the residence of the sisters and their workplace of service to the students, priests, and brothers, and nearby was a recently constructed student infirmary. Behind and to the east of the college building was the Professed Brothers' House and St. Francis Home, a residence for retired priests and perhaps needy elderly laymen. Further to the south stood the Music Hall, used for vocal and instrumental music exercises, with a recreation facility on the ground floor for the Junior Department, and also Washington Hall, used for elocution and theatrical productions, with a similar recreation facility on the ground floor for the Senior Department students. To the west of the college building stood the university church, with an independent, two-story bell tower in front with the heavy carillon Father Sorin had purchased in France. South of the church was the Manual Labor School where the apprentices learned their trades. At the entrance to the campus were two small structures: Father Sorin's post office, usually manned by one of the brothers, and a porter's lodge where a brother could assist and even control visitation to the campus. Further to the south and west was the university farm with its barns and sheds and storage facilities, a farm sufficiently extensive that hired laborers were needed to assist the brothers in peak seasons. Off the main campus, the brothers' novitiate stood on the "Island" between the lakes, a priests' novitiate had been built on the hill overlooking Saint Mary's Lake, and the Missionaries' Retirement Home overlooked Saint Joseph's Lake from its north bank.[1]

The curriculum now offered two distinct tracks. The Classical Course was still a six-year program (two preparatory and four collegiate), emphasizing Greek, Latin, and English languages, theoretical and moral philosophy, mathematics and natural sciences. The Commercial Course was a two-year program for students with a satisfactory background in grammar and arithmetic and included courses in advanced grammar and mathematics, bookkeeping, commercial law, German, geography, and history. Holy Cross sisters also continued to teach traditional grammar school subjects to the minims, and the apprentices could take basic courses in grammar, arithmetic, and catechism.[2]

With the increases during the Civil War, student enrollment remained high, close to five hundred, although it would decline gradually over the next few years as these wartime enrollees finished and departed. The faculty remained constant, numbering thirty-nine: twenty priests and seminarians, seven brothers (four comprising the faculty of the Preparatory Department), and twelve laymen. Seven other brothers served as prefects or assistant prefects of discipline.[3]

A recent undertaking of which Father Sorin had to be particularly proud was the founding the year before of the *Ave Maria*, a journal dedicated primarily to increasing devotion to the Blessed Virgin among American Catholics. Several bishops tried to discourage him, some because they thought it would prove a financial failure, others because they feared that non-Catholics might interpret it as bestowing on Mary the worship and adoration due only to God, and others perhaps because they saw it as a competitor to their own diocesan newspapers. But Father Sorin was adamant and the first issue appeared on May 1, 1865. The initial editorial announced that it was to be a family magazine for both old and young; it would emphasize devotion to the Blessed Mother and it would be addressed directly to Catholics since others would not understand and perhaps even mock some of its Catholic professions. The first issue printed an excerpt from a sermon of Cardinal Nicholas Wiseman on devotion to Mary and began a multipart series entitled "The Virgin and the Priest." Subsequent issues contained brief biographies of saints and reviews of books on the Blessed Virgin and other religious topics. The sixth issue (June 17, 1865) inaugurated a "Children's Department" of information and short articles of interest to them, and the following issue began a weekly column of "News from Rome." With his other responsibilities, Father Sorin was not able to devote much time to the magazine, although his interest in it never lagged, and he appointed Father Neal Gillespie, Notre Dame's first graduate and later vice president of the university, as its editor, but the major editorial and publishing work was done by Mother Angela, aided by other Holy Cross sisters who also stitched and put the journal together each week. The magazine changed over the years, with features added and dropped, but it continued until 1970.[4]

With the resignation of Father Dillon as Notre Dame's president in the late summer of 1866, Father William Corby was named successor. As earlier noted, Father Corby had been born into a relatively well-to-do family in Detroit, had received a better-than-average education there, had entered Notre Dame in 1853, and was ordained a priest in 1860. For one year he taught at the university and served as director of the Manual Labor School. In December 1861, he volunteered as chaplain in a New York regiment of the Army of the Potomac where he gained fame for granting general absolution to his Catholic soldiers at the Battle of Gettysburg. Returning to Notre Dame at the end of the war, he was named pastor of Saint Patrick's Church in South Bend, then vice president and director of studies at Notre Dame, and finally president in August 1866.[5]

Notre Dame's growth and progress during the six years of Father Corby's first presidency were steady if, in the academic area, not as striking as the growth and progress in the presidencies of many of his successors. And how much of that steady progress was due to Father Corby and how much to Father Sorin, now his provincial superior or superior general, or to Father August Lemonnier, his vice president and director of studies, is uncertain. But steady growth and progress it was.

Even with students transferring out of the safe location of northern Indiana after the Civil War, and others selecting institutions closer to the former battlegrounds, Notre Dame's enrollment remained high. Figures can be only an approximation since students continued to come and go throughout the year, but enrollment seemed to remain generally between 400 and 450. The number of degrees or citations awarded rose steadily, from thirty in 1867 to forty six years later. The degrees awarded in the regular Collegiate or Classical Course remained constant—with five bachelor of arts and four master of arts degrees in 1867 and four bachelor of arts and two master of arts degrees in 1872—with the largest concentration of students completing their education in the commercial or mercantile area that Father Dillon had earlier been instrumental in developing. In 1864, during Father Dillon's vice presidency, the recognition awarded to those completing the two-year program was changed from a diploma in the Commercial Course to a degree of master of accounts, although it was the same program and in no way a postgraduate degree, and the number receiving this master of accounts degree from 1866 to 1872 never dropped below fourteen in any year and twice reached a high of thirty.[6]

In addition to the ongoing Classical and Commercial Courses, a Scientific Course, announced only a year before in 1865–1866, emerged as a stable and popular option during the presidency of Father Corby. It was a full six-year program, two preparatory and four collegiate. Many of the requirements of the Classical Course were retained, but classes in Greek and Latin grammar and literature, approximately twenty in all, were dropped and classes were added in higher arithmetic, geography, modern and United States history, natural history, astronomy, calculus, botany, surveying, chemistry, geology, mineralogy, and constitutional law.[7]

The chief promoter of the new course was probably Father Joseph Carrier, recently discharged from his chaplaincy in the Civil War. He had been born in France in 1833, was attracted to books and reading at an early age, especially in the areas of the physical or natural sciences, studied French, Latin, and Italian under private tutors, and entered the Collège de Belley at age nine and graduated with high honors at sixteen. He taught briefly at his alma mater before immigrating to the United States, was ordained a priest at Notre Dame in 1861, and shortly thereafter was assigned to General Grant's army at Vicksburg. He traveled back to France in 1866 to acquire scientific laboratory equipment and specimens for the university museum, and apparently was successful, even procuring an excellent telescope from Emperor Napoleon III himself. Father Carrier told an interesting story of his visit to the emperor's palace:[8]

On my arrival at the entrance to the palace, I was met by one of the guards who demanded to know my business. "I wish to see the Emperor," said I. "Are you a soldier?" asked the guard. "Greater than that," I responded. "Perhaps you are a lieutenant?" "Greater than that," said I. "Can it be that you are a general?" "Greater than that!" said I, drawing myself up to my full height. "Are you a prince?" questioned the guard. "Greater than that," I again replied. "Surely you are not a king," said the mystified guardian of the palace. "Ah, far greater than that," I replied. "Pray, then who are you?" asked the much-puzzled man. Looking him in the face, I answered with all the dignity at my command, "I am an American citizen!" It is needless to say that I was soon piloted into the private apartments of his majesty; and that later on when I related the joke I had played on the guard, the Emperor enjoyed it quite as much as I did myself.

Father Sorin's Americanism had clearly rubbed off on his associates.

A very interesting member of the science faculty, arriving at Notre Dame at about this time, was Father Louis Neyron. According to his own testimony, he had been born in France in 1791, studied medicine and surgery, was drafted into the French army, and served with Napoleon at the Battle of Waterloo. He was there captured by the British, attempted to escape twice and was sentenced to death for the second attempt, but the decree was rescinded when, with a shortage of doctors, his services were needed in nearby hospitals. He eventually decided to become a priest, was ordained in 1828, and happened to hear Bishop Bruté's plea for missionaries on his visit to France in 1835. Father Neyron returned to Vincennes with Bishop Bruté, labored throughout the Midwest, and attempted to reach the dying Father Deseille in Father Badin's log cabin in 1837 but arrived a few days too late. His medical background could be of service also, as an item from the *Northwestern Chronicle* published in the *Scholastic* in 1878 noted:[9]

> We remember Father Neyron nearly thirty years ago making a long and tiresome journey to a stranger's house in Kentucky, where some dozen doctors were quarrelling over a broken leg, one half saying it was broken, the other half that it was out of joint. . . . The moment Father Neyron saw and touched the limb, he solved the trouble—the thigh socket bone was broken. He relieved the suffering patient and went his way. The wife of the gentleman pressed upon him a sum of money when he took his leave—but every cent of it was returned the next day. He would receive no remuneration whatever.

Father Neyron continued his priestly labors throughout Indiana and the Midwest until 1863 when, afflicted with rheumatism, he asked Father Sorin if he might reside in the Retired Missionaries' Home then under construction. Soon after his arrival, he began offering classes in human anatomy and other premedical sciences, and one of his early students graduated from the Philadelphia University of Medicine and Surgery in 1868 with "highest graduating honors." Needing to provide his own food in his early priesthood, he had become an excellent outdoor marksman, and he was an avid walker, on one occasion walking the sixteen miles from Elkhart when a train was delayed by bad weather. Age eventually took its toll and he had to transfer to the Infirmary where the Holy Cross sister-nurses took excellent care of him and where he died peacefully in January 1888.[10]

Father Neyron's contribution to the Scientific Course was significant. He, Father Carrier, and Professor A. J. Stace apparently taught all the classes needed, assisted at times by advanced students, like the future priest-scientists Alexander Kirsch and John Zahm. But the program remained small. The strictly science classes were taught almost exclusively in the final two years of the program, and in 1867 two students received the degree of bachelor of science and one received a medical certificate. Receiving this medical certificate was apparently good preparation for a student desiring to continue on elsewhere for a university MD degree. Over the next five years, only eleven degrees of bachelor of science were awarded, and fourteen medical certificates, approximately two and three a year.[11]

The Scientific Course also apparently acquired its own building about this time. At the end of the Civil War, Father Sorin, always interested in music, and especially church music, purchased a new organ for the church, only to discover that the chancel ceiling was not high enough to contain it. A second building was added to the back of the church in 1865–1866, about half as long as the church itself and of the same width but twenty feet higher, to accommodate the larger organ. It was built of old bricks salvaged from four college chimneys recently torn down when steam heat was installed, and one professor later admitted that it "was never a very 'pretty' building . . . but it used to suggest the idea of the old church having got its back up."[12] When the old church was demolished a few years later and the new one erected, the addition was retained and became Old Science Hall. In 1876 it was renamed Phelan Hall in honor of William Phelan, stepfather of Father Neal Gillespie and Mother Angela and Notre Dame's greatest benefactor up to that time. It continued to serve the science program until it was demolished in the mid-1880s to make room for the Lady Chapel and the apsidal chapels of the new university church.[13]

Writing of these six years of Father Corby's presidency, Timothy Howard in his *A Brief History of the University of Notre Dame du Lac, Indiana, from 1842 to 1892* states that "during this period, also, the societies of the university, in which so much of its life centers, showed a marked increase of activity."[14] One of these societies was the Scientific Association founded by Father Carrier in the spring of 1868 to complement classroom instruction and promote scientific research. Its main interests were in natural science, physics, and mathematics; it boasted its own scientific library; student membership numbered about twenty-five; and, according to its constitution, "it will be the earnest endeavor of the members of the U.S.A. [United Scientific Association] to aim *high*, both in the estimation of their superiors and fellow-students, by their irreproachable behavior and gentlemanly deportment, and in the pursuit of knowledge by a diligent application to their respective studies."[15] At its weekly meetings, faculty and student papers on "The Origin of Ideas," "The Utility of the Sciences," "The Harmony of Nature," "Botany," "Physiology," etc., were presented and discussed, and the society published numerous articles of a scientific nature in the student press on ginseng, asbestos, petroleum, tobacco, the microscope, and "A Few Thoughts on Science and the Age in which we Live." The society also sponsored short research trips, occasionally collecting botanical specimens for the university museum.[16]

The Saint Aloysius Philodemic Society had been founded in 1851 to further the study of history and to provide opportunities for elocution and debate. It numbered about twenty members, possessed a library of three hundred books in 1868, sponsored a moot court, and occasionally published a small paper, *The Two Penny Gazette*. At its weekly meetings, it held debates ranging from "Resolved, the death of Caesar was beneficial to Rome" to "Is absolute monarchy the best form of government" and "That the Press of the present day is productive of more evil than good."[17]

The Saint Edward's Literary Association was similar, and it also had about twenty members, but it held two meetings each week—one a business meeting and the other a meeting to sponsor a debate or the presentation of a scholarly essay. Debate topics included: "Resolved that the present system of common schools is injurious to the morals of the rising generation"; "Resolved that the United States Government would be justified in executing Jefferson Davis"; and "Are wealth, rank, and personal beauty better passports in society than education?"[18]

These two latter societies were probably reserved to students in the Senior Department, and thus the Saint Cecilia Philomathean Association had been established in 1865 "for the purpose of improving the musical and dramatic talent of the Junior Department." It sponsored debates, public readings, essays, declamations, and a moot court. It had its own library and a membership of approximately forty.[19]

Two other student associations were the Thespian and Philharmonic Societies. Father Sorin thoroughly enjoyed plays and theatrical exhibitions, and many of these were put on by members of the Thespian Society. In addition to acting in dramatic presentations, the members strove "to cultivate in the students of the University a taste for classical drama, by presenting plays of the most able writers, whenever they can be adapted without too great a change of plot, to male characters only."[20] The Philharmonic Society, numbering about twenty members who met twice a week, sought "to afford its members the opportunity of perfecting themselves in the theory and in the practice of sacred and secular vocal music, and to give dignity and spirit, by their performances, to the celebration of our religious, national and literary festivals."[21]

If these academic and literary societies grew in influence in the years following the Civil War, the same may not be true of the religious societies. The Archconfraternity of the Blessed Virgin Mary was the university's first such society, formed in 1845 with the stated goal of the sanctification of its members and the conversion of sinners through the intercession of the Blessed Mother, and with its practice of gathering at Mass and receiving Holy Communion the first Saturday of each month. But membership in this and other religious societies declined after the war in part probably because Father Granger, the director and inspiration behind many of them, was named provincial superior in 1868 and had less time to devote to them because of other duties.[22]

The Sodality of the Holy Angels was probably founded in the late 1840s. Its membership was limited to grade school and high school students (minims and the Junior Department) and its purpose was to provide altar servers for all religious ceremonies throughout the year. The sodality met for instruction each Sunday morning at 9:00 a.m. and before all major feasts and festivals. The members took the holy angels as their patrons because the angels serve around the throne of God in heaven and as an encouragement to live lives of purity and holiness. Its membership appeared to decline over the years also.[23]

The Society of the Holy Childhood was organized among the minims in 1866–1867 to pray for infidel children in China and other non-Christian countries, and perhaps make small donations to assist missionary efforts. Membership numbered more than thirty-five each year and Father Granger served as director. The Saint Gregory Society was formed in 1871, also by Father Granger, and was open to students of all ages and to priests and brothers. Its members, in cassocks and surplices, were to provide correct liturgical music at High Masses and Vespers. They rehearsed twice a week and held a regular monthly meeting. In 1868 Father Granger also organized the Sodality of Our Lady of the Sacred Heart for Junior Department students who pledged to recite the rosary and Litany of the Blessed Virgin together each Tuesday evening for the intention of living pure and sinless lives, and to attend Mass and Benediction each Saturday morning with members of other religious societies.[24]

Of great benefit to these literary and religious societies was the founding of the student publication *The Scholastic Year* in the fall of 1867. There had been attempts at student publication before this—*Literary Gazette*, *Progress*, *Olympic Gazette*, and *Weekly Bee*—but all were short-lived. The semimonthly *Progress* in the late 1850s was the best remembered of these in later years and offered a writing outlet for students Timothy Howard and Arthur Stace, later longtime Notre Dame professors, but the *Scholastic* was the only one that endured.[25]

The first issue of the *Scholastic* stated its purpose:[26]

It has been undertaken in order to give to parents frequent accounts of the institutions in which they have placed their children; institutions in which the parents' hearts must be, so long as their children remain, and of which all who have visited it retain, we hope, a pleasing remembrance.

We wish to convey to parents, in a less formal way than by the Monthly Bulletin of Classes and Conduct, which is sent to the parents of each student, all the news that may concern their children.

We should give an account of all the arrivals at the College and Academy [Saint Mary's], both of students and of friends; of the general and relative progress of the classes; of those students who distinguish themselves in class, in study, in athletic sports—and many other interesting items, which, though not of importance in the great world, are of great moment in the "*Student World*," and will be extremely interesting to parents. . . .

As the year goes on we shall also give, either entire, if short, or in part, if long, the best compositions from the classes.

The editors apparently changed with each issue but the journal carried out its stated purpose well. It publicized the meetings of each society, printed student essays and poetry, had a column of happenings at Saint Mary's, listed members of the Tables of Honor and winners of premiums, printed notices of coming lectures and visits of prominent personages, injected occasional humor, noted intramural sports scores (chiefly baseball at this time), accepted paid advertising, and once a year published the complete rosters of Notre Dame and Saint Mary's students. For the first few months, parents who subscribed to the *Scholastic* ($2.50 a year) also received a copy of the *Ave Maria*, but this could be discontinued if any parent, Catholic or non-Catholic, so requested.[27]

A second major, and lasting, innovation of these six years of Father Corby's presidency was the founding of the Notre Dame Law School in 1869, the first in any Catholic university in the United States. The university's charter in 1844 stated explicitly that it could grant "degrees and diplomas in the liberal arts and sciences, in law and medicine," and Father Sorin may have had a Department of Law in mind as early as 1854. A class in constitutional law was added to the curriculum in 1858 and eventually was required in the final year of the Scientific Course. Finally, at "a meeting of the Board of Trustees of the University of Notre Dame [Fathers Sorin, Granger, Corby, Gillespie, and Lemonnier], held on the 5th inst. [October 1868] . . . the question of Law Studies at Notre Dame and the propriety of opening a class for that purpose was discussed, and a resolution to the effect of beginning said class at an early opportunity was passed unanimously."[28] The official announcement of the new program was printed in the *Catalogue* at the end of the academic year:[29]

> The complete course will be made in two years, the terms, of which there are four, corresponding with those of the other faculties of the University. At the end of the course, students who have passed a successful examination, and who have in other respects satisfied the requirements of the University, will be entitled to receive the degree of LL.B.
>
> Students presenting themselves for matriculation in the Department will be expected to have a good liberal education. Those, however, who may not have completed their studies in the Faculty of Arts, will have an opportunity of doing so, without extra charge, while prosecuting their legal studies. . . .
>
> As it is a matter of highest importance to a young Lawyer, that on being admitted to the practice of his profession he should be able to express himself clearly, fluently, and in a methodical manner, ample opportunities will be afforded to cultivate the art of public speaking.

Although no specific academic background was required for admission except "a good liberal arts education," that could be interpreted as at least some serious study in a normal collegiate or classical program. The fact that a student could complete his collegiate program during his two years of law studies seems to imply that he should already be well along in those studies. The books that the students were urged to purchase both for their classes and as references in their later law practice presuppose a level of academic maturity even at the start of the program: "Blackstone's Commentaries, Pothier on Obligations, Bishop on Criminal Law, Cooper's Justinian, and Burrell's Law Dictionary . . . Kent's Commentaries, Parson's on Contracts, Storey's Equity Jurisprudence, Story on Constitutional Law, Greenleaf on Evidence, Stephen on Pleading, and Domat on the Civil Law." The student apparently took five classes each term, attending lectures for two hours each weekday and for three and a half hours on Saturday.[30] The faculty in the first year included only L. G. Tong as professor of commercial law, M. T. Colovin as professor of law, and A. A. Griffith as professor of elocution, but that was probably sufficient for the few students enrolled. One historian suggests that Colovin served as first head or principal of the new department. The following year a Chicago attorney, P. Foote, was hired and named principal, Father F. P. Battista was named professor of ethics and civil law, and T. A. Moran was named professor of constitutional and criminal law. The first three students received the LL.B. degree in the commencement of 1871.[31]

At the same time that the law program was being inaugurated, another major project was under serious consideration—replacing the college church with a larger one. The college church, built in 1848 to supersede the early log chapel, was ninety feet by thirty-eight feet, but with close to five hundred students in the late 1860s, close to one hundred Holy Cross religious, plus Catholics in the surrounding area for whom it served as their parish church, it was clearly too small. The earliest mention of a new church may be a reference in the October 1868 minutes of the Notre Dame local council, presided over by Father Corby as superior and president, noting: "A petition for building a church is ordered to be drawn up."[32] A petition to whom? Since it would involve a major expense and also serve as the Congregation of Holy Cross church, possibly to the provincial superior (Father Granger) and his council or the new superior general (Father Sorin). Another impetus had come from Father Sorin himself. He was in Europe at the time and had been in serious discussions with Bollée et Fils of France about purchasing a new and larger carillon for Notre Dame. But the present carillon was already too heavy for the church and a two-story bell tower had been built in front of the church to house it. A new church would obviously be needed to support an even heavier carillon. It was noted in early 1869 that the "project of building a church and getting a new chime was brought before the Council, and a letter of Rev. Father General who originated the idea was read. It was proposed to sell the old chime by lottery and realize if possible $10,000." No action was taken at this time, however, since no one had shown interest in purchasing the old carillon and it was difficult to borrow money during that period of Reconstruction after the Civil War.[33]

But a new church was still needed, large enough to accommodate the growing student and parish population, and now to accommodate the new carillon, with one bell weighing twelve hundred pounds, that Father Sorin so desired. Father Granger, provincial superior and also pastor of the church, submitted an advertisement in Catholic papers, urging donations for the building of a new church and promising a remembrance at daily Mass for five years for a donation of five dollars, a remembrance for ten years for a ten dollar donation, and a remembrance for fifty years for fifty dollars. The church would be dedicated to Our Lady of the Sacred Heart. By early 1870, plans called for the new church to seat two thousand, with one thousand in the nave, four hundred in each of the two transepts, and two hundred in the sanctuary. The aisles were to be eight feet wide and each pew eight feet long. It was also resolved that a residence for the superior general be construed behind the new church.[34]

Father Sorin had returned to the United States by April 1870, and it was decided to dig the foundation and begin construction immediately. It was to be built in front of the 1848 church, which would remain for the present and continue to serve as the college and parish church. The new church was actually constructed in three stages, probably as money became available. The first stage was conducted under the day-to-day direction of Brother Charles Borromeo (Patrick Harding). He had been born in Ireland in 1838, immigrated to the United States, came to Notre Dame in 1862, and was professed as a brother of Holy Cross in 1866. His father had been a carpenter and he may have learned something of the building trade from him. He may have gained additional experience working with Father Dillon in the construction of the second Main Building in 1865 and the first college building at St. Mary's that same year. A well-known church architect, Patrick Charles Keely, had submitted a plan for the church patterned after the Baroque Church of the Gesù in Rome, but when this was rejected, Brother Charles apparently submitted a plan for a Gothic structure that was then, with modifications, accepted. Under his supervision in this first stage, the façade with its three entrances (symbolic of the Trinity), the long nave, and the two transepts were constructed from 1870 to 1875, with the cornerstone blessed by Archbishop John Purcell of Cincinnati on May 31, 1871, the Feast of Our Lady of the Sacred Heart.

The elaborately ornate Gothic altar was purchased from Froc-Robert and Fils of Paris, and the back wall of the church was, temporarily, a plain brick wall adorned only by a floor-to-ceiling black cross. The former church, now almost hidden from view by the larger new one, was then demolished, and the new church came into use.[35]

In February 1870 the local council had approved the building of a residence for the superior general behind the new church, and the Presbytery building was constructed immediately. It was a plain boxlike structure of three stories, a full basement, and a mansard roof. Father Sorin lived (and died) there as superior general, and the building over time served as the residence and office for both the provincial superior and the Sacred Heart Parish pastor, the residence of the editor of the *Ave Maria* magazine, and the residence for numerous Holy Cross and other priests on the Notre Dame faculty.[36]

Another innovation at the university at this time, and eventually a very important one, was the organization of an alumni association. The first public mention of it probably occurred in the *Scholastic* in January 1868:[37]

> Notre Dame has nearly reached her twenty-fifth, or silver, anniversary. During those twenty-five past years, numbers have left her fostering care, to enter on the active business of life. Those who have fought their way successfully through the first bustle and struggle of making a name and a reputation, in the sphere of activity their genius has prompted them to select, are beginning again to revert in thought to the *Alma Mater* where the foundation of their success was laid, and to the comrades who shared their studies in those long past days. Accordingly we have received suggestions from various sources, to form an association of the *alumni* of Notre Dame, in which mutual acquaintance can be formed and kept up among those already united by a common bond—their attachment to the college in which their studies were pursued.

The editors then asked the alumni to send suggestions, along the lines of the following questions: 1) Notre Dame graduates would be members but what of those students who left the university before the full six-year course had been completed? 2) What should be the name of the proposed organization? 3) What literary or scientific benefits should the association hope to provide for its members? 4) How often should meetings be held? And suggestions did come. On April 8, Father Corby called a meeting in the president's parlor of the *resident* alumni, and appointed a committee of Father Neal Gillespie and Professors Timothy Howard, Joseph Lyons, Arthur Stace, and Michael Baasen to draft a constitution embodying answers to the above questions. The committee met, the drafted constitution was approved by resident or local alumni, and all alumni were invited to return to campus for a general meeting on June 23, 1868, commencement weekend.[38]

At that first general meeting, under the chairmanship of Father Corby, the proposed constitution, after a few amendments, was approved. The new organization was to be called the "Associated Alumni of the University of Notre Dame," and its annual meetings were to be held on the Tuesday preceding commencement. The membership included all graduates of the university, all officers of the university (president, vice president, and director of studies), and all holding honorary degrees from the university. Professors and former students who did not graduate could be elected by a three-fourth vote of the membership. Father Gillespie and Professors Howard and Lyons were elected officers of the association and Father Carrier was elected as a member.[39]

The association held its second meeting the following year on June 22. Minutes were read, new elections were held, miscellaneous business was conducted, and a special banquet was enjoyed, with the bishop of Fort Wayne and superior general Father Sorin in attendance. Various toasts and responses were in order—to the country, to the hierarchy and clergy, to the press, to the bar, to the medical and academic professions, to the university, and to the alumni—and Father Sorin was then asked to speak on this, the Silver Jubilee of the university's charter. The members were invited to tour the college, noting especially Father Carrier's library, the college museum, and the new telescope from France. That evening the alumni joined the students and invited guests for musical presentations, speeches in English, Greek, and Latin, and a theatrical performance in four acts. The format adopted at this 1869 meeting seems to have been followed in succeeding years, and, surprisingly, the question of possible financial contributions to the university in these early years was apparently never raised.[40]

The general chapter of the Congregation of Holy Cross met at Notre Dame in late summer 1872, the first time a general chapter of any religious congregation had been held in the New World.[41] For the past two years Father Corby had been serving as both provincial superior of all Holy Cross religious in the United States and superior-president of the University of Notre Dame, and at the close of the general chapter several changes were made. The Congregation decided to open a "new establishment" in Watertown, Wisconsin—College of Our Lady of the Sacred Heart—and Father Corby was assigned to be its founding president and the pastor of a parish church the Congregation would found the following year. Father Granger, who served as provincial superior from 1868 to 1870 (replacing Father Sorin when he became superior general) was named provincial superior again, and Father Augustus Lemonnier, vice president and director of studies under Father Corby, was named Notre Dame president.[42]

Father Lemonnier was Father Sorin's nephew, the son of his eldest sister. He had been born in 1839 in Ahuillé, France, Father Sorin's birthplace also, entered the *collège* at Précigné at age thirteen, and at twenty began the study of law. He had an older brother studying for the priesthood, and two years later he also decided to enter the seminary at Le Mans. Interested more in the foreign mission, he transferred to the seminary in Paris in 1860 where he had a conversation with his uncle on one of Father Sorin's many trips back to Europe. Father Sorin convinced him that, if he was interested in missionary work, he should come to America, and this he did in 1861. He completed his seminary studies and was ordained two years later. He mastered English quickly, became president or director of various student associations (Saint Aloysius Philodemic Society, Saint Edward's Literary Association, Philharmonic Society, the Thespians, and the Notre Dame Boating Club), was appointed prefect of discipline and then prefect of religion, and, in 1866, vice president and director of studies under Father Corby.[43]

Father Lemonnier was apparently loved by all. Professor Timothy Howard, who knew him well, later wrote enthusiastically:[44]

> What a gracious presence, what kindness, what ease, what exquisite taste, what goodness! In him met most perfectly the priest, the scholar, and the gentleman. But he was even more than this: he was an artist in the broadest sense of the term, having a true appreciation of music, poetry, landscape gardening, and general scenic effect. . . . He was, besides, a most genial companion, possessed of a delicate and ready wit and a neverfailing fund of good humor.

Unfortunately, his presidency was limited to two years—he died at the age of thirty-five, but much was accomplished in the short time.

One of Father Lemonnier's first goals was to raise the academic standards of the university and tighten its regulations. He began his administration by visiting—with his director of studies—each classroom, getting to know firsthand what was being taught and how well it was being received. He seemed pleased with what he observed, but he realized that more was needed. He added a third year to the former two-year Preparatory Course and required passing a comprehensive examination before a student could progress from the Preparatory into the Collegiate or Classical Course. The Classical Course itself was strengthened, especially with increasing the mathematics and science requirements, adding botany, geology, and physics to the former chemistry and human physiology requirements. Some kind of comprehensive written and oral examination in all branches was instituted before the degree of bachelor of arts could be awarded. Even the Manual Labor School was strengthened academically. Up until this time, the students spent approximately three-fourths of their time learning a trade and one-fourth taking elementary classes, but with recent changes, the students now worked at their trades five hours each day and spent four hours in studies, providing more consistency and continuity to their early learning.[45] Under Father Lemonnier, the university took another major step out of the French boarding school format toward the American university model.

If the academic standards were to be raised, however, sufficient resources had to be available, and Father Lemonnier turned his attention early to establishing a circulating library. Books, of course, were already available. Many of the academic societies, such as the Saint Aloysius Philodemic Society and the Saint Edward's Literary Association, had their own libraries, and many professors, Father Carrier for one, had personal collections that they could loan to students, but an established and supervised lending library was needed. Soon after taking office, Father Lemonnier collected a small lending library of less than three hundred volumes, charged students one dollar for the privilege of borrowing books, and used the money to purchase more books.[46] He did not have time, of course, to remain as librarian himself, and that same fall turned the project over to Professor James Farnham ("Jimmy") Edwards.

Edwards had been born in Toledo, Ohio, in 1850, the son of Irish immigrants. His father was successively co-owner of a billiards franchise, proprietor of a theater, toll collector on a local canal, and state inspector of tobacco, snuff, and cigars. Father Peter Cooney, C.S.C., had been a neighbor to the Edwards family in Toledo and, in 1859, apparently suggested that young Jimmy be sent as a minim to Notre Dame since there was no Catholic school in Toledo. Edwards progressed through the Minim, Preparatory, and Collegiate Departments, with a slight interruption to recover from a bout of bad health, and then joined the Notre Dame faculty in 1872. He first taught Latin and rhetoric in the Preparatory Department, received a bachelor of law degree in 1875, and then taught history in the Collegiate Department. He remained at Notre Dame until his death in 1911, one of the best known and most approachable of the lay faculty. Parents wrote to him about their sons spending too much money or suffering a toothache;

other schools asked his advice on plays proper for a Catholic campus; Catholics across the country wrote for blessed rosaries or papal blessings or to complain if the *Ave Maria* did not arrive on time; and hearing that the drinking water at Notre Dame had medicinal qualities, one person wrote to ask Edwards if the water was from a mineral spring or if the iron was put into it by the sisters.[47]

In selecting Professor Edwards, Father Lemonnier had selected well. A couple of years before, just as a hobby, Edwards had begun collecting photos and other memorabilia of American bishops, and now he turned his attention also to books—spiritual books, history, biography, literature, etc., almost exclusively in English. Some of these were gifts he begged and others were purchased. Within five years the library numbered approximately five thousand volumes.[48]

At the same time, Edwards began seriously collecting unpublished records and documentation, thus beginning the University of Notre Dame Archives. As a historian, he realized that diocesan records and episcopal letters were valuable and worth preserving, and if the bishop or the diocese did not have the personnel to care for them, he agreed to preserve them at Notre Dame. Eventually numerous bishops and dioceses entrusted their records to him, and he occasionally sought material from outside the United States. He might also request some material remembrance to complement the papers—a miter, crozier, zucchetto, surplice—and these all eventually found their way into the Bishops' Memorial Hall.[49]

Much of the work that Father Lemonnier and Professor Edwards began that fall of 1872 would burn in the great fire of 1879, but Edwards would simply begin again and, for decades, the library would continue to be known for its originator, the Lemonnier Library.

Father Lemonnier loved the students, and was loved by them, but he could be strict and forceful as needed. He once put a notice in the South Bend paper, warning local merchants:[50]

> Permit me to avail myself of the publicity of your columns to inform all persons engaged in the sale of liquor in the city of South Bend and vicinity that I shall prosecute those who shall hereafter sell or give liquor or any other intoxicating drink to any one of the students of the College, and that I will have such persons punished with the heaviest penalties of the law.

A final achievement of Father Lemonnier's short presidency was the inauguration of the course or program in engineering in 1873, apparently the first such program in any American Catholic university. The years after the Civil War saw population expansion across the country, a need for increased surveying and the building of bridges and railroads, and a demand for professionals with such engineering skills. The Engineering Course began as a two-year program and the applicant for admission apparently should have completed the first two years of the Scientific Course or at least demonstrated that level of knowledge through examination. The list of classes was impressive—isometry, blending and shading, linear perspective, mechanics, geodesy, plans and elevation in engineering construction, stonecutting, civil engineering, roads and bridges, resistance of building materials, and hydraulics—but it is unclear how many students were actually enrolled or how many of these classes initially were taught. Arthur Stace taught surveying and civil engineering, Father Carrier taught physics and chemistry, Brother Albert taught drawing, and seminarian John Zahm assisted in chemistry, physics, and natural science. The first graduate in engineering was Cassius Proctor of Elkhart, Indiana, in 1875, but only two others received the degree in the next ten years.[51]

The university indeed made significant strides during Father Lemonnier's brief presidency. He added a year to the Preparatory (high school) Course, making the total a seven-year rather than a six-year program, and comprehensive examinations were required for completion of the Preparatory and Bachelor Programs. The four collegiate years were now designated as freshman, sophomore, junior, and senior. A circulating library had been established and was being well used by students, and the archives begun by Professor Edwards would soon be one of the very best in the world for Catholic Americana. With the inauguration of the Engineering Program, the university was organized into five major academic areas—Classical Course (Arts and Letters), Commercial, Science, Law, and Engineering—the five major divisions of the university for decades.

But Father Lemonnier's health had not been good even before he was named president. In the fall of 1871 he had left Notre Dame temporarily to seek rest and regain his strength, and he did the same the following year. Whatever the illness, it had returned with a vengeance by mid-1874. The students and faculty were notified that fall of its serious nature and were asked for prayers. His death that October 29, at age of only thirty-five, was most edifying. To those assisting around his bed he remarked: "I brought nothing with me into this world—and I carry nothing with me from this world; I am attached to nothing. I ask for nothing but the grace of God." Saying good-bye to some associates, he said: "If I get better, I will go and see you; if not, you must come and see me." His final words before his death were reported: "Be good to the students."[52]

He was so respected and beloved that the anniversary of his death in succeeding years was always commemorated in the *Scholastic* with a simple note, a poem, or a request for prayerful remembrance.[53] His life and work may have been best summarized by a close associate:[54]

> For him the term University was a word of marked significance: he would have all departments of study in prosperous condition, the sciences, the arts, the languages, the professions; he would have the various societies active and harmonious; he would have the officers and professors working together with one mind; he would have the students contented and rapidly advancing in all knowledge; he would have the surroundings as comfortable and beautiful as they were good and useful; and finally he would have all sanctified by a pervading spirit of Christian piety and virtue.

It was a tragedy that Father Lemonnier died so young, dimming the promise he embodied of steady academic progress in a thoroughly Catholic religious environment, and only a slightly smaller tragedy that there seemed to be no one his equal to replace him. It was Father Sorin's choice to make, and he took the chance on a bright young priest in Canada, Father Patrick Colovin. About the same age as Father Lemonnier, Father Colovin had been born in Ontario in 1842 of Irish parents. Apparently well schooled in the seminary, he soon gained a reputation as a serious theologian and accomplished public speaker, and Father Sorin appointed him religious superior of the community in Montreal at the age of twenty-eight—the same age as Father Sorin when he founded the university. He apparently was not a complete success in that position, several religious were not happy with his administration, and he may have turned to drink on occasion. At least that was the report Father Sorin was given at the time, as he confided to Father Corby:[55]

> I am very sorry to learn here such an unpleasant account of poor Father Colovin. A regular and scandalous drunkard; a proud and merciless censor and natural enemy of anyone above him in office; a lazy, irregular, and piousless sort of Religious, whose spirit is [recalled?] as subversive of all authority. They predict he will surely prove equally dangerous anywhere else.

He was a scholar, however, and Father Lemonnier wanted a scholar with him, and Father Sorin appointed him Notre Dame's vice president and director of studies in early October 1874. With Father Lemonnier's early death, Father Sorin had a difficult decision to make, and he delayed two months in making it. As vice president and director of studies, Father Colovin continued to oversee the daily working of the university but it was not until January 1, 1875, that Father Sorin announced that he "was now definitely appointed President of the University."[56]

With that delay, and with earlier differences with Father Sorin, Father Colovin knew he did not have the superior general's full confidence, but the years of his presidency were not unsuccessful. Father Lemonnier's reforms remained in place, Father Colovin himself taught dogmatic theology, presumably a course of scholarly rigor, and he constantly urged the faculty to higher academic standards. He lamented that "the commercial course was more thorough than either the classical or scientific," he "hoped the day would come when the classical course would be the glory of the University," and he urged that examinations be more demanding "so as to form an accurate idea of where each student should be placed."[57] The Engineering Course was reduced from two years to one, but the small number of applicants seemed to justify this. Overall student enrollment did decline but this may have been the result primarily of the weak national economy in the 1870s, and several members of the faculty spent at least part of the summer of 1875 canvassing for students. Recognized as a public speaker, the president was invited to lecture in Chicago, South Bend, and elsewhere, and at home he remained popular with the students.[58]

As time went on, however, Father Sorin grew more discontented with the president, and with his ability to lead what Father Sorin still considered his own school. As a bright, self-confident young man, Father Colovin's views probably clashed on occasion with those of Father Sorin. Declining enrollment must have been a concern. Father Colovin was also Irish, and was proud of it (he had actually been ordained on Saint Patrick's Day), and Father Sorin could be suspicious of the Irish. He considered them too unstable, too independent minded, and too critical of authority. Finally, the rumors remained of excessive drinking on occasion. But when accusations of intemperate language and contempt for authority were raised, many prominent religious at Notre Dame—future president Thomas Walsh, Daniel Hudson, John Zahm, Daniel Spillard, Thomas Carroll, and others—signed a statement questioning the allegations.[59] After two and a half years, however, Father Sorin had apparently seen enough, and decided to make a change. He recalled Father Corby from his post as founding president of the two-year-old Our Lady of the Sacred Heart College in Watertown, Wisconsin, named him president of Notre Dame for the second time, and assigned Father Colovin to replace him in Wisconsin.[60]

It may seem strange that, if Father Sorin removed Father Colovin from the presidency at least in part because he thought him too outspokenly Irish, he would replace him with someone forever associated with the Irish Brigade in the Civil War. But the choice was not surprising. First, Father Corby had served successfully as Notre Dame's president only a few years before and could easily step in again. Second, Father Corby's parents may have emigrated from Ireland but he had been born in the United States and the early Catholic influence of his youth in Detroit and at Notre Dame may have been more French than Irish. Third, during the 1850s, Father Sorin had appointed him to his various positions of influence at Notre Dame, and thus he had Father Sorin's confidence, as Father Colovin had not.[61]

Father Corby's second presidency began well. Father Lemonnier's reforms were still in place, Father Colovin, scholar that he was, may have even strengthened them, and Father Corby continued. Finances remained a major concern, as they would throughout the century and beyond, and the weekly meetings of the local administrative council always reviewed that week's revenues, expenses, and cash on hand. Purchases were often postposed, and efforts were made to utilize Holy Cross religious in the classrooms rather than more costly laymen. But student enrollment increased steadily, from approximately three hundred in 1877–1878 to over four hundred four years later, and that was a benefit.[62]

One of the significant achievements at the university during Father Corby's second term as president, although most of the credit clearly belongs to Father Sorin as superior general and perhaps Father Granger as provincial superior and church pastor, was the addition of the apsidal chapels to the recently constructed Sacred Heart Church and the impressive decorating of the whole interior. When the first Mass was celebrated in the new church on August 15, 1875, the building extended only a few feet beyond the transepts. Shortly thereafter—and as money became available—the apsidal chapels were begun, dedicated to the Holy Angels, Our Lady of Victory, the Passion of Christ (Stations of the Cross Chapel), the Holy Family, the Blessed Mother, and one as a Reliquary Chapel for the preservation of relics.[63]

The beautiful stained glass windows were produced in France by a manufacturing company founded by the Carmelite Sisters of Le Mans, the company that had probably produced the circular rose windows that had graced the first Sacred Heart Church on campus. It went through changes in ownership while the windows were being made for the new church in the 1870s and 1880s but the Carmelite Sisters continued their supervision and the principal artist, Eugène

Hucher, remained throughout. The windows are one of the glories of the campus and reflect much of nineteenth-century French spirituality and religious sentiment. There had been four major apparitions of Mary in France at this time— Our Lady of the Miraculous Medal in 1830, Our Lady of LaSalette in 1846, Our Lady of Lourdes in 1858, and Our Lady of Pontmain in 1871—and the windows of the transepts are devoted especially to the Blessed Mother. Other windows depict Fathers and Doctors of the Church, appropriate for an educational institution, founders of religious communities (Saint Dominic and Saint Clare), numerous men and women martyrs, and national patrons Saint Elizabeth of Hungary, Saint Patrick of Ireland, Saint Louis of France, and Saint Rose of Lima.[64]

While Father Sorin was visiting Rome in the summer of 1873, a friend showed him some fine portraits he possessed, and mentioned that the artist might be an excellent recruit for Notre Dame. His name was Luigi Gregori. Gregori had studied at the Bologna Academy of Fine Arts in the 1840s, had been curator at the Museum Campana for fifteen years, a professor at the Royal Academy of Bologna, and more recently cataloger/curator for the Vatican's invaluable collection of art. Father Sorin was interested, contacted him immediately, and offered him a position at Notre Dame. Before giving a definite answer, Gregori left Rome and returned to Bologna to confer with his wife and seventeen-year-old daughter. Father Sorin wrote Father Lemonnier that July 12: "Father Ferdinando will send you next week, the written contract: $10,000 for ten years. Prepare your young artists. You should have 3 or 4 from among our own Religious, placed under his tuition." An agreement was reached the following year, but only for three years, and primarily to paint the fourteen Stations of the Cross for the new church.[65]

Gregori arrived at Notre Dame on July 30, 1874, fifty-five years old, "of medium stature, of fine appearance, with fiery, black eyes and white hair," apparently with little or no knowledge of English. It would be a year before the first Mass would be celebrated in the new church, but he began immediately painting the Stations of the Cross that would eventually hang there. With brush in hand Gregori could work rapidly, but he was also a perfectionist and delayed between each station until inspired as to exactly what the next station might contain. In the meantime, he produced other works—life-sized portraits of Father Sorin and Father Lemonnier, others of Father Gillespie and Judge Thomas Stanfield of South Bend—and in the fall of 1875 he began a series of lectures on art criticism at the university. The lectures were free of charge, open to all, and students were encouraged to attend, although it is not clear if Gregori lectured in English or Italian. He lectured and had exhibits in Chicago also, and was elected a lifetime member of the Chicago Academy of Design. But the Stations of the Cross were his primary and, overall, probably his best work. All fourteen were completed by the summer of 1877 and solemnly erected by Father Sorin on the Feast of the Seven Sorrows, September 15. Two of the stations, the fourth and twelfth, won awards at the World's Columbian Exposition in Chicago in 1893.[66]

The new church was much larger than the Stations of the Cross, of course, the interiors of nineteenth-century churches needed decorating, and Gregori was asked to extend his visit beyond three years and undertake the work. With Father Sorin's devotion to the Blessed Mother, it is not surprising that the murals (and windows) of both transepts were devoted to major events of her life: her birth, her presentation in the Temple, praying with Saint Anne, the Annunciation, the Visitation, her marriage to Saint Joseph, the birth of Christ, the flight into Egypt, the finding in the Temple, and the Assumption. The ceiling where the nave and transepts meet was divided into eight panels, depicting the four evangelists and four prominent figures of the Old Testament—Moses, David, Isaiah, and Jeremiah. The spangled murals on each side of the nave depicted the sainted companions of Jesus, John the Baptist and Mary Magdalene, the founders of religious communities, Saint Dominic and Saint Francis, Church scholars Saint Thomas Aquinas and Saint Bonaventure, and Father Granger's patron, Saint Alexis. Taken together, as authors Thomas O'Meara and Thomas Schlereth have suggested, the new church's windows and murals showed influence of the Italian Baroque of the sixteenth century, the French Baroque of the seventeenth, and the Neo-Gothic of the nineteenth, revealing much of the Catholic spirituality of those decades.[67]

The great event of the late 1870s, however, was the devastating fire of 1879. It occurred on a Wednesday, April 23, at 11:00 in the morning. The minims, playing in their yard east of the college building, noticed the flames on the building roof and began the cry: "College on Fire! College on Fire!" Workmen had been repairing the roof that morning, perhaps with tar and pitch, but had finished by 10:00 a.m. and had locked the door to the roof behind them when they departed. The cause of the fire was never determined. Did the workmen overlook and leave a burning ember? Did a spark from the steam-house chimney blow over and set the roof's dry timber dust on fire? Was it the heat of the sun or even spontaneous combustion? The destruction was so extensive that an answer was never found.[68]

Father Corby took charge immediately (Father Sorin being absent) and the university community united in action. Students began a bucket brigade up six floors to the roof but the fire had spread too fast. Other students rushed into rooms, even the private quarters of the faculty, and tried to rescue what they could. Beds, desks, and chairs were thrown out of windows, some breaking when they hit the ground. Library books and museum specimens were thrown down also, but not far enough to escape loss when the walls collapsed on them. Two students remained on the roof fighting the blaze too long, and one was slightly injured jumping from floor to floor to escape. A sister was able to run out the back door just before the porch roof collapsed behind her. A volunteer from town suffered from heat prostration after carrying heavy beds to safety, but, fortunately, no one died or was even seriously injured. It was reported at one time that the fire spread so rapidly because the two-thousand-pound statue of Mary atop the dome crashed to the ground and carried burning embers in its wake to all the lower floors, but this theory was later repudiated. Three horse-drawn hose carts and firemen arrived from South Bend at 11:45 a.m. but by then it was too late to save the building.[69]

The wind that morning was from the southwest and thus the new church, the Presbytery, and the buildings to the northwest of the college building were saved, but, to the east, the Infirmary, the Music Hall, the minims play-hall, and the St. Francis Home were all destroyed. Since it took some time for the flames to spread that far, however, the contents of many of those buildings, including the trunks of the students, were saved. Not so with the college building. Many of the beds, desks, and chairs were rescued, but little else. The building itself, except for fragments of the bare outside walls, was gone, the museum and library were destroyed, as were the personal belongings of many of the faculty. When Professor Arthur Stace was asked what he had been able to save, he smiled and pointed to the shirt he was wearing. An ad was printed in the *Scholastic* that September: "Wanted immediately a complete set of human bones. Apply to Dr. Neyron (professor of anatomy)."[70] The museum loss can be indicated from an item in the *Scholastic* just a year before:[71]

Very Rev. President Corby lately purchased a large number of zoological and mineral specimens for the Museum and Cabinet of Natural Sciences. The value of the collection is seven thousand five hundred dollars, and is well worth the money expended. The minerals are gold and silver quartz, green felspar, opalized wood, wood jasper, chalcedony, agates, fluorspar, and many others, to name which would take up too much space in our columns. Among the stuffed specimens of animals are five buffaloes—from the calf two days old to the largest sized bull; three mountain sheep of various sizes; four antelopes, two black-tailed deer; one white-tailed deer; one black bear; one cinnamon bear; three grizzly bears; three mountain lions; one Bengal tiger; besides wolves, foxes, beavers, and other smaller animals. In the collection are specimens of every variety of birds known in the Rocky Mountain section of our country.

The university's loss was estimated at $250,000, and only $40,000 was insured.[72]

Father Sorin was in Canada at the time, preparing for a trip to Europe, and Professor Edwards was dispatched immediately to bring him the tragic news in person. After meeting with his advisors, Father Corby decided to end the school year immediately, notify the parents, and send the students home, but assure everyone that the university would reopen in September. Brief commencement ceremonies were held on Thursday and Friday after the fire, and degrees were awarded to seniors in the Collegiate, Commercial, Science, and Law Departments. The minims and manual labor apprentices were allowed to remain through the summer, the minims sleeping in Washington Hall, which they referred to as "Hotel de Washington." The public responded generously: residents of South Bend had hurried to the scene and helped rescue what was possible, others offered their homes for temporary shelter, the telegraph office sent telegrams to the parents gratis, railroads gave reduced fares to students forced to leave, and General Sherman in Washington offered to send army field tents as needed. Alexis Coquillard, Notre Dame's first student in 1842, sent $500. Aid came from Chicago, mindful that Notre Dame students had organized a concert and sent the proceeds to Chicago after its devastating fire in 1871. The students at Saint Mary's held a meeting and agreed to send all their pocket money to Father Corby as a pledge of additional assistance to come. Father Zahm went on a fundraising trip to Fort Wayne, Cleveland, Toledo, and Columbus, Professor Howard to Detroit, Albany, and Buffalo, and two Holy Cross sisters, Valeria and Bridget, sailed to Ireland to seek assistance.[73]

Father Sorin returned to Notre Dame with Professor Edwards on Sunday, April 27, and called the community together in the new church, as Professor Howard remembered:[74]

> I was then present when Father Sorin, after looking over the destruction of his life-work, stood at the altar steps of the only building left and spoke to the community what I have always felt to be the most sublime words I ever listened to. There was absolute faith, confidence, resolution in his very look and pose. "If it were ALL gone, I should not give up!" were his words in closing. The effect was electric. It was the crowning moment of

his life. A sad company had gone into the church that day. They were all simple Christian heroes as they came out. There was never more a shadow of a doubt as to the future of Notre Dame.

Work began immediately. The *Scholastic* in early May noted that "everyone agrees that Very Rev. Father General can wheel off a load of bricks with great grace and dignity," but then added: "we do not wish to discourage the efforts of a conscientious worker, but, still regard for historical accuracy compels us to state our conviction that Very Rev. Father Granger would scarcely command a large salary among the horny-handed sons of toil." Eight architects had submitted proposals by May 10, and a cornerstone had already been blessed. The architectural plan accepted was that of Willoughby J. Edbrooke of Chicago, later the architect of the Georgia State Capitol, the Grand Tabor Opera House in Colorado, and the Federal Post Office in Washington. Rubble from the old building was cleared away by mid-May; the architect, Brother Charles, and Professor William Ivers began running lines, driving stakes, and mapping out foundations; and by the end of the month the outside walls were beginning to rise. By that time, twenty-six bricklayers, plus their necessary attendants, were employed each day, and that number rose to fifty-six a month later. The building was to be 224 feet in length, with two wings to be added in the future, 155 feet in depth, and a height of 170 feet from ground to roof, with a tower and dome to be added later; 556 floor-to-ceiling windows would provide sunlight and fresh air; and an estimated 4,350,000 bricks would be needed to finish the project. Two dining rooms, for the seniors and juniors, would be on the ground floor; on the floor above (the main floor) would be the study halls, twelve classrooms, the university parlor, and offices of the president and vice president; and ten more classrooms, dormitories, and private rooms for faculty were on the floors above. The building was equipped with indoor plumbing, gas lighting, and steam heat. Mr. Edbrooke visited frequently throughout the summer, and in his absence Brother Charles and Brother Alfred supervised the day-to-day construction, always under the eye of President Father Corby who only a few years before had overseen the construction of the impressive Saint Bernard's Church in Watertown, Wisconsin. The overall architectural style might be called "Modern Gothic" or "Eclectic Gothic." One viewer thought it "a monstrous example of decorative impulses running riot in brick, wood, paint and plaster." Others dubbed it simply "Modern Sorin."[75]

Fire protection was an obvious concern. The roof of the new building was slate, with nothing to burn, and the chimneys of all buildings were cleaned. Father Zahm was commissioned to found a university fire department, and the *Scholastic* noted that "the church and the college fairly bristle with lightning rods." Money was requested of the provincial council to rebuild the Infirmary and the Music Hall, and no more elderly residents were accepted until a new St. Francis Home could be built. With these priorities, no other expenditures could be undertaken without the explicit permission of Father Corby, and tuition was lowered from $150 per session to $125 to attract new students. Father Corby had promised that classes would reopen in early September, and reopen they did. The central portion of the new building, absent the wings and dome, was completed; the refectories, classrooms, study halls, and dormitories were ready for use; the library and museum still awaited fixtures; and the Infirmary was completed. The *Scholastic* noted: "Very Rev. President Corby deserves great credit for the energetic manner in which he has pursued the work of constructing the new building. He did it all in the quiet way peculiar to himself, without much talk, but with every order well weighed and matured before giving it utterance." After such a devastating fire and recovery, some awarded him the title "the second founder of Notre Dame."[76]

CHAPTER 6

A New Notre Dame

In the aftermath of the devastating fire of April 23, 1879, appeals were made to alumni and others in various cities to assist with the immediate rebuilding of the college. Father Corby addressed such a gathering in Chicago, and many responded favorably. However, a letter to the editor appeared in the *Chicago Tribune* questioning whether Notre Dame actually deserved such assistance:[1]

> There are many claims just now pressing on public attention, and some over-zealous people are pushing up too much the so-called University of Notre Dame. What are its special claims on the public? It has been in existence forty years, yet literature or oratory is silent about the claims of one single scholar it produced, or one book that ever came forth under its patronage. As a University no one knows it; its claims as a school for teaching ultramontane doctrines is certainly well founded. I wonder will they solicit from those of other or no denominations subscriptions to replace the large image of the Virgin Mary which was heretofore so conspicuous and so useless? Its claims for practical education may be judged from this fact. How many of our distinguished medical men, how many mechanics, how many engineers—in short, how many useful members of society—has it turned out in forty years?

As was to be expected, an anonymous supporter of the university was quick to reply:[2]

"What has Notre Dame done for the past forty years?" Chicago is not the place to ask such a question, but Chicago is the place to answer it. No city in the nation knows so well what Notre Dame has done as does Chicago, for they have grown up together from the untamed wilds of Nature, and Chicago has at all times availed herself largely of advantages she fancied Notre Dame presented for the education of youth,—as many as one hundred students being present at one time from that city. But "it has produced no scholar, and no book has come forth under its patronage." Shall we then reckon up the colleges and universities of the country, and wherever we find one that has produced no scholar, no book, of which literature and oratory are boastful, cast that aside as unworthy of the name? What college west of the Alleghenies has produced this scholar or this book that literature and oratory laud so highly? Who, pray, are the scholars, and what are the books, of even so renowned an institution as the University of Michigan? And yet who will dare say that that great University has not been doing noble work during the past forty years? . . .

Notre Dame has produced her fair share of books, periodicals, writers, orators, and scientists, but she has done something far better than all this. In the thirty-five years that have passed since she received her charter from the Legislature of Indiana, she has sent forth an army of young men as highly moral and intelligent as any institution can boast in the same time and with the same advantages. . . . Her cause is the cause of liberal and Christian education; and, so long as there are parents who believe in the Christian education of their children, so long will Notre Dame prosper, all detraction to the contrary notwithstanding.

To another correspondent who criticized the university as chiefly a proselytizing arm of the church, a local judge replied:[3]

Notre Dame is truly a Catholic institution, as I believe many other notable institutions of learning have been and presently are, but nothing can be further from the truth than that it was established for the purpose of "making converts to Catholicism from among its Protestants [*sic*] students," and this is not done "under the pretense of furthering the cause of education," nor any other pretense. Notre Dame is not a theological school, nor does it seek exclusively, or mainly, or in any partial sense, to benefit Catholicism. Its curriculum is liberal and elevating, its processes conformable to the progressive tendencies of the day, and its results gratifying to enlightened minds. Self-righteous bigotry alone disputes its superiority or laments over its success. . . . I am not, sir, nor have I ever been, nor do I expect to be a Catholic, but I am a friend of honesty and truth. I am, also, yours truly, T. G. Turner.

As usual in controversies of this kind, the institution was not as bad as some of its critics claimed, nor as good as some of its defenders insisted. But with its main college building and four of its auxiliary buildings now destroyed by fire, and with new and more impressive buildings rising to replace them, a new era in the university's life might now begin, and in a sense it did.

The new era began with a new president. Thomas E. Walsh had been born in Canada in 1853, attended common grammar school and then entered the College of St. Laurent in Montreal, founded by the Holy Cross fathers. On graduating in 1873, he decided to become a priest and entered the Holy Cross novitiate there. As superior general, Father Sorin had visited the College of St. Laurent several times, noticed the brilliant scholastic record young Walsh was making, and eventually decided to send him to the College de Ste. Croix in France for his theological studies. After three years in Paris, Father Sorin reassigned him in 1876, not to Canada, but to Notre Dame. Walsh was a young man of excellent intellectual and administrative potential, and Notre Dame always ranked first in the heart of Father Sorin.[4]

Walsh arrived at Notre Dame at a difficult time. Father Colovin was president but was clearly losing favor with Father Sorin. Walsh, a serious student with a very bright mind, admired Father Colovin's intellectual interests and scholarly goals, yet he respected and owed much to Father Sorin also. He was assigned to continue his theological studies for an additional year, and also teach advanced classes in Greek and Latin. The following year, 1877, Father Sorin, whatever his reasons, decided to make a change at Notre Dame and recalled Father Corby to replace Father Colovin as president. Father Corby, not primarily an intellectual himself, had the insight to ask that young Walsh, still twenty-four, be named the university's vice president and director of studies. He was ordained that summer, was appointed to the position, and was successful in organizing classes and re-establishing the academic program after the fire of 1879. In 1881, at age twenty-eight, he was named president.[5]

The reasons for the change were complex and not at all clear. In late 1880 the Vatican had notified Father Corby that he should not be serving both as provincial superior of all Holy Cross priests and brothers in the United States and as president and local superior at Notre Dame, because that lodged too much authority and responsibility in the hands of one man. The Vatican allowed Father Corby to decide which office to vacate and which to retain, and on January 21, 1881, Father Corby notified the community of his resignation as provincial superior.[6] Shortly thereafter, however, Father Sorin decided to replace Father Corby as president with Father Walsh, and Father Corby was reassigned to Watertown, Wisconsin, to the impressive church he had constructed a few years before. Father Sorin may have been displeased that Father Corby had seemed to side at times with Father Colovin in that priest's recent conflict with the superior general. He may also have thought that Father Corby had assumed too much initiative in rebuilding the campus after the tragic fire, without seeking the approval of the founder. Moreover, Father Sorin, more under the influence now of Father Walsh, Father John Zahm, and other young priests, may have wanted the university guided in a slightly different direction, with more emphasis on the collegiate division. Whatever the reason, Father Corby was apparently no longer the person Father Sorin wanted to be president of what he still considered *his* university.[7]

Father Walsh served as Notre Dame's president for twelve years, until his early death in 1893 at age forty, and he fully justified Father Sorin's faith in him. A statement in the *Catalogue* of 1882–1883 expressed his goal:[8]

> Its [Notre Dame's] officers, its Faculty, and all connected with it are determined that it shall continue onward and upward, ever directed and stimulated by the laudable motives and enthusiastic zeal of its venerable founder.

Father Walsh decided, for the first few years at least, to retain the office of director of studies himself, and as president and director of studies he could have greater impact on this "onward and upward" progress of the university. Under his guidance and leadership, progress was made in increased numbers, in developing programs, in building expansion, and in student life.

After the disappointing enrollment numbers of the 1870s, when even faculty members were sent on summer recruiting trips to attract more students, there was a steady growth in enrollment in the 1880s. Fewer than four hundred students were enrolled when the decade began but the number increased throughout the decade and over six hundred were enrolled in Father Walsh's final year. Much of this increase seems to have been in the Senior or Collegiate Department, as the number of collegiate degrees awarded annually increased during the decade from fifteen to thirty-three. The faculty also increased by one-fourth over the decade, with almost all of the additions Holy Cross religious. Since these did not receive full salaries, just their daily maintenance, this was a major financial benefit for the university, and two of the recent additions later became influential Notre Dame presidents: Fathers John W. Cavanaugh and James A. Burns.[9]

Academically the university continued to progress. In 1865, the name of the four-year Collegiate Course had been changed to Classical Course, and the subjects required remained consistent throughout the 1880s: Greek, Latin, English, history, mathematics, philosophy, political economy, and natural and physical science. By 1882, the Preparatory and Classical Courses were clearly separate divisions.[10]

The Commercial Course continued to attract students also, although probably not proportionately as many as in earlier years. Notre Dame had a class in bookkeeping as early as 1851, and courses in bookkeeping, penmanship, and arithmetic composed at least the beginnings of a Mercantile Department in 1853. Four commercial diplomas were awarded in 1861, and it was made a full two-year program in 1863, probably due to the initiative of Father Patrick Dillon, recently reassigned to the university. For the most part, the classes remained constant throughout the 1880s—bookkeeping, penmanship, arithmetic, algebra, English grammar, composition, elocution, history, German, and commercial law—and it was still primarily a high school program, with only a diploma, not a degree, awarded after completion of the required two years of study.

In 1882 a new course was added, the Belles-Lettres or English Course, leading to the degree of bachelor of letters. The new course retained most of the classes of the Classical Program, with two major exceptions: in the Belles-Lettres Course, Greek and Latin were dropped and modern languages inserted, and the final year was composed exclusively of English courses (Principles of Literary Criticism, Philosophy of Style, Oratorical Composition and Elocution, Literature of the Nineteenth Century, and Aesthetics of Literature). In establishing the program, the university was following a national trend, and the annual *Catalogue* that year explained the reason:[11]

The Faculty of the University of Notre Dame, recognizing the fact that the exclusive study of the ancient languages and of pure science is not in itself sufficient for a liberal education, have determined to institute a course which shall provide for a more than ordinarily thorough acquaintance with the English language and with English and American literature. At the same time, all that is most serviceable in the Classical and Scientific Courses will be made an indispensable requisite.

The person Father Walsh tapped to be the head and mainstay of this new Belles-Lettres Program was the well-known writer Charles Warren Stoddard. A direct descendent of the Stoddards who arrived in colonial Boston in 1639, he was born in Rochester, New York, in 1843 and spent part of his youth in New York City and part in San Francisco. He began writing verse at an early age and sent it to local newspapers anonymously. He attended a few college classes, acted briefly on stage but did not like it, and in 1864 visited Pacific islands that he wrote about in *South-Sea Idyls*. He converted to Catholicism in 1867, began writing for the *San Francisco Chronicle*, and continued his travels throughout Europe and the Middle East, meeting Ambrose Bierce, Joaquin Miller, and Mark Twain along the way. He contributed pieces occasionally to the *Ave Maria* and began a long correspondence with Father Daniel Hudson, the magazine's editor. It was Father Hudson who recommended him to Father Walsh.[12]

Stoddard accepted the position with some hesitation, even misgivings. In a letter to Father Hudson, he wanted to know how much he would be expected to teach, what ages his students would be, and whether there would be restrictions on his free time. He admitted that he was a "free liver," drank with his friends ("sometimes . . . more than was good for me"), smoked "sigarettes" [*sic*] but never "chowed" [*sic*], and was a "confirmed misspeller . . . which is beyond all human aid." He remained at Notre Dame less than two years, 1885–1886. He found Indiana's climate less agreeable than San Francisco's, he bridled at some restrictions (not sharing his "sigarettes" with students), his health was not good, and his lifestyle was out of step with Catholic teachings. Although retaining his friendship with Father Hudson, he departed Notre Dame in late 1886, as he wrote, "full of disgust and malaria."[13]

With the failure of the Stoddard appointment, Father Walsh then turned to Maurice Francis Egan. Egan had been born in Philadelphia in 1852 and grew up devoted to both literature and Catholicism, influenced by his mother who was supposedly often seen "with a rosary in one hand and a novel of Jane Austen's in the other." He published his first essay in *Appleton's Journal* at age seventeen, graduated from La Salle College in 1873, and studied and taught philosophy at

Georgetown University for three years. His first love was writing, and prolific he was. He contributed to local newspapers, wrote novels, and published sonnets. He held editorial positions at *Magee's Weekly*, *The Illustrated Review*, the *Catholic Review*, and *The Freeman's Journal*, of which he became part owner.[14]

Father Walsh paid him a visit in New York in 1888 and offered him the chair of English literature. Egan and his wife were at home in the East Coast culture of New York and Boston, but they were not sure that New York was the best place to raise their three young children, and Egan was confident that he could live comfortably in South Bend with an independent income. The university built a large home for him, "The Lilacs," just off the campus, and the building still stands. Egan continued his writing, became close friends with Father Walsh, Father Zahm, and Father Hudson, and attracted distinguished guests at times to his home and to Notre Dame, including theatre personalities Augustin Daly, Anne Hartley Gilbert, and Ada Rehan, and the bishop of Peoria, John Lancaster Spalding, whose prose Egan admired, but not his efforts at poetry. Egan left Notre Dame in 1896 for the Catholic University of America in Washington, DC, served as minister to Denmark from 1907 to 1918, and then returned to the United States to continue his writing and lecturing. He died in Brooklyn in 1924.[15]

If there was a silver lining to the disastrous fire of 1879, it was that it necessitated the construction of new, and better, educational facilities, and the fine arts were one area that profited. A freestanding exhibition hall had been constructed a little to the northeast of the first Main Building in the early 1860s, and was possibly already named Washington Hall.[16] The ground floor served as an indoor recreation facility for the Senior Department and the upper two floors for student assemblies, exhibitions, theatrical performances, and similar gatherings. A smaller Music Hall was constructed close by in 1865, with an indoor recreation room for the Junior Department, and this building was one of those destroyed in the fire. A new Music Hall was constructed in 1880, the present north section of Washington Hall. The old Washington Hall (exhibition hall) was demolished in 1882 and the present building constructed, with the tower and the main steps of stone not completed until 1889. The architect was Willoughby Edbrooke who had recently designed the new Main Building, Luigi Gregori painted much of the interior, and the Gothic building was to balance and mirror on the east side of the Main Building the new Sacred Heart Church on the west side. The building had a total floor space of thirty thousand feet, a large main stage, auxiliary rehearsal and recitation rooms in back, and a seating capacity, on the floor and in the balcony, of over a thousand. The total cost was close to $30,000. Commencement exercises were to be held there, and musical performances, oratorical contests, and theatrical productions throughout the year. For the commencement exercises in 1882, *Oedipus Rex* was performed entirely in Greek, with costumes Professor Gregori helped to design, and the following year *Antigone*, the first plays ever performed in Greek west of the Allegheny Mountains.[17]

The university's science program improved throughout the 1880s also. The program had been inaugurated in the mid-1860s, possibly as a result of the needs and demands of the Civil War, and Father Joseph Carrier had taken the lead in developing and promoting it. Students in the Scientific Course took the basic classes of the then Collegiate Course, with the exception of Greek and Latin, and added comparative anatomy, botany, zoology, human physiology, theoretical and analytical chemistry, physics, geology, minerology, and four years of mathematics. The program grew throughout the 1870s but suffered a devastating loss with the destruction of the laboratories with their equipment and the museum with its scientific specimens when fire destroyed the Main Building in 1879.[18]

Fortunately for the university, the person to rebuild the science program was at hand. Father John Zahm had been born in New Lexington, Ohio, in 1851, and received his elementary education in a one-room log schoolhouse where classes were taught at times convenient for young farm boys to attend. The Zahm family moved to Huntington, Indiana, in 1863 where young John continued his education at the parish school of Saints Peter and Paul. During these years he began thinking of the possibility of becoming a priest and, in 1867, he wrote for advice to an aunt, Sister M. Praxedes, who was a Sister of Holy Cross at Saint Mary's. Sister Praxedes showed the letter to Father Sorin and, after discovering what English and Latin he had studied and what tuition he could pay, he admitted John Zahm to the university.[19]

Because he was interested in the priesthood, Zahm enrolled in the Classical Course and was a superior student, most of the time. He was often seated at the Table of Honor in the refectory, but he also failed German and mathematics in his sophomore year. He was a member of the Saint Aloysius Philodemic Society, the Scientific Association, the Archconfraternity of the Immaculate Heart of Mary, the student choir, and the Juanita Baseball Club. He served as officer and librarian for the Saint Aloysius Society, taking part in the numerous scholarly debates it sponsored, but he was especially active in the Scientific Association, chaired at that time by Father Carrier. When one of the university professors suggested that the growth of the Science Department was having a deleterious effect on the university's classical and liberal education program, student Zahm answered with praise of the progress made through such inventions as Watt's steam engine, Morse's telegraph, and printing in general, and insisted that science was "the highest exponent of power and intellectual superiority . . . and . . . the most reliable touchstone of the progress and tendency of the age in which we live."[20]

Zahm graduated from Notre Dame in 1871 and immediately entered the Holy Cross novitiate. To assist the university financially, he was also assigned to teach courses in English grammar and Greek during his novitiate year. In succeeding years in the seminary he assisted Father Carrier in his physics and chemistry classes and served as assistant librarian and curator of the museum. In 1875, Father Carrier was named president of Saint Mary's College in Galveston, Texas, and Zahm, not yet ordained, was named professor of chemistry and physics and a member of the university's all Holy Cross board of trustees. He was ordained to the priesthood in 1875 and the following year was given a one-year appointment as both vice president of the university and director of studies, and, for some reason, president of the Lemonnier Boat Club. He remained professor of chemistry and physics, and he spent free time travelling to purchase new scientific equipment and museum specimens. Most of this was lost in the tragic fire, and it fell to Zahm, as vice president and professor of chemistry and physics, to rebuild it.[21]

Approximately half of the students' courses were in the humanities or liberal arts: English grammar and literature, various periods of history, modern or classical languages, political economy, philosophy, and so on. As was customary among Catholic colleges at the time, no religion classes were required, or offered, in any of the college programs. Students were required to attend Mass on Sundays and Wednesdays, confessions were heard weekly, spiritual conferences were given periodically, and these religious exercises were apparently considered sufficient. Religion classes were not included in the curriculum until 1920.

Basic science courses were all offered. In mathematics, the student took algebra; plane, solid, and analytical geometry; trigonometry; and calculus. There were four semesters of chemistry and four of physics, two of botany and two of astronomy, and one each of zoology, geology, and physiology. As new instruments were purchased, microscopic work in biology was added. Bordering on engineering, the scientific program offered courses in mineralogy, mechanics, telegraphy, and photography. The faculty offering the courses seems quite respectable: Father John Zahm, Father Louis Neyron, Father Alexander Kirsch, Brother Celestine in telegraphy, and Father Zahm's younger brother, Albert, who later gained international fame through his work in aerodynamics.[22]

The main advance in science education, however, was the construction of a new, freestanding science building. The earliest science courses had been taught in the Main Building, as was everything else. After 1876 they were taught in

Phelan Hall, called "Old Science Hall," behind the campus church, but with the loss of the science classrooms, laboratories, equipment, and museum specimens in the fire of 1879, Father Zahm campaigned for a new building with greater space, and his request was heard. His first task, of course, was to locate funding. He procured an eight-hundred-pound electromagnet and began a lecture tour to demonstrate the marvels of science. Of his lecture in South Bend, the local *Daily Register* wrote: "His language was well suited to the popular style of lecturing, through its simplicity and succinctness, and the lecture was so profusely illustrated by experiments that the audience was kept awake to every point introduced." According to the Fort Wayne *Sentinel* two weeks later, his audience there "had the pleasure of witnessing some of the most brilliant and interesting experiments in connection with the subject-matter." The money raised was specifically for the new building. Father Sorin had written in October 1879: "Our Father Zahm is hereby fully authorized to keep for the building of the eastern wing, as marked in the place, for a Scientific Hall, all donations and moneys he may, from this day, solicit and receive for that purpose."[23]

The new building (later the LaFortune Student Center), was designed also by Willoughby Edbrooke—after much consultation with Father Zahm—and opened in 1884. Built in the neoclassical style and situated just south or in front of the recently constructed Washington Hall, it was 131 feet by 104 feet and included a basement and two upper stories, with twenty-five rooms in all. The basement contained the boiler room, a storeroom, the metallurgical laboratory, and room for dynamo-electric machines. The first floor held rooms for the professors and lecture rooms, laboratories, and cabinets for both chemistry and physics. The second floor housed the university museum and lecture and laboratory rooms for biology, geology, and mineralogy. With this added space, professors' rooms, and newer facilities, Father Zahm had to be pleased.[24]

Although it was called the Science Hall for the first seventy or more years of its existence, the new building at first also served the Engineering Program. That course had begun in 1873 as a two-year program in civil engineering for students in their junior and senior years of college. For a time the program was apparently reduced to one year, but in 1889–1890 this Civil Engineering Program was elevated to a full four-year course. Classes in the first two years included English, history, foreign languages, mathematics, drawing, and natural sciences, and in the final two years pure and applied mathematics, drawing, foreign languages, philosophy, and natural and physical sciences. Economics was added from 1890 to 1892. It seems probable that courses in geology and mineralogy were included under the natural and physical sciences.[25]

A second engineering program, mechanical engineering, was inaugurated in 1886, in the words of one author, "to teach design and functions of steam engines, boilers, and condensers." The curriculum for the first two years of study was probably the same as in civil engineering. In the third year, however, the students studied Analytical Mechanics, Materials of Engineering, Machinery and Millwork, Kinematics, Machine Drawing, and Shop Practice. The fourth-year classes included Prime Movers, Machine Drawing, and Design and Experimental Machines. Foreign languages, logic, and metaphysics were also taken in the third and fourth years.[26]

The engineering programs were not large and there were several professors on the faculty to offer the courses: Arthur Stace continued to teach surveying and civil engineering until his unfortunate death in 1890 at age fifty-eight, Michael O'Dea taught electricity, John Kivlan machine shop, Brother Celestine telegraphy, Brother Stanislaus photography, and young Martin McCue, later dean of the College of Engineering, civil engineering. But the most accomplished of the engineering professors in the 1880s was Father Zahm's younger brother, Albert.[27]

Albert Zahm was born in 1862 and enrolled in the Classical Course at Notre Dame in 1879. As an undergraduate, he won Freshman, Sophomore, Junior, and Senior Medals, a medal in philosophy of history, and First Honor Gold Medals for conduct. Captivated by science and technology, especially aeronautics, he tried to invent a perpetual motion machine, only to discover it contravened the law of conservation of energy; he made a toy boat with a wind screw that activated an opposing water screw that enabled it to sail directly into the wind; he tried to pad the feet of a dog so it could gallop across Saint Mary's Lake; he invented a toy gun he hoped could shoot around a corner; he demonstrated why a spinning baseball curved; and he built a wind tunnel in his junior year to compare the lift and drag of aeronautic models. He received his BA degree in 1883, an MA in 1885, an MS degree in 1890, eventually another MS in mechanical engineering from Cornell in 1892, and a PhD from Johns Hopkins in 1898.[28]

He taught mathematics and mechanics at Notre Dame in the 1880s and, in his research, launched man-carrying gliders from the roof of the new Science Hall, always at night to avoid publicity. He hoped also to launch a glider from a hot-air balloon at a much higher altitude but the university administration refused permission. He did construct a foot-powered flying machine that he suspended by rope from the ceiling of the Science Hall museum and that could then circle around within the museum high above the ground. The driver's feet would gently push the machine away from the walls as it came close. Seeing those footprints high on the walls the next morning, the brother building manager reportedly felt they could only have been made by the devil himself and sprinkled the museum with holy water. Zahm was a pioneer in discovering ways to launch airplanes from the ground and to control them in flight by rotating wing parts and double tails. He eventually left Notre Dame, taught for a time at the Catholic University of America in Washington, DC, became director of the United States Navy Aerodynamical Laboratory, and then became holder of the Guggenheim Chair of Aeronautics at the Library of Congress. On his death in 1954, his body was returned to Notre Dame and buried in the Holy Cross community cemetery where his brother, Father John Zahm, had been buried thirty-two years before.[29]

Since most of the engineering classrooms and laboratories were in the basement of the new Science Hall, most of the engineering classes were taught there also—except for Albert Zahm's higher-flying experiments—but with the inauguration of mechanical engineering classes in 1886 and electrical engineering in 1889, additional space was needed. As vice president, Father Zahm convinced the administration to construct a small Institute of Technology building just south of the Science Hall. The architect was Brother Charles Borromeo Harding again, certainly with major, and probably constant, input from Father Zahm himself. It was a three-story structure, one hundred feet by forty, housing classrooms, drawing rooms, a machine shop, a foundry, and a forge, and it opened for use in the fall of 1891. It served the Engineering Program well until that department moved into other quarters in 1902, and it then became home successively for chemistry and pharmacy, law, architecture, psychology, and music.[30]

The program that made the greatest progress in the 1880s was undoubtedly the course in law. Founded in 1869, it was a two-year program offering the standard courses of that time: Introduction to Roman Law, Principles of Legislation, Criminal Law, Procedure, Constitutional Law, Civil Jurisprudence, Contracts, Evidence, and similar. "A good liberal education" was the only requirement for admission, and, at times, it was not clear who was actually in charge of the program. But all this changed when Father Walsh in 1882 invited William J. Hoynes to join the law faculty.[31]

Hoynes had been born in Callan, County Kilkenny, Ireland, in 1846, and through his grandmother he was a direct descendent of Daniel O'Connell. His family immigrated to America, and Wisconsin, when he was seven, and at age twelve he began working as a printer's apprentice. After being rejected the year before, he was accepted into the Twentieth Wisconsin Infantry in June 1862, at fifteen certainly one of the younger volunteers in the Union Army. He saw action in Missouri and Arkansas, lost the sight of his right eye from a kick in the head by a recalcitrant mule, and a rebel bullet grazed his skull in the Battle of Prairie Grove, leaving a furrow deep enough to hold a pencil. It bled profusely, caused him considerable pain, and left some debilitating aftereffects for a time. Honorably discharged on November 11, 1863, he returned to the printer's office in Wisconsin but dizziness and limited movement of his head rendered this work impossible. Desiring to continue his education, he enrolled in Notre Dame in 1867 and, after two years, transferred to the University of Michigan to study law, receiving the degree in 1872. For the next few years he alternated between law and journalism. He served as editor of the New Brunswick, New Jersey, *Daily Times* and of the Peoria *Daily Transcript*, and as chief of staff for Mark Pomeroy's Chicago *Democrat*. He was successful in law also and was admitted to practice before the Supreme Court of Michigan, the Supreme Court of Illinois, the United States Circuit Court, and the Supreme Court of the United States. Notre Dame had awarded him a master of arts degree in 1877 and he was invited to return to campus in 1883 as dean of law, in fact if not yet in name.[32]

Hoynes remained at Notre Dame until his death in 1933, as dean until 1918, and was undoubtedly the university's best known "character" in all fifty years. He had a great love of the military, was well read in strategy and tactics, and could regale listeners for hours with stories of Civil War battles. A student remembered that he began one lecture at 7 p.m. with the firing of a shell on Fort Sumter on April 12, 1861, and when the lecture ended at 10 p.m. the shell had not yet landed. He formed and drilled a small band of military cadets on campus, known affectionately as "The Hoynes Light Guards," and, although he had been mustered out of the Union Army as a private, his cadets dubbed him "Colonel," and he remained Colonel Hoynes the rest of his life. A staunch Republican, he was nominated for Congress in 1888 but was defeated, was appointed by President Benjamin Harrison to head the commission that successfully negotiated a land treaty with the Turtle Mountain Chippewa Natives in 1890, and in 1895 he served on an Indiana commission to plan the centenary celebration of that state's admission as a territory. A big man of over two hundred pounds, he enjoyed being the center of attention, wore an army uniform on military occasions, a cravat and ascot on legal ones, a top hat and long coat for student assemblies, and he loved to pose for pictures in all of them. He invariably arranged to enter an auditorium after everyone was seated and inserted as many polysyllabic words in a sentence as it could hold. Smiling at his own pomposity, he began one address: "Socrates is dead; Demosthenes is dead; ah-hem and I am not feeling so good myself." He attended Mass almost daily and could not refuse a small donation to anyone in need. Scrupulously honest, he housed his Turtle Mountain Indian Commission in second- and third-class hotels and returned the money saved back to the government—much to the surprise of Washington officials! He was a bundle of idiosyncrasies, students and colleagues could laugh at his foibles, but he was deeply loved. When someone, mistakenly or not, dumped a bucket of water on him as he exited the residence hall where he lived, the university added a porch and a roof to prevent it happening again.[33]

He was a "character" but not a buffoon, and the law program greatly improved under his leadership. The course had been lengthened to a full three-year program the year before he arrived, and it has remained that ever since. Enrollment was small, with ten or twelve students in each class. Ten graduated in 1889, the largest class of the decade. Lecturing was emphasized, allowing also for class participation, but the standard law textbooks were also assigned. In the first year, only one hour of law class was required each day, allowing the students to continue or complete their liberal arts education. The class was based on the *Commentaries* of Blackstone and Kent, but other works were also utilized: Walker's *American Law*, Smith's *Elementary Law*, Munson's *Elementary Practice*, Holland's *Elements of Jurisprudence*, and Fishback's *Manual of Elementary Law*. In the second year, the students studied Common and Statutory Law, Contracts, Torts, Criminal Law and Procedure, Medical Jurisprudence, Evidence, and Common Law Pleading. Third-year students took classes in Equity Jurisprudence, International Law, Constitutional Law, Private and Municipal Corporations, and Personal and Real Property. There were two or three lecture classes each day, with perhaps an additional class for quizzes and recitation. Debates were held every Wednesday evening, and moot court on Saturday, trying actual or hypothetical cases and giving students familiarity with and practice in a full court setting. Many of the classes were taught by Hoynes himself, although three others were listed on the law faculty in 1882 and seven others in 1892.[34] The *Chicago Law Journal* in 1886 had high praise for the program:

> Within the past three or four years, the Law Department of the University of Notre Dame . . . has taken rank among the very best law schools in the country. Not one of its graduates, during that time, has failed to pass a credible examination for the Bar in any of the States; while its diploma admits the holder, without examination, to the Bar of Indiana, yet in other states prevails the general rule applying to all law schools outside

of their respective jurisdictions, and an examination is necessary. But it is worthy of note that the graduates of Notre Dame have not only successfully passed the test in every case, but also have, on several occasions, been highly complimented by the examiners.

The university began a graduate program in 1890, leading to the degree of master of laws. It was a one-year program, emphasizing legal writing, taking depositions, examination of witnesses, preparation of briefs, and the making of deeds and mortgages. Moot court sessions were again required.[35]

As the law program both improved and expanded throughout the 1880s, new facilities were required. When it was founded in 1869, the Law Department was housed in the Main Building, but that building burned ten years later. It found quarters in the new Main Building when it was constructed but the allotted space soon became too small. In 1888 the university administration decided to build a student residence hall, name it for Father Sorin, and reserve space in it for the law program.[36]

Sorin Hall was one of the first residence halls on a Catholic college campus with private rooms for students, in the belief that at least older students, for whom the hall was being built, could study more seriously there than in the common study hall. But whose idea what it? Professor Ralph Weber, in his fine biography of Father John Zahm, says that Albert Zahm claimed it was his brother's idea, and that Father Walsh either opposed it or was at least hesitant. Father Zahm then convinced Father Sorin of the project, Father Walsh was sent to Europe to attend the meeting of the International Catholic Scientific Congress, and during his absence, Mr. Edbrooke was commissioned to design the building and the cornerstone was dedicated on May 27, two days before Father Walsh disembarked from Europe. Weber speculates that Father Walsh may not have been pleased and eventually replaced Father Zahm as vice president with Father Andrew Morrissey, and it was then Father Morrissey who would succeed him as president.[37]

Much of this may be true. It could have been Father Zahm's idea and he could have convinced Father Sorin of it since the two were becoming close. But the date of May 27 probably had nothing to do with Father Walsh's absence but was the exact date on which Father Sorin had been ordained a priest fifty years before and the blessing of the cornerstone of the new Sorin Hall was an appropriate part of that Jubilee celebration, and Father Sorin would certainly have been involved in Father Zahm's replacement as vice president and it was probably not for an action in which he had been a part.

Sorin Hall was 144 feet by 112 feet, with sixty private rooms, each measuring 14 feet by 12 feet. It was situated south and a little to the west of the campus church, to mirror and balance the new Science Hall to the east across the developing quadrangle. The rooms were intended to be "large enough to encourage study and at the same time small enough to discourage visiting," although no college room can ever be that small. The south half of the first floor was assigned to the law program. Dean Hoynes had his residence there, the classes were held there, and there was space for the law library. The *Columbia Law Times* called the facility a "magnificent structure" and added: "The moot court library and lecture rooms are spacious, well lighted, well ventilated and exceptionally comfortable rooms and afford pleasant quarters for the students of the law courses."[38] The journal was particularly complimentary of Hoynes:[39]

> He introduced a system of instruction somewhat eclectic in its general features, in that it combined the most approved methods of teaching followed in other law schools. Since then the number of students has steadily increased. The average ratio of increase has been from eight to ten a year. Prof. Hoynes has labored so assiduously and effectively to promote the interests of the school that it now ranks favorably with the best law schools of the country. Since he assumed charge, the studies have been raised to the most approved plane, and an excellent library comprising about twenty-five hundred volumes has been procured.

Sorin Hall, the Science Hall, and the Institute of Technology were not the only constructions that changed the face of the campus in the 1880s. In fact, Sorin Hall was not even the first student residence hall on the campus. The Minim Department, schooling and boarding for young boys aged six to thirteen, had been housed in the Main Buildings since its inauguration in the mid-1850s, but when their numbers reached to more than a hundred, that age group needed its own daily schedule, closer supervision, and more time for play, and a separate building was constructed for them in 1882, named for Father Sorin's patron, Saint Edward. The building, ninety feet by forty feet, was designed by Father Sorin himself and Brother Charles Borromeo Harding, and was situated a little to the northeast of the Main Building, north of and behind the Music or Washington Hall. Four floors in height, washrooms and storage rooms were on the ground floor, the chapel, study hall, and classrooms on the floor above (main floor), and the top two floors held dormitories and additional classrooms. A beautiful garden was laid out in the front, and large indoor and outdoor recreation facilities were provided just to the east. Sister Aloysius Mulcaire, C.S.C., was the beloved principal for more than forty years. She and other Holy Cross sisters taught most of the classes—reading, spelling, history, grammar, geography, arithmetic, penmanship, and catechism (for Catholics)—and Brother Cajetan Gallagher (Brother "Caj") and several other brothers oversaw the youngsters' study time and recreation.[40]

The two most noticeable construction changes on the campus were the final additions to both Sacred Heart Church and the new Main Building. Construction of Sacred Heart Church, originally intended to be called the Church of Our Lady of the Sacred Heart, was begun in 1870 and the first stage of the project—the nave, transepts, and sanctuary as far as the first bay window beyond the transepts—was completed five years later, in 1875. The older church, directly behind the new one, was then demolished, and six apsidal chapels were added at the north end of the new church. These chapels were completed by 1886. Phelan Hall, formerly directly behind and to the north of the old church, was then torn down, and the Lady Chapel was constructed, completing the interior of the church by 1888. Three people had major input into the design of the church over the years—Father Sorin (the superior general), Father Granger (the provincial superior), and Brother Charles Borromeo Harding (community architect)—and the eclectic nature of the overall design might be symbolized in the majestic Gothic high altar by Froc Robert of France and the flowery Baroque altar of the Italian school of Gianlorenzo Bernini in the Lady Chapel. The church was consecrated to the Sacred Heart of Jesus by Bishop Joseph Dwenger of Fort Wayne on August 15, 1888, although the main spire and home for Father Sorin's impressive carillon was not completed until 1892.[41]

If adding the impressive spire and the Lady Chapel to the new church was a striking enhancement to the campus view, adding the wings and especially the Golden Dome to the Main Building was even more so. The original plans for the reconstructed building after the fire of April 1879 called for the extended east and west wings and impressive dome, but there was not enough time (or money) for those if the building was to be ready for occupancy by September. The central core of the building and the roof were all that could be completed in five months. But enrollment was increasing and further steps had to be taken. Plans were made to build a new residence for the minims (Saint Edward's Hall), the science classrooms and laboratories were relocated in the new Science Hall, the law program needed additional classroom and library space, and the dormitories and study halls for both the juniors and seniors were overcrowded. By the mid-1880s, wings on both the east (named Brownson Hall) and west (named Carroll Hall) sides of the Main Building were added, lengthening the building from 224 feet to 320.[42]

When the second Main Building burned in 1879, a boxlike structure topped by a small dome and white-painted statue of the Blessed Mother, Father Sorin resolved that its successor would have an even more impressive dome and statue. And he knew what he wanted. The model for the statue was to be the statue of the Immaculate Conception standing in the Piazza di Spagna in Rome that Father Sorin had seen on almost every visit to that city since it was adjacent to the offices of the Congregation of the Propagation of the Faith. This doctrine of the Immaculate Conception, that in the light of her selection to be the mother of God, Mary was freed from original sin from the moment of conception, had been solemnly defined by Pope Pius IX less than thirty years before. Father Sorin had first thought of having a copy of that statue commissioned in Rome but discovered it would be much more expensive there, and so he asked a Chicago sculptor, Giovanni Meli, to craft it here. The sisters, students, and graduates of Saint Mary's had asked for the privilege of financing the statue, and this they did. The statue was completed in 1880 but, since construction on the dome had not even begun by that time, the statue was placed over the porch of the Main Building for the first years.[43]

Much of this construction in the 1880s took place at an almost haphazard pace, with periodic halts in work as money, supplies, and laborers became available. The central core of the Main Building was completed by the fall of 1879, the east and west wings were not added until 1884, and in the meantime Washington Hall was constructed, Saint Edward's Hall was built for the minims in 1882, the new Science Hall the year following, and Father Sorin still had his mind set on a majestic dome to support the statue of Our Lady. Work began on the dome in the fall of 1882, and almost every issue of the *Scholastic* over the next few years listed recent donors and their contributions to the construction. By the following spring, 1883, the initial brickwork for the dome (it was estimated to require 500,000 bricks in all) had progressed sufficiently that it was visible from the ground. Eight iron frames, forming the corners of the octagonal structure, were in place by the summer, and the work was completed and the scaffolding removed by the fall. The dome had not yet been gilded but the statue was removed from the Main Building porch roof and hoisted to its place on the dome in a two-day operation by the feast of Saint Edward, October 13, 1883. The statue was sixteen feet in height and weighed 4,400 pounds.[44]

Gilding the dome produced a major crisis. With so much other costly construction on campus, many in the Holy Cross leadership, to save money, wanted the dome simply painted, perhaps yellow or gold, but Father Sorin insisted it be gilded with actual gold, regardless of the expense. When his council balked, he packed his few belongings and moved to Saint Mary's. The council could not validly meet without its chairman and thus much university and community business had to be deferred. At the urging of Father Walsh, the council eventually relented, the gilding was approved, and Brother Frederick and several assistants completed the work in 1886. Twelve electric lights were placed around the head of the statue, forming a halo, and another twenty-seven lights as a crescent under her feet, all powered by a thirteen horsepower steam engine. A narrow metal ladder, becoming a little rickety over time, was installed on the back of the dome and statue, and periodically one of the brothers would climb up and replace any burned-out bulbs.[45]

While construction on the exterior of the Main Building continued—adding the wings, the dome, the gilding, the statue, and the lighting—Professor Gregori was commissioned to paint murals for the main corridor and the inside of the dome. The twelve murals of the main corridor, each eleven feet in height and varying from five-and-a-half to nineteen feet in length, and painted from 1882 to 1884, depict major scenes in the life of Columbus: his departure from Palos on August 3, 1492, the mutiny at sea, the discovery of land, his return and reception at court, and, finally, his death in Valladolid. The arrival of the Catholic Columbus in America was an appropriate theme for an institution striving to show itself publicly as both Catholic and American. Gregori used Father Walsh as his model for Columbus in all the paintings except the deathbed scene where he turned to the aging Father Sorin; Professors Edwards, Lyons, and Stace were models for the seamen in the *Discovery of Land*; Father Neyron is seen as the Franciscan monk at the feet of the dying Columbus; and Gregori painted himself peering out from behind a drape in the *Return of Columbus and Reception at Court*. This latter scene was chosen by the United States Post Office as the design for a commemorative stamp at the time of the Columbian Exposition in 1893.[46]

The paintings on the inside of the dome represented the work or goals of the university as a Catholic institution of learning. In the center was a representation of the muse of religion, with an open book, eyes raised to heaven, her white, green, and red robes suggesting faith, hope, and charity, and the Holy Spirit in the form of a dove inspiring overhead. The allegory of philosophy is depicted directly beneath her, holding two open books to represent natural and moral philosophy. Next to it is history, a winged woman in white, representing truth, and Father Time holding a book in which she is writing. The symbol of science is robed in the gold and purple of power and majesty and holds a scepter with the sun that dispels the darkness of ignorance. Fame is depicted in flight, suggesting its shortness of life. Music seems lost in the seven-stringed instrument she is playing. And poetry is depicted with an upraised quill as she writes the words *Numine afflor* (I am touched by the breath of God).[47]

The lighting around the statue on the dome was only one step in the electrification of the campus that took place in the 1880s, in all probability due chiefly to the efforts of Father John Zahm. In 1881, Father Zahm proposed illuminating the campus grounds with arc lights, purchased a dynamo-electric machine, had it connected to the steam plant, and it produced the lighting power of 2,500 candles. That October the student cadets could drill outdoors in the evenings, and the minims played a game of night football. In the buildings themselves, the university first experimented with gasoline lamps but in 1885 turned to the incandescent lamp recently developed by Thomas Edison. Two companies, the Edison Electric Light Company and the Armington and Sims Company, donated the dynamo and the high-speed engine that produced the power. Lights were first installed in the corridors and study halls of the Main Building, then around the statue on the dome, and gradually in almost all the campus buildings. The student magazine in 1887 reported that there were close to seven hundred such lights throughout the campus—three hundred in the Main Building, ninety in the Science Hall, eighty in Washington Hall, sixty-seven in Saint Edward's Hall, etc.—and most were of ninety-five volts and sixteen candlepower. It seems probable that Notre Dame was the first American university with electric lighting. In March 1887 a student at Bowdoin wrote that Bowdoin was going to be the first college illuminated with electricity, but the *Electrical Review* responded that Notre Dame had been employing arc lights since 1881 and the incandescent lamp since 1885.[48]

Almost from the start Father Sorin seemed to have had at least a general plan for the physical growth of his college, and the fire of 1879 gave him the opportunity to implement it. He had already decided that the center of his university, Notre Dame du Lac, would not actually be on the lake where the original Log Chapel and his first building, Old College, stood but would be on higher ground, maybe five hundred feet to the northeast, where he built his first (and second and third) Main Building. Those Main Buildings, and the new church, all faced south, not toward the lake, and the campus was to grow in two parallel lines south from the Main Building and the church. Washington Hall, the Science Hall, and the Institute of Technology were constructed on the east side, Sorin Hall and eventually Walsh Hall would be built on the west side, and at the south entrance to the campus stood the porter's lodge on the west side and the post office on the east. Near the post office and the Institute of Technology also stood the Observatory, housing the telescope given to Father Carrier by Emperor Napoleon III in the late 1860s, nine and a half feet in length and with an object glass of six inches.[49]

The land between, in front of the Main Building, was to be park or garden of some kind. The two roads or paths leading out from the Main Building, in front of the buildings on each side and coming together again close to the porter's lodge and the post office (and where the majestic statue of Father Sorin would eventually be placed) were laid out in the shape of a heart, reflecting perhaps the Sacred Heart of Jesus to whom the new church had recently been dedicated. Brother Philip Kunze, a native of Silesia, was given the task of developing the park in the center, and this he did very well. Along the paths he placed flower urns, benches, fountains, and statues, and hoped to plant there a specimen of every tree, shrub, and vine indigenous to North America. In this central arboretum, he introduced a shingle oak, the European beech, the paper birch, the Camperdown elm, the Schwedler maple, the saucer magnolia, and others, approximately fifty-three species in all. In the early 1890s it was decided to erect a statue of the Sacred Heart of Jesus on a pedestal on the lawn directly in front of the Main Building. A little to the east of the Main Building, a second and smaller garden was laid out in front of Saint Edward's Hall. It was heart-shaped also, four hundred feet by one hundred feet, containing fountains and urns, a statue of King Saint Edward high on a pedestal, and various flowers planted to spell out "Ave Maria" and "Saint Edward's Park."[50]

As impressive as the expansion and beautification of the physical plant of the university was after the fire of 1879, a development taking place inside the Main Building was at least equally impressive: the rebuilding of the university's library and archives by Professor James Edwards. The collections that he had acquired under the direction of Father Lemonnier in the early 1870s had been almost totally lost in the fire, but Edwards began again with renewed enthusiasm. He purchased books with whatever funds the university could make available and he published the need widely and urged both individuals and libraries to donate any volumes they could spare. He was successful, and by the end of the century the library numbered more than 55,000 books. He contacted bishops across the country, volunteering to preserve their personal and diocesan papers at Notre Dame if they did not have the facilities or personnel to preserve them themselves, and he begged each of them for some personal memento, which he wished to retain for a "Bishops' Gallery" or "Memorial Hall" that he intended to establish. He accumulated over time a large collection of chalices, mitres, crosiers, vestments, walking sticks, pairs of sandals, locks of hair, and similar. On his visits he was often accompanied by Professor Paul Wood, who endeavored to paint the portrait of each bishop for the "Bishops' Gallery."[51]

Preserving the personal and diocesan papers of various bishops (and others) may have been Professor Edwards's most significant and lasting contribution. The collection from the diocese of New Orleans measured thirty-four linear feet and included the correspondence of all the bishops of the diocese from 1793 on. The three feet of records from Baltimore contained autographed letters of Archbishop John Carroll and Charles Carroll of Carrollton, the latter the only Catholic to sign the Declaration of Independence. The papers of the diocese of Detroit included the correspondence of Father Gabriel Richard, co-founder and vice president of the University of Michigan and territorial delegate to Congress. Edwards's visits to New York, Cincinnati, Cleveland, Philadelphia, Hartford, Vincennes, and Fort Wayne were equally successful. When meeting with Archbishop Michael Corrigan of New York, he also asked if he might have a lock of his hair. The archbishop located a pair of scissors and suggested he cut it himself. But bishops were not the only persons Edwards contacted. He acquired the papers of Orestes Brownson, convert and founder of the *Brownson Quarterly Review*, including correspondence with Comte de Montalembert, Lord Acton, Louis Veuillot, Cardinal Newman, Ralph Waldo Emerson, and Henry David Thoreau. John Gilmary Shea contributed the manuscripts of his *History of the Catholic Church in the United States*. The William J. Onaham papers include material on the American Catholic Congress of Baltimore of 1889 and the Columbian Catholic Congress in Chicago four years later, in both of which he figured prominently. James A. McMaster was owner and editor of New York's *Freeman's Journal and Catholic Register* and entrusted his papers to Edwards. Persons associated with Notre Dame, of course, left their papers and correspondence also—Charles Warren Stoddard, Maurice Francis Egan, Father Sorin, Father Daniel Hudson of the *Ave Maria*, and Edwards himself. The collection of materials he acquired soon became recognized as one of the most important repositories of Catholic Americana anywhere in the world.[52]

It was apparently Professor Edwards also who suggested that Notre Dame might honor in a singular way a prominent Catholic layman or woman who had made significant contributions to the American church or to American public life. Such an honor might encourage others in the laity to take a more active role in church and public affairs. For centuries the Vatican had been accustomed to bestow an honor, the Golden Rose, on a prominent member of a Catholic royal family each year on Laetare Sunday, the fourth Sunday of Lent, and, taking Profes-

sor Edwards's suggestion, Father Walsh in 1883 decided to institute a similar practice at Notre Dame, honoring an outstanding American Catholic with the Laetare
Medal that same Sunday. A university publication explained the rationale:[53]

> It is intended as a recognition of service rendered by the laity in behalf of
> religion, education and morality. The University of Notre Dame bestows
> her degrees on the young men who worthily finish their studies in her
> halls, and they go forth into the world crowned with her laurels, and as-
> sured of her cherished hopes and cordial wishes for their success and wel-
> fare. But, not content alone with this, she seeks also to reach, according
> to her own method of University extension, in helpfulness and good of-
> fices to the great world outside—to the body of the Church, or to mem-
> bers of the laity whose zeal for the faith, and achievements in the arts,
> sciences, literature, law, medicine, etc., entitle them to appreciative rec-
> ognition and encouragement.

The first recipient of the Laetare Medal, in 1883, possibly at the urging of
Professor Edwards again, was the well-known historian John Gilmary Shea, an
appropriate choice for an academic institution. (Orestes Brownson had died in
1876 or he undoubtedly would have been the first so honored.) In 1885, the third
year of its existence, the Laetare Medal was awarded to a woman, Eliza Allen Starr,
poetess, artist, religious writer, and friend of both Mother Angela and Father
Sorin. William Onahan, Chicago publicist and organizer of successful public
celebrations to emphasize the compatibility of Catholicism with American patriotism, received the honor in 1890, and the award continues to the present.[54]

The most memorable event of this decade of the eighties was the celebration of Father Sorin's Golden Jubilee as a priest in 1888. The Jubilee was actually
two celebrations: one for the students and the campus community, and one for
the American church at large. There had been some discussion of postponing any
major celebrations until 1892, the fiftieth anniversary of the university's founding,
or even 1894, the anniversary of receiving its official charter, but Father Sorin's
priesthood was so central to his life and work—and his strength was showing
signs of weakening—that the anniversary of his 1838 ordination in France could
not be overlooked.[55]

The first celebration took place toward the close of the 1887–1888 school
year, May 26 and 27, 1888. On Saturday afternoon, the 26th, the university community gathered in Washington Hall at four o'clock, the university orchestra

opened with *Le Diadem*, tributes were delivered in prose and poetry by representatives of the senior, junior, and minim divisions, interspersed with piano duets and a rendition of "Remember Me" by the Saint James Vocal Quartette of South Bend, and then the classical ode "A Patriarch's Feast" by Eliza Allen Starr was proclaimed. At the close, Father Sorin rose and made a reply, thanking God for the gift of his priesthood, for the 18,000 Masses he had been privileged to offer, and for his fifty years of ministry at Notre Dame. At the close of dinner that evening, Father Sorin and other university officials assembled on the Main Building porch, the students gathered around on the lawn, and a beautiful carriage with two coal-black horses drove up, a Jubilee present to Father Sorin from the faculty. Father Sorin expressed his gratitude again to the faculty and, with acting university president Father Zahm, his close collaborator Father Granger, and Professor James Edwards, he drove off in the direction of Saint Mary's.[56]

The celebration continued the following day, May 27, the precise date of his ordination fifty years before. Father Sorin officiated at a Solemn High Mass in the university church, with the sermon preached by Father Corby, the provincial superior. After Mass a procession formed and Father Sorin blessed the cornerstone of the new building just under construction, Sorin Hall. At noon, a Jubilee banquet was held for all, using both the junior and senior refectories, with a menu of Turtle Soup, Fish with Sauce Tartare, Roast Chicken, Filet of Beef, Potatoes Parisianne, Creamed Asparagus, Assorted Cakes, Ice Cream, Strawberries, and Coffee. Various toasts were offered—to the pope, to Father Sorin, to the United States, and to alma mater—and responses were made. The festivities closed that afternoon with boat races on Saint Joseph's Lake and competitive drills by companies of Colonel Hoynes's Light Guards.[57]

The second, and public, Jubilee celebration took place on August 15, the Feast of the Assumption of the Blessed Virgin, and preparations for it were elaborate. The avenue leading to the university was lined with American and papal flags; a log cabin had been constructed at the entrance to the campus, a reminder of the university's humble beginnings and a contrast to what had been accomplished; arches had been placed in prominent places around campus, adorned with papal, American, and Notre Dame colors; a double-arched canopy in front of the church was decorated with golden roses; American flags waved from windows of the Main Building, and an evergreen arch in front boldly proclaimed: "Welcome" and "1838–1888." Father Walsh, who had been absent in Europe at the time of the campus celebration in May, had returned, and welcomed each distinguished visitor on arrival: Archbishops John Ireland of Saint Paul and William

Elder of Cincinnati, Bishops Joseph Dwenger of Fort Wayne, Richard Gilmour of Cleveland, John Watterson of Columbus, John Keane of Richmond, John Lancaster Spalding of Peoria, James Ryan of Alton, Maurice Burke of Cheyenne, Henry Richter of Grand Rapids, Stephen Ryan of Buffalo, John Janssen of Belleville, Richard Phelan of Pittsburgh, and His Eminence James Cardinal Gibbons of Baltimore. The cardinal's arrival on the 14th had been delayed due to the funeral of General Philip Sheridan in Washington, DC, at which the cardinal preached, and the students had cheered heartily the arrivals of Archbishop Ireland and Bishop Gilmour, mistakenly thinking each had been the cardinal, but the presence of Gibbons, America's only cardinal, demonstrated the esteem in which Father Sorin was held throughout the American, and universal, church.[58]

The ceremonies began early on the 15th. At six o'clock, Bishop Dwenger, accompanied by other prelates in a liturgy not open to the public, consecrated the new church to the Sacred Heart. Some had thought it was to be consecrated to the Blessed Mother under the title "Our Lady of the Sacred Heart." In fact, Father Corby, the provincial superior, in a letter to all the priests and brothers in the United States less than three months before the event, referred to the coming "consecration of the New Church—a monument to the honor of God and to the glory of Our Lady of Sacred Heart," but Bishop Dwenger, or Father Sorin, must have thought otherwise, and it was consecrated to the Sacred Heart of Jesus. Father Sorin confirmed this in a Circular Letter less than a week later: "What a joy to kneel in that new sanctuary consecrated to the Sacred Heart, with the beautiful chapel of Our Lady of the Sacred Heart" [the present Lady Chapel].[59] Bishop Burke of Cheyenne, a former Notre Dame student, then blessed the mammoth seven-ton Saint Anthony and other bells in the carillon. Father Sorin offered Mass for the Holy Cross community at 9:00 a.m., and later an impressive procession formed and led into the already crowded church—the Ancient Order of Hibernians, Knights of Saint Casimir, Saint Hedwig Society, assembled priests and bishops, and Cardinal Gibbons, the celebrant of the solemn Jubilee Mass. The music of the Mass was Haydn's Third, sung by the choir of the Jesuit Church of Chicago. Archbishop Ireland extolled the contributions of Father Sorin in his sermon, based on the Gospel verse, "Well done, good and faithful servant:"[60]

Fifty years ago the Republic of the West was but emerging from her age of infancy, though her features plainly bore the lineaments of greatness and majesty. The vast regions encircling the Lakes and lying westwards toward the Mississippi gloried in their primeval forests and wild uncultured plains.

Traders, hunters, venturesome pioneers, in small knots, hundreds of miles apart, divided the boundless territory with the aboriginal Indian. Cleveland, Detroit, Chicago, giant cities of today, were villages, mere outposts of civilization. The Church was at work. Bruté, Badin, Mazzuchelli, were sowing the seed in the Master's vineyard amid privations and long journeys. To others at a later day, they felt, was it reserved to put the sickle into the rich harvest. . . .

Toward America the young levite of fifty years ago, soon after his ordination, turned longing eyes. He came to us from France. I thank thee, fair France! We owe to thee our political freedom. Lafayette and Rochambeau were partners with Washington in liberating us from the yoke of foreign oppression. We owe to thee most saintly and bravest missionaries, heralds of the faith to our forefathers, when few others dared to penetrate the wilderness, founders and fathers of the Church in America. I need not go back to the heroic wanderings among Indian tribes of a Jogues, an Allouez, a Marquette. I have but to recall names, which in tender love and gratitude living generations yet murmur,—Cheverus, Flaget, Dubois, Bruté, Loras, Cretin—names made to be immortal in the annals of America. . . .

In August, 1841, Father Sorin, accompanied by six brothers of the order of the Holy Cross, of which he himself had become a member shortly after his ordination, departed to the new world. The year following he was on the banks of the St. Joseph River, famed in annals of early missionary labors in America. Here he resolved to remain and to spend himself in the Master's service. . . .

We need but look around us—*Si monumentum vis, circumspice.* In 1842 we had the log hut and the wilderness. In 1888 there are the stately buildings of Notre Dame and St. Mary's, admired for their proportions and shapeliness, and, far more, for the wondrous works done within their halls, and loved by tens of thousands throughout the country for the sweet influences that have gone forth from them. The one priest and the few brothers are multiplied more than a hundredfold. There is a whole legion of laborers gathered together by the patient hand and inspired by the generous spirit of the venerable founder. . . .

Brethren, permit a glance into the future. Fifty years hence—what will the Church in America be? With the forces to day at work, the opportunities spreading out before her,—what ought she not be? Upon whom does it devolve to decide her destinies? Upon our own selves, upon the bishops, the priests, the lay Catholics of America. God works if we work with Him.

What a responsibility! But what encouragement, in the grandeur of our mission and the nearness of triumph. Let us live and work as Father Sorin has lived and worked, and all will be well.

The Jubilee banquet followed the Mass at one o'clock, with the visiting Church dignitaries, university and Holy Cross officials, and prominent personages of the city and state attending. The menu was again appropriately elaborate for the occasion and the usual toasts were offered, but only with water, in deference to the goals of the Catholic Total Abstinence Society that both the hierarchy and the university were furthering at that time. Later that afternoon, Bishop Watterson blessed several buildings on the campus, rededicating the university to the Blessed Mother, and Bishop Spalding delivered a half-hour address from the porch of the Main Building on the subject of "Christian Education." After Benediction of the Blessed Sacrament in the newly consecrated church and an evening meal in the refectory, Bishop Keane presented Cardinal Gibbons with the pallium he had brought from Rome for Archbishop Ireland, and the cardinal solemnly bestowed it on the archbishop, confirming his appointment to the See of Saint Paul. The celebration was brought to a close with a light musical program featuring soloists, duets, and quartets, and a fireworks display on the grounds in front of the Main Building. The dignitaries departed the next day, except Bishop Keane. He remained at Notre Dame for several weeks to profit from the advice and experience of Father Sorin as he drafted the statutes of the recently established Catholic University of America in Washington, DC, of which he had been named first rector.[61]

If 1888 was one of the most joyous and satisfying years in the early history of Notre Dame—Father Sorin's Golden Jubilee, the dedication of the majestic new church, and the laying of the cornerstone of Sorin Hall—the year 1893 was one of sadness and loss. Father Walsh, the university's young president, Father Granger, longtime pastor and prefect of religion, and Father Sorin himself all passed away within five months of each other that summer and fall.

Father Walsh's health had been declining over the preceding two years but he told very few and carried on despite the pain. He presided at the university's commencement exercises in June and greeted visitors with his usual good grace and smile. Once the school year was completed, however, accompanied by Brother Paul and Professor Edwards, he retired to Waukesha Springs, Wisconsin, to profit from the water at Colonel Dumbar's Bethsaida Springs and to seek relief from the heat of the Indiana summer. After two weeks, his health continuing to deteriorate, he transferred to Saint Mary's Hospital in Milwaukee to be under the care of an eminent specialist and the devoted Sisters of Charity. His decline continued and he faced the end religiously. He asked Brother Paul for a copy of the Congregation's Directory of Prayers in order to recite the prayers for the dying. Informed that there was no directory at hand, he replied: "Well, do not mind. I can recollect myself. I know what I must do and can prepare myself." He made his confession to the hospital chaplain and received the Last Sacraments. Other priests arrived from Notre Dame and Canada, a few local clergy were present, and several sisters and nurses were at his bedside when he breathed his last in the early morning of July 17. He was only forty.[62]

His body was brought back to Notre Dame by train, accompanied by Brother Paul and Fathers Patrick Condon, Moses McGarry, and Daniel Spillard. The casket was placed in the parlor of the Main Building and the following day hundreds of clergy, religious, townspersons, former students, and friends filed past to pay their final respects. At nine-thirty Wednesday morning, the 19th, the Holy Cross community gathered in the parlor for final prayers, a procession formed, and the body was carried into the main church where Bishop James Rademacher, newly appointed bishop of Fort Wayne, offered the funeral Mass and Bishop John Lancaster Spalding preached. Interment in the community cemetery did not take place until later that afternoon, awaiting the arrivals of Father Walsh's sister, Ellen, from Montreal and his brother, John, from New York. Father Corby, provincial superior and two-time former university president presided at the last rites at the cemetery.[63]

As sad as Father Walsh's death was for Father Sorin, an even greater loss was the death of his close friend and longtime collaborator, Father Alexis Granger, just nine days later. Ordained for the diocese of Le Mans in 1840, he had been encouraged by young Father Sorin to join the newly founded Congregation of Holy Cross, which he did in 1843. The following year he was sent to the United States where he worked closely with Father Sorin for almost fifty years. At various times he served as university vice president, director of novices, pastor of the university church, provincial superior, and almost continuously prefect of religion and moderator of many of the university's religious associations. A quiet, shy, and deeply religious priest who never completely lost his French accent, he had a lasting influence on generations of Notre Dame students as their confessor, spiritual adviser, and trusted confidant. He received letters throughout his life from grateful alumni acknowledging the lasting impact he had had on their lives.[64]

Although still superior general, Father Sorin had taken no prominent role in the funeral services for Father Walsh or Father Granger. He simply was not well. Despite showing his age, he had been able to take full part in his Golden

Jubilee celebrations five years before, but his health began to deteriorate shortly thereafter. In the summer of 1890 he, Father Granger, and Father Walsh spent some time together at Sacred Heart College in Watertown, Wisconsin, in part to regain their failing health. He also made two trips to Europe in the early 1890s, one with Father Zahm, hoping "that a sea-voyage will restore my enfeebled health," but the decline continued. A specialist from Chicago diagnosed the condition as Bright's disease, a failing of the kidneys, but could recommend no remedy. Occasionally bedridden, he did preside at the general chapter in August 1892, participated in a ceremony that November 26 to commemorate the arrival at Notre Dame fifty years before, composed his last Circular Letter the following February, and even welcomed the apostolic delegate, Archbishop Francesco Satolli, to Notre Dame in June. On October 13 he was too ill to commemorate his patronal feast of Saint Edward, and on the 28th, the death watch began. He received the Last Sacraments and his final Eucharist on the 30th, and his "little princes," the minims, went to the chapel to pray for him. His community gathered around his bed in the Presbytery and, with no sign of struggle, he breathed his last on the morning of October 31.[65]

Father Sorin had given explicit directives for his funeral:[66]

When I die, the Community shall not be disturbed by extra preparations or invitations to strangers for my obsequies. On the contrary, I wish the community to remain completely at peace, exclusively occupied with the needs of my poor soul. I want nothing more than is prescribed by the Rule: a simple wood coffin, with simplest purple vestment. No strangers of any sort are to be disturbed by any telegraphic announcement, no invitations whatsoever to attend; none present but my own dear children of the Holy Cross around my bed.

Most of this, of course, was ignored. He belonged to Holy Cross certainly but, as the presence of fourteen bishops at his Golden Jubilee indicated, he belonged to the wider American Church also. The day after his death was the Feast of All Saints and thus funeral arrangements had to be delayed. After Vespers on November 1, a catafalque was placed in the center aisle of the church, with the raised coffin, and crowds of visitors passed by on the 2nd. The funeral Mass was celebrated on the 3rd by Bishop Rademacher, and Archbishop Elder preached, noting the appropriateness of Father Sorin dying in October and being buried in November—October, the month of the holy rosary, one of Father Sorin's favorite devotions, and November, dedicated to the Poor Souls, another of his deep devotions, as he had urged students to pray for them often to have them eventually as their intercessors in heaven. The long cortege then made its way up to the community cemetery where Father Sorin was laid to rest with his fellow religious, obeying at least that part of his final directives.[67]

The year 1893 clearly marked the end of an era in the life of Notre Dame, and Fathers Sorin, Walsh, and Granger could look back on the era with a sense of satisfaction. Those original 524 acres of mostly uncleared wilderness in 1842 had expanded to 1300. Twenty-four buildings dotted the campus and at least two of them, the Main Building and the university church, were among the most impressive in all the Midwest. The faculty numbered fifty-two and at least a few on the faculty—John Zahm, Albert Zahm, Charles Warren Stoddard, and Maurice Francis Egan—were professors other universities would have been proud to claim as their own.[68] Student enrollment exceeded five hundred and Notre Dame graduates were achieving success in various careers and professions across the country.

And Father Sorin himself had grown and changed. He had founded Notre Dame fifty years before as a French *collège*, a combination high school and college, although many of the early students were not even of high school caliber. But as time went on, Father Sorin wanted to become more American, and he wanted his institution to become more American, more like other American universities, more like a true university. Father Walsh may have been an influence here, and almost certainly Father Zahm. Father Arthur Hope, Father Morrissey's secretary in 1916 (when Father Zahm was still alive), remarked in an Oral History interview: "Another funny thing that strikes me about Zahm was that he had a great influence over Sorin."[69] It was probably Father Zahm who convinced Father Sorin of the need for the Science Hall and the Institute of Technology for more advanced classes and research, and for Sorin Hall with private rooms for older and more serious students. Father Zahm dedicated *Sound and Music* to Father Sorin: "For more than Fifty Years the Friend and Promotor of Higher Education."[70] As Notre Dame had grown and changed through the years, so may have Father Sorin. In 1893 the institution was not yet a true university but, under the leadership of Father Walsh, Father Zahm, and Father Sorin, progress had been made, and it was becoming a new Notre Dame.

CHAPTER 7

The 1890s

A Contest for Identity

When university president Father Thomas Walsh left the university in the summer of 1890 to seek relief from his health problems in cooler and calmer Wisconsin—and when news of his trip became public—speculation must have begun about who might succeed if the president were forced to resign, or if worse occurred. And if a successor had to be named, a further question might be asked: Whose decision would that be? For the last forty years, that second question had been easy to answer: Father Sorin. But the superior general's own health was obviously declining, and it was no longer clear how much control or influence he could, or even desired, to exert. Fortunately, Father Walsh already had two strong candidates in his administration, Father John Zahm and Father Andrew Morrissey.

Father Zahm was the university's brightest star at the time. He had been ordained in 1875 and was immediately appointed professor of chemistry and physics, curator of the museum, a member of the university's board of trustees, and, in 1885, Father Walsh appointed him the university's vice president, presiding over the university whenever Father Walsh was absent, as at Father Sorin's first Jubilee celebration in 1888.[1]

Father Andrew Morrissey had been born in County Kilkenny, Ireland, in 1860. A cousin of his, Patrick Leo Foley from County Leitrim, had earlier immigrated to the United States and had joined the Congregation of Holy Cross as Brother Bernard. At the age of twelve, young Andrew decided to follow in his cousin's footsteps, immigrated to the United States, and entered the high school seminary at Notre Dame to study for the priesthood. He progressed through his novitiate training and seminary studies well and, as he was a very bright young man, he also found time to teach mathematics while still a student himself. He was ordained a priest in 1884 and was immediately named director of studies at Sacred Heart College in Watertown, Wisconsin, the institution founded by Father Corby in 1872. After one year he was reassigned to Notre Dame, probably at Father Walsh's request, and was named director of studies in the same year that Father Zahm was named vice president for the second time. In 1889 he was also appointed the first rector of the newly opened Sorin Hall.[2]

The contrast between these two close assistants to Father Walsh could hardly have been greater. Where Father Zahm was of average height and weight, Father Morrissey was short and rather pudgy. Father Zahm could be critical, blunt, and sharp at times, while Father Morrissey was genial, welcoming, and diplomatic. A young priest who knew them both, and strongly favored Father Zahm, admitted that Father Zahm had "annoying peculiarities" and acknowledged that Father Morrissey was "broad-minded, liberal, energetic, talented, with winning personal qualities."[3] Both men had good minds and while Father Zahm spent a large part of his life in study, teaching, research, and writing, Father Morrissey had been assigned to administrative positions almost from the day of his ordination. After working closely with them for several years—with one as vice president and the other as director of studies—Father Walsh apparently decided that Father Morrissey, because of his winning personality and perhaps greater administrative talents, should be his successor. In 1892 Father Morrissey was named university vice president in place of Father Zahm and on Father Walsh's death the following year Father Corby, the provincial superior, named him university president.[4]

Eighteen ninety-three was not an auspicious year for Father Morrissey to be taking on this new responsibility. The preceding twelve years had been a period of growth and expansion—a new Main Building, the completion of the church, Saint Edward's Hall, Washington Hall, Science Hall, the Institute of Technology, Sorin Hall, the electrification of the campus, the hiring of higher-salaried professors—and the university finances had been strained. Its indebtedness had dropped from a high of $139,000 in 1880, after the fire, to $17,420 in 1893, but even that amount was worrisome. It was not a good time to be in any debt since the country itself that year was falling into the greatest depression in its history to that time. Agriculture profits were weak due to the high tariff; money, based on gold, was tight; and the nation was afflicted with natural disasters of drought, dust storms, and grasshoppers. Mary Ellen Lease urged farmers to "raise less corn and more Hell" and the farmers did unite under the Populist Party of 1892. Railroads had overexpanded since the end of the war, overconfident businesses had borrowed too heavily and banks had loaned too freely, a Rockefeller or Carnegie could reap millions a year while the salaries of workers were too low to raise a family—and the government seemed indifferent. As expansion slowed and loans were called in, confidence was shaken and panic spread. Major railroads declared bankruptcy in 1893, as did five hundred banks and sixteen thousand other businesses. It was only the start and the depression lasted throughout the decade. Unemployment across the country stood at less than 4 percent in 1892 but never dropped below 10 percent for the next six years.[5]

Father Morrissey was understandably concerned but still confident. His goal was to keep the university solvent in these difficult times—to balance expenses with revenues and keep the debt at least manageable—and to continue to provide a good Catholic education to all the young men entering. This might mean, at least for the present, continuing the university as it generally had been: a college program certainly, but with the majority of students in the sub-college programs (the prep or high school, the Manual Labor School, and the minims). If Notre Dame were to continue to grow, it would be chiefly on those sub-college levels. More young men were seeking a high school than a college education, education at that level was less expensive since classes could be larger and their faculty not as high salaried, and educating Catholic young men of any age was an important Church goal. For financial and other reasons, Father Morrissey was convinced that Notre Dame was not able to compete with schools such as the University of Michigan, Harvard, and other institutions of the East, and it would be unwise to try.[6]

Such a view did put Father Morrissey in conflict with Father Zahm. Father Zahm was primarily a scholar. An accomplished linguist, he read Latin and Greek, knew French and German, his Spanish carried him through several trips into Latin America, and for relaxation he read Dante in the original Italian. At the time of his death in 1921, he had accumulated Dante materials in more than thirty languages and dialects, and the Dante books in his library numbered more than five thousand.[7] His own writings earned national and international acclaim, some published under his own name and some under a pseudonym, H. J. Mozans. His best-known and his most controversial work, *Evolution and Dogma*, published under his own name in 1896, traced the various theories of evolution from Aristotle to Charles Darwin, insisting that belief in the evolution of the human body from lower creation was wholly compatible with Catholic dogma as long as the direct and immediate creation of the human soul by God was accepted. He was convinced that science and revelation could not conflict since God was the author of both. The book was praised at home and abroad but fell afoul of the Vatican, which quietly ordered it out of circulation since it still seemed problematic to reconcile evolution from a lower creature with the Biblical story of creation of Adam and Eve. Surprisingly, although most of these then controversial views had been expounded in Father Zahm's Summer School lectures over the preceding four years, Pope Leo XIII in 1895 had still awarded him an honorary doctorate of philosophy, one of only two such degrees apparently ever awarded.[8]

Father Zahm was not only a scholar himself but he wanted Notre Dame to be an institution of serious scholarship as well, not abandoning the minim or high school programs but devoting major efforts to the collegiate and even postcollegiate programs. He had earlier urged the construction of the new Science Hall and the Institute of Technology to promote student research, and he hoped Sorin Hall, with its private rooms, would encourage more serious study among the older students. Contrary to the views of Father Morrissey and provincial superior Father Corby, he favored the establishment of a house of theology, Holy Cross College, in Washington, DC, in the late 1890s to prevent the Congregation's seminarians, then studying at Notre Dame, from being recruited to teach undergraduate courses in addition to their studies, as he had taught during his seminary years, and permitting the seminarians and newly ordained priests to enroll in additional classes at the recently founded Catholic University of America for advanced degrees. In fact, many young priests did pursue advanced degrees in Washington, DC, in those years and returned to influential positions at Notre Dame—Fathers James Burns, Julius Nieuwland, Matthew Schumacher, Leonard Carrico, Charles O'Donnell, and Mathew Walsh, among others.[9] Father Zahm was eager to make Notre Dame a true university, the equal of most others across the land, but Father Morrissey did not agree. He considered Father Zahm's plans too costly and too risky in that decade of the depression—and Father Morrissey was now president.

The twelve years of Father Morrissey's presidency were not years of regression certainly, but they were years of limited growth and progress. Finances, of both the nation and the university, were an ever-present concern. The university's indebtedness varied each year throughout the 1890s but was usually in the $20,000 range, and its "cash on hand," which usually varied between $3,000 and $15,000 each week, dropped to $385.78 on one occasion in 1895, and to only

$5.64 in December 1900.[10] But despite these financial worries, the physical plant of the university did expand.

One need was for a residence facility for the increasing number of priests and brothers teaching at and staffing the university. Until this time they had been living in scattered residences across the campus—the Main Building, Sorin Hall, Old College, the Presbytery behind the Main Building—but these were proving inadequate. In 1895 a new residence was constructed just to the west and connected with the university church. Probably designed by Brother Charles Borromeo Harding and originally called the "Community House" or the "Professed House" (for those having professed religious vows), it was situated on the brow of Saint Mary's Lake and close to both the new church and the Main Building, with approximately one hundred individual rooms in its basement and three upper floors, a comfortable and convenient religious house for the Holy Cross community at Notre Dame.[11]

The building did have one other immediate use, however. After Father Sorin's Golden Jubilee celebration in 1888, there was talk of a second Golden Jubilee, this one of the university itself. The university had been founded in 1842, and 1892 would have been the appropriate year—or 1894, the fiftieth anniversary of Notre Dame's official charter—but Father Sorin and Father Walsh were not in good health in 1892, and after their deaths in 1893 it seemed too hurried to plan a celebration for the following year. Thus the dates selected were June 11–13, 1895. A number of bishops, priests, and brothers were invited for the occasion, private rooms were needed to house them, and the new Professed House was sufficiently completed that they could all reside there. As time went on and enrollments increased, additional student housing was needed and in 1899 this Professed House was transformed into a student residence, probably for younger college students, and was renamed Corby Hall after Father Corby, who had died in late 1897. It remained a student residence into the 1930s.[12]

Even before this Professed House was recommissioned as a student residence, another step was taken to keep pace with increased student enrollment. In 1897 it was decided to construct east-west wings on both the north and south ends of Sorin Hall, adding forty-some private rooms to the building. With its four cone-shaped turrets at the corners of the then expanded building, one professor remarked: "That monstrosity, Sorin Hall! It looks like an old-fashioned ice-box turned upside down!"[13] But it did fulfill a student residence need.

That same year, a new Manual Labor School building was also constructed. The school was then located in a building on what was later referred to as "Badin

Bog," built after fire destroyed the earlier one in 1849, but the building had deteriorated after almost forty years of teenagers' use. It was decided in 1897 to build a new Manual Labor School a little further to the southwest, larger to accommodate increased numbers and closer to some of the shops and farm buildings. The new structure was of brick, three stories high, with a refectory and washrooms on the first floor, a study hall and private rooms on the second, and dormitories on the third. It was appropriately called Saint Joseph's Hall, as was its predecessor, after the carpenter, Saint Joseph, the foster father of Jesus. A chapel was eventually located in the building and Mass was celebrated every morning. This building remained the home of the Manual Labor School until the program was abolished in 1917. That year two wings were added, it was converted into a residence hall for younger college students, and the name was changed to Badin Hall.[14]

While Corby Hall (the Professed or Community House) and Saint Joseph's Hall were being built, and the wings were being added to Sorin Hall, another construction project was also taking place, more famous than these others, but one in which Father Morrissey apparently had little input. That was the construction of the Notre Dame Grotto in 1896. In 1854, Pope Pius IX had promulgated the dogma of the Immaculate Conception, that Mary, the one chosen to be the mother of Jesus, the Son of God, was "preserved free of all stain of original sin" from the moment of conception. Four years later, in 1858, it was reported that the Blessed Mother appeared to young Bernadette Soubirous on eighteen occasions at the grotto of Massabielle in Lourdes, in southern France, declaring herself to be the Immaculate Conception. A church was eventually built there, numerous cures were reported, and it soon became a center of worldwide pilgrimage. Father Sorin himself visited the site on several of his trips to Europe, as did Mother Angela, inspiring each of them with a desire to have a facsimile of that Grotto on the Notre Dame or Saint Mary's campuses.[15]

The present Grotto at Notre Dame was not the first. Apparently in the early 1870s Mother Angela had a grotto constructed at Saint Mary's, as there is mention of the "Grotto of Lourdes" in the Saint Mary's section of a student publication in 1874. A later publication suggests its location:[16]

After leaving the State road, leading from South Bend to Niles, for more than a quarter of a mile, maples, sycamore and poplars shade . . . the broad carriage drives and pleasant walks that lead to St. Mary's Academy. . . . Passing the Grotto of Our Lady of Lourdes which separates the Academy from the Convent.

The first permanent building at Saint Mary's, Bertrand Hall, had been built in 1865 under the supervision of Notre Dame vice president Father Patrick Dillon, and the second building, Lourdes Hall, in 1872. It may be presumed that that first grotto was erected in the vicinity of those two almost side-by-side halls. It was eventually demolished and the statues of the Blessed Virgin and Saint Bernadette were placed reverently in an alcove on the third floor of Lourdes Hall, with a kneeler, inviting any passerby to pause and pray.[17]

Father Sorin had the first "grotto" built at Notre Dame in 1878. It was not a cave-like grotto at all but was composed of a glass-paneled octagonal structure at the northwest corner of the then uncompleted Sacred Heart Church, later between the sacristy steps and the first apsidal chapel on the west side. The structure was approximately fifteen feet in height and seven in diameter, on a three-foot pedestal, with a life-size statue of the Blessed Virgin within, facing west. In front of this octagonal structure, on the incline leading toward the lake on the south side of the Presbytery (and toward the rear of what was later Corby Hall), was a small wall of rock, a fountain, perhaps a garden, and the statue of the kneeling Saint Bernadette. A campus visitor described it:[18]

> Our path has now led us to the foot of a little hill, and we are agreeably surprised, as we are brought face to face with a facsimile representation of the Grotto of Lourdes, beautifully sculpted out of the side of the declivity. The rocks are there portrayed, while underneath is the gurgling fountain. To one side, lifted on high, is a beautiful statue of Our Lady of the Immaculate Conception, encased in an octagonal frame, the sides of which are glass, supported by stone pillars. At a little distance is the kneeling figure of Bernadette, in her quaint, pleading Breton dress, praying to the Virgin of the Apparitions. To the left of this lovely spot is a square, three-story building—the residence of the Very Rev. Father General Sorin and his assistants.

The present Grotto at Notre Dame, constructed in 1896, owes less to Father Sorin and more to two other priests, Father William Corby and Father Thomas Carroll.

An intriguing notice appeared in the June 1896 issue of the *Annals of Our Lady of Lourdes*:[19]

> About a year and a half ago our Provincial, Father Corby, desired a great favor for the benefit of his Community in the United States. He started

at once for Europe, and after attending to some important business in Rome, directed his steps to Our Lady of Lourdes, France, where he celebrated Holy Mass, said some fervent prayers, and then placed his desired request in the hands of Our Lady of Lourdes. Then and there he promised, with God's help and the help of friends of Mary, to build at Notre Dame a Grotto in honor of the Immaculate Conception, if Mary would grant him his request. On the first day of May, 1895,—Mary's own Month—he was informed by cable that his request was granted.

There may be different opinions about this "favor" of Father Corby, but the following explanation, suggested by excellent researcher Dorothy Corson, seems the most accurate.[20]

Father Moreau had founded the Congregation of Holy Cross with three branches—priests, brothers, and sisters—but in 1857 the Vatican gave official approval of the union of priests and brothers in one congregation and insisted that the sisters be a separate community. Efforts were made over the next several years to acquire official Roman approval of the sisters, but there were complications and delays. There were two novitiates, one at Saint Mary's and another at Notre Dame, which Father Sorin had established precisely to form sisters who would work at Notre Dame. Each house of the sisters had its own sister superior, but Father Sorin remained the ecclesiastical superior of all the Holy Cross sisters in the United States. A resolution was finally reached and by 1890 Rome officially approved the Sisters of the Holy Cross in the United States as a separate, recognized congregation, with three recommendations: 1) that there be only one novitiate, not two; 2) that the sisters ministry at Notre Dame be closed (or that they receive satisfactory financial compensation for their service); and 3) that the period of novitiate and scholasticate for the sisters be lengthened.[21]

Mother Augusta (Anderson) was elected superior general, and Father Sorin's name soon ceases to appear on any of the sisters' documents. The sisters' novitiate at Notre Dame was closed and the novices and scholastics were transferred to Saint Mary's, but Mother Augusta requested a delay in terminating the sisters' ministry at Notre Dame—there was simply not enough room at the time at Saint Mary's to house the more than one hundred sisters who were working at Notre Dame. Father Corby, provincial superior of the priests and brothers, did not want the sisters to move at all, of course. While in Europe in 1894, at about the time of his visit to Lourdes, he wrote to Professor Edwards back at Notre Dame: "Keep the Sisters question quiet just for the present. Without Sisters we cannot run

N.D. and from all I can learn here it depends on St. Mary's. No Bishop or even Cardinal can help us unless St. Mary's is willing to hold the place at N.D."[22]

That the sisters be permitted to remain at Notre Dame seems to be the request Father Corby made of the Blessed Virgin at Lourdes. Mother Augusta was also willing to permit the sisters' ministry to continue, a satisfactory financial compensation was agreed upon, and on April 23, 1895, Cardinal Miecislaus Ledochowski of the Congregation of the Propaganda in Rome notified Father Sorin's successor as superior general, Father Gilbert Français, that the sisters' mission at Notre Dame did not have to close but could continue. Father Français cabled this message to Father Corby and he probably received it around the first of May.[23]

With his requested favor at Lourdes now granted, Father Corby looked to fulfill his promise to build a Grotto at Notre Dame. Fortunately, a generous benefactor was at hand. Thomas Carroll had been born in Longford, Ireland, in 1834, graduated from Notre Dame in 1855, entered the seminary, and was ordained a Holy Cross priest in 1859. He served for a time at Saint Patrick's Church in South Bend, and was one of those defending Father Colovin against allegations of intemperance and disobedience in the early 1870s. He eventually left the Congregation of Holy Cross, joined the diocese of Erie, and was the longtime pastor of Saint Joseph's Church in Oil City, Pennsylvania.[24]

Father Carroll never lost his affection for Notre Dame, and on one of his return visits when he and Father Corby were walking from the seminary on the bank of Saint Mary's Lake toward Sacred Heart Church, Father Carroll mentioned that he would like to donate money to build a Grotto of Our Lady of Lourdes at Notre Dame and Father Corby suggested that the quiet spot behind the Presbytery and Professed House (Corby Hall) might be perfect. They hoped that everyone who would pray there would include a prayer for a happy death for each of them. Work began in the spring of 1896 and continued into the summer, large boulders were brought in to duplicate the cave in France, the statue of the Blessed Mother was transferred from its niche in the former "grotto" nearer the university church to the new one, and the Grotto was impressively blessed on the Feast of Our Lady of Snows, August 5, 1896. It was remarkable that in digging the land in front of the Grotto, a spring of water was discovered, another likeness to the shrine in France. Within two years, Father Corby and Father Carroll had both died, Father Carroll happily surrounded by his friends and parishioners in Pennsylvania and Father Corby by his beloved community members at Notre Dame.[25]

While Father Morrissey was not involved in the construction of the Grotto, he was quite instrumental in the building of the gymnasium in 1898. Because of the spring and autumn rains and the bitterly cold winters in northern Indiana, indoor recreational facilities must have been provided for the students from the very beginning, both in Old College and in the first Main Building. Recreational rooms were apparently available for the juniors in the Music Hall and the seniors in the Exhibition Hall in the 1860s, and, after the fire of 1879 destroyed the Music Hall, a gymnasium was built a little to the east of the new Washington Hall. By the late 1890s, however, Father Morrissey was convinced that a larger facility was needed, as the local council minutes note in early 1898:[26]

> The President of the University pointed out to the members of the council the great necessity of a new Gymnasium. The continued increase in Students demands more room for recreation and it was the unanimous consent of the council that a Gymnasium be built the cost to be about ten thousand dollars.

The new gymnasium was built, and it was dedicated on March 11, 1899. At the time, and at dimensions of 225 feet by 110 feet, it was thought to be one of the largest college gymnasiums dedicated exclusively to athletics. The front section had two floors, with offices, showers, training rooms, and lockers on the ground floor and a gymnastics room on the second floor. The gymnastic apparatus was for the use of all the students. The rest of the building, with a twenty-five-foot ceiling, was a facility for track, basketball, handball, and baseball practice, with a gallery seating three hundred. An announcement noted that the president and faculty "realize that the development of the body must go hand in hand with the training of heart and head, otherwise the education would be incomplete."[27]

Unfortunately, in less than two years, on November 9, 1900, the gymnasium caught fire and was destroyed, at a total loss of approximately $40,000. The fire had apparently begun in the basketball area and spread quickly. The university's hose and ladder company poured four streams of water on it and South Bend firefighters arrived in fifteen minutes, but the walls began to crumble and the roof fell. Father Morrissey and the administration decided to rebuild immediately, despite additional costs. As the *Scholastic* noted: "A delay until spring would mean a saving of money—and a large saving at that,—for an unusual demand for labor and battling with foul weather perforce call for a greater expenditure of capital." But construction began immediately anyway. The new building had a castellated appearance in front, brick and steel replaced lumber in some places, the lighting was improved, including large skylights, and the track area was extended, with a twelve-lap track rather than thirteen and a longer run for pole vaulters. Six thousand spectators could be crowded into the gallery. The building was officially opened with an intermural meet on February 8, 1901, less than three months after the fire.[28]

If the growth of the university's physical plant in the 1890s was commendable, only moderate were any changes in its academic programs during Father Morrissey's presidency. A significant change was made in the high school or Preparatory Department, however. The university had been founded on the six-year French educational model, with four years of college courses and two of preparatory work. Father Lemonnier added a third year of preparatory work in 1873, and Father Walsh in 1882 separated the Preparatory and the Collegiate Departments into two distinct departments of the university. In 1902, Father Morrissey added a fourth year to the Preparatory Department, finally making it a high school similar to most other high schools in the United States.[29]

On the collegiate level, the Classical Course (the basic humanities program) seems to have changed little. The core courses still included Greek and Latin, English, history, mathematics, philosophy, political economy, and the natural and physical sciences. A new class might be added one year and another dropped, and the content of each course might vary, especially if the professor teaching it were changed, but the overall curriculum remained quite stable. Since this Classical Course curriculum was heavy with English classes, the Belles Lettres or English Course followed the Classical Course curriculum closely for the first three years of study and had its own concentrated literary program in the fourth year: Principles of Literary Criticism, Philosophy of Style, Oratorical Composition and Elocution, Literature of the Nineteenth Century, and Aesthetics of Literature. Literature of the United States seemed slighted in both programs.[30]

The Commercial Course, a two-year program leading to a diploma rather than to a degree, continued throughout the 1890s and, as business became more prominent during these heyday years of the Rockefellers, Carnegies, and Morgans, additional business classes were added—shorthand, typewriting, office work, business practice, and so on. However, it seems that this Commercial Course may have been de-emphasized during Father Morrissey's presidency. Enrollment figures do not separate commercial from other post–high school students, but the number of degrees and diplomas granted seems to indicate a relative decline. At the commencement exercises in 1893, Father Walsh's last year as president, forty-six degrees or diplomas were awarded (five bachelor of arts, five bachelor of letters, six bachelor of science, one degree of engineering, seven bachelor of laws, and twenty-two commercial diplomas) with almost half being commercial diplomas. Twelve years later, in Father Morrissey's final year as president (1904–1905), thirty-eight degrees or diplomas were awarded, and only twelve were for the Commercial Course—less than one-third. Figures for the year before were even more telling: of the sixty-six degrees or diplomas awarded, only fifteen were commercial diplomas. The four-year degree-granting programs seemed to be making progress at the expense of the two-year Commercial Course.[31]

The Scientific Course remained strong throughout the 1890s with Father Zahm, the Kirsch brothers (Fathers Alexander and Joseph), and young Father James Burns (later president) on the faculty. The program also continued to expand. By the mid-1890s, the title was changed to "General Science Course," and more specialized programs developed. The science museum, most of whose specimens had been burned in the fire of 1879, had been re-established in the new Science Hall, as had the herbarium, and it had been greatly expanded through the efforts of Father Zahm. A specialized course in biological science was established, with classes in human anatomy, botany, zoology, bacteriology, comparative embryology, cytology, and cellular pathology. Degrees in pharmaceutical biology were also granted toward the end of the decade.[32]

The Engineering Course seemed to mirror the Scientific Course in the 1890s, with some growth as enrollments increased and with some revisions in the curriculum. Engineering remained a four-year program throughout the decade, with core classes in English, history, foreign language, mathematics, natural science, and drawing in the first two years, and philosophy, natural and physical sciences, and advanced classes in pure and applied mathematics, drawing, and languages in the final two years. In 1895, the title was changed from Engineering Course to Engineering School, and additional courses in surveying, highway engineering, sanitary engineering, roofs and bridges, and hydraulics gradually appeared in the curriculum.[33]

A significant addition to the engineering faculty was the hiring of Jerome Green in 1895. He had studied engineering at Ohio State University, could not find a job during the early years of the depression, taught night classes in Chicago for $2.50 a night, and was hired by Father Morrissey and Father Corby while they were on a visit to Chicago. His expertise was in wireless telegraphy. He built his own apparatus, "a wire running from the induction coil to a galvanized iron ball suspended from a high object." He experimented first inside a classroom of the Science Hall; then he sent a message from the Science Hall to the flagpole; and, finally, with a crowd of students, South Bend reporters, and assorted passersby attending, he sent a message from Notre Dame to Saint Mary's, almost two miles away, the first such wireless message ever sent in the United States. He was not only a boon to electrical engineering at Notre Dame; he also did valuable research in the area of X-ray, and local doctors often brought their patients to Notre Dame to obtain pictures of bone fractures and other mishaps. But it was not all serious research. William Benitz joined the engineering faculty about the same time as Green. He was an excellent teacher and popular with students. On one occasion a student wrote "We love our teachers" on a stair riser, and the following day Professor Benitz wrote "Like Hell you do" on the next riser. His tobacco chewing was legendary and he was said to be able to hit a spittoon at ten feet.[34]

The most significant addition to the curriculum in the 1890s was the introduction of a program in architecture in 1898, the first such program in the state of Indiana and the first in any Catholic college in the United States. The university had been offering courses in drawing, both mechanical and artistic, for several years, and beginning a program in architecture may have been an easy next step since the decade of the 1890s was a period of architectural flowering across the country, spurred on by the Columbian Exposition in Chicago in 1893. Henry John Schlacks, a noted church architect in Chicago, travelled to Notre Dame once a week to teach and supervise student work, and Francis Xavier Ackerman continued to offer courses in drawing. Courses were all taught on the fifth floor of the Main Building and were not considered part of the Engineering School. Gradually other classes were introduced: Orders of Architecture, Theory of Arches, Masonry, Iron Construction, etc. The first degree in architecture was awarded in 1904 to a young man from Cuba, Eugenio P. Rayneri y Piedra.[35]

The year after the program in architecture was inaugurated, Father Morrissey also introduced a graduate program in journalism. The students would first have to complete the four-year English Course for the bachelor of literature degree, taking classes in history, theology, economics, philosophy, and politics to give substance to their later writings, and also shorthand and typing. The postgraduate year would continue courses in history and economics but would also provide lectures by an experienced newsman on reporting, news gathering, proofreading, and editorial writing. Students were required to submit their writings to the *Scholastic* and various national journals.[36]

The law program continued its respectable course under "Colonel" William Hoynes, with a few major changes. The name was changed from "Department of Law" to "School of Law" in 1898, and a shorter, two-year program for those with an advanced educational background was dropped. The principal method of instruction was no longer the lecture and the use of textbooks and especially the case study method were becoming more prominent. The faculty continued to expand and by the mid-1890s eight full-time instructors were employed. The three-year curriculum remained consistent: the study of Blackstone's and Kent's *Commentaries* in the first year; Contracts, Torts, Criminal Law, Evidence, Sales, Insurance, Common Law, and Medieval Jurisprudence in the second year; and Equity, Corporations, Property, Wills, Executors, International Law, and Negotiable Instruments in the third year.[37]

Notre Dame's reputation after fifty years was such that prominent persons in religious, political, and academic life were attracted to visit and speak to the campus community. Two apostolic delegates of the Vatican to the United States, Archbishops Francesco Satolli and Sebastiano Martinelli, visited in 1893 and 1899, and Archbishop Diomede Falconio, the apostolic delegate to Canada (and later to the United States) arrived in 1902. William Jennings Bryan, the presidential nominee of both the Democratic and Populist Parties in 1896, visited on his way to the Democratic Party convention in Chicago. Professor Henry Van Dyke of Princeton University, author of *The Other Wise Man*, lectured on Tennyson, and F. Marion Crawford lectured in 1897 on Pope Leo XIII and the Vatican. William Butler Yeats, the Irish poet and playwright, spent three days discussing Irish literature, and Henry James, author of *The Golden Bowl* and other works, spoke on Honoré de Balzac. In 1904, William Howard Taft, secretary of war and future president of the United States, delivered three lectures on his work as recent governor of the Philippines.[38]

But if Father Morrissey was successful in attracting distinguished lecturers to the campus, he was much less successful in attracting distinguished academics to the permanent faculty. Jerome Green in electrical engineering certainly added luster to the university during his twenty years on the faculty, and Dr. Austin O'Malley was an excellent choice to succeed Maurice Francis Egan as the chair of the Belles Lettres Department. Dr. O'Malley had degrees in both literature and medicine (having studied medicine at Georgetown and in Vienna and Berlin), was bacteriologist for the U.S. Marine Hospital in Washington, DC, wrote widely on literary and medical ethics subjects, and F. Marion Crawford thought him "the best educated man in America."[39] A third distinguished scholar, Charles Veneziani, Father Morrissey was sorry he had hired.

Professor Veneziani had been born in Italy, was fluent in English, Italian, French, and German, and received his PhD from the University of Heidelberg. After holding temporary teaching positions at St. Mary's Academy in Washington, DC, Johns Hopkins, Boston University, the University of Texas, and the University of California, Father Morrissey offered him a position at Notre Dame in 1896. There were misunderstandings from the very beginning, with faults on both sides. He was hired to teach French, perhaps thinking it was a department in itself, and was annoyed when it was announced that he would be teaching in the "Department of Romance Languages," a broader responsibility perhaps and a "department" that actually did not exist. He was promised a future "chair" in mathematics but discovered that Father Morrissey meant only an appointment in mathematics, not a prestigious "chair" as major universities provided for their most distinguished faculty. He was surprised that most of the students were not "university" students at all, they were much younger. He was informed that his salary of $600 a year was the highest ever given to a first-year hire, but discovered that there was at least one higher. (For comparison, Professor Woodrow Wilson was hired by Princeton University in 1890 at a salary of $3,000.)[40] He was disappointed to be told that, because of the university's financial constraints, he could receive no salary increase his second year. Finally, he was to be paid extra for a German course he was scheduled to teach, but the university either cancelled it for low enrollment or located a Holy Cross religious to teach it, and Veneziani was denied that additional class and income.[41]

Father Morrissey soon realized that the appointment had been a mistake, that Veneziani was apparently not a successful teacher at the level of Notre Dame students—and he certainly was not happy—and Father Morrissey urged him to apply for positions elsewhere. Veneziani replied that public universities would not hire professors from Catholic universities since their reputations were so low, and Father Morrissey finally notified him that his contract would not be renewed after 1899, even withholding $140 of his salary until he would agree that the university owed him nothing further.[42]

By this time, major changes had taken place within the governing Congregation of Holy Cross. On Father Sorin's death in 1893, Father Gilbert Français had been elected superior general. An academic, he had been a teacher and a superior of the Holy Cross college at Neuilly in France for several years. In late 1897, Father William Corby, the provincial superior of the priests and brothers in the United States, died unexpectedly, and Father Français appointed Father Zahm his successor.[43] When his contract was not renewed by Father Morrissey in 1899, Professor Veneziani appealed the decision to the university's board of trustees, four Holy Cross priests and one Holy Cross brother, with Father Zahm now as chairman. Father Zahm replied that faculty hiring was exclusively the prerogative of the president and the issue would have to be resolved with Father Morrissey. Veneziani replied that he found that Father Morrissey's "heart is blacker than his robe," that he could have gotten a fairer hearing before "four saloon keepers and one gambler," and he continued:[44]

> No Asiatic court ever prostituted so low its sacred functions of dispensing justice, as did the Board of Trustees of Notre Dame with such an infamous answer.
>
> Far from accepting the President of the University of Notre Dame as my judge, I denounce him before you as a first-class liar, a faithless man, a scoundrel, an unjust despot, and a low deadbeat.

Father Morrissey explained his side of the story in a letter to Father Zahm, his provincial superior; Father Zahm forwarded the letter to Archbishop William Elder of Cincinnati, the prelate overseeing ecclesiastical affairs throughout much of the Midwest; and for some reason the archbishop shared the letter with Professor Veneziani. Father Morrissey's words were equally strong. He described Veneziani as an "incomprehensible person . . . gesticulating and muttering incoherent menaces, precisely as might an escaped inmate of an insane asylum . . . utterly unfit to have charge of students." He referred to his "puerile inanities . . . his vituperative and vindictive ravings . . . [statements] too suggestive of the ravings of a madhouse," and concluded:[45]

> The incomprehensible and tortuous course followed by the deluded man seems to indicate that he is either mentally a wreck and irresponsible or knavishly striving to compel the University to buy peace from his wild and malignant misrepresentations. If he has any reasoning power in reserve he ought to know that he cannot compel me to submit to blackmail, and the mantle of charity and silence has been permitted to cover him over and his ravings under a strong belief in the former alternative, viz., that he is not mentally or otherwise responsible for what he says or does.

In the midst of this controversy, Professor Veneziani published two broadsides against the university. In the first, *A Plea for the Higher Education of Catholic Young Men of America, with an Exposure of the Frauds of the University of Notre Dame, Ind*, he reiterated his allegations against the university in his hiring and dismissal and went on to chastise the university for both its overall dishonesty and its mediocrity as a university. Notre Dame, he charged, attracted students under false pretenses, Holy Cross brothers were ill-prepared for classroom teaching, priests could be better employed in parishes, lay faculty salaries were embarrassingly low, advertised academic programs did not exist, and religious congregations were simply not qualified to administer respectable colleges or universities.[46]

The second publication, *Frauds of the University of Notre Dame, Notre Dame, Indiana, or How the Catholic University of Notre Dame with Her Fraudulent Doctor's Degrees, Courses, etc., Prostitutes the Prestige, Which a Religious Order Enjoys in the Eyes of Catholics to Obtain Their Money Under False Pretenses*, echoes some of the same charges: that degrees were advertised that could not be awarded, that the *Ave Maria* falsely advertised such programs also, that lay faculty salaries were scandalously low, that the university recruited athletes to lure other students to campus, that the press was complicit in concealing Notre Dame's abuses, and that the Congregation of Holy Cross used student tuition money for its other ministries. The final thirty-five pages of the document spelled out in detail the inaccuracies and exaggerations he alleged in Father Zahm's recently published *Catholic Science and Catholic Scientists.*[47]

There was obviously some truth in Professor Veneziani's accusations—Notre Dame's publicity often did outrun the reality, most students were not at "university" level, and salaries for lay faculty were embarrassingly low—but his criticisms were also exaggerated and perhaps mean-spirited. Through the efforts of Father Français, he was eventually awarded $417.20 in back salary and interest but he also wanted vindication of the charges against him and a retraction of the accusations contained in Father Morrissey's letter to Zahm. Receiving no relief from Notre Dame, he appealed to four successive apostolic delegates in Washington, DC, also unsuccessfully. Those appeals continued into 1924 but by that time both Father Morrissey and Father Zahm had been dead for three years and, as far as Notre Dame officials were concerned, the case had long been closed.[48]

In criticizing the university for the low salary he was paid, Professor Veneziani complained that Notre Dame somehow "has money to erect a fine gymnasium, and has money for many other purposes,"[49] but Notre Dame was primarily a residential university, student population had nearly doubled since the close of the Civil War, and the administration was necessarily concerned about student life. Enrollment had been approximately 450 in the early 1870s, declined after the fire in 1879, but then increased steadily in the 1880s and 1890s as new buildings—the Main Building, Washington Hall, Science Hall, Saint Edward's

Hall, Sorin Hall, and Corby Hall—helped to make the university more attractive. Enrollment was 550 in 1895 and approached 700 ten years later. The majority of the students were from the Midwest—Indiana, Illinois, Ohio, Michigan, and Wisconsin—but the institution was attracting Catholic students from all across the country. It was a diverse lot, as was the Catholic Church in America. The student population in 1872 was identified as 183 Irish, 155 American, 75 German, 21 French, 3 Spanish, 1 English, and 1 Italian. Probably only one-fourth of the students were enrolled in the collegiate programs and were strictly "university" students. The minims numbered between 80 and 100 each year, about 15 or 16 percent of the totally enrollment. The other 60 percent were the Preparatory (high school) and Commercial Course students, and the numbers here fluctuated widely. In 1894–1895, for example, there were 97 prep students and 223 in the Commercial Course, but in 1899–1900 the numbers were almost reversed, with 288 in the Preparatory Department and only 103 in the Commercial Course. The diversity in the ages and maturity of the students—and the faculty—may be indicated from two items in the faculty council minutes in the 1880s. In one, the prefect of discipline "requested Profs to do all in their power to prevent the spitting of tobacco on the floors," and another entry notes: "As the warm season was now at hand, the younger and giddier members of the faculty should be warned not to throw chalk or spitballs at their pupils in the classrooms. Other and more legitimate methods of keeping students awake can be devised."[50]

The student's day was still closely regulated. Rising was now at 6:30, followed by morning prayer or Mass, and breakfast at 7:30. After a short break, the morning was occupied with classes or study, with a brief period of relaxation or recreation in the middle. Dinner was at noon, classes and study resumed after a short break, then a period for afternoon games or exercise, and a return to study hall. A period of spiritual reading or a spiritual conference preceded supper, a brief break, a study period, and retiring at 10:00. During at least part of the meals, a spiritual or exemplary book was read aloud by one of the students and, to be sure attention was being paid, students could be quizzed about what was being read. The minims' schedule varied slightly, with snacks served in midmorning and midafternoon, with no more than two hours in the classroom or study hall without a break, and with retiring set at 8:30. The religious character of the institution was always paramount, as the 1893–1894 *Catalogue* noted:[51] "While persons of all religious denominations participate in the privileges of the University, it is nevertheless a strictly Catholic institution, and all students are required to attend divine services at stated times."

University regulations sought to preserve the students, as much as possible, from temptation and moral harm:[52]

1. Students were required to come to campus immediately on arriving at the South Bend station and not loiter in the city.
2. Students were forbidden to leave the campus grounds without the permission of the president or vice president.
3. No courses or classes could be dropped except with the approval of the director of studies.
4. The use of tobacco was prohibited except for those older students in Sorin and Brownson Halls who had the written permission of their parents.
5. Intoxicating liquors were absolutely prohibited to all.
6. Students were not permitted to receive boxes of eatables except for fruit.
7. Students were expected to write home once a week, and the president reserved the right to review all incoming and outgoing mail.
8. Visiting between student rooms was prohibited.
9. Unescorted young women were not welcome on the campus, and students were permitted to visit at neighboring Saint Mary's College only if a sister or cousin were enrolled there. (Understandably, students were constantly attempting to manufacture new "cousins" they were seeking permission to visit, sometimes successfully.)

Professors or prefects (priests and brothers) were apparently with the students most of their waking hours, and the importance of the regulations was stated clearly:[53]

> The aim of the authorities of the University of Notre Dame is to secure for each student that quiet and to promote that mental concentration which are absolutely necessary to a thorough college course. Although the rules made and enforced with this intention are more stringent than is usual in American Colleges, there is nothing required by them to which any earnest student can reasonably object. . . . [The] causes of expulsion are not more numerous than in any well-organized club of gentlemen. There can, for instance, be no mitigation of the extreme penalty for flagrant disobedience of authority, the use of intoxicating liquors, immorality, the habitual use of profane or obscene language, unauthorized absence from college limits, etc.

For less serious infractions, students could be given demerits—twenty-five demerits for breaking silence in the study hall, fifty demerits for festooning the lava-
tory with toilet paper, and so on. Demerits could be worked off through good
behavior, and three hundred demerits could be reason for dismissal.[54]

Professor Veneziani questioned the wisdom of building a gymnasium (and
a second one when the first burned to the ground) but the university recognized
the need for recreation, exercise, and sports in the lives of growing young men.
With so much property, opportunities abounded, and indoor facilities were
needed for inclement weather.

The minims, Father Sorin's little "princes," had what must have seemed to
most of them their own private park. Their playground was a level five-acre field
just behind (north of) Saint Edward's Hall, suitable for organized games like baseball or football but with space available also for impromptu footraces and other
youthful challenges. It was generously equipped with swings, ladders, rings, turning poles, sliding boards, parallel bars, etc., to encourage activity and healthy exercise. The playground was exclusively for them, the older students had their
recreational facilities elsewhere, and a brother or sister was always present during
their recreation periods.[55]

In 1888, a connecting indoor facility was constructed on the east side of
Saint Edward's Hall, where the west wing of Zahm Hall was later built. It was approximately two hundred feet in length and probably a story and a half in height.
It provided additional dormitory space, a library and reading room, a gymnasium,
handball and basketball courts, a roller-skating area, and a game room. The
grounds in front of Saint Edward's Hall were manicured into an attractive park,
with walking paths among fountains, trees, and flower gardens. A low iron fence
suggested that this little park was for the exclusive enjoyment of the minims. With
the then up-to-date lighting, heating, and plumbing in Saint Edward's Hall,
Father Sorin could truly call it a "palace for his princes."[56]

There were similar recreational facilities for the high school and college students. Their outdoor playing fields were separate and were to the east and south
of the Science Hall and Institute of Technology, and were adaptable to baseball,
football, track, and other sports. Marbles were a popular recreation for students
of all ages, tournaments were held, and, in his younger days at least, Father Sorin
was said to be quite skilled. Father Sorin also sent a velocipede back from Paris in
1868, and bicycling had grown into a popular pastime. Baseball, however, seemed
to be the most popular sport. The first intermural games were played in the 1860s
and by the 1880s there were probably a dozen campus teams with such strange-

sounding names as Juanita, Fashion, Pickwick, Star of the East, Star of the West, and Quick-Step. Only rarely were games scheduled with outside teams. A game was played against the South Bend Green Stockings in 1885, and a team from a Catholic parish in Philadelphia played a game on a visit to the university the following year. The most famous of the Notre Dame baseballers was undoubtedly Adrian "Cap" Anson, who later starred for the early Chicago Cubs, batted .334 in over twenty seasons in the major leagues, and was elected to the Baseball Hall of Fame, his plaque in Cooperstown reading: "Greatest Hitter and Greatest National League Player-Manager of the 19th Century." He was a staunch opponent of integrating major league baseball and had a caustic tongue, telling an opposing pitcher, "If I had the money you think I have, I would buy your release from Pittsburgh, trade you for a yellow dog and shoot the dog."[57]

Football gradually overtook baseball as the most popular sport on campus. It was played among the students as early as the late 1860s, with the rival teams being the "Reds" and the "Blues," although it is not clear under what rules the games were played. Notre Dame's first intercollegiate football game was against the University of Michigan in 1887. Two former Notre Dame students were then studying (and playing) at the University of Michigan and, on a trip Michigan was making to play against teams further west, they suggested they stop and play a game at Notre Dame. It was a friendly affair: Notre Dame students met the Michigan team at the train station, gave them a brief tour of the surroundings, and the visitors then explained the rules of the game to the Notre Dame players. Games were still measured in "innings," this first inter-collegiate game lasted only one "inning," and Michigan won 8–0. The visitors were then invited to dinner, Father Walsh thanked them for coming, they departed for the train station in Niles, and the next day, Thanksgiving, they defeated the Chicago alumni of Harvard and Yale 26–0.[58]

From these beginnings, football grew as both an intermural and an intercollegiate sport. Uniforms were purchased, some with black trimmings and some with brown, the early teams were called the "Blacks" and the "Browns," but the names were then changed, for some unknown reason, to the "Specials" and the "Anti-Specials." Notre Dame lost two intercollegiate games to Michigan in 1888, although the second defeat was challenged since Michigan scored while a dispute was going on among the players. In the only other game that year, Notre Dame defeated the Harvard alumni of Chicago 20–0, and the following year Notre Dame defeated Northwestern 9–0 in Notre Dame's first away game. By 1894, Notre Dame had hired a coach—James Morrison, the left tackle on the 1893 Michigan team—and the team compiled a four and one record against Hillsdale, Wabash, Rush Medical of Chicago, and Albion twice. Morrison may have coached for only one game and then left to coach at Hillsdale. Frank Hering, formerly the quarterback for Amos Alanzo Stagg at the University of Chicago, was recruited to coach in 1896. He also played on the team, coached baseball and basketball in their seasons, and even found time to study law. In a speech in late 1904 he suggested that a day be set aside each year to honor mothers, and thus he is often considered the "Father of Mother's Day." There were certainly abuses in intercollegiate football at that time—players played for different teams and were not always full-time students—and in 1897 Notre Dame adopted these athletic regulations:[59]

I. No student shall be allowed to play on any team for a period longer than six years; four of which shall be as undergraduate, two of which shall be as post-graduate.

II. No person shall be a member of any athletic team representing the University unless he be a *bona fide* student taking the full course of studies. All persons who have received compensation for athletic services shall be debarred from the athletic teams. . . .

III. No student whose class standing during the current session shall fall below 75 shall be a member of any athletic team.

Although he did establish a faculty board of athletics in 1898, Father Morrissey was never enthusiastic about intercollegiate sports, chiefly because of the expenses involved, but countenanced them probably because they did assist in attracting other students to Notre Dame.[60]

Track and field events were also popular. They played a prominent part in Father Sorin's Saint Edward's Day celebration each October, and intermural competition was a major part of the inauguration of the new gymnasium, but only rarely did these develop into intercollegiate competition. Notre Dame's best runner was Hal Jewett. He and three others travelled to Ann Arbor for a meet in 1890, he did well enough there to be invited to join the Detroit Athletic Club, and in succeeding years he defeated several United States and international champions. His numbers were impressive: 5 feet 10 inches in the running high jump, 21 feet 4 ¾ inches in the running broad jump, 10.2 seconds in the hundred-yard dash, and 35 feet 8 ¾ inches in the sixteen-pound shot put. He later served in the Spanish-American War and eventually was CEO of the Paige-Detroit Motor Car Company.[61]

With two lakes on the campus itself, and a moderately sized river less than a mile away, boating also became a popular pastime. The Saint Joseph's Boating Club was formed in 1867 "for the physical, as well as the mental education of its members, both in the art of rowing and sailing."[62] Two four-oared boats were purchased at about that time, the *Pinta* and the *Santa Maria*, and occasionally the boats would be carried to the Saint Joseph River and rowed downstream to Niles, about twelve miles distant, not actually races but pleasant outings with a picnic lunch at the end. In 1874 the boating club was officially named the Lemonnier Boating Club in honor of the recently deceased and popular president, a new boathouse was built on the north shore of Saint Joseph's Lake in 1888, with a small gymnasium on the second floor for exercise and training in winter, and new boats were regularly purchased—the *Evangeline, Minnehaha, Montmorency, Yosemite, Ferdinand, Columbus, Silver Jubilee*, and *Golden Jubilee*—as the sport attracted more adherents.[63]

There were also indoor facilities for leisurely recreation and relaxation and for more strenuous exercise when winter snows or spring and fall rains made outdoor activity less desirable. The ground floor of Washington Hall was given over to student recreation, with the north end for the prep or high school students and the south end for the collegians. The rooms included newspapers, periodicals, billiard tables, and games of various kinds. There was a room in the basement of Sorin Hall, and probably also in Corby Hall, where residents could gather to chat, play table games, sing, or simply relax. The new gymnasium in 1901 provided generous space for intramural track competition on the ground floor, plus facilities for handball, and the second floor housed gymnastic and other exercise equipment. For a time at least there was also a well-equipped gymnasium on the top floor of the Institute of Technology.[64]

Many students got additional exercise through military drill. In the 1850s some of the older students had organized a military company called the "Continental Cadets," and shortly thereafter the younger students, the minims, asked for a similar organization, and their company was called the "Washington Cadets" or the "Sorin Cadets."[65] Some of these Continental Cadets volunteered and served with honor in the Civil War. After the war, and with the support of Professor Arthur Stace, the students organized a military company they called the Notre Dame Zouaves, and twenty-five attended the first meeting in 1869. In 1880, Father Corby considered asking the federal government to assign a military officer to supervise military training at Notre Dame, and two years later, Colonel Elmer Otis, commanding officer of the 7th U.S. Cavalry, spent six months at Notre Dame, educating the students in modern drills and tactics. After his departure, the company's name was changed to the "Otis Light Guards." The company may have been in decline for a year or two but it was revived in 1885 through the efforts of Col. William Hoynes of the Law School, and the name was changed again to the "Hoynes Light Guards." There were then at least two military companies, one for the high schoolers and one for the collegians, and the minims still boasted of their "Sorin Cadets." It is not clear how many students were enrolled but the troops drilled twice a week, took part in local parades and civic celebrations, and performed drills and demonstrations as requested.[66]

Another form of student relaxation and entertainment—and education—was the frequent presentation of theatrical productions and oratorical exhibitions, chiefly in Washington Hall. The Thespian Society sponsored many of these but the Senior, Junior, and Minim Departments also produced their own, especially on Father Sorin's feast day, commencement weekend, and other special occasions. Both fencing and dancing lessons were often conducted in preparation for these, and plays and declamations were occasionally presented in foreign languages. Musical renditions by the university's bands and orchestra could be part of each exhibition as well.[67]

Father Morrissey will never be ranked among Notre Dame's greatest presidents. He probably did not possess the charm and charismatic personality of his successor, Father John W. Cavanaugh, nor did he have the scholarly vision of his predecessor, Father Walsh, or of his predecessor as vice president, Father Zahm, but Notre Dame continued to prosper during the twelve years of his presidency. Student enrollment increased, the faculty remained stable, and the physical plant expanded. Father Morrissey was concerned about the university's finances during the depression years of the 1890s, and this may explain why student enrollment increased more on the high school than on the collegiate level: high school (and minim) education was often income-producing, but collegiate education was an expense. The figures may be deceiving, however. As overall enrollment increased in the 1890s, collegiate enrollment increased proportionately, remaining at a steady 23 percent. High school enrollment did increase from 97 to 288, from 18 percent to 46 percent overall, but the figures for the two-year Commercial Course are almost the reverse, from 223 students to approximately 100, from 41 percent down to 16 percent. It may be that, under Father Morrissey's presidency, fewer students were encouraged to select the two-year Commercial Course track and more therefore entered the less professional but more academic prep courses that, on completion, could lead directly into the four-year Classical Course. Thus Father Morrissey's academic vision may have been more advanced than is often considered.[68]

A further complication emerged, of course, when Father Corby, the provincial superior, died in 1897 and Father Zahm, Father Morrissey's archrival in planning Notre Dame's future, was named his replacement. Father Zahm was now Father Morrissey's immediate superior. Father Morrissey knew he did not enjoy Father Zahm's confidence and full support and, fearing that Father Zahm would eventually remove him, he asked the provincial chapter in 1905 to accept his resignation. This the chapter did, and it named Father John W. Cavanaugh to succeed him.

CHAPTER 8

The First Father John Cavanaugh

The appointment, and election, of Father Zahm as provincial superior of all Holy Cross religious and institutions in the United States in 1898, and the resignation of Father Morrissey as Notre Dame's president in 1905, might have clarified and confirmed the aspiration of the university to become a true institution of higher learning, with less emphasis on high school, grade school, and Manual Labor School students, but it did not. The new president, Father John W. Cavanaugh, C.S.C., was a close friend and admirer of Father Zahm (which helps to explain his selection as president) and would remain so for the rest of Father Zahm's life, but the following year, 1906, Father Zahm had lost the confidence and support of Father Gilbert Français, Father Sorin's successor as superior general, and Father Zahm was replaced as provincial superior—by Father Morrissey! Throughout his presidency, Father Cavanaugh might owe his educational philosophy more to Father Zahm, but his religious obedience was to Father Morrissey.[1]

John Cavanaugh had been born in 1870 in Leetonia, Ohio, a small town twenty-five miles south of Youngstown, only a few miles from the Pennsylvania border. His father, Patrick Cavanaugh, hailed from Tyrone, Ireland, and his mother, Elizabeth O'Connor, from Armagh. They had married in Ireland and had four children before deciding to immigrate to the United States, probably shortly after the American Civil War. Young John attended the local parish school and, when not in school, probably worked in the nearby coal mines, as did his father and older brothers. A bright young man with a flair for oratory, while working alone in the family garden he used to pause and declaim aloud, perhaps imitating priests and politicians he had witnessed moving their listeners. The pastor of the local Saint Barbara's Parish was Father E. W. J. Lindesmith, a former army chaplain who may have come to know one or several of the Holy Cross priest-chaplains in the Civil War, and it was probably he who recommended Notre Dame to young John when he expressed a desire to continue his education further. At the age of sixteen he entered the recently constructed Holy Cross Seminary,[2] set a little distance from the main Notre Dame campus and to the west of Saint Mary's Lake, and began his studies for the Holy Cross priesthood.[3]

Father Cavanaugh's years in the seminary, 1886–1894, were eventful. He was able to take classes from, or at least attend lectures of, both Charles Warren Stoddard and Maurice Francis Egan; Father Daniel Hudson, editor of the *Ave Maria*, lectured at times in his literature classes, and his command of the English language, written and spoken, continually improved. He was an officer in the seminary's literary society, took part in debates, and wrote occasionally for the *Scholastic*, the Notre Dame student magazine. He enjoyed playing the violin until he discovered that the seminary superior, Father Stanislaus Fitte, had a deep aversion for violin music. Young Cavanaugh served as a prefect in Sorin Hall for a time, and he spent one year teaching English at the Congregation's Saint Joseph's College in Cincinnati. He was present at the joyful celebrations of Father Sorin's Golden Jubilee of priestly ordination in May and August 1888, and also at the sorrowful funerals of Father Walsh, Father Granger, and Father Sorin in 1893. He made a lifelong friendship with James Burns, a Manual Labor School apprentice learning the printing trade and a catcher on the Notre Dame baseball team. Cavanaugh himself was not an athlete, preferred nothing more strenuous than walking for exercise, and, at age eighteen, could write critically of college sports:[4]

> One of the evils of the day is the mania of the student for athletic sports. A student should positively be a man of thought and mental application, and in an education, the diligent pursuit of learning should be the paramount idea. Nothing renders a man so unfit for study as excessive exercise. It strains every muscle and exhausts every particle of mental energy, thus excluding study from the mind of the wretched enthusiast. The number of those who can confine themselves within proper limits in athletic sports is small indeed; and the college man who is at once a dunce and a baseball fiend is a standing disgrace to the college world.

Was some of this written tongue-in-cheek, perhaps as a humorous prod for his good friend Jimmy Burns and his athletic success? In any case, it is interesting coming from the man who would later hire Knute Rockne as head coach and inaugurate the heyday of Notre Dame football nationally.

John Cavanaugh was ordained a priest on April 20, 1894, and the following day he offered his first Solemn High Mass before his family and hometown friends in Saint Patrick's Church in Leetonia, with Father Morrissey, recently appointed Notre Dame president, as preacher. The choice of Father Morrissey may be surprising. Father Cavanaugh would eventually be much closer philosophically to Father Zahm than to Father Morrissey, but in 1894 that public controversy may still have been a few years in the future. As a prefect in Sorin Hall, seminarian Cavanaugh had undoubtedly gotten to know both of them, but the Notre Dame president was the much better preacher (and Father Cavanaugh always appreciated fine oratory), he had a very genial and winning personality, and, like the Cavanaugh family, he was also very proudly Irish. The newly ordained priest was then reassigned to Notre Dame. He continued as a prefect in Sorin Hall, teaching rhetoric, moderating the student Philodemic Society, and serving as assistant to Father Daniel Hudson, editor of the *Ave Maria*.[5]

Father Hudson had been born in Nahant, Massachusetts, a suburb of Boston, in 1849, of a Methodist father and Irish Catholic mother, was one of ten children, and was raised Catholic by his mother. As a teenager he worked first in an antique bookstore and then in a publishing house, where he was fortunate to have met Longfellow, Lowell, Holmes, Whittier, Emerson, and Hawthorne on occasion. When he once mentioned to Longfellow that he hoped to become a priest and an Indian missionary, the poet gave him encouragement. After graduating from Holy Cross College in Worcester, he happened to meet Father Paul Gillen on a train heading west and told him of his desire to be a priest. Father Gillen persuaded him to detrain with him in South Bend and he immediately entered the seminary at Notre Dame. He was ordained a priest in 1875, was named editor of the *Ave Maria*, and for the next fifty-nine years rarely left the campus. He felt he was too busy with the magazine even to attend his mother's funeral, and when he spent two days with his close friend, Bishop John Lancaster Spalding, his Holy Cross colleagues thereafter would humorously refer to "the summer he spent in Peoria." He could remain at work until two o'clock in the morning and still get up at five to assist at community morning prayer. In winter the heat was turned off at ten o'clock and he stuffed straw in his large rubber boots to keep warm. He solicited articles from the best American Catholic writers of the time and translated and reprinted the best of European authors also. It was from Father

Hudson and his experience with the *Ave Maria* that Father Cavanaugh honed his own literary style, that he learned to be meticulous and errorless, and that he learned that rewriting (often more than once) was necessary to achieve the precision desired.[6]

Father Cavanaugh's life changed in 1899. Father Corby had died unexpectedly shortly before, Father Zahm, the Congregation's procurator general in Rome, had been appointed provincial superior to succeed him, and Father Frederick Linneborn, superior of Holy Cross Seminary at Notre Dame, was named to replace Father Zahm in Rome. Young Father Cavanaugh, only twenty-eight years old, was named superior of Holy Cross Seminary.[7]

Father Linneborn had emigrated from Westphalia, Germany, had received a doctorate in theology in Rome, and had administered the seminary with something like German military precision, deviating rarely from established regulations. Father Cavanaugh was a welcomed change. During the five years of his superiorship, the number of seminarians increased from less than thirty to eighty-four, and a two-story annex had to be added to the rear of the seminary building. Seminarians were encouraged to mingle with other Notre Dame students, some went to Chicago to see Sarah Bernhardt on her final tour, they enjoyed opera in South Bend, and seminarian John Farley was permitted to continue on the Notre Dame football team. Discipline was not neglected. When a few seminarians slept in and missed morning prayer, Father Cavanaugh announced that some situations could be remedied only by prayer and fasting, and since others had been praying, the culprits would fast, and go without breakfast. Father Cavanaugh continued his work with the *Ave Maria*, taught seminarians to be careful proofreaders, and read much of John Ruskin and Thomas Babington Macaulay to improve his own literary style. Many seminarians who later contributed much to Notre Dame's and the Church's success were initiated into the religious life by Father Cavanaugh—Father Charles O'Donnell in literature, Father Julius Nieuwland in science, Father Matthew Walsh in history, Father Ernest Davis in chemistry, Father Michael Mathis in scripture and liturgy, and two later bishops, George Finnigan and Timothy Crowley—and throughout their lives they could refer to themselves as "Father Cavanaugh boys." Father Cavanaugh was personable, popular, handsome (six feet tall, close to two hundred pounds, sandy hair, and a wide smile), and a very successful administrator, and when Father Morrissey resigned as Notre Dame president in 1905, it was no surprise that Father Cavanaugh was named to succeed him.[8]

This background had prepared Father Cavanaugh well for the Notre Dame presidency. He had been teaching rhetoric on campus for five years and, for part of that time, served as director of the English or Belles-Lettres Course. He spent much time working on the *Ave Maria* magazine, which was housed very close to the Main Building, and he must have crossed paths frequently with students, faculty, and University administrators. As seminary superior he was a member of the minor chapter along with the president of Notre Dame and other local religious superiors, and thus he was part of the financial and expansion discussions for all the religious houses—including Notre Dame. By this time, he was well aware of the debates among the supporters of Father Morrissey and Father Zahm over the future course of Notre Dame, and these debates surely helped clarify his own educational philosophy and goals.[9]

Someone has described him as "studious but not scholarly,"[10] and it may be accurate. Though highly respected by Father Zahm, the provincial superior did not send him on to pursue graduate studies, as he had sent his classmate James Burns, but he seemed to have been selected for administrative posts early on. On one occasion, when the University of Ottawa awarded him an honorary doctorate of divinity and clothed him with the appropriate crimson gown, he could smile and say: "Even my robes are blushing!"[11] But he was remarkably well read and in one public lecture entitled "A Plea for the Classics," he could mention Homer, Pindar, Aeschylus, Euripides, Aristophanes, Horace, Chaucer, Dante, Milton, Shakespeare, Holmes, Sienkiewicz, Newman, Emerson, Brownson, and Harriet Beecher Stowe, and there is no indication he was unfamiliar with any of them.[12] And he was an outstanding public speaker. One who knew him in his later years has written:[13]

> Father John W. Cavanaugh, C.S.C., stands in Notre Dame history as its most eloquent President. Many were fine orators. Many spoke with force and persuasion. But throughout the presidency of Father Cavanaugh, from 1905 to 1919, he spoke on many occasions, of great diversity in goals and audiences. The collection of these addresses indicates the range of his mind, the mastery of his words and the lasting effect upon his hearers. He became one of the nation's great orators. The printed word cannot convey the music of his voice, or the aura of culture and confidence that were there even before the first word was spoken. . . . Ex-presidents at Notre Dame tend to follow the path of humility, rather than the corporate path of chairmanship of the board. And because he overshadowed anyone on a platform where he spoke, it was not good public relations for the University to find its new "establishment" overshadowed.

If on occasion he became too dramatic or flowery, his friend (and preacher at his first solemn Mass) Father Morrissey could smile and say: "Smell those flowers!"[14] Another has written that "his pose and dignity of bearing can justly be described as majestic. No one who ever saw him sweep onto a platform or into a room, or who listened to one of his sermons or talks, could ever forget him."[15]

In early December 1905, only a few months after the new president had assumed his office, the student body assembled to honor him on his feast day, and he took the opportunity to share a little of his hopes and vision for the university. He praised the work the university was already doing, the training of fine Christian gentlemen in and outside the classroom, and this he obviously would continue:[16]

> But you will permit me to say . . . that this glorious old college with its sixty years of sincere and laborious effort for the best in education and the best in human life, is as worthy of the love and loyalty of her children as any in the land. Where else do so many hundreds of young men live in such close and peaceful communion? Where else is the standard of manly morality so high? Where else are obedience, purity, kindliness, labor—the noblest lessons of life—so persistently inculcated and so willingly received? Where else are learned professors so unassuming, so companionable, so sympathetic with students? Where else is notoriety seeking so rare and honest teaching so common?

But he also acknowledged that more was needed, especially academic enhancements: "We need two residence halls handsomer and better equipped than either Sorin or Corby. We need a great fire-proof library, we need a great school of technology and new laboratories, professorships and scholarships."[17]

In his numerous speeches, lectures, and even sermons over the years, Father Cavanaugh was able to enunciate a rather clear philosophy of Catholic education. Influenced by the teachings of Father Moreau and the examples of Fathers Sorin, Walsh, Zahm, and Morrissey, he viewed education as the development of the whole person, as he stated in a sermon opening the new school year in 1909: "The theoretically perfect education, therefore, is that which most fully develops all the capabilities of action that are latent in man, education of the body, the mind, and the heart."[18]

Perhaps the most basic of all was development of the body and the achievement and maintenance of good health:[19]

Your body is the instrument with which you labor. It must be strong and supple, quick to respond to the direction of your mind. Hence the hollow-chested boy who sits on the bleachers, his only exercise breathing languidly through a cigarette and feebly applauding a good play, does not do his whole duty to himself. He needs to be told that his life work will make severe demands on his physical energies and that these must be abundant if he is not to break down.

"Next," Father Cavanaugh proclaimed, "your mind must grow strong by hard study, as muscles grow strong by exercise." His ideal was the development of all areas of the mind, not some narrow specialization:[20]

Suppose you had the memory of a Mezzofanti (who is said to have learned a new language in one night), and the logic of an Aquinas, and the philosophical judgment of a Plato and the artistic faculty of a Raphael, and the musical genius of a Mozart, and the scientific knowledge of a Pasteur—suppose you had every faculty of the intellect as perfectly developed as it has ever been in any man, and suppose all these developed faculties were united in a single individual, you would have the ideal educated mind.

The mind was to be developed, not for any pragmatic or utilitarian goals, but because it is a reflection of God's own mind and, like God's mind, it can grasp and appreciate God's work and creation:[21]

[God] has given us the kingdom of intellect, and He bids us go forth with lamps to search its confines. And our Heavenly Father looks down on His children as they delve and dig in this mine of knowledge, unearthing His Mysteries, explaining His plans, unfolding His works adoringly, and He is filled with complacence. . . . Hence, I find the dignity of culture in this; that the more active our minds, the broader and deeper our knowledge, the closer we approach to the divine ideal, the clearer becomes the image of God impressed on our souls in creation. All this, education does for us.

In an address before the faculty and student body at the Catholic University of America in 1910, he stressed the need for persons who were both competent scholars and committed believers:[22]

It is true that research is in large part the end and object of the University; it is true that you must have the specialist's knowledge in order to interpret the great scholar and the great scientist to the world. But what I plead for is a tribe of writers who shall take their stand in this middle field [both popular and scholarly], and by a brilliant presentation of the great questions of scholarship, win back the world to a respect for the supernatural and for Revealed Religion.

To do this you must acquaint yourselves thoroughly with the contents of modern science. You must know the present status of those questions about which there is controversy, or if you take philosophy or Scripture or sociology or economics for your field you must be familiar with the farthest-going questions in these great fields. But whatever the matter you select, what the Church expects of the University is a skilled body of intellectual swordsmen ready to leap to her defense at a moment's notice.

But education of the mind and body itself was not sufficient. "Above all you must cultivate character," Father Cavanaugh insisted at the Mass opening the new school year in the fall of 1907.[23] He had proclaimed this same message the year before:[24]

A third lesson that you must learn is that the conquest of life is to be wrought by character. . . . There have been great temples with towering domes and splendid façades and immortal frescoes that have tumbled down into dust and rubbish because there was a flaw in the foundations. So, too, powerful men of brilliant parts are every day sinking into failure and disgrace and death because of a fundamental flaw in their character. This University is based upon the theory that education is chiefly moral; that character is more than culture.

Your *Alma Mater* will surround you with every strengthening influence that makes for character, but she can work no improvement in you without your active co-operation. . . .

Your school years are indeed a preparation for life, but forget not that they are also a part of life, and that they must be lived conscientiously and profitably if you would escape condemnation in the day of final accounting.

Very importantly, Notre Dame offered students "the opportunity to grow in the knowledge and practice of . . . religion:"[25]

By God's grace you have the gift of faith. You have it because your fore-fathers held to it through poverty and persecution, and you appreciate it as the most precious possession of your lives. To that holy faith your *Alma Mater* stands dedicated. Her mission is to nourish and strengthen it while providing you with all the knowledge of the modern as well as the ancient world. For this great opportunity you must also render an account in the day of final reckoning. Let it not be said of you that familiarity with sacred things has brought a want of reverence for the Church, for the prayers you say in common every day and above all for the Holy Mass which is the center, the life of our faith.

With his friend Father Zahm as his provincial superior, Father Cavanaugh did not hesitate to begin a strong presidency. In 1906, his first year as president, he and Father Zahm requested of the archbishop of Cincinnati that the body of Father Badin, then resting in that cathedral city, be transferred back to Notre Dame, the acreage he had originally purchased. To provide a suitable final resting place, it was decided to rebuild Father Badin's original Log Chapel, which had burned down in the fire of 1856. Rather detailed floor plans of Father Badin's 1832 chapel were available and an architect familiar with that type of early construction was sought. A black American former slave, William Arnett of Kentucky, was selected, but then a second difficulty arose. A broadax was needed to shape the logs correctly, but apparently no stores in South Bend still stocked them. Two elderly settlers in the South Bend area had retained theirs and loaned them to Notre Dame for the project. With local assistance certainly, Mr. Arnett then constructed the present Log Chapel, close to the spot where Father Badin's original chapel had stood.[26]

May 3, 1906, the Feast of the Finding of the Holy Cross, was the day selected for the re-entombment, but another ceremony was scheduled for earlier that day: the unveiling and blessing of a statue of Father Sorin at the then entrance to the campus. The eight-foot bronze figure had been sculpted by Ernesto Biondo, and the pedestal was of Vermont granite, at a total cost of $25,000, contributed by students, alumni, and friends of the university. The celebration began in the university church with a Solemn High Mass sung by Bishop Herman Alerding of the diocese of Fort Wayne, and the sermon was preached by Archbishop John Keane of Dubuque. A procession formed in front of the church—students, faculty, Holy Cross religious, and the university band—and made its way slowly to the veiled monument where a crowd of perhaps two thousand had gathered.

Father Cavanaugh addressed the assembly in words that reminded some of the Gettysburg Address:[27]

> Three score years and more have passed since a young missionary first looked in hope and affection on the wilderness where now blooms this beautiful garden. . . . Often he was carried half frozen from the sled in which he made his missionary journeys to the Indians and the scattered white men for one hundred and fifty miles in every direction; more than once the horses were unyoked from the plow and sold for debt. . . .
>
> Rich only in the zeal of his fervent soul, strong only in the courage of his noble heart, he labored on, till today the work he directed is the pride of America and the glory of the Church. . . . Notre Dame is Father Sorin's monument.

He closed with a dramatic invocation:

> Therefore, in the name of the sainted apostles who carried the Roman cross into countries over which the Roman eagle never passed; in the name of the holy missionaries of every age, the evangelizers of every land, who have ventured for God where the merchant would not venture for gold nor the soldier for glory; in the name of those Christian educators who believe, as he believed, that the heart of culture is the culture of the heart, and that the soul of improvement is the improvement of the soul; in the name of humanity whom he loved and served without distinction of race or creed; in the name of America, the scene of his labors and the land of his predilection; in the name of generations of young men whose lives have been touched and sanctified by his consecrated hands; in the name of *Alma Mater* whose foundation stones were cemented with his sweat and blood; in the name of the noble army of priests, brothers, and sisters of Holy Cross who with him bore the burden of a long day and are now trembling in everlasting ecstasy; in the name of venerable religious here present into whose souls come rushing back so many holy memories today; in the name of the Holy Catholic Church whose loyal and faithful priest he was; in the name of St. Joseph and the Blessed Virgin whose names he magnified; in the name of Him, the Savior of us all, whom he served and loved with almost perfect love and service—I say, unveil the statue of Sorin.

It was Father Cavanaugh's oratory at its finest.

At four o'clock that afternoon, the remains of Father Badin were then solemnly brought into the main church, the seminary choir sang the *Miserere* psalm, and a brief prayer service was held, closing with the singing of the *Benedictus* canticle. A procession then formed and the casket was placed on a hearse and slowly carried to the recently constructed Log Chapel close to the Old College building and Saint Mary's Lake. Years earlier Father Badin had expressed the wish that such a cabin be built for him in which he could spend his final days but Father Sorin decided that he could not spare a brother to care for and nurse him that independently, and he then returned to Cincinnati where he died in 1853. Father Zahm, the provincial superior, had celebrated Mass in the chapel that morning, and now Father Badin's remains were interred there as he had wished. A commemorative plaque on the chapel wall extolled him as the first priest ordained in the United States, missionary in the Mississippi Valley for sixty years, builder of a mission chapel on this site, and generous donor of the land on which the University of Notre Dame was built. In attendance at the ceremony that afternoon were Mother Mary of the Compassion, who as a young sister had known and spoken with Father Badin more than fifty years before, and Father Louis Letourneau, who as an early Notre Dame student had served Father Badin's Mass.[28]

One of Father Cavanaugh's early goals was to increase student enrollment. The student body stood at more than 600 when he assumed office and in one of his first addresses to the students and faculty, in December 1905, he asked student assistance in increasing that number:[29]

> Why should not this University count 1500 students on its roll instead of half that number? Why should not the city of which organically if not geographically we are a part, why should not South Bend and her sister cities send us 200 earnest day scholars next year? Why can not every man here today make it a point of honor and of loyalty to bring at least one worthy student back with him after the holidays? Show us of the Faculty how we can help towards this result without sacrificing anything essential to the character or efficiency of this college, and I pledge you my honor that no effort will be spared to accomplish it.

Slightly more than fifty additional students arrived each year over the next three years and the enrollment figure reached 850 by the fall of 1908. Still not satisfied, Father William Moloney was commissioned to go to Chicago, canvass the area, and recruit as many qualified students as he could interest in Notre Dame. Precise figures are impossible to come by because students, at all levels, continued to come and leave throughout the academic year, but enrollment was probably close to 1,000 by 1912 and 1,500 by 1917.[30]

With the increased student enrollment, additional housing was also needed. The university administration was always concerned about students living in town with less daily supervision and more exposure to distractions and temptations. Father Cavanaugh had announced as early as December 1905 that "we need two residence halls handsomer and better equipped that either Sorin or Corby"[31] and by 1908 he was ready to act. Father Deseille had apparently been given some property in the Chicago area to continue the mission work of "Ste. Marie des Lacs," Father Sorin had inherited this land for the mission, and a portion of it may have been sold in 1908 to finance the new building, Walsh Hall.[32] It was to be 230 feet by 41 feet, four stories plus a basement, and able to accommodate slightly more than one hundred freshmen, with Brownson, Corby, and Sorin housing older students. The rooms on the back, or west, side of the building and all the rooms on the top floor (or "attic" as it was called) were single rooms, 14 feet by 10 feet, with common baths and toilets on each floor. On the other floors, the rooms on the front, or east, side of the building were three-room suites, each with a study in the center flanked by a bedroom on each side, and some with private baths. There was a chapel on the north end of the first floor, an auditorium, billiard room, and smoking room in the basement, and a freight elevator in the center, perhaps the first such convenience at Notre Dame. The rooms had hardwood floors, the corridors were mosaic tile, and the exterior was yellow brick trimmed in Bedford stone. Construction began in April 1909 and the cornerstone, containing medals and relics, lists of Holy Cross religious and all current students, and the most recent issues of the *Scholastic* and the *Ave Maria*, was in place and blessed in May. Construction continued throughout the summer, the building was ready for occupancy in October, and it was solemnly blessed by the apostolic delegate, Archbishop Diomede Falconio, in early November.[33]

The new hall was clearly the Gold Coast, as Father Cavanaugh wrote to a parent that summer:[34]

> Replying to your letter dated August 16th I desire to say that the price of a double room suitable for your boys will be anywhere from $160.00 to $500.00 per year. A suite of rooms costing $500.00 will contain a center study room with three windows forming a bay, well lighted and equipped, and a bedroom on either side of the study room. The bedrooms will be

furnished with hot and cold water. The room costing $160.00 for two boys would be a large single chamber which would conveniently hold a bed, table, and wash-stand for each boy.

As enrollment continued to increase, even more beds were needed, and in 1917 a convenient solution was found. The Manual Labor School, chartered in 1844, had been housed successively in the first college building, then in a separate structure behind the college, after the fire of 1849 in a new wooden building in front of what was later Corby Hall, and finally, in 1897, Father Morrissey had constructed a brick building on the southwest corner of the then campus for this St. Joseph's Industrial School. As the number of apprentices declined in the early years of the twentieth century, Father Cavanaugh decided to terminate the Manual Labor School, add wings on the north and south ends of the building, convert it for use as a residence for university freshmen, and rename it Badin Hall. A cafeteria was also provided on the ground floor and students then had the option of enrolling in a meal plan in the Main Building refectories or purchasing meals individually in the Badin cafeteria.[35]

Student life seems to have been pleasant in the early years of the twentieth century. Varsity football victories were a source of pride, interhall competition in football and baseball stirred campus interest, broad fields allowed for pickup games of almost every sort, and marbles remained a popular pastime. In addition to the meals in the Main Building and the cafeteria in Badin Hall, students could get an inexpensive lunch at Hullie and Mike's in downtown South Bend or purchase a snack at Brother Leopold's (Brother Leep's) little store, especially "lemonade and fours" for a nickel—a glass of lemonade and two vanilla-marshmallow-chocolate cookies listed as Number 4 at his counter. Born in Germany, Brother Leopold had taught violin to the students before retiring to his little confectionary. He lived to be ninety-eight and once remarked: "I don't know why I have lived so long! I was such a beautiful baby!" Cigarette smoking was still frowned upon but pipes and cigars were becoming more common among older students. Rules were still broken and pranks abounded, and on one occasion, after some fights and other unpleasant incidents on the Hill Street streetcar that served Notre Dame, a few students one evening commandeered the car as it approached the university and they set the car on fire, destroying it completely. Good relations with the city were eventually restored.[36]

Having succeeded in increasing student enrollment, and usually keeping them contented, Father Cavanaugh also wanted to encourage graduates to remain close to and interested in the university. From the university's earliest days, many alumni were accustomed to return to campus for commencement ceremonies each year, and in 1868 they were organized into the "Associated Alumni of the University of Notre Dame."[37] The purpose of the organization was "to preserve and strengthen the common tie that binds us to each other and alma mater, by means of yearly reunions and by literary correspondence."[38] They met and renewed friendships each year during commencement week, enjoyed "a sumptuous banquet," and elected new members—chiefly professors and others connected with the university who were not alumni (Father Carrier, for example)—but there seemed to have been no intention to offer tangible or financial support to the university. The institution was still small, most of the faculty and staff were vowed religious, and financial contributions from the alumni may not have seemed urgent.[39]

Over the course of years, the alumni in individual cities—New York, Chicago, Boston—began to meet among themselves for similar reasons, but the national organization went into decline. Father Cavanaugh hoped to resurrect it and, on February 10, 1908, addressed a letter to all the alumni, inviting them to return to the university during commencement week that year, "for the purpose of drafting a constitution and perfecting an organization" of the alumni.[40] One hundred thirty-six alumni returned on June 17 and, except for those classes where all the graduates were deceased, only seven classes were unrepresented. The members adopted the name "Alumni Association of the University of Notre Dame," William Breen of Fort Wayne, class of 1877, was elected the first president, annual dues were set at five dollars, and the stated mission of the organization was "to promote friendly relations among the Alumni of the University and to further the interests of Alma Mater in such ways as may be considered best."[41]

The alumni continued to meet each year. They received information of faculty and administration changes, attended Mass for deceased members, reviewed the success of the athletic teams, and considered ways to "further the interests" of the university. By the association's sixth meeting in 1913, the treasury showed a balance of more than $2,500 and it was decided to begin soliciting funds to construct an Old Students' Hall or Alumni Hall on campus where graduates might reside when they returned to visit the university. By Father Cavanaugh's last year as president, the association had collected $75,000 in the Old Students' Hall fund, in addition to $5,000 in its general treasury. Alumni Hall would eventually be built on campus, although for students rather than returning alumni, and the Alumni Association would continue to be a major means of financial support for the university in succeeding years.[42]

Shortly after the statue of Father Sorin had been unveiled and blessed in late spring of 1906, a campaign to honor a second Holy Cross dignitary, even legend, was begun. Father William Corby had died unexpectedly in December 1897. He had been president of Notre Dame twice, pastor and president of Sacred Heart College in Watertown, Wisconsin, provincial superior of Holy Cross priests and brothers in the United States on three occasions, and won national fame as a chaplain in the Civil War when he gave general absolution to the troops of the Irish Brigade at the Battle of Gettysburg. Soon after the turn of the century, Father Corby's friend and former officer in the Irish Brigade, General St. Clair Mulholland, sought to interest various persons of means, and Civil War veterans, to contribute funds for a monument to be erected on the Gettysburg battlefield. His early efforts were not successful. "I started the movement here by going to see some wealthy people, but I was so discouraged I gave it up," he wrote. "The surviving officers and men of our faith throughout the country are poor. Hardly one of them has a cent."[43]

But the general continued to lecture across the country, emphasizing Father Corby's heroic ministry at Gettysburg, and the Catholic Alumni Sodality of Philadelphia undertook to promote the erection of a suitable monument on the battlefield. General Mulholland agreed to lead the fundraising effort, and this time he was successful. Samuel Aloysius Murray of Philadelphia was commissioned to craft the bronze, life-size statue of the bearded priest with his right hand raised in absolution. Father Cavanaugh was one of those invited to the dedication ceremony in October 1910 and he spoke, but unfortunately General Mulholland had passed away a few months earlier.[44]

When reports of the 1910 monument at Gettysburg reached Notre Dame, the students of Corby Hall called a meeting to discuss whether a similar monument might be erected on campus. Father Thomas Irving, the hall rector, was enthusiastic, Father Cavanaugh approved, and the students selected a committee of eight to contact present and former residents of Corby Hall for contributions. The campaign was not a complete success and the university eventually had to solicit funds from other sources.[45]

Samuel Murray, who had crafted the original statue at Gettysburg, was commissioned to make the replica, the rock on which it was to stand was imported from the Gettysburg battlefield itself, and Memorial Day, May 29, 1911, was selected for the dedication. A Solemn High Mass was celebrated in the main church at eight o'clock, followed by the dedication ceremonies presided over by Colonel William Hoynes, dean of the Notre Dame Law School and Civil War veteran.

An official proclamation from the governor was read, as was President Lincoln's Gettysburg Address, and the principal speech of the day was delivered by Father John Chidwick, the surviving chaplain of the USS *Maine* sunk in Havana harbor at the start of the Spanish-American War in 1898.[46] His words in part:[47]

> Few of those whose names the awful conflict of '61 to '65 placed upon the world's roll of honor and imperishable fame deserve better than Father Corby, the gratitude of our country. . . . In the long, tedious and trying marches on the peninsula, in cold and drizzling rain and under parching and blistering sun he bore fatigue and hunger and was a stay and comfort to his men. In the deadly swamps of the Chickahominy where the poisoned air swept strong men to their graves by the thousands, he himself was laid low by exhaustion and disease.
>
> At Chancellorsville he was warned, "You will stay here till you are killed," but yet he remained and at immortal Gettysburg, which will live in our people's memory as the salvation of our Union and in the records of all people as one of the bloodiest, bravest, and most important battles of any war, he reached to the height of heroic and self-sacrificing devotion to God and man when fearless of danger he sprang up on a rock in front of his men while the battle swelled and roared about him to speak of heaven's trust and their sacred duty, of the worthy ends for which they were fighting and then imploring them to recommend themselves to God in a fervent act of contrition, he raised his hand in aid and making the sign of forgiveness imparted what was for most of them their final absolution. . . . It is a scene which neither the painter nor the poet, the orator or the patriot will ever let die.

General John C. Black, commander of the Grand Army of the Republic, arrived belatedly from Washington and also spoke. Miss Nellie Mahoney, president of the senior class at Saint Mary's College, was then asked to pull the cord to release the giant flag draping the monument, the statue of Father Corby was revealed to great applause, and Father Morrissey, the provincial superior, gave the statue its solemn blessing. The ceremony closed with the joyful singing of "Holy God," and the assembly then processed to the cemetery where flowers were placed on the graves of all G.A.R. veterans.[48]

One further war memorial was erected on campus a few years later. John H. Shillington enrolled as a student in the 1890s, was a fine athlete, and had travelled to Chicago with the baseball team in the spring of 1897 for an intercollegiate game. For reasons not clear, he decided not to return to campus with the team but to remain in Chicago overnight. This was a serious infraction of the rules, for which he was subsequently expelled. He was not bitter over the university's decision, his affection for the college remained strong, and, perhaps to put the sad incident completely behind him, he decided to join the Navy. Assigned to the battleship USS *Maine*, he wrote to a friend from shipboard:[49]

> I often think of Notre Dame. I can picture her daily, and in my reminiscences of her a tear is often brushed away. . . . I suppose "Shilly" is forgotten by people at the old college, and I don't blame them. Though forgotten, I shall always hold Notre Dame near and dear to me.

When the USS *Maine* was destroyed in Havana harbor on February 15, 1898, "Shilly" was one of those who lost their lives. Six weeks later, university president Father Morrissey offered Mass for the repose of his soul, with his mother present at the service. The university wanted a more lasting memorial and, through the offices of a Cuban alumnus, obtained one of the shells from the ship after it had been raised. Secretary of the Navy Josephus Daniels was invited to speak at the dedication, first reviewing the student military groups, including the young khaki-clad minims whom Father Cavanaugh said were too small to be called "minute men" and thus should be called "second men," and he presented awards of gold, silver, and bronze medals to those meriting them. He then delivered the dedicatory address, and the monument, a ten-inch shell on a base of bronze and a pedestal of Wisconsin granite was revealed and blessed. The small memorial later appropriately graced the main entrance of the Pasquerilla (ROTC) Center.[50]

Father Cavanaugh was successful in making Notre Dame a larger university, but was he successful in making it a better one? The answer is "yes," but perhaps a hesitating "yes." He had not been assigned to pursue a higher education degree himself, and he may not have preferred to do so. But he had a scholarly vision. The quality he sought in the priest-teacher on the Notre Dame faculty was a solidly broad education with a specialization. He wrote in 1905:[51]

> To develop a body of priests who shall know something about everything and everything about something—to produce a catholic and symmetrical culture that shall be crowned with a specialist's knowledge of a particular field in the kingdom of learning—is the aim of the course of studies in the Congregation.

"To know something about everything and everything about something" was an expression he returned to frequently throughout his life, and thanks to the efforts and decisions of Father Zahm, the provincial superior before 1907, several talented young priests were sent on to higher studies at this time and then returned to Notre Dame with their specializations.

The first of these was Father Matthew Walsh, a future president of Notre Dame. He had been born in Chicago in 1882, the seventh of ten children of David Walsh from County Cork, Ireland, and his wife, Joanna Clogan of Troy, New York. After completing grammar school, young Matthew attended a Holy Cross brothers' high school for one year and then entered Holy Cross high school seminary at Notre Dame. He graduated from Notre Dame in 1903, one of the "Father Cavanaugh boys," and was assigned to the recently opened Holy Cross College in Washington, DC, to study theology and pursue doctoral studies in history at the Catholic University of America. He received his PhD in history in 1907, writing his dissertation on "The Political Status of Catholics in Colonial Maryland," spent one summer at Columbia University in New York, took classes at the Johns Hopkins University in Baltimore, was ordained a priest in 1907, and returned to join the faculty at Notre Dame that year.[52]

A second priest was Charles L. O'Donnell, also a future president of Notre Dame. He was born in central Indiana, son of Neil O'Donnell and Mary Gallagher, both originally from Donegal. Completing his grade school education at his parish school in Kokomo, he entered the high school seminary at Notre Dame in 1899, another of the "Father Cavanaugh boys." He loved to write, he had a good literary style, and Father Cavanaugh was an excellent mentor as both his prose and poetry improved. He graduated from Notre Dame in 1906, which was the year that the students and the university administration decided to begin publishing an annual yearbook, the *Dome*, and Charles O'Donnell was chosen first editor-in-chief. At the commencement exercises, he was chosen to compose and read the class poem, and he was awarded the Quan Medal for the best record in classical studies and the Meehan Medal for the best English essay. Assigned to Holy Cross College in Washington, DC, that fall to begin theological studies, he also enrolled in literature classes at the Catholic University of America, especially classes on Francis Thompson. He spent one summer at Harvard studying Anglo-Saxon, received his doctorate from Catholic University in 1910 after completing his dissertation, "A Study of the Prose Works of Francis Thompson," and then returned to Notre Dame. He was assigned to a student residence hall briefly, taught classes in literature, and assisted Father Hudson at the *Ave Maria*, contributing and evaluating poetry.[53]

A third priest was Father Julius Nieuwland. He had been born in Hansbeke, Belgium, in 1878 and had been brought to the United States by his parents, John Baptiste and Philomena Van Hoecke Nieuwland, while still an infant. The family settled in South Bend, which had a strong Belgian community at the time. (Saint Bavo's Church in nearby Mishawaka may have been the only church in the United States dedicated to that Belgian saint.) After completing high school, Nieuwland entered the University of Notre Dame, joined the Congregation of Holy Cross, and received his AB degree in 1899. He went on to theological studies at Holy Cross College in Washington, DC, and was ordained a priest in 1903. He remained in Washington the next three years, received a doctorate in chemistry from the Catholic University of America in 1906, and joined the Notre Dame faculty that same year. He was best known throughout his life, and later, for his experiments with acetylene gas and cuprous and alkali metal chlorides, resulting in a kind of synthetic rubber. A positive side to his studies is that DuPont Laboratories became interested, developed the process further into neoprene, and paid the university handsomely for Father Nieuwland's discoveries. On a less positive side, Father Nieuwland had a raincoat made out of the early stuff and it smelled so bad that other community members would not let him in their rooms if he was wearing it. Brilliant scientist that he was, there was a light side to him also. He read murder mysteries for relaxation, enjoyed circuses, especially in the company of children, would stop and take a few swings with the bat or catch a few flies if he happened to pass a baseball team at practice, and appreciated good music. He once defined a gentleman as a fellow who was able to play the saxophone but would not.[54]

But less known is the fact that, while working on his doctoral dissertation at Catholic University in the early 1900s, his early experiments with acetylene gas had another result. On one occasion, he released pressurized acetylene into arsenic trichloride, and when nothing happened he added aluminum chloride. When he poured the mixture into water, it set off such a putrid and nauseating odor that he became ill from breathing the fumes and eventually spent several days in the hospital, never telling his superiors for fear they might terminate his studies, but never attempting that experiment again. But the story did not end there. With the United States' entrance into World War I in 1917, President Woodrow Wilson called a group of scientists to Washington to work in the area of poison gas as a deterrent to any possible enemy use. One of the scientists, Winford Lewis of Northwestern University, heard of Father Nieuwland's earlier experiments with arsenic trichloride and acetylene and contacted Father Nieuwland's mentor, who was still at Catholic University. Lewis duplicated Father Nieuwland's experiment and also landed in bed for three weeks. But he and another scientist, James Conant, later president of Harvard University, began varying the experiment slightly, desensitizing it in some ways, and developed the terrible poison gas now known as lewisite, after Professor Lewis. If American investigators ever succeed in discovering poison gas stored up in rogue countries, they may be surprised to learn that the original and essential research into building that terrible product may have accidentally been conducted by a young Holy Cross priest from Notre Dame working less than two miles from the White House itself.[55]

As the university grew, gained faculty, and became stronger, it also at times lost members and was diminished.[56] In 1911, Professor James Farnham ("Jimmie") Edwards, a faculty member since 1872, passed away. Born in 1850, he had been a minim, a junior, and a senior at Notre Dame, and he became a close enough associate of Father Sorin that it was he who was selected to hurry to Montreal in 1879 and inform Father Sorin in person of the devastating fire that had destroyed so much of his university. But his major contribution was the founding of the Notre Dame library in the early 1870s, its rebuilding after the tragic fire, and the collecting of personal papers, diocesan records, correspondence, and other documentation pertinent to American Catholicism, making the Notre Dame Archives an indispensable research source for anyone studying the history of the American Church.[57]

Professor Timothy Howard passed away a few years later. He had graduated from Notre Dame in 1862 and immediately joined the Union Army. A serious wound at Shiloh eliminated any possibility of a future military career. He returned to Notre Dame in 1864, applied for a teaching position, and was listed among the faculty for the next fifty years. He taught English literature, astronomy, Latin, Greek, and mathematics; he then studied law and became a professor of law. He wrote *A Brief History of the University of Notre Dame du Lac, Indiana, From 1842 to 1892* and the majestic two-volume *A History of St. Joseph County, Indiana*. A highly respected public citizen, he also served on the South Bend City Council, as both city and county attorney, as state senator, and as a member of the Indiana Supreme Court. Notre Dame awarded him the Laetare Medal in 1898, and Father Cavanaugh borrowed from Shakespeare as he closed his eulogy:[58] "His word was wisdom, his spirit joy, his friendship almost a sacrament. The elements were so mixed in him that nature might stand up and say: 'Here was a man.'"

The university suffered another loss, a deeply personal one, with the death of Sister Aloysius. She had come to America from Ireland as a young woman in

1873 to join the Holy Cross sisters, and from the day of her religious profession she had been asked to take charge of the minims, a position she filled with love and care for forty-three years. One who knew her wrote that "she made young boys from six to twelve who entered the grammar school at the University gentle and thoughtful, strong, studious and resourceful."[59] She cared for them when they were sick and taught them to work and learn when they were well. If sad news had to be reported to a minim, it was Sister Aloysius who was invariably asked to report it in her kind, understanding, and motherly way. In his funeral sermon, Father Cavanaugh proclaimed:[60]

> I have known most of the great figures in the development of Notre Dame. They were saintly, they were talented, they were zealous, they were consumed with a divine enthusiasm. In none of them was the union of these qualities more evident than in Sister Aloysius, in none of them was the spirit of the founder more exquisitely crystallized. . . .
>
> It is my deliberate judgment that there has never been among the Sisters of the Holy Cross at Notre Dame any to whom the University owes so much. When she began her work St. Edward Hall was only a small room on the first floor of the Infirmary; it is due almost entirely to her that it is now the best school for young boys in America. . . . Her rich gift of Celtic humor kept her sane and beautifully poised in all her intensities and enthusiasms. During the more than forty years of her work in St. Edward Hall between four and five thousand boys have felt her influence. Their lives have been touched and consecrated by her teaching, her counsel and her piety. . . .
>
> Her faith and her piety, though evident always, was never more impressive than during the last moments of her life. When her noble mind had yielded to the weakness of the body, and delirium of death had come upon her, in that unconscious condition her lips repeated the beautiful words of the prayers for her departing soul, which she must have memorized and uttered habitually in the days of her health and strength and preoccupation. It was a beautiful and holy ending to a beautiful and holy life.

Progressive Judge Ben Lindsay of Denver, a non-Catholic and former minim, offered his tribute:[61]

> I need scarcely tell you that in common with thousands of men who had the privilege of spending a part of their boyhood days at Notre Dame, I

had for her the greatest affection. She was to me a source of great inspiration and seemed to have discovered whatever small talents I had, and really opened the way to their development into any service that I may have helped to render in this world. I feel under a lasting debt of gratitude to her and to those wonderful influences that came into my life at St. Edward Hall where she presided so beautifully and helpfully for more than a generation.

There were few major changes in the university's academic programs during Father Cavanaugh's early years as president. Engineering was one area that did expand. Engineering programs had been housed in the Institute of Technology since the early 1890s, and in 1902 they were moved into a new Engineering Hall located approximately where Dillon Hall was later built. A first-floor room in it also provided space for the university's undertaking, embalming, and coffin-making service. The Institute of Technology building was then given over to chemistry and pharmacy.[62]

A Department of Mining Engineering was established in 1908, as the *University Bulletin* stated, "to give the student sufficient training in the various branches of mining to enable him to project and successfully carry through a mining enterprise."[63] The program included a semester course of English, the various basic science and engineering courses, and specialized courses in Mining Engineering, Crystallography, Mineralogy, Petrography, Principles of Geology, Physical and Chemical Geology, Metallurgy, and Assaying. The program and course offerings and requirements remained much the same until the department was terminated in 1941.[64]

A Department of Chemical Engineering was established about that same time. It was an important addition and grew over time, but it required few new faculty or new courses since most classes were drawn from the already established Departments of Chemistry, Mathematics, Mechanical Engineering, Physics, English, and Modern Languages. From arts and letters the student took a year of English and of modern language; from mathematics he took basic mathematics through Calculus; from physics he took General Physics, Heat, Magnetism, and Electricity; chemistry courses included Quantitative, Elementary, and Advanced Organic Chemistry, Technical Chemical Analysis, and Physical, Electro, and Industrial Chemistry; the mechanical engineering courses were Analytic Mechanics, Mechanics of Materials, Kinematics, Hydromechanics, Machine Design, Valve Gears, Steam Boilers, Shopwork, and Drawing.[65]

In the area of science, minor changes were made in the course in pharmacy. The program had begun in 1897 and it was soon divided into two programs: a three-year program leading to the degree of pharmaceutical chemist (PhC) and a two-year program leading to the degree of graduate in pharmacy (GPh). Candidates had to be seventeen to be admitted, and each program included a small number of basic arts and letters courses. In 1910, a four-year course was introduced, leading to the degree of bachelor of science in pharmacy, but the classes were quite similar to those in the three-year program, except that the students had more time to grasp and discuss the material on the way to the more impressive degree.[66]

The start of a significant new program occurred on a rather uncertain foundation in 1912 when a Jewish lawyer and businessman in Chicago offered to endow a professorship in journalism at Notre Dame. Max Pam had lectured occasionally at the university in the past and decided that Notre Dame was an excellent location for a school or department of journalism since it already embraced the high standards of honesty and integrity on which the profession of journalism should be based. He stated:[67]

> A press that is prejudiced, unreliable or that has a personal or selfish interest to serve, cannot produce the right kind of public opinion on any given subject. To get the right kind of journalism, viz: men of conscience and character, animated by high ideals and a high sense of the responsibilities attached to their profession, legislative penalties and criminal statutes are not sufficient safeguards. We need conscience and the elements that make for conscience, the old-fashioned ideas of right and wrong, the high regard for truth and justice and the abhorrence of untruth and injustice which are instilled in the religious atmosphere of such an institution as yours.
>
> We are a newspaper reading people and it has been asserted more than once that we are less affected by what is said in the pulpit, on the lecture platform and in the schools than we are by what is said in the press. Such being the case, it is important, yes vital, that serious attention should be paid to the formation and training of journalists to the end that the man who makes public opinion should by education, by conviction and by habit in all he does be led to conscience and to truth, courage and honesty born of conscience.
>
> The danger to reputation, to property, to happiness, to even the very foundation of government flowing from lack of conscience in journalism,

is so great a peril that I deem it prudent and wise to establish this foundation in an institution which keeps religion in the foreground, the spirit of which if followed I believe will so ennoble the profession that public opinion will express the concepts of justice and righteousness. The University of Notre Dame possesses the facilities and elements making possible a realization of these hopes and wishes.

It is to me a source of great satisfaction to feel with confidence that the purpose of this foundation will be fulfilled and will find fruition through the inspirations, ideals, and religious influence that prevail in this University.

His intention was to give the university $5,000 each year for five years, hoping that the $25,000 endowment could provide the salary for a professor of journalism. After the first $5,000, Mr. Pam ran into difficult times and the rest of the $25,000 did not arrive until 1922. However, the program began. Father Cavanaugh asked Professor John M. Cooney, a former newspaperman from Kentucky and already on the Notre Dame faculty, to begin offering journalism classes. To give the new program additional prestige, Mr. James Keeley, managing editor of the *Chicago Tribune*, was asked to accept the position as first dean, and this he did. He would visit the campus approximately once a week and offer a class on the more practical aspects of current publishing and journalism.[68]

A Notre Dame education continued to gain respect. In a letter to Keeley in early January 1913, H. L. Sayler of the Chicago City News Association noted:[69]

I would like to add that Notre Dame for some reason I never quite understood has furnished us a higher percentage of reportorial successes than any other school from which we draw applicants. . . . Father Cavanaugh . . . had no theory to explain it himself unless it might be that the school's literary journal was of high grade and really literary. . . . I think you have the best body of men in the West to work on.

At about this same time, a major change was made in the Commercial Course, but it was short-lived. The Commercial Course had been reduced to a two-year and then a one-year college program, and in 1909 the title was changed to Commercial High School and it was included as one of the four-year tracks in the Preparatory Department. The program offered courses in bookkeeping, shorthand, typewriting, penmanship, and the history of commerce, among others. In 1913, a four-year college Commercial Course was introduced into the College of

Arts and Letters, offering classes, in addition to some of the above, in banking, finance, advertising, accountancy, and probably business management. Each program continued only to 1920. That year the high school or prep department was closed and a College of International and Domestic Commerce was established separate from the College of Arts and Letters.[70]

The year 1917 was a climactic year in the presidency of Father Cavanaugh, at least in campus construction. Due to decreasing numbers, he closed the Manual Labor School, added wings to the former St. Joseph's Hall, renamed it Badin Hall, and added it to the list of student residence halls with Sorin, Corby, Walsh, (and St. Edward's). With Father Nieuwland's chemistry programs expanding, a new Chemistry Hall was begun that year but, due to the shortage of building materials during World War I, the structure was not completed until 1920. Finally, an impressive new library was constructed and dedicated.

The new library filled a major need. The lending library begun by Father Lemonnier and Professor Edwards in the early 1870s was still housed on one of the upper floors of the Main Building, but more space was needed and that Main Building space could be more efficiently used for other academic purposes. As early as 1914, Father Zahm, whose advice Father Cavanaugh always welcomed, wrote from Washington, DC:[71]

> The great, crying need of Notre Dame is a library, and it should now take precedence of every other building. I should have put it up years ago had not the more important work of putting Holy Cross Seminary and Holy Cross College here on a proper footing, prevented it. These two buildings were indispensable for the proper training of our young priests and for supporting Notre Dame with a faculty worthy of the name.
>
> Now that you have such a splendid teaching corps, you should have a library before anything else. You need it not only for your increasing number of collegiate students, but also for your young doctors and seminarians if you wish to encourage them to do real scholastic work. For them, a literary workshop is even more important than your chemical and physical laboratories are for your students of science. . . .
>
> I spent several years in making plans for such a library as I conceived was needed by Notre Dame. The plans and specifications were drawn only after I had examined the best libraries of Europe and America and after I had consulted the most successful librarians—those who know the best wants of a modern library in the United States.

A few months later came a reminder:[72]

Don't forget the library. Be sure to begin it without fail in the spring. In the meantime, it will be well to begin the work of preparation—getting specifications, bids, etc., etc. Anything I can do to help you, I shall gladly do.

As a man who appreciated good literature, Father Cavanaugh did not need encouragement. Plans were drawn, construction began, and the new building was completed by the late spring of 1917, in time for commencement weekend and the Diamond Jubilee Celebration of the university's founding. It was constructed of Indiana limestone, the only stone building on campus at the time, and it was situated on former farmland at a short distance from the Main Building and residence halls, in part to be out of danger if fire should break out again in any of those structures. It offered two large reading rooms, shelf space for 500,000 volumes (the university's holdings at that time comprised 100,000 volumes), and was home for various specialized collections: medieval manuscripts, the University of Notre Dame Archives, Father Zahm's impressive Dante collection, and the Wrightman Art Gallery.[73]

The dedication of the building was indeed impressive, combined with commencement weekend and the Diamond Jubilee. The celebration began on the evening of June 9, 1917, with the awarding of that year's Laetare Medal to Admiral William Shepherd Benson, United States Chief of Naval Operations. After reading the citation, Father Cavanaugh handed the medal to Cardinal James Gibbons to do the honors. The cardinal beckoned Mrs. Benson to the stage from the audience, and together they pinned the award on the admiral.[74]

On Sunday morning, in the presence of Most Reverend Giovanni Bonzano, the Vatican's apostolic delegate to the United States, Cardinal Gibbons presided at a Solemn High Mass in the university church, with Archbishop George Mundelein of Chicago preaching and Chicago's Paulist Choir providing the music. The new library was blessed that afternoon by Bishop Thomas Shahan, rector of the Catholic University of America in Washington, DC, and the dedicatory address was delivered by the Honorable Bourke Cockran, one of the great Irish-American orators of the day. His theme was the complete compatibility between democracy and Catholicism, and he traced the relationship through the centuries. "Charity administered by the state has always degraded its objects," he suggested, but "Charity administered by the monastery has always improved, and, in many instances, ennobled its recipients." He reminded his audience that the United States was then in a war "to make the world safe for democracy," and Catholics have always been willing to fight for freedom, liberty, and democracy.[75]

Commencement exercises were held the following day, and the recently re-constituted Alumni Association met.[76] Father Cavanaugh had to be the most pleased. As a brilliant speaker himself, he appreciated fine oratory, and thirteen public addresses and sermons were delivered over the weekend. And as a lover of books, he could be justifiably proud of the magnificent library before him.

CHAPTER 9

World War I and the
"Burns Revolution"

When Father Sorin arrived in the United States in the early 1840s, he discovered that the country was indeed a melting pot of various ethnic and national groups— English-speaking residents whose families had been here for generations, the French who had colonized the Midwest in the seventeenth and eighteenth centuries, German immigrants seeking affordable farmland, and the Irish. Father Sorin had little respect for the Irish, as noted earlier in his *Chronicles*:[1]

> The former are by nature full of faith, respect, religious inclinations, and sensible and devoted; but a great defect often paralyzes in them all their other good qualities: the lack of stability. They change more readily than any other nation.

Father John Cavanaugh was a man of an entirely different stripe and mind. Both his parents had been born in Ireland, they had met and married there before immigrating to the United States, and they imbued their son with a deep love of Catholicism and a deep love of almost anything Irish. These two, with his love of the United States, were three major characteristics of his life.

Father Cavanaugh was an avid reader of English and Irish literature, and in 1905 he began a correspondence with Seumas MacManus, a popular poet, dramatist, and author at that time who wrote *In Chimney Corners: Merry Tales of Irish Folklore; The Bewitched Fiddle and Other Irish Tales;* and *Donegal Fairy Stories.* MacManus sent Father Cavanaugh a couple of books written by his wife and Father Cavanaugh had them reviewed in the *Ave Maria.* Their friendship and correspondence continued, and in 1908 MacManus visited and took charge of the university's English classes for a month, and this was not his only visit.[2]

At about this same time, Father Cavanaugh decided to build up an Irish collection in the university library and he wrote to a prospective benefactor in Watertown, Wisconsin, for assistance:[3]

> It is my desire to have an Irish section in the University library which shall contain all the books written about Ireland and Irishmen, either in Irish, English or German, or whatever language. . . . It is a source of profound regret to me to find so many of our young men, the sons of good Irish fathers, growing up without the pride in their race which they ought to have. This is due, I believe, to the fact that they do not understand what Ireland and Irishmen have been in the history of the world. . . . It will require $5,000.00 at least to carry out my plan, and it is for this reason that I address myself to you. <u>It is not pleasant for me to go begging</u>, and it is contrary to the training of my whole life. Nothing less than my great interest in this important work could have induced me to make this proposal.

This Dr. Johnson had earlier contributed some $17,000 to the Congregation's works in Watertown (St. Bernard's Parish and College of Our Lady of the Sacred Heart) but unfortunately, and unbeknownst to Father Cavanaugh, the relations between Dr. Johnson and the Holy Cross priests there had soured, and, in reply, he complained of the "barbarous treatment" he had received at the hands of the priests recently, and he insisted he would not contribute another penny to anyone or any community connected with that parish. Father Cavanaugh wrote back and apologized for whatever had happened, and admitted that at times some priests could be "peculiar."[4] The "barbarous treatment" was never fully explained.

It is not surprising that, as president of a major Catholic institution, an outstanding orator, and an unabashed lover of all things Irish, Father Cavanaugh would be widely in demand for Saint Patrick's Day addresses. He spoke to an Irish

Catholic group in Detroit in 1912, recounting the history and legends of Ireland from the time of Saint Patrick, through trial and oppression and persecution, down to the present, but always preserving the faith that Saint Patrick first brought. He emphasized that Ireland was not only a land of saints but also of scholars and that many from continental Europe made pilgrimage to Ireland to study under masters there, and Irish scholars emigrated throughout the rest of Europe and left education and learning in their wake. Father Cavanaugh urged Irish parents of his day to be worthy of these ancestors, not to be satisfied to let their sons be day laborers as their fathers and grandfathers may have been before them, but to take full advantage of the educational opportunities available in America, become leaders in business, public life, religion, and the professions through education, and be the saints and scholars their ancestors were.[5]

In all of his addresses, year after year, he stressed the contributions the Irish had made to America, especially their spiritual contributions: their faith in God, their acceptance of Christ and His teachings, their conviction of the sacredness of marriage and their devotion to family, their loyalty to the church, their love of liberty and opposition to tyranny, and their honesty and dedication to hard work. Father Cavanaugh could be bitterly critical of King Henry VIII for leading so many English-speaking Europeans away from Catholicism:[6]

> You remember that day, the saddest I believe since the crucifixion of Christ, when that King Henry, who never spared man in his anger nor woman in his lust, flung defiance into the face of Christ. The so-called Reformation was well under way. . . . The Holy Catholic Church, once the Lady of Kingdoms, sat down in the dust to weep over what seemed her dead greatness, and amid this universal desolation and apostasy, there arose that mightiest emperor of Europe to declare that unless he were given permission to put away his wife and marry another, England too would be added to the apostate nations. England the one uplifted arm in all the world that still held a sword for Christ; England that by her chain of colonies was to gird around the world; England that by her wonderful literature was to color with prejudice the intellect of the world,—England would be added to the apostate nations.

Speaking of King Henry on another occasion, he declared that "it would take three generations of Christian culture to raise him to the level of total depravity!"[7]

With such deeply held and contrasting sentiments toward Ireland and England, Father Cavanaugh's loyalties were challenged when World War I broke out in 1914 and tensions between England and Ireland increased:[8]

> I think I may fairly speak for men of Irish blood and extraction. Let me begin by saying that love of Ireland and her people has been one of the great passions of my life. Among the millions of the scattered children of the Gael, I doubt if there are many who love with more impassioned ardor the old country, the old people, the old tales, the old saints and scholars, the old glories and traditions of that beautiful people. I believe I would do as much as any man to liberate Ireland from her ancient thralldom. I hate (that is exactly the word I want to use) England for her treatment of Ireland, and the hardest duty I ever had to perform was to line up with England in this war.
>
> But all this has nothing to do with the case. America is my country first, last and always. In all that relates to this world, America is my holy land, Washington is my sacred city. America has no rival in my allegiance and affections, there is no second and no third. America is above and beyond comparison with any other.

At the end of the war, when President Wilson was about to depart for Europe to negotiate a final peace treaty, Father Cavanaugh sent the president a telegram, urging that freedom for all of Ireland be included in such a treaty:[9] "The Faculty of the University of Notre Dame in regular session assembled sends respectful greetings to President Wilson, prays for him a happy voyage and safe return, and expresses the hope that Ireland through his genius and friendship may attain to self-determination in government and share in the blessings of liberty for which men of Irish blood in America fought so heroically in the Great War."

Ireland, of course, was not included in the Treaty of Versailles, and Father Cavanaugh probably never expected that it would be. In fact, he had little respect for or confidence in the president personally. As early as 1914, he had heard reports that the president seemed hostile to Catholicism at times, and this was confirmed in a letter he received from his close friend, Father James Burns, in Washington, DC:[10]

> In regard to your inquiry, I have to say that the facts are substantially as you heard them. Cardinal Gibbons, Cardinal Farley, Archbishop Ireland, and the Apostolic Delegate visited the White House, on separate occa-

sions, and none of them was invited to take a seat. I have this from un-questionable authority. I need not say that they were all surprised at this seeming lack of courtesy. . . . The priests in the city here have, of course, been discussing the matter: some are indignant; others are mystified; still others hope that some sufficient explanation of the matter may appear in time.

As President Wilson campaigned for reelection two years later, Father Ca-vanaugh wrote to former president Theodore Roosevelt, urging him to visit Notre Dame and deliver an address to American Catholics—and more:[11] "Notre Dame is a superb pulpit from which to reach our people, and of all Americans you are the one best suited to utter a ringing address to them. I may add that though I am a hereditary Democrat, and though I have long had what I thought was an ineradicable prejudice against a third term, I should welcome the opportunity of stumping the country in favor of your reelection as President." He even wrote to Vice President Thomas Marshall (from Indiana) that he would eagerly vote for him in the coming election if President Wilson were not on the ticket also.[12]

By the time of World War I, Notre Dame was a much better known univer-sity than it had been when Father Cavanaugh assumed the presidency in 1905, and at least one of the reasons for this was the increasing publicity he was receiv-ing as a public speaker. The *Scholastic* regularly noted where the president had most recently been invited to speak, and often the special occasion for it—major cities such as New York, Philadelphia, Washington, DC, Providence, Detroit, Cincinnati, Chicago, and San Francisco, and smaller ones closer to home such as Fort Wayne, Indiana; Peoria, Illinois; Louisville, Kentucky; Bourbonnais, Illinois; Oldenburg, Kentucky, and many others. No earlier president, not even Father Sorin, was ever invited to address such audiences, and the university Father Cavanaugh represented became more widely known as a consequence. Distin-guished visitors were pleased to come and address the university community: Governor Thomas Marshall, Senator Albert Beveridge, poet Thomas Walsh, medical doctor and historian James J. Walsh, and from England the novelist and apologist Msgr. Robert Hugh Benson, biographer and man of letters Wilfrid Ward, and Cecil Chesterton, brother of Gilbert K. Chesterton.[13]

When World War I broke out, it was obvious that a university campus com-posed so heavily of young men of military age would be deeply affected. Military training had been part of Notre Dame life for more than fifty years, with the Con-tinental Cadets, the Washington Cadets, the Notre Dame Zouaves, the Otis Light Guards, and the Hoynes Light Guards.[14]

Weeks and months after war broke out in Europe, more and more Notre Dame students enrolled in the campus military cadets, in preparation for what might come. President Woodrow Wilson had won reelection in 1916 on the slogan "He kept us out of the war," but there was little he could do when Germany declared unrestricted submarine warfare on all ships destined for Great Britain, and American merchant ships were attacked and sunk, with the loss of American lives. In response, the United States declared war in April 1917.

Some students dropped out of school and entered the military. If they were seniors missing the final month or two of classes, they would still be awarded their degrees in June. The students who remained on campus did their part for the effort also. They cooperated with United States Food Administrator Herbert Hoover's program to conserve food with the establishment of "Meatless Tuesdays" and "Wheatless Wednesdays" on campus, although, if the students protested, chicken or mutton might be served on Tuesdays, and cornbread could replace the usual Notre Dame bun on Wednesdays. Students collected money for various worthy causes and the senior class decided to finance an ambulance to assist the medical personnel in Europe. The war wound down before the ambulance could be purchased but it was eventually sent to Cardinal Désiré Mercier in Belgium to assist in caring for the needy and refugees in that war-torn country. On it was inscribed: "From the men of Notre Dame to Cardinal Mercier of Belgium, the noblest moral figure manifested in this war."[15]

In urgent need of officers as the military expanded, the government established the Students' Army Training Corps (SATC), a program to permit young men to join the military and receive officer training while continuing their education on a college campus. With the loss of student enrollment due to enlistments in the army, Father Cavanaugh requested that a branch of the SATC be established at Notre Dame. This request was at first rejected, the War Department deciding that Notre Dame's military training programs were not of sufficiently high caliber, and Father Cavanaugh immediately protested to government officials. Eventually, the program was established at Notre Dame for the fall semester of 1918, one of forty-two Catholic schools selected.[16]

Any young man who was a high school graduate, was accepted at Notre Dame, and could pass the physical examination could enter the program. Such students were then considered full members of the United States Army, the War Department paid their tuition, they were given an additional thirty dollars a month for subsistence, and Captain William Murray was assigned as commander. These students' academic schedules had to be revised, and even limited, to allow for required drills, military exercises, and special studies. Army discipline ruled. Rising might be at 5:30, followed by drill, marching, and exercises, with breakfast at 7:30, and arriving even a minute late could result in KP duty for a week or the cleaning of the barrack's latrines. The army's priorities, however, were not always Notre Dame's. Father Cavanaugh often complained to Captain Murray that excessive noise in the Main Building disturbed the priests and students living there, that smoking regulations were being ignored (and these regulations were lowering the university's insurance costs), and that the quality of some of the women visiting the cadets was suspect. Father Cavanaugh admitted the challenge in a letter only a couple of weeks into the program:[17]

> I wonder if anybody has suffered more in this war than I have. Believe me, the effort to make an old University, like this one, over into a barracks, without destroying it, is a subtle trick. As I said to the boys in my opening sermon, "Where one Louvain has been criminally destroyed in Europe, let us look to it that one hundred Louvains may not be innocently destroyed in America."

The program lasted little more than two months, since the Armistice was signed on November 11 and demobilization began shortly thereafter. Father Cavanaugh was happy to see the program go. In late November, when it was still unclear when the program would be officially terminated, he wrote to a young seminarian:[18]

> The S.A.T.C. has made military obsession very unpopular here. . . . There is some possibility that we may take advantage of the Government's willingness to send the S.A.T.C. about its business. We will have a consultation about this today or tomorrow.
>
> Meanwhile all of us are possessing our souls in patience, hoping for the day of redemption. Anything will look good to us after these musketeers banish.

In all, more than 600 Notre Dame students had enrolled in the military, chiefly seniors and juniors, and close to 1,500 alumni also, and 46 lost their lives in the line of duty. But despite the campus disruptions and the academic-military tensions, the presence of the SATC on this and other Catholic campuses also demonstrated again the patriotism of American Catholics and their continuing acceptance into American public life. Father Sorin would have approved.[19]

Another reason to welcome the end of hostilities was the return of several priest-professors who had volunteered to serve as chaplains during the war. Eighteen Holy Cross priests had volunteered (although Father Cavanaugh lists twenty-four in a letter to a priest-friend)[20] and eight were eventually selected, including at least five from the Notre Dame faculty. Father Edward Finnegan, ordained in 1910, was serving as prefect of discipline at Notre Dame when he was selected; he served in France and Luxembourg, was discharged with the rank of first lieutenant, and went on to serve as professor of Church history at Holy Cross College in Washington, DC. Father John McGinn, also ordained in 1910, taught sociology at Notre Dame before being commissioned as a chaplain, and he served with the 35th Division of the AEF in France before returning to the faculty of Notre Dame. Father Ernest Davis was a popular and well-respected professor of chemistry at Notre Dame; he saw action during the war at the Marne and Velse Rivers and the Argonne Forest, on one occasion offered Mass with German prisoners of war, was gassed at the Argonne, and spent time recovering in a hospital before his discharge and return to Notre Dame.[21]

Father Charles O'Donnell was a poet, a professor of rhetoric, and later the provincial superior of all Holy Cross priests and brothers in the United States and the president of the university. He received his commission and left Notre Dame in February 1918 and, without any chaplain's training in the United States, sailed immediately to France and arrived at the front in March. He was assigned to an engineering group whose main responsibilities were to build roads and trenches, lay wire entanglements, etc., but who often fought side by side with the infantry whenever attacked. The majority of the company was not Catholic but Father O'Donnell ministered to all, consoling the wounded, burying the deceased, and writing letters to bereaved families. He offered Mass daily and three times on Sundays, often within the sound of booming cannons, and he heard confessions whenever and wherever a soldier asked. He was billeted for a time in the same locality as was Joyce Kilmer, the author of "Trees," and the two became friends. In August 1918, he was reassigned to the 332nd Infantry Regiment, was the first American chaplain to enter Italy, and saw action at the battle of Vittorio Veneto, for which service he was awarded the Italian War Service Ribbon by the Italian minister of war. He remained in Italy for five months after the Armistice, caring for the wounded in hospitals, and did not return to the United States until April 1919.[22]

Father Matthew Walsh, professor of history and university vice president, was the first Holy Cross priest to be commissioned, on January 10, 1918. After a departure ceremony in Washington Hall, he was sent to Camp Sheridan in Montgomery, Alabama, where his immediate superior officer was Ray Miller, a recent graduate of Notre Dame. A few years before, he had to approach Father Walsh as vice president for special permissions, and now Father Walsh had to approach him for permissions to leave the base. Of his experience at Camp Sheridan, Father Walsh wrote to Father Morrissey: "The chaplain must keep an open house and furnish cigarettes to all callers," but he did not complain: "I have a bunch of fellows in my quarters every night and after they have smoked a little more will try and get them to go to Confession." He was in France by early June and saw heavy fighting at the Marne, and he spent much of his time ministering to the wounded. On one occasion, a former Notre Dame student who had left the university early to enter the military was considered for promotion in the intelligence division but was not eligible because he did not have a college degree. Father Walsh decided, as university vice president and in the absence of the president and faculty, that he could award the degree on the spot. He did so, and the young man received his commission. On another occasion a near riot erupted among American soldiers imprisoned for various offenses—larceny, desertion, cowardice, etc.—and Father Walsh was asked to address the crowd. He offered his priestly ministry to any Catholic among them (which many of them immediately accepted), and the prison calmed. By the time of the Armistice, the United States government had decided to establish a university in Beaune, France, where soldiers might take courses while awaiting ships to take them home, and Father Walsh was assigned to the faculty for a time. He was finally decommissioned on May 6, 1919, and returned to Notre Dame.[23]

The influenza epidemic that broke out toward the end of World War I did not spare the university—or its chaplains. Father Davis wrote from France in October 1918 that he had spent a couple of weeks in a hospital, due in part "to a severe attack of influenza," and Father McGinn was hospitalized in Vichy a couple of months later for what he called "a slight attack of influenza," but which may have been only "bronchitis and grippe." The disease struck the campus when the students returned in the fall of 1918. Some classes were apparently cancelled and the infirmary staff was overworked. That October, Father Cavanaugh confided in a letter to Father Zahm: "We have had an extraordinary siege of sickness here, but, thank God, nothing like what other parts of the country are experiencing. The doctor thinks that we had probably 100 cases of Spanish influenza, and we have had just six deaths among the students. In every case the final trouble took the form of pneumonia." Looking back a year later, Father Cavanaugh revised the final figures upward. In a letter to the Dominican theologian Father Francisco Marin-Sola, he confirmed: "The influenza was almost the death of all human joy.

We had more than two hundred cases of the disease and there were nine deaths among the students."[24]

Despite the disruptions among both the students and the faculty due to the war, and the uncertainties caused by the spread of influenza, three new academic programs were inaugurated during this World War I period. The first of these was a Department of Medicine. By the charter of 1844 the university was empowered to award degrees in "the liberal arts and sciences, and in law and medicine." Courses in anatomy, physiology, and premedical science were offered off and on through the years, and one science track did lead to the awarding of a medical certificate, apparently a satisfactory preparation for entering medical school.[25] But it was not until 1917 that a Department of Medicine was established. That summer the *South Bend Tribune* described the contemplated program:[26]

Rev. Matthew Schumacher, CSC director of studies at Notre Dame has just been notified by Dr. W. T. Gott, secretary of the Indiana State Board of Medical Registration and Examination, that the proposed medical course to be opened in September at Notre Dame will receive due recognition. The secretary assures Fr. Schumacher that the mere compliance with the published requirements for medical schools will suffice at the start, and that when the school has been under way a short time, a committee from the state board will visit Notre Dame to make an inspection of the work and that official recognition will then be considered.

Only two years of medicine will be given at Notre Dame, at least for the time being. Though the isolation of Notre Dame offers many desirable features not obtainable at schools located in larger centers, still the lack of adequate clinical facilities, so necessary in the latter half of a medical course, has deterred the university from establishing a full four years' program. The new medical school will have its own board of directors as soon as plans mature. The board will be composed of physicians who, besides acting in an advisory capacity, will also give special lectures in the school. The appointments to this board have not yet been announced, but they will be made public shortly. This will be somewhat of a new departure at Notre Dame as all other college faculties in the university have been composed of men who are active professors in the school. All facilities will be of the most up-to-date and serviceable. Thoroughness will be the goal sought in the new school and no effort will be spared to make its graduates the best trained in the country.

It was eventually to be a four-year program: two years of preparatory or premedical classes and two years of medical education itself. The student could then transfer to an established medical school for his final two years of study and the MD degree. Father Schumacher gave the reasons for establishing the program: "first, the cultivation of science to a marked degree by our own men; second, to help the young men over the first two years of Medicine, which are considered the most important; third, Notre Dame as I can see her place in education ought to comprise every field of knowledge." He noted also that the relationship between science and religion was being more and more publicly debated, and Notre Dame needed to be highly qualified to enter that debate.[27]

Despite the early plans and preparations, the program was cancelled after two years. With approximately half the student population preparing for war service through the SATC, it did not seem an appropriate time to inaugurate the program. Father Cavanaugh confirmed in August 1918:[28]

> As regards to the Medical School, I have announced that, on account of war conditions and in conformity with the wishes of the United States Government, we have delayed the establishment of our Medical School. The Government wants no unusual expense contracted except where necessary, and we would have to use a lot of money establishing our Medical School. For the present, therefore, medics, like politics, is adjourned.

The students already admitted into the program in 1917 probably completed the first two years of premedical studies and then matriculated elsewhere for their full medical courses, as did the students who entered the university before the program was announced.

In 1917 the university also established a Department of Agriculture, the first such program on an American Catholic campus. The university seemed well qualified to do so. The brothers had taught farming to Manual Labor School students for decades, several hundred acres of productive farmland surrounded the campus, and the 1,600-acre Saint Joseph's Farm, purchased in the 1860s and also worked by the brothers, lay only eight miles to the northeast. The director of the Notre Dame farm was Brother Leo Donovan, an Indiana native who had become a Holy Cross brother in 1897, and who had studied agriculture at both the University of Illinois and the University of Iowa. Through better use of fertilizing techniques, crop rotation, and the planting of legumes, crop production doubled and tripled year after year, and his Hereford steers, Belgian stock horses, and Hampshire hogs won prizes at the state fair annually. He was sought out as an adviser throughout the state and even across the country.[29]

Actually two academic programs in agriculture were begun, one of four years and one of two. The four-year program had a heavy core of liberal arts courses (English, history, economics, philosophy, sociology, and politics) and basic science courses also (chemistry, geology, physics, bacteriology, botany, zoology, and entomology). The specialized agriculture courses in both tracks were numerous, and one wonders how often each was taught: Judging Livestock, Horticulture, Breeding, Marketing, Forage Crops, Farm Mechanics, Grain Growing, Agricultural Engineering, Soil Fertility, Feeding Farm Animals, Vegetable Gardening, Poultry, Dairying, Farm Management, and so on. The program over the years was divided into specialized tracks, and other courses were added. The hope at one time seemed to be to attract three hundred students into the program, but it never reached that number and was eventually terminated in 1932.[30]

The third innovation, and this a lasting one, was the inauguration of a summer session, and this innovation was chiefly on the initiative of Father Matthew Schumacher, the director of studies. It began in the summer of 1918, in part to profit from the additional income the program would generate, and in part to provide priests, brothers, sisters, and lay men and women who were teaching in Catholic schools the opportunity to pursue or complete a college degree even though they were busy teaching during the regular academic year. Father Cavanaugh sent out letters to numerous bishops and superiors of religious communities, announcing the summer session and urging them to send interested persons to the program. The matriculation fee was ten dollars and tuition twenty-five dollars, with additional charges for courses in music, painting, and elocution. Close to two hundred courses were offered in thirty-one different areas—accounting, biology, chemistry, history, modern language, etc.—and the faculty numbered sixty-three: twenty-four priests, nine brothers, and thirty laymen. The sisters lived in Walsh Hall, priests and brothers in Badin, and lay men and women in different places. There were Masses and various religious exercises provided in the main church, recreational facilities were open to all, and cultural presentations were arranged for those interested. Approximately two hundred attended the first session, and almost all seemed pleased. One sister wrote:[31]

> Whatever you are doing here,—whether mopping your brow over tasks in lecture room or laboratory, or, if in sentimental mood you stroll away

to see the sunset on the lovely little lakes, or perhaps stop to watch the landscape gardening of old Brother Philip . . . —or if you are privileged to chat with reverend, busy Father Hudson, or with Father O'Neill of the *Ave Maria*, whose famous pedometer has evolved a cult of pedestrianship,— everywhere and always you find in Notre Dame that delightful human quality, which takes on its finest flavor when suffused with sincere religion. And you return to your student desk just as Our Lady away upon the big dome begins to flash out her crescent of electric lights; and you feel that life is a big thing, and that there is a power in you too to make it worth while.

In early 1919, Father Cavanaugh knew that his time as president was coming to a close. Church regulations and national customs law had been growing and changing over the centuries and in the first decade of the twentieth century it was decided that these various strands needed to be collected, reviewed, sifted, and a revised Code of Canon Law made public. The new Code was promulgated by Pope Benedict XV in May 1917 and was to take effect in May 1918. The Code decreed that religious superiors should hold office no longer than six years (without special dispensation), the president of Notre Dame was also the religious superior of the priests and brothers assigned to the campus, and thus Father Cavanaugh, after fourteen years, knew he would be replaced.[32] He informed Father Zahm that February: "Of course, you know that I am to lay down the burden of office this year. I shall do my best to see that no other office is ever put in my way." To a seminarian in Washington he wrote:[33]

> I hope to send you this afternoon a copy of the papers announcing my resignation. My only idea was to get the odious publicity over before the end of the year. . . .
>
> This old Canon Law is a dandy institution. It is good to the school since it removes the decrepit and it is good to the decrepit as it removes them from trouble. Next summer is going to be a great little summer all around.
>
> I believe my health is at least as good as it has been at any time in the past five years, and when I get the harness off I want you to watch me kick around and roll over like a young colt.

Despite his assurances, his health was still a concern. He wrote to that same seminarian in July:[34] "I come to Holy Cross in Washington, as I understand it, to do a bit of good wherever I can, but chiefly for a rest until my health is restored. I don't know when I will reach Washington as yet, but I think it will be necessary for me first to go to a hospital and get fixed up. That will take some weeks, and after that, if I have my way, I will rest for a while in Ohio on the way."

His health improved and he lived another sixteen years.

The person selected to succeed him in the provincial chapter of 1919 was his close friend Father James Burns. Father Burns had an earned doctorate in education, had written widely on Catholic education in the United States, and was a founding member of the Catholic Educational Association. He was also available since he had been religious superior of Holy Cross College in Washington, DC, since 1900 and, according to that same Canon Law, had to be moved as well. Most importantly, serious discontent had broken out within the Congregation of Holy Cross in recent years, and several priests at Notre Dame had signed a petition sent to Rome, over the head of the superior general, urging drastic changes in the Congregation's governing structure. They proposed that the majority of delegates to general chapters, the highest legislative authority in the Congregation, be elected by the members and not be *ex officio* superiors and administrators, and that in elections priests vote only for priests and brothers only for brothers, tending perhaps toward two separate congregations. Several dissenting priests had been removed from Notre Dame for their part in this, including director of studies Father Schumacher, and it was apparently thought that Father Burns, a religious superior for nineteen years, might be able to return the Notre Dame community to harmony and greater conformity with the rest of the Congregation.[35]

Father Burns had been born in Michigan City, Indiana, only thirty miles from Notre Dame, in 1867. He attended the local St. Ambrose Academy, run by the Holy Cross sisters, for grammar school, and at age thirteen he entered the Manual Labor School at Notre Dame to learn the trade of printing. In 1884, he transferred to the Collegiate or Classical Department, was catcher on the varsity baseball team, and his swollen knuckles the rest of his life gave credence to the report that catchers at that time played without a mask, pads, or a glove. On graduating from Notre Dame in 1888, he entered the Congregation of Holy Cross as a seminarian, continued his theological studies at the university, and was ordained a priest in 1893. He also took science courses at Notre Dame, became a close friend and protégé of Father John Zahm, and taught science and was a prefect at Notre Dame in the early years after his ordination. In 1900 he was appointed the first superior of the newly opened Holy Cross College in Washington, DC, a position he held until his selection as president of Notre Dame in 1919.[36]

Father Burns's doctoral dissertation at the Catholic University of America was a study of the history of the Catholic school system in America from the early mission schools down to the 1770s. Although the dissertation concentrated on Catholic elementary school education (almost all there was throughout most of the colonial period), Father Burns's interest soon turned to the movement for Catholic central high schools. The Catholic school system had usually consisted of six years of parish elementary schooling and six years beyond, including years of preparation and perhaps some years of actual college courses. Most Catholics halted their formal education after elementary school either because there was no Catholic high school in the vicinity or because high school was too expensive. Father Burns (and others) saw the need for a central high school system in each diocese, four years of education between the six (or eight) years of parish grammar school and the four years of true college. Such high schools would be separate from the college but would prepare interested students for college and would also serve as a satisfactory conclusion of formal education for others, probably the majority. Many colleges opposed the plan since they had prep departments, as did Notre Dame, and needed the income to remain solvent. Staffing might change. Sisters were teaching in many of the parish grammar schools at this time but there was opposition to women teaching boys in high school and thus the high school ministry could open for religious orders of brothers. Bishops would also have to be in favor of the program and urge each parish to contribute financially to the local central high school. Discussions continued in Catholic educational circles throughout the early years of the twentieth century, with more and more parish grammar schools extending to eight years and more and more dioceses establishing central high schools.[37] The number of such high schools for boys, the only ones surveyed at the time, increased from 295 in 1911 to 438 in 1915, a gain of almost 50 percent. Thus by 1919 when he was appointed president of Notre Dame, Father Burns had clear convictions about what he thought the American Catholic education system, and Notre Dame, should be.[38]

In the Father Zahm–Father Morrissey controversy, Father Burns was clearly on the side of Father Zahm. He confided in his diary in 1896:[39]

Father Morrissey is sincerely anxious for Notre Dame's advancement, but it is his and our misfortune that he is not himself a "university" man. He is broad-minded, liberal, energetic, talented, with winning personal qualities. But he lacks the substance as well as the polish of higher education, and is himself, I think, sensible of his own limitations. He doesn't seem to believe in higher education—University education for college teachers.

When Father Zahm was assigned to Rome as the Congregation's new procurator general in 1896, Father Burns wrote:[40] "It is certain that Father Morrissey can retain Dr. Zahm if he wishes. It is equally certain that he is glad to be rid of him. I can realize and sympathize with his position; but I think he should have taken a broader view of the matter and overlooked Dr. Zahm's annoying peculiarities for the sake of the University."

A major problem—or perhaps benefit—that Father Burns encountered on assuming the presidency was a large increase in enrollment. In 1915, the last year before the war, the student population stood at 1,079, but in 1919, the first year after the war, that figure jumped to 1,422.[41] The major increase was among the older students, the collegians, many of whom were war veterans, and they now numbered over a thousand, a majority of the total. Even with Badin Hall recently converted into a student residence, 250 students were forced to live in town. This Father Burns found unfortunate, since students living off campus missed much of the campus academic and religious life and some parents might decline to send their sons to Notre Dame if they could not be guaranteed lodging on campus. Father Burns was planning a million-dollar fund drive at the time, but he needed to be debt-free to conduct it and thus could not construct a new residence hall. He hesitated also to double up students in private rooms since that seemed less healthy after the recent spread of influenza.[42]

A possible solution was close at hand, and a solution that Father Burns had undoubtedly favored for some time—the closing of the preparatory or high school department and the use of those facilities for the college students. From his days with the Catholic Educational Association he had been advocating that all Catholic colleges should eliminate their preparatory departments and that dioceses should establish central Catholic high schools to meet that need of their students. Having a prep school on a college campus seemed disadvantageous for the high school since the institution's best resources would most often be allocated to the college, and it also seemed disadvantageous for the college to have the younger high school students, and their culture, on a more serious college campus. Although he agreed with Father Burns's goal of upgrading the collegiate programs, Father Zahm, possibly for financial reasons, apparently thought "the idea of throwing away a good ready-made prep school" was "folly." There was also danger of alienating many of the alumni who had been sending their sons to the prep department for years.[43] But Father Burns was adamant. He wanted Notre Dame to be a highly respected institute of higher learning, but he was convinced that a prep school contributed little to that, and he needed those facilities to house and educate increasing numbers of true college students. Father Burns announced that in the fall of 1920 the first two years of the high school or preparatory department would be eliminated, and the department would close completely when the students in the final two years had graduated in 1922.[44] It was a risky step because it not only deprived the university of an important source of income but the intended increase in college enrollment would add further expenses with the hiring of additional higher salaried professors. But Father Burns had an answer for that also—a million-dollar fund drive, the first such drive in Notre Dame's history.

Seeking outside financial assistance had been considered previously. As early as 1908 Father Cavanaugh had apparently visited the General Education Board of the Rockefeller Foundation in New York to inquire about a possible grant to Notre Dame, but nothing came of it.[45] Others had similar ideas. In 1916, James Ryan Hayden, an alumnus, former seminarian, and friend of Father Cavanaugh wrote the president to ask approval for him and two other alumni to undertake a million-dollar fund drive for a Notre Dame endowment fund. One of the three was an advertising executive and they were confident the drive would be a success. They outlined their proposal in detail:[46]

1. The money collected would be for buildings, endowed chairs, scholarships, and other aid to university growth and development.
2. Ten percent of the money collected would be used for advertising and other expenses.
3. A full-page appeal would appear in the *Chicago Herald* each Sunday.
4. All publicity would have the prior approval of Father Cavanaugh before publication.
5. All publicity would be prepared by the O'Shaughnessy Advertising Agency of Chicago. (James O' Shaughnessy was one of the three originators of the proposal.)

Father Cavanaugh was never shy about making decisions on his own, but this time he discussed the proposal with fellow priests. Father Paul Foik, librarian, opposed the idea, suggesting that an advertisement in only one paper seemed too limited and an advertisement in any paper seemed undignified. Father Michael Quinlan feared that such a drive would also detract from the present campaign for funds for Old Students' Hall. Another priest simply called it a "scheme . . . too wild for consideration." Father Cavanaugh eventually decided it was not a good idea and on April 24, 1916, notified Mr. Hayden: "Let us therefore consider that question closed."[47]

In March of the following year, 1917, Father Cavanaugh asked Father Burns, still superior of the Holy Cross College in Washington, DC, to accompany him to New York to renew acquaintance with the General Education Board of the Rockefeller Foundation and to visit with officials of the Carnegie Corporation also. The meetings went well, the officials asked pertinent questions about the university, but no promises were made. The United States entered World War I the following month and future plans, and money needs, had to be put on hold, but valuable contacts had been made.[48]

The war ended in late 1918, the provisions of the new Canon Law became effective, necessitating Father Cavanaugh's removal as president and religious superior of Notre Dame, and Father Burns was named his successor. Having already decided to terminate the high school program, with the important income it provided, and to increase the collegiate enrollment, with the added expense that would entail, Father Burns contacted officials at the General Education Board again that fall. The board had been set up in 1905 with a gift of $10 million from John D. Rockefeller, and he had only recently added another $50 million to it, chiefly for increases in faculty salaries, clearly one of Notre Dame's greatest needs. Dr. Wallace Buttrick, president of the General Educational Board, visited Notre Dame that winter and apparently had two suggestions, and only suggestions, to make: that the Law School might be strengthened academically, and that a lay board of trustees might be established to supervise any endowment investments.[49]

The Law School almost certainly needed attention. Founded in 1869, the first Catholic law school in the United States, it was originally a two-year program, and apparently a high school diploma was the only requirement for admission. When "Colonel" William Hoynes was appointed dean in 1882, a third year of classes was added, standards were raised, and the Law School acquired a respectable reputation. But Hoynes was seventy years old in 1917, the school had recently been denied membership in the Association of American Law Schools, and there was probably validity in at least some of the criticisms leveled by one of the professors in a letter to Father Cavanaugh in 1918:[50]

1. Law courses were taught similarly to other undergraduate courses, which seemed to denigrate their professional status.
2. The Law School no longer had an active and respected head.
3. There was little uniformity or coordination of teaching methods among the law faculty.

4. The grading system could allow some unqualified students to pass and even receive degrees.
5. The physical facilities and law library in Sorin Hall were inadequate.

That final criticism was no longer valid in 1919 because the new chemistry building had recently opened and the Law School had moved into the larger facility, the original Institute of Technology building. Father Burns also moved and replaced the elderly Hoynes as dean with Francis Vurpillat, the author of the above critical letter, and insisted that at least one year of college liberal arts courses be required before beginning law studies. The school would be admitted into the American Association of Law Schools in 1925.[51]

Notre Dame's board of trustees at that time consisted of the provincial superior, the university president, and four other Holy Cross religious, all with a vow of poverty and none with extensive experience in managing large investments. The university's productive endowment was listed as only $22,000, with an additional income of $1,000 a year from scholarships, and $75,000 in Chicago property that, because of taxes and other expenses, produced no income. In such discussions, however, Father Burns also included what he called Notre Dame's "Living Endowment." In fact, Indiana seemed about to require an endowment of $500,000 for certification as a teacher-training institution, which Notre Dame was, and Father Burns always pointed out that there were forty-seven Holy Cross religious working at Notre Dame without salaries. If they were paid salaries equal to the lay faculty, the total would be $93,800, equal to the 5 percent interest on an endowment of $1,876,000. Father Burns made frequent mention of this "Living Endowment" in any discussion of the status of Notre Dame's finances.[52]

But Father Burns did agree that if Notre Dame was going to undertake a major fund drive, benefactors would be much more amenable if they were confident that the funds would be managed well. As a student of the American educational system, he also knew that many colleges and universities, in addition to a board of trustees, had a separate board simply to manage the institution's endowment and finances. Harvard had a similar arrangement with a board of fellows and a board of overseers, and Father Burns contacted Harvard president Abbott Lowell for information and advice. He then asked William Breen, a Notre Dame alumnus and former president of the American Bar Association, to draft bylaws establishing a board of lay trustees whose primary responsibilities would be to manage the university's investments and to issue an annual report on the state of its finances. As established, it was a fifteen-member board with six Notre Dame alumni, six non-alumni, and three *ex officio* members (the provincial superior, the university president, and the university treasurer), these three Holy Cross religious. It was a board worthy of public confidence. The alumni members were William Breen as chairman, Joseph Byrne (Newark stockbroker), James Callery (Pittsburgh industrialist), Samuel Murdock (Indianapolis businessman), Clement Mitchell (Chicago banker), and Warren Cartier (Michigan financier). The non-alumni members included Edward Hurley (chairman of the United States Shipping Board), J. W. Johnson (president of Kokomo Brass Works), Solon Richardson (vice president of Libbey Glass Company), Francis Reitz (Evansville manufacturer), and soon Albert Erskine (president of the Studebaker Corporation). The board met for the first time on January 25, 1921.[53]

President Buttrick's visit in late 1919 kept the General Education Board's interest alive. Otis W. Caldwell of the General Education Board visited Notre Dame in the spring of 1920 and was quite impressed with the physical plant, the dedication of the faculty, and the sincerity of the students, but the board was not yet ready to make an offer. Father Burns prepared a detailed report of the university's financial status, including the small endowment, the value of the 184-acre campus ($180,000) and the physical plant ($3,914,495), and the current indebtedness of $73,516. President Buttrick and board secretary Trevor Arnett visited in February 1921 and were gratified with the financial report and the recent decisions to upgrade the Law School, terminate the first two years of the high school, and establish a lay board of trustees to oversee the institution's finances. As Mr. Arnett wrote:[54]

> Dr. Buttrick and I were favorably impressed with the attitude of the president towards the problems of the University and the service which he thought the University could render to the community at large; and we felt that any contribution which the General Education Board might make would be carefully guarded by the Lay Board of Trustees and would be rendering a real service toward education.

Notre Dame immediately notified the General Education Board of its plan for a million-dollar fund drive and asked for General Education Board assistance. The board always preferred matching grants, matching some percentage of what the institution itself collected, and on February 24, 1921, it agreed to contribute $250,000 if the university could raise $750,000 on its own. The terms of the agreement were that the full amount of $750,000 had to be donated or pledged by June 30, 1922, the total amount had to be collected and in hand by June 30, 1925, and none of the General Education Board money could be used for theological purposes. The board also promised an additional $12,500 annually to increase faculty salaries immediately. Notre Dame's grant was the largest the General Education Board awarded that year, and it was the only one awarded to a Catholic college.[55]

Such a campaign would be difficult at any time, but especially in 1921. The country was in the midst of a serious post–World War I recession, the alumni were already being canvassed, with little success, for contributions for an Old Students' Hall, and several other Catholic colleges and universities were undertaking fund drives at just this time, including Holy Cross's own Saint Edward's College in Texas. The time did not seem propitious. Father Burns consulted with officials at Cornell and Ohio State, he immediately put the drive for Old Students' Hall on hold, and, to assist the university, the provincial superior requested that Saint Edward's postpone its major drive.[56]

Father Burns launched the campaign with a dinner in a South Bend hotel on May 23, with most of the city's leading citizens present. Father Burns explained the need: at the moment every student bed at the university was occupied and five hundred more applicants were expected in the fall. New facilities and additional professors were needed, or many students would have to be turned away and fewer students would receive the education they deserved. Studebaker Company president Albert Erskine, soon to be appointed to Notre Dame's board of lay trustees, pledged $10,000, as did three other Studebaker officials, and the company itself promised $50,000. Mr. Erskine also assigned two of his experienced financial people to assist Notre Dame in setting up a modern and professional accounting system. Father Burns did not hesitate to seek pledges from South Bend businesses from whom Notre Dame bought food and other supplies, and he reminded local business leaders of the major financial benefit of Notre Dame football to the city of South Bend. Vice President Father Matthew Walsh, born and raised in Chicago, was assigned to open the campaign there in January, and similar campaigns were launched in New York, Boston, Cleveland, and elsewhere. A pep rally was held on campus and head football coach Knute Rockne gave one of his patented motivational speeches. Slogans like "Put your dollars where you put your boys—Notre Dame" and "Sign your name for Notre Dame" were common. Brochures were published and mailed, letters were sent to all alumni, and other letters were mailed to business and industrial leaders, emphasizing Catholicism's strong defense of private property and its long-standing opposition to communism and socialism.[57]

As June 1922 approached, thirteen months from the campaign's launching in South Bend, the goal had not been reached, but the Indiana Knights of Columbus pledged $50,000 and the Alumni Association contributed the $60,000 it had collected for Old Students' Hall. By the end of June the goal was passed, with total pledges reaching $824,765. Of this amount, $252,000 came from South Bend, $197,000 from Chicago, and $22,000 from the student body. The Carnegie Corporation contributed $75,000.[58]

As a condition of the General Education Board grant, the university was not permitted to take on any debt, and thus Father Burns was prevented from undertaking much new construction during his presidency. However, he was already planning a second million-dollar fund drive, this one chiefly for buildings, and the Alumni Association had been willing to contribute the $60,000 in the Old Students' Hall fund because they hoped this building would be included in that second drive. Unfortunately, as one historian noted, "the drive for the second million never came close to reaching the goal."[59]

Eliminating the high school, upgrading law studies, establishing a board of lay trustees, and conducting a successful million-dollar endowment drive were not Father Burns's only innovations during his short three-year presidency. In 1920, he decentralized the university's top administration, appointing strong deans (including laymen)—Father Leonard Carrico for Arts and Letters, Father Julius Nieuwland for Science, Professor Martin McCue for Engineering, and Professor Francis Vurpillat for Law—and giving them authority to govern, with the aid of faculty councils and meetings. He appointed chairmen over each department and supported their decisions. George Shuster was named chair of the English Department and enjoyed Father Burns's backing even in conflicts with Holy Cross religious. Academic departments were reorganized and streamlined. Arts and Letters absorbed the separate programs of Music and Library Science, Engineering absorbed Architecture, and in 1921 Commerce was separated from Arts and Letters and made an independent college with Father John O'Hara as first dean. A twelve-member University Council was established with authority over admissions, graduation requirements, class absences, etc., but always subject to the approval of the president. A similar Committee on Graduate Studies was established, with membership varying from five to ten. A major innovation was the extent of lay participation in the university's governance, with two of the five deans being laymen, fourteen of the twenty-two department chairmen, five of the twelve on the University Council, and two on the Committee on Graduate Studies.[60]

Father Burns's decentralization efforts reached down even into student life when he set up, or at least greatly strengthened, the Student Activities Committee. It was a nineteen-member board that included the four class presidents, an off-campus president, and fourteen elected members (eight seniors, four juniors, and two sophomores), and its responsibilities were to supervise such student activities as interhall sports, to serve as student liaison with the administration, and to survey and implement student requests and opinions, although the president could always decline SAC proposals. The committee oversaw the few dances that were permitted: one all-campus dance each year, one dance each for the senior, junior, and sophomore classes each year, and, beginning in 1922, a dance before each home football game. The Student Activities Committee also established the Blue Circle, a campus service organization called on to assist with various administration or student projects. The committee's one failure may have been the founding of a campus newspaper, the *Daily*, in 1923. It appeared five times a week, but early editorials could be critical of administration policies, it reviewed books that the faculty considered objectionable, and, rather than be self-supporting, it lost $1,200 the first year. A faculty publication committee soon ordered the paper dissolved.[61]

The curriculum at a Catholic college did not change as much, or as radically, as at many nonreligious colleges, for reasons that Father Charles Miltner, the second dean of the College of Arts and Letters, suggested in the *Scholastic*:[62]

> In educational matters Notre Dame has always been conservative. That is tantamount to saying that she has never given up the traditional Catholic concept of education which, including as it does a definite and settled conviction about the nature of man and his purpose in life, shuts out all possibility of any really radical change in educational philosophy.

Thus the changes Father Burns introduced into Notre Dame's curriculum proper seem minor compared with the other changes he made. He did introduce physical education courses into the freshman year—perhaps, as a former catcher on the varsity baseball team, he saw clear academic advantage in a strong and healthy body. He also added six semesters of religion as a requirement for graduation for Catholics. Until this time, religion was not required as an academic subject since the whole campus seemed permeated with religion. Further, various two-year or "short courses" in pharmacy, commerce, agriculture, engineering, and architecture were eliminated. The requirements for graduate degrees were regularized and strengthened. For the master's degree, a bachelor's degree was required, plus one year of residence, thirty-two hours of class, one foreign language, and a final written examination. For the PhD degree, a bachelor's degree was again required and, in addition, three further years of study, a reading knowledge of both French and German, and final oral and written examinations. These requirements may not always have been adhered to, but they were at least a start toward raising the graduate standards.[63]

In the summer of 1922, the provincial chapter of the Congregation of Holy Cross was scheduled to meet again, and one issue on the agenda was whether or not to reappoint Father Burns for a second three-year term. There were good reasons on both sides. He clearly had been a successful president. The university had a $73,000 debt when he entered office, due in part to the recently constructed chemistry and library buildings, and in three years the university was debt-free and had successfully completed a million-dollar endowment drive. The university's enrollment was increasing, new and more qualified faculty members had been hired, and the academic programs had been strengthened. No new construction had been undertaken, but that was because construction would have entailed indebtedness that was prohibited by the terms of the General Education Board grant. The university's higher administration had been reorganized, and more laymen were included. It is possible, however, that Father Burns did not want another term. There are indications that he so informed Father Walsh of this during the first year of his presidency. He was uncomfortable with some of the public relations responsibilities of the office, and he hoped to devote himself almost exclusively to collecting the donation pledges before the June 1925 deadline. Further, if he had been elected originally because a strong religious superior was needed at the time of community discontent, and even revolt, among some of the priests, that situation no longer existed. And undoubtedly some of his decisions (for example, closing the high school) did not find favor with all of his fellow religious. After serious deliberation, the chapter delegates named him president emeritus to continue his work of collecting those pledges, and appointed his vice president, Father Matthew Walsh, to succeed him as president.[64]

CHAPTER 10

The Emergence of Football

Father John Cavanaugh had given Notre Dame at least the beginnings of truly national fame and publicity. He was Notre Dame's greatest orator-president. For fourteen years as president he was called on to speak at conventions, conferences, and similar occasions throughout the East and Midwest, and even occasionally on the West Coast, and he did not disappoint. Most years found him delivering Saint Patrick's Day addresses in the nation's major cities, and his reputation, and Notre Dame's, was enhanced each year. Father James Burns, his successor in office, laid a solid foundation for Notre Dame's financial security with his million-dollar fund drive. The alumni and others pledged $800,000, the General Education Board of the Rockefeller Foundation contributed $250,000, and the Carnegie Corporation added another $75,000. With this endowment, Notre Dame was not only more financially secure but was poised for future growth and expansion. A third major contributor to both Notre Dame's national fame and its financial security, of course, was Coach Knute Kenneth Rockne and his extraordinarily successful football teams.

Football began at Notre Dame in the 1880s, but it had been around for at least twenty years before that. It began in the East, with the Ivy League. Princeton students seemed to have been playing a game of "balldown" as early as the 1820s, and Harvard had an annual game called "Bloody Monday" that same decade, but it was not until the 1860s that some general rules were in place. The first intercollegiate game was probably Rutgers versus Princeton in 1869, and the rules were clearly adapted from soccer. There were twenty-five men on a team, throwing or running the ball was forbidden, points were scored by batting or kicking the ball through a goal post, tripping and holding were the only fouls, and the team that scored six points won. These soccer-like rules remained in place for some years in several eastern schools, where baseball and rowing remained the most popular student sports. When Harvard played McGill University in 1874, rugby rules, more familiar to McGill, were played: the ball could be advanced by running with it, passing the ball laterally was permitted, tackling was approved but only above the waist, and the rugby scrummage was employed to put the ball into play each time. By the 1880s, chiefly under the influence of Walter Camp of Yale, rules were standardized. The scrummage was replaced by the scrimmage to start a play, a center (or someone) throwing or kicking the ball to a quarterback, a team had three downs to make five yards, and the earlier rules permitting running with the ball, passing it laterally, and tackling only above the waist remained. Yard marks were painted on the field every five yards, making the field resemble a "gridiron." John Heisman recalled the game of 1885: "Of rules we observed few, having few. Signals we had none—needed none, wanted none. We butted the ball, punched it, elbowed it and kicked it."[1]

As time went on, the game became more brutal. The plays were chiefly mass power runs, the ballcarrier trying to advance behind four to six linemen pushing and shoving the opposing linemen in any way they thought effective. "Nearly all linemen," Heisman recalled, "lined up squarely against those who played the same position on the opposing team. They didn't crouch or squat or play low. They mostly stood bolt upright and fought it out with each other, hammer and tongs, tooth and nail, fist and feet. Fact is, you didn't stand much chance of making the line those days unless you were a good wrestler and fair boxer." The players wore no helmets or padding, and injuries were common. The flying wedge was introduced in the 1890s, with linemen, especially on kickoff, forming a V, interlocking arms perhaps, and charging down the field, mowing down everyone in front of them, with the ball carrier close behind. Against the wedge, Yale's Hall of Fame lineman William "Pudge" Heffelfinger was reported to charge, jump, and crash feetfirst into the chest of a lead blocker. In a game against Harvard, a Yale tackler grabbed the ballcarrier by the throat, choking him in an effort to make him fumble. No penalty was called. Yet "from 1880–1905 there were more than 325 deaths reported in college football, plus 1,149 serious injuries." Because of the violence and disagreements over rules and eligibility requirements, Harvard and Columbia each dropped football for a time, and President Andrew White of Cornell refused to watch a game. The field was just beneath his window but he would pull the shades and remain at his desk. He refused to allow the team to play at Michigan, stating: "I will not permit thirty men to travel 400 miles to agitate a bag of wind."[2]

In 1905, the football coach at Columbia University remarked casually: "The number of deaths from football this season was nineteen. The number last season was about the same, and I don't think there has been any increase in the death list for many years. When you consider that during the football season probably 100,000 players are engaged in the game, the death rate is wonderfully small." His was clearly a minority view. The outcry against the violence was so widespread that President Theodore Roosevelt, a Harvard graduate and fan of this "manly sport," called representatives of Harvard, Yale, and Princeton to the White House and requested that they devise ways to reduce the game's violence and injuries. It was not going to be easy. Not all schools agreed on what changes were needed, or even who had the authority to make them. Three groups vied for influence—the Intercollegiate Rules Committee, the Advisory Committee (composed of graduates of different colleges), and the University Athletic Club of New York. The Intercollegiate Rules Committee was the most respected, but it was powerfully ruled by Walter Camp of Yale and he opposed several rule changes. Under the leadership of Harvard, a meeting was called for New York in January 1906 with representatives of Harvard, Yale, Princeton, Chicago, Army, Navy, Cornell, Haverford, Pennsylvania, Texas, Dartmouth, Nebraska, Oberlin, and Minnesota in attendance, and sweeping rule changes were approved. A team now had four downs to make ten yards, rather than three downs to make five. The forward pass was approved, but with restrictions: it had to be thrown from five yards behind the line of scrimmage, it had to be thrown at least five yards to either side of the center, and it could not be longer than twenty yards. It was hoped that these first two changes would make it a more wide-open game, with passes and end sweeps rather than the constant mass power running game. Six players were required on the line of scrimmage, and the offensive and defensive lines had to be separated by the length of the football. The length of a game was reduced from seventy to sixty minutes, with two halves of thirty minutes each. Finally, a new rules committee was established at this New York meeting, and in 1910 it adopted the name National Collegiate Athletic Association (NCAA).[3]

The new committee amended or fine-tuned the 1906 rules over the next several years: a field goal was reduced from four to three points in 1909, seven men had to be on the line of scrimmage in 1910, receivers could not be touched until after the pass was caught, passes of any length and in any area were approved by 1912, hiding the ball under clothing was prohibited, the field was shortened from 110 to 100 yards, the shape of the ball was less round and more aerodynamic, and a touchdown was six rather than five points. The violence, unfortunately, was not eliminated, and twenty-six players were killed in 1909.[4]

While all this was taking place in the East, football was gaining in popularity at Notre Dame. Baseball was still the most popular sport on campus (not counting marbles), but there seem to have been pickup games of "football" in the 1860s and 1870s, although it is not clear under what rules the games were played. The winners were usually rewarded with a bushel of apples or a barrel of cider. The first intercollegiate game was with Michigan in 1887, and three or four similar games were scheduled annually in succeeding years. The university hired its first coach in 1894, James Morrison from the University of Michigan, but he may have coached only one game. The university then hired Frank Hering of the University of Chicago in 1895 for two years. Over the next fourteen years, nine different men served as coaches, often acting as team captain and quarterback at the same time. The most famous of these "player-coaches" was Louis "Red" Salmon from 1902–1904. An all-around athlete, best in track and football, he punted, kicked off, and was a breakaway ball carrier. He graduated with honors in civil engineering in 1903, coached again in 1904, and from this relatively little-known school in the Midwest was named to Walter Camp's third team of All-Americans.[5]

In 1897 and 1908, Notre Dame applied for admission into the recently formed Western Conference (today's Big Ten), but their admission was denied on both occasions. With coaches changing so often and with some uncertainty over how much authority Father Morrissey's board of athletics actually had, some conference leaders feared that conference rules and regulations might not be strictly enforced. Actually university vice president Father Thomas Crumley oversaw the athletic program and apparently did it conscientiously. But there were questions of eligibility standards also. Notre Dame at that time generally accepted almost every student who applied and simply placed each one in whatever grade in the Prep or Collegiate Department that seemed most appropriate. Students occasionally came at different times during the year, and left at different times, depending on needs at home or financial ability. On one occasion when such an accusation became public, the *New York Times* undertook an investigation and declared that all disputed players were in fact full-time students and eligible. The anti-Catholic American Protective Association was influential in the 1890s, and religious prejudice may have played a part in the decisions. Finally, Notre Dame was getting stronger athletically, and some conference teams might have preferred not to play them regularly. As a result, Notre Dame had to seek opponents outside the Midwest and eventually gained popularity all across the country.[6]

The Western Conference boasted of strong teams and, denied the opportunity to schedule them, Notre Dame was left to turn to other nearby colleges—Adrien, Saint Viator, Wabash—with (often) weaker teams. Such contests rarely drew large crowds, the games did not pay for themselves, and the sport was adding to the university's deficit. Football reportedly cost the university $2,300 in 1911 and $500 in 1912. An alumnus from Crawfordsville, Indiana, the home of Wabash College, mentioned to Notre Dame president Father Cavanaugh that Jesse Harper, the coach of the Wabash football team, was convinced that college football could and should pay for itself. Wabash had narrowly lost to Notre Dame two years before, six to three, and this on a controversial play. Wabash had passed for a touchdown but it was eventually decided that the pass had travelled more than twenty yards, which the rules prohibited at that time, and the points were disallowed. Harper had proven himself a successful coach with limited material, was conscious of the need to make football more productive financially, and, at the end of 1912, Father Cavanaugh hired him to coach football, baseball, basketball, and track, and serve as athletic director for a salary of $2,500 a year.[7]

Jesse Harper had been born in East Paw Paw, DeKalb County, Illinois, in 1883, but at age ten his family moved to Mason, Iowa, after a fire destroyed the family farm. His father continued in farming and in breeding and raising cattle, Jesse and his two brothers assisted with chores, and all three boys excelled in sports, especially baseball. Jesse completed grammar school and the first two years of high school in Mason, and then he transferred to Morgan Park Academy in Chicago and eventually to the University of Chicago itself. As he said later: "We lived in Iowa and my father was in the cattle business. I could always get a free ride into Chicago on a cattle train. For that reason I went to Morgan Park Academy, a Chicago prep school, and then on to the University of Chicago." He majored in philosophy at the university and was also a star on Amos Alonzo Stagg's baseball team, playing both in the outfield and catching, fast enough to be a constant base stealing threat and batting over .300 in each of his three seasons. Suffering from rheumatism, he played no football in his first two years at the university and was the substitute quarterback behind the great Walter Eckersall in his final year, 1905. That year the team was clearly "Champions of the West," never losing a game and defeating Michigan 2 to 0 in the final game of the season, Michigan's first loss in five years. Twenty-seven thousand fans attended that game, marked by controversy when Michigan's Fielding Yost accused Coach Stagg of using ineligible players.[8]

Degree in hand, Harper took a part-time job selling books in Kansas, but Alma College in Michigan was looking to hire its first coach and offered him the position. Alma was a small, four-year, Presbyterian liberal arts college, and Harper was asked to coach football, baseball, basketball, track, and gymnastics, and also teach history. None of his first players had ever played college football before. It was a teaching and learning process, and his record in his two years was 7–3–3 against the likes of Kalamazoo, Hillsdale, Ferris, Olivet, Mount Pleasant, Albion, and Michigan Agricultural College (later Michigan State). Toward the end of the 1907–1908 academic year, his father asked him to return to Iowa and assist with the family farm, and this he did—temporarily. But coaching was in his blood and after several months he contacted his former mentor, Amos Alonzo Stagg, who recommended him highly to Wabash College in Crawfordsville, Indiana. The college offered him the position, and he remained there for four years. Wabash was an independent, nonsectarian liberal arts college and, as at Alma, he also coached baseball and track. In his first year, his football team lost to Notre Dame, Butler, Purdue, and Saint Louis, but in his second year the team defeated Saint Louis, Purdue, Butler, and Georgetown in a season cut short when one of his players died from injuries sustained when his head crashed against the knee of an opponent. His dying words reportedly were: "Did Wabash win?" The year 1911 was a good year for Wabash, losing to Notre Dame only by a 6 to 3 score on that controversial pass play, and the following year Wabash defeated Moore's Hill, DePauw, Butler, Earlham, and Rose Polytechnical.[9] Harper had learned under the best, Amos Alonzo Stagg, although he did not absorb Stagg's dislike of Notre Dame. Like Stagg, he had a firm grasp of the fundamentals and the technical aspects of any sport he coached. He was an innovator as well, shying away from the more brutal power-plunging offensive game of others and preferring wider sweeps and the use of the forward pass, teaching his players to make it spiral. He was also a disciplinarian, stressing character and forbidding smoking and drinking. He valued academic progress over athletics, sportsmanship over winning, and preferred only two hours of practice a day rather than four, hoping to keep athletics in proper perspective. All of these qualities appealed to the administration at Notre Dame, in addition to his goal of making football pay its own way, and Father Cavanaugh was pleased to offer him the open Notre Dame position.

Coach Harper fulfilled his contract with Wabash College to the end of the 1912–1913 academic year, but he also spent some time preparing for his first year at Notre Dame. If football was to break even financially, or even make a profit, major opponents needed to be added to the schedule to attract more fans into the stadium. Several games with traditional foes were already on the schedule, but he had some openings as well. On December 18, 1912, he wrote to the United States Military Academy at West Point to see if they had any open dates for the next year and were interested in scheduling a game. It happened that Yale's game with Army had just been cancelled, the date of November 1 was open, and many at the Academy thought it would be an easy tune-up for the final games on the schedule. As one student manager remarked: "We needed a 'breather' before our annual meeting with Navy." Army also guaranteed Notre Dame $1,000.[10]

When he accepted the position at Notre Dame, Coach Harper was well aware that his team had talent. After all, Wabash had lost to Notre Dame that year 41 to 6, and most players were returning. If the team had a star, it was probably Ray Eichenlaub, the fullback. At 210 pounds, 48 pounds heavier than Elmer Layden, the Four Horsemen's fullback ten years later, "Iron Eich" was a bruising runner, able to plunge for a two- or three-yard gain almost anytime he was called upon. The halfbacks were "Sam" Finegan and Joe Pliska, both quick on end sweeps and fast enough to get open as pass receivers. The quarterback was Charles "Gus" Dorais from Chippewa Falls, Wisconsin. Less than 150 pounds, he was a speedy runner, a smart field general, and eventually an extraordinarily accurate passer. At one end had emerged Knute Kenneth Rockne. Born in Norway, he had emigrated with his family at age five, grown up in Chicago, and entered Notre Dame as a freshman in 1910 at age 22.[11]

In the summer of 1913, while Coach Harper was developing strategies for the coming season, Gus Dorais and Knute Rockne (and other college students) took summer jobs at Cedar Point amusement park in north central Ohio, chiefly as lifeguards, room clerks, food servers, etc. They had taken a football with them and, in their off hours, would practice passing and receiving along the beach. Harper was trying to teach Dorais to throw the ball in a spiral, with a smooth overhand motion, and he was trying to teach Rockne to catch it, not with his arms and against his stomach, but over his shoulder with his back to the passer. Many passers at the time threw the ball underhand, some threw it overhand but end over end, and most threw to a standing target. Harper wanted his receivers to catch it on the run. As the *New York Times* wrote later: "The forward pass had been used before . . . but this ball had been thrown by an underhand method. No one had ever seen the likes of Dorais' long arching overhand tosses." The two, with other receivers, continued to practice when they returned to campus for the fall semester. The forward pass, when used before by other teams, had usually been a desperation play when the team was far behind. Coach Harper intended to make it an integral part of every game.[12]

In the first game that fall, at home against Ohio Northern, Dorais passed continuously and Notre Dame won 87 to 0. The second game, against South Dakota, was much more difficult. The South Dakota line outweighed the Notre Dame line by thirty-five pounds per man, and Rockne was injured and could not play. Despite the weight disadvantage, Notre Dame was able to score on the ground, winning 20 to 7, with only one touchdown through the air. The next game, the third and last home game of the season, was against Alma. Harper used it as a tune-up for the games to come. He experimented with new formations and hoped to utilize speed to overcome the weight advantage of his coming opponents. Rockne returned to the lineup and played superbly on both offense and defense. Dorais passed for four touchdowns, and Eichenlaub, Pliska, and Finegan ran for more scores in the 62 to 0 victory. The weekend was also touched with sadness when the university dedicated a plaque to a player on the 1910 team who had died soon after, and because of, injuries suffered in an alumni game.[13]

The next opponent was Army, on November 1. Although the cadets felt confident of victory, they prepared thoroughly, inviting alumni greats to return and help drill present players in techniques. They were one of the strongest teams in the East, and the following year they would go undefeated and be declared national champions. Notre Dame sent only nineteen players, and only fourteen pairs of cleats. When a starting halfback broke a shoestring during the game, Coach Harper asked his substitute to lend him his shoe. The substitute refused and Harper had no choice but to send in the substitute, "Bunny" Larkin, to play in his place. Each player carried his own gear and equipment on the train, and a box lunch prepared by the nuns in the dining hall. The trip's only "luxuries" were "a roll of tape, a jug of liniment and a bottle of iodine."[14]

Notre Dame won the toss and elected to receive. Eichenlaub gained little on the first play and Notre Dame fumbled on the second, with Army recovering. Army's heavier line, about fifteen pounds per man, assured cadet gains on the ground but they were not able to push over for a score. Coach Harper noticed that the Army backs were bunched up close to the line to halt fullback plunges and halfback sweeps before they could get up to speed, and he told Dorais to begin passing. His first three short passes were completions, with Rockne a decoy on each. Rockne later confided that he faked a limp on all three passes—he had missed a game with an injury two weeks before—and the defenders guarded him rather loosely. Dorais then called his number, he started off the line with his slight limp, and when he reached the defender he shifted into full speed (he also ran track), left the defender far behind, and Dorais hit him on the run with a forty-yard pass, and it was an easy jog into the end zone. Dorais's forty-yard toss was one of the longer passes thrown from scrimmage in college football to that time. Army scored twice in the second quarter, chiefly on the ground, but they missed one extra point. Notre Dame retaliated with Dorais's accurate passing to Rockne and halfback Pliska and went into halftime with a 14 to 13 lead.[15]

Neither team scored in the third quarter, Dorais stopping one Army drive with an interception in the end zone. But the fourth quarter belonged to Notre Dame. The Notre Dame players felt that they were in better physical condition than Army, and perhaps they were. As one player remarked: "We had two, sometimes three scrimmages every week—rough ones. . . . The scrimmages were harder than the game, and longer. We were always glad when the day of the game arrived because it meant a respite from scrimmages." Finegan and Eichenlaub made large gains around and through the Army line, and Notre Dame widened the lead to 21 to 13. The next time he got the ball, Dorais reverted to a passing attack, culminating in a short pass to Pliska in the back of the end zone, 28 to 13. Then, with the Army line tiring, Dorais turned to Eichenlaub and the big fullback made gain after gain until finally plunging in for Notre Dame's final touchdown, 35 to 13. Dorais had completed 14 of 17 passes for 243 yards, and Eichenlaub had run for 200 more.[16]

The game was given wide publicity. It was the ever-popular David defeats Goliath theme. Notre Dame had won football games every year and had a reputation for success in the Midwest, but its level of play had always been considered inferior to that of the powerhouses of the East—Harvard, Yale, Army, etc. It was a remarkable upset victory. The forward pass had also played an important role. Had it been an old-fashioned running game, Notre Dame, even with Eichenlaub, might not have been a match for Army. The forward pass not only gained yards and scored touchdowns but spread the defense and opened up the field for a more effective running game. With a forty-yard pass an ever-present threat, defenses, and the game, had to change. Finally, the game was played in the East, covered by New York City and most eastern newspapers, and the news spread nationwide. Both Notre Dame and the forward pass were frequent subjects of conversation all across the country.

The final three games of the season were in no way letdowns or anticlimactic. The following week's game was at Penn State, and Penn State had not even been scored upon at home in the last five years. Notre Dame broke that streak.

Its first score came on a Dorais to Rockne pass of forty yards, and the second on a long run by Eichenlaub, allowing Notre Dame to emerge with a 14 to 7 victory. Notre Dame was scheduled to play Wabash the following week but, realizing they were no match for Notre Dame, Wabash decided to cancel. Coach Harper was not displeased since it gave his team an extra week to recover from bruises sustained in the Army and Penn State contests, and extra time to prepare for the final two games against Christian Brothers in Saint Louis and the University of Texas at Austin. The coach still wanted to play the best, and reap the profits from a full stadium, and tried to schedule a postseason game in Chicago against Nebraska, another power of the Midwest. Nebraska was willing, but with the Notre Dame team in Austin over Thanksgiving and end-of-term academic demands looming, the logistics became too complicated and the plan had to be dropped. Dorais was injured in practice before the game with Christian Brothers in Saint Louis, and Coach Harper kept him and Eichenlaub out of the starting lineup. Christian Brothers, coached by Notre Dame alumnus Luke Kelly, played Notre Dame evenly for a time, and then Harper inserted his stars into the game and Notre Dame went on to win 20 to 7. The following day, the team boarded the train for Austin. Texas was clearly the strongest team in the Southwest, having defeated Kansas A&M by forty-eight points the week before. Coach Harper took no chances, even carrying the team's drinking water with them. He had heard that Texas water had a high sulfur and mineral content and he wanted the team to drink none of it, at least until after the game. It was one of Dorais's best performances. He completed ten out of twenty-one passes for two hundred yards, passed for one touchdown and ran for another, and converted all his extra points. Final score: Notre Dame 29, Texas 7. With an undefeated season and victories over football powers Army, Penn State, and Texas, Notre Dame had a claim to be national champions, but eastern writers and coaches still felt that football played in the Midwest was inferior to that in the East, and recognition had to be delayed a little longer.[17]

Jesse Harper coached Notre Dame football for five seasons, but 1913 was the most successful season. Dorais and Rockne both graduated in 1913. Harper hired Rockne as his assistant coach at Notre Dame and Dorais moved west as head coach at the College of Dubuque, later Loras College. Harper was also able to include Yale on the schedule. If Western Conference (Big Ten) teams refused to play Notre Dame, landing Yale, a power in the powerful East, earned them some national respect. The first two games of 1914 were not competitive. Notre Dame defeated Alma 56 to 0, with Rockne coaching the team while Harper traveled to

New Haven to scout Yale. Against Rose Polytechnical the next week, Harper cleared the bench, let everyone play, threw no passes, and still won 102 to 0. But the Yale game demonstrated that Notre Dame still had a way to go. Eichenlaub was slightly injured, and although Notre Dame outgained Yale 408 yards to 287, Yale was victorious 28 to 0. Yale had one play where each of the four backs would lateral the ball to another just before being tackled, and Notre Dame did not seem able to cover all four backs. Notre Dame won the next two games, South Dakota 33 to 0 and Haskell Institute 21 to 7. Next was Army, anxious to avenge last year's defeat. Eichenlaub and halfback Finegan were both injured and could not play, and Army won 20 to 7 and went on to be acclaimed national champions. The final two games were Notre Dame victories, 46 to 6 against Carlisle and 20 to 0 against Syracuse. Jim Thorpe had already left Carlisle by this time, and it was the only time the two schools met. Syracuse had defeated Michigan the week before but could not duplicate it against Notre Dame. It was a 6 and 2 season against the toughest schedule Notre Dame had ever played.[18]

The next three years in many ways were repetitions—strong schedules, good victories, but no undefeated seasons. Nebraska was on the schedule in 1915—Notre Dame's only defeat, 20 to 19, when Notre Dame missed an extra point. Eichenlaub had now graduated and the stars of the team were Arthur "Dutch" Bergman in the backfield and J. Hugh O'Donnell, the future Notre Dame president, at center. The Army game was difficult, as usual. The cadets were led by Elmer Oliphant, who had played four years at Purdue before entering the Academy, but Bergman scored on a twenty-yard pass and Notre Dame won 7 to 0. In 1916 Notre Dame was victorious, and even unscored upon, in eight of its nine games, but the Army passing combination of Oliphant to Eugene Vidal (father of Gore Vidal) proved too much and Army emerged a 30 to 10 victor. The 1917 season was Jesse Harper's final year as coach, and he also saw many of his regulars leave school and join the military with the United States entrance into World War I. Coach Harper's father-in-law needed assistance on his cattle ranch in Kansas and promised to match Harper's Notre Dame salary. The pressure to win every game was also taking its toll on the coach. Wisconsin broke rank with other Western Conference (Big Ten) schools that year and scheduled Notre Dame, the game ending in a 0–0 tie. Nebraska gave Notre Dame its only defeat, 7 to 0, but other games were close—Army 7 to 2 and Washington and Jefferson 3 to 0. Notre Dame's score against Army came when sophomore George Gipp devised a new play, with the halfback running directly toward Elmer Oliphant's area rather than away from him as had been the strategy all game.[19]

George Gipp would be in the Notre Dame backfield—off and on—over the next three years. He had been born in Laurium, in the far Upper Peninsula of Michigan, on February 18, 1895, the seventh of eight children. With six brothers and sisters before him, he may not have received large amounts of his parents' attention and grew up independent and self-sufficient. Never particularly interested in books and learning, he enjoyed spending much of his youth at the local YMCA, playing baseball, basketball, football, and shooting pool. He became a master at all of them. He was frequently suspended from high school for pranks, rule violations, and skipping class, and was finally expelled for smoking in the hallways. He took on various odd jobs but could frequently support himself through billiards and poker, reportedly making up to $100 a night on occasion. Good-natured as he was, he generally gave away most of his winnings to some persons in need, and he rarely had much money to his name. And he continued playing baseball and even semipro football.[20]

A friend from Michigan's Upper Peninsula and a member of Notre Dame's baseball team, William "Dolly" Gray, suggested Gipp apply for a baseball scholarship at Notre Dame. Gipp was not certain. He was already twenty-one years old and had no high school diploma, but it was also the best offer he had. He passed the entrance examination and entered the freshman class in the fall of 1916. The story goes that Rockne was walking across campus one afternoon and saw Gipp and a friend kicking a football back and forth, was impressed with the length of Gipp's kicks, and invited him to try out for the football team. The raw talent was there and Rockne undertook to teach him proper form and technique. The self-confidence and independent streak were still there also. Toward the end of a freshman football game, he was told to punt from his own thirty-eight yard line and preserve a tie but, instead, he dropkicked a sixty-some-yard field goal for the victory. In a baseball game he was told to bunt on one occasion, but instead he swung away and hit a towering home run, explaining that "it was too hot to run around the bases."[21]

The man chiefly charged with harnessing and channeling this extraordinary talent, of course, was Notre Dame's new head football coach, Knute Rockne. He had been born in Voss, Norway, on March 4, 1888. For some reason, many Americans of that time called anyone born in a Scandinavian country a "Swede," and that occasionally happened with Rockne. There is a story told that after Jim Crowley, one of the Four Horsemen and of Irish background, made a particularly egregious mistake, Rockne asked sarcastically, "Is there anything dumber than a dumb Irishman?" and Crowley answered, "a smart Swede." Rockne's father was a carriage maker, and a very good one. The German Kaiser on one occasion purchased one. In 1893 Mr. Rockne came to the United States to exhibit his workmanship at the World's Columbian Exposition in Chicago. He decided to stay, and so he sent for his wife and four children to join him in America. Knute was five. As a young boy in Chicago, Knute played both football and baseball, boxed and ran track, and his lifelong flattened nose resulted not from a football collision but from a baseball bat in a particularly hard-fought game. He left high school before graduating, worked at a series of odd jobs, eventually took the civil service exam, and applied for and was given a position in the Chicago post office. He continually received promotions until he was earning $1,000 a year, a fine salary for that time. Two friends from Chicago were entering Notre Dame in the fall of 1910 and urged Knute to join them. As a Lutheran from Norway, already twenty-two years old, he was not sure he would fit in but, with an older sister's strong encouragement, he decided to take the chance. He joined the football team, in the backfield at first and then at end, had a significant role in many of Coach Harper's victories, and was team captain in his senior year. He also ran track and at times probably boxed for small purses. His success on the football field was more than matched by his success in the classroom. He received a bachelor of science degree in pharmacy with a four-year average of 90.50. His grades were 98 in anatomy, 99 in bacteriology, and 97 in chemistry. Chemistry professor Father Julius Nieuwland reportedly considered him one of his finest students. He was also one of the yearbook editors, played flute in the university orchestra, and took part in theatrical productions, occasionally assuming a female part. Later known for his fiery pep talks, he was not a natural public speaker. His close friend Gus Dorais recalled:[22]

> You must remember about Knute that he came to school about four years older than the rest of us. His thoughts tumbled out in such bursts that he was inclined to stammer. This was the reason for his machine-gun oratory of later on—but he had trouble becoming a speaker. He seemed to have more problems than the rest of us.

The first three years of Notre Dame football under head coach Knute Rockne could accurately be called the years of George Gipp. Gipp had been on the team in 1917 but played in only three games, missing the first two of the season because he did not report to campus until mid-October and the last three because of a serious leg injury. The leg was still injured when he reported for his draft physical the following spring and he was granted a deferment from World War I. Not so for other players. Some that Rockne was counting on for the 1918 season had left school to enroll in the military, and others were in the Students' Army Training Corps (SATC) and their football practice time was limited. Influenza also struck during the fall football season, and government travel regulations forced major changes in the schedule. The games with Army and with Washington and Jefferson were cancelled due to travel limits, and two others were cancelled because of the flu. Wabash was hurriedly added to the schedule as other teams cancelled. One bright spot was that Gipp had convinced a friend from Michigan, Heartley "Hunk" Anderson, to join him at Notre Dame and go out for football. When Rockne first met him, he asked what position he played. "Fullback," he replied. "We don't need fullbacks," said Rockne, "We need guards." The young man countered: "You're looking at the best guard you'll ever see." And perhaps he was. Grantland Rice called him "the toughest man, pound for pound, I have ever known." Anderson worried that his father, a Presbyterian and a Mason, might not approve of him attending a Catholic school, but there was no problem. "I don't care if you come back a priest," his father said, "Just get an education."[23]

Because of the wartime restrictions, only six games were played in 1918, and Rockne's record was three wins, one loss, and two ties. The wins and losses were often influenced by Gipp's health and availability. In a 26 to 6 win over Case Technical, he scored two touchdowns, gained 88 yards rushing and 101 yards passing, completing five out of twelve passes. In the hurriedly arranged game versus Wabash, a 67 to 7 victory, Gipp again scored 2 touchdowns, and he gained 119 yards on 19 carries. The next game was with Great Lakes, with ex-collegians George Halas of Illinois and Paddy Driscoll of Northwestern, and it ended in a 7 to 7 tie, with Gipp gaining 69 yards on 15 carries but missing a 40-yard field goal that could have won the game. Gipp was injured for the Michigan A&M game (later Michigan State), and the Aggies won 13 to 7. Gipp recovered enough to play against Purdue next, scoring 2 touchdowns and gaining 137 yards on 19 carries in a 26 to 6 victory. The final game was a 0 to 0 tie with Nebraska, with Gipp gaining 76 yards on 15 attempts, passing for 65 yards, and returning a kickoff 40 yards. It was not a great year for either Rockne or Gipp, but considering the loss of regulars to the war, disruptions in the schedule, and injuries, it was probably as successful as could have been expected. Football profits for the year were $234.[24]

The following year was Gipp's best. Kalamazoo was the first game, and during pregame warm-ups Gipp walked out to the fifty yard line carrying two footballs. He drop-kicked one through the goalpost at one end, turned, and drop-kicked the other through the other goalpost. Notre Dame won the game 14 to 0 with Gipp rushing for 148 yards. He also had runs of 68 and 80 yards called back, leading him, a story goes, to suggest to the referee on his way back to the huddle: "Next time give me one whistle to stop and two to keep going." Notre Dame defeated Mount Union, defending champions of Ohio, 60 to 7; Nebraska, 14 to 9; Western Normal, 53 to 0; Indiana, 16 to 3; Army, 12 to 9; Michigan Aggies, 13 to 0; Purdue, 33 to 13; and Morningside College 14 to 6. Gipp for the season gained 729 yards on the ground and an almost-identical 727 yards in the air. It was not an easy year for Rockne, however. Gipp was living in the Oliver Hotel in town, close to his billiards and poker profits. Many returning veterans were difficult for the young coach to discipline, and several on the team were also playing semipro football on Sundays under assumed names. Rockne ordered center George Trafton, whom Red Grange called "the toughest, meanest, most ornery critter alive" and who later starred for the Chicago Bears, to give up semipro ball or leave school, and Trafton departed. Notre Dame was undefeated that year, 9 to 0, but Harvard at 9–0–1 was declared national champions.[25]

The year 1920 was a year of triumph and tragedy, triumph because it was Notre Dame's second consecutive undefeated season and the team was finally acclaimed national champions, but tragedy because of the early and unexpected death of its young star, George Gipp. Gipp had become more and more a source of concern. Living in the downtown hotel, he was missing classes more frequently, he may have been smoking two or three packs of cigarettes a day, and he had met a young woman in Indianapolis and was trying to spend more and more time with her. Father Burns, in his first year as university president, finally spoke with him on March 8 and expelled him from the university, apparently chiefly for missing too many classes. When the news became public, Michigan under Fielding Yost, Pittsburgh under Glenn "Pop" Warner, and West Point under its new superintendent, Douglas MacArthur, all reportedly invited him to transfer, and both the Chicago White Sox and the Chicago Cubs offered him $4,000 to play baseball. South Bend business leaders, envisioning a successful and profitable football season, urged Father Burns to reconsider, and Father Burns probably realized that a successful season would also assist the million-dollar fund drive he was planning. On April 29 Gipp was reinstated, but he apparently took no exams that spring and the academic semester was lost.[26]

Gipp spent the summer of 1920 working and playing baseball in Flint, Michigan, batting .375 and fielding .964, and he returned to Notre Dame in late September. In the opening game, Notre Dame defeated Kalamazoo 39 to 0, with

Gipp gaining 183 yards in 16 carries. Against Western Normal, a Notre Dame 42 to 0 victory, Gipp gained 123 yards, scored two touchdowns, and kicked three extra points. Notre Dame defeated Nebraska next, 16 to 7, with Gipp accounting for 218 yards of Notre Dame offense. Against Valparaiso, Rockne started his second team, the "shock troops," and when the opposition had tired, inserted his first team and won 28 to 3. By the time of the Army game, Gipp was feeling ill effects from his infected tonsils, but he had refused to have them removed over the summer since he wanted to continue playing ball. The Army game was close. Army led at halftime, 17 to 14, and with Gipp enjoying a cigarette, Rockne reportedly asked him if he had any interest at all in the game. Gipp was said to reply: "I got $400 bet on this game, and I'm not about to blow it." Notre Dame eventually pulled it out, 27 to 17, with Gipp rushing for 150 yards, passing for 123, and returning kicks for 207, for a total of 480 yards. Notre Dame next defeated Purdue 28 to 0 and Indiana 14 to 10. Rockne did not want to play Gipp against Northwestern in Chicago but the fans clamored for him, and Rockne relented in the fourth quarter. Notre Dame won 33 to 7 and ended the year by defeating Michigan A&M on Thanksgiving Day 25 to 0, with Gipp now ill in the hospital. It had been a marvelous football season. In only his third year as head coach, Rockne had enjoyed his second consecutive undefeated season and Notre Dame was finally acclaimed national champions.[27]

By the season's end, however, most attention was turning toward Gipp in the hospital. He continued to lose weight, the infected tonsils perhaps making eating difficult, and rallies and relapses alternated. His mother and siblings arrived to be with him, Rockne spent time at his bedside, Father Pat Haggerty visited often, and Father John O'Hara, later Notre Dame president and cardinal-archbishop of Philadelphia, gave him the last rites. Rockne, of course, has told the story that on one of his visits Gipp whispered a final request: "Rock, I know I'm going to die. I'm not afraid. But someday, Rock, when things on the field are going against us, tell the boys, Rock, to go out and win just one for the Gipper. Now, I don't know where I'll be then, Coach. But I'll know about it, and I'll be happy." Rockne related this story to his team at halftime of the Army game in 1928 and they went on to upset the Cadets, but did that deathbed conversation take place as described? Questions and concerns have been raised over the years. First of all, on no other occasion, apparently, did he ever refer to himself as the "Gipper." Second, to some it seems almost too sensitive and sentimental for one as hardscrabble as Gipp usually was. Third, why would Rockne wait eight years to mention or use it? And finally, it is certainly the type of story that Rockne could make up to inspire his team to victory. But the consensus is that it did happen, that Gipp did say something to that effect, that Rockne may have elaborated on it somewhat, or maybe that was simply the way he remembered the incident eight years later. Early in the morning on December 14, 1920, George Gipp, at age twenty-five, breathed his last.[28]

The funeral was one of the most impressive in South Bend up to that time. The body was first laid in state at McGann's Funeral Home, viewed by five hundred of Gipp's fellow students and hundreds of South Bend residents and civic officials. Others admitted they stayed away, preferring to remember him in his physical prime. Classes were cancelled on Wednesday, the 15th, and the funeral Mass was celebrated in the college church, with the sermon preached by Father O'Hara, prefect of religion, reminding those present that Gipp had had all the blessings of a happy death and had faced it calmly and with religious faith. A procession then formed, beginning with a police escort, then the football team in offensive formation, with the left halfback position left vacant. The Monogram Club followed, and the student body and faculty four abreast, about 1,400 in all. Behind them came the hearse, flanked by the six student pallbearers—close friends and teammates Hunk Anderson, Norman Berry, Joe Brandy, Frank Coughlin, Fred "Ojay" Larson, and Percy Wilcox. The Gipp family rode in three automobiles behind the hearse. Flags at Notre Dame and the county court house were at half-staff. As the casket was placed on the train, the students all bared their heads, despite the snowy cold, as a final mark of respect for their departed classmate. The train went first to Chicago where the casket was transferred to a train for northern Michigan. Stores in Laurium and nearby Calumet closed Saturday afternoon for the funeral, and a Protestant service was held in the Calumet armory, the only structure large enough to hold the crowd. Teammate and captain Frank Coughlin delivered a eulogy for Notre Dame:[29]

> He was a man among men, brilliant and unassuming, and has endeared himself to the heart of every Notre Dame student by his athletic prowess, magnetic personality, keen mind, and his great love for the old school. He will be forever remembered as a friend, a student, an athlete, and a gentleman, for to know him was to love him.

Tributes flowed into Notre Dame from all across the country, one of the finest perhaps from Warren Brown of the *Chicago Herald and Examiner* after watching California defeat Ohio State in the 1921 Rose Bowl:[30]

I saw California trounce Ohio State, the Western Conference champions, 28–0. I saw Brick Muller of California's team throw the longest completed forward pass on record. I thought then I had seen everything. I know now I had seen nothing at all. I hadn't seen Gipp of Notre Dame.

It was a mark of Rockne's coaching that Notre Dame was able to continue its winning ways in the early 1920s without a star of Gipp's magnitude. Rockne by this time had perfected the Notre Dame "shift." Despite an early story, it was not something he devised while watching a ballet. Coach Harper, among others, had used it and Rockne simply improved and fine-tuned it. The backfield would line up in the single-wing or Notre Dame box formation, and then all shift to one side or the other just before or as the ball was being centered. The ends might shift also. Whichever back received the ball might run with it, pass it, or hand it off to another going in the same or the opposite direction, and always a step or two ahead of the opposition. Rockne's teams were often outweighed by their opponents, but they were quicker, and the shift gave them an even faster start. Eventually the shift was outlawed and all backs, except one man in motion, had to be stationary before the ball was centered, but it was a winning technique while it lasted.[31]

The team, now beginning to be called the "Fighting Irish" by the students, had a record of 10 and 1 in 1921, losing only to Iowa. Against Purdue, Hunk Anderson, a guard, scored two touchdowns in three minutes, one a fumble recovery and the second a blocked kick. Against Marquette, one of the Marquette subs who got into the game was a Pat O'Brien, later the actor who played Rockne in the movie *Knute Rockne—All American*. Although it was the first ten-win season in Notre Dame history, several players admitted having played in a professional game on Thanksgiving, they were suspended from further football, and Notre Dame declined any postseason bids. Football that year showed a profit of $14,875. The following year the team went 8–1–1 and returned a profit of $32,020. Although the new university president, Father Matthew Walsh, had strengthened the Faculty Board in Control of Athletics, all prospective players were scrutinized for eligibility and one was declared ineligible. In the locker room before the Georgia Tech game in Atlanta, Rockne pulled from his pocket a crumpled telegram he said was from his six-year-old son Billy, seriously ill in a hospital back in South Bend. He read it to the team: "Please win this game for my daddy. It's very important to him." Notre Dame won, 13 to 3, and when the team arrived back at the train station in South Bend, recalled Jim Crowley, there was "little

Bill Rockne, rushing up, whooping and hollering. . . . You never saw a healthier kid in all your life. He hadn't been in a hospital since the week he was born." It simply had been Rockne's effort to motivate the team. In the game against Butler, Paul Castner, the All-American fullback, broke his hip in a pileup, Rockne shifted Elmer Layden, his 164-pound left halfback, to fullback, inserted Jim Crowley at the vacant halfback spot, and thus created, with this all-sophomore backfield, the Four Horsemen.[32]

The quarterback of the famous backfield was Harry Stuhldreher. He had been born in Massillon, Ohio, a hotbed of early professional football, in 1901. His father owned a grocery store, and an older brother, Warren, had preceded him at Notre Dame. In 1915 and 1916, Notre Dame assistant coach Rockne and Gus Dorais occasionally played for the professional Massillon Tigers on Sundays, while Jim Thorpe starred for the neighboring Canton Bulldogs. Young Stuhldreher used to attend the games and, at times, assist Rockne by carrying his gear to and from the field. He was a bright lad, getting good grades at Massillon's Washington High School, and he was a scrappy football player but, at less than 140 pounds, he did not start until his senior year when the first team quarterback was injured. He led the team to several victories, and he was a smart field general and a quick and elusive runner, but he still seemed too small for college football. After graduating from high school, he decided to enroll for one year at Kiskiminetas Springs School near Pittsburgh to prepare himself better, academically and athletically, for college. While not a military school, it did offer military exercises and regular inspections, and it had a proud football tradition. Stuhldreher excelled there, a "whiz of an athlete and a scholar" the yearbook called him, he increased his weight to close to his college playing weight of 151 pounds, and he chose to follow his brother by enrolling at Notre Dame in the fall of 1921.[33]

The right halfback was also an Ohioan, from Defiance, Don Miller. The Millers were one of the best known of Notre Dame's football families. Don's oldest brother, Harry or "Red" Miller, starred at Notre Dame from 1906 to 1909, captained the team in 1908, and played such a prominent role in Notre Dame's victory over Michigan in 1909 that one Detroit paper wrote simply "Miller defeats Michigan." His younger brother Ray enrolled next in 1910 and was a substitute end behind Rockne. He was bright and an excellent debater, served in the National Guard and saw action in World War I, returned to public life, and was eventually elected mayor of Cleveland. The year he graduated, 1914, his brother Walter entered as a freshman. He played fullback next to George Gipp in 1917 and 1919, and sat out the influenza-shortened season of 1918. In the fall of 1921,

Gerry and Don Miller arrived at Notre Dame together, Gerry being older but having lost time due to illness, especially typhoid fever. And the line did not stop there. Harry's two sons, Tom and Creighton, enrolled at Notre Dame in the early 1940s. Tom was a fine halfback and Creighton even finer, an All-American and eventually a member of the College Football Hall of Fame.[34]

Don Miller was born in 1902 and starred at left halfback at Defiance High School, scoring five touchdowns in a game against Bowling Green in his senior year. At only 160 pounds, Rockne considered him the greatest open-field runner he ever had. Quieter and more serious than his brother Gerry, he was made business manager of the high school paper and was elected senior class president at Notre Dame. Working one summer at Cedar Point amusement park, as had Knute Rockne and Gus Dorais before him, he heard a cry for help from a woman about to drown about three hundred feet out from shore. Don and another bystander dove into the water immediately, reached her in time, and carried her back to safety where she was revived with a lung motor.[35]

Opposite Miller at the other halfback spot, and also playing at 160 pounds, was Jim Crowley, born in Green Bay, Wisconsin, in 1902 and coached in high school by Earl "Curly" Lambeau, a former Notre Dame student and later a founder of the Green Bay Packers. Jim's father died of consumption when Jim was small and, with many young men away in World War I, Jim was able to find work during his high school years to assist the family financially. A gifted athlete, it is said that he made the eighth-grade baseball team as a third grader, and after one tryout in 1920, the Cincinnati Reds offered him a contract. The money was attractive but he eventually declined. His football debut as a high school sophomore was not particularly promising. Sent into a game as an emergency substitute, he found himself open for a pass. But in the rush to get on the field, he had put his helmet on backward, it slipped down over his eyes, and the ball bounced off the helmet incomplete. That may have been the origin of his reputation as slow, befuddled, and inattentive, earning the nickname "Sleepy Jim." But, as opponents learned, the opposite was true. As one author described him:[36]

> Watch him stand in the backfield, seemingly asleep—his eyelids add to the illusion. Listen to the quarterback call signals—no sign from Jimmy. The backfield heps into the first step of the shift—Jimmy reluctantly moves with them. The ball is snapped—whiz! The emotional switch has been pulled. Off around the end quicker than you thought. When a tackle hit—Jimmy hits too—and let the tackle worry. When a man

obstructs his pathway—Jimmy plows into him and does a swan dive through space for a touchdown, if the play is within five yards of the goal. He just has football instinct. He has a fearless drive, and angelic courage.

Elmer Layden was the fullback, and at 162 pounds he was the heaviest of the four. Born into a close-knit family in Davenport, Iowa, in 1903, he had an older brother, a younger brother, and two sisters. Youngsters could always find places to play, and Elmer excelled in football, basketball, and track. The Layden children all attended the parish grade school and the boys attended Davenport public high school. The University of Iowa, his father's alma mater, expressed interest in Elmer for a time but wavered when he suffered a leg injury in basketball. Walter Halas, brother of George Halas and Layden's high school coach, had recently joined Rockne's staff as an assistant, and he urged Rockne to take a chance with him and he did. Layden's first days were not happy. He was not comfortable in his assigned three-man room in the basement of Sorin Hall, so he slept on the floor of a friend's room in Badin Hall for the first two weeks, and he missed his family terribly. Coach Halas invited him to his home one evening for dinner, and Elmer called his father to say that he was thinking of coming home, that Notre Dame was not for him. His father suggested he give it more thought, that he sleep on it and call him again in the morning. Rockne himself showed up at the Halas residence that evening and mentioned to Elmer that he had never lost a freshman from his team yet. Layden replied: "Mr. Rockne, your record is about to be broken." Layden stayed, although it was never certain he would return after each vacation, and at one time he seriously considered transferring to Wisconsin where a girlfriend was enrolled—and where he thought he would have more playing time. Rockne finally inserted him at left halfback and then switched him to fullback when Paul Castner was injured. In the backfield's first full game together, quarterback Stuhldreher changed the play at the last minute, the backfield shifted, Layden was caught unprepared, and the ball from center bounced off his knee and landed near the goal line where a Notre Dame lineman landed on it for a touchdown. The Four Horsemen's first touchdown was not their prettiest.[37]

As the young backfield began to attract national attention, other issues also emerged. The new president, Father Matthew Walsh, and a strengthened board of athletics were understandably concerned about the number of classes some athletes had been missing and whether some were also playing professional or semi-professional games while still students. Coach Rockne was enjoying his success and relative freedom and chafed a little at the regulations, and it was well known that Northwestern, Iowa State, Cincinnati, and Minnesota had made him attractive offers to leave Notre Dame. Father Walsh finally put a halt to much speculation by signing the coach to a ten-year contract at the very impressive salary of $10,000 a year.[38]

Prefect of religion Father John O'Hara was also becoming a more influential person on campus. He had been ordained in 1916 and was appointed prefect of religion in 1918. Both deeply religious and personable, he had a way of relating well with students, he was in great demand as a campus confessor, and students referred to him affectionately as "The Pope." There was a growing sense of anti-Catholicism throughout much of the Midwest, especially since the founding of the second Ku Klux Klan in 1915, and Father O'Hara thought that the example of the manly religious practices of the Notre Dame football team might help to counteract this. When the schedule made time for the players to attend Mass as a team in a distant city the weekend of an away game, Father O'Hara sought to have it given publicity. His *Religious Bulletin*, begun in late 1921, publicized whenever the team received Holy Communion as a body. Before the Army game in 1923 he distributed a medal of Saint Joan of Arc to each player to wear during the game, and the practice continued for every game and was given wide publicity, often noting what saint's medal was given at each game. Catholics across the country, and non-Catholics also, began to take the Notre Dame team to heart, to cheer when this small underdog school upset the older and powerful teams of the East, and they could not help but notice that Mass and Holy Communion and devotion to saints were part of the players' lives. Father O'Hara hoped that the Notre Dame football team might be attractive ambassadors for Catholicism in this age of rising anti-Catholic feeling.[39]

Nineteen twenty-three was a good but not perfect year for Notre Dame football. In the opening game, the Irish defeated Kalamazoo 74 to 0, with Kalamazoo making no first downs, and the teams decided not to play each other again. Rockne played mostly substitutes in the second game in order not to show much to the Army scouts who were present, and Notre Dame won over Lombard 14 to 0. The Army game was played at Ebbets Field in Brooklyn because the Yankees and Giants were playing the World Series at the Polo Grounds, and Notre Dame won 13 to 0. Princeton had not been defeated since 1921, but they fell next 25 to 2. Notre Dame won next over Georgia Tech and Purdue by almost identical scores of 35 to 7 and 34 to 7. Nebraska proved too strong once again and defeated Notre Dame 14 to 7. The Irish rallied the following week to defeat Butler 34 to 7, although Don Miller broke a rib and was through for the season. Carnegie Tech fell next, 26 to 0, and Notre Dame defeated Saint Louis in the season's finale, 13 to 0. Rockne rarely scheduled Catholic school opponents because, if there were allegations or suspicions of ineligible players, he never wanted to challenge or embarrass a Catholic school publicly. The season ended successfully at 9 and 1, and with a profit of $70,000, but the Nebraska game was unpleasant to remember.[40]

Rockne had an excellent team the following year, and he knew it. In the backfield, Don Miller had been an All-American in 1923, and the other three—Stuhldreher, Crowley, and Layden—would be All-Americans in 1924. They had been playing together as a unit for a year and a half, they knew each other's moves and tendencies well, and they ran Coach Rockne's "shift" almost to perfection. And the front line, now christened "The Seven Mules," was quick and laden with talent, especially with Adam Walsh at center and Joe Bach and Edgar "Rip" Miller at tackles. The schedule was the toughest the university had yet played, with games against Army and Princeton in the East, and against Wisconsin, Northwestern, and powerful Nebraska closer to home. The team was heavy with seniors, they realized it was their last chance, and they, and their coach, wanted to win it all.

The first two games were warm-ups. Rockne started the substitutes, the "shock troops," inserted the first team only later, and defeated Lombard 40 to 0 and Wabash 34 to 0. It was the last meeting between Wabash and the Irish. Army was next and sportswriters and fans throughout the East were anxious to see how good Rockne's eleven truly were. The game was played at the Polo Grounds before a crowd of 55,000, almost twice the attendance of any previous Notre Dame game. It was a low-scoring contest, with Notre Dame winning 13 to 7. Adam Walsh played part of the game with two broken hands and still returned an interception twenty yards, but it was the smooth precision running and blocking of the backfield that captured the most attention. Walter Eckersall of Chicago wrote: "Notre Dame's slashing attack, directed at the Army flanks, was the turning point of the game. The cadet ends and tackles failed to shift fast enough with the westerner's backfield shift."[41] Francis Wallace for the Associated Press was equally impressed: "The brilliant Notre Dame backfield dazzled the Army line today and romped away with a 13 to 7 victory in one of the hardest fought of the intersectional series between the two teams."[42] But it was Grantland Rice who gave the backfield a name and a kind of sports immortality:[43]

> Outlined against a blue-gray October sky, the Four Horsemen rode again. In dramatic lore they are known as Famine, Pestilence, Destruction and Death. These are only aliases. Their real names are Stuhldreher, Miller,

Crowley and Layden. They formed the crest of the South Bend cyclone before which another fighting Army football team was swept over the precipice at the Polo Grounds yesterday afternoon, as 55,000 spectators peered down on the bewildering panorama spread on the green plain below.

A cyclone can't be snared. It may be surrounded, but somewhere it breaks through to keep on going. When the cyclone starts from South Bend, where the candle lights still gleam through the Indiana sycamores, those in the way must take to storm shelters at top speed. Yesterday the cyclone struck again, as Notre Dame beat Army, 13–7, with a set of backfield stars that ripped and crashed through a strong Army defense with more speed and power than the warring cadets could meet.

Notre Dame won its ninth game in twelve Army starts through the driving power of one of the greatest backfields that ever churned up the turf of any gridiron in any football age. Brilliant backfields may come and go, but in Stuhldreher, Miller, Crowley and Layden, covered by a fast and charging line, Notre Dame can take its place in front of the field. Coach McEwan sent one of his finest teams into action, an aggressive organization that fought to the last play around the first rim of darkness, but when Rockne rushed his Four Horsemen to the track they rode down everything in sight. It was in vain that 1,400 gray-clad cadets pleaded for the Army line to hold. The Army line was giving it all it had, but when a tank spears it with the speed of a motorcycle, what chance has flesh and blood to hold?

The game the following week was at Princeton but the university administration requested the team to return to campus after the Army game and attend class for a few days before boarding the train again for the East. Although Notre Dame was clearly the superior team, gaining twenty first downs to Princeton's four, the final score was only 12 to 0. Georgia Tech and Wisconsin were next to fall, 34 to 3 and 38 to 3. The team had been looking forward to the Nebraska game since the defeat the year before, and the year before that, and it was more than ready. Notre Dame made 24 first downs to Nebraska's 3, 566 yards of total offense to Nebraska's 76, and 8 completed passes to Nebraska's 1, leading to a final score of 34 to 6. The final two victories of the regular season were over Northwestern, 13 to 6, and Carnegie Tech, 40 to 19.[44]

Such a season merited a bid to play in the Rose Bowl, and the university administration accepted. The opponent was Stanford, coached by Glenn "Pop" Warner. Warner had played football at Cornell and then coached successively at

Carlisle Indian School, the University of Pittsburgh, and now Stanford. After Rockne, he was probably the best-known college coach in the United States. Their coaching philosophies were different. Warner preferred a possession game, grinding it out three or four yards at a time, keeping the ball out of the hands of the opponent for much of the game, and he had one of the greatest college full-backs, Ernie Nevers, six foot three and 235 pounds, to do most of the grinding. Rockne's philosophy was the opposite. For him, every play could be the "perfect play," every play could be a touchdown. If every player blocked his opponent according to plan, every runner ran the correct route, or every passer hit the correct receiver, every play would be a score. With both teams undefeated, it seemed an exciting end to an exciting season.[45]

Since it was Christmas vacation, Rockne planned a leisurely trip to California. The team left South Bend by train on December 18 for Chicago, then they headed south, with stops at Memphis (for Mass), then New Orleans, Houston, and Tucson for four days of sunshine, dry fields, and practice. They arrived in Los Angeles and Pasadena in time for the required receptions, banquets, Rose Bowl parade, and the game itself, finally, at 2:15 p.m. on January 1. The game was played as many expected. Nevers received the ball on almost every play, to run, pass, or punt as the situation dictated. The statistics all favored Stanford. They gained 316 yards to Notre Dame's 186, 17 first downs to Notre Dame's 7, and 138 yards passing to Notre Dame's 56. But Notre Dame was quicker and capitalized on Stanford mistakes, recovering three fumbles and intercepting five passes. Layden intercepted two Nevers passes and ran them back for touchdowns of 78 and 70 yards, leading one wag to suggest that the most productive play of the game was the Nevers to Layden combination. The final score was Notre Dame 27, Stanford 10.

It was a fitting end to an outstanding season. The team had notched ten victories without a loss, and they had defeated the best teams on both the East and West Coasts. Several players were named All-Americans, Rockne was recognized as the nation's best college coach, and Notre Dame was unanimously voted national champion.[46]

The next four years must have been disappointing for Rockne—no national championships—but they were successful financially for the university. There were a few outstanding players—Christie Flanagan and Jack Elder were two—but there were weaknesses most years also. Rockne started an entirely new team in 1925 since all eleven regulars of 1924 had been seniors and had graduated, although many of the 1925 starters had gained good experience as the "shock troops" the year before. The team went 7–2–1, losing to Army and Nebraska and tying Penn State, 0–0. At the end of the year, Columbia University offered Rockne $25,000 a year to be their coach and Rockne signed a contract, then he realized it was a mistake since he still had a ten-year contract with Notre Dame and he and Columbia agreed to cancel. Before the 1926 season began, the Notre Dame "shift" was outlawed and every backfield player had to be stationary for one second before the ball was centered, but Rockne seemed to adjust to the new regulation well. However, he skipped the Carnegie Tech game to go to Chicago on business and perhaps to scout out the Navy team for next year, and Carnegie Tech upset the Irish, 19 to 0. It was the only mishap in an otherwise undefeated season. The following year Notre Dame tied Minnesota, led by the great Bronko Nagurski, 7 to 7, and lost to a powerful Army team 18 to 0. The season's final game was against Southern California in Chicago's Soldier Field before an estimated 125,000 spectators, the largest crowd to witness a college football game up to that time. Notre Dame won, 7 to 6. Rockne's worst year was 1928, as he won only five games and lost to Wisconsin, Georgia Tech, Carnegie Tech, and Southern California. The Army game was memorable since, tied at halftime, Rockne recounted George Gipp's deathbed conversation and urged the team to "win one for the Gipper." Win they did. Rockne sent in Johnny "One Play" O'Brien as a substitute and he immediately caught the winning touchdown pass. Despite falling below fans' hopes each year, football profits were impressive: $190,000 in 1925, $251,000 in 1926, $331,000 in 1927, and close to $500,000 in 1928.[47]

Two other issues were occupying the minds of the university administration—and of Knute Rockne—at this time. The first was Notre Dame's application, again, to be admitted into the Big Ten in 1926. Notre Dame was playing Big Ten schools regularly now—Wisconsin, Indiana, Purdue—and was abiding by Big Ten eligibility rules and regulations. But there was still opposition, led chiefly by Fielding Yost at Michigan. He insisted that Notre Dame's well-organized interhall football program also prepared athletes for four years of varsity football, and that Rockne was still fielding ineligible players. Many at Notre Dame thought that anti-Catholicism also played a large role in the opposition, and Notre Dame's application was denied. The second issue was the need for a new stadium. Cartier Field seated 20,000, but new stadiums at other schools held more: Michigan held 101,000, Ohio State 81,000, and Illinois 71,000. More and more fans wanted to see Notre Dame play—125,000 filled Soldier Field for the 1927 Southern California game—and thus Rockne preferred to play games on the road before larger crowds and with increased profits, leading some to call his team (in addition to the "Horrible Hibernians") the "Nomads" or the "Ramblers." Rockne on one occasion even threatened to resign if a new stadium were not built but Father Matthew Walsh, president from 1922 to 1928, was convinced that, at least for the present, other building needs, especially additional residence halls, were more pressing, and a new stadium had to be postponed.[48]

Knute Rockne's final two teams, in 1929 and 1930, may have been his best. He lost only one regular from the 1928 team, tackle Fred Miller, later of Miller Brewing Company. The backfield both years was certainly Rockne's deepest and possibly his finest. Rockne always spoke of Frank Carideo at quarterback on the same level as Dorais and Stuhldreher. In 1929 Jack Elder, the fastest man on the squad, was at one halfback and Marty Brill, a transfer from the University of Pennsylvania, was at the other. When Elder graduated in 1930, he was replaced by Marchy Schwartz. At fullback was Larry "Moon" Mullins, backed up by Joe Savoldi. The "shift" had now been outlawed, speed and quickness were not so necessary, and the 1930 backfield outweighed the Four Horsemen by approximately twenty pounds per man. The quarterback was now using spins and fake handoffs to confuse the opposition, somewhat similar to the veer offenses developed later. In 1930, all four in the backfield—Carideo, Brill, Schwartz, and Mullins—were named All-Americans, an honor apparently not achieved even by the Four Horsemen in 1924. Three of the seven linemen were named All-Americans also, including Bert Metzger, an outstanding guard weighing only 149 pounds. An All-American tackle in 1929, Jack "Boom-Boom" Cannon, was reportedly the last lineman to play without a helmet.[49]

The 1929 season was unique for two reasons. First, in 1928 the six-year term of Father Matthew Walsh as president and religious superior came to an end, and he was succeeded by Father Charles O'Donnell. Father Walsh had overseen the construction of five student residences and most students were now living on campus. Money was available (much of it from football) and Father O'Donnell approved the construction of a new stadium. Cartier Field was being demolished and, as a consequence, there were no home games in 1929, every game was somewhere on the road. Second, early in the 1929 season Rockne contracted phlebitis, with serious swelling of the legs. The danger of a blood clot moving to his heart was real and he was warned to slow down and reduce his commitments. He missed six games that year, all away, of course, but McGann's Funeral Parlor was able to outfit one of its hearses with a kind of hospital bed and Rockne could attend practices and even a couple of away games. One of the assistant coaches directed the team in Rockne's absence.[50]

Some of the games in 1929 were close but Notre Dame won them all. Carnegie Tech was still a nemesis and Notre Dame won only 7 to 0. Georgia Tech had been national champions the year before but they fell 26 to 6. The Southern California game was played at Soldier Field in Chicago, this time before 112,000 spectators, and Notre Dame won narrowly, 13 to 12. Rockne worried about a letdown the following week against Northwestern, again in Chicago, and sent a message asking the team to win this one since it would be his one hundredth victory. The team won, only to discover later that it was not his hundredth victory at all. The Army game was especially close and the only score was a ninety-five-yard interception return for a touchdown by Jack Elder. In all, Notre Dame scored 145 points that season to their opponents' 38, and was declared national champions. The stock market had begun its crash in late October, between the Carnegie Tech and Georgia Tech games, but it did not seem to have any major impact on the football season.[51]

Rockne once called the 1930 team his greatest and, with seven of the eleven named All-Americans, perhaps it was. It had a new stadium to play in also. In the first game there, Notre Dame defeated Southern Methodist University 20 to 14 in what was intended to be, in part, a warm-up for the Navy game and the dedication of the stadium the following week. The crowd at the SMU game was smaller than predicted (14,751) and traffic and parking around the new stadium proved to be no problem, but over 10,000 hot dogs and buns went unsold. The following Friday evening, the varsity band marched around the campus, collecting students behind it, each carrying a lighted torch, and led them into the stadium for the dedication. Professor Clarence Manion of the Law School was the first speaker, with G. K. Chesterton in attendance in the front row, and he was followed by Coach Rockne and President Father O'Donnell. A fireworks display closed the evening. Forty thousand attended the game the following day, a 26 to 2 victory for Notre Dame. Victories continued over Carnegie Tech, Pittsburgh, Indiana, and Pennsylvania. Marty Brill had originally enrolled at Penn but was told he was not quite good enough for the football team and transferred to Notre Dame. Quarterback Carideo kept calling his number and he scored three touchdowns before being replaced. About this time it was discovered that fullback Joe Savoldi had been secretly married and was then in the process of divorcing. He was expelled from the university but later won fame as a professional wrestler. Notre Dame defeated Army 7 to 6 on a fifty-four-yard touchdown run by Marchy Schwartz behind blockers led by undersized pulling guard Bert Metzger. The final game of the season was in Los Angeles against Southern California, which had defeated its last three opponents by a combined score of 158 to 0. Seventy-four thousand fans attended and Notre Dame won a surprisingly easy victory, 27 to 0. In the final minutes, Rockne substituted for all his seniors individually and hugged each one as he reached the sidelines. For the season, Notre Dame outscored its opponents 265 to 74, and Rockne had to be most pleased: his team was named national champions again, the first time in history a team was so honored two years in a row.[52]

This 1930 season was probably Rockne's most satisfying, but it was also, unfortunately, his last. He had recovered satisfactorily from his bout of phlebitis, but his health was still a concern. The stress to win mounted with each successive victory, and second best was never good enough. He was also in the pay of South Bend's Studebaker Corporation and gave motivational talks to its employees across the country. Invitations to speak arrived almost daily—from football clinics to parish Communion breakfasts—and he too often said "yes." At the end of the 1930 season, he decided to go to the Mayo Clinic over Christmas break for a thorough examination and rest from the exhaustion he was increasingly feeling. He asked one of his senior tackles, Frank Leahy, to accompany him, and they shared a hospital room in Rochester for several days. Leahy used the opportunity to probe Rockne's mind on any number of football issues, and the coach was willing to spend hours in the conversations. The work ethic, the precision, and the success of Rockne's program were later reflected in young Leahy's own national championships.[53]

Returning to Notre Dame by the start of the new year, Rockne did try to cut back on his speaking engagements and other commitments, but he could not eliminate them all. He was invited to Los Angeles to assist in the production of a proposed movie, *The Spirit of Notre Dame*, and he explained to Father O'Donnell, university president, that he wanted the film to be instructional and a credit to the university. He took the train to Chicago where he visited with his mother and sister, and then took another train to Kansas City where he hoped to see his sons who were studying at the Pembroke School. On March 31, he, five other passengers, and a pilot and copilot boarded the Fokker F-10-A Trimotor for Wichita and eventually Los Angeles in weather that was cold and cloudy but not prohibitive. While others were still leery of airplane travel, Rockne was not. He insisted that it was as safe as any other mode of transportation. The plane took off satisfactorily, climbed into the clouds, maybe met some turbulence or began icing, and descended again, perhaps to get below the clouds. Turning could be difficult that close to the ground. Local residents heard the plane circling, and some thought they saw it lose a wing, and it eventually crashed in a field near Bazaar, Kansas. Rockne and three others were apparently thrown out of the plane by the force of the crash, and the other four were found still inside the wreckage. One report had it that Rockne had his rosary clutched in his hand.[54]

As the news spread across the wires, the nation was shocked. Years later people could still remember where they were and what they were doing when they first heard the report. University vice president Father Michael Mulcaire was called to the telephone in the Badin Hall basement recreation room for a long-distance call, heard the message, and turned to his fellow priests shakenly: "Rockne's killed." It was Tuesday of Holy Week. The body was brought back to Notre Dame by train, and when it had to be transferred from one station to another in Chicago, more than ten thousand crowded the terminals or lined the streets in tribute. The funeral service was scheduled for Saturday afternoon since no Requiem Mass could be offered on Holy Saturday. Many stores in South Bend closed for the day, or at least for the afternoon, and flags were lowered to half-staff. The campus church was filled to capacity, hundreds stood solemnly outside, and the Columbia Broadcasting System aired the proceedings over the radio. Pall-bearers were members of Rockne's final team—Frank Carideo, Marchy Schwartz, Marty Brill, "Moon" Mullins, Tom Conley, and Tom Yarr—and the Moreau Seminary choir provided the music. Father O'Donnell's sermon was eloquent:[55]

> In this Holy Week of Christ's passion and death there has occurred a tragic event which accounts for our presence here today. Knute Rockne is dead. And who was he? *Ask* the president of the United States, who dispatched a personal message of tribute to his memory and comfort to his bereaved family. *Ask* the king of Norway, who sends a special delegation as his personal representatives to this solemn service. *Ask* the several state legislatures, now sitting, that have passed resolutions of sympathy and condolences. *Ask* the thousands of newspapermen whose labor of love in his memory has stirred a reading public of millions of Americans. *Ask* men and women from every walk of life, ask the children, ask the boys of America. *Ask* any and all of these, who was this man whose death has struck the nation with dismay and has everywhere bowed heads in grief. . . .
>
> I would not dare the irreverence of guessing. But I find myself in this hour of piteous loss and pained bewilderment recalling the words of Christ: "Thou shalt love the Lord thy God with thy whole heart. This is the first and greatest commandment. And the second is like unto this: thou shalt

love thy neighbor as thyself." I think, supremely, he loved his neighbor, his fellow-man, with genuine deep love. In an age that has stamped itself as the era of the "go-getter"—a horrible word for what is all too often a ruthless thing—he was a "go-giver"—a not much better word, but it means a divine thing. He made use of all the proper machinery and legitimate methods of modern activity to be essentially not modern at all: to be quite elementarily human and Christian, giving himself, spending himself, like water, not for himself, but for others. And once again, in his case, most illustriously is verified the Christian paradox—he has cast away to keep, he has lost his life to find it. This is not death, but immortality.

It is fitting that he should be brought here to his beloved Notre Dame and that his body should rest awhile in this church where the light of Faith broke upon his happy soul. . . . He might have gone to any university in the land and been gladly received and forever cherished there. But he chose Our Lady's school, he honored her in the monogram he earned and wore, he honored her in the principles he inculcated and the ideals he set up in the lives of the young men under his care. He was her own true son.

To her we turn in this hour of anguish and of broken hopes and hearts laid waste. She is the Mother of Sorrows and the Comforter of the Afflicted. O Mother of God, and Mother of God's men, we give him into thy keeping. Mary, Gate of Heaven, we come to thee, open to receive him. Mary, Morning Star, shine upon his sea. Mary of Notre Dame, take him into thy House of Gold. Our Life, Our Sweetness, and Our Hope, we lay him in thy bosom.

He was then carried to rest in Highland Cemetery, less than two miles from his beloved Notre Dame.

Tributes poured in from across the country and beyond. President Herbert Hoover wired the family: "I know that every American grieves with you. Mr. Rockne so contributed to a cleanness and high purpose and sportsmanship in athletics that his passing is a national loss." King Haakon VII of Norway sent a similar message. Lou Little, the football coach at Columbia, stated: "They have taken our leader away." "I have lost a true friend," wrote Howard Jones of Southern California, "I shall always cherish the memories of the years of our association." Major General Douglas MacArthur, superintendent of West Point, sent his condolences, as did Babe Ruth, Lou Gehrig, and Jack Dempsey. Westbrook Pegler, often critical of Rockne, could praise him in death: "I read that youth has no idols nowadays. But they had one at Notre Dame." And finally, Will Rogers:

"We thought it would take a President or a great public man's death to make a whole nation, regardless of age, race or creed, shake their heads in real, sincere sorrow. . . . Well, that's what this country did today, Knute, for you. You died one of our national heroes. Notre Dame was your address, but every gridiron in America was your home."[56]

The tributes were well deserved. He had begun coaching in 1913 when football, especially in the Midwest, was still in its infancy, and he coached at a school with a limited college enrollment. In thirteen seasons as head coach, he won 105, lost 12, and tied 5, for a winning percentage of .881, the highest of all Notre Dame coaches of the modern era. Notre Dame's margin of victory was over sixteen points per game, and the opponent was held scoreless in 50 of the 122 games Rockne coached. Rockne had five undefeated seasons and four national championships, coached George Gipp, probably Notre Dame's greatest individual player, and had perhaps the most famous college backfield in the Four Horsemen. Notre Dame played and won games on both the East and West Coasts—Army, Princeton, Penn, Rutgers, Southern California, Stanford—and gained fans and favorable publicity, especially among Catholics, nationwide. The financial impact of Rockne's successes on Notre Dame is difficult to gauge with any certainty because it is not always clear if the figures are gross or net (with expenses deducted). But it seems that football earned a net profit of $234 in 1918 and $540,000 after expenses in 1930, thus probably increasing the university's revenue by some $2,000,000 throughout the 1920s.[57] The victories may also have encouraged benefactors to fulfill their financial pledges more promptly, or even contribute additional funds, to a university emerging into prominence in the public estimation. Notre Dame would suggest different things to different persons in succeeding years—a beautiful campus, academic achievement, a center of Catholicism—but football would rarely be absent from the public image. Knute Rockne began it.

CHAPTER 11

The 1920s

The president of Notre Dame during the major portion of Coach Rockne's successful years of the 1920s, the coach's strong supporter at times and his quiet but firm adversary at others, was Father Matthew Walsh. Born of Irish parents in Chicago on May 14, 1882, he was a member of a predominantly Irish parish, Saint Columbkille's, and was taught in the parish school by the Holy Cross brothers. At age fifteen, desiring to become a priest, he entered Holy Cross Seminary, across Saint Mary's Lake on the Notre Dame campus. He completed high school, made his novitiate, and began his four years of college, again in Holy Cross Seminary, at that time under the direction of its young and genial superior, Father John W. Cavanaugh. Graduating from Notre Dame in 1903, he was assigned to study theology at Holy Cross College in Washington, DC, then under the direction of Father James Burns, and he took additional classes in history at the Catholic University of America. He was ordained a priest and received his doctorate in history, both in 1907. After four years of teaching at Notre Dame, he was named its vice president under Father John Cavanaugh in 1911, spent much of 1918–1919 as chaplain in the American Expeditionary Force in Europe for World War I, and then returned as vice president under both Father Cavanaugh and his successor, Father Burns. The provincial chapter of 1922, deciding not to reappoint Father Burns to a second term, named Father Walsh to succeed him.[1]

There were striking similarities and differences between Father Burns and his successor. Both had graduated from Notre Dame, both had earned doctorates from the Catholic University of America in 1907, both had spent time at non-Catholic educational institutions—Father Burns at Cornell and Harvard, and Father Walsh at Columbia and Johns Hopkins—and both had backgrounds in educational administration, Father Burns as superior of Holy Cross College in Washington, DC, for nineteen years and Father Walsh as Notre Dame's vice president for eleven. But there were differences also. Father Walsh by nature was more outgoing and gracious and made friends more easily. But he was not the educational theorist Father Burns was and generally simply followed the academic direction Father Burns had established. He was deeply concerned over the number of students living off campus and was determined to return them to campus, constructing five residence halls and a massive dining facility to accommodate them.

Father Walsh could hardly have assumed the presidency of the university at a more auspicious time. Student enrollment was high, 1,727 students, the highest it had ever been, and these were all collegians. They were spread satisfactorily throughout the colleges—346 in Arts and Letters and Journalism, 132 in Science, 329 in Engineering and Architecture, 55 in Agriculture, 320 in Law, and 543 in Commerce. The 128 high school students at Holy Cross Seminary and the 100 minims in Saint Edward's Hall were not included, and if the summer session students were added, the total would have been close to 2,500.[2] Classroom space was obviously at a premium. Every classroom in the Main Building was used, plus basement rooms in Sorin and Corby Halls and recitation rooms in the new Lemonnier Library. The faculty was at its highest in 1922 also. It had numbered 62 in 1900, with Holy Cross religious outnumbering laymen 33 to 29. Twenty-two years later, the faculty had almost doubled to a total of 114, the number of available religious had not doubled, and the lay faculty outnumbered the religious 68 to 46. The Holy Cross religious received no salaries, only their basic maintenance and living expenses, and thus the increases in the lay faculty presented a strain on the budget, but fortunately, from Father Burns's fundraising and Knute Rockne's football receipts, additional money was available.[3]

Father Burns had reorganized the university's academics, part of the so-called "Burns Revolution," and Father Walsh and the recently established Academic Council undertook only some tweaking or fine-tuning. The College of Arts and Letters in 1922 housed ten departments—Classics, Letters (English), Philosophy, Modern Languages, Economics, History, Education, Journalism, Music, and Library Science—and awarded seven different undergraduate degrees: bachelor of arts, bachelor of letters, bachelor of philosophy, bachelor of philosophy in journalism, bachelor of philosophy in education, bachelor of library science, and bachelor of music. The content of individual courses changed throughout the decade, depending on who was available to teach in a particular year, and the number of courses offered and the size of the faculty increased as enrollment grew. To cite just one example, the Department of English numbered twelve faculty members in 1922, Father Walsh's first year, and that had doubled by 1928. A few other changes had been introduced: the number of departments had been reduced from ten to eight; politics was included with economics in one department; religion and sociology were added as separate departments; all arts and letters graduates received a single degree, bachelor of arts; and separate Schools of Education, the Fine Arts, and Journalism were established. After 1927, courses and degrees in library science were offered only in the summer session.[4]

The College of Science, begun in the 1860s with Father Carrier, prospered through the decades under Father Zahm and Father Nieuwland, and, under deans Father Nieuwland (1921–1923) and Father Francis Wenninger (1923–1940), the college made few changes in the 1920s. It numbered seven departments when Father Walsh assumed the presidency in 1922—Zoology, Botany, Chemistry, Physics, Mathematics, Pharmacy, and Agriculture—but it awarded nine distinct degrees: bachelor of science, bachelor of science in zoology, bachelor of science in botany, bachelor of science in chemistry, bachelor of science in physics, bachelor of science in mathematics, bachelor of science in pharmacy, bachelor of science in agriculture, and pharmaceutical chemist (PhC). Very little changed over the next six years. The number of departments remained the same, although botany and zoology were combined into a single Department of Biology and a Department of Astronomy was added. The science faculty increased only from 19 to 23, and the degree of pharmaceutical chemist was eliminated. With the closing of the once contemplated Department of Medicine in 1919, premedical students were encouraged to take a program of foundational courses in the newly formed Department of Biology. Some thought it ironic that it was Father Nieuwland as dean of the College of Science who thus began the university's formal premedical program, while he personally had limited faith in doctors, preferring at times to concoct his own medical cures from the chemicals and herbs he knew so well.[5]

Business courses had taken a rather convoluted path in Notre Dame's early decades. A few commerce or mercantilist courses were inserted in the humanities curriculum as early as the 1850s, a commercial track was at times a one-year and at times a two-year program, then a four-year program in the Preparatory (high school) Department in the early twentieth century. In 1913 it was included within the College of Arts and Letters and in 1921 established as the separate College of Foreign and Domestic Commerce, with more than five hundred students, the largest college of all. It was comprised of four departments in 1922—Accounting, Advertising and Marketing, Finance, and Foreign Trade—and offered three undergraduate degrees: bachelor of philosophy in commerce, bachelor of commercial science, and engineering administrator. Over the next few years, finance and accounting would merge into one department, marketing and business administration would comprise another department, and foreign commerce a third. By 1928, the degree of engineering administrator had been dropped, and all undergraduate students received one of two degrees: bachelor of philosophy in commerce or bachelor of commercial science.[6]

The College of Engineering remained relatively stable throughout the 1920s. Civil engineering had begun in 1873, possibly the first engineering program in a Catholic university in America, mechanical engineering in 1886, electrical in 1895, mining engineering in 1908, and chemical in 1910. A program in architecture was established in 1898 and was at least associated with the College of Engineering until 1920 when it became a department within the college. In 1918, a program in industrial engineering was inaugurated to give engineering students a basic education in business as well, but the program was terminated in two years. The most significant achievements of the college until that time were probably the experiments in aeronautics and wind flow by Albert Zahm and the advances in wireless technology of Jerome Green. By 1922, the college was comprised of six departments and awarded degrees in all six: bachelor of science in civil engineering, bachelor of science in mechanical engineering, bachelor of science in electrical engineering, bachelor of science in mining engineering, bachelor of science in chemical engineering, and bachelor of architecture. Francis Kervick and Vincent Fagan, who had joined the Architecture Department in 1909 and 1921 respectively, were the chief designers of some of the major buildings constructed on campus throughout the 1920s.[7]

The Law School saw many changes in the 1920s. Colonel Hoynes had been dean since 1883, his direction of the Law School had become more lax as he aged into his seventies, the General Education Board had indicated that changes were in order, and Hoynes had been replaced as dean by Professor Francis Vurpillat. Vurpillat's tenure as dean was brief and not successful. He asked the university to support him in a dispute with one of his faculty, and also to grant him as dean the additional degree of master of law, both of which the administration declined, and in 1923 Thomas Konop, a former prosecuting attorney, member of the House of Representatives, and public utilities consul, was named dean in his place. In 1919, the Law School had moved from its location in Sorin Hall into the recently vacated Institute of Technology or chemistry building. With the additional space, the library was expanded and in 1925 the first law librarian was hired. Two years of undergraduate college were required in 1925 for admission to the Law School. This was increased to three years in 1928, and by that date students were given greater freedom in the selection of courses. Also by 1928, any student entering the Law School already possessing a bachelor's degree and completing Law School with an average of 85 or above could be awarded the degree of juris doctor (JD) instead of a bachelor of law degree.[8]

Graduate studies at Notre Dame were not well organized from the very beginning and, unfortunately, little improvement was made in the 1920s. In 1905, a Committee of the Faculty on Graduate Studies was set up and requirements for graduate degrees were stipulated: for the master's degree, one year of residency, one major and two minor fields of study, a reading knowledge of one foreign language, a written final examination, and a dissertation of not less than five thousand words; for the doctorate, three years of postgraduate study (at least two at Notre Dame), one major and two minor fields of study, competence in both French and German, a comprehensive examination, and a defense of the dissertation before the faculty. In 1925, thirty-two credit hours were required for the MA degree, ninety-six for the doctorate, and a special section of the annual *Bulletin* was devoted to Graduate Studies. In the course of the 1920s, including the summer sessions, more than two hundred graduate degrees were awarded in fourteen departments but, considering the quality of the faculty and the limits of the library, the program was undoubtedly overly ambitious.[9]

Father Walsh's presidency, 1922–1928, was not a period of significant academic advancement. Among the faculty, Professor Charles Phillips's literary works may have been read and Father Nieuwland's scientific discoveries won him national and even international recognition, but most of the faculty were little known off the campus. With the great increase in student enrollment, the administration's emphasis was primarily on finding faculty and classrooms and student residences to carry on as in the past. Father Walsh may have preferred a period of academic calm after Father Burns's "revolution" and not a time for creative change and innovation. His priorities seemed elsewhere.

At least one faculty member lamented the lack of academic progress. English professor George Shuster confided to his wife in late 1923:[10]

And so I don't mind telling you that as matters are now, I should really very much like to get away from Notre Dame. Even though I love the place and love the purpose to which it has been dedicated, I must admit that it seems impossible to expect of Notre Dame anything like what I had once hoped for from it. We have an administration now without any vision or sense of scholarship—much less poetry. It has deteriorated so far that the candid opinion of all the lay faculty is very pessimistic. And of course I saw the future as it could be seen under Father Burns—a new Louvain, with dreams steadily coming true. I have spent many a bitter hour beside the ashes of a dying dream.

Shuster had been born of German-American parents (the original spelling of the name was "Schuster," and his parents and sisters retained it) in Lancaster, Wisconsin, in 1894. He graduated from Notre Dame in 1915, served in World War I, received a Certificat d'Aptitude in French culture from the University of Poitiers, and taught at Notre Dame from 1919 to 1924, earning an MA in 1920 and chairing the English Department from 1920 to 1924. In 1924 he moved to New York, began writing for the recently founded magazine *Commonweal,* and the following year published two articles critical of Catholic higher education in the United States. In the first article, entitled "Have We Any Scholars?" in *America* magazine, he wrote:[11]

> It appears to me, however, that if we try to view Catholic academic life as a whole, we shall find that during the past seventy-five years it has produced not a single great literary man or writer on literary subjects; not a scientist, excepting possibly two or three chemists and seismologists, who has made an original contribution to the vast catalogue of recent discoveries; not an historian whose study of a definite field has resulted in a new orientation of our minds toward the past; and, with one exception, no economist whose leadership has divined new and better social directions. If we are honest, we must admit that during seventy-five years of almost feverish intellectual activity we have had no influence on the general culture of America other than what has come from a passably active endeavor to spread to the four winds knowledge accumulated either by our ancestors or by sectarian scholars.

He found scholarly research in Catholic universities deficient:[12]

I can only say that a relatively careful examination of some twenty-five doctorate theses prepared in Catholic colleges on the subjects relating to English literature forced me to conclude that not a single one would have been accepted, simply as research, at a university of the first rank. Almost every one revealed a meager knowledge of historical background or linguistics; scarcely any were even comparatively original studies; and only three disclosed on the part of the authors a trained aptitude for investigating a problem.

In his second piece, an unsigned editorial in *Commonweal*, he made it clear that he included Notre Dame, his undergraduate alma mater and his teaching home for five years, in his criticism:[13]

But, on our part, we believe that for the colleges the problem is not going to be settled by merely haranguing about social duties and the obligations of citizenship. What is needed is an awakening of the student's intellectual life—the culture of a mind for its own sake, with which will come a sympathetic realization of those broad issues upon which the stability of our human world ultimately depends. So long as Catholic education refuses to concede that its goal is not quantity—not buildings and "splurge," but quality—excellent quality achieved at no matter what cost—it will talk in vain about "Christian brotherhood." Leadership is the by-product of intellectual exercise and fidelity to moral obligations. We have not developed such leadership. Why? Because we have not led in education: apart from a number of good professional schools, we have superimposed upon a splendid system of elementary training little more than excellence—in football! There is the rub.

This was the year of the "Four Horsemen," the Rose Bowl victory over Stanford, and the national championship. The editorial was also critical of the religious program of Father O'Hara, Notre Dame's popular prefect of religion, and some at the university never forgave Shuster for this public criticism.

Father Walsh's priorities at the time were focused on student life outside the classroom. Student enrollment was approaching two thousand, and more than six hundred were living off campus. Father Walsh preferred that everyone live on campus where Mass and religious exercises were readily available, where priests were closer at hand with counsel and advice, and where the temptations of bars and dance halls were further distant. The rate of absenteeism from class of off campus students was twice that of on campus students, and their overall academic average was lower. In addition, the food and lodging money of off campus students stayed off campus, and was of no benefit to the university. The problem could be ameliorated on other campuses by the presence of fraternity houses, but Notre Dame was not interested.[14]

Father Walsh certainly wanted all first-year students, freshmen, living on campus, and as more and more high school seniors applied and were accepted for the fall of 1922, increasing overall enrollment further, new lodging needed to be found, and quickly. Father Walsh had been appointed president only in June and there was not sufficient time to review competing architectural plans, put out bids to contractors, and construct a four-story residence hall similar to Sorin, Corby, or Walsh before September. A wooden frame building, two stories high, two hundred seventy feet in length and forty-five in depth, was constructed early that summer, north of and perpendicular to the east end of the gymnasium, able to accommodate one hundred seventy-six students in double rooms. Called Freshman Hall, it was located approximately where Breen-Phillips was later built and was at least a start toward the east campus of the university.[15]

But these students would return the following fall as sophomores and additional lodging was needed for them. At a right angle to the north end of Freshman Hall, stretching roughly from the later location of Zahm Hall toward the area where Farley Hall was later built, a second hall was built in the summer of 1923 to accommodate one hundred eighty-six of these sophomores. This "Sophomore Hall" was three hundred by thirty-seven feet and the exterior was a cover of pebble-dash stucco over the lathing. These two new buildings, called the "Cardboard Palaces" by the students, were not meant to be permanent, but the accommodations were adequate and they provided for an additional three hundred sixty students to reside on campus, which was where Father Walsh wanted them.[16]

Those two halls addressed part of the problem temporarily, but as enrollment continued to rise, a more permanent solution had to be found. Three new residence halls were planned, to be designed by Notre Dame architecture professors Francis Kervick and Vincent Fagan. In Father Sorin's original plan, on the axis leading south from the Main Building, academic buildings were on the east—Washington Hall, Science Hall, the Institute of Technology, and (a little behind) Chemistry Hall—and residence halls were on the west—Sorin Hall, Corby Hall, Walsh Hall, Badin Hall, and even Old College. Professor Kervick wanted to remain on the west side of Father Sorin's central axis but did not want to continue southward, too far from the lake. After all, the university was named Notre Dame du Lac, Our Lady of the Lake, and the lake should remain integral to the campus plan. There was an east-west county road (St. Joseph's Road, later Dorr Road) running just south of Badin Hall, the Father Sorin statue, and the post office, and Kervick would build along it. The three buildings were thus designed to begin immediately west of Badin Hall (and immediately south of the Lemonnier Library) and continue to the west, remaining close to the lake.[17]

The first hall built, in 1924, was Howard Hall. It was originally to be called Old Students' Hall, in part a student residence hall and in part a convenient residence for alumni, "old students," returning to campus for any reason, but the Alumni Association had generously contributed the $60,000 collected for the Old Students' Hall to Father Burns's million-dollar fund drive. During construction it was usually referred to as Old Students' Hall but eventually it was decided to name it for Timothy Howard, longtime Notre Dame professor and South Bend and Indiana public official. It was the first truly Gothic building on campus and the first named for a layman (if one excepts Washington Hall).[18]

The hall, built immediately to the south of the Lemonnier Library, was constructed of two wings, with a two-story arch dividing the two and leaving the lake visible to Badin Hall on the central axis. The structure was 204 feet in length and 87 feet in width at the widest and was constructed of buff brick and Bedford stone that harmonized with the surrounding buildings. Professor Fagan's artwork decorated the exterior near the arch—the football player and a squirrel on the east side representing autumn and a statue of Saint Timothy (for Timothy Howard) and an owl, representing wisdom, peering at a crying boy on the west side. The main entrance to each wing was under the central arch, although other doors opened to the sidewalk encircling the building. The hall held ninety-one rooms, mostly singles but with several doubles also, and a central tower over the arch that one author called the hall's "most compelling feature." The prefects resided in rooms under the tower. For the first time there were lounges at the ends of each corridor, and there was also a chapel on the first floor and a room in the basement for smoking and games. It could accommodate as many as 156 students and opened in the fall of 1925.[19]

As Howard Hall was being completed, a second hall was constructed immediately to the west and set back several feet so as not to block Howard Hall's view of the lake. It was the largest of the three halls, with one hundred twenty-seven rooms to accommodate two hundred fifty students, and was named for Father Andrew Morrissey, Notre Dame's president from 1893 to 1905 and provincial superior from 1906 to 1920. Architecturally it harmonized well with Howard Hall, with individual characteristics. Four stories in height, built Gothic style in brick, with reinforced concrete and limestone trim, it too was surmounted by a tower, this one with a copper flèche in the center. However, the front door was off-center and the roof lines were mismatched. An x-shaped cross on the front represented the crucifixion of Saint Andrew, the main door opened onto an oak-paneled lobby and large fireplace, and there was a balcony on the west wing, per-haps for viewing passing processions along the lake. The hall was not ready for occupancy until the fall of 1926 due to bad weather the previous winter.[20]

The third hall, constructed closest to the lake, was Lyons Hall, named for another longtime lay professor, Joseph Lyons. Similar to Howard Hall, an arch-way separated a north and south wing and allowed a view of the lake from the rest of campus on the east. Begun in the fall of 1925, it was to accommodate two hundred students, most of them in private rooms, and some rooms in the smaller northern wing were reserved for professors. In fact, one or two bachelor dons re-sided there over the next fifty years. The hall contained a comfortable lounge for students, a smoking room, and a large quiet chapel in the basement that reminded some of a castle dungeon. A statue of Saint Joseph, the patron saint of Professor Joseph Lyons, crowned the archway.[21]

Father Walsh was successful in relocating close to eight hundred students back on campus, but he also had to feed them. Students at that time had two choices: eating in the refectory on the ground floor of the Main Building, the food having been prepared by the sisters in the French Quarter and rushed into the Main Building refectory, or paying to eat in Clark's cafeteria, which had opened in 1917 in the basement of Badin Hall. Students were charged $350 per year to eat in the Main Building refectory, so most students preferred to eat in Clark's cafeteria and pay by the meal, and by 1922 only one hundred twenty-five students were eating in the Main Building. The university realized it was losing thousands of dollars and Father Walsh was determined to have a new and larger dining facility available when Mr. Clark's lease expired in a couple of years. It was not to be renewed, and the noted American architect, Ralph Adams Cram, who had re-cently received an honorary doctorate from Notre Dame, offered to submit plans for a new dining hall gratis. He visited campus in late 1925, surveyed various pos-sible sites, and drew up plans for a large and most impressive dining hall. It was eventually judged too expensive and, with the aid of Notre Dame architects Fran-cis Kervick and Vincent Fagan, the scale was reduced.[22] The site selected was on the farmland south of Badin Hall, across the east-west Saint Joseph's or Dorr

Road, and was the beginning of a new quadrangle with Howard, Morrissey, and Lyons Halls on its north side. It was two hundred thirty-two feet in length and two hundred four in width, with the main entrance facing the rest of campus to the north. The exterior bricks were a distinctive reddish-brown, three arches graced the main entrance, lancet windows allowed light throughout the building, and a thirty-foot flèche mirrored the one on Morrissey Hall. Two large, two-story dining rooms, one at each end, could accommodate one thousand students each, and a public cafeteria between the two could seat three hundred. Behind the cafeteria was the massive kitchen. The second floor held a faculty dining room, a private room for trustee lunches, and business offices. The basement contained restrooms, a smoking room, a cloakroom, refrigerated storage areas, vegetable preparation rooms, a butcher shop, and a freezing room. The facility was designed to serve up to two thousand at a seating, and did so efficiently.[23]

With the continued increase in student enrollment—Father Walsh set a limit of 2,500 but it was not respected—other facilities clamored for enlargement also. One of these was the gymnasium, and not only for the increased student enrollment. The gymnasium did not have a satisfactory wooden basketball floor, seating was so limited that only one-half of the student body could be admitted to any game, and for two years the basketball team played its home games on the South Bend YMCA court because visiting teams refused to play on the Notre Dame court. In 1925 an extension was built onto the east end of the gymnasium. It was one hundred thirty by one hundred feet, with wings on each side for stands. The removable hardwood basketball floor was ninety-eight feet by fifty-four and the facility could now seat five thousand. Under the stands on the south wing were the locker rooms, showers, two handball courts, and the office of the director of athletics. The area under the stands of the north wing was used for storage.[24]

The construction project that was particularly close to Father Walsh's heart was the addition of the Memorial Door to Sacred Heart Church. Father Walsh had been a chaplain in World War I, he had seen war firsthand, he had seen soldiers die, and he was eager to see Notre Dame honor students and graduates who had lost their lives in that conflict. Under the direction of Professor Kervick again, a small extension was built onto the eastern entrance of the church. The addition was Gothic, to harmonize with the rest of the church, plaques on each side listed the forty-six who had lost their lives, a statue of Saint Joan of Arc adorned one side of the entrance and a statue of Saint Michael the Archangel the other side. Above the door was placed the seal of the university and in three distinct lines were carved the words "In Glory Everlasting," "Our Gallant Dead," and "God,

Country, Notre Dame." The shade covering the inside ceiling light was—and is—the doughboy helmet worn by Father Charles O'Donnell as chaplain during World War I.[25]

Two other construction projects, that were most important but seldom seen, were also undertaken about this time. The first was a new well. With the expansion of the university, approximately 450 gallons of water were being drawn from Saint Joseph's Lake each minute, and the level of the lake was dropping considerably. To remedy this, a new source of water was sought. A well was dug close to the new Moreau Seminary on the north side of the lake, the well yielded approximately 500 gallons a minute, and the level of the lake rose 45 inches in a few months. The second project was necessitated by the start of the new quadrangle on the south side of campus—Howard, Morrissey, Lyons, and the new dining hall. How could sufficient heat and electricity be supplied that far from the power plant behind the Main Building? Father Thomas Steiner, professor of civil engineering and soon to be named dean of the College of Engineering, recommended a series of underground tunnels to carry the utilities to each campus building. Father Steiner had graduated from Notre Dame in 1899, had been a member of the varsity basketball team and a monogram winner, and had worked for a time with the Illinois Central and Big Four Railroads. He joined the Notre Dame faculty in 1911, entered the seminary in 1914, and was ordained a priest in 1918. The campus was torn up quite inconveniently as tunnels were dug to every building, with frequent manholes to allow for easy access for maintenance, and since then the campus utilities have been preserved from the vagaries of the weather.[26]

Another project, which was begun under Father Walsh but completed under his successor, was the Notre Dame golf course. Mr. William J. Burke, president of the Vulcan Golf Company of Portsmouth, Ohio, volunteered to build a golf course at Notre Dame at his own expense with his own engineers if the university would provide the land. Land Notre Dame had aplenty. The sport was becoming increasingly popular in the 1920s and it could provide wholesome recreation and exercise for the students, so the university accepted the offer and designated farmland south and southwest of the campus for its construction. The university still had hundreds of acres of farmland north, east, and southeast of the campus, and the brothers also worked Saint Joseph's Farm eight miles to the northeast. The course was ready for play by the fall of 1929, but Mr. Burke had died before its completion and so the course was named the Burke Memorial Golf Course.[27]

Golf was not the only sport on campus coming into its own in the 1920s. Varsity basketball also took a giant step forward during the early years of the decade, between Knute Rockne's 1920 team with George Gipp and his 1924 team with the Four Horsemen, and Rockne himself deserves much of the credit. As director of athletics, in 1923 he hired George Keogan as Notre Dame's basketball coach. Basketball had already been played on campus for decades. The first varsity game apparently took place in 1897 against the Fort Wayne YMCA, with Notre Dame the victor 26 to 11. The new fieldhouse was built in 1899, burned to the ground in 1900, and then was rebuilt in 1901 with a clay floor for basketball, making dribbling always an uncertain challenge. Jesse Harper was hired in 1912 to coach football, baseball, track, and basketball, and he moved home games to gyms in South Bend for their wooden floors. In 1914–1915, two players, Rupe Mills and "Dutch" Bergman, won monograms in four sports, a feat not duplicated until Johnny Lujack in 1943–1944. Whenever Harper was occupied with one of his other sports, his assistant, Knute Rockne, coached basketball, and in 1918, the year Rockne replaced Harper as head football coach, Rockne's former teammate, Gus Dorais, was named Notre Dame basketball coach. Basketball was going through a dry spell at the time. Rockne was one and five in games he coached, in 1919 Notre Dame lost all five games to other Indiana teams (Western State Normal, DePauw, Wabash, Franklin, and Indiana) by an average of twenty points each, and the record from 1918 to 1923, under coaches Dorais and Walter Halas (brother of George) was 32 and 63.[28]

George Keogan had earlier coached at several high schools and at Superior State Teachers College in Wisconsin, Saint Thomas College in Saint Paul, Minnesota, Alleghany College in Pennsylvania, and Valparaiso University in Indiana, compiling a record at these last three stops of close to 140 and 10. In his twenty years as head coach at Notre Dame, he compiled an equally commendable record of 327 wins and 94 losses, with excellent seasons of 19–1 in 1925–1926 and 1926–1927, 20–3 in 1936–1937 and 1937–1938, and 22–2–1 in 1935–1936, and he never had a losing season. In 1925–1926 he suffered only one defeat while Knute Rockne in football suffered two. Two of his stars on the 1924 team were Clem Crowe and Noble Kizer, two of the Seven Mules blocking for Rockne's Four Horsemen, and Keogan often had to arrange a softer schedule in the fall when some of his best players were on the football field. His greatest player of all also spent each fall playing football: Ed "Moose" Krause, 1931–1934. Standing six foot three and bulky, Krause could plug up the keyhole and dominate the backboards. Win or lose, he normally scored one-third of Notre Dame's total points each game, and most games were wins, with a record of 54 and 12 during his three years. He was named All-American all three years, despite playing only in the spring. In his most memorable feat, he was knocked to the floor in a struggle for a rebound in the Butler game in 1933, somehow corralled the ball while lying on his back, threw it at the basket, and tied the score as time expired. When Coach Keogan arrived at practice the next day, several players were lying on their backs, practicing Krause's shot, but the coach was not amused. Keogan is often credited with designing "pivot" plays (still used today) to take advantage of Krause's dominance and designing the "shifting man to man defense" to counter anyone else using it. He was not the only coach, of course, who had to compete with football or other sports for players. In 1937 Notre Dame lost to an Illinois team led by future baseball star Lou Boudreau and in 1941 defeated a Northwestern team led by future Hall of Fame footballer Otto Graham. In 1939, Notre Dame lost to a Purdue team led by South Bend's own Johnny Wooden. Not to be completely outdone by Wooden, four of Keogan's own players went on to successful coaching careers: George Ireland at Loyola in Chicago, Ray Meyer at DePaul, and "Moose" Krause and John Jordan back at Notre Dame. The 1930s witnessed other remarkable basketball incidents in addition to Krause's shot from his back. In early 1935, the timekeeper in a game against Pittsburgh forgot to start the clock for the half. Over ten minutes elapsed before it was noticed, the clock was finally started, and the game eventually played for fifty-two and a half minutes instead of forty. One year the team played two doubleheaders (two games the same day) and in at least one doubleheader Keogan fielded two entirely different teams and still won both. That same year, the game against Northwestern ended officially in a tie when a postgame review reportedly revealed that a Notre Dame foul shot had gone unrecorded, mistakenly giving Northwestern a 20–19 victory, but the tie could not be broken since both teams were already taking showers. Doc Carlson, the Pittsburgh coach, insisted that in the closing seconds of his game at Notre Dame in 1931, an elderly lady tapped the timekeeper on the shoulder, asked him to wait, and during the delay Notre Dame scored the tying basket.[29]

With consistently winning seasons, All-American players "Moose" Krause, Johnny Moir, and Paul Nowak to watch, and such unusual incidents to experience, the student body usually crowded into the five-thousand-seat gymnasium, leaving few seats for townspeople and resulting in almost no gate from visiting team fans (Notre Dame students entered free). Because of the phenomenal success and national publicity of Knute Rockne's football teams, Notre Dame athletics in the eyes of many in the 1930s still meant football, but thanks to George Keogan, his winning record, the players he developed, and his fine representation of the university, when he died unexpectedly in the midst of the 1942–1943 season (on February 17, 1943), basketball at Notre Dame had been firmly established.

Relocating more and more students on campus throughout the 1920s probably reduced some of the tension between Notre Dame and the city, but the most celebrated conflict between the two occurred in the spring of 1924. Catholics across the country were becoming openly proud of this still relatively small college in Indiana. Father John Cavanaugh's oratory had given the university national publicity, every football fan knew the name Geroge Gipp, and Catholics were pleased that Rockne's teams were proving equal to or better than any in the country. American Catholics, clergy and laity alike, could look to Notre Dame with a sense of deep pride—pride in the university, pride in their religion, and pride in themselves.

But there were those who did not approve of this growing sense of Catholic pride, and one of those groups in Indiana was the Ku Klux Klan. The first Ku Klux Klan had been founded in Pulaski, Tennessee, in 1866, after the close of the Civil War. Many Southern leaders had been disenfranchised and barred from public office because of their part in the war, Northern whites with various motives hurried into former Confederate states to take advantage of the political vacuum, and former slaves, often with little education and even less experience with democracy, were now eligible to vote and hold public office. It was a goal of the Klan to so intimidate these recent freedmen (and occasionally white Northerners) that they would not exercise these rights. The Klan held power in several states for three or four years through threats, acts of violence, and ready access to law enforcement officials, judges, and members of juries. The Federal Force Act of 1870 and the Ku Klux Klan Act of 1871 curbed their activities, and with the removal of the federal troops from the South and the end of Reconstruction after the election of 1876, local white leaders returned to power and the disenfranchisement of black Americans was achieved through discriminatory legislation.[30]

The Klan was revived in 1915, this time in Stone Mountain, Georgia, but it was different. The members still dressed in white robes and covered their faces with hoods, and still resorted at times to intimidation and violence, but in addition to black Americans, their targets now were Catholics, Jews, immigrants, and at times organized labor. The Klan numbered close to five million in the mid-1920s and its influence and activities were no longer centered in the South but were strongest in the rural Midwest—Indiana, Ohio, Michigan, and Illinois—and, surprisingly, Oregon in the far Northwest. In Oregon it was successful in passing legislation mandating attendance at public schools, but Catholic nuns challenged the law to protect their own schools and the law was invalidated. The Klan was especially strong in Indiana. David C. Stephenson was northern Grand Dragon for a time and was a most successful salesman. With emphasis on patriotism, Christian (Protestant) virtues, and fear of foreign contamination, he recruited religious ministers, business leaders, and politicians to his cause. To show off Klan strength, and to recruit new members, he sponsored parades and rallies in cities throughout the state, and by 1924 Klan membership in the state may have reached four hundred thousand. Said Stephenson: "We're going to klux Indiana as she's never been kluxed before!"[31] But there was a problem, as one historian noted:[32]

> Steve [Stephenson] was concerned over a persistent weak spot in the kluxing of Indiana—a pocket where the Klan had had much difficulty. The area was South Bend, the state's second largest city. The publisher of the South Bend *Tribune*, Frederick Miller, was stridently anti-Klan. The city had a thriving chapter of the Unity League and a sizable population of immigrants and Catholics. But the biggest problem was that "mackerel-snapping" Notre Dame University. The legendary Knute Rockne was in charge of its famous football team, and recently, the celebrated George "the Gipper" Gipp had converted to Catholicism on his deathbed. Notre Dame was quickly becoming the state's most popular instrument of nationwide publicity, and the St. Joseph Valley Klavern was at a loss over what to do about it. One of its members volunteered to fly over the university in a helium balloon and dynamite it from the air. That idea had been shelved.

Stephenson was confident that he knew what to do. He would hold a state convention, or Klonkave, in South Bend, almost at Notre Dame's front door. The date set was the weekend of May 17–19. On May 16, Notre Dame's prefect of discipline, Father J. Hugh O'Donnell, met with the South Bend police chief to express concern that if any public, anti-Catholic Klan parade took place, Notre Dame students, heavily Catholic and probably outnumbering the Klansmen, might want to respond. The chief assured Father O'Donnell that there would be no parade because the request for a parade permit had been denied. Father O'Donnell was grateful, but the 17th was a Saturday, and would all the students remain on campus? Father Walsh issued a directive that was pinned on bulletin boards in all residence halls and other prominent places across campus:[33]

It has been rumored that the Ku Klux Klan is to hold some sort of gathering in the vicinity of South Bend, this evening. There is also a rumor to the effect that there may be a parade of the Klan in South Bend. Notre Dame is interested in the proposed meeting of the Klan, but not to the extent of wishing to interfere with whatever plans may have been made for a demonstration. Similar attempts of the Klan to flaunt its strength have resulted in riotous situations, sometimes in the loss of life.

However aggravating the appearance of the Klan may be, remember that lawlessness begets lawlessness. Young blood and thoughtlessness may consider it a duty to show what a real American thinks of the Klan. There is only one duty that presents itself to Notre Dame men, under the circumstances, and that is to ignore whatever demonstration may take place today. This suggestion should be taken in all seriousness. It is my wish that the Klan be ignored, as they deserve to be ignored, and that the students avoid any occasion of coming into contact with our Klan brethren during their visit to South Bend. Let the South Bend authorities take care of the situation. The place for Notre Dame men, this afternoon and tonight, is on the Notre Dame campus. Any injury, or even a more serious mishap, to a single Notre Dame man would be too great a price to pay for a protest, which in the nature of things is unnecessary and highly undesirable to the authorities of both the University and South Bend.

As off campus students arrived on campus the afternoon of the 16th and the morning of the 17th, they spoke of the increasing number of visitors on the streets, presumably arriving Klansmen. On campus students may have wanted to see for themselves, or perhaps wanted to assure the visitors they were not welcome, and they boarded the streetcar heading for town. When they met a man carrying what looked like a bundle of clothes, they presumed it was a Klan robe, grabbed it, and ran. Some waited at the train station, asked arriving gentlemen if they were here for the rally, led them down a side street, stole their robes, maybe roughed them up a bit, and ran away. The local Klan headquarters were on the third floor of a downtown building, and a grocery store was nearby. Some students helped themselves to a few potatoes and then threw them to break windows in the Klan offices. Rumor had it that Harry Stuhldreher, quarterback on the 1923 and 1924 football teams, clearly had the most accurate throwing arm. Klansmen thought it better to remain off the streets.[34]

The next day, Sunday, was quiet. Hiram Evans, the Klan's Imperial Wizard, called a meeting of Indiana Klansmen in Indianapolis in an effort to heal a breach between the national Klan and the state branch. It was not successful. The chief of police thought he had done his part by preventing a public parade, and yet the students had gotten out of hand. Local citizens did not like being accosted on the street and asked if they were Klan members, and they deplored the broken windows, unsafe streets, and even physical harm to some visitors. Students had taken things into their own hands and seemed to have the run of the city, the disturbance had kept local residents away from the downtown area, and they were not pleased.[35]

Monday started out a quiet day. The students attended classes and the Klansmen held their meetings in town. But after dinner that evening, someone called the public telephone in Freshman Hall and said, apparently falsely, that the Klansmen had apprehended and were beating a Notre Dame student on the courthouse lawn. Word spread quickly and over a hundred students began running into town to rescue their companion. Fearing trouble, and smarting from criticism of his handling of the Saturday confrontation, the police chief had his force assembled but out of sight. When their meeting ended at nine o'clock, the Klansmen emerged from their building, only to see the band of students gathered before them. One student hurled a potato or other object at the lighted cross in the third-floor Klan window and, as other students began to look for similar projectiles, the police moved in. The students were caught between the police behind them and the Klansmen in front. The students may have had the advantage of numbers but they knew better than to fight the police. Trying to avoid a conflict, someone had called Father Walsh to come and assist. Father Walsh waited on the courthouse lawn and Father O'Donnell, prefect of discipline, met with students and urged them to repair there. To be better seen and heard, Father Walsh mounted one of the memorial canons and addressed the students as he must have addressed soldiers during his years as army chaplain in World War I. His words were conciliatory but direct:[36]

Whatever challenge may have been offered tonight to your patriotism, whatever insult may have been offered to your religion, you can show your loyalty to Notre Dame and to South Bend by ignoring all threats. The constituted authorities have only the desire to preserve order and peace and protect everyone. That is their duty. Others can well leave to their hands the maintenance of peace and punishment of anything that is wrong. If tonight there have been violations of law, it is not the duty of you and your companions to search out the offenders.

I know that in the midst of excitement, you are swayed by emotions that impel you to answer challenge with force. As I said in the statement issued last Saturday, a single injury to a Notre Dame student would be too great a price to pay for any deed or any program that concerned itself with antagonisms. I should dislike very much to be obliged to make explanations to the parents of any student who might be injured—even killed—in a disturbance that could arise out of any demonstration such as has been started tonight.

There is no loyalty that is greater than the patriotism of a Notre Dame student. There is no conception of duty higher than that which a Notre Dame man holds for his religion or his university. I know that if tonight any of the property of the university or any of its privileges were threatened, and I should call upon you, you would rise to a man to protect it. It is with the same loyalty to Notre Dame that I appeal to you to show your respect for South Bend and the authority of the city by dispersing.

This the students did, and it was the last confrontation. The following year, Stephenson was convicted of assault and second-degree murder, and his disgrace hastened the decline of the Klan, certainly in Indiana but also throughout the Midwest.[37]

If the 1920s saw this rise in anti-Catholic sentiment throughout the Midwest, it also witnessed an increase in religious fervor and religious practice on the Notre Dame campus. The person chiefly responsible for this increase was the prefect of religion, Father John O'Hara, whom, for his religious prominence, the students affectionately called "The Pope." Father O'Hara had been born in Ann Arbor, Michigan, in 1888, but the family moved within two years to Peru, Indiana, and enrolled in Saint Charles parish. It was a German parish, as were many in the Midwest at that time, and the sermon each Sunday was delivered in both English and German. The English speakers were expected to say their rosary during the German sermon. Young John attended the parish grade school and was taught by the Sisters of Providence, the order founded by Father Jacques Dujarié in France a century before, and he then attended the city's public high school. In 1905, President Theodore Roosevelt appointed John's father United States consul in Montevideo, Uruguay, and John, at age seventeen, went along as secretary. He attended the Jesuit Colegio del Sagrado Corazón but also withdrew for a time to work on a ranch in Argentina, hoping the fresh air and exercise would be good for his health. In 1907, Mr. O'Hara was transferred to the consulate in Santos, Brazil, and John accompanied him again.[38]

John returned to the United States in the summer of 1908 and, desiring to continue his education, entered the University of Notre Dame the following January. With his transcripts from the Colegio del Sagado Corazón, he graduated from Notre Dame in 1911 and entered the Holy Cross Novitiate to begin preparation for the priesthood. He studied theology at Holy Cross College in Washington, DC, where Father Burns was rector, attended classes at the Catholic University of America in Latin American history, and was ordained a priest in 1916. He remained in Washington for a fourth and final year of theology, spent some time at the Wharton School of Finance and a commercial house in New York, joined the Notre Dame faculty in 1917, and was named its first dean of the College of Foreign and Domestic Commerce in 1921. As dean, he was personally acquainted with the prominent business leaders and Catholic philanthropists W. R. Grace and Edwin F. Hurley, and they or their families became major benefactors to the university. He also made trips through Latin America to recruit students, perhaps in imitation of Father Zahm. But Father O'Hara had also been named prefect of religion in 1918, and in 1924 he resigned his position as dean to devote himself full-time to his prefect of religion responsibilities.[39]

When the O'Hara family returned to the United States from South America, they settled in Indianapolis, and Saints Peter and Paul Cathedral became their home parish. The pastor was Auxiliary Bishop Joseph Chartrand, a strong advocate of frequent Confession and frequent Communion, as the Holy Father, Pope Pius X, was advocating at the time. Bishop Chartrand urged everyone, especially youths, to attend Mass frequently, he spent hours during the day in the confessional, and he would often leave the confessional to distribute Holy Communion to anyone who had been unable to attend Mass that morning. John O'Hara was one of the youths Bishop Chartrand befriended, he was deeply influenced by the bishop's devotion to Confession, Mass, and Communion, and this influence was to be reflected in the religious program he established at Notre Dame as prefect of religion.[40]

At this time, university regulations required that all students attend Mass on Sunday and one other day each week. Some sodalities, like the Archconfraternity, added Mass on Saturday, and members of the Angel Guardians of the Sanctuary and other Mass-serving groups assisted at Mass as scheduled. To encourage a more meaningful and more frequent attendance at Mass, Father O'Hara in

1921 began a series of weekly conferences on the Mass and had pamphlets on the Mass readily available to all students. He urged the use of the missal as early as 1923. Daily Mass attendance in the 1920s was high, and it rose throughout the decade, increasing from approximately 37 percent in 1922–1923 to 45 percent in 1928–1929.[41]

The practice that Father O'Hara may have been best known for—and often criticized for—was his advocacy of the reception of Communion even outside of Mass. He certainly preferred that Communion be received within Mass and, as a student, had helped to organize in 1911 the Daily Communion or Eucharistic League where students could add their names to a list and be awakened early each morning for Mass. But if a student, for whatever reason, did not attend Mass in the morning and still wished to receive Communion, Father O'Hara was available to distribute Communion throughout the morning, whenever asked. The student, of course, always had to be fasting since midnight. In fact, Father O'Hara's room was eventually wired so that a student could press a buzzer in the chapel that would sound in the prefect's room, one buzz for Communion and two for Confession. Father O'Hara was convinced that the frequent reception of Communion, in Mass or outside, was a strong help to keep the students in the state of grace. His efforts bore fruit. In 1922–1923, it was estimated that 38.9 percent of Catholic students received Communion daily (666 out of 1,709) and in 1930–1931, 51 percent (1,504 out of 2,946). Since never more than 13 percent of these Communions were received outside of Mass, Father O'Hara insisted that the practice did not discourage attendance at Mass but actually encouraged it:[42]

> Time is proving to well-intentioned critics who have condemned the University for its free administration of Holy Communion outside of Mass that devotion to Holy Communion breeds devotion to the Mass. Each passing year has marked the increase in attendance at the Holy Sacrifice; the current year particularly has witnessed a diminution in the number of late communicants, although there has been an increase of 107 in the total number of communicants (during the fall months of 1927).

Opportunities for Confession were similarly available. In the main church's basement chapel, called the Brownson Memorial Chapel because Orestes Brownson was buried there, confessions were heard each morning before breakfast and each evening after dinner, and they were heard each evening in the residence halls also. The prefect of religion was available in his office throughout most of the day for Confession or Communion. But the most accessible time and place for Confession was before and even during Sunday Masses in the main church. As Father O'Hara noted:[43]

> The most-used opportunity for confession . . . is during the four Sunday Masses; and while confessions at this time are condemned by many lovers of order the practice is again justified by results. A sermon, for instance, or a request for prayers for some urgent intention, may determine a lax student to go to confession. This determination may grow weak if the prospective penitent has to wait until evening to carry out his resolution, and it will almost of necessity vanish if the wait is until the following Saturday night. Furthermore, there is a compelling force in the example of the great throngs of communicants who receive Sunday after Sunday, and invariably, when the students rise at the *Domine, non sum dignus* to approach the Holy Table, others make their way to the confessionals.

Father O'Hara realized, of course, that Confession was not only a preparation for receiving Holy Communion but was an important sacrament and means of grace in itself:[44]

> There is a little tendency on the part of the frequent communicants to abolish the Sacrament of Penance. Frequent instructions are given on the confession of devotion, which is little understood by the student on entrance. The student soon comes to realize that the Sacrament of Penance, which is so frequently regarded as simply a preparation for Holy Communion, is a sacrament in itself with its own peculiar graces.

Devotion to Mass and Holy Communion led naturally to adoration of the Blessed Sacrament. Forty Hours devotion was celebrated from the very founding of the university, as was Exposition on Holy Thursday (since students did not leave campus for Holy Week and Easter), and Benediction of the Blessed Sacrament was always popular. In 1921 Father O'Hara began public Exposition and adoration of the Blessed Sacrament all-day on the first Friday of each month. He encouraged students to vest in cassock and surplice and kneel in the sanctuary for agreed-upon hour or half-hour periods. He had hopes for a perpetual adoration chapel on campus someday but realized that the university was not yet ready for that.[45]

Novenas, nine consecutive days of prayer, became prominent religious devotions on campus in the 1920s. Two novenas of Communions (receiving Communion on nine consecutive days) were sponsored during World War I, asking God's protection on Notre Dame students then in the military. Other novenas followed. Throughout the decade there were novenas for parents, for students' families, for deceased friends and relatives, for success in exams, for purity, for vocations, for happy marriages, even occasionally for the football team. During Father O'Hara's tenure as prefect of religion, there was an average of seventeen nine-day novenas each year, occupying approximately 65 percent of the school year. In 1925–1926, twenty-one novenas were scheduled, occupying 80 percent of the time.[46]

Few devotions or religious practices seemed to slip past Father O'Hara's attention. At a university dedicated to the Blessed Mother, the rosary had long been a part of official May and October devotions, and perhaps one in six students recited the rosary daily in the 1920s. In public devotions, the Litany of the Blessed Virgin held a prominent place. A few students made daily visits to the Grotto also. The Way of the Cross was a popular devotion each Lent, and the outdoor Stations of the Cross along Saint Joseph's Lake were erected in 1923. Periodic retreats were held for individual student groups, and spiritual conferences by different priests abounded. Father O'Hara put pamphlet racks in the back of each hall chapel and kept them supplied with pertinent reading material. In 1924–1925, an estimated five thousand religious medals were distributed through his office.[47]

These religious programs and periodic devotions were publicized across campus through Father O'Hara's *Religious Bulletin*. He was the first dean of the College of Foreign and Domestic Commerce, he had studied marketing, advertising, and salesmanship, and he knew the importance of making his religious program, or any program, known and accessible to its patrons. The 1920s was the great age of print advertising, and Father O'Hara turned to print. He began the *Bulletin* in the fall of 1921, during a three-day mission or retreat opening the new school year, to encourage all to attend the mission and to remind students of the mission's daily schedule. The *Mission Bulletin* proved successful and Father O'Hara decided to continue it, at first a couple of times a week and then daily. After the first four issues, the name was changed from *Mission Bulletin* to *Religious Bulletin*. It was a one-page sheet, typed on Father O'Hara's own typewriter between Communion and Confession calls each day, and it was pinned up on residence hall bulletin boards or slipped under each student's door.[48]

The *Bulletin* listed prayer requests, mentioned who was sick, and noted deaths of alumni and former faculty.[49] Very often, the number of Communions received that morning was noted, and how that number compared with the day or week before.[50] If the number were down, a gentle rebuke might be in order. Father O'Hara was pleased that the number of Communions was high on December 14, 1921, the first anniversary of George Gipp's death. But the main block of the *Bulletin* was most often an exhortation to virtue or an encouragement to avoid the occasions of sin. He wrote frequently on safeguards to purity.[51] Daily Communion was at the top of the list, Confession as necessary, devotion to the Blessed Mother, keeping busy throughout the day, practicing modesty of the eyes, choosing companions well, avoiding improper literature ("Best Smellers" he often called them), and certainly staying away from the local dance halls and some of the women who gathered there.[52]

He also often made suggestions for a happy marriage. Keeping oneself pure was a first step, and dating only someone of whom one's mother and father would approve was another. He urged students to have the same goals and ideals for their girlfriends as they had for their mothers. Religion and prayer should hold a high priority in her life. Most wives at the time were mothers and homemakers, and Father O'Hara wrote very little about careers beyond that.[53]

Other topics were the importance of prayer or an explanation of the Mass.[54] He decried drinking and the evil of overindulgence.[55] He might summarize a book he encouraged every student to read, or pose questions students often asked about religion and answer them as convincingly as he could.[56] He could ridicule those who left Mass early to be first in line at the cafeteria or who waited until the last minute to approach the confessional. His comments could be humorous at times, and even sarcastic. "If your need is desperate," he once wrote, "get Badin Hall to pray for what you want. When God hears a strange voice He answers at once."[57] He expressed his views on smoking. "There is no law against smoking before receiving Communion," he said, but added: "Neither is there a law against dancing at your grandmother's funeral."[58] Later he asked: "Is it a sin for a girl to smoke?" He answered: "It might be for the cigarette—bad company."[59]

Not everyone approved of what he wrote, of course. George Shuster in the *Commonweal* article noted earlier lamented the fact that so much in the culture of the 1920s was defined by numbers, measurements, and statistics, and that Father O'Hara seemed especially pleased with the number of Communions, confessions, mission sermons, etc., that he was able to compile. Shuster wondered whether this made religion too individualistic and whether these figures indicated any increase in charity and concern for others, especially the less fortunate.[60] Others protested that fine young women also found enjoyment and relaxation in the city's dance halls and should not be referred to in derogatory terms.[61] Some students in Badin Hall went so far as to produce their own *Irreligious Bulletin* to take issue with some of Father O'Hara's comments and criticisms and even questioned some of his devotional practices.[62]

In order to understand the students better, Father O'Hara also undertook an annual survey of their backgrounds, attitudes, and future goals. The surveys were heavy with numbers, measurements, and statistics, although as the decade progressed, more and more personal comments were included, and replies of frequent and infrequent communicants were constantly compared. For the first survey, in 1921, 1,200 questionnaires were sent out, only to Catholic students, and 550 were returned. None of the questions touched on matters of conscience, all answers were anonymous, and Father O'Hara thought only five "showed a spirit of levity or bad taste."[63] The first several questions were mostly informational: religion of parents, attendance at Catholic grade or high school, reading habits, summer occupation, favorite recreation, and frequency of religious practices.[64] The final thirteen questions, not surprisingly considering the author, concerned frequent Communion. If the respondent was a frequent communicant, when did he begin the practice, has it increased his respect for the Blessed Sacrament, has it lessened temptations, has it made his conscience more sensitive, and how much time is spent in preparation for Communion and in thanksgiving. If the respondent was not a frequent communicant, why: laziness, fear of routine, scruples, inconvenience, fear of Confession, or habit of receiving only monthly.[65]

Most responses were not surprising. Eighty-five percent responded that both parents were Catholic, two-thirds attended Catholic grade school, but only slightly more than half attended Catholic high school. The vast majority went to Confession and received Communion at least monthly at home. Approximately 75 percent belonged to either the Knights of Columbus or the Holy Name Society, about one-third found their Notre Dame companions better than their companions at home, and almost half judged them about the same. In answer to the question "How many Catholic books have you read in college?," 268 respondents said "None." Despite this response, athletics, dancing, and reading ranked high among favorite diversions. In religious practices, 18 percent were daily communicants during the year and 50 percent were daily communicants during Lent. Half of the students had completed the nine First Fridays, half said the rosary at least weekly, and half never visited the Grotto. The vast majority who answered acknowledged that frequent Communion had lessened temptation in their lives and made their consciences more sensitive.[66]

By mid-decade, Father O'Hara was addressing seriously what he called the "Girl Question."[67] The five or six questions under this heading were the most answered questions of all, and he often listed answers from frequent and infrequent communicants separately.

The first question asked was "Is your girl an inspiration?" Almost half the respondents replied that they had no girl. Of the others, 75 percent of the frequent communicants answered "yes," but only 60 percent of the infrequent communicants answered "yes." The comments ranged from "She is the nearest thing to mother I have been able to find" and "A girl friend at home says her rosary for me" to "I have never met one who was an inspiration."[68] Most responses were positive, however.

To the question "Is your girl impeding or furthering your religious progress?," approximately 50 percent thought the influence was positive, 10 percent thought it was negative, and 40 percent thought that any influence was indifferent. Responses ranged from "I am striving to be as good as she is. She's perfect," to "The home girl is furthering them, whereas the South Bend one is impeding them," to "I have no girl, and will follow my dad's advice and not get one until I finish school."[69]

The third question asked: "If you marry, do you intend to choose a wife who can give your children sound Catholic training?," and more than 90 percent, frequent and infrequent communicants alike, answered "Yes." Still, the comments varied. One answered: "It depends. If I'm in love, and she has money, a firm and sweet character, and is pretty, I'll marry her." Another responded: "My mother is a Protestant. I feel that my father has given his three children a good Catholic training and if he was able to do it, certainly I should be able to."[70]

To another question, "What type of girl do you want to marry?," more than one hundred fifty qualities were suggested, from convent-bred and brilliant down to half-modern, ability to cook, and not too religious. "Of good character" and "Catholic" led the list of preferred qualities, although "pretty" and "Irish" were in the top fifteen.[71]

Toward the end of the decade, 1927–1928, Father Walsh's final year as president, the survey downplayed "The Girl Question" and sought information primarily on religious attitudes and activities. As might be expected, the first topic was the Holy Eucharist. "The center of the religious life of the students at Notre Dame," wrote Father O'Hara, "and the groundwork of their spiritual development, is daily Holy Communion."[72] There were 311,226 Communions received during the 1927–1928 year, an increase of 43,334 over the preceding year, and

1,381 Communions were being received each day in the spring of 1928. Sixty-two percent of those who had attended Catholic grade school and public high school received Communion daily but, surprisingly, only 47 percent of those who had attended both Catholic grade and high schools. The most popular way of assisting at Mass was with a prayer book, followed by the rosary, and then the missal.[73]

The favorite religious devotions outside of Mass were the rosary, visits to the Grotto, and visits to the Blessed Sacrament. More than 1,000 blessed rosaries were given to the students in the fall semester of 1927. The Grotto was the students' favorite place to pray, followed by Sacred Heart Church and the basement chapel. Surprisingly or not, 35 percent of the students responding acknowledged that the sermons heard did not help form their ideals or strengthen their faith. Favorite Lenten mortifications were abstaining from tobacco, from sweets, and from movies, attendance at daily Mass, and receiving Communion daily. One student noted that he had adopted no mortification practices but tried "to do more good things." Critic George Shuster would have been pleased with that priority of charity.[74]

In the summer of 1928 when Father Walsh's term as president came to an end, the United States and Notre Dame both seemed prosperous. Calvin Coolidge was approaching the end of his presidency as well, and there was evidence that "Coolidge prosperity" was real. The gross national product had increased from $86 billion to $104 billion during his presidency, savings deposits from $20 billion to $28 billion, and corporate incomes from $8 billion to $11 billion. The number of chain stores grew from 30,000 to 160,000 in the 1920s, and corporate dividends increased 65 percent. And the prosperity was not only in materials. The country boasted of literary giants H. L. Mencken, Walter Lippmann, John Dewey, and Reinhold Niebuhr; novelists F. Scott Fitzgerald and Sinclair Lewis; playwright Eugene O'Neill; poets Carl Sandburg and Robert Frost; painters Grant Wood, Thomas Hart Benton, and John Steuart Curry; composers Aaron Copland and Samuel Barber; and conductors Leopold Stokowski and Arturo Toscanini. National prosperity was not spread evenly, of course, and farmers, factory workers, black Americans, women, and immigrants were often left behind.[75]

The Notre Dame of 1928 seemed equally prosperous. Five new residence halls had been added over the last six years but enrollment had continued to increase and hundreds still lived off campus. The added enrollment, however, helped balance the budget. The university was not hurting financially because Father Burns's million-dollar fund drive pledges were being fulfilled and football gate receipts continued to climb. Rockne's 1924 backfield of the Four Horsemen only added to Notre Dame's national fame. If Father Walsh did not undertake significant academic innovations, he did maintain Father Burns's "revolution" and saw it continue and progress. The religious program of the campus, orchestrated by prefect of religion Father John O'Hara, was the envy and model of many Catholic institutions across the country. Father Walsh attempted to limit enrollment but requests for admission were so great that his limit never held. Both Notre Dame and the nation seemed prosperous in the summer of 1928 but there was no guarantee how long that prosperity would last.

The Depression Years

The summer of 1928 was not a propitious time for a university president to assume office. In less than a year and a half the stock market would crash, and the rest of the economy would follow. Banks would close their doors, endowments plummet, industrial production slow to 48 percent of capacity, farm income drop 60 percent, and unemployment pass 20 percent. Families would live in makeshift shacks ("Hoovervilles") on the outskirts of cities, former white-collar workers sell apples on street corners, and hoboes hitch rides on freight trains looking for work and food.

The priest assuming the reins at Notre Dame at this unpropitious time was Father Charles L. O'Donnell. He was not unprepared. Born of Irish immigrant parents near Indianapolis in 1884, he had graduated from Notre Dame in 1906, serving as first editor of the student yearbook, the *Dome*, and winning the university's Quan Medal for the best record in the Classical Course and the Meehan Medal for the best English essay. He had entered the Holy Cross Novitiate the same year, studied theology in Washington, DC, spent one summer learning Anglo-Saxon at Harvard, was ordained a priest in 1910, and that same year received his PhD in English from the Catholic University of America. He taught English literature, rhetoric, and poetry at Notre Dame, served as army chaplain during World War I, and was named provincial superior of all Holy Cross priests and brothers in the United States in 1920 (and as provincial superior he was also chairman of Notre Dame's board of trustees) and university president in 1928.[1]

Father O'Donnell was also a poet, and a good one. One student of his poetry has written:[2]

> Reading these poems, one is apt to think of the lyrics of George Herbert rather than, for example, the religious lyrics of Alice Meynell, although the latter poet is more akin to O'Donnell's Mariology than Herbert could ever have been. There is evident in both Herbert and O'Donnell a sweet, almost naïve, sense of divinity that brings to their styles an eminent child-like dependence. Both men, of course, were priests and sacerdotal imagery as well as Biblical themes and scenes infuse many of their lyrics. Neither poet avoided the long form, and both mastered the sonnet. O'Donnell's sonnets are among his finest poems, the subjects handled deftly within the short form and his pacing often controlled by a fine sense of enjambment to keep his rhythm conversational.

His collected poems number approximately three hundred. "A Rime of the Road" may be his best, but "At Notre Dame" is probably his most popular, at least on the Notre Dame campus:[3]

> So well I loved these woods I half believe
> there is an intimate fellowship we share;
> so many years we breathed the same brave air,
> kept spring in common, and were one to grieve
> summer's undoing, saw the fall bereave
> us both of beauty, together learned to bear
> the weight of winter—when I go otherwhere—
> an unreturning journey—I would leave
> some whisper of a song in these old oaks,
> a footfall lingering till some distant summer
> another singer down these paths may stray—
> the destined one a golden future cloaks—
> and he may love them, too, the graced newcomer,
> and may remember that I passed this way.

Father O'Donnell did have to grapple at times with the inroads of the Depression, but these were not devastating. The million-dollar endowment fund Father Burns had accumulated was first invested in Liberty Bonds issued to help finance the efforts of the United States in World War I with an interest rate of 4.85 percent. Such bonds were obviously safe. In 1923, these bonds were sold and the money was then invested in real estate bonds and preferred stock. By 1925, two-thirds of the endowment was in real estate bonds and one-third in preferred stock. Although some on the board of lay trustees were not in favor of the stock investments, in 1927–1928, Father Walsh's final year, the endowment made $28,000 in stock transactions and earned more than 7 percent interest on its bonds. On the recommendation of Albert Erskine, president of South Bend's Studebaker Corporation and chairman of Notre Dame's board of lay trustees, some money was invested in the Pierce-Arrow Motor Car Company, and close to $50,000 was lost when the market collapsed, although Mr. Erskine generously decided to cover most of this loss personally.[4]

A decision that had at least an indirect impact on the university's finances was the termination of the minims program in 1929. The minims program, educating young boys aged six to thirteen, had begun in the 1850s and, under the guidance and direction of dedicated religious like Brother Cajetan and Sister Aloysius, had trained thousands of young men through the years. The boys numbered close to a hundred much of the time, Saint Edward's Hall had been built for them, and the open spaces behind the hall served as their playing fields. But the Manual Labor School had been closed in 1917 and the prep or high school in 1922, and the minims were out of place on a campus slowly developing into a true university. With the termination of the program, Saint Edward's Hall was transferred to a college residence hall, additional students were admitted, and the added revenue was welcomed. Enrollment reached a temporary peak near 3,200 in 1930–1931 and then, due to the impact of the Depression, began a steady decline. Enrollment in 1933–1934 was closer to 2,600.[5]

Notre Dame's financial situation was positive throughout the six years of Father O'Donnell's presidency. University expenses in 1929, Father O'Donnell's first year in office, were $922,466. Tuition receipts of $590,106 covered about 65 percent of these expenses and $63,000 from the endowment for faculty salaries covered a little more. Football profits of more than $500,000 easily made up the rest. In fact, with the building of the new dining hall and the termination of the Clark cafeteria lease, and with profits from football, the university had a surplus in the late 1920s of $775,000. Because of this, the United States Province of the Congregation of Holy Cross, which was running a deficit of $20,000 each year, requested an increased assessment. The province had been given $300 per priest per year and there were discussions of raising this to $450 but it was eventually decided that one-third of the university's surplus each year would be given to the Congregation, and this amounted to $265,000 in 1933.[6]

Father O'Donnell did carry out one additional fundraising effort, although it was not successful at the time. In Father Walsh's last year in office, a Chicago banker and alumnus, Francis H. Hayes, suggested the establishment of a "living endowment" similar to those established at Yale, Dartmouth, and Northwestern. Rather than asking the alumni to contribute large sums to the endowment, of which the university would spend only the annual interest, ask them simply to make an annual contribution of the amount of that interest, and retain the capital themselves. An annual contribution of $100 would represent the interest on an endowment of $2,000 at 5 percent. If one thousand alumni would agree to this, it would represent an endowment of $2 million. Father O'Donnell agreed to put it before the Alumni Association in 1930, but with the Depression beginning, it received little enthusiasm, and the death of Knute Rockne the following year raised more interest in some kind of memorial for him. Some preferred simply naming the newly built stadium for him, and others preferred an independent memorial. A fund drive was begun for a Rockne Memorial but money arrived slowly and the building was not built until 1938.[7]

If the memorial building dedicated to the deceased coach had to be delayed throughout the 1930s, a structure the living coach early sought could be delayed no longer—a new stadium. Rockne had been lobbying for a new and larger stadium through the whole of Father Walsh's presidency, but with little success. Cartier Field held less than 30,000 fans, its facilities were outdated, and the financial rewards so limited that major universities declined to play there. Rockne's teams could draw twice that number elsewhere, and they could draw 120,000 in Chicago's Soldier Field with a corresponding increase in revenue. It was no wonder that Rockne preferred to play his games on the road, giving rise to the nickname "Rockne's Ramblers" before Father Walsh in 1927 officially accepted the name "Fighting Irish." With games on the East and West Coasts, punsters were beginning to suggest that the players were spending more time in Pullmans than in classrooms. Rockne pushed his case harder and harder throughout the decade and even threatened to resign. In 1928, he seemed prepared to accept a position at Ohio State, but his resignation threats may have hurt him more than helped. Notre Dame could fill a larger stadium as long as Rockne was coach, but if there was danger of his leaving, Cartier Field with 30,000 seats might be sufficient. Father Walsh's main goal was always to bring off campus students back to campus where religious and academic assistance was more accessible, and a new stadium, to be used only five or six Saturdays a year, did not have priority over Freshman,

Sophomore, Howard, Morrissey, and Lyons residence halls and the new dining hall. In 1927, however, Father Walsh did appoint a committee to look into the feasibility of a new stadium and to recommend means to finance it, but he decided to let his successor in a few months make the final decision since it would be the successor's responsibility to see it to completion.[8]

The committee soon divided itself into two subcommittees, one on finances and one on construction. The subcommittee on finances considered several options for financing the structure, with an estimated cost of $600,000. One possibility was to issue bonds. Michigan and Iowa State had done this but Michigan had been able to sell less than a quarter of its bonds, and its alumni were more numerous than Notre Dame's. The university would also be taking the risk that the money generated by the new stadium might not cover the amount of the bonds. Taking out a mortgage presented the same risk. The subcommittee eventually recommended the advance selling of premium box seats before construction began. Thus the money would be available before the first shovel was turned. The proposal was to provide 250 boxes with six seats in each, in a prime location, for a cost of $2,000 per box for ten years. This would raise $500,000 of the $600,000 needed for the full construction, leaving only $100,000 to be found from other sources, and Rockne's teams were clearing at least twice that a year. After ten years, the purchaser could repurchase the box for another ten years at the market price. Father O'Donnell announced the project on April 15, 1929, and by September, $400,000 had been collected.[9]

The subcommittee on construction recommended the Osborn Engineering Company of Cleveland as the architects. The company had designed White Sox Park in Chicago, Fenway Park in Boston, and Yankee Stadium in New York, and football stadiums for Purdue, Indiana, Minnesota, and Michigan. The provincial council of the Congregation of Holy Cross approved the project in July 1929, with the provision that the total cost not exceed $900,000. Excavation and construction began immediately, although some details were left for later decision. Total capacity, for example, would vary depending on whether the seats were 18 or 17 or 16.8 inches wide. Despite winter snow and fall and spring rain, construction progressed satisfactorily, although disagreements did arise among engineering, construction, and Notre Dame officials. Father Michael Mulcaire, university vice president and Father Thomas Steiner, dean of the College of Engineering, oversaw the project for the university, and their decisions carried.[10]

When it was completed in October 1930, the stadium was 670 feet in length and 480 feet in width, and it was 1.5 miles to walk around outside. The seats, one historian has written, were "the smallest college football seats in the country."[11] At its busiest, six hundred men worked on the construction at a time, with wages ranging from twenty cents to a dollar an hour, depending on the skill demanded. Eventually two million bricks were required. The recently constructed dining hall provided lunch for workers at seven cents each, and most were impressed with the quality of the food. Providing lunch on campus also circumvented the need for workers to seek lunch off campus, with the temptation of having a few beers and perhaps returning to work somewhat impaired. There had been discussions of providing lights for the field, but these would have had to be mounted on poles along the outside of the stadium, marring the beauty of the structure. Father Steiner wanted the press box glass-enclosed and other officials feared that such heavy glass might break loose and injure spectators below, but a way was eventually found to solidify it. The first grass was brought in sod rolls from Cartier Field since Rockne, always a little superstitious, had won on it often. Twenty thousand fans attended the dedication ceremonies the evening before the Navy game on the weekend of October 10, and forty thousand attended the game itself. Notre Dame won 26 to 2, and the gate receipts were the highest ever for a home game to that time.[12]

While the major construction on campus that spring and summer, the stadium, was continuing, a second, smaller building was rising not that many yards away—a new Law School. The Notre Dame Law School, founded in 1869, had been housed successively in the second Main Building, the first floor of Sorin Hall, and in 1919 in larger quarters in the old Institute of Technology. As the number of law students increased to close to 150 throughout the 1920s and the library shelving became inadequate, a new building was required. The site selected was on the east side of Notre Dame Avenue close to the entrance to the university and on a line with the dining hall, marking the southern edge of Professor Kervick's new quadrangle. The architects chosen were Maginnis and Walsh of Boston, whose Gothic style, towers, flèches, statues, and gargoyles could harmonize well with other recent buildings on campus. The university *Bulletin* called it:[13]

> A fine three-story structure of the Gothic type and of first-class construction. This building, 157 feet long and 104 feet wide, has an assembly hall for 350 persons, four classrooms, four seminar rooms, a courtroom, a discussion room, and a library reading room, 50 by 100 feet, in which is a working library of 10,000 volumes readily accessible to the students, an additional stockroom for 25,000 volumes, offices for the dean, the librarian, members of the faculty, and the *Notre Dame Lawyer*, the quarterly

review of the law school. The new building [was] erected at a cost of more than $400,000.

With the erection of the stadium and the Law School building in 1930, Father O'Donnell's construction project had just begun. There was a huge space now between the dining hall and the Law School and Father O'Donnell knew what he wanted there. Despite the five residence halls Father Walsh had constructed, the ever-increasing student enrollment still left more than eight hundred students living off campus. Father O'Donnell wanted to bring them back, and two additional residence halls would at least be a start. At first they were designated simply as halls "A" and "B" but eventually they were named Dillon Hall and Alumni Hall. Residence halls had already been named for university presidents Fathers Sorin, Corby, Walsh, and Morrissey, and one of the new halls was named for Father Patrick Dillon, Notre Dame's second president. The alumni had collected money for years for what was to be called Old Students' Hall but the money was eventually contributed to Father Burns's fund drive in order to help it attain the $1 million goal. Alumni Hall was to be a student hall but also the headquarters for alumni reunions, as Old Students' Hall was intended to be.[14]

Ground was broken for the two halls in early 1931 and work progressed well, despite poor weather at times. The architects were again Maginnis and Walsh and the buildings combined the majestic beauty of medieval times with truly modern conveniences. Alumni Hall was built in the form of a "U" and Dillon in the form of an "H," they were characterized by the familiar towers, flèches, statues, niches, and gargoyles, and they had modern amenities earlier residence halls lacked: slots to dispose of used razor blades, an electric elevator, and a laundry slide. If the students were calling Howard, Morrissey, and Lyons the "Gold Coast," they called these two the "Platinum Coast." Juniors from off campus began moving into Alumni Hall by the second week of October, and freshmen into Dillon by the end of the month. Neither chapel was completed by that time, and work continued on them, the Dillon chapel eventually adding an altar dedicated to Saint Olaf in memory of the recently deceased Knute Rockne of Norway. When both halls were completed, at a total cost of approximately $950,000, 85 percent of the student body was living on campus and only two hundred still lived in South Bend.[15]

Within a month of the dedication of the stadium and the new law building, and before ground was turned for the construction of Dillon and Alumni Halls, Father O'Donnell received a letter from Edward Hurley (a friend of Father

O'Hara, a member of the university's board of lay trustees, and the recipient of the Laetare Medal in 1926). The letter said in part:[16]

> The University of Notre Dame is rendering valuable service to American industry by educating young men in its School of Foreign and Domestic Commerce, particularly because the University features the great importance of foreign trade to the future industrial development of our country. In recognition of this service, I wish to contribute to the University the sum of two hundred thousand dollars for the erection of a new building to be known as the College of Foreign and Domestic Commerce.

It is not clear when Father O'Hara first met Edward Hurley. Perhaps it was through Father O'Hara's father, John Walter O'Hara, since he and Mr. Hurley were both active in promoting trade with Latin America. Mr. Hurley had been born in Galesburg, Illinois, in 1864, he worked for a time as a farmhand and then as a railroad engineer, and he eventually originated and developed the pneumatic tool industry in the United States. He founded the Hurley Machine Company, was a member of the United States Trade Commission to Latin America, a member of the Federal Trade Commission in 1914, chairman of the United States Shipping Board in 1917, a member of President Herbert Hoover's Advisory Shipping Commission, and a member of Chicago's Council on Foreign Relations. Even before becoming dean, Father O'Hara had been writing to Mr. Hurley about his hopes and plans for the future business college. Contacts continued throughout the 1920s, and Father O'Donnell was most pleased to receive his offer.[17]

The site chosen for the building was slightly to the east of the post office near the entrance of the university on a line with Badin and Howard Halls and across the new quadrangle from the Law School. Hurley suggested a Chicago architecture firm to design the building, the firm that had designed Chicago's Museum of Natural History, the Shedd Aquarium, and the Wrigley Building, and an artist's conception appeared in the *Scholastic* that same month. It was to be an E-shaped, two-story building with classrooms and faculty and administrative offices on each floor, and a most impressive two-story central lobby surrounded by a second floor balcony. In the center was a slightly sunken eight-foot revolving globe marking the world's most important international trade routes, and murals on the four walls depicted the major trading nations, principal seaports, and shipping lanes. Over the main entrance was mounted a miniature three-mast schooner to emphasize international trade, leading some students to name the college

"The Yacht Club." The college was officially called the College of Foreign and Domestic Commerce, and the building, named for its benefactor, was dedicated on May 13, 1932.[18]

Hurley Hall of Commerce was the first university building named for a benefactor, but Cushing Hall of Engineering was a close second. Like commerce, engineering needed a permanent setting. Engineering classes, like law classes, had been offered in various locations through the years: in Phelan Hall, behind the first main church; in Science Hall, later LaFortune Student Center; in the Institute of Technology; and finally in a two-story Engineering Hall, constructed in 1905 on the quadrangle in front of the present Dillon Hall and housing also some Manual Labor School shops and the casket-making and undertaking office. That building unfortunately was struck by lightning in 1928 and the whole second floor was lost. The building may not have been adequate anyway because one of the professors remarked: "Isn't it too bad that the fire department got here too soon." Engineering classes continued to be taught in the partially damaged first-floor classrooms and in the basement of Badin Hall until John Cushing came to the rescue.[19]

John Cushing had been born in Arapahoe, Nebraska, in 1882, he served as a blacksmith's apprentice for a time, and he was a student at the University of Nebraska for two years before transferring to the University of Notre Dame. There is a tradition that after one year at Notre Dame he notified Father Morrissey, president at that time, that he intended to leave the university because he could no longer afford the tuition but Father Morrissey convinced him to remain and repay the money if it became possible in the future. He graduated in 1906, the same year as Father O'Donnell, joined the Great Lakes Dredge and Dock Company as a timekeeper, and eventually worked his way to the top and was named president in 1926. In 1931, in part in gratitude for Father Morrissey's earlier kindness, he offered the university $300,000 for a new engineering building.[20]

The new building was designed by Francis Kervick, Notre Dame professor of architecture. He had assisted in the laying out of the new quadrangle, with the dining hall, Dillon and Alumni Halls, and the Law School to the south, and Lyons, Morrissey, Howard, Badin, and the Hurley building to the north, and he would continue the quad by placing the engineering building just east of the Law School and directly across from the commerce building. It was a neo-Gothic three-story building with classrooms and drafting rooms, laboratories and machine shops, offices, and an assembly hall to hold five hundred. There was hope that the exterior might have paneling representing and honoring Catholic scientists of the past—Ampère, Volta, Ohm, Roentgen, and others—but this was never completed. What was left of old Engineering Hall was demolished and the new building was dedicated on June 4, 1932.[21]

With seven new residence halls, three academic buildings, and a large dining hall recently completed or under construction, heating the campus buildings in the harsh Indiana winters and providing them with water year-round became a challenge, and Father O'Donnell answered it with a new power plant in 1931. In the early days, heat was provided by stoves or furnaces in each building. The first heating plant was built behind the Main Building in 1881, a larger one in back of Saint Edward's Hall in 1899, and this new one on the northeast shore of Saint Joseph's Lake. Due to Father Steiner's initiative, all the buildings were now connected through underground tunnels, three major wells at the north end of campus supplied sufficient water, and the power plant circulated the water throughout the campus.[22]

The new $250,000 power plant was one hundred by fifty feet, made of sturdy brick but with numerous windows to let in light and avoid the dreary appearance of similar power plants. There were four four-hundred horsepower boilers on the first floor, with two at work all the time and the other two dormant. There was space to hold 460 tons of coal inside the building, and 1,500 tons outside it, and the plant burned up to 100 tons of coal a day during the winter season. Gauges on each boiler recorded the pounds of pressure and the amount of carbon dioxide, and water was automatically sprayed on the ashes to reduce the dust. The plant operated 24 hours a day, 365 days a year, with three teams working eight-hour shifts. It also solidified Father O'Donnell's reputation as one of the great builders in Notre Dame's history: seven major buildings in less than six years, at a total cost of $2,800,000, during the early years of the Great Depression.[23]

Father O'Donnell was eager not only for the physical growth of the campus but also for its intellectual enhancements, and, as a poet and man of letters himself, he invited some of the English language's best to visit and address the students and faculty. In his first autumn as president, he wrote to invite Hilaire Belloc, the noted British historian, poet, essayist, and apologist, to lecture at the university. Father O'Donnell offered him $5,000 for a series of lectures but he was too committed in England at the time to accept. He attempted to come the following year, but he took sick in New York and was unable to travel further.[24]

Father O'Donnell's major success in this recruitment area was in attracting Gilbert Keith Chesterton to Notre Dame in 1930 for a series of eighteen lectures on the history and literature of the Victorian period. Chesterton, a convert to Catholicism, was a poet, novelist, short-story writer, controversialist, and author of *Orthodoxy*, the *Everlasting Man*, and the *Father Brown* series. His lectures, given to a packed Washington Hall audience, sparkled with wit. He began his opening lecture by asking if there actually was a Victorian period, and the large, overweight man answered. "If there is no such period, then to my considerable and your enormous relief we may betake ourselves to lighter pleasures and let there be a vast yawning chasm where I now stand."[25] He lectured on Thomas Carlyle and Thomas Babington Macaulay, on Dickens and Thackeray, and even drew a couple of caricatures for the *Juggler*, the student fine arts journal. He received an honorary degree that extolled him as "a man of letters recognized as the ablest and most influential in the English-speaking world of today, and defender of the Christian tradition, whose keen mind, right heart, and versatile literary genius have been valiantly devoted to the eternal truth, goodness and beauty in literature and in life."[26] His wife and secretary accompanied him since he was not adept at making practical decisions without them. With forty thousand others he attended the football game dedicating the new stadium that fall, and he later defended Notre Dame as an academic institution and blamed the media for overemphasizing its athletic prowess. He could view even embarrassing moments with humor. When he had difficulty entering one of the narrower doorways on campus, the university chauffeur is reported to have suggested that he turn sideways, to which the rotund Chesterton is said to have replied: "I have no sideways." Chesterton was scheduled to return to the university in the fall of 1936 but unfortunately took sick and died that summer.[27]

A third literary giant, William Butler Yeats, was invited to the campus for a second time in early 1933. Primarily a poet and a dramatist, he had been awarded a Nobel Prize in 1923 and was a co-founder of the Irish Academy of Letters, but he was also Protestant and his views, the *Scholastic* wrote diplomatically, did "not always mesh perfectly with the more developed Irish Catholic mind."[28] In his lecture, he spoke of the background for the Irish literary renaissance, of Berkeley, Swift, and Burke, of the Irish love of liberty and freedom, of Lady Gregory and John Synge, and of England as "the origin of all evil." His fit on Notre Dame's campus, so devoted to Catholic Ireland, was not perfect and, in a letter to a friend, Father O'Donnell admitted as much:[29]

> He read a few things of my own, mostly early Irish pieces, which he termed charming. Some of my later things he said he couldn't follow, and indeed as he read them—out loud, of course—I found them quite incomprehensible myself. The fellow, by the way, is positively "hipped"

on psychical research, but on the whole he was much more human and agreeable than the somewhat snobbish and esoteric freak that he appeared to me thirty years ago.

Other distinguished personages visited the campus in the early 1930s, and the fiftieth anniversary of the Laetare Medal in 1933 was one occasion. The awardee that year was the renowned Irish tenor John McCormack. McCormack had been born in Ireland but had become an American citizen (and thus eligible for the Laetare Medal) in 1919. Previous Medal winners were invited to the golden anniversary celebration, and seven returned, including Alfred E. Smith, the Democratic nominee for president in 1928 and Laetare Medalist in 1929. Mr. McCormack's citation read:[30]

Unheard beauties you have made audible. Simple, homely things you have taken from kitchen and fireside to the whiteness and brightness of the theaters. You have captured Irish ballads from cross-roads and country-sides, and by a wizardry of times have transformed them into new, beautiful essences. You have made Ireland's voice audible to millions who have never seen Ireland's face.

In his reply, McCormack admitted that he was both grateful for the honor and nervous in the presence of such illustrious others. He thanked this university of the "Fighting Irish" with such Gaelic names as Carideo, Savoldi, and Schwartz, and added: "In no sense of false modesty do I now confess that I never thought that I would stand as I do here tonight with this precious medal on my breast. . . . Words are futile things at such a moment. . . . It would be so much easier for me to sing my thanks."[31] He then sang "The Prayer Perfect" of James Whitcomb Riley, one of Father O'Donnell's favorite poets:[32]

Bring unto the sorrowing
All release from pain,
Let the lips of laughter
Overflow again.
And with the needy,
O divide, I pray,
This vast treasure of content
That is mine today!

Notre Dame had been founded by Father Sorin and the brothers of the Congregation of Holy Cross, and the interests and activities of the school and the religious community for years were hard to untangle. With Father Burns's fund drive and the establishment of the board of lay trustees, steps were taken to clarify the separation and quasi-independence of the two, and Father O'Donnell thought that a new official seal or coat of arms for the university would assist in this. To this time, the seal of the Congregation and the college were quite similar. He commissioned Pierre de Chaignon la Rose of Harvard to design an appropriate seal, and his design was accepted. An outer ring contains the words "Sigillum Universitatis Dominae Nostrae a Lacu" ("Seal of the University of Our Lady of the Lake"). Within that ring is a clear blue shield with a cross of gold, blue and gold being colors associated with the Blessed Mother. At the base of the shield are two wavy lines of silver, representing the "of the Lake" of the official title, and in the upper left corner a silver star representing Mary, Star of the Sea. The central cross represents the Congregation of Holy Cross that founded the university. The open book across the stem of the cross signifies Notre Dame as an educational institution, and the words "Vita, Dulcedo, Spes" ("Life, Sweetness, Hope") on the pages of the book are from a hymn to the Blessed Mother.[33]

Like many other universities, Notre Dame lost revenue in the early years of the Depression due to a decline in enrollment, from 3,200 in 1930–1931 to 2,600 three years later, and it faced the danger of losing additional revenue with the drop in football fortunes following the death of Coach Rockne in the spring of 1931. Many thought that, as both head coach and athletic director, Rockne had become too powerful, almost autonomous, and Father O'Donnell and his vice president, Father Michael Mulcaire, were determined to bring the Athletic Department more fully under administration control by separating the two positions. They asked Jesse Harper in May 1931 to come out of retirement and resume the duties of athletic director, one of which was to reduce the department's spending. Harper became so conscientious in his implementation that one manager said that to please him "You would've had to get a receipt from a pay toilet." Figures are not clear, but it seems that while full athletic scholarships for football were reduced, other work options on campus given preferentially to football players may have reduced the impact to a minimum. In 1934, for example, sixty-seven players were still receiving full grants and thirty-five others were receiving smaller assistance.[34]

Selecting a successor to Rockne as a coach was an even more important decision and time was short. Soon after hiring Harper as athletic director, Father

O'Donnell announced that no one could realistically replace Rockne as "head coach" and thus his first assistant, Hartley "Hunk" Anderson, was named senior coach and Jack Chevigny, who had called "There's one for the Gipper" when he crossed the goal line against Army in 1928, was named junior coach. Eventually, Anderson was named head coach but he and Chevigny did not always see eye-to-eye and this was a source of difficulty. Anderson had been an excellent player—along with Adam Walsh he was probably one of the two best linemen Rockne ever coached—and an excellent assistant coach, but he lacked Rockne's charm and diplomacy, and this hurt seriously in recruiting and in finding off campus employment for athletes without full scholarships.[35]

Anderson's first year was not wholly successful. Rockne's 1930 team may have been his best and many of the players returned, but many had also graduated. Notre Dame won six games that year, but they lost to Southern California and Army and they tied Northwestern. (After defeating Notre Dame, Coach Howard Jones took his Southern California team to visit Rockne's grave.) The following year Notre Dame won seven, but they lost to Pittsburgh and Southern California again. The team seemed poorer as Rockne's recruits continued to graduate, and 1933 was a disaster. In six of the nine games, Notre Dame did not score a point, going scoreless for sixteen consecutive quarters at one stretch. The opponents outscored them 80 to 32, and their final record was 3–5–1, Notre Dame's first losing season since 1888. It was clear that Anderson had to go. Alumni Jimmy Crowley of Fordham, Harry Stuhldreher of Villanova, "Slip" Madigan of St. Mary's in California, Gus Dorais of Detroit, and "Rip" Miller of Navy were all considered, but the final choice was Elmer Layden, another of the Four Horsemen, a very successful coach at Duquesne, and even a distant cousin of Father O'Hara.[36]

Layden's selection, however, was not the only significant athletic hire in 1934. Baseball also received a new skipper. In the preceding forty years, Notre Dame had had fourteen different baseball coaches; in the succeeding forty years there was only one, Clarence "Jake" Kline. Several well-known Notre Dame officials had held the position earlier, at least part-time: Frank Hering, football coach and reputed "Father of Mother's Day," 1897–1899; Jesse Harper, athletic director and football coach, 1914–1918; Charles "Gus" Dorais, Rockne's teammate and quarterback, 1919–1920; Walter Halas, brother of George Halas, 1921–1923; George Keogan, head basketball coach, 1923–1926; and Tommy Mills, Rockne's assistant football coach, 1927–1929. All had commendable records. Hering had an overall winning percentage of .708; Harper also .708; Dorais .730; Halas .688;

Keogan .521; and Mills .740. Harper won 17 and lost only 5 in 1914, Halas was 19 and 4 in 1922, and Mills 24 and 8 in 1928. These coaches produced some memorable players also. From 1906 to 1912, John "Red" Murray ranked among the top five in the major leagues in both home runs and stolen bases, a feat equaled only by Honus Wagner, Ty Cobb, Willie Mays, and Henry "Hank" Aaron. In 1916, George Gipp enrolled at Notre Dame on a baseball scholarship, and he shifted to football later. Football star John Mohardt, in his only plate appearance in the majors, collected a base hit in 1922, leaving him with a lifetime batting average of 1.000, and that same year he was sent in to run for Ty Cobb, one of the great base stealers of all time. With the Chicago Cubs in 1923, Cy Williams led the National League in home runs with forty-one, the same number Babe Ruth belted to lead the American League.[37]

Jake Kline had been one of Notre Dame's finest athletes. He hailed from Williamsport, Pennsylvania, later home of the Little League World Series, monogrammed in baseball from 1915 to 1917, batted over .300 each year, and captained in 1917. He joined the infantry in World War I, played and managed baseball throughout the West and the Midwest in the 1920s, returned to Notre Dame as freshman baseball coach in 1931, and succeeded Keogan as head coach in 1934. His overall record was 522–436–5, for a winning percentage of .558, eight of his teams made the NCAA playoffs, and in 1957 his team played in the College World Series finals. Notre Dame produced at least two excellent major leaguers in the Kline years, Carl Yastrzemski and Ron Reed. Yastrzemski won three American League batting titles, played in eighteen All-Star games, was voted Most Valuable Player in 1967, and was elected to the Hall of Fame in 1988, and Reed is remembered as one of the very few who played successfully both major league baseball (sixteen years) and NBA basketball (six years). Kline can probably claim little credit for either of these, however, since Yastrzemski spent only his freshman year at Notre Dame (and freshmen were not then eligible for varsity competition) and Reed played only in his senior year, concentrating on basketball earlier. Another former student accomplished the unusual feat of winning a major league game without throwing a pitch. Frank Carpin was called in to relieve a tie game with two outs, before the first pitch he threw out a runner attempting to steal, and his teammates scored in their half of the inning, making him the winning pitcher. Kline's record was commendable, given his difficulty in recruiting top players. Baseball could only be played in northern Indiana six months of the year, and in three of these months students were away for summer vacation; in the sports world, Notre Dame was known primarily for its football program, especially in those years of Frank Leahy and Ara Parseghian; and the university awarded very few baseball grants-in-aid. Kline also taught mathematics, represented the university well, and ran an honest athletic program, finally retiring at age eighty-one.[38]

Although football, basketball, and even baseball attracted more fans, track and field in the 1930s produced two of the university's finest athletes, Alex Wilson and Greg Rice. Track and field dated back to the late 1880s, along with baseball and football, and all-around athlete (football, baseball, and rowing) Harry Jewett in 1890 defeated America's fastest in the 100-yard dash and set a record in the hop, skip, and jump. Knute Rockne ran and coached track in the early decades of the new century and was said to be outstanding in the pole vault. Gus Desch won a bronze medal in the 1920 Olympics in the 220-yard low hurdles, and Tom Lieb won a bronze medal with the discus four years later. John Nicholson succeeded Rockne as coach in 1928 and is credited with innovating the starting block for sprinters and hurdlers. Alex Wilson received All-American honors in 1930, 1931, and 1932, and he won silver in the 800 meter and bronze in the 400 meter while competing for his native Canada in the 1932 Olympics. J. Gregory Rice went undefeated in sixty-five meets in three years at Notre Dame, was All-American in 1937, 1938, and 1939, and was awarded the Sullivan Trophy as the nation's top amateur athlete in 1940. Outstanding in the mile, two-mile, and three-mile distances, he never competed in the Olympics due to the outbreak of World War II. Alex Wilson returned to Notre Dame in 1950, and in his twenty-two years as track coach developed the likes of Aubrey Lewis (also a football star), Ron Gregory (brother of comedian Dick Gregory), Bill Clark, Bill Hurd, and Sullivan Award–winner Rick Wohlhuter. Coach Wilson was succeeded by Joe Piane in 1970, and his finest was probably miler Chuck Aragon late in that decade.[39]

Although Father O'Donnell had preached an eloquent sermon at Knute Rockne's funeral in April 1931, it soon became clear that the president's own health was failing. He had contracted a streptococcus infection of the inner ear as chaplain in World War I, and it had begun to spread and left him partially deaf. He underwent treatments and spent more and more time in the hospital or in the Holy Cross infirmary. He was able to preside at commencement ceremonies in June 1933, and at the awarding of the Laetere Medal that evening to John McCormack, but he was clearly a very sick man. Preparations had to be made for the worst and Vice President Michael Mulcaire did not seem the man to take over higher responsibilities, so Father O'Hara was named to replace him as vice president that July. Retaining his position as prefect of religion, he presided over the university as acting president during most of the 1933–1934 academic year while

Father O'Donnell was either at the Mayo Clinic or in the Holy Cross infirmary. Father O'Hara kept in touch with the president as much as the latter's health would permit, and Father O'Hara always insisted that it was Father O'Donnell's decision to replace both Jesse Harper and Hunk Anderson after the disastrous 1933 season. Doctors at Mayo Clinic recommended that he spend the winter of 1933 in Florida, and this he did. When he returned to South Bend the following April, one leg was already paralyzed and the paralysis was spreading. He entered the hospital immediately and remained there until the day after commencement Sunday (which was presided over by Father O'Hara) when he peacefully breathed his last.[40]

The provincial chapter had been scheduled to meet at Notre Dame later that month and, to no one's surprise, Father O'Hara was named president of the university. No administrative transition could have been smoother since Father O'Hara had already been serving as acting president for much of the year. As the replacement for Father O'Donnell, he had delivered talks to alumni and others in Chicago, Boston, South Bend, and Providence, Rhode Island. He attended the funeral of Edward Hurley, represented the university at the annual meeting of the National Collegiate Athletic Association in Columbus, and presided at the visits to Notre Dame of Wiley Post and Guglielmo Marconi. He presided also at the Washington Day Exercises in 1934, made preparations for commencement that year, and was at least an important voice in the football coaching change from Hunk Anderson to Elmer Layden.[41]

Also in late 1933, Henry S. Pritchett (president-emeritus of the Carnegie Foundation for the Advancement of Teaching) published a report, *A Slump in the Football Trade*, in which he questioned some of Notre Dame's activities and decisions, and Father O'Hara, with some assistance from the recently appointed coach and director of athletics, Elmer Layden, responded. Doctor Pritchett had suggested that Notre Dame's emphasis on football at the expense of intellectual achievement made it a most attractive opponent for other college football teams, with very profitable gate receipts, he questioned the wisdom of the recent three-year home and home football contract between Notre Dame and the University of Southern California, two thousand miles apart, in the midst of a Depression, and he wondered where those football profits eventually went.[42]

Father O'Hara's rejoinder was courteous but to the point:[43]

> We believe that he has started with a false assumption that highly publicized football is inimical to the intellectual interests of the university. We wish to reiterate that if we ever found it to be the case we would drop football

without a moment's hesitation. The present report asks for information on the advancement of intellectual pursuits at Notre Dame. We have 20 priests, whose theological studies are completed, studying for advanced degrees in six universities. During the last decade, advanced studies have been pursued by our priest-teachers at Vienna, Rome, Oxford, Paris, and Madrid in Europe, and at the University of California, California Institute of Technology, Catholic University of America, Yale, Harvard, Columbia, Johns Hopkins, and other universities in the United States.

The record of Notre Dame in protecting its lay professors during the depression has perhaps been unique. Although student attendance has dropped 600 during the last two years, no professor has been dismissed and no salary has been decreased as a result of the depression; on the contrary, the usual advances in salary, due to promotions, have been made.

It will interest the Carnegie Foundation to hear that of the $4,000,000 increase in the material plant at Notre Dame during the last 12 years, only 20 per cent is devoted to athletic purposes.

Father O'Hara insisted also that the Notre Dame–Southern California series was not exclusively about money:

Aside from the fact that the University of Southern California furnishes decidedly worthwhile competition, we have a large alumni group on the Pacific coast. I doubt if another school in the eastern half of the country has so large a proportion of its alumni and old students residing in that important section of the country. And if our interest in this game were largely commercial, the university would yield to the heavy pressure that is exerted every time Southern California comes east, and play the game in Chicago where the number of spectators would be 70,000 or 80,000 larger than it is here.

Father O'Hara was undoubtedly pleased with the opportunity to emphasize Notre Dame's academic programs over its athletic achievements because one of his principal goals was to strengthen the university's academic life by adding to its graduate programs. Notre Dame had been offering graduate degrees since the very early days. Precise figures are not available since it is uncertain which graduate degrees in the early decades were earned and which were honorary, but for a time at least graduate degrees were awarded after one or more years of postbaccalaureate study, or when the person was accepted into one of the learned professions—law or teaching, for example. With the inauguration of Summer Session classes in 1918, the demand for graduate classes increased since some, already in possession of a bachelor's degree, desired graduate courses to aid their advancement in the teaching profession. A graduate committee was set up in the 1920s to oversee graduate studies but it seems that most departments continued their own policies, usually requiring some kind of comprehensive examination and a thesis of original research. Father O'Hara knew that an early step in strengthening the graduate program was to recruit nationally and internationally recognized scholars to the faculty, and, fortunately for Notre Dame, such scholars were becoming available from troubled Europe.[44]

The future was indeed uncertain for academics in Europe at this time. Benito Mussolini had been ruling Fascist Italy since 1922, Joseph Stalin had been ruling Communist Russia since 1924, and Adolf Hitler was then in the process of gaining complete control in Germany. Fascism, Communism, and Nazism were all dedicated to state control of public life, including the arts, science, teaching, and scholarly research, and each leader was further bent on expanding his control into other lands and nations. University professors throughout Europe were uneasy, some were forced to flee as Nazism and Communism advanced, and others chose voluntary exile while time permitted. Father O'Hara, accompanied by Father James Donahue, the Congregation's then superior general, made a trip to Europe in the spring of 1935, Father O'Hara's first spring after his election as president, precisely to recruit European scholars for Notre Dame, either as visiting lecturers or as permanent members of the faculty. In both goals he proved quite successful.[45]

One of the first of these to come was Waldemar Gurian. Born of Jewish parents in Russia in 1902, he and his sister were taken to Germany when he was nine and they both became Catholic. He studied at the Universities of Munich, Breslau, Bonn, and Cologne, receiving his PhD in 1923 at the age of twenty-one. He edited a newspaper and lectured in Cologne for several years and fled Hitler's Germany for the United States, and Notre Dame, in 1937. He never lost his interest in nor his love of his native Russia and, in his writings, sought to warn the American people of the evils and deceitfulness of Soviet Bolshevism. He published *Bolshevism: Theory and Practice* in 1932, *The Future of Bolshevism* in 1936, *Hitler and the Christians* that same year, and *The Rise and Decline of Marxism* in 1938. He founded *The Review of Politics* in 1939 and remained its editor until his death in 1954. In his article "The Catholic Publicist," he insisted that the Catholic writer or editor had an obligation not only to defend the church against false and unjust attacks but to contribute positively to its mission:[46]

> The Catholic publicist has the task of showing that all times may be embraced by the Church, that Church life and Church teaching, as the timeless objectification of the absolute, cannot be separated from and contrasted to the flux and changes of time. The Catholic publicist must be concerned with the actual moment of existence, or fail to be a publicist; he must see in Christ and His Church the fullness of life and truth, or fail to be a Catholic. He may never forget that he, even as a child of time, must explain its meaning sub *specie aeternitatis.*

He retained many Old World ways throughout his life, he seemed to have more idiosyncrasies than most, and he could at times be gruff and indifferent to the feelings of others. Sitting in the front row before a visiting lecturer on one occasion, he showed his disdain for a position the speaker held by standing up, turning his chair around, and, with his back to the speaker, reading a book for the rest of the lecture. Hannah Arendt was probably correct in calling him "an extraordinary and extraordinarily strange man," but for almost two decades he was Notre Dame's brightest star in the area of international relations, highly respected at home and throughout Europe.[47]

A second recruit to the Department of Political Science was Professor Ferdinand Hermens. Born in Germany in 1906, he studied at the Universities of Münster, Berlin, Bonn, Freiburg, and Rome, and the London School of Economics. He taught and conducted research in Kiel and Berlin, Germany, and at the Catholic University of America, was a Guggenheim fellow in Germany in 1937, and joined the Notre Dame faculty in 1938. His publications included *Demokratie und Kapitalismus* in 1931, *Demokratie und Wahlrecht* in 1933, and *Der Staat und die Weltwirtschaftskrise* in 1936 in German; *Democracy or Anarchy* in 1941 and *The Tyrants' War and the Peoples' Peace* in 1944 in English; and numerous articles and reviews in *The Review of Politics,* on whose editorial board he also regularly served.[48]

The Department of Mathematics could have profited the most from the arrival of émigré professors, but two remained only one year. Karl Menger remained the longest. He was born in Austria in 1902, and when he was an undergraduate student at the University of Vienna, a professor in class noted that there was no satisfactory definition of a particular curve and that the problem seemed unsolvable. Within a few days, young Menger had found a solution. He received his doctorate in 1924, was a member of the celebrated "Vienna Circle" of philosophers, scientists, and mathematicians, and taught at Amsterdam University, the University of Vienna, Harvard University, and Rice Institute before coming to Notre Dame in 1937. He authored *Dimensionstheorie* in 1928, *Kurventheorie* in 1932, and *Algebra of Analysis* in 1944. He earned worldwide recognition for his work in mathematical axiomatics, the theory of curves, and the geometry of points, and his major contribution to the field of mathematics was his construction of the Menger Sponge in 1926. He chaired Notre Dame's Department of Mathematics from 1938 to 1946. Seymour Kass called him "a peerless mathematician."[49]

Kurt Gödel spent only one year at Notre Dame, 1939. He was born in Austria-Hungary in 1906, at age twelve he became a Czechoslovakian citizen when the Austro-Hungarian Empire was broken up, he automatically became a German citizen in 1938 when Germany annexed Austria and Czechoslovakia, and he eventually became an American citizen in 1947. At first interested primarily in physics, he switched to mathematics and philosophy at the University of Vienna and received his doctorate in 1930. He taught principally at the University of Vienna, with occasional lecture trips to the Advanced Institute of Princeton, and when Hitler overran Austria he decided to flee as he was fearful of being drafted into the German army. Rather than risking an Atlantic crossing, he went by rail through Russia, then to Japan, and on to the United States. After one year at Notre Dame, he moved on to Princeton and his close friend, Albert Einstein. To Einstein's theory of relativity, Gödel added both his belief that time was a human construct and an illusion, and his own cosmology of rotating universes. His collected works filled five volumes. Toward the end of his life, Einstein is supposed to have remarked to a friend that his "own work no longer meant much, that he came to the Institute merely . . . to have the privilege of walking home with Gödel." During his citizenship interview in 1947, the presiding judge stated that the United States Constitution prevented the rise of a dictator here. Gödel responded that there was actually a logical flaw in the Constitution and a dictatorship could be possible, but Einstein, one of his sponsors, immediately motioned to him to pursue it no further. Gödel was a deeply troubled man, always fearful of being poisoned, and would only eat food prepared by his wife. When his wife was hospitalized and not available to prepare his meals, he neglected to eat, eventually dying, in part, of malnutrition.[50]

A third émigré mathematician in the 1930s was Emil Artin. He was born in Vienna in 1898, studied at the Universities of Vienna, Leipzig, and Göttingen, and received his doctorate in 1921. Offered positions also in Münster and Zurich, he chose to teach in Hamburg. In 1929, he married Natalia (Natascha) Naumovna Jasny, a former student and Russian émigré. She was half-Jewish, and when Hitler solidified his power, Artin decided to leave. He had already been forced from his teaching position and was convinced the government was spying on him. He taught at Notre Dame for only one year, 1939, and then moved on to Indiana University in Bloomington and eventually to Princeton. "For Artin," Richard Brauer has written, "to be a mathematician meant to participate in a great common effort, to continue work begun thousands of years ago, to shed new light on old discoveries, to seek new ways to prepare the developments of the future. Whatever standards we use, he was a great mathematician." A well-cultured gentleman, he was a student of astronomy and biology also, and he played the flute, harpsichord, and clavichord.[51]

Physics was a third department that profited significantly from the arrival of émigré scholars. Arthur Haas was born in Moravia, later part of the Czech Republic, in 1884, studied at the Universities of Vienna and Göttingen, and received his PhD in 1906. His primary interest was the history of physics, but his examination committee at Vienna requested that he do additional work in pure physics itself. Becoming interested in black-body radiation, he may have been the first to apply a quantum formula to the clarification of atomic structure. His published works included *Der Geist des Hellenentums der Modernen Physik* in 1914 and the two-volume *Einfuhrung in die Theoretische Physik* in 1919–1921. He taught at both the University of Leipzig and the University of Vienna, immigrated to the United States in 1936, and taught at Notre Dame until his death in 1941. In one of his first public lectures at Notre Dame, he stated his belief that there was no conflict between science and religion, that science can reveal much about the universe, but beyond that there is much that can be explained only by the existence of God:[52]

> A new path from physics to religion seems to open in such a way that physics of itself sees the necessary limits of its own claims. If this is the case, then from the very outset the conclusions of those writers become meaningless, who, in advocating atheistic ideas, revert wrongly to physics.

Of the various émigré professors joining the Notre Dame faculty in the 1930s, Eugene Guth may have ranked with Waldemar Gurian as the best known. He was born in Budapest, Hungary, in 1905, studied at the Universities of Vienna and Leipzig and the Institute of Technology in Zurich, and immigrated to the United States in 1937. He joined the Notre Dame faculty that same year and worked closely with fellow émigré Arthur Haas, Haas a Catholic and Guth a Jew. Notre Dame was an appropriate location for him. He was interested in researching the integration of high-energy electrons with matter and Notre Dame possessed a Van der Graaf atom-smasher, and he was also interested in the elasticity of rubber and Father Nieuwland had done outstanding research in that area. In addition to establishing and directing the Polymer Physics Laboratory at Notre Dame, he was director of the Office of Rubber Research Project, technical advisor to the director of the Oak Ridge National Laboratory, and visiting professor at Rice University and the University of Tennessee. His research made significant contributions in the areas of nuclear and solid state physics, he was the recipient of the University of Vienna's Distinguished Alumnus Award, he was elected an honorary member of Sigma Pi Sigma, the national physics honor society, and he was awarded the Cross of Honor of Science and Arts by President Rudolf Kirschläger of the Republic of Austria. His favorite pastimes were chess, iceskating, and ping-pong.[53]

A final émigré scholar at this time, if that is what he may be called, was Yves Simon of the Department of Philosophy. Different from the others, he was probably not fleeing from Nazi encroachments but simply accepted the invitation of Father Leo R. Ward of the Philosophy Department to come as a visiting professor in 1938—and he remained for ten years. He had been born in France in 1903, studied at the University of Paris and at the Institute Catholique under Jacques Maritain, and was a firm follower of the philosophy of Saint Thomas Aquinas. He rejected the idea, quite common in France, that Catholic theology favored a monarchy, and he insisted that the philosophy and theology of Saint Thomas was wholly compatible with the liberal democracies of the west. He wrote on logic, ethics, epistemology, metaphysics, and the philosophy of science, but his main interest was in political philosophy. He published *Introduction à l'ontologie du connaître* in 1934 and *Philosophy of Democratic Government* in 1951. He remained a staunch friend and disciple of Maritain throughout his life, was often present at Maritain's public lectures, and at times offered to clarify what Maritain's accent may have left obscure, although Simon's accent occasionally seemed only slightly superior. For ten years, until he left for the University of Chicago in 1948, he added solid strength to Notre Dame's Department of Philosophy.[54]

Students at times referred to these European scholars as "Father O'Hara's Foreign Legion" or, because of their accents, as "the Department of Fractured English," but John U. Nef of the University of Chicago was close to the truth when he called them "a Notre Dame Renaissance." That is what they were. Each was an international scholar and their Notre Dame affiliation gave the university valuable recognition abroad. They attracted more qualified graduate students to the university and raised the level of each department's scholarship. Cooperating with Father O'Hara, they also organized outstanding scholarly colloquia: a symposium on "Calculus of Variations," hosted by Karl Menger and Arthur Haas, attracted such notables as the president of the American Mathematical Society and Marston Morse of the Institute of Advanced Study; Waldemar Gurian organized a "Symposium on Political and Social Philosophy" in late 1938 with participants Jacques Maritain and Mortimer Adler; and that same year a symposium on "the Physics of the Universe and the Nature of Primordial Particles," organized in part by Eugene Guth, offered papers by Arthur Compton of Chicago, Harlan Shipley of Harvard, and Carol Anderson of California. Twenty years before, the minims and prep students had been a majority. It truly was a renaissance.[55]

These European scholars were of great assistance in Father O'Hara's efforts to strengthen the university's graduate program. The Department of Chemistry was already offering respectable doctoral degrees under Professor Henry Froning and Father Nieuwland, and the Department of Biology was beginning to do the same with Professors James Reyniers, Theodore Just, and Father Francis Wenninger. Father Philip Moore, with a recent doctorate from the Catholic University of America and three additional years of study at the École des Chartes in Paris, was appointed secretary of the graduate committee in 1933, and five additional doctoral programs were added throughout the decade. The basic requirements for all doctorates were three years of postbaccalaureate study, a reading knowledge of French and German, a final written and oral examination, and a dissertation approved by the department.[56]

With the opening of the new Cushing Hall of Engineering in 1932 and its up-to-date equipment and laboratories, a Department of Metallurgy was established the following year, with a doctoral program. The program relied on other departments for courses in geology, physics, chemistry, and quantitative analysis but offered its own classes in Ferrous and Nonferrous Metallurgy and Metallography, Alloy Steel, and Alloy Systems, among others. Dr. Edward Mahin chaired the department from 1933 to 1953.[57]

In 1936 the Department of Philosophy introduced a doctoral program. Philosophy in the tradition of Plato and Saint Augustine, and of Aristotle and Saint Thomas Aquinas, had long been at the heart of Catholic higher education, and much of Catholic theology was expressed in Aristotelian and Thomistic terminology. The graduate courses offered reflected this tradition—Problems of Matter and Form, Problems of Substance, the System of Plato, the System of Aristotle, the System of St. Thomas Aquinas. To enter the doctoral program, the student needed some background in logic, general and rational psychology, metaphysics, ethics, epistemology, and cosmology. The student could concentrate in one of two areas: a historical study of twelfth and thirteenth century texts or an analytical study of the philosophy of Saint Thomas. Father Leo R. Ward, Yves Simon, and Francis McMahon were the most respected of the faculty.[58]

With the arrival of Professors Arthur Haas and Eugene Guth from Europe and the return of Father Henry Bolger from four years of study at the California Institute of Technology, the Department of Physics offered a doctoral program in 1938. In addition to the usual advanced physics courses, specialized instruction was available in the physical properties of rubber and similar substances, atomic physics, and theoretical mechanics and wave-mechanics. The presence of the university's atom-smasher and Father Nieuwland's experiments with synthetic rubber clearly influenced these specializations.[59]

The doctoral program in mathematics, also established in 1938, followed a similar path. Almost all graduate courses offered were taught by émigré professors Karl Menger and Emil Artin and reflected their interests and contributions: Topology, Calculus of Variations, Complex Variables, and Advanced Algebra and Geometry. Professor Menger also inaugurated an annual mathematical colloquium, similar to one that he was familiar with in Vienna, to showcase recent research at Notre Dame and elsewhere, and its published proceedings were well received.[60]

The following year, the Department of Political Science (or Politics as it was then called) began the final doctoral program added in the 1930s. As might be expected, the bulk of the graduate courses were offered by Waldemar Gurian and Ferdinand Hermens, with assistance from Father Francis Boland and young Paul Bartholomew. There were graduate courses in the governments of Latin America, Chinese-Japanese relations, the history of political philosophy, the American Constitution, state and municipal government, and Marxism.[61]

Another program that Father O'Hara established was the Bureau of Economic Research. At the suggestion of Martin Gillen, an economic theorist and Notre Dame benefactor, and with the assistance of Frank Walker, Notre Dame alumnus and member of the university's board of lay trustees, Father O'Hara met in late 1934 with Orlando Weber, chairman of Allied Chemical Corporation in New York. Weber apparently committed close to $50,000 to the project, and

Father Edward Keller was assigned as principal investigator. Father Keller, a Holy Cross priest, had been ordained in 1931, did two years of postgraduate study at the University of Minnesota, and then returned to Notre Dame to teach economics. His first book, *A Study of the Physical Assets, Sometimes Called Wealth, of the United States, 1922–1933*, published in 1939, was a defense of the American capitalistic system against the claims of serious unequal distribution of wealth in the United States. Father O'Hara contributed the preface and defended it against criticism from Father Raymond McGowan of the National Catholic Welfare Conference in Washington, DC. Father Keller published several books through the bureau over the years—*The Church and Our Economic System* in 1947, *Christianity and American Capitalism* in 1953, and *The Case for Right to Work Laws* in 1956—and Father (later Bishop and Cardinal) O'Hara consistently came to his defense. As president, Father O'Hara was also a strong supporter of the conservative theories of Dean James McCarthy of the Business College and Dean Clarence Manion of the Law School.

As successful as Father O'Hara was in recruiting émigré scholars to join the faculty in the 1930s, he was equally successful in attracting others as temporary and visiting lecturers. In the fall of 1934 Jacques Maritain delivered a lecture in Washington Hall entitled "The Historical Ideal of a Renewed Christianity." Maritain, a convert to Catholicism, was professor of philosophy at the Institute Catholique in Paris, authored *An Introduction to Philosophy* and *Art and Scholasticism*, and was generally considered the world's most outstanding Thomistic philosopher. Étienne Gilson, philosopher, historian of philosophy, and professor at the Sorbonne in Paris, delivered three lectures on the history of Thomistic philosophy from the Middle Ages to the present. He would later be instrumental in the establishment of the Medieval Institute at Notre Dame. Frank Sheed, prominent Catholic author and publisher, delivered a lecture that October, and his wife, Masie Ward, lectured the following month. Shane Leslie, convert, author, former editor of the *Dublin Review* and first cousin of Britain's future prime minister, Winston Churchill, spoke on "The Oxford Movement," the title of a book he had published the previous year.[62]

Invited lecturers the following year were equally impressive. Étienne Gilson returned and delivered lectures on "Forerunners of the Renaissance in Medieval England" and "The Problem of the Theoremata and the Meaning of Scotism." Arnold Lunn, British convert, apologist, and author of *Now I See* and *The Flight From Reason* (and the originator of slalom skiing) lectured on "The Joy of Controversy" and "Science and the Supernatural." Christopher Hollis, the brilliant

British economist, delivered fourteen lectures in the fall of 1935 on "The Standard of Living of Our Ancestors," "The Founding of the Bank of England," "English Capital in America," "Karl Marx," "Booms and Slumps," "Economic Nationalism," and "The Last Ten Years." Desmond FitzGerald also lectured that fall. He had fought the British in the 1916 uprising and was captured and jailed along with William Cosgrave and Éamon de Valera, but he presently was a member of the Dáil of the Irish Free State. His six lectures were on Richard Crashaw, Coventry Patmore, Gerard Manley Hopkins, Joseph de Maistre, Ernest Hello, and Léon Bloy. Shane Leslie returned that fall for a series of weekly lectures, one on the Catholic sympathies of William Shakespeare.[63]

Christopher Hollis returned in 1936 to lecture on Karl Marx and on his and Thomas Jefferson's concepts of society, and later that year Arnold Lunn spoke on "Physical Research in England and Some of My Experiences with Conan Doyle." Monsignor Fulton Sheen and Father James Gillis, editor of the *Catholic World*, also visited and spoke. Desmond FitzGerald returned for six weeks in 1938 to lecture on "The Philosophy of Politics," the title of a book he was then completing. Shane Leslie in 1936 left a poem, "Notre Dame Farewell," that included the following two verses:[64]

> From the day Freshman landeth
> Where thy golden beauty standeth
> High above the morning campus
> Stars of thine have come to lamp us
> Till Commencement bids us going
> Gather harvest from our sowing.
> One by one the eager classes
> Rise from work and play and Masses—
> Athletes, scholars, strong and clever
> Rise and march away for ever.
> Notre Dame the beautiful, the wonderful!
>
> All the men who knew thy grotto
> Guard through life thy sacred motto.
> Lift the night away from morrow
> Unto all in toil and sorrow
> They are thine and thine for ever
> When their lives are in the twilight

Shed thy glory in their eyelight.
Let them glimpse thy golden phantom
Let them hear thy victory's anthem—
Let them join the Notre Dame legion
In thine everlasting region!
Notre Dame the beautiful, the wonderful!

It is difficult to evaluate Father O'Hara's intellectual leadership of the university. There is no question that the undergraduate programs established by Fathers Burns, Walsh, and O'Donnell remained strong. He strengthened graduate programs and the university's scholarly research with the hiring of world-renowned émigré professors, and he complemented them with an impressive series of scholarly lectures from well-respected philosophers, theologians, poets, economists, and scientists from home and abroad. Yet Father O'Hara always remained prefect of religion at heart and his primary concern was with the spiritual welfare of his boys. He inspected the library shelves regularly and often removed sociology and anthropology books he thought a temptation to students, tearing out the title page and giving it to the director of libraries to allow him to remove such titles from the card catalogue. Several popular American novelists were also victims. He continued an earlier ban on *Time* magazine, and he rejected *Life* magazine's request for an article on Notre Dame because "bare legs and bare backs are spread over the pages for their sales appeal." Librarian Paul Byrne may have summed it up best:[65]

> Surely no one can say that Father O'Hara was anti-intellectual. . . . He was in my judgment a highly intelligent man—though he was no great scholar—with a quick mind. . . . He could be very broad on some topics when you felt he might not be, and very narrow on others when you felt he should not be. Anyway, I am sure that whatever he did he felt it was the right thing to do.

Two other visitors arrived in the 1930s to attend special convocations and receive honorary degrees: President Franklin Roosevelt in 1935 and Vatican Secretary of State (and future Pope Pius XII) Cardinal Eugenio Pacelli in 1936. The president's visit was almost, but not quite, an afterthought. The Commonwealth of the Philippines was to inaugurate its first president, Manuel Quezon, after independence in the fall of 1935 and a friend of Notre Dame in the Philippines suggested that the university have a celebration to mark the occasion. The Philippines was a Catholic country, Notre Dame was a leading Catholic institution, and Philippine students were enrolled at Notre Dame every year. The suggestion was made that the celebration should include the awarding of an honorary degree to Carlos Romulo, publisher of a Philippine newspaper syndicate, a practicing Catholic, and a possible candidate for the presidency of the University of Manila. Father O'Hara embraced the idea enthusiastically but met with some early disappointments. Cardinal Dennis Dougherty of Philadelphia, formerly a bishop in the Philippines, declined to attend since he feared that the new Philippine government might eventually turn anti-Catholic. Theodore Roosevelt, Jr., former governor general of the Philippines, was invited to give an address but could not be excused from an earlier commitment. Former governor Al Smith of New York, a strong supporter of Philippine independence, also declined to come.[66]

Father O'Hara had originally intended to invite President Roosevelt to send a message that might be read at the convocation, but after the earlier rejections he decided to invite the president to attend in person. He sent the invitation through alumnus Frank Walker, then secretary of President Roosevelt's executive council (where he once said his job was "to coordinate the incoordinatable and unscrew the inscrutable"). The president accepted the invitation and said he could be available on December 9, after a speech earlier that day in Chicago. The president's acceptance, however, did open another controversy. The Knights of Columbus that fall had petitioned the president to intervene in the Mexican persecution of the Church and protect the religious liberty of the American citizens living there. The president replied, publicly, that it would not be proper for the American government to intervene in the internal affairs of another country, although at that time United States Ambassador Josephus Daniels was in fact in secret negotiations with the Mexican government. President Roosevelt did not want to make it public and seem to be responding to Catholic pressure. The Catholic press was generally critical of Roosevelt's non-interventionist reply, and for Notre Dame to offer him an honorary degree at just that time seemed, said one historian, "almost treason to the Catholic cause." The *Brooklyn Tablet*, the *Catholic Review* of Baltimore, and *America* magazine all expressed opposition. Father O'Hara was embarrassed by the opposition because he feared it would distract from the convocation's goal of honoring the Philippines, and he himself had publicly opposed United States intervention in Mexico in a *New York Times* article earlier.[67]

The convocation went off without a hitch, but narrowly. Presidential speech-writer Raymond Moley prepared notes for the president's remarks and, thinking Notre Dame was a Jesuit university, included several references to the Jesuits' dedication to both liberty and science, but a Catholic member of the administration noted the slip in time. Nearly 100,000 people lined the streets of South Bend from the railroad station to the campus. The president was accompanied by Postmaster General James Farley, Governor Henry Horner of Illinois, and Mayor Edward Kelly of Chicago, and he was met on arrival by Indiana Governor Paul McNutt, Cardinal George Mundelein of Chicago, Bishop John Francis Noll of Fort Wayne, and numerous other civic, religious, and Holy Cross officials. Father O'Hara opened the convocation in the gymnasium with a greeting of welcome and read the citations for the honorary degrees. Mr. Romulo responded first with eloquent words on the importance of faith and liberty to the people of the Philippines, but he violated propriety slightly by speaking longer than the president, much longer in fact. Cardinal Mundelein then introduced the president, praising his courage in overcoming personal hardships and commending his early legislation to assist the poor and the forgotten. Roosevelt expressed his gratitude at being "a new alumnus of the University of Notre Dame," reflected on the Philippines' forty-year progress to independence, commended both Notre Dame and the Philippines for their espousal of the principles of religious freedom, and thanked Father O'Hara and the assembled congregation especially for their continued prayers. The president later wrote that "that day shall always stand out as one of the greatest days of my life."[68]

The Vatican secretary of state visited the following year. When news was released that Cardinal Eugenio Pacelli was coming to the United States that fall, Father O'Hara immediately invited him to Notre Dame. The cardinal's schedule was already quite full and such a visit at first seemed impossible. Bishop Francis Spellman, auxiliary bishop of Boston and close acquaintance of Cardinal Pacelli from his days in Rome, apparently interceded, and an hour's visit on the cardinal's way from New York to Chicago was arranged. The cardinal's plane landed in South Bend at about 1:30 p.m. on Sunday, October 25, a motorcade drove immediately to Sacred Heart Church where the cardinal was welcomed by Father O'Hara and several Indiana bishops, and after a few minutes of prayer, kneeling in the church sanctuary, all processed to Washington Hall for the convocation and honorary degree. The cardinal expressed his gratitude in understandable English, blessed all in the name of the Holy Father, and, if superiors did not object, granted the students a holiday, including the students of Saint Mary's. Within three years he would be governing the Church as Pope Pius XII.[69]

Father O'Hara continued the work of his predecessors Father Matthew Walsh and Father Charles O'Donnell in expanding the campus physically as well. Money was available—from Father Burns's million-dollar fund drive, from Knute Rockne's football profits, and from tuition as enrollment rose. The University Council voted to limit student enrollment to 3,000, but that limit apparently was too difficult to maintain. When Father O'Hara was named president in 1934 the student body numbered approximately 2,600, but by 1940, when he left office, the number had grown to 3,200. Building costs were lower and unemployment high during the economic slump of the continuing Depression of the 1930s and it was a favorable time to build.[70]

The first building that Father O'Hara added, in 1934, was a modern laundry, erected next to the sisters' quarters and close to Saint Joseph's Lake. It comprised a full laundry to serve the students, priests and religious, the dining hall, and athletic teams, and also a dry cleaning facility. With the increase in student enrollment over the years, the larger facilities were needed.

Also of benefit to the students was a new infirmary in 1935, behind Saint Edward's Hall and a little to the northeast of the Main Building. It was designed by Maginnis and Walsh of Boston, the architects of the Law School and Dillon and Alumni Halls, and it was to face west, with a clear view of Saint Joseph's Lake, and perhaps the beginning of a new quadrangle on that northeast portion of the campus. The three-story collegiate Gothic structure could accommodate 125 persons with several guest rooms, a chapel, and a modern, well-equipped clinic. The infirmary was open twenty-four hours and was staffed by two doctors, four Holy Cross sisters, and two registered nurses. The total cost of the building was $250,000.[71]

The Department of Biology, housed at that time in the basement of the Science Building (later LaFortune Student Center), was expanding, especially in the relatively new area of germ-free research, and larger quarters were needed. The cornerstone of a new biology building was laid on commencement weekend, June 1936, and honored at the ceremony were Francis Garvan of the Allied Chemical Corporation and brothers Doctor William and Doctor Charles Mayo of the Rochester, Minnesota, clinic. The building's architecture was modern, not collegiate Gothic, a few rooms were air-conditioned and others were ventilated by special air ducts, and the building was set at the far end of the then northeast playfields, close to the power plant on which it would rely for proper steam and water pressure. It also marked the northern end and effectively closed off the new northeast quadrangle that was being developed. The $500,000 structure had two stories plus a basement and held classrooms, laboratories, offices, and a large auditorium.[72]

As former dean of the College of Commerce, Father O'Hara kept an eye on profit and loss, and as a former prefect of religion he always had the students' spiritual and religious welfare in mind; as enrollment continued to increase by approximately a hundred a year, he was concerned that off campus students lived too far away from campus Masses and other religious exercises—and their board and room money was remaining off campus also. It was decided to build three new halls, forming the northeast quadrangle between the university gymnasium on the south and the recently constructed biology building on the north. The temporary wooden and stucco "Cardboard Palaces" (Freshman and Sophomore Halls) and the one-story eastern wing of Saint Edward's Hall had to be demolished. The first new hall, constructed in 1936, was named for Father John W. Cavanaugh, university president from 1905 to 1919, who had died only a year before. The second hall, built in 1937 just to the north, was named for Father John Zahm, the brilliant priest-scientist who had also served as Notre Dame's vice president for a time and made several scientific trips into Latin America, one with former president Theodore Roosevelt in 1913. The third building was built in 1939 and was named for two alumni and important donors, William Breen and Frank Phillips, and was situated at the east end of the gymnasium and began the eastern side of the northeast quadrangle. The three halls were quite similar, all of neo-Gothic architecture but less elaborate than Alumni and Dillon, all of brick with limestone trim, each having four stories with at least a partial basement, and each accommodating between 180 and 200 students, mostly in double rooms. In the basement and first floor of the southern wing of Breen-Phillips Hall, the Athletic Department administration and ticket manager had their offices.[73]

With these new residence halls able to accommodate hundreds of additional students, Father O'Hara turned his attention to another of his concerns—a central location for the prayer, meals, and community life of the Holy Cross priests residing at the university. Many lived in the residence halls, but not all, and Father O'Hara decided to renovate Corby Hall and turn it into a Holy Cross community residence, providing lodging for priests and brothers not living in student halls, and providing a kitchen, dining room, chapel, and social space to enable all Holy Cross religious to come together regularly.[74]

The final building constructed during Father O'Hara's presidency was also the longest in preparation. With the sudden and unexpected death of Knute Rockne in the spring of 1931, there was a groundswell of support for some kind of memorial on the campus. Students, alumni, and others began contributing immediately but, in the midst of the Depression, the contributions never reached the level the administration hoped. An altar dedicated to Saint Olaf, the patron saint of Norway, Rockne's birthplace, was constructed in the Dillon Hall chapel, and a bas-relief of the coach was added to the east wall of the recently erected Alumni Hall. By the fall of 1937, $135,000 had been contributed, and the accumulated interest had brought the total up to $150,000, and the administration decided to add $200,000 and begin construction.[75]

The building would undoubtedly have pleased the coach who believed that every student should be involved in games and sports and exercise. The semi-Gothic building, designed by Maginnis and Walsh, was situated on the former site of the ninth and eighteenth greens, just to the south of Lyons Hall, and closed off to the west the south quadrangle of Alumni, Dillon, the dining hall, Badin, Howard, and Lyons. Over the main entrance were plaques honoring Sieur de La Salle and Chief Pokagon, early Christian visitors to this area. Over the north entrance was the seal of the university, and over the south that of the United States. The coat of arms of France was placed over one door, of Norway over another, and the shields of the United States Military Academy and of the Naval Academy, two traditional football opponents, were placed over other entrances. Sealed in the cornerstone were copies of the 1930 and 1931 football reviews, Rockne's autobiography, various newspaper clippings, including one from the *Lordages-Avisen* of Tonsberg, Norway, and the speech of Will Rogers on the occasion of Rockne's death.[76]

The building's main floor contained a memorial foyer with a bust of Rockne, a trophy room, and faculty and student lounges. The swimming pool was 75 feet by 45 feet, and a beginners' pool measured 45 feet by almost 12 feet. The water, drawn from Saint Joseph's Lake, was pumped and preheated by the power plant, and was filtered at a rate of 27,000 gallons per hour. The water temperature was maintained at 75 degrees and the room temperature at 80 degrees. The building contained three basketball courts, twelve handball or squash courts, wrestling and boxing rooms, more than 2,000 small and large lockers, and a sun porch on the third floor overlooking the slightly shortened golf course.[77]

If the students were proud of the Rockne Memorial and the new facilities for non-varsity athletes, they were equally proud of the varsity football team's success throughout the decade under new coach Elmer Layden. The team had a 3–5–1 record in 1933, Hunk Anderson's final year as coach, which was Notre Dame's first losing season in forty-five years. The new coach seemed able to turn the program around immediately and the team won six and lost three in 1934. Tragedy struck the next spring, however, when Joe Sullivan, the starting left tackle, died of pneumonia. For the rest of the decade, the team never lost more than two games a season, was eight and one in 1938, and had at least one All-American every year. The 1935 game with powerful Ohio State before 81,000 in Columbus was voted the "game of the century" by the Associated Press in 1969. Down 13 to 0 at halftime, the Irish slowly crawled back. They scored two touchdowns but missed both extra points, remaining behind 13 to 12 with less than three minutes to go. After the second score the Irish tried an onside kick but Ohio State recovered. The Buckeyes tried to run out the clock but a hard tackle by Andy Pilney jarred the ball loose. Notre Dame's substitute center fell on it, and Notre Dame had a final chance. With less than thirty seconds left, Notre Dame faked a reverse, and Billy Shakespeare threw a pass to Wayne Millner in the end zone for the winning score. The stadium crowd was understandably stunned but the celebration back on campus lasted for hours. Nuns across the country wrote to Father O'Hara and told him of their prayers for victory during the game, and most never knew (not that it would matter) that Shakespeare was a Protestant and Millner was Jewish.[78]

One final campus celebration was slightly tinged with sadness, at least for Father O'Hara. On December 11, 1939, the Vatican representative in the United States announced that Father O'Hara was being appointed bishop in charge of all Catholic military chaplains of the United States throughout the world. The choice was understandable. Father O'Hara's six-year term as president and religious superior was coming to a close. He had proven himself a very effective administrator, and he had wide experience and success in caring for the religious and spiritual needs of young men of college age, the age of most men in the military. The archbishop of New York had traditionally been given the responsibility of assuring that there were a sufficient number of military chaplains at any time and the responsibility of overseeing their work, and this was not a heavy burden during peacetime when the military was small. But with the outbreak of World War II in Europe in September 1939, and with Japan's invasion of China two years before, the American military was being increased. Francis Spellman, former auxiliary bishop of Boston, had recently been named archbishop of New York, and he wanted an assistant bishop to whom he could delegate all responsibility for the military chaplain ministry. He asked for Father O'Hara.[79]

Father O'Hara arranged to be away from campus, in Los Angeles, when the appointment was announced, and he did not return until December 21, Christmas vacation, so as not to disturb the academic schedule. After the usual round of celebrations and congratulatory meetings, the episcopal ordination was set for January 12 in the campus church. The consecrating bishop was Archbishop Spellman, assisted by Bishop Joseph Ritter of Indianapolis and Bishop John Noll of Fort Wayne. The bishop-elect's mother, still living in Indianapolis, was unable to attend, but the church was filled with visiting bishops, priests, religious, students, faculty, and civic dignitaries. At the banquet following, Archbishop Spellman put the day in a wider context:[80]

> It is not that Notre Dame loses Father O'Hara. It is not that Notre Dame gives up Bishop O'Hara forever. It is that Notre Dame, through the personality of Bishop O'Hara, widens the university's scope, and brings the spirit of Notre Dame into the Army and Navy, brings the spirit of Notre Dame into our country, and the spirit of Notre Dame is a spirit of patriotism, the spirit of devotion to our country, the spirit of love for the church.

Ever the prefect of religion, Bishop O'Hara asked for a residence in a New York parish where, even as bishop, he could hear confessions from six to nine each morning and from four-thirty to five-thirty each afternoon. The rest of his day would be devoted to his military ordinariate ministry. The day after his episcopal ordination, he published a final *Religious Bulletin* for the students:[81]

> The typewriter is a bit rusty from disuse, and perhaps the fingers move more slowly than they once did, but the heart begs the Prefect of Religion for a chance to do one more <u>Bulletin</u> before the separation. . . .
>
> Retrospect is easy—especially when in three decades of work with Notre Dame men you can't recall one who was really evil. Retrospect is pleasant when you know that thousands of penitents have gone out with resolution strong enough to withstand temptations, when you know that daily Communion has turned good intentions into good deeds, has made weak infants into strong men, and strong men into saints of God. . . .
>
> Your problem is of the present and of the future. It is yours to say whether Notre Dame shall be for your brother and your children and for your children's children, the shrine of our Blessed Lady, the haven of peace it has been for you. . . .

Daily Communion is the Food of Sacrifice—never let its tradition weaken or fade. Daily Mass is the sacred core of Sacrifice. Daily visits to Mary, the Mother of God—at the Grotto, telling your beads, in a goodnight smile to the Lady of the Dome—these means of grace keep you close to God.

To the students of today and tomorrow I entrust Notre Dame.

Good-bye, boys. God bless you.

CHAPTER 13

Notre Dame, the Navy, and World War II

Father J. Hugh O'Donnell seemed well prepared to succeed Father O'Hara as president of Notre Dame in the summer of 1940. He had been born of Irish ancestry in Grand Rapids, Michigan, in 1895, and graduated from Notre Dame in 1916. Serious efforts were being made to organize a Glee Club during his student days, he joined as a tenor, and he apparently assumed direction of the club during his senior year while awaiting the appointment of a permanent director. A well-built, raw-boned young man, he was also the center on the football team. The rumor persisted throughout his life that somehow he was responsible for Notre Dame's loss to Yale in 1914, perhaps because of a fumble he caused. When students later observed him walking across campus, someone could sing out "Who lost the Yale game?" and another in sing-song would reply "J. Hugh O'Donnell!" The final score of the game was 28 to 0 and thus one miscue, no matter how serious, did not cause the defeat. In fact, summaries of the game indicate that he did not play at all that afternoon. Graduating in 1916, he entered the Congregation of Holy Cross, spent one year in the novitiate, studied theology (and American history) in Washington, DC, and was ordained a priest in 1921. The following year he received his PhD in American Church history from the Catholic

University of America. He taught history at Notre Dame, served as rector of Badin Hall and prefect of discipline throughout the 1920s, and in 1931 was appointed president of Saint Edward's University in Austin, Texas. Saint Edward's had been founded by the Congregation of Holy Cross in 1876 and named for Father Sorin's patron saint. When Father O'Hara was named president of Notre Dame in 1934, he asked that Father O'Donnell be appointed vice president, and he held this position for six years, serving as acting president when Father O'Hara was absent from campus on university, Church, or government assignments. Student, professor, prefect of discipline, college president, and Notre Dame vice president, he had excellent preparation for the university's highest office.[1]

The university was in a comfortable situation as the new academic year began in the fall of 1940. The student body numbered over 3,100 and the faculty was slightly over or under 300, depending on how graduate student-teachers were counted. The dining hall was large enough to feed everyone, the student infirmary could care for any sick, the new power plant and system of tunnels kept all buildings comfortable during the harsh northern Indiana winters, the stadium, gymnasium, and Rockne Memorial were more than adequate for varsity and interhall athletic activities, and the eleven residence halls accommodated most students on campus. The university certainly had needs—additional faculty office space, more modern science laboratories, more classrooms, and at least one additional residence hall—but the university community could live with these deficiencies, at least for a time.[2]

One of the first decisions of his presidency, the hiring of Father John A. O'Brien to the faculty, soon began one of the major controversies of Father O'Donnell's tenure. Father O'Brien had been born in 1893 in Peoria, Illinois, of a well-to-do family. He attended Saint Patrick's Parish grade school there, Spalding Institute for high school, the College of Holy Cross in Massachusetts, Saint Viator's College in Bourbonnais, Illinois, and was ordained a priest for the diocese of Peoria in 1916. He spent a year studying philosophy—which he did not like—at the Catholic University of America in Washington, DC, and was then assigned as pastor of Saint John's Church and Newman Club chaplain at the University of Illinois in Champaign. While there, he also found time to study for and receive a PhD in educational psychology in 1920, with a specialization in speed-reading and comprehension. He and other religious ministers on the campus eventually received approval to offer religion classes for which students received academic credit as long as the classes were not taught on university property and the professors had PhD degrees. Father O'Brien, a man of some family wealth, immediately acquired a building close to campus and began offering religion classes to Catholic students. He and the Knights of Columbus, with aid from the diocese, soon erected a most impressive Newman Club Center, with residence and dining facilities, at a cost of $750,000. Father O'Brien urged dioceses and religious communities to consider establishing similar academic programs on state university campuses across the country since he felt that there would never be sufficient places in Catholic universities to accommodate the Catholic population of the United States. This opinion met with strong opposition from various bishops and religious congregations, especially the Jesuits, who had invested personnel and millions of dollars in Catholic universities. Father O'Brien was obliged to tone down his rhetoric.[3]

That was not Father O'Brien's only controversy. He was not a serious research scholar but a popularizer and apologist, dedicated to making even difficult Catholic doctrines understandable to the average Catholic churchgoer and interested non-Catholics, and he published articles on the Ogino-Knaus system of family planning through the rhythm method, wrote favorably of evolution, and questioned the reality and duration of hellfire. His principal interest however, was in making and instructing converts. He scheduled convert instruction classes at the University of Illinois and spent summers street preaching throughout the southern states, explaining Catholic beliefs to interested listeners. He published pamphlets on dating and courtship, marriage and the family, Confession and Holy Communion, the Mass and priesthood, and short lives of individual saints, and in 1938 he authored *The Faith of Millions*, a primer of Catholic teachings suitable for use in convert instruction, and it eventually went through twenty-seven editions and was translated into nine languages. By the end of the 1930s, his more controversial writings had become the source of some embarrassment to the diocese, and although the debt on the Newman Club Center had recently been paid, in part through Father O'Brien's royalties and personal wealth, a newly appointed bishop of the diocese questioned the prudence of involving the diocese in such a debt at all. Father O'Brien realized that it was probably time to move on—but where? His views on education had alienated many among the Jesuit community and his controversial views on hell had raised opposition among theologians at the Catholic University of America in Washington, DC. In 1939 he approached Father O'Hara and asked if a place could be found for him at Notre Dame. Father O'Hara was agreeable but Father O'Brien first wanted to spend a year at Oxford, continuing his reading and writing. When he returned in the fall of 1940, Father J. Hugh O'Donnell had succeeded Father O'Hara as president but he followed his predecessor's commitment and signed a contract with Father O'Brien for $2,500 a year. This was only the second visit Father O'Brien ever made to Notre Dame. The first had been in 1913 when he captained the Saint Viator's College debate team and defeated Notre Dame, Notre Dame's first defeat in debate in approximately twenty years.[4]

The year Father O'Brien spent in England was a very important one. Germany invaded Poland on September 1, and England and France retaliated by declaring war on Germany two days later. From England Father O'Brien saw Germany overrun the Low Countries and invade France, and he cheered the narrow escape of British troops at Dunkirk. He made friends with Joseph P. Kennedy, the American ambassador in London at the time (and father of the future president), and he and the ambassador seemed to have the same depressing view of the European situation: Germany had long prepared for war and possessed Europe's most powerful fighting machine; England began preparing too late and was no match for the German military; England would have little chance once Germany completed its conquest of the continent and turned its might across the channel; even with American aid, Britain could not win, and thus any American aid—ships, guns, planes—could eventually fall into German hands and be used against future German foes, even the United States; and therefore the best resolution was for England to seek a negotiated peace with Hitler and for the United States to withhold all aid to Britain and build up its own defenses at home.[5]

This was the message Father O'Brien wanted to sound on his return to the United States but, of course, his voice was not the only one. The country was divided over two major issues—President Roosevelt's decision to break tradition and run for a third term against Wendell Willkie in November and the stance of the United States toward the war in Europe—and the two could be related. Franklin Roosevelt was convinced that Adolf Hitler had to be stopped and turned back, and at least for the moment he was willing to give Great Britain whatever assistance he could to accomplish this. Many others, confident that two wide oceans had kept European and Asian troubles far from American shores throughout most of its history, hoped to remain aloof and let the war in Europe remain the concern only of the Europeans. American aviation hero Charles Lindbergh and the famed "radio priest" of Royal Oak, Michigan, Charles Coughlin, were leading spokesmen for this view, and Congress itself had passed Neutrality Acts from 1935 to 1939 to implement it. From his year's experience in England, Father O'Brien was eager to add his voice to the isolationist chorus.[6]

Within weeks of his return to the United States, Father O'Brien joined the America First Committee, a committee formed in the late summer of 1940 to counter an earlier group, the Committee to Defend America by Aiding the Allies under the chairmanship of Kansas editor William Allen White. This White Committee, as it was often called, was organized in May 1940 and it strongly supported President Roosevelt's internationalist foreign policy, including efforts to revise the Neutrality Acts and find ways to supply Great Britain with aid, including needed destroyers. The America First Committee, originally the "Emergency Committee to Defend America First," opposed any United States involvement in the European conflict, espousing four basic principles:[7]

1. The United States must build an impregnable defense for America.
2. No foreign power, or group of powers, can successfully attack a *prepared* America.
3. American democracy can be preserved only by keeping out of the European war.
4. "Aid short of war" weakens national defense at home and threatens to involve America in war abroad.

Father O'Brien's first published article on the world situation was isolationist but moderate:[8]

> An America at first merely benevolently neutral, later an active participant, is the prize for which propagandists of Europe and their agents in this country are working overtime. Can we resist their wiles? This is the supreme question facing the people of America today. . . .
>
> The traditional policy of non-intervention in the quarrels of Europe does not mean that America is without sympathy for the victims of unjust aggression or unwilling to succor them. It means simply that in the present state of international anarchy, America will help them most effectively, not by spreading the flames of war to our continent, but by using her good offices ceaselessly and untiringly to bring peace and give generously of her means to all the victims of the madness of war. . . . Can America stay out of war? Yes, we answer. American not only *can* but *must*.

In December, he delivered a speech in Washington Hall that was more fiery. By that time President Roosevelt had been re-elected for his third term and had announced his intention to send fifty "overaged" destroyers to Great Britain. Five Notre Dame faculty members, identified as such by a reporter, had also signed a letter to the *New York Herald Tribune* favoring Britain's tight blockade of Europe and continued fighting, and Father O'Brien may have wanted to clarify that all at Notre Dame did not support the president's pro-British policy. He was critical of America's entrance into World War I, of the Treaty of Versailles that ended that war, and of the efforts of internationalists to aid the Allies presently at war:[9]

That treaty [Versailles], imposed at the point of a sword, sunk the fangs of hatred into a prostrate foe, sowed the seeds of future wars, and paved the way for the rise to dictatorships in Europe. Our entrance paved the way, too, for the worst depression in our history. . . .

Shall we pour out our blood and treasure to guarantee the ever shifting boundary lines in Europe and try to dictate to foreign nations the kind of government they must have? That way lies futility, war, tragedy; in short, national suicide.

The propaganda pouring into our country from the broadcasting companies and the cables of Great Britain that our frontiers are in Europe, and that we must put the European household in order before we can be safe in America, is unmitigated buncombe. Never in our national history were we less in danger of attack from Europe than at the present time.

The Committee to Defend America by Aiding the Allies should be called the mass murder committee. Their concern is first with Great Britain, only secondly with America. To perpetuate Britain's hold on one-fifth of the world's surface they would sacrifice the blood of uncounted millions of American boys and bring bankruptcy to our nation.

Are the American people going to be led like sheep to the slaughter for a second time? If not they should thunder in the ears of Congress and of the President their protest against the efforts to drag us into the flames of Europe's strife.

His criticisms of the Treaty of Versailles, which had established the later borders of Poland, Hungary, Czechoslovakia, and other European nations, met with heated opposition from numerous residents in the South Bend area with backgrounds in Eastern Europe, and Father O'Brien hurried to offer clarification. He insisted that he had no love for Hitler and condemned his invasions of Eastern Europe, and he clarified that he had great affection for the peoples of Poland, Czechoslovakia, and their neighboring countries and was happy that the Treaty of Versailles had given them independence. But he still insisted that the treaty had been conceived in hate and revenge and had numerous unfortunate provisions—

"Very Reverend Basil Anthony Mary Moreau
Founder of the Congregation of Holy Cross."

Father Basil Moreau, C.S.C., founder of the Congregation of Holy Cross in France in 1837

Father Jacques Dujarié, founder of the Brothers of Saint Joseph, later the Brothers of Holy Cross

Log Chapel, the 1906 replica of the original chapel built by Father Stephen Badin in 1832

Father Edward Sorin, C.S.C., with seven Holy Cross brothers, founded the University of Notre Dame du Lac in 1842

Notre Dame's Main Building, with its nationally recognized Golden Dome

Sacred Heart Basilica, the spiritual center of the Notre Dame campus

Statue of Father William Corby, C.S.C., as he granted general absolution to the Irish Brigade at the Battle of Gettysburg

Father John A. Zahm, C.S.C., professor, scientist, explorer, and controversial author

Artist Luigi Gregori, whose paintings graced the Main Building, Sacred Heart Basilica, and Washington Hall

Sister M. Aloysius Mulcaire, C.S.C., who for forty years cared for the grammar school minims

Professor "Colonel" William Hoynes, teaching class in a law school classroom in Sorin Hall in the 1890s

Notre Dame Grotto, a favorite campus location for quiet prayer for students and visitors alike

Babe Ruth and Knute Rockne on the baseball star's visit to Notre Dame in 1926

Holy Cross brothers and lay workers periodically changed light bulbs around the statue on the Golden Dome; this was probably taken in the 1920s

Father James Burns, C.S.C., university president from 1919 to 1922 and organizer of the first million-dollar fund drive

The 1924 "Four Horsemen" backfield: Don Miller, Elmer Layden, Jim Crowley, and Harry Stuhldreher

Father Julius Nieuwland, C.S.C., brilliant biologist and chemist, and one of the discoverers of synthetic rubber

V-12 Midshipmen in formation on the south quad during World War II

Holy Cross brothers manned the university's fire department from the 1880s into the twenty-first century

The university's main library, named for Father Theodore Hesburgh, C.S.C., features the 132-foot "Word of Life" mural

(opposite-top)
University of Notre Dame Board of Trustees leadership, 1967: Paul Hellmuth (secretary), Father Theodore Hesburgh, C.S.C. (university president), Edmund Stephan (chairman), and Father Howard Kenna, C.S.C. (provincial superior)

(opposite-bottom)
Four Notre Dame presidents. Seated: Fathers John O'Hara, C.S.C. (1934–1940) and Matthew Walsh, C.S.C. (1922–1928). Standing: Fathers Theodore Hesburgh, C.S.C. (1952–1987) and John J. Cavanaugh, C.S.C. (1946–1952)

Badin Hall rector
Kathy Cekanski and
several of the first
undergraduate women,
1972–1973

Future university president
Father Edward "Monk" Malloy,
C.S.C., enjoying cotton candy
at a university picnic in the
spring of 1986

forcing Germany to accept all responsibility at the point of the sword, stripping Germany of its colonies, depriving her of her navy, mandating the occupation of the Rhineland—and that these helped prepare the way for a new conflict twenty years later.[10]

Father O'Brien continued to speak out—against the Treaty of Versailles, against aid to Britain, and against the Committee to Defend America by Aiding the Allies. He spoke in Chicago, Cincinnati, Trenton, and West Lafayette. In December 1940, President Roosevelt advocated a Lend-Lease plan, an effort, despite the provisions of the Neutrality Act of 1939, to supply arms and ammunition to Great Britain without immediate payment. Father O'Brien delivered an especially forceful speech in Dubuque. He began with a criticism of the treaty ending World War I. "Hitlerism is the cancerous product of the Versailles Treaty," he said, a treaty to bring "economic strangulation" to Germany, a treaty filled with "vengeance, hatred and rancor—a treaty that outlawed Christ." "While I despise Hitler's cruelty and his ruthless invasion of the small countries," he added, "I feel that the processes that caused him should be understood." He opposed aid to Britain: "They tell us that Britain says she does not want men now, but 15 million men will be needed from America to help Britain invade Europe." He added that "thinking Americans" wonder if "we are living in America or are we a colony of Britain." The Lend-Lease bill, then under consideration, he called a "war dictatorship bill with all the sinister rumblings of war. . . . We should have national or state referendums which would allow the people to say to their senators and representatives: 'We're against this war and we demand (not plead) that you cast your vote against this measure that will lead us into war.'" He addressed one Iowa senator specifically: "If you are not going to be a second Judas Iscariot, you will cast your vote against the measure every honest man knows is leading us into war." He called the White Committee the "Drag America into the War Committee . . . a saccharine, insidious and deeply entrenched minority" leading America into war as President Wilson did in 1917.[11]

By this time, Father O'Brien was becoming America First's most prominent Catholic spokesperson and, as his fame spread—the *Scholastic* referred to his "renown"—others at Notre Dame stepped forward to oppose him, especially professor of philosophy Francis McMahon.[12] Professor McMahon had been born in Chicago in 1906, attended his parish grade school, Saint Mel High School, and DePaul University. He received his PhD in philosophy from the Catholic University of America in Washington, DC, in 1931, spent two years on a postdoctoral scholarship in Belgium and Rome, and joined the Notre Dame faculty in 1933.

He also became an active member of the Catholic Association for International Peace, an organization founded in 1927 "to help American public opinion, and particularly Catholics, in the task of ascertaining more fully facts of international life and of deciding more accurately what ought to be done that the relations between nations may become just, charitable and peaceful."[13] In a pamphlet he published in early 1940, *The Rights of Man*, Professor McMahon questioned whether the United States, or any country, could remain indifferent to the atrocities being perpetrated by aggressor nations:[14]

> A problem that affects humanity as a whole is one that morally obligates all of humanity. A nation, such as the United States, with its great power, prestige and resources is *a fortiori* charged with a heavy responsibility to promote this work. . . . If a spirit of extreme isolationism prevails in the policy and actions of the United States it is very likely that the problem will remain unsolved. . . . Dominant majorities have not scrupled to violate basic natural rights: the right to life itself, to education, to religious worship, and the right to work. Great masses of people have been reduced virtually to the status of slaves, and brought to the brink of starvation. The problem of ethical minorities was perhaps never graver in modern history than it is at the present time.

By his own admission, what galvanized Professor McMahon into taking a more aggressive stance was the Washington Hall speech of Father O'Brien in December of that year. McMahon was present that evening, challenged Father O'Brien's characterization of the White Committee as a "mass murder" committee from the floor, and was chagrined with the national publicity Father O'Brien's speech was given. Later that month he signed a telegram, with 168 others, urging President Roosevelt to continue his efforts to aid Great Britain and thwart the extension of dictatorships. In public speeches he reminded hearers that another advocate of isolationism, similar in that respect to the America First Committee, was the Communist Party and the Communist paper, the *Daily Worker*. That paper also insisted that the European war was no concern of ours and that the United States should remain aloof.[15] (Russia and Germany had recently signed a nonaggression pact and at the time were carving up Eastern Europe together.)

In early 1941, another controversy entered the debate, the desire of Great Britain to have use of southern Irish ports in its fight against German submarines. Relations between Ireland and England had long been strained, even bitter. Ireland was neutral in the war at that time and hoped to remain so. British Prime Minister Winston Churchill was hoping that Irish Americans might use their influence to convince Ireland to reverse its negative policy. In May 1941, McMahon sent a letter to Irish Prime Minister Éamon de Valera, and he also sent a copy to the *New Republic*. In the *New Republic*, he was identified as a Catholic and a professor at Notre Dame. Of Irish ancestry himself, he deplored England's centuries-old oppression of the Irish ("If we forgive, it is too much to ask that we forget"), but he insisted that England was the only defense against Nazism now and must be aided:[16]

> The waters of the North Atlantic are the danger zone. So long as England carries on, the rest of the world has hope. England's ability to carry on depends on effective delivery of food and munitions. But the present rate of sinking exceeds the tonnage now under construction in the combined yards of Britain and the United States. . . .
>
> What do we ask of the Irish people? Merely the use of three naval bases—Cobb, Berehaven and Lough Swilly. The Treaty of 1921 reserved to England these ports. They were and are vital to her defense. In 1938, however, Prime Minister Chamberlain gave them back as a gesture of friendship, hoping that in any future hour of trial England would not be denied access to them. . . .
>
> Centuries ago Eire rolled back a tide of barbarism, as her scholars and saints spread over Europe instructing the ignorant in faith and sound philosophy. It was Eire that preserved the learning of the ancients when the rest of Europe was in darkness, and imparted the truths of divine and human wisdom to the hungry minds of England and continental Europe. Today a new tide of barbarism has arisen, far worse than the old. Again, it is Eire that can help to turn it back. It is unthinkable that she will fail humanity at this crisis.

At about the same time, Professor McMahon authored a small piece for Fight for Freedom, Inc., warning Americans against six provisions of current Nazi propaganda that needed to be rejected:[17]

1. That it is unethical to go to war when America has not been attacked or provoked;
2. That Hitler is a bulwark against the spread of Communism;

3. That wars settle nothing and the United States should stay out;
4. That the present war is being fought simply to preserve the British Empire;
5. That the war was brought on by international Jewry;
6. That President Roosevelt is misusing his authority in his present favoritism toward Great Britain.

Congressional consideration of the Lend-Lease bill in the early months of 1941 heightened further the debate between the two outspoken professors. In his speech in Dubuque, Father O'Brien categorized Lend-Lease as a major step toward war, and Professor McMahon felt the opposite, that "no decision of the Senate in its history has been weighted with more awesome factors. It is in its power to decide that the world shall be saved from the forces of nihilism; it is also in its power to decide that peoples of the world shall succumb to one of the most destructive forces of human history."[18] By this time, alumni and other friends of the university thought the debate between the two unseemly, and even embarrassing for the university itself, and complaints flowed into the president's office. He early on answered that neither one spoke for the university, that each was expressing only his personal opinions, but he realized that the public dispute was causing some embarrassment. Father O'Donnell decided to intervene and meet with each one.

He met with Father O'Brien on April 26, 1941. Although no memorandum or record of the meeting remains, only Father O'Donnell's preliminary notes, the session seemed to go satisfactorily. Father O'Brien agreed to apologize to the Iowa senator whom he likened to Judas Iscariot if he voted for Lend-Lease. Father O'Donnell had no objection to Father O'Brien speaking when both sides were represented on the program, said he and his vice president, Father John J. Cavanaugh, were willing to review any speeches before their delivery, and, although he would not oppose Father O'Brien writing for scholarly journals, he would discourage him from writing for newspapers. Father O'Brien seemed to accept the conditions, he sent a short apology to the offended senator, but continued his public speaking.[19]

The president's meeting with Professor McMahon did not take place until mid-May, close to final examinations, and it may not have gone well. Although no official record of the meeting remains, Father O'Donnell's secretary wrote that the professor was ordered not to discuss the European war situation in public speeches, and that was the report that circulated. A few days later Father O'Donnell denied that he had put any kind of ban on the professor, and Professor McMahon himself declared that he "was free to speak and write without any hindrance."[20]

Whatever transpired in those meetings, both Father O'Brien and Professor McMahon continued to speak out, always clarifying that they were private citizens and in no way representing the university. They disagreed over President Roosevelt's decision to convoy shipping through the submarine-infested North Atlantic, Professor McMahon insisting that it was necessary to guarantee that Lend-Lease aid would reach its destination and Father O'Brien sure that any sinking of an American ship could only bring the United States closer to war. When Germany declared war on the Soviet Union in the summer of 1941, Professor McMahon was in favor of extending aid to the latter, while Father O'Brien echoed Pope Pius XI, who in speaking of Communism in the encyclical *Divini Redemptoris* said that "no one may collaborate with it in any undertaking whatsoever." When President Roosevelt later announced the Allied policy of "unconditional surrender" at the Casablanca Conference in early 1943, Professor McMahon thought it both appropriate and ethical but Father O'Brien considered it immoral and likely to prolong the war. But with the Japanese attack on Pearl Harbor on December 7, 1941, the isolationist position collapsed. Father O'Brien pledged his loyalty and support to the war effort and spoke rarely about foreign affairs. As one historian has suggested, it was ironic that "the outbreak of the war brought political peace to the campus."[21]

If American entrance into the war left the isolationists, including Father O'Brien, with little to say, the interventionists could carry on as usual, with even greater confidence. On September 24, 1942, as the Soviet Union was bracing for the bitter battle of Stalingrad, Professor McMahon sent a cablegram to Premier Joseph Stalin in the name of Irish-Americans, pledging Irish-American support in this hour of trial and even implying that the United States was soon to open a second front in the West to assist the Soviet Union in the East. The following April he was asked if he thought American Catholics would be sympathetic if Spain attempted to intervene and negotiate a peace, and McMahon answered in the negative, that Franco himself was fascist and American Catholics wanted nothing less than unconditional surrender of the Axis. When American planes bombed rail centers and military locations in and around Rome on July 19, 1943, some bombs hit the Basilica of San Lorenzo outside the walls, about five hundred yards from a rail center. Several in the American hierarchy criticized this attack on Rome, the center of Catholicism, but Professor McMahon stated that as a military objective it was no different than any other Italian city and the bombing could be justified.[22]

More and more of Professor McMahon's remarks were making higher church officials nervous, if not actually displeased. On August 3, 1943, the Vatican's apostolic delegate in Washington, DC, Archbishop Amleto Cicognani, wrote to Father O'Donnell, stating that the Vatican was disturbed by Professor McMahon's recent criticism of Francisco Franco of Spain, calling him fascist, and that Archbishop Cicognani himself was displeased with the professor's very favorable attitude toward Communist Russia and his easy acceptance of the recent bombing of Rome. The archbishop concluded: "I would ask you to take whatever measures may be dictated by prudence and charity to obviate a recurrence of these difficulties."[23] Father O'Donnell took counsel, met with Professor McMahon and, without ever hinting at Archbishop Cicognani's letter (at the archbishop's request), stated that, as a *modus agendi* for the future, the professor should submit to Vice President Father John Cavanaugh for prior approval all speaking invitations the professor received and copies of the proposed speeches themselves. Father O'Donnell insisted that this was not censorship (not until a speech was actually rejected) but Professor McMahon considered the imposition of such irregular conditions tantamount to firing because he felt no respectable faculty member could ever accept them, while Father O'Donnell judged his subsequent departure for the University of Chicago a resignation.[24]

What one historian called a "firestorm" then erupted. Twenty-nine prominent members of the faculty signed a letter asking for clarification and justification, but Father O'Donnell chose not to prolong the controversy and did not reply. Some faculty members, of course, did side with the president. Newspaper columns were generally critical of the president, as were professors at most public universities, including Catholic alumnus George Shuster, president of Hunter College in New York. Of the American Catholic hierarchy who expressed an opinion, the majority favored the president, although a few favored the professor. By late 1943, the Navy had taken over much of the university to train its officers, very few regular students remained, and the Navy had its own concerns. Professor McMahon continued his public activities from Chicago and the controversy passed over, but hard feelings remained among many on the Notre Dame faculty.[25]

Father O'Donnell's personal views in the debate between Professor McMahon and Father O'Brien are not known, although as president of a university with an enrollment of three thousand young men of military age, he must have favored keeping the war far from America, whether by aiding the Allies or not. But once war was declared, he pledged his and the university's complete loyalty and cooperation:[26]

Today, Notre Dame is one. She has known the grim horrors of past wars. . . . In accordance with her strong tradition of patriotism, the University pledges unswerving loyalty and devotion to the Commander-in-Chief of our country and places her facilities at his disposal. We stand united behind him and pray hourly to God to strengthen his arm during the perilous days that lie ahead. We also bespeak Divine Guidance for Congress and all military and civil authorities in the execution of their trust so that in due time our country may be victorious and peace may be restored to the people of the world who love and cherish it.

He urged the students to remain calm and continue their studies as before. He admitted that there would be rumors of who would be called into service and when, but he advised everyone simply to wait for official information from Washington, DC. On January 13, 1942, the start of the new semester and one month after the attack on Pearl Harbor, he revealed in detail the steps that the university had already taken, his hopes to assist in the winning of the war in any way asked, and his hopes to permit as many students as possible to complete their education, enabling them better to assist in the winning of the war and in the reconstruction that would follow. There would be necessary changes on campus but he hoped much would remain the same:[27]

Let the usual social and recreational programs continue. Of course there should be a senior ball, junior prom, and other social events. Of course there should be intercollegiate and interhall athletics. Such programs are necessary for good morale at a time like this. But, through it all, don't forget to pray unceasingly.

Some changes, however, had already taken place. Sixty college-level courses in defense had begun for industrial workers in the St. Joseph Valley area, and 150 students had completed ground courses at the university in the Civilian Pilot Training Program. Some faculty members in the army reserves had already been called into service, several priests had volunteered as military chaplains, and numerous alumni and students had enlisted. To date (1942), eight alumni had already lost their lives. Other changes were envisioned. The university would transfer immediately to a three semester per year schedule to enable students to graduate in less than three years. Additional courses in mathematics were planned to help students qualify for specialized positions in the Navy, and a five hour a week course in radio technology also was inaugurated. Further courses in languages and other areas would be offered as needed. Naval officers had visited the campus to determine if they wished to establish Navy training programs here and, if they so decided, the university promised consent. That would cause sacrifices for many, but regular students would be able to remain and on campus housing would be available to them. Despite changed conditions, the fundamental goals of the university would remain the same:[28]

> Notre Dame is not going to operate under a new dispensation. Any changes that she may make in your interests, and in the interests of our common cause, are matters of policy that do not affect the character, purposes, and integrity of the University. Notre Dame can make no changes in principle. As long as there is a Notre Dame she will continue to train, in her own way, engineers, lawyers, chemists, accountants, teachers, linguists, and philosophers. For the present, she is putting special stress upon work being done in the Colleges of Science and Engineering because of its immediate importance to the task at hand, which is winning the war. But Notre Dame insists today, as she has always insisted, upon the education of the whole man. Notre Dame still emphasizes the discipline of the spiritual, the intellectual, and the moral. At Notre Dame you will always find the first principles from which all intellectual development proceeds. You will also always find importance given to the training of the will.

The world was being challenged by aggressor nations espousing a Godless view of man, and that view could be countered by the Christian philosophy, accompanied by prayer, as a Notre Dame education professed.

As Father O'Donnell acknowledged in this January address, changes had taken place on campus even before America's entrance into the war. The Selective Training and Service Act of September 1940 mandated the registration of all men between the ages of twenty-one and thirty-five, and thus most Notre Dame students were not affected. However, some young men were enlisting rather than waiting to be called, and others hesitated to begin college, fearing that the war would interrupt their education anyway. In an effort to keep enrollments from falling, Father O'Donnell contacted the Army about the possibility of establishing a training program on campus similar to the Students' Army Training Corps (SATC) of World War I. When the Army declined, Father O'Donnell turned to the Navy, although some believed the Navy was the university's preference because of the higher academic requirements in math, physics, and engineering for its officers. Congress in the spring of 1941 approved the establishment of eight additional Naval Reserve Officers Training Corps branches, and Notre Dame, along with Princeton, Harvard, Yale, and other eastern universities, had been selected.[29]

The Naval ROTC was a four-year program that allowed students to complete their college education before serving in the military. The program imposed strict requirements for admission: the student must be between fourteen and twenty-four years of age; must be an American citizen; must pass a rigid physical examination; must pass an Applicant's Selective Test given to all NROTC applicants; must agree to be immunized from typhoid fever and smallpox (if not already done); must agree to be fingerprinted for naval records; and must agree to wear the uniform at stated times and submit to naval discipline. The Notre Dame program was established in the fall of 1941, 450 freshmen applied for admission but only 165 were admitted, most of the others failing to pass the physical exam. NROTC enrollment remained constant although the number of regular civilian students entering Notre Dame declined each year throughout the war. The Navy students enrolled in regular four-year degree programs, and twenty-four hours of naval science courses were required for graduation, substituting for twenty-four other hours in the students' schedules. Pre-theology, pre-medical, and pre-dental students were excluded from the program since they were preparing for further study after graduation. The courses in the first two years for NROTC students were Naval Gunnery, Seamanship, Naval History, and Elementary Navigation, and in the final two years courses included Marine Steam Engineering, Navigation, Astronomy, and Strategy and Tactics. Four-week summer cruises for the advanced students (those in the final two years) were required, and they were encouraged but optional for those in the first two years. The cruises were planned for battleships or cruisers off the Atlantic coast but at times had to be transferred back to Lake Michigan. The NROTC unit took part in extracurricular activities, sponsoring dances, often with Saint Mary's students, organizing interhall football and basketball teams, and its rifle team, practicing beneath the stands in the stadium, competed with ROTC units from other universities. On completion of the program, the students were to serve for five years in the Naval Reserve, not necessarily on active duty. At the beginning, the NROTC staff of twelve officers and sailors was headquartered in the Rockne Memorial.[30]

The NROTC program was so successful, and the Navy Department was so pleased, that it decided to expand its cooperation with the university. A Naval Reserve Midshipmen's School, or V-7 program, was established in March 1942.

This was an accelerated three- or four-month program to train recent college graduates for command positions as deck officers in the Navy's surface fleet. The program was actually divided into two stages: a one-month indoctrination experience to give the candidate some familiarity with naval life and naval discipline, and a three-month period of intensive classes, giving rise to the derisive name they were sometimes given, "ninety day wonders." At first Notre Dame was selected only for that first, month-long stage, but it soon became apparent that transferring the seamen to another location for the further three months was both costly and a loss of time, and thus the full program was inaugurated on campus.[31]

Since the earlier NROTC program was never large and since these students took mostly regular university courses each semester, the program required few changes in campus structures or routine, but the V-7 program was different. There were approximately a thousand trainees in each four-month program, and Badin, Howard, Morrissey, and Lyons Halls were eventually assigned as barracks exclusively for them. Renovations had to be undertaken in some halls, chapels were converted into classrooms, and some single rooms were increased to doubles, and triples into quads. Some facetiously wondered if the sleeping space allotment in submarines was used as the measure. Actually, one measure was the plumbing, the standard being one toilet for every fifteen men and one urinal for every ten men. Until 1942 meals in the dining hall had been served sit-down family style, but the Navy changed it to cafeteria style to feed the approximately 1,300 trainees in the limited time the daily schedule allowed. Marching and drilling took place on the south quadrangle in front of Badin, Howard, Morrissey, and Lyons Halls, and the seamen lined up and marched into the dining hall for meals three times a day in order. The university did construct, at the Navy's expense, two new buildings for the Navy's use: a large cavernous Drill Hall just east of the gymnasium (where the Hesburgh Library now stands) for inside drilling, calisthenics, and all-hands addresses, and an office and classroom building just west of the Rockne Memorial. V-7 classes, chiefly in mathematics, physics, seamanship, navigation, ordinance, naval gunnery, and damage control were taught by naval officers themselves and were not given Notre Dame credit. The trainees came from all forty-eight states and approximately 90 percent of them were not Catholic, just the reverse of the regular student enrollment. In another change, members of the Navy's auxiliary corps for women—the WAVES—were also assigned to duty on campus. Trained for the Navy at Smith College or Mount Holyoke, they lived in the Oliver Hotel in South Bend and served as drivers, secretaries, and assistants in naval offices. Reaching close to fifty by 1945, they were a noticeable increase in the presence of women on the campus.[32]

The NROTC and V-7 programs proved to be successful, but not sufficient. American industry rose to the occasion during World War II and, along with planes, tanks, jeeps, and guns, produced almost six thousand ships in that five-year period. One of Henry Kaiser's West Coast shipyards, as a publicity stunt, assembled a ship, complete with life jackets and coat hangers, in less than five days. Some nicknamed him "Sir Launchalot." A joke made the rounds that a governor's wife was invited to christen one of his ships. She arrived at the dock and was handed a bottle of champagne, but then, perplexed, asked where the ship was. She was told: "Just start swinging. The ship will be there." With ships coming into service as rapidly as they were, ever more crews were needed, and in 1943 the Navy inaugurated an even larger officer training program, the V-12 program.[33]

The purpose of the V-12 program was to produce more college-educated naval officers than the United States Naval Academy in Annapolis could graduate at the time. The program was open to high school graduates, college transfer students, and naval officers seeking additional education. It was a four-year program at Notre Dame, the student could select any major of his choice (although math and engineering majors were in greatest demand), additional naval courses were required each semester, and the Navy paid board, lodging, and tuition, but the student could be called into active service as needed. It was soon the largest navy program on campus, numbering over 1,300 at its peak, and the students were housed in Alumni, Dillon, Cavanaugh, Zahm, and Walsh Halls. Courses were taught by the regular Notre Dame faculty, the freshman courses were the standard mathematics, English, history, and science courses, and specialized courses were offered beginning in the sophomore year to meet each student's interest—candidate training, supply corps, chaplain assistant, etc. Since the students' morning schedule was so crowded, weekday Masses in those residence halls were transferred to late afternoon. The trainees, as full Notre Dame students, took part in all extracurricular activities, including intercollegiate sports. Angelo Bertelli entered Notre Dame as a freshman in 1941, quarterbacked the football team that year and in 1942, was accepted into the V-12 program when it was established in July 1943, was called into active service after six games of the 1943 season, and was still awarded the Heisman Trophy as the outstanding college football player in the nation. In some ways the V-12 program seemed a replacement for the NROTC program then in decline since the regular student or civilian enrollment at Notre Dame had dropped to seven hundred students who were housed in Sorin and Saint Edward's Halls and the Brownson Hall and Carroll Hall wings of the Main Building.[34]

One famous trainee who found the academic program especially difficult was the former child movie star, Jackie Cooper. Growing up in Los Angeles, he was an extra in movies before he was five, at age seven he began acting in *Our Gang* movies, and at age nine he was nominated for an Academy Award for his leading role in *Skippy* in 1931, the youngest ever nominated to that time. He continued making movies—*Teacher's Pet, The Champ, Treasure Island, Syncopation*, and so on—until World War II, and after a short stint at Loyola College in Los Angeles he transferred to Notre Dame and the V-12 program. The V-12 was an accelerated program (eight semesters in less than three years) and Cooper admitted that he had had only three years of regular schooling—kindergarten, one year in grade school, and one year in high school—and the rest with private tutors, and he was not prepared for college mathematics and physics. With his celebrity status, he had no difficulty attracting companions and admitted to spending many of his liberty nights in the Oliver Hotel or in Chicago. Eventually his poor grades and collection of demerits got him transferred out of the V-12 program and into the regular navy at Great Lakes. He wrote:[35]

> Everybody told me that if I thought Notre Dame was tough, I should be prepared for something REALLY tough—boot training. But it was just the opposite. Compared to Notre Dame, boot training was a breeze.

Cooper apparently never got deeply involved in campus life because he always referred to the campus priests as Jesuits.[36]

Cooper's academic difficulties, his unorthodox lifestyle, and even occasional abuse from other trainees were an exception. The pride most young men felt in the military, whatever their background, was captured in a poem by a trainee and printed in the *Scholastic*.[37]

> I'm a graduate of West Point, and I came up from the ranks;
> And I've never had a dollar, and I own a dozen banks.
> I'm a corporal, lieutenant, sergeant, major, brigadier,
> I'm an ensign, captain, private, pilot, gunner, bombardier.
> I'm a boilermaker's helper; I was fullback for the Bears;
> I'm an auction bridge instructor, and I worked a farm on shares;
> An Annapolis Midshipman, by the Severn I was taught;
> And I got my wings at Randolph, and I learned to fly at Scott;
> I'm a fellow at old Harvard; and I never went to school;

I'm a fine white-collar worker; and I used to skin a mule.
I'm a seven-hitch Coast Guardsman, and a boot-camp-fresh Marine;
I'm a grocery clerk from Brooklyn, and a logger from Racine.
I'm a salesman from Milwaukee, and a butcher from St. Joe';
I'm a bartender from Reno, and a pug from Kokomo.
I'm a transient cotton-picker, I'm an engineer from 'Tech;
I'm a French-Italian-English-Irish-Swedish-Polish-Czech.
I'm Mormon, Catholic, Buddhist, Presbyterian, Methodist;
I'm a Lutheran, Judaic, Baptist, Christian Scientist.
I'm a ringtailed catawampus when it's time to start a scrap.
I'm a walking, talking nightmare to a Nazi, or a Jap.
I'm ten thousand different fellows, multiplied a thousand times;
And you'll find me at the moment in a dozen different climes.
I'm the roughest, toughest hombre since the day that time began;
I am youth; I'm strength; I'm manhood; I'm the U. S. fighting man.

A major contribution the V-12 and NROTC programs made to the university was the desegregation of its student body. Notre Dame apparently had no black American students prior to World War II. The majority of black Americans were not Catholic and probably preferred to enroll elsewhere, and tuition cost would discourage others. But Notre Dame's official policy was not to accept black Americans. Many Notre Dame students were from southern states where segregation was strict and the university wanted to avoid any embarrassing conflicts. But the Navy did send several black American trainees to Notre Dame—Frazier Thompson, Carl Coggins, Alexander Poindexter, and Samuel L. Dean, Jr. Unfortunately, little is known of most of these, except for Frazier Thompson. He was born in Philadelphia, attended John Bertram High School there, and enrolled in Lincoln University. In July 1944, the Navy assigned him to the V-12 program at Notre Dame, and he also joined the Notre Dame track team, posting times of ten seconds in the one-hundred-yard dash and twenty-two seconds in the two hundred. When the V-12 program was terminated, the university offered him an athletic scholarship and he remained and competed for two more years, although he was asked to live off campus, and graduated in June 1947. Carl Coggins came to Notre Dame in either the V-12 or the NROTC program in February 1945, graduated in June 1947, and returned for a second bachelor's degree, in civil engineering, in 1952. A fifth black American student, Rev. Edward Burrell Williams of South Bend, middle-aged and Notre Dame's first non-military black American student, earned a bachelor's degree in journalism in August 1947 and served as an AME minister in Philadelphia and Milwaukee.[38]

Two other programs, not strictly military but still contributing to the war effort, were the Civilian Pilot Training Program and the Engineering, Science, and Management Defense Training Program. The Civilian Pilot Training Program was provided for by the Civil Aeronautics Act of 1938 and was established the following year in thirteen colleges with the goal of training twenty thousand pilots a year. The Army and Navy were not producing sufficient pilots to meet their needs. The college-trained pilots were licensed chiefly to train others, continuing the production of qualified pilots, but approximately 10 percent of them did join the military directly after licensing. The program was established at Notre Dame in 1940 and was divided into two parts. The first or primary course included seventy-two hours of groundwork instruction and thirty-five to fifty hours of flying, both dual and solo. The groundwork classes familiarized the student with airplane mechanics, the principles of takeoff and landing into the wind or in a crosswind, the handling of stalls and accidental spins, meteorology, and civil air regulations. Time in the air, both dual and solo, put this learning into practice. In the advanced or secondary course, the pilot practiced more complicated maneuvers—snap rolls, steep climbs, barrel rolls, vertical reverses, etc.—that might be necessary in combat. The students learned on Piper Cubs and similar planes, flew chiefly from Bendix airport in South Bend, and were trained by instructors from Indiana Air Service and Homer Stockert Flying Service, two local businesses. It was never a large program at Notre Dame since the number of civilian students continually declined.[39]

The Engineering, Science, and Management Defense Training Program, established at Notre Dame in 1941, was an effort to assist industrial workers in management positions in South Bend and the surrounding areas. The classes were all taught at night, some in electrical engineering and aeronautics, others in personnel training and management skills, and the goal was to make defense industries run more efficiently. Close to thirty different classes were taught by forty-five instructors from Notre Dame and industry, and nine hundred workers from seventy-nine industries in twelve different cities took advantage of the program. The program was open to all, regardless of race, sex, religion, or age, tuition was not charged, although each worker had to purchase assigned textbooks, and the government paid them for each hour they spent in class. The training of women was especially important since they were increasingly replacing men who were called into active service. The fact that seventy-nine industries were represented in the program suggested its need and popularity.[40]

The regular students and faculty were assisting in the war effort in their own ways as well. The Physics Department continued its research into atomic energy, both for the atomic bomb itself and for the peaceful use of atomic energy after the war. Professor Bernard Waldman, later dean of the College of Science, was one of four scientists who flew in the military plane following the *Enola Gay* to photograph the detonation of the first atomic bomb at Hiroshima.[41] Scientists were also continuing the research of Father Nieuwland into synthetic rubber. The Biology and Chemistry Departments were investigating methods to control malaria in tropical areas, and the Biology Department was researching the nutritional needs of men in the military. Father O'Donnell himself served on a government committee whose work led to the establishment of the National Science Foundation, whose funding has supported much Notre Dame research. Professor James Reyniers and Father Theodore Hesburgh eventually served on the National Science Foundation governing board. Students also contributed. The Knights of Columbus and other student clubs sponsored an annual four-night War Charities Carnival to raise money for dependent children of men in the military. Some students took part-time evening jobs in local South Bend and Mishawaka industries, and the university made allowances for their late hours off campus. Some halls undertook to plant Victory Gardens to supplement the food available in the dining hall but apparently these were not successful. The fact was that shortages occurred—the dining hall could not always procure the amount of meat, milk, and butter it desired, and students had to accept the sacrifices. Laundry service was much slower due to the daily needs of the Navy and the desire to reduce water consumption. The most noticeable campus change was the decision to leave the golden dome dark at night.[42]

As might be expected with former university president and now Bishop John O'Hara responsible for recruiting priests to serve as military chaplains, Notre Dame and the Congregation of Holy Cross answered the military ordinariate's call generously. Twenty-five priests eventually served in the military, ten of whom had or would have a Notre Dame connection. Others were from the Mission Band, local parishes, and even the foreign missions. Father Robert Woodward of Notre Dame's Philosophy Department and rector of Morrissey Hall was the first Holy Cross priest to enlist, in late February 1941, ten months before the attack on Pearl Harbor. He remained stateside, rose to the rank of major, and was supervisor of approximately three hundred chaplains in the United States, the Caribbean, Greenland, and Iceland. He was discharged in 1946, returned to the Department of Philosophy, and was instrumental in establishing an Army ROTC unit at Notre Dame in 1951. Another priest entering before Pearl Harbor was Father Joseph Barry, pastor of Saint Joseph's Parish in South Bend. He saw action in Sicily, Salerno, Anzio, southern France, and Germany, and he was present when the gruesome Dachau concentration camp was liberated, saw piles of naked, skeleton-like dead, and witnessed the starving but still alive captives walk into freedom. Discharged from the Army in 1946, he was appointed rector of Farley Hall and later Notre Dame's prefect of discipline.[43]

Two Holy Cross priests from Notre Dame entered the military in 1942, Fathers Joseph Corcoran and Edmund Murray. Father Corcoran was with the 32nd Regiment of the 7th Infantry Division in the Central Pacific during the liberation of the Southern Philippines and the capture of the Ryukyu Islands, and on his discharge he returned to Saint Edward's Hall and the Department of Religion. Father Murray was commissioned a lieutenant in the 104th Army Division, rose to the rank of full colonel, and accompanied the 104th as they fought across Germany until they reached the Russian army at the Elbe River. On discharge, he studied for his PhD in history at the University of Dublin and taught Irish history at Notre Dame until his retirement.[44]

All the above served in the regular army but others, beginning in 1943, enlisted in other services. Father Norman Johnson, a member of the English Department and an assistant prefect of religion, joined the Army Air Force and served in the Asiatic-Pacific Theater. Father Francis Boland, prefect in Cavanaugh Hall, member of the Department of Politics (as it was then called), and co-author of a textbook in political science, was commissioned a captain in the Navy and served on attack transports. After his discharge, he was named president of Stonehill College in Massachusetts. Father John Dupuis, rector of Freshman Hall and member of the Religion Department, served with the 4th Marine Division in the Marshall Islands and returned to Notre Dame to be rector of Howard Hall. Father James Norton, from Saint Edward's University in Austin, Texas, served with Marine Aircraft Group 45. On his discharge, he resided in Farley Hall, taught economics, and was vice president of academic affairs for a time. Father John J. Burke, rector of Zahm Hall and also instructor in economics, served as chaplain on the U.S.S. *Pennsylvania* in the battles of Wake Island, Saipan, and Okinawa, and on his return he served as vice president of business affairs at Notre Dame. Another priest had served on the Mission Band and, when stationed in Iceland, decided to build a small chapel. He pilfered lumber and other resources from various army installations and, for that reason, eventually dedicated the chapel appropriately to Saint Dismas, the Good Thief.[45]

Daily life changed for almost everyone in the United States during World War II, but President Roosevelt hoped to keep those changes to a minimum. In establishing the various college navy programs like the V-7 and V-12, one goal, in addition to producing qualified naval officers, was to allow colleges and universities to continue functioning with as few interruptions as possible. All residence halls at Notre Dame were occupied, classes were being taught, experiments continued in science laboratories, the laundry was busier than before, and the dining hall was probably serving more meals since all trainees, unlike regular students, had to rise for breakfast. College life still included dances, interhall sports, smokers, evening card games, and intercollegiate athletics. But a major change had taken place in Notre Dame football. At the close of the 1940 respectable seven and two season, head football coach and director of athletics Elmer Layden announced his resignation to become commissioner of the National Football League. Two prominent candidates to succeed him were Buck Shaw of Santa Clara and Frank Leahy of Boston College, and vice president Father John Cavanaugh happened to be in California on university business when Layden announced his resignation. Father Cavanaugh spoke with Father O'Donnell on the telephone and it was agreed that he should at least meet with Coach Shaw and see if there was any interest. Father Cavanaugh recalled that they met in Salinas, between Los Angeles and San Francisco, in a driving rainstorm in an automobile at the far end of the city. Coach Shaw was interested, wanted to talk with his wife, and agreed to send Father Cavanaugh a telegram signed something like "Georgie Obstreperous" to keep the contact secret. The telegram asked that he not be considered, and Father Cavanaugh then telephoned him from Marcellus, Michigan, (again to keep the contact secret) to learn the reasons. The coach said he and his wife were well established in California, their friends were there, they enjoyed the weather, and despite their respect and love for Notre Dame, they would remain at Santa Clara. Father O'Donnell then asked Father Cavanaugh's younger brother, Father Frank Cavanaugh, to go to Albany, New York, under an assumed name and meet secretly with Frank Leahy, a Notre Dame graduate and very successful young head coach at Boston College.[46]

Leahy had been born in O'Neill, Nebraska, in 1908 and moved with his family to Winner, South Dakota, while still a child. He soon learned to ride horses and rope steers, he was a successful amateur boxer, and in his senior year at Winner High School he captained the football, basketball, and baseball teams. He played halfback on the football team and his high school coach, Earl Walsh, a teammate of George Gipp at Notre Dame in 1919–1920, thought him good enough to recommend him to Rockne. He entered Notre Dame in the fall of 1927, and Rockne shifted him from halfback to center and then to tackle. He was a starter on the 1929 team but a dislocated elbow and damaged knee seriously limited his playing time. He remained a member of the 1929 and 1930 national championship teams, observing Rockne from the bench because of his injuries and learning much about successful coaching. During his senior year, he accompanied Rockne to Mayo Clinic where both underwent operations and, in beds side by side, he could bombard the coach with additional football questions. Graduating in 1931, he was hired as line coach at Georgetown, then he transferred to Michigan State for a year, and finally he went to Fordham for five years with head coach and former Four Horseman Jimmy Crowley. One of the undersized guards on Fordham's line, nicknamed "The Seven Blocks of Granite," was Vince Lombardi, later Hall of Fame coach of the Green Bay Packers. Leahy was hired as head coach at Boston College in 1939, took them to the Cotton Bowl in his first year, and defeated Tennessee in the Sugar Bowl after an undefeated season in 1940. That year, Boston College won the Lambert Trophy as "the finest team in the East." He was rewarded with a five-year contract that he may have broken to sign with Notre Dame.[47]

Leahy's first year at Notre Dame set the tone for a brilliant tenure. He had excellent players returning: Bernie Crimmins, a future Notre Dame line coach, and Bob Dove were fixtures on the line, and the backfield included Steve Juzwik, Angelo Bertelli, Creighton Miller, and Dippy Evans, if space could be found for all of them. Although Rockne's shift was now illegal, Leahy retained the Notre Dame box formation, with Bertelli usually a left halfback receiving the ball from center and running, passing, or handing it off to another. The passing of Bertelli, nicknamed "The Springfield Rifle" after his hometown, and the running of Juzwik and Evans brought easy victories in the first five games, as Notre Dame outscored opponents 142 to 27. In heavy rain and on a sloppy field in Yankee Stadium they then fought Army to a 0–0 tie. After defeating Navy 20 to 13, they eked out a 7–6 victory over Northwestern and the great Otto Graham when Wally Ziemba, another future Irish line coach, blocked an extra point conversion. In the final game, Southern California missed two extra point conversions and Notre Dame won 20 to 18. With a first-year record of eight wins and one tie, and with Bernie Crimmins and Bob Dove named All-Americans, Frank Leahy, and all Notre Dame fans, had to be pleased.[48]

As successful as the season was, Leahy still wanted to make changes the following year. He decided to drop Knute Rockne's single-wing or box formation and, after conversations with George Halas and Sid Luckman of the Chicago Bears and Clark Shaughnessy of Stanford, decided to install the new T-formation. Bertelli would be the quarterback—"the finest passer and worst runner I have ever coached," Leahy once remarked. The season did not start well. The opening game was against Wisconsin in Madison; Bertelli apparently boarded the wrong train somehow, soon discovered it, switched to the correct train, and arrived just in time for the game, which ended in a 7–7 tie. A loss to Georgia Tech followed, after which an illness struck Leahy and sent him to Mayo Clinic, and Ed McKeever coached the team for the next three games, all of which were victories. Leahy returned to win against Navy and Army, lost to Michigan (the first the teams had met since a disputed Notre Dame victory in 1909), won the next two games and tied the Great Lakes Naval Base in the finale. Leahy continued with the T-formation in 1943, with Bertelli an even more experienced field general. In the first six games, with Bertelli passing and Creighton Miller running, Notre Dame outscored their opponents 261 to 31. Misfortune could have struck because Bertelli was then called into active service with the Marines and saw action in the Pacific, including Iwo Jima, but his replacement was the exceptionally talented sophomore, Johnny Lujack. Lujack led the team to victories in the next three games and lost only to the star-laden Great Lakes, 19–14. It was a season of firsts: Coach Leahy's first national championship and, after playing only six games, Notre Dame's first Heisman Trophy winner, Angelo Bertelli.[49]

The next two seasons were heavily influenced by the war and by the military academies. Leahy joined the Navy in May 1944, Lujack was also in the service (as was Bertelli), and Creighton Miller had graduated. Ed McKeever again took over the coaching reins and Frank Dancewicz was the starting quarterback. The season started well, with Notre Dame outscoring their first three opponents 148 to 0 and defeating everyone else but Army and Navy. Both service academies were heavy with players from other colleges, including Notre Dame. Navy defeated the Irish 32 to 13, and Army, with Glenn Davis and Doc Blanchard and so many others, won 59 to 0, the worst defeat in Notre Dame history. At the end of the season, Coach McKeever moved to Cornell and Hugh Devore agreed to coach until Leahy returned. Nineteen forty-five was a repeat of the previous year. The season ended 7–2–1, every opponent defeated except the service academies. The Navy game ended in a tie when Navy's Clyde "Smackover" Scott ran an interception back for a touchdown and Notre Dame's Phil Colella's feet crossed the goal line but officials ruled that the ball had not. Army was just as powerful as the year before and won 48 to 0. In the final game, Great Lakes defeated the Irish 39 to 7, with former Irish quarterback George Terlep directing the opposition. It was as good a season as could be expected, but in 1945 the war ended and the dominance of the service academies was coming to an end. Coach Leahy was decommissioned and heading for the sidelines, players were returning to their colleges, and Notre Dame fans could look forward to an especially bright future.[50]

As the end of the war approached, the university administration began preparations for the postwar years. One area that needed to expand was the graduate program. The Graduate School had been officially organized in 1921 as an outgrowth of graduate courses offered in the summer sessions, and by the early 1930s, university publications listed seven doctoral programs (chemistry, metallurgy, philosophy, physics, mathematics, biology, and politics) and thirteen masters programs (social work, economics, politics, education, English, history, philosophy, sociology, biology, chemistry, metallurgy, physics, and mathematics). Several of the doctoral programs—physics, mathematics, and politics—had been greatly strengthened with the addition of the émigré professors fleeing Nazi Europe throughout the decade. Graduate programs all declined during World War II due to lack of students, but the university was proud of the fact that no faculty members had to be relieved. The university prepared for the influx of students, especially from the military, after the war, and in August 1944 the university officially announced:[51]

> After a consideration of a survey made by the Committee on Postwar Problems, the Rev. J. Hugh O'Donnell, C.S.C., president of the University of Notre Dame, last Monday, announced the reorganization of the Graduate School. This important administrative change had been made, Father O'Donnell said, because of the rapid development of the Graduate School in pre-war years, and in anticipation of even greater expansion in the postwar period. . . .
>
> The armistice will undoubtedly bring a resurgence of graduate study. In this anticipation and in preparation for the many problems that the future rapid development will raise, Notre Dame at this time takes this step in its reconversion program and reorganizes the Graduate School, making it an autonomous body within the University.

Father Philip Moore, medievalist and member of the Philosophy Department, was named dean, and a Graduate Council of priests and laymen was appointed to assist him. The influx of students would not begin until the fall of 1946 and by that time Father O'Donnell would no longer be president, but he had satisfactorily prepared the way for the academic growth that was to follow.[52]

An additional question was where to put this influx of students when it arrived. Some of them had been Notre Dame students before being called into service and were eager to return, some had been on campus for a time in one of the navy programs, and some had heard of Notre Dame and preferred it for its academic programs and reputation. Single undergraduate students could be housed in the residence halls and many of those halls in fact had been reconfigured to hold more, with single rooms converted into doubles, and doubles into triples, etc. But what of older and now married students, some with children? Before the war, Notre Dame students were not allowed to marry, and trainees during the war who were married lived off campus. Convenient off campus housing was not that plentiful and could be expensive. A solution was at hand, however. The federal government had earlier built thirty-nine prisoner-of-war barracks in Weingarten, Missouri, that were now of no use with all prisoners released, and the Federal Housing Authority was willing to appropriate $400,000 to dismantle, transport, and reassemble them at Notre Dame if the university requested. The site Notre Dame selected was at the northeast corner of the campus, adjacent to the Navy Drill Hall, the power plant, and the biology building. The university spent approximately $40,000 to clear the site and provide roads and sewer and water mains. Each barrack was divided into three units or apartments, making 117 in all. Each unit had a small porch, a kitchenette, two bedrooms, a living room, and a bath. Telephones were installed only in every third unit. The floors were linoleum and the walls a drab white, although the university offered free leftover paint if the residents wished to paint them themselves. Rent was $27 a month and preference was given to those with children. Most were veterans but not all. Thus when students in greater numbers returned for class in the fall of 1946, housing was available, the faculty was intact, with some returning from the service, and a new president, Father John J. Cavanaugh, had that summer been appointed to succeed Father O'Donnell at the close of his permitted six-year term.[53]

CHAPTER 14

The Postwar Years and the Second Father John Cavanaugh

In his early years, John J. Cavanaugh would have seemed a most unlikely candidate for college president—he had never attended high school. He was born on a forty-acre farm in Bennington Township, Shiawassee County, Michigan, on January 23, 1899, one of three sons and one daughter of Michael and Mary Ann (Keegan) Cavanaugh. His father died when John was five and, at their pastor's suggestion, his mother moved the family to nearby Owosso where, for a time, she took in boarders to help cover expenses. The children all had jobs early on— peddling papers or working in hardware or grocery stores. After graduating from Saint Paul's Parish grammar school, John enrolled immediately in a secretarial program, learning typing, dictation, spelling, grammar, shorthand, etc. Several temporary jobs followed—timekeeper at a sawmill in Manistee, car checker for the Lake Shore and Michigan Southern Railroad, and secretary to a coal mine owner in Owosso. For a time he also served as secretary or typist for Henry Ford's secretary. The secretary would take dictation from Mr. Ford, and John and a couple of others would type the letters in proper form. By this time John's younger brother, Frank, had entered the high school seminary at Notre Dame and, on a visit to see his brother in 1917, John was introduced to the university president,

Father John W. Cavanaugh (no relation). John mentioned that he was an experienced secretary and if the president ever needed one, he would be happy with the position. Father Cavanaugh admitted that he did need a secretary, so John hurried home to quit his job and returned to Notre Dame.[1]

John spent two years as secretary to Father Cavanaugh, 1917–1919. Toward the close of Father Cavanaugh's presidency, John, realizing that he seemed as bright as some of the students he was meeting, asked Father Cavanaugh if he could be accepted as a student if he passed an entrance examination, even without attending high school. Father Cavanaugh agreed, John passed, and he was offered a scholarship if he would serve as assistant resident hall prefect to Father O'Hara, allowing Father O'Hara to spend more time as prefect of religion. John majored in commerce (where Father O'Hara also served as dean for a time), took a heavy load of liberal arts courses, served as student government president in his senior year, and graduated in 1923. He did some secretarial work for Father Burns, then president, during this time, and he also did some secretarial work for Father Cavanaugh when he returned to Notre Dame in retirement in 1922. It was through Father Cavanaugh that he made the acquaintance of Albert Erskine, president of the Studebaker Corporation in South Bend and a member of Notre Dame's board of lay trustees, and Erskine offered him a position. He learned everything he could about the making of a Studebaker, visited dealers across the Northwest and in California, and was eventually named assistant advertising manager at Studebaker. But he had been considering the priesthood for some time and decided to enter the Holy Cross Novitiate in January 1925. When he did, his patron Father Cavanaugh, mindful of John's ambition, reminded him that he was joining a religious community, not founding one. After a year of novitiate in the former Missionaries' Retirement Home on the north bank of Saint Joseph's Lake, he was assigned to Notre Dame for one year, received a master's degree in English in 1927, went on to Holy Cross College in Washington, DC, for four years of theology, and was ordained to the priesthood in 1931. His younger brother had been ordained four years earlier.[2]

Father John J. Cavanaugh was then sent to Rome to study philosophy at the prestigious Gregorian University—although he called some of his courses "very uninspiring"—and received his licentiate degree in 1933. He wanted to remain another year, but Father O'Hara had recently replaced Father Mulcaire as Notre Dame vice president while retaining his position as prefect of religion, and Father Cavanaugh was recalled to work with Father O'Hara as assistant prefect of religion. He retained that position until 1938, offering Masses, hearing confessions, and sending out some 14,000 *Religious Bulletins* each day. In the 1938 provincial chapter, Father Thomas Steiner was named provincial superior, and he selected Father Cavanaugh as his assistant provincial. When Father Hugh O'Donnell was appointed to succeed Father O'Hara as president in 1940, he in turn asked that Father Cavanaugh be named vice president, and he held this position throughout Father O'Donnell's six-year term. When that term was completed in the summer of 1946, Father Cavanaugh was the clear choice to succeed him. The postwar years were a challenging time—the university had to reconvert from a primarily military to a civilian regime, thousands of veterans, older and some five years removed from high school, sought admission, and the world of 1946 was far different from the world of 1939 and universities needed to adjust to the changes—and Father Cavanaugh, despite his slow start of never attending high school, met the challenges well. One author has written of him: "To too many today, the late Holy Cross priest is simply 'the one before Hesburgh.' But to those who worked for him and learned from him, John J. Cavanaugh was the man who set Notre Dame on its modern course."[3]

The first step on this modern course was to prepare for the crowds of new students who would seek admission, many of them, under the Servicemen's Readjustment Act or G. I. Bill of Rights, financed fully by the federal government. In the fall of 1946, student enrollment was close to 3,200, with perhaps a thousand of these still in the Navy programs. As the students in the Navy programs graduated or the programs terminated, additional applicants were at hand to take their places. Enrollment increased year by year during the postwar period, and by the fall of 1952 it had reached a maximum of slightly over 5,000. The Navy had demonstrated that the resident halls could accommodate many more students than had been assigned to each hall before the war, and Notre Dame simply retained some of those heavily crowded conditions. Still, additional lodging was necessary. In the spring of 1946, Father O'Donnell had announced that a new student residence hall would be built just north of Breen-Phillips. Originally it was called only "Project F," but later it was announced it would be named for the legendary Holy Cross priest and rector, Father John "Pop" Farley. An outstanding athlete as a student, he won four letters in football, additional letters in baseball and track, and he captained the football team in his senior year. He was never assigned to the classroom and reportedly never preached a sermon in the campus church, but he counseled thousands of students as hall rector and was a campus favorite. Farley Hall, designed for approximately 180 first-year students but able to accommodate up to 70 more if some rooms were doubled, opened in 1947.[4]

A second hall, donated by the widow of Fred Fisher (the founder of Fisher Body Corporation of Detroit), was originally intended to be built next to and north of Farley Hall (where the North Dining Hall was eventually constructed), but that was later changed to just west of the (south) dining hall. Mrs. Fisher donated $1 million, three-fourths of which was for the building and the remaining $250,000 for loans to qualified and needy students. The hall was constructed in the shape of a T, but due to rising costs, the original plans had to be modified. The east wing, containing most of the student rooms, had four floors, while the west wing, housing the chapel, had only one floor. The north-south wing, also containing student rooms, had only two stories, but two more stories were added a few years later. The hall was for upperclassmen, and it contained 120 single rooms and 18 doubles, with the single rooms measuring 12 feet by 7 feet 4 inches and the doubles 15 feet by 12 feet. It was equipped with a lounge near the front entrance, a study room, a recreation room for Ping-Pong or billiards, and a large storage room. The total cost of the building was $762,000 and it opened in the fall of 1952.[5]

The most noticeable change in student housing on campus, however, was Vetville. All 117 units were occupied by mid-December 1946, with preference given to couples with children. Most residents were military veterans, but not all. The units were divided geographically into six wards, with roads dividing and connecting them all. Each ward elected a representative to the Vetville Council, and a mayor was elected for a six-month term by popular vote. The community published a weekly, the *Vetville Herald* (originally the *Vetville News*), that contained household hints, "stork report" news, birthdays, anniversaries, lost items, recipes, requests for improved services, and a column from the Vetville chaplain. Bridge games were a favorite pastime but the main social event of the week was the Saturday night dance in the recreation center. A student band would usually provide the music and other students might volunteer to babysit (for kitchen privileges). Longer skirts were the new style after the war, but the first Vetville chaplain, young Father Theodore Hesburgh, asked the wives to remain with the shorter wartime skirts in order not to embarrass the women who could not afford the newer fashions. He even offered a prize for the worst-dressed couple to discourage the veterans from overspending on new clothes. He also offered a course on the Catholic religion for non-Catholic wives, not precisely to convert them but primarily to help them understand better the religion of their husbands and the university. If their schedules permitted, some husbands and wives also held part-time jobs on campus or in South Bend, the men as engineers at Bendix, perhaps, or night monitors in residence halls, and the women at Saint Joseph's Hospital or as secretaries in the Main Building. Vetville served the married students well until 1962 when it was demolished to make room for the new library, and an even larger facility, the Married Student Housing complex, was constructed northwest of the campus on the main South Bend–Niles highway. But the memory remained, as one resident recalled:[6]

> Yes, Vetville has become a permanent part of Notre Dame history. Long after our present homes are torn away, the Spirit of Vetville will remain. As you leave us, keep a memory niche for the days you spent here. In later years we'll look back on them as the best and happiest days of our lives.

But housing was not the only challenge the influx of students provided. Additional faculty members were needed to teach them, and the hiring of new faculty seemed to indicate where student interests lay. Approximately seventy new faculty positions were added in the six years following the war. The largest number of these were in the College of Commerce, with faculty positions in accounting, finance, and marketing almost doubling and positions in business administration increasing by a third. The numbers remained about the same in most College of Arts and Letters departments, although in classics they declined from nine to five and in history they increased from fourteen to twenty-two. The mechanical engineering faculty increased from six to ten, but surprisingly aeronautical engineering declined from six to three. There was some slight shifting in the College of Science, but overall the numbers remained approximately the same, despite Notre Dame's solid wartime research into atomic physics.[7]

With the increase in student enrollment, the faculty both expanded and deepened, especially with the arrival, again, of internationally acclaimed émigré scholars, this time mostly from Eastern Europe and fleeing what threatened to be Russian domination of their homelands. They contributed in a wide variety of fields: Ernest Brandl in architecture, Elias Denisoff in philosophy, Ernest Eliel in chemistry, Ky Fan in mathematics, E. K. Francis in sociology, and George Kuczynski in metallurgical engineering.[8]

The émigré faculty member from this wave who may have contributed most to Notre Dame was medieval historian Canon Astrik Gabriel, O. Praem. Canon Gabriel was born in Pecs, Hungary, in 1907, studied at the École des Chartes in Paris, was ordained a priest in the Premonstratensian order in 1931, and received his doctorate from the University of Budapest in 1936. He was founder and director of the French College in Gödöllő, Hungary, but when the Communist coup took place in 1947 he fled first to Canada and then to Notre Dame in 1948. Notre Dame's Medieval Institute had been established in 1946 with the strong support of medieval philosopher Father Philip Moore and with Professor Gerald Phelan of Toronto as first director. Canon Gabriel succeeded Phelan as director in 1951 and published *Robert de Sorbonne* in 1953 and *Student Life in Ave Maria College, Mediaeval Paris* in 1955. In addition to his teaching and writing, he was most successful in building the valuable collection of manuscripts and first editions of the Medieval Institute, making it second only to Toronto in the Western Hemisphere as a center of medieval research.[9]

Another medieval historian who joined the faculty in the postwar years was Gerhart Ladner, an expert in the field of medieval art. He was born in Vienna in 1905 and received his PhD from the University of Vienna in 1930. He was on the staff of Monumenta Germaniae Historica in Berlin and Munich, was a fellow of the Instituto Storico Austriaco in Rome, and a lecturer at the University of Vienna when the Anschluss took place and forced him to flee to Canada, where he was given a position of assistant professor of medieval history and archaeology at the Pontifical Institute of Mediaeval Studies and the University of Toronto. He was recruited to Notre Dame in 1946, taught a course on the cultural history of the Middle Ages, won a Guggenheim Fellowship to the Institute for Advanced Study at Princeton, and in 1951 left Notre Dame for a position at Howard University in Washington, DC.[10]

A third historian, Boleslaw Szczesniak, joined the Notre Dame faculty in 1948. Born in Polska Wola, Poland, in 1908, he studied at Warsaw's Institute of Oriental Studies and Waseda University in Japan, and received a PhD from the University of Ottawa in 1950. He lectured on Eastern European history at Rikkyo University in Japan and spent World War II in London. At Notre Dame he offered courses in Russian, Japanese, and Chinese history, the history of Eastern Europe, and even world naval history. His experiences in both Eastern Europe and the Far East enabled him to speak out on diplomatic issues facing the world in the aftermath of World War II.[11]

Helmut Gordon, an Eastern European physiologist and medical doctor, came to Notre Dame in 1947 to undertake research at the university's recently established germ-free laboratory, LOBUND (Laboratory of Bacteriology, University of Notre Dame). Gordon was born in 1908 in Malinska, then Austria, later Croatia. Early in his life, his family moved to Budapest where he began his studies, eventually receiving an MD degree from the University of Budapest and, after six months of postgraduate studies in Rome, returned to the University of Budapest as assistant professor of physiology. He traveled widely in Europe to attend scientific conferences in France, Germany, Russia, and Scandinavia, could read and write five languages, and could speak four others. He received a Rockefeller Foundation fellowship in 1937 for a year of research at New York University, and then he returned to Denmark to work with a Nobel Prize–winning physiologist there. When war broke out in Europe in September 1939, he returned to Budapest but was soon conscripted by the conquering Germans to help staff the bombed and battered hospitals in their homeland. As the end of the war approached, he reported to the American forces around Munich, offered his assistance as a doctor, and, after a careful examination, was put in charge of public health in one of the counties in Upper Bavaria, at times taking care of former inmates of the terrible Dachau concentration camp. His work won him praise from the United Nations Relief and Rehabilitation Administration. In early 1947, now married and the father of a baby girl, he was relieved of his duties with the American forces and allowed to immigrate to the United States. Gordon contacted a close friend at New York University, and the friend advised him to seek a position at the University of Notre Dame. He was immediately hired as LOBUND's chief pathologist and physiologist and remained at Notre Dame until 1962, his one regret being that he could not conveniently indulge his favorite hobby of mountain climbing in Indiana.[12]

The Department of Politics, or Political Science, profited immensely from émigré professors arriving before the war, especially Waldemar Gurian and Ferdinand Hermens, and it profited after the war also, especially with the coming of Stephen Kertesz. Kertesz's World War II background was even more harrowing that that of Dr. Gordon. Kertesz was born in Putnok, Hungary, in 1904, he progressed through an excellent Hungarian educational system, and he received a doctor of law degree from the University of Budapest in 1926. He spent two years studying at the Institut des Hautes Études Internationales in Paris, and subsequently at the Academie de Droit International at The Hague, and then he had research years at Yale, Oxford, and Geneva. He began his career as a lawyer at the Tribunal of Budapest and then joined the Office of Foreign Ministry, representing Hungary at the Mixed Arbitral Tribunals and the Permanent Court of International Justice in The Hague. He was one of a group of officials who were attempting to end Hungary's participation in the war, and who were offering aid to Dutch and British officers who had escaped from German prisons. He was arrested by the Hungarian Nazi party in October 1944 and was transferred from jail to jail as the Russian army approached. At one of these jails, sixteen prisoners were executed each day. Kertesz had been able to get word to his wife to burn any personally incriminating documents, but he was still in danger on his release, so he hid in a private hospital, receiving periodic hypodermic injections to keep his fever high. Life in the early postwar years under Russian occupation was equally harrowing, with danger of arrest and shipment to Russia and forced labor, and with lack of food and other necessities in devastated Hungary. When the new government was established in 1945, Kertesz was recalled to its Foreign Office, was put in charge of preparations for the Paris Peace Conference, spent months in Paris as minister-counselor and secretary general of the Hungarian peace delegation, and at the close of the conference he was appointed minister to Italy. When the Communist coup overthrew the Hungarian government in June 1947, the new regime announced that Kertesz would be the new foreign minister, but he refused to return to Budapest and eventually fled to the United States. He spent two years as visiting professor of law at Yale and then joined the Notre Dame faculty in 1950.[13]

The immediate postwar period was not a propitious time for academic innovation and advance. There were too many uncertainties. Thanks to the G. I. Bill of Rights, the number of students enrolling at Notre Dame increased every year, and at various ages and grade levels. Faculty members were returning from the war, new faculty members were hired, and some faculty left for other universities. Increased student housing was needed, dining hall facilities were renovated, and additional classroom and laboratory space was required. And the uncertainty spread beyond the campus. Serious depression usually followed major wars and the future of the American economy was not clear. Europe and Asia were already in serious depression, and the dropping of the two atomic bombs and the dawn of the atomic age put the future of the whole world in question. If academic innovation thrived in a period of calm and stability, the postwar years were not ideally suited. But Father Cavanaugh seemed determined that it would not be a period of stagnation or simply holding the line. Changes were made, in addition to the hiring of impressive professors from abroad, and Notre Dame began to take important steps toward becoming a major university of the twentieth century.

One of the innovations Father Cavanaugh long had in mind was some revision of the undergraduate curriculum. He had never been fully satisfied with his own education, undergraduate or graduate, for two reasons. First, he disliked the lecture method of teaching that was then prevalent in most college and university classrooms. He was personally very gregarious, loved to share his opinions, enjoyed bantering about topics great and small, and sitting still in a classroom, listening to a lecturer, taking notes, and submitting those same ideas back to the teacher on a test was not the best learning methodology in his opinion. Second, he felt that the undergraduate curriculum lacked unity; it was too random, with each course in English, history, philosophy, mathematics, science, and economics doing its own thing with almost no relation to the other courses the students were taking. Some integrating principle was needed and he thought he had found it in the study of the Great Books.[14]

The Great Books program had been founded by John Erskine, professor of literature and humanities at Columbia University in 1920. His goal was to revitalize and strengthen the liberal arts tradition in the university. At that time, it was generally the professors who read the original great works of Western culture— Homer, Plato, Thucydides, Virgil, Dante, Goethe, Gibbons—and then explained them to the class, perhaps using textbooks the professors themselves had written. Erskine's plan was to have the students read and discuss these great works themselves. Approximately one hundred Great Books of Western Culture eventually comprised the standard list, and the seminar method of teaching was adopted, with perhaps two professors of different educational backgrounds leading the discussions, and with the seminars being complemented by pertinent connecting lectures in philosophy, history, science, etc. The goal was that each student would emerge from the course with a unified view of Western culture through the ages. The program met with partial success at Columbia University, it was brought to the University of Chicago in 1929 by Professors Robert Hutchins and Mortimer Adler, and it eventually went to Saint John's College in Annapolis and elsewhere. Father John Cavanaugh learned of it through the University of Chicago, was fascinated by it, and decided to adopt a program at Notre Dame.[15]

Notre Dame's first Great Books seminar actually took place in the Law School in 1947. Appellate Judge Roger Kiley, a classmate and fellow graduate of John Cavanaugh in 1923, was familiar with the program through the Great Books Foundation in Chicago and he and Father Cavanaugh began conducting a seminar in the Great Books one day a week for the first and second year law students. Three years later the program was added to the offerings in the College of Arts and Letters under the directorship of Otto Bird, who had been an associate of Mortimer Adler in Chicago. It was first titled the General Program of Liberal Studies and begun as an elective major with a faculty of five and student enrollment of forty-nine. The students took their courses together in two sections to keep class sizes in the twenties; they studied languages, history, mathematics, science, philosophy, and theology; and this study especially included the reading and discussing of the Great Books. The basic core of the Great Books was retained but important substitutions were also made—Books of the Bible, Saint Augustine, Venerable Bede, Saint Thomas Aquinas, later Thomas Merton, and so on. From daily contact with the same classmates and faculty, students became familiar with each other and comfortable discussing books and ideas, challenging each other's views, and adjusting their own opinions and ideas. Although a small program, it had an influence on the rest of the college. Other departments experimented more with the seminar method of teaching, original texts were assigned more often, and outside speakers were invited to lecture on topics of their expertise (as in the General Program of Liberal Studies), on Saint Augustine or Dante or Newton. It began as a full four-year program, and there is some question whether Father Cavanaugh thought it might eventually comprise the whole College of Arts and Letters, but it never did and, with many alterations through the years, it remained one department major within the college, always a very popular one among its students.[16]

The increase in student enrollment was not only on the undergraduate level in the postwar years but on the graduate level also. Graduate enrollment increased from less than a hundred in 1946 to more than five hundred in 1952. The university had prepared, however. As noted earlier, Father O'Donnell in 1944 had appointed a dean of the Graduate School, Father Philip Moore, and a Graduate Council to advise him, and outstanding faculty members from home and abroad were joining the university. The number of doctoral programs doubled from seven to fifteen, including English, history, sociology, education, mechanical engineering, and medieval studies, and doctorates were also offered now in both botany and zoology. Master's degree programs were introduced in aeronautical, chemical, civil, electrical, and mechanical engineering, and in art, medieval studies, music, religion, business administration, and speech. Over time, the scholarly research and publications flowing from some of these departments proved impressive, including, by mid-century, the *Review of Politics*, Publications in Medieval Studies, Texts and Studies in Medieval Education, the *Notre Dame Journal of Formal Logic*, the *American Midland Naturalist*, and the *Natural Law Forum*.[17]

Two recently founded institutes were also making significant contributions to scholarship. The Medieval Institute, established in 1946, had its origin in 1933 when young Father Philip Moore returned to Notre Dame from the École des Chartes in Paris and began offering graduate courses in the philosophy of the Middle Ages. Courses expanded into medieval theology, history, literature, and education, and students were free to select specializations. Father Gerald Phelan of Toronto was named the first director in 1947, and he was then succeeded by Canon Astrik Gabriel, with Father Joseph Garvin as assistant director. The institute soon took its place among the best in the United States. A solid knowledge of Latin was needed for student admission, two years of residency was required for the master's degree and five years for the doctorate. Classes in a single year might include Middle English Dialects, Chaucer I and II, The Thirteenth Century, The Later Middle Ages, Patristic-Medieval Philosophy, and Liturgy of the Middle Ages. The institute library was one of the best in the Western Hemisphere and, thanks to the Michael A. Grace, II, Trust, centuries-old documents, additional first editions, and priceless engravings were regularly added to the collection, especially from libraries of Eastern Europe. Advanced undergraduate students might take classes in the institute but the program was chiefly for specially selected graduate students.[18]

A second institute was LOBUND (Laboratory of Bacteriology, University of Notre Dame). LOBUND began as a hope in the mind of James Reyniers. As an undergraduate majoring in biology at Notre Dame in 1928, young Reyniers became especially interested in the presence and function of bacteria, and on his graduation in 1930 he was hired by the College of Science to offer courses in biology and to continue his research in bacteriology. From the time of Louis Pasteur in the late nineteenth century, bacteriologists had first studied a disease and then searched for the bacterial cause, but Reyniers and others hoped to find a way to isolate and study bacteria directly. The problem was contamination, how to prevent other and unwanted bacteria from contaminating the cultures being researched. What Reyniers needed, and what every bacteriologist before him needed, was the creation of a germ-free environment, something that had not yet been successfully accomplished. Reyniers's first effort, with limited success, was a glass bell jar that could be sterilized with a germicide, equipped with cotton air filters and sealed with a rubber glove at the top. He was eventually to raise a germ-free guinea pig in that apparatus for twenty-two days. As time went on, he was able to build larger and more sophisticated equipment, and when the new biology building was opened in 1937, he was given laboratory space on the first floor and in the basement. Reyniers and his few assistants had to build their germ-free tanks or cages themselves, often with materials they could beg or borrow from others, and a major breakthrough occurred when they discovered that steam under pressure was a better sterilizer than germicides.[19]

After almost ten years, Professor Reyniers's research process had been refined. A pregnant animal—guinea pig, rabbit, mouse, rat—was stripped of its hair, sterilized in a germicide bath, and through a series of trap doors was lowered into a cage or tank totally germ-free. The offspring was delivered by Caesarian section from the germ-free womb, placed in its own germ-free tank, and fed by germ-free artificial "pig milk" developed by Reyniers. As it grew, the animal was transferred to ever-larger cages, given (germ-free) fresh food and water, and lived like any other animal, except in a totally germ-free environment. Eventually one bacterium could be introduced into the specimen and the impact and progress of that culture could then be followed.[20]

Some of this research was halted during World War II as Reyniers was called into the Navy, but it was recommenced postwar. LOBUND researched the causes of tooth decay with the University of Chicago's Zoller Clinic, sent nutritional findings to the Kellogg Company, studied diseases in chickens for the U.S. Regional Poultry Research Laboratory, undertook vitamin studies for Parke-Davis and Company, and researched prevention of airborne epidemics among infants. The institute was established as a research agency, distinct from the Department of Biology, and with no classroom teaching responsibilities.[21]

Another teaching and research program inaugurated in the late 1940s was the School of Liturgy, spearheaded by Father Michael Mathis. Father Mathis had been born in South Bend in 1885, was ordained a priest in 1914, and had hoped to be assigned as a Holy Cross missionary in India. That assignment never came but his interest remained strong: he founded *The Bengalese* magazine in 1919 to publicize the work of the Holy Cross missionaries, he oversaw the building of the Holy Cross Foreign Mission Seminary in Washington, DC, in 1924, and, with Dr. Anna Dengel, he co-founded the Medical Mission Sisters in 1925. In 1936 he began reading Pius Parsch's multivolume work *The Church's Year of Grace* and decided that liturgy was "the real stuff." If he could not go to the foreign missions, he would be a missionary for the liturgy here at home.[22]

In 1939 he began to gather a small group of undergraduate students for daily study of the missal and for a Recitated Mass. With Father Cavanaugh's approval, this expanded into a modest undergraduate program in the summer of 1947. Father Mathis insisted that the liturgy had to be both studied and celebrated, and thus the students attended Mass and prayed much of the breviary in common each day, in addition to attending classes. Classes covered the whole gambit of liturgical studies—History of Liturgy, Gregorian Chant, The Sacramental Way, Ecclesiastical Places, Station Churches and Latin Masses, Liturgy and Catholic Action, and The Scriptural Background for the Liturgical Year. Father Mathis made contact with the best liturgical scholars in Europe and, with the financial aid of Michael Grace, one of his early undergraduate followers, he recruited them to his summer session faculties: Louis Bouyer, Jean Daniélou, Balthasar Fischer, Joseph Goldbrunner, Johannes Hofinger, Josef Jungmann, Christine Mohrmann, and Ermin Vitry, in addition to American scholars Godfrey Diekmann, Gerald Ellard, Martin Hellriegel, and Reynold Hillenbrand. Hundreds of priests, sisters, brothers, and lay men and women enrolled in the summer programs over the years and brought the liturgical message home to their parishes, schools, monasteries, and convents. To give the program wider impact and spread the message further, many of the summer lectures were published in a series called Liturgical Studies, and some became classics: Bouyer's *Liturgical Piety*, Jungmann's *The Early Liturgy*, and Daniélou's *The Bible and The Liturgy*. Because of the program's academic quality and wide influence, Father Mathis ranks with Dom Virgil Michel and Father Godfrey Diekmann as the foremost leaders of the American Catholic liturgical movement.[23]

As student enrollment and the size of the faculty continued to increase, and as academic programs continued to expand, new sources of income were also needed. Father Cavanaugh, who had familiarity with business from his time in advertising with the Studebaker Corporation, was desirous of putting the university's fundraising on a solid, continuous basis, and he was fortunate that he did not have to start from scratch. At the urging of alumnus Francis Hayes, the university had established the so-called "living endowment" in 1928, a program in which each alumnus would be asked to contribute something to the university each year, fifty dollars, a few or many hundreds, contributed in monthly, quarterly, or yearly installments. Rather than making a capital donation to the university, an alumnus could retain the principal himself and contribute the interest or dividend to the university each year. Dartmouth had a similar program and had received $97,000 in gifts the year before, the equivalent of the profit from a $2 million endowment. Each donation could also be directed to the individual college of the alumnus's choice.[24] The program brought in a few thousand dollars the first year, but then declined during the Depression years of the 1930s. The university was also seeking money for a chair in organic chemistry in honor of Father Nieuwland and for a memorial building to honor Knute Rockne, but neither of these were fully successful. A Centenary Fund Drive was announced for 1942 and it garnered $100,000, the "living endowment" was then transferred into the annual fund drive, and each of these from 1942 to 1946 brought in close to $100,000.[25]

Father Cavanaugh and Harry Hogan, a banker from Fort Wayne and a member of the alumni board, wanted to transform all of this into a permanent fundraising arm of the university in 1947. The office was established as the "University of Notre Dame Foundation" and, although it was to be under the university president, his assistant, Father Robert Sweeney, was the effective director. They set a goal of adding $25 million to the endowment over a ten-year period, all alumni club presidents were briefed on the program that summer, it was explained to the faculty in the fall, and the board of lay trustees gave it full approval. The university's endowment at that time was close to $5 million. Father Cavanaugh publicized particular needs of the university and explained the benefits of the additional money. One early strategy was the "Give or Get $200" program, which asked each alumnus to give $200 annually to the university or request it successfully from a local business, industry, or acquaintance. By 1950, the foundation had collected $484,356 for a new Science Hall, Mrs. Sally Fisher had donated $1 million for a new residence hall and student aid, I. A. O'Shaughnessy had given a second $100,000 for liberal arts at the university, the Rockefeller Foundation donated $69,000, alumnus Ernest Morris contributed $79,000, the Kresge Foundation $25,000, and there were other similar gifts. The foundation was a success from the start, a major contribution of Father Cavanaugh to the growth of Notre Dame.[26]

Another source of income to the university in these postwar years, of course, was football. If Knute Rockne and the 1920s marked the "Golden Age" of Notre Dame football, Frank Leahy and the post–World War II years were the "Silver Age." Although the war had been over for more than a year in 1946, it still had an impact on Notre Dame since players returning from the military were older and more mature. Of the seventy players who made the 1946 squad, fifty had served in the military. The other twenty were predominantly freshmen. Freshman Terry Brennan was only seventeen when the season opened that fall, but five of his teammates were already twenty-five. Emil Sitko, the starting right halfback, had been on the Great Lakes team that defeated Notre Dame the year before. Coach Leahy himself had been discharged from the Navy in mid-November 1945, had followed the team in its remaining games of the season, familiarizing himself with the players who would be returning, and he conducted a brutal practice the next spring to get everyone into the football shape he desired. He reportedly had one practice in a heavy spring downpour, even demanding extra laps: "You never know what kind of weather we could have on any Saturday."[27]

It was Leahy's second national championship season. Lujack, a veteran of the 1943 team, was the quarterback, running backs were Sitko, Brennan, and Jim Mello, with Jim Martin, Ziggy Czarobski, and George Connor anchoring the line. Freshman Leon Hart was a substitute. Leahy worried about the opening game against Illinois—"Leahy Gloomy About Illini Game" read the *Scholastic* headline—but Notre Dame won easily, 26 to 6. Pittsburgh fell the next week, 33 to 0. The offense came fully alive the next two weeks, defeating Purdue 49 to 6 and Iowa 41 to 6. Navy had now lost many of its starters who had defeated Notre Dame 32 to 13 in 1944 and tied them 6 to 6 in 1945, and Notre Dame won easily, 28 to 0. Leahy had called a very conservative game, not willing to reveal much to Army scouts who he knew were in attendance.[28]

The Army game has also been called "the game of the century," and perhaps it was. It featured some of the best all-time collegiate players, older and more experienced than in other years—Army's Doc Blanchard and Glenn Davis and Notre Dame's Johnny Lujack and George Connor—and the teams were evenly matched. The game was played mostly between the twenty-yard lines since neither team was able to make large gains. Terry Brennan had one twenty-yard run for Notre Dame, as did Blanchard for Army, but they were the longest. Blanchard's was the play of the game because he broke free and seemed headed for the goal line when Lujack, playing safety on defense, brought him down with a classic one-on-one tackle at the thirty-six yard line. Notre Dame did have an eighty-five-yard drive that was stopped on the three yard line, and Notre Dame halted an Army effort on the five yard line. The game ended in a 0–0 tie with Army still never scoring against a Leahy team in four attempts, but neither team, and neither coach, was fully satisfied.[29]

The final three games were predictable victories. Northwestern fell 27–0, with Notre Dame backs combining to gain 423 yards. The Irish travelled to New Orleans and defeated Tulane, 41–0, although Coach Leahy then suffered a bout of bad health and his assistant, Ed "Moose" Krause, had to take over for the final game against Southern California. Notre Dame won 26–6 with little-used running back Coy McGee gaining 146 yards in six carries. Leahy reportedly phoned Krause often during the game and inquired why McGee was playing rather than the lineup Leahy had drafted. Several starters were named All-Americans and, when Army narrowly eked out a victory over Navy, 21–18, in their last game, Notre Dame was declared national champions.[30]

If the 1946 team was good, and indeed it was, the 1947 team was even better. Respected sports writer Gene Schoor called it "Notre Dame's Greatest Team," and *Sport* Magazine's Bill Furlong entitled an article "The Year South Bend Had an NFL Franchise."[31] Furlong was not far wrong. He noted that forty-two players on the team went on to professional football: "Art Statuto, a third- or fourth-string center played three years of pro football. Zeke O'Connor, an end who didn't win a letter, was named to the College All-Star team. Vince Scott, a fourth-string guard, didn't play in a game that year, yet went on to play a year in the old All-America Conference, and many more in Canadian football."[32] Some first-stringers, of course, like Terry Brennan, passed on professional football and went immediately into coaching. Another sports writer wrote that Michigan, Oklahoma, Alabama, or Texas might dispute who was the greatest, "but you can be sure that no school ever had a stronger second team, or a third team, or a fourth team."[33] Coach Leahy lost a good right end from his 1946 team but had a replacement in young Leon Hart, a three-time All-American and Heisman Trophy winner. Another change, important but not that noticeable to the public, was that Ed "Moose" Krause was named athletic director before the season began to enable Leahy to concentrate exclusively on football. Krause—large, outgoing, and jovial, often with a cigar in his mouth—seemed friendly to everyone. Public relations improved. One West Point veteran remarked:[34]

> When Rockne was alive, Army seldom beat Notre Dame, but it was different. You didn't hate to lose. Rock would come up to the Point every spring, stay around two or three days with Biff James or whoever was coaching, and renew and strengthen relations. Losing to Leahy is just the same as losing to a concrete mixer.

Frank Leahy might not always have been gracious in his victories, but there was no doubt that he would have many in 1947. He had recruited and assembled a remarkable group of athletes. The quarterback and field general was Johnny Lujack, an excellent all-around athlete—he could pass, kick, placekick, pass on the run, and play defense—and such a good runner that there was some thought that he might move to halfback where he could do more than hand off and pass. He was also so famous, and respected, that he averaged close to fifty fan letters a day. In a later interview, Lujack humorously made light of his athletic achievements:[35]

> "I made All-County, and they found out later that we were the only high school in the county. . . .
>
> That [Blanchard tackle] was supposed to be a highlight, although I didn't think much of it at the time because that's what you were back there for—to tackle. . . .

We played against the Iowa Seahawks, and I went up against an All-Pro end. I went up to knock the pass down one-handed, and the ball actually stuck in my hand, so it was a one-handed interception, and it was written up as a great interception. But I went up to knock it down and it just stuck. . . .

The reason I was able to play all four sports is that I was in the service, so I didn't have to go out for spring practice. My first baseball game I got two singles and a triple out of four times up. In between innings I won the high jump and javelin in track, so my roommate, being a very comical guy, said, 'if you get dressed real quick, I know where there's a swimming meet.'"

Joining Lujack in the backfield was John Panelli at fullback. At 185 pounds, he was heavy enough to gain a necessary three or four yards plunging, but fast enough to take a lateral and sweep around the end. He had a five-and-a-half-yard average for his collegiate career. With him were halfbacks Emil Sitko and Terry Brennan. Not exceptionally fast, Sitko had an explosive start and was hard to bring down until he had gained six or seven yards. Brennan was not particularly fast either, and did not have Sitko's power, but as one writer said, he "couldn't do anything but get the job done."[36] There was great depth at the halfback position. Notre Dame had recruited the 1945 All-City backfield from Chicago—Billy Gay and Mike Swistowicz from Tilden, Larry Coutre from St. George, and Roger Brown from Fenwick—and others returned from the war. One author wrote that "Leahy got a little thin at half back when he reached down to the sixth and seventh string."[37]

At one end was Leon Hart, only a sophomore but already considered by many the finest end in the country. At six foot four and close to 230 pounds, he was a devastating blocker and almost impossible to bring down when he got up speed after a catch. Used as fullback in short-yardage situations, he could gain four or five yards before enough of the defense could assemble to gang-tackle him. On the opposite end was Jim Martin who played almost any line position. In World War II, he had gone ashore at Tinian in the South Pacific to get valuable information to aid the Allied invasion that followed, and for this he received a presidential citation. Big, blond, with a crew cut and no fear, he looked every inch a marine, and would likewise be a recognized All-American before his graduation. The tackles were George Connor and Ziggy Czarobski, dissimilar in almost everything but football talent. Handsome and well built at six foot three and 225 pounds, Connor was at one time considered as a possible Tarzan in future movies. He was a superb blocker, a natural team leader, respected by all, and on defense almost impossible to block one-on-one. He was a two-year All-American. Another All-American, Ziggy Czarobski anchored the other tackle position. Lighthearted and seemingly always happy, he was the team jokester, and for a time he wrote a weekly column in the *Scholastic* under the byline "It Behooves Me Greatly," but overall he was an excellent football player, difficult to move out or get through on offense and a sure tackler of anything he reached. He loved to eat and gained weight off-season but he was always in shape and ready to play when the new season opened.[38]

The guards were Marty Wendell and Bill Fischer. Wendell, at five-eleven and 198 pounds, was an in-between size. Over three years he changed positions from fullback to center to guard, and he won monograms at all three, only the second person till then to do that. Fischer was young, big (six foot two and 230 pounds), easygoing but durable, and in 1947 led all linemen with three hundred minutes played. He was a consensus two-time All-American and, in his senior year, the Outland Trophy winner as the best lineman in the country. At center, Leahy had two choices, George Strohmeyer and Bill Walsh, both good enough to start anywhere. Strohmeyer was named to two All-American teams in 1946, and Walsh had been a first-stringer in 1945 and had already won two monograms. Before the season began, even Coach Leahy, ever the gloomy pessimist, had to admit that the team looked "darn good."[39]

The season itself was "darn good" also, not spectacular with a "game of the century" or one won for "the Gipper," but a highly efficient combination, rolling over each opponent, often with second- and third-stringers allowed to do much of the rolling. In the first game Notre Dame overwhelmed Pittsburgh 40–6, with Lujack throwing three touchdown passes. The next week the Irish defeated Purdue 22–7, with Lujack throwing for one touchdown and running for another. The next three games, against Nebraska, Iowa, and Navy, were shutouts, with Brennan carrying much of the running load and Frank Tripucka substituting frequently for Lujack. Army was next and it had already been announced that this would be the last meeting of these two teams since the public spectacle seemed to be getting too large. Notre Dame scored twice in the first three minutes, with Brennan taking the opening kickoff ninety-five yards for a touchdown, and the final score was 27–7. Notre Dame next edged Northwestern 26–19, with Lujack throwing two touchdown passes and Tripucka one. With Leahy in California scouting the Trojans, Ed Krause coached the next game against Tulane, used fourth- and fifth-stringers in the backfield, and still won 59–6. Due to wartime restrictions, Notre Dame had not played on the West Coast since 1942, so the season's final game at Southern California was a new experience for many of the players, and the 38–7 victory made it even more enjoyable. Lujack won the Heisman Trophy, he and four teammates were named All-Americans, it was Leahy's third national championship, and one sports writer stated that he could have won it with his second team.[40]

Coach Leahy must have considered the 1948 season a disappointing one, although not wholly unexpected. He had lost three crucial All-Americans from 1947—Lujack, Connor, and Czarobski—and several other starters, and the replacements were of lesser caliber. In the opening game against Purdue it was defense, a blocked punt and an interception run for a touchdown, that earned a narrow 28–27 victory. Most other victories were less stressful: Pittsburgh, 40–0; Michigan State, 41–7; Indiana, 42–7; Northwestern, 12–7; and Washington, 46–0. Against Southern California in the final game, Tripucka got hurt, Bob Williams replaced him and threw an interception, Sitko fumbled once, and USC led 14–7 with thirty-five seconds to go when Sitko managed to score, tying the game at 14. At season's end, Hart, Fischer, Sitko, and Wendell were named All-Americans, the tie with Southern California was the only blotch on the record, and Notre Dame's unbeaten streak had reached twenty-eight, but Michigan was voted national champions.[41]

In 1949 the national championship returned to South Bend. Bob Williams was the quarterback, Emil Sitko in his final year did most of the ball-carrying, and Hart and Martin still anchored the line, Martin now moved to tackle. The first nine games were not close, with Notre Dame outscoring its opponents 323 to 66. The final game against Southern Methodist was a thriller, and could have been more so, but Doak Walker, SMU's best, was injured and unable to play. His colleague Kyle Rote, however, played the game of his life. In the second half, Leahy moved 250-pound Leon Hart to fullback and, as the defense concentrated on him, sent speedy halfbacks around the end. The strategy worked. Notre Dame won 20–14 but had to intercept a pass from Rote on the five-yard line to preserve the victory and the national championship. Leon Hart was awarded the Heisman Trophy, the first lineman ever to win it.[42]

The next three years were not up to the standards or successes of the past. In some ways they were rebuilding years because the last members of those early postwar teams—Hart, Martin, and Sitko—had graduated, the younger recruits seemed more prone to mistakes, and Coach Leahy's health was declining. Nineteen-fifty was Leahy's worst season, with a record of 4–4–1. In the second game, Purdue halted Notre Dame's winning streak at thirty-nine with a 28–14 loss, and that was followed by other losses to Indiana, Michigan State, and Southern California, and a tie with Iowa. The following year, Notre Dame lost to Southern Methodist and Michigan State, and again tied Iowa, for a 7–2–1 record. The record was the same in 1952, with high points and low points. There were a total of twenty-one fumbles in the Purdue game, eleven by Purdue and ten by Notre Dame, with Notre Dame recovering fifteen. Oklahoma boasted a superb running back in Billy Vessels, the lead in that game changed several times, and Notre Dame eked out a 27–21 victory. The play of the game was a kickoff after a Notre Dame score: Oklahoma's Larry Grigg caught it on the six yard line and started up the field at full speed where Dan Shannon met him head-on. Grigg did a half loop in the air and lost the ball and Shannon was knocked unconscious. The next week Notre Dame lost seven fumbles and the game to Michigan State. The team lost an average of one fumble per quarter that year (1952), forty in all.[43]

By 1953 the young recruits had matured and the backfield of Ralph Guglielmi, Johnny Lattner, Joe Heap, and Neil Worden was one of Notre Dame's finest. In the first game, Lattner and Heap each fumbled early but Notre Dame eventually won 28–21. Then came victories over Purdue, 37–7, and Pittsburgh, 23–14. Georgia Tech was the No. 1 team in the country and was on a thirty-one-game winning streak but Notre Dame won 27–14, without Coach Leahy in the second half since he had been rushed to the hospital with gastroenteritis. Notre Dame next defeated Navy, 38–7, Pennsylvania, 28–20, and North Carolina, 34–14. The Irish salvaged a 14–14 tie with Iowa only because players faked injuries to gain an extra time-out at the end of the first half and at the end of the game. With the two extra plays, Notre Dame scored both times. There was much criticism of the "Fainting Irish," and rules were eventually altered to prevent it. The season ended with victories over Southern California, 48–14, and Southern Methodist, 40–14. Lattner won both the Heisman and the Maxwell Trophies, and many writers voted Notre Dame national champions, although some favored Maryland, perhaps because of the fake injury controversy. Coach Leahy had missed six games in recent years for poor health and his doctor warned him that the stress of coaching was shortening his life. Only forty-five years old, he announced his resignation at the end of the season. It was also the end of an era. Notre Dame won five national championships (1943, 1946, 1947, 1949, and 1953) and had four Heisman Trophy winners (Bertelli, Lujack, Hart, and Lattner) under Leahy, and his record at Notre Dame was 87–11–9, for a winning percentage of .855, second only to Knute Rockne's among Notre Dame's major coaches. He was the best of his time.[44]

The extensive construction programs and physical expansion of the campus under his three predecessors had come to a halt during the presidency of Father Hugh O'Donnell. Those previous eighteen years had been a period of remarkable growth and construction—Howard, Morrissey, Lyons, Dillon, Alumni, Cavanaugh, Zahm, Breen-Phillips, a dining hall, Hurley Commerce Building, Cushing Hall of Engineering, the student infirmary, the fire station, the power plant, and the football stadium—but wartime restrictions had put an end to such building. The Navy Drill Hall and a Navy office and classroom building across from the Rockne Memorial had been built and were still in use by the university after the war, but that was the extent. As student enrollment increased after the war, Farley and Fisher residence halls were constructed and, with a growing faculty, additional academic space was also needed, especially for science and the liberal arts since commerce, engineering, and law already had individual buildings.

Science had been taught at Notre Dame since at least 1865, first in the Main Building, then in Phelan Hall, in Science Hall (later LaFortune Student Center), and, after 1917, in Chemistry Hall (later the Riley Hall of Art), where most of Father Nieuwland's chemical experiments took place. After Father Nieuwland's early death in 1936, money was contributed for some way to honor him, but the donations were never large during the years of Depression and World War II, and a larger and more modern science hall was critically needed after the war. It was hoped that the new Notre Dame Foundation could successfully locate the money, and plans for the new building were announced in April 1949. Completed and dedicated in the fall of 1953, Nieuwland Science Hall was situated between the fieldhouse and the 1917 chemistry building, "thus eliminating one of the most used softball and touch football fields in northern Indiana," according to *Scholastic*. The cost of the building was $1.75 million, more than the cost of Cavanaugh, Zahm, Breen-Phillips, and Farley combined, and the university had only $350,000 on hand at ground-breaking. The Notre Dame Foundation was able to solicit the rest. The building housed the Departments of Physics, Chemistry, and Mathematics, as did the old Science Hall, it contained a library on the second floor, large and small lecture rooms, a dark room, a microfilm room, a faculty lounge, four polymer laboratories, an electronics laboratory, and laboratories for elementary chemistry, advanced chemistry, organic chemistry, and nuclear physics, plus offices for the dean and the faculty. It was a fitting tribute to Notre Dame's outstanding priest-chemist.[45]

As great as the need was for a new science building, the need for a liberal and fine arts building may have been greater. That college had been centered in the Main Building for most of the university's history, crowded as that building was at times, and after the war, social science offices and classes were transferred to the Navy's military office building close to the Rockne Memorial, referred to then as the Social Science Building. The classrooms were not perfect for all classes since some did not have individual student desks but instead had long tables especially suited to reading naval maps. Realizing the university's needs in the area of the liberal arts, Mr. I. A. O'Shaughnessy, president of Globe Oil in Minneapolis, had earlier donated $300,000 for the university's uses. In 1952 he gave the university close to $2 million for a building devoted to the liberal and fine arts. The ground-breaking ceremony took place on May 24, with the board of lay trustees, of which Mr. O'Shaughnessy was a member, present, and Mortimer Adler of the University of Chicago delivering the principal address. The three-story building was in the Tudor-Gothic style, with faculty offices (and telephones) on the third floor, classrooms on the first and second floors, and the dean's office on first floor. There were soundproof rooms in a wing of the second floor for the Music Department and vocal and instrumental practice, and the first floor had rooms for the Art Department and a gallery. In the basement were a lounge and an air-conditioned storage room for the university's works of art. The building encouraged liberal and fine arts students and faculty to come together for formal and informal communication.[46]

Another building project begun during Father Cavanaugh's presidency—after Farley, Fisher, Nieuwland, and O'Shaughnessy—was the Morris Inn. Ernest Morris, a young Presbyterian from Valparaiso, Indiana, graduated from Notre Dame in 1906, but for a time did not think he would. He completed his law courses at the university but had not been able to pay his bills, and he felt sure he would receive no degree until those bills were paid. But the president, Father John W. Cavanaugh, gave him his degree and simply asked him to pay the remaining bills whenever he was able. He was deeply grateful. He eventually went into banking, founded Associates Investment Company, was president of the First Bank and Trust Company of South Bend, and decided to express his gratitude to Notre Dame in a very concrete way. Although he admired Notre Dame's Catholic character, he thought it could also benefit from a more neutral facility where non-Catholics like himself could feel totally comfortable meeting and speaking with university personnel, and he thought it also needed a place to lodge visitors outside of guest rooms in Catholic residence halls. He donated $1 million for a modern hotel to be built near the entrance to the university campus.[47]

The three-story structure opened in the spring of 1952, with the young women visiting the university for the junior prom its first guests. There were ninety-two guest rooms, all with baths, and the rates were six dollars and up for single rooms and nine dollars and up for doubles. The hotel opened in back onto the university's golf course and male guests of the hotel could play the course for a $1.50 fee. (Women at the time were not permitted to play the course.) Off the large lobby was a dining room that seated 125, three private dining rooms were available on the first floor, and there was an auxiliary lounge or dining room in the basement. The hotel employed sixty-five, and some of these employees were students part-time.[48]

With these five new buildings—Farley, Fisher, Nieuwland, O'Shaughnessy, and the Morris Inn—an upgrading of the heat and power plant was also necessary. Two new pressure boilers were installed, each with a capacity of more than 70,000 pounds of steam per hour, and a third boiler was updated. The three together could produce 180,000 pounds of steam per hour, double the earlier capacity. A new six-foot by six-foot tunnel was dug from the power plant to Farley Hall, and a large water tower was constructed. At a cost of $138,000, the new water tower, 183 feet high, held 500,000 gallons of water, taken entirely from three campus wells. This water tower allowed there to be pure drinking water from the faucets in all buildings, whereas in the past some water had been taken from the lakes and used only for cleaning purposes. It was a major improvement and convenience.[49]

Father Cavanaugh had taken business courses as a student at Notre Dame, although he did not rate them very highly, and he experienced firsthand how a successful business was run during his months as an executive with the Studebaker Corporation. He thought there were ways in which Notre Dame might be a more efficient and successful operation. He liked to ask deans which departments in their colleges were the strongest, and which the weakest, and ask department chairs who their best professors were, and who were below standard. He would ask the same questions and seek the same information from scholars and other professionals outside the university, to see if the evaluations of the outsiders were the same, or if Notre Dame administrators might be blind to some weaknesses. He thought the university should always be improving, always getting better, and he wanted to get as many opinions and recommendations as he could from outside experts. For this reason he established advisory councils for each of the five colleges. Each council was composed of twenty or thirty members, some alumni, some not, but all were recognized experts or successful practitioners in a particular field. The Law Advisory Council, for example, was composed of prominent lawyers, judges, and law school professors and deans from across the country. Each council met at least once a year (usually on a football weekend in the fall), spoke with students and faculty, attended classes, and made a report to the president and/or dean: Which departments seemed strong, and which weak? Which areas in the discipline might the university be overlooking or neglecting? What modern equipment might the university be lacking? Is a department offering too many classes, or too few? Should a dean or department chair be removed? Father Cavanaugh relied heavily upon the councils. The final decisions on hiring, promoting, and allotting the university's relatively meager financial resources were his, and he felt more comfortable, and more confident, after reading the reports of these councils. If a council's recommendation was going to involve an added expense on the part of the university, occasionally the council members, or a small number of them, might make donations to cover the costs.[50]

One of the changes outside observers were recommending, and a change Father Cavanaugh realized was necessary from his own observation, concerned the Law School. Clarence Manion had been dean since 1941. He had been born in Kentucky in 1896 ("My Old Kentucky Home" was played at his funeral), graduated from St. Mary's College in his home state, received a master's degree in philosophy from the Catholic University of America in Washington, DC, and a law degree from Notre Dame. After a brief practice of law in southern Indiana, he joined the Notre Dame faculty in 1924, and with the resignation of Dean Thomas Konop in 1941, Manion was named his successor. Strongly conservative in politics, he had a well-modulated speaking voice and was invited to address conferences and conventions across the nation and on the radio. These began to occupy more and more of his time, his travels took him away from the university ever more frequently, and the Law School did not seem to be making significant progress. Father Cavanaugh and his new executive vice president, Father Theodore Hesburgh, decided in 1952 that the school needed a dean who could spend more time guiding the school and less as a public spokesman. A search committee was appointed, twenty names emerged as leading candidates (most members of law schools across the country), and each was examined and interviewed thoroughly. Supreme Court Associate Justice Wiley Rutledge then recommended to a Notre Dame alumnus that Joseph O'Meara, a practicing lawyer in Cincinnati, should also be considered. He was not on the list of twenty but was interviewed by the committee. "What do you think of our Law College?" he was asked. "You have night school operating in the day time," he answered. "Would you like to be Dean?" "You wouldn't like me," he replied. "I'd be very difficult and demanding." His credentials were excellent, and he was hired. When once asked as dean if he might consent to be considered for the Supreme Court, he answered: "I came here to do a job and, God willing, I mean to stay and finish it." It was one of the final decisions of Father Cavanaugh's presidency, and a very important, successful, and correct one.[51]

An even more important change Father Cavanaugh made was the reorganization of the university's higher administration. When he assumed the presidency in 1946, the higher administrative structure consisted of the president, the vice president, the director of studies, the prefect of religion, the prefect of discipline, the director of faculty, the business manager, the purchasing agent, and the registrar. In practice, all of these positions under the president were appointed by him and reported to him, but their relations to each other were not always clear. Some order among them seemed necessary, and not all needed to report directly to the president.[52] In the summer of 1949, Father Thomas Steiner, the Holy Cross provincial superior, clearly at the recommendation of Father Cavanaugh, announced the creation of five new vice presidencies at the University of Notre Dame—vice presidents of academic affairs, of student affairs, of business affairs, and of public relations, and an executive vice president to coordinate their offices. The university vice president at the time, Father John Murphy, was named vice president of public relations. He would no longer be in line to succeed as president. Father Howard Kenna was appointed vice president of academic affairs. He had been ordained in 1930, did three years of graduate studies in mathematics at Johns Hopkins, had been superior of Moreau Seminary, and at the time was the university's director of studies. Father Joseph Kehoe, a member of the Economics Department and, since 1944, the prefect of discipline, was named vice president of student affairs. Father John J. Burke, former prefect of discipline and business manager, was named vice president of business affairs. For executive vice president, Father Cavanaugh had asked for, and was given, the thirty-two-year-old head of the Religion Department, Father Theodore M. Hesburgh.[53]

CHAPTER 15

The Early Presidency of
Father Theodore M. Hesburgh

When Father John Cavanaugh's six-year term as president came to an end in the summer of 1952, the university was in as fine a condition as it had ever been. Student enrollment had reached five thousand and all indications were that it would remain there. The "Baby Boom" generation was already five or six years old. More students were entering graduate school for advanced degrees—graduate school enrollment at Notre Dame had increased five-fold over the last six years—and there was an abundance of new faculty to recruit. Holy Cross Seminary enrollment was high, a larger college seminary would soon be needed, and there seemed to be no shortage of priest-professors for the future. With Nieuwland and O'Shaughnessy Halls underway, soon each college would have its own building for classes and administrative and faculty offices. The Notre Dame Foundation was functioning well and seemed to assure that funding would be available as needed. The present administrative structure of president, vice-presidents, deans, and chairs was efficient and well adapted for university growth. In almost every area, the future did indeed seem bright, and there was a new, young president in charge.

Father Theodore M. Hesburgh had been born in Syracuse, New York, on May 25, 1917, just four days before another president, John F. Kennedy, was born in Brookline, Massachusetts. He had an older sister and two younger sisters, and a younger brother sixteen years his junior. He attended Most Holy Rosary grade and high schools in Syracuse, played some competitive sports but was never very good at them, nor interested, joined the Boy Scouts, attended summer camps, and won numerous badges. His favorite sports were hunting and fishing, and at least this love of fishing remained with him for the rest of his life. He did well in all his classes (less well in science) and graduated third in his high school class. Deeply religious, the Hesburgh family recited the rosary together frequently, young Ted attended weekday Mass often before class, and he formed the desire to become a priest during his grade school years. Holy Cross priests preached a parish mission at Most Holy Rosary when Ted was in the seventh grade. He confided to one of the priests that he wanted to be a priest also, and the priest suggested to his parents that he might attend the high school seminary at Notre Dame rather than risk losing his vocation by delaying. His mother answered that if there was danger of losing a vocation being raised in a Catholic family and attending daily Mass, it must not be much of a vocation. He remained at home for high school.[1]

In the fall of 1934, the Hesburgh family drove young Ted, a recent high school graduate, out to Holy Cross Seminary at Notre Dame. He had kept in contact with one of those retreat preachers, Father Thomas Duffy, since the seventh grade, and he had never wavered in his desire to become a priest. Some classes that first year were taught in the seminary and some on the university campus, and his favorite course was Philosophy of Literature taught by Father Leo L. Ward. Hesburgh had a tendency to use polysyllabic words, and Father Ward warned him of the danger: "If you don't learn to simplify your style, you'll wind up being a pompous ass."[2] The young seminarian took the advice. After that first year at Notre Dame, Hesburgh and his classmates were sent for a year of novitiate in Rolling Prairie, Indiana, about twenty miles from the campus. Twenty-two hours a day were spent in silence, in prayer, and in spiritual reading; the director of novices gave daily conferences on the theology of the vows, the history of the Congregation of Holy Cross, and different methods of prayer; and several hours each day were spent in manual labor, chiefly farming. He returned to Notre Dame in 1936 and continued his studies, majoring in philosophy. He expected to be there for three years, until graduation, but after his sophomore year he and a classmate were sent to Rome to complete their philosophical studies and take four years of theology at the Pontifical Gregorian University. Classes were all taught in Latin, with oral exams in Latin, and much of the conversation in the seminary where they lived was in French, but Hesburgh had taken both Latin and French in high school and had a facility for picking up languages quickly. Summers were spent in northern Italy, the South Tyrol, formerly part of Austria, where most people still spoke German, and Hesburgh learned at least a smattering of that language. Spanish he learned conversing between classes with students from Spain and Latin America, and with other students he spoke Italian. He received his bachelor's degree in philosophy in 1939 and pronounced his final vows of poverty, chastity, and obedience as a member of the Congregation of Holy Cross that same year. He began his studies in theology that fall, just about the time Germany invaded Poland to begin World War II, and in May 1940 the American consul urged the American seminarians to leave Italy because Mussolini was about to lead his country into war on the side of Hitler. Hesburgh and others hurried to Genoa and boarded the USS *Manhattan*, possibly the last ship to leave Italy for the United States.[3]

On his arrival in New York, Hesburgh was allowed a ten-day vacation with his family, whom he had not seen for three years, and was then assigned to Holy Cross College in Washington, DC, to complete his theological studies. This he did in three years, working also with delinquent youths at the National Training School for Boys and helping to start a Newman Club at all-black Howard University. On June 24, 1943, having completed their theological studies, Hesburgh and his classmates were ordained to the priesthood in Sacred Heart Church on the Notre Dame campus. Hesburgh had earlier expressed the desire to serve as a military chaplain with the Navy in the Pacific but the provincial superior, Father Thomas Steiner, instead assigned him to return to Washington, DC, to study for a doctorate in theology at the Catholic University of America. He completed the doctorate in only two years, in part because he could study and research in Latin, French, Italian, and German sources with greater facility than most of his classmates. He offered Mass and assisted with confessions at Saint Patrick's Church in midtown Washington, and, with classmate Father Charles Sheedy, he also found time to write inspirational booklets for Catholic men and women in the service. These became so popular that he estimated that the U.S.O. distributed close to three million of them. His doctoral dissertation was on the position of the laity in the Church, entitled "The Relation of the Sacramental Characters of Baptism and Confirmation to the Lay Apostolate," insisting that, although Catholic Action was defined as the participation of the laity in the work of the hierarchy, through the indelible characters of Baptism and Confirmation that participation was essential in the Church's mission. The laity, he claimed, formed[4]

> a link between the hierarchy and a secularized world which is, in many ways, inaccessible to the hierarchy. The lay apostolate disposes others to be taught, governed and sanctified, thus extending the hierarchy's sphere of influence. The layman thus intimately participates in the hierarchical apostolate, most especially in the function of teaching, bringing the truth of Christ to those who would never come in direct contact with the official teachers of this truth. . . . The lay apostle is united to Christ, and living in a world which does not know Christ. In many cases, the Christian layman is the sole point of contact between the saving message of Christ and the secularized world which cannot be saved without Christ. Hence the dignity, necessity and providential nature of the lay apostolate today . . . "that in every way . . . Christ be proclaimed." (Phil. 1:18)

Father Ted, as he was then called, defended his dissertation in the late spring of 1945, received his doctoral degree, and despite asking again to serve as Navy chaplain in the Pacific, was assigned to return to Notre Dame, to be a prefect for chiefly returning veterans on the third floor of Badin Hall and to teach several classes of theology. Mindful of his desire to be a Navy chaplain, and noting the large number of V-12 students still on campus, the provincial superior remarked that "we've got more Navy at Notre Dame than any ship in the Pacific."[5] Since the veterans were older and more mature than traditional college students, Father Ted relaxed the rules and allowed extra freedoms, decisions that were not always popular with the other prefects. Soon after he was assigned to Badin Hall, the university procured some former prisoners-of-war barracks from the government to house married students. One hundred and seventeen couples, many with children, moved in, and Father Ted soon found himself acting as their unofficial chaplain. It was a work he loved: hearing confessions, offering Mass, giving convert instructions, baptizing, counseling, arranging social events, and being available in myriad ways as needed. In 1948 he was reassigned to Farley Hall as rector of approximately three hundred freshmen, although he admitted he preferred working with the older students and veterans. That same year, he was named chairman of the Department of Religion, one of the university's largest departments, and continued his teaching. He discovered that there were not many satisfactory textbooks written for college students 18 to 22 years of age, and he and two other young priests in the department decided to write their own. Father Joseph Cavanaugh wrote a book on apologetics, *Evidence for Our Faith*, Father Charles Sheedy wrote one on moral theology, how to live according to Catholic teachings, entitled *The Christian Virtues*, and Father Hesburgh wrote on dogmatic theology, the study of God, and creation and man's place in creation, and he entitled it *God and the World of Man*. All three were written quickly, among numerous other responsibilities, and Father Hesburgh admitted that they had their weaknesses, but there was little competition and they met an important need at Notre Dame, and the authors hoped at other Catholic colleges also.[6]

When Father Hesburgh accepted the position of chair of the Department of Religion, he must have had a suspicion, or even a fear, that this could be a first step to other and higher administrative positions. Father Cavanaugh had once asked how he would feel about being appointed dean of the College of Arts and Letters. Both of them knew that the present dean, Father Cavanaugh's brother Frank, needed to be replaced but Father Hesburgh insisted it should not be him. He was too young on the faculty and he was also in the midst of writing his textbook. But Father Cavanaugh kept trying to convince him that administration could be very satisfying also. It was in the summer of 1949 that Father Cavanaugh decided to reorganize the university's higher administration, creating four new vice president positions, and when the Holy Cross assignments were announced, Father Hesburgh had been named executive vice president, second only to the president in the university's administration.[7]

Father Cavanaugh immediately assigned him two major responsibilities. The first was to write articles of administration for all five new vice presidencies, including his own. He encountered some opposition since a couple of the new vice presidents had been working in their areas of expertise—academic, student, financial affairs—even longer than he had been a priest, and now he was suggesting how their new offices should operate. Eventually he completed the task. The second responsibility he was to undertake was to oversee the new construction on campus. Four buildings were under construction at that time, in various stages: Nieuwland Science Hall, O'Shaughnessy Hall of Liberal and Fine Arts, the Morris Inn, and Fisher Hall. He immediately hired a young engineer to assist him but remained, under the president, the final decision-maker. He said his principle was "function before form," making sure the building fulfilled its purpose within the university the best it could. Form and appearance came after that. He also chaired the Faculty Board in Control of Athletics and, on one occasion, had a serious disagreement with Coach Leahy. The board had approved thirty-eight players to make a trip to an away game but Leahy wanted forty-four. Father Hesburgh insisted that the list be reduced to thirty-eight or six players would be suspended from school for unexcused absences from class. Reluctantly, the coach relented.[8]

Father Hesburgh was executive vice president for only three years, but they were important years. He worked closely with Father Cavanaugh, witnessed his successful administrative principles and techniques, and absorbed many of them. He learned an enormous amount about the university's higher, and lower, administration from drafting the articles of administration for each vice presidential area. He oversaw the construction of four major buildings and became familiar with that important area. He stood in for Father Cavanaugh at campus meetings, spoke at alumni gatherings across the country, and became acquainted with leaders of most of the alumni clubs and with most of the university's major benefactors. When he was named president of the university at the close of Father Cavanaugh's six-year term in the summer of 1952, he was much better prepared for the responsibility than he or anyone might have been three years before.

Father Hesburgh's appointment was not a surprise, to him or to anyone else. The last three presidents—Fathers John O'Hara, Hugh O'Donnell, and John J. Cavanaugh—had all succeeded from the vice presidency, and Father Hesburgh had been the top vice president. He must have given the presidency some thought, set some goals, and considered ways to achieve them. One goal clearly was to raise Notre Dame's standards, to make Notre Dame the best university it could be, in fact, the best Catholic university in the world. But he also knew it had a long way to go, as he later reflected:[9]

> Our student body had doubled, our facilities were inadequate, our faculty quite ordinary for the most part, our deans and department heads complacent, our graduates loyal and true in heart but often lacking in intellectual curiosity, our academic programs largely encrusted with the accretions of decades, our graduate school an infant, our administration much in need of reorganization, our fund-raising organization nonexistent, and our football team national champions.

One of his earliest mantras was "God is not glorified by incompetence."[10] God deserved man's very best, and incompetence in a Catholic university dedicated to God seemed an insult. Father Hesburgh hoped to recruit only the best students, hire only the best faculty, build the best facilities, and have a beautiful campus. The university must be strong in its Catholic mission also. The majority of the faculty were Catholics at that time but if any were out of harmony with Notre Dame's Catholic goals, or were in opposition to them, he would be happy to see them move elsewhere. As a former chairman, he knew there were some weak professors in the Department of Religion, and he hoped to replace them with stronger ones.

He saw an important niche in American higher education that he thought Notre Dame could fill. There had been great Catholic universities in the past—Paris, Bologna, Louvain, Chartres, Oxford, Cambridge—and they had deeply influenced medieval society, but they had gradually lost their religious essence. The United States had never had a truly great Catholic university, and the Church and the nation were the poorer because of it. But Father Hesburgh was optimistic in an address to the faculty in the fall of 1954:[11]

> Here is a demanding spiritual task of the highest order, in fullest accord with the rich age-old tradition of Christian wisdom. Here is an apostolate that no secular university today can undertake—for they are largely cut off from the tradition of adequate knowledge which comes only through faith in the mind and faith in God, the highest wisdom of Christian philosophy and Catholic theology.
>
> Here is a task that requires that we be conscious of our past heritage, and enthusiastic in bringing new insights of Christian wisdom to the present. Here is a task for the greatest minds, and the most devoted hearts and completely dedicated lives.
>
> I know of no other spot on earth where we might make a better beginning than here at Notre Dame, where we might inaugurate a new center of Christian culture to effect a re-awakening of the potential of Christian wisdom applied to the problems of our age.
>
> This is no work of defense, no declaration of war, no practice in isolation, but a move to revitalize our own understanding of the treasure of supreme intellectualism and divine faith, wedded in strength and beauty. It means working together, each with our own particular talents to exploit the full power of Christian wisdom to order what is disordered, to complete what is good but incomplete, to meet insufficient knowledge with the fullness of truth, to give a new direction and a wider, saner perspective to all that is good and true in our times.
>
> The time is ripe. The old errors are sunk in frustration and pessimism and disorder. Men of good will are not wanting. Darkness awaits a light. We

have done, and are doing, a wide variety of good things at Notre Dame. If we do everything else and fail in this, our proper task, our high calling, our providential mission, then as we pray in the presence of God here today, we will be unworthy servants, and a failure as a Catholic university.

He found American higher education increasingly lacking in the essential qualities of values, ethics, character, and justice, and he believed only a religious university could supply them. In his opening sermon to the faculty and students in the fall of 1952, three months after assuming the presidency, he spoke of the need for wisdom, a proper understanding of the priorities of human life under God:[12]

> Do Americans think better, read better, write better today? Do they have a better married and family life, are wars diminishing and prayers more fervent, are lives more righteous in the sight of God? Or is God even granted sight? . . .
>
> What are the challenges of the spirit that face our civilization, our country, and our University today? Certainly, a prime challenge is the need for wisdom, not merely the pragmatic prudence of day-to-day decisions, but the age-old Christian wisdom that understands the whole pattern of creation and man's place in this pattern. Our work is the perfecting of human beings, drawing out and developing all the human potentialities of our students. Certainly this requires of us as educators some clear concept of what is good for men, for his body and for his soul, for his mind and his will, for only what is good for man will perfect man and assure him of a good life.
>
> It is the work of wisdom to recognize the true human perfections and to order them rightly, so that we do not place the goods of the body above those of the soul, those of time against those of eternity. Wisdom gives us a pattern of ordered education, because it gives us an ordered view of the world and of man.

There was no true understanding of man without a belief in God, and thus an education without God had to be woefully incomplete.

Knowing what he wanted to accomplish, Father Hesburgh assembled an administration he was confident would assist him. As his executive vice president he selected Father Edmund "Ned" Joyce. Father Joyce had been born in British Honduras on January 26, 1917, almost four months to the day older than Father Hesburgh. His father was working at that time for United Fruit Company but the family soon settled in Spartanburg, South Carolina, where Ned played varsity basketball throughout high school. Encouraged by his pastor, he entered Notre Dame in 1933, and he believed he was the first South Carolinian to do so. He worked part-time in the students' dining hall, and he graduated magna cum laude from the College of Commerce in 1937. He worked for five years in an accounting firm, passed the CPA exams in 1939, and returned to Notre Dame to enter the seminary in 1942. Ordained a priest in 1949, he spent a year at Oxford studying philosophy, political science, and economics, and he was then called back to Notre Dame to assist in the business affairs office. He was named vice president of business affairs in 1952 and Father Hesburgh's first (and only) executive vice president that same summer. Although different in so many ways, he complemented Father Hesburgh well and together they functioned as an efficient team for thirty-five years. Father Hesburgh was a northerner, Father Joyce a southerner; Father Hesburgh in most things liberal, Father Joyce conservative; Father Joyce was comfortable in the world of business, finance, and athletics, areas in which Father Hesburgh had little interest; Father Hesburgh felt very much at home in the limelight while Father Joyce preferred to remain at his desk with his schedules and ledgers. Father Joyce was a brilliant financier and effective administrator, and Father Hesburgh rarely overturned a decision in the areas of business, finance, and athletics.[13]

Most of the other vice presidents, like Father Joyce, were carryovers from Father Cavanaugh's administration. For vice president of academic affairs, Father Hesburgh selected Father Philip Moore, at the time dean of the Graduate School. The oldest of the vice presidents, he had been born in 1900, graduated from Notre Dame in 1924, was ordained a priest in 1928, received advanced degrees from both the Catholic University of America and the École des Chartes in Paris, and served as both head of the Philosophy Department from 1942 to 1948 and dean of the Graduate School from 1944 to 1952. His academic field was medieval philosophy, he was one of the founders of the Medieval Institute, and he was recognized for his scholarly achievements. The vice president of student affairs was Father James Norton. A native of Indianapolis, he had graduated from Notre Dame in 1929, was ordained a priest in 1933, received a master's degree from the Catholic University of America in 1934, and taught economics at both St. Edward's University in Austin and the University of Notre Dame. Father Cavanaugh appointed him vice president of academic affairs in 1950 and Father Hesburgh transferred him to student affairs in 1952. Father John Hoey Murphy was vice president of public relations during the final three years of Father Cavanaugh's administration and retained that position when Father Hesburgh assumed the presidency. Graduating from Notre Dame in 1933, he continued his studies for six years at the Gregorian University in Rome, was ordained a priest in 1938, received an advanced degree in sacred scriptures from the Pontifical Biblical Institute in Rome, and was superior of Moreau Seminary from 1943 to 1946. He was fascinated with the work and dedication of firemen and showed up at fires throughout the city of South Bend whenever he was free. Father Hesburgh selected Father Jerome Wilson, a seminary classmate of Father Joyce, for vice president of business affairs. Born in Pittsburgh in 1911, he graduated from Notre Dame in 1932, worked for nine years for Bendix-Westinghouse in Elyria, Ohio, was ordained a priest in 1949, and taught accounting at Notre Dame until 1952. The story is told that once a large bill arrived at the university on a Friday afternoon, Father Wilson told Father Hesburgh he hesitated to sign a check to pay it since there was not enough money in the bank to cover it, but Father Hesburgh told him to go ahead and sign it and he would get the money to cover it over the weekend.[14]

Satisfied with his vice presidential team, Father Hesburgh felt other administrative changes were necessary if academic standards were to be raised. One significant change had been made during Father Hesburgh's final year as executive vice president, a change he had strongly encouraged. That year, Dean Clarence Manion of the Law School was asked to resign and he was replaced by Joseph O'Meara, a prominent Cincinnati lawyer. The effects of the change were seen almost immediately. The new dean wanted a smaller law school, limiting total enrollment to three hundred. Lecturing to large classes was abandoned and the Socratic method of questions and answers in seminar-size classes was installed. Elective classes were discontinued in order to concentrate on basic core courses. The elective system, O'Meara felt, assumed "that students know more about what it takes to make a lawyer than their professors do."[15] The case method of teaching was limited to first-year classes, and second- and third-year students learned by problem solving, research in the law library, and working on concrete legal questions. Comprehensive examinations were imposed on first-, second-, and third-year students. First-year applicants were required to take the Law School Admission Test administered by the Law School Admission Council, and military veterans, who had previously been admitted after two years of college, were now required to have three. In the new dean's first year, 40 percent of the first-year students were dismissed for failing grades, and attrition rates for second- and third-year students were similarly high. But the dual purpose of the program remained constant:[16]

Drawing inspiration, as it does, from the Christian tradition, the Law School, while aiming first of all at technical proficiency, aims at more than that. . . . The School believes that a lawyer is best served, and the community as well, if he possesses not only legal knowledge and legal skills but also a keen sense of the ethics of his profession—and something else, which this sequence of courses is likewise designed to cultivate: pride in the legal profession and a fierce partisanship for justice.

A second long-term dean who the new administration soon felt was too set in his ways and not keeping abreast of the changing times was Dean James McCarthy of the College of Commerce. He had been a close friend of and successor to Father John O'Hara as dean of the college in 1924 and, nicknamed "Gentleman Jim" for his impressive appearance, he had been the face of the college for thirty years. The actual break was of his own making. Father Cavanaugh had recruited a tenured professor from Harvard to the faculty, he introduced an experimental program in the college with the administration's approval, and the dean was not comfortable with this and other changes. He apparently expressed his discontent to a group of faculty members:[17] "We've had two bad presidents in a row. We can't stand a third. But we probably won't have to worry about that because we'll outlast Hesburgh." When he admitted that he had made the remark, his days as dean were over. Father Hesburgh appointed the Harvard recruit, James Culliton, as dean, his experimental program became standard in the college, and humanities courses soon comprised one-half the college curriculum. Because of his long service to the college and university, McCarthy was kept on as a fundraiser and public relations consultant at his dean's salary.[18]

One of the more delicate decisions that had to be made was in the College of Arts and Letters. The dean was Father Francis Cavanaugh, younger brother of Father Hesburgh's predecessor, but he too had grown too comfortable in the position, the college was progressing little, and it was operating efficiently chiefly through the efforts of the assistant dean, Devere Plunkett, and secretary Loretta Brennan. But Father Frank was a very popular Holy Cross priest and was assistant superior of all Holy Cross priests and brothers on campus. Father John Cavanaugh realized that a change needed to be made but it was too delicate to fire his own brother and he left the move up to Father Hesburgh. In his first months as president, Father Hesburgh asked Father Frank to step down, and he replaced him with his close friend, Father Charles Sheedy. Father Sheedy, not a research scholar himself, may not have encouraged research and publication among the faculty to the extent Father Hesburgh envisioned, but he was a fine undergraduate dean, encouraged wide interests and wide reading among students, enjoyed being a popular campus figure, and proved to be an informal but effective administrator.[19]

Two other important changes were made early in the new administration, but they had little effect on the rest of the university. They were made chiefly to tighten up the administration and bring the institutes closer under vice presidential control. Professor James Reyniers, a Notre Dame alumnus and longtime member of the faculty, was the founder of LOBUND (Laboratory of Biology, University of Notre Dame) and he and his institute had made excellent contributions in the area of germ-free research. The institute operated through different sources of funding, the new administration wanted it brought more directly under the Controller's Office, and the new procedures seemed to require a new director. A similar change was made in the Medieval Institute. Father Gerald Phelan had been one of the founders and the first director of the institute, the institute was doing excellent work, and its library and manuscript collection was becoming one of the most respected in the country. But some fundraising and spending had drifted away from direct administration oversight, and in reasserting that oversight and control, Canon Astrik Gabriel was asked to replace Father Phelan. In his memoirs, Father Hesburgh admits that he probably could have made these two changes with greater sensitivity.[20]

A final important administrative change, and by far the one most publicized across the nation, was the replacement of Frank Leahy as football coach. Notre Dame had hired Leahy in 1941, he was one of the most successful coaches of his era, and, after Rockne, Notre Dame's greatest. In ten seasons, he had won 87, lost 11, and tied 9, and he had won four national championships. But in recent years he had been running his very successful program with little direct oversight or control from higher administration, and some incidents, like a player faking an injury to stop the clock when Notre Dame had no time-outs remaining, received public criticism and were somewhat embarrassing. The new administration's efforts to raise academic standards were not making competitive recruiting any easier, and the stress to win began taking a toll on Leahy's health. Over the years he had missed six games due to illness, he sometimes walked hotel floors the nights before important games, and he collapsed in the locker room at halftime of the Georgia Tech game in 1953. At the end of the season, his doctors gave him a choice: continue coaching or continue living. He was only forty-five years old and had a wife and eight children. Father Hesburgh asked two of Leahy's close friends—the director of public relations, Art Haley, and sports writer Arch

Ward—to meet with the coach and convince him that further football victories were not worth his life. He announced his retirement in January 1954 and was replaced by his freshman football coach and popular Notre Dame alumnus Terry Brennan.[21]

Whatever lofty visions a university president might have for his institution, there will always be unexpected interruptions that will intrude and absorb his attention, at least for a time. This happened to Father Hesburgh in the first few months of his presidency. The national presidential election was scheduled for November 4, 1952, four months into his own presidency, with Republican Dwight Eisenhower running against Democrat Adlai Stevenson, governor of Illinois. Eisenhower was clearly a hero to most Americans, Catholics and non-Catholics alike. He had been supreme Allied commander in Europe in World War II, defeated Hitler and Nazi Germany, returned as first commander of North Atlantic Treaty Organization (NATO) forces after the war, and had a personality and broad smile that made him almost everyone's favorite uncle or grandfather. If Eisenhower's personal popularity was not a sufficient obstacle for the witty, well-educated, and urbane Stevenson to overcome among Catholic voters, he faced two additional challenges. First, Republican Senator Joseph McCarthy of Wisconsin, a well-known Catholic, had achieved some success in chastising the Democratic Party, Stevenson's party, for harboring Communists and other radicals hostile to Catholicism's traditional values. Second, Governor Stevenson was divorced (although not remarried), the Catholic Church generally opposed divorce, and the nation had never elected a divorcé to the presidency before. The majority of Catholics were probably leaning toward Eisenhower, maybe influenced in some part by Senator McCarthy and Stevenson's marital status.[22]

Perhaps to counteract such thinking, sixty-five Notre Dame professors, sixty-four laymen and one priest, signed a statement drafted by popular professor Frank O'Malley, also a Democratic precinct chairman, favoring the election of Governor Stevenson. It spelled out five reasons:[23]

First: Governor Stevenson offered a realistic foreign policy intent on "the strength of our own nation and leading to the peace and security of all free nations."

Second: He had a domestic policy "devoted to the achievement of justice and prosperity for all groups."

Third: He would be "forthright and dauntless in combatting the twin tyrannies" of Communism and McCarthyism.

Fourth: He would be active in challenging political corruption.

Fifth: "Above all, we admire Governor Stevenson for his profound spiritual insight into the crises—social, political and economic—of our time. . . . He grasps the mystery of the existence of man in the midst of time and time's tasks."

The statement closed with the acknowledgement that the signers had subscribed to it "as individuals and as citizens" and that it "in no way commits the University of which we are members."

Professor O'Malley sent the statement, with the signatures, to a Stevenson campaign official, and the National Volunteers for Stevenson then decided to circulate it as a paid advertisement in city newspapers across the country. It appeared on October 29. The impression given was that Governor Stevenson was highly respected and championed on the Notre Dame campus, and thus Catholics, and others, should have no hesitation in casting their votes for him. Most of the signers did not know that the statement was going to be given such publicity but none seemed to object either.[24]

Father Hesburgh immediately felt the need to refute the impression that Notre Dame seemed to favor Stevenson. He issued the following statement:[25]

The University of Notre Dame strenuously objects to the paid political advertisement which has been placed by the Volunteers for Stevenson organization in several metropolitan newspapers in an attempt to identify the University of Notre Dame with one side of the present political campaign. . . .

The professors who signed the statement were perfectly free to do so as private citizens but had no right whatever to involve the name of the university which has been, and remains, absolutely nonpartisan in this campaign.

The University of Notre Dame has encouraged its faculty and student body to take an intelligent interest in the present campaign by inviting both presidential candidates to speak at the university on spiritual and moral issues which face the nation today.

Both candidates did speak at Notre Dame; both were well received.

To diminish the impact of the statement further, Father Hesburgh noted that those sixty-five professors comprised less than 12 percent of the university faculty, and his rejoinder eventually appeared in approximately two hundred papers.[26]

A second unpleasant intrusion crossed the president's desk two years later, this time an objection to an article on church-state relations written by Jesuit Father John Courtney Murray for a book published by the University of Notre Dame Press. The traditional Catholic view of proper church-state relations had been expressed most explicitly in Pope Leo XIII's encyclical *Immortale Dei* in 1885, and in Pope Pius IX's *Quanta Cura* and Syllabus of Errors in 1864. In that view, the proper goal and purpose of government was the common good, the general welfare of all, and since every human was a political, economic, moral, and religious being, the goal and purpose of government must be to promote welfare in all these areas, promoting peace in the political area, prosperity in the economic area, opposing immorality in the moral area, and promoting religion, the one true Catholic religion, in the religious area. The government could and should pass laws restricting immorality and immoral lifestyles, and it could and should positively aid the practice of the true religion. Sin and error were contrary to the common good and therefore should be restricted. Since human beings were social beings, they should practice religion, and worship, not only as individuals but as social beings, as families, as local churches, as a nation. This ideal might not be realizable in deeply pluralistic societies (like the United States) but it was still the Church's ideal, and anything less than this was to be only tolerated.[27]

Father Murray espoused a different view. He had been born in New York in 1904, entered the Society of Jesus (Jesuits) at age sixteen, was ordained a priest in 1933, and was named editor in 1941 of *Theological Studies*, the journal in which many of his articles appeared from 1945 to 1954. He acknowledged that there were papal documents rejecting the separation of church and state but he insisted that these were written either in the Middle Ages when all Europeans were Catholics and lived in one wholly Christian society or in the nineteenth century, after the French Revolution, when civil governments were often hindering the practice of the true religion. For Father Murray the American context was entirely different. He based his theory on the famous letter of Pope Gelasius I, *Duo Sunt*, to the emperor in the late fifth century: "Two there are, August Emperor, by which the world is ruled on title of original and sovereign right—the consecrated power of the priests and the royal power." Thus the church and state were each supreme in their own spheres, with jurisdiction coming from God and natural law. The First Amendment to the United States Constitution, "Congress shall make no law respecting an establishment of religion," clearly established the principle of separation of church and state, but it did much more. Murray made a distinction among society, the state, and the government, where "society" is all the people of a nation (the importance in the Constitution of "We, the People . . ."), the "state" is the subsidiary of society whose goal is the preservation or promotion of the common good, and the "government" is the arm of the state that implements this. Thus, for Murray, the First Amendment took religion out of the hands of the state and the government and left it in the hands of society, of the people, where it belonged. The people were free to worship as individuals or as groups as they wished, and thus American separation of church and state was wholly acceptable.[28]

The principal opponents of Father Murray's theory, and especially of his interpretation of papal documents, were Father Joseph C. Fenton, dean of the theology faculty at Catholic University of America in Washington, DC, and Cardinal Alfredo Ottaviani, brilliant canon lawyer and head of the Vatican Department of the Holy Office in Rome, and they feared that, in defending America's separation of church and state, Murray's theory could also be approving America's secular, nonreligious culture. As Father Murray continued his writings, Rome finally stepped in and asked, through his Jesuit superior, that he cease his writing on the church-state question. This Father Murray did. However, he had already taken part in a symposium at Notre Dame, and his address, "On the Structure of the Church-State Problem," and those of the other participants, had been accepted for publication in a book by the University of Notre Dame Press, with his as the lead chapter.[29]

When Cardinal Ottaviani learned of the book and Father Murray's chapter, possibly informed by Father Fenton, he contacted the superior general of the Congregation of Holy Cross in Rome, Father Christopher O'Toole, and informed him that he did not wish the book to go on sale. Father O'Toole relayed the message to Father Hesburgh, adding that no one was to know of his or the cardinal's part in the decision. Father Hesburgh reacted strongly. He insisted that such a step would be a clear violation of academic freedom and it was too late anyway since the book was already in the hands of reviewers, had been publicized, and had even been selected by the Catholic Book of the Month Club. Father Hesburgh convinced the superior general to make excuses and delay any action for a month, and by that time six thousand copies had been sold. Some copies remained on bookstore shelves, however, and in storage, and Cardinal Ottaviani requested the Jesuit superior general to buy up all unsold copies. Father Hesburgh said he would not accept the Jesuits' money and had the five hundred copies still in the hands of Notre Dame Press stored away on campus until the storm blew over and they could be sold again. Cardinal Ottaviani himself visited Notre Dame a few years later, was deeply impressed with the university and its Catholicity, and remarked, as Father Hesburgh recalled: "Give me a place like this and I'll convert all of Italy." He added: "Padre, you probably have difficulties from time to time. Whenever you do, a letter is all I need, and I will take care of them for you." The controversy ended satisfactorily and apparently no hard feelings remained.[30]

Despite these distractions, Father Hesburgh held true to his goal of raising Notre Dame's academic standards. That meant better students, better faculty, and better facilities, and all this was going to cost money. Thanks to the Notre Dame Foundation, now headed by Father Cavanaugh, the money was becoming available. In addition to revenue from room, board, and tuition, the Notre Dame Foundation announced that close to $2 million had been received through gifts and grants in 1952. Seven thousand alumni had contributed $963,000, with a 40 percent participation rate; 1,350 non-alumni had contributed $352,000; and grants from government and industry amounted to $580,300. The total could have been larger but there was no football television revenue that year due to NCAA restrictions on television broadcasts. But Notre Dame's budget at the time was under $6 million and its endowment a low $7.5 million, and thus the $2 million was a significant amount.[31]

The fundraising continued to improve year by year. Total gifts to the university in 1953 were $2,170,000, with 47 percent of the alumni contributing, 7 percent higher than the preceding year. Non-alumni contributed $462,340, and grants from government and industry reached $602,000. The foundation announced that gifts in kind, whatever they were, added another $42,000. The figures showed an increase again the following year. In 1954, $2,290,000 was contributed in all, with slightly more than 50 percent of the alumni contributing. Non-alumni friends contributed $675,000, government and industry $710,000, and parents of students $64,000. By 1958 the total had climbed to $3 million annually.[32]

With student enrollment increasing year by year, and with funds available, the postwar campus construction program begun under Father Cavanaugh continued. The first major project was a renovation. Nieuwland Science Hall opened in mid-1952, the science equipment in old Science Hall was transferred to its new home, and the old hall was converted into a student union building. Joseph La-Fortune, an alumnus from Oklahoma, an oil executive, and a member of Notre Dame's board of lay trustees, donated $135,000 to cover the major costs, and agreed to match whatever funds the students could raise through Mardi Gras and other festivities for further improvements. That brought in an additional $50,000.

The renovated building held offices for the vice president of student affairs and officials of Student Government, Student Senate meeting rooms, student publications offices, meeting rooms for campus clubs, a television room, a lounge, a photo lab, a ballroom on the second floor, and two balconies overlooking a central court. Pool and Ping-Pong tables were relocated from the ground floor of Washington Hall, 480 basement lockers were available for off campus students, and the Huddle, the campus snack shop, was moved from its previous location in a small building next to Washington Hall to the rear extension of the new La-Fortune Student Center.[33]

A new bookstore was next on the list of building priorities. The campus bookstore had originally been housed in the Main Building, and then it was transferred to the ground floor of Badin Hall in the fall of 1931. That site had earlier been a student refectory and then, after the dining hall was built, it was a lounge and recreation room for priests and brothers serving on campus. It was there that Father Mulcaire received the telephone call informing the campus of Coach Rockne's death. Mr. and Mrs. Romy Hammes of Kankakee, Illinois, donated $250,000 for a new bookstore to be situated between Badin Hall and the post office, on part of the old Badin bog. It was a two-story bookstore with bowling lanes in the basement and a clothing store adjacent, and it provided not only additional revenue for the university but also a wider variety of products for sale to students and much more efficient service than the long lines necessitated by its predecessor.[34]

In 1955, the university constructed its own television station, WNDU-TV, just to the east of Breen-Phillips Hall. Regular television broadcasting had begun in the United States before World War II, but the war had then limited civilian production. Wartime restrictions were removed in 1946 and television grew rapidly across the country. By 1949 there were one million receivers in use, ten million by 1951, and fifty million by the end of the decade. The televising of the political conventions and the Army–Senator McCarthy Senate hearings showed the educational benefits of the new medium. The university dedicated its WNDU-TV building in October 1955 with Brigadier General David Sarnoff, Chief Executive Officer of RCA, giving the main address and receiving an honorary degree. The popular Eddie Fisher show *Coke Time* was broadcast that week from the campus.[35]

The major construction projects of the first six years of Father Hesburgh's presidency, however, were three new residence halls and a new dining hall. Each year, more and more students were living, and eating, off campus. Enrollment had increased from 5,000 after the war to 5,425 in the fall of 1954, to 5,600 two years later in 1956, and to more than 6,000 by 1957. Most of these were traditional undergraduate students and no longer military veterans coming under the G. I. Bill of Rights. In the fall of 1954, Thomas and John Pangborn and their foundation contributed $800,000 for a new residence hall constructed between Fisher Hall and the Rockne Memorial. The L-shaped hall had a basement and three upper floors, a flat roof, approximately one hundred double rooms for two hundred upperclassmen, a pleasant lounge, and a chapel in front. At about this same time, the third and fourth floors were added to the north-south wing of Fisher Hall, providing rooms for forty more students at a cost to the university of $100,000. Although flat-roofed and not built in the traditional collegiate Gothic style of most other residence halls on campus, Fisher and Pangborn added balance to the south quadrangle, located to the west of the dining hall while Alumni and Dillon were to the east.[36]

In 1957, two additional residence halls were constructed on the north side of the campus, between Zahm Hall and the Wenninger-Kirsch Biology Building, just east of the student infirmary. Keenan Hall, closest to Zahm Hall, had four stories, rooms for close to 300 students, an attractive foyer in front, a second-floor study hall, and a student lounge in the basement. Stanford Hall was very similar, and was connected to Keenan on the first and second floors. Also four stories tall, Stanford held 136 rooms to accommodate 278 students, had its own second-floor study space, a TV lounge, and shared with Keenan Hall a chapel seating four hundred. A large mahogany crucifix by émigré East European sculptor Ivan Meštrović hung over the altar. Although the buildings had two front doors side by side, and two entrances to the chapel, a tradition developed of Keenan students always using only the Keenan entrances and the Stanford students only using the Stanford entrances.[37]

With the addition of three new residence halls on the north quadrangle since the close of the war (Farley, Keenan, and Stanford), housing close to nine hundred students, a new and more convenient dining facility seemed desirable, and in 1957 it was constructed in the space between Farley Hall and the Wenninger-Kirsch Biology Building. The structure could be divided into smaller, individual eating spaces or opened up into one large dining area, accommodating approximately two thousand diners at a sitting. Architecturally, it was closer to the Keenan and Stanford model than the collegiate Gothic of Breen-Phillips and Farley, but it did complete the north quadrangle, with Cavanaugh, Zahm, Keenan, and Stanford on the west side and Breen-Phillips, Farley, and the new dining hall on the east. Some, of course, did not approve of the break with the traditional collegiate Gothic of these recent buildings—Fisher, Pangborn, Keenan, Stanford, the new dining hall—and one critic wrote:[38]

> All were highly utilitarian, coldly institutional, and aesthetically bland, interiorly and exteriorly. All were totally inconsistent with the character, mood and sensitivity of previous structures and therefore represent the worst collective response to architectural design compatibility at Notre Dame.

A final major construction project of these first six years of Father Hesburgh's presidency, although it was just off campus, still concerned the university. This project was the new Moreau Seminary. The old seminary, built in the 1920s, was too small for the more than one hundred seminarians living there, and it had serious weaknesses as a house of study—a small library, no conference or meeting rooms, and few rooms with private baths for the faculty. Father Hesburgh announced to the university that the new building would cost in the vicinity of $3 million, that adequately trained young Holy Cross seminarians were necessary for the continuing growth and excellence of Notre Dame, and that the university had thus pledged to collect $1 million for its construction. The very impressive-looking building, with Notre Dame artist Father Anthony Lauck's stained glass chapel window facing the campus on the opposite side of Saint Joseph's Lake, was completed in 1958 and was built to accommodate up to two hundred seminarians.[39]

The collecting of money and construction of new facilities was geared to the raising of the academic standards of the university, and this was going on apace. With the appointment of Dean Joseph O'Meara in 1952, the regulations and requirements of the Law School changed immediately. More classes were required, examinations were strengthened, and less qualified students were requested to leave. Changes in other colleges may have been less dramatic but the requirements and regulations were strengthened and the academic standards were nudged upward.

A new dean, Father Charles Sheedy, had been appointed in the College of Arts and Letters in 1953, an extensive self-study had been undertaken in the college, and a revised curriculum was announced for the 1954–1955 academic year. The goal of the new program was two-fold: to reduce the number of courses required of each student each semester and to provide greater coherence and integration among the courses taken, especially through the pervasive influence of philosophy and theology.[40] The College of Arts and Letters *Bulletin* elaborated:[41]

> Liberal education . . . has had a long and successful history at Notre Dame. But the new program is not just a rearrangement or revision of the old. It represents a true strengthening, pointing, illuminating and structuring of the values of liberal education in the university. The new program has an active form—a focus and a direction—not quite so clear before. . . .
>
> The program of studies is centered in a trinity: *God, Man,* and *the World*. Theology and philosophy, history, literature and art, the natural and social sciences—these are the broad fields of liberal knowledge in which the various ways of knowing are exercised. Naturally, Christian theology and philosophy are seen and studied not only as areas of knowledge profoundly important in themselves but also as furnishing the liberally disciplined mind with certain governing principles for the unification of knowledge and life. Christian theology and philosophy, giving a perspective into all knowledge and existence, are not just another field or fields on a plane with all others; they compose a wisdom that penetrates and animates the other studies, a wisdom whose values descend into the mind and dynamize it and its work.

Each college applicant was now required to take the college entrance examination, whereas earlier this was not required of students graduating from an accredited high school. Students were also required to take a comprehensive examination at the close of the sophomore year covering all material taken in the first two years, and a departmental seminar was required of all students in the senior year. Twelve credits in philosophy and twelve in theology were required of every student. The purpose of the first year of studies (philosophy, theology, English, mathematics, history, and language) was to introduce the student to college work and help develop basic intellectual skills. The sophomore year (philosophy, theology, English, natural science, social science, and history) was to investigate significant ideas in science, history, and theology. The junior year (philosophy, theology, collegiate seminar, courses in the major, and an elective) enabled the student to begin major courses and introduce him to the masterpieces of Western culture in the seminar. The senior year (philosophy, theology, departmental seminar, major courses, and an elective) continued major courses and required a department seminar and seminar paper. It was a tighter and more focused curriculum, with fewer courses each class could be more demanding, and it was envisioned that Christian (Thomistic) philosophy and theology would permeate all other courses and shed light on questions raised and answered.[42]

The dean of the College of Engineering, Karl Schoenherr, was appointed in 1945 and remained in office until 1957, but other changes took place. In 1954, a combined five-year arts and letters–engineering program was established with other colleges, with the first three years of arts and letters courses taken on other campuses and the two years of engineering taken at Notre Dame. Some of the participating colleges were St. Francis College of Loretto, Pennsylvania; St. Thomas College of St. Paul, Minnesota; St. Vincent College of Latrobe, Pennsylvania; Villa Madonna College of Covington, Kentucky; and St. Benedict College of Atchison, Kansas. The students received an arts and letters degree after four years and an engineering degree after the fifth.[43]

The following year, the Carnegie Corporation gave the university a grant for a self-study of its engineering curriculum. "The general purpose of this self-study," Father Hesburgh announced, "would be to define what is, in our best judgment, the finest and most basic type of engineering study for undergraduates here at the University of Notre Dame." A committee of faculty, students, and outside consultants was appointed, a questionnaire was sent to three thousand engineering alumni, and twelve hundred responded. The committee recommended that both the traditional four-year engineering program and the five-year combined arts and letters–engineering program be retained, but that there be less specialization and fewer options. Greater emphasis on mathematics, physics, and chemistry was recommended, and it was also recommended that courses in history and the social sciences be added to the heavily liberal arts curriculum of the first two years. The philosophy course was revised, a course in public speaking was recommended but not required, and greater attention was given to effective writing.[44]

Under James Culliton, appointed dean by Father Hesburgh in 1955, the programs of the College of Commerce became stronger, more practical, and more academically challenging. Former dean James McCarthy had once said that the "aim of the College of Commerce is to produce the well-rounded Catholic gentleman," and this it did successfully, but Father Hesburgh and Dean Culliton also thought that the college could do a better job preparing its students for leadership positions in the business world. The liberal arts component of the curriculum remained intact—theology, mathematics, history, science, English—and the overall number of courses each student took was reduced. The "case study" method of teaching was emphasized, giving students hypothetical situations to address and having them initiate and grapple with possible solutions. "We stopped teaching 'today's' practices," Dean Culliton remarked, "because by the time the students would get into the business world, 'today's' practices would be obsolete. So we tried to instill a way of thinking, an attitude. . . ." In religion classes they were challenged to explain why they belonged to a Church that demanded a lifestyle at times in opposition to American culture. An important goal was to develop self-confidence and an ability to lead. The university had a policy that if a professor did not arrive within the first ten minutes of a class, the students could leave. Not in the College of Commerce. The students were taught to assume initiative and get the class started without the professor. Successful business leaders take the initiative and see the work to completion. The students took a senior seminar of Great Books because, as Dean Culliton noted, "great books don't offer answers, but they ask the right questions." A final goal was to increase faculty salaries and hire more faculty members with PhDs.[45]

The new administration seemed quite satisfied with the College of Science and few changes were made. Lawrence Baldinger remained dean throughout the 1950s and the five departments—Biology, Chemistry, Geology, Mathematics, and Physics—remained constant, although courses and requirements within each department could change and be strengthened.[46]

Even more important than money, buildings, and programs in improving the academic standards of the university was the hiring of a stronger faculty, and this Father Hesburgh did. Current faculty members, he thought, may have been qualified for the Notre Dame of the 1920s when they were hired, but some could be thirty years out of date in the 1950s. The university was also growing. Throughout the 1950s, ten or twelve new faculty positions were created each year and, with forty or fifty retiring or terminated, the university hired between fifty and sixty new faculty each year, most with terminal degrees. With the money the Notre Dame Foundation was attracting, more and more "distinguished professors" were hired, a program announced by Father Cavanaugh a few years before to recruit internationally recognized and respected scholars in the various fields. (This program preceded the later endowed chairs program.) In 1954, four distinguished scholars were recruited for lecture series on campus: the eminent natural law scholar A. P. d'Entrèves, Supreme Court Associate Justice William O. Douglas, renowned scholar of ancient Greece Sir Richard Livingstone, and distinguished British historian Arnold Toynbee. That year five equally distinguished scholars were hired for the full semester: noted physicist Joseph Becker, economist and presidential adviser Robert Turner, British philosopher and theologian

Father Martin D'Arcy, S.J., Church historian Father Philip Hughes, and German historian Fritz Fischer. Added to the permanent faculty that year were distinguished mathematician Vladimir Seidel, biologist Charles Brambel, chemist G. F. D'Alelio, and celebrated sculptor Ivan Meštrović, for whom an eighty foot by forty foot studio was constructed, seventeen feet in height to accomodate his large religious sculptures, and connected by a breezeway to O'Shaughnessy Hall. Two years later, parish sociologist Father Joseph Fichter, S.J., and French historian Father Guillaume Bertier de Sauvigny were added to the list of distinguished professors. Father Hesburgh's goal was to have sixty distinguished professors in all.[47]

Another step to improve the academic programs on campus was the appointment of Father Arthur Harvey as director of the university theater program in 1955. Dramatic presentations had been held at Notre Dame from its founding since Father Sorin himself was a strong devotee. An exhibition hall was constructed in the early 1880s, even before the third Main Building was completed, and few campus feasts or celebrations were organized without an evening theatrical performance, with Father Sorin always prominently in the first row. He seemed particularly to enjoy the efforts of the minims. The tradition that Father Sorin started continued after his passing. In the second decade of the twentieth century, with no women enrolled at Notre Dame, female roles were played (convincingly?) by the likes of students Knute Rockne and future Notre Dame professor Cecil Birder. Student clubs also sponsored productions, and Professor Frank Kelly brought organization and structure to them under the university theater program in the 1920s. The theater prospered under his direction (he retired in 1951) and then under Professors Cecil Birder, William Elsen, and John Tumpane. The early 1950s witnessed the fine student acting of Reginald Bain, future Notre Dame drama professor; Phil Donohue, future talk show host; and Eugene Gorski, future Holy Cross priest and member of the theology faculty. Very popular musicals, written and directed at times by Saint Mary's College professor Natalie White, were performed principally by nuns during the summer sessions.[48]

Father Harvey had been born in Washington, DC, in 1911, graduated from Notre Dame in 1947, was ordained a Holy Cross priest in 1951, and received an MA degree in drama from the Catholic University of America in 1953. At Catholic University he came under the influence of Dominican Father Gilbert Hartke, director of that university's nationally respected theater program. Until this time, Notre Dame's theater program had functioned chiefly under the office concerned with student life (whatever its official name) and often featured student-written plays. Father Harvey envisioned a different direction. He wanted to make the theater a highly respected academic program, with introductory workshops and formal speech and drama classes, although plays were also open to non-drama students. He de-emphasized plays written by students and emphasized Broadway musicals and literary productions that had passed the test of time. He often said that reading a Shakespeare play in class but never seeing one on stage was similar to reading the notes of a Mozart concerto but never hearing them played.[49]

Father Harvey was a meticulous theater director. Rehearsals lasted six or seven weeks, absences were not excused or tolerated, every position had to be blocked, and each performer had to agree to accept whatever part he or she was assigned. Father Harvey oversaw costuming, lighting, and even ticket sales. He "demanded 100 percent," one student remarked, "but he gave 150 percent." On his watch, Washington Hall became almost exclusively a theater, with new seats, carpeting, curtains, and heating. The interior was repainted in gray, amid some controversy, covering over Gregori's portraits of Shakespeare, Molière, Mozart, and Beethoven, the emblematic figures representing Tragedy, Comedy, Music, and Poetry, Gregori's chiaroscuro portraits of Cicero and Demosthenes, and even the central portrait of George Washington for whom the building was named. The building had previously served as a venue for lectures, concerts, panel discussions, and commencements, but now it was to be almost exclusively a theater. And under Father Harvey's direction, it was an excellent theater. He selected *Detective Story* as his first play, with its delicate abortion theme, and followed over the years with *The Caine Mutiny Court-Martial*, *Death of a Salesman*, *Hamlet*, and *King Lear*, and popular musicals *Camelot*, *Seventeen*, *Oklahoma!*, *South Pacific*, and *My Fair Lady*. In 1966, with the co-exchange program with Saint Mary's well under way, the drama departments of the two schools merged and the larger and more modern O'Laughlin Auditorium at Saint Mary's had a distinct advantage. Father Harvey was named director of the combined department, but he soon resigned to accept the position of assistant to the executive vice president, Father Joyce. The university theater program continued without him but his influence was lasting.[50]

In an effort to make Notre Dame more respected among other universities, and to bring it more fully into the twentieth century, the university adopted a faculty manual in 1954. Before this, the rights and duties of university officials and faculty members were often what a higher administrator decided, but now they were written and in some ways guaranteed. Most academic authority was still in the hands of the president. He appointed the deans and department chairmen, institute directors and members of the Committee on Appointments and Promotions, and decisions of the Academic Council needed his approval. But after three years on the faculty in rank, professors and associate professors now had tenure; faculty children were given two-thirds scholarships; and the TIAA-CREF insurance plan was spelled out in detail. Tenured faculty could still be released if their department was abolished, and dismissal was possible for failure to meet scholarly standards, lack of cooperation, grave offenses against Catholic doctrine or morality, or (in this age of Senator McCarthy) engaging in subversive activity. An appeals process was outlined fully but the decision of the president was always final. It was not on a par with manuals at major universities but it was an important first step.[51]

If the university administration was pleased with the progress it was making in enlarging the endowment, building up the campus, and raising the academic standards, it had to be disappointed with the football program. The administration had eased Frank Leahy out as head football coach in early 1954 and replaced him with young Terry Brennan, former Notre Dame football star and successful Chicago high school coach. Brennan's first year was a good one. Inheriting much of Coach Leahy's team of the year before, he finished with nine wins and one loss, almost duplicating Coach Leahy's final year record of nine wins and one tie. Quarterback Ralph Guglielmi was an All-American. The next year, more of Leahy's starters had graduated, Paul Hornung and speedster Aubrey Lewis were future stars, but the guards and center averaged only two hundred pounds. The team won eight but lost to Michigan State and Southern California. The following year, 1956, with most of Leahy's recruits absent, was, for Notre Dame, a disaster. Hornung was outstanding—running, passing, kicking, tackling, intercepting—and, with much self-confidence and a flair for the limelight, he reminded many of George Gipp, and he was awarded the Heisman Trophy as college football's best player. But football is a team sport, not a one-man show, and Brennan did not have the team. It won only two games, losing to Michigan State 47 to 14, to Iowa 48 to 8, and to Oklahoma 40 to 0, and was outscored by opponents 289 to 130. At the close of the season the Faculty Board in Control of Athletics voted to change coaches, but Father Hesburgh overruled the board and allowed Brennan to continue. The next year was better, seven wins and three losses, an excellent achievement considering the young rebuilding team Coach Brennan had. The high point of the season was a 7–0 victory over Coach Bud Wilkinson's Oklahoma Sooners, ending their forty-seven-game winning streak. But the progress did not continue into 1958. The team won six but lost to Army, Purdue, Pittsburgh, and Iowa. With the university's renewed emphasis on raising its academic standards, there was suspicion that Father Hesburgh might be de-emphasizing football, but this he denied. Brennan's overall record of 32 victories and 18 losses seemed unacceptable after Leahy, the trend into the future did not seem promising, and that December it was announced that Brennan would not be returning and would be replaced by Joe Kuharich, Notre Dame graduate and Professional Coach of the Year with the Washington Redskins in 1955.[52]

The timing of the dismissal of the young coach, only a few days before Christmas, was criticized by many. *Sports Illustrated* published an article entitled "Surrender at Notre Dame," speculating that the administration, for all its talk that winning was not everything, gave in to complaints from benefactors and influential alumni and fired Brennan because he had not totaled up enough victories. Father Hesburgh took the criticism seriously and issued a detailed response. He admitted that Notre Dame strove for excellence in everything it did, including athletics, but insisted that to achieve excellence in athletics there would be "no softening of admission standards, no lowering of scholastic average for eligibility each year, no amending of scholarly requirements or numbers, in a word, NO University athletic policy change at all." The coaching change was made, not from any alumni pressure (he had received only two negative letters) but simply from that commitment to excellence. The timing of the announcement he had discussed with Brennan and it was decided not to wait longer in order to give assistant coaches better opportunity to apply for coaching positions that were still open. All coaches' salaries would continue for three months, or until they found new positions. He then reversed the criticism:[53]

> One last word. While I can appreciate the wide national interest in sports, I think it somewhat of an inversion of values that a university can appoint twenty distinguished professors, make broad and significant changes in academic personnel to achieve greater excellence, without attracting more than a slight ripple of attention. But let the same university make a well-considered change in athletic personnel for the same reason, and it sparks the ill-considered charge that it is no longer a first-rate academic institution and must henceforth be considered a football factory. . . . At least we are grateful that *Sports Illustrated* and others are so interested that we keep our goals in proper perspective. There has indeed been a surrender at Notre Dame, but it is a surrender to excellence on all fronts, and in this we hope to rise above ourselves with the help of God.

As Notre Dame's reputation as an institution of higher learning increased throughout the 1950s, so did the personal reputation of the president. There was no doubt that he was both the brains and the brawn behind the university's progress. Father Cavanaugh's fundraising success as head of the Notre Dame Foundation was an essential element, as was the cooperation of all the deans, those newly appointed and those remaining. But the overall guidance, encouragement, and final decision-making were Father Hesburgh's. As Notre Dame's and Hesburgh's reputations increased, Hesburgh was tapped for membership on various national and international agencies and commissions.

In 1954, President Eisenhower appointed him a member of the National Science Board (succeeding Professor James Reyniers), a twenty-four-person board overseeing the work of the National Science Foundation and approving the foundation's major grants. Father Hesburgh admitted he knew little about science, but the president thought there should be someone on the board to offer a clear moral perspective. Father Hesburgh was also a quick learner, and one historian has written: "thus began his education in quantum mechanics, relativity theory, positivist psychology, cybernetics, atomic technology, and their effects on social and cultural life." He became acquainted with some of the country's most outstanding scientists, he sought their advice both on how to improve the study of science at Notre Dame and on who the best scientists to hire were, and their advice was not ignored.[54]

In 1955 Father Hesburgh was appointed to the United States Naval Academy Board of Visitors. The relations between Notre Dame and the Naval Academy had been close since World War II. More than ten thousand naval officers had been trained at Notre Dame during that war, some for as long as four years and some for only four months, and the government's room, board, and tuition money had helped to keep the university in session. As a sign of this friendship, the two schools continued to play each other in football every year. The USNA Board of Visitors was a panel of fifteen appointed by the president, vice president, speaker of the house, and Senate and House Armed Services Committees "to inquire into the state of morale and discipline, the curriculum, instruction, physical equipment, fiscal affairs, academic methods, and other matters relating to the academy which the Board decides to consider. . . . The President of the United States receives an annual written report of the Board's findings and recommendations."[55]

Two years later Father Hesburgh was named one of two representatives of the Vatican to the International Atomic Energy Agency ("Atoms for Peace"). The agency had been established in October 1956, it was foreseen that there would be differences between the United States and its allies on one side and the Soviet

Union and its allies on the other over the question of inspections and trust, and the then secretary of state, John Foster Dulles, was looking for countries that he thought would be favorable to the positions of the United States. The Vatican was one possibility but Pope Pius XII had declined to join, claiming that the Vatican had no atomic energy experts. Dulles contacted Cardinal Francis Spellman of New York, who in turn spoke with the pope, and Pius XII agreed to appoint representatives if the cardinal would select them. The cardinal then called Father Hesburgh. Father Hesburgh admitted that he probably owed the cardinal a favor since the year before he had turned down the cardinal's request that Notre Dame play Maryland in a postseason football game to benefit a New York charity, and the cardinal also assured him that the assignment need not be that time-consuming. As the other representative, Father Hesburgh recommended Marston Morse, a world-class mathematician at Princeton who was also fluent in French. Father Hesburgh insisted that he and Professor Morse be given full freedom to vote according to their own insights and conscience and not have some other Vatican official looking over their shoulders. This freedom was granted, Father Hesburgh was to remain with the agency for thirteen years, much of that time with Frank Folsom, the CEO of RCA, as his associate, and it remained one of the most satisfying positions he was called upon to fulfill.[56]

In September 1957, three years after the landmark *Brown v. Board of Education* civil rights decision and two years after the Montgomery, Alabama, bus boycott that was begun by Rosa Parks and led by Rev. Martin Luther King, Jr., Congress passed the country's first civil rights law in more than seventy-five years. The act gave persons recourse if they were denied the right to vote, established a civil rights division within the Department of Justice under an assistant attorney general, and established a Civil Rights Commission to investigate and report on civil rights conditions in the United States. By statute, the members were to be three Democrats and three Republicans, and President Eisenhower also appointed three northerners and three southerners. Father Hesburgh, one of the original six members, declared himself an independent in politics, and was thus listed as either a Democrat or a Republican according to the preference of the president considering a new appointment. From 1969 to 1974, Father Hesburgh would serve as commission chairman.[57]

By the summer of 1958, Father Hesburgh had been serving as president of Notre Dame and religious superior of the Holy Cross priests and brothers on campus for six years, and according to canon law the term of a religious superior was limited to six years. The triennial chapter of the Indiana Province of Holy

Cross priests met that summer at Notre Dame to review the various ministries of the province, approve all budgets, and make personnel assignments. The members were impressed with the progress Notre Dame was making under Father Hesburgh's leadership, and with the national reputation and influence the university, and its president, were achieving. Its growing acclaim was confirmed two years later when President Dwight Eisenhower agreed to deliver the university's commencement address in the spring of 1960, and Cardinal Giovanni Montini, the future Pope Paul VI, preached the baccalaureate sermon. Not wishing to lose Father Hesburgh as president, the chapter decided to separate the office of president from that of religious superior and to reappoint Father Hesburgh as president but another priest religious superior. Father Hesburgh would remain Notre Dame's leader for the next twenty-nine years.[58]

The 1960s

Progress and Controversy

Notre Dame had witnessed significant changes in the 1950s, a new president and four new deans, two football coaches hired and two relieved, new buildings dotting the campus—Fisher, Pangborn, Keenan, and Stanford Halls, the North Dining Hall, Nieuwland Science and O'Shaughnessy Halls, and the Morris Inn— increases in student enrollment and the size of the faculty, and another change that was probably little noticed by most students but in the long history of Notre Dame was most significant. For more than a century, the Holy Cross sisters had ministered at Notre Dame, and now that ministry was almost coming to an end. The first four sisters, at Father Sorin's request, had arrived at Notre Dame in the second half of 1843, a year before Notre Dame first acquired a charter as a university. They lived for a time in that early log cabin that also housed the chapel. They assisted the small community wherever help was needed: cooking, baking, washing laundry, sewing, gardening, caring for the sick, picking fruit, caring for the chickens and other farm animals. Soon a few other young women came to join them, but since Bishop de la Hailandière did not want another sisters' novitiate in his diocese (the Sisters of Providence had already opened one in Terre Haute), Father Sorin decided to move the novitiate to Bertrand, Michigan, which was across the state line, approximately five miles from Notre Dame, and in a different diocese. The sisters opened a school for the youths of the area, visited the sick, and began caring for the local Potawatomi Indians. They lived on fare regularly brought from Notre Dame, and at times they assisted the sisters still at Notre Dame with their cooking, sewing, and laundry duties. A horse-drawn wagon usually made the trip between the two locations each day, but if it did not, the sisters or novices, as necessary, made the trip on foot. After a few years, the sisters opened an academy for girls in Bertrand, and more and more young women asked to be enrolled. In 1854, however, the bishop of Detroit seemed less favorable to their presence in his diocese, and the new bishop in Vincennes was willing to welcome them back to Indiana. They transferred the academy to Mishawaka that year and, in 1855, to the former Rush property across the highway from Notre Dame.[1]

Thus there were two groups of sisters in the vicinity, one at the new Saint Mary's Academy and one at Notre Dame, eventually with a novitiate on each campus. Notre Dame might not have survived without the sisters, and certainly not in the way it did. The sisters moved their residence frequently as new buildings were constructed or fire damaged old ones, but their work never ceased—preparing meals daily for the priests, brothers, and students; baking bread; doing the laundry, often by the side of the lake; mending clothes; operating the infirmary; preparing the vestments and sacred vessels for liturgies; proofreading and binding at the *Ave Maria* magazine; assisting the brothers and lay farmhands with planting, harvesting, and caring for the livestock as needed; and so many other services that the young institution required. A major ministry, in cooperation with the brothers, was the daily care of the minims, the grade school boys, instructing them in the classrooms, supervising their recreation, cleaning and mending their clothes, selecting what each should wear each day, teaching the youngest to lace their shoes and comb their hair, and explaining the catechism in a way that each could understand. And through it all, they lived lives of prayer and religious observance, assisting at Mass daily, being present at community devotions, finding time for spiritual reading, and constantly asking God's blessing on the work they were doing and on the people they were serving. They did heroic work when fire struck the campus—the fire in the apprentice workshop and sacristy in 1849 and the blaze that destroyed the Main Building in 1879—and many served heroically as nurses near the battle lines during the Civil War. Toward the close of the nineteenth century there were more than one hundred sisters laboring in various ministries at Notre Dame, and when the Vatican ordered the novitiate at Notre Dame closed, there was genuine fear that all the sisters would be recalled to the motherhouse at Saint Mary's, and at Notre Dame Provincial Superior Father Corby was deeply concerned for the university's future if that should occur. The sisters were permitted to remain and continue serving at Notre Dame, but the need for them declined throughout the new century. The Manual Labor School was closed in 1917, the high school in 1922, and the school for minims in 1929, and the new dining hall, opened in 1927, relieved the sisters of their cooking responsibilities. Furthermore, the sisters were increasingly needed in the schools and hospitals that the Sisters of the Holy Cross were opening throughout the country. In May 1958, a final Solemn High Mass was celebrated in the sisters' chapel behind the Main Building for the few sisters who remained, and Father Hesburgh read the following citation:[2]

> While you leave the campus which has been your home for so many years, you can never leave the hearts and affectionate memory of the priests and Brothers of Holy Cross and the administrators, faculty and students of the University of Notre Dame. You have been golden threads woven forever into the tapestry of her life.

Thirteen sisters then departed for Saint Mary's and only five remained, living and serving in the student infirmary and caring for the altar linens, but for 115 years, the dedicated service of the Holy Cross sisters had contributed mightily to making Notre Dame a successful university.[3]

Once Father Hesburgh was relieved of his duties as religious superior of the Holy Cross priests and brothers on campus in 1958, and reappointed without limit as president of Notre Dame, he could confidently make longer-term plans in his effort to raise Notre Dame to the level of the very best universities in the nation. This goal would demand money, large sums of money, for distinguished faculty, student scholarships, modern laboratories, and a world-class library, and fortunately the Ford Foundation came to his assistance. The Ford Foundation had earlier given the university $25,000 for a self-study and revision of its arts and letters curriculum, and it was pleased with the result. In 1960, it announced a $46 million Special Program in Education, offering matching grants to five universities in which it saw the potential to take the next step toward elite academic status. Stanford was offered $25 million, Johns Hopkins University and Notre Dame $6 million each, the University of Denver $5 million, and Vanderbilt $4 million. The purpose, said the president of the Ford Foundation, was "to assist institutions in different regions of the country to reach and sustain a wholly new level of academic excellence, administrative effectiveness and financial support." It was a two-to-one matching grant, with Notre Dame receiving $6 million if it could raise $12 million on its own over the next three years. It was "an answer to our deepest hopes," Father Hesburgh declared, enabling Notre Dame "to take a great leap forward in its striving for academic excellence."[4]

The university organized a fund drive immediately, called "Challenge 1960–1963." A nationwide kickoff celebration was scheduled for the evening of October 17, 1961, with radio or television connections to alumni clubs in 175 cities. The alumni were addressed by Father Hesburgh, honorary chairman I. A. O'Shaughnessy, and general appeal chairman Joseph O'Neill. The goal was to contact every alumnus personally. Chairmen and assistants were appointed for every city, and regional chairmen over them. Pledge cards were distributed and each solicitor was given directions on how to approach a prospective donor. The major needs of the university were stressed: a new library, additional distinguished professors, enhanced academic programs, increased student aid, and one or two residence halls for graduate students. Early in the campaign, Father Hesburgh announced that he hoped the university could raise not just the required $12 million but actually $18 million because the university's needs and opportunities were that great. Periodic reports were circulated to campaign leaders, noting what regions seemed to be progressing well and which regions might be lagging. Father Hesburgh, Father Joyce, Father John Walsh (director of the Notre Dame Foundation in 1961), and other university officials spoke at various alumni club gatherings, and a monthly newsletter was published to show both progress and needs. Mr. O'Shaughnessy, who had earlier donated in excess of $2 million for the building of O'Shaughnessy Hall of Liberal and Fine Arts, pledged another $1 million for the library fund in the campaign, and Frank Freimann, president of Magnavox, pledged $500,000. The final total collected in the campaign was $18,602,000, not counting the money from Ford.[5]

The centerpiece of the fund drive was a new memorial library, at one time projected to cost $6 million, then $8 million, and eventually close to $14 million. A library is the academic heart of a university. Cartier Field was relocated to make room for it, Vetville was torn down, and the Vetville families were moved to the new University Village. The new library rose to a height of 180 feet, slightly lower than the statue on the dome and the cross on the steeple of Sacred Heart Church. The 1917 library had been built when student enrollment was 1,200 and volumes in the library numbered 100,000. Student enrollment in 1960 was 6,000 and the library was filled to capacity with 475,000 volumes. The new library had shelf space for two million volumes on its thirteen floors, and it also housed the Medieval Institute, the university archives, the Jacques Maritain Center, a rare book room, an audio-visual area, an auditorium, and more than two hundred faculty offices in the basement. The building had air-conditioning throughout. The mosaic mural on the front, 132 feet by 65 feet, was financed by trustee Howard Phalin (executive vice president of Field Enterprises) and depicted Christ in the center, surrounded by saints, scholars, and cultural leaders throughout the centuries. Architecturally it did not seem to harmonize with the rest of the campus—fourteen stories, flat roof, and almost no windows above the second floor—but direct sunlight could be harmful to the books and the administration felt it necessary to build up rather than out in order to keep Notre Dame a walking campus as it expanded. The dedication of the building in May 1964 was one of the most impressive academic celebrations of the decade. After a day filled with scholarly addresses and symposia, Cardinal Eugene Tisserant, dean of the college of cardinals in Rome, presided at a Solemn Pontifical Mass, Cardinal Albert Meyer of Chicago preached, fifteen university presidents from across the country received honorary degrees at the academic convocation, and the building was solemnly blessed by Cardinal Joseph Ritter of St. Louis.[6]

The library, however, was only one of several buildings financed by the Challenge campaign. Mrs. Frank Lewis, in memory of her husband, donated money for a residence hall on campus for nuns studying for graduate degrees. Nuns had been studying during Notre Dame's summer session since 1918, and approximately seventy were studying during the regular academic year. With accommodations in the new Lewis Hall, on the shore of St. Joseph's Lake north of the Main Building, that number could easily double. Alfred Stepan donated $350,000 for an all-purpose building with a distinctive geodesic dome at the north end of the campus. The circular building accommodated three thousand persons at a time, had 22,000 square feet of unobstructed floor space, and was suitable for concerts, convocations, dances, conventions, and informal student activities such as tennis, basketball, volleyball, and badminton. The Atomic Energy Commission, at a cost of $2.2 million, financed the Radiation Research Building just southwest of the new library. Facing the Radiation Research Building was a new Computer Center and Mathematics Building just southeast of the library, a $3 million structure financed by Sperry Rand, the Alfred P. Sloan Foundation, the National Science Foundation, and the Ford Foundation.[7]

Not all of the money in the Challenge campaign was directed to buildings. Three and a half million dollars was for faculty advancement, hiring better and more distinguished teachers, researchers, scientists, and engineers, and raising faculty salaries overall. An additional $340,000 had been allocated to raise faculty salaries the year before, 1962–1963, and a permanent endowment of $10 million had been established precisely for faculty development. Two million dollars of Challenge money was devoted to student aid, to provide more scholarships, loans, and student employment opportunities for qualified but less wealthy undergraduate students, and to provide additional scholarships and fellowships to attract more highly qualified graduate students. Challenge money was also channeled into a fund for medical and retirement benefits for non-teaching university employees. The faculty already had such retirement benefits and $600,000 was set aside for non-teachers, so that with Social Security a staff employee could retire with half of his or her former salary for the rest of his or her life. A medical plan for faculty and staff was also begun. Finally, a small sum was earmarked for the recently established Center for the Study of Man in Contemporary Society, presided over by George Shuster (Notre Dame graduate, English professor in the 1920s, and then president of Hunter College in New York for twenty years). The mission of the center was to sponsor study of areas of crucial concern such as education, population, and ecumenical relations, as well as conditions in Africa and Latin America. It would be difficult to overestimate the impact the Ford Challenge grant had on the overall progress of the university in the early 1960s.[8]

In fact, the campaign was so successful that the Ford Foundation agreed to renew the program in 1963, offering a second $6 million if the university could solicit another $12 million in gifts and donations. This campaign was entitled "Challenge II," the campaign slogan was "Extending the Tradition of Great Teaching," and Father Hesburgh announced that he hoped the university could attract $14 million rather than the required $12 million, making the total (with the $6 million from Ford) $20 million. The campaign was organized after the model of its predecessor, with kickoff dinners in most major cities, with thousands of volunteers, with city and regional chairmen, with monthly reports and published newsletters, and with the goal that every alumnus would be contacted personally or by personal letter and pledge card. The campaign was a complete success. The alumni contributed $5.8 million, non-alumni $3.7 million, corporations and foundations $6.6 million, and Ford the final $6 million, for a total of $22.1 million.[9]

The largest amount of the funding, $6.5 million, went for faculty development and new academic programs. The faculty then numbered approximately 600, up from 439 in 1955; $350,000 had been added to faculty salaries annually over the preceding three years, but more needed to be done. Salary increases from Challenge II funding would bring Notre Dame salaries a little closer to those in major universities across the country, sponsored leaves of absence were instituted, summer research grants provided, and teaching loads reduced. Additional "distinguished" faculty members were hired on a visiting or a permanent basis. Historian James Silver, who had just authored *Mississippi: The Closed Society*, was one of these, and also scripture scholar Father John McKenzie, S.J., historian Julius Pratt, and Father Ivo Thomas of the Program of Liberal Studies. Close to 65 percent of the faculty had PhD or similar degrees, as compared to 50 percent eleven years before. An American Council on Education study noted that 50 percent of Notre Dame's new faculty had graduate degrees from "attractive" or "extremely attractive" universities.[10]

The money earmarked for new academic programs had a significant impact on the university's undergraduate and graduate education. A Department of Psychology was established. Psychology classes had been taught in the past, but within the Philosophy Department. This new department put the growing field of psychology on the same level as other departments. Doctoral programs were established in the Department of Theology in the three areas of systematic theology, biblical theology, and liturgy. A master of business administration (MBA) program was inaugurated, a graduate program in microbiology, and a graduate program in West European studies under the direction of former Hungarian ambassador to Italy Stephen Kertesz. New programs were begun in the Departments of Anthropology and Sociology, and also in African and Latin American studies. The university had established an international study opportunity in Innsbruck in 1964 and it added one in Angers, France, in 1966. A Committee on Academic Progress (CAP) was begun in 1964, enabling select superior students to be dispensed from some curricular regulations, enroll in more advanced and specialized courses, and shape a course of study adapted more specifically to their potential and goals, always under the direction of a personal mentor from the faculty. Finally, in the mid-1960s a co-exchange program was established with Saint Mary's College, permitting students from each school to enroll in classes on the opposite campus, the first step toward merger talks between the two administrations in the early 1970s.[11]

After faculty development and new academic programs, the next largest amount of funding in the Challenge II campaign, $5,5 million, went to student aid. It was clearly necessary if Notre Dame hoped to attract the very best students. Only 12 percent of undergraduates at the time had scholarships, 6 percent had loans, and one out of eight held campus jobs. In the last year, 2,040 students had received a total of $1,466,000 in undergraduate aid, but with close to 6,000 students enrolled, a large majority were left with no financial aid at all. The $5.5 million earmarked in the campaign would significantly increase the amount of student financial aid the university could offer.[12]

Five million dollars was allocated for building and construction, but from the beginning it was clear that that figure was much too low. The centerpiece of the building campaign was a new Athletic and Convocation Center. The old gymnasium could accommodate five thousand for basketball, the track and field and convocation area had a dirt floor, and the locker rooms were quite primitive. Although the need was great, Father Hesburgh had not wanted this athletic building to have priority over the new library in the first Challenge campaign. The double-domed Athletic and Convocation Center had twin arenas, one a 12,500-seat arena for basketball, convocations, concerts, and cultural events, and the other for track and field, hockey, recreational skating, and exhibition space. It was envisioned to cost in the area of $8 million, with part of that from the Challenge II campaign and part from a special campaign throughout South Bend and the surrounding area since the facility would also be available for the use of local people not affiliated with the university. A second building was the Center for Continuing Education, financed by the W. K. Kellogg Foundation of Battle Creek, Michigan. The structure, close to the entrance to the campus and designed by Notre Dame architect Frank Montana, held twenty-two seminar rooms, each with closed circuit television, a four-hundred-seat auditorium, and it opened up to the university the whole field of continuing and adult education, becoming an attractive facility for national and international scholarly conferences. The College of Business was growing and an addition was built onto the north end of the Hurley Building. The addition, named the Hayes-Healy Center, had classrooms, laboratories, and faculty offices. The Architecture Department was given the former Lemonnier Library building, and it was renovated for $250,000 to provide the needed classrooms, studios, office space, study carrels, and drafting areas. In 1965, a new post office was constructed across from the Morris Inn at the entrance to the university, and the former post office building was given to the local chapter of the Knights of Columbus. With eight hundred students still living off campus, two new residence halls were also envisioned in the campaign, but these were not constructed at the time.[13]

Having successfully completed these two major fund drives in six years, and proud of the progress these funds permitted the university to attain in faculty development, physical plant expansion, and improved student social life, the administration in 1967 announced the inauguration of a third campaign, this one without matching financial support from the Ford Foundation.[14] It was a five-year drive with a goal of $52 million. Some referred to it in the beginning as Challenge III, but the official title was "SUMMA: Notre Dame's Greatest Challenge." A few changes had taken place in the university's administration before the campaign began. Father Chester Soleta, vice president of academic affairs, had resigned his post in the summer of 1965, Father John Walsh, vice president of public relations and development, was transferred to academic affairs, James Frick was named vice president of public relations and development, and Francis McGuire was appointed to the newly created position of vice president of special projects. Frick had entered Notre Dame after World War II as a freshman under the G. I. Bill of Rights, and after he graduated, he began working under Father John Cavanaugh in the Notre Dame Foundation. He and McGuire were the first lay vice presidents ever at Notre Dame.[15]

The campaign was organized, in many ways, after the model of Challenge I and Challenge II. Since 80 percent of the funds collected in those two campaigns had come from the country's forty largest cities, the new drive concentrated on those, with kickoff dinners scheduled for each one. Two teams of speakers were sent out from the university to these cities, one team comprised of Father Hesburgh, trustee Dr. O. C. Carmichael, James Frick, dean of science Frederick Rossini, and student body president Christopher Murphy, III, and the other comprised of Father Joyce, trustee Thomas Carney, assistant to the president George Shuster, assistant vice president of public relations Frank Kelly, associate vice president of academic affairs Thomas Stewart, and a student (David Tiemeier or Coley O'Brien).[16] Two other teams, under Father John Walsh, the new vice president of academic affairs, and Father Charles Sheedy, dean of the College of Arts and Letters, visited other cities. The country was again divided into geographical regions, with regional and city campaign captains, campaign materials were mailed out frequently, a monthly report (*SUMMAry*) and newsletters were generated, and seven hundred volunteers assisted with the campaign. Twenty million dollars of the $52 million was earmarked again for faculty development, including forty endowed chairs; $9 million was for three new residence halls to accommodate fifteen hundred students; $6 million was for the improvement of graduate education; and much of the rest was for general development, reducing overcrowded conditions in the residence halls, expanding the North Dining Hall, and similar.[17]

When all the money was counted, $62,408,825.47 had been contributed, which was $10 million above the original goal. It was almost unprecedented to have three major capital fund drives in ten years, and to succeed in all. The university had raised approximately $2 million in the first hundred years of its history, and in the ten years of the 1960s it raised over $100 million. Its fundraising had grown more efficient also. It spent 2.6 cents to raise a dollar in Challenge I, 1.7 cents in Challenge II, and 1.5 cents in SUMMA. The donations, of course, did not always meet the university's specific priorities. A major goal had been $20 million for faculty development, chiefly forty endowed chairs at approximately $500,000 each, but the campaign raised a little less than $10 million for that. The Graduate School of Theology, an urban studies program, the Center for the Study of Man in Contemporary Society, and graduate education in general were all underfunded, but student financial aid was oversubscribed, and money for two of the five high-rise residence halls, Flanner and Grace, was available. Joining Flanner and Grace on the land between the new library and Stepan Center was to be at least one additional high-rise residence hall, perhaps a graduate hall, and a modern circular church, but these were never built. However, SUMMA money did contribute to the construction of the Galvin Life Science Building, including LOBUND, and the Center for Continuing Education and the University Club, both across from the Morris Inn.[18]

The money from Challenge I, Challenge II, and SUMMA had certainly set Notre Dame on a new path, a path toward becoming one of the major institutions of higher learning in America. The faculty, the heart of any university, had greatly improved. In the ten years from 1959 to 1969, the size of the faculty had jumped from 438 to 628, teaching loads had been reduced, more endowed professors were hired every year, and the percentages of faculty members with a PhD or similar terminal degrees had increased significantly. Salaries had increased each year but were still lower than major schools in the Midwest. Student enrollment had also increased since 1960, undergraduates from 5,474 to 6,194, and graduates from 748 to 1,381. The Office of Undergraduate Admissions could be more selective, but progress was slow. In 1959, 3,726 high school students had applied, the university accepted 71 percent of them, and 60 percent of those accepted actually enrolled. In 1968, 4,496 candidates applied, the university accepted 60 percent of them, but only 56 percent of those accepted enrolled. The students were more qualified, however, with the average Student Aptitude Test (SAT) scores of entering freshmen jumping from 960 to 1,180. More than 80 percent of the first-year class in 1968 graduated in the first quintile, the top 20 percent, of their high school class. Seventy-one percent of them had graduated from Catholic high schools in 1960, but only 64 percent in 1969. With the new library, the university was adding over forty thousand volumes to its collections a year, ten thousand more than in the former library. The progress of the graduate program was similar to that of the undergraduate program, with average Graduate Record Examination (GRE) scores increasing from 589 to 613. The university was honored in 1964 also when Congressman William E. Miller, a graduate of the class of 1935, was nominated for the vice presidency on the Republican Party ticket with presidential nominee Senator Barry Goldwater, the first Notre Dame graduate ever named to a presidential ticket.[19]

Another building constructed at this time, although not with money from these three drives, was the Ecumenical Institute for Advanced Theological Studies in Tantur, Israel. On one of Father Hesburgh's visits to the Vatican as president of the International Federation of Catholic Universities, Pope Paul VI asked that he and the International Federation take responsibility for establishing a center where Catholic, Protestant, Jewish, and Muslim scholars could meet and discuss common theological issues. The pope thought the Holy Land would be the most feasible location and the Vatican eventually purchased thirty-five acres there at a cost of $300,000. Professor Frank Montana of the Notre Dame Architecture Department designed the building and I. A. O'Shaughnessy, chairman of the Globe Oil and Refining Company and a member of Notre Dame's board of trustees, donated over $4 million to construct the building, and another $6 million for an endowment to cover operating expenses. The building opened and was dedicated in November 1971.[20]

Despite all the progress and success, the 1960s were also a decade of controversy and even conflict. One of these controversies concerned, of all things, a movie. Early in the decade, William Peter Blatty, a Catholic and later author of *The Exorcist*, wrote a book (published in hardcover by Doubleday and Company and in paperback by Fawcett Publications) and a screen script (in cooperation with Columbia Pictures) entitled *John Goldfarb, Please Come Home*. It was the fictional story of a Jewish-American U-2 pilot, John Goldfarb, who parachuted from his disabled plane over the mythical Arab country of Fawzia (U-2 pilot Francis Gary Powers, of course, had actually been shot down over the Soviet Union in 1960) and was blackmailed into forming and coaching a football team that the king hoped could play and defeat Notre Dame. The king was angry because his son had not been accepted onto the Notre Dame team. The king notified the American State Department that he would renew the lease on an important air base in his country only if the department arranged such a game, and thus the game was scheduled. The Notre Dame players flew to Fawzia and the night before the game the king provided a banquet for them at which they were entertained by dancing harem girls, plied with wine, and served stuffed mongoose that was intended to make them ill. It had its intended effect. At the game the next day, the Notre Dame team was nauseous, vomiting frequently on and off the field, and the Arab team eventually won when a female magazine reporter (played by Shirley MacLaine), who had earlier been smuggled into the king's harem for a story, donned a uniform, got possession of the football, and scored the winning touchdown.[21]

In May 1962, Columbia Pictures sent the screenplay of the movie to Father Joyce and asked permission to use the Notre Dame name. Father Joyce and Father Hesburgh both read the script and notified Columbia that, despite any financial benefits the university might receive, they could not authorize the use of the university's name in such a picture. Columbia Pictures then dropped the project, but two years later Twentieth Century Fox decided to make the movie. Executives of Twentieth Century Fox agreed to let Notre Dame officials review the film and in October 1964 Father Joyce and two Notre Dame trustees flew to California for a screening. After the viewing, they insisted that Notre Dame could not give its approval, the company made a few changes, a second screening was held at Notre Dame for other university officials and trustees, but their decision remained the same: no approval. Twentieth Century Fox had invested $4 million in the film and decided to go ahead, scheduling the movie to open in twenty-two theaters across the country in late December.[22]

Notre Dame immediately went to court to halt the showing. The suit charged that the film and the book "knowingly and illegally misappropriate, dilute and commercially exploit for their private profit the names, symbols, football team, high prestige, reputation and goodwill" of the university without its permission. "Logically," the suit continued, "the plot depends in no way upon the American team being that of the University of Notre Dame and could as easily be that of a mythical American college," except that the Notre Dame name would bring the company greater profit. The argument concluded:[23]

> The team is of some renown, in keeping with the renown of the University. It is part of the University's constituency and its prestige, good name and reputation are assets to the University. The unwarranted liberty taken in the gross depiction of the team, its coach and its players in the motion picture and book is not only a misappropriation and exploitation of University property but cheapens and degrades the University name, insignia, and student body.

Judge Henry Clay Greenberg of the New York Supreme Court agreed with the university in his decision:[24]

> The script is ugly, vulgar and tawdry. Its justification is difficult to find even with a most liberal concept and with a most indulgent and elastic imagination.
>
> The gravamen of the legal wrong allegedly perpetrated against Notre Dame consists of the unauthorized appropriation and commercial exploitation of that private institution's name, and symbols and reputation, in a manner which inflicts irreparable injury upon the high prestige of the University and to the value of its name and symbols—all to the end that defendants might privately profit from such misappropriation and use. . . .
>
> Plaintiff Notre Dame thus postulates, as an indispensable element of its cause of action, a legally protected property right in its name, symbols and reputation with the attendant dominion and control over the exercise of that right. . . .
>
> Whatever difficulty may be encountered in other cases in drawing a line of demarcation between the permissible and the forbidden, the defendants unconscionable conduct has far transgressed any justifiable bounds of legal license. . . . This is a clear case of commercial piracy.

Twentieth Century Fox appealed the decision and the five justices of the appellate court unanimously overturned the decision and struck down the ban. Presiding justice Bernard Botein wrote:[25]

> Whether "John Goldfarb, Please Come Home," is good burlesque or bad, penetrating satire or blundering buffoonery, is not for us to decide. It is fundamental that courts may not muffle expression by passing judgment on its skills or clumsiness, its sensitivity or coarseness; nor on whether it pains or pleases. It is enough that the work is a form of expression.

The justice concluded that there was "no possibility whatever" that anyone would think such a zany and farcical movie actually represented the prestigious University of Notre Dame, that it was a legitimate exercise of free expression and art, and thus the banning injunction was reversed.[26] The university had realized that bringing the case to court would give the film greater publicity, and more persons would pay to see it for that reason, but it felt that preserving its good name and reputation was worth the risk, a risk that, ultimately, it lost.

The major campus controversies and conflicts of the 1960s, however, did not concern movies but student demands and student unrest. Such student protests might be said to have begun in February 1960 in Greensboro, North Carolina, when black students at North Carolina Agricultural and Technical College staged a sit-in at a local Woolworth store to protest its policy of seating only whites at its coffee counter. Demonstrations erupted on campuses across the country throughout the decade, each with its own unique cause or issue: free speech at the University of California at Berkeley and campus expansion at Columbia in New York. At Notre Dame, the discontent had many sources. The university had raised its academic standards over the past eight years, and students feared that that entailed a de-emphasis on football. The fact was that the university had recently changed from a percentage grading system to a six-point system, with an overall average of 2.0 required for varsity athletics eligibility, approximately an 80 percent average when before 77 percent was the minimum requirement. The students were convinced that the more demanding academic expectations caused greater stress in all, and some relaxation of traditional rules was needed: elimination of the midnight (or any) curfew, termination of morning check three days a week, all-night lights, and an easing of dance regulations. They demanded more appealing dining hall food, and better dining hall service.[27]

The first public protest took place on the Tuesday before Thanksgiving, November 22, 1960. Approximately 1,500 students, after the evening meal in the dining hall, marched over to Corby Hall, the priests' residence on campus, chanting "Down with Excellence," "We Want Football Players," and "Burn the Books." Some shouted "We want Jesuits." Father Hesburgh happened to be away from campus that evening but Father Leonard Collins, the prefect of discipline, came to the porch and spoke with the students, but in vain. The demonstration was eventually interrupted when the marching band paraded by on the way to the fieldhouse and the pep rally before the Southern California football game that Saturday in Los Angeles, and most of the protesters left to follow the band and cheer for the team.[28]

The protest, in fact, may have had an effect—and maybe not. Several changes in student regulations were made the following summer, but Father Hesburgh and some of the priests on campus, especially younger ones, may have realized that some regulations were no longer appropriate in the Notre Dame they were attempting to create. Morning check, the regulation that students had to be up and sign in outside the chapel door before morning Mass three days a week, was abolished. There had been no obligation to attend Mass, although the dining halls did not open for another half hour. All-night lights were now permitted, and the dean of students or his assistant would no longer patrol South Bend and visit local bars to see if any Notre Dame students were drinking illegally. Perhaps to signal the change, a new vice president of student affairs was appointed, Father Charles McCarragher.[29]

But the fact that Father Hesburgh was not on campus the evening of the "Thanksgiving" protest suggested another source of student discontent. Not only were many decades-old regulations still in place but the president himself, the only person who could finally change them, was often absent from the campus. The students were proud that the president of their university was so highly respected—a member of the National Science Board and the Civil Rights Commission, the Vatican representative on the International Atomic Energy Agency, and the subject of a *Time* magazine cover in early 1962—but his national and international commitments, some students thought, kept him away from the university too often. Maybe he did not understand the present-day student or realize how out-of-date some campus regulations still were. One solution the editors of the *Scholastic* recommended was to name Father Hesburgh university chancellor and appoint someone else president to run the university day to day. The editorial began:[30]

> Now that the student romance with Fr. Hesburgh is over, the necessity of evaluating the administrative power structure and prevailing modes of thinking is evident. For reasons that will become obvious we feel that it is imperative that Fr. Hesburgh be removed from his post as president and be designated as Chancellor. For the Presidency we would advocate that a renowned lay educator of the stature of George N. Shuster, presently special Assistant to the President, be appointed to govern the internal affairs of the University.

The editorial then listed several (at least rumored) incidents of recent abuse of presidential authority by Father Hesburgh: that he vetoed an Academic Council recommendation to change the academic calendar and begin the school year earlier; that he rejected a "no lights out" policy for freshmen advocated by rectors; that he dismissed a student proposal to inaugurate a stay-hall policy on campus; that in part because of the university's centralization of authority, some professors were transferring to other schools; and that all authority to alter student regulations resided in the president's hands alone, even when he was absent from the university. The fundamental problem, in the eyes of the editors, was that Father Hesburgh was a member of a religious congregation:[31]

> The Congregation of Holy Cross is governed by a Rule which permeates all aspects of an individual's private and public life, linking the members together in a hierarchically-structured community and bound by religious oaths: the priests make a voluntary compact with a certain way of life that, once entered into, is forever binding and continually directs their lives. Elemental to this Rule is an orientation of submissiveness to authority and an emphasis on moral righteousness. . . . The nature of this fundamental order within the community of priests presents grave difficulties when it comes to the operation of a university which, today at least, necessarily comprises many persons who are and must be outside the religious jurisdiction (sanction) of the priestly community. We believe that the notion of a religious order as model image of The Way to salvation and the notion of a religious order as ruler of men who are not priests are incompatible on the theoretical and operational level.

Thus the editorial proposal that George Shuster be named president.

The movement did not progress far because in the following issue of the magazine Dr. Shuster definitely took his name out of contention. He noted, first of all, that he had no desire to be a college president since he had been president of Hunter College in New York for twenty years and could have continued had he been interested. Second, a successful university president must travel widely, to absorb information from other sources and to represent the university at important meetings, conferences, and celebrations. As Shuster remarked on one occasion: "The president who is not seen away from campus is probably not worth seeing on campus either." Third, the Congregation of Holy Cross founded the university in 1842, staffed it through the decades without full pay, and it is a major reason why benefactors are willing to make contributions to continue Notre Dame's progress. Finally, laymen do hold numerous administrative positions at the university and "by and large . . . are in charge of instruction at Notre Dame."[32]

Once Professor Shuster declined the *Scholastic*'s offer of the presidency, and students saw no evidence that the Congregation of Holy Cross was considering any administrative changes, student leaders realized they would have to bring their criticisms and complaints back to Father Hesburgh and his vice president of student affairs, Father McCarragher. The first salvo, drafted by the student body president and at least some senators, was a "Declaration of Student Rights and Grievances" introduced into the Student Senate in March 1963. There was opposition to it, some objecting that it was too harsh, and it got bogged down in parliamentary procedures, but eventually it did pass. However, the university administration apparently forbade the publication of the declaration, at least *in toto*, in the *Scholastic*, and probably also forbade its circulation across campus. All student senators had copies of the declaration, of course, and Father Hesburgh was certainly informed of its contents.[33]

The university at the time was administered more as a family than a juridical body, and proudly so. Permission was needed for students to be away from campus overnight, a rector could impose penalties for disciplinary violations within a residence hall, consumption of alcohol was forbidden, student publications were censored, students could be suspended or expelled from the university without formal due process, and women were permitted in the residence halls only in specific time periods and places, and almost never in student rooms. In many ways, the university administration considered itself *in loco parentis*, almost a substitute parent while the student was at the university. The first part of the declaration was a rejection of this principle:[34]

> *In Loco Parentis* doctrine denies the fact that a man must decide how he wishes to live, that no one can decide this for him. In purporting to inculcate the Catholic way of life into a student, it actually engrains him with a habituated, pressured response, an unthought worship, and unquestioned principles that cease as a motivating force when challenged, or never motivate the individual at all except in providing a comforting, amorphous assurance.
>
> The over-protective attitude of the administration promotes a secure atmosphere thoroughly incompatible with the idea of a university as a forum for the free conflict and critical interchange of ideas, where none purports to have all the truth, but where each is searching for it in a community of scholars. . . . When decisions are made for the individual in areas pertaining to his private life, immaturity, conformity, and lack of interest are promoted and reinforced, and he is deprived of the opportunity for mature self-development.

The second section enumerated various student "rights" that the declaration urged the administration to formally and officially recognize:[35]

1. To clear and concise written statements of all rules and regulations pertaining to student life, and to be informed of any change in previous policy.
2. To be advised in writing of any charges that might lead to his expulsion, suspension, or other disciplinary measure prior to action in his case.
3. To trial by a body including equal voting representatives of the students, the faculty, and the administration.
4. To express whatever ideas he wishes without fear of disciplinary action.
5. To determine his own daily schedule in its entirety.
6. To choose food and housing, on or off-campus, as he sees fit.
7. To establish or be a member of any student group which does not use the name of Notre Dame in its constitution or activities, thereby gaining freedom from university control of any kind.
8. To establish and issue regular student-directed publications free from any . . . censorship or other pressure designed to control editorial policy and staff appointments and removals, provided that these publications do not transgress the code of common decency, and civil or criminal laws against libel, pornography, or indecency.

The third section listed various student grievances and requests for changes. Some of the most important of these, noted by Joel Connelly and Howard Dooley in *Hesburgh's Notre Dame: Triumph in Transition*, were the "removal of all priests from the dormitories and their replacement with professional counselors; abolition of curfew; the granting of parietal hours for women visitors; ending of restrictions on cars and off campus apartments; elimination of restrictions on class cuts; and termination of censorship."[36]

With the student body president, probably a majority of the Student Senate, and the editorial staff of the *Scholastic* all in public opposition to his administration and to Notre Dame's regulations, Father Hesburgh decided it was time to reply, even to take a stand. He issued his (later famous) "Winter of Discontent" letter on April 8, 1963. The letter began by citing President John Kennedy's comment that in some ways recent months had been a winter of discontent for America, and Father Hesburgh admitted that they had certainly been a winter of discontent at Notre Dame. He attempted to plumb the causes: a long and harsh winter that bred cabin fever in many (which he had experienced on a recent trip to Antarctica), a malaise throughout the country because President Kennedy was not moving at a faster pace, university regulations that some felt were too restrictive, and student publications that aggravated any campus discontent. But Father Hesburgh insisted that there were even greater reasons for optimism, confidence, and pride. Student social facilities had been increased in recent years with the addition of LaFortune Student Center, Stepan Center, bowling alleys in the bookstore basement, and enlarged outdoor playing fields. Academic life had been enhanced with the building of Nieuwland Science Hall and O'Shaughnessy Hall of Liberal and Fine Arts, and a new library was on the drawing board. With the annual budget increasing from $8 million to $23 million over the past ten years, distinguished professors had been hired and the education imparted had improved year by year. There was also now, for the first time, a functioning student government. The letter admitted that criticism can be healthy, and that all can profit from it, but it has to be civil, kept in perspective, and not indifferent to all the progress recently made. Finally, some regulations and traditions would remain:[37]

> Beyond the normal griping, if anyone seriously believes that he cannot become well educated here without a car, or girls in his room, or if one really thinks that his personal freedom is impossibly restricted by curfew, or State laws on drinking, or the presence of priests in the residence halls, then I think the only honest reaction is to get free of Notre Dame, not to expect Notre Dame to lose its unique character and become just another school with just another quality of graduates. Notre Dame has changed greatly, and will change more, for the better, one hopes. But set principles must guide the change. Permanent values must remain. And, benighted though it may appear to some, we do see permanent educational value in the few essential rules and regulations that were retained when all the non-essentials were dropped two years ago. The dropping is now over as we catch our breath in this exhilarating new freedom of abridged discipline.
>
> I can work up a good case of anger against anyone or anything that tries to divide those who must grow together on this campus—faculty and students, priests and laymen. Neither do I consider faculty and students equal partners in the educative process here, since students by definition are here to study under the direction of the faculty, and to learn. Nor do I consider student leaders to be makers of broad University policy or wielders of pressure, except in their own domain. I am ready to admit that we of the faculty and administration can learn some valuable lessons from students as we walk this road together. Nonetheless, your primary role as students here is to learn, not to teach. Students who think otherwise should go out, found their own universities, and then take lessons from their students.

Despite the general theme of the letter, Father Hesburgh closed on a positive note:

There is no real cause for discontent here that could not be dissipated by more intelligent, more understanding, more dedicated people on every level, including my own. If a few stalwarts among you make this move, the positive deed will outshine the negative word, and the winter of our discontent may be forgotten in the flowering of a new Springtime of hope.

This discontent, of course, continued, and the students now had an additional medium through which to express it. The *Voice*, a student weekly newspaper, had begun on March 22, just a few days before Father Hesburgh's letter. The four-page paper carried campus news and commentary—the first issue discussed a football coaching change, student efforts to assist in Notre Dame's Challenge (I) fundraising, a critique of Lionel Trilling's recent address on campus, and a review of the religious art exhibit in the O'Shaughnessy Art Gallery—but it also had a self-proclaimed mission of stimulating serious communication among students, faculty, and administration. The administration was too aloof, the faculty totally tied up with their teaching and other academic responsibilities, and the students too isolated from the other two to have any real influence on policy. Thus it was to be a voice, a voice for students, faculty, and even administrators to comment and suggest changes in administration policy. It was financed in part by Student Government but it hoped to attract income-producing advertising. As time went on, it became a twice-weekly paper and expanded on occasion to eight pages. It provided the needed service of bringing campus news to all students, and it also kept many student interests before the administration—curfew, cars, stay-hall, too many lecture classes and too few discussion seminars, limits on class cuts, censorship of student publications, and an honor code. In early 1966 it published an article exposing what it thought was a double standard in dealing with athletes, claiming that there were easy courses for athletes, scheduling preferences for them, grade changes, and academic cheating among athletes. The charges were serious but the author gave no substantiating evidence. Professor Mike DeCicco, the fencing coach and also the academic advisor to the student athletes, wrote a reply, explaining that only the Admissions Office, not the Athletic Department, decided which prospective athletes would be admitted to Notre Dame, that athletes took a wide variety of classes, all of them open to all students, and that athletes were expected to take advantage of the tutoring and study hall options available to remain eligible. By this time, the paper had started to decline. As a weekly or biweekly, the news was often well-known across campus before the paper reported it, its finances were always uncertain, and too few students seemed interested in staffing the paper. The *Voice* presses stopped in late October 1966.[38]

One issue that emerged to prominence during the life of the *Voice* was the question of stay-hall. The residence halls at this time were divided by classes, with three or four halls assigned exclusively to freshmen, another three exclusively to sophomores, and similarly for juniors and for seniors. With class halls, tighter class spirit was thought to develop. But many students were advocating a stay-hall system, with students permitted to remain in the same hall all four years. Students insisted that this would develop stronger hall or community spirit over a four-year period and it would produce an efficient hall government with only a 25 percent turnover each year caused by graduation. The administration at first was not convinced. It felt that many freshmen still needed special residential consideration—earlier curfew, regular quiet or study hours, etc.—in order to adjust more successfully to college life. The university was also in the process of establishing a special First Year of Studies program and this did not seem the time to alter the freshman living situation. But after weighing the advantages and disadvantages, the administration inaugurated the stay-hall system on an experimental basis in the fall of 1965 in Alumni, Dillon, and Farley Halls. The experiment was successful. Hall governments were set up with section representatives and an elected hall president, but year after year other halls rejected the system, preferring not to have freshmen living in them. In 1967, Zahm and Breen-Phillips established stay-hall, and other halls eventually followed until it became campus-wide.[39]

A similar major change in student academic life occurred in the fall of 1964 with the implementation of a university-wide honor code. Father Hesburgh had been urging it for some time as a demonstration of student maturity and responsibility, and student leaders were anxious to embrace it to prove that same maturity. Under the code, each student pledged to be honest in all academic work and professors were urged not to be present in classrooms during tests and examinations. Students violating the code were urged to self-report, or a faculty member or other students could report them. A first violation was to be handled by the professor of the class. A second violation was to be tried before an honor council, and penalties varied according to the seriousness of the violation. Unfortunately, the students never fully embraced the concept and they were hesitant ever to report on a classmate. The code was revised periodically to make it more effective, and it did not live up to early expectations.[40]

Additional changes came in the summer of 1965 when Father Joseph Simons, ordained only four years, replaced Father Leonard Collins as dean of students. That spring had furnished Father Collins with one final incident. On April 20, a sixteen-year-old South Bend young woman entered the basement of the student center with some friends and, probably at the suggestion of others, began to dance. There was a band playing upstairs, and they all repaired there where she continued her dancing. The band struck up the then popular song "The Stripper" and her dance became more exotic. She promised to return the following night, which she did, and the night after. The students had given her the name "Lola," probably after Lola Montez, famed nineteenth-century courtesan and dancer, and by the third evening several hundred students had assembled to watch. However, the young woman was intercepted by campus security between the bus stop and the student center, much to the chagrin, protests, and catcalls of the students. She was taken to the security office to be interviewed and was eventually driven to her home. Spring rites were taking place on college campuses all across the country after the long cold winter, and perhaps this was Notre Dame's.[41]

In addition to the appointment of Father Simons, the students noticed two other changes when they returned to campus that fall. First, curfew regulations had been relaxed. Freshmen could now be out until midnight on Fridays and 12:30 a.m. on Saturdays. Saint Mary's curfew was midnight and this gave the freshmen time to walk back from Saint Mary's on Saturday nights. Curfew was 1:00 a.m. on Friday and Saturday for sophomores, 1:30 a.m. for juniors, and 2:00 a.m. for seniors. A second change was the appointment of Dr. Peter Grande as assistant dean of students. Dr. Grande was a member of the University Counseling Service and the emphasis of the Dean of Students Office was now to be less heavy on discipline and more focused on counseling and on developing a sense of maturity and responsibility among the student body. The earlier change of the prefect of discipline to the dean of students was not only in name but in spirit and in fact.[42]

If there was a bright spot on the campus during the turbulent 1960s, it was clearly football, although not at the beginning. Joe Kuharich had replaced Terry Brennan as football coach in 1959, and he had impressive credentials: born and raised in South Bend, he was a starting guard under Coach Hunk Anderson in the 1930s, he played professionally with the Chicago Cardinals and Pittsburgh Steelers, he was head coach at the University of San Francisco for four years, with an undefeated season in 1951, he then coached the Chicago Cardinals and the Washington Redskins and was named Professional Coach of the Year in 1955. He had been an excellent professional coach, emphasizing a complex passing game from a variety of formations, but in 1959 he inherited a young team with only twelve monogram winners. The best Kuharich could do that first year was five and five. The following year was worse, with eight consecutive losses and an overall record of two and eight. The 1961 season was a little better, a five and five record again, but the year was memorable for the controversial field goal at the end of the Syracuse game. Notre Dame attempted a winning field goal as time ran out and it was not successful but a defensive lineman ran into the holder. The officials marched off a fifteen-yard penalty, awarded Notre Dame a second try, and it won the game. Many felt that Notre Dame may have been awarded that second attempt incorrectly because once the kicked ball was in the air, it was not clear which was the offensive team and which the defensive, and time may also have run out (and the game ended) before the foul occurred, but the university did not consider forfeiting. The following season was no better, five and five. After four years, Coach Kuharich's record was seventeen wins and twenty-three losses, much below Brennan's record of thirty-two and eighteen, and much below his own expectations. Realizing that his days at Notre Dame were probably numbered, he resigned in the spring of 1963 and accepted a position as supervisor of National Football League officials. Since it was only two weeks before the start of spring practice, there was no time for a full search and Hugh Devore was asked to step in for a year, as he had done in 1945 while the university awaited the return of Frank Leahy from the service.[43]

It had been ten years since the glory years of football victories under Frank Leahy, and Notre Dame needed a consistently winning coach again—and it found one a hundred miles away. Ara Parseghian, of Armenian ancestry and named for a ninth-century Armenian king, was born in Akron, Ohio, and excelled as a youth in baseball, basketball, and football. His mother only reluctantly permitted him to play football in high school, and she did not go to games. After time in the Navy during World War II, he enrolled at Miami University in Ohio, was drafted by the Cleveland Browns in 1947, and played one year under Coach Paul Brown until a hip injury ended his playing days. He returned to Miami University as an assistant coach under Woody Hayes and succeeded him as head coach in 1951. In five years there he compiled a record of thirty-nine wins, six losses, and one tie, and he was then recruited away to Northwestern. In eight years at Northwestern, he was thirty-six, thirty-five, and one in the powerful Big Ten Conference and, with much less talent, defeated Notre Dame in four consecutive meetings from 1959 to 1962. Parseghian was not a Catholic nor a Notre Dame graduate but he had learned football under the best—Paul Brown, Woody Hayes, and Sid Gilman—and he had the knack of getting the best out of the talent he had. He seemed precisely what Notre Dame needed.[44]

Parseghian's first year was a Cinderella year. He brought three coaches with him from Northwestern and added five graduates of Notre Dame. Their first mission was to select a quarterback and they had four, most with limited game experience, from which to choose. Parseghian decided on John Huarte, low enough on the depth chart that, although a senior, some coaches had difficulty pronouncing his name, but he was probably the best passer of the group, although he threw with a peculiar three-quarter sidearm motion. If Huarte was going to pass, someone had to catch, and Parseghian decided on six-foot-two, 220-pound senior Jack Snow. The rest of the team was young but solid because Devore had recruited well, including seven future All-Americans. The season opened with a 31–7 victory at Wisconsin, followed by successive wins over Purdue, Air Force, UCLA, Stanford, Navy, Pittsburgh (a close 17–15 win), Michigan State, and Iowa. The final game in Los Angeles was a classic Notre Dame–Southern California confrontation. The scoring shifted back and forth throughout the game, with Southern California scoring late with 1:34 left in the game and walking away a 20–17 victor. But the season was a remarkable success: from a two and seven record the year before to less than two minutes from an undefeated season, and with a young, dynamic, charismatic coach that some students thought might be able to walk on water, the students had a reason to be proud, confident, and contented.[45]

That first year might have been exceptional but it was no fluke. Notre Dame had talent and a coaching staff that used it well. Nineteen sixty-five in some ways was a rebuilding year since both John Huarte (Heisman Trophy winner) and Jack Snow (All-American) had graduated. It was a season of seven wins, losses to Purdue and Michigan State, and a tie at Miami. But if 1965 was something of a disappointment, the following year was 1964 all over again, but with a happier ending. The team had a solid core of veterans: Nick Eddy at halfback, Jim Lynch at linebacker, and an excellent defensive line, but the passing game had to be rebuilt. Parseghian found it in the sophomore class. Two young quarterbacks vied for the starting position—Coley O'Brien and Terry Hanratty—and Hanratty won by the narrowest of margins. At end the sophomore class had Jim Seymour, from Father Charles Coughlin's famous Shrine of the Little Flower parish in Royal Oak, Michigan, a high school star in football, basketball, and track. In his junior and senior years, he was never beaten in either low or high hurdles. Parseghian decided to start the duo in the opening game against a Purdue team led by Bob Griese, although neither had yet played a down of college football, since freshmen were not eligible in 1966. Parseghian admitted he was nervous, and was surprised at how calm Hanratty and Seymour were—and at how much they could eat before the game! Everyone was surprised during the game. Seymour had a knack for getting open in the seams between two defenders, and Hanratty could find him with bullet passes. If he was not open, Hanratty could throw it high and hurdler Seymour could outjump his defenders. Notre Dame won that opening game 26 to 14 but the headlines were Hanratty and Seymour. In his first game, Hanratty had completed sixteen of twenty-four passes for 304 yards, and Seymour had caught thirteen of them for 276 yards, more than any previous Notre Dame receiver, including Knute Rockne, Leon Hart, and Jack Snow. The aerial show continued game after game but they were not the whole team. Nick Eddy, Larry Conjar, and Rocky Bleier provided a balanced running attack and the defense often held opponents scoreless. In the first eight games, Notre Dame outscored its opponents 301 to 28, but it was still Hanratty and Seymour who had captured the public's imagination. Sports writers dubbed them the "Dynamic Duo," the "Teen Terrors," the "Super Sophs," and the "Kiddie Korps," they were on the cover of *Time* and the magazine claimed that Hanratty's passes travelled faster than Johnny Unitas's, and Don Klosterman of the Baltimore Colts stated that Jim Seymour "could make any professional team in the country right now." Parseghian could only shake his head: "Good Lord, they are only babies."[46]

The test was to come, everyone knew, at Michigan State late in the season, on November 19. The Spartans were undefeated also, and boasted an outstanding defensive unit led by George Webster and Bubba Smith. Nick Eddy somehow hurt himself getting off the train in Lansing, Bubba Smith knocked Hanratty out of the game in the first quarter, and All-American center George Goeddeke sprained his ankle two plays later. Coley O'Brien replaced Hanratty, Tim Monty replaced Goeddeke, and Bob Gladieux replaced Eddy. It was fortunate that the three had practiced together as the second team all year. Michigan State scored first, a touchdown and then a field goal, before O'Brien hit Gladieux with a thirty-four-yard pass and a touchdown, leaving Michigan State ahead 10–7 at halftime. Notre Dame was concerned because O'Brien was a diabetic, munching candy bars on the sidelines when the offense was off the field, and the team doctor worked to balance his blood sugar at halftime. Both defenses came out of the locker rooms strong and the second half soon descended into a duel between punters. Notre Dame converted one field goal, and missed another by less than a foot. O'Brien seemed to be tiring and losing strength as the game went on, and on the last series of plays in the game, Parseghian called only runs. The final play was a quarterback sneak simply to run out the clock and settle for the tie. Parseghian was highly criticized for playing it safe, some alumni wrote to remind him that the goal of every game was to win, and people he had never met sent him ties for Christmas. But the coach had thought ahead. Notre Dame and Michigan State would have to be tied at the top of the national polls, and this was Michigan State's final game, but Notre Dame still had to play Southern California over the Thanksgiving weekend. Even with key injuries, Notre Dame overwhelmed the Trojans 51 to 0, and the Irish were awarded the national championship. The team had included eleven All-Americans, and eighteen of the twenty-two starters went into professional football.[47]

Parseghian's teams were good for the rest of the decade but they could not match the excitement of 1964 to 1966. In 1967, Notre Dame was only 2–2 after the first four games, having lost to Purdue and Southern California. Opponents were putting two or three defenders on Seymour, and Hanratty had to find other receivers. Discouraged, he wrote a letter to his hero, Johnny Unitas, and received a two-page reply of encouragement. Notre Dame did not lose again the rest of the season. The record was 7–2–1 in 1968, with losses to Purdue and Michigan State and a tie with Southern California. Hanratty was hurt in the game against Navy and did not play in the last three games, but he and Seymour were still named All-Americans, Seymour for the third time. Nineteen sixty-nine was an exciting season because Notre Dame announced that, if invited, it would accept a bid to play in a bowl game, its first since 1925, with the profits going to minority scholarships. The season ended with eight wins, a loss to Purdue, and a tie with Southern California. In an exciting Cotton Bowl contest, Notre Dame lost to Texas 21–17.[48] After six years, and with Parseghian at the helm, it was clear that winning football was back.

One of the issues stirring Catholic campuses across the country, including Notre Dame, in the 1960s was the question of academic freedom and free speech. In the spring of 1963, the Catholic University of America barred Fathers Godfrey Diekmann, Hans Küng, John Courtney Murray, and Gustave Weigel from speaking on campus, and two years later Saint John's University in New York terminated thirty-one faculty members for what the administration called using the classroom for propaganda purposes but what the professors said was for teaching something other than strictly Thomistic philosophy and theology. At Notre Dame in the early 1960s, the administration rejected a student request to invite *Playboy* publisher Hugh Hefner to speak on campus, insisting that it would not have academic value but would be a publicity coup for the magazine to have *Playboy* bunnies photographed under the Golden Dome. In February 1966, conservative traditionalist priest Father Gommar De Pauw was also denied permission to speak or offer Mass on campus. Father De Pauw was an outspoken critic of the liturgical changes of the Second Vatican Council and Cardinal Lawrence Shehan of Baltimore had suspended him "from any and all exercise of the sacred ministry." The *Scholastic*, unfortunately, mistakenly referred to him as a "defrocked priest" and he threatened to sue, but the magazine printed a retraction and apology. But he was still barred from appearing.[49]

One priest who did speak on campus was Father James Kavanaugh of the nearby diocese of Lansing in Michigan. He had recently published a book entitled *A Modern Priest Looks at His Outdated Church* and the student academic commission invited him to discuss his book on campus. In his talk, he denounced the Church and revealed his intention to resign the priesthood and marry: "I don't know how I, as a man, can find God and meaning without marriage. I need it and I intend to have it. Therefore, I renounce my priesthood, and as far as I am concerned, the institutional church can go to hell!"[50] His publisher took out an advertisement in the *New York Times* ten days later, quoting Father Kavanaugh:[51]

> I am resigning from the Catholic priesthood in personal protest against the refusal of the hierarchy of the institutional church to bring about reform. I announced my resignation before an assembly of students of Notre Dame University because this great University, a short distance from my hometown, represents to me the greatest Catholic center of learning in the country. I can no longer wear the collar nor accept the title of 'Father,' when the institution I represent can cut off from communion the divorced and remarried, can refuse to admit its error in the matter of birth control, can ignore the plea of priests for marriage, can continue to reduce the principles of Christ to instruments of fear and guilt.

An editorial in the *Scholastic*, the student news magazine, reviewed the speech and the speaker:[52]

> Father James Kavanaugh's recent lecture at Notre Dame was as unsophisticated as a Huey Long harangue: repeatedly emotional, continuously negative and consistently gross. He claimed to be in search of a more authentic Christianity, but not a single grace note of Christian joy relieved the torrent of vindictive hatred that poured from his lips for more than an hour. . . .

The speaker did more than castigate the institutional and impersonal Church, mock old bishops and cardinals, and ridicule celebrate [*sic*] priests and nuns. He also chose this drab and public occasion to expose some of the most personal decisions of his life: he has decided to reject basic dogmas touching even the real Presence and the Trinity itself, he has determined to cut himself off from the church and the priesthood.

His remarks found some echo in the titters and applause of his overflow audience, but he failed to win their unanimous approval. Perhaps it was the shock of his naked hatred, perhaps it was revulsion from uncalled-for vulgarity, and perhaps it was perception of continued contradiction, but something kept a third of his hearers from ever catching fire.

In response to the *New York Times* piece, the university submitted a rejoinder, quoting much of the *Scholastic*'s editorial. The controversy generated additional responses, some criticizing the university for inviting such a controversial figure to campus, and others criticizing it for such an elaborate defense of its image in a small matter of academic freedom.[53]

The second half of the 1960s was a period of serious challenges in American public life and of at times well-intentioned but uncertain responses from public authorities. Urban riots broke out across the country: Watts in 1965, Chicago in 1966, and Newark and Detroit in 1967. National leaders were assassinated: President John Kennedy in 1963, Malcolm X in 1965, George Lincoln Rockwell (leader of the American Nazi Party) in 1967, and Martin Luther King, Jr., and Robert F. Kennedy in 1968. Radical students took over campuses at Berkeley, Cornell, and Columbia. The Democratic National Convention in Chicago in 1968 saw confusion and hostility within the convention hall and confrontations between police and protestors outside it. The country was not sure if the Richard Nixon who succeeded Lyndon Johnson after the election of 1968 was a "new Nixon" or the same Nixon as in the past. The country was not sure either if the Woodstock gathering in New York in 1969 was a celebration of love and life or simply youth culture gone amuck.

All this uncertainty and unrest seemed to be reflected on the Notre Dame campus with the protests and demonstrations and articles critical of the administration. At the same time, the university was continuing to grow—increased student enrollment, additional faculty, expanded physical facilities, and a larger budget year by year. As both the problems and the opportunities of the university increased throughout the decade, Father Hesburgh realized that his administration could only profit from additional outside and professional counsel. With fund drives becoming so important, it was also advantageous to have persons assisting who had knowledge of and contacts in the corporate and political worlds. Furthermore, the Second Vatican Council of the early 1960s had recommended that the Catholic laity have more of a leadership role in the Church's works and ministries, and Father Hesburgh realized that Catholic education was one area where they could make significant contributions. In the summer of 1965, therefore, Father Hesburgh first broached the idea with both his provincial superior and the superior general of the Congregation of Holy Cross of restructuring the higher government of the university and creating a predominantly lay board of trustees. With their assent, he next discussed the idea with Edmund Stephan, a noted Chicago attorney and member of Notre Dame's board of lay trustees. Stephan drafted a set of statutes incorporating such a board of trustees and also, over it, a board of fellows composed of six Holy Cross religious and six lay members whose primary responsibilities were to preserve the Catholic character of the university and to make all decisions involving the alienation of university property.[54]

The process of approving this major transfer of university authority and control went more smoothly than Father Hesburgh might have feared. First, Notre Dame sought and received Rome's approval, believing that transferring university control from the religious community to a predominantly lay board was in reality alienating church property and thus required Vatican approval. Saint Louis University at this time did not seek Vatican approval since it held that Catholic universities and hospitals did not truly belong to religious communities (monies donated to them could not be taken by the religious community for other purposes) and thus were not strictly church property but were only held in trust. Father Hesburgh and Mr. Stephan then explained the proposition to the Holy Cross community at Notre Dame, where a small minority raised objections, fearing the loss of the Catholic character of the university. An extraordinary provincial chapter was called for January 1967 and, after some opposition, it approved the restructuring by a vote of 38 to 4. Father Howard Kenna, provincial superior, had probably summed up the convictions of at least some who approved in his letter to the Holy Cross community in December 1966:[55]

> This is not primarily a Holy Cross institution: it is a Catholic institution which Holy Cross has been privileged to found, to build, and to cement through its labor, its sacrifices and, indeed, its heart's blood, but it has

been done for the Church and for God and his people. . . . Holy Cross has traditionally been open; it has traditionally been ready to go along with the changes which seem to make more effective its apostolate. I think this one is now necessary.

The current board of trustees, six Holy Cross religious, met on March 28, 1967, and formally approved the new statutes and the transfer of authority to the new board. That new board met for the first time on May 6, 1967, and officially assumed control over the university. Father Hesburgh always insisted that this restructuring was one of the two most important decisions made in the thirty-five years of his presidency, the other being the admission of undergraduate women into the university in 1972.[56]

Academic freedom, however, and what Hesburgh considered abuses of it at the Catholic University of America, at St. John's College, and at his own institution in the Francis McMahon and John Courtney Murray incidents, continued to be bothersome concerns.[57] He was at the time president of the International Federation of Catholic Universities, and at its meeting in Tokyo in 1965 the delegates adopted the nature and role of the contemporary Catholic university as its theme for its next meeting in Kinshasa in 1968 and recommended that regional discussions be scheduled to prepare for it. Father Hesburgh organized such a meeting on Notre Dame property in Land O'Lakes, Wisconsin, in July 1967. Nine university presidents attended, two bishops, and high officials of several religious orders. After four days of serious deliberation, they issued the so-called "Land O'Lakes Statement" on the position of a Catholic university in the contemporary world.[58] The opening paragraph proved to be the most controversial:[59]

1. *The Catholic University: A True University with Distinctive Characteristics*
The Catholic University today must be a university in the full modern sense of the word, with a strong commitment to and concern for academic excellence. To perform its teaching and research functions effectively the Catholic university must have a true autonomy and academic freedom in the face of authority of whatever kind, lay or clerical, external to the academic community itself. To say this is simply to assert that institutional autonomy and academic freedom are essential conditions of life and growth and indeed of survival for Catholic universities as for all universities.

The second paragraph insisted that the university must still remain Catholic:[60]

The Catholic university participates in the total university life of our time, has the same functions as all other true universities and, in general, offers the same services to society. The Catholic university adds to the basic idea of a modern university distinctive characteristics which round out and fulfill that idea. Distinctively, then, the Catholic university must be an institution, a community of learners or a community of scholars, in which Catholicism is perceptibly present and effectively operative.

This Catholicity was to be preserved primarily through the central and pervading influence of theology. Professors of theology at a Catholic university must be well qualified and academically respected to color and influence other academic disciplines, the physical and social sciences, for example. With this pervasive theology, the Catholic university must confront the major problems of the time, offer Catholic-inspired solutions, and allow the Church itself to benefit from its counsel. Students at a Catholic university should take part in the Church's public liturgies and should be involved personally and experientially in the problems afflicting society.[61]

The statement, of course, was not the final word on the relation of the Catholic university with the institutional church, and much was presumed or left unsaid, but it was an effort to prevent unwarranted interference into the personal teachings and writings of individual professors at a Catholic university.

As the stay-hall system progressed, with responsible hall governments and hall judicial boards, and with increased requests for more student and faculty input into university decision-making, Father Hesburgh, with the approval of the board of trustees, in 1968 announced the establishment of a tripartite Student Life Council. The council was to be made up of twenty-four members, eight from the faculty, eight from the student body, and eight from the administration. Six were *ex-officio* members: the chair of the Faculty Senate and the chair of the senate's Student Affairs Committee, the student body president and vice president, and the vice president of student affairs and the dean of students. The council was empowered to make rules and regulations in the area of student life, and if the president could not accept what the council passed, it would go to the board of trustees for a final decision. The council normally met every week, deliberations were governed by Robert's Rules of Order, and decisions were made by majority vote. Students and administrators often (but not always) voted as blocks, with the faculty casting deciding votes. If the council did not eventually measure up to everyone's expectations, it did succeed in making changes in student life over time (eliminating some car restrictions early on) and providing a forum where student requests and complaints could be officially and openly heard.[62]

The Student Life Council had been meeting for less than six months when it was thrust into its first major campus crisis. The Student Union had organized what it hoped would be a serious discussion of pornography and censorship for early February 1969. The Supreme Court, and much of the country, had been wrestling with the issue for several years, often debating what kinds of literature the post office might legally refuse to carry. Justices attempted to set standards such as primarily "appealing to prurient interest" or being "utterly without redeeming social value," and Justice Potter Stewart admitted that he could not define pornography but knew what it was when he saw it. Student Union leaders questioned whether nine male lawyers on the Supreme Court were the best panel to determine what was art and what was pornography, and wondered whether a Catholic university, with faculty specialists in art, moral theology, law, literature, and sociology might not have something worthwhile to contribute to the discussion.[63]

Student Union leaders had spent much time planning the conference. The LaFortune Student Center ballroom would house an exhibit of erotic art, an off-Broadway troupe would present *Lady Godiva* in Washington Hall, Allen Ginsberg was scheduled to read his poetry in the library auditorium, several films were to be shown in the Center for Continuing Education, representatives of the conservative Citizens for Decent Literature in California were present to take part, and various panels were scheduled to discuss the issues raised. Unfortunately, there were problems from the start. The company that was to transport the art from New York, owned by alumni of Notre Dame, refused to follow through, fearing legal complications in carrying such material across state lines. Students then rented a truck and brought the material themselves. Tickets to view the art were to be limited to Notre Dame persons and a few others, but some distributed their tickets more widely. One of the films to be shown, *Flaming Creatures*, had been barred in Michigan and, on appeal to the Supreme Court, Justice William Brennan had upheld the ban. The weekend of the conference was also the centenary of the Notre Dame Law School (founded in 1869), and Justice Brennan was to be the keynote speaker. The Student Union leaders agreed not to show the controversial film while the justice was on campus and not until it was clear whether it was in violation of Indiana decency laws.[64]

The conference began without major slips. Allen Ginsberg read his poetry, the art exhibit opened, and faculty and others took part and prepared for later panel discussions. Trouble began the second day, Thursday, February 6. Either the projectionist at the Center for Continuing Education made a mistake, or someone intentionally violated the agreement with the administration, but the banned film, *Flaming Creatures*, was put on the screen, at least until the mistake was recognized. The representatives of the Citizens for Decent Literature were convinced that it had not been an honest mistake and they had an affidavit to have the film confiscated if shown. By this time, another group of students began protesting the presence of pornography on campus at all, but a few of the more radical students on campus decried the censorship and announced that they would show at least one of the films in Nieuwland Science Hall. When the film was put on the screen, plainclothes policemen arrived. A Saint Mary's student tried to hide the film but the police retrieved it and then attempted to leave. The officer carrying the film was knocked to the ground, and some students were maced as the police beat a retreat to their cars and drove away. Thankfully, at no time did the officers, all armed, draw their guns. With the campus in such disarray, and with the Law School Centenary in progress, the Student Union officials announced the cancellation of the conference on Friday at 6:00 p.m.[65]

Father Hesburgh then called an emergency meeting of the Student Life Council. After some discussion of how open the meeting should be and who should be allowed to address the council, two decisions were taken: first, the council members would repair to the police station and view the controversial film that had been confiscated, and second, a subcommittee of six would be elected from the council to investigate the controversy and attempt to determine what went wrong. The subcommittee met several times over the next four weeks, numerous people were interviewed, including the county prosecutor, and more than 1,400 pages of testimony were compiled. The report stated that the conference should have been better planned by the Student Union leaders, especially in light of the legal issues involved, that the vice president of student affairs should have taken a greater part in the planning, that he and the dean of students should have been more present as difficulties emerged, that the more radical students should not have attempted to screen the films in Nieuwland Science Hall, that the university administration should have been more forceful in discouraging the sending of police to the campus, that the police should not have employed mace, and that the Citizens for Decent Literature, especially as invited visitors to campus, should not have sought outside police intervention in this campus controversy. The report shied away from evaluating the actions of most individual students because the council did not want to prejudice any judicial proceedings the dean of students might wish to undertake. Some faulted the report for not criticizing the students more. One lawyer on the council said it was the first time in his experience that a jury returned and found the *judge* guilty.[66]

The decade of the 1960s ended with maybe the most controversial student incident in the thirty-five years of Father Hesburgh's presidency—his famous fifteen-minute rule. Students had been protesting various issues since the Corby Hall protest in 1960 but they seemed to be getting more serious as the decade progressed and that culminated in the public confrontation with the police at the Pornography and Censorship Conference. Radical students the year before had taken over Columbia University and occupied the president's office, and Father Hesburgh decided it was time to take a stand. He asked for and received advice from various university constituents—the Academic Council, Student Life Council, Faculty Senate, college councils, the alumni board, and numerous individual faculty members and students—and on February 17, 1969, he addressed a letter to the faculty and student body outlining the university's policy in the face of the present campus unrest across the nation.[67]

The letter acknowledged that there were numerous evils in the world that needed to be confronted and remedied, but in a constructive way. "The last thing a noisy, turbulent, and disintegrating community needs," Father Hesburgh noted, "is more noise, turbulence, and disintegration." Protests, demonstrations, and expressions of dissent on campus were acceptable as long as they did not violate the rights of others or impede the "normal operations of the University." If a demonstration did violate the rights of others or impede the normal operation of the university, the new policy was clear:[68]

> Anyone or any group that substitutes force for rational persuasion, be it violent or non-violent, will be given fifteen minutes of meditation to cease and desist. They will be told that they are, by their actions, going counter to the overwhelming conviction of this community as to what is proper here. If they do not within that time period cease and desist, they will be asked for their identity cards. Those who produce these will be suspended from this community as not understanding what this community is. Those who do not have or will not produce identity cards will be assumed not to be members of the community and will be charged with trespassing and disturbing the peace on private property and treated accordingly by the law. The judgment regarding the impeding of normal University operations or the violation of the rights of other members of the community will be made by the Dean of Students.

Father Hesburgh justified the new policy by saying that he sensed a "revulsion on the part of legislatures, state and national, benefactors, parents, alumni, and the general public for much that is happening in higher education today." He feared that if universities themselves were not successful in curbing the violence and disruptions spreading across college campuses, the public authorities would step in, and universities needed to remain free of such outside interference. His final sentence stated clearly: "we rule ourselves or others rule us, in a way that destroys the university as we have known and loved it."[69]

The letter drew an immediate response. In opposition, an administrator at San Fernando Valley State College declared: "If we had taken that stand, the place probably would have burned down." A dean at Brown University added: "You need a completely intimidated student body to make that sort of statement and get away with it. I think it will come back to haunt him." Student body president Richard Rossie criticized the letter since it had not been passed by the Student Life Council. Former student Robert Sam Anson wired: "Will succeed only in provoking further disruption. For good of all, sadly but strongly suggest your immediate resignation." On the other hand, Father Hesburgh received hundreds of letters praising his stand, many from alumni. President Nixon wrote "to applaud the forthright stand you have taken" and asked him to write Vice President Agnew with any advice on how the federal and state governments might assist in combatting campus disorder. From Bogota, Colombia, Father Hesburgh wrote the vice president:[70]

> The best salvation for the university in the face of any crisis is for the university community to save itself by declaring its own ground rules and basic values and then enforcing them with the widest and deepest form of moral persuasion for the good life of the university.
>
> Assume for a few months that the university community—faculty, students, administration, and trustees—is capable, in most cases, of laying down its own guidelines and effectively maintaining them in its usual free and independent university style. Things will be messy from time to time, but we will make it as universities if we determine strongly to maintain our freedoms and our values.
>
> Where special help is needed, let all assume it will be asked for and given quickly, effectively, and as humanely as possible, given the provisions that surround the need for such outside help, as a last alternative to internal self-correction. But let it be understood that the university, and only the university, public or private, makes this determination.

Minnesota Senator Eugene McCarthy treated it lightly and suggested that warning Notre Dame students not to disrupt the campus was like warning an all-girl band not to chew tobacco.[71]

The policy outlined in the letter was put to the test nine months later. In the fall of 1968 the Central Intelligence Agency and the Dow Chemical Company had been scheduled to visit campus in the same week to recruit students for future employment. Several students had protested their visit, the CIA for its part in destabilizing and even overthrowing national governments the administration considered hostile or too leftist, and Dow Chemical because it manufactured the napalm that was being used to destroy much of the environment in Vietnam and was causing numerous civilian deaths. In their protest, some students laid down in front of the Career and Placement Office, forcing interested students to step over them to enter for their interviews. To avoid a confrontation, both the CIA and Dow Chemical cancelled their interviews.[72]

Despite this confrontation, the Career and Placement Office again scheduled their interviews for the same week the following November, only a few months after Father Hesburgh's letter. Students again collected around the rotunda outside the Career and Placement Office in the Main Building, many lying on the floor. They viewed it more as a picket line and hoped that most students would not step over them to reach their interviews. Father Hesburgh and the dean of students judged this to be impeding the operation of the university since they insisted that no secretary or other office employee should have to step over a student to get to her or his office. Without its staff, that office could not open. Father James Riehle, the dean of students, approached the demonstrators, warned those in front of the entrance that they were in violation of university policy, gave them fifteen minutes to consider, and then invoked the recently announced policy, collecting the ID cards of ten students and officially suspending them from the university. (In fact, some were expelled and some suspended, but the expulsions were all later reduced to suspensions.)[73]

It may have been the greatest threat to the university's good order in the 1960s, but it ended successfully. The majority of the suspended students returned to Notre Dame and received their degrees, and the lesson was learned. There would be other demonstrations for other causes in the future, but the fifteen-minute rule never needed to be invoked again.

CHAPTER 17

The 1970s

Coeducation, Vietnam, and More

Despite the support of the new predominantly lay board of trustees and the assistance of the Student Life Council, the year 1969 had been a very trying one for Father Hesburgh. The enforcement of the fifteen-minute rule and the Pornography and Censorship Conference had been major campus disruptions, the inauguration of President Nixon did not offer assurance that the Vietnam War would wind down soon, his membership on the Civil Rights Commission was keeping Father Hesburgh absent from the university more often, and the students were once again calling for his resignation. "It is said around Corby Hall," a *Scholastic* editorial stated, "that Father Hesburgh realizes that 17 years of administrative work have squelched the creativity of his leadership, that he senses the moral distance between himself and the students and that he wants [to] retire but has no successor. Perhaps both a president and a chancellor are needed."[1] The editors went no further and apparently had no one in mind to replace Father Hesburgh as president, but a young Notre Dame alumnus, recently appointed to the faculty, did have a candidate, Professor Willis Nutting.[2]

Professor Nutting had been born in a place that he called "the center of the world," but that everyone else called Iowa, in 1900. His father taught marine biology at the University of Iowa and young Willis grew up in an educational environment, familiar with both the achievements and the foibles of academics. After graduation from the University of Iowa, he spent three years at Oxford as a

Rhodes scholar. "At that time you had to know Greek to get a Rhodes," he later remarked, "and since I was the only one in the state who knew Greek, I got it." He studied Christianity at Oxford, received BA and BLitt degrees, and was ordained an Anglican priest. He had also become somewhat disillusioned with the formal education he had received at Iowa and at Oxford: "The most valuable education I could get only by ignoring the advice of all the official teachers of the university. In this situation I came to appreciate the value of unofficial teachers." Returning to the United States, he served for a time in an Episcopalian parish in Colorado, left the Anglican Church in 1930 and became a Catholic, returned to the University of Iowa for a PhD, married in 1934, and joined the faculty of history at Notre Dame in 1936. At Notre Dame, he was also one of the early faculty members in the Program of Liberal Studies or the Great Books program. He could still be critical of academic regulations—syllabi, examinations, assigned papers, periodic grades, class attendance—but he became a very popular classroom instructor. Outside of the classroom, he was a lover of nature, taking early morning walks to bird-watch, and living on a farm to till the soil and care for animals and remain close to nature. For students opposed to strict regulations, Professor Nutting seemed an ideal choice for the Notre Dame presidency.[3]

The "Nutting for President" movement survived longer than the earlier campaign for George Shuster, but it eventually faded also. It did spawn one concrete result, however, the "Free City Day." Professor Nutting published *The Free City* in 1967, noting defects in the current education system of class assignments, standardized tests, grading, and large lecture halls, and championing an education of more dialogue between teacher and student, and among students themselves. He argued that every human being—before being a doctor, lawyer, merchant, or whatever—was first of all a person, and that only a liberal education educated a person simply as a person. Current education, he lamented, trained a person to be a specialist—in chemistry, in physics, in literature, in history, in finance, in metallurgy, and so on. He asked: "Is the specialist scholar . . . the highest and best example of the man whose intellect is fully and rightly developed?" His answer was a resounding "No."[4]

The following year a group of students organized a "Free University" on campus. Professors and students were invited to offer classes in whatever areas they felt competent to teach, and students could attend as they wished. Courses in beginning guitar, North Indian music, and draft counselor's training were some of the offerings. There were no grades, just the opportunity to learn.[5] In early 1970, several students and faculty members organized a "Free City Day," with informal lectures and discussions offered at various outdoor locations across the campus. Some of the titles offered were Black History, The Irrelevancy of Education, Christian University—Contradiction in Terms?, and Resistance and Contempt. The "Free City Day" was described as follows:[6]

> The Free City Day is a day of learning and living in a free environment. The Free City Day is essentially a spontaneous educational experience. The Free City is free food, Pepsi, music, and thought. The Free City is getting together and asking about God, Man, Society, and the universe. The Free City is tuning into nature and tuning into what education really ought to be. The Free City is taking one day in four years to think and speak about whatever is important to you; and to listen to others do the same thing. The Free City is loving and living in a free Christian contact.

Overall, it was a peaceful illustration of the antiestablishment sentiment of many students.

Father Hesburgh himself became convinced that some administrative changes were in order. The most significant of these was the appointment of Father James Burtchaell to the position of provost, the position created by the board of trustees at its meeting of June 22, 1970, to replace the office of the vice president of academic affairs. Father Burtchaell, thirty-six years old at the time, one year older than Father Hesburgh when he was named president in 1952, had been born in Portland, Oregon, had attended a high school there founded and staffed by the Congregation of Holy Cross, and had graduated from Notre Dame in 1956. He earned degrees in theology from the Gregorian University in Rome and the Catholic University of America, a licentiate in sacred scripture from the Pontifical Biblical Institute in Rome after research at the École Biblique et Archéologique Française in Jerusalem, and a PhD in divinity from Cambridge University in 1966. Ordained in 1960, he joined the Notre Dame faculty in 1966, celebrated evening Mass before large crowds in Dillon Hall where he resided, published widely, and was appointed chair of the Department of Theology in 1968. He was undoubtedly brilliant, a gifted linguist, supremely self-confident, unembarrasingly frank, dictatorial at times but charming and diplomatic at others. Father Hesburgh explained that the provost "is directly in charge of the total academic enterprise and indirectly supervises student affairs. He is Acting President in the absence of the President, a Fellow and Trustee of the University. . . . The Executive Vice President will supervise everything else and will, as

Treasurer of the University, give special attention to all financial affairs."[7] Thus Father Burtchaell was suddenly the second most important person in the administration, and his influence would be felt, often amid controversy, in almost every area of university life over the next seven years.

The new administrative structure, however, did not cause all student demonstrations to subside or all student requests to be satisfied. The requests of black American students were clearly an area that needed to be addressed. These requests and demonstrations had to be particularly embarrassing for Father Hesburgh as a member and now chairman of the federal Civil Rights Commission with a national reputation as a champion of black American rights. Congress had established the Civil Rights Commission in 1957, President Eisenhower had appointed Father Hesburgh one of its original six members, and President Nixon in 1970 named him chairman. But at the same time, black students were protesting their treatment at his own university.[8]

Notre Dame had enrolled no black American students in the first hundred years of its existence, and that was not by accident. Many of its students hailed from the South where strict segregation ruled, and the university feared that the presence of black students might be a source of friction and conflict or might deter southern white students from applying. Many non-Catholic black students might not feel comfortable at a Catholic university, and many others might not be able to afford the tuition. The first black student, Frazier Thompson, was assigned to Notre Dame in the Navy's V-12 program in World War II and he graduated in June 1947 along with another black student, Carl Coggins of Warren, Ohio. Once the door had opened, others applied and were accepted, including several athletes—in 1950 Joe Bertrand and Entee Shine in basketball, Wayne Edmonds and Aubrey Lewis in 1952 and 1954 in football, and Ron Gregory, brother of comedian and activist Dick Gregory, in track in 1957. In a student body of over five thousand, there were only sixteen black students in 1962 and almost no black faculty. Black students were discontented and knew that the university could do better.[9]

Most of their demands seemed reasonable and justified. They wanted a scholarship fund for black students, the hiring of a full-time black recruiter, an increase in black student enrollment to 10 percent, the hiring of black counselors, additional black faculty and administrators, expansion of the tutoring program, and the inauguration of a Black Studies Program. To put teeth in their demands, several students threatened a demonstration at the nationally televised basketball game against UCLA in the fall of 1968, and Father Hesburgh agreed to appoint a student-faculty University Committee for Afro-American Students to recommend improvement in university procedures. The demonstration was cancelled.[10]

The administration probably agreed with most of the student requests but insisted that it was all going to take time. Ten percent black enrollment would be a challenge since approximately 5 percent of black Americans were Catholic and Notre Dame wanted a student body that was predominantly Catholic. With the high inflation of the late 1960s and early 1970s ("stagflation" some called it), the budget had few opportunities for additional recruiters or even faculty. The students themselves stepped up and organized a Committee on Negro Enrollment (CONE) and, with the administration's encouragement, visited high schools to urge black students to consider Notre Dame. They sponsored various concerts and entertainments to help finance their trips but their recruitment trips did not match their hopes. The university did set up a Black Studies Program in 1968 and recruited Professor Joseph Scott to head it. A black sociologist, Professor Scott had earned a PhD from the University of Indiana, spent several months in Argentina on a Fulbright grant, spoke Spanish fluently, and, at the time, held a faculty position at the University of Toledo. In a major about-face, the university also announced that it was reversing its seventy-year ban on postseason football games and would accept a bowl bid for January 1970, with the resulting revenue devoted to black student scholarships. Texas defeated Notre Dame in that Cotton Bowl, but of the $340,000 the game grossed, $130,000 went for expenses (band and football team), $160,000 for minority scholarships, and $50,000 for Professor Scott and the Black Studies Program. Future bowl revenues were also earmarked for minority scholarships. In the fall of 1969, the university also announced the appointment of Bayard Rustin, a black social activist and companion of Martin Luther King, Jr., to the board of trustees. At the board meeting the following spring, he could both sympathize with and moderate student demands.[11]

These initial steps did not remedy all the problems, however. With so few black students on campus, each hall might have one or two at most if they were spread over the seventeen residence halls, emphasizing their minority status. At the students' request, the administration established sections of "black concentrations" in a couple of the halls, but this proved unsatisfactory also. The solution was obviously to enroll more black students and these efforts gradually bore fruit. As black enrollment increased, a second problem emerged: the lack of black women. In a student body of approximately fifteen hundred, Saint Mary's numbered twelve or fewer black students, and thus the social life for black students on both campuses was far from normal. Finally, the Black Studies Program developed problems also. It was a program, not a department, and could not hire and promote its own faculty. Faculty members were hired through other departments, as Professor Scott was through sociology, and they cross-listed their courses under black studies. The needs and priorities of the other departments might differ from those of black studies, but the program had to be satisfied with whomever the department hired. The administration responded to the problem by saying that in the fall of 1971 no faculty hires would be approved until two black faculty were hired, and the same requirement would hold for the fall of 1972. Progress was further indicated in the spring of 1970 when David Krashna was elected the first black student body president.[12]

The poor social conditions and limited social opportunities afflicted not only black students but all students. The lack of feminine companionship had been criticized on campus for years, probably going back to the days of Father Sorin, but, as in other areas, progress had been made in the 1960s. In fact, Notre Dame administrators were becoming more and more convinced that young men and young women should be educated together, for a number of reasons. The university was striving to improve year by year, and improving meant attracting both better faculty and better students, yet the university was recruiting students from only half of the human race. If women were included, the recruiting pool would increase, and the academic level of the student body should rise. Furthermore, high schools were changing also. In the past, Notre Dame attracted many of its students from single-sex college prep or parish high schools, but parish high schools by this time were very often giving way to coeducational Central Catholic high schools. In addition, more Catholic students, for various reasons, were attending public high schools, and after attending coeducational grade and high schools, single-sex Notre Dame might seem less attractive to many. Women were also assuming more and more prominent places in business, education, politics, and all of the professions, and if men were going to be working closely with them for the rest of their lives, they should probably begin working with them in college. Finally, small Catholic women's colleges were struggling. Without large graduate programs, it was difficult to attract government and foundation funding, tuition could be raised only so high, and many excellent Catholic women's colleges were forced to close their doors. If Catholic education was to remain available to women, all-male schools like Notre Dame needed to open their doors to them.[13]

The university considered inviting one or several Catholic women's colleges, Barat College and Rosary College among them, to relocate on Notre Dame property adjacent to the campus, forming a broad and diverse Catholic intellectual community with Notre Dame as its capstone. After initial discussions, all colleges declined. The most logical affiliation, of course, was less than a mile away—Saint Mary's College. Throughout the 1960s across the country, affiliation discussions were taking place between several prominent universities and nearby women's colleges—Harvard and Radcliffe, Brown and Pembroke, Yale and Vassar, Columbia and Barnard—and most of these negotiations eventuated in at least closer cooperation if not a formal affiliation. Close affiliation with Saint Mary's College might have financial benefits for both institutions also, eliminating some of the costly duplication in classes, buildings, supplies, and even personnel.[14]

The two instituted a limited co-exchange program in 1965. Saint Mary's students could take chiefly language and science classes at Notre Dame, and Notre Dame students could enroll primarily in education courses at Saint Mary's. If the classes were taught immediately before or after lunch, such students could eat on the opposite campus, and a shuttle bus service was begun between the two institutions. For the time being, no money was exchanged between the two schools. The program was a success from the start, and it expanded, with two hundred students participating that first year and two thousand participating by 1971. An official Notre Dame–Saint Mary's College Co-Exchange Committee was appointed in 1966, and it drafted a questionnaire to gauge the sentiment of the faculties at both schools on closer cooperation or affiliation. The questions included:[15]

> Do you prefer single-sex classes or are you comfortable teaching students from the other campus?
> Do you favor a combined or coordinated admissions office for both schools?
> Would you favor an "experimental" college for women on the Notre Dame campus?
> Do you favor joint faculty meetings?
> Is there danger that Saint Mary's College could be totally absorbed into Notre Dame, and would you be opposed to this?
> What kind of affiliation would you prefer [and several options were listed]?
> How soon would you like affiliation to happen?

Many faculty at Saint Mary's were unhappy with the questionnaire and with the status of the discussion, sensing that the movement toward complete merger had already begun with no assurance that Saint Mary's identity would be preserved or that Saint Mary's faculty would be retained.[16]

Despite the misgivings, negotiations continued. The two Speech and Drama Departments easily united into one since the men and women had been acting together in plays for years. The two Sociology Departments agreed to make only joint appointments when vacancies occurred, and Notre Dame's Psychological Services Center and Placement Bureau were also open to Saint Mary's students. The *Observer* listed Saint Mary's students on its staff, and four Saint Mary's women became Notre Dame cheerleaders.[17]

On May 2, 1969, the two schools released a "Statement of Principles," beginning with the statement that "The University of Notre Dame and Saint Mary's College, which have grown side by side for more than 125 years as separate institutions of Catholic higher learning, today announce initial steps which will eventually make them substantially co-educational with each other."[18] Notre Dame would limit its freshman enrollment to 1,500 and Saint Mary's College would admit 450–500 first-year students in the fall. The goal was a three-to-one ratio of men to women between the two institutions. Two hundred fifty first-year students from each school would share four classes together—Humanities Seminar, World Civilization, Political Science, and Introductory Sociology—and the co-exchange program would expand for sophomores, juniors, and seniors. Joint dining room privileges and joint seating at athletic contests were under discussion.

As collaboration continued, the two schools hired consultants in the spring of 1970 to advise on further steps and an ultimate goal. Dr. Rosemary Park was professor of education at the University of California in Los Angeles and former president of Barnard College in New York, and Dr. Louis Mayhew was professor of education at Stanford University. After several months of study, their report, dated December 29, 1970, recommended that Saint Mary's adopt the official name of "Saint Mary's College in the University of Notre Dame," but it also recommended for the present that the two schools "function cooperatively while still retaining separate corporate identity and . . . separate interests."[19] The report also recommended that the president of Saint Mary's be appointed a vice president of Notre Dame, that the registrar's offices, admissions staffs, and security forces be merged, and that academic departments be united over time, with due protection of all faculty rights. No women undergraduate students should be admitted to Notre Dame, nor men to Saint Mary's, without the approval of the other, and only Saint Mary's would offer undergraduate degrees in education. The report considered but rejected the options of the two schools remaining completely separate, as before the co-exchange program, or of Notre Dame totally absorbing Saint Mary's College.

Neither Father Hesburgh nor Sister Alma Peter, acting president of Saint Mary's, commented publicly on this *Park-Mayhew Report*, but Father Burtchaell, Notre Dame's provost, took issue with some of the presumptions he saw underlying it. He insisted that the two schools were in no way equal partners in any collaboration or affiliation: Notre Dame's budget was ten times that of Saint Mary's, Notre Dame had more freshmen than Saint Mary's had total students, and Notre Dame had an endowment while Saint Mary's was tuition-driven. "As an alternative to the Park-Mayhew proposal," Father Burtchaell continued, "I would ask the trustees of both schools to agree to effectuate a complete incorporation of Saint Mary's College into the University of Notre Dame."[20]

Ten days later, Father Burtchaell released his own alternative proposal to the *Park-Mayhew Report*. He noted that the co-exchange program was costing Notre Dame approximately $250,000 annually and insisted that this could not continue indefinitely. In his proposal, men and women would live on both campuses but not in co-residential dormitories. All parallel academic departments should merge, tenured Saint Mary's faculty would retain tenure, and all Saint Marys' faculty salaries would gradually be upgraded to Notre Dame's. One overall Department of Social Sciences would be created, and the social sciences, law, and fine arts would be housed on the Saint Mary's campus. Science, engineering, business, and the humanities would remain at Notre Dame. Holy Cross sisters, finally, would hold places on Notre Dame's board of fellows and board of trustees.[21]

Despite clear and fundamental differences, negotiations progressed over the next several weeks and, on May 14, 1971, the two schools signed an agreement to unify fully within the next four years. Academic departments were to begin merging immediately, Sister Alma Peter, president of Saint Mary's, was named vice president of Notre Dame, men and women were to be housed on both campuses but not in co-residential dormitories, and all women undergraduates would matriculate through Saint Mary's College. One unresolved challenge was the reconciliation of the two schools' diverse and complicated finances, and Father Joyce, Notre Dame's executive vice president and treasurer, and Sister M. Gerald Hartney, secretary of Saint Mary's board of trustees, were commissioned to draft an overall financial plan.[22]

Discussions continued throughout the summer and early fall on all levels—academic, business, financial, and student affairs—with the smoothest progress accomplished in student affairs. The male and female students clearly wanted to be together and, in this era of student unrest and protest, student affairs administrators were not reluctant to transfer into another area if displaced. In theory, almost everyone seemed in favor of a merger, but, as an adage says, the devil is in the details and, as the negotiating teams wrestled with those details, agreements seemed more and more elusive. There were rumors that discussions were not going well in some areas but hopes remained high until November 30, 1971, when the chairs of the two boards of trustees announced the termination of the merger talks and acknowledged that "it is not possible to accomplish complete unification at this time." The only explanation given was that "we are unable to solve financial and administrative problems." The thorny issues were thought to be the division of property between the college and the Sisters of the Holy Cross on the Saint Mary's campus, the fundamentally different financial situations of the two schools, and the inability to arrive at a satisfactory way to preserve the name and identity of Saint Mary's College. The co-exchange program between the two schools was to continue, but Notre Dame would also admit undergraduate women, both first-year and transfer students, into its student body in the fall of 1972.[23]

Students reacted to the news harshly, even bitterly, especially at Saint Mary's, and with reason. With the announcement of intended unification in May 1971, some students entered Saint Mary's that fall for programs that only Notre Dame offered, and now those courses might not be available to them. To show their displeasure, some students at Saint Mary's boycotted classes, others threatened to withhold tuition for the spring semester, still others announced their intention to transfer, and a few first-year students considered suing the college for breach of promise. Signs hung from Saint Mary's windows: "Welcome to Screw U"; "SMC Minus ND Equals Zero"; "Combine or Resign"; "Will the last person out of Saint Mary's please turn out the lights." Merger talks did resume on a very limited basis in February 1972 but they came to nothing. Quite a few Saint Mary's students transferred to Notre Dame, and the two schools continued on their separate ways, cooperating as feasible to both.[24]

The decision to admit undergraduate women into Notre Dame in the fall of 1972 had been made quickly, and some would say too quickly. More time might have been taken to prepare. But the university was convinced that men and women should be educated together, that Notre Dame should be admitting and educating women also, and, once the unification with Saint Mary's proved unfeasible, admitting undergraduate women into Notre Dame seemed the natural step. But preparations did have to be accelerated. The Provost's Office set the number to be admitted at 325, with 125 first-year students and 200 transfers, many of the transfers possibly from Saint Mary's. The movement into coeducation had to be gradual, a few hundred women a year, to allow the university to adjust faculty hiring in case most women selected the College of Arts and Letters and fewer chose science, business, or engineering.[25]

How and where to house these students was the responsibility of the Office of Student Affairs. The vice president of student affairs and the director of student residence visited four universities in Chicago with co-residential dormitories, two Catholic and two not, to compare advantages and disadvantages of co-residential and single-sex housing in areas of academic progress and success, alcohol and drug use, destruction of property, assaults, overall maturity, and so on. Unfortunately, little useful information was garnered. Each university had its own unique reasons for opening co-residential dormitories, and the advantages and disadvantages were not yet clear in the relatively short time available. With no reason to change, Notre Dame remained with single-sex housing. One of the larger residence halls could have accommodated the 325 women but student affairs preferred two smaller halls, with two women rectors and two women hall presidents. The vice president had asked three students from Saint Mary's to advise him in preparing for coeducation, and they stressed the need for common social space and larger closets. Walsh Hall was the only residence hall with built-in closets, and it also boasted a full basement of social space, and thus Walsh, centrally located and with few security concerns, seemed a logical choice. Badin, Howard, and Lyons qualified as candidates for the second hall but the numbers fit best for Badin, it had single rooms to complement Walsh's doubles, and it was close enough for the women to enjoy the basement social space Walsh provided. Each of the remaining men's halls was given a quota to admit of the men displaced from Badin and Walsh, from ten in Holy Cross Hall to thirty each in Flanner and Grace.[26]

The university community in general welcomed the young women with open arms, although not universally. The two hall rectors were young: Joanne Szafran, a graduate student in medieval history and former rector of a residence hall at Saint Mary's, and Kathleen Cekanski, a second year law student. Sister John Miriam Jones, with a recent Notre Dame PhD in microbiology, was appointed assistant provost to oversee the women's transition into the Notre Dame community over the summer. Walsh and Badin Halls underwent $150,000 of renovations: new outside doors and locks, new locks and safety chains on inside doors, laundry rooms, renovated bathrooms, new mirrors and medicine cabinets, larger dressers, and a complete paint job. Wards were set aside for women in the student infirmary and both dining halls were open to them. There were hitches, of course. Some professors preferred not to have women in their classes, others occasionally called on them "for the women's point of view," and it could be uncomfortable to find oneself the only woman in a class. It took time to construct equal shower and locker-room facilities for women in athletic buildings, and on occasion male students resorted to crude comments or gestures. But the overall experience was positive. Those who contributed to *Thanking Father Ted* in 2007 remembered those years with gratitude: a fine education, lifelong friendships, and the school they hoped their daughters would also select.[27]

Although most Notre Dame students were pleased with the coeducation decision, other sources of discontent remained—or emerged. Students still chaffed at regulations on cars and alcohol, and they could be highly critical of some of the influential banking and business leaders on the board of trustees, even attempting to disrupt the board's meeting on campus in the spring of 1970. As in most universities since Mistress Eaton was accused of putting goat dung in early Harvard's hasty pudding, students found reason to complain about the food and service in the dining halls, and they demanded that a Student Government dining hall committee assist in planning overall improvements.[28] A more public controversy erupted when a student group invited Ti-Grace Atkinson to speak on campus. A strong advocate of women's rights and author of *Radical Feminism* in 1969, she attacked the Church's positions on abortion, marriage, motherhood, and sex. She scoffed at the Virgin Birth, accused the Church of oppressing women, saw no reason for the Church's tax-exempt status, and sprinkled her talk throughout with four-letter words. Unfortunately, in covering her visit, the *Observer* repeated the vulgarities directly, the local bishop and the editor of the diocesan newspaper both protested, and Father Hesburgh responded, noting the university's open speaker policy, the validity of women's liberation as a topic of discussion on a university campus, that Atkinson's earlier writings were not that provocative, that her language was indeed an abuse of her invitation, and that the students should not have quoted her directly.[29]

In a controversy in early 1971 that occupied much of the administration's attention but little of the students' attention, the mayor of South Bend attempted to annex Notre Dame, Saint Mary's College, and Holy Cross Junior College to the city. He reasoned that annexation would allow South Bend to claim approximately ten thousand additional residents, receive increased revenue from the state, and perhaps allow for the annexation of land north of the university (Roseland) that would then be contiguous. Notre Dame opposed annexation, fearing it might lose some of its freedoms and be subject to municipal taxation. Notre Dame also pointed out the additional costs to the city in providing police, fire, and other required services to the university. The city council voted against annexation 6 to 3.[30]

The issue of deepest concern to the students during these years was, of course, the war in Vietnam. The students were of military age and that war, as it began to absorb larger and larger forces, could have a major impact on any or all of their lives. Student sentiment across the campus probably supported the war in the early 1960s. The only Americans involved were a relatively few military advisors to the South Vietnam regime, the government trumpeted the war as a fight to prevent the spread of Communism into the South (as the Berlin Airlift and the Korean War had earlier checked Communist encroachments), Notre Dame graduate and American hero Dr. Tom Dooley warned of the Communist threat in Southeast Asia, and President John Kennedy, immensely popular among college students, favored American involvement. But Kennedy was assassinated in late 1963 and Vice President Lyndon Johnson succeeded him. President Johnson sent combat troops into the area after the killing of American advisors at Pleiku in February 1965, ostensibly to protect the advisors there, and began bombing supply lines from the North in what was named Operation Rolling Thunder.[31]

With this escalation, students at the University of Michigan probably held the first teach-in that March, a gathering of students and faculty to learn about the war and discuss American involvement. Most of the speakers opposed American participation. A few months later, in October 1965, the Farley Hall Academic Commission sponsored a similar teach-in of students and faculty at Notre Dame, and assured that both sides of American participation were represented. Opposing American participation, history professor Samuel Shapiro decried the indiscriminate use of force and Professor James Bogle of the Political Science Department feared that our participation in the war was only straining relations with China and the Soviet Union with whom we needed to cooperate to halt nuclear proliferation. On the other side, Professor Gerhart Niemeyer insisted that if South Vietnam fell to Communism, the other countries of Southeast Asia would soon follow, and visiting history professor Charles Tull viewed American participation in the context of the successful containment doctrine espoused by President Truman in 1947.[32]

The debate continued over the next two years. In November 1965, one month after the Farley Hall teach-in, 3,100 students signed a petition supporting United States policy in Vietnam, and two months later 105 students donated blood for wounded American soldiers. Author, reporter, and Indochina expert

Bernard Fall lectured at Notre Dame in February 1966 and submitted to an extensive interview in the *Scholastic*. A "Day of Prayer for Peace" was also declared for February 27, with interfaith prayer services in each residence hall. ROTC numbers remained high—535 in the Army, 250 in the Navy, and 410 in the Air Force—although attrition rates were also high. Robert Sam Anson (soon to found the *Observer*), in a *Scholastic* article in October, lamented the one-sided reporting of the war—Viet Cong's atrocities but not America's, the war's constant progress despite rising deaths, and President Johnson's characterization of South Vietnam's Premier Ky as a "courageous battler for democracy." A *Scholastic* article a month later discussed the dilemma of the conscientious objector. Every citizen had an obligation to serve the common good, and if war was declared to defend the country or its principles, every citizen had an obligation to serve. If conscience does not permit the objector to serve, he or she must either renounce citizenship (and its obligations) and depart the country or accept the consequences of the decision by being jailed or even executed. The following year, the *Scholastic* solicited faculty views on the Vietnam War and published a few of them. Professor Norling of the History Department thought no one could oppose the war on "moral" grounds since Communism was clearly immoral. Professor John Williams of the same department described the war as a "brutal and degrading use of force against a poor and small nation" for our own self-interests. Professor James Dougherty of the English Department feared that the United States was supporting a government that no longer represented the will of the people. Professor Joseph Duffy of the same department characterized the war as "the adventure of a corrupt president and his equally corrupt advisors." Professor Walter Nicgorski of the Government Department disagreed: "My opinion is that President Johnson is leading the nation in a judicious and heroic effort to fight and win a limited war." Another cited the vast number of refugees fleeing North Vietnam as a justification for halting the spread of Communism.[33]

If the student body broke fairly evenly on American participation in the war, or even if the majority favored participation, that all seemed to change with the Tet Offensive in January 1968. In a well-coordinated surprise attack during the New Year holidays, the Viet Cong successfully attacked over thirty provincial capitals throughout the South, killed hundreds of city officials, and even breached the United States embassy compound in Saigon. American and South Vietnamese forces retook all those capitals within weeks and President Johnson called the offensive a Viet Cong defeat, alleging that the enemy had amassed all its resources to drive the Americans out of the country but they were still there.

But after billions of dollars and thousands of deaths, American forces had had difficulty defending even the embassy, and there seemed to be no early end to the war, no "light at the end of the tunnel." If the war did not seem winnable in the near future, all students could see themselves called into service in a war that was rapidly losing popular support. The senior class's annual "Patriot of the Year" award strikingly mirrored this change in sentiment. In 1967, the award was given to General William Westmoreland, commander of United States forces in Vietnam, and two years later, after the Tet Offensive, the 1969 award was voted to Senator Eugene McCarthy, the strong anti-war candidate who challenged President Johnson and his policies in the tumultuous election of 1968. In early May 1968, approximately 150 anti-war demonstrators attempted to block the march of 1,500 ROTC students in the annual President's Review, but the units simply marched around them.[34]

As the sentiment on campus began to swing against the war, a group of forty or fifty student leaders met with Father Hesburgh and asked that a program in nonviolence be established on campus. Father Hesburgh agreed with the proposal and noted that such studies had already been inaugurated at such respected places as Stanford University and the Woodrow Wilson Institute at Princeton. He added his opinion that "we are coming to a point where we are reaching the ultimate in violence. Violence is no longer, even physically speaking, a viable answer to any human conflict because it destroys all the people involved in it." He insisted, however, that any such program be "rigorously intellectual and the spirit of nonviolence would have to be practiced by the members." As the discussions continued, agreement was reached that it be an autonomous program, with authority to hire and release its own faculty, but also be interdisciplinary and be open as a minor to any student. The student leaders accepted the responsibility for generating faculty support for the program and Father Hesburgh promised to seek the necessary finances.[35]

That same week a vice president of Gulf Oil Corporation called to make an appointment to see Father Hesburgh and, after their conversation, offered Notre Dame $100,000 for any use he might desire. Father Hesburgh responded that he had an excellent use, this program in the study and practice of nonviolence. The students had been successful also in attracting faculty support for the program, with 80 percent of those contacted in favor. Professor Charles McCarthy, with degrees in both theology and law, was named head of this new Program for the Study and Practice of the Non-Violent Resolution of Human Conflict, and Gordon Zahn, an authority on the sociology of religion, Allard Lowenstein, a newly elected congressman from New York, and David Riesman, author of *The Lonely Crowd*, all agreed to visit and address the campus that spring. Close to three hundred students attempted to enroll in the program that fall but only eighty could be accepted because only four core seminars could be staffed and a limit of twenty was set for each one. Students took other courses in the Departments of Theology, History, Sociology, Anthropology, Literature, and Political Science.[36]

October 15, 1969, had been declared National Moratorium Day by those who wanted to demonstrate against the Vietnam War. Organized by supporters of Senator Eugene McCarthy, the anti-war candidate in the campaign of 1968, millions across the country participated. A reported 90,000 turned out in Boston where Senator George McGovern spoke, 50,000 in Washington, DC, 30,000 in New York, 10,000 in Chicago, and even in England young Rhodes scholar Bill Clinton and his companions organized a demonstration. At Notre Dame, the administration announced that the university would remain open but faculty members could suspend classes if they wished for attendance at Moratorium events, and students could absent themselves from class for the same reason. Faculty members were asked not to penalize students who missed class to attend the Moratorium, and the Student Life Council, in a special session, echoed the same request.[37]

Moratorium events actually began the night before when a group of more than two hundred Notre Dame and Saint Mary's students gathered for a vigil service for peace. The service began in Sacred Heart Church with prayer and hymns, then a visit to the Grotto for further prayer, followed by a procession around the campus with candles and folk singing, and a return to the church to continue the vigil. The main ceremony of the Moratorium, however, was a Mass celebrated on the library mall at noon the following day, with approximately two thousand in attendance. Archbishop Thomas Roberts, a strong anti-war advocate from England, presided, concelebrants included Fathers Amen, Bartell, Burrell, Gerber, Lewers, and others from the Notre Dame faculty, and five students from Moreau Seminary provided music. Father Hesburgh attended but did not concelebrate. At the offertory of the Mass, two professors and four students, including one woman, publicly tore up draft cards, and Professor James Douglass of the Program for the Study and Practice of the Non-Violent Resolution of Human Conflict spoke:[38]

> We believe that conscience in obedience to God and to the dignity of man must resist a law which enforces murder. . . . We can no longer cooperate

with a system which makes objects of men and which deepens the exploitation of the poor and the blacks in America by sending them first to fight a war against the Vietnam poor. . . .

We therefore refuse all cooperation with the institution of killing, and in this Mass of Peace we signify our non-cooperation with evil by tearing up our draft cards.

All of the events of the day were peaceful and nonviolent. A rally was held that afternoon on the main quadrangle at which various faculty members and students spoke. The rally organizers attempted to lower the flag on the main quadrangle but several first-year law students, who were also Navy veterans, immediately raised it again. The organizers insisted that they had meant no disrespect to those who were serving and risking their lives for their country. Father Hesburgh praised the demonstration, especially its religious character, although he was not sure it was appropriate to tear up draft cards at the offertory. He thought that President Nixon could not ignore the demonstrations across the country, and he stated his own opinion that a temporary cease-fire should be called and free elections held, and if South Vietnam objected, the United States should withdraw. He opposed sending more troops, adding: "If I had the wisdom and the power, I would stop the war tonight." His remarks were followed by twenty seconds of applause.[39]

The climax of the anti-war movement on campus came in May 1970. The Nixon administration, promising to wind down the war, had begun withdrawing thousands of troops each month since Nixon's inauguration the previous year, but it had also been discovered that North Vietnam was sending troops and supplies to the Viet Cong along the Ho Chi Minh Trail through Cambodia, and storing such arms and ammunition just across the border from South Vietnam, easily accessible to the Viet Cong. The administration had authorized a secret bombing mission against these Cambodian sanctuaries in March 1969, and in late April 1970 the administration approved an outright invasion. This apparent widening of the war gave rise to protests and demonstrations on campuses across the country, and on the Kent State campus in northeast Ohio on Tuesday, May 4, nervous national guardsmen opened fire on protesting students, killing four. Protests increased on college campuses and became more strident, but President Nixon defended the guardsmen and characterized protesting students as "bums."[40]

Notre Dame students reacted with outrage, and a protest rally was organized for the main quadrangle for that same afternoon. Father Hesburgh addressed the crowd of a thousand and repeated his opposition to the war:[41]

I have successfully read and re-read the President's statement, and I hope you have, and I recognize both his sincerity and his courage in deciding as he did. But I do not agree with him . . . even though he knows more about all this than I do and he has the responsibility of decision. . . . I have tried to understand the recurrent military logic that the war must be widened to be narrowed, escalated to be de-escalated, but with all the good will in the world, I find it difficult to follow a logic that has grown more barren, more illogical and more self-defeating in promising victory through defeat. . . . Military logic reached its highpoint when we were told of Vietnamese villages and villagers: We had to destroy them to save them.

He insisted that expanding the war into Cambodia was a mistake, that "moral righteousness is more important than empty victories," and that "no force of arms from North, East, West, or South can create stable governments and stable societies in Southeast Asia. Only the people themselves can do this."[42]

Students had begun boycotting classes across the country and Father Hesburgh urged the crowd before him not to follow. "Striking classes as some universities are doing," he declared, "in the sense of cutting off your education, is the worst thing you can do at this time, since your education and your growth in competence are what the world needs most, if the leadership of the future is going to be better than the leadership of the past and present." He added his opinion that "we are living in an age of midgets, I want you to prepare to be giants," and that the goal should be to "commit our persons and our future to a better America and a better world."[43]

Student body president David Krashna followed Father Hesburgh to the podium and, despite Father Hesburgh's eloquent plea, urged the students to strike and boycott classes. The protest, he declared, was not only against war but against a pervading racism, sexism, and militarism. Succeeding speakers echoed Mr. Krashna, the crowd seemed in enthusiastic agreement, and the Student Life Council, meeting in special session, recommended that "the student body through its officers, the officers of the administration, and the faculty . . . plan and set aside Wednesday and Thursday, May 6 and 7, as days for speeches, teach-ins, and liturgical ceremonies to express deep feelings and reservations about our government's recent actions in Indo-China." The days were to be set aside for "an intensive study of all sides of this profound and complicated problem which involves the moral and spiritual, as well as the intellectual, quality of our national life and public policy."[44]

Approximately one thousand students took part in a Mass on the main quadrangle Wednesday afternoon, with readings from the works of Thomas Merton, and an estimated three thousand marched to Howard Park on the north side of South Bend for a rally. Several persons spoke, including a young woman who had witnessed the shootings on the Kent State campus, but most student leaders, although impressed with the size of the march, expressed disappointment with the quality of the speeches. Different speakers protested different issues and the rally seemed to lose its focus. Another rally was held that evening to debate whether the boycott of classes should continue for another week. After some confusing discussion, 250 voted not to extend the boycott, 1309 voted to extend it, and 1013 voted to postpone a final vote. Student body president Krashna then announced, amid additional confusion, that the vote would be delayed.[45]

On Monday, May 11, the Academic Council, meeting in special session, decided that all class absences from May 4 to May 11 would be excused, and that a general referendum of faculty and students would be held on October 2 to determine if classes should be suspended for ten days before the coming November election, allowing faculty and students to campaign on the important issues facing the country. For the present, individual students could continue the semester's classes if they wished or they could terminate the semester early if they wished to participate in "organized activities" elsewhere, and in doing so they would accept their present grade for the class or accept a pass-fail grade. A student could also withdraw from a class (with a grade of "W") if the professor determined that no honest grade could be given at the time, or a grade of "I" (Incomplete) could be given if essential work had not been completed.[46]

In his address to the students on the afternoon of May 4, Father Hesburgh had outlined a six-point program he was recommending to bring the war to a close:[47]

1. The earliest possible withdrawal of American troops
2. Full repatriation of all American prisoners of war, whatever the cost
3. The allotment of personnel and finances to rebuild Vietnam, so damaged by wars
4. Allowing the peoples of Southeast Asia to select the form of government and society that they wish to have
5. End divisions at home with priorities that are human, not military
6. Commit ourselves, our talents, and our efforts to achieve this

The students resonated with these sentiments and undertook to collect thousands of signatures that Father Hesburgh agreed to send directly to the president.

Canvassing South Bend, the students accumulated 16,000 signatures by May 11, and 23,000 by May 15, with approximately 35 percent of the contacted residents approving. By that time, however, many students had departed campus for anti-war projects at home, and those remaining were giving full attention to classes and final examinations, but Father Hesburgh did send the signatures on to the Oval Office.[48]

Disagreements over the wisdom and morality of the Vietnam War certainly continued. Shortly after the Cambodian invasion and the resulting student protests, twenty-two faculty members signed a statement supporting President Nixon's policies. In response, forty-four members of the Theology Department faculty and the Graduate Theological Union criticized the war and expressed disappointment that the university had not condemned the war outright, basing their stands on the encyclical *Pacem in Terris* ("Peace on Earth") and *Gaudium et Spes* (the Pastoral Constitution on the Church in the Modern World). A professed religious at Moreau Seminary answered in a letter praising them for their adherence to papal pronouncements and hoping they were equally sincere in championing *Humanae Vitae*, Pope Paul VI's recent encyclical opposing artificial birth control.[49]

Other campus concerns of the time were far less strident. In the midst of preparations in the spring of 1972 for the entrance of undergraduate young women that fall, and with continued demand for greater student input in the passage of campus rules and regulations, eight students entered the race for student body president. Each had his own platform for dealing with the administration, from harmonious negotiations to aggressive confrontation. Each insisted that his program was the best, and the debates at times were intense. At almost the last moment, junior Bob Kersten announced his candidacy. He did it with humor, in part to mock what he thought were the overly serious platforms of the other candidates. He proposed to abolish all Student Government offices and set up an oligarchy of himself and his friends. He would take over the *Observer* to guarantee harmony between the paper and his administration. He announced that prices should be raised in the bookstore and that the pass-fail option in classes should be replaced with an A-B option. He favored the recruitment of Yanamamo Indians from southern Brazil and the distribution of scholarships by lottery. He insisted that he was running for office because he "never had any close friends in childhood."[50]

He ran his campaign with humor also. He selected a cat for vice president on his ticket, UnCandidate the Cat. He held press conferences fully dressed sitting in a bathroom stall in his residence hall, and he would occasionally address the crowds from a fourth-floor window in Walsh Hall, reminiscent of Mussolini's harangues sixty years before. At rallies his friend Walt Patulski, an All-American defensive end, would insist he had been a ninety-eight-pound weakling until he met Bob Kersten. Kersten stated that he was not running to be student body president but king; he wore a crown, and would later march into the stadium before football games wearing the crown, with a purple cape, two bodyguards, and often a cigar.[51]

Joke or no joke, he won in a runoff election. He was a premedical student from a well-respected medical family, and he had no interest in spending time with day-to-day student body president duties. He selected another student to be vice president, and a second student to be chief of staff to run his office on a daily basis. He won the approval of his fellow students for his lighthearted antics but he could be serious when needed, showing up on ceremonial occasions and representing the university well. He seemed to many a welcomed break in an overly serious situation.[52]

The majority vote for Bob Kersten indicated that many students had daily concerns higher than regulations about cars, alcohol, and visiting hours in residence halls and what Student Government might do to address them. A small, but for a time growing, number of students had become increasingly concerned with their religious life, and the benefits of the young Pentecostal or Charismatic movement. Although the Pentecostal movement was not young—it was as old as the New Testament—the Catholic Pentecostal movement in the United States apparently had its origin in Pittsburgh in 1966 when several members of the Duquesne University faculty began coming together to deepen their lives of prayer. They realized that their personal efforts, good as they were, were insufficient, and they needed the aid and influence of the Holy Spirit whom Christ promised to send to His Church. They each prayed daily the Sequence of the Mass of Pentecost, "Come Holy Spirit"; they began meeting with Episcopalian and Presbyterian Pentecostals; and a Duquesne theology professor described one of the sessions:[53]

> It ended when we asked to be prayed with for the baptism in the Holy Spirit. They broke up into several groups because they were praying over several people. They simply asked me to make an act of faith for the power of the Spirit to work in me. I prayed in tongues rather quickly. It was not a particularly soaring or spectacular thing at all. I felt a certain

peace—and at least a little prayerful—and truthfully, rather curious as to where all this would lead.

In February 1967, four faculty members had received the Baptism of the Spirit and joined approximately twenty-five students on retreat for what has been called the "Duquesne Weekend." They were inspired to hold an all-night prayer session and the Holy Spirit seemed to touch them all: some spoke in tongues, a few wept in joy, others sang.[54]

At approximately that same time, a graduate of Duquesne pursuing doctoral studies at Notre Dame met with his friends Kevin and Dorothy Ranaghan in South Bend. He explained the movement and the accompanying phenomena to them, but they remained skeptical. A Duquesne professor then visited and, on March 4, attended a prayer meeting with about thirty friends in the Ranaghan home. Intrigued by what they were hearing, nine of these met again the following evening and prayed over each other with the "laying on of hands," but there was no prophesying or speaking in tongues. The Ranaghans have described the experience:[55]

> Only each one can adequately relate what happened to him or her that night. In general, we all experienced and witnessed in one another the breakthrough of the love of Christ in our lives. With this love came the peace and joy, the faith and boldness and all those things we call the fruit of the Holy Spirit.

Regular prayer meetings were scheduled and, although skeptical at first, students and faculty from Notre Dame and Saint Mary's began to attend—priests, sisters, brothers, lay men and women—and they too experienced the same gifts of peace, joy, love, faith, and occasionally prophesy and speaking in tongues. Meetings were held at the Old College building on campus, and on one occasion, forty students from Michigan State University, introduced into the movement by friends at Duquesne, asked to join. The building being too small, the forty Michigan State students and forty Notre Dame students met instead in a large classroom and attended Mass together at the Grotto on this so-called "Michigan State Weekend." As their numbers increased, South Bend businessman Herb True offered them one of his homes for their meetings (True House) and the movement soon had regularly scheduled prayer sessions on campus and in South Bend, where the community became known as the People of Praise.[56]

Although the Charismatic movement probably never numbered more than a hundred adherents on campus, Notre Dame summer sessions helped to spread the movement across the country. Upwards of two hundred students—priests, nuns, lay men and women—attended prayer sessions in the summer of 1967 and carried word of the movement when they returned home. The movement was spreading rapidly, from different sources. In 1969, the Ranaghans estimated the number of Catholic Pentecostals across the nation at five thousand. National Charistmatic Renewal Conferences were held each summer in the early 1970s, and the conference at Notre Dame in 1973 attracted more than 20,000, with the keynote address delivered by Cardinal Leon Suenens of Belgium.[57]

The rise of the Catholic Charismatic Movement was only one indication of the continued interest in religion on campus in the 1970s. In 1976, with financial assistance from the Provost's Office, Professor Jay Dolan of the Department of History established a center to encourage the study of American Catholicism, to sponsor conferences and seminars, to encourage research and award travel grants, to finance publications, and to assist in the collection of pertinent resource materials for the archives and library. It functioned with its own limited university budget until 1981, when the Charles Cushwa family of Youngstown, Ohio, agreed to endow it and it was renamed the Charles and Margaret Cushwa Center for the Study of American Catholicism, eventually one of the country's major centers for American Catholic Church studies.[58]

The major extracurricular interest of the majority of students throughout the 1970s probably remained the fortunes of the football team. The decade had its ups and downs, with the ups clearly in the majority. Ara Parseghian remained as coach until 1975 and his record during those final five years was forty-five wins and seven losses. The 1970 team, with Joe Theismann and Tom Gatewood leading the offense, won ten and lost only to Southern California, 38–28. In the Cotton Bowl against Texas, Parseghian faced the wishbone as he had the year before, but this year he was ready. He devised a "mirror defense," with each linebacker shadowing a Texas back on each play, forcing the Texas offense to commit first and not take advantage of any specific defensive alignment. Notre Dame won 24–11 but the one defeat cost them the national championship.[59] The following year, without Joe Theismann, the offense rarely jelled. With a strong defense, the team won eight games, but they lost to Southern California and Louisiana State and finished out of the top ten for the first time in Parseghian's Notre Dame career. Parseghian's next year was no better: eight victories, losses to Missouri and Southern California, and a humiliating 40 to 6 defeat at the hands of Nebraska and Johnny Rodgers in the Orange Bowl.[60]

Redemption came the following year, however. The offensive line was anchored by Dave Casper, Gerry DiNardo, and Frank Pomarico; the backfield boasted of Tom Clements, Eric Penick, and Wayne Bullock; Luther Bradley roamed the defensive secondary; and the young defensive front four of Ross Browner, Steve Niehaus, Mike Fanning, and Willie Fry would eventually rank with Notre Dame's best. The Irish won all ten regular season games, with only the Michigan State and Southern California contests being close, 14–10 and 23–14. Overall, Notre Dame outscored its opponents 358 to 66. The most memorable game was the victory over Alabama's Crimson Tide coached by Bear Bryant in the Sugar Bowl. Notre Dame gained a 24–23 lead with four minutes to play, but on the succeeding exchange, Notre Dame was backed up near its own goal line. Alabama hoped to force a punt from the end zone, almost certainly giving them a chance for a game-winning field goal. But on third and eight, quarterback Clements dropped back into the end zone and threw a perfect pass to little-used tight end Robin Weber, giving Notre Dame four more downs and an opportunity to run out the clock. Only Dave Casper and Mike Townsend were named All-Americans but the 11–0 record made the team the unanimous choice as national champions.[61] But winning consecutive national championships is always difficult and the 1974 season was especially disappointing for Coach Parseghian. Not only had Casper, Townsend, and Pomarico graduated but four other starters (three future All-Americans) were suspended for violating university regulations. The season started well, with victories in seven of its first eight games, but after that eighth game, a narrow 14–6 victory over Navy, Parseghian let it be known that he was retiring at the end of the year. He had family concerns to consider, the stress of winning each year was taking its toll, and the game was becoming more of a job than fun. The team went on to defeat Pittsburgh and Air Force, and they lost to Southern California, but they defeated Alabama again in the Orange Bowl, 13 to 11. Coach Parseghian's overall record at Notre Dame was 95–17–4, a winning percentage of .836, third behind only Knute Rockne and Frank Leahy.[62]

Father Joyce, Notre Dame's executive vice president and chairman of the Faculty Board in Control of Athletics, had had his eye on Coach Dan Devine since at least 1964, and that attraction increased after Devine's Missouri team upset a highly favored Notre Dame in South Bend in 1972. Born in 1924, Devine, after service in the Army Air Corps, had graduated from the University of Minnesota at Duluth in 1948, coached East Jordan High School in Michigan to two undefeated seasons, and then joined Clarence "Biggie" Munn's staff at Michigan

State in 1950. Michigan State was dominant at the time, defeating Notre Dame three out of four games and winning the national championship in 1952. Devine went to Arizona State College (now University) as head coach in 1955 and in three years compiled an excellent record of 27–3–1. Missouri lured him away in 1958 and, in thirteen years, he won ninety-three, lost thirty-seven, and tied seven, making him the second-winningest coach at the university to that time. Attracted to the challenge of the professional game, he accepted the head coaching position in Green Bay in 1971 but, despite a 10–4 record in 1972, could do no better than 25–27–4 in four seasons. By his final year, both fans and players had lost confidence.[63] His college record, however, remained impressive.

Devine had to rebuild the offense in his first year at Notre Dame. Ernie Hughes and Ken MacAfee anchored an inexperienced line, Tom Clements had graduated, Rick Slager won over young Joe Montana at quarterback, but the defense could still boast of Browner, Niehaus, Bradley, and Fry. The season was moderately successful, with eight victories and losses to Southern California, Michigan State, and Pittsburgh, but it also witnessed the start of Joe Montana's reputation as "The Comeback Kid." With six minutes to play and with Notre Dame losing to North Carolina, Montana replaced Slager, and in five plays and with a two-point conversion pass tied the score. With less than ninety seconds left, Montana noticed his split end with single coverage, called an audible, and, with a short pass, Ted Burgmeier outran the secondary for an eighty-yard winning touchdown.[64] In the final home game of the season, against Georgia Tech, Coach Devine inserted scout-team player Daniel Eugene "Rudy" Ruettiger into the game and he made one tackle. The inspiring story of his life was later told in the movie *Rudy* in 1993.[65]

The 1976 season was more of the same: an 8 and 3 record with Joe Montana out with a shoulder injury and a 20–9 victory over Penn State in the Gator Bowl. Expectations were high the following year and the team surpassed them all. Montana had recovered fully but started the season on the third team. Notre Dame defeated Pittsburgh and Purdue but lost to Mississippi in its first three games; the team did not jell under the starting quarterback; his replacement, Gary Forystek, broke his collarbone; and Montana started against Michigan State. The team went undefeated the rest of the season, donned green jerseys at halftime during the Southern California game, and defeated Texas and Heisman Trophy–winner Earl Campbell in the Cotton Bowl. MacAfee won the Walter Camp Award; Browner the Maxwell and Lombardi Awards; Bradley, Hughes, Bob Golic, Fry, and Burgmeier were All-Americans; and Notre Dame was the unanimous choice as national champions.[66]

The 1978 season was memorable for the way it began and for the way it ended. Notre Dame lost its first two games, the first time since 1963, with one shutout, the first time Notre Dame was shut out since 1965. The next eight games were victories. In the final game against Southern California, Joe Montana brought Notre Dame back from a 24 to 6 deficit to a 25–24 lead with forty-five seconds to play. After an official's controversial call on what Notre Dame claimed was a fumble, Southern California kicked a thirty-five-yard field goal for a 27–25 victory. Despite the loss, Notre Dame was still invited to play Houston in the Cotton Bowl. The weather was terrible, with an icy rain keeping thousands of fans at home, and it may have affected both coaches since both sent out their kicking teams to start the game. The fans that braved the weather witnessed a series of fumbles, interceptions, slips, and incomplete passes, and a Joe Montana suffering from hypothermia. He sipped hot chicken soup at halftime and returned to the field toward the end of the third quarter, with the team behind 34 to 12. He engineered two touchdown drives and passed twice for two-point conversions, bringing the score to 34 to 28. The Notre Dame defense held, taking over the ball with twenty-eight seconds to play, and after a completion and two incompletions, Montana hit Chris Haines in the corner of the end zone with two seconds to go. The drama continued, however, when Notre Dame was called offside on the extra-point attempt, which backed them up five yards, but the second attempt was also true. It was a memorable season, but Joe Montana was left off the All-American team again.[67]

Coach Devine's final two seasons lacked the excitement of the previous two. The 1979 team went 7–4 with the final game a 40 to 15 victory over a Jim Kelly–led Miami team in Tokyo. Before the 1980 season, Devine announced that it would be his last season. With freshman Blair Kiel directing the Irish in most games, the season unfolded with seven consecutive wins before a tie with Georgia Tech, two more victories, and a final loss to Southern California. The Michigan game early in the season provided the most suspense and exhilaration when young Harry Oliver kicked a 51-yard field goal into a fifteen-mile-an-hour wind with four seconds remaining. Before this, his longest had been 38 yards in a junior varsity game. In the Sugar Bowl, Notre Dame outgained Georgia 328 yards to 127, despite the running of Georgia freshman sensation Herschel Walker, and held the Bulldogs to one-of-twelve passing, but Notre Dame still lost 17 to 10. Before the Southern California game, Father Joyce announced the hiring of Gerry Faust, the phenomenally successful coach at Moeller High School in Cincinnati, to succeed Devine. Although Devine lacked the personality and charisma of Parseghian, and he never won fan affection as had his predecessor, his record at Notre Dame was a commendable 53–16–1.[68]

But if Coach Devine's personality at times seemed bland, his counterpart in basketball, Richard "Digger" Phelps, was the opposite, at times over-the-top, loving the limelight, and eager to keep Notre Dame basketball in the limelight.[69] Basketball at Notre Dame had been on a roller-coaster ride in the thirty years since World War II—near the heights one year but in the valley the next. Ed "Moose" Krause coached the team those first five years and, with Kevin O'Shea as a recognized All-American, compiled an acceptable 98–48 record, with impressive victories over Saint Louis and "Easy" Ed McCauley in 1947, over Kentucky with Alex Groza, Ralph Beard, and "Wah-Wah" Jones in 1948, and over NYU and Dolph Schayes that same year. Krause's team was 20–4 in 1946–1947 but only 13–11 in 1950–1951. He took on director of athletics duties in 1949, and he later suggested that one of his smartest moves as director of athletics was to fire himself as basketball coach.[70]

Krause selected alumnus John Jordan as his successor. Like Krause, Jordan put together some good seasons (22 and 3 in 1953–1954 and 24 and 5 in 1957–1958) and some poor ones (9 and 15 in 1955–1956 and 7 and 16 in 1961–1962), compiled an overall record of 199 and 131, and was named Coach of the Year in 1952–1953. In December of his first year, 1951, Jordan started two black Americans, Joe Bertrand and Entee Shine—the first ever to play on a Notre Dame basketball team. With three players ineligible for academic reasons, another injured, and a fifth out on fouls, the coach inserted Johnny Lattner late in the 1952 game against NYU in Madison Square Garden, and the future Heisman Trophy winner scored the winning two points in overtime. Because some top teams were reluctant to play in Notre Dame's small, crowded, noisy fieldhouse, it was difficult to recruit top players (although Dick Rosenthal and Tom Hawkins were legitimate All-Americans), and Coach Jordan announced his retirement at the end of the 1963–1964 season.[71]

As Jordan's successor, Notre Dame chose Johnny Dee, a Notre Dame alumnus and a successful coach at the University of Alabama, the AAU Denver Truckers, and the Kansas City Steers, the last champions of the now-defunct American Basketball League. Dee inherited a solid nucleus in Ron Reed, Jay Miller, Larry Sheffield, and Walt Sahm, but he was an outstanding recruiter himself, attracting the likes of Bob Arnzen, Bob Whitmore, and three blue-chippers from the Washington, DC, area—Austin Carr, Collis Jones, and Sid Catlett. Dee's seven-year record was 116–80, but the period is probably best remembered as "The Era of

Austin Carr." Freshmen were not eligible to play in 1967–1968, but the freshman team with Carr, Jones, and Catlett scrimmaged against the varsity and won seven of eight. Carr averaged 22 points a game in his sophomore year, 38.1 his junior year, and 37.9 his senior year, often when double-teamed. Dee was occasionally accused of running up the score, but Carr was such a magician with a basketball and so fascinating to watch that fans booed when he was taken out. In the 1971 game against UCLA, Coach John Wooden assigned All-American Sidney Wicks to guard him, but Carr still scored 46 in Notre Dame's 89–82 victory. He scored 1,000 points in two different seasons, a feat only Pete Maravich had achieved before him, he was a unanimous All-American his senior year, was named Player of the Year, and was selected first in the NBA draft.[72] Kentucky's Adolph Rupp paid him high tribute:[73]

> The fact that he could go inside or outside and his ability to shoot with either hand is what made him such a great player. . . . We used to put four different men on him during a game, but he was too quick for the big men and had the ability to post the smaller boys down low. When we went to a zone to force him outside, he'd hit those damn 30 footers better than he did the baseline shots. . . . I tried everything to stop Carr but nothing ever worked.

The administration asked Dee to resign after the 1970–1971 season. With the graduation of Carr, Jones, Catlett, and their classmates the immediate future did not look promising and Dee hoped that his assistant, Gene Sullivan, would succeed him. Instead, the administration selected the twenty-nine-year-old Phelps, the Fordham coach for only one year who had upset Notre Dame 94 to 88 that February. His first season was brutal, with a top-flight schedule but few top-flight players. He won 6 and lost 20, with embarrassing losses at Indiana (94 to 29) and UCLA (114 to 56). At the end of the football season, football players Willie and Mike Townsend joined the team, and Willie finished third in scoring. The following year freshmen were eligible for the first time since 1952, the team boasted a six-foot-seven Gary Novak and a six-foot-nine healthy John Shumate, compiled a record of 18 and 12, and lost to Virginia Tech in the NIT finals, 92–91.[74]

The following year, 1973–1974, saw Notre Dame in the national spotlight. The team had a 26–3 record that season, and the centerpiece was the January 15 contest with UCLA. The Bruins, led by everyone's All-American, Bill Walton, were ranked No. 1, Notre Dame was ranked No. 2, and UCLA was riding an 88-game winning streak. UCLA led 43–34 at halftime and 70–59 with 3 minutes and 22 seconds to go. But Notre Dame managed to score the game's final twelve points, with remarkable clutch shooting and thanks to some poor ball handling by the Bruins. With twenty-nine seconds left, Dwight Clay, nicknamed "The Iceman," put Notre Dame ahead from the corner, and UCLA missed its final five attempts. Shumate finally grabbed a rebound and threw it into the air, knowing that time would run out before it came down. Fans stormed the court and the team gathered to cut down the nets, an exercise Coach Phelps had had them practice the day before to give them confidence.[75]

The 1973–1974 season might have marked the end of UCLA's 88-game winning streak but it also marked a beginning at Notre Dame, the beginning of the Adrian Dantley era. In his three years at Notre Dame, the team won 68 and lost 19, and he averaged 25.8 points a game, second only to Austin Carr. Phelps installed his four-corner offense in 1975–1976, with the ball in the hands of either Ray Martin or Dantley, and almost no one could guard either player one-on-one. Dantley would break for the basket and would either make a layup or two free throws. He entered the hardship draft at the end of his junior year, but he returned and earned his degree in the summer of 1978. The year 1976–1977 might be remembered for one of the longest non-baskets in NCAA history. In the last second before the half in the game against Pittsburgh, Billy Paterno took the ball out-of-bounds under the Pitt basket and attempted a full-court pass to Toby Knight to tip in at the opposite end, but the pass swished through the net, not counting because Paterno was out-of-bounds when he threw it. Johnny Dee's recruiting class of 1967 (Carr, Jones, Catlett, John Pleick, Tom Sinnott, Jim Hinga, and Jackie Meehan) may have been Notre Dame's best, but Phelps's class of 1977 had to rank a close second—Kelly Tripucka, Stan Williams, Orlando Woolridge, and Tracy Jackson—and that class compiled a record of 92 and 26. Losing that firepower in 1981–1982, Phelps often elected to play stall-ball since there was no twenty-four-second clock. At one point in a 34–28 loss to Kentucky, Notre Dame made more than two hundred consecutive passes before taking the shot. The games seemed boring to most, opposing fans booed, and a television executive, justifying his decision not to televise the Notre Dame–Michigan game, called it a "worthless game between two worthless teams." But after that disappointing 10–17 season, prospects improved. John Paxson still had a final year in 1982–1983, David Rivers arrived the following year, and LaPhonso Ellis in 1988. In Phelps's final eight years, his teams compiled a record of 152 and 86, went to the NCAA tournament six times, and went to the NIT once.[76]

Sports writer Jim Murray once suggested that Phelps "did for Notre Dame basketball what Rockne did for football."[77] It was clearly an exaggeration since, thanks especially to Austin Carr, Notre Dame was already a popular national power when Phelps arrived. But when he retired in the spring of 1991, he could certainly look back on his twenty years with pride. He had compiled an overall record of 393–197, for a winning percentage of .666, all the more commendable considering he was 24–32 in his first two years with the players he inherited. He could count fourteen 20-win seasons, he defeated seven teams ranked number 1 at the time Notre Dame played them, and, most laudably, he saw every one of his four-year students receive his degree.[78]

If the basketball and football teams experienced periods of both success and disappointment throughout the 1970s, so did the university's striving for academic excellence. Father Hesburgh had created the office of provost, and had recommended Father James Burtchaell, with a twofold purpose. One was to put another administrator between himself and some of the unrest on campus. When students were dissatisfied with an Office of Student Affairs decision, the matter was immediately appealed to the president. If a Mass was to be offered or a speech to be delivered on the Vietnam War, organizers immediately asked Father Hesburgh to do so. His door was always open and any student knew he or she could walk through it with whatever issue he or she happened to have. It was taking too much time, and if Father Hesburgh made a mistake, it was made at the highest level. He once confided to an interviewer: "It was an agony. I remember getting up every morning with a knot in my stomach, and saying 'What are they going to do today?' and then 'What am I going to do?' You never knew the answer to either of these, so you went through day-by-day. . . . I think I had a perpetual knot for about three or four years. You were always under pressure."[79] He needed someone who could share the responsibility. But he also needed someone who could continue the goal of creating a great Catholic university, an institution of higher learning on the academic level of the most respected institutions in the country, and an institution that was thoroughly Catholic—in its mission, in its classrooms, in its faculty, and in its students. In Father Burtchaell he hoped he had that man.

Father Burtchaell was more than willing to take some of the spotlight, and some of the responsibility, from Father Hesburgh. Unlike Father Joyce, he enjoyed the attention. While Father Hesburgh drove a Ford, Father Burtchaell drove a Mercedes, and while most priests in the administration wore black suits and Roman collars, Father Burtchaell was seen more often in blue or brown suits and a bow tie. He openly criticized Pope Paul VI's encyclical on birth control, *Humanae Vitae*, declaring that on the issues of ecclesiastical authority and contraception the encyclical was "grossly inadequate and largely fallacious." He questioned the pope's distinction between what is natural and what is artificial—why the rhythm method with its tapes and tubes and thermometers was natural while methods of biochemical control were unnatural. What the pope must not do, he added, "is attempt to bring closure on a discussion which he cannot successfully bring to conclusion."[80] More directly concerned with academic life, he spoke out against the government's affirmative action policies, insisting that sufficient numbers of women and minorities were not available for hiring:[81]

> The recent Carnegie Council study, soon to be published, indicates that there is no significant supply of qualified women or ethnic minorities unsuccessfully seeking appointments at colleges and universities. . . . I would venture to suggest that if affirmative action plans of all the colleges and universities in this country were put beside one another, and their goals added up, the sum of them would ludicrously exceed the possible supply of women and minorities . . . in the various fields.

The solution, he suggested, was for the government to provide more fellowships and other financial aid for these groups.

In the area of student affairs, Father Burtchaell strongly supported *in loco parentis*, the concept that the university could and should oversee student life, pass regulations, and even penalize violations. He insisted that individual student halls could not make their own regulations since there needed to be uniformity across campus, that a university needed campus order to accomplish its goals, and if students declined to enforce regulations (which they had not made), the university administration itself had no choice but to enforce them.[82] In his formal speeches and informal conversations, Father Burtchaell could speak with supreme confidence and self-assurance. A friend once stated that he "wished he was as sure of anything as Father Burtchaell seemed of everything."[83] If Father Hesburgh was willing on occasion to step out of the spotlight, Father Burtchaell was clearly willing to step into it.

Father Burtchaell's self-assurance and his willingness, even eagerness, to lead, often led to conflict with faculty or students, or both, although over time most of his decisions seemed correct. An early disagreement resulted from his effort to revise the academic calendar. Father Burtchaell objected to the tradition of beginning the school year after Labor Day and terminating that first semester in mid-January, approximately two weeks after Christmas vacation. He considered those two weeks in January poorly used, preparing for final examinations chiefly by reviewing what the students had unfortunately forgotten over Christmas break. Father Burtchaell recommended that classes for the fall semester of 1973 begin in late August and terminate before Christmas, with a week's break for Thanksgiving, but the Academic Council rejected this, preferring a post–Labor Day start, termination before Christmas, and no extended break within. In fact, classes could not have begun earlier that fall because a mobile home show, scheduled for late August, was occupying necessary campus facilities. The following year, 1974–1975, did provide for a pre–Labor Day start for classes, a midterm break, and a pre-Christmas end of the semester. Minor alterations were made throughout the year—for example, adding a day to Easter break so that students would not have to travel back to campus on Easter itself.[84]

Having experienced the pre–Labor Day start in the fall of 1974, the Faculty Senate spoke out against it and against the fact that the senate had had no part in determining it. The major objection was the difficulty it posed for faculty with children on that final Labor Day holiday weekend of the summer. Even Father Burtchaell was concerned that the schedule did not include a full seventy-two days of class, and as a result the Academic Council in early 1975 voted to return to a post–Labor Day start. That did not satisfy either. In fact, 92 percent of three thousand students surveyed that fall claimed they favored the pre–Labor Day start, although ten months before 74 percent had voted the opposite. The pre–Labor Day start was then approved again by the Academic Council, but to reach a satisfactory number of days, classes were scheduled for the Friday after Thanksgiving. In the realization that most students would probably remain home the whole Thanksgiving weekend, that Friday was changed to a free day and the registrar was charged with adding one Saturday to any fall semester with too few class days. To the comment that "no calendar was going to please everyone," a student rejoined that "every calendar should please at least someone."[85] The "Burtchaell calendar" was ultimately accepted and survived the test of time.

The Teacher-Course Evaluations (TCEs) proved another source of disagreement between the Provost's Office and the faculty. They were introduced into the College of Arts and Letters in 1968 as a way for students to evaluate the classes they were taking and their professors. Each professor might learn which texts he or she assigned seemed most satisfactory and which teaching methods most effective. In 1970, Father Burtchaell extended the practice to the other colleges as well.

In the beginning, only the individual professors, the department chairs, and the college deans were given summaries of these evaluations, but Father Burtchaell eventually requested that these summaries be sent to the Provost's Office also, to be considered in the final decisions to retain, promote, or tenure a faculty member. Some faculty feared that the TCEs could be given too much weight in denying tenure—Was a student truly competent to evaluate a textbook if it was the only one he or she had ever seen?—but the major criticism was that it had been decided by the Provost's Office without consultation with the faculty.[86]

A similar disagreement arose over the scheduling of departmental and other examinations. Some departments, and individual professors if they were offering multiple sections of the same course, scheduled examinations for the evening hours in order to give the same exam to all and not interfere with other class times. Father Burtchaell opposed evening examinations because they deprived students of concerts and lectures and other evening events. Father Burtchaell decided that, beginning in the fall of 1976, no classes would be scheduled between 8:00 and 9:30 on Tuesday and Thursday mornings, and departmental and other examinations could be scheduled at those times. The Faculty Senate opposed the directive, insisting that each department or each professor could better decide what was best educationally for his or her classes. Eventually the Academic Council voted with Father Burtchaell, 30 to 19, to eliminate the evening examinations, although 53 percent of the students seemed to favor them.[87]

Father Burtchaell also saw a need to make individual academic departments more efficient and productive. In early 1972 he spoke before the local chapter of the American Association of University Professors (AAUP) and announced that an effective department should have between one-half to two-thirds of its members tenured—that is, generally on the associate or full professor level. In some departments, this figure was exceeded. Tenure, he insisted, was good and necessary since it protected academic freedom and prevented dismissal of a professor for espousing an unpopular stand. That percentage of one-half to two-thirds was needed to provide stability in a department, he said, but if a higher percentage were tenured, it prevented new hires, new ideas coming into the department, and the ability to adjust teaching to changing student needs.[88]

The provost was also concerned that the teaching loads of a number of faculty had wandered from the norm over the years. He considered the basic teaching load to be twelve hours per week, although that would be reduced to nine if the faculty member was involved in research, as he presumed almost all should be. If a member's research activity required a further reduction in teaching, a subvention from an outside source should be sought to cover part of the salary. But in early 1972, he discovered that 68 members of the faculty were teaching only three hours, another 40 only four or five hours, and another 152 only six hours, making a total of 260 faculty members teaching six hours or less. He noted that this was not fair to colleagues since at times it was necessary to hire new professors to teach the required classes, leaving less money available for faculty raises.[89]

Father Burtchaell was clearly shaping academic life more and more from the Provost's Office, often without consultation of the faculty, but in one area he desired more consultation. In arriving at final decisions on renewal, promotion, and tenure, the provost and the president relied heavily on the departmental Committees on Appointments and Promotions (CAPs), the college deans, and student evaluations, but in 1977 Father Burtchaell created another board of advisors, the Provost's Advisory Committee (which included six appointed faculty members), to meet with the deans and the provost and deliberate with them. That year he asked the deans and the appointed faculty members to vote separately on each case, the two agreed on all but three cases, and Father Burtchaell followed the recommendation of the faculty in all three cases.[90] The Provost's Advisory Committee became a permanent fixture in the university administration.

There can be little doubt that the faculty standards were raised during Father Burtchaell's tenure as provost. He was convinced that the faculty had grown too fast in preceding decades and, with regulated teaching loads, rapid growth need not continue. The regular faculty numbered 774 in 1970–1971 and grew to only 795 seven years later. But it did improve in quality. The percentage of the faculty with doctoral degrees increased from approximately 67 percent in 1972–1973 to close to 77 percent in 1977–1978. Many of those retiring had been hired in the 1930s and 1940s without terminal degrees, but almost all new hires had them.[91]

The faculty was also upgraded through the creation of endowed chairs. These were faculty positions held by especially distinguished scholars whose salaries came from endowed gifts and not from the annual operating budget, leaving more money for regular faculty raises. The first five endowed chairs were announced in 1971, one for each college—Science (Biology Department), Engineering (Electrical Engineering Department), Arts and Letters (Philosophy Department), Business Administration, and Law. When an endowed chair was assigned to a department, the department itself usually had the option of awarding it to one of its own distinguished members or recruiting a scholar from elsewhere. Each of these first chairs was endowed at $800,000, and within six years the university could boast of eighteen, although not all of them had been filled.[92]

One area of academic life that Father Burtchaell strove to improve, but with only limited success, was faculty compensation. Notre Dame salaries had lagged behind those of other universities for years, and Father Burtchaell admitted as much. In 1972 he noted that, although faculty salaries had risen steadily over the preceding decade, they still remained below those of comparable or "peer" universities. Of those, Notre Dame's salaries surpassed those of one school but lagged behind those of Emory, Pittsburgh, Southern California, Iowa, Vanderbilt, Indiana, Duke, Cornell, and Northwestern. Furthermore, the provost was not optimistic. The creation of endowed chairs would release some money in the operating budget for faculty raises, but the university was also contending with rising fuel costs, new computer expenses, recently mandated unemployment compensation contributions, additional coeducation costs, and overall inflation. The Faculty Senate asked that any new monies be devoted to faculty raises rather than the endowment, but Father Jerome Wilson, vice president of business affairs, countered that the present endowment of $72 million should be five or six times as large for an operating budget of Notre Dame's size. The administration was able to channel an additional $300,000 into faculty raises in 1974, and it added $300 to every faculty salary the following year, but that was not sufficient. According to the AAUP, Notre Dame's median salaries in 1974–1975 were $1,400 below Big Ten schools and $600 below the "peer" group; in 1975–1976 they were $1,600 below the Big Ten and $800 below the "peers," and in 1976–1977, Father Burtchaell's last year as provost, they were $1,700 behind the Big Ten and still $760 behind the "peers." For all their efforts, it was a challenge Father Hesburgh and Father Burtchaell could not meet.[93]

Father Burtchaell's most significant contribution to the university was undoubtedly his leadership in the overall advancement of its academic life, but a close second must be his leadership and direction on the Committee on University Priorities. Appointed by Father Hesburgh in September 1972, it was at first a twelve-member committee, all male and with no members from student affairs, and after a minor protest from the two women rectors, Father James Flanigan, associate vice president of student affairs, and Sister Madonna Kolbenschlag, assistant professor of American studies, were added. The committee was charged "to study the present and, especially, the future of Notre Dame, in an effort to determine what are the most important and indispensable elements of our total mission, the most essential as contrasted with that which might have seemed desirable under other circumstances." The committee met thirty times in plenary session, and also appointed four task forces to study four major areas of university life—academic disciplines, research and instruction, enrollment, and physical facilities—and incorporated many of their findings in their final report.[94]

The first section of the report was appropriately devoted to Catholic character. "The University's highest and also its most distinctive priority," it began, "is to understand and to adhere to its evolving Catholic character."[95] The report then spelled out how this was to be achieved, recommending:[96]

That the University continue its traditional commitment to freedom of inquiry and thought. The Catholic university should be especially open to all truth and to every human insight, more, even, than other universities. . . .

That the University have a faculty and a student affairs staff among whom committed Catholics predominate. . . .

That appointment to the faculty and staff continue to be offered by preference to competent members of the Congregation of Holy Cross, whose contribution to the University is a special guarantee of its Catholic character.

In the area of finances, the university's annual operating budget had grown since 1946 from $4 million to $54 million, and its endowment from $4 million to $73 million. Despite these successes, the future was not rosy. The federal government had cut its educational support, student protests had made universities less attractive to donors, the 1969 Tax Reform Act reduced some benefits to benefactors, and many foundations were shifting their support to urban problems and the plight of minorities. With the financial future thus uncertain, the report recommended that the "endowment have the highest priority. Gift income, unless otherwise restricted, should be allocated to the endowment, upon which the future of the University depends." The report also recommended that new programs be undertaken "only if they are central to Notre Dame's purpose and identity"; that "student tuition, room, board and other fees be related to the University's fiscal needs but that the University continually monitor increases to insure that continued rises do not drastically affect the character of the student body"; that present physical facilities be well maintained since future building might be limited; and that "a Budget Review Committee, representative of the whole University" should be appointed.[97]

Turning to enrollment, the report recommended that the present student population of approximately 6,600 be maintained into the future. An increase would be costly in adding faculty and new residence halls, and a decrease would create a deficit since maintenance costs could not be similarly reduced. The committee did recommend, however, that the percentage of women and minority groups be increased, that the co-exchange program with Saint Mary's be continued, that more women be hired in administrative and faculty positions, and that enrollment in the College of Science and Engineering be maintained to guarantee quality education.[98]

Almost four-fifths of the student body lived on campus and the committee thus addressed the question of residentiality:[99]

> Education at Notre Dame takes place in and out of classrooms and laboratories, and the University encourages students to develop into complete Christians. The University offers many encouragements to the practice of Christianity, but the opportunity is especially found in the residence halls, through the conversation, moral guidance and example of peers and the hall staff.

The committee further recommended "steps to eliminate overcrowding and to make life in the halls more congenial . . . [and] exploration of specific ways of enhancing the intellectual role of the rector," programs "to meet the special needs of off-campus students," . . . and "residence facilities for advanced students, unmarried and married."

In the area of academic disciplines, the report urged continued support for strong departments and the upgrading of weaker ones, more interdisciplinary teaching and research, and increased international education and foreign study programs. "Also," it stated, "in the light of Notre Dame's character as an independent Catholic University transcending merely parochial or national interests, special priority should be given to those programs which seek understanding of Third World and non-Western peoples, especially those wounded by poverty."[100]

The committee acknowledged that teaching and research constituted the primary functions of a university but lamented that the system had developed few means to evaluate teaching. Universities educate future teachers in graduate classes but the emphasis is on developing research skills rather than classroom techniques. The report encouraged the university to institute ways to support good teachers and assist others to become good teachers, and to revise evaluation processes to recognize teaching competence better in promotion and tenure decisions. But the report also admitted that without research an institution was a college and not a university. "Research," it stated, "is concerned with the enlargement of knowledge, art and understanding through the discovery of what was previously unknown, the invention of what previously did not exist and the development through synthesis of insights, models or theories for better understanding of what is known." Research was not only essential but also expensive, and it was recommended that the university should seek additional ways of assisting researchers in locating outside financial support.[101]

The discussion of research flowed smoothly into the consideration of advanced studies. On the bright side, student aid was extensive. The university remitted tuition for 70 percent of all graduate students and offered stipends to 40 percent. Outside aid provided tuition remission and stipends for another 20 percent. On the less bright side, stipends started at a comparatively low $2,400, prospects for increasing this significantly seemed slim, and graduate enrollment had shown a slight decline over the past five years. Weaker graduate programs needed to be strengthened or (only as a very last resort) eliminated. The report recommended that "within the next five years, every unit in Advanced Studies should do a self-study, according to a schedule set up by the vice president for Advanced Studies. This will be followed by a thorough review performed by an outside board reporting to the vice president and to the dean of the appropriate college . . . [and] a task force on the Summer Session . . . constituted in order to draw up a realistic, innovative, ten-year plan."[102]

The final section included the library and auxiliary enterprises. The library needed serious attention: "Among the 84 academic libraries belonging to the Association of Research Libraries (ARL) our library's rank is so low that the possibility of losing ARL membership is real." The most recent annual book budget of $512,000 was only $12,000 above the minimum needed for ARL membership. The recommendations that the university both find ways to increase the library budget and undertake a study to assure that the budget was being well spent caused no surprise.[103]

Turning to other enterprises, the report urged the continuation of intercollegiate athletics:[104]

> Because of our national prominence and religious character, we have been for half a century in a unique position to be a leader in the ethics of organized sport. We should continue to work against any exploitation of athletes; to guard against the danger of brutalizing participants and spectators; to remember athletics are only a *part* of our total endeavor; to adhere scrupulously to, and even surpass, the ethical norms of the Na-

tional Collegiate Athletic Association; to push vigorously for equal participation of women in all athletics; finally, to do all this without isolating either player or coach from the University as a whole.

The physical plant had expanded rapidly during the last two decades but the building boom had to halt. Such monies were not available and an increased endowment held higher priority. Still, several buildings needed renovation—the Main Building, the power plant, the bookstore, the former biology building, LaFortune Student Center, and the old Institute of Technology—and enlarged facilities were needed for chemical research, the fine arts, faculty offices, engineering research, classroom instruction, laboratory teaching, and the art gallery.[105] Computing was a special concern since, although not every student or faculty member needed a computer at the time, the future was uncertain and computing was highly expensive. The university housed an IBM 370-158 computer and some forty-five terminals across the campus, and the report recommended that an outside team be recruited to advise the university on future needs and directions.[106] The report also recommended an expansion of audio-visual education across campus and praised the scholarly journals the university published, but it requested that an editorial board be appointed for the University of Notre Dame Press to improve its focus and the quality of the books published.[107]

The report concluded with a summary of its ten strongest recommendations:[108]

1. That the university continue its commitment to freedom of inquiry and thought.
2. That committed Catholics predominate on the faculty and student affairs staff.
3. That the endowment enjoy highest priority in the allocation of unrestricted income.
4. That the university continue to support good teachers and assist others to become such.
5. That the university allocate resources to increase excellence in all disciplines.
6. That the library book budget be increased.
7. That graduate education be improved and a self-study of advanced studies be undertaken.
8. That overcrowding in the residence halls be reduced and the intellectual role of the rector be enhanced.

9. That an outside committee of consultants be utilized to advise on computer needs and direction.
10. That the university undertake long-range planning for physical plant and facilities needs.

Notre Dame was scheduled for its ten-year accreditation review the following year by the North Central Association of Colleges and Secondary Schools, and the ten-member evaluation team's report was positive overall. Some areas of concern were noted, and the university's renewed accreditation was unanimously recommended. The visiting team felt that the new governance structure did not lessen the Catholic character of the university, and it was "favorably impressed with the Catholic dedication, alertness, thoughtfulness and all-around capability of the Board of Trustees." The recent move to coeducation was also a success: "Present female undergraduates seem to be quite euphoric about Notre Dame, considering it a special honor to be enrolled there. And they have been well accepted." The university still needed more women in administrative positions and among the tenured faculty, however. The faculty was dedicated and accomplished, but it had concerns. The members sought more input in academic decision-making, they felt their salaries were lower than salaries at comparable universities, they questioned the limited percentage of tenured faculty permitted in any department, and non-Catholic members seemed nervous over the renewed emphasis on the institution's Catholic mission. The university's central administration was given high praise, as was the university's financial management and investment strategy, and the new library had "splendid potential" but its holdings were deficient in some areas. Admitting that athletics are "a bright spot in the Notre Dame picture," the report noted that "athletes are students first, members of the Notre Dame community second, and athletes third." Overall Notre Dame impressed the North Central evaluation team "as an institution with a clear and strong sense of purpose, outstanding leadership, academic and financial strength, high morale, and a strong sense of community."[109]

The year following Notre Dame's accreditation review, Father Burtchaell was due for his own formal five-year review as provost. The *Academic Manual* stated that the provost was elected by the board of trustees for an indefinite period but was "subject to formal review every five years."[110] At its first meeting of the 1975–1976 year, the Academic Council elected a six-member committee to review the provost, and the committee met eighteen times in the spring of 1976. It interviewed the provost himself, twelve other administrators, members of the faculty, several student representatives, and it received approximately seventy written responses from other faculty. The final report was submitted to the president and only he and the chairman of the board of trustees had access to it. The report unanimously recommended that Father Burtchaell continue in office as provost, Father Hesburgh discussed it with the board of trustees at the board meeting in November 1976, and the board voted to have Father Burtchaell continue as provost.[111]

Despite this commendation from the review committee and his reelection by the board of trustees, Father Burtchaell surprisingly announced his resignation from the Office of the Provost on August 28, 1977.[112] Criticisms of his administrative style had certainly been building—his lack of consultation with faculty before initiating changes in the academic calendar, before inaugurating wider use of the Teacher-Course Evaluations, before eliminating evening examinations, before assigning new faculty positions to individual departments, and, in general, centralizing more authority and initiative in the Office of the Provost. The discontent was sufficiently deep that the faculty began considering the possibility of unionization as a remedy, and in the spring of 1977, 34 percent of the faculty wanted the local AAUP to move toward a vote to determine if a majority favored collective bargaining. Most faculty probably opposed unionization at the time but even the discussion indicated the depth of the discontent. Earlier, fearing that Father Burtchaell might be the heir apparent, the Faculty Senate had even voted to ask the trustees to drop the provision that the university president had to be a Holy Cross priest.[113] It is possible that the board of trustees wanted Father Burtchaell to continue as provost but also decided that he was not to be Father Hesburgh's successor, and the confidential report of the Provost Review Committee may have recommended the same. Learning of the board's negative feelings about his future advancement, Father Burtchaell may have decided to return to teaching. Someone remarked, "Jim is not a lame duck kind of person." Said another: "The resignation is a sign that he won't be it, the position was created as a testing ground for the presidency. Obviously he lost out."[114]

Father Hesburgh had only praise for Father Burtchaell's work and accomplishments as Notre Dame's provost and chief academic officer:[115]

It is difficult to find words adequate to thank Father Burtchaell . . . for [his] seven years of superlative service. . . . He has set a standard of service that will be difficult, if not impossible, to match.

Under Father Burtchaell, the provost's office has been characterized by a style that reflected his high intelligence, broad vision and constantly courageous dedication to academic excellence. He has attracted many talented scholars to Notre Dame, and has inaugurated new academic programs and procedures to better the University for many years yet to come. In particular, he has been actively engaged both in the current improvement of faculty salaries and in the amassing of permanent endowment to assure continuing progress in faculty compensation.

In creating the Office of the Provost, Father Hesburgh had envisioned a close associate who could relieve some of the responsibility and stress engulfing him in that difficult decade, and also carry on, and even strengthen, steps toward true academic excellence, and for seven rather turbulent years Father Burtchaell had eagerly undertaken and accomplished both commissions.

CHAPTER 18

The 1980s

Father Hesburgh's Homestretch

With the sudden and unexpected resignation of Father Burtchaell as provost, Father Ferdinand Brown, the associate provost, was named acting provost until a more permanent successor could be found. As required by the *Academic Manual*, the Academic Council met and elected a search committee "charged with recommending to the President of the University candidates who could assume the office of Provost."[1] The committee elected Professor Timothy O'Meara of the Department of Mathematics as chairman and took out an announcement in the *Chronicle of Higher Education*, asking applicants to submit curricula vitae by December 8, 1977. The committee narrowed the list of submissions to eight and invited each candidate to campus for a two-day visit. Each candidate met with the search committee twice, with deans, faculty members, students, and the president, and the committee then submitted its own evaluations to the president. Father Hesburgh was grateful for the committee's work but was convinced that there were equally or better qualified candidates among Notre Dame's own faculty, and urged Professor O'Meara to allow his name to go forward. The committee approved and Father Hesburgh then selected Professor O'Meara as the university's second provost.[2]

Timothy O'Meara was born in Cape Town, South Africa, on January 29, 1928, one of five children of an Italian mother and Irish father, and he described himself at times as "half Irish, half Italian, all South African." He received his early education from Irish Christian Brothers, a bachelor's degree in science from the University of Cape Town in 1947, and a master of science degree in the following year. He taught for one year at the University of Natal and then earned his doctorate in mathematics from Princeton University in 1953, studying principally under Professor Emil Artin, an émigré professor who had taught at Notre Dame in 1939. After teaching at the University of Otago in New Zealand for three years, O'Meara returned to Princeton in 1957 as a member of both the Department of Mathematics and the Institute for Advanced Study. Encouraged by Marston Morse, a professor at the Institute for Advanced Study and Father Hesburgh's Vatican associate at the Atoms for Peace Conference, O'Meara accepted Father Hesburgh's invitation to join the Notre Dame faculty as professor of mathematics in 1962. He served as the department's director of graduate studies, chaired the department from 1968 to 1972, was named Howard J. Kenna Professor of Mathematics in 1976, and became an American citizen in 1977. He served as visiting professor at the California Institute of Technology in 1967–1968 and at the University of California at Santa Barbara in 1976, as Carl Friedrich Gauss Professor at the Göttingen Academy of Sciences and Humanities in 1978, and as visiting scientist at the University of Toronto that same year. O'Meara asked that his appointment as provost be for four years since the presumption was that, upon reaching the age of sixty-five in 1982, Father Hesburgh would retire after thirty years as Notre Dame's president.[3]

O'Meara proved an excellent choice. An internationally respected mathematician for his work in number theory, linear groups, and quadratic forms, his scholarly articles had appeared in mainline professional journals, accrediting agencies called on him to review college and university mathematics departments, and he served frequently as evaluator of grant proposals for the National Science Foundation. He agreed wholeheartedly with Father Hesburgh's goal of making Notre Dame a truly great university, and a Catholic one, and when he insisted on continued high scholarly standards in departmental promotion and tenure decisions, colleagues knew he had long practiced what he advocated. On the Notre Dame faculty for sixteen years, he knew department needs and challenges well and understood faculty criticisms of the administration over salaries and university governance, but his leadership style was much less confrontational than Father Burtchaell's. O'Meara prepared well for meetings and appointments, familiarized himself with objections before they were raised, and presented his replies step-by-step, similar to mathematical proofs. Father Hesburgh could talk around a subject at times but O'Meara was a man of fewer but well-chosen words. His policies did not veer far from Father Burtchaell's but the faculty accepted them more favorably. If there was any gap in his preparation for his new position, it was his lack of close familiarity with the area of student affairs, an area the Office of the Provost also oversaw. He was undoubtedly interested—life outside the classroom affected success inside the classroom, and O'Meara's own children were Notre Dame students—but, unlike Father Burtchaell, he had never lived in a student residence hall nor had he been elected to student life committees. But he had a fine associate in the vice president of student affairs, Father John VanWolvlear. Father Van, as he was affectionately called, had had several years' experience in student life at Notre Dame and the University of Portland, was a classmate of Father Joyce, was outgoing with an attractive personality, and Provost O'Meara rarely felt obliged to overturn a decision. Like Father Burtchaell before him, Provost O'Meara did not hesitate to make decisions in academic and even student affairs, and thus relieved Father Hesburgh of some of his burdens and responsibilities, precisely what Father Hesburgh desired in the position.

Five months after O'Meara's appointment, on October 9, 1978, Father Hesburgh delivered his annual address to the faculty in Washington Hall and met with the Faculty Senate that evening to respond to questions. Notre Dame's goal, he insisted, was still to be one of the top universities in the country, and to achieve this, the university's higher administration, including deans and a few trustees, had met for four days that summer at the university's secluded retreat in northern Wisconsin to plan for the immediate future. A major challenge was the rising inflation. Grace and Flanner Halls together had cost $6.5 million in 1969 but they would cost more than twice that in 1978. Fuel costs jumped approximately $4 million per year, Blue Cross Blue Shield insurance costs rose 10 percent, and he characterized increases in Social Security contributions as "monumental." On the positive side, the Congregation of Holy Cross had contributed close to $8 million to the university over the last ten years, and the recent $130 million "Campaign for Notre Dame" had been successful. Father Hesburgh suggested that the university probably had too many committees and that some could be eliminated "if all administrators worked harder." He raised the question of a possible moratorium on additional courses, that students might be carrying too many, and that it might be better educationally to delve more deeply and devote more time to fewer classes. When questioned about faculty salaries, he noted that they had increased 24 percent over the preceding three years, much higher than the average nationally, and he hoped to reach the AAUP's number 1 ranking within five years.

He admitted that the university had not met its earlier affirmative action goals of eighty-nine women and seventy-nine minority faculty members, numbering at the time (in October 1978) eighty-five women and only forty-seven minority teachers. Criteria for promotion and tenure, he insisted, had not changed, although teaching and research were weighted more heavily than service. In the matter of student participation in university governance, he favored student membership on the Academic Council, the college councils, the curriculum committee, and the Campus Life Council, but not on hiring or promotion committees, trustees committees, or judicial committees with authority of expulsion. Future construction priorities, he outlined, were an office building for Arts and Letters faculty, an engineering building, a chemistry building, and a women's residence hall if the university desired to enroll an additional five hundred women. In all the planning, the goal remained the same: to make Notre Dame a truly great Catholic university, with an excellent faculty, an excellent student body, and excellent academic facilities.[4]

Unfortunately, in the midst of this early planning for the future, Father Hesburgh and Provost O'Meara had also to turn their attention to two pressing lawsuits.

A professor of chemistry who had received his bachelor of science degree in 1933, a master of science in 1934, and a PhD in organic chemistry in 1936, all from Notre Dame, had joined the Notre Dame faculty in 1951 as assistant professor in the General Program of Liberal Studies, and was promoted to associate professor in the Department of Chemistry in 1956.[5] When he reached the age of sixty-five in the spring of 1977, he was notified that he would be retired, according to the provision of the *Faculty Handbook*: "a member of the faculty ordinarily retires and becomes emeritus on the first day of July following his sixty-fifth birthday. . . . When a member is permitted to continue in active service beyond the date prescribed for retirement, service beyond that date will be on the basis of a year-to-year appointment."[6] The chairman of the Chemistry Department defended the retirement procedure since it allowed for younger scholars with newer ideas to be recruited continually into the department, but the professor challenged the decision in court.

The case was transferred to Knox, Indiana, in Stark County, away from South Bend and Notre Dame, and the professor's lawyers made three strong points: that the university did not actually have a mandatory retirement policy since twenty-seven of the most recent eighty-one members reaching the age of sixty-five had continued full-time employment, that the university did not have a clear and consistent procedure for handling reappointment requests, and that the university's procedures actually violated the Fourteenth Amendment's requirement of due process of law. The university responded that faculty members "ordinarily" did retire at age sixty-five but that exceptions could be made in individual circumstances. It added that, although the university did not have *written* guidelines for requesting reappointment outside the *Faculty Handbook*, the professor had followed the university's normal procedure in his petition. Finally, his petition was considered in the usual and accepted manner by the departmental committee on appointments and promotions, the dean of the college, the Office of the Provost, and the university president. There was no lack of due process. The judge ultimately decided in the university's favor, stating that the university did have "a uniform policy for ending contracts," that the university could retire faculty at age sixty-five, and that the university had followed the provisions of the *Faculty Handbook* in this case. The professor was also charged the court costs and, since he did not receive any financial support from the American Civil Liberties Union or the American Association of Retired Persons, he decided not to appeal.[7]

A second suit was especially embarrassing since it involved charges of sex discrimination just at the time when the university was making its first efforts to become a fully coeducational institution. An assistant professor in the Department of English claimed that she had been denied promotion to associate professor and tenure because she was a woman, and an associate professor in the Department of Theology filed suit that she had been denied promotion to full professor for the same reason. They were filed as class action suits, although 62 of the eligible 130 present and former nontenured faculty women eventually opted out of the first suit, and 4 of the 6 eligible tenured women opted out of the second. As Father Hesburgh had admitted, and lamented, the university was not meeting its early affirmative action goals. In 1978–1979, for example, the College of Arts and Letters had hired as new faculty twenty-two men and eight women, the College of Business eight men and zero women, the College of Engineering ten men and one woman, and the College of Science twenty-two men and two women. After several hearings before District Court Judge Allen Sharp, much maneuvering, and much negative publicity, the administration on July 31, 1981, decided to settle out of court.[8] According to the agreement:[9]

1. There was no determination that the university had violated any law or regulation on discrimination (and the university denied any such violation).

2. The assistant professor in the English Department would be promoted to associate professor with tenure and receive back pay from September 1, 1980.
3. The associate professor in the Theology Department would be promoted to full professor and receive back pay from September 1, 1980.
4. Notre Dame agreed to pay "a reasonable amount" of the plaintiffs' legal fees.
5. Notre Dame also agreed to make good faith efforts to renew, promote, and tenure women at the same rate as men.
6. An appeals committee, consisting of Professors David Leege and Charles Wilber of Notre Dame and Sister Ann Ida Gannon of Mundelein College in Chicago, was established to hear discrimination cases of any others in the suits.
7. A second appeals procedure would be established to hear any future cases.
8. The university would file an affirmative action report with the EEOC annually for at least the next three years.

The settlement was not popular with many. The professor in the Theology Department had been denied promotion three times by her department, and the professor in the English Department had been denied promotion four times. Upon receiving news of the settlement, several members of the English Department's Committee on Appointments and Promotions resigned from the committee. One member said: "I don't like the way they handled it. Giving her tenure after she was turned down by four committees, by the dean four times, and by the provost four times undermines the Committee. . . . I feel, and other people feel, that there is no merit to the case. I don't like being called unfair and unjust. That's what the University giving her back to us is saying."[10] The administration agreed to the settlement in the summer of 1981, and soon after the opening of the new school year that fall, Provost O'Meara explained the administration's reasoning in a letter to the faculty:[11]

1. There was no admission or determination of discrimination.
2. The outcome of any such class action discrimination suit was always uncertain.
3. There would have been disruption of academic life and divisiveness on campus had the suit been allowed to continue.

4. If the case proceeded, confidential letters and information would have become public.
5. The university wanted to avoid anything like a recent court consent decree involving the University of Minnesota:
   a. A quota for women was set there for the Department of Chemistry.
   b. There was to be automatic preference for women across the whole university.
   c. A master of the court would have jurisdiction over all discrimination claims until 1989.
6. The heightened publicity of the court case would have deterred women from applying to Notre Dame, the opposite of what the university was seeking.

Controversial though it was, it was a decision the administration felt it had to make.[12]

The challenging lawsuits may have garnered the most publicity in the first years of the new decade, but two other occurrences had, or could have had, equal notice. The first was the intention of Father Hesburgh in 1982, at the age of sixty-five and after thirty sometimes turbulent years, to retire as Notre Dame president. The board of trustees, which he had created, was functioning well, coeducation had proved successful, and Professor O'Meara had stepped into the Provost's Office smoothly and effectively. The timing seemed perfect but there was a hitch—no clear successor had emerged. According to the statutes of the university, the president had to be a Holy Cross priest and that eliminated Provost O'Meara; Father Joyce was sixty-five years old, the same age as Father Hesburgh; Father Burtchaell may have been groomed for the position originally but could no longer be considered; and no one else seemed to have sufficient higher administration experience, at least at Notre Dame. Acknowledging the dilemma, the board of trustees contemplated dividing the office, appointing a new, if inexperienced, president, and naming Father Hesburgh to a new position of university chancellor responsible for public relations and fundraising and being nearby to advise and assist the new president as needed.[13] But a satisfactory successor still had not surfaced, Father Hesburgh's health remained good, and he agreed to accept an additional five-year term. The board of trustees also decided to appoint to significant high-level university positions four younger Holy Cross priests "whose scholarly credentials and administrative potential commend them for future University leadership but who need further administrative experience."[14] Father

Ernest Bartell, age fifty and with a PhD in economics from Princeton, was named executive director of the Helen Kellogg Institute for International Studies; Father E. William Beauchamp, age forty, was named administrative assistant to Father Joyce; Father Edward Malloy, age forty-one, was named associate provost to succeed the retiring Father Ferdinand Brown; and Father David Tyson, age thirty-four, was named executive assistant to Father Hesburgh.[15]

Father Hesburgh accepted the decision with his usual good grace but he was clearly disappointed. He thought he had given his "thirtieth and final annual speech as president" to the faculty in October 1981, and he admitted that he was not "jumping for joy," that it had been a good time "to get out," and that he had "pretty much psychologically prepared myself to be Chancellor and someone else President."[16]

At the same time that discussions were taking place over a possible successor to Father Hesburgh, a high-level committee of university professors and administrators debated future goals and priorities of the university. Ten years had passed since the *Committee on University Priorities (COUP) Report*, and it seemed time for another self-evaluation and vision for the future. Father Hesburgh requested Provost O'Meara to draft such a report and the advisory committee he appointed to assist and advise him worked on the project for two years. The final report, released in the fall of 1982 and called *PACE* for *Priorities and Commitments for Excellence*, comprised five sections: The Mission of The University, Teaching and Research, The Faculty, The Student Body, and Support Functions.

The first section acknowledged that the times were changing, that the period of educational expansion of the 1960s was over, that the economic malaise and uncertainty of the 1970s posed serious challenges to the nation and to the world, and that university education was even more in demand because of these challenges. Notre Dame had unique contributions to make if it remained strong in teaching, strong in research, and strong in its Catholic character and mission. "The University of Notre Dame finds itself on the threshold of becoming a great university," the report stated, "and all our efforts should be directed towards crossing that threshold."[17]

The report noted academic challenges that needed attention. Student interests were changing. In 1962, the College of Arts and Letters held 43 percent of Notre Dame students, the College of Engineering 24 percent, the College of Business Administration 19 percent, and the College of Science 15 percent, but in 1981, Arts and Letters comprised only 30 percent, Engineering 25 percent, Business also 25 percent, and Science 20 percent. Faculty hiring needed to be adjusted accordingly. The job market was demanding more engineers and fewer humanities graduates. Notre Dame was also experiencing serious grade inflation and a declining interest in classwork among seniors. But there were bright spots also. While average SAT scores nationally had declined from 973 to 893 over the recent eighteen years, Notre Dame students' scores remained fairly constant at 1190. With the fluctuation in student majors, the curriculum could profit from a re-evaluation but there appeared to be no need to assign quotas or gates for each college. The report recommended that the core curriculum for every student— English, social science, history, natural science, philosophy, theology—should remain intact and be permeated with Christian evaluations and judgments. The Radiation Laboratory, the Kellogg Institute for International Studies, the Center for Continuing Education, the Institute for Pastoral and Social Ministry, and other centers and institutes should continue but strive to be more self-supporting. The library needed serious attention. According to the Association of Research Libraries, of its 101 members, Notre Dame ranked 27th in volumes per student, 23rd in volumes per PhD awarded, 21st in volumes per doctoral program, 43rd in current serials per student, 30th in current serials per PhD awarded, 42nd in current serials per doctoral program, and 52nd in staff per student. In 1980–1981, Notre Dame ranked 96th out of 101. Improvement would take time but it was recommended that the university should begin by building further in collections where it had strength.[18]

The report insisted that "every member of the faculty should be strong as a teacher and strong as a researcher." Some felt that Notre Dame students were too homogenous but good teaching could broaden their views and interests. Every teacher must remain a learner also, researching, publishing, and keeping abreast of current developments in the discipline. Diversity among the faculty contributed to a broad education, but Catholicism must continue to remain strong, as the report succinctly stated: "The University, therefore, seeks a diversity of individuals concerned with values on a faculty in which dedicated and committed Catholics predominate." The university's sacramental, communal, and intellectual life demanded a sufficient number of priests, brothers, and sisters; the Congregation of Holy Cross should encourage qualified religious to consider academic careers, especially in theology and philosophy; and departments should give such candidates special consideration. The warning was unmistakable: "The evidence suggests that if Notre Dame is not more successful in attracting Catholics, it will cease to be a Catholic university in a generation or two."[19]

The report was complimentary of the student body. According to a recent American Council on Education and UCLA joint report, Notre Dame ranked in the top-level "private university, highly selective" category. The average SAT verbal score of Notre Dame applicants in 1982 was 530, of accepted applicants 566, and of enrolling freshmen 559; the average SAT mathematical averages were 590 for applicants, 632 for accepted applicants, and 625 for enrolling freshmen. The report recommended that undergraduate enrollment remain at 7,300 throughout the 1980s and that standards continue to rise, admitting all the while that there were challenges. The number of college-age students nationwide was declining, federal aid was being cut, and more students were attending public high schools. On the positive side, Notre Dame's reputation was high; it would be even more attractive with a better male-female balance; room, board, and tuition costs were competitive; the endowment was satisfactory; and ROTC brought in substantial revenue. However, student financial aid needed to be tripled by 1990, and the quality of student life needed attention. Some residence halls were overcrowded, lacked social space, and needed to be more comfortable and attractive, especially for upperclassmen. Social facilities were no longer adequate for a coed institution, spontaneous social events were becoming more popular than planned ones, social life was shifting out of the residence halls, and student affairs needed to adapt to those changes. Alcohol was a major concern on almost every campus and a top-level committee needed to carefully examine the situation at Notre Dame. The university had long been proud of its athletics program and should continue to abide by all governing body regulations, use the same admission criteria for athletes as for all other students, should house athletes with other students and not in a separate residence hall, and should compete against only those schools with similar goals and practices.[20]

In the area of support functions, the report noted, finally, that computers were changing rapidly, that Notre Dame needed a long-range plan to keep abreast of developments, and that special attention should be given to what support could and could not be supplied efficiently by the mainframe computer.[21]

The report ended, as it had begun, with its three fundamental recommendations:[22]

1. we must excel as a university in the full sense of the word, actively engaged in teaching and research;
2. we must maintain our Catholic identity;
3. we must remain conscious of and faithful to our mission in all our actions and decisions.

Provost O'Meara also encouraged continuation of the university's program of strengthening the faculty by recruiting outstanding professors to endowed chairs. In 1979, Roger Schmitz of the University of Illinois, later to be dean of Notre Dame's College of Engineering and associate provost, accepted a chair in chemical engineering, and Denis Goulet, a senior fellow with the Overseas Development Council, a chair in education for justice. Similar hires followed in succeeding years: Father Richard McBrien of Boston College in theology, Alvin Plantinga of Calvin College in philosophy, Walter Nugent of Indiana University in history, Gerald Bruns of the University of Iowa in English, John J. Gilligan, former governor of Ohio, as Francis J. O'Malley University Professor, Father Charles Kannengiesser, S.J., of the Institut Catholique de Paris in theology, William Wilkie of the University of Florida in marketing, and Father Richard McCormick, S.J., of Georgetown as professor of Christian ethics.[23]

The faculty was growing in size also. The full-time teaching and research faculty numbered 660 in 1980 and grew to 808 in 1988.[24] The increase was reflected in almost all departments. Art, Art History, and Design grew from 15 to 19, Government and International Relations from 22 to 28, History from 20 to 25, Philosophy from 31 to 36, Accountancy from 19 to 24, Biology from 27 to 39, Physics from 27 to 34, Chemical Engineering from 9 to 11, Electrical and Computer Engineering from 17 to 23, and the Law School faculty from 33 to 44. The number of women on the faculty increased from 35 to 63. The faculty grew in respectability and reputation sufficiently that the number of successful research proposals grew from 111 in 1977 to 197 in 1988, with the research monies increasing from $6,836,962 to $27,552,535.[25]

Faculty salaries were on the rise also, a much-needed rise. In 1976, Notre Dame's faculty compensation had ranked below that of peer institutions Emory, Pittsburgh, Iowa, Southern California, Vanderbilt, Indiana, Duke, Northwestern, and Cornell.[26] Two years later, Notre Dame salaries were still given a number 3 ranking by the AAUP, putting them in only the 60th percentile. Salaries of full professors ranked 94th in the nation, associate professors 62nd, and assistant professors 90th. Average ranking of all levels was 90th. A faculty survey in 1979 evidenced discontent. More than four hundred members of the total faculty (58 percent) responded to the survey, and of these 75 percent disagreed with the statement that "salaries at Notre Dame are adequate"; 80 percent disagreed that "my salary increases in recent years at Notre Dame kept pace with inflation"; and more than one-third thought "the Notre Dame faculty should organize into a collective bargaining unit."[27]

Progress was made in the early 1980s. Salaries increased 7.7 percent overall in 1978–1979, 6.9 percent in 1979–1980, 8.9 percent in 1980–1981, 12.7 percent in 1981–1982, 11.6 percent in 1982–1983, 9.4 percent in 1983–1984, and 8.2 percent in 1984–1985. That year, Notre Dame reached the AAUP number 1 ranking at all faculty levels. Salaries of full professors at Notre Dame ranked 38th in the nation, of associate professors 14th, and of assistant professors 12th. And this was in northern Indiana where the cost of living was favorable.[28] To finance these increases, however, tuition unfortunately had to be raised even faster. Student tuition increased 7.9 percent in 1978, 8.3 percent in 1979, 12.2 percent in 1980, 12.3 percent in 1981, 13.4 percent in 1982, and 8.4 percent in 1983.[29] Enrollment remained steady but there was understandable concern that Notre Dame was becoming too much a school for the wealthy, a far cry from Father Sorin admitting almost anyone with land or grain or livestock to pay.

Even with the more or less satisfactory increases in salaries, disagreements between the faculty and administration continued. With the rising national inflation in the 1970s and early 1980s, the faculty requested higher retirement benefits, including those for spouses of deceased members. Some faculty desired increased tuition benefits for faculty children attending other colleges. Arts and Letters faculty were pleased with the announcement of a new faculty office building but also wanted a role in selecting the architect. Although revised periodically, the Teacher-Course Evaluations always met with criticisms: that they could not be adapted equitably to each department or college, or that they were weighted too heavily by the administration in promotion and tenure decisions. The faculty also desired greater input in the university's budget process. After a faculty member was removed from teaching a freshman class due to complaints from students and parents about his inappropriate language, some faculty requested clarification of how and when such terminations could take place.[30]

The majority of the faculty were probably also in agreement with the PACE committee's recommendation that a committee be appointed to review and, if necessary, revise the university's basic undergraduate curriculum of studies. In early 1983, Provost O'Meara appointed a twelve-person faculty committee with the mandate:[31]

> to report and make recommendations to the Academic Council on the following matters: the overall structure of the undergraduate curriculum; the general education requirements; the role of philosophy and theology in the general education requirements; academic standards, academic advising, and career counseling; the quality of undergraduate intellectual life on campus.

The committee met regularly from May 1983 to April 1984, reviewed the curricula of fifteen peer institutions, met formally with the four college councils, and heard from numerous individual members of the university community. The committee commended the First Year of Studies for the "high quality of the academic counseling that takes place and for the genuine interest shown in each student," but it expressed concern that the student might be left without satisfactory counseling in the sophomore year until he or she declared a major and entered officially into a department. Addressing the question of the quality of undergraduate intellectual life, the committee recommended additional smaller classes, more informal space for student-faculty dialogue, and wider cultural events, although it also recognized the advantage of large lecture courses if taught by a department's strongest teachers and the more efficient use of department resources that these larger classes permitted. Noting that much intellectual growth occurs outside the classroom, the committee urged the vice president of student affairs and rectors to consider ways to better foment the intellectual life in the residence halls. The committee did not address the problem of classroom cheating but they recommended that a second committee be appointed to investigate.[32]

The committee looked most intently at the undergraduate curriculum itself but recommended few significant changes. The current curriculum included a semester of Composition and Literature, a semester of Freshman Seminar, and required two semesters of either Physical Education or ROTC in the first year, and the committee recommended no change. The curriculum also mandated that two semesters of mathematics be taken in the freshman year and the committee suggested that one semester be taken in the freshman year and the second in either first or second year. The student currently was required to take two semesters of natural science, normally in the freshman year, and the committee recommended that they be taken within the first two years. The present requirement called for two semesters of philosophy to be taken within the first two years, and the committee added only that they should be taken in consecutive semesters. Two semesters of theology were required of each student, normally beginning in the first two years, and no change was recommended. Each student was currently required to take one semester of either history or a social science, normally in the freshman year, but the committee extended that to two semesters, to be satisfied at any time and in any way—two histories, two social sciences, or one of each. Finally, the committee recommended the addition of one semester of fine arts or literature, to be taken anytime.[33]

The report reviewed each requirement individually, noting how it conveyed desired knowledge and helped develop the basic skills of reading, writing, analyzing, judging, and discussing effectively. It then turned to explaining why some courses were not included. Most members of the committee would have preferred a foreign language requirement but it was not included because it would have overloaded some professional majors, and the Department of Modern and Classical Languages was not equipped to handle such a demand. The two colleges (Business and Engineering) that did not have a language requirement, however, were encouraged to find ways to include it. The committee was highly appreciative of experiential learning and its growth at Notre Dame in recent years, and urged its inclusion in courses wherever feasible, but did not add a requirement since sufficient resources were lacking and voluntary participation in some ways seemed preferable. The committee saw no need for a computer science requirement since incoming students would be increasingly familiar with computer use and would adapt it to their individual needs successfully. Each college should make computers available for the students, however.[34] The Academic Council discussed the report in four meetings from December 1984 to April 1985 and accepted it with only two substantial changes—that the two-semester history or social science requirement must be fulfilled by one semester of history and one of social science, and that the two philosophy courses need not be taken sequentially but the first must be taken by the end of sophomore year.[35]

Acting on the recommendation of this curriculum committee, the provost in the fall of 1985 appointed a special committee to investigate the question of academic cheating on campus. The committee was composed of nine members, five faculty members and four students, with the mission, according to the chairman and associate provost Father Edward Malloy, "to try to find out what the extent of cheating is, what circumstances promote cheating, and to try to cultivate respect for honesty." A major concern another committee member noted was "students who don't cheat. They don't want to turn in other students. They're in an awkward position. They don't think it's fair for others to get away with it. Ultimately, they get a lower grade." Another committee member noted that "there's no big cheating ring around the school. People are more or less casually cheating."[36]

The committee divided itself into subcommittees—one to survey other schools, a second to interview faculty, and a third to seek student opinion—and it submitted an early report in March 1986. The report noted that there was "more cheating at Notre Dame than any of us wants," but recommended against establishing an honor code. Students would simply not report on each other. Professors were encouraged to clarify in class what was permitted and what was not in preparing individual assignments, a pledge of honesty should accompany all work, and examinations should normally be proctored. If cheating occurred, the professor was empowered to decide on the penalty personally, or the case might be referred to the college honesty committee (which replaced all department honesty committees), and a notice was sent to the dean. The penalty for any second violation was to be suspension or dismissal, but any notice to the dean was to be destroyed at the student's graduation. Effort was to be made to reduce environmental and other factors that might facilitate cheating—crowded classrooms, short-answer examination questions, identical tests, etc.[37]

The initial report was then submitted to the Student Government and the four college councils for comments and suggestions, and it was returned to the Academic Council for final decision. In early 1987 the council decided to set up an experimental honesty program for four years. The freshman year dean would designate a number of first-year courses to be taught under the honor system, and other professors could volunteer to teach their courses under the system with their dean's approval. No upper-class student was obliged to take a course under the honor system. A professor on the first day of the semester might survey the class, and if all were willing, the course could then be taught under the honor system. If even one student demurred, it could not be taught that way. In a course taught under the honor system, all exams were to be unproctored, each student would pledge not to give or receive any inappropriate aid, and each student was obliged to report violations. Alleged violations were to be reported to the dean and from there referred to the university honesty committee composed of both faculty and students. If found guilty, the student would receive an F for the assignment, and a second violation would result in dismissal. It was decided that this experimental program should continue until 1992 and the Academic Council would make a final decision then. Although the earlier honor code had been abandoned in 1969 for lack of student cooperation, Father Oliver Williams, then associate provost and chair of the university honesty committee, was hopeful: "There seems to be a feeling that people are more interested in making it work. Moral development is a primary mission of the University. Faculty members want to use every educational tool available to help students grow."[38]

The university undertook two new academic initiatives in the mid-1980s. In December 1985, Mrs. Joan Kroc, widow of the founder of the McDonald's restaurant chain, gave the university $6 million to establish an Institute for International Peace Studies. She had recently heard Father Hesburgh speak in San Diego on the need to find nonviolent means of solving world problems, and his ideas harmonized with her interests in international peace and the halting of nuclear proliferation. The primary purpose of the institute was to provide graduate fellowships to twelve students, six from the West and six from Russia and China, to study together for a full year and receive a master's degree in peace studies. Father Hesburgh hoped that each year twelve new students would come to study together, and on their return home they would exert peacekeeping influence in the areas of business, labor, politics, and education in their native countries. Courses were to be offered in political science, history, sociology, theology, anthropology, and related disciplines. Other monies from the donation would be used to invite eminent scholars to the university to lecture, to sponsor seminars and workshops, to develop interdisciplinary research programs, and to consolidate studies into an undergraduate program. John Gilligan, Francis J. O'Malley University Professor and former governor of Ohio, was named institute director.[39]

Two years later, Mrs. Kroc visited Notre Dame to see how the programs were progressing, and Father Hesburgh noted that what would still be helpful was a central location where the students might live together, get to know each other better, and where classes, conferences, and lectures could be conveniently held. Mrs. Kroc reminded Father Hesburgh that she gave money for programs, not buildings, but he explained that living together would be an important part of the program. On her return home she telephoned Father Hesburgh, told him she had thought about his request further, and that he could have an additional $6 million for the building if he named it the Hesburgh Center for International Studies. Father Hesburgh pleaded that he already had the main library named for him, and a public policy program, and that the new building should carry the Kroc name. When she repeated that she did not want her name on the building either, Father Hesburgh rejoined "Then we're even." She said, "Not quite. I have the money." Father Hesburgh eventually consented, and the Theodore M. Hesburgh Center for International Studies was dedicated on September 14, 1991.[40]

In late 1986, the Exxon Education Foundation awarded Notre Dame a three-year $300,000 grant to establish an interdisciplinary academic program in public service. This Hesburgh Program in Public Service was to honor the university's president for his numerous commitments to public welfare. Father Hesburgh was grateful: "There will always be a need for public servants whose understanding of complex issues is informed by a keenly Catholic insight, and this gift will help our university to respond to it." Professor David Leege of the Department of Government and International Studies was named director, and the program was scheduled to begin in the fall of 1987. It was intended to sponsor between ten and twenty summer government internships, invite professionals to campus to interact with students, and establish a five-course minor concentration in public service. Students enrolled in the minor had a number of courses from which to choose, chiefly in government, economics, and history, with a new course, unique to the program, Introduction to Public Policy. "The concentration provides a way of looking at the broad foundations and principles which should guide a democracy," said Nathan Hatch, associate dean of the College of Arts and Letters. "We're not just interested in the technical concerns, but also the moral aspects."[41]

Notre Dame attracted national news coverage in the area of public policy when New York governor Mario Cuomo delivered a major address in Washington Hall the evening of September 13, 1984. The hall was packed, and seven hundred people watched on closed-circuit TV from elsewhere on campus. The governor and Senator Edward Kennedy were the two most prominent Catholics in American political life at the time, and the governor had been invited by Father Richard McBrien, chair of the Department of Theology, to speak on his role as both Catholic and public official, and especially on how he confronted the question of abortion that the Supreme Court had declared permissible. The governor was not only an influential public official and possible presidential candidate but also an outstanding orator, and his speech was reprinted or summarized in major newspapers across the country.[42]

He began with a clear profession of his Catholic faith:[43]

> I speak here as a politician. And also as a Catholic, a lay person baptized and raised in the pre–Vatican II church, educated in Catholic schools, attached to the Church first by birth, then by choice, now by love. An old-fashioned Catholic who sins, regrets, struggles, worries, gets confused, and most of the time feels better after Confession. The Catholic Church is my spiritual home. My heart is there, and my hope.

He admitted that America's secular and consumer culture of the late twentieth century posed serious challenges to every Catholic striving to live true to his or her faith:[44]

> In addition to all the weaknesses, dilemmas, and temptations that impede every pilgrim's progress, the Catholic who holds public office in a pluralistic democracy—who is elected to serve Jews and Moslems, atheists and Protestants, as well as Catholics—bears special responsibility.

He or she undertakes to help create conditions under which *all* can live with a maximum of dignity and with a reasonable degree of freedom; where everyone who chooses may hold beliefs different from specifically Catholic ones—sometimes contradictory to them; where the laws protect people's right to divorce, to use birth control, even to choose abortion.

He insisted that every American—priest or layman, Catholic or Protestant, Jew or Muslim—had the right to advocate for any position he or she believed the government should espouse and enact:[45]

> I can, if I wish, argue that the state should not fund the use of contraceptive devices, not because the Pope demands it but because I think that the whole community—for the *good* of the whole community—should not sever sex from an openness to the creation of life.
>
> Surely I can, if so inclined, demand some kind of law against abortion, not because my bishops say it is wrong but because I think that the whole community, regardless of its religious beliefs, should agree on the importance of protecting life—including life in the womb, which is, at the very least, potentially human, and which should not be extinguished casually.

He stated his personal opinion clearly:[46]

> As Catholics, my wife and I were enjoined never to use abortion to destroy the life we created. We never have. We thought Church doctrine was clear on this and, more than that, we felt it in full agreement with what our hearts and our consciences told us. For me, life or fetal life in the womb should be protected, even if five of nine justices of the Supreme Court and my neighbor disagree with me. A fetus is different from an appendix or a set of tonsils. The full potential of human life is indisputably there. That by itself should demand respect, caution, indeed reverence.

He came then to the heart of the problem facing the Catholic politician:[47]

> I accept the Church's teaching on abortion. Must I insist you do? By law? By denying you Medicaid funding? By a constitutional amendment? If so, which one? . . .

Our public morality, then—the moral standards we maintain for everyone, not just the ones we insist on in our private lives—depends on a consensus view of right and wrong. The values derived from religious belief will not—and should not—be accepted as part of the public morality unless they are shared by the pluralistic community at large.

There is no Church teaching that mandates the best political course for making our belief everyone's rule, for spreading this part of our Catholicism. There is neither an encyclical nor a catechism that spells out a political strategy for achieving legislative goals. So the Catholic trying to make moral and prudent judgments in the political realm must discern which, if any, of the actions one could take would be best.

The latitude of judgment is not something new in the Church, not a development that has arisen only with the abortion issue. Take, for example, the question of slavery. It has been argued that the failure to endorse a legal ban on abortions is equivalent to refusing to support the cause of abolition before the Civil War.

The truth of the matter is, few if any Catholic bishops spoke for abolition in the years before the Civil War. It wasn't that the bishops endorsed the idea of some humans owning and exploiting other humans; Pope Gregory XVI, in 1840, condemned the slave trade. Instead, it was a practical political judgment that the bishops made. They weren't hypocrites; they were realists. At the time, Catholics were a small minority, most immigrants, despised by much of the population, often vilified, the object of sporadic violence. In the face of public controversy that aroused tremendous passions and threatened to break the country apart, the bishops made a pragmatic decision. They believed their opinion would not change people's minds. . . . They concluded that under the circumstances arguing for a constitutional amendment against slavery would do more harm than good. So they were silent—as they have been generally in recent years on the question of birth control. . . . The decision they made to remain silent on a constitutional amendment to abolish slavery or on the repeal of the Fugitive Slave Law wasn't a mark of moral indifference. It was a measured attempt to balance moral truths against political realities. Their decision reflected their sense of complexity, not their diffidence. Lincoln behaved with similar discretion.

The governor emphasized his conviction that an amendment outlawing abortions would not be effective, even if it could pass: "Given present attitudes, it would be Prohibition revisited, legislating what cannot be enforced, and in the process creating a disrespect for law in general." The Hatch Amendment (declaring the right to abortion not protected by the United States Constitution), he stated, "by returning the question of abortion to the states, would give us a checkerboard of permissive and restrictive jurisdictions. In some cases, people might go elsewhere to have abortions." Denying Medicaid funding for abortions "would burden only the already disadvantaged." If they could be enacted, laws might "put most abortions out of sight [but only] return them to the back rooms where they were performed for so long." He was not advocating complacency. The nation could and should pass laws enabling impoverished mothers to bring to term and raise their children in decency, could and should provide better medical care for all children, and could and should reduce our infant mortality rate, then ranked 16th in the world, but there was no consensus on the abortion question at present and, without that consensus in a pluralist society, no legislation could be enacted, nor could any enacted legislation be effective.[48]

Reaction to the governor's speech on campus, of course, was immediate. Father McBrien viewed it with favor:[49]

> Governor Cuomo's lecture set a new standard for discussion of his topic. Rarely if ever has a public official—Catholic or otherwise—addressed the issue of religious belief and public morality in so sophisticated and nuanced a manner.
>
> He asked all the right questions—without pretending to have all the right answers. . . .
>
> Unlike many other liberal-leaning public figures, Cuomo offers explicit reasons for his own unequivocal moral opposition to abortion. The question for him is not moral but political: What should be done about abortion in the public forum?
>
> The governor correctly insists that the Catholic Church has not set down any "inflexible moral principle which determines what our *political* conduct should be," on this or any other issue. In fact, the American bishops themselves have often exercised political judgment in determining when and where to apply their moral and institutional resources. Even on the abortion issue, the bishops have changed their own tactics as political circumstances have changed.

Two weeks later, Representative Henry Hyde, a Republican from Illinois and a strong pro-life advocate, was invited to give an address at the Notre Dame

Law School. He responded to the governor's speech directly, insisting that Catholics in the Democratic (Cuomo's) Party faced a serious challenge:[50]

> Their dilemma is that they want to retain their Catholic credentials but realize that in today's Democratic Party to be upwardly mobile is to be very liberal, and to be very liberal is to be very feminist, and to be a feminist is to be for abortion. . . .
>
> The Constitutional separation of church and state is thus a question of institutional distinctiveness and integrity. It was never intended to rule religiously-based values out of order in the public arena. Yet that is precisely what some among us would do: disqualify an argument or public policy from constitutional consideration if its roots are "religious." . . .
>
> In my view, there is nothing unconstitutional or inappropriate in a president making clear his or her understanding that religiously-based values have had, and will continue to have, a crucial, formative role in our democratic experiment.

Father Hesburgh gave his reflections on the governor's address in a syndicated column for United Press International. He acknowledged that he had grown up in the 1920s and 1930s in an age of racial segregation sanctioned by the Supreme Court decision of *Plessy v. Ferguson* in 1896. After years of struggle that unfortunate decision was finally overturned in the *Brown v. Board of Education* decision in 1954. With 1.5 million abortions-on-demand performed each year in the United States at that time, polls indicated that most Americans supported some restriction to abortion access. He then continued:[51]

> If it was patriotic, just and noble to work for the repeal of *Plessy v. Ferguson* and apartheid, why should it now seem un-American to work for fewer legally sanctioned abortions when there is already a moral consensus that finds our present legal permissiveness on abortion excessive and intolerable?
>
> In fairness, it must be said, as Governor Cuomo and others committed to politics, the art of the possible, have pointed out, there is not a consensus in America for the absolute prohibition of abortion. But there is and was a moral consensus, one ignored by the Supreme Court in *Roe v. Wade*, for a stricter abortion law. A remarkably well-kept secret is that a minority is currently imposing its belief on a demonstrable majority. It is difficult to explain how a moral America, so brilliantly successful in confronting racial injustice in the sixties, has the most permissive abortion laws of any Western

country. . . . In West Germany, the highest federal court, mindful of the Holocaust, struck down abortion-on-demand as violating right-to-life provisions of the country's constitution. The only countries that agree with our laws are mainly the Communist countries, especially Russia and China.

Is making common cause with all those against truly permissive abortion a Catholic position? The bishops' support of the Hatch Amendment was a move in this direction. But generally, the pro-life movement has been for an absolute prohibition of abortion. If such a total solution is not possible in our pluralistic society, and, in fact, was voted down by national referendum in Catholic Italy, will Catholics cooperate with other Americans of good will and ethical conviction to work for a more restrictive abortion law? One might hope so. This would not compromise our belief in the sanctity of all human life. We should continue to hold ourselves to a higher standard than we can persuade society-at-large to write into law.

Governor Cuomo and Representative Hyde, of course, were only two of the innumerable public figures invited to campus during the final decade of Father Hesburgh's administration. Former president Gerald Ford, defeated by Jimmy Carter in the election of 1976 but respected for restoring decency to government after the Watergate scandal, addressed 3,000 in the Athletic and Convocation Center in 1979. The Catholic political theorist and theologian Michael Novak lectured on campus in 1980, and George W. Bush, the future president, visited that same year. The university inaugurated a Distinguished American Women Lecture Series in the fall of 1981 with an address by actress Helen Hayes. She was followed the following year by Jane Cahill-Pfeiffer, former chairman of the board of the National Broadcasting Company; Marina Whitman, vice president and chief economist of General Motors; Jane Pauley of NBC's *Today* program; Mrs. Barbara Bush, wife of the then vice president and herself the future first lady; Jean Wilkowski, former United States Ambassador to Zambia; and Sister Helen Flaherty, president of the Sisters of Charity. Arousing controversy in 1983, Christie Hefner, daughter of *Playboy* founder Hugh Hefner and herself president of Playboy Enterprises, Inc., was invited to speak as a woman business executive. Representative Romano Mazzoli, congressman from Kentucky and a Notre Dame alumnus, spoke in 1984. Abbie Hoffman, radical protest leader of the 1960s, was invited to campus the following year and urged students to continue their protests against university policies with which they disagreed. That same year, Cardinals Joseph Bernardin of Chicago and John O'Connor of New York spoke jointly on the American bishops' pastoral letter on the economy. Various other national leaders arrived to take part in the university's mock political conventions in 1980, 1984, and 1988.[52]

Many of these visitors championed liberal positions—including Christie Hefner and Abbie Hoffman—but the nation itself was trending conservative in the 1980s, as the election and reelection of Ronald Reagan confirmed, and the younger generation seemed part of that conservative trend. In a survey taken of incoming freshmen by the Cooperative Institutional Research Program of the American Council on Education in 1980, 21 percent of students nationwide professed a liberal point of view, compared with 34 percent in 1972, and 28 percent claimed a conservative point of view, compared with only 17 percent in 1972. Among Notre Dame freshmen, 21 percent in 1980 claimed a liberal point of view, down from 29 percent in 1972, and 29 percent espoused a conservative point of view, up from 24 percent in 1972. On social issues, Notre Dame freshmen were also more conservative than their classmates across the country. Only 20 percent of them favored legalized abortion (the national figure was 65 percent), 21 percent at Notre Dame approved of living together before marriage (65 percent approved nationally), only 19 percent desired more liberal divorce laws (41 percent favored them across the country), and 25 percent favored legalizing marijuana (against 41 percent nationally). Only on the death penalty might Notre Dame students seem more liberal, with 41 percent in favor of abolishing it while only 37 percent favored its abolition nationally. Compared to their own 1972 classmates, more freshmen in 1980 hoped to be authorities in their field (71 percent to 63 percent), raise a family (76 percent to 73 percent), have administrative responsibilities (41 percent to 28 percent), and be very well off financially (56 percent to 45 percent). On the other hand, they were less interested in developing a philosophy of life (66 percent to 78 percent), in participating in community action (26 percent to 34 percent), and in being involved in environmental cleanup (22 percent to 42 percent).[53]

Incoming students continued to be bright, and also slightly more diverse. In 1977, 67 percent of the incoming freshmen ranked in the top 10 percent of their high school class, with mean SAT scores of 1187, and in 1988, 80 percent ranked in that top decile, with a mean SAT score of 1210.[54] The number of black Americans in the first-year class rose from forty-six in 1978 to ninety-six ten years later, Asian students from twenty-five to fifty-four, and Hispanic students from fifty-six to ninety-four. The university's selectivity remained about the same throughout the decade. The university sent acceptances to 35 percent of those who applied in 1980 and 33 percent of those who applied in 1988, but the rate of those who actually enrolled dropped from 66 percent to 56 percent. Each year the admission rate was lower for women but the enrollment rate higher. In 1980, 83 percent of the freshman class had an A or A– average in high school and 86 percent in 1988; 93 percent of the freshman class in 1980 selected Notre Dame for its academic reputation and 96 percent in 1988; 89 percent had Notre Dame as their college of first choice in 1980 but surprisingly only 84 percent in 1988. The attrition rate in the freshman year dropped throughout the 1980s from 1.6 percent to 0.4 percent.[55]

Unfortunately, many of those incoming freshmen each fall confronted the problem of overcrowding in the residence halls. The situation had existed since the early 1970s, with more students committing to enroll than the Office of Undergraduate Admissions had anticipated and fewer students moving off campus or leaving school. In the fall of 1983, forty-one freshmen had to be housed initially in the study lounges of Flanner, Grace, and the Pasquerilla Halls, but thirty-eight were relocated into permanent rooms within two weeks. In the following year, temporary lodging had to be found for 128 freshmen as the semester began. One student lamented the inconvenience: "Our mail is late and, with four in the room, it is really crowded. Worst of all, we have no control over when or where we are moved. We can't get settled because we don't know when we will be moved." Leaving their temporary home when a room opened also had a downside, as another student noted: "I wish we were able to have a say in where we are moved. It would be better if we could choose our roommates before they move us. Personally, I would like to stay here. . . . I think the people in charge of housing need more foresight." Unfortunately, fifteen of those students that year, eight men and seven women, were forced to remain in their temporary housing the whole first semester, and they were relocated only the following January. The next year, temporary lodging was initially needed for forty-one freshmen, and in 1986 for eighty-four, all men, and that year study lounges in Sorin Hall were utilized in addition to those in Flanner and Grace.[56]

The students seem to have tolerated the overcrowding reasonably well, but there were other issues that they decided to protest, or at least publicly oppose. In 1978, the Notre Dame–Saint Mary's community voted to boycott all Nestlé products because of reports that the company was giving free samples of its infant formula to hospitals and homes of newborn babies and lobbying doctors to prescribe the product, to lead mothers to believe that bottle-feeding was superior to breast-feeding. Nestlé denied the allegations but evidence indicated it might be occurring in some developing countries. The students renewed the boycott every two years, with no Nestlé products used or for sale in the dining halls, Huddle, bookstore, or other university facilities, although a couple of the residence halls continued to sell Nestlé candy bars in their food sales.[57]

The students organized a second boycott in early 1980 against the Campbell Soup Company at the urging of the Farm Labor Organizing Committee (FLOC). Ceci Schickel, FLOC president, insisted that Campbell farmworkers "live in inhuman conditions, are treated unjustly, and deserve improvements in living and working conditions, wages, and safety." No Campbell products were sold or used anywhere on campus. This boycott was also renewed every two years by the student body until it was finally called off in 1986 when the Farm Labor Organizing Committee and the Campbell Soup Company signed a contract granting FLOC union recognition and preparing the way for major improvements in working and living conditions. The FLOC president gave much credit to Notre Dame, the first major educational institution to join the boycott: "When you boycott a product for six years, and you have students who can lead this and carry on the tradition, I think that's phenomenal, and a credit to the students at Notre Dame."[58]

Throughout the decade, students expressed deep concern over any university financial investments in South Africa that might be aiding that country in its continued policy of apartheid. Notre Dame's policy had been formulated, after much discussion, by the board of trustees in 1978. The university, first of all, held no investments in South African companies themselves. Secondly, it did have investments in approximately thirty companies (perhaps 10 percent of the endowment) that had business dealings in South Africa. Thirdly, each of those companies had signed and agreed to abide by the so-called Sullivan Principles, named for their author, Philadelphia Baptist minister Rev. Leon Sullivan. According to these principles, a company had to adopt a no-segregation policy, award equal pay for equal work, strive for additional nonwhite management, permit free movement of black workers from job to job, work to improve quality of life outside the workplace (in schools, medical facilities, etc.), and take an active part in urging revision of apartheid laws. In addition, Notre Dame invested in no company selling to the South African government, police, or military, and in no banks loaning to the South African government. Each company was audited annually by Arthur D. Little, Inc., and the audit was made public. Father Hesburgh noted that "one corporation said they would not be bullied by the Sullivan Principles, so we divested them." It was Notre Dame's position not to divest of all companies doing business in South Africa since investors in other countries would simply buy up what Notre Dame divested, with perhaps little concern for apartheid, and Notre Dame would have lost all influence in that country. Father Hesburgh explained: "The day you divest . . . you're out of the ball game. We wouldn't have any base from which to operate. . . . I don't believe in running away from a fight." Professor Peter Walshe of the Department of Government and International Studies spoke strongly in favor of full divestment, and a visiting priest-professor from South Africa went on a hunger strike for twenty-nine days to urge it, but the board of trustees agreed to divest only if conditions deteriorated further or if it became clear that Notre Dame and other right-minded investors were having no influence at all.[59]

The less serious side of student life continued throughout the 1980s also. The decade began with the usual Mardi Gras celebration in the spring of 1980. Mardi Gras had been inaugurated on campus in the 1940s, usually featuring at that time a big band and dancing, and gradually developed into a New Orleans casino night theme. In the spring of 1980, Mardi Gras recorded a profit of approximately $30,000, with 60 percent of that going to on campus volunteer service groups such as Big Brothers Big Sisters, Logan Center (for special-needs children), Neighborhood Study Help programs, and the World Hunger Coalition. Unfortunately for Mardi Gras, that fall Bishop William McManus of the diocese of Fort Wayne–South Bend ordered Catholic parishes and other organizations in his diocese to put a halt to all gambling activities (raffles, bingo, cards, dice, wheels) even if for charitable causes. Since this would seriously cut into Mardi Gras participation and profits, the university asked the bishop for an exception, but he declined, insisting that Catholic institutions abide fully by state no-gambling laws. The bishop allowed for one year of adjustment before full conformity, and Mardi Gras in 1981 made approximately $28,000 for charity. The spring celebration continued into succeeding years but on a smaller scale. In 1984, it sponsored a "Roommate Game" to see which pair of contestants knew his or her roommate best, a dance-a-thon, a square dance, and the films *The Jazz Singer* and *Showboat*. The organizers hoped to clear $6,000 for charity. The following year, a Mardi Gras primarily featuring dancing brought in $5,000. Without the games, participation continued to decline, and other campus activities soon took its place.[60]

An Tostal (Irish for "the festival") fared much better. It was begun in 1967 and by the mid-1980s covered six days—Timid Tuesday, Wicked Wednesday, Thirsty Thursday, Frivolous Friday, Sunny Saturday, and Serene Sunday. A golf tournament opened the festivities on Tuesday, with competitions ranging from longest drive to tackiest attire. Weeklong events began that day also—voting for Ugly Man on Campus, with the penny per vote charge going to charity; mud volleyball; men's and women's Bookstore Basketball; and tuck-ins (for fifty cents a student would be tucked in bed at night, read a bedtime story, and brought a glass of water). Wednesday featured decathlon and slam dunk contests. Canoe racing, a dunking booth, and jello wrestling highlighted events on Thursday. Friday's events included a donut-eating contest, a hot pepper–eating contest, watermelon seed spitting, an egg toss, a trivia bowl, cow chip throwing, and an impersonation contest. Saturday featured kite flying, a sack race, a three-legged race, Frisbee golf, croquet, and the mud volleyball finals. The men's and women's Bookstore Basketball finals concluded on Sunday. Events were scheduled on both the Notre Dame and the Saint Mary's campuses, the fire department assisted in providing mud pits, rectors took steps to prevent mud from clogging shower drains, and a fun time was had by almost all.[61]

Campus frivolity may have reached its height—or depth—with the Cap'n Crunch weekend organized by the sophomore class in the fall of 1983. Quaker Oats, the manufacturer of the popular breakfast cereal, agreed to sponsor the event, offered prizes, and promised to make no commercials from the week. A Cap'n Crunch eating contest featured teams of five students—five men, five women, or any combination—with each team member running the length of the quad, consuming two bowls of cereal there, and returning to the original end to tag another member to do the same. The team consuming the ten bowls first was the winner. If a contestant spilled any cereal while eating, that person had to consume a penalty bowl, almost eliminating any chance of winning. Each member of the final winning team was rewarded with a free trip to Ft. Lauderdale for spring break. The week also sponsored a Cap'n Crunch look-a-like contest and a scavenger hunt for 125 Cap'n Crunch t-shirt certificates hidden around the campus. No record was kept of how many penalty bowls of the crunchy cereal were consumed or the final times, some contestants admitted that the contest had been a little hard on the roof of the mouth, and others expressed uncertainty when they might be hungry for a bowl again, but all agreed it was a fun week. A team from Fisher Hall won the eating contest and four women from Breen-Phillips won for best costumes, dressed as a spoon, milk, a piece of cereal, and Cap'n Crunch.[62]

At least equally juvenile was the traditional once-a-year panty raid of Notre Dame males charging across the highway to Saint Mary's College on either the Wednesday evening before the first home football game or some spring evening. The students occasionally did break into residence halls and cause damage but later usually apologized and paid for any losses. All admitted it was immature, and even degrading, but most students took it lightly. One Saint Mary's residence hall attempted a fundraising undergarment sale the week before, but it was halted, and a Notre Dame freshman acknowledged: "We're fortunate to be old enough to know better, yet young enough to enjoy ourselves."[63]

In the 1960s and 1970s a drug culture spread across college campuses around the country—marijuana and beyond—and Notre Dame did not escape. Penalties were handed out to drug users, plus mandatory counseling, and drug sellers or providers were suspended or dismissed. But at Notre Dame the drug of preference was clearly alcohol. The use of alcohol on campus in the earliest years had been banned, students at times were forbidden to enter South Bend bars and taverns, and shop owners were warned not to serve them. Compliance and enforcement were never perfect, of course, but the policy was clear and violations were weighed seriously.[64]

World War II brought many changes to the campus—the Navy's V-7 and V-12 programs, overcrowded residence halls, cafeteria lines in the dining halls—and in the immediate postwar years, some relaxation in alcohol enforcement. In the postwar years, the majority of students were veterans and had spent two, three, and four years risking their lives in defense of their country and enjoying whatever freedoms the military permitted. They were older and more mature than regular college students, and it was difficult to treat them the same as eighteen-year-olds recently out of high school. Rectors overlooked their drinking at times, as long as it did not become public or out of hand. In his autobiography, Father Hesburgh admitted that he assisted veterans in sobering up before he would let them back in the residence hall. In 1972, the administration finally at least tacitly approved drinking in private residence hall rooms, but that soon led to abuses. Students might hang a blanket at the end of a corridor, call the whole section a private room, and provide a party for scores. Post–football game celebrations, lubricated with alcohol, could get destructive. Death marches, Irish wakes, and Polish weddings—all with alcohol—were inaugurated and had to be curbed. Alcohol was present in much of the negative behavior on campus—vandalism, sexual assault, theft, even absences from class and poor academic performance. Following the recommendation of the PACE committee report, Provost O'Meara in the spring of 1983 appointed a University Committee on the Responsible Use of Alcohol with tasks "to draw up a public statement on responsible drinking, to consider whether present practices and policies on alcohol are conducive to responsible drinking, and to recommend new policies where appropriate." The chair of the committee was Father William Beauchamp, assistant to the executive vice president, with other members Brian Callaghan, student body president; Michael Carlin, chairman of the Hall Presidents Council; Angie Chamblee, assistant dean of the Freshman Year of Studies; Sister John Miriam Jones, assistant provost; Father Edward Malloy, associate provost; Professor Kenneth Milani of the Department of Accountancy; Joni Neal, assistant director of student activities; Father Mark Poorman, rector of Dillon Hall; and Father David Tyson, executive assistant to the president.[65]

The committee met regularly over the next twelve months and consulted with Psychological Services, campus security, the dean of students, residence hall staffs, parents, legal counsel, students, and members of the Saint Mary's College community. The discussions were guided by three parameters—the moral evil of drunkenness, the social life of the campus, and state law, and the final report was issued in April 1984. The committee summarized its findings succinctly: "It is the conviction of the University that drunkenness and public intoxication are unacceptable. Certainly, students in need of counseling and therapy should receive it. However, sanctions should be imposed on those students found intoxicated." Drinking was still permitted in private rooms, but no parties or happy hours unless all were twenty-one. Alcohol was prohibited in all public areas except for restricted tailgates. Each hall was permitted two semiformal dances with wine and beer. The hall rector was to handle a first incident of intoxication or policy violation, and all others were to be sent to the dean of students. No advertising of alcohol was permitted on campus, social space on campus was to be improved to better social life, and an Office of Alcohol Education was to be established.[66]

To the students, the policy seemed a major curtailment. A bold-print *Observer* headline blared "The Party Is Over." Banners hung from windows proclaimed "We Secede" and "N.D., the B.Y.U. of the Midwest." Fifteen hundred students marched to Corby Hall that evening, chanting "We Want Ted," and "Give Beer a Chance." Two thousand students stormed the Main Building the following day, heard speeches from the newly elected student body president and vice president, and the dean of students promised to meet with student leaders and discuss how the new regulations might best be implemented. Father Hesburgh defended the policy as moderate, not as open as before but not dry either. Some feared it might lead a few toward marijuana or other drugs, and bar and tavern owners worried about a possible flood of false ID cards. Other schools wrote for copies of the policy, and protests subsided as discussions commenced over implementation and as final exams and summer vacation approached.[67]

The students even found football discouraging in the early 1980s. Gerry Faust, who had been hired to succeed Dan Devine at the end of the 1980 season, had had a sensational record at Moeller High School in Cincinnati (174 wins, only 17 losses, and 2 ties), he was an outstanding motivational speaker, a deeply committed Catholic, and a gentleman in every way. His first season started superbly, with a 27 to 9 victory over powerful Louisiana State, and an immediate No. 1 ranking in the college football world. But the bubble burst the next week with a loss at Michigan, followed by a second loss at Purdue. Faust shifted players around, seeking the right combination, but the team never seemed to jell. There was a nucleus of good players—Blair Kiel, Tony Hunter, Bob Crable, John Krimm, and Dave Duerson—but the season ended with a disappointing 5–6 record. Succeeding seasons showed only marginal improvement: 6–4–1 in 1982, 6–5 in 1983, 7–4 in 1984, and 5–6 again in 1985. With a victory over Boston College in the Liberty Bowl in 1983 and a loss to Southern Methodist in the Aloha Bowl in 1984, he announced his resignation before the last game of the 1985 season. Characteristically, he did it with class:[68]

> I called Father Hesburgh this morning in Baltimore, Maryland, and told him of my decision to resign. I'm a fighter to the end. It was tough for me to do this. But I think it is for the best—for me and for Notre Dame. You don't quit. You just change directions for the good of both.
>
> I felt this would be the best time because it gives them the opportunity to get another coach before recruiting starts next week. I also wanted the pressure off the players. . . .
>
> I love this place and I love what it stands for. I would have liked to have won more than we did. If you're going to put the blame somewhere, you've got to put it on the coach, and that's where it should be.

He also wrote a letter to the student body:[69]

> It has been a great five years for me here at Notre Dame, and I will cherish the memories all the rest of my life. There have been many fun times, some joys and some sorrows, but they were shared with a class student body from a class institution, and that means a lot to me. I regret that you are limited to only four years here, while I was fortunate in being able to have five. Cherish those four years. Get the most out of your education and take advantage of all that Notre Dame has to offer in so many ways.

Many doors will be opened to you throughout your future because you are part of this great institution. . . . God bless you always.

One of the students wrote a letter to the editor in reply:[70]

Take a look, a close look, at our head football coach Gerry Faust. This man has been teaching an intensive course for five years. It has nothing to do with engineering, business, or physics; but, rather with how to be a decent, honest, courageous, loving human being. I need not go through the details of the course, since we all have good notes already. I suggest, however, that we study these notes, because most of us will have our 26 defeats and we will be hard-pressed to shine as Faust has. Thanks, for a lesson well taught.

If Notre Dame's football fortunes were disappointing under Gerry Faust, they improved impressively under his successor Lou Holtz. Lou was born in Follansbee, West Virginia, in January 1937, grew up in East Liverpool, Ohio, played linebacker at Kent State University, and graduated in 1959 with a degree in history. He served as assistant coach at several schools, including Ohio State when it won the national championship in 1968, before serving successively as head coach at William and Mary, North Carolina State, the New York Jets (for ten months), Arkansas, and Minnesota (from 1984 to 1986). The day after Gerry Faust's resignation, Father Joyce announced the signing of Holtz.[71]

Holtz's first season had its heartbreaking moments. With Steve Beuerlein and Tim Brown leading the offense and Wally Kleine and Cedric Figaro the defense, the team lost four of the first five games, two of them by one point each, later losing to Louisiana State by two points and finishing the season five and six. The following season showed the improvement the fans were expecting. Tony Rice entered the fourth game after quarterback Terry Andrysiak broke his collarbone, and Holtz installed the option football he always preferred. The team improved to eight and three, with season highlights of Tim Brown returning two punts for touchdowns of 71 and 66 yards in the first quarter against Michigan State and being awarded the Heisman Trophy, Notre Dame's seventh, at the end of the season.[72]

Although Tim Brown and the previous year's whole offensive line were gone, hopes for the 1988 season were high. The team featured the passing of Tony Rice to Derek Brown, the running of Ricky Watters and Tony Brooks, the explosive speed of "Rocket" Ismail, and the defense of Wes Pritchett, Frank Stams, Mike Stonebreaker, and Chris Zorich. The hero of the opening game was five-foot-five Reggie Ho, who kicked the winning field goal in the last two minutes for a 19–17 win over Michigan. Victories followed over Michigan State (20–3), Purdue (52–7), Stanford (42–14), and Pittsburgh (30–21). The hero of the next game, against Miami, was defensive back Pat Terrell, who batted down a last-minute pass in the end zone to preserve a 31–30 victory. Succeeding games were won by comfortable margins: Air Force (41–13), Navy (22–7), Rice (59–14), Penn State (21–3), and USC (27–10), although the USC game was played without the two best running backs, who had been sent home for violating team rules. Victory over West Virginia in the Fiesta Bowl, 31–21, completed the undefeated season. Notre Dame was awarded the national championship; Andy Heck, Wes Pritchett, Frank Stams, Mike Stonebreaker, and Chris Zorich received All-American honors; but any celebration was marred a few days after the Fiesta Bowl by the sudden and shocking death by cardiac arrest of defensive back Bobby Satterfield.[73]

Winning two national championships in a row is difficult but Notre Dame almost accomplished it in 1989. The team was victorious in its first eleven games, although some victories were close—Michigan (24–19, with "Rocket" Ismail running back two kickoffs for 89-yard and 92-yard touchdowns), Michigan State (21–13), and USC (28–24). That meant twenty-three consecutive victories over a two-year span, a school record. The final game of the season, unfortunately, was a loss to Miami, 27–10, and Miami was named national champions with Notre Dame second in the voting.[74]

Changes took place throughout the 1980s, not only in academic programs, student demonstrations, and football fortunes, but also in the physical appearance of the campus. One building, the large fieldhouse near the center of campus, was finally torn down. It had been constructed in 1901 for track, field, and basketball but was no longer needed with the erection of the Athletic and Convocation Center in 1968. It might have been demolished at that time but several faculty members and students of the Department of Art, Art History, and Design moved in and transformed it into their studios. No repairs were made, the upkeep was neglected (intentionally), and it was finally demolished in April 1983. In its place a mall was constructed, with two sidewalks leading from LaFortune Student Center and Cavanaugh Hall to the Memorial Library, and with crosswalks where student traffic dictated. Five hundred bricks were saved and a small monument was built around the old cornerstone as a permanent memorial of the venerable building.[75]

A second landmark building, after multiple uses, was also eliminated at the end of the decade. Holy Cross Hall, across Saint Mary's Lake from the main campus, had been constructed in 1889 as Holy Cross Seminary, the principal semi-nary for young men studying for the priesthood in the Congregation of Holy Cross, taking courses in both philosophy and theology. After Holy Cross College was opened in Washington, DC, in 1895 and Moreau Seminary across Saint Jo-seph's Lake in 1920, Holy Cross Seminary was used exclusively as a seminary for high school students. That program was terminated in 1967 and the building was leased to the university and converted into a student residence hall named Holy Cross Hall, and the student residents proudly called themselves the Hogs. With the building in serious need of repairs and with two new residence halls recently constructed, the lease was not renewed in the late 1980s and the building was finally demolished after the 1989–1990 school year.[76]

Construction on campus had been limited in the turbulent decade of the 1970s—the O'Hara-Grace townhouses in 1976 and Fitzpatrick Hall of Engineer-ing in 1979—but major building projects in the 1980s included new indoor sports facilities, the Snite Museum of Art, Stepan Chemistry Hall, two new residence halls for women, and Decio Faculty Hall.

The often-inclement northern Indiana weather made indoor sports facilities a necessity, both for the recreation of the student body in general and for practice and competition in the varsity sports of baseball, football, soccer, lacrosse, track, and tennis. In 1987, the Loftus Center was constructed near the Athletic and Convocation Center and included the Meyo astroturf athletic field, the Haggar Fitness Center, locker rooms, a first aid station, conference rooms, and a 154-seat auditorium. Close by was the Eck Tennis Pavilion, constructed the same year, with six tennis courts, locker rooms, and a small visitors gallery, the benefaction of alumnus Frank Eck of Columbus, Ohio.[77]

Except for the period of Luigi Gregori, the fine arts at Notre Dame had lagged behind the other academic disciplines, and an art gallery or museum was needed to give the arts their due prominence. The Snite Museum of Art, do-nated by the Fred B. Snite family in honor of their son, Frederick, Jr., and opened in 1980, was designed by Professor Ambrose Richardson of the Notre Dame Architecture Department and was a seventy-thousand-square-foot addition to O'Shaughnessy Hall (including the now-connected Meštrović Studio Gallery) that enabled the university to exhibit more of the impressive art collection it had acquired over the years.[78]

Stepan Chemistry Hall was a $9 million addition on the east side of Nieuw-land Science Hall to house faculty offices, classrooms, and laboratories formerly located in the old (1920) Chemistry Hall. During construction, some on campus thought it leaned a little to the east and referred to it as the "leaning tower of

Notre Dame," but construction officials insisted that the foundation was solid and the walls perfectly straight.[79]

Two new residence halls to serve undergraduate women, Pasquerilla West and East, were financed by Frank Pasquerilla, chairman of Crown American Realty Trust. One hall opened in January 1981 and the second the following fall, with each hall accommodating approximately 250 students. The halls contained single rooms, doubles, triples, and quads, a study lounge in each section, typing rooms, a kitchen and dining rooms, large storage areas, social areas with vending machines, a chapel area, and a furnished apartment for a campus visitor. The buildings were flat-roofed and not in the collegiate style of nearby Farley and Breen-Phillips Halls, and some architects voiced criticisms.[80]

The new arts and letters faculty office building met a genuine need. The faculty had been housed in the basement of the Memorial Library since its construction in the mid-1960s, with no windows and only limited access by students. The new office building, conveniently located just east of the O'Shaughnessy Hall of Liberal and Fine Arts, was a $6.2 million gift of Arthur Decio, chairman of Skyline Corporation in Elkhart, Indiana, and a Notre Dame trustee. A four-story structure divided into three distinct sections, it contained offices for 250 faculty members, conference and seminar rooms, a faculty lounge, a mail room, a secretarial pool, a copy center, a computer terminal room, and offices for the Helen Kellogg Institute for International Studies and 1st Source Travel. Each faculty office was carpeted and furnished with a desk, two chairs, a worktable, a filing cabinet, a built-in bookcase, a corkboard, an individually controlled heating/cooling unit, and a large window. Close to O'Shaughnessy Hall and the library, it was easily accessible to students. It housed arts and letters faculty from all departments except art, music, and psychology, which had their own buildings and offices. The dedication of the building in April 1984 was organized around a special convocation with the awarding of eight honorary degrees and an academic symposium on the topic: "The Liberal Arts and the University."[81]

Other buildings were expanded or renovated. An Olympic-sized pool, the benefaction of Thomas J. and Robert T. Rolfs, was added to the east side of the Athletic and Convocation Center in 1984. A pool had originally been planned for the building twenty years before but had been eliminated for financial reasons. The new pool was fifty meters long and twenty-five yards wide, with two movable bulkheads to make it a multipurpose facility. "We could have diving at one end of the pool, recreational swimming in the middle, and water polo at the other end," noted physical plant director Don Dedrick. The $4 million addition provided three one-meter diving boards and two three-meter diving boards, lockers for students, faculty, staff, and varsity teams, a balcony for 350 spectators, and twelve new administrative offices.[82]

That same year the university announced plans for a $3 million addition to the east side of Galvin Life Science Center. A complication arose because the expansion would bring the building too close to Juniper Road and a zoning variance was needed. The new addition was to house the animal research center, an expanding university program but one also governed by ever-changing and detailed government guidelines. The two-story addition provided 24,000 square feet of space and increased the size of the building by 20 percent. A teaching and research facility, it was equipped with an automatic watering system, easily sanitized floors, a washing area, a quarantine section for newly arrived animals, and an air-filtering system that allowed for fifteen changes of air per hour.[83]

The following year, the university announced plans for a $4 million expansion of the Law School, chiefly on the southern side. With one level underground and three stories above, it would almost double the capacity of the library, in addition to providing space for classrooms, offices, and moot court.[84]

The major expansion and renovation project of the decade was probably the renewal of Saint Edward's Hall. In June 1980 the hall suffered serious damage from a fire that swept through the fourth floor and the roof. The cause was never determined but workers were using blowtorches in the area, ironically to install a new sprinkling system. The fire began about nine o'clock in the morning, ten pieces of fire equipment from campus and South Bend worked on it, and the fire was extinguished by eleven-thirty that morning. Only the rector was living in the building during the summer and he was away at class, but most of his personal belongings were saved, including his pet Moluccan Cockatoo, and two prized hall possessions were also saved: a late 1800s fresco on the second floor and a stained glass window of Father Sorin. Although the insurance coverage for the damage was only $1 million, the university decided on a major renovation at double that cost. The two-story annex on the north side of the building, badly in need of repairs, was demolished and replaced by a four-story addition that included a mansard roof and a fourth floor to match the rest of the building. Students assigned to Saint Edward's Hall for the 1980–1981 academic year were housed in study lounges in Grace and Flanner Halls and in the annex at nearby Columba Hall (the annex was called Vincent Hall). Construction continued through the fall and winter of 1980 and the spring and summer of 1981. The renovated hall boasted of smoke detectors and sprinklers in every room, smoke alarm doors, an emergency generator, an elevator in the new addition, refurbished rooms and corridors, and it could accommodate 188 students, 50 more than its predecessor.[85]

In another important renovation, the former WNDU radio and television building adjacent to the library was converted into the Center for Social Concerns, equipped with a large classroom, a hospitality room, a coffeehouse, a reflection room, a reading room, and ten offices. Father Don McNeill, with Sister Judith Anne Beattie, C.S.C., and a few others established the center in 1983 as an outgrowth of Father McNeill's earlier Center for Experiential Learning. The CSC, as it was often called, oversaw a variety of service learning projects (Urban Plunge, Neighborhood Roots, Head Start, Big Brothers Big Sisters, etc.) and cooperated effectively with other programs—Council for the International Lay Apostolate (CILA), Holy Cross Associates, and Catholic Committee on Urban Ministry. Most of the students who participated in volunteer service projects during their undergraduate days, hundreds each year, were sponsored by the Center for Social Concerns, and many continued volunteer service in the years after graduation.[86]

Other buildings underwent similar renovations. In the summer of 1987, minor changes were made in Howard Hall and it was converted into a women's dormitory to accommodate 150 additional women the university intended to admit that fall. A statue of Dr. Tom Dooley was placed near the entrance of the Grotto in 1985 for the twenty-fifth anniversary of his death. A 1948 Notre Dame graduate, he spent most of his short adult life as a medical doctor in Southeast Asia, leading President Eisenhower to remark: "There are few, if any, men who equaled his exhibition of courage, self-sacrifice, faith in his God, and his readiness to serve his fellow men." Closer to the center of campus, where the former fieldhouse once stood, a new memorial fountain was constructed to honor the estimated five hundred Notre Dame alumni who lost their lives in World War II, Korea, and Vietnam. The major benefactor was Mrs. John Clarke of Chicago, the principal architect was Notre Dame alumnus John Burgee, and the commemorative plaque read: "This is our prayer, that all living Notre Dame men and women dedicate themselves to the service of their country and world peace."[87]

The most unexpected renovation of the decade took place in the fall of 1985 when the Grotto of the Blessed Virgin caught fire. Flames had broken out in the Grotto five years earlier when hot wax from the candles fell on stored cardboard boxes, but damage had been minimal and the fire was extinguished quickly. The fire in 1985 was more serious. Thousands of visitors had arrived on September 21 for the Notre Dame–Michigan State football game, the wrought-iron racks were filled with lighted candles, and visitors began putting new ones on the ground under the racks. The heat from those candles on the ground may have caused the candle holders above to melt, fuse, and break into flames. The interior rocks of the Grotto were blackened, as was the statue of the Blessed Virgin, trees and shrubs above the Grotto were scorched, and even the lock on the donation box melted. An anonymous caller notified the fire department at about three o'clock that Monday morning, and the fire was extinguished in a little over thirty minutes. More than five hundred gallons of water were needed, and foam was also needed since water could be ineffective on the hydrocarbons and wax from the candles. The Grotto was closed for a week while the heavy rocks were inspected for damage, the area was thoroughly washed, new candle racks were purchased, and by October 1, the Grotto was reopened to visitors.[88]

The most significant change at the university in the 1980s, of course, was the retirement of Father Hesburgh in 1987 and his replacement by Father Edward "Monk" Malloy as president. Father Hesburgh had served as president for thirty-five years and it is likely that none of that year's students—even graduate students—had been born when he assumed the presidency in 1952. Father Marvin O'Connell dedicated his brilliant biography of Father Sorin to Father Hesburgh, the "Second Founder of Notre Dame."[89] It was hardly an exaggeration. Father Sorin had founded a very successful educational institution, Father Burns had made it a true college, and Father Hesburgh had made it an organized research university.

The university had made remarkable progress during Father Hesburgh's thirty-five years. The new president had begun by replacing all five deans, signifying that academic life was taking a different direction.[90] Good teaching would remain essential but faculty research and publication were also required. Nationally and internationally respected chaired professors were recruited to help raise academic standards in each department. SAT scores rose each year and admissions became more selective. Foreign study programs were introduced to offer broader educational opportunities, and a quasi-honors program, the Committee on Academic Progress, was inaugurated for brighter and more creative students. Six new academic centers were begun: Center for the Study of Human Society (formerly the Center for the Study of Man in Contemporary Society), Helen Kellogg Institute for International Studies, Center for Civil and Human Rights, Cushwa Center for the Study of American Catholicism, Joan B. Kroc Institute for International Peace Studies, and the Ecumenical Institute for Advanced Theological Studies in Tantur, Israel. Two years after his retirement, Notre Dame would be recognized as one of the top twenty-five universities across the country.[91]

In the area of student life, an area that caused scores of university presidents to lose their positions in the 1960s and 1970s, Father Hesburgh had not only survived but led Notre Dame into a more attractive and comfortable living environment. Longstanding regulations of nightly curfew, no cars, rector's permission for weekend absences, no female visitors in residence halls, and areas of South Bend that were out-of-bounds for Notre Dame students were gradually abolished as inappropriate for post–World War II generations of students. Student Government garnered more authority campus-wide and in individual residence halls, and students held places on most judicial boards. Despite state regulations, the university took a more lenient stand on the use of alcohol. Students generally responded maturely, though not always. The fact that Father Hesburgh sympathized with, and even agreed with, many of the students' demands, especially their growing opposition to the war in Vietnam, kept protests from becoming excessive. They were proud of their president's confrontation with the Nixon administration over civil rights.

Change was most noticeable in campus growth. Student enrollment increased from 5,000 to 9,600, the faculty from 390 to 800, the annual budget from $10 million to $176 million, and the endowment from $9 million to $350 million. Close to forty buildings were erected—more than one a year. New residence facilities included Pangborn Hall, Stanford and Keenan Halls, University Village, Lewis Hall, Flanner and Grace Halls, the O'Hara-Grace townhouses, and Pasquerilla East and West. Strengthening academic life were the new library, Radiation Laboratory, Meštrović Studio Gallery, Computer Center and Mathematics Building, Center for Continuing Education, Galvin Life Science Center, Fitzpatrick Hall of Engineering, Hayes-Healy Center, Snite Museum of Art, Stepan Chemistry Hall, Decio Faculty Hall, and a permanent home for the Center for Social Concerns. Other buildings might be considered auxiliary enterprises but they were much more—North Dining Hall, the Athletic and Convocation Center, WNDU, Hammes Bookstore, Stepan Center, the new post office, Rolfs Aquatic Center, Loftus Center, and Eck Tennis Pavilion.

Father Hesburgh would probably have acknowledged that his three most important achievements were his successful handling of the student protests and riots that rocked most universities across the nation in the 1960s and 1970s, the transfer of the ultimate governance of the university to a predominantly lay board of trustees in 1967, and the decision to admit undergraduate women into the university in 1972. After the final two at least, the university could never be the same again.

CHAPTER 19

A President Called "Monk"

The First Five Years

Father Edward "Monk" Malloy, Father Hesburgh's successor as president of Notre Dame, was born in Washington, DC, on May 3, 1941. His father worked as a claims adjuster for the DC Transit Company and was conservative in both religion and politics. A fourth degree Knight of Columbus, he went to Confession frequently, attended parish missions and retreats, gathered the family on occasion to say the rosary, and was deferential to any pronouncements emanating from the Vatican. A Republican in politics, he favored the anti-Communism of Senator Joseph McCarthy, worked with the Committee to Re-elect the President in 1972, and was invited to one of President Richard Nixon's inaugural balls the following January. Father Malloy's mother walked a different path. A convinced liberal Democrat, she attended President Nixon's inaugural ball with her husband only out of a sense of duty. In religion, because she may have been cured of a physical ailment through prayer as a young girl, she retained a strong devotion to Our Lady of Victory. She held fast to basic Catholic teachings but was also open to the beliefs of others, and saw good in other religions and in persons with no religion at all.[1] Father Malloy admired and was strongly influenced by both.

The future president attended Saint Anthony's Grade School in the District, taught by the Benedictine Sisters, and it was at Saint Anthony's that he first developed his lifelong love of reading, began to broaden his vocabulary, and followed his parents in their devotion to crossroad puzzles. It was in the third or fourth grade at Saint Anthony's also that he acquired a new name. A fellow student had been nicknamed "Bunky" but young Malloy had shortened it to "Bunk," and "Bunk" retaliated by calling him "Monk" since it seemed alliterative with his last name. Others began adopting it also, much to his mother's chagrin, but his mother eventually relented, and he remained "Monk" Malloy ever after. At Saint Anthony's he also excelled in sports, having grown taller than most of his schoolmates, and he played fullback in football, was a catcher in baseball, and developed a good set shot in basketball. The nearby public park where most games took place was called Turkey Thicket, and young Malloy spent sufficient time there that he was declared "The Mayor of Turkey Thicket."[2]

His love of reading and his basketball skills developed further when he entered Archbishop Carroll High School in the fall of 1955, an all-male school opened by the archdiocese in 1951 and operated by the Augustinian friars. Ten to fifteen percent of the students were black. By his senior year, Malloy had been elected student body president, head of a student political party, member of the honor society, assistant editor of the yearbook, and assistant editor of the student newspaper. In this last position, he contributed a column every Friday, developing his writing style further and sharpening his early fascination with words. But influenced by an excellent teacher of physics, and influenced also by the new world of space Sputnik had opened, his major academic interest had turned to engineering.[3]

In basketball, the coach at the time was determined to build a championship team. Malloy was a student at Archbishop Carroll all four years, but the coach actively recruited outstanding players from other areas: John Thompson and George Leftwich in their sophomore year and Tom Hoover as a junior. The coach located scholarship funds for those who could not afford the tuition. Malloy was the only white starter in his junior year and one of only two in his senior year. He was too slow to run the fast break and his hands were too small to handle the dribbling demanded of a point guard, but he possessed a deadly outside shot. Unfortunately, he arrived too early for the three-point line. The team went 22–4 in his junior year, with one of those losses to the Georgetown University freshmen, and 28–0 in his senior year.[4] Basketball furnished lessons off the court also. As an integrated team, the players could encounter hostile crowds when playing all-white or all-black schools, and an eatery in Delaware once refused to serve the black players, causing all to leave to seek another restaurant. Throughout his senior year, Malloy received more than fifty college scholarship offers. He turned down Harvard, Princeton, and Yale (not Catholic), Georgetown and the Catholic University of America (too close to home), and eventually narrowed the choice to Villanova, Santa Clara, and Notre Dame, with Notre Dame finally the winner. It was Catholic, had an engineering school, and was far from home—but not too far.[5]

Malloy's undergraduate years at Notre Dame were successful, but not at all as he intended. Still interested in engineering, he enrolled in mathematics and engineering drawing in his freshman year, and he failed both. He thoroughly disliked his math professor and simply stopped going to class, and in engineering drawing he had difficulty plotting images from different angles. After a meeting with his academic counselor, he transferred his major to English, an excellent choice given his love of reading, and he compiled a fine academic record over the final seven semesters.[6] His basketball career did not progress as well. Coach John Jordan's offense featured guards with quickness and ball-handling skills who could orchestrate picks and cuts and backdoor passes, and Malloy's talents lay elsewhere. He played enough to letter but he spent most of the time on the bench, witnessing less than inspiring season records of 17–9, 12–14, 7–16, and 17–9. Football was equally disappointing, with Coach Joe Kuharich's 17–23 record over those four years. But successes abounded in other areas. Malloy was elected president of Badin Hall in his junior year, was a member of the respected Blue Circle service organization, and narrowly lost the election for senior class president. Most important of all, on a trip to Mexico with Notre Dame's Council for the International Lay Apostolate (CILA) to drain ditches, mix cement, and distribute surplus food in the summer after his junior year, he visited the mountaintop basilica of Cristo Rey outside the town of Guanajuato, and there he felt a clear call to become a priest. He had been giving thought to a possible vocation for several years, but the call seemed unmistakable now, and after four years at Notre Dame and the favorable impressions of Holy Cross priests Ernest Bartell, Joseph Garvin, and Herman Reith, he decided to enter the Congregation of Holy Cross.[7]

Malloy began his years of preparation for the priesthood at Notre Dame in the late summer of 1963. He spent the first year at Saint Joseph Hall (the new name of the former Moreau Seminary after the new Moreau Seminary was built in the late 1950s) and he spent the next year in the novitiate in Jordan, Minnesota, studying the religious life in general and the Congregation of Holy Cross in particular, spending time in spiritual reading and silent prayer (and afternoon manual labor), and discerning whether the priesthood and religious life were truly his calling. He professed his first vows at the end of that year, and he returned to Moreau

Seminary for a year of additional classes in Latin and philosophy as preparation for future studies of theology. He was assigned to Holy Cross College in Washington, DC, his hometown, in the fall of 1966, began classes in Moral and Systematic Theology, Sacred Scripture, and Canon Law, did volunteer work at Saint Elizabeth's Hospital for the mentally ill, received a master's degree in English for summer studies at the University of Notre Dame, took part in an anti–Vietnam War protest in 1967, and witnessed the city's turbulence after the assassination of Martin Luther King, Jr., in April 1968. The theology program at Holy Cross College closed in the summer of 1968, and Malloy and his classmates returned to Notre Dame and enrolled in its recently established master of divinity program. He came under the influence of Father Louis Putz, seminary superior and leader of the national Christian Family Movement and Young Christian Students movement, and Father Henri Nouwen, the brilliant Dutch spiritual writer, and from the safety of the other side of the lake he witnessed the various student protests, the imposition of Father Hesburgh's fifteen-minute rule, the pornography conference debacle, and the national protests over the birth control encyclical *Humanae Vitae*. He pronounced his final vows in 1969 and was assigned to Flanner Hall as assistant rector. Ordained a priest in Sacred Heart Church in April 1970, he chose Vanderbilt University for graduate studies in Christian ethics, relaxed at the Grand Ole Opry on occasion, played basketball a couple of afternoons a week with other graduate students, taught a course at Aquinas Junior College in Nashville one year, and received his PhD in 1975.[8]

After completing all his classes at Vanderbilt, and having begun work on his dissertation, in 1973 he was assigned to teach in the Theology Department at Notre Dame and live in Moreau Seminary as director of the college seminary program. This continued for four years and was followed by a year living in Corby Hall on campus, a sabbatical year in Berkeley in 1978–1979, a return to campus and a room in Sorin Hall, and finally his appointment as associate provost in 1982. Notre Dame underwent major changes and experienced major progress in the fourteen years from 1973 to 1987, and Father Malloy witnessed them closely or took part in some of them. The university was adjusting to undergraduate women on campus for the first time; football fortunes fluctuated under the leadership of Ara Parseghian, Dan Devine, and Jerry Faust; a young Digger Phelps orchestrated the basketball program; the *COUP* and *PACE* reports were released and acted upon; Father Burtchaell resigned as provost; Governor Cuomo delivered a controversial address as a Catholic public official struggling with complex moral issues; fire struck both Saint Edward's Hall and the Grotto; the campus debated an honor code (that Father Malloy strongly supported); new buildings continued to grace the campus; and as associate provost, Father Malloy was an influential member of the Provost's Advisory Committee and the university's officers' group, and he made the effort to schedule personal meetings with every member of the faculty.[9] When he assumed the presidency in 1987, Father Malloy knew the university well—as student, professor, and administrator—and he assumed responsibility easily, delivered precise and articulate speeches without the aid of notes, and preferred to govern through consultation and consensus, listening quietly to advice from various (and competing) sources, deciding himself, and then convincingly explaining the decision to others. He certainly entered the office more qualified through experience than many presidents before him.

The ceremonies inaugurating Father Malloy as sixteenth president of the university were both impressive and unique. Unique because Notre Dame presidents had not been inaugurated before. Prior to 1967, the university was controlled by the Congregation of Holy Cross and the presidency of Notre Dame was a priestly assignment similar to other assignments as parish pastor, foreign missionary, or seminary superior. Father Hesburgh recalled that when he was appointed president, his predecessor, Father John Cavanaugh, simply handed him the keys to the office and told him the president was committed to deliver a talk to a religious group on campus that evening.[10]

The inauguration ceremonies began with a morning Mass in the basketball arena of the Athletic and Convocation Center, and that was followed by a formal luncheon for university officers, trustees, and visiting dignitaries. Early in the afternoon an academic procession of approximately eight hundred faculty members, a score of trustees, and official representatives of more than 150 universities formed on the library mall and proceeded into the Athletic and Convocation Center. Thousands of students, close to 350 alumni from across the country, and hundreds of visitors also attended. Donald Keough, chairman of the university's board of trustees, made the formal transfer of authority:[11]

> Father Malloy, on behalf of the trustees of the University, I commend to you the presidential leadership of the University of Notre Dame and officially invest you as its 16th president. We welcome you to the rights and responsibilities of this office.

In his response, Father Malloy listed areas where he felt continued progress needed to be made—more women on the faculty and in administration, better computer facilities, increased library support, additional graduate and under-graduate student housing—and he outlined clearly his vision for the university's future:[12]

> Notre Dame will continue self-consciously and proudly proclaiming itself to be a Catholic university. . . . The essential character of the University as a Catholic institution of higher learning shall at all times be maintained. . . .
>
> It is not acceptable at Notre Dame to engage in (teaching) in a per-functory or indifferent fashion. Our students deserve total commitment of their mentors to providing a lively and stimulating educational environ-ment. . . .
>
> We must enthusiastically embrace our potential as a major research institution and we must define those areas of scholarly pursuit where we at Notre Dame are especially well suited to make a lasting contribution. . . .

Father Malloy retained almost all of the administration he inherited. Father Joyce, the executive vice president, retired with Father Hesburgh, and he was replaced by Father William Beauchamp, but Professor Timothy O'Meara as pro-vost, Professor Roger Schmitz as associate provost, Father David Tyson as vice president of student affairs, Thomas Mason as vice president of business affairs, Professor William Sexton as vice president of university relations, and Professor Robert Gordon as vice president of advanced studies all agreed to remain in their positions.[13]

Several months before assuming the presidency, Father Malloy, in keeping with his penchant for seeking wide advice before reaching decisions, had four task forces appointed to examine and report on what he called "important areas of University life:"

1. Marriage, Family and Other Life Commitments
2. Whole Health and the Use and Abuse of Alcohol
3. The Quality of Teaching in a Research University
4. Residentiality

Task force reports were due in March 1988.[14]

The Task Force on Marriage, Family, and Other Life Commitments was given the broad mandate to examine how the university was fulfilling its mission of preparing students for marriage, singleness, parenthood, and vowed life, to evaluate male-female relations on campus, to review present support structures, and to propose pertinent policy changes. Through circulated surveys and personal interviews, the fifteen-person task force collected information on the social environment for both graduate and undergraduate students, male-female relations, child care, parental leave, sexual harassment, homosexuality, family sick leave, the tenure clock, and concerns of single individuals. The group discussed its findings in regular meetings throughout the year, and agreed on forty-two recommendations, among them the following:[15]

7. The University should strive to achieve a sex-blind admission process.
9. The University should create some form of coeducational residence living arrangement to improve male/female relationships among undergraduates and to decrease sex stereotyping.
10. The President should charge student groups . . . to promote more creative, non-alcoholic events and coeducational programs.
22. Child care should be included in a University flexible benefits program as one of the options available to those individuals who could benefit from such a service.
24. The University should adopt a parental leave policy which is more generous in paid time off than the present policy for birth mothers, [and which] includes some provision for fathers and for adoptive parents.
29. A stopped tenure clock option should be included in the segment of a parental leave policy that pertains to faculty.
37. The University should be as attentive to the needs of single persons as it is to families in planning activities and social functions.
38. The University should vigorously pursue a program of affirmative recruitment and promotion of women . . . [and] protected minorities to achieve greater representation on the faculty [and] in administrative ranks.
39. The University should develop [both] a policy statement which defines and prohibits sexual harassment [and] . . . a formal complaint procedure for students, staff, and faculty.
42. The University should include "sex" and "sexual orientation" as part of its nondiscrimination policies.

The report of the Task Force on Whole Health and the Use and Abuse of Alcohol began with a detailed history of the university's policy on the use of alcohol from the 1860s (expulsion for any use) down to the recommendations of the University Committee on the Responsible Use of Alcohol chaired by Father William Beauchamp in 1984. The report next reviewed federal and Indiana laws pertinent to alcohol use and outlined Notre Dame's possible liability as "supervisor," as "property owner," as a "seller of alcohol," and as a "social host." The policies and procedures of a few other colleges and universities were considered, with apparently no other institution permitting alcohol to be purchased with university funds and then provided to minors as Notre Dame was allowing at all-hall parties (SYRs). The task force mailed a survey to eight hundred randomly selected students, two hundred from each academic class, and received responses from 45 percent of those students. The results indicated that 90 percent of Notre Dame students did drink; 43 percent (more males than females) drank two or three times a week; 78 percent of students believed present university policy led students to drink off campus; 20 percent of freshmen admitted drinking off campus; 76 percent favored a facility on campus where underage students could experience responsible drinking; only 5 percent favored the establishment of an alcohol-free dormitory; 86 percent agreed that a student drinking too much should be challenged by other students; and 28 percent would enroll in a three-credit elective course on the use of alcohol.

The task force recommended:[16]

1. Establishment of a required course for freshmen on alcohol education.
2. Prohibition of advertisements glamorizing alcohol or an alcoholic lifestyle.
3. Provision of funds for "creative social alternatives to the use of alcohol."
4. Permission for hall parties only if 70 percent of residents enroll and no alcohol is provided with hall funds.
5. Drunkenness should not be tolerated at tailgates on football weekends and consumption of alcohol should be forbidden in the "inner part of the campus."
6. Drunkenness should not be tolerated on Alumni Reunion weekends and hours of serving alcohol in refreshment tents should be limited.
7. To better the social life of the campus itself, hours in recreational facilities should be extended, additional lights should be installed on outside basketball courts, alternative uses of Stepan Center should be considered, and a major performing arts center should be investigated for the future as well as the development of a commercial center in the area surrounding campus.

8. Kitchen and living room areas should be provided when residence halls are renovated.

In two minority reports, one recommended the banning of all alcohol at hall-sponsored parties, and a second recommended the prohibition of the public use of alcohol at football weekend tailgates.

The Task Force on the Quality of Teaching in a Research University, appointed and commissioned by Provost O'Meara, stated in its report that "we found that the Notre Dame faculty does a good job of teaching" and acknowledged that "it has continued to do so while upgrading the quality of its research. Indeed, there is a connection between the two. The intellectual content of courses at Notre Dame has never been better. This is one of the ways in which the increased emphasis on research at the University has improved teaching."[17] Among the report's seventeen recommendations were the following:

1. With the reduction in teaching loads and greater emphasis on research, additional faculty are needed.
2. Chaired and full professors should be fully involved in undergraduate teaching.
3. The use of adjuncts in teaching should be minimized, and those used should be paid respectably.
4. A Center for the Improvement and Support of Teaching is needed.
5. Notre Dame needs more and better classrooms.
6. The campus bookstore needs upgrading.
7. Departmental procedures for reappointing and promoting faculty need to be reviewed and possibly revised.
8. Each academic department should have a mentoring system for junior faculty.

The Task Force on Residentiality, appointed and commissioned by the vice president of student affairs Father David Tyson, stated the university's residential goal succinctly: "Residence life at Notre Dame must provide more than the necessities of room and board; it must encourage and foster students' spiritual, moral, intellectual and social growth." To achieve this goal, the task force offered recommendations to address the following:[18]

1. A clearer definition of the responsibilities of the rector is needed.
2. Salaries should be sufficient to hire highly qualified persons as rectors.

3. Student-faculty contacts outside the classroom should be encouraged.
4. More classes should be taught in the residence halls.
5. The number of undergraduate women needs to be increased.
6. More minority students and staff persons are needed.
7. Campus Ministry should make special efforts to meet the religious needs of minority students.
8. *Du Lac* should be revised and reasons for the regulations should be better explained.
9. Additional residence halls should be constructed to house interested students presently living off campus.
10. A co-residential housing option should be available.
11. All residence halls should be handicapped accessible.

A majority of the task force also favored additional priests living in the women's residence halls, but a minority agreed only if women were added to the staffs in men's residence halls.

Influenced by the task force reports, Father Malloy decided to inaugurate a series of thematic years dedicated to exploring and addressing what he considered particular concerns of the university community. On the recommendation of the Committee on Minority Students appointed by the provost in November 1986, Father Malloy declared the first of these thematic years, 1988–1989, the Year of Cultural Diversity.[19] Diversity was clearly a university concern. In a student body of close to 8,000 in the fall of 1988, black Americans numbered only 4 percent, Hispanics 4 percent, Asians 2 percent, and Native Americans 0.04 percent. Thirty-five percent of undergraduates were women. The faculty needed attention also. In a teaching and research faculty of 855, there were only 128 women (15 percent), 15 black Americans, 13 Asians, 35 Hispanics, and 1 Native American.[20] To broaden the educational experience of all students, the university needed to find ways to attract both students and faculty of more diverse backgrounds and cultures and make them feel comfortable and at home on the Notre Dame campus.

From his years growing up in the nation's capital, Father Malloy realized that his fellow citizens held a variety of views on race and diversity, some contradictory to others, but he remained optimistic:[21]

> The Year of Cultural Diversity is a step in what I hope will be a process
> of exchange and bonding across such divisions. I think only if the mi-

nority population increases will there be enough opportunity for that to continue as part of everybody's experience here. I do not think that a year of cultural diversity is sufficient, but we have to begin somewhere, and I think everyone would agree that this is a good place to begin.

The committee organizing events invited a series of prominent speakers throughout the year. The first two were African American business executives: Carl Ware, vice president of Coca-Cola, speaking on "Minorities, Markets, and Corporate Strategies," and Roy Roberts, vice president of Navistar, on minorities in American corporations. Dr. Jawanza Kunjufu, educational consultant with African American Images in Chicago, spoke on "Countering the Conspiracy to Destroy Black Boys." Professor Donald Fixico, historian of Native Americans, lectured on "Urban American Indians since World War II," and Professor Deborah White of Rutgers University lectured on the status of African American women in the United States. Miriam Makeba, renowned singer from Johannesburg, performed a concert with Hugh Masekela, and the Ballet Folklorico Azul y Oro danced on Mexican Independence Day.[22]

The following year was announced as the Year of the Family. The family was clearly deteriorating nationally. A recent study indicated that 60 percent of all children born in the 1980s would spend at least one year in a single-parent house, and almost a third of these would live with a stepparent.[23] For this celebration, the university defined "family" broadly, including the traditional family, residence hall communities, and the Notre Dame family as a whole. In early September, the university welcomed the L'Arche Daybreak community, a Canadian group where "the mentally handicapped and their assistants live together in the spirit of the beatitudes."[24] The executive counsel to an Indiana senator lectured on family values as influenced by state and federal legislation. The University Health Center sponsored lectures on the dangers of smoking and unprotected sex. The Office of Drug and Alcohol Education presented a lecture on the impact of alcoholism on the family, and Notre Dame Security discussed how women can protect themselves from spousal abuse. Tying in with the year before, one lecturer spoke on "The Importance of Maintaining Family Ties in African American Families." As commencement speaker that year the university selected Bill Cosby, star of the premier family television program, *The Cosby Show*, although Cosby's honorary degree was later revoked.[25]

The Year of Women followed in 1990–1991. Motivation for the year was twofold. First, Notre Dame had admitted undergraduate women for the first time in the fall of 1972, women made up 37 percent of the undergraduate student body by 1990, women had joined the undergraduate faculty in the mid-1960s and still comprised less than 18 percent of the faculty, and Notre Dame needed to decide if the undergraduate increases would continue incrementally as in the past or if the goal should be gender-blind admissions. Second, campus security had become a major concern. The number of reported sexual assaults was increasing, date rapes were also increasing but they were not always reported, and there was concern that these numbers might increase as more undergraduate women were admitted to campus.[26] The events of the year were impressive. A special committee was appointed to study and report to Father Malloy on future enrollment policy. Two movies were shown: *Story of Women*, about the last woman guillotined as an abortionist during the French Revolution, and *Camille Claudel*, the model of several of Auguste Rodin's sculptures. Two theatrical productions, *The Trojan Women* and *The Good Woman of Setzuan*, were produced by the Department of Communications and Theatre. Prominent speakers addressed the campus community—Rosa Parks, Geraldine Ferraro, Maya Angelou, and Alicia Ostriker—and the Indigo Girls, an all-woman rock group, played to a sold-out crowd. Margaret O'Brien Steinfels, prominent Catholic and spokesperson for women's issues, delivered the commencement address.[27]

The 1991–1992 school year marked the 150th anniversary of the founding of the university and the whole year was planned as a sesquicentennial festival, celebrating Notre Dame's achievements over the century and a half and celebrating the role of Catholic education in the history of the United States. The school year opened with a multimedia Mass in the Athletic and Convocation Center followed by a picnic for all and a fireworks display. The weekend of November 1 was declared Homecoming Weekend, with a parade-float competition among the halls and campus organizations. Rocky Bleier, Notre Dame graduate and member of the Super Bowl champion Pittsburgh Steelers, spoke at the pep rally. Former president Jimmy Carter and comedian Howie Mandel addressed the student body in March, Senator Daniel Patrick Moynihan received the university's Laetare Medal, and President George H. W. Bush delivered the commencement address.[28]

The task force reports and the thematic year organizing committees recommended excellent projects but, unfortunately, they also increased the budget. Operating a growing university continued to be more expensive each year. After long discussions throughout the spring of 1988, the administration announced an 8.9 percent increase in tuition for the following year and a 6.9 percent increase in room, board, and laundry, bringing the total cost to $13,400. Father Malloy noted that the increases were needed because of higher faculty and staff salaries, a rise in insurance premiums, new faculty and student affairs positions, and additional library and computer technology needs.[29] The cost of a Notre Dame education took an even higher jump the following year. Tuition for 1989–1990 was $11,315, an increase of 9.6 percent, and room, board, and laundry was $3,275, up 6.5 percent. The increases continued the following year, with tuition rising 8.7 percent to $12,390 and room and board rising $200 to $3,475, bringing the total to $15,865. Similar increases were announced for 1991–1992: a 9 percent rise in tuition to $13,505 and a 6 percent rise in room and board to an average of $3,575, bringing the total to $17,080. The increases announced the final year of Father Malloy's first five-year term were slightly lower. Tuition for 1992–1993 was set at $14,605, an increase of 8.5 percent, and room and board was set at $3,790, a 6 percent increase. The university also announced its intention, and hope, to reduce those increases in the coming year.[30]

Various academic changes took place during Father Malloy's first years in office. The undergraduate grading system itself was revised. The grading system at the time consisted of grades A, A–, B, B–, C, D, and F, and the system was criticized on two counts: evaluations might be more accurate and precise if there were more grade levels, and the minus grades in the system (A– and B–) without corresponding plus grades might give transcripts a more negative tone than intended. After serious discussion and debate, the Academic Council on February 16, 1988, voted almost unanimously to add the grades B+, C+, and C–, stabilizing the system at A (4.00), A– (3.67), B+ (3.33), B (3.00), B– (2.67), C+ (2.33), C (2.00), C– (1.67), D (1.00), and F (0.00).[31]

In the College of Arts and Letters, more and more students were taking languages, and a restructuring of the language program seemed warranted. In those years, all courses were offered under the single Department of Modern and Classical Languages, although the goals and levels of each language taught could vary. After much discussion, the department was divided into three—a Department of German and Russian Languages and Literatures, a Department of Classical and Oriental Languages and Literatures, and a Department of Romance Languages and Literatures. This realignment permitted each language group to more easily establish its own goals and levels of classes, determine its own best class sizes, and offer more opportunities for student advising, but it was not a perfect solution. German and Russian faculty and students had few common interests, and the same was true for Classical and Oriental Languages.[32]

Also in the College of Arts and Letters, and at about the same time, the Department of American Studies voted to eliminate its concentrations in communications and journalism. These seemed to overlap with courses in the Department of Communications and Theater. With the change, American Studies students could now select two concentrations among American literature, history, government, and social sciences, taking three courses in each. The department chair explained that writing and journalism courses would still be offered in the Department of American Studies, especially print journalism, but it would all be taught in the context of American history and culture.[33]

Restructuring took place in the College of Engineering also. The Department of Materials Science and Engineering was abolished over the summer of 1990 and replaced by a Department of Computer Science and Engineering. The Department of Electrical and Computer Engineering was also changed to simply the Department of Electrical Engineering. Provost Timothy O'Meara explained: "Significant and continuing changes in technology and how it serves society, combined with a shift in the interests of Notre Dame's engineering faculty and our desire to best use the resources of the College and the University, all contributed to this decision, which is overdue." The reorganization required no new equipment, some professors transferred between departments, and only two or three new faculty members were hired.[34]

In the fall of 1991, the university announced the establishment of a program leading to a doctorate in juridical science (JSD) in the Law School. "This is a research degree parallel to the Ph.D.," explained the program director. "The difference is that students will come with eight years of university experience rather than six. The usual candidate will have an undergraduate degree, a professional law degree (J.D.) and a LL.M. (master of laws degree)." The program was designed to serve those interested in academic careers especially well. Harvard, Yale, Columbia, Virginia, Pennsylvania, and perhaps ten other highly acclaimed law schools offered the degree and the director felt it would be difficult for the Notre Dame Law School to be recognized as a top research law school without such a program. Though prestigious, the program was intended to attract only two or three students at any one time.[35]

Studying abroad continued to be an important part of a Notre Dame education for many, but changes were taking place there also. The program in Jerusalem, inaugurated in 1985, had to be cancelled for the spring of 1988 due to increased tensions and violence in the area. Twelve students had registered for the program but Associate Provost Isabel Charles, after speaking with people in the Holy Land and with State Department officials, explained that "the situation was just too tense to send a group of young people." The program met a similar fate three years later. Because of renewed political tensions in the Middle East, only five students applied for the program in the spring of 1991, and a minimum of ten was required. Safety and security were again major concerns. "Five is not a sufficient number of students to make a viable program," Charles noted, "but that is not to say that we would have offered the program even if ten had applied."[36]

Low enrollment also caused the cancellation of the summer program in Tianjin, China, in 1989. The eight-week program had been introduced in 1984, and fifty students had participated in its first five years. The six-credit program included six weeks of intensive language classes at the Tianjin Foreign Language Institute, with lectures and tours to further explain Chinese history and culture, and a final ten days of rail and air travel to Hong Kong and other places of interest. Distance from the United States and the $3,000 cost of the program may have contributed to the low enrollment.[37]

To compensate for these disappointments, the university offered two new full-year foreign study abroad programs in the fall of 1990. The Japanese program was transferred from Sophia University in Tokyo to Nanzan University in Nagoya. Nanzan University had been founded by the Society of the Divine Word in 1949 and its president at the time held a doctorate in sociology from Notre Dame. Participating students needed one year of Japanese before entering the program, and they took one intensive Japanese language course and three or four other courses in Japan. The second new program was in Toledo, Spain, about forty miles south of Madrid. Students had to have attained intermediate proficiency in Spanish to enter the program, and they enrolled in fifteen credit hours each semester in Toledo, including at least one course each semester in Spanish language or literature (from Spain or Latin America). Students also had the option of living in a residence hall or with a Spanish family.[38]

In two important areas of academic support the university had fallen well behind its peers in recent years, and these needed attention. Notre Dame had originally been slow in appropriating sufficiently large sums for computing services, and various faculty members, especially in science and engineering, had used personal grant money to procure individual computers, with the result that various computers could not easily communicate with each other and the university found it difficult to maintain and service the different makes. Some of the early problems had been remedied but more needed to be done. In the fall of 1988, the university announced its intention to budget $17 million over the next four years for computer improvement—to upgrade computers in O'Shaughnessy and LaFortune Halls for student use, to add more public computers across campus, and to purchase a mini-supercomputer to replace the IBM mainframe that the university had acquired in 1984 but that had not been state of the art even then and that could not run some up-to-date programs. The $17 million price tag would have to come out of higher tuition over the next four years.[39]

The library was still clamoring for assistance also. The Association of Research Libraries had recently rated the Notre Dame library 74th out of 105. Only five of its schools had lower library budgets than Notre Dame ($6,208,325) and only fourteen had a smaller library staff. Notre Dame had added 72,403 volumes to its collections the preceding year, while Harvard had added 313,922, Berkeley 195,012, Yale 156,767, and Stanford 161,451. Notre Dame officials pointed out that such figures were misleading. Other schools needed larger libraries to service their larger number of departments and programs, and Notre Dame's library was geared more to Notre Dame's fewer departments and programs. But the library was weak in several areas—languages, for one—and Provost O'Meara, acknowledging that the ranking had come down from 97th a few years before, insisted that more was needed and would be done, although no specific financial increment was revealed.[40]

The university administration and the faculty knew quite well the academic progress the university was making during Father Malloy's first term in office, but friction was developing between the administration and the Faculty Senate. The Faculty Senate had been striving to increase faculty participation in university governance since its establishment in 1967 but it had been difficult to challenge someone esteemed so highly nationally and internationally in education as Father Hesburgh. Father Malloy did not have that same prestige. In the spring of 1989, Father Malloy's second year as president, a member of the senate brought the issue to the fore in an open letter to his colleagues. He insisted that the Faculty Senate, although the official representative of the faculty, had little influence on university policy, and membership in the senate was considered by some a waste of time. He stated that senate proposals sent to the Academic Council in the past had been ignored; that faculty surveys on health and other benefits had been dismissed as "unrepresentative"; that administrators often referred to the administration as the "University," as if the faculty were "peripheral appendages"; that university officers often came to the senate to answer questions but never to engage in constructive dialogue; and that faculty members serving as administrators represented the administration, not the faculty. The author saw three options open to the senate: it might continue as is, without much influence; it might disband (probably without much public notice); or the faculty might unionize and acquire significant influence.[41]

At the next meeting, the final one of the academic year, the senate instructed the next year's executive committee to investigate the feasibility of unionization at Notre Dame, the costs and benefits of such a step, who might be the best bargaining agent (AAUP, etc.), and what conditions the National Labor Relations Board might require for such a vote. Although some expressed opposition to unionization, chiefly because going on strike seemed unfair to students, a survey was drafted that fall and mailed to all faculty. Approximately 70 percent of the teaching and research faculty returned the survey, a commendable percentage. Eighty-six percent agreed that there was a lack of faculty participation in university decision-making; 85 percent agreed that elected faculty bodies should have greater roles to play; and more than 50 percent considered the Academic Council, the Graduate Council, and the college councils ineffective. Of the three options the senate had before it, 18 percent wanted to continue the situation as it was while 41 percent did not; 15 percent would dissolve the senate but 39 percent opposed; 32 percent wanted to pursue collective bargaining while another 32 percent did not. Seventy-one percent wanted some restructuring of present mechanisms for greater faculty participation in university governance.[42]

The executive committee of the senate met with Father Malloy and Provost O'Meara in early June 1990 but no agreement was reached on increased faculty participation. The president and provost agreed to submit the whole question to the Academic Council but this was not acceptable to the senate since the recent faculty survey seemed to reveal widespread lack of confidence in the council. The executive committee proceeded to have an ad hoc committee elected by and from the faculty to examine the issue and make recommendations. After six months of deliberations, the committee made its recommendations: that the Academic Council be restructured to be composed of fourteen ex-officio members and eighteen elected members; that it be empowered to deliberate all matters "affecting the quality of academic life;" that it be divided into standing committees with the right of agenda; that it meet six times a year; and that its executive committee be composed of ten members, including five elected faculty members and the chair of the Faculty Senate.[43]

The report was submitted to the Academic Council in early 1992, was seriously debated, and eventually passed with a vote of 21 to 12. Father Malloy declared that he could not accept such a major restructuring of the university's highest academic body, but his veto could be appealed to the board of trustees. The Faculty Senate considered taking a no-confidence vote in the president. Before the division could widen further, however, the administration and the Faculty Senate negotiated a compromise in the spring. In a joint statement of Father Malloy, Provost O'Meara, and the executive committee of the Faculty Senate, the Academic Council would be restructured to include appropriate committees with right of agenda (but not a budget committee), the Provost's Advisory Committee would be enlarged by five elected faculty members, the graduate and college councils would be strengthened, the administration would be more open about university finances, the executive committee would recommend that any plans for a no-confidence vote be dropped, the administration would investigate ways in which the faculty might participate more effectively in the university's strategic planning, and the senate would study faculty participation in preserving the Catholic character of the university. It was a compromise document with the university itself the major winner: the faculty acquired a greater role in university decision-making and the controversial options of a no-confidence vote and faculty unionization were avoided.[44]

Another cause of distress for Father Malloy and the Congregation of Holy Cross, and for the university as a whole, was the necessary resignation of Father James Burtchaell, former university provost, from the faculty. Father Burtchaell had been a popular classroom teacher, a brilliant scholar, and an efficient administrator, but accusations had been brought forth of serious improprieties in his counseling relations with both graduate and undergraduate students over the years. The university appointed a panel of one theologian and two lawyers to investigate the charges, Father Burtchaell admitted that they were true, and he offered his resignation from the faculty effective the summer of 1992. His resignation was accepted. The provincial superior of the Congregation of Holy Cross stated: "We acknowledge the serious nature of this matter and apologize to those who may have been hurt." He noted that Father Burtchaell "was asked to undergo psychological evaluation and treatment and is doing so." Father Burtchaell added that he had apologized to those he had hurt and was receiving forgiveness.[45]

As the university continued to grow, Father Malloy wanted it to continue to diversify also. He had designated the first thematic year of his administration as the Year of Cultural Diversity and, growing up in a widely diverse Washington, DC, diversity was an area where he felt comfortable and at home. But increasing diversity among the Notre Dame student body posed serious challenges. Even Father Hesburgh, chairman of the Civil Rights Commission, had fallen short of achieving his goals. Less than 6 percent of black Americans were Catholic and might be attracted to Notre Dame, and the university's high tuition forced many to look elsewhere. Increased financial aid was essential. However, the stock market had recently taken a heavy hit, and that could have an impact. Notre Dame had been fairly well positioned at the time, with 50 percent of the endowment in bonds, but many donors may still have preferred to hold on to what they had for the present.[46]

The total amount of student financial aid in 1986–1987, Father Hesburgh's final year in office, had been $43 million, but that figure increased to $50 million in Father Malloy's first year. Federal programs contributed $18 million of this, mostly in guaranteed loans; nonfederal sources provided $26 million; and ROTC scholarships provided $6 million. Sixty-eight percent of Notre Dame students received financial aid. In an effort to increase minority enrollment from 11 percent to 15 percent, a $12 million endowment was established for minority student aid, and academic support systems were set up for minority students who could profit from them. Financial aid jumped 12 percent the following year, with 69 percent of all students receiving a total of $61 million. The university stated that its future goal was to meet the financial need of every admitted student. The increase continued in succeeding years. In 1990–1991, $66.5 million was awarded to 70 percent of the student body, and $72.6 million to 71 percent of the students in 1991–1992. The administration announced that $5 million had been set aside for special scholarships: Holy Cross Scholarships for minority students and Notre Dame Scholarships for the most highly qualified students. The board of trustees also announced that the student aid endowment would be increased by $100 million over the next ten years.[47]

Despite the progress being made, many considered it too slow. Around the time of Martin Luther King, Jr., Day, January 21, 1991, a group of minority students came together as "Students United for Respect" (SUFR). Its members included black Americans, Native Americans, Hispanics, and others. They requested passage of the clear and strong racial harassment policy that was before the Academic Council at the time but whose passage was delayed over efforts to preserve freedom of speech while prohibiting discriminating speech and verbal abuse. Other student demands included a multicultural gathering space, the hiring of additional faculty for Black Studies and Latin American Studies, a larger staff in the Office of Minority Student Affairs, and greater access to reserved space in LaFortune Student Center. An early meeting had been scheduled with Patricia O'Hara, the vice president of student affairs, but it was subsequently cancelled since SUFR was not a recognized student organization. SUFR took this as a lack of respect. Informal conversations were held over the next several weeks, and some progress was made in allotting space in LaFortune Student Center, but delays also continued in the drafting of a new racial and sexual harassment policy.[48] On April 16, the Academic Council finally approved a Discriminatory Harassment Policy, which prohibited "discriminatory harassment" while defending "free expression and advocacy of ideas." Its precise wording:[49]

2. DEFINITION

For purposes of this policy:

a. Harassment. Harassment is any physical conduct intentionally inflicting injury on the person or property of another, or

any intentional threat of such conduct, or

any hostile, intentional, and persistent badgering, addressed directly at another, or small group of others, which is intended to intimidate its victim(s) from any University activity, or

any verbal attack, intended to provoke the victim to immediate physical retaliation.

b. Discriminatory Harassment. Conduct as described in a., above, constitutes discriminatory harassment, if, in addition, it is accompanied by intentionally demeaning expressions concerning race, sex, religion, sexual orientation, or national origin of the victim(s).

3. PROHIBITION

All discriminatory harassment is prohibited.

The statement then outlined to whom allegations of discriminatory harassment, whether involving faculty, staff, students, administrators, or others, were to be reported.

Two days later, sixty students connected to SUFR staged a sit-in on the first floor of the Main Building from eight o'clock in the morning until they were asked to leave at seven o'clock that evening. The demonstration highlighted two principal demands—a meeting with Father Malloy and a stronger anti-harassment policy. Father Malloy met with seven student leaders of SUFR in Sorin Hall chapel shortly after midnight but the students considered it unproductive. Father Malloy urged SUFR to seek and receive recognition as a registered student group and he was confident that present university structures could satisfactorily address their concerns. He declined to commit himself on the hiring of additional faculty for Black Studies or Latin American Studies, a larger staff in the Minority Student Affairs Office, or more meeting space.[50] The students called the recently passed anti-harassment policy "unacceptable" and demanded a policy that "offers a better definition of harassment, a central department in which discriminatory issues are handled, as well as concrete fines and punishment for offenders."[51] Discussions continued, once with a representative of the National Association for the Advancement of Colored People attending, and Father Malloy repeated his commitment to greater cultural diversity, urged SUFR to apply for and receive official recognition, promised to form a committee that "will engage in constructive dialogue" on the outstanding issues, and confirmed that those participating in the recent sit-in would suffer no academic or other reprisals. The students wanted outside, third-party arbitration or involvement but Father Malloy insisted that the committee would include only members of the university community.[52] SUFR leaders immediately applied for and received official recognition, Father Malloy began the process of appointing this new committee on cultural diversity, with SUFR represented, and fruitful discussion continued. Moderation had prevailed on both sides and a satisfactory conclusion had been reached.[53]

In order to increase the diversity of the student body even further, the university adopted a near gender-blind admissions policy in 1992–1993, resulting in a 7 percent increase in the number of women in the first-year class, 823 women out of 1,879, 44 percent of the total. That brought the number of women in the student body overall to 2,938 out of 7,618, which was 39 percent of the total student population.[54] To provide residence space for the increased number of women, Pangborn Hall was converted from a men's to a women's hall. Over the summer, the hall pool room was turned into a laundry room, a kitchenette was installed, bathrooms and showers were redone, a handicapped bathroom was added to each floor and a ramp in front, carpets were replaced, and stops were added to all ground floor windows for security. The former residents found rooms in Sorin and other male halls.[55]

With the number of women increasing on campus, campus safety continued to be a major concern. Student-operated SafeWalk, an escort service to assist anyone walking across campus, was established in the spring of 1990 and it operated from 7:00 p.m. to 1:00 a.m. on weeknights and until 2:00 a.m. on Friday and Saturday nights. The escorts worked in pairs, with at least two pairs on duty each evening and each escort wearing a blue reflective vest and carrying a flashlight and a radio connected to campus security. To request an escort, a student could call, ask at the Information Desk in LaFortune Student Center, or simply encounter a pair of escorts patrolling the campus. The service employed forty-eight paid escorts and several volunteers, and each escort received a two-hour security briefing and was familiar with the SafeWalk handbook of policies and guidelines.[56]

At about the same time, the Weekend Wheels bus program was resurrected to transport students from local bars back to campus on weekends. Using residence hall funds, the service first began in 1988 and employed local school buses and drivers, but a recent Indiana law had prohibited school buses from being used on state highways as anything but school buses. The local United Limo Service agreed to supply the buses and drivers but at approximately twice the former cost. The Office of Student Affairs refused to contribute, fearing that the service would encourage drinking even more. The service functioned from midnight to 3 a.m. Fridays and Saturdays, bringing students back to campus or to Campus View Apartments from bars on Notre Dame Avenue and the Five Corners area. The stated purpose was to reduce the number of students walking or driving back to campus from the bars, and to decrease the number of assaults and robberies.[57]

The university also increased the number of varsity sports for women at this time—with some juggling. Softball, soccer, and golf were raised to varsity level in 1988–1989, with soccer and softball each receiving two full scholarships. Women's tennis received two additional scholarships also, as did men's tennis, soccer, and hockey. On the negative side, field hockey was dropped as a varsity sport. Field hockey was not a popular sport in the Midwest—Purdue University had eliminated its program a month before and no Indiana high school provided it—and the money seemed better spent elsewhere. A couple of years later, men's wrestling met the same fate. The sport had been inaugurated in 1955–1956, had had some good years (the team was 10–3 in 1988–1989, with two All-Americans), but its overall record was 254–245–8. The program offered eleven scholarships, in part funded through an endowment, but it had little fan support and, once again, the money seemed better spent elsewhere.[58]

Not unrelated to concerns over campus safety was the continuing problem of alcohol consumption among students. It affected class attendance, thefts, auto accidents, incidents of sexual assault, and hall vandalism. In early September 1987, only three months into Father Malloy's administration, Father Tyson, the vice president of student affairs, addressed one aspect of the problem and announced a new policy dealing with students stopped for driving while intoxicated. The new policy was prompted by a number of alcohol-related accidents in recent years in which Notre Dame students were either drivers or victims. The policy applied to any student driving on or off campus with a blood alcohol level above the legal limit. For the first offense, the student's parking privileges would be revoked and the student might be required to participate in an alcohol education program. For a second offense, the student would be suspended for a semester and would have to receive clearance from the university's alcohol counselor to be readmitted. On readmission, the student's parking privileges would be revoked and he or she might be required to participate in an alcohol counseling program. If injury or death resulted from an alcohol-related accident, additional penalties might be imposed. On campus arrests by Notre Dame Security would be reported to state authorities, and off campus arrests would be handled by local civil authorities.[59]

The earlier Task Force on whole Health and the Use and Abuse of Alcohol, after a yearlong study, made its report to the administration on March 15, 1988, the pertinent university offices studied it, a new policy was developed at a five-day meeting at the university-owned research center in Land O'Lakes, Wisconsin, in July, and the new policy was announced in late August. The policy noted that the legitimate drinking age was now twenty-one nationwide, the only alternative to the new policy seemed to be a dry campus, and the university preferred to educate students about the responsible use of alcohol. The new policy stipulated that each hall could sponsor only one all-hall or SYR dance each semester instead of two,[60] that 70 percent of the hall residents had to purchase dance tickets, that no university or hall funds could be used to purchase alcohol, that there be no open containers of alcohol in public places, that the hall must provide funds for food and nonalcoholic beverages, and that there be no advertising of events with alcohol present.[61]

The hall rectors contacted at the time felt that the policy actually changed very little but did give needed consistency to halls across the campus. "In terms of residentiality," one rector stated, "the policy remains essentially the same." Another rector noted that the "difference is the prohibition of the purchase of alcohol by the hall and the consumption of alcohol in public places." She added: "I think the hall semi-formals now will be an opportunity for people to focus on the real reason for semi-formals, which is to enjoy one another's company and not focus on alcohol." A third rector hoped it "will force more creative thinking about alternative social activities."[62] The students were not pleased with the reduction of all-hall dances from two to one each semester and the required 70 percent participation, but they realized that the university could not approve the public consumption of alcohol by persons under twenty-one contrary to state law.[63]

In the fall of 1991, the student handbook, *du Lac*, tightened and clarified the alcohol policy further. Large quantities of alcohol (kegs, cases, etc.) were still being openly transported on campus, a campus on which the vast majority of residents were under the legal age for drinking. The new provision in *du Lac* stated that "those of legal age may possess or transport in any public area of campus an amount of alcohol which is consistent with the concept of responsible individual consumption," and the alcohol must be in a closed container—a bag or box. The policy stated also that "alcohol may not be provided for those who are underage" and defined "providing" as selling, lending, giving, exchanging, bartering, or furnishing "in any way." Further, "no underage person may possess or transport alcoholic beverages in any public area of the campus." The rector was to handle a violation if it occurred in the residence hall, and the Office of Residence Life if it occurred elsewhere. The policy again seemed preferable to a totally dry campus.[64]

One of Father Malloy's hopes, from his early days as a student, was to see the establishment of an effective academic honor code. Plagiarism was a serious problem on campuses across the country. A study in 1988 suggested that 25 to 40 percent of students at major schools had plagiarized at one time or another, and the number probably reached 65 percent at some.[65] The number may have been lower at Notre Dame but it still posed a problem. Plagiarized grades did not accurately reflect what the student actually learned and knew, and honest students could receive lower grades and lower standing because others had cheated. In an honor system, each student pledged not to be dishonest in his or her academic work and not to tolerate dishonesty in the work of fellow students, even if this meant confronting a plagiarizing student or reporting the violation to authorities. Honor codes had failed in the past because students proved unwilling to confront or report on a classmate.[66]

In late April 1987, the Academic Council had passed a resolution establishing an experimental honor code for four years, beginning in 1988. The new code was in force in a number of freshman courses selected by the dean, and in any upper-division courses in which both students and professor agreed to abide by it. No student would be enrolled in such a course against his or her will. All exams in such classes would be unproctored, and students would sign pledges that all work was their own, no illegitimate help had been given or received, and that they would confront or report any discovered code violations. Students were also to be involved in any investigation and judgment of an alleged violation. Alleged violations were to be reported to the dean of the college and then turned over to the appropriate honor committees in the department, the college, or university-wide. A record of violations was preserved in the Provost's Office. The penalty for an initial violation was normally an F for the specific assignment or for the course, and the penalty for a second violation was dismissal.[67] At the close of the four-year experiment in 1993, the Academic Council approved the honor code permanently, with the modifications that each student would take the honor pledge only once, on entering the university, that departmental honor committees were to be composed of three students and two faculty, and that any accuser could remain anonymous during the investigation into an alleged violation but not at a formal hearing where the accused had a right to know his or her accuser.[68]

As the student body continued to increase, especially with the admission of additional women, and as the faculty continued to grow in both size and quality, further and better physical resources were needed. Like most university presidents, Father Malloy entered office in the fall of 1987 with high hopes and expectations. He was unfortunately met by a serious drop in the stock market that fall and a subsequent lack of confidence in the state of the American economy. Whatever that lack of confidence, renovations and expansion continued during the new president's first term.

Two new residence halls stood high on the university's list of priorities. Female applicants were confirming at a higher rate than men and the university was seeking a more equitable male-female balance. Pasquerilla East and West had been built in the early 1980s to accommodate an additional five hundred women, and two further halls were needed toward the end of the decade. Knott and Siegfried Halls opened in the fall of 1988, each built to accommodate approximately 235 students. Patterned somewhat after the Pasquerilla Halls, they were L-shaped and flat-roofed, with each floor divided into two sections. The majority of rooms on second, third, and fourth floors were doubles, with a few quads and singles, and the first floor held the chapel, typing and computer rooms, group study areas, a social and recreation room, and service facilities. When Grace and Flanner Halls were transformed into office buildings in 1996 and 1997, the men from Flanner Hall moved into Knott and Siegfried and the women from Knott and Siegfried relocated to the newly constructed McGlinn and Welsh Family Halls located just to the south of the South Dining Hall. The men from Grace Hall had moved into Keough and O'Neill Halls on that same new quad the year before.[69]

In the summer of 1988, as the furniture was being moved into Knott and Siegfried Halls and the landscaping around the halls was beginning to take shape, an elaborate scaffolding was being constructed around the Main Building for the regilding of the Golden Dome. Over time, weather wears through the gold, making a regilding necessary approximately every twenty-five years. This was the ninth regilding since the first in 1886. The process is complicated. The old oxidized and weathered gold has to be scraped off, the whole dome washed down with a solvent, a slightly sticky substance painted on, the gold, on three-and-a-half-inch-wide strips of tissue paper, then carefully applied, and the whole dome finally hand-buffed. The dome covers 3,500 square feet and the 23 karat gold leaf is so thin (0.4 micron thick) that the president of Conrad Schmidt Studios, overseeing the regilding of the dome, noted, "you can see through the leaf if it is held to the light." The gilding cannot take place in high humidity, rain, or wind, and the heat around the dome could get so intense that the workers often labored only from 5:30 to 10:30 a.m., and then again from 5:00 p.m. until dusk. The total cost of the project approached $300,000, with $96,000 for the scaffolding, $122,000 for labor, and $70,000 for the gold itself, only a couple of pounds in all.[70]

As Knott and Siegfried Halls were opening, one of the older structures on campus was being renovated—Sacred Heart Church. The slate roof had been replaced in 1986 as part of the $300 million "Strategic Moment" campaign, and the interior was given a major makeover in 1989–1990. The goal was to restore the 117-year-old church to its 1888 condition as authentically as possible. All 42 stained glass windows, with their 114 life-size figures and 106 smaller ones, were removed, repaired, and cleaned. After the devastating bombings in Europe in World War II, these may be the finest examples of nineteenth-century French stained glass in existence. Luigi Gregori's ceiling frescoes were touched up, as were his paintings high on the walls and his Stations of the Cross. An updated sound system was installed, and also a safety sprinkling system, air conditioning throughout, and a new electrical system to better illuminate the restored frescoes. New floor tiles were laid, and new carved pews provided both comfort and beauty. Two years later, because of its international reputation, its position as a center of prayer, pilgrimage, and devotion, and the richness of its liturgies, the church was raised by the Vatican to the rank of minor basilica. There are four major basilicas, all located in Rome (Saint John Lateran, Saint Peter's, Saint Mary Major, and Saint Paul Outside the Walls). Minor basilicas display the papal coat of arms over the main door and possess both a basilica bell (tintinnabulum) to be carried in processions and the umbrellum or special canopy. The number of minor basilicas is limited throughout the world and it was an honor for Notre Dame to be selected.[71]

At the same time that the church was being renovated for the future, another building was lost to fire. Flames broke out in the campus laundry, not far from the church, at about two o'clock on the morning of November 16, 1989. Fire trucks from Notre Dame and South Bend arrived quickly, but by two-thirty the fire had burned through the roof. The collapse of the roof over one section sent a fireball a hundred feet into the air, and several explosions were heard and seen. Nearby Lewis and Brownson Halls were evacuated, and Breen-Phillips, Knott, Siegfried, and other halls found room for the evacuees. The front or south section of the building, housing the offices and student records, suffered little damage, and the dry cleaning facility in the back or north section escaped almost unscathed. Windows of the Earth Science Department in Brownson Hall next door were broken and some floors were flooded. The fire was contained by 4:10 that morning and the cause was never determined. Apparently no one was in the building at the time but many flammable cleaning materials were stored there. In the aftermath, the university arranged to have its institutional laundry (sheets, towels, etc.) cleaned at Saint Joseph's Medical Center, students were reimbursed for clothing lost at about three-fifths of the cost of new garments, and the university sought to find positions for the now unemployed laundry workers in the food service operation, the cleaning and maintenance department, and the medical center laundry. The university also made plans for a new laundry building north of the campus and near the credit union on Douglas Road, with optional service for both men and women. (The former building had had no facilities for women's garments, but washers and dryers had been installed in all women's residence halls.)[72]

The southeast section of the campus, near the stadium and the Athletic and Convocation Center, had over time become the location for other athletic and extracurricular buildings—the Loftus Center and Eck Tennis Pavilion—and so when an alumnus wanted to donate money for a band rehearsal building, that location seemed particularly appropriate, especially as it was near open fields for outdoor practice. The former band building had been a small structure near La-Fortune Student Center, with rehearsals scheduled for the large music room in Washington Hall. The new building was home to the then 226-member marching band, the 60-member concert band, three smaller varsity bands, and two jazz bands. It included a large rehearsal room, a storage area for instruments, offices for band directors, and a sheet music library. The original donor eventually met financial reverses but the university decided to finance the $3.5 million building itself until another donor, the Kenneth Ricci family, generously came forward.[73]

Near this new band rehearsal building, but closer to the Hesburgh Library, the new Pasquerilla Center was constructed to house the three military units of the Reserve Officers Training Corps (ROTC).[74] The Navy had established a ROTC program at Notre Dame in 1941, the Army had returned in 1947 after an absence since World War I, and the Air Force established a program in 1951. Notre Dame numbered 681 cadets in 1990, about one-tenth of the student population. The new building was thought to be the largest ROTC center in the country. The first floor held classrooms for between forty and seventy students each, and lounges for each of the services. On the second floor, the Air Force had a four-office complex, the Army had five offices, and the Navy had seven offices. There were also cadet offices and a three-person dormitory suite.[75]

In its efforts to become a truly great university, the administration hoped to build what Graduate School dean Nathan Hatch referred to as a "small but superb" graduate school. To further attract superb graduate students, the university desired to offer convenient and comfortable housing, and one of the university's alumni, Charles Fischer of Fort Worth, came forward with funds for graduate apartments. The new construction was a complex of 33 two-story units, with each unit comprised of 6 two-bedroom apartments, thus accommodating 400 students in total. A community center and chapel were also included. The university itself contributed approximately half of the total $12 million cost, but this would be made up through rents. The Fischer Graduate Residences opened for occupancy in 1991.[76]

In the early 1990s, construction began to change the face of the campus entrance as well. Joan Kroc, widow of the founder of McDonald's, had earlier given the university $6 million to establish a master's degree program in peace studies, and in 1988 she gave another $6 million for a building to house this and other programs. Completed and dedicated in the fall of 1991, it was built across Notre Dame Avenue from the Morris Inn and, at her insistence, was named the Theodore M. Hesburgh Center for International Studies. The building comprised three connected units surrounding a pleasing courtyard. The first unit, close to the main entrance and a 1,200-square-foot great hall, included a 123-seat auditorium, 40- and 50-seat classrooms, a dining area to seat 100, and a 900-square-foot kitchen. The second, or academic and administrative, unit held conference rooms and faculty and staff offices for the Joan B. Kroc Institute for International Peace Studies on the first floor and similar facilities for the Helen Kellogg Institute for International Studies on the second and third floors. The third, or residence, unit contained 12 one-bedroom apartments, 4 two-bedroom apartments, a reading room, and laundry facilities.[77]

As the university continued to grow, more and more classrooms in the Main Building and in O'Shaughnessy, Nieuwland, and other halls had been converted into office space for new administrators and their staffs, and the university faced a serious shortage of classroom space, especially at the popular hours between nine-thirty in the morning and two in the afternoon. Edward DeBartolo of Youngstown, Ohio, a Notre Dame graduate of 1933 and a most successful builder of shopping malls throughout the country, came to the rescue with a donation of $33 million for a classroom building and later a performing arts center to honor his deceased wife. The DeBartolo Classroom Building, which opened in the summer of 1992, included eighty-four classrooms, some seating 20, 30, or 50 students, six classrooms seating 100, three classrooms seating 250, and a main auditorium accommodating 450. All classrooms were equipped with stereo sound systems, overhead projection facilities, and television monitors or large-screen projection units. One computer cluster with seventy-eight workstations was open twenty-four hours, and two others, with thirty workstations each, were closed at night. The workstations were connected to campus-wide, national, and international networks. At a cost of $22 million, it was at the forefront of technologically advanced classrooms across the country.[78]

As Father Malloy's first five-year term approached its close in early 1992, he could look back to both disappointments and successes. He had weathered conflicts with students over alcohol regulations and disagreements with the Faculty Senate over university governance, but overall the record was positive. Student SAT scores continued to rise, as did faculty salaries, additional endowed chairholders were hired each year, new buildings dotted the campus, the number of women and black Americans on the faculty and in the student body increased, and the university's Catholic mission retained its high priority. Unfortunately, the most lasting memory of these first five years in office had to be the tragedy that struck the women's swimming team in January 1992. In the early hours of January 24, thirty members of the team, plus coaches and managers, were returning by chartered bus from a meet with Northwestern in Chicago. The winter weather was bad but the toll road remained open, and about two miles from the Notre Dame exit the bus hit a patch of ice and began to slide off the road. It fishtailed, went down the embankment into a shallow ravine, and rolled over, almost upside down. The bus had not been equipped with seat belts. Windows were smashed open, several young women were thrown out, and the bus rolled over on at least two. Truck drivers stopped and sheltered the young women in their cabs, emergency personnel were called, and thirty-two injured were rushed to four nearby hospitals. Unfortunately two of the young women, Meghan Beeler of South Bend and Colleen Hipp of Saint Louis, were killed in the accident, and a third, Haley Scott, was severely paralyzed. As soon as the news of the accident reached campus, several priests and other rectors rushed to the scene, Father Malloy hurried back from a conference in Washington, DC, and the men's swim team members began visiting all the women individually in the hospitals. A memorial Mass was held that evening in an overcrowded Sacred Heart Basilica, with hundreds of students standing outside in the cold. Father Malloy presided at the Mass; Father Beauchamp, executive vice president and chairman of the Faculty Board in Control of Athletics, delivered the homily; and the recovering women's swim team members, some in arm slings or on crutches, sat together in the front pews. Most of the injured had suffered broken bones or serious bruises and spent time in the student infirmary to recover further. Haley Scott, told she would never walk again, eventually underwent five back operations and not only walked again but swam and, after marriage and two children, became a motivational speaker. Meghan Beeler was laid to rest in Cedar Grove Cemetery on Notre Dame Avenue in the shadow of the Golden Dome after a funeral Mass in Sacred Heart Basilica, and Colleen Hipp was returned to Saint Louis for funeral services among family and friends and a large contingent from Notre Dame. It was a tragedy the members of the Notre Dame community remembered the rest of their lives.[79]

The 1990s

Father Malloy began his second five-year term as president, 1992–1997, with what he hoped was a clear vision of what the university could and should be by the close of the decade. In the fall of 1991 he appointed four high-level self-study committees to assist him in developing such a plan. The committees numbered more than one hundred members of the faculty, administration, staff, and student body, others submitted written recommendations or joined in panel discussions, ideas were solicited from the college councils, and approximately three hundred alumni also sent letters. From all the information collected, Father Malloy drafted the final report, *Colloquy for the Year 2000*, as his personal vision of the university's priorities and goals as it moved toward and into the new millennium. The document was released in May 1993.[1]

The colloquy began with a mission statement describing the university "as a place of teaching and research, of scholarship and publication, of service and community."[2] Its character "as a Catholic academic community presupposes that no genuine search for the truth in the human or cosmic order is alien to the life of faith," it "welcomes all areas of scholarly activity as consonant with its mission," and the "Catholic identity of this University depends upon, and is nurtured by, the continuing presence of a predominant number of Catholic intellectuals." Discussing this mission further in its first section, which focused on Catholic character, the colloquy again recognized the special role played by the members of the Congregation of Holy Cross on the faculty, in the administration, in the residence halls, and in Campus Ministry, but acknowledged also that, while it sees Catholics predominantly in those positions, the university also "benefits and brings to public recognition the contribution of its individuals from a wide variety of other backgrounds, religious or not."[3]

Turning to academic life, the document expressed the goal to "seek educational excellence at all levels, baccalaureate and postbaccalaureate, by attracting and enrolling students of high quality, by offering demanding programs, and by providing an excellent environment in which students can learn."[4] To maintain high academic standards, the university sought to recruit teacher-scholars to the faculty who were at least equal to those of the top twenty-five universities in the country. Within the next ten years, the university intended to add 150 members to the faculty, 50 of them senior endowed chairs, 50 junior endowed chairs, and 50 regular hires. Those hiring were directed to be attentive to the university's need for additional Catholics, women, and ethnic minorities. Each academic department was commissioned to adopt a plan explicating its position and goals within the overall mission of the university. The colloquy noted that a great university required not only an outstanding faculty but also excellent students and, to attract these, Notre Dame needed to set a goal of providing aid packages meeting full financial need, with only moderate dependence on loans and work, and offer especially attractive packages to the top 10 percent of applicants. For the next ten years, enrollment should remain steady at 7,625. Financial aid should be enhanced for graduate, law, MBA, and MDiv students also. Architecture and fine and performing arts should play a prominent role in undergraduate education, and library and computer resources required greater financial support.[5]

Notre Dame strove to educate not only the minds of its students but also their hearts and souls, and responsibility for this area, student life, was entrusted primarily to the Office of Student Affairs. As a residential university, Notre Dame housed most of its students on campus, and the residence halls and graduate housing were staffed with priests, brothers, sisters, and dedicated laymen and women who assisted in the students' religious, spiritual, and moral development. The colloquy acknowledged that the student body had continued to change—the numbers of women, members of ethnic minorities, and graduate students steadily increased—and the university must adapt to these new challenges and opportunities. Changes in student life and culture must be kept in mind as new residence halls were constructed and old ones renovated.[6]

Addressing athletics, the colloquy noted both benefits and concerns. The university had consistently sought to abide by NCAA regulations, even living by more stringent ones; athletes had added to Notre Dame's national reputation through the years; and athletic revenues, over and above expenses and chiefly from football and men's basketball, added several million dollars to the university's academic budget. But the colloquy expressed concerns also. Athletic costs were rising at a faster rate than revenues and additional revenue sources would be necessary, including expanding licensing permissions and broader marketing; meeting Title IX guidelines would require additional funds as enrollment of women increased; and alumni requests always outstripped supply for football tickets.[7]

In its efforts to attract and retain a more qualified faculty and student body, the university might have paid insufficient attention to its staff who, in addition to the faculty, served the university with dedication and were essential to its success. The staff numbered more than two thousand. The colloquy sought ways to improve communications, to provide the staff members with a greater collective voice in the decision-making, and to assure that compensation was at least equal to comparable positions in the wider labor market.[8]

Despite the recent recession, the colloquy found the university's finances to be "in good shape overall." The budget had been balanced each year, the endowment remained stable, salaries were rising, the physical plant continued to expand, and the university enjoyed a Triple-A bond rating. But the document also noted three challenges: 1) Expenditures must be reduced since revenues are limited; 2) tuition must be controlled and stay in line with the value of the education received; and 3) the budget must be increased to the level of those universities that Notre Dame wished to emulate.[9]

In the colloquy epilogue, Father Malloy summarized his goals and priorities as maintaining the university's Catholic character, fostering excellence in teaching and scholarly research, expanding library resources, strengthening international education, increasing diversity among the faculty and the student body, and enhancing residential life. It was a clear if general guide for the whole university community to follow.[10]

The colloquy had acknowledged that athletics, especially football, had given Notre Dame national publicity over the years, and that was clearly illustrated with the filming of *Rudy* as Father Malloy's second term began. Since the making of *Knute Rockne: All-American* in 1940 (with Ronald Reagan playing George Gipp), Notre Dame had declined all requests to make movies on campus, but this one seemed different, and the university gave permission for the filming throughout the fall of 1992. The film presented the inspiring story of Notre Dame student Daniel E. "Rudy" Ruettiger. One of fourteen children born in a deeply Catholic but not wealthy family in Joliet, Illinois, the household listened on the radio almost religiously to Notre Dame football games every Saturday, and young Rudy used to memorize and mimic the halftime speeches of Notre Dame coaches. Although a better-than-average athlete in grade and high school, at five-foot-seven and not built for speed, college football seemed out of the question. In addition, due to dyslexia his grades were below average. Still, he dreamed of entering and playing for Notre Dame. After high school and service in the Navy, he labored for two years in a local power plant where a young friend was killed without the chance to realize his dreams, and Rudy decided then and there that he would not let his own dream die. He was eventually accepted into Holy Cross Junior College, located adjacent to the Notre Dame campus, he succeeded well enough to transfer to Notre Dame in the fall of 1974, and he joined the football team as a walk-on, spending practices on the scout team, often being run over by the varsity as they practiced for their next opponent. But as often as he was knocked down, he invariably jumped back up. Finally, in the last home game of the 1975 season, with the game clearly in the victory column against Georgia Tech, he was sent in for the last twenty-seven seconds and made the final tackle. His teammates erupted into cheers and carried him off the field on their shoulders.[11]

Ruettiger had campaigned to have his story made into a movie for years. He finally convinced director David Anspaugh and screenwriter Angelo Pizzo, who had collaborated on *Hoosiers* in 1986, of its merits. The university administration was reluctant at first, but after three rewrites the script became less of a football story and more of a human-interest story. Twenty-two-year-old Sean Astin played the lead, surrounded by Ned Beatty, Charles Dutton, Robert Prosky, and Lili Taylor. Father Hesburgh and Father Joyce made brief appearances, and Father Jim Riehle led a locker-room Hail Mary. The film was shot in the stadium, on the practice field, in Corby Hall, Sacred Heart Basilica, and O'Shaughnessy Hall on the Notre Dame campus, at Holy Cross (Junior) College, and in Corby's Bar in South Bend. But if the scenes were accurate, some liberties were taken. Coach Dan Devine insisted that the scene showing seniors prepared to quit in order to force his hand and let Ruettiger suit up for the last game never took place but he also agreed to take no legal action. Hundreds of Notre Dame students, and others, were recruited as extras, and the final climactic scene was filmed during the halftime of the Notre Dame–Boston College game on November 7, 1992, to take advantage of a full stadium crowd.[12]

Although there was some concern about how it would be received, the film proved a major success. The premier was scheduled for October 6, 1993, in the Morris Civic Auditorium in South Bend, the university's marching band staged an outdoor concert from 6:30–7:00, celebrities began to arrive at 7:10, including Sean Astin and his mother Patty Duke, and the showing opened at 7:30. The film made the rounds of theatres across the country in the weeks and months that followed and was acclaimed by moviegoers as one of the finest sports films ever. Twenty-five years later it still appeared on national television. One early review stated:[13]

> "Rudy" is not simply a movie about football. It is a story that uses football as a metaphor for life. Its universal theme of holding on to your dreams, working hard to achieve them and the general feel-good attitude about an underdog coming out on top, elevate the film to a higher level with mass appeal.

Notre Dame had won eight games and lost three (for a winning percentage of .727) in 1975, the year Rudy had played his memorable twenty-seven seconds, and Notre Dame almost matched that winning percentage throughout the 1990s. With All-Americans "Rocket" Ismail, Todd Lyght, Mike Stonebreaker, and Chris Zorich, the 1990 team compiled a record of nine and three, with last-second losses to Stanford and Penn State and a one-point loss to Colorado in the Orange Bowl. The record improved to ten and three the following year, with losses to Tennessee, Penn State, and Michigan (before a record crowd at that time of 106,138 fans), and a victory over Florida in the Sugar Bowl. In 1992, the Irish won ten, lost to Stanford, and tied Michigan 17–17. The following year ranked near the top of any list of heartbreak seasons. With All-Americans Jeff Burris, Aaron Taylor, and Bryant Young, Notre Dame won its first ten games with combined scores of 364 to 153, setting another attendance record of 106,815 in Ann Arbor, Michigan, along the way. The Florida State game could have been the most memorable game of the season. Both teams were undefeated, both were riding sixteen-game winning streaks, the teams were ranked 1–2, and ESPN's College Gameday for the first time travelled to the site of the game to be broadcast. Notre Dame held on to a 31–24 victory when Shawn Wooden batted away Heisman Trophy–winner Charlie Ward's last-ten-second pass in the end zone. But, unfortunately, the season was not over. In the final game, Boston College defeated the Irish 41–39 on a field goal as time expired. Defeating Texas A&M in the Cotton Bowl and finishing second to Florida State in the national championship poll could not erase the bitter disappointment.[14]

Unfortunately, the disappointment lingered. The record slid to 6–5–1 in 1994, Coach Holtz's worst record since his first season (5–6–0) in 1986. The team improved to 9 and 3 in 1995, with losses only to Northwestern and Ohio State in the regular season, and to Florida State in the Orange Bowl. The following year, Lou Holtz's last as an Irish coach, saw the team win eight, including a victory over Navy in Ireland, lose to Ohio State, and suffer two close overtime losses to Air Force and Southern California. The change in coaches, unfortunately, did not inaugurate a change in fortunes. Coach Bob Davie compiled a 7–6 record in 1997, 9–3 in 1998, and 5–7 in 1999. At the game at Stanford in 1997, the Stanford band put on a show to mock its opponent, but the ridicule went too far. The Stanford president apologized: "Our students should know better than to insult others' religions and ethnic heritage. The band's purported satire was uncivil and improper." He further announced that the band would not be permitted to perform when Notre Dame returned to Stanford in 1999. Notre Dame had already banned the unit from performing in South Bend because of a similar incident in 1991.[15]

When Bob Davie was appointed to succeed Lou Holtz in late 1996, one of his first desires, as is normal for coaches, was to shape his own coaching staff, retaining some coaches and hiring others. One of the coaches he decided not to retain was Joe Moore. Moore had been an extraordinarily successful coach. He had joined Lou Holtz's staff in 1988, was named offensive line coach in 1989, and throughout the years had developed outstanding offensive linemen and sent many into the National Football League. Davie may not have agreed with Moore's coaching techniques and their personalities may not have meshed, but in informing Moore of his decision, he also said he wanted a younger staff and, at sixty-four, Moore was probably too old to remain the full five years of Davie's contract. Moore was disappointed and acknowledged that he had "had the greatest nine years of my life here at Notre Dame." Desiring to retain his position, he brought a lawsuit against the university, charging age discrimination. Negotiations began in early 1998 to settle the matter out of court, with Moore reportedly asking for reinstatement or $1.3 million to make up for the money he could have made if he had coached for an additional seven years, as he intended, and the university countering with a much-smaller offer. With no agreement, the case went to court. A couple of players admitted that Moore had struck them but admitted also that such instances were rare. Additional uncomplimentary allegations were brought up against each side. In the end, the court ordered the university to pay close to $200,000 for back and anticipated salaries, plus all legal fees.[16]

As the controversy over the termination of Coach Moore was making its laborious way toward resolution, a more serious scandal erupted in the football program. In February 1998, the university administration learned that seven former and five current players over a four- or five-year period had received possibly illegal benefits from a South Bend businesswoman, and the university reported the matter to the NCAA. A month later, the story hit the papers that the NCAA was investigating a report that a young female employee of a local business in South Bend had embezzled approximately $750,000 from the company she worked for and had spent much of it on jewelry, clothing, trips to Chicago, flights to Minneapolis and Las Vegas, car repairs, meals, and other gifts to individual players. She may also have paid for players' families to attend games, she had given money to a player to pay an agent who threatened to reveal the player's illegal contact, and she had a daughter by one of the players. In June 1995, for twenty-five dollars, she had also joined the university's Quarterback Club, entitling her to purchase a ticket to a football luncheon on the Fridays before every home football game, raising the question of whether this made her an official representative of the university. The university, of course, said it did not since anyone, even an opposing football coach, could pay twenty-five dollars to become a member. It was also never clear whether the players knew the source of the money being expended.[17]

After several months of deliberation by the court and by the NCAA, the young woman was sentenced to four years in prison for the embezzlement, was ordered to pay back the amount stolen, and was prohibited from seeing any of the players, except the father of her daughter whom she could see with court approval. The NCAA decided, in a split 5–4 decision, that the membership in the Quarterback Club did make her an official university representative or booster, and thus it was concerned only with activities since June 1995 when she had joined the Quarterback Club. (The university immediately abolished the Quarterback Club and opened the Friday luncheon to the paying public.) But the NCAA considered the activities since June 1995 major violations since the benefits had continued over an extended period of time, some of the gifts were extravagant, and an assistant coach had learned of the gifts weeks earlier and had not reported immediately. Each player was ordered to donate to charity the cost of the benefits he received and the university was put on probation for two years and was also denied one scholarship in each of those years. The university insisted that no penalty was warranted since the young woman was in no way an official representative of the university, but others charged that, if the violations were indeed determined to be major, the penalties were far too light.[18]

Other sports—happily for the university's reputation—were able to avoid such negative publicity. In men's basketball, John MacLeod succeeded Digger Phelps as coach in 1991 and had several excellent players throughout the decade, but he compiled an overall winning percentage of under .500. He had only three winning seasons—his first, 1991–1992 (18–15); 1994–1995 (15–12); and 1996–1997 (16–14)—but individual players ranked with Notre Dame's finest. Monty Williams (1989–1994) sat out a couple of years with a heart irregularity but averaged twenty points a game during his final two years, scored 28 points in Notre Dame's upset victory over No. 4 UCLA in 1994, and after graduation went on to a successful professional coaching career. On Williams's graduation, Pat Garrity took over as team leader, averaged 18.8 points per game, and then played ten years in the National Basketball Association. Troy Murphy arrived the year Garrity left and perhaps outplayed his predecessor, averaging 21 points per game and leaving after his junior year to play professionally. He eventually completed his senior year at Columbia University in New York. Some of the others who played during MacLeod's years at Notre Dame, including Elmer Bennett (1988–1992), Daimon Sweet (1988–1992), Ryan Hoover (1992–1996), and David Graves (1998–2001), had excellent games but, unfortunately, could never lead the team to the championship level.[19]

Women's basketball boasted both excellent players throughout the 1990s and excellent teams—as well as an excellent coach. Muffet McGraw had arrived from Lehigh in 1987, succeeding Mary DiStanislao, and (through the year 2000) compiled a record of 322 and 117, for a winning percentage of .733. Led by Karen Robinson, Margaret Nowlin, and Coquese Washington, the team won 23 and lost 9 in 1990–1991. The team was 29 and 29 over the next two years, but with Letitia Bowen and Beth Morgan it improved to 44 and 17 over the following two years. Katryna Gaither succeeded Bowen in 1995, and she and Morgan led Notre Dame into the NCAA tournament in 1995–1996 and into the Final Four in 1996–1997. The overall record the next four years was an outstanding 109 and 22 (.832), and the team went to the NCAA tournament each year.[20]

National championship trophies were not limited to football. Notre Dame had had a successful fencing program since the close of World War II and it became one of the nation's best under legendary coach Mike DeCicco from 1962 to 1995. He was Coach of the Year in 1966, 1975, and 1992, and his teams had a winning percentage of .938. Yves Auriol was hired as the women's fencing coach in 1986 and he succeeded DeCicco as the men's coach ten years later. In the 1990s, the combined men's and women's team finished third in the nation three times

(1990, 1991, and 1995), second four times (1996, 1997, 1998, and 1999), and won the national championship in 1994. Throughout the decade, the team boasted of three- and four-year All-Americans Myriah Brown, Magda Krol, Luke LaValle, Bill Lester, Jeremy Siek, and Sara Walsh. Fencing was clearly Notre Dame's winningest sport.[21]

The women's soccer team won the national championship the year after the fencers. Chris Petrucelli was hired as the women's coach in 1990, coached for nine years, and was succeeded by Randy Waldrum in 1999. The team compiled a .882 winning percentage throughout the decade, was invited to the NCAA tournament the last seven years, and was runner-up for the NCAA championship three times. In 1995 the team won its way into the final four, defeated North Carolina on an own-goal 1–0 in the semifinal game (North Carolina's first tournament loss since 1985), and defeated the University of Portland by an identical 1–0 score in the final game for the national championship. Among the three- and four-year All-Americans were Cindy Dawes (who scored the winning point against Portland in the final game), Jen Grubb, Anne Mäkinen, Holly Manthei, Kate Sobrero, and goalkeeper Jen Renola. In 1996, Dawes was also awarded the Hermann Trophy as the nation's best women's collegiate soccer player.[22]

The men's soccer team did not reach the same level of success, in part because of the limited number of scholarships. Federal law required some equitable distribution of scholarship aid between men and women athletes on campuses receiving federal aid, and with football receiving approximately eighty-five male scholarships annually, scholarships in the other male sports were limited. Mike Berticelli was hired as coach in 1990 and remained throughout the decade, the team's overall record was 94 wins and 80 losses, and the best year was Berticelli's second with a record of 13 and 5. The team was invited to the NCAA tournament in 1993, 1994, and 1996, but lost in the first round in the first two years and in the second round in 1996.[23]

Baseball was one of the earliest sports on campus—along with marbles— and it compiled successful seasons in the 1990s under coaches Pat Murphy (1988–1994) and Paul Mainieri (1995–2006), despite northern Indiana's often-inclement spring weather. The team's overall record for the decade was 440 victories and 169 defeats for an impressive winning percentage of .720. The program produced major leaguers Craig Counsell, Aaron Heilman, Brad Lidge, Chris Michalak, and others.[24] Softball was not far behind. Coached by Brian Boulac through 1992 and then by Liz Miller, the team won 380 and lost 202 for a winning percentage of .650 and was invited to the NCAA tournament in five of those years. Pitcher Terri

Kobata (1993–1996) won 79 and lost 15 (.840), with 14 no-hitters. Her battery mate, Sara Hayes, played in 232 games, the most in Irish history at the time, and batted .338, and Meghan Murray batted .380 in 227 games over four years.[25]

In other sports throughout the 1990s, men's lacrosse won 87 and lost 49, and was selected for the NCAA tournament in eight of the ten years, but only in 1995 did it make it to the second round. Women's lacrosse became a varsity sport in 1997 and had three winning seasons of 5–4, 7–6, and 9–6, but it was never selected for the NCAA tournament. Men's swimming had an overall record of 79 and 52 throughout the decade, for a winning percentage of .600. With more scholarship aid, the women's program had greater success. The team compiled a 132–35 record throughout the decade and boasted of consensus All-Americans Carrie Nixon, Linda Gallo, Shannon Suddarth, Erin Brooks, and Tanya Williams. In men's golf, Notre Dame came in second in the Midwestern Collegiate Conference each year from 1990 to 1994, won the title in 1994–1995, and after the team moved to the Big East Conference they captured that title from 1995 to 1998. The women's golf program had just gained varsity status in 1988 and it improved throughout the 1990s from a four-player stroke average of 333.83 in 1991–1992 to a 319.88 average in 1997–1998. The men's tennis team was invited to the NCAA tournament every year of the decade and, led by All-American David DiLucia, made it to the final round in 1992. The women's tennis team compiled a winning percentage of .673 throughout the decade, was represented in the NCAA singles every year, and in the doubles every year from 1993. Women's track and field in the 1990s was led by JoAnna Deeter, Liz Grow, and Dominique Calloway, and the men by distance runners Ryan Shay and Luke Watson and by dash men Raghib Ismail, Allen Rossum, and Errol Williams.[26]

Mike DeCicco was not only a popular and respected professor of mechanical engineering and a phenomenally successful fencing coach but from 1964 on was also academic advisor to student athletes. After several athletes were dismissed from the university for failing classes in 1963, Executive Vice President Father Joyce asked DeCicco to take on the new position, the purpose of which was to assist athletes in achieving success in their classes while maintaining high academic standards and integrity. DeCicco had the authority to withhold athletes from practice if he judged they needed the time for study, and he made sure each student-athlete attended classes regularly and on time.[27] He had the respect of the student athletes, his fellow coaches, and the faculty.

The university grew steadily throughout the decade. The undergraduate student enrollment increased by close to 500, from 7,545 in 1990 to 8,014 in

1999, and the faculty grew at an even faster rate, permitting smaller classes, closer faculty-student relations, and more leave time for faculty research and publication. During the decade, the Department of English grew from a faculty of forty to fifty-six, History from thirty to thirty-nine, Biology from thirty-three to forty-five, Chemical Engineering from fourteen to seventeen, and Finance from twenty-four to twenty-seven. Some departments remained steady, depending on student needs and demands, but the trend was toward growth. Approximately twenty departments awarded doctoral degrees throughout the decade, and the number of degrees increased from sixty-nine in 1990 to ninety-nine in 2000. The number in philosophy rose from two to five, in theology from three to nine, in mechanical engineering from two to six, and in chemical engineering from four to eight. The Department of Chemistry consistently awarded the highest number each year, twelve in 1990 and thirteen in 2000.[28]

A further indication of the university's continuing progress was its national rankings. In the *U.S. News'* rankings, Notre Dame was ranked twenty-fifth in 1993, climbed to nineteenth in 1994, tied with Brown for seventeenth in 1996, dropped to nineteenth the following year, and remained at eighteenth or nineteenth the rest of the decade. In *The Rise of American Research Universities*, published by the Johns Hopkins University Press in 1997, Hugh Davis Graham and Nancy Diamond noted that Notre Dame was ranked twenty-second among the top twenty-five private universities in science according to the Top-Science Index (no other Catholic school was listed) and ranked twelfth according to the Arts and Humanities Index (Marquette was twenty-first, the Catholic University of America was twenty-second, and Fordham was twenty-fourth). Combining all three areas, Notre Dame ranked twentieth among all private universities, again the only Catholic university listed among the top twenty-five. Stanford, Princeton, Chicago, Harvard, Yale, and Columbia were the top six.[29] Academic achievement among students showed progress also. National academic awards won by graduating seniors increased irregularly throughout the decade from three in 1990 and four in 1991 to twenty-three in both 1999 and 2000, with Fulbright and National Science Foundation grants leading the way.[30]

Among academic programs, the School of Architecture witnessed the most noticeable changes in the 1990s. Courses in design had been offered from the earliest days of the university, degrees were awarded in 1898, and it became the College of Architecture in 1906, but it was reduced to the Department of Architecture within the College of Engineering in Father Burns's reorganization in 1920. It was renamed the School of Architecture in the 1980s but remained within the College of Engineering. Professor Thomas Gordon Smith assumed the chairmanship in 1989 and re-emphasized the centrality of classical architecture studies. In 1994 the School of Architecture was finally separated from the College of Engineering and became a "free-standing academic entity." At the time, it had a faculty of 16, a student enrollment of 220, and it retained its departmental structure but reported directly to the provost. With its separation from the College of Engineering, the school was given its own advisory council, it introduced a furniture design program in 1994, and it inaugurated a two-year master's course specializing in classical architecture. From 1995 to 1997, the architecture building itself, formerly the Lemonnier Library, was renovated. The exterior changes were minimal—a small addition to the back and a renewal of the main steps in the front—but the interior received a major makeover. The architecture library was positioned in front on the main floor, the north reading room was converted into an auditorium, the reading room on the south was transformed into offices, faculty offices on the upper floors were on outside walls with windows, freshman and sophomore studios were in the basement, fourth-year studios were on the mezzanines, and fifth-year studios were on the top floor.[31] The basement also housed the computer cluster. The renovation was the gift of William and Joanne Bond of Memphis and the building was rededicated as Bond Hall.[32]

Although the university had accepted the characterization of itself as the "Fighting Irish" as far back as 1927, although classes in Irish history and literature had been taught on campus for decades, and although every Notre Dame president except Father Sorin and Father Lemonnier could claim Irish background, no formal Irish studies program was established at Notre Dame until the 1990s. In 1991–1992, Trinity College Dublin was added to the list of approved foreign study programs for sophomores, with the possibility of taking classes in any of five areas—humanities, letters, business and social studies, science, and engineering systems. Later a program at University College Dublin was added and by the end of the decade approximately seventy students were studying in Ireland annually.[33] In 1993, an Irish studies program was officially established on campus, with a gift of $2.5 million from Donald Keough (Notre Dame trustee and retired president of Coca Cola Bottling Company) and his wife Marilyn. Seamus Deane, one of Ireland's most respected literary scholars, was recruited to direct the program, and money was devoted to building up Irish studies resources in the library. Most of the courses offered were in Irish literature, although Irish history was not neglected, and within four years at least fifty students were enrolled in Gaelic language classes. In 1997 the university expanded the program further, thanks to a generous $13 million gift contributed by Donald and Marilyn Keough, Thomas O'Donnell of Oppenheimer, Dr. Michael Smurfit of the Jefferson Smurfit Group in Ireland, and Martin Naughton of Glen Dimplex. The Irish studies program was able to add three endowed professorships, provide additional Irish collections for the library, renovate the Irish studies administrative offices in Flanner Hall, and take a lease on the historic Newman House at No. 86 Saint Stephen's Green in Dublin to house the Keough-Notre Dame Study Centre. The building had been the original site of the Catholic University of Ireland, which had opened in 1854 with John Henry Newman as its first rector.[34]

In late 1997, the university also announced the establishment of an Erasmus Institute, named for Desiderius Erasmus, pivotal sixteenth-century Catholic humanistic scholar and reformer, and funded in part by a gift of $1.5 million from an anonymous benefactor, the Pew Charitable Trusts, and the university itself. It adopted as its mission: "to bring resources from Catholic thought of any period to bear on current problems in the humanities and social sciences (broadly understood as including the arts and professional fields such as law), rather than to advance the study of the Church or Catholic theology as such. . . . The Institute also supports parallel work grounded in the intellectual traditions of other Christian faiths, of Judaism, and of Islam."[35] The institute brought nine or ten scholars to the university each year—from dissertation writers to senior professors—to continue their research, to discuss among themselves, and to share their interests with regular Notre Dame faculty. It also sponsored academic conferences, summer programs for faculty and advanced graduate students, and the publication of books and scholarly articles. It tackled contemporary topics like the just war theory, examining its development from Saint Augustine and Saint Thomas down to modern theologians Bernard Lonergan and John Courtney Murray and debating its validity in an age of atomic bombs and total warfare. The institute professed that there could be no contradiction between theology and science, between faith and reason, and its goal was to bring them all into closer harmony.[36]

As Notre Dame's foreign study program in Dublin prospered and expanded, the program in Jerusalem struggled. In 1964, Pope Paul VI had asked Father Hesburgh, then head of the International Federation of Catholic Universities, to take the lead in setting up a center of comparative theology that the pope hoped to establish in Jerusalem, a city holy to Christians, Jews, and Muslims. Through the generosity of Mr. I. A. O'Shaughnessy, president of Globe Oil Company and Notre Dame trustee, the center was built in Tantur (located on the road from Jerusalem to Bethlehem), and religious scholars from around the world were invited to use the facility for research seminars, conferences, and other scholarly discussions.[37] In 1985, the university made use of the facility to establish an additional undergraduate foreign study program. "Notre Dame believes strongly in the international dimensions of education," the director of international studies noted. "The more students know about other cultures, the better they will be able to cope with today's world."[38] Four students attended that first year and the classes available included Hebrew and Arabic, Old and New Testament, Holy Land Geography and Archeology, Middle East Politics, Religion and Peace, and similar offerings. The program had to be suspended in 1987 due to insufficient enrollment. Seventeen students enrolled in the spring of 1989 but the program was suspended again in 1991, this time for the turbulent political situation in the Middle East. In 1996 the program had to be cut short on May 1 because of political turmoil, although the students themselves were never in direct danger. In 2000, escalating violence in the area led the university to suspend the program again, and it was not resurrected until 2008. Students majoring in theology, history, sociology, or government found the program especially worthwhile and the university always did its best to keep it open.[39]

The Alliance for Catholic Education (ACE), one of the most successful and innovative of the Notre Dame programs that began in the 1990s, was established in 1994. The founder, Father Timothy Scully, vice president and associate provost at the time, expressed highest regard for his Catholic grade and high school education: "I'm a product of Catholic education, and I consider the Catholic education I received to be the greatest gift I have received from the Church. . . . I think our educational system is the greatest source of grace in action the Church has."[40] But the Catholic educational system clearly faced a crisis. Vocations to the priesthood, sisterhood, and brotherhood had declined precipitously since the 1960s, parishes did not have the funds to hire full-time lay teachers (often with families), and Catholic schools were being closed across the country, especially in poorer areas. Father Scully continued: "We, at all costs, can't see our greatest institutional legacy in this country as a church—which is our Catholic school system—weakened or even destroyed by this shift."[41] Sister of Mercy Lourdes Sheehan, director of education for the National Catholic Conference of Bishops, had the same lament, and asked Father Scully if Notre Dame might inaugurate a pilot program to train teachers to serve in understaffed areas, especially in the South. Father Scully put an ad in the student newspaper: "Tired of getting homework? Then give some. Be a teacher." He thought he might get four or five responses, but, to his surprise, two hundred Notre Dame and Saint Mary's College students showed up for an information session. The program was on its way.[42]

As developed, the program stipulated that the college graduates would spend one summer enrolled in education courses at Notre Dame, then teach for a year under supervision in a selected grade, middle, or high school. They would then return to Notre Dame for a second summer of classes, then go back to their school for a second full year of supervised teaching, and finally receive a master's degree in education at the close of the two-and-a-half-year program. Notre Dame at the time did not have a Department of Education, so Father Scully recruited faculty from the University of Portland in Oregon, another university staffed by the Congregation of Holy Cross. The basic and fundamental courses taught in the first summer included techniques in teaching primary, middle, and high school grades, the uses of the computer, and the teaching of religion. The more specialized courses in the second summer were the teaching of reading, language arts, mathematics, science, and social studies, and courses in moral education and exceptionality in childhood and adolescence. Forty students were chosen in the first group, selected from different backgrounds and majors since the teaching needs varied from school to school. Notre Dame eventually established its own education faculty, housed in the Institute for Educational Initiatives.[43]

In the beginning, the teachers were needed most urgently in the states and dioceses of the South and Southeast: Mobile in Alabama, St. Augustine in Florida, Oklahoma City, and Alexandria, Baton Rouge, Lake Charles, and Shreveport in Louisiana. Between two and five teachers might be assigned to the same city, although generally never more than one or two to the same school. Each group lived together as a community, often in a vacated convent or rectory, usually praying together daily and eating and cooking together as schedules permitted. Each participating school contributed $4,000 annually, AmeriCorps awarded the program an early grant of $100,000, and each teacher received a monthly stipend of $650.[44] In succeeding years, other grants flowed in from the W. K. Kellogg Foundation, the Annenberg Trust, the UPS Foundation, the Our Sunday Visitor Foundation, the MCJ Foundation, the Mathile Family Foundation, the Arthur Vining Davis Foundations, the Christel DeHaan Family Foundation, the Koch Foundation, and the Helen Branch Family Foundation.[45] By the end of the decade, close to 400 student teachers in the program had taught more than 30,000 students in approximately 140 schools in over 50 cities in 12 states. The retention rate in the two-year program was a remarkable 95 percent, and 75 percent of graduates remained in education after their two-year commitment.[46] Said one:[47]

People enter the ACE program because they want to make the world a better place. Teaching allows them to learn how to teach. ACE teachers enter with the passion and desire, learn the skills along the way, and leave with experience, and a charge to continue the mission.

Another said:

> The spirituality of ACE presents itself in a communal way, a way of celebrating Christ and meditating together on His ideas. This encouragement to explore and develop my relationship with God has led me to a deeper, more personal understanding of my faith and its relevance to my whole life.

Despite notable success in the expansion of architecture, the establishment of the Irish studies program, the popularity of the Alliance for Catholic Education, and the rise in national academic rankings, disagreements between the administration and the Faculty Senate remained. One issue concerned describing the Catholic character of the university. The committee drafting the proposed *Colloquy for the Year 2000* agreed that the faculty had a central and critical role in maintaining that Catholic identity, and the early 1993 draft stated that "all who participate in hiring faculty must be cognizant of and responsive to the need for dedicated and committed Catholics to predominate in numbers among the faculty."[48] After much debate, the Faculty Senate objected to this on four accounts. First, it felt that the colloquy should be a joint faculty-administration statement, not ultimately a pronouncement of the president. Second, it would strike the word "predominate" since it seemed to overemphasize number. Some departments might indeed need additional Catholics to maintain their Catholic mission but other departments might accomplish this with fewer. Third, the senate feared the implementation of this recommendation might lower the priority of hiring the very best candidates available, especially women and racial and ethnic minority candidates. Finally, the senate envisioned difficulty in recognizing a "dedicated and committed Catholic" at the time of first hiring. Some senators did agree with the draft as written, admitting the challenges presented but confident that the university could resolve them, but the majority preferred a rewording:[49]

> All who participate in hiring faculty must be cognizant of and responsive to the need to recruit a faculty that achieves the highest level of excellence and that includes a proportion of Catholics sufficient to foster the Catholic intellectual tradition.

Despite the objections, the original wording remained.

This issue was brought up again the following year when some in the senate raised the question of whether the administration purposely delayed approval of non-Catholic hires. A senate subcommittee circulated a survey among department chairs that asked: "Has it been your experience that the administration takes longer to approve your recommendation to hire a non-Catholic than a Catholic candidate?" Eleven chairs answered "Yes" and thirteen chairs answered "No." After discussion, the senate passed by voice vote the following resolution:

WHEREAS there is serious reason to believe that the preferential treatment given to Catholic candidates by the Administration works to the detriment of the University's academic advancement:

WHEREAS there are profound and widespread reservations among the faculty about the wisdom of such a policy,

BE IT RESOLVED:

That the Faculty Senate express its deep concern over the possibility that the Administration takes longer to approve recommendations to hire non-Catholic than Catholic candidates and urges that if such a policy does in fact currently exist, it be openly stated and subject to review and debate by the faculty of the University before continuing its implementation.

Both Father Malloy and Provost O'Meara declared that they did not delay non-Catholic appointments, but they also noted that only 30 percent of new hires for 1993–1994 were Catholics, an all-time low.[50]

Another controversy over hiring procedures erupted the following year when the *National Catholic Reporter* alleged that Bishop John D'Arcy of Fort Wayne–South Bend had intervened several years earlier to block the appointment of a noted theologian to the faculty.[51] The Faculty Senate undertook to investigate. Two prominent chair holders in the Department of Theology had approached Father Malloy with the suggestion that Father Charles Curran, recently removed from the Catholic University of America for his dissent against some Church moral teachings, be appointed to a tenured position in the Kroc Institute for International Peace Studies. Cardinal Joseph Bernardin of Chicago, seeking reconciliation between American bishops and theologians, confided that he would support such an appointment if the local bishop did not oppose. One senator objected that, in a concern over outside intervention, it seemed irregular that the process originated outside the Kroc Institute itself, and it was also irregular that Cardinal Bernadin, someone outside the university, was involved.[52] Bishop John D'Arcy did consider such an appointment pastorally harmful to the diocese, but the senators could not agree on any resolution after Provost O'Meara assured them that the university would submit to no outside interference in its hiring procedures.[53] No appointment was made, and Father Malloy closed the discussion with a letter to the senate on April 29, 1994:[54]

> I say unequivocally that Bishop John D'Arcy, in my seven years as President, has never influenced, or had any role, in hiring decisions at the University. This is in conformity with my understanding of the autonomy of the University in such matters. This position has been clearly articulated in Notre Dame's official response to the proposed Ordinances of Catholic Higher Education.

A similar controversy broke out about the same time when the university announced that Father Timothy Scully was being appointed vice president and associate provost as of July 1, 1995, and that the current associate provost, Father Ollie Williams, would leave that position and, after a year's sabbatical for research, return to full-time teaching. Two objections were raised. First, the provost certainly had the right to select his own staff, his associate provosts, but to create a new vice presidency in that area and make a new appointment seemed to merit faculty participation.[55] Second, Father Williams's removal seemed at least shabby, if not unjust. To the first objection, Father Malloy countered that he and the trustees were concerned that the university needed to groom additional younger Holy Cross religious (like Father Scully) for university leadership positions, that Professor O'Meara would be resigning as provost in two years, and Professor Schmitz as vice president and associate provost perhaps before that, and thus change needed to be made quickly. He expressed sorrow and regret that Father Williams was offended in the switches.[56]

Father Williams was indeed offended. He explained before the Faculty Senate that he had earlier agreed with Provost O'Meara to accept the position of associate provost on two conditions: that he be given a year's notice before termination and that he be permitted to continue teaching. He actually had been given only two weeks' notice before leaving office. He was assured that his work was not unsatisfactory but that Father Malloy felt the need to restructure his administration. He admitted that Father Malloy may not have known of his one-year agreement with the provost when he decided on a change, but it was still a violation of his agreement or contract.[57]

For a time it seemed that the controversies might never cease. Next came the hiring of a Holy Cross priest, Father Michael Baxter, ordained in 1985, a strong supporter of Dorothy Day and the Catholic Worker Movement, with a doctorate from Duke University under Professor Stanley Hauerwas who had departed from Notre Dame's Theology Department a few years before. He applied for a position at Notre Dame in February 1996 and, desiring more Holy Cross priests on the faculty, the administration agreed to add a budget line in the department for him. He delivered a public lecture and met with the faculty, but the Theology Department did not consider him sufficiently qualified and rejected his application. In May, the provost asked the department to consider him for a visiting assistant professorship, but the department rejected this proposal also. The following month, Father Malloy overruled the department and extended an offer of a three-year visiting assistantship to the candidate, and he accepted.[58]

That fall, the executive committee of the Faculty Senate introduced a resolution expressing "grave concern" over the manner in which the appointment was made, although all agreed that the president held the final decision in all hiring cases and possessed the authority to overrule a department recommendation, either positive or negative. Father Malloy appeared before the senate on October 14 and answered questions for an hour. He would not address the specific hire, but he stressed that in every decision, he considers, as does every department, the candidate's teaching potential, research promise, contribution to the university's Catholic mission, and, where pertinent, the statement in the university statutes on the importance of the presence of Holy Cross priests in the Departments of Theology and Philosophy.[59] Heated debate continued through the next two senate meetings, with Father Baxter's strongest champion admitting that he was "young, brash, and irreverent toward his intellectual elders" but also "bright, well-read, and articulate." A letter appeared in the *Chronicle of Higher Education* that said "we think he [the candidate] is more than well-qualified academically for the position to which he has been appointed" and "we fully understand how President Malloy came to the conclusion that he is well-qualified for a position at Notre Dame," and it was signed by, among others, professors Philip Gleason and George Marsden of Notre Dame, Alasdair MacIntyre of Duke, Ruth Marie Griffith at Northwestern, and Leigh Schmidt and Robert Wuthnow of Princeton.[60] But the opposition was not convinced. A resolution was presented to the Faculty Senate with eight "whereas" statements and the following three resolves:

Be It Resolved that the Faculty Senate wishes to express its strong disapproval of President Malloy's handling of the "special relationship" and its strong disapproval of his decision to appoint a Visiting Professor for a term of three years to the Theology Department against the unanimous negative vote by the department's ATP committee and the negative recommendations of the department chair; and

Be It Further Resolved that a President who makes such decisions seriously erodes the confidence that a faculty ought to have in a President; and

Be It Further Resolved that the Faculty Senate sends a copy of this resolution to President Malloy as an expression of its strong disapproval.

The resolution passed with twenty-nine in favor, five opposed, and three abstentions.[61]

The major controversy of the decade, however, did not originate among the faculty but among the students and the Office of Student Affairs. In January 1995, the Gays and Lesbians of Notre Dame and Saint Mary's College (GLND/SMC) were informed that they could no longer hold meetings in the University Counseling Center. The group had been organized in 1986 and had been holding meetings in the center since then, but apparently without the university administration's knowledge. In the fall, the group had advertised the time and place of its meeting and the Office of Student Affairs determined that, since the group was not an officially recognized university organization, it was not permitted to advertise or hold meetings in university facilities. The office admitted that gay and lesbian students were underserviced on campus and it was investigating ways to assist them further but university regulation still needed to be enforced.[62]

The Campus Life Council raised the issue in its first meeting in February and asked that the group be officially recognized and invited the vice president of student affairs, Professor Patricia O'Hara, to its next meeting to explain the nonrecognition policy. A week later, more than three hundred students, faculty, and staff marched peacefully to the steps of the Main Building to demonstrate support for the gay and lesbian students. Vice President O'Hara met with the Campus Life Council later that month and explained that, in its application for recognition in 1992, "GLND addressed homosexual acts neutrally, and urged the University towards encouraging monogamous homosexual relationships . . . not consistent with the teachings of the Church." She stressed that "Notre Dame is different than many places. It articulates individual behavioral expectations of their students, especially with sexuality, and it is also expected to be reflected, philosophically and conceptually, in recognized student organizations."[63] On March 6, Vice President O'Hara wrote an open letter to the Campus Life Council, confirming that "we value our gay and lesbian students, as we value all students who are members of this community. We want the University to be a safe and inclusive environment in which every student can pursue the educational endeavor to which we are all committed—free from harassment of any kind." She repeated her opposition to recognition of GLND/SMC because of its "value-neutral approach toward a variety of ways in which gays and lesbians may live out their orientation." She appointed an ad hoc committee of nine faculty and staff, the student body president and vice president, and two gay or lesbian students to advise student affairs how better to assist gay and lesbian students in supporting each other in conformity with Catholic teachings and how to assure an environment free of harassment for everyone.[64]

This ad hoc committee submitted its final report on February 29, 1996, with twelve recommendations:[65]

1. That assistant rectors and resident assistants participate in workshops to better assist gay and lesbian students.
2. That hall rectors be provided with continual professional education to better support gay and lesbian students.
3. That hall rectors be provided resources to sensitize hall staffs better to assist gay and lesbian students.
4. In orientation addresses, that hall rectors declare their openness to assist gay and lesbian students.
5. That a gay and lesbian student group be formed, with one or two faculty or administrative facilitators, for gay and lesbian mutual support.
6. That a standing committee be established to advise the Office of Student Affairs on matters of interest to gay and lesbian students.
7. That the University Counseling Center continue its role in assisting gay and lesbian students.
8. That Campus Ministry continue to provide counsel, support, and assistance to gay and lesbian students.
9. That the Office of Student Affairs provide forums for discussion among homosexual and heterosexual students.
10. That official university publications explicitly prohibit all harassment, and welcome gay and lesbian students.

11. That new faculty and students be informed of the university's no harassment, nondiscrimination policy.
12. That the administration consider including sexual orientation in the university's official nondiscrimination policy.

Vice President O'Hara accepted all twelve recommendations, with the stipulation that the faculty or administration facilitators of the new group, to be named "Notre Dame Gay and Lesbian Students," be selected for the present by the vice president of student affairs, and that requests for funding, meeting places, etc., be channeled through the facilitators.[66] Some were pleased with the vice president's acceptance but others opposed the inclusion of the facilitators (it was not an exclusively student group) and the influence they could exert. Father David Garrick, a Holy Cross priest and faculty member in the Communications and Theater Department, published a full-page letter in the student newspaper, acknowledging that he was gay but also celibate. He insisted that, according to Church teachings, homosexual orientation, as distinct from homosexual activity or lifestyle, was not morally wrong, and thus students of homosexual orientation should be permitted to assemble as they wished, as did heterosexual students, with no faculty or administration facilitators present.[67]

The twelfth recommendation of the ad hoc committee had urged the administration to consider adding sexual orientation to the university's nondiscrimination clause. The administration considered this throughout the next year, sought advice of theologians, lawyers, and other university administrators, and toward the end of the summer of 1997 Father Malloy issued an official statement, "The Spirit of Inclusion at Notre Dame":[68]

> The University of Notre Dame strives for a spirit of inclusion among the members of this community for distinct reasons articulated in our Christian tradition. We prize the uniqueness of all persons as God's creatures. We welcome all people, regardless of color, gender, religion, ethnic, sexual orientation, social or economic class, and nationality, for example, precisely because of Christ's calling to treat each other as we desire to be treated. We value gay and lesbian members of this community as we value all members of this community. We condemn harassment of any kind, and University policies proscribe it. We consciously create an environment of mutual respect, hospitality and warmth in which none are strangers and all may flourish.

Father Malloy explained that the administration had agreed on this statement rather than adding "sexual orientation" in the university's nondiscrimination clause because American culture and the court system do not always distinguish between "homosexual orientation" and "homosexual lifestyle," and including sexual orientation in such legal documents might be interpreted to accept homosexual lifestyle and activity that Church and university policies oppose.[69]

The controversy, however, would not end. The following March, Father Garrick resigned his position on the Notre Dame faculty in protest against the administration's handling of the gay and lesbian situation. He called it "my last, best chance to help my alma mater." He believed that Father Malloy's "Spirit of Inclusion" statement was too weak and that sexual orientation still needed inclusion in the university's nondiscrimination clause. He revealed also that he was no longer being asked to preside at Masses in Sacred Heart Basilica, and he claimed that some had protested his homilies, perhaps because of his defense of gay and lesbian rights and the need for further support.[70] Two hundred fifty persons gathered on Fieldhouse Mall in support, and Father Garrick pleaded:

> Nobody has secure rights until everyone has equal rights. This applies to people we don't agree with in their outlook, ethnic background and sexual orientation. . . . We need to be proud of our minority sexuality and we need all of you, the majority sexuality who are gathered here. Without your help, we can't get equal rights.

He then asked a "blessing on Notre Dame and Saint Mary's . . . that good fruit may come out of this, with equal rights for everyone."[71]

Father John Jenkins, the Holy Cross religious superior at the time (and later the university president) clarified that "Father Garrick has always had and continues to have the full faculties to preside at the Eucharist and hear confession, or perform any other priestly ministry, wherever he is invited."[72] The rector of Sacred Heart Basilica, Father (later Bishop) Daniel Jenky, admitted that Father Garrick had no longer been invited to preside over basilica Masses, not because of his views on homosexuality, but simply because his homilies were too long and, outstanding theater actor that he was, overly dramatic, reaching at times to twenty or twenty-five minutes and causing complaints from those attending.[73]

The Faculty Senate reentered the fray, voting 32 to 3 that, in light of Father Garrick's resignation, the "Spirit of Inclusion" statement was clearly inadequate, and the senate urged again the addition of sexual orientation in the nondiscrimination clause.[74] The Academic Council acknowledged that risks were involved, but they judged the risks worth taking and, in a close vote of 19 affirmative and 15 negative, with 2 abstentions, recommended that sexual orientation be added to the clause.[75] Father Malloy announced he could not accept the council's decision and referred the matter to the board of trustees. The fellows of the university in December voted with Father Malloy not to include sexual orientation in the university's nondiscrimination clause, the full board of trustees reaffirmed that decision, and there the matter rested for the time.[76]

The student body did not change that significantly throughout the 1990s, at least according to annual surveys conducted by the American Council on Education. As in other decades, Notre Dame first-year students seemed slightly more conservative in some areas, but slightly more liberal in a few others, and in most were out of step with their cohorts nationwide, as the figures in table 20.1 suggest.[77]

Table 20.1. Information from Surveys Conducted by the American Council on Education

	ND 1992	ND 2000	Nationwide 2000
Caucasian	89.5%	86.6%	81.2%
African American	1.6%	3.5%	8.9%
Central and Latin Americans and Puerto Ricans	6%	8.5%	5.4%
A or A+ high school average	59.9%	71.1%	16.4%
Attended religious service last year	97.1%	97.3%	80.6%
Participated in a demonstration	22.1%	26.4%	45.9%
Smoked cigarettes	1.4%	2.2%	14.2%
Drank beer	52.2%	45.9%	50.7%
Drank wine or liquor	49.9%	49.1%	53.8%
Did volunteer service	87.8%	96.1%	75.3%
Should legalize abortion	45.4%	32%	52.7%
Premarital sex accepted if in love	25.1%	20.9%	40.6%
Should legalize marijuana	13.7%	22.0%	22.9%
Racial discrimination no longer a problem	9%	17.7%	23%
Wealthy should pay more taxes	65.7%	42.9%	55.4%

Source: UDIS 310/7-8 and 248/7-8, Freshman Attitude Survey, vols. 1 and 2, UNDA; and *The American Freshman National Norms for Fall 2000*, American Council on Education, University of California, Los Angeles, 2000.

Individual students, of course, stood out from the crowd and were long remembered. Less than two years after the devastating swimming team bus accident in 1992, tragedy struck again with the death of first-year student Mara Fox in an automobile accident on November 13, 1993. Fox and four others had decided to walk back to campus along Douglas Road after waiting extensively for the arrival of a taxi on a foggy and rainy night. Fox was apparently walking on the shoulder or perhaps the road itself when she was struck by a car driven by a Notre Dame law student. The driver then left the scene but was later apprehended when passengers in the car notified the police. Fox had made numerous friends across campus and had been involved in various service projects, and her residence, Lyons Hall, began sponsoring an annual two-and-a-half mile fun run to provide scholarship aid for a student desiring to study in Spain, as Fox had hoped to do. The driver was eventually acquitted because Fox may have been on the road, rain and fog may have blinded him to Fox's presence, and the alcohol test machine slightly malfunctioned during the test that showed the driver's blood alcohol content in excess of the legal limit.[78]

But there were very positive and inspiring moments also. On October 28, 1993, Haley Scott, less than two years after the swimming bus accident that left her partially paralyzed, returned to intercollegiate competition for the first time and, before a battery of newsmen and photographers and a packed seating gallery, won her meet in the 50-yard freestyle with an excellent time of 25.04 seconds.[79]

Molly Kinder faced less daunting odds. Not easy to overlook at six-foot-three and red hair, she sought to join the Notre Dame Marching Band's Irish Guard. The guard, which paved the way for the marching band through crowds, had been exclusively male and had developed a macho image, including at times overindulging in alcohol and the antics that followed, but Kinder met the height requirement (six foot two inches) and was not deterred. She practiced marching, twists, and turns throughout the summer, even on the streets of Chile during a summer research project. Some opposed her application but she eventually succeeded, and further successes followed her graduation—Jesuit Volunteers, the World Bank in India and Pakistan, the Clinton Global Initiative, the U.S. Agency for International Development, and ONE, the anti-poverty advocacy organization.[80]

Few success stories could top Alex Montoya. Born in Colombia with one leg and no lower arms, he was sent to San Diego at age four to live with an aunt and uncle. He learned English by watching baseball on television, was voted prom king in high school, lived on the first floor of Saint Edward's Hall (no stairs), and carried the torch in the 1996 Olympics. He admitted that "the faculty as well as the general population of this University make it a very happy and lovable environment to live in" but also that doorknobs, bathroom fixtures, and Indiana snows posed challenges, but never challenges he could not overcome. He eventually authored two books, *Swinging for the Fences* and *The Finish Line*, and his love of baseball led him to the position of manager of Latino affairs for the San Diego Padres.[81]

If campus construction had been slowed by the stock market blip in 1987, it picked up in the 1990s. The first major construction project of Father Malloy's second term was the Frank Eck Baseball Stadium, replacing the older Cartier Field and funded by Mr. Eck, a 1944 graduate of Notre Dame and the president and chairman of Advanced Drainage Systems, Inc., of Columbus, Ohio. The new stadium housed comfortable locker rooms for home and visiting teams, meeting spaces and coaching facilities, a VIP room and press box, a three-thousand-seat grandstand, and a lighted and well-manicured playing field. Four batting and pitching cages completed the complex.[82]

Saint Mary's College had established the Early Childhood Development Center on its campus in 1971 to serve both the Saint Mary's and the Notre Dame communities, and in 1994 Notre Dame constructed a branch of that ECDC on the north side of its own campus, on Bulla Road across from the Fischer O'Hara-Grace townhouses. The center's activities included children's literature, art, music, creative dramatics, play, and field trips, and each activity was supervised by a full-time lead teacher and an assistant. Notre Dame and Saint Mary's students majoring in education, psychology, sociology, and nursing served as assistants. Breakfast, lunch, and morning and afternoon snacks were available. The facility could accommodate 165 youngsters aged two through six (two-and-a-half through nine in the summer) and tuition varied according to gross family income. The center publicized its philosophy:[83]

> The learning environment, activities, and daily schedule foster social, emotional, physical, cogitative and creative development through experience-based, hands-on activities and play. A central goal is the promotion of children's self-confidence and the love of learning.

Four new undergraduate residence halls were constructed in 1996–1997, chiefly to accommodate the students relocated from Grace and Flanner Halls when those were converted mainly into faculty and institute offices. Building funds were donated by Notre Dame trustees Donald Keough, Terrence McGlinn,

Joseph O'Neill, and Robert Welsh. McGlinn Hall and Welsh Family Hall housed women, initially those women transferring from Knott and Siegfried, and O'Neill Hall and Marilyn Keough Hall accommodated men. The halls were similar in construction, each with a capacity of between 265 and 282 on four floors, and 15 percent of their rooms were singles, 70 percent were doubles, and 15 percent were three-room quads. Each hall was air-conditioned, had an exercise room, laundry facilities, study rooms, kitchen access, a chapel, elevator, and modular furniture. The floor plans of McGlinn and Keough were identical, as were those of O'Neill and Welsh Family, leading one female student to remark that it was clear that the university was run by celibate priests who did not realize that women needed more closet space than men! The chapels were dedicated to Our Lady of Guadalupe (Keough), Saint Bridget of Kildare (McGlinn), Saint Joseph the Worker (O'Neill), and Blessed (now Saint) Kateri Tekawitha (Welsh Family).[84]

While the new residence halls were being constructed, on the same south side of the campus a new College of Business Administration building was rising to succeed the Hurley College of Commerce building erected in 1932. The 153,000-square-foot collegiate Gothic complex housed four connected branches or buildings and a central lobby and auditorium. The Donald P. Kelly Building included undergraduate administrative offices on the first floor, the dean's suite on the second, and faculty offices on the third. The Terrence J. McGlinn Building held offices and classrooms for the Master of Science in Administration program on the ground floor and faculty offices on the second and third floors. The Vincent J. Naimoli Building comprised offices, classrooms, and group study facilities for the Executive Master of Business Administration program on the first floor and faculty offices on the second and third floors. The Raymond H. Siegfried Building contained offices and classrooms for the MBA program on the first floor and faculty offices on the second and third floors. The John W. Jordan II Auditorium accommodated 350 people in theater-style seating and boasted a state-of-the-art sound system and cutting-edge technology. Each of the complex's twenty-one classrooms and seminar rooms featured advanced computer, audio, and video technology.[85]

University Village, constructed on U.S. 33 between the Notre Dame and Saint Mary's campuses in 1962, accommodated some 132 families with 150 children in the 1990s. Common social space was limited, and in the fall of 1997 a new Rev. Paul E. Beichner Community Center was opened, a four-thousand-square-foot building housing computer facilities, lounges, a playroom, a communal kitchen and dining room, a chapel, and a large multipurpose room. It was fittingly named for Father Beichner, a scholar of Medieval English and longtime dean of the Graduate School who had assisted graduate students in so many ways but was little-known outside the campus and the field of Chaucerian studies. He once described himself: "I may have lived somewhat like a hippopotamus, mostly below the surface of the water, but with eyes and ears and nose above—a calm and undisturbed life. . . . I think that a hippo keeps his mouth shut and lives low most of the time, and so should I."[86]

Constructed in 1999, and donated by the same Frank Eck of Columbus, Ohio, the Eck Center at the entrance to campus just south of the Morris Inn filled three important university needs—a visitors' center, larger Alumni Association offices, and an expanded bookstore. The visitors' center housed an information desk and sponsored student-led guided tours of the campus, two each weekday during the academic year and seven each weekday during the summer. Specialized tours for larger groups could also be conveniently arranged. The offices of the Alumni Association shared the same building. On two floors, it provided office space for twelve professional workers, a support staff of thirteen, and eighteen part-time student employees. The building also contained an attractive one-hundred-seat auditorium to serve both the Alumni Association and the visitors' center. The Hammes Notre Dame Bookstore was in a separate building, covering 65,000 square feet and holding 75,000 reference works and titles of general reading. The ground level featured general-interest books, a café, reading areas, religious articles, jewelry, Notre Dame apparel, novelties, and souvenirs. The second level included school and personal supplies, college text and reference works, music selections, and a multimedia section.[87]

In order to build the four new residence halls in 1996–1997—McGlinn, O'Neill, Marilyn Keough, and Welsh Family—land had been taken from the Burke Golf Course, reducing it to nine holes. William K. Warren, Jr., a graduate of 1956 and chairman of Warren American Oil Company of Tulsa, came to the university's assistance with a gift of $7 million to underwrite the construction of a new course. The course was designed by professional golfer Ben Crenshaw and his partner Bill Coore, and it was situated on 250 acres of wooded land on the northeast corner of the campus property. The course measured 6,744 yards from the back tees, included eighty-six bunkers, and there were water hazards on six holes. Juday Creek ran through the course and required special environmental consideration, at an eventual cost of $500,000. Approximately 4,400 native hardwood trees and shrubs were planted to increase the stream's canopy cover; boulders, gravel, and logs were added to the stream's slopes to enhance fish habitat; filtration techniques were employed to minimize the impact of fertilizers and pesticides; and 2,200 feet of new stream was created to relocate two sections of the original creek. The course also included a 7,000-square-foot clubhouse, a pro shop, a driving range, and a putting green.[88]

In the area of athletics, a major renovation project of the decade was the expansion of the football stadium. South Bend winters had been hard on the concrete flooring and as the alumni increased, stadium seating did not, and by the early 1990s more money was being returned to alumni for unfulfilled ticket requests than was retained by the university from alumni ticket sales. The board of trustees in the spring of 1994 agreed to expand the stadium on two conditions: 1) that no money be diverted from any other university priority and 2) that all financial benefits from the expansion be applied to the educational mission of the university. The decision was made to expand the old stadium rather than build a new one. As Executive Vice President Father Beauchamp remarked, "I don't want to be remembered in history as the man who tore down 'the house that Rockne built.'" Rockne's stadium remained intact. The expansion was a circular addition around the old stadium, adding approximately 20,000 seats, a new press box, and more restrooms and concession stands. The renovation began in November 1995 and was completed for the first game in the fall of 1997, at a cost of approximately $50 million, financed chiefly through new bonds. Unfortunately, a major problem surfaced during the opening game against Georgia Tech on September 2. A valve on one of the two major water mains into the stadium had apparently been closed over the preceding winter and had not been reopened. The water pressure dropped and when toilets flushed the pressure was not sufficient to shut off, so the toilets overflowed—at a rate of about 1,200 gallons a minute—flooding the concourse with two inches of water. It took time for the plumber to locate the source of the problem but the culprit valve was eventually reopened and toilets returned to normal.[89]

The often-delayed renovation of the Main Building also took place in the 1990s. The building had been given patchwork repairs over the years but much more was needed. Its demolition and replacement was considered, but no drawings for a modern building with a golden dome seemed acceptable, so total renovation was decided upon, the first since its construction in 1879. The project took place in two phases: the exterior renovation in 1995–1996 and the renovation of the interior from 1997 to 1999.

For the exterior renovation, scaffolding was constructed around the structure in the summer and fall of 1995, the outside bricks were cleaned, and the roof was replaced. Window hoods, the base around the statue of the Blessed Virgin, and all exterior wood was repainted in tan, medium, and dark brown, as in the original. The external fire escapes were removed since a new sprinkling system made them unnecessary. The dome and statue were left untouched since they had been regilded in 1988.[90]

A campus protest erupted just as the exterior renovations began. On October 10, 1995, representatives of various minority groups on campus, especially Native Americans, protested the presence of the Columbus murals on the second or main floor of the Main Building. The murals had been painted by Luigi Gregori in the 1880s and the students stressed that they depicted Indian culture inaccurately and from an exclusively Western European point of view. The protesters marched to the Main Building with placards reading: "Take down the murals. End the disgrace," and "A great people inhabited the land long before 1492." The protest was well timed because Columbus Day was only two days away and the building was being renovated anyway. Said one Native American student: "We're celebrating a day of disgrace to us because Columbus got credit for only stumbling on a culture that was already strong." Said another: "Tradition doesn't make it right. Notre Dame is supposed to be our home, but as long as these murals remain, we can never be part of the Notre Dame family." Both the undergraduate Student Senate and the Graduate Student Union called the murals unacceptable, admitting they did not have a specific solution but requesting that the administration address the issue. After much discussion, the administration announced that the murals would remain, a brochure would be drafted and available near the murals that depicted them in their historical context, and other university displays would be organized to celebrate cultural diversity.[91]

The second and final phase of the renovation began in the summer of 1997 and was complete in August two years later. (The student newspaper pointed out that the renovation took twenty-five full months, while it had taken only four months for Father Sorin to build it originally!) The university's top administration moved temporarily into classrooms and offices in Hayes-Healy Hall and other buildings, the upper floors of the Main Building were gutted, and the crawl space under the building was expanded into a seven-foot-high tunnel. Parts of the building were restored to their original look and use, and offices were all modernized. The fifth floor had been closed since after World War II due to structural weakness and it was reopened for the Graduate School offices. Some floor beams had to be replaced since, in the rush of 1879, green lumber had been utilized from nearby woods and the beams had shrunk over time. Ornate hanging lamps and intricate banisters duplicated the earlier ones, air-conditioning and two elevators were installed, the marble-tile second floor was repaired, and a back porch was added on the north side. Space was reserved for three classrooms (there were more in the original), and a Wall of Honor was added on the ground floor to celebrate those who through the years had contributed to the growth and success of the university.[92]

The university approached the end of the decade—and of the century and of the millennium—with some concerns, as did the rest of the country. It was called the Y2K problem. Could the binary computer systems handle the change to 2000 smoothly or would they revert to 1900 again? Would the campus experience power outages, database collapses, blackouts of electricity, shutdowns of power plant boilers—the malfunctioning of all things regulated by computers? In the weeks and months leading to the deadline, university officials examined more than 1,200 items they considered critical and all were Y2K compliant. Students were asked to unplug computers and other electrical appliances before leaving for Christmas vacation in order to allow university generators to direct all electricity to more essential areas if problems developed. A team of university experts remained on campus throughout the night on December 31, keeping an eye on the situation in other countries as the international dateline was crossed, but only a few small glitches emerged on campus. These were corrected in minutes, and none of the contingency plans had to be invoked. It had come and gone as smoothly as campus officials had hoped.[93]

Toward the close of the decade, Notre Dame had the opportunity to join the Big Ten Conference in athletics and the Conference on Institutional Cooperation in academics that was coupled with it. The Conference on Institutional Cooperation included the University of Chicago in addition to the eleven Big Ten schools and, in the words of a Faculty Senate report, was "easily the most important intellectual force in the Midwest and one of the most significant in the country."[94] By sharing library and research facilities more closely, it could significantly benefit faculty and graduate student research at Notre Dame and, since all schools of the CIC were members of the Association of American Universities (AAU), the presumption was that their lobbying would gain admission of Notre Dame into that prestigious association. The CIC also sponsored programs to increase minority graduate student enrollment and facilitate opportunities for graduate students to study abroad, and Notre Dame could benefit from these also. Both the Faculty Senate and a general faculty forum arranged by the senate favored Notre Dame's joining.[95]

On the other hand, the Student Life Council and the undergraduate student body seemed in opposition. Both apparently feared that the resulting emphasis on graduate education and graduate research would diminish the priority on undergraduate education and classroom teaching. Concern was expressed also that Notre Dame might become more regionalized than national and its Catholic character might also be diluted. The athletic coaches who spoke publicly seemed neutral. Some Big Ten schools did not field hockey or men's soccer teams but that was not prohibitive. Playing more regional, midwestern schedules might make recruiting nationally more challenging, but the coaches felt they could adjust. Travel distances might be shorter, but teams might prefer an air flight to Baltimore to a bus ride to Bloomington. The Big East schools had welcomed Notre Dame into their conference a few years ago, and loyalty to them was another consideration.[96]

At its winter meeting in early February 1999, the board of trustees accepted the administration's recommendation and voted not to join the Big Ten. The university had sought to join the Conference on Institutional Cooperation without joining the Big Ten but this was not possible. Board chairman Andrew McKenna explained that Notre Dame had always enjoyed its association with Big Ten and CIC schools in the past and hoped to expand these associations in the future, and acknowledged that it had been a privilege to explore the possibility of joining the CIC. Father Malloy echoed these sentiments and noted that several current deans and numerous faculty members had come to Notre Dame from Big Ten schools, that finances were not an issue, but that Notre Dame would be the smallest school in the Big Ten, the only religiously affiliated school, and one of only two private schools. Every university has its unique identity, he explained, Notre Dame's is that it is Catholic, private, and independent, and it decided to remain that way. Addressing the Big Ten directly, however, the president concluded: "Our relationship with you over more than a century—our competition in sports and cooperation in research and scholarship—have greatly enriched Notre Dame, and we look forward to maintaining and deepening those relationships—not as a member of the family but as, we hope, an old and close family friend."[97]

Thus, having ridden out the Y2K challenge successfully and having decided against joining the Big Ten and CIC, Notre Dame entered the new millennium as it always had been, and as the *Colloquy for the Year 2000* had envisioned—Catholic, private, and independent.

Entering the New Millennium

The new millennium began with a challenge for Notre Dame and for all Catholic universities, and it was a challenge from the highest source possible, Pope (now Saint) John Paul II. His apostolic constitution on higher education, *Ex Corde Ecclesiae*, and its official application to the United States went into effect on May 3, 2001. Since 1987, Father Malloy had had a part in drafting both the constitution and the application, but its background stretched even further back. The International Federation of Catholic Universities (IFCU) had been recognized by the Vatican in 1949 and from that time held discussions on the relationship between Catholic universities and the Church's magisterium, the official teaching authority of the Church. The Land O' Lakes Statement in 1967 was a critical contribution to the ongoing discussions, insisting that "the Catholic university must have a true autonomy and academic freedom in the face of authority of whatever kind, lay or clerical, external to the academic community itself," and emphasizing the importance of all branches of human knowledge, the centrality of the study and teaching of theology, and the need for a strong and attractive liturgical and sacramental life.[1] The Vatican issued a document, *Sapientia Christiana*, in 1979, detailing regulations for the study and teaching of what it called "ecclesiastical" disciplines (theology, philosophy, canon law, etc.), but this document applied only to pontifical universities, those "canonically erected or approved by the

Apostolic See . . . and which have the right to confer academic degrees by the authority of the Holy See."[2] Notre Dame was not one of those. In 1983 the revised Code of Canon Law was promulgated, including a section on Catholic universities that noted that no university could bear the title "Catholic" without the consent of competent Church authority, and that no one was permitted to teach theological discipline in a Catholic university without "a mandate from competent ecclesiastical authority."[3]

While one Vatican office was preparing the final draft of the revised Code of Canon Law, another office, the pontifical Congregation for Catholic Education, in 1980 began composing an extensive document on Catholic education that would apply to all Catholic universities throughout the world. An early draft of this schema was circulated among bishops, university presidents, and other educational experts throughout the 1980s. Father Malloy took part in discussions organized by Father Hesburgh in 1987, and he joined an advisory committee of Vatican officials, bishops, university presidents, superiors of religious communities, and educators at large that met for the first time in Rome in 1989. Most university presidents probably felt that no document was necessary, while Vatican officials were convinced that official guidelines were required to guarantee the authenticity of Catholic teachings throughout the world. Further discussions were held throughout the year, and each draft emerged less legalistic and more pastoral, much to the liking of university presidents. The final document, *Ex Corde Ecclesiae*, promulgated by Pope John Paul II on August 15, 1990, was composed of three sections: a personal introduction by the Holy Father, emphasizing his longtime interest in Catholic education; a section on the "Identity and Mission" of a Catholic university; and a listing of approximately thirty general and transitional norms. The main themes enunciated by the document were that Catholic universities should clearly and proudly identify themselves as Catholic; that their mission was, through teaching, research, and pastoral ministry, to contribute to the overall mission of the Church, the salvation of souls; that in carrying out this mission, harmony and cooperation must prevail between the universities and the hierarchy, the official teachers of the Church; and that theologians especially must be faithful to the teachings of the Church's magisterium.[4]

Each national hierarchy was commissioned to draw up a specific application of the apostolic constitution for implementation in its own country. In the United States, the National Conference of Catholic Bishops (NCCB) immediately appointed a committee of approximately equal numbers of bishops and university presidents to begin the work, but only the bishops on the committee were empowered to vote on the final draft, and the document would then need to be sent to Rome for final approval. Meetings continued throughout the decade, with deadlines constantly missed, and the divisions remained the same, bishops preferring a more legalistic document and tighter regulations on universities, and university presidents urging a more pastoral approach with fewer limitations and greater freedom. *Ex Corde Ecclesiae* had stated that theologians "fulfill a mandate received from the church," and this became the thorniest issue. After some twenty-odd meetings and conference calls throughout the decade, the committee reached a compromise with the concept of a "presumed mandate," that a mandate might be presumed if the theologian met the approval of the Catholic university and its president who were hiring him or her. The completed application gained acceptance of the bishops on the committee with a vote of 24 to 2 and the document made its way to Rome for final approval, but some of the more conservative bishops apparently exerted influence and the Congregation for Catholic Education returned the document for further revision. A subcommittee of bishops reworked the document, recommended stricter and more canonical language, and in this form it was accepted by the American hierarchy with a vote of 223 to 31 and subsequently approved by Rome to take effect on May 3, 2001.[5]

In its final and approved form, the application stated clearly that "Catholic universities enjoy institutional autonomy: as academic institutions their governance is and remains internal to the institution."[6] It further acknowledged that "academic freedom is an essential component of a Catholic university."[7] The document emphasized the concept of "communion," the union of God with His people, and the union of peoples among themselves as children of God, and with God. Catholic institutions participate in this communion: "Every Catholic University is to maintain communication with the universal Church and the Holy See; it is to be in close communion with the local Church and in particular with the diocesan bishops of the region or the nation in which it is located."[8] Bishops hold overall responsibility for the pastoral care of the people, a Catholic university shares in this ministry on its campus, and thus the university must remain in harmony with the teachings of the hierarchy.[9] To assure the Catholic character of a university, the document stated that "the university president should be a Catholic" and that "the university should strive to recruit and appoint Catholic professors so that, to the extent possible, those committed to the witness of the faith will constitute a majority of the faculty."[10] About the controversial mandate, the application decreed the following:[11]

Catholics who teach the theological disciplines in a Catholic university are required to have a *mandatum* granted by competent ecclesiastical authority. . . .

The competent ecclesiastical authority to grant the *mandatum* is the bishop of the diocese in which the Catholic university is located. . . .

Without prejudice to the rights of the local bishop, a *mandatum*, once granted, remains in effect wherever and as long as the professor teaches unless and until withdrawn by competent ecclesiastical authority.

The *mandatum* should be given in writing.

Bishop John D'Arcy of the diocese of Fort Wayne–South Bend subsequently met with Notre Dame's Theology Department but the number of faculty members who accepted or were denied a mandate remained private.[12]

Ex Corde Ecclesiae aroused little discussion or concern on campus when it went into effect that May. Commencement followed and both students and faculty began to drift away for the summer. Soon after the new semester opened in the fall, however, the whole world was shaken by the terrorist attack on the World Trade Center in New York and the Pentagon in Washington, DC. Word spread rapidly across campus. Classes were immediately cancelled, the administration asked that it be a day of prayer, students visited the Grotto in large numbers, and those from New York and Washington rushed to call their families, with limited success. Many lined up to donate blood to meet the critical need. The administration was able to ascertain that everyone in the Notre Dame semester program in Washington was safe. Approximately six thousand students, faculty, and staff, some with families, attended a Mass on the south quad that afternoon, presided over by Father Malloy. Campus security was increased that day, and access to the campus moderately limited, not in fear of a local attack but simply because of the increased crowd at the Mass.[13]

The normal schedule of classes resumed the following day. Returning to a familiar daily routine helped reduce the stress and worry many felt but professors were also encouraged to allow students to express their feelings and share their concerns publicly with others. All extracurricular lectures and concerts, and all athletic events, were cancelled for the week, but panel discussions of faculty and others were organized for those desiring to attend. The football game with Purdue scheduled for September 15 was postponed to December 1, and football practice was cancelled to allow players to readjust at their own pace. Notre Dame and Saint Mary's students studying in France worried at first if it was safe to speak English on the streets but professors and students from other countries offered sympathy and support and one French newspaper proclaimed "We are all Americans." Students in London attended a prayer service in St. Paul's Cathedral, attended also by Queen Elizabeth, and the American embassy supplied them with daily phone calls and news dispatches. On Sunday evening, September 16, a thousand students gathered at the Grotto on campus for scripture reading and prayer, and then with lighted candles marched in silence to the reflecting pool at the library for additional prayer and hymns. At the Michigan State football game on September 22, where the two university bands performed together at halftime in a sign of unity, students canvassed through the stands and collected over $270,000 in donations for families of police and firefighters killed in the attacks.[14] The day was commemorated each succeeding year.

If *Ex Corde Ecclesiae* had provided no immediate challenge to the university, other matters did require attention. Grade inflation was one. Grade levels had risen steadily over the past thirty or forty years but debate continued over the causes and whether to judge it good or bad. Father Joseph Walter noted that in his Analytical Chemistry class in 1967–1968, nineteen students had received a C, four a D, and two an F. In the class in 1987, twenty years later, no student received a C, D, or F. He added that the average grade point average entering medical school nationwide in the 1960s was approximately 2.7 but it was 3.4 in 2004. Notre Dame was not exempt. The percentage of classes in which half or more of the students received grades of A or A– in the College of Arts and Letters was 51.3 percent in 1994 but 74.1 percent in 2003; in the School of Architecture the percentage jumped from 16.7 percent to 47.1 percent; in the College of Business from 29.2 percent to 47.1 percent; and in the College of Engineering from 25 percent to 42.1 percent. Across the colleges, the percentage rose from 43.6 percent to 64 percent.[15]

Grades were clearly on the rise, but why? In the early years, some blamed the Vietnam War. Students needed good grades to remain in school or they could easily be drafted into the war. Grade inflation had invaded universities all across the country, and if Notre Dame grades remained low, Notre Dame students could be at a competitive disadvantage when applying for medical, law, and graduate schools. In fact, many graduate, law, and medical schools were relying more and more on standardized GRE, LSAT, and MCAT scores to determine admission for precisely this reason. Some were also concerned that the increased importance the administration was attaching to the Teacher-Course Evaluations might be leading some in the classroom to give higher grades. But others did not decry grade inflation at all. They argued that Notre Dame was admitting brighter students every year and they should be getting better grades than their predecessors. Further, professors were carrying lighter teaching loads, were teaching smaller classes, could spend more time with individual students, and the students should be learning more. Deans and department chairs admitted that they kept an eye on the situation and would speak with individual professors whose grades seemed out of line, not to request changes but simply to review the situation more thoroughly. In light of the grade inflation, however, the university adopted the policy of awarding *summa cum laude* honors to students graduating in the top 5 percent of their college, *magna cum laude* to those in the top 10 percent, and *cum laude* to the top 30 percent, rather than the earlier respective cutoffs of 3.8, 3.6, and 3.4.[16]

By the turn of the century, faculty, students, and the administration agreed that the honor code also needed revision. Under the current code, all cases of alleged violation were to be heard by a departmental or college honesty committee, and a report then filed in the Office of the Provost. This was simply not happening. Faculty and students both felt that the hearings were unnecessarily complicated, and thus faculty members often simply imposed a penalty and no report was filed. A student might be guilty of plagiarism in more than one class with no one knowing of the multiple offenses. The inefficiency of the system seemed especially bothersome if instances of plagiarism were on the rise due to increased use of the computer and internet, and that seemed to be the case across the country. Class assignments and final papers could be cribbed from a computer with even a minimal knowledge of cutting and pasting.

To alleviate that final problem, the university arranged to make Turnitin.com available to all faculty. If a faculty member had reason to question whether a student's paper was original or not, he or she could submit it to Turnitin.com and within twenty-four hours a report would be returned that detailed whether all or parts of the material had previously appeared elsewhere. The administration urged that this procedure be used only if reason existed to believe that the material was not the student's original work. To submit every assignment routinely to Turnitin.com seemed a violation of at least the spirit of the honor code.[17]

But the system itself needed revision. Cheating may have been more widespread in high school, but it was common enough at Notre Dame that students acknowledged it openly and casually. Some speculated that incidents probably numbered a thousand, or even more, a year, although only forty-two cases were reported in 2003–2004 and forty the year before. The academic environment itself might have been contributing to the problem. Students were seated too close together in crowded classrooms, professors gave the same exams semester after semester, and true-false and other objective exams were easy to correct but also easy to plagiarize. Students would rarely report on another, especially a friend or roommate, and a hearing was time-consuming and cumbersome. The Academic Council in April 2005 approved several changes recommended by the University Code of Honor Committee. Allegations of honor code violations could now be handled by the professor if the professor and student reached an agreement on the student's guilt and the penalty imposed. In such a case, a report would then be filed in the Provost's Office. If the student then had second thoughts, he or she could appeal within the next seven days and the case would then be heard by an honesty committee. If the student did not want the case handled by the professor, or if the student and professor could not agree on the degree of guilt or an appropriate penalty, the case would then be heard by an honesty committee. A report was always sent to the Provost's Office, and that office could also alter a penalty. The normal penalty for a minor offense was zero for the assignment; for a major offense, zero for the course; and for a flagrant offense, premeditated and especially egregious, suspension or expulsion from the university. All incoming students were required to read a pamphlet explaining the honor code and sign a statement pledging to abide by it, and all departmental honesty committees, under the new policy, were required to have a majority of student members.[18]

Although the faculty and administration could agree on many issues, including that both grade inflation and the honor code needed attention and that there was a need for an additional 150 new faculty, differences still remained. In 2000, the Faculty Senate asked that the minutes of the university's board of fellows' and board of trustees' meetings be made public as a step toward improving campus-wide communications. Father Malloy acknowledged that because of so-called sunshine laws, the board minutes of public universities were published, but it was a privilege of private institutions to retain them as confidential. Confidentiality allowed for honest and open discussion of at times sensitive questions and the university benefited greatly from such discussions. Public press releases provided pertinent and necessary information to faculty, students, and the public at large.[19] No change was made.

Two more disagreements arose that year when the administration appointed a new director of the Medieval Institute without the full participation of the academic department of which he would also be a member, and when the board of trustees extended Father Malloy's term an additional three years without faculty consultation or recommendation.[20] In the wake of these and other controversies, the Faculty Senate in the spring of 2001 formally voted to disband. Faculty colleagues seemed to consider the senate pointless, many declined to stand for election, and the administration often disregarded its opinions. The resolution to disband required the approval of the Academic Council, the president, and the board of trustees (since it was established in the academic articles), and that fall Father Malloy asked the senate to reconsider its decision. He insisted that the university needed, and benefited from, a body that represented and expressed faculty opinion as a whole. The senate had also been considering a possible restructuring to make it function more efficiently, and that restructuring was then undertaken and completed the following spring. The number of senators was reduced, with one senator elected from each academic department, making the body more representative, and a few others from other constituencies—emeriti faculty, professional specialists, etc. The senate retained the right to place issues on the Academic Council agenda, and the senate chair and the four standing committee chairs became *ex officio* members of the Academic Council.[21]

Academic changes continued during the final five years of Father Malloy's administration. The most noticeable one, and the most controversial, was the division of the Economics Department into two departments, one a Department of Economics and the other a Department of Economic Thought and Policy. They were later renamed, respectively, the Department of Economics and Econometrics and the Department of Economics and Policy Studies. The principal reason for the split seemed to have been that mainstream economics nationwide had been trending in a more mathematical direction and the department at Notre Dame had not followed. In the most recent comprehensive review of the College of Arts and Letters, the Department of Economics had been the only department ranked in the fourth (lowest) quartile. Most of the more senior professors remained with the Department of Economics and Policy Studies, but the majority of more recent hires joined the Department of Economics and Econometrics. Graduate programs were housed primarily in the latter department, and between five and seven new positions were given to strengthen that department even more. Not everyone was pleased with the decision—the Arts and Letters College Council had voted 25 to 14 against it—but after months of discussion, this solution seemed the best compromise to allow the department to grow and gain respect nationwide while also permitting each professor to continue his or her teaching and research in complete freedom.[22]

In 2003, Joan Kroc, widow of McDonald's Corporation founder Ray Kroc, died and left in her will $50 million for Notre Dame's Kroc Institute for International Peace Studies. She had given Father Hesburgh $6 million to begin the program in 1985, another $6 million to construct the Hesburgh Center for International Studies, which was constructed in 1991, and for the past six years had sent him an additional $1 million for the institute each year on his birthday. The peace studies program at the time numbered twenty-four graduate students from seventeen different countries, and this most recent gift, the largest single bequest in Notre Dame history to that time, allowed the institute to expand from a one-year program to a two-year program, providing additional courses, more time for reflection and discussion, and especially a semester of research and supervised fieldwork. In the words of the program's director: "[This will] prepare our students to work at the governmental, non-governmental and local grass roots levels to resolve conflicts nonviolently and to provide education for peace and justice."[23]

In the fall of 2005, Indiana University and Notre Dame combined to open a new medical education center at the corner of Notre Dame Avenue and Angela Boulevard, adjacent to the Notre Dame campus. This cooperative program had begun in 1972 and had been located in the basement of Haggar Hall, formerly the Wenninger-Kirsch Biology Building. Between twenty-five and thirty-five Indiana University students took the first two years of medical classes at Notre Dame, classes taught mostly by Notre Dame faculty of the College of Science but some Indiana University faculty taught classes as well. After the two years at Notre Dame, the students transferred to the Indiana University campus at Indianapolis for additional classes and, chiefly, for specialized work in Indianapolis that South Bend hospitals at that time did not provide. As the program grew, larger facilities were called for, and the new Raclin-Carmichael Hall was constructed in 2004–2005. The building housed the W. M. Keck Center for Transgene Research on the second floor, a collaborative research study into the causes of cancer, infectious diseases, and blood maladies. Faculty offices, classrooms, and research laboratories were located on the first floor, and in the basement was a 300-gallon aquarium for trout and a highly secure room for genetically altered mice.[24]

As new programs developed or were expanded, old ones were abandoned or revised. In 2003, the twenty-year-old two-semester sophomore Core course was dropped in the College of Arts and Letters and replaced by a one-semester College Seminar in the freshman year. The Core course had been required of all Arts and Letters sophomores, it had carried an approved reading list for all sections, and thus all sophomores in the college had had a common foundation of books and topics for discussion, even outside of class. The required reading list did not please everyone, professors felt less qualified to lead discussions on some readings, and reaction to the course varied widely. For the new one-semester College Seminar, each professor selected the readings for his or her own section, but since it was a first-year course it was hoped that each section would introduce the students into the humanities, social sciences, and creative arts.[25]

Violence at home and abroad also necessitated changes at times. The semester abroad program in Jerusalem had to be cancelled in the spring of 2000 due to heightened violence in the West Bank and the Gaza Strip. The Ecumenical Institute for Advanced Theological Studies at Tantur, where the students lived, was on a hilltop road between Jerusalem and Bethlehem and seemed safe, but the students had to be sequestered there at times and they were not able to experience fully the cultures of the Jews and the Palestinians. Closer to home, the Center for Social Concerns canceled a seminar scheduled for the 2002 fall break in Washington, DC, due to random sniper attacks that killed ten people in the DC area. The center felt that students would not be able to walk the streets alone and too much of the Washington experience would have to be curtailed.[26]

The Notre Dame community saw many of its members honored in the new millennium. Father Thomas Streit of the Department of Biology received a grant of $5.2 million from the Bill and Melinda Gates Foundation to fight lymphatic filariasis in Haiti, the disease that causes elephantiasis. Lymphatic filariasis is a mosquito-transmitted disease afflicting approximately 120 million people throughout the tropical world, and Father Streit, in cooperation with the Center for Disease Control and the World Health Organization, researched, here and in Haiti, ways to prevent and control the disease. Unfortunately, the ouster of President Jean-Bertrand Aristide in early 2004 left parts of the country in turmoil and some workers had to be relocated. But progress continued. The year before, volunteers had administered medicines to nearly 500,000 people, a preventative medicine that warded off the infection for one year.[27]

James Wetherbee, a 1974 graduate in aerospace engineering, achieved fame in 2002 by commanding the space shuttle *Endeavor* on an eleven-day mission to the international space station in orbit 240 miles above the Earth. This was Wetherbee's sixth space mission and his fifth as a commander, a record at the time. After joining NASA in 1984, he had logged approximately 1,200 hours in space by 2002, had commanded the first flight with a woman pilot and the first flight to exchange crew members with the space station, and he had been awarded the Distinguished Flying Cross, the Navy Achievement Medal, two Meritorious Unit

Commendations, six Space Flight Medals, two Outstanding Leadership Medals, and four Distinguished Service Medals.[28]

Chemistry professor Dennis Jacobs received national recognition in 2002 when he was named Professor of the Year by the Council for the Advancement and Support of Education (CASE) and the Carnegie Foundation for the Advancement of Teaching. An innovative teacher, Professor Jacobs's courses combined lectures and demonstrations with class discussions and on-site learning. Students in one class did research in South Bend homes, checking the lead content in paint, and students in another class tested samples of dust and soil for harmful components. Students seemed more engaged and passionate, and prouder of their accomplishments.[29]

Another innovative teaching program scored a victory when Alliance for Catholic Education (ACE) successfully turned back a court challenge to its federal funding. In the fall of 2002, the American Jewish Congress brought suit in federal court, claiming that ACE members were teaching religion in Catholic schools while being funded by government money through AmeriCorps and that this violated separation of church and state. ACE teachers received a stipend of close to $12,000 from the schools in which they taught and were eligible for an additional $9,000 from AmeriCorps if they completed 1,700 hours of service inside or outside the classroom. The American Jewish Congress stressed that it had no objection to the fine work ACE was performing; the only objection was that government money was funding the teaching of religion. ACE administrators acknowledged that some members did teach religion, but they clarified that that activity was not funded by AmeriCorps. In the summer of 2004, a federal district judge agreed with the American Jewish Congress and declared the line between ACE's secular and religious activities to be "completely blurred," but she also postponed any implementation of her decree until Notre Dame could appeal. ACE and Notre Dame eventually emerged victorious when the federal court of appeals in Washington, DC, in a 3–0 decision, agreed that ACE teachers receiving AmeriCorps funding were accumulating 1,700 hours teaching secular subjects—mathematics, history, literature, chemistry, etc.—and any religion courses need not be included.[30] The AmeriCorps grants were especially important for those ACE members still in debt from their college education.

If the federal government looked favorably on Notre Dame in the Alliance for Catholic Education decision, it turned the other way in a faculty recruitment effort. The Kroc Institute for International Peace Studies had invited Swiss Muslim scholar Tariq Ramadan as Henry R. Luce Professor of Religion, Conflict and

Peacebuilding. Nine days before his scheduled departure from Geneva in July 2004 and after his furniture had been sent ahead, his visa was revoked by the Department of State at the request of the Department of Homeland Security. Most American scholars praised him as a moderate, although some Jewish groups considered him anti-Semitic, and his grandfather had founded the Muslim Brotherhood in 1928. Scotland Yard and Swiss intelligence had found charges against him groundless, and the Chicago-based Jewish Council on Urban Affairs supported his admission. He had lectured in the United States some twenty times in the past without complication, and he had visited Notre Dame on four occasions, and no reasons were given for the revocation in 2004. After several months of delay, and needing to enroll his children in school somewhere, Ramadan in December officially resigned the position offered him at Notre Dame and eventually accepted a teaching position at St. Anthony's College at Oxford.[31]

As the new millennium opened, the Athletic Department also experienced both highs and lows. On the low side, on January 19, 2000, as noted earlier, the National Collegiate Athletic Association found Notre Dame guilty of a major violation for several players accepting financial benefits from a member of the university's Quarterback Club and sentenced the university to two years of probation. One month later, Mike Wadsworth, Notre Dame's director of athletics since 1995, submitted his resignation. In May, the board of trustees extended Father Malloy's presidency an additional three years to 2005 but did not reappoint Father Beauchamp as executive vice president and chairman of the Faculty Board in Control of Athletics, naming Father Timothy Scully instead. Kevin White had been named director of athletics replacing Wadsworth in March. Matt Doherty had been hired to succeed John MacLeod as men's basketball coach in early 1999, but he resigned after one year when North Carolina, his alma mater, offered him its head coaching position. Led by consensus All-American Troy Murphy, Doherty compiled a 22–15 record during his only year at Notre Dame, the university's first twenty-win season in ten years. Sadly, the millennium had begun with the sudden and unexpected death in January 2000 of Mike Berticelli, Notre Dame's men's soccer coach for the previous ten years, and he was not replaced until Bobby Clark of Stanford was named the new coach in January 2001.[32]

At the close of the 2001 football season, Kevin White, the new director of athletics, informed Bob Davie that his position as head coach was being terminated even though he had been given a five-year extension only the year before. His record at Notre Dame was 35 victories and 25 defeats, for a winning percentage of .583, well below the .765 winning percentage of his predecessor, Lou Holtz.

The highest rankings Davie's teams had achieved were 22nd in 1998 and 16th in 2000, and his record was only 5 and 6 in 2001, his final year. Kevin White did not see signs of progress for the future and decided that a change was needed.[33] Unfortunately, good fortune did not smile on the new athletic director in his next decision. He had formerly served in that position at Loras College, the University of Maine, Tulane University, and Arizona State University, and he knew the athletic landscape well. After only seven days, he decided that George O'Leary, head coach at Georgia Tech, was the man he wanted as football coach. As reporters scurried to learn more about the new coach, questions arose, and O'Leary admitted that the personal resume he had put together twenty years before and was still using had inaccuracies. It stated that he had won varsity letters as a student at the University of New Hampshire and that he had received a master's degree from a university in New York, both of which he admitted were false. Georgia Tech and other employers had not caught the mistakes either, but such dishonesty seemed unacceptable in a university setting where students were taught to be honorable in the classroom and outside it, and after only four days O'Leary submitted his resignation.[34]

The university then turned to Tyrone Willingham, the very successful seven-year coach at Stanford University. He had compiled a 44–36–1 record there with a Pacific-10 Conference championship in 1999, he had been named conference Coach of the Year twice, and he had defeated Notre Dame in three of their five meetings. A graduate of Michigan State, he had previously coached at Central Michigan, at North Carolina State, and with the Minnesota Vikings. He was Notre Dame's first black American head coach. His first season started phenomenally well. The team was victorious in the first eight games, with wins over Michigan, Michigan State, and Florida State. He lost two of the final four, and the Gator Bowl, but his 10–3 record easily surpassed his predecessor's final year of 5 and 6. His record reversed in his second year, losing six of the first eight games, and concluding with a record of 5 and 7. The third year showed only slight improvement, six wins and six losses,[35] the university decided to replace him, and Charlie Weis, a Notre Dame graduate and offensive coordinator for the New England Patriots under Bill Belichick at the time, was eventually named his successor.

When the men's basketball coach, Matt Doherty, left Notre Dame for North Carolina in the summer of 2000, the university reached out to Mike Brey of the University of Delaware. Brey had graduated from DeMatha High School in Hyattsville, Maryland, where he had played for and then coached under the legendary Morgan Wootten. He had then served as assistant coach at Duke under Mike Krzyzewski from 1987 to 1995 before moving to Delaware. In his first five years at Notre Dame, he compiled a record of 102 wins and 56 losses, with appearances in two NIT and three NCAA tournaments, reaching the Sweet Sixteen in 2003. He was the only coach in Notre Dame history to lead his teams to NCAA appearances in his first three years. In 2001, Troy Murphy was named Big East Player of the Year, and in 2002 Chris Thomas was named National Freshman of the Year.[36]

The women's basketball team began the millennium even stronger. With a starting five of guards Niele Ivey and Alicia Ratay, forwards Kelley Siemon and Ericka Haney, and led by consensus All-American Ruth Riley, the team won 34 and lost only 2 in the 2000–2001 season and was declared national champions after a thrilling 68–66 victory over Purdue in the NCAA finals. Muffet McGraw was named Coach of the Year and Ruth Riley Player of the Year. Only Alicia Ratay returned the next year, but Jacqueline Batteast arrived in the fall of 2001, Megan Duffy arrived the following year, and Charel Allen arrived in 2004. Victories continued. The women won 20 and lost 10 in 2001–2002, were 21 and 11 in both 2002–2003 and 2003–2004, and improved to 27 and 6 in 2004–2005. They received an NCAA Tournament bid every year. The team's overall record for the first five years of the new century was an impressive 123 victories against 40 defeats, for a winning percentage of .751.[37]

Women's basketball did not win Notre Dame's only national championship in the final years of Father Malloy's presidency. Led by men Michal Sobieraj and Ozren Debic and women Andrea Ament and Alicja Kryczalo, Notre Dame won the national championship in fencing in 2003, and with Mariel Zagunis and Valerie Providenza joining Ament and Kryczalo and Patrick Ghattas joining Sobieraj, the team repeated in 2005.[38] Boasting All-Americans Jen Buczkowski, Candace Chapman, Melissa Tancredi, and Katie Thorlakson, the women's soccer team brought the national championship trophy back to Notre Dame in 2004 (a repeat from 1995), defeating Santa Clara in the semifinals and UCLA on penalty kicks in the final.[39]

Women rose to the top not only in basketball and soccer during these years but also in Student Government. Junior Brooke Norton was elected student body president for 2001–2002, the first woman elected to that position. Norton had served as student body vice president the year before, as had other women in the past, but she was the first elected to the top post. The following year, Elizabeth "Libby" Bishop was elected student body president, and with Molly Kinder already selected for the Irish Guard and Tambre Paster named first black

American and second female drum major, coeducation was continuing to gain full acceptance.[40]

One area in which gender equality did not meet with universal approval was in women's boxing. Men had been boxing in the Bengal Bouts since 1931, raising money for the Holy Cross missions in South Asia under the slogan "Strong Bodies Fight That Weak Bodies May Be Nourished." The university did not want women participating against men and in 1997 began a program in women's boxing, although at that time there were no matches in public. Only Notre Dame and the service academies sponsored women's boxing at the time. In the spring of 2003, six exhibition bouts of women were permitted to open the Bengal Bouts, each with two rounds of one minute and forty-five seconds, the first public exhibitions. One hundred women tried out and twelve were selected. The women trained two hours a day for five weeks, with sessions featuring jumping jacks, push-ups, sit-ups, an hour of punching and footwork, and an hour of sparring. For some the emphasis was more on form and style than on winning. Eventually the program separated from the men, it took the name Baraka Bouts, and all proceeds were sent to Holy Cross schools in Uganda.[41]

Another student volunteer accomplishment was the Holy Cross Associates program, which celebrated its twenty-fifth anniversary in 2003. Founded in 1978 by Fathers Jerome Wilson and Timothy Scully, the program offered college graduates the opportunity for one (domestic) or two (international) years of volunteer service in education, care of the homeless, domestic violence services, parish ministry, family programs, and HIV/AIDs services. The program began in Portland, Oregon, but it gradually expanded into Phoenix, Colorado Springs, Brockton (Massachusetts), Wilkes-Barre (Pennsylvania), and Santiago and Pocuro in Chile. The program adopted four pillars for the associates' everyday life: commitment to service, desire to live and share community, a simple lifestyle and option for the poor, and a commitment to spirituality, prayer, and Christian living. The associates not only provided welcomed services but profited themselves from the experience. Said one, returning from Chile:[42]

> It was a difficult decision to leave the United States, but looking back at Notre Dame, you realize what a gift it is when you get to go to a poorer country. It was the best decision I made in my life. It made me rethink who I am and what I believe in. I am very grateful for the experience.

"The Shirt" also exemplified the students' willingness to assist those in need. The idea originated with Sister Jean Lenz, assistant vice president of student affairs, in 1989. A graduate student from China, Zheng de Wang, had been seriously injured by a hit-and-run driver on a dark, rainy night on Notre Dame Avenue, and Sister Jean sought a way to raise money for his medical expenses and to permit his parents to travel to Notre Dame. A special short-sleeved pullover shirt was designed in collaboration with the Student Union Board and the Hall Presidents Council, and sales ultimately totaled over $100,000 for the family. A new "Shirt" was then designed in secret each year, was unveiled in a well-publicized ceremony, and the proceeds were directed to pertinent charities, aid to needy students, and to student organizations, and more than $2 million was raised during the first twelve years.[43]

The whole Notre Dame community was saddened by two youth deaths in 2002. That spring, Melissa Cook, a 1994 graduate and former member of the varsity softball team, died tragically in Chicago. She and another young woman had stopped for a red light and part of some scaffolding at the John Hancock Center collapsed and fell on the car, killing both young women in the front seat and injuring their mothers in the rear seat. The wind may have been primarily to blame but the companies involved settled for several million dollars. Miss Cook's parents used part of the money for scholarships for students from northern Indiana (their home had been in Michigan City) and donated more than $3 million to Notre Dame for a new softball stadium. Melissa's mother remarked: "From the beginning of the lawsuit, we didn't think that money belonged to us. Melissa paid the ultimate price for that money and that money actually belonged to her. We wanted the money to live on." Melissa's body was later reburied in Cedar Grove Cemetery on Notre Dame Avenue, and the softball stadium was named the Melissa Cook Stadium.[44]

The campus was saddened by another death later that year, the death of Fisher Hall freshman Chad Sharon. He attended an off-campus party with other students on the evening of December 12 but declined to ride back to campus with them. He was reportedly seen by several people in town but he may have lost his way and did not return to his hall that evening. Wide searches were made for him, he missed his final exams, and he did not return home for Christmas break. Two months later his body was found in the Saint Joseph River, the victim of drowning, and the bells of Sacred Heart Basilica tolled the news that afternoon.[45]

Controversies with students over free speech and the use of alcohol continued in the early years of the new millennium. In 2002, the play *The Vagina Monologues* by Eve Ensler was performed on campus, a series of short episodes with speakers elucidating the challenges and opportunities of a gay and lesbian lifestyle. It was performed again two years later as part of a four-day Queer Film Festival sponsored by the Gender Studies Program, the Gay and Lesbian Alumni of Notre Dame and Saint Mary's, and the Departments of English and Film, Television, and Theatre. Bishop John D'Arcy of the diocese of Fort Wayne–South Bend called the play "offensive to women" and "antithetical to Catholic teaching on the beautiful gift of human sexuality and also to the teachings of the Church on the human body relative to its purpose and to its status as a temple of the Holy Spirit."[46] But it was also defended. "We are in an academic institution that has a whole [range] of classes, seminars and conferences," said a university spokeswoman, "and that is what we are all about."[47] When the Queer Film Festival was held the following year, the bishop again expressed his disapproval, calling it "an abuse of academic freedom," and he lamented that there was "no place given to the presentation of Catholic teaching on the matter of homosexuality." He asked: "What about the rights of the Church to have its teachings properly presented? What about the rights of parents of those students at Notre Dame who find the contents of this seminar offensive?" The founder of the festival responded that he had made the effort to recruit others to join the panels but all refused, and he added that those opposing the festival had no obligation to attend.[48]

In the midst of the campus discussion and controversy in the spring of 2004, a group named the Gay-Straight Alliance distributed orange shirts emblazoned with the wording "Gay? Fine by Me" throughout the campus. Three hundred were distributed within the first forty-five minutes. The supporters explained that the purpose was "to raise awareness of the homosexual population on campus and to help the homosexual population feel welcome." Others objected that the words could be a welcoming of either homosexual orientation or homosexual lifestyle, the latter being contrary to Catholic moral teaching. Some opposed even the ambiguity, preferring that students stand openly behind whatever opinions they held.[49]

Alcohol continued to be a major concern for university administrators across the country, and Notre Dame confronted it directly in the spring of 2002. Father Mark Poorman, the vice president of student affairs, announced a revised policy that March that banned all hard alcohol in residence halls, eliminated all in-hall dances, and revised the tailgate policy to allow of-age students to drink in designated parking lots on home football weekends. Father Poorman stated that his office had been studying the alcohol situation on campus over the past two years and had discovered that many students drank in moderation or not at all, but too many students drank to excess. "I want a campus culture that is creative,"

Poorman said, "that finds lots of alternatives [to drinking] and that isn't completely rooted in alcohol use." Campus culture, he noted, was becoming too centered on alcohol.[50]

The barring of in-hall dances met with immediate student opposition. Some objected that such a major decision was taken without any student input, but most emphasized the loss of hall spirit that could result from their termination. The in-hall dance, said the student body vice president, "is a major part of Notre Dame tradition and it's a huge part of the residential community that we try to foster here at Notre Dame."[51] Six hundred students gathered near the Peace Memorial (Clarke Memorial Fountain) on the north quad to protest the decision, and they then marched to the Main Building where incoming student body president Libby Bishop promised to work with the administration throughout the summer to revise the policy. Student senators noted that larger residence halls could afford venues off campus for hall dances but smaller halls, Badin for example, might not have sufficient participants to justify the extra cost of the facility and transportation. Father Poorman met with students at an open meeting of the Campus Life Council and insisted that the policy would stand, emphasizing student safety as a major concern, and citing incidents of drunken driving, sexual assault, and alcohol poisoning.[52] Father Malloy joined the discussion a month later when a panel on which he was a member released a paper from the National Institute on Alcohol Abuse and Alcoholism that publicized the facts that drinking by college students aged eighteen to twenty-four contributed each year to an estimated 1,400 student deaths, 500,000 injuries, and 70,000 cases of sexual assault. Also, 400,000 students reported having unprotected sex as a result of drinking. National experts recommended the scheduling of classes and examinations on Fridays and Saturday mornings and the designation of alcohol-free residence halls as partial solutions. By the end of the spring semester, however, more than 4,000 Notre Dame students still signed a petition that the new alcohol policy be revised.[53]

The issue was brought before the board of trustees the following year and the trustees decided to retain the ban on in-hall dances, at least for the present. However, the board did pass a resolution that each residence hall be given an additional $1,000 to assist with dances outside the hall, that the Office of Student Affairs draft plans to make popular dance locations on campus more available to residence halls, and that the Office of Student Affairs work with Food Services to lower costs and increase food options for hall dances.[54]

As the National Institute on Alcohol Abuse and Alcoholism report indicated, excessive drinking was also a major factor in sexual assaults, and this was clearly the case on the Notre Dame campus. Reported incidents of sexual assault had been given wider publicity in recent years and yet the majority of assaults had almost certainly been unreported. The reported statistics for the year 2000, for example, were two forcible rapes and four forcible fondlings. In the fall of 2000, the university decided to alter the current reporting policy to make it simpler and more comfortable for victims to come forward. First, student victims would not be subject to disciplinary action in connection with alcohol or parietal hours violations relating to the assault incident. Second, brochures would be published and circulated, detailing the resources and courses of action available to assault victims. Third, a committee of students, faculty, and administrators would be appointed to advise university officials on issues and procedures pertaining to sexual assault incidents. Fourth, a staff or faculty member would be appointed as an official resource person for campus victims of sexual assault.[55]

Campus construction in the new millennium kept pace with the changes and progress in the university's academic and student life. The first of these new buildings was the Coleman-Morse Center, housing both the Coleman Family Center for Campus Ministry and the James and Leah Rae Morse Center for Academic Services. The $14 million building was funded by Thomas Coleman, a Notre Dame graduate of 1956 and university trustee since 1984, and by James and Leah Rae Morse, James a graduate of 1957, captain of the football team, and private investor in Muskegon, Michigan. A chapel, satellite Campus Ministry offices, offices for Academic Services for Student-Athletes, and a twenty-four-hour social space occupied the first floor. The second floor contained the First Year of Studies offices, the Writing Center, two conference rooms, and six classrooms. Principal Campus Ministry offices occupied the third floor, with one classroom and two conference rooms, and one large and three smaller rehearsal rooms for university choirs. The building was dedicated in May 2001.[56]

Later that same year, the Edward A. Malloy, C.S.C., Hall was dedicated with an academic symposium and the awarding of honorary degrees on participants Father Gustavo Gutiérrez, Notre Dame professor and strong supporter of liberation theology; Cardinal Avery Dulles, S.J., son of former secretary of state John Foster Dulles, prolific author, and Laurence J. McGinley Professor of Religion and Society at Fordham University; Father Ernan McMullin, former chair of Notre Dame's Philosophy Department; and Bas van Fraassen, Dutch-born Catholic professor of philosophy at Princeton University. The building contained the administrative offices of the Departments of Theology and Philosophy, 150 private offices for the faculties of both departments, and the Chapel of Mary, Seat of Wisdom where Mass was celebrated regularly and the Blessed Sacrament reserved. Donald Keough, former chairman of the board of trustees, was the principal benefactor. The building was conveniently annexed to Decio Faculty Hall, which contained the offices of other Arts and Letters faculty, and close to other departmental administrative offices in the nearby I. A. O'Shaughnessy Hall of Liberal and Fine Arts.[57]

Thanks to the generous gift of Richard and Peggy Notebaert, a major renovation of the Senior Bar took place in 2003. Appropriately renamed Legends of Notre Dame at its renovation, the building was located close to the stadium, the site of so much football lore and tradition. The revamped building could accommodate slightly more than eight hundred people in a restaurant, pub, and nightclub. The restaurant served lunch and dinner from 11:00 a.m. to 9:00 p.m., the pub boasted of sixty-four bottled beers and twenty-two on tap, and the nightclub featured a stage for performances, $200,000 worth of sound and lighting equipment, video games, a pool table, and an available 144-inch television screen for viewing Saturday and Sunday football games. Some areas were restricted to those twenty-one years of age, and those people were identified with special colored wrist bracelets.[58]

The major construction project of Father Malloy's final years in office was the Marie P. DeBartolo Center for the Performing Arts. With a price tag of $64 million, much of that donated by 1932 graduate Edward J. DeBartolo in memory of his wife, it housed five performance spaces—the 900-seat Judd and Mary Lou Leighton Concert Hall, the 350-seat Patricia George Decio Mainstage Theatre, the 100-seat Regis Philbin Studio Theatre, the 200-seat Michael Browning Family Cinema, and the 100-seat Chris and Ann Reyes Organ and Choral Hall. Also included were classrooms, editing studios, costume and prop shops, and state-of-the-art technology. The facility was greatly needed but a long time in coming. The university had made progress in both academics and athletics throughout the decades, but the performing arts had lagged behind. Music and drama had formerly been located in Washington Hall, which was adequate for the 1800s when it was built but not for a century later. The new center was not as large as commercial theaters because, although the local community was invited to join the performances, it was constructed primarily for the educational benefit and use of the Notre Dame students and faculty.[59]

Hammes-Mowbray Hall, home to the Notre Dame Post Office and Notre Dame Security/Police, opened in early 2005 after some delay. Ground had been broken in 2002 but the slow economy and the stock market decline had forced a temporary postponement in construction. Building projects were allowed to continue only if they were directly related to academics or student life. When completed in 2005, the security side of the structure accommodated approximately one hundred people, twenty-six of whom were sworn police officers. Although equipped with modern technology, some older methods still worked best. "The bicycle patrol has been huge for us," noted the director of security. "They're the fastest to get to a called location. They beat squad cars every time."[60] The post office, on the west side of the building, was about the size of its predecessor across from the Morris Inn but it provided more parking, a twenty-four-hour lobby with postal boxes, a stamp vending machine, a copy machine, and an electronic scale. Approximately twelve thousand pieces of mail were picked up or delivered on campus each day, in addition to the service to the local community that the post office also provided.[61]

The Golden Dome on the Main Building needed regilding in 2005, for the tenth time in its history. As it had been the last time, in 1988, the 3,500-square-foot surface area was regilded with several ounces of 23.9-karat gold, at an approximate cost of $300,000. This time a controversy arose. In order to complete the project over the summer, the scaffolding had to be erected in the spring. The senior class petitioned that the scaffolding be removed for commencement weekend in order not to interfere with graduation photographs, and the scaffolding was removed down to the base of the Dome for that weekend and rebuilt the following week.[62]

Two other buildings that occupied much of the administration's time during Father Malloy's final years as president, although they were not completed until he had left office, were the Jordan Hall of Science and the Saint Liam Hall medical facility. At 202,000 square feet, the Jordan Hall of Science was the largest classroom building on campus. It housed a majestic Great Hall featuring twelve glass-enclosed display cases of scientific materials, forty undergraduate teaching laboratories, a greenhouse, an observatory, two 250-seat lecture halls, and a state-of-the-art multimedia visualization center—the only one on a university campus at the time—to create a spectacular 360-degree visual and auditory experience of the heavens. The building was dedicated by President Father John Jenkins on September 14, 2006.[63]

Saint Liam Hall was a thorough renovation of the University Heath Center that had been built in 1935 under President Father (later Cardinal) John O'Hara. The $8 million renovation was home not only to the University Health Services but also to the University Counseling Center and the Office of Alcohol and Drug Education. It included a large triage area and procedure room; new plumbing, electrical, security, and fire-protection systems; up-to-date medical equipment; an X-ray machine; and a satellite office for physical therapy. Said the vice president of student affairs, Father Mark Poorman: "The new facility helps us to provide students with the very best services available, such as 24/7 health care, on-site counseling services, and education, outreach and prevention for alcohol and drug use." The building was largely funded by the William K. Warren Foundation of Tulsa, and it was dedicated by Father Jenkins in February 2007.[64]

Father Malloy's presidency came to a close in 2005. He had asked the board of trustees in 2004 to review his administration. "I have no idea myself how it'll go," he remarked. "I'm happy with whatever the outcome is because I asked them to do it. . . . I'm not seeking to stay on because I think that should be the decision of the Board—but I will do whatever the Board wants in terms of what the future has in store."[65] After eighteen years, he was the third-longest-serving Notre Dame president (after Father Hesburgh and Father Sorin), the trustees had a desired successor close at hand in Associate Provost Father John Jenkins, and they decided to make a change.[66]

Father Jenkins and the board of trustees also decided to replace Ty Willingham as head football coach after three years of his six-year contract. Father Malloy had not agreed—Notre Dame had traditionally let athletic coaches, even unsuccessful ones, serve out their full first contracts—but he felt that he should allow Father Jenkins to shape his own incoming administration. After Urban Meyer at Utah declined Notre Dame's overtures and accepted the invitation to coach at the University of Florida, Director of Athletics Kevin White was reported to have narrowed the search to graduates Tom Clements, offensive coordinator of the Buffalo Bills, Greg Blache, defensive coordinator of the Washington Redskins, and Charlie Weis, offensive coordinator of the New England Patriots. The final choice was Weis, and Coach Willingham signed almost immediately as head coach of the University of Washington Huskies.[67]

The university, the Congregation of Holy Cross, the South Bend community, and much of the nation recognized that Father Malloy, although in the difficult position of following a legend, had been a very successful president. Tributes and testimonials poured in from all quarters. Among his major achievements during the eighteen years of his presidency, the university had continued strong in academics, athletics, and public esteem; over the last ten years it had ranked consistently among the top twenty universities according to *U.S. News and World Report*; and it had retained its fundamental Catholic character. The faculty had gained greater influence in university governance, the percentage of women on the faculty had increased from 10 percent to 24 percent, and the percentage of women in the student body had increased from 30 percent to 47 percent. Study-abroad programs had expanded from nine to twenty-five, and the Alliance for Catholic Education had assisted numerous Catholic grade, middle, and high schools to survive and prosper. The campus expanded with construction of the DeBartolo Hall classroom building and the DeBartolo Performing Arts Center, the Mendoza College of Business, the Coleman-Morse Center, and four new residence halls on the west quadrangle, and the Main Building, Sacred Heart Basilica, and the stadium underwent major renovations. The university had reacted well to the Y2K challenge, *Ex Corde Ecclesiae*, and the 9/11 terrorist attack. When appointed president in 1987, Father Malloy was asked if it made him nervous to realize that the final decisions were now his, that the success or failure of the university was in his hands, often his hands alone, and he answered, No, that as a basketball player, when the game was on the line, he always wanted to take the last shot, confident that he could make it. In eighteen years as president, he had made it.

In fact, through 175 years, the university itself had made it, and at times when other schools had not. Historian of education Frederick Rudolph estimated that there were approximately 250 colleges in the United States in 1860 but another 700 might have opened—or attempted to—and failed. "Between 1850 and 1866," he noted, "fifty-five Catholic colleges were started, of which twenty-five were abandoned by 1866."[68] Notre Dame had certainly faced challenges. It was founded in a period of anti-Catholic hostility but, fortunately for Notre Dame, that opposition was less aggressive in the Midwest than in the East. Finances were a serious problem for at least the first seventy-five years, with cash-on-hand occasionally dropping to less than forty dollars. Several wars disrupted normal campus life. Enrollment accelerated during the Civil War due to Notre Dame's favorable location far from the battle lines, but faculty and staff numbers declined as many departed for war service; the Students' Army Training Corps in World War I and the Naval Reserve Officers' Training Corps and the V-7 and V-12 programs in World War II permitted the university to continue many academic programs; and the Vietnam War was one of several causes of student discontent and protest in the 1960s and 1970s. Fires posed serious problems in the early years. In fact, the devastating fire of 1879 could easily have caused the university to close, but with quick and determined action it managed to survive. Early Notre Dame copied the *Ratio Studiorum* curriculum already in place at Saint Louis, Georgetown, and Holy Cross, but it also became the first Catholic university to open Schools of

Engineering, Law, and Architecture. In these and most other areas, however, it lagged far behind the nation's major public and private universities. But, like most successful Catholic institutions, Notre Dame survived because the founding religious community, in this case the Congregation of Holy Cross—priests, brothers, and sisters—would not let it fail, and because a devoted lay faculty was willing to serve for minimal salaries in their dedication to Catholic education.

Notre Dame not only survived, but prospered and impacted American public life. Jerome Green made significant contributions in wireless telegraphy, Father Nieuwland in synthetic rubber, James Reyniers in germ-free biological research, and George Collins and Bernard Waldman in nuclear energy. The *Review of Politics*, the *American Midland Naturalist*, and the *Notre Dame Journal of Formal Logic* have been respected scholarly journals. As Notre Dame's president, Father Hesburgh was often listed among the top three people in national influence in education (with the secretary of education and the president of Harvard) and in religion (with Rev. Billy Graham and the general secretary of the World Council of Churches). Notre Dame graduates have graced legislative chambers across the country and embassies around the world; since the days of Knute Rockne, the university has played an important role in intercollegiate athletics; and its alumni/ae have been prominent in law, medicine, politics, communications, finance, education, industry, labor organizations, and the military through the years.

Father Hesburgh often stated that a Catholic university was where the Church did its thinking, and indeed it is. The Kellogg Institute for International Studies, the Cushwa Center for the Study of American Catholicism, and the Kroc Institute for International Peace Studies sponsor scholarly conferences; faculty publications examine critical Church issues; and controversial topics—from evolution under Father Zahm through Governor Cuomo's wrestling with abortion to *The Vagina Monologues* during Father Malloy's presidency—have been presented and debated, and issues were clarified and beliefs strengthened from the discussions. Father Hesburgh's fifteen-minute rule and the Land O' Lakes Statement were discussed for decades, and Notre Dame's Laetare Medal is given national, and even international, publicity each year. Thousands of graduates have entered seminaries and convents, and numerous alumni have been elevated into significant positions in the hierarchy and have influenced Church policy at home and abroad.

The university had accomplished much throughout its history, but as a living institution it had no plans to stop when Father Malloy left office in 2005. His successor, Father John Jenkins, declared in his inaugural address:[69]

With respect and gratitude for all who embraced Notre Dame's mission in earlier times, let us rise up and embrace the mission for our times: to build a Notre Dame that is bigger and better than ever—a great Catholic university for the 21st century, one of the pre-eminent research institutions in the world, a center for learning whose intellectual and religious traditions converge to make it a healing, unifying, enlightening force for a world deeply in need. This is our goal. Let no one ever . . . say that we dreamed too small.

N O T E S

<hr />

Chapter 1.   Background in France, 1789–1841

1. Rev. Edward Sorin, C.S.C., Letter XXXI, October 18, 1878, *Circular Letters of the Very Reverend Edward Sorin*, vol. I (Notre Dame, IN, 1885), p. 122.

2. Rev. Edward Sorin, C.S.C., *The Chronicles of Notre Dame du Lac*, trans. John M. Toohey, C.S.C., ed. James T. Connelly, C.S.C. (Notre Dame, IN, 1992), p. 9.

3. The best biography of Father Sorin is Marvin R. O'Connell, *Edward Sorin* (Notre Dame, IN, 2000). The following quotation is from *Scholastic*, Vol. XXII, No. 1 (August 25, 1888), p. 7.

4. The hardships faced by the poor are discussed in Simon Schama, *Citizens: A Chronicle of the French Revolution* (New York, 1989), pp. 71–79; Owen Connolly, *The French Revolution and Napoleonic Era*, 2nd ed. (New York, 1991), pp. 17–18 and 51–52; and William Doyle, *The Oxford History of the French Revolution*, 2nd ed. (New York, 2002), pp. 9–17. For the nation's serious indebtedness, see Connolly, *French Revolution*, pp. 18–19, 41–43, and 59–62; Doyle, *Oxford History*, pp. 130–32; Francois Furet, *Revolutionary France, 1770–1880* (Cambridge, MA, 1988), pp. 33–40; and Schama, *Citizens*, pp. 60–87. The impact of the Enlightenment is discussed by Connolly, *French Revolution*, pp. 25–32, and Furet, *Revolutionary France*, pp. 14–17. The increasing unpopularity of Queen Marie Antoinette is described in Doyle, *Oxford History*, pp. 176–77; Furet, *Revolutionary France*, pp. 30–33; and Schama, *Citizens*, pp. 203–27.

5. Ralph Gibson, *A Social History of French Catholicism, 1789–1914* (London and New York, 1989), pp. 1–29, and Adrien Dansette, *Religious History of Modern France*, vol. I (New York, 1961), pp. 2–33 and 100–102.

6. C. S. Phillips, *The Church in France, 1789–1848* (London, 1929), p. 8. A livre was about the equivalent of a franc, about five to a dollar.

7. Phillips, *Church in France*, pp. 8–10; Gibson, *Social History*, pp. 34–36; Dansette, *Religious History*, pp. 43–47; and Thomas Kselman, *Conscience and Conversion: Religious Liberty in Post-Revolutionary France* (New Haven, CT, 2018), pp. 13–17.

8. Phillips, *Church in France*, pp. 10–19; Gibson, *Social History*, pp. 36–38; Dansette, *Religious History*, pp. 56–63; Joseph F. Byrnes, *Catholic and French Forever* (University Park, PA, 2005), pp. 5–6; and Kselman, *Conscience and Conversion*, pp. 36–37.

9. Gibson, *Social History*, pp. 38–41, and Phillips, *Church in France*, pp. 19–24.

10. The most complete biography of Badin is J. Herman Schauinger, *Stephen T. Badin: Priest in the Wilderness* (Milwaukee, 1956).

11. Phillips, *Church in France*, pp. 26–40; Gibson, *Social History*, pp. 41–47; Schama, *Citizens*, pp. 779 and 789; and Dansette, *Religious History*, pp. 71–111.

12. Dansette, *Religious History*, pp. 121–28; Doyle, *Oxford History*, pp. 387–90; and Phillips, *Church in France*, pp. 71–72. Relations between the emperor and the pope deteriorated further when the pope refused to annul the marriage of Napoleon's brother or permit Napoleon to divorce Josephine and marry another, and Napoleon eventually captured the pope and imprisoned him in Savona. See also Frank McLynn, *Napoleon: A Biography* (New York, 1997), pp. 301–5 and 433–627; Alan Schom, *Napoleon Bonaparte: A Life* (New York, 1997), pp. 334–49 and 458–761; and Phillips, *Church in France*, pp. 83–144.

13. Phillips, *Church in France*, pp. 150–285; Furet, *Revolutionary France*, pp. 269–359; and Dansette, *Religious History*, pp. 171–234. The following quotation is from Dansette, *Religious History*, pp. 189 and 196.

14. Accessible biographies of Father Dujarié are Tony Catta, *Father Dujarié*, trans. Edward L. Heston, C.S.C. (Milwaukee, 1960); Brother Ephrem O'Dwyer, C.S.C., *Curé of Ruillé* (Notre Dame, IN, 1941); Rev. Phileas Vanier, C.S.C., *Le Chanoine Dujarié* (Montreal, 1948); and Basil Moreau, "Sketch of Life and Works of M. L'Abbé Jacques-François-Dujarié, Pastor of Ruillé-sur-Loire," in *Circular Letters of the Very Reverend Basil Anthony Mary Moreau*, vol. I, trans. Edward L. Heston, C.S.C. (Notre Dame, IN, 1943), pp. i–xxvi. See Catta, *Father Dujarié*, pp. 1–4; Vanier, *Le Chanoine Dujarié*, pp. 11–15; and O'Dwyer, *Curé of Ruillé*, pp. 35–46.

15. Vanier, *Le Chanoine Dujarié*, pp. 15–22, and Catta, *Father Dujarié*, pp. 4–7. Tonsure was the rite of initiation into the clerical state involving the cutting of a small portion of the candidate's hair.

16. Vanier, *Le Chanoine Dujarié*, pp. 23–27; Catta, *Father Dujarié*, pp. 10–14; and Rev. James T. Connelly, C.S.C., *Basile Moreau and the Congregation of Holy Cross* (Portland, OR., 2007), pp. 17–18.

17. Vanier, *Le Chanoine Dujarié*, pp. 27–31, and Catta, *Father Dujarié*, pp. 17–21.

18. Moreau, "Sketch," in his *Circular Letters*, vol. I, pp. ii–iii; Vanier, *Le Chanoine Dujarié*, p. 30; O'Dwyer, *Curé of Ruillé*, pp. 42–45; and Catta, *Father Dujarié*, pp. 21 and 36n.15.

19. Quoted in Catta, *Father Dujarié*, p. 23.

20. Catta, *Father Dujarié*, pp. 21–29; Moreau, "Sketch," in his *Circular Letters*, vol. I, pp. ii–iv; and Vanier, *Le Chanoine Dujarié*, pp. 31–34 and 181.

21. Quoted in Catta, *Father Dujarié*, p. 30.

22. Quoted in Catta, *Father Dujarié*, p. 30.

23. Catta, *Father Dujarié*, p. 32.

24. Moreau, "Sketch," in his *Circular Letters*, vol. I, pp. iv–v; and Catta, *Father Dujarié*, pp. 30–35.

25. The confusion came about when the mayor, knowing that the parishioners could be bitterly divided among those favoring a juring, a non-juring, or a retracting priest, first requested that a new and wholly unfamiliar priest be appointed, but he later changed his mind and requested the appointment of Father Dujarié. See O'Dwyer, *Curé of Ruillé*, pp. 68–70.

26. Quoted in Catta, *Father Dujarié*, p. 46.

27. Quoted in Catta, *Father Dujarié*, p. 44. See also Vanier, *Le Chanoine Dujarié*, p. 47.

28. O'Dwyer, *Curé of Ruillé*, pp. 61–72; Catta, *Father Dujarié*, pp. 39–51; and Vanier, *Le Chanoine Dujarié*, pp. 45–52.

29. Vanier, *Le Chanoine Dujarié*, pp. 52–66; James Connelly, *Basile Moreau*, pp. 19–20; Moreau, "Sketch," in his *Circular Letters*, vol. I, pp. vi–viii; O'Dwyer, *Curé of Ruillé*, pp. 73–87; and Catta, *Father Dujarié*, pp. 53–77. For additional information on the Sisters of Providence, see *History of the Sisters of Providence of Saint Mary-of-the-Woods*, vol. I by Sister Mary Borromeo Brown, PhD (New York, 1949) and vol. II by Sister Eugenia Logan, S.P. (Terre Haute, IN, 1978); J. F. Alvic, S.J., *La Congrégation de la Providence de Ruillé-sur-Loir* (Tours, 1923); and Catta, *Father Dujarié*, pp. 80–104.

30. O'Dwyer, *Curé of Ruillé*, pp. 88–102. The quotation is from pages 95 and 96. See also Vanier, *Le Chanoine Dujarié*, pp. 81–89, and Catta, *Father Dujarié*, pp. 105–13.

31. O'Dwyer, *Curé of Ruillé*, pp. 103–15. The quotation is from Catta, *Father Dujarié*, p. 129.

32. O'Dwyer, *Curé of Ruillé*, pp. 116–21; Vanier, *Le Chanoine Dujarié*, pp. 89–94, 239–40, and 248–49; and Moreau, "Sketch," in his *Circular Letters*, vol. I, p. xv.

33. O'Dwyer, *Curé of Ruillé*, pp. 122–39. The quotation is on page 139. At its peak membership in 1828, according to O'Dwyer, p. 148, the brothers numbered 105, serving fifty schools.

34. O'Dwyer, *Curé of Ruillé*, pp. 140–45, and Catta, *Father Dujarié*, pp. 185–257. The quotation is from Catta, *Father Dujarié*, pp. 227–28.

35. Connelly, *Basile Moreau*, pp. 25–28; O'Dwyer, *Curé of Ruillé*, pp. 157–99; and Catta, *Father Dujarié*, pp. 240–67. After the transfer of the brothers to Father Moreau in Le Mans, Father Dujarié returned to his parish in Ruillé, but he was clearly too weak to continue. He resigned as pastor in April 1836 and a few months later accepted Father Moreau's repeated invitation to come and live in Le Mans, close to his beloved brothers. There the Sisters of Providence cared for his needs also. His health continued to decline, he received the last sacraments from Father Moreau, and he died peacefully on February 17, 1838. Tony Catta penned a beautiful eulogy of his final months: "His greatest distraction was to have his armchair placed in the recreation yard. The children crowded around him, like garden sparrows around the plants on which crumbs of bread had been thrown. He distributed to the children any sweets he had been able to get. Until the very end, he remained the friend of children. He had met up with youth, abandoned, suffering, and

threatened, in the far-off days of the beginning of his ministry along the roads of Ruillé-sur-Loir. In the evening of his life, he found this same youth, again cared for, educated, and cultivated by the Brothers who were carrying on his work. Certainly in these days of grace, he must have had a foretaste of his reward" (*Father Dujarié*, pp. 278–79).

36. The best biographical studies of Father Moreau are Canon Etienne Catta and Tony Catta, *Basil Anthony Mary Moreau*, 2 vols., trans. Edward L. Heston, C.S.C. (Milwaukee, 1955); Rev. John W. Cavanaugh, C.S.C., *The Priests of Holy Cross* (Notre Dame, IN, 1905), pp. 9–33; Gary MacEoin, *Basil Moreau: Founder of Holy Cross* (Notre Dame, IN, 2007); and Thomas Barrosse, *Moreau: Portrait of a Founder* (Notre Dame, IN, 1969). See Etienne and Tony Catta, *Basil Anthony Mary Moreau*, vol. 1, pp. 3–17; Connelly, *Basile Moreau*, pp. 26–27; MacEoin, *Basil Moreau*, pp. 27–33; and Barrosse, *Moreau*, pp. 12–13.

37. Etienne and Tony Catta, *Basil Anthony Mary Moreau*, vol. 1, pp. 18–27, and MacEoin, *Basil Moreau*, pp. 33–38.

38. Etienne and Tony Catta, *Basil Anthony Mary Moreau*, vol. 1, pp. 27–68; Barrosse, *Moreau*, pp. 19–33; and MacEoin, *Basil Moreau*, pp. 39–50.

39. Etienne and Tony Catta, *Basil Anthony Mary Moreau*, vol. 1, pp. 69–117; Barrosse, *Moreau*, pp. 34–75; and MacEoin, *Basil Moreau*, pp. 51–76.

40. Etienne and Tony Catta, *Basil Anthony Mary Moreau*, vol. 1, pp. 319–37; Connelly, *Basile Moreau*, p. 27; and MacEoin, *Basil Moreau*, pp. 80–87.

41. Etienne and Tony Catta, *Basil Anthony Mary Moreau*, vol. 1, pp. 339–70; Connelly, *Basile Moreau*, pp. 27–28; and MacEoin, *Basil Moreau*, pp. 85–86.

42. Etienne and Tony Catta, *Basil Anthony Mary Moreau*, vol. 1, pp. 379–81, and Connelly, *Basile Moreau*, pp. 36–37.

43. Etienne and Tony Catta, *Basil Anthony Mary Moreau*, vol. 1, pp. 431–37; Sister M. Georgia Costin, C.S.C., *Priceless Spirit: A History of the Sisters of the Holy Cross, 1814–1893* (Notre Dame, IN, 1994), pp. 2–9; and Moreau, *Circular Letters*, vol. I, pp. 43–44.

44. Etienne and Tony Catta, *Basil Anthony Mary Moreau*, vol. 1, pp. 457–89.

45. Moreau, *Circular Letters*, vol. I, pp. 161–62. See also Rev. James B. King, C.S.C., *Holy Cross and Christian Education* (Notre Dame, IN, 2015).

46. Basile Antoine Marie Moreau, *Excerpts from "Christian Education,"* trans. Brother Edmund Hunt, C.S.C. (n.d.), p. 9.

47. Joseph M. White, *Worthy of the Gospel of Christ* (Fort Wayne, IN, 2007), pp. 7–9; Etienne and Tony Catta, *Basil Anthony Mary Moreau*, vol. 1, pp. 492–503; Rev. Charles Lemarie, C.S.C., *De La Mayenne a l'Indiana: le Pere Edouard Sorin (1814–1893)* (Angers, 1978), pp. 6–11; and Rev. Arthur Hope, C.S.C., *Notre Dame: One Hundred Years* (Notre Dame, IN, 1943), pp. 11–20.

Chapter 2.   The Founding, 1841–1844

1. O'Connell, *Sorin*, pp. 6–9; Etienne and Tony Catta, *Basil Anthony Mary Moreau*, vol. 1, p. 501; and Lemarie, *De La Mayenne a l'Indiana*, pp. 5–6. The quotation is from Lemarie, page 6, and the translation is the author's.

2. Quoted in O'Connell, *Sorin*, p. 44.

3. O'Connell, *Sorin*, pp. 43–49, and Lemarie, *De La Mayenne a l'Indiana*, pp. 6–10.

4. Brother Kilian Beirne, C.S.C., *From Sea to Shining Sea: The Holy Cross Brothers in the United States* (Valatie, NY, 1996), pp. 21–27; Brother Aiden O'Reilly, "Brother Aiden's Extracts" (manuscript preserved in the University of Notre Dame Archives), pp. 710–25; Brother Garnier Morin, *From France to Notre Dame* (Notre Dame, IN, 1952), pp. 31–35; Marvin R. O'Connell, "The Magnificent Six" (convocation address, Holy Cross College, Notre Dame, IN, March 7, 2002), copy in possession of the author; and George Klawitter, ed., *Adapted to the Lake: Letters by the Brother Founders of Notre Dame, 1841–1849* (New York, 1993), p. xix.

5. Beirne, *Sea to Shining Sea*, pp. 27–28, and O'Reilly, "Extracts," pp. 290–91.

6. Beirne, *Sea to Shining Sea*, pp. 28–30; O'Reilly, "Extracts," pp. 332–34; and Klawitter, *Adapted*, pp. xix–xx.

7. Beirne, *Sea to Shining Sea*, pp. 31–33, and O'Reilly, "Extracts," pp. 213–17.

8. Beirne, *Sea to Shining Sea*, pp. 33–37; O'Reilly, "Extracts," pp. 16–18; and Klawitter, *Adapted*, pp. xx–xxii.

9. Beirne, *Sea to Shining Sea*, pp. 37–39, and George Klawitter, *After Holy Cross, Only Notre Dame: The Life of Brother Gatian (Urbain Monsimer)* (Lincoln, NE, 2003).

10. Sorin, *Chronicles*, pp. 2–8; Sorin, *Circular Letters*, vol. I, p. 8; O'Reilly, "Extracts," p. 725; Morin, *France to Notre Dame*, pp. 45–54; and O'Connell, *Sorin*, pp. 55–60.

11. Sorin, *Chronicles*, pp. 9–10. The quotation is from page 9.

12. Sorin, *Chronicles*, pp. 9–10; O'Connell, *Sorin*, pp. 60–63; and Hope, *Notre Dame*, p. 20.

13. O'Reilly, "Extracts," pp. 711, 722, and 725, and Beirne, *Sea to Shining Sea*, p. 22.

14. Sorin, *Chronicles*, pp. 11–13; O'Connell, *Sorin*, pp. 62–72; and Hope, *Notre Dame*, pp. 21–23. The total cost of the trip from New York was approximately 950 francs, or about $200. See O'Connell, *Sorin*, p. 62n.15. For the attempted robbery, see Fr. Sorin to Madam Pasquier, October 1, 1844, Sorin Papers, box 1, folder 5, University of Notre Dame Archives (hereafter abbreviated UNDA), and John T. Wack, "The University of Notre Dame du Lac: Foundation, 1842–1857" (PhD. diss., University of Notre Dame, 1967), p. 19.

15. Sorin to Moreau, October 14, 1841, Holy Cross Generalate Archives (hereafter CSCG), Manuscripts, UNDA.

16. Sorin to Moreau, October 14, 1841, CSCG, Manuscripts, UNDA.

17. Sorin, *Chronicles*, p. 16–17.

18. Sorin, *Chronicles*, pp. 17–20; O'Connell, *Sorin*, pp. 84–88; and Klawitter, *After Holy Cross*, p. 94. They had farm animals also. Father Sorin asked Father Moreau to send along a brother who could make shoes since they killed cows for food but no one could make shoes from the leather. Sorin to Moreau, November 13, 1841, CSCG, Manuscripts, UNDA.

19. O'Connell, *Sorin*, pp. 89–96; Sorin, *Chronicles*, pp. 17–20; and Hope, *Notre Dame*, pp. 28–31. A good summary of these early months at St. Peter's is contained in Sorin's letter to Moreau, February 21, 1842, and to Moreau and the Society for the Propa-

gation of the Faith, February 2, 1844, CSCG, Manuscripts, UNDA. See also Sorin to Augustus Martin, January 3, 1842, Sorin Papers, box 1, folder 2 (CSOR 1/2), UNDA.

20. O'Connell, *Sorin*, pp. 96–100; Sorin, *Chronicles*, pp. 21–22; and Hope, *Notre Dame*, pp. 32–33.

21. Cecilia Bain Buechner, "The Pokagons," *Indiana Historical Society Publications*, vol. 10, no. 5 (Indianapolis, IN, 1933), pp. 298–99; R. David Edmunds, *The Potawatomis: Keepers of the Fire* (Norman, OK, 1978); George Pare, "The St. Joseph Mission," *The Mississippi Valley Historical Review* XVII (June 1930 to March 1931), pp. 24–54; Everett Clasby, *The Potawatomi Indians in Southwestern Michigan* (Dowagiac, MI, 1966), pp. 3–14; and Rev. Thomas T. McAvoy, C.S.C., *The History of the Catholic Church in the South Bend Area* (South Bend, IN, 1953), pp. 1–7. For the suppression of the Jesuits, see Raymond A. Schroth, S.J., "Death and Resurrection: The Suppression of the Jesuits in North America," *American Catholic Studies* 128, no. 1 (Spring 2017), pp. 51–66.

22. As noted in chapter 1, the best biographical study of Badin is Schauinger, *Stephen T. Badin: Priest in the Wilderness*. See also Rev. Thomas T. McAvoy, C.S.C., "Father Badin Comes to Notre Dame," *Indiana Magazine of History* XXIX (1933), pp. 7–16.

23. Badin to M., September 30, 1830, *Annales de l'Association de la Propagation de la Fois*, vol. IV (Lyon, 1830), p. 547, English translation in Rev. William McNamara, C.S.C., *The Catholic Church on the Northern Indiana Frontier, 1789–1844* (Washington, DC, 1931), p. 25.

24. Schauinger, *Badin*, pp. 215–63; Hope, *Notre Dame*, p. 51; and *Catholic Telegraph* (Cincinnati), July 14, 1832, cited in McAvoy, "Father Badin," p. 10.

25. Schauinger, *Badin*, pp. 243–63; McNamara, *Catholic Church*, pp. 42–68; and Shirley Willard and Susan Campbell, *Potawatomi Trail of Death: 1838 Removal from Indiana to Kansas* (Fulton County Historical Society, 2003), pp. 15–25.

26. The Removal Act is reprinted in Anthony F. C. Wallace, *The Long Bitter Trail: Andrew Jackson and the Indians* (New York, 1993), pp. 125–28. See also Matthew Warshauer, *Andrew Jackson in Context* (New York, 2009), pp. 119–22; Robert Remini, *Andrew Jackson and the Course of American Freedom, 1822–1832*, vol. II (New York, 1981), pp. 259–64; and the thoroughly researched doctoral dissertation of W. Benjamin Secunda, "In the Shadow of the Eagle's Wings: The Effects of Removal on the Unremoved Potawatomis," University of Notre Dame, 2008.

27. Benjamin F. Stuart, "The Deportation of Memominee and his Tribe of the Pottawattomie Indians," *Indiana Magazine of History* XVIII (1922), pp. 257–58.

28. Col. Abel C. Pepper to Deseille, May 16, 1837, in "Documents: Correspondence on Indian Removal, Indiana, 1835–1838," *Mid-America* XV (1932–1933), pp. 185–86; Willard and Campbell, *Potawatomi Trail*, pp. 15–26; and McNamara, *Catholic Church*, pp. 68–69.

29. Petit to his family, January 1838, *Annales de l'Association de la Propagation de la Fois*, vol. XI (Lyon, 1839), p. 387, English translation in Willard and Campbell, *Potawatomi Trail*, p. 52.

30. Willard and Campbell, *Potawatomi Trail*, pp. 26–28 and pp. 87–88n.21; Petit to Bruté, June 20 and 23, 1838, and Gen. John Tipton to Petit, September 2, 1838, in Willard and Campbell, *Potawatomi Trail*, pp. 77–81 and 201–2.

31. Willard and Campbell, *Potawatomi Trail*, pp. 114–16; Petit's hurried journal entries are reprinted in Willard and Campbell, *Potawatomi Trail*, pp. 129–31; and Petit to Bishop Bruté, November 13, 1838, *Annales de l'Association de la Propagation de la Fois*, vol. XI (Lyon, 1839), p. 408, English translation in Willard and Campbell, *Potawatomi Trail*, p. 105.

32. O'Connell, *Sorin*, pp. 105–6; Hope, *Notre Dame*, pp. 51–52; and Thomas J. Schlereth, *The University of Notre Dame: A Portrait of Its History and Campus* (Notre Dame, IN, 1976), pp. 6–8. The Fathers of Mercy, officially the Congregation of the Priests of Mercy, were founded by Jean Baptist Rauzau in Lyon, France, in 1808 and were invited to the United States by Archbishop John Hughes of New York in 1839.

33. Klawitter, *Adapted*, pp. 347–48; Sorin, *Chronicles*, p. 23; O'Connell, *Sorin*, pp. 101–2; and Beirne, *Sea to Shining Sea*, p. 10.

34. Sorin, *Chronicles*, pp. 21–22; O'Connell, *Sorin*, pp. 101–3; and Hope, *Notre Dame*, p. 34. There is some uncertainty over the exact date of arrival, and Hope, *Notre Dame*, p. 35n.3, provides a good discussion of the conflicting evidence.

35. Sorin to Moreau, Dec. 5, 1842, in Sorin, *Circular Letters*, vol. I, pp. 260–61.

36. Sorin, *Chronicles*, p. 24.

37. Sorin, *Chronicles*, pp. 23–24; Schlereth, *University of Notre Dame*, pp. 10–12; Hope, *Notre Dame*, pp. 51–52; and O'Connell, *Sorin*, pp. 103–4. Father Sorin and the brothers did not actually have legal title to the land since Father Bach did not return the legal papers to the bishop until the following year. See Hope, *Notre Dame*, pp. 51–52.

38. Sorin, *Chronicles*, pp. 24 and 30; Klawitter, *Adapted*, pp. 347–48; Sorin, *Circular Letters*, vol. II (Notre Dame, IN, 1894), p. 30.

39. Sorin, *Chronicles*, pp. 30–31, and Schlereth, *University of Notre Dame*, pp. 10–12. For that February trip north, see also Sorin to Moreau, March 20, 1843, CSCG, Manuscripts, UNDA, and Brother John to Father Moreau, February 1843, in Klawitter, *Adapted*, pp. 21–24. The quotation is from Klawitter, *Adapted*, p. 23.

40. Sorin, *Chronicles*, p. 34, and Wack, "University of Notre Dame," p. 53.

41. Sorin, *Chronicles*, pp. 34–35; Wack, "University of Notre Dame," pp. 50–53; Schlereth, *University of Notre Dame*, pp. 26–28; Joseph A. Lyons, *Silver Jubilee of the University of Notre Dame, June 23, 1869* (Chicago, 1869), p. 19; and Timothy Howard, *A Brief History of the University of Notre Dame du Lac, Indiana, From 1842 to 1892* (Chicago, 1895), p. 57.

42. Sorin, *Chronicles*, 32–34, and Wack, "University of Notre Dame," pp. 49–50. On the trip from New York, the group had stopped in Detroit and Father Cointet had fallen from the bishop's balcony there, barely escaping serious injury. Brother Eloi and Sister Mary of Calvary remained with him a few days in Detroit until he was able to travel again. See Sorin, *Chronicles*, pp. 32–33. For the brothers' novitiate, see Sorin, *Chronicles*, pp. 39–43; Beirne, *Sea to Shining Sea*, pp. 40–44; and Wack, "University of Notre Dame," p. 78.

43. Wack, "University of Notre Dame," pp. 62–64 and 87, and Borders Ledger No. 2, 1849–1852, UNDA.

44. Schlereth, *University of Notre Dame*, p. 29; Wack, "University of Notre Dame," p. 68; Hope, *Notre Dame*, p. 67; and Sorin, *Chronicles*, pp. 43–45. According to Father Sorin's *Chronicles*, page 45, no orphans were admitted under the age of twelve, although very shortly an elementary school education was provided for young boys aged six to thirteen, the "Minims' Department." This program would be formally established in 1854 and would be housed in its own residence hall in 1882. See also Minutes of the Council for the Direction of Trades, Notre Dame du Lac, accession number 1970-15, folder 2, p. 1, United States Province of Priests and Brothers Provincial Archives (hereafter abbreviated USPA). See also Beirne, *Sea to Shining Sea*, pp. 67–80.

45. Register of the Council of Professors, vol. I, January 7, 1844, to April 1, 1846, UFMM, UNDA. The offerings were quite similar to those in other American schools at the time. See Gerald L. Gutek, *Education in the United States* (Englewood Cliffs, NJ, 1986), pp. 114–15.

46. Council of Professors, vol. I, UFMM, UNDA, January 7, 1844. The order of the day was similar to that at Saint Louis University a few years earlier. See William Faherty, S.J., *Better the Dream: St. Louis University and Community* (St. Louis, MO, 1968), p. 28.

47. *South Bend Free Press*, December 2, 1843, reprinted in Schlereth, *University of Notre Dame*, p. 15. See also Hope, *Notre Dame*, pp. 59–60.

48. Council of Professors, vol. I, January 7, 1844, to April 1, 1846, UFMM, box 1, vol. I, UNDA, first (introductory) page.

49. Council of Professors, minutes of January 7 and 12 and May 31, 1844, UFMM, UNDA. Mr. Riley taught grammar, reading, and spelling.

50. Sorin, *Chronicles*, pp. 49–50, and Wack, "University of Notre Dame," p. 83. The quotation is from Sorin, *Chronicles*, p. 50. See also Sorin to Moreau, July 6, 1845, CSCG, Manuscripts, UNDA.

51. Costin, *Priceless Spirit*, pp. 11–15; Sister Mary Immaculate Creek, C.S.C., *A Panorama, 1844–1977: Saint Mary's College, Notre Dame, Indiana* (Notre Dame, IN, 1977), pp. 8–9; Sister M. Eleanore Brosnahan, C.S.C., *On the King's Highway* (New York, 1931), pp. 116–28; Sorin, *Chronicles*, p. 32; and Register of the Council of Administration of the Brothers of St. Joseph, St. Mary's of the Lake, South Bend, Indiana (1841–1845), acc. no. 1970-15, folder 1, USPA, esp. December 16, 1844, and April 1, 1845. In the book itself, Sister M. Eleanore does not use her last name.

52. Sorin, *Chronicles*, pp. 46–48; Costin, *Priceless Spirit*, pp. 16–18; Creek, *A Panorama*, pp. 10–11; Brosnahan, *On the King's Highway*, pp. 128–36; and Sorin to Moreau, July 2, 1844, CSCG, Manuscripts, UNDA.

53. Costin, *Priceless Spirit*, pp. 19–21; Creek, *A Panorama*, pp. 11–12; Sorin, *Chronicles*, pp. 48–49; Brosnahan, *On the King's Highway*, pp. 133–36; and Sorin to Moreau, June 6, 1844, CSCG, Manuscripts, and Sorin to Martin, June 21, 1844, CSOR 1/2, UNDA.

54. Beirne, *Sea to Shining Sea*, pp. 100–101; O'Connell, *Sorin*, p. 172; Brosnahan, *On the King's Highway*, pp. 137–39; Wack, "University of Notre Dame," pp. 43 and 50; and Mother M. Angela, C.S.C., *Life of the Rev. F. Cointet, Priest and Missionary of the Congregation of Holy Cross* (1855), copy in UNDA, pp. 32–35. Some brothers were also

teaching in other parish schools throughout the diocese: See Wack, "University of Notre Dame," p. 77.

55. Sorin, *Chronicles*, pp. 37–38, and Wack, "University of Notre Dame," p. 75. The quotation is from Sorin, *Chronicles*, p. 38.

56. Wack, "University of Notre Dame," p. 32.

57. Sorin, *Chronicles*, pp. 34 and 36, and Wack, "University of Notre Dame," p. 51; and Council of Administration, USPA, November 27, 1843.

58. Wack, "University of Notre Dame," pp. 32, 48–76, and 101; Sorin, *Chronicles*, p. 36; and Hope, *Notre Dame*, p. 71. The financial records of these early years are understandably unclear. Money sent by Father Moreau may have come from the Society for the Propagation of the Faith and should not be counted twice; Father Sorin often accepted land or livestock in lieu of tuition dollars; and on particularly hectic days some transactions may never have been recorded.

59. *Laws of a Local Nature . . . of the State of Indiana*, 1844, chap. 34, pp. 61–62 (1844, In. Acts, 61–62).

Chapter 3. *Toward an American Institution, 1845–1854*

1. Sorin to Moreau, December 5, 1842, in Sorin, *Circular Letters*, vol. I, pp. 261–62.

2. Ibid., p. 262. For why these Native Americans remained after the Indian removal efforts, see James A. Clifton, *The Pokagons, 1683–1983* (Landam, MD, 1984), pp. 43–51.

3. Sorin to Chappé, no date, but "about the same time," in Sorin, *Circular Letters*, vol. I, p. 264.

4. Sorin to Moreau, March 20, 1843, in CSCG, 1843, March, III, Manuscripts, UNDA.

5. O'Connell, *Sorin*, p. 117; Sorin to Rev. Augustus Martin, January 31, 1843, Sorin Papers, box 1, folder 2 (CSOR 1/2), UNDA; and Clifton, *Pokagons*, pp. 73–76. The complicated question of land possession and government annuities, and Father Sorin's involvement, is detailed in Clifton, *Pokagons*, pp. 77–90.

6. O'Connell, *Sorin*, pp. 149, 237, 251, and 319–22; Costin, *Priceless Spirit*, pp. 52, 64–65, and 98; Beirne, *Sea to Shining Sea*, pp. 100–101; *The Metropolitan Catholic Almanac and Laity's Directory*, 1851, p. 86, 1852, pp. 127–28, 1853, p. 172, 1854, p. 133 (Baltimore, 1850–1854); Louis Baroux, "Seventeen Years in the Life of a Missionary Apostolic in Europe, Africa, Asia, and America," vol. I, chaps. III and V, unpublished manuscript, UNDA; Secunda, "Shadow," pp. 477–652; and Sorin, *Chronicles*, pp. 48–49. Bro. Joseph to Wm. Richmond, October 1, 1845, National Archives Microcopy, Michigan Superintendency 1, roll 59, images 276–81, National Archives and Records Administration (NARA); Sorin et al. to Richmond, October 22, 1846, roll 60, image 395, NARA; and Sorin to Richmond, December 13, 1848, roll 62, image 377, NARA. See Sorin to Martin, October 9, 1843, CSOR 1/2, UNDA; Sorin to Moreau, July 6, 1845, CSCG, UNDA; and also Sorin, *Chronicles*, pp. 312–13, for another visit of Sorin to the Indians a few miles from Pokagon's village. Notre Dame continued to send baskets of food annually to the

Potawatomi Nation near Dowagiac, Michigan, into the twenty-first century. The dispute between Father Sorin and Father Moreau is discussed later in this chapter, pages 59–61.

7. CSOR, Sorin Papers, UNDA.

8. Ray Allen Billington, *The Protestant Crusade, 1800–1860* (New York, 1952), pp. 53–57, 68–76, 92–95, 120–25, and 220–37; Mark S. Massa, S.J., *Anti-Catholicism in America* (New York, 2003), pp. 18–29; and Faherty, *Better the Dream*, p. 98.

9. C. Walker Gollar, "Early Protestant-Catholic Relations in Southern Indiana and the 1842 Case of Roman Weinzaepfel," *Indiana Magazine of History* 95 (September 1999), pp. 233–54. See also Sorin to Moreau, July 6, 1845, CSCG, Manuscripts, UNDA.

10. Sorin, *Chronicles*, p. 25.

11. Reprinted in Wack, "University of Notre Dame," p. 99n.42.

12. Mr. M. R. Keegan in the *Philadelphia Catholic Herald*, August 7, 1845, reprinted in Howard, *Brief History*, p. 65.

13. O'Connell, *Sorin*, pp. 180–81; Hope, *Notre Dame*, p. 77; Wack, "University of Notre Dame," pp. 99–100; and Sorin to Moreau, July 6, 1845, quoted in Etienne and Tony Catta, *Basil Anthony Mary Moreau*, vol. 1, p. 568.

14. "Notre Dame Thirty-Four Years Ago—A.D. 1845," by "An Old Boy," *Scholastic*, Vol. XIII, No. 7 (October 18, 1879), p. 99, and Schlereth, *University of Notre Dame*, pp. 26–28.

15. "Notre Dame Thirty-Four Years Ago," *Scholastic*, Vol. XIII, No. 7 (October 18, 1879), pp. 99–100; Schlereth, *University of Notre Dame*, pp. 28–32; Howard, *Brief History*, pp. 68–73; Wack, "University of Notre Dame," pp. 110–12; and Rev. James J. Trahey, C.S.C., "Dujarié Hall," *Scholastic*, Vol. XXXIX, No. 24 (March 31, 1906), pp. 399–400.

16. Sorin, *Chronicles*, p. 57; Schlereth, *University of Notre Dame*, p. 28; and "Notre Dame Thirty-Four Years Ago," *Scholastic*, Vol. XIII, No. 7 (October 18, 1879), p. 99. See also Costin, *Priceless Spirit*, p. 16, and Register of the Council of Administration of the Brothers of St. Joseph (1841–45), acc. no. 1970-15, folder 1 (hereafter abbreviated A.N. 1970-15, F1), USPA, December 12, 1844. Mark Pilkinton, in *Washington Hall at Notre Dame* (Notre Dame, IN, 2011), p. 22, speculates that the structure behind and to the east of the college building may be the first music building.

17. Sorin, *Chronicles*, pp. 57–58 and p. 57n.4, and Costin, *Priceless Spirit*, p. 16.

18. Sorin, *Chronicles*, pp. 74 and 86–87; Minutes of the Minor Chapter, A.N. 1970-15, F2, USPA, August 29, 1847; Wack, "University of Notre Dame," pp. 176–77; Schlereth, *University of Notre Dame*, pp. 37–39; and Thomas J. Schlereth, *A Spire of Faith: The University of Notre Dame's Sacred Heart Church* (Notre Dame, IN, 1991), pp. 6–8. Bishop de la Hailandière resigned as bishop of Vincennes in 1847, he was succeeded by Bishop John Basin who unfortunately died the following year, and Bishop Basin was succeeded by Bishop Maurice de Saint Palais.

19. Schlereth, *A Spire of Faith*, pp. 7–8.

20. Register of the Council of Professors, UFMM, box 1, vol.1, UNDA, April 14, 1844, and October 1, 1845, and Register of the Council of the Prefect of Discipline, A.N. 1970-15, USPA, June 1, 1844.

21. Sorin, *Chronicles*, pp. 44–45, and Schlereth, *University of Notre Dame*, pp. 134–37. Minutes of the Council for the Direction of Trades, A.N. 1970-15, F2, USPA, summarizes the production in each trade each week. This council apparently only existed during the 1845–1846 school year.

22. Sorin, *Chronicles*, p. 88.

23. Sorin, *Chronicles*, p. 89.

24. Sorin, *Chronicles*, pp. 88–89, and Schlereth, *University of Notre Dame*, pp. 134–37.

25. Minor Chapter Minutes, A.N. 1970-15, F2, USPA, May 24, 1853; Schlereth, *University of Notre Dame*, p. 26; and Wack, "University of Notre Dame," pp. 267 and 275.

26. Minor Chapter Minutes, A.N. 1970-15, F2, USPA, May 1853, and Wack, "University of Notre Dame," p. 267.

27. Howard, *Brief History*, p. 65; Council of Professors, UFMM, box 1, vol. 1, UNDA, January 7, July 1 and 24, 1843; John W. Cavanaugh, "Notes on Early History of Notre Dame," University of Notre Dame Archives, http://archives.nd.edu/research/texts/notes.htm; Wack, "University of Notre Dame," p. 267; Schlereth, *University of Notre Dame*, pp. 100–102; Pilkinton, *Washington Hall*, pp. 20–22; and *The Band of the Fighting Irish, Memory Book*, vol. 1 (Notre Dame, IN, 2002), pp. 142–45. Brother Basil was so well respected that Father Charles O'Donnell wrote one of his major poems, "The Dead Musician," in his honor. See Klawitter, George, C.S.C., ed., *The Poems of Charles O'Donnell, C.S.C.* (New York, 2010), pp. 1–3.

28. Council of Professors, UFMM, box 1, vol. 1, UNDA, January 1 and 12, March 14, and May 15, 1844. Father Sorin may have dropped that sixth level of the French system since he realized that no students at that time qualified for it.

29. Council of Professors, UFMM, box 1, vol. 1, UNDA, March 15 and September 2, 1844, and June 5 and July 21, 1845. See also Wack, "University of Notre Dame," p. 67.

30. Council of Professors, UFMM, box 1, vol. 2, UNDA, April 15, May 6, and July 16, 1846, and Wack, "University of Notre Dame," p. 89.

31. UFMM, box 1, vol. 2, UNDA, October 1, 1846. See also Faherty, *Better the Dream*, pp. 28–29.

32. Council of Professors, UFMM, box 1, vol. 2, UNDA, January 14 and 18, 1847.

33. Sorin, *Chronicles*, pp. 83–84; Hope, *Notre Dame*, 67–68; Wack, "University of Notre Dame," p. 193; and Brother Gatian's Journal, CCIJ, UNDA, paragraph before August 29, 1848, page 25 in original. See also Faherty, *Better the Dream*, pp. 95–116, and George E. Ganss, S.J., *The Jesuit Tradition and Saint Louis University* (St. Louis, MO, 1969), pp. 25–39.

34. *Catalogue of the Officers and Students of the University of Notre Dame, Indiana, 1854–1855* (Chicago, 1855), pp. 4–5; Wack, "University of Notre Dame," p. 195; and O'Connell, *Sorin*, pp. 247–48. The above is one of the earliest descriptive catalogues and it is a valid description of the 1849–1855 curriculum.

35. Robert Emmett Curran, *A History of Georgetown University*, vol. I (Washington, DC, 2010), pp. 44–46; Anthony J. Kuzniewski, S.J., *Thy Honored Name: A History*

of the College of the Holy Cross (Washington, DC, 1999), p. 38; and Frederick Rudolph, *The American College and University: A History* (Athens, GA, 1962), pp. 131–35. Father Cointet, of course, could teach some of these Latin and Greek courses.

36. Logan Esarey, *History of Indiana from its Exploration to 1922*, vol. II (Dayton, OH, 1923), pp. 995–96.

37. Lyons, *Silver Jubilee*, pp. 75–98 and 169–70. The Corby quotation is from Lawrence Frederick Kohl, *Memoirs of Chaplain Life* (New York, 2001), p. xi.

38. Lyons, *Silver Jubilee*, pp. 75–80 and 94–95, and Minor Chapter Minutes, A.N. 1970-15, F2, USPA, June 8, 1849.

39. Father Julian Benoit to Sorin, November 4, 1848, CSOR 1/55 (1848), UNDA.

40. Wack, "University of Notre Dame," pp. 199–200, and Sorin, *Chronicles*, p. 84.

41. Council of Professors, UFMM, box 1, vol. 1, UNDA, March 14, 1844, October 10, 1845, and March 4, 1846; and vol. 2, UNDA, March 19, October 2 and 20, 1846.

42. Council of Professors, UFMM, box 1, vol. 3, UNDA. There is brief mention of a "jail" in 1847 but this was probably just temporary isolation during a recreation period for someone seriously disrupting good order. See UFMM, box 1, vol. 3, UNDA, February 4, March 4, May 6, 11, and 20, 1847, and March 2, April 7, and May 26, 1848.

43. Council of Professors, UFMM, box 1, vol. 2, UNDA.

44. Council of Professors, UFMM, box 1, vol. 2, UNDA, January 18, 1847.

45. Council of Professors, UFMM, box 1, vol. 1, UNDA, December 7, 1844.

46. Council of Professors, UFMM, box 1, vol. 1, UNDA, February 21, 1845.

47. Council of Professors, UFMM, box 1, vol. 1, UNDA, March 7, 1845.

48. "Evaluations of Students by Father Cointet, 1844–1845," UNDR, 2/01, UNDA, November 3, December 1, 8, and 14, 1844.

49. Council of Professors, UFMM, box 1, vol. 1, UNDA, December 7, 1844. See also Wack, "University of Notre Dame," p. 76.

50. Council of Professors, UFMM, box 1, vol. 3, UNDA, May 10, 1847.

51. Council of Professors, UFMM, box 1, vol. 2, UNDA, April 15, 1846.

52. Council of Professors, UFMM, box 1, vol. 2, UNDA, June 17, 1846.

53. Council of Professors, UFMM, box 1, vol. 2, UNDA, August 1, 1846.

54. Council of Professors, UFMM, box 1, vol. 2, UNDA, October 1, 1846.

55. Council of Professors, UFMM, box 1, vol. 3, UNDA, May 11, 1847.

56. Wack, "University of Notre Dame," pp. 76, 93, and 103.

57. Wack, "University of Notre Dame," pp. 156–57 and 234, and the quotation is from Lyons, *Silver Jubilee*, pp. 35–36.

58. *Catalogue*, 1854–1855, p. 7. See also Council of Professors, UFMM, box 1, vol. 1, UNDA, August 31, 1844.

59. Council of Professors, UFMM, box 1, vol. 1, UNDA, January 12, March 14, June 8, August 31, and November 10, 1844, and December 18, 1845; vol. 2, UNDA, June 17 and October 1, 1846; and vol. 3, UNDA, March 4, July 1, and October 5, 1847, and March 31 and May 26, 1848. Rising was probably a half hour later on Sundays and festivals.

60. Rev. Thomas Patrick Jones, C.S.C., "The Development of the Office of Prefect of Religion at the University of Notre Dame from 1842 to 1952" (PhD diss., Catholic University of America, 1960), pp. 187–94, and Lyons, *Silver Jubilee*, pp. 242–43. Lyons dates the Society of Holy Angels from 1848 and Jones from 1858. Since Lyons was a student at Notre Dame from 1852 to 1858, his dating may be more accurate.

61. Lyons, *Silver Jubilee*, pp. 80–82, and Sorin to Granger, October 12, 1855, Granger Papers, box 1, folder 1855-59, USPA.

62. Sorin to Granger, August 31, 1840, and Novitiate Notes of Father Granger, 1843–1844, both in Granger Papers, box 1, folder 1832-44, USPA.

63. William Adderly to Granger, August 4, 1857, Granger Papers, box 1, folder 1855-59, USPA.

64. Sorin, *Chronicles*, pp. 41–43; Schlereth, *University of Notre Dame*, pp. 19 and 50; and Beirne, *Sea to Shining Sea*, pp. 40–46.

65. Sorin, *Chronicles*, pp. 65–73, and Raymond A. Schroth, S.J., *Fordham: A History and Memoir* (Chicago, 2002), pp. 11–15.

66. O'Connell, *Sorin*, pp. 214–31; Sorin, *Chronicles*, pp. 65–73; Etienne and Tony Catta, *Basil Anthony Mary Moreau*, vol. 1, pp. 553–64; and Wack, "University of Notre Dame," pp. 137–51 and 168–74. This issue has been presented at some length since the question can be raised whether Father Sorin ever considered moving his university from Indiana to Kentucky. The Kentucky school already enrolled more students than did Notre Dame, and a move would also free him from the jurisdiction of Bishop de la Hailandière.

67. O'Connell, *Sorin*, pp. 314–18 and 358, and Sorin, *Chronicles*, pp. 71, 91–95, 108–9, 112–15, and 155–58.

68. The best study of Brother Gatian is Klawitter, *After Holy Cross*. It is Klawitter's opinion that Brother Gatian's struggles with his homosexual yearnings were a major source of his discontent. The quotation is from Timothy Howard, *A History of St. Joseph County*, vol. II (Chicago, 1907), p. 629.

69. Hope, *Notre Dame*, p. 90.

70. Minor Chapter Minutes, A.N. 1970-15, F2, USPA, April 19 and October 11, 1847, November 3, 1848, January 29, 1849, and May 3, 1852; Ledger A, UNDA; Etienne and Tony Catta, *Basil Anthony Mary Moreau*, vol. 1, pp. 553–64; and Wack, "University of Notre Dame," pp. 119 and 148–50.

71. See Minor Chapter Minutes, A.N. 1970-15, F2, USPA, throughout, esp. June 6, 1854.

72. Drouelle to Moreau, Sorin Papers, CSCG, November 20, 1848, UNDA.

73. Drouelle to Moreau, CSCG, November 1, 1848, UNDA.

74. Drouelle to Moreau, CSCG, November 1, 1848, UNDA.

75. Drouelle to Moreau, CSCG, November 20, 1848, UNDA.

76. Drouelle to Moreau, CSCG, November 20, 1848, UNDA.

77. Father Drouelle's visit is discussed in Brother Gatian's Journal, CCIJ, UNDA, September 1 to November 2, 1848; Sorin, *Chronicles*, pp. 78–79; Etienne and Tony Catta, *Basil Anthony Mary Moreau*, vol. 1, pp. 927–34; O'Connell, *Sorin*, pp. 236–39; and Wack, "University of Notre Dame," pp. 182–83.

78. A.N. 1970-15, F2, USPA.

79. The best study of this California venture is Franklin Cullen, C.S.C., *Holy Cross on the Gold Dust Trail* (Notre Dame, IN, 1989), see esp. pp. 1–5. See also O'Connell, *Sorin*, pp. 253–62, and Wack, "University of Notre Dame," pp. 210–16. The quotations are from Howard, *History of St. Joseph County*, vol. II, p. 629, and Sorin, *Chronicles*, pp. 90–91.

80. Cullen, *Holy Cross*, pp. 8–19. The quotation is on page 16. See also Brother Gatian's description quoted in Beirne, *Sea to Shining Sea*, pp. 156–61.

81. Cullen, *Holy Cross*, pp. 29–31; O'Connell, *Sorin*, pp. 261–62; Wack, "University of Notre Dame," pp. 214–16; and Moreau to Sorin, March 30, 1851, CSCG, UNDA.

82. Etienne and Tony Catta, *Basil Anthony Mary Moreau*, vol. 1, pp. 886–89, and O'Connell, *Sorin*, pp. 289–90.

83. Council of Professors, UFMM, box 1, vol. 1, UNDA, July 18 and 25, 1845, and Sorin, *Chronicles*, p. 59.

84. Etienne and Tony Catta, *Basil Anthony Mary Moreau*, vol. 1, pp. 887–95 and 954, and O'Connell, *Sorin*, pp. 291–92.

85. O'Connell, *Sorin*, pp. 292–93. The quotation is on page 292.

86. Etienne and Tony Catta, *Basil Anthony Mary Moreau*, vol. 1, pp. 891–983, and O'Connell, *Sorin*, pp. 293–318. Archbishop Blanc's quotation is in O'Connell, *Sorin*, p. 298.

87. Etienne and Tony Catta, *Basil Anthony Mary Moreau*, vol. 2, pp. 3–25, and O'Connell, *Sorin*, pp. 318–26.

88. Sorin, *Chronicles*, p. 100; O'Connell, *Sorin*, pp. 278–82; Hope, *Notre Dame*, pp. 73–74; Beirne, *Sea to Shining Sea*, p. 191; and Wack, "University of Notre Dame," pp. 224–26; See also Council of Professors, UFMM, box 1, vol. 2, UNDA, July 1, 1846; Minutes of Particular Council, 1841–1845, A.N. 1970-15, F1, USPA, May 26, 1845; Visa of Father Sorin, CSOR, 5/9, oversize box 1, UNDA; and records of the steps in Father Sorin's naturalization process, 1843 and 1846, St. Joseph County Court *Order Books*, 6/1842–10/1845 and 10/17/1845–9/1848, St. Joseph County Archives and Records. The mutual benefit of roads to colleges and colleges to roads is noted in Kenneth H. Wheeler, *Cultivating Regionalism: Higher Education and the Making of the Midwest* (Dekalb, IL, 2011), pp. 14–15.

89. Sorin, *Chronicles*, p. 101.

Chapter 4. The End of An Era (?), 1855–1865

1. Sorin, *Chronicles*, pp. 57–58; Brother Gatian's Journal, CCIJ, UNDA, March 28, 1847; Wack, "University of Notre Dame," pp. 96–97 and 160–62; and O'Connell, *Sorin*, p. 206.

2. Sorin, *Chronicles*, pp. 126–32, and Wack, "University of Notre Dame," pp. 279–85. The quotations are from Sorin to Mother Theodore Guerin, October 16, 1854, Sorin Correspondence, 2001/05, box 1, F6, USPA, and Moreau, *Circular Letters*, vol. I, p. 322.

3. Minor Chapter Minutes, A.N. 1970-15, F2, USPA, November 9, 1847, April 3, 1848, March 26 and September 10, 1849, November 11, 1850, and October 4, 1852; Sorin, *Chronicles*, pp. 56–57 and 132–34; and Wack, "University of Notre Dame," pp. 188–89 and 287–89.

4. Sorin, *Chronicles*, pp. 135–38; Hope, *Notre Dame*, pp. 84–86; and Wack, "University of Notre Dame," pp. 288–90. The historian mentioned is Hope, *Notre Dame*, p. 85.

5. Sorin, *Circular Letters*, vol. I, p. 261.

6. Creek, *A Panorama*, pp. 11–13, and Brosnahan, *On the King's Highway*, pp. 131–43.

7. Quoted in Creek, *A Panorama*, pp. 13–14. See also Brosnahan, *On the King's Highway*, pp. 156–258.

8. Creek, *A Panorama*, pp. 15–16.

9. Creek, *A Panorama*, pp. 21–24, and O'Connell, *Sorin*, p. 319. In late 1854, the orphans and the sisters' school had been transferred from Bertrand to a house in Mishawaka, just to the east of South Bend, and these were relocated to the former Rush property in 1855 also. See Creek, *A Panorama*, p. 27.

10. Creek, *A Panorama*, pp. 16–19; Anna Shannon McAllister, *Flame in the Wilderness* (Notre Dame, IN, 1944), pp. 1–85; and Brosnahan, *On the King's Highway*, pp. 165–69. See also Thomas Blantz, C.S.C., "James Gillespie Blaine, His Family, and 'Romanism,'" *The Catholic Historical Review* XCIV (October 2008), pp. 695–716.

11. Creek, *A Panorama*, pp. 20–21; McAllister, *Flame in the Wilderness*, pp. 86–90; and Neal Gillespie to "Lidie," February 19, 1853, MAC, box 4.6, Holy Cross Sisters Archives, Saint Mary's, Indiana.

12. McAllister, *Flame in the Wilderness*, pp. 90–95.

13. Creek, *A Panorama*, pp. 21–24; McAllister, *Flame in the Wilderness*, pp. 95–101; and Brosnahan, *On the King's Highway*, pp. 169–73.

14. Sorin, *Chronicles*, pp. 152–78. Lowell (or New Lowell) was a small community less than two miles from South Bend, and St. John's was about eighty miles southwest of South Bend. In 1857, the Congregation of Holy Cross in the United States was divided into two geographical vicariates, Indiana and Louisiana, and Father Sorin was named vicar for Indiana.

15. Sorin, *Chronicles*, pp. 224–41, 250, and 262–63.

16. James M. Schmidt, *Notre Dame and the Civil War: Marching Onward to Victory* (Charleston, SC, 2010), pp. 83–84. Figures are lower in Sorin, *Chronicles*, pp. 192, 246, and 288.

17. *Catalogue of the Officers and Students of the University of Notre Dame*, 1855–1856, p. 9.

18. *Catalogue*, 1855–1856, p. 9; *Catalogue*, 1857–1858, pp. 37–38; and *Catalogue*, 1863–1864, pp. 59–60

19. *Catalogue*, 1862–1863, p. 13.

20. Marion T. Cassey, "The Minims of Notre Dame: Underpinnings of Sorin's University, 1842–1929," *American Catholic Studies* 127, no. 1 (Spring 2016), pp. 45–72;

Schlereth, *University of Notre Dame*, pp. 88–89; Hope, *Notre Dame*, p. 221; and O'Connell, *Sorin*, pp. 351 and 671.

21. *Catalogue*, 1855–56, pp. 5–6; *Catalogue*, 1857–1859, pp. 5–6; and *Catalogue*, 1863–1864, p. 13. The faculty roster for 1863–1864 lists five Holy Cross priests, two non–Holy Cross priests, one brother (Basil), thirteen laymen, five brothers as "Teachers in the Preparatory Department," and seven brothers as "Assistant Prefects of Discipline." *Catalogue*, 1863–1864, pp. 3–4.

22. *Catalogue*, 1863–1864, p. 14. This classical program was not that dissimilar from the one favored in the influential *Yale Report of 1828*: see Rudolph, *American College*, pp. 131–34.

23. *Catalogue*, 1857–1858, pp. 5–6; *Catalogue*, 1863–1864, pp. 15 and 34; and *Catalogue*, 1860–1861, pp. 22–39.

24. *Catalogue*, 1863–1864, p. 15, and Philip S. Moore, C.S.C., "Academic Development: University of Notre Dame Past, Present and Future" (privately published, 1960), p. 97.

25. *Catalogue*, 1859–1860, p. 19; *Catalogue*, 1860–1861, p. 19; and *Catalogue*, 1863–1864, p. 34.

26. *Catalogue*, 1863–1864, pp. 17–18, and Lyons, *Silver Jubilee*, p. 246.

27. *Catalogue*, 1863–1864, pp. 18 and 19, and Lyons, *Silver Jubilee*, pp. 251 and 252.

28. *Catalogue*, 1863–1864, p. 18. Literary and other societies were increasing in colleges all across the country at this time: Rudolph, *American College*, pp. 136–44.

29. Council of Professors, UFMM, box 1, UNDA, February 15, May 3, and September 26 and 30, 1857, February 14, 21, and 27, and June 12, 1858, September 22 and October 6, 1860, September 5 and November 23, 1861, May 24, 1862, February 8, 1863, March 10, 1864, and February 3, 1865. The Council of the Faculty name seems to have replaced Council of Professors beginning in 1856. The archives store the Council of the Faculty minutes with the Council of Professors minutes, under the Council of Professors label.

30. *Catalogue*, 1854–1855, p. 6; *Catalogue*, 1858–1859, p. 25; *Catalogue*, 1863–1864, p. 34; Lyons, *Silver Jubilee*, pp. 109–15; and Moore, "Academic Development," pp. 131–32.

31. Sorin, *Chronicles*, pp. 37–38 and 88.

32. Sorin, *Chronicles*, pp. 190–91; "The Arson at Notre Dame," *St. Joseph County Forum*, December 27, 1856, p. 3, col. 1; Hope, *Notre Dame*, pp. 111 and 182; and Wack, "University of Notre Dame," pp. 321–22.

33. O'Connell, *Sorin*, pp. 284–86, notes that Rome had approved a similar request from another congregation a few years earlier and the sisters subsequently complained that they were not treated equitably and fairly by the male administrators.

34. Etienne and Tony Catta, *Basil Anthony Mary Moreau*, vol. 2, pp. 166–69, and O'Connell, *Sorin*, pp. 284–86 and 377–80. See also Moreau, *Circular Letters*, vol. I, May 25, 1856, pp. 345–46.

35. Quoted in Moreau, *Circular Letters*, vol. II, July 3, 1857, p. 10. It is not clear why the original document has "Maria Basilio Moreau" rather than "Basilio Maria."

36. Costin, *Priceless Spirit*, pp. 136–53; Sorin, *Chronicles*, pp. 192–93; and Etienne and Tony Catta, *Basil Anthony Mary Moreau*, vol. 2, pp. 241–57.

37. Etienne and Tony Catta, *Basil Anthony Mary Moreau*, vol. 2, pp. 275–304.

38. Moreau, *Circular Letters*, vol. II, September 25, 1857, pp. 31–37; Sorin, *Chronicles*, pp. 193–94; Etienne and Tony Catta, *Basil Anthony Mary Moreau*, vol. 2, pp. 304–18; Costin, *Priceless Spirit*, pp. 140–43; and O'Connell, *Sorin*, pp. 284–92. There was a disagreement over whether $3,000 that Father Sorin had sent to France at a time of financial crisis there had been a gift or a loan, but the difference was resolved satisfactorily. See O'Connell, *Sorin*, pp. 387–88.

39. Moreau, *Circular Letters*, vol. II, September 25, 1857, pp. 38–39.

40. This idea was first suggested to the author by Father Thomas McAvoy, C.S.C., historian of American Catholicism and longtime archivist at the University of Notre Dame.

41. Sorin, *Chronicles*, p. 29. See also Beirne, *Sea to Shining Sea*, pp. 55–66.

42. Minutes of Minor Chapter, A.N. 1970-15, F1, USPA, March 11, 1844; F2, November 27, 1848, and January 7, 1856.

43. Minor Chapter Minutes, A.N. 1970-15, F1, USPA, January 7 and March 10, 1856, and October 23, 1865; Brother Donald Stabrowski, C.S.C., "Brickmaking at Notre Dame" (paper delivered at the Holy Cross History Conference, July 5–7, 1991), pp. 2–3; and Hope, *Notre Dame*, p. 74. In the late 1860s the kilns were leased out to private contractors, a Mr. McCabe and Mr. Kavanaugh, who may have paid the community approximately six dollars per thousand bricks made: Minor Chapter Minutes, A.N. 1970-15, F1, USPA, January 2, 1866 and December 12, 1868, and Beirne, *Sea to Shining Sea*, pp. 55–61.

44. Sorin, *Chronicles*, p. 276.

45. Sorin, *Chronicles*, p. 277.

46. *Summary Report to Father Moreau*, box Aug. 1860–Nov. 1861, folder 1861, April (IX), CSCG, UNDA.

47. *Summary Report*, box Aug. 1860–Nov. 1861, folder 1861, IV, CSCG, UNDA.

48. Council of Professors Minutes, UFMM, box 1, UNDA, April 20, 1861.

49. *Catalogue*, 1860–1861, pp. 13–18; *Catalogue*, 1861–1862, pp. 12–17; *Catalogue*, 1862–1863, pp. 13–20; *Catalogue*, 1863–1864, pp. 21–32; *Catalogue*, 1864–1865, pp. 21–32; and *Catalogue*, 1865–1866, pp. 20–32. On pages 83 and 84 of his well-researched and attractively written study, *Notre Dame and the Civil War*, James M. Schmidt suggests even larger numbers: 203, 220, 274, 405, 543, and 659.

50. Sorin, *Chronicles*, p. 285. For the exhibition hall, see Pilkinton, *Washington Hall*, pp. 41–42.

51. Schmidt, *Notre Dame*, pp. 83–84.

52. Sorin, *Chronicles*, pp. 285–86. That Christmas date is noted on page 286.

53. James McCormack, unpublished paper on "Life at Notre Dame during the Civil War and After," CNDS, 17/15, UNDA, p. 2.

54. McCormack, "Life at Notre Dame," CNDS, 17/15, UNDA, p. 2.

55. Orville Chamberlain to his family, the Joseph W. and Orville T. Chamberlain Papers, box 1, folder 8, Indiana Historical Society, Indianapolis, IN, quoted in Schmidt, *Notre Dame*, p. 13.

56. *Scholastic*, Vol. V, No. 19 (January 13, 1872), p. 5.

57. Howard, *Brief History*, p. 93.

58. Howard, *History of St. Joseph County*, vol. II, p. 637; Howard, *Brief History*, p. 93; *Scholastic*, Vol. XXXIII, No. 11 (November 18, 1899), pp. 176–77; and Hope, *Notre Dame*, pp. 116–17.

59. Schmidt, *Notre Dame*, pp. 24–27, 59–60, 78–80, and 102–3. The quotation is from page 102.

60. Hope, *Notre Dame*, pp. 118–21.

61. Quoted in Robert J. Miller, *Both Prayed to the Same God* (Lanham, MD, 2007), p. 97.

62 Schmidt, *Notre Dame*, pp. 33–35, and William Corby, C.S.C., *Memoirs of a Chaplain Life* (New York, 1992), pp. 286–98.

63. Schmidt, *Notre Dame*, pp. 31–33; Corby, *Memoirs*, pp. 307–11; and David Power Conyngham, *Soldiers of the Cross, the Authoritative Text: The Heroism of Catholic Chaplains and Sisters in the American Civil War*, edited by David J. Endres and William B. Kurtz (Notre Dame, IN, 2019), chap. XIV, pp. 197 and 199.

64. Schmidt, *Notre Dame*, pp. 37–39, and 103–6; Rev. Thomas McAvoy, C.S.C., "The War Letters of Father Peter Paul Cooney of the Congregation of Holy Cross," *The Records of the American Catholic Historical Society of Philadelphia* XLIV (1933), pp. 47–69, 151–69, and 220–37; Conyngham, *Soldiers of the Cross*, chap. XVI; Sean Fabun, "Catholic Chaplains in the Civil War," *The Catholic Historical Review* XCIX, no. 4 (October 2013), pp. 682–97; and Garret Kuhls, "Fr. Peter Paul Cooney, C.S.C., Civil War Chaplain" (senior seminar paper, University of Notre Dame, 2008), in possession of the author. The quotation is from McAvoy, "The War Letters," p. 232.

65. Schmidt, *Notre Dame*, pp. 35–37 and 93–98; Hope, *Notre Dame*, pp. 132–33, and Conyngham, *Soldiers of the Cross*, chaps. IV, V, VI, and VII.

66. Schmidt, *Notre Dame*, pp. 39–40, 55–57, 73–77, and 100–101; Fabun, "Catholic Chaplains," pp. 683–99; Conyngham, *Soldiers of the Cross*, chap. XVIII; and Corby, *Memoirs*, esp. pp. 182–83 for the quotation.

67. Schmidt, *Notre Dame*, pp. 127–30. With Father Corby's hand raised almost above his head, the Notre Dame students have named the statue "Fair Catch Corby" after the familiar punt receiver's signal in football.

68. An excellent study of the Holy Cross sisters in the Civil War is Barbara Mann Wall, "Grace under Pressure: The Nursing Sisters of the Holy Cross, 1861–1865," *Nursing History Review* I (1993), pp. 71–87. See also *A Story of Fifty Years: From the Annals of the Congregation of the Sisters of the Holy Cross, 1855–1905* (Notre Dame, IN, n.d.) pp. 89–113; Sister Mary Denis Maher, *To Bind Up the Wounds* (New York, 1998), pp. 36, 69–91, 101, 106, and 116; Sorin, *Circular Letters*, vol. I, pp. 304–6; Costin, *Priceless Spirit*, pp. 155 and 179; Brosnahan, *On the King's Highway*, pp. 233–68; Sorin, *Chronicles*, pp. 276–77; Schmidt, *Notre Dame*, p. 43; Conyngham, *Soldiers of the Cross*, chaps. XXXIII–XXXIV; and Mother Angela to Anna Harmon, December 4, 1861, Mother Angela Collection, MAC Box E4.6, Holy Cross Sisters Archives, Saint Mary's, IN.

69. Quoted in Schmidt, *Notre Dame*, p. 44.

70. Quoted in Costin, *Priceless Spirit*, pp. 180–81.

71. Sorin, *Chronicles*, p. 280, and Costin, *Priceless Spirit*, p. 155.

72. Costin, *Priceless Spirit*, pp. 180–94; Sorin, *Chronicles*, pp. 276–284; Schmidt, *Notre Dame*, pp. 41–50. The quotation is from Wall, "Grace under Pressure," p. 82.

73. The best study of this subject is Dorothy O. Pratt, "Notre Dame and the Civil War Draft: Fact or Fiction" (graduate seminar paper, University of Notre Dame, 1995), in possession of the author. See also James McPherson, *Battle Cry of Freedom* (New York, 1988), pp. 600–603; O'Connell, *Sorin*, pp. 496–99; Schmidt, *Notre Dame*, pp. 93–95; and Sorin to Cardinal Barnabo, May 5 and 7, 1864, CSCG, 1864 May (V), UNDA.

74. Pratt, "Notre Dame," pp. 8–10; Schmidt, *Notre Dame*, p. 97; and Thomas Low Nichols, *Forty Years of American Life, 1821–1861* (New York, 1937), p. 276.

75. Pratt, "Notre Dame," p. 10, and Minor Chapter Minutes, A.N. 1970-15, F2, USPA, November 7, 1864.

76. Pratt, "Notre Dame," pp. 10–13; Schmidt, *Notre Dame*, pp. 97–98; O'Connell, *Sorin*, pp. 501–3; and McPherson, *Battle Cry of Freedom*, pp. 809–11.

77. Anna McAllister, *Ellen Ewing: Wife of General Sherman* (New York, 1936), pp. 284–91; and Mrs. Phelan to Neal Gillespie, June 12, 1864, CEWI, box 3, F4, UNDA. Charley's older brother, Willy, who had earlier been a student at Notre Dame, had died before his tenth birthday of what was then called "camp fever" after the Battle of Vicksburg and was buried temporarily near the family home in Lancaster, Ohio. See Philemon Ewing to his son, Tom, October 11, 1863, CEWI, box 2, F3, UNDA.

78. Reproduced in Wilson D. Miscamble, C.S.C., *Go Forth and Do Good* (Notre Dame, IN, 2003), pp. 46–47, and Hope, *Notre Dame*, p. 122.

79. William Sherman to Sorin, February 28, March 1 and 9, 1867, reel 1, frames 532, 534, 536, Sherman Family Papers, UNDA.

80. O'Connell, *Sorin*, pp. 283–328, 361, and 514–15; Sorin, *Chronicles*, pp. 250–54; and "A Chronological Outline: The Congregation of Holy Cross in the United States, 1841–1978," USPA.

81. Lyons, *Silver Jubilee*, pp. 75–77; Hope, *Notre Dame*, p. 115; and McCormack, "Life at Notre Dame during the Civil War and After," CNDS, 17/15, UNDA.

82. Costin, *Priceless Spirit*, pp. 155–58; Creek, *A Panorama*, pp. 25–27; Brosnahan, *On the King's Highway*, p. 269; Hope, *Notre Dame*, p. 138; and Howard, *History of St. Joseph County*, vol. II, p. 705.

83. Sorin, *Chronicles*, pp. 274–76 and 303; *Ave Maria* 1, no. 4 (June 3, 1865), pp. 63–64; O'Connell, *Sorin*, pp. 449–51, 495, 523–24, 531, and 650; and Schlereth, *University of Notre Dame*, p. 94.

84. Schlereth, *University of Notre Dame*, pp. 37–38; Thomas J. Schlereth, *A Dome of Learning: The University of Notre Dame's Main Building* (Notre Dame, IN 1991), pp. 4–6; and O'Connell, *Sorin*, pp. 518–19. The quotation is found on page 6 of Schlereth, *A Dome of Learning*.

85. O'Connell, *Sorin*, pp. 519–20; Lyons, *Silver Jubilee*, p. 76; Hope, *Notre Dame*, pp. 141–42; Howard, *History of St. Joseph County*, vol. II, p. 639; Council of Professors

Minutes, UFMM, box 1, 1863–1868, UNDA, January 27, 1866; and McCormack, "Life at Notre Dame during the Civil War and After," CNDS, 17/15, UNDA.

86. Etienne and Tony Catta, *Basil Anthony Mary Moreau*, vol. 2, pp. 708–19; Sorin, *Chronicles*, pp. 300–302; and O'Connell, *Sorin*, p. 544. See also Sorin to Granger, December 9, 1868, CSCG, 1868-XII-9, UNDA. In a note on page 714, the Cattas suggest that Father Dillon may have made an intervention during the chapter's deliberations.

87. Howard, *History of St. Joseph County*, vol. II, pp. 638–39.

88. Sorin, *Chronicles*, p. 302, and O'Connell, *Sorin*, p. 521.

Chapter 5.   *Father Corby to Father Corby, 1866–1881*

1. *A Guide to the University of Notre Dame and the Academy of St. Mary of the Immaculate Conception* (Philadelphia, 1865), pp. 12–46; Sorin, *Chronicles*, p. 294; Schlereth, *University of Notre Dame*, pp. 37–39; Pilkinton, *Washington Hall*, pp. 31–47; *Catalogue*, 1867–1868, pp. 10–11; and Matthew Hovde, "The History of the Old College" (senior seminar paper, University of Notre Dame, 2010), in possession of the author.

2. *Catalogue*, 1865–1866, pp. 13–15.

3. *Catalogue*, 1865–1866, pp. 3–4.

4. *Ave Maria* 1, no. 1 (May 1, 1865), pp. 1–4, 7–8, and 12–14, no. 6 (June 17, 1865), pp. 95–96, no. 7 (June 24, 1865), p. 107, and no. 8 (July 1, 1865), p. 123; O'Connell, *Sorin*, pp. 503–10; McAllister, *Flame in the Wilderness*, pp. 229–37; and Rev. Thomas McAvoy, C.S.C., "The Ave Maria after 100 Years," *Ave Maria* 101, no. 18 (May 1, 1965), pp. 6–9 and 21.

5. Lyons, *Silver Jubilee*, pp. 77–80, and see also the preceding chapter.

6. *Catalogue*, 1863–1864, p. 34; *Catalogue*, 1864–1865, pp. 34–35; *Catalogue*, 1866–1867, pp. 23–38; *Catalogue*, 1867–1868, pp. 29–44; *Catalogue*, 1868–1869, pp. 29–40; *Catalogue*, 1869–1870, pp. 29–40; *Catalogue*, 1870–1871, pp. 24–34; and *Catalogue*, 1871–1872, pp. 22–33.

7. *Catalogue*, 1865–1866, pp. 13–15.

8. Conyngham, *Soldiers of the Cross*, chap. IV; Schmidt, *Notre Dame*, pp. 35–37; *Scholastic*, Vol. XXVIII, No. 5 (October 6, 1894), pp. 75–77, and Vol. XXXVIII, No. 10 (November 19, 1904), pp. 160–61. The quotation is from Vol. XXVIII, No. 5 (October 6, 1894), p. 76.

9. *Scholastic*, Vol. III, No. 18 (May 14, 1870), p. 42; Vol. XI, No. 31 (March 30, 1878), p. 490; Vol. XX, No. 2 (August 21, 1886), pp. 31–33; and Vol. XXI, No. 17 (January 14, 1888), pp. 264–67. The quotation is from Vol. XI, No. 32 (April 6, 1878), p. 506.

10. *Scholastic*, Vol. I, No. 31 (April 4, 1868), p. 3; and Vol. XXI, No. 17 (January 14, 1888), pp. 264–67. The quotation is from Vol. I, No. 31 (April 4, 1868), p. 3.

11. *Catalogue*, 1865–1866, pp. 34–35; *Catalogue*, 1866–1867, p. 37; *Catalogue*, 1867–1868, p. 43; *Catalogue*, 1868–1869, pp. 39–40; *Catalogue*, 1869–1870, p. 40; *Catalogue*, 1870–1871, p. 34; and *Catalogue*, 1871–1872, p. 33. See also *Scholastic*, Vol. I, No. 31

(April 4, 1868), p. 3; Vol. III, No. 1 (September 18, 1869), p. 4; Vol. VI, No. 2 (September 21, 1872), p. 13; and Vol. XI, No. 3 (March 30, 1878), p. 292.

12. *Scholastic*, Vol. IX, No. 24 (February 12, 1876), pp. 373–74.

13. *Scholastic*, Vol. IX, No. 30 (March 25, 1876), p. 495; Vol. XVII, No. 24 (February 23, 1884), p. 379, and No. 27 (March 15, 1884), p. 427; and Vol. XVIII, No. 37 (May 23, 1885) p. 593.

14. Howard, *Brief History*, p. 105.

15. *Scholastic*, Vol. II, No. 3 (September 19, 1868), p. 21. The original name, "United Scientific Association," was changed to simply "Scientific Association" by November 1869. See *Scholastic*, Vol. III, No. 5 (November 13, 1869), p. 38.

16. *Catalogue*, 1868–1869, p. 23, and *Scholastic*, Vol. I, No. 35 (May 2, 1868), pp. 1–2; Vol. II, No. 18 (January 9, 1869), p. 140, No. 19 (January 16, 1869), pp. 146–47, No. 20 (January 23, 1869), pp. 157–59, No. 22 (February 6, 1869), pp. 173–75, No. 24 (February 20, 1869), pp. 190–91, No. 27 (March 12, 1869), pp. 211–12; Vol. III, No. 5 (November 13, 1869), p. 38, No. 20 (June 11, 1870), p. 158; Vol. IV, No. 15 (April 8, 1871), p. 6, No. 19 (May 27, 1871), pp. 7 and 12, No. 20 (June 3, 1871), p. 8, and No. 21 (June 14, 1871), p. 8.

17. Lyons, *Silver Jubilee*, p. 246, and *Scholastic*, Vol. I, No. 5 (October 5. 1867), p. 5, No. 6 (October 12, 1867), p. 4, No. 17 (December 28, 1867), p. 8; and Vol. II, No. 4 (November 5, 1870), p. 6.

18. Lyons, *Silver Jubilee*, p. 247, and *Scholastic*, Vol. I, No. 4 (September 26, 1867), p. 4, No. 6 (October 12, 1867), p. 4, No. 24 (February 15, 1868), p. 7; and Vol. II, No. 6 (October 10, 1868), p. 47, and No. 11 (November 14, 1868), p. 87.

19. Lyons, *Silver Jubilee*, p. 248, and *Scholastic*, Vol. I, No. 2 (September 11, 1867), p. 5.

20. Lyons, *Silver Jubilee*, p. 251.

21. Lyons, *Silver Jubilee*, p. 252.

22. Jones, "Development of the Office," pp. 187–91, and *Scholastic*, Vol. I, No. 3 (September 21, 1867), p. 6; Vol. III, No. 6 (November 27, 1869), p. 45; Vol. V, No. 15 (December 16, 1871), p. 56, and No. 25 (March 2, 1872), p. 7.

23. Jones, "Development of the Office," pp. 193–94; *Scholastic*, Vol. IV, No. 22 (June 21, 1871), p. 8; *Catalogue*, 1867–1868, p. 23; and *Catalogue*, 1871–1872, p. 16.

24. Jones, "Development of the Office," pp. 197–202; *Scholastic*, Vol. I, No. 10 (November 9, 1867), p. 67, and No. 34 (April 25, 1868), p. 4; Vol. II, No. 3 (September 19, 1868), p. 19, and No. 35 (May 8, 1869), pp. 277–78; Vol. IV, No. 11 (February 11, 1871), p. 7, and No. 14 (March 25, 1871), pp. 5–7; and Vol. V, No. 26 (March 9, 1872), p. 5; *Catalogue*, 1867–1868, p. 23; and *Catalogue*, 1871–1872, p. 16.

25. *Scholastic*, Vol. I, No. 14 (December 7, 1867), pp. 3–4; Vol. V, No. 26 (March 9, 1872), pp. 4–5; and Vol. XXXI, No. 34 (June 4, 1898), pp. 578–81 and 586–87. The first issue of *Progress* was reprinted on pp. 578–81 of *Scholastic*, Vol. XXXI, No. 34. *The Scholastic Year* changed names several times in these early years and it is referred to in this work simply as the *Scholastic*.

26. *Scholastic*, Vol. I, No. 1 (September 7, 1867), p. 2.

27. *Scholastic*, Vol. I, No. 9 (November 2, 1867), pp. 2 and 4–5, No. 11 (November 16, 1867), pp. 2–3, No. 14 (February 7, 1867), pp. 7–8, No. 15 (December 14, 1867), p. 8, No. 21 (January 25, 1868), pp. 7–8, and No. 26 (February 29, 1868), pp. 7–8; Vol. II, No. 31 (April 10, 1869), pp. 241–43; Vol. III, No. 1 (September 18, 1869), pp. 5–6, No. 2 (October 2, 1869), pp. 14–16; Vol. V, No. 4 (September 30, 1871), pp. 6–7, No. 7 (October 21, 1871), p. 7, No. 11 (November 18, 1871), pp. 7–8, and No. 35 (May 11, 1872), p. 7.

28. The only full-length history of the Notre Dame Law School is Rev. Philip S. Moore, C.S.C., *A Century of Law* (Notre Dame, IN, 1969); *Catalogue*, 1854–1855, p. 6; *Catalogue*, 1858–1859, p. 6; and *Catalogue*, 1865–1866, pp. 14–15. The quotation is from *Scholastic*, Vol. II, No. 6 (October 10, 1868), p. 47.

29. *Catalogue*, 1868–1869, p. 20.

30. *Catalogue*, 1868–1869, pp. 20–26, and *Scholastic*, Vol. I, No. 17 (January 2, 1869), pp. 129–30, and No. 40 (June 12, 1869), pp. 313–14. Father Moore, in *A Century of Law*, pages 3 and 4, suggests that Notre Dame's admission requirements were higher than those of some other well respected schools.

31. *Catalogue*, 1868–1869, p. 21; *Catalogue*, 1870–1871, p. 34; *Scholastic*, Vol. II, No. 43 (September 5, 1869), p. 348; and Vol. III, No. 3 (October 16, 1869), p. 21; and Moore, *A Century of Law*, pp. 2–3. The quotation is from *Catalogue*, 1868–1869, p. 21.

32. Local Council Minutes, 1865–1875, CCIJ, October 5, 1868, UNDA. See also Minutes, 1855–1865, CCIJ, August 15 and 19, 1864, UNDA.

33. Minutes, 1865–1875, CCIJ, January 2 and April 10, 1869, UNDA. See also O'Connell, *Sorin*, pp. 616–17.

34. Schlereth, *A Spire of Faith*, pp. 16–20, and Minutes, CCIJ, 1865–1875, February 12, 1870, UNDA. Mother Angela had intended to have a church dedicated to Our Lady of the Sacred Heart built at St. Mary's, but when she learned that Father Sorin wanted that dedication for his new church at Notre Dame, she deferred to him and actually donated $1,400 for Notre Dame's new church: Schlereth, *A Spire of Faith*, p. 17.

35. Schlereth, *A Spire of Faith*, pp. 17–20 and 24–26. The best study of Brother Charles Borromeo is by Brother James Newberry, C.S.C., "Brother Charles Borromeo Harding, 1838–1922: American Architect" (paper delivered at Holy Cross History Conference, Holy Cross College, Notre Dame, IN, 2010).

36. Schlereth, *University of Notre Dame*, pp. 44–45, and Local Council Minutes, CCIJ, 1865–1875, February 12, 1870, UNDA.

37. *Scholastic*, Vol. I, No. 20 (January 18, 1868), p. 1.

38. *Scholastic*, Vol. I, No. 20 (January 18, 1868), p. 1, No. 22 (February 1, 1868), pp. 5–6, No. 32 (April 11, 1868), p. 5, and No. 37 (May 16, 1868), p. 7. See also the very thorough study of the Alumni Association by James E. Armstrong, *Onward to Victory* (Notre Dame, IN, 1973), pp. 30–31.

39. *Scholastic*, Vol. I, No. 43 (June 27, 1868), pp. 1–2.

40. *Scholastic*, Vol. II, No. 42 (July 3, 1869), pp. 330–32 and 340, and Armstrong, *Onward to Victory*, pp. 32–36.

41. Earlier general chapters had been held in either France or Rome. See Howard, *Brief History*, p. 127.

42. *Scholastic*, Vol. VI, No. 1 (September 14, 1872), p. 12, and Vol. VII, No. 4 (September 20, 1873), p. 27. See also *Sadlier's Catholic Dictionary*, 1873 (New York, 1873), p. 229, and Beirne, *Sea to Shining Sea*, pp. 225–27.

43. Lyons, *Silver Jubilee*, pp. 90–92; Hope, *Notre Dame*, pp. 158–59; and O'Connell, *Sorin*, pp. 494–95. See also *Scholastic*, Vol. I, No. 22 (February 1, 1868), p. 6; Vol. III, No. 2 (October 12, 1869), p. 15, and No. 11 (February 5, 1870), pp. 88; Vol. IV, No. 3 (October 22, 1870), p. 8, and No. 11 (February 11, 1871), p. 8; and Vol. V, No. 5 (October 7, 1871), p. 7.

44. Howard, *Brief History*, p. 129.

45. *Catalogue*, 1872–1873, pp. 12–13; *Catalogue*, 1873–1874, pp. 12–17; *Catalogue*, 1874–1875, p. 10; *Scholastic*, Vol. VI, No. 8 (November 2, 1872), pp. 60–61, and Vol. VII, No. 44 (July 4, 1874), p. 357. See also Schlereth, *University of Notre Dame*, pp. 65–66.

46. Sister Damien Tambola, O.S.B., "James F. Edwards, Pioneer Archivist of Catholic Church History in America" (MA thesis, University of Notre Dame, 1958), pp. 39–40.

47. Tambola, "James F. Edwards," pp. 1–41 and 145; Rev. Thomas Blantz, C.S.C., "The Founding of the Notre Dame Archives," *American Catholic Studies Newsletter* 32, no. 1 (Spring 2005), pp. 1 and 7–10; and in the James F. Edwards Papers (CEDW) UNDA the following letters: E. B. Rhodes to Edwards, March 23, 1902, B10, F22; Joseph Hayes to Edwards, September 17, 1907, B14, F9; Henry Frawley to Willie, September 3, 1906, B13, F20; Fr. Herman Alerding to Edwards, January 11, 1891, B6, F2; Fr. Joseph Haas to Edwards, December 6, 1894, B6, F31; Fr. Maurus Brink, O.S.F., to Edwards, September 12, 1894, B2, F28; Fr. Otto Zardetti to Edwards, December 7, 1886, B2, F14; Fr. Clement Lau to Edwards, July 10, 1889, B4, F6; John Reinhood to Edwards, December 23, 1889, B4, F11; Mary K. Ryan to Edwards, April 5, 1900, B9, F22; and Sister Albertine to Edwards, February 12, 1891, B5, F3. See also Schlereth, *University of Notre Dame*, pp. 65–66, and Hope, *Notre Dame*, p. 164.

48. Tambola, "James F. Edwards," pp. 42–54; Alan D. Krieger, "Notre Dame Library Collections of the Nineteenth Century: The Legacy of the Fire of 1879," in *What Is Written Remains*, ed. Maureen Gleason and Katharina Blackstead (Notre Dame, IN, 1994), pp. 7–9; and *Catalogue*, 1874–1875, p. 29.

49. Tambola, "James F. Edwards," pp. 51–54; "The Lemonnier Library of the University of Notre Dame," *Scholastic*, Vol. XXIII, No. 40 (June 14, 1890), pp. 629–32; Blantz, "The Founding," p. 8; and Moore, "Academic Development," pp. 153–54.

50. *Scholastic*, Vol. VII, No. 39 (May 23, 1874), p. 317.

51. Anne Klimek, *The Zahms' Legacy: A History of Engineering at Notre Dame, 1873–1993* (Notre Dame, IN, 1993), pp. 5–7; Lyons, *Silver Jubilee*, pp. 121–23; and Moore, "Academic Development," p. 72.

52. *Scholastic*, Vol. V, No. 7 (October 2, 1871), p. 4; Vol. VIII, No. 7 (November 7, 1874), p. 73, No. 8 (November 14, 1874), p. 91, No. 15 (January 2, 1875), p. 195, and No. 37 (May 25, 1872), p. 4. Father Corby's eulogy for Father Lemonnier is preserved in the Lemonnier Papers, CPLE, B3, F16, UNDA.

53. *Scholastic*, Vol. IX, No. 9 (October 30, 1875), p. 139; Vol. X, No. 10 (November 11, 1876), p. 154; Vol. XI, No. 11 (November 3, 1877), p. 154; Vol. XIII, No. 8 (October 25, 1879), p. 113; Vol. XV, No. 8 (October 29, 1881), p. 112; Vol. XVI, No. 9 (November 4, 1882), pp. 137–38; and Vol. XVII, No. 9 (November 3, 1883), p. 138.

54. *Scholastic*, Vol. VIII, No. 7 (November 7, 1874), p. 73.

55. Materia Generale, USPA; *Scholastic*, Vol. IV, No. 9 (January 14, 1871), p. 4, and No. 25 (August 12, 1871), p. 5; Vol. VIII, No. 3 (October 17, 1874), p. 29, and No. 8 (November 14, 1874), p. 91; and Vol. XXI, No. 1 (August 27, 1887), p. 12; O'Connell, *Sorin*, pp. 627–29; and Hope, *Notre Dame*, pp. 170–71. The following quotation is from Sorin to Corby, September 17, 1871, Corby Papers, 1970-3(b), B1, F1, USPA.

56. *Scholastic*, Vol. VIII, No. 2 (October, 3 1874), p. 13, No. 4 (October 17, 1874), p. 29, and No. 16 (January 9. 1875), p. 212.

57. Faculty Council Minutes, UFMM, box 2, UNDA, February 17, 1876, and September 6, 1875.

58. Faculty Council Minutes, UFMM, box 2, UNDA, February 3 and 17 and November 2, 1876, and January 18 and February 15, 1877; *Scholastic*, Vol. VIII, No. 3 (October 10, 1874), p. 22, No. 8 (November 14, 1874), p. 91, and No. 13 (December 19, 1874), p. 171; Vol. IX, No. 18 (January 1, 1876), p. 283; Vol. XI, No. 26 (February 23, 1878), p. 410; and Vol. XXI, No. 1 (August 27, 1887), p. 12; and O'Connell, *Sorin*, p. 629. According to the university's official *Catalogues*, 1874–1875, pp. 30–38, and 1876–1877, pp. 32–38, the enrollment dropped from approximately 345 to approximately 270. For the canvassing, see Local Council Minutes, CCIJ, UNDA, June 25, and July 2 and 9, 1875.

59. Sorin, *Chronicles*, p. 16, and Hope, *Notre Dame*, p. 170. That defense of Colovin is in Sorin Papers, 1970-1, Correspondence 1879–1883, box 6, USPA. See also Granger to Colovin (n.d.), Sorin Era Box, folder 2, USPA.

60. *Scholastic*, Vol. XI, No. 1 (August 25, 1877), p. 8.

61. Kohl, *Memoirs of Chaplain Life*, pp. xviii–xix.

62. Local Council Minutes, CCIJ, UNDA, December 26, 1873, April 13, 1877, June 1, 1877, and May 16, 1879; *Catalogue*, 1877–1878, pp. 37–43; and *Catalogue*, 1881–1882, pp. 48–56.

63. Schlereth, *A Spire of Faith*, pp. 16–21 and 58.

64. Schlereth, *A Spire of Faith*, pp. 33–37, and 60–67.

65. Sorin to Lemonnier, July 12, 1873, B1, F4, CPLE, UNDA; Schlereth, *A Spire of Faith*, p. 34; and *Scholastic*, Vol. LIV, No. 8 (November 13, 1920), p. 113.

66. Schlereth, *A Spire of Faith*, p. 34; *Scholastic*, Vol. IX, No. 5 (October 2, 1875), p. 72; Vol. XI, No. 4 (September 22, 1877), p. 59; and Vol. LIV, No. 8 (November 13, 1920), p. 114.

67. Schlereth, *A Spire of Faith*, pp. 33–42, 60–61, and 64–65. It might be surprising that there is nothing of Saint Edward or Saint William, the patrons of the superior general and the university president.

68. *Scholastic*, Vol. XII, No. 35 (May 10, 1879), pp. 539–40.

69. *Scholastic*, Vol. XII, No. 34 (April 26, 1879), p. 533, and No. 35 (May 10, 1879), p. 539.

70. *Scholastic*, Vol. XII, No. 34 (April 26, 1879), p. 533–34, and No. 35 (May 10, 1879), pp. 539–41. See also Schlereth, *A Dome of Learning*, pp. 7–10, and Howard, *Brief History*, pp. 138–47.

71. *Scholastic*, Vol. XI, No. 31 (March 30, 1878), pp. 491–92.

72. *Scholastic*, Vol. XII, No. 35 (May 10, 1879), p. 539.

73. *Scholastic*, Vol. XII, No. 34 (April 26, 1879), pp. 534–36, and No. 35 (May 10, 1879), pp. 539–48; and Schlereth, *A Dome of Learning*, p. 12.

74. Howard to Father Hudson, n.d., quoted in Hope, *Notre Dame*, p. 186.

75. *Scholastic*, Vol. XII, No. 37 (May 24, 1879), pp. 576–77, No. 38 (May 31, 1879), p. 592, No. 39 (June 7, 1879), p. 608, and No. 41 (June 21, 1879), p. 640; Schlereth, *University of Notre Dame*, p. 58; Schlereth, *A Dome of Learning*, pp. 21–25; Beirne, *Sea to Shining Sea*, pp. 123–24; and Kerry Temple, "The Day Notre Dame Burned," *South Bend Tribune*, April 22, 1979, Michiana Section, pp. 3–6.

76. Local Council Minutes, CCIJ, UNDA, May 16 and 27, and November 5 and 21, 1879, and October 8, 1880; and *Scholastic*, Vol. XII, No. 43 (July 5, 1879), p. 672, and Vol. XIII, No. 1 (August 23, 1879), p. 8, and No. 2 (September 13, 1879), p. 28.

Chapter 6. A New Notre Dame

1. *Scholastic*, Vol. XII, No. 36 (May 17, 1879), pp. 557–59, and letter of William Francis, *Chicago Tribune*, May 18, 1879, p. 6.

2. Reprinted in *Scholastic*, Vol. XII, No. 37 (May 24, 1879), pp. 577–78.

3. *Scholastic*, Vol. XII, No. 37 (May 24, 1879), p. 573; see also Vol. XII, No. 39 (June 7, 1879), pp. 608–9.

4. Hope, *Notre Dame*, pp. 202–3, and *Scholastic*, Vol. XXVII, No. 1 (July 29, 1893), p. 3, and Vol. XXVIII, No. 1 (August 18, 1894), p. 1.

5. Howard, *Brief History*, pp. 177–78; Hope, *Notre Dame*, pp. 198 and 203–4; and *Scholastic*, Vol. XXVII, No. 1 (July 29, 1893), p. 4, and No. 14 (December 16, 1893), pp. 230–31.

6. Letters of Cardinal Simeoni and Father Corby in Corby Papers, 1970/3, box 1, folder 3, USPA.

7. Sorin to Fernando Battista, September 8, 1881, CSCG, 1881, Early Documents Arranged Chronologically, 1780–1909, UNDA, and O'Connell, *Sorin*, pp. 672–74.

8. *Catalogue*, 1882–1883, p. 11.

9. *Catalogue*, 1880–1881, pp. 50–54; *Catalogue*, 1881–1882, pp. 5–9 and 48–56; and *Catalogue*, 1892–1893, pp. 4–8 and 82–96.

10. Moore, "Academic Development," pp. 6, 17–19, and 97–98; Hope, *Notre Dame*, p. 141; Lyons, *Silver Jubilee*, p. 76; and Kerry Temple, *O'Hara's Heirs: Business Education at Notre Dame, 1921–1991* (Notre Dame, IN, 1992), p. 5.

11. *Catalogue*, 1886–1887, p. 40, and Moore, "Academic Development," pp. 19–20.

12. Rev. Daniel Hudson, C.S.C., Papers, UNDA; Hope, *Notre Dame*, pp. 212–13; Matthew J. Flaherty, "Charles Warren Stoddard," in *Catholic Encyclopedia*, vol. 14 (New

York, 1913), pp. 298–99; and Robert L. Gale, "Charles Warren Stoddard," in Garraty and Carnes, *American National Biography*, vol. 20 (New York, 1999), pp. 815–16.

13. Stoddard to Hudson, September 12, 1884, Hudson Papers, UNDA; Hope, *Notre Dame*, pp. 213–14; and Roger Austen, *Genteel Pagan* (Amherst, MA, 1991), pp. 103–14.

14. Kimberly Markowski, "Maurice Francis Egan," in Garraty and Carnes, *American National Biography*, vol. 7 (New York, 1999), pp. 344–45.

15. Maurice Francis Egan, *Recollections of a Happy Life* (New York, 1924), pp. 157–79.

16. Pilkinton, *Washington Hall*, p. 13, and Sorin to Fr. Auguste, February 23, 1864, CSCG, UNDA.

17. Pilkinton, *Washington Hall*, pp. 25–44, 88–93, 106–41, and 344–45; Schlereth, *University of Notre Dame*, pp. 100–104; and *Scholastic*, Vol. XV, No. 41 (July 1, 1882), pp. 641–42.

18. Moore, "Academic Development," pp. 47–48, and Hope, *Notre Dame*, pp. 225–26.

19. Ralph E. Weber, *Notre Dame's John Zahm* (Notre Dame, IN, 1961), pp. 1–3.

20. Weber, *Notre Dame's John Zahm*, pp. 5–7.

21. Weber, *Notre Dame's John Zahm*, pp. 7–16. A very worthwhile intellectual biography of Zahm is David B. Burrell, C.S.C., *When Faith and Reason Meet: The Legacy of John Zahm, CSC* (Notre Dame, IN, 2012).

22. *Catalogue*, 1881–1882, pp. 5–9 and 29–33; *Catalogue*, 1891–1892, p. 43; and *Catalogue*, 1892–1893, pp. 4–8. On the absence of religion classes at the time, see Philip Gleason, *Contending with Modernity* (New York, 1995), pp. 142–45.

23. Weber, *Notre Dame's John Zahm*, pp. 16–18. The Sorin quotation is from Patrick J. Carroll, "Mind in Action," *Ave Maria* LXIII (January 1946), p. 82, and the other two from the South Bend *Daily Register*, January 10, 1880, and the *Fort Wayne Sentinel*, January 24, 1880. The new science facility may at first have been thought of simply as an added east wing of the Main Building.

24. *Catalogue*, 1884–1885, pp. 53–57, and Schlereth, *University of Notre Dame*, pp. 104–5.

25. Moore, "Academic Development," pp. 72–73.

26. Klimek, *Zahms' Legacy*, p. 8.

27. *Catalogue*, 1881–1882, pp. 5–9; *Catalogue*, 1892–1893, pp. 4–8; and Klimek, *Zahms' Legacy*, p. 6.

28. Klimek, *Zahms' Legacy*, pp. 9–11, and "Dr. A. F. Zahm, As Pioneer in Aeronautics" (unpublished manuscript, University of Notre Dame Hesburgh Library, 1942), pp. 2–5.

29. Klimek, *Zahms' Legacy*, pp. 9–11, and "Dr. A. F. Zahm, As Pioneer in Aeronautics," pp. 6–10.

30. *Scholastic*, Vol. XXIV, No. 2 (September 13, 1890), p. 28, and Vol. XXV, No. 2 (September 12, 1891), p. 33; Schlereth, *University of Notre Dame*, pp. 108–11; and Klimek, *Zahms' Legacy*, p. 14.

31. Moore, *A Century of Law*, pp. 1–11.

32. Thomas A. Lahey, C.S.C., *Colonel Hoynes of Notre Dame* (Notre Dame, IN, 1948), pp. 3–12; Moore, *A Century of Law*, pp. 12–19; *Catalogue*, 1867–1868, p. 34; *Catalogue*, 1868–1869, p. 33; and *Scholastic*, Vol. V, No. 29 (March 30, 1872), p. 4; Vol. VIII, No. 19 (January 30, 1875), p. 266; Vol. IX, No. 31 (April 1, 1876), p. 489; Vol. X, No. 19 (January 13, 1877), pp. 297–98, and No. 31 (April 7, 1877), p. 490; Vol. XV, No. 22 (February 11, 1882), p. 333; and Vol. XVI, No. 4 (September 30, 1882), p. 58.

33. Lahey, *Colonel Hoynes*, pp. 28, 31–36, 38, 43–44, 56, and 72–74, and Moore, *A Century of Law*, pp. 16–18.

34. Moore, *A Century of Law*, pp. 19–24 and 36–37, and Howard, *Brief History*, pp. 122–27. The following quotation is from Howard, *Brief History*, pp. 124–25.

35. Moore, *A Century of Law*, p. 27.

36. Moore, *A Century of Law*, p. 29.

37. Weber, *Notre Dame's John Zahm*, pp. 34–35. A more complete discussion is in Ralph E. Weber's doctoral dissertation, "The Life of Reverend John A. Zahm, C.S.C., American Catholic Apologist and Educator" (University of Notre Dame, 1956), pp. 86–87. See also *Scholastic*, Vol. XXI, No. 26 (March 17, 1888), p. 413, No. 36 (May 26, 1888), p. 510, and No. 37 (June 2, 1888), p. 592.

38. Schlereth, *University of Notre Dame*, pp. 112–15; Hope, *Notre Dame*, pp. 219–21; and Howard, *Brief History*, p. 182. The quotation is from Howard, *Brief History*, p. 125.

39. Quoted in Howard, *Brief History*, p. 125.

40. Schlereth, *University of Notre Dame*, pp. 88–92; Hope, *Notre Dame*, pp. 196 and 221; and Howard, *Brief History*, p. 178.

41. Schlereth, *University of Notre Dame*, pp. 39 and 44; Schlereth, *A Spire of Faith*, pp. 16–20 and 26; *Scholastic*, Vol. XVII, No. 27 (March 15, 1884), p. 428; Vol. XIX, No. 14 (December 12, 1885), p. 227, and No. 28 (March 27, 1886), p. 453; Vol. XX, No. 39 (June 11, 1887), p. 641; Vol. XXI, No. 35 (May 19, 1888), p. 552; Vol. XXII, No. 1 (August 25, 1888), pp. 11–12; and Vol. XXVI, No. 8 (October 29, 1892), p. 125; and Hope, *Notre Dame*, pp. 216–18.

42. See pages 114–18 of the preceding chapter; see also Schlereth, *University of Notre Dame*, p. 58, and *Scholastic*, Vol. XVII, No. 30 (April 5, 1884), p. 472.

43. Schlereth, *A Dome of Learning*, pp. 12 and 25; *Scholastic*, Vol. XII, No. 42 (June 28, 1879), p. 659, and Vol. XIV, No. 1 (August 14, 1880), p. 10; Sorin to Father Pietrobattista, August 18, 1879, CSCG, 1879 August (VIII), UNDA; Creek, *A Panorama*, p. 38; and Costin, *Priceless Spirit*, pp. 214–15.

44. *Scholastic*, Vol. XVI, No. 7 (October 21, 1882), p. 109, No. 12 (November 25, 1882), p. 184, No. 35 (May 12, 1883), p. 556, and No. 38 (June 2, 1883), p. 603; Vol. XVII, No. 2 (September 15, 1883), p. 28, No. 6 (October 13, 1883), p. 88, No. 8 (October 27, 1883), p. 122, and No. 33 (April 26, 1884), p. 525.

45. *Scholastic*, Vol. XIX, No. 11 (November 26, 1885), p. 182; Schlereth, *A Dome of Learning*, p. 25; and O'Connell, *Sorin*, p. 658.

46. Schlereth, *University of Notre Dame*, p. 242, and Schlereth, *A Dome of Learning*, pp. 30 and 41.

47. Schlereth, *University of Notre Dame*, pp. 242–43, and Schlereth, *A Dome of Learning*, pp. 30–31 and 41.

48. Hope, *Notre Dame*, pp. 227–28; Weber, *Notre Dame's John Zahm*, pp. 18 and 34; and *Scholastic*, Vol. XV, No. 8 (October 29, 1881), p. 112; Vol. XIX, No. 1 (August 25, 1885), p. 10, No. 2 (September 19, 1885), p. 28, No. 17 (January 9, 1886), pp. 272–73, No. 21 (February 6, 1886), p. 337; and Vol. XX, No. 28 (March 26, 1887), pp. 460–61. Despite all the construction of the 1880s—Washington Hall, Saint Edward's Hall, the Science Hall, the Institute of Technology, the completion of the Main Building and Sacred Heart Church, and the electrification of the campus—the university's finances remained satisfactory and its indebtedness dropped from $139,000 in 1880 (with losses from the fire) to $17,420 in 1893. Annual Financial Statement Book, 1880–1905, ULDG, B13, F5, UNDA.

49. Thomas J. Schlereth, "A Place, Its Plantsmen, and Its Plants," in Barbara J. Hellenthal, Thomas J. Schlereth, and Robert P. McIntosh, *Trees, Shrubs, and Vines on the University of Notre Dame Campus* (Notre Dame, IN, 1993), pp. 25–33; and *Scholastic*, Vol. I, No. 31 (April 4, 1867), p. 2; Vol. III, No. 16 (April 16, 1870), p. 126; and Vol. XIX, No. 29 (March 13, 1886), pp. 420 and 468.

50. Schlereth, "A Place, Its Plantsmen, and Its Plants," in Hellenthal, Schlereth, and McIntosh, *Trees, Shrubs, and Vines*, pp. 33–34; Beirne, *Sea to Shining Sea*, pp. 201–2; and Local Council Minutes, 1970-15, B2, F6, USPA, April 29 and December 23, 1892.

51. Tambola, "James F. Edwards," pp. 39–40; Blantz, "The Founding," pp. 1, 7–10; Krieger, "Notre Dame Library Collections," pp. 4–20.

52. Descriptions of the various collections in the University of Notre Dame Archives can be found on the archives website: http://www.archives.nd.edu/findaids/ead. See also Thomas T. McAvoy, C.S.C., "Manuscript Collections Among American Catholics," *Catholic Historical Review* XXXVII (October 1951), pp. 281–95.

53. "Origin of the Laetare Medal," *Scholastic*, Vol. XXXI, No. 25 (March 26, 1898), pp. 425–27. The quotation in from pages 426 and 427. See also Tambola, "James F. Edwards," pp. 69–71; Howard, *Brief History*, pp. 192–94; and Hope, *Notre Dame*, pp. 232–34.

54. Howard, *Brief History*, pp. 193–94. For brief biographies of these recipients, see, for Shea, Garraty and Carnes, *American National Biography*, vol. 19 (New York, 1999), pp. 761–62; for Starr, *Catholic Encyclopedia*, vol. XIV (New York, 1912), p. 250; and for Onaham, *New Catholic Encyclopedia*, 2nd ed., vol. 10 (Washington, DC, 2003), pp. 599–600.

55. Howard, *Brief History*, pp. 207–8, and Hope, *Notre Dame*, p. 235.

56. *Scholastic*, Vol. XXI, No. 37 (June 2, 1888), pp. 593–95; O'Connell, *Sorin*, pp. 700–701; Howard, *Brief History*, pp. 208–11; and Hope, *Notre Dame*, pp. 235–36.

57. *Scholastic*, Vol. XXI, No. 37 (June 2, 1888), pp. 595–98; O'Connell, *Sorin*, pp. 701–2; Howard, *Brief History*, p. 211; and Hope, *Notre Dame*, p. 236.

58. *Scholastic*, Vol. XXII, No. 1 (August 25, 1888), pp. 8–11; Howard, *Brief History*, pp. 211–15; Hope, *Notre Dame*, pp. 236–37; and O'Connell, *Sorin*, pp. 702–4.

59. For the quotations, see Sorin, *Circular Letters*, vol. II, pp. 64 and 120–21. Hope, *Notre Dame*, p. 238, refers to "the consecration of the new Church of Our Lady of the Sacred Heart."

60. *Scholastic,* Vol. XXII, No. 1 (August 25, 1888), pp. 2–12; *South Bend Daily Times,* August 16, 1888; *Chicago Tribune,* August 16, 1888; Howard, *Brief History,* pp. 215–36; Hope, *Notre Dame,* p. 238; and O'Connell, *Sorin,* pp. 703–7.

61. *Scholastic,* Vol. XXII, No. 1 (August 25, 1888), pp. 12–15; O'Connell, *Sorin,* pp. 707–8; Hope, *Notre Dame,* p. 239; Patrick Ahern, *The Life of John J. Keane* (Milwaukee, 1955), p. 87; and John Tracy Ellis, *The Formative Years of the Catholic University of America* (Washington, DC, 1946), p. 304. The pallium is a white woolen band with pendants worn by the pope and archbishops as a symbol of full episcopal authority. See also Sorin, *Circular Letters,* vol. II, p. 71.

62. *Scholastic,* Vol. XXVII, No. 1 (July 29, 1893), pp. 1–2, and Vol. XXVIII, No. 1 (August 18, 1894) pp. 1–3; and Hope, *Notre Dame,* pp. 250–51.

63. *Scholastic,* Vol. XXVII, No. 1 (July 29, 1893), pp. 2–8.

64. *Scholastic,* Vol. XXVII, No. 1 (July 29, 1893), pp. 10–11. Letters Father Granger received are preserved in the Father Granger Papers, boxes 1 and 2, USPA.

65. Sorin, *Circular Letters,* vol. II, pp. 84, 90, and 92; *Scholastic,* Vol. XXIV, No. 1 (August 21, 1890), p. 11, and Vol. XXVII, No. 9 (November 11, 1893), pp. 129–31; O'Connell, *Sorin,* pp. 713–15; and Hope, *Notre Dame,* p. 255.

66. CSOR (Sorin Papers), B5, F14, Burial Instructions, UNDA.

67. *Scholastic,* Vol. XXVII, No. 9 (November 11, 1893), pp. 132–41; O'Connell, *Sorin,* p. 716; and Hope, *Notre Dame,* pp. 256–57.

68. Albert Zahm was still featured in the eighth edition of *American Men of Science,* edited by Jacques Cattell, in 1949 (Lancaster, PA: Science Press), page 2797, and the other three in John A Garraty and Mark C. Carnes, eds., *American National Biography* (New York, 1999).

69. Oral History Interview by the author, July 2 and 29, 1969, and March 18, 1970 (p. 10), Holy Cross House, UNDA.

70. Dedication page, *Sound and Music* (Chicago, 1892). See also O'Connell, *Sorin,* p. 713, and Weber, "Life of Reverend John A. Zahm," pp. 101–3.

Chapter 7.   The 1890s

1. Weber, *Notre Dame's John Zahm,* pp. 1–52, and Burrell, *When Faith and Reason Meet,* pp. xxii–liv.

2. Joseph Kehoe, C.S.C., "The Legacy of Father Andrew Morrissey, C.S.C." (paper delivered at the Sixth Annual Holy Cross History Conference, 1987), pp. 5–6, a copy in the University of Notre Dame Library; Hope, *Notre Dame,* pp. 252–53; Klawitter, *Adapted,* p. 363; and *Scholastic,* Vol. XVI, No. 1 (August 5, 1882), p. 10, and Vol. XX, No. 3 (September 18, 1886), p. 48.

3. James Burns Diary, the James Burns Papers, 1991/27, USPA, February 18 and March 3, 1896.

4. Hope, *Notre Dame,* pp. 257–62; Kehoe, "Legacy of Father Andrew Morrissey," pp. 1–6; Weber, *Notre Dame's John Zahm,* pp. 134–38; and *Scholastic,* Vol. XXVII, No. 1 (July 29, 1893), p. 10.

5. All standard textbooks describe the Depression of 1893, and a more detailed discussion can be found in Harold U. Faulkner, *Politics, Reform and Expansion, 1890–1900* (New York, 1959), pp. 141–62, and David O. Whitten, "The Depression of 1893," EH.Net Encyclopedia, ed. Robert Whaples, August 14, 2001, https://eh.net/encyclopedia/the-depression-of-1893. See also Annual Financial Statement Book, ULDG, B13, F5, UNDA.

6. Kehoe, "Legacy of Father Andrew Morrissey," pp. 7–9; Hope, *Notre Dame*, p. 257; and Weber, *Notre Dame's John Zahm*, pp. 134–37.

7. Weber, *Notre Dame's John Zahm*, pp. 138 and 192–93.

8. Other significant works by Zahm were *Sound and Music* (1892), *The Bible, Science, and Faith* (1894), *Up the Orinoco and Down the Magdalena* (1910), *Along the Andes and Down the Amazon* (1911), and *Women in Science* (1913). For *Evolution and Dogma*, see Burrell, *When Faith and Reason Meet*, pp. 15–35, and Weber, *Notre Dame's John Zahm*, pp. 75–87.

9. Weber, *Notre Dame's John Zahm*, pp. 95–96 and 141–45, and Rev. James Doll, C.S.C., "The History of Graduate Training for Holy Cross Priests," *Educational Conference Bulletin of the Priests of Holy Cross* XXV (December 1957), pp. 24–42. Because of his important contributions, Father Zahm might even be counted among the founders of Notre Dame as a true university.

10. Local Council Minutes, B2, F6, December 27, 1895, and F7, December 21, 1900, USPA, and Annual University Financial Statement Summary Book, 1880/1881–1898/1905, ULDG 13/5, UNDA. The figures from the local council minutes also include the Holy Cross seminaries, novitiates, Saint Joseph's Farm, etc., but the university was clearly the largest source of both income and expenses.

11. *Scholastic*, Vol. XXVIII, No. 33 (May 18, 1895), p. 541, and Schlereth, *University of Notre Dame*, p. 233.

12. *Scholastic*, Vol. XXIII, No. 33 (May 18, 1895), p. 541; Vol. XXVIII, No. 33 (May 18, 1895), p. 9; Vol. XXXII, No. 3 (June 14, 1899), p. 9; Vol. XXXIII, No. 1 (August 1899), p. 12; Local Council Minutes, B2, F6, May 17, 1895, USPA; Faculty Council Minutes, UFMM, October 9, 1894, and October 24, 1900, UNDA; and Hope, *Notre Dame*, pp. 263–64.

13. Local Council Minutes, B2, F6, January 8 and 22, 1897, USPA; *Scholastic*, Vol. XXX, No. 28 (April 24, 1897), p. 472; and Hope, *Notre Dame*, pp. 257–58.

14. "The New St. Joseph's Hall," *Scholastic*, Vol. XXXI, No. 12 (November 27, 1897), pp. 196–97; see also Vol. XXX, No. 28 (April 24, 1897), p. 472, and No. 32 (May 22, 1897), p. 535; and Vol. XXXIII, No. 3 (September 23, 1899), p. 6; Schlereth, *University of Notre Dame*, pp. 138–39; and Hope, *Notre Dame*, pp. 264–65.

15. O'Connell, *Sorin*, p. 618; Schlereth, *University of Notre Dame*, p. 54; and Dorothy Corson, *A Cave of Candles* (Nappanee, IN, 2000), p. 13. Ms. Corson's extraordinarily well researched book is a must read for anyone seriously investigating the Notre Dame Grotto.

16. *Scholastic*, Vol. VIII, No. 14 (December 26, 1874), p. 189, and *Class Day Book of 1880*, PNDP 100-1880, pp. 80–81, UNDA.

17. Costin, *Priceless Spirit*, p. 211, and Corson, *A Cave of Candles*, p. 14.

18. *The Columbian Jubilee*, vol. II (Chicago, IL, 1892), p. 493, PNDP, 101-1890, UNDA; Corson, *A Cave of Candles*, p. 24; and *Scholastic*, Vol. XI, No. 4 (September 22, 1877), p. 59, No. 5 (September 29, 1877), p. 75, No. 32 (April 6, 1878), p. 506; and Vol. XX, No. 1 (August 14, 1886), p. 15.

19. The *Annals of Our Lady of Lourdes* XII, no. 6 (June 1896), p. 92.

20. Corson's website is http://www.nd.edu/~wcawley/corson.htm.

21. Costin, *Priceless Spirit*, pp. 229–30, and Creek, *A Panorama*, p. 41.

22. Corby to Edwards, October 2, 1894, CEDW XI-I-L, UNDA. See also Corson's website, http://www.nd.edu/~wcawley/corson.htm; Creek, *A Panorama*, p. 41; and Costin, *Priceless Spirit*, pp. 229–30. Apparently the 105 sisters ministering at Notre Dame had received an annual salary of $6,500 since 1890 (Costin, *Priceless Spirit*, p. 230).

23. Ledochowski to Français, April 23, 1895, Mother Augusta Papers, E4.9, K-I-4, Holy Cross Sisters Archives, Saint Mary's, Indiana, and Costin, *Priceless Spirit*, pp. 229–30.

24. *Scholastic*, Vol. XXXII, No. 2 (September 17, 1898), pp. 47–48; Vol. XCI, No. 25 (May 12, 1950), pp. 12–13; and Hope, *Notre Dame*, p. 264. See also page 111 in chapter 5.

25. *Scholastic*, Vol. XXX, No. 1 (August 20, 1896), pp. 14–16, No. 3 (September 26, 1896), p. 47, No. 6 (October 17, 1896), p. 93; Vol. XXXI, No. 15 (January 15, 1898), p. 239, No. 33 (May 28, 1898), p. 570; Vol. XXXII, No. 2 (September 17, 1898), pp. 47–48; Vol. XCI, No. 25 (May 12, 1950), pp. 12–13; Schlereth, *University of Notre Dame*, pp. 54–55; Corson, *A Cave of Candles*, pp. 71–86; and Corson's website, http://www.nd.edu/~wcawley/corson.htm.

26. Pilkinton, *Washington Hall*, pp. 43–44 and 73–74, and *Scholastic*, Vol. XV, No. 37 (May 27, 1882), p. 575; Vol. XVI, No. 2 (September 16, 1882), p. 28; Vol. XVII, No. 13 (December 1, 1883), p. 204, and No. 17 (January 5, 1884), p. 265; and Local Council Minutes, B2, F6, HCPA, February 25, 1899.

27. *Scholastic*, Vol. XXXI, No. 25 (March 26, 1898), p. 434; Vol. XXXII, No. 1 (August 1898), p. 34, and No. 22 (March 4, 1899), pp. 391–92. The quotation is from *Scholastic*, Vol. XXXIII, No. 1 (August 1899), p. 10.

28. *South Bend Daily Times*, November 9, 1900; *Scholastic*, Vol. XXXIV, No. 12 (November 24, 1900), p. 199, No. 16 (January 19, 1901), pp. 278 and 280, No. 19 (February 9, 1901), p. 330; and John Cackley, "Irish Gymnasium Dedicated in 1898 Swept by Flames and Destroyed in 1900," *Scholastic*, Vol. LXIX, No. 10 (December 6, 1935), pp. 17 and 22.

29. Moore, "Academic Development," p. 6.

30. Moore, "Academic Development," pp. 19–21.

31. See Moore, "Academic Development," p. 97; Hope, *Notre Dame*, p. 67; Temple, *O'Hara's Heirs*, p. 5; *Catalogue*, 1892–1893, pp. 110–11; *Catalogue*, 1903–1904, pp. 199–201; *Catalogue*, 1904–1905, pp. 203–4; and Kehoe, "Legacy of Father Andrew Morrissey," pp. 7–10.

32. *Catalogue*, 1899–1900, pp. 192–94; *Catalogue*, 1901–1902, pp. 194–96; *Catalogue*, 1903–1904, pp. 199–201; *Catalogue*, 1904–1905, pp. 203–4; Moore, "Academic Development," pp. 46–49; and Rev. Joseph L. Walter, C.S.C., *History of Premedical Stud-*

ies at Notre Dame (privately printed at the University of Notre Dame), chap. 1 (pages are not numbered). The name "General Science Course" was used for only a few years. The name was changed to the "School of Science" in the early 1900s, and eventually to the "College of Science."

33. Moore, "Academic Development," pp. 72–74, and Klimek, *Zahms' Legacy*, pp. 13–16.

34. Hope, *Notre Dame*, pp. 258–60, and Klimek, *Zahms' Legacy*, pp. 17–21. The quotations are from Klimek, pp. 17–19.

35. John W. Stamper, "Between Two Centuries: A History of the School, 1898–1998," in *100 Years of Architecture at Notre Dame*, ed. Jane A. Devine (Notre Dame, IN, 1999), pp. 6–8; Klimek, *Zahms' Legacy*, pp. 19–20; and Moore, "Academic Development," pp. 79–81.

36. Hope, *Notre Dame*, p. 270, and *Scholastic*, Vol. XXXII, No. 35 (June 10, 1899), p. 610, and Vol. XXXIII, No. 1 (August, 1899), pp. 6–7.

37. Moore, "Academic Development," pp. 118–21, and Moore, *A Century of Law*, pp. 25–26 and 35–37.

38. *Scholastic*, Vol. XXVII, No. 3 (September 23, 1893), pp. 43–44; Vol. XXX, No. 2 (September 19, 1896), p. 26; Vol. XXXI, No. 11 (November 20, 1897), p. 178; Vol. XXXII, No. 31 (May 13, 1899), p. 542; Vol. XXXIV, No. 13 (December 1, 1900), p. 215; Vol. XXXV, No. 15 (January 11, 1902), p. 242; Vol. XXXVII, No. 16 (January 23, 1904), pp. 276–77; Vol. XXXVIII, No. 4 (October 8, 1904), pp. 64–65, No. 5 (October 15, 1904), pp. 69–74, No. 6 (October 22, 1904), pp. 86–91, No. 7 (October 29, 1904), pp. 101–7, No. 22 (March 11, 1905), p. 360; and Hope, *Notre Dame*, pp. 273–74.

39. For Professor Green, see pages 160–61 in this chapter. For Dr. O'Malley, see *Scholastic*, Vol. XXIX, No. 29 (April 25, 1896), p. 482; James J. Walsh, MD, PhD, "Dr. Austin O'Malley," *The Catholic World* CXXXV, no. 806 (May 1932), pp. 157–65; and *The Guide to Catholic Literature, 1888–1940* (Detroit, 1940), p. 875.

40. A. Scott Berg, *Wilson* (New York, 2013), p. 114.

41. An excellent and thorough discussion of this controversy is in Robert E. Burns, *Being Catholic, Being American*, vol. 1, *The Notre Dame Story, 1842–1934* (Notre Dame, IN, 1999), pp. 41–66. See also Charles Veneziani, *A Plea for the Higher Education of Catholic Young Men of America: With an Exposure of the Frauds of the University of Notre Dame, Ind* (Chicago, IL, 1900), pp. 11–22 and 30.

42. Burns, *Being Catholic, Being American*, vol. 1, pp. 43–46, and Veneziani, *A Plea*, pp. 14–17.

43. Weber, *Notre Dame's John Zahm*, pp. 129–32, and Etienne and Tony Catta, *Basil Anthony Mary Moreau*, vol. 2, pp. 1042–44.

44. Veneziani, *A Plea*, pp. 22 and 83–88.

45. Morrissey to Zahm, March 22, 1900, and related materials, in UBVP 63/16, reel 3, envelope 176, UNDA. See also Veneziani's A.M.D.G., in PNPD 100-1912, Charles Veneziani, An Appeal, UNDA.

46. Veneziani, *A Plea*, pp. 26–56.

47. Charles Veneziani, *Frauds of the University of Notre Dame* (Chicago, 1901). A copy of this publication is in the possession of the author.

48. Burns, *Being Catholic, Being American*, vol. 1, pp. 50–60.

49. Veneziani, *A Plea*, p. 20.

50. *Scholastic*, Vol. V, No. 35 (May 11, 1872), p. 4; Kehoe, "Legacy of Father Andrew Morrissey," pp. 7 and 9; Faculty Council Minutes, UFMM, B2, February 5, 1880, and March 24, 1886, UNDA. The manual labor students are probably not included in these figures.

51. *Catalogue*, 1893–1894, pp. 17 and 61, and Hope, *Notre Dame*, p. 193.

52. *Catalogue*, 1893–1894, pp. 17–18 and 66, and Hope, *Notre Dame*, p. 229.

53. *Catalogue*, 1893–1894, p. 16.

54. Hope, *Notre Dame*, p. 275.

55. *Catalogue*, 1893–1894, pp. 62–63 and 66.

56. Schlereth, *University of Notre Dame*, pp. 88–89 and 97.

57. Hope, *Notre Dame*, pp. 149, 244–45, and 302–3; Schlereth, *University of Notre Dame*, pp. 31–91 and 136–37; Cappy Gagnon, *Notre Dame Baseball Greats* (Chicago, 2004), pp. 9–15; Hon. James O'Brien, "Notre Dame Fifty Years Ago and Today," *Scholastic*, Vol. XLI, No. 36 (Alumni Number, 1908), p. 2; and *Scholastic*, Vol. II, No. 19 (January 16, 1869), p. 149. Before they were called the "Cubs," the Chicago baseball team was known as the "White Stockings" and the "Colts." The quotation is from Gagnon, *Notre Dame Baseball Greats*, p. 13.

58. *Scholastic*, Vol. XXI, No. 8 (October 29, 1887), p. 125, and No. 12 (November 26, 1887), p. 190; and Hope, *Notre Dame*, pp. 240–42.

59. Hope, *Notre Dame*, pp. 242–44 and 278; *Scholastic*, Vol. XXXI, No. 3 (September 25, 1897), p. 55; Frank Maggio, *Notre Dame and the Game that Changed Football* (New York, 2007), pp. 32–34; and Murray Sperber, *Shake Down the Thunder* (Bloomington, IN, 2002), pp. 11–12.

60. Hope, *Notre Dame*, pp. 278–79; *Catalogue*, 1893–1894, p. 17; and *Bulletin* (formerly called *Catalogue*), 1904–1905, p. 25. See also Faculty Council Minutes, UFMM, October 27, 1898, UNDA.

61. *Scholastic*, Vol. XXIII, No. 7 (October 19, 1889), p. 109; Vol. XXIV, No. 1 (August 21, 1890), p. 13, and No. 4 (September 27, 1890), pp. 61–62; and Vol. LVI, No. 9 (November 25, 1922), p. 275; and Hope, *Notre Dame*, p. 248.

62. *Catalogue*, 1866–1867, p. 21.

63. Hope, *Notre Dame*, pp. 245–46, and *Scholastic*, Vol. XXI, No. 41 (June 30, 1888), pp. 663–64.

64. *Catalogue*, 1893–1894, pp. 12–13.

65. See chapter 4, pp. 80–81, and Schmidt, *Notre Dame*, pp. 19–22.

66. *Scholastic*, Vol. II, No. 18 (January 9, 1869), pp. 143–44; Vol. XVIII, No. 24 (February 21, 1885), p. 385; Vol. XIX, No. 8 (October 31, 1885), p. 133, No. 11 (November 21, 1885), p. 180, No. 21 (February 6, 1886), p. 340, and No. 29 (April 3, 1886), p. 469; Hope, *Notre Dame*, pp. 197 and 207; and Philip Mauro, "Early Military Training

at Notre Dame: As Seen Through Student Publications" (senior seminar paper, University of Notre Dame, 2007), in possession of the author.

67. Hope, *Notre Dame*, pp. 147–48, 153–54, and 165.

68. This position is stated most clearly by Kehoe, "Legacy of Father Andrew Morrissey," pp. 6–10. See also *Catalogue*, 1895–1896, pp. 22 and 72–74.

Chapter 8.   The First Father John Cavanaugh

1. After Father Corby's death in December 1879, Father Français appointed Father Zahm as his successor in January 1898, and the general chapter later that year elected him to a full term. However, over time his personality alienated many, the brothers felt neglected under his administration, and he was replaced by Father Morrissey at the general chapter of 1906; Weber, *Notre Dame's John Zahm*, pp. 129–70.

2. The building was probably still called Saint Aloysius Seminary at that time, and the name was changed to Holy Cross Seminary in 1889. See J. W. Cavanaugh, "A Sketch of St. Aloysius Seminary, Notre Dame, Ind," *Scholastic*, Vol. XXII, No. 37 (May 18, 1889), pp. 606–7.

3. The best study of Father Cavanaugh's life is a manuscript of Father Arthur Hope, C.S.C., "Life of John W. Cavanaugh, C.S.C.," a copy of which is in both the Notre Dame Archives and the Holy Cross Provincial Archives. See especially pages 1–5. See also Edward B. Kunkle, "Father John W. Cavanaugh" (unpublished student essay, University of Notre Dame Hesburgh Library, 1941), pp. 1–3; Richard Sullivan, *Notre Dame: Reminiscences of an Era* (Notre Dame, IN, 1961), pp. 170–82; and Schlereth, *University of Notre Dame*, pp. 18–20.

4. Hope, "Life of John W. Cavanaugh," pp. 7–47. The following quotation is from *Scholastic*, Vol. XXII, No. 12 (November 10, 1888), p. 189.

5. Hope, "Life of John W. Cavanaugh," p. 47; Diary of James Burns, C.S.C., March 24, 1895, March 6, 1896, and December 31, 1897, A.N. 1991/27, USPA; *Catalogue*, 1894–1895, p. 6; and *Catalogue*, 1895–1896, p. 6. For some reason, the patron of the church in Leetonia was changed from Saint Barbara to Saint Patrick between 1883 and 1884. See the *Official Catholic Directory* for those two years.

6. Rev. John W. Cavanaugh, C.S.C., *Daniel E. Hudson, C.S.C., A Memoir* (Notre Dame, IN, 1934), pp. 5–22.

7. Weber, *Notre Dame's John Zahm*, pp. 106–21. Father Cavanaugh had been named to replace Father Linneborn in the summer of 1898 but, since Fr. Linneborn did not leave for Rome until several months later, Father Cavanaugh did not assume his new position until January 1899. Father Arthur Hope, C.S.C., "Oral History Interview," p. 11, UNDA.

8. Hope, "Life of John W. Cavanaugh," pp. 78–102, and "Changes at Notre Dame," *Scholastic*, Vol. XXXIX, No. 1 (Midsummer, 1905), pp. 10–11. See also letters to Cavanaugh from Ernest Davis (July 2, 1908), Stephen Gavin (September 19, 1907), James Gallagher (November 14, 1909), James Donahue (December 8, 1909), and George Finnigan (August 8, 1913) in the John W. Cavanaugh Papers, CJWC, UNDA.

9. "Changes at Notre Dame," *Scholastic*, Vol. XXXIX, No. 1 (Midsummer, 1905), pp. 10–11.

10. Moore, "Academic Development," p. 12.

11. Hope, "Life of John W. Cavanaugh," p. 121.

12. "A Plea for the Classics," Father John W. Cavanaugh, C.S.C., Papers, CJWC 11/61 folder B1, UNDA.

13. Armstrong, *Onward to Victory*, p. 117.

14. Hope, "Oral History Interview," p. 11, UNDA.

15. Moore, "Academic Development," p. 12.

16. *Scholastic*, Vol. XXXIX, No. 13 (December 22, 1905), p. 225.

17. *Scholastic*, Vol. XXXIX, No. 13 (December 22, 1905), p. 225.

18. *Scholastic*, Vol. XLII, No. 4 (October 2, 1909), p. 49. See also Sister M. Ruberta Callahan, C.S.C., "The Educational Contributions of Reverend John William Cavanaugh, C.S.C." (MA thesis, University of Notre Dame, 1942).

19. "Education and Character," *Scholastic*, Vol. XLI, No. 3 (September 28, 1907), pp. 33–34.

20. The first quotation is from *Scholastic*, Vol. XLI, No. 3 (September 28, 1907), p. 34, and the following is from *Scholastic*, Vol. XLIII, No. 4 (October 2, 1909), p. 50.

21. "A Plea for the Classics," CJWC 11/61 folder B1, UNDA.

22. "Witness to Christ," *Scholastic*, Vol. XLIII, No. 29 (April 30, 1910), p. 467.

23. *Scholastic*, Vol. XLI, No. 3 (September 28, 1907), pp. 34–35.

24. "The Conquest of Life," *Scholastic*, Vol. XL, No. 3 (September 29, 1906), p. 36.

25. "A Day of Visitation," *Scholastic*, Vol. XLII, No. 2 (September 26, 1908), pp. 35–36.

26. *Scholastic*, Vol. XXXIX, No. 24 (March 31, 1906), pp. 397–401; Schlereth, *University of Notre Dame*, p. 13; and Hope, *Notre Dame*, p. 284.

27. *Scholastic*, Vol. XXXIX, No. 29 (May 12, 1906), pp. 482–93; Schlereth, *University of Notre Dame*, p. 124; Hope, *Notre Dame*, pp. 282–83; and Armstrong, *Onward to Victory*, pp. 118–19. The address is printed in *Scholastic*, Vol. XXXIX, No. 29 (May 12, 1906), pp. 489–91.

28. *Scholastic*, Vol. XXXIX, No. 29 (May 12, 1906), pp. 491–93; Schlereth, *University of Notre Dame*, p. 10; and Hope, "Life of John W. Cavanaugh," pp. 125–29.

29. *Scholastic*, Vol. XXXIX, No. 13 (December 22, 1905), p. 226.

30. Cavanaugh to Burns, October 3, 1908, UPWC, 106/05; Cavanaugh to Moloney, September 19, 1910, UPWC, 206/106, and various others between them in that folder, UNDA; *Bulletin*, 1911–1912, pp. 226–49; and *Bulletin*, 1916–1917, pp. 255–86.

31. *Scholastic*, Vol. XXXIX, No. 13 (December 22, 1905), p. 225.

32. Hope, "Life of John W. Cavanaugh," p. 248, and Minutes of the Provincial Council, 1906–1927, USPA, October 27, 1907, and October 7, 1908.

33. *Scholastic*, Vol. XLII, No. 27 (April 17, 1909), pp. 476–77, No. 31 (May 15, 1909), p. 540, No. 32 (May 22, 1909), p. 559; Vol. XLIII, No. 1 (Midsummer, 1909), p. 12, and No. 9 (November 6, 1909), pp. 140–41; Cavanaugh to Burns, October 3, 1908,

UPWC 106/05, and Cavanaugh to Rev. John Boland, April 22, 1909, UPWC, 1960–1909, A-CO, Boland, UNDA.

34. Cavanaugh to Mrs. J. P. Birder, August 19, 1909, UPWC, 1906–1910, A-CO, Birder, UNDA.

35. *Scholastic*, Vol. XXXI, No. 12 (November 27, 1897), pp. 196–97, and Vol. LI, No. 4 (October 20, 1917), pp. 58–59; Schlereth, *University of Notre Dame*, pp. 138–39; and Hope, *Notre Dame*, pp. 264–65. A Badin cafeteria menu is printed in Kelly Hanratty, ed., *Badin Hall, 1897–1997*, p. 9 (copy in Special Collections, University of Notre Dame Hesburgh Library, 1997).

36. Hope, *Notre Dame*, pp. 154, 303–5, and 314; Hope, "Life of John W. Cavanaugh," pp. 389–92; Schlereth, *University of Notre Dame*, pp. 100 and 158–60; and Cavanaugh to Burns, February 9, 1916, UPWC, A/Folder Rev. James A. Burns, UNDA.

37. Armstrong, *Onward to Victory*, pp. 30–32, and chapter 5 in this book.

38. Armstrong, *Onward to Victory*, p. 31.

39. Armstrong, *Onward to Victory*, pp. 34–36.

40. *Scholastic*, Vol. XLI, No. 21 (February 15, 1908), p. 349.

41. *Scholastic*, Vol. XLI, No. 36 (Alumni Number, 1908), pp. 19 and 22, No. 18 (February 22, 1908), p. 349; and Cavanaugh to George Anson, March 21, 1907, B134, F19, UPWC, UNDA.

42. *Scholastic*, Vol. XLV, No. 37 (June 1912), p. 601; Vol. XLVI, No. 37 (June 1913), p. 603; and Vol. LII, No. 31 (June 21, 1919), p. 553.

43. Schmidt, *Notre Dame*, pp. 127–28. The quotation is in Mulholland to Brother Leander, December 23, 1907, SGAR, GAR Correspondence, 1897–1931, UNDA.

44. Schmidt, *Notre Dame*, pp. 129–30.

45. *Scholastic*, Vol. XLIV, No. 23 (March 18, 1911), pp. 371–72, No. 34 (June 3, 1911), p. 546, and No. 36 (Commencement, June 1911), pp. 604 and 606.

46. *Scholastic*, Vol. XLIV, No. 34 (June 3, 1911), p. 548, and *South Bend Times*, May 30, 1911, p. 8.

47. *South Bend Times*, May 30, 1911, p. 8.

48. *Scholastic*, Vol. XLIV, No. 34 (June 3, 1911), p. 548, and *South Bend Times*, May 30, 1911, p. 8.

49. *Scholastic*, Vol. XXXI, No. 20 (February 19, 1898), p. 356.

50. *Scholastic*, Vol. XXXI, No. 25 (March 26, 1898), p. 437; Vol. XLVIII, No. 34 (June 3, 1915), pp. 563–65; Hope, *Notre Dame*, p. 267; Hope, "Life of John W. Cavanaugh," p. 368; and Schlereth, *University of Notre Dame*, p. 103.

51. Cavanaugh, *The Priests of Holy Cross*, p. 96.

52. Hope, *Notre Dame*, pp. 356–58, and Todd Tucker, *Notre Dame vs. The Klan* (Chicago, 2004), pp. 1–13. Father Hope used to join Father Walsh at the latter's late breakfasts, listen to the elder priest's recollections and reminiscences, and then return to his room and write them down for the Notre Dame histories he thought he might write. This information came from conversations between the author and Father Hope.

53. Hope, *Notre Dame*, pp. 397–400, and Klawitter, *Poems of Charles O'Donnell*, p. xv.

54. Hope, *Notre Dame*, pp. 286–87; Hope, "Life of John W. Cavanaugh," pp. 275–76; Kenneth E. Filchak, "In Homage to Our Founder: A Brief Biography of Reverend Julius Aloysius Nieuwland, C.S.C.," *American Midland Naturalist* 161, no. 2 (April 2009), pp. 178–88; and Walter, *History of Premedical Studies*, chap. 3.

55. Hope, *Notre Dame*, p. 287, and Joel Vilensky, "Dew of Death," *Washingtonian* (March 2003), pp. 97–99.

56. On a light note, when a member of the Notre Dame community died, the priest-poet Arthur Barry O'Neill would dash off a sonnet in their memory, thus, in the inimitable phrasing of Father Cavanaugh, "adding a new terror to death." Hope, *Notre Dame*, p. 337.

57. For Professor Edwards's life and work, see chapter 5 in this book.

58. Hope, *Notre Dame*, pp. 306–7; *Scholastic*, Vol. L, No. 1 (September 23, 1916), p. 10, and No. 6 (October 28, 1916), pp. 86–87. The quotation is from *Scholastic*, Vol. L, No. 6 (October 28, 1916), p. 87.

59. *Scholastic*, Vol. XLIX, No. 16 (January 15, 1916), p. 258. See also Brosnahan, *On the King's Highway*, p. 366.

60. *Scholastic*, Vol. XLIX, No. 16 (January 15, 1916), pp. 259–60, and Hope, *Notre Dame*, pp. 307–8.

61. *Scholastic*, Vol. XLIX, No. 28 (April 8, 1916), p. 452.

62. Schlereth, *University of Notre Dame*, pp. 108–10 and 157.

63. *Bulletin*, 1908–1909, p. 87.

64. Moore, "Academic Development," pp. 86–87 and Klimek, *Zahms' Legacy*, p. 20.

65. Moore, "Academic Development," pp. 84–85, and Klimek, *Zahms' Legacy*, p. 20. By this time, the Classical or Collegiate Course had been renamed the College of Arts and Letters.

66. Moore, "Academic Development," pp. 53–55.

67. Max Pam to Cavanaugh, June 9, 1912, UPWC, Journalism, Max Pam School of, UNDA. For Pam's lectures on campus, see *Scholastic*, Vol. XLIII, No. 16 (January 22, 1910), p. 260; Vol. XLIV, No. 31 (May 13, 1911), p. 499; and Vol. XLV, No. 37 (Commencement, June 1912), pp. 583–87.

68. Hope, "Life of John W. Cavanaugh," pp. 270–73, and Hope, *Notre Dame*, p. 289.

69. Sayler to Keeley, January 2, 1913, in *Scholastic*, Vol. XLVI, No. 14 (January 11, 1913), p. 222.

70. Moore, "Academic Development," pp. 97–98.

71. Zahm to Cavanaugh, August 14, 1914, CJWC 10/22, Zahm, UNDA.

72. Zahm to Cavanaugh, January 15, 1915, CJWC 10/23, Zahm, UNDA.

73. Schlereth, *University of Notre Dame*, p. 139. Some of these had different titles at that time, and later. For a dispute between Father Paul Foik and Father Michael Quinlan over the selection of the architect for the new library, see Burns, *Being Catholic, Being American*, vol. 1, pp. 86–95.

74. *Scholastic*, Vol. L, No. 35 (Diamond Jubilee Number), pp. 579–82.

75. *Scholastic*, Vol. L, No. 35 (Diamond Jubilee Number), pp. 597–612.

76. *Scholastic*, Vol. L, No. 35 (Diamond Jubilee Number), pp. 625–56.

1. Sorin, *Chronicles*, p. 16.

2. MacManus to Cavanaugh, November 28, 1905, and April 17, 1908, CJWC, B6, F14 and 15, UNDA; *Ave Maria* LXI, no. 26 (December 23, 1905), p. 824; and *Scholastic*, Vol. XLII, No. 4 (October 10, 1908), p. 76.

3. Cavanaugh to Johnson, April 8, 1907, UPWC [from old boxes 160A–160F], UNDA.

4. Johnson to Cavanaugh, April 10, 1907, and Cavanaugh to Johnson, May 8, 1907, UPWC [from old boxes 160A–160F], UNDA.

5. "Ireland—The Old and the New," in *The Hour: Supplement*, Papers of Rev. John W. Cavanaugh, 1987-49, 1/1, USPA.

6. "Spiritual Contributions of the Irishmen to America," CJWC, 11/106, UNDA.

7. Quoted in Hope, "Life of John W. Cavanaugh," p. 321.

8. "The Irishman's Gift to America," CJWC, 11/105, UNDA.

9. *Scholastic*, Vol. LII, No. 9 (December 7, 1918), p. 136.

10. Burns to Cavanaugh, February 12, 1914, CJWC, 1/72 UNDA. Burns mentions that several explanations for the president's actions have been offered but none seem to him fully convincing.

11. Cavanaugh to Roosevelt, September 18, 1916, UPWC, General Correspondence, N–RO, UNDA.

12. Cavanaugh to Marshall, September 18, 1916, UPWC, AC/06/05/1, UNDA.

13. Another reason for this national publicity was the growing success of the university's football team after its upset victory over Army in 1913, and this will be treated in the following chapter. For the distinguished visitors, see *Scholastic*, Vol. XLIII, No. 35 (June 25, 1910), p. 564, No. 4 (October 2, 1909), p. 60; Vol. L, No. 6 (October 28, 1916), p. 9; Vol. XLII, No. 29 (May 1, 1909), p. 509; Vol. XLVII, No. 25 (April 25, 1914), p. 614; Vol. XLVIII, No. 21 (February 27, 1915), p. 349; and Vol. XLVIII, No. 17 (February 6, 1915), p. 298.

14. See chapter 7, pp. 171–72.

15. Cavanaugh to Brother Onesimus, November 20, 1917, UPWC, Gen. Corresp., N–RO, UNDA; Hope, *Notre Dame*, pp. 323–24; Hope, "Life of John W. Cavanaugh," pp. 7–8 (second supplement); and *Scholastic*, Vol. LII, No. 5 (November 7, 1918), pp. 74–75.

16. Gleason, *Contending with Modernity*, pp. 72–75; Hope, *Notre Dame*, pp. 317–18; and Cavanaugh to Raymond Ruffing, November 23, 1917, UPWC, AC/06/05/2, UNDA.

17. *Scholastic*, Vol. LII, No. 1 (October 12, 1918), pp. 8–9; Hope, *Notre Dame*, pp. 332–33; Hope, "Life of John W. Cavanaugh," p. 6 (second supplement); and Cavanaugh to Rev. W. D. O'Brien, October 8, 1918, UPWC, Gen. Corresp., N–RO, UNDA.

18. Cavanaugh to Vincent Mooney, November 22, 1918, UPWC, Gen. Corresp., Mi–My, UNDA. For the SATC at Notre Dame, see also Gleason, *Contending with Modernity*, pp. 75–77.

19. *Scholastic*, Vol. L, No. 27 (April 21, 1917), p. 462; Hope, *Notre Dame*, p. 335; and Gleason, *Contending with Modernity*, pp. 77–80.

20. Cavanaugh to Rev. John Scheier, December 7, 1917, UPWC, Gen. Corresp., R–T, Folder Scheier, UNDA.

21. George J. Waring, *United States Catholic Chaplains in the World War* (New York, 1924), pp. 63, 99, and 186; Hope, *Notre Dame*, pp. 324 and 331; and Davis to Morrissey, May 21 and October 23, 1918, Father Morrissey Administration Papers, 1970-05, 6/10 and 7/3, USPA.

22. Waring, *United States Catholic Chaplains*, pp. 236–37; *Scholastic*, Vol. LXIII, No. 1 (September 21, 1934), p. 10; and Hope, *Notre Dame*, pp. 324 and 331. In the Father Morrissey Administration Papers, 1970/05, USPA, there are about a dozen wartime letters of Father O'Donnell to Father Morrissey (provincial superior), but almost all concern routine matters of his health (which was good), his present location, rumors of his next destination, and how best to send his salary check back to the Congregation in the present uncertain state of the mail service.

23. Waring, *United States Catholic Chaplains*, p. 309; *Scholastic*, Vol. LI, No. 14 (January 26, 1918), pp. 232–33, and No. 18 (February 23, 1918), p. 306; Tucker, *Notre Dame vs. The Klan*, pp. 61–72; Hope, *Notre Dame*, pp. 324–31; and letters of Walsh to Morrissey in Father Morrissey Administration Papers, 1970/05, USPA. The quotation is from a letter of January 31, 1918, in 6/8. Another chaplain, serving on the Holy Cross Mission Band rather than on the university faculty, was Father George Finnigan, later bishop of Helena, Montana: *Province Review* L, no. 5 (December 2002), p. 2.

24. Davis to Morrissey, October 23, 1918, and McGinn to Morrissey, February 4, 1919, Father Morrissey Administration Papers, 1970/05, 7/3 and 7/5, USPA; Cavanaugh to Zahm, October 26, 1918, UPWC, Gen. Corresp., T–Z, Folder Zahm, and Cavanaugh to Marin-Sola, August 26, 1919, UPWC, 1916-1010, Marin, Rev. Francisco, O.P., UNDA; Hope, *Notre Dame*, p. 333; and *Scholastic*, Vol. LII, No. 3 (October 26, 1918), pp. 41–42.

25. See pages 96–97 in chapter 5 of this book.

26. *South Bend Tribune*, July 13, 1917, and Moore, "Academic Development," pp. 59–61.

27. Schumacher to Cavanaugh, June 20, 1918, UPWC, Gen. Corresp., R–T, Schumacher, UNDA; Cavanaugh to Sisters of Mercy, Saginaw, Michigan, April 25, 1917, quoted in Hope, "Life of John W. Cavanaugh," p. 22 (first supplement); and *Bulletin*, 1917–1918, pp. 78, 87, and 215–19.

28. Cavanaugh to Schumacher, August 19, 1918, UPWC, Gen. Corresp., R–T, Schumacher, UNDA.

29. Schlereth, *University of Notre Dame*, pp. 150–54.

30. Moore, "Academic Development," pp. 61–62; *Bulletin*, 1917–1918, pp. 79, 88–89, and 147–58; and Schlereth, *University of Notre Dame*, p. 152.

31. *Scholastic*, Vol. LI, No. 25 (April 20, 1918), pp. 425–26; Vol. LII, No. 2 (October 12, 1918), pp. 22–23, and No. 7 (November 16, 1918), pp. 103–4. The quotation is from the October 12, 1918, issue of *Scholastic*. Bishop Thomas Lillis of Kansas City to Cavanaugh, May 3, 1918; Bishop Henry Althoff of Belleville to Cavanaugh, May 3, 1918; and Cavanaugh to Mother Superior, December 24, 1918, UPWC, 41/44, Summer School, 1918–1919, UNDA; Cavanaugh to Zahm, July 14, 1918, UPWC, Gen. Corresp., T–Z,

Zahm Folder, UNDA; *Bulletin*, Summer Session, January 1918, pp. 8–13; and Hope, *Notre Dame*, p. 291.

32. For a brief summary of the 1918 Code of Canon Law, see the *New Catholic Encyclopedia*, 2nd ed., vol. 3 (Washington, DC, 2003), p. 55.

33. The earlier quotation is from Cavanaugh to Zahm, February 8, 1919, UPWC, Gen. Corresp., T–Z, Zahm Folder, and the following one from Cavanaugh to J. Hugh O'Donnell, April 15, 1919, UPWC, Gen. Corresp., N–RO, UNDA.

34. Cavanaugh to J. Hugh O'Donnell, July 8, 1919, UPWC, Gen. Corresp., N–RO, UNDA.

35. Anna Rose Kearney, "James A. Burns, C.S.C., Educator" (PhD diss., University of Notre Dame, 1975), pp. 108–13, and David Joseph Arthur, "The University of Notre Dame, 1919–1933: An Administrative History" (PhD diss., University of Michigan, 1973), pp. 84–99.

36. Hope, *Notre Dame*, pp. 341–44, and Kearney, "James A. Burns," pp. 1–25.

37. Rather than expanding to eight years of grammar school, some parishes established junior high schools to keep the students within the parish even longer. Kearney, "James A. Burns," p. 95.

38. See the excellent study by Kearney, "James A. Burns," pp. 59–109.

39. Father Burns Diary, James Burns Personal Papers, A.N. 1991/27, February 18, 1896, USPA.

40. Father Burns Diary, A.N. 1991/27, March 6, 1896, USPA.

41. Thomas T. McAvoy, "Notre Dame 1919–1922: The Burns Revolution," *Review of Politics* 25, no. 4 (October 1963), p. 438.

42. Arthur, "University of Notre Dame," pp. 207 and 269–73.

43. Arthur, "University of Notre Dame," pp. 207–11, and Hope, *Notre Dame*, p. 347. The quotation is from Hope. The fact that there was apparently no thought at the time of eliminating the minims program and using Saint Edward's Hall for the collegians might suggest that Father Burns's motivation was in large part philosophical, that he believed that diocesan central Catholic high schools should replace Catholic college prep schools all across the country.

44. Arthur, "University of Notre Dame," pp. 209–12, and McAvoy, "Notre Dame 1919–1922," p. 441.

45. Kearney, "James A. Burns," p. 124.

46. Hope, "Life of John W. Cavanaugh," pp. 14–15 (second supplement).

47. Hope, "Life of John W. Cavanaugh," pp. 15–17; Arthur, "University of Notre Dame," pp. 121–22; Kearney, "James A. Burns," p. 124; and McAvoy, "Notre Dame 1919–1922," p. 432.

48. McAvoy, "Notre Dame 1919–1922," p. 434, and Kearney, "James A. Burns," p. 125.

49. Arthur, "University of Notre Dame," pp. 124–25, and Kearney, "James A. Burns," pp. 125–27.

50. Moore, *A Century of Law*, pp. 47–50.

51. Academic Council Minutes, March 6, 1920, UACO, B1, F1, UNDA; Arthur, "University of Notre Dame," pp. 53–57; Moore, *A Century of Law*, pp. 50–51; and Kearney, "James A. Burns," p. 116.

52. McAvoy, "Notre Dame 1919–1922," pp. 441–46, and Kearney, "James A. Burns," p. 122.

53. Arthur, "University of Notre Dame," pp. 158–63, and Kearney, "James A. Burns," pp. 118–20. A couple of the non-alumni members were not appointed the first year.

54. Kearney, "James A. Burns," pp. 127–28. The quotation is from Trevor Arnett, Report of February 11, 1921, visit to University of Notre Dame, February 1921, UPGE at AC 7/2/4 box 1, folder: Visit to UND Report, UNDA.

55. Arthur, "University of Notre Dame," pp. 124–30, and Kearney, "James A. Burns," pp. 128–29.

56. Arthur, "University of Notre Dame," pp. 131–33, and Kearney, "James A. Burns," p. 131.

57. Arthur, "University of Notre Dame," pp. 133–37, and Kearney, "James A. Burns," pp. 121 and 133–36.

58. Arthur, "University of Notre Dame," pp. 137–38, and Kearney, "James A. Burns," pp. 138–39.

59. Arthur, "University of Notre Dame," pp. 141–43, and Kearney, "James A. Burns," p. 156. The quotation is from Arthur, p. 142.

60. Arthur, "University of Notre Dame," pp. 216–17 and 244–46; Kearney, "James A. Burns," pp. 112–18; and Moore, "Academic Development," p. 135. See also Thomas Blantz, C.S.C., *George N. Shuster: On The Side of Truth* (Notre Dame, IN, 1993), p. 34.

61. Arthur, "University of Notre Dame," pp. 378–84.

62. *Scholastic*, Vol. LVII, No. 5 (January 1924), p. 303. (This issue is also listed as "New Series, Vol. I.")

63. Academic Council Minutes, March 21 and 23, 1921, UACO, B1, F1, UNDA; Arthur, "University of Notre Dame," pp. 216–17 and 247–50, and Kearney, "James A. Burns," pp. 116–17.

64. Kearney, "James A. Burns," pp. 140–41; McAvoy, "Notre Dame 1919–1922," pp. 448–49; and Arthur, "University of Notre Dame," pp. 139–40.

Chapter 10. The Emergence of Football

1. Mark Bernstein, *Football: The Ivy League Origins of an American Obsession* (Philadelphia, 2001), pp. 5–19, and Maggio, *Notre Dame and the Game*, pp. 23–28. The quotation is in Maggio, p. 28.

2. Bernstein, *Football*, pp. 24–79, and Maggio, *Notre Dame and the Game*, pp. 29–42. The quotations are from Maggio, pp. 29 and 42, and Bernstein, p. 9.

3. Bernstein, *Football*, pp. 79–89, and Maggio, *Notre Dame and the Game*, pp. 42–50. The quotation is from Maggio, p. 42.

4. Bernstein, *Football*, pp. 89–92, and Maggio, *Notre Dame and the Game*, pp. 51–61.

5. *Scholastic,* Vol. XXI, No. 8 (October 29, 1887), p. 125; Maggio, *Notre Dame and the Game,* pp. 32–39; and Chet Grant, *Before Rockne at Notre Dame* (Notre Dame, IN, 1968), pp. 46–105. Those coaches may have been, in order, James McWeeney, Patrick O'Dea, James Faragher, Louis Salmon, Henry McGlew, Thomas Barry, Victor Place, Frank Longman, and John Marks.

6. Maggio, *Notre Dame and the Game,* pp. 34–36, and Sperber, *Shake Down the Thunder,* pp. 17–20 and 29–33.

7. Maggio, *Notre Dame and the Game,* pp. 32–40.

8. Jim Lefebvre, *Coach for a Nation* (Minneapolis, 2013), pp. 127–29, and Maggio, *Notre Dame and the Game,* pp. 63–71. The quotation is from Maggio, p. 65.

9. Maggio, *Notre Dame and the Game,* pp. 74–80.

10. Maggio, *Notre Dame and the Game,* pp. 86–87, and Sperber, *Shake Down the Thunder,* pp. 38–39. The quotation is from Maggio, p. 87.

11. Lefebvre, *Coach,* pp. 117–20; Maggio, *Notre Dame and the Game,* p. 79; and Sperber, *Shake Down the Thunder,* p. 35.

12. Lefebvre, *Coach,* pp. 148–49; Maggio, *Notre Dame and the Game,* pp. 98–101; and Ray Robinson, *Rockne of Notre Dame* (New York, 1999), pp. 40–41. Another young person working at Cedar Point that summer was Bonnie Skiles of Kenton, Ohio. She and Rockne began dating and were married on July 15, 1914.

13. *Scholastic,* Vol. XLVII, No. 3 (October 11, 1913), pp. 47–48, No. 5 (October 25, 1913), pp. 77–79, No. 6 (November 1, 1913), pp. 94–95; and Maggio, *Notre Dame and the Game,* pp. 91–96.

14. Maggio, *Notre Dame and the Game,* pp. 101–8 and 115.

15. *Scholastic,* Vol. XLVII, No. 7 (November 8, 1913), pp. 107–8; Maggio, *Notre Dame and the Game,* pp. 108–13; and Robinson, *Rockne of Notre Dame,* p. 45.

16. *Scholastic,* Vol. XLVII, No. 7 (November 8, 1913), pp. 108–9; Maggio, *Notre Dame and the Game,* pp. 114–17; and Lefebvre, *Coach,* pp. 154–55.

17. *Scholastic,* Vol. XLVII, No. 8 (November 15, 1913), pp. 126–27, No. 10 (November 29, 1913), pp. 158–59 and 157–58; Maggio, *Notre Dame and the Game,* pp. 123–31; and Lefebvre, *Coach,* pp. 157–60.

18. *Scholastic,* Vol. XLVIII, No. 4 (October 10, 1914), pp. 61–63, No. 5 (October 17, 1914), pp. 78–79, No. 6 (October 24, 1914), pp. 92–96, No. 7 (October 31, 1914), pp. 109–11, No. 8 (November 7, 1914), pp. 125–26, No. 9 (November 14, 1914), pp. 141–42, No. 10 (November 21, 1914), pp. 158–59, No. 11 (November 28, 1914), pp. 173–75; Maggio, *Notre Dame and the Game,* pp. 133–50; and Lefebvre, *Coach,* pp. 175–208.

19. *Scholastic,* Vol. XLIX, No. 5 (October 9, 1915), pp. 77–78, No. 6 (October 16, 1915), pp. 94–95, No. 8 (October 30, 1915), pp. 124–27, No. 9 (November 6, 1915), pp. 142–43, No. 10 (November 13, 1915), pp. 158–59, No. 11 (November 20, 1915), pp. 173–75, No. 13 (December 4, 1915), pp. 204–6 and 206–7; Vol. L, No. 3 (October 7, 1916), p. 46, No. 4 (October 14, 1916), pp. 60–61, No. 5 (October 21, 1916), p. 78, No. 7 (November 4, 1916), pp. 110–11, No. 8 (November 11, 1916), pp. 125–27, No. 9 (November 18, 1916), pp. 141–42, No. 10 (November 25, 1916), pp. 156–58, No. 11 (December 2, 1916), pp. 172–73, No. 12 (December 9, 1916), pp. 194–97; Vol. LI, No. 3 (October 13, 1917), p. 47, No. 4 (October 20, 1917), pp. 62–64, No. 5 (October 27, 1917), pp. 78–79,

No. 6 (November 3, 1917), pp. 94–95, No. 7 (November 10, 1917), pp. 107–11, No. 8 (November 17, 1917), p. 127, No. 9 (November 24, 1917), p. 143, No. 10 (December 1, 1917), pp. 170–73; Maggio, *Notre Dame and the Game*, pp. 151–87; and Lefebvre, *Coach*, pp. 175–208.

20. Lefebvre, *Coach*, pp. 194–96, and Burns, *Being Catholic, Being American*, vol. 1, pp. 186–89.

21. Lefebvre, *Coach*, pp. 196–202.

22. Robinson, *Rockne of Notre Dame*, pp. 9–36, and Lefebvre, *Coach*, pp. 11–49 and 63–160.

23. Lefebvre, *Coach*, pp. 216–20; Sperber, *Shake Down the Thunder*, pp. 85–86; and Michael R. Steele, *The Fighting Irish Football Encyclopedia* (Champaign, IL, 1996), p. 48.

24. *Scholastic*, Vol. LII, No. 1 (October 12, 1918), p. 12, No. 5 (November 9, 1918), p. 77, No. 6 (November 16, 1918), pp. 91–92, No. 7 (November 23, 1918), p. 109, No. 9 (December 7, 1918), pp. 140–41 and 141–42; Lefebvre, *Coach*, pp. 219–24; Sperber, *Shake Down the Thunder*, pp. 84–86; and Steele, *Fighting Irish*, p. 48.

25. *Scholastic*, Vol. LIII, No. 3 (October 11, 1919), pp. 46–47, No. 4 (October 18, 1919), p. 62, No. 5 (October 25, 1919), pp. 77–78, No. 6 (November 1, 1919), pp. 94–95, No. 7 (November 8, 1919), pp. 109–10, No. 8 (November 15, 1919), pp. 126–28, No. 9 (November 22, 1919), pp. 141–42, No. 10 (November 29, 1919), pp. 157–59, No. 11 (December 6, 1919), pp. 178–79; Sperber, *Shake Down the Thunder*, pp. 92–93; and Steele, *Fighting Irish*, pp. 48–49. The quotations are from Lefebvre, *Coach*, p. 231, and Sperber, *Shake Down the Thunder*, p. 93.

26. Lefebvre, *Coach*, pp. 235–36, and Patrick Chelland, *One for the Gipper* (Chicago, 1973), pp. 128–39.

27. *Scholastic*, Vol. LIV, No. 3 (October 9, 1920), pp. 46–47, No. 4 (October 12, 1920), pp. 62–63, No. 5 (October 23, 1920), pp. 77–79, No. 6 (October 30, 1920), pp. 92–93, No. 7 (November 6, 1920), pp. 107–9, No. 8 (November 13, 1920), pp. 125–26, No. 9 (November 20, 1920), pp. 141–43, No. 10 (November 27, 1920), pp. 158–59, No. 11 (December 11, 1920), pp. 198–200; Lefebvre, *Coach*, pp. 238–43; and Steele, *Fighting Irish*, pp. 50–52. The quotation is from Lefebvre, *Coach*, p. 239.

28. Gene Schoor, *100 Years of Notre Dame Football* (New York, 1988), pp. 43–44; Sperber, *Shake Down the Thunder*, pp. 111–12; and Chelland, *One for the Gipper*, pp. 191–92. Father Pat Haggerty believed he had an indication from Gipp that he wanted to be baptized, and he baptized him conditionally. See Chelland, p. 192.

29. Chelland, *One for the Gipper*, pp. 194–99.

30. Quoted in Chelland, *One for the Gipper*, p. 205.

31. Robinson, *Rockne of Notre Dame*, pp. 54–55.

32. Lefebvre, *Coach*, pp. 249–61; Steele, *Fighting Irish*, pp. 53–54; Sperber, *Shake Down the Thunder*, pp. 114–37; and Jim Lefebvre, *Loyal Sons: The Story of the Four Horsemen and Notre Dame Football's 1924 Champions* (Minneapolis, 2008), pp. 46–50. The quotation is from Sperber, *Shake Down the Thunder*, p. 135.

33. Lefebvre, *Loyal Sons*, pp. 26–33; Steele, *Fighting Irish*, pp. 387–88; and Schoor, *100 Years*, p. 47.

34. Lefebvre, *Loyal Sons*, pp. 14–15; Schoor, *100 Years*, dedication page; and Steele, *Fighting Irish*, pp. 371–72.

35. Lefebvre, *Loyal Sons*, pp. 15–21; and Steele, *Fighting Irish*, pp. 371–72.

36. Lefebvre, *Loyal Sons*, pp. 33–40; and Steele, *Fighting Irish*, pp. 338–39. The quotation is from Lefebvre, *Coach*, pp. 269–70.

37. Lefebvre, *Loyal Sons*, pp. 21–25; and Steele, *Fighting Irish*, p. 364.

38. Sperber, *Shake Down the Thunder*, pp. 114–55.

39. Sperber, *Shake Down the Thunder*, pp. 157–58; Jones, "Development of the Office," p. 11; and Thomas T. McAvoy, C.S.C., *Father O'Hara of Notre Dame* (Notre Dame, IN, 1967), pp. 110–15.

40. *Scholastic*, Vol. LVII, No. 1 (September 1923), pp. 59–60 and 60–61, No. 2 (October 1923), pp. 116–19 and 119–24, No. 3 (November 1923), pp. 183–87, 187–88, and 189–90, and No. 4 (December 1923), pp. 249–50, 250–51, and 251–52; Sperber, *Shake Down the Thunder*, pp. 138–50; and Steele, *Fighting Irish*, pp. 56–58.

41. The best study of the 1924 team is Jim Lefebvre's *Loyal Sons: The Story of the Four Horsemen and Notre Dame Football's 1924 Champions*. The quotation is from page 125. See also *Scholastic*, Vol. LVIII, No. 1 (October 1924), p. 24, No. 2 (October 1924), pp. 56–57, and No. 3 (October 1924), pp. 87–88.

42. Quoted in LeFebvre, *Loyal Sons*, p. 125.

43. *New York Herald Tribune*, October 19, 1924, quoted in Robinson, *Rockne of Notre Dame*, pp. 152–53.

44. *Scholastic*, Vol. LVIII, No. 4 (October 1924), pp. 119–24, No. 5 (November 1924), pp. 153–54, No. 6 (November 1924), pp. 183–84, No. 7 (November 1924), pp. 216–17, No. 8 (November 1924), pp. 248–49, No. 9 (December 1924), pp. 281–82; and Lefebvre, *Loyal Sons*, pp. 132–211.

45. Steele, *Fighting Irish*, p. 61.

46. *Scholastic*, Vol. LVIII, No. 11 (January 1925), pp. 345–47; and Lefebvre, *Loyal Sons*, pp. 235–39. The Rose Bowl, of course, was the Four Horsemen's last game, the end of an era, and Grantland Rice touched on the loss in a hurried poem:

> There will be stars who are still paradin'
> Out in front with the flare of fame,
> But Stuhldreher, Miller, Crowley, and Layden
> Are playing their final game
>
> Soon they rise and as soon are fadin'
> Others will come from the laurelled glen;
> But I want to see Miller and Crowley and Layden
> Taking that ball again.

Scholastic, Vol. LVIII, No. 8 (November 1924), p. 249.

47. Steele, *Fighting Irish*, pp. 62–70; Sperber, *Shake Down the Thunder*, pp. 183–295; Lefebvre, *Coach*, pp. 353–405; and Schoor, *100 Years*, pp. 53–66.

48. Sperber, *Shake Down the Thunder*, pp. 207–12 and 269–72.

49. Steele, *Fighting Irish*, pp. 329–30, 333–34, 344, 374, and 383; and Schoor, *100 Years*, p. 370.

50. Sperber, *Shake Down the Thunder*, pp. 294–95 and 313–16; and Lefebvre, *Coach*, pp. 420 and 430.

51. Steele, *Fighting Irish*, pp. 70–73; Sperber, *Shake Down the Thunder*, pp. 312–21; Schoor, *100 Years*, p. 372; and Lefebvre, *Coach*, pp. 419–27.

52. Steele, *Fighting Irish*, pp. 73–77; Sperber, *Shake Down the Thunder*, pp. 323–45; Lefebvre, *Coach*, pp. 428–36; and William E. Reifsteck, *Two Million Bricks in 160 Days* (Notre Dame, IN, 2012), pp. 246–48.

53. Lefebvre, *Coach*, pp. 438–39.

54. Lefebvre, *Coach*, pp. 450–53; Sperber, *Shake Down the Thunder*, pp. 350–52; and Robinson, *Rockne of Notre Dame*, p. 264. Rockne was baptized a Catholic in November 1925: See Hope, *Notre Dame*, pp. 425–26.

55. Robinson, *Rockne of Notre Dame*, pp. 269–72; and Hope, *Notre Dame*, pp. 426–28. Father O'Donnell's sermon is in the *Scholastic*, Vol. LXIV, No. 23 (April 17, 1931), pp. 725 and 743. There was also a Mass in the campus church on Wednesday, the morning following the crash, that almost all students attended. *Scholastic*, Vol. LXIV, No. 23 (April 17, 1931), p. 722.

56. *Scholastic*, Vol. LXIV, No. 23 (April 17, 1931), pp. 724, 733, and 746. See also Sperber, *Shake Down the Thunder*, pp. 354–56; Robinson, *Rockne of Notre Dame*, pp. 266–69; and Lefebvre, *Coach*, pp. 454–58.

57. Sperber, *Shake Down the Thunder*, pp. 86 and 345.

Chapter 11.   The 1920s

1. Hope, *Notre Dame*, pp. 356–59, and Tucker, *Notre Dame vs. The Klan*, pp. 1–15.

2. At its height in 1919, the Prep Department or high school numbered 464.

3. *Notre Dame Alumnus* I, no. 2 (March 1923), pp. 34–37.

4. Academic Council Minutes, December 10, 1923, UACO, B1, F1, UNDA; *Bulletin of the University of Notre Dame*, 1922–1923, pp. 42–43 and 63–130; *Bulletin*, 1927–1928, pp. 58–126; Moore, "Academic Development," pp. 17–42; and *Alumnus* II, no. 7 (April 1924), pp. 203–11. The *Bulletin* was formerly called the *Catalogue*.

5. *Bulletin*, 1922–1923, pp. 43 and 131–215; *Bulletin*, 1927–1928, pp. 132–59; Moore, "Academic Development," pp. 46–68; *Alumnus* II, no. 6 (March 1924), pp. 171–72, and no. 7 (April 1924), pp. 203–11; and Walter, *History of Premedical Studies*, pp. 23–25. Father Nieuwland had also founded the *American Midland Naturalist* in 1909.

6. *Bulletin*, 1922–1923, pp. 44 and 318–40, and *Bulletin*, 1927–1928, pp. 196–210.

7. *Bulletin*, 1922–1923, pp. 216–17; *Bulletin*, 1927–1928, pp. 161–63 and 181; *Alumnus* II, no. 5 (February 1924), pp. 131–43; Moore, "Academic Development," pp. 72–83; and Stamper, "Between Two Centuries," pp. 7–15.

8. *Bulletin*, 1922–1923, pp. 286–317; *Bulletin*, 1927–1928, pp. 186–94; Moore, "Academic Development," pp. 114–27; and Moore, *A Century of Law*, pp. 47–84.

9. Moore, "Academic Development," pp. 131–37.

10. George to Doris Shuster, December 22, 1923, box 20, Shuster Papers, UNDA. The most complete biography of Shuster is Blantz, *George N. Shuster: On the Side of Truth*.

11. George Shuster, "Have We Any Scholars?," *America* XXXIII (August 15, 1925), p. 418.

12. Shuster, "Have We Any Scholars?," p. 418.

13. George Shuster, "Insulated Catholics," *Commonweal* II (August 19, 1925), p. 338.

14. Schlereth, *University of Notre Dame*, p. 140.

15. *Alumnus* II, no. 1 (October 1923), p. 1; Hope, *Notre Dame*, pp. 359–60; Schlereth, *University of Notre Dame*, p. 140; Campus map, 1928, PNDP 10-Aa-05, UNDA; Freshman Hall, PNDP, 10-22-20, UNDA; and *Scholastic*, Vol. LXXII, No. 22 (April 21, 1939), p. 5.

16. *Alumnus* II, no. 1 (October 1923), p. 1; Hope, *Notre Dame*, pp. 359–60; Schlereth, *University of Notre Dame*, p. 140; Campus map, 1928, PNDP 10-Aa-05, UNDA; and Sophomore Hall, PNDP, 10-20-4, UNDA.

17. Kervick to Burns, April 14, 1920, and "Report Upon Submitted Plan," UPWL, 15/66 ND Data, UNDA.

18. *Scholastic*, Vol. LVIII, No. 1 (October 1924), p. 16, and No. 16 (February 1925), p. 491, and *Alumnus* IV, no. 2 (November 1925), pp. 39–40.

19. PNDP, 10-H0-02, Howard Hall, UNDA; *Scholastic*, Vol. LVIII, No. 1 (October 1924), p. 16; and Vol. LIX, No. 1 (September 25, 1925), p. 6; Francis Kervick, *Architecture at Notre Dame* (Notre Dame, IN, n.d.), p. 5; and Kenneth William McCandless, "The Endangered Domain: A Review and Analysis of Campus Planning and Design at the University of Notre Dame" (MA thesis, University of Notre Dame, 1974), pp. 51–55.

20. *Alumnus* IV, no. 1 (October 1925), pp. 5–6, and no. 2 (November 1925), pp. 39–40; *Scholastic*, Vol. LIX, No. 1 (September 25, 1925), p. 15, and No. 14 (January 22, 1926), p. 422; PNDP, 10-M0-3 Morrissey Hall, UNDA; Kervick, *Architecture at Notre Dame*, p. 5; and McCandless, "Endangered Domain," pp. 51–55. The balcony on the west side was balanced by another balcony on the east side.

21. *Scholastic*, Vol. LIX, No. 11 (December 4, 1925), p. 328; PNDP, 10-LY-1 Lyons Hall, UNDA; Kervick, *Architecture at Notre Dame*, p. 5; and McCandless, "Endangered Domain," pp. 51–55.

22. Hope, *Notre Dame*, pp. 361–62, and Arthur, "University of Notre Dame," pp. 277–79.

23. *Scholastic*, Vol. LVII, No. 12 (December 15, 1925), p. 358; Vol. LX, No. 9 (November 19, 1926), pp. 264–66; and Vol. LXIII, No. 4 (October 11, 1929), pp. 112–13; and McCandless, "Endangered Domain," pp. 53–55. See also Kervick to Burns and enclosed "Report," April 14, 1920, UPWL, 15/66 ND Data, UNDA.

24. *Alumnus* IV, no. 1 (October 1925), pp. 13–14.

25. Schlereth, *A Spire of Faith*, pp. 18 and 56; Schlereth, *University of Notre Dame*, pp. 43–44; and Hope, *Notre Dame*, pp. 364–65.

26. Hope, *Notre Dame*, pp. 363–64; Klimek, *Zahms' Legacy*, pp. 29–30; McCandless, "Endangered Domain," p. 224.

27. Hope, *Notre Dame*, p. 364, and Schlereth, *University of Notre Dame*, pp. 150 and 154.

28. George Keogan, UDIS 109/32, UNDA, and Tim Neely, *Hooping It Up: The Complete History of Notre Dame Basketball* (Notre Dame, IN, 1985), pp. 7–37. The records for some years are not complete. Dutch Bergman might also have a football record because he once ran a kickoff back 105 yards—and did not score—the field then being 110 yards: Gagnon, *Notre Dame Baseball Greats*, p. 72.

29. *Scholastic*, Vol. LXIV, No. 12 (January 9, 1931), p. 384; Vol. LXV, No. 20 (March 18, 1932), p. 21; Vol. LXVI, No. 12 (January 13, 1933), p. 23, No. 18 (March 3, 1933), p. 22; Vol. LXIX, No. 12 (January 10, 1936), pp. 15 and 17; Vol. LXXI, No. 13 (February 6, 1942), p. 22; Vol. LXXVIII, No. 3 (February 19, 1943), p. 3, and No. 4 (February 26, 1943), pp. 16–17; and Neely, *Hooping It Up*, pp. 38–90. Coach Keogan's pre–Notre Dame record is approximate. His record at those three colleges plus one high school, according to one newspaper account, was 151 and 10: Keogan, UDIS 109/32, UNDA.

30. There are many fine studies of the Klan. Two very accessible ones are David Chalmers, *Hooded Americanism* (New York, 1965), pp. 8–27, and Wyn Craig Wade, *The Fiery Cross* (New York, 1987), pp. 9–111.

31. Chalmers, *Hooded Americanism*, pp. 28–38 and 162–74, and Wade, *Fiery Cross*, pp. 140–204 and 215–47. The quotation is from Wade, p. 235.

32. Wade, *Fiery Cross*, p. 235.

33. Hope, *Notre Dame*, pp. 373–74, and Tucker, *Notre Dame vs. The Klan*, pp. 155–56. Robert Burns in *Being Catholic, Being American*, vol. 1, has an extensive discussion of this whole incident on pages 265 to 425. The directive is printed in Tucker, *Notre Dame vs. The Klan*, pp. 149–50.

34. Tucker, *Notre Dame vs. The Klan*, pp. 156–62, and Hope, *Notre Dame*, pp. 374–75.

35. Tucker, *Notre Dame vs. The Klan*, pp. 163–66.

36. Hope, *Notre Dame*, pp. 375–77; Tucker, *Notre Dame vs. The Klan*, pp. 166–72; and *South Bend Tribune*, May 20, 1924. Father Walsh's words are quoted in all three.

37. Chalmers, *Hooded Americanism*, pp. 171–72, and Wade, *Fiery Cross*, pp. 245–47.

38. McAvoy, *Father O'Hara*, pp. 1–16; Hope, *Notre Dame*, pp. 442–43; and Temple, *O'Hara's Heirs*, pp. 1–4.

39. McAvoy, *Father O'Hara*, pp. 17–89; Hope, *Notre Dame*, p. 443; and Temple, *O'Hara's Heirs*, pp. 4–21.

40. McAvoy, *Father O'Hara*, pp. 19 and 79–80.

41. Most of the material on the religious program of the university in the 1920s is taken from Rev. Thomas Patrick Jones, C.S.C.'s detailed and well-researched dissertation, "The Development of the Office of Prefect of Religion at the University of Notre Dame from 1842 to 1952," pages 38–50. For Mass attendance figures, see pages 59 and 75. Also, McAvoy, *Father O'Hara*, pp. 90–123.

42. Jones, "Development of the Office," pp. 52–80, esp. p. 59. The following quotation is from Father O'Hara's *Religious Survey, 1927–1928*, p. 10, reprinted in Jones, p. 74.

43. *Report of the Prefect of Religion*, p. 11, as quoted in Jones, "Development of the Office," pp. 92–93. See also Jones, pp. 90–97.

44. *Religious Survey, 1922–1923*, pp. 29–30.

45. Jones, "Development of the Office," pp. 81–87.

46. Jones, "Development of the Office," pp. 103–15.

47. Jones, "Development of the Office," pp. 116–25 and 138.

48. Jones, "Development of the Office," pp. 144–47.

49. *Religious Bulletin*, November 11, 1921, February 12, 13, and 16, 1923, and March 6, 1923.

50. *Religious Bulletin*, November 30, 1921, February 15, October 3, and November 10, 1922, June 5 and October 13, 1924, March 2, 1925, and February 3, 1927.

51. *Religious Bulletin*, December 4, 1922, November 6, 1923, October 28 and November 28, 1924, December 1, 2, 3, 6, and 8, 1924, March 12, 13, and 17, 1925, and February 14, 1927.

52. *Religious Bulletin*, December 14, 1921, May 12, 1923, December 13, 1924, and February 11, 1927.

53. *Religious Bulletin*, January 30 and April 20, 1923, and March 9, 1925.

54. *Religious Bulletin*, February 20, 1923, November 6, 1924, January 22 and February 26, 1925.

55. *Religious Bulletin*, February 13 and May 11, 12, and 24, 1923.

56. *Religious Bulletin*, May 10, 12, 17, 20, 21, 23, and 24, 1927.

57. *Religious Bulletin*, February 26, 1923.

58. *Religious Bulletin*, October 23, 1922.

59. *Religious Bulletin*, November 23, 1922.

60. Shuster, "Insulated Catholics," pp. 337–38.

61. *Religious Bulletin*, November 9 and 16, 1923, and February 15 and 18, 1927.

62. *Religious Bulletin*, February 17, 18, and 21, 1925.

63. *Bulletin of the University of Notre Dame: Religious Survey, 1921*, "Introduction." The quotation is from the second (unnumbered) page.

64. *Religious Survey, 1921*, pp. 1–18.

65. *Religious Survey, 1921*, pp. 19–28.

66. *Religious Survey, 1921*, pp. 1–5, 9–13, and 19–21.

67. *Religious Survey, 1925–1926*, p. 88.

68. *Religious Survey, 1925–1926*, pp. 88–91.

69. *Religious Survey, 1925–1926*, pp. 91–94.

70. *Religious Survey, 1925–1926*, pp. 95–100.

71. *Religious Survey, 1925–1926*, pp. 101–5.

72. *Religious Survey, 1927–1928*, p. 7.

73. *Religious Survey, 1927–1928*, pp. 7–34.

74. *Religious Survey, 1927–1928*, pp. 35–64. The quotation is from page 64.

75. Any standard American history textbook would treat of the 1920s in detail. William E. Leuchtenburg's *The Perils of Prosperity* (Chicago, 1958) is a very readable account.

1. Hope, *Notre Dame*, pp. 397–403, and Klawitter, *Poems of Charles O'Donnell*, pp. xv–xvii. From 1926 to 1928, Father O'Donnell served as assistant general in the Congregation of Holy Cross.

2. Klawitter, *Poems of Charles O'Donnell*, p. xvii.

3. In Klawitter, *Poems of Charles O'Donnell*, p. 90.

4. Minutes of the Board of Lay Trustees, November 19, 1929, UPCO 10/129, Charles O'Donnell Papers, and Erskine to O'Donnell, December 14, 1931, UPCO 7/80 Charles O'Donnell Papers, UNDA.

5. Hope, *Notre Dame*, p. 408; *Bulletin*, 1930–1931, pp. 257–312; and *Bulletin*, 1933–1934, pp. 346–407.

6. Arthur, "University of Notre Dame," pp. 197–202, and Hope, *Notre Dame*, 408–9.

7. Arthur, "University of Notre Dame," p. 196, and Hope, *Notre Dame*, pp. 409–10.

8. Reifsteck, *Two Million Bricks*, pp. 67–93 and 120–24, and Lefebvre, *Coach*, pp. 205, 354–355, 372, and 395–96. The Cartier Field stadium was expanded with additional seats until it reached approximately 30,000 by the end of the decade.

9. Reifsteck, *Two Million Bricks*, pp. 84–93.

10. Reifsteck, *Two Million Bricks*, pp. 101–47. Brother Irenaeus Stackhouse assisted in connecting the utilities with the rest of campus.

11. Reifsteck, *Two Million Bricks*, p. 1.

12. *Scholastic*, Vol. LXIII, No. 1 (September 20, 1929), p. 14, and No. 4 (October 11, 1929), p. 116; and Vol. LXIV, No. 2 (October 3, 1930), p. 49; Reifsteck, *Two Million Bricks*, pp. 181–248; and Hope, *Notre Dame*, pp. 403–4.

13. *Scholastic*, Vol. LXIV, No. 2 (October 3, 1930), p. 38; Moore, *A Century of Law*, pp. 73–74; McCandless, "Endangered Domain," p. 57; *Bulletin*, 1931–1932, p. 218–19; and Kervick to Burns, and enclosed "Report," April 14, 1920, UPWL, 15/66 ND Data, UNDA.

14. *Scholastic*, Vol. LXIV, No. 22 (March 27, 1931), pp. 691 and 697.

15. *Scholastic*, Vol. LXIV, No. 22 (April 24, 1931), p. 764; Vol. LXV, No. 1 (September 25, 1931), p. 5, No. 2 (October 2, 1931), p. 8, No. 3 (October 9, 1931), p. 12, and No. 4 (October 16, 1931), p. 10; and Hope, *Notre Dame*, p. 405.

16. Hurley's letter is quoted in Temple, *O'Hara's Heirs*, p. 27. See also agreement of gift, UPCO, Hurley papers, 4/75, 1929–1930, UNDA; and *Scholastic*, Vol. LXIV, No. 21 (November 21, 1930), p. 229.

17. O'Hara to Hurley, November 15, 1919, Hurley Papers, Personal Letters – 62, UNDA; *Scholastic*, Vol. LXIV, No. 8 (November 21, 1930), p. 229; *Alumnus* IV, no. 6 (March, 1926), pp. 163–65; and McAvoy, *Father O'Hara*, pp. 70–75.

18. Temple, *O'Hara's Heirs*, pp. 27–32; *Scholastic*, Vol. LXIV, No. 8 (November 21, 1930), pp. 229 and 247, and No. 27 (May 15, 1931), p. 860; and Vol. LXV, No. 1 (September 25, 1931), p. 5, No. 25 (May 13, 1932), p. 7, and No. 26 (May 20, 1932), p. 5; and Kervick, *Architecture at Notre Dame*, p. 6.

19. *Scholastic*, Vol. LXII, No. 1 (September 21, 1928), p. 14; Klimek, *Zahms' Legacy*, pp. 3–30. The quotation is in Klimek, p. 30.

20. Klimek, *Zahms' Legacy*, pp. 3–31; Hope, *Notre Dame*, pp. 406–7; and *Scholastic*, Vol. LXIV, No. 24 (April 24, 1931), pp. 755 and 778, and Vol. LXIX, No. 3 (October 11, 1935), pp. 5 and 22.

21. *Scholastic*, Vol. LXIV, No. 24 (April 24, 1931), pp. 755 and 778; Vol. LXV, No. 1 (September 25, 1931), p. 5, and No. 23 (April 25, 1932), p. 5; and Klimek, *Zahms' Legacy*, p. 31.

22. *Scholastic*, Vol. LXXII, No. 16 (February 17, 1939), pp. 8–9, and Vol. LXXIV, No. 13 (January 24, 1941), p. 18.

23. *Scholastic*, Vol. LXV, No. 5 (October 23, 1931), p. 14, No. 11 (January 8, 1932), p. 15; Vol. LXXIV, No. 13 (January 24, 1941), p. 18; and Hope, *Notre Dame*, p. 407. The main church was also renovated in 1931, an automated clock was installed in the church tower, and a bell would mark each quarter hour: Hope, *Notre Dame*, p. 404.

24. Hope, *Notre Dame*, pp. 415–16.

25. *Scholastic*, Vol. LXIV, No. 2 (October 3, 1930), p. 27, and No. 3 (October 10, 1930), p. 74. The quotation is in Vol. LXIV, No. 3 (October 10, 1930), p. 74.

26. *Scholastic*, Vol. LXIV, No. 7 (November 7, 1930), p. 203.

27. *Scholastic*, Vol. LXIV, No. 5 (October 24, 1930), p. 135, No. 6 (October 31, 1930), p. 170, No. 8 (November 21, 1930), p. 230, No. 11 (December 12, 1930), p. 328, No. 17 (February 20, 1931), p. 531; and Vol. LXX, No. 1 (September 25, 1936), p. 10. The incident with the chauffeur was told to the author by Father John J. Cavanaugh.

28. *Scholastic*, Vol. LXVI, No. 12 (January 13, 1933), p. 14.

29. The above quotation is from *Scholastic*, Vol. LXVI, No. 12 (January 13, 1933), p. 14, and the following one is from Hope, *Notre Dame*, p. 419. For mention of Yeats's earlier visit, see chapter 7, page 162 in this book.

30. *Scholastic*, Vol. LXVI, No. 22 (March 31, 1933), p. 5. The quotation is from Hope, *Notre Dame*, p. 414.

31. Hope, *Notre Dame*, p. 414.

32. Hope, *Notre Dame*, p. 415.

33. R. W. Rauch, "Notre Dame's New Coat of Arms," *Alumnus* IX, no. 6 (February 1931), p. 195; Schlereth, *University of Notre Dame*, p. 170; and "History of the University Seal" (Office of the Registrar, University of Notre Dame, 2012), in possession of the author.

34. Sperber, *Shake Down the Thunder*, pp. 271–375, The quotation is on page 373.

35. Sperber, *Shake Down the Thunder*, pp. 375–78.

36. Steele, *Fighting Irish*, pp. 78–82; and Sperber, *Shake Down the Thunder*, pp. 399–418.

37. Gagnon, *Notre Dame Baseball Greats*, pp. 42–44, 66, 73, and 83; *Notre Dame Baseball Guide, 1980*, PATH, UNDA, pp. 18 and 21; and Jenny Marten, "A Tradition is Born: Irish Baseball in the Early Years," *Observer*, Vol. XXVI, No. 99 (February 28, 1994), p. 14.

38. Gagnon, *Notre Dame Baseball Greats*, pp. 109, 110, and 114–15; *Notre Dame Baseball Guide, 1980*, PATH, UNDA, pp. 11, 12–14, and 21–22; and Jenny Marten, "Jake Kline's Impact on Irish Baseball Spanned a Lifetime," *Observer*, Vol. XXVI, No. 100 (March 1, 1994), p. 14.

39. The fine study of A. J. Andrassy, "The History of Notre Dame Track and Field" (senior seminar paper, University of Notre Dame, 2005), in possession of the author; *Scholastic*, Vol. XXIV, No. 1 (August 21, 1890), p. 13, No. 4 (September 27, 1890), pp. 61–62; Vol. LXXII, No. 4 (February 3, 1939), p. 17; and Vol. LXXIII, No. 2 (September 29, 1939), pp. 13–14; and *Notre Dame Track and Field Media Guide, 2008*, pp. 64–75, PATH, UNDA.

40. McAvoy, *Father O'Hara*, pp. 123–44, and Hope, *Notre Dame*, pp. 439–41.

41. McAvoy, *Father O'Hara*, pp. 123–45.

42. *Twenty-Eighth Annual Report of the President and the Treasurer of the Carnegie Foundation for the Advancement of Teaching, 1933* (Boston, 1933), pp. 31–34.

43. *Chicago Daily Tribune*, February 20, 1934.

44. Moore, "Academic Development," pp. 131–37, and Hope, *Notre Dame*, pp. 451–52.

45. McAvoy, *Father O'Hara*, pp. 153–54. For personal remembrances of most of these émigré professors, see Thomas Stritch, *My Notre Dame* (Notre Dame, IN, 1991), pp. 200–210.

46. *Who's Who in America*, vol. XXVI, *1950–1951* (Chicago, 1950), p. 1088, and *Review of Politics* XVII, no. 1 (January 1955), pp. 5–23, 33–43, and 80–81. Gurian's quotation is on pages 11 and 12 of *Review of Politics* XVII, no. 1.

47. *Review of Politics* XVII, no. 1 (January 1955), p. 33. The present author attended the lecture described.

48. *Scholastic*, Vol. LXXI, No. 22 (April 8, 1938), p. 8, and Vol. LXXII, No. 7 (November 4, 1938), p. 13; and *American Catholic Who's Who*, vol. XIII, *1958–1959* (Grosse Pointe, MI, 1959), p. 202. The name of that department does change throughout the years.

49. *Scholastic*, Vol. LXX, No. 12 (January 15, 1937), p. 6; *American Catholic Who's Who*, vol. VIII, *1948–1949* (Grosse Pointe, MI, 1949), p. 314; Illinois Institute of Technology, IIT Social Media Directory, Karl Menger; Seymour Kass, "Karl Menger," *Notices of the American Mathematical Society* 43, no. 5 (May 1996), pp. 558–61.

50. *Biographical Encyclopedia of Scientists* 2 (New York, 1998), pp. 520–23; John W. Dawson, *Logical Dilemmas: The Life and Work of Kurt Gödel* (Wellesley, MA, 1997); and Kenneth M. Sayre, *Adventures in Philosophy at Notre Dame* (Notre Dame, IN, 2014), pp. 34–35.

51. *Dictionary of Scientific Biography* I (New York, 1920), pp. 306–8, and Richard Brauer, "Emil Artin," *Bulletin of the American Mathematical Society* 73, no. 1 (January 1967), pp. 27–43. The quotation is on page 40 of Brauer, "Emil Artin."

52. *Dictionary of Scientific Biography* V (New York, 1972), pp. 609–10, and *Scholastic*, Vol. LXX, No. 8 (November 20, 1936), p. 5. The quotation is from the *Scholastic*.

53. *Scholastic*, Vol. LXXI, No. 2 (October 1, 1937), p. 5; Eugene Guth Papers, UDIS 105140, Dr. Eugene Guth, UNDA, and homepage of Dr. Eugene Guth, http://michael guth/family/eugeneguth.htm.

54. *New Catholic Encyclopedia*, 2nd ed., vol. 13 (Washington, DC, 2003), pp. 127–28, and "Yves Simon," *Fondazione Rui's*, VII European Seminar of Philosophical Studies, July 18–23, 2004.

55. *Scholastic*, Vol. LXX, No. 20 (April 9, 1937), p. 4; Vol. LXXII, No. 7 (November 4, 1938), p. 12; and McAvoy, *Father O'Hara*, pp. 176 and 181.

56. Hope, *Notre Dame*, pp. 452–53; Moore, "Academic Development," pp. 137–39; and *Bulletin*, 1938–1939, pp. 357–61.

57. *Bulletin*, 1938–1939, pp. 303–8.

58. *Bulletin*, 1938–1939, pp. 118–20.

59. Hope, *Notre Dame*, p. 455, and *Bulletin*, 1938–1939, pp. 254–55.

60. Hope, *Notre Dame*, p. 455, and *Bulletin*, 1938–1939, pp. 261–62.

61. Hope, *Notre Dame*, pp. 455–56, and *Bulletin*, 1938–1939, pp. 166–69.

62. *Scholastic*, Vol. LXVII, No. 22 (April 20, 1934), p. 5; Vol. LXVIII, No. 4 (October 12, 1934), p. 4, No. 6 (October 26, 1934), p. 1, No. 8 (November 16, 1934), p. 2, and No. 9 (November 23, 1934), p. 1.

63. *Scholastic*, Vol. LXVIII, No. 17 (February 22, 1935), p. 3; Vol. LXIX, No. 2 (October 4, 1935), pp. 6 and 9, No. 3 (October 11, 1935), pp. 6 and 9, and No. 5 (October 25, 1935), p. 5.

64. *Scholastic*, Vol. LXIX, No. 23 (January 10, 1936), p. 8; Vol. LXX, No. 1 (September 25, 1936), p. 8; and Vol. LXXII, No. 2 (September 30, 1938), p. 3. The verses are from Vol. LXX, No. 1 (September 25, 1936), p. 8.

65. McAvoy, *Father O'Hara*, pp. 145–95. The first quotation is on page 185, and the second is on page 159.

66. McAvoy, *Father O'Hara*, pp. 161–63.

67. McAvoy, *Father O'Hara*, pp. 151 and 163–66. The Walker quotation is from Robert H. Ferrell, ed., *FDR's Quiet Confidant: The Autobiography of Frank C. Walker* (Niwot, CO, 1997), p. 85, and the historian's quotation is from McAvoy, p. 165.

68. *Scholastic*, Vol. LXIX, No. 11 (December 13, 1935), pp. 3, 8–9, and 12–13, and McAvoy, *Father O'Hara*, pp. 166–68. The quotation is from McAvoy, p. 168.

69. *Scholastic*, Vol. LXX, No. 1 (October 30, 1936), pp. 3 and 23; McAvoy, *Father O'Hara*, pp. 173–74; and Hope, *Notre Dame*, pp. 463–64.

70. McAvoy, *Father O'Hara*, p. 177; *Bulletin*, 1933–1934, pp. 354–410; and *Bulletin*, 1939–1940, pp. 429–86.

71. *Scholastic*, Vol. LXIX, No. 1 (September 27, 1935), p. 7, and Vol. LXXV, No. 3 (October 10, 1941), p. 24. In "The Endangered Domain," Kenneth McCandless questions whether the infirmary is the start of a new quadrangle since it faces west, away from later buildings on the quadrangle. Facing west ties it closer to Saint Joseph's Lake, for *Notre Dame du Lac*.

72. *Scholastic*, Vol. LXIX, No. 22 (May 29, 1936), p. 5; Vol. LXX, No. 1 (September 25, 1936), p. 9, and No. 9 (November 27, 1936), p. 6; Vol. LXXII, No. 13 (January 13,

1939), p. 10; Schlereth, *University of Notre Dame*, pp. 189–91; and McAvoy, *Father O'Hara*, p. 170.

73. *Scholastic*, Vol. LXX, No. 1 (September 25, 1936), p. 9, and No. 20 (April 9, 1937), p. 7; and Vol. LXXII, No. 21 (March 24, 1939), p. 7, and No. 25 (May 12, 1939), pp. 5 and 7.

74. McAvoy, *Father O'Hara*, pp. 171–72.

75. *Scholastic*, Vol. LXXI, No. 6 (October 29, 1937), pp. 3 and 22.

76. *Scholastic*, Vol. LXXI, No. 6 (October 29, 1937), p. 3; and Vol. LXXII, No. 5 (October 21, 1938), p. 8; and Schlereth, *University of Notre Dame*, p. 144.

77. *Scholastic*, Vol. LXXII, No. 1 (September 23, 1938), p. 5, and No. 18 (March 3, 1939), pp. 10 and 23.

78. Steele, *Fighting Irish*, pp. 81–100; Schoor, *100 Years*, pp. 99–104; and Sperber, *Shake Down the Thunder*, pp. 435–36.

79. McAvoy, *Father O'Hara*, p. 195.

80. McAvoy, *Father O'Hara*, pp. 196–202. The following quotation is from page 202.

81. *Religion Bulletin*, January 13, 1940.

Chapter 13.   *Notre Dame, the Navy, and World War II*

1. *Scholastic*, Vol. XLVIII, No. 6 (October 24, 1914), pp. 92–96; Vol. LXV, No. 1 (September 25, 1931), p. 6; Vol. LXVIII, No. 1 (September 21, 1934), p. 1; and Vol. LXXIV, No. 1 (September 20, 1940), p. 5; *South Bend News Times*, December 5, 1916; and Hope, *Notre Dame*, pp. 465–66.

2. *Bulletin*, 1939–1940, pp. 13–40 and 428–86, and *Official Catholic Directory*, 1940, p. 368.

3. John Whitney Evan, *The Newman Movement* (Notre Dame, IN, 1980), pp. 78–81, and Burns, *Being Catholic, Being American*, vol. 2, *The Notre Dame Story, 1934–1952* (Notre Dame, IN, 2000), pp. 33–34.

4. Burns, *Being Catholic, Being American*, vol. 2, pp. 28–30 and 36–65, and *Scholastic*, Vol. LXXIV, No. 1 (September 20, 1940), p. 10.

5. Richard Whalen, *The Founding Father* (New York, 1964), pp. 281–311 and 321–48; David Kosoff, *Joseph P. Kennedy* (Englewood Cliffs, NJ, 1974), pp. 187–295; and Michael Beechloss, *Kennedy and Roosevelt* (New York, 1980), pp. 157–233.

6. David Kennedy, *Freedom from Fear* (New York, 1999), pp. 393–434; A. Scott Berg, *Lindbergh* (New York, 1998), pp. 384–412; and Sheldon Marcus, *Father Coughlin* (Boston, MA, 1973), pp. 196–204.

7. Wayne Cole, *America First* (Madison, WI, 1953), pp. 3–16. The four principles are listed on pages 15–16. See also Mark Lincoln Chadwin, *The Warhawks* (New York, 1968), pp. 74–86. By far, the most complete and detailed discussion of the conflict involving Father O'Brien and Professor Francis McMahon is in Burns, *Being Catholic, Being American*, vol. 2, pp. 28–339. This present work relies heavily upon Burns's book.

8. Quoted in *Scholastic*, Vol. LXXIV, No. 2 (September 27, 1940), p. 8. There do not seem to be copies of Father O'Brien's early speeches in his collected papers, COBR, UNDA.

9. *South Bend Tribune*, December 17, 1940, sec. 2, p. 1.

10. *South Bend Tribune*, December 20, 1940, sec. 2, p. 1.

11. *Scholastic*, Vol. LXXV, No. 1 (January 26, 1941), p. 6, and *Dubuque Telegraph-Herald*, March 5, 1941, p. 1.

12. *Scholastic*, Vol. LXXV, No. 1 (January 26, 1941), p. 6.

13. *A Catholic Program for World Peace*, published by the C. A. I. P. (Washington, DC, n.d.), p. 1.

14. *Scholastic*, Vol. LXXIV, No. 5 (October 10, 1940), p. 10.

15. Francis McMahon, *A Catholic Looks at the World* (New York, 1945), pp. 95–97, and Burns, *Being Catholic, Being American*, vol. 2, p. 140.

16. *New Republic* CIV, no. 19 (May 12, 1941), pp. 661–62.

17. "On Your Guard" in Fight for Freedom, Inc., *Midwestern Scholars Take Their Stand* (Chicago, 1941).

18. McMahon, *A Catholic Looks at the World*, pp. 97–98.

19. Notes of meetings with both in UPOH, McMahon Folder, 110/2, UNDA, and Burns, *Being Catholic, Being American*, vol. 2, pp. 144–45.

20. Arthur O'Leary to O'Donnell, May 12, 1941, and attachments, UPHO, War Controversy, #2, 86/16, UNDA, and Burns, *Being Catholic, Being American*, vol. 2, pp. 151–52.

21. Charles Foley to O'Donnell, August 11, 1942, UPHO, McMahon Folder, 110/2, UNDA; Burns, *Being Catholic, Being American*, vol. 2, pp. 145–48, 161–62, 216, 231, 250, and 254; and *South Bend Tribune*, May 2, 1941.

22. Burns, *Being Catholic, Being American*, vol. 2, pp. 166, 227, 234–36, 255, 263–66; *New York Times*, April 25, 1943, p. 25, col. 5; and McMahon, *A Catholic Looks at the World*, p. 91.

23. Cicognani to O'Donnell, August 3, 1943, UPHO, 97/8, UNDA.

24. Press Release, November 8, 1943, PNDP 83-RR-45, Press Releases 1940–1945, UNDA, and Burns, *Being Catholic, Being American*, vol. 2, pp. 268–81.

25. Burns, *Being Catholic, Being American*, vol. 2, pp. 282–330, and Sullivan, *Notre Dame*, pp. 223–27.

26. Announcement of December 8, 1941, in *Scholastic*, Vol. LXXV, No. 11 (December 12, 1941), p. 5.

27. *Scholastic*, Vol. LXXV, No. 11 (December 12, 1941), p. 5, and No. 12 (January 16, 1942), pp. 7–8 and 21–22, the quoted material is taken from Father O'Donnell's address to the students on January 13, 1942. See also *Scholastic*, Vol. LXXVI, No. 9 (October 14, 1942), p. 9.

28. *Scholastic*, Vol. LXXV, No. 12 (January 16, 1942), pp. 7–8 and 21–22, this quoted material is also taken from Father O'Donnell's January 1942 address to the students. See also *Scholastic*, Vol. LXXVI, No. 9 (October 14, 1942), p. 9.

29. Memorandum from Robert Riordan to O'Donnell, July 23, 1940, UPHO, box 82, Defense-1940 File, UNDA; Hope, *Notre Dame*, p. 466; and *Bulletin*, 1942, pp. 225. This discussion on the Navy at Notre Dame during World War II has benefitted greatly from research papers presented in the author's seminar on Notre Dame history by Mary Conroy, Jaimie Feltault, Karl Kadon, Thomas Kleiber, John Mulflur, and Baraem Nah.

30. See *Bulletin*, 1942, pp. 225–36, and *The Irish Pennant*, 1945, for photos and brief articles.

31. *Scholastic*, Vol. LXXVI, No. 1 (June 5, 1942), pp. 12–13; and Vol. LXXXIV, No. 3 (March 29, 1945), p. 11; and O'Donnell to Rear Admiral John Downes, U.S.N., September 1, 1942, UPHO 95/6, V-7 File, UNDA.

32. *Scholastic*, Vol. LXXVI, No. 1 (June 5, 1942), pp. 12–13; and Vol. LXXXIV, No. 3 (March 29, 1945), p. 11; Father John Cavanaugh to Commander Webb, August 8, 1942, UPHO 95/6, V-7 File, UNDA; *South Bend Tribune*, April 15, 1942, for Lieut. Commander Gene Tunney (former heavyweight boxing champion) speaking to first V-7 trainees; W. K. Thompson, "Our Changing Armed Forces," *Journal of Educational Sociology* 16, no. 9 (May 1943), pp. 557–61; "WAVES at Notre Dame," University of Notre Dame Archives, July 20, 2012, http://www.archives.nd.edu/about/news/index.php/2012/waves-at-notre-dame; and issues of *Capstan* for each V-7 graduating class.

33. Kennedy, *Freedom from Fear*, pp. 650–53.

34. James G. Schneider, *The Navy V-12 Program* (Boston, 1987), pp. 1–62 and 472–73; *Scholastic*, Vol. LXXVIII, No. 5 (March 12, 1943), p. 10; "What the V-12 is Like at Notre Dame," p. 8, and "The Purpose of the V-12 Program," pp. 15 and 27, in *Scholastic*, Vol. LXXXII, No. 1 (July 7, 1944); and Jaimie Feltault, "God, Country, Notre Dame: The Navy on Campus during World War II" (senior seminar paper, University of Notre Dame, 2005), in possession of the author.

35. Jackie Cooper, *Please Don't Shoot My Dog* (New York, 1981), pp. 116–24. The quotation is on page 124.

36. Cooper, *Please Don't Shoot My Dog*, p. 121.

37. *Scholastic*, Vol. LXXVIII, No. 7 (March 26, 1943), p. 15.

38. Schneider, *The Navy V-12 Program*, p. 158; "Negroes at Notre Dame," *Ebony Magazine* (February 1950), pp. 21–24; Pete LaFleur, "Irish Trailblazers," https://www.und.com/ot-60bca-champions-blazers-html; and Margaret Fosmoe, "1947 Saw First Black Notre Dame Grads," *South Bend Tribune*, February 26, 2009.

39. James Gardner Birch, *They Flew Proud* (Nappanee, IN, 2007), pp. 17–26 and 48, and *Dome* (yearbook) 1942, pp. 250–53. Astronaut John Glenn was a product of the national Civilian Pilot Training Program.

40. *Dome* (yearbook) 1942, pp. 254–57.

41. *Scholastic*, Vol. LXXXVII, No. 3 (April 5, 1946), p. 3.

42. Raymond Donovan, "Notre Dame's Contributions in World War II," *Illinois v. Notre Dame* program, September 29, 1945, p. 21; Gleason, *Contending with Modernity*, pp. 215–19; and *Scholastic*, Vol. LXXVIII, No. 2 (February 5, 1943), p. 21, No. 3 (February 19, 1943), p. 5, and No. 10 (April 23, 1943), pp. 9 and 29.

43. Rev. Joseph Kehoe, C.S.C., "Holy Cross Military Chaplains in World War II" (paper delivered at Holy Cross History Conference, 1995), pp. 2–5. Although Father Kehoe's paper is not footnoted, he knew all of these men personally, and his discussion of them should be accurate. *Bulletin*, 1940, pp. 10 and 33; *Bulletin*, 1947, p. 11; and John F. Wukovits, *Soldiers of a Different Cloth* (Notre Dame, IN, 2018), esp. pp. 43, 125–46, 218, and 253–320.

44. Kehoe, "Holy Cross Military Chaplains," pp. 8–10; *Bulletin*, 1940, p. 30; *Bulletin*, 1947, p. 15; and Wukovits, *Soldiers*, pp. 21–30 and 253–85.

45. Kehoe, "Holy Cross Military Chaplains," pp. 4–5 and 14–17; *Bulletin*, 1940, pp. 10, 14, 34, and 35; *Bulletin*, 1947, pp. 13 and 26; and Wukovits, *Soldiers*, pp. 172–85 and 227–305.

46. Ed Fitzgerald, "Frank Leahy: The Enigma," in Fred Katz, *The Glory of Notre Dame: 22 Great Stories on Fighting Irish Football from the Pages of Sport Magazine* (n.p., 1971), p. 99; Sperber, *Shake Down the Thunder*, pp. 493–94; and John J. Cavanaugh Oral History Interview, pp. 213–15, UORL, UNDA.

47. Fitzgerald, "Frank Leahy," pp. 93–98; Schoor, *100 Years*, pp. 112–16; and Steele, *Fighting Irish*, pp. 103–4.

48. Steele, *Fighting Irish*, pp. 103–6, and Schoor, *100 Years*, pp. 119–23.

49. Steele, *Fighting Irish*, pp. 110–12 and 327–28, and Schoor, *100 Years*, pp. 123–32.

50. Steele, *Fighting Irish*, pp. 112–17.

51. Moore, "Academic Development," p. 138, and *Scholastic*, Vol. LXXXII, No. 7 (August 25, 1944), pp. 5 and 11. The quotation is from the *Scholastic*.

52. Moore, "Academic Development," p. 138, and *Scholastic*, Vol. LXXXII, No. 7 (August 25, 1944), p. 5.

53. Schlereth, *University of Notre Dame*, pp. 190–93, and Catherine Lawlor, "The Life and Times of Vetville" (senior seminar paper, University of Notre Dame, 2005), in possession of the author, pp. 3–6.

Chapter 14.   The Postwar Years and the Second Father John Cavanaugh

1. John J. Cavanaugh Oral History Interview, pp. 1–24, UORL, UNDA; *Current Biography*, 1947, pp. 101–2; and *American National Biography* 4 (New York, 1999), pp. 589–90.

2. Cavanaugh Oral History, pp. 25–46, UORL, UNDA; *Current Biography*, 1947, p. 102; and *American National Biography* 4, p. 590.

3. Cavanaugh Oral History, pp. 46–53, UORL, UNDA; *Current Biography*, 1947, p. 102; *American National Biography* 4, p. 590; *Time Magazine*, April 28, 1952, pp. 78–79; and the quotation is from John Powers, "The Charm President," *Notre Dame Magazine* (Spring 1992), p. 14.

4. *Supplement to the General Bulletin*, 1946, p. 96; *Student Directory*, 1952–1953, pp. 11–87; and *Scholastic*, Vol. LXXXVII, No. 4 (April 12, 1946), pp. 17 and 18.

5. *Scholastic*, Vol. XCI, No. 13 (January 13, 1950), p. 9; Vol. XCIII, No. 21 (March 21, 1952), p. 9; and Vol. XCV, No. 7 (November 19, 1954), p. 12.

6. Lawlor, "Life and Times of Vetville,"pp. 6–19; Rev. Theodore Hesburgh, *God, Country, Notre Dame* (New York, 1990), pp. 48–53; and copies of the *Vetville Herald*, PNDP, UNDA. The quotation is from the title page of Lawlor.

7. *Bulletin*, 1946, pp. 18–85, and *Bulletin*, 1952, pp. 14–85.

8. Rev. E. C. Stibili, "Refugee Professors at Notre Dame, 1930–1960" (graduate seminar paper, University of Notre Dame, 1970), in possession of the author, pp. 28–30.

9. *Scholastic*, Vol. XCVI, No. 4 (October 22, 1954), p. 3; Vol. XCVII, No. 9 (December 9, 1955), pp. 14–16; Vol. XCVIII, No. 6 (November 2, 1956), p. 32; and Vol. CIII, No. 21 (May 11, 1962), pp. 18–21; and Sayre, *Adventures in Philosophy*, pp. 151–56.

10. *Scholastic*, Vol. LXX, No. 17 (February 24, 1939), p. 6; Vol. LXXXVII, No. 6 (May 3, 1946), p. 17; and Vol. XCI, No. 23 (April 28, 1950), p. 33.

11. *Directory of American Scholars* I (New York, 1969), p. 503, and *Scholastic*, Vol. XCVI, No. 5 (October 29, 1954), p. 10.

12. *Scholastic*, Vol. LXXXVIII, No. 12 (January 10, 1947), p. 22.

13. Stephen Kertesz, *Between Russia and the West: Hungary and the Illusions of Peacemaking, 1945–47* (Notre Dame, IN, 1984), pp. 3–28; Kenneth W. Thompson, *Diplomacy and Values* (Lanham, MD, 1984), pp. 25–28; and *Scholastic*, Vol. XCI, No. 23 (April 28, 1950), p. 28.

14. Cavanaugh Oral History, pp. 29, 45, and 145–61, UORL, UNDA.

15. Nicholas Ayo, C.S.C., "The Beginning of Great Books in the Cavanaugh Years, 1946–1952," in *Notre Dame's Program of Liberal Studies: The First Fifty Years*, ed. Nicholas Ayo, Micheal Crowe, and Julia Marvin (Notre Dame, IN, 2000), p. 1.

16. Otto Bird, "The General Program," in Ayo, Crowe, and Marvin, *Notre Dame's Program*, pp. 4–5; and Moore, "Academic Development," pp. 43–44.

17. Moore, "Academic Development," pp. 139–41, and Hope, *Notre Dame*, rev. ed. (Notre Dame, IN, 1948), p. 469.

18. "Mediaeval Institute: Echo from the Past," *Scholastic*, Vol. XCVII, No. 9 (December 9, 1955), pp. 14–16; "The Medieval Institute," *Scholastic*, Vol. CIII, No. 21 (May 11, 1962), pp. 18–21; Moore, "Academic Development," pp. 139–41; and *Graduate Bulletin*, 1951–1952, pp. 29–75.

19. *Scholastic*, Vol. LXVIII, No. 26 (May 24, 1935), p. 7; Vol. LXXI, No. 15 (February 11, 1938), pp. 7 and 20; and Vol. LXXXVII, No. 4 (April 12, 1946), pp. 11–13.

20. *Scholastic*, Vol. LXVIII, No. 26 (May 24, 1935), p. 7; and Vol. LXXI, No. 15 (February 11, 1938), pp. 7 and 20.

21. *Scholastic*, Vol. LXXXVII, No. 4 (April 12, 1946), p. 14; Vol. LXXXIX, No. 24 (April 30, 1948), p. 29; and Vol. XCII, No. 1 (September 11, 1950), p. 24.

22. Rev. Michael Mathis Papers, 1998/05, D-16, USPA; Rev. George Schidel, C.S.C., "Never Too Much: In Memoriam: Rev. Michael Ambrose Mathis, C.S.C. (1885–1960)," *Yearbook of Liturgical Studies* 3 (Notre Dame, IN, 1962), pp. 1–11; and Robert J. Kennedy, *Michael Mathis: American Liturgical Pioneer* (Washington, DC, 1987), pp. 1–11. The quotation is from Kennedy, p. 4.

23. Kennedy, *Michael Mathis*, pp. 11–28, and Schidel, "Never Too Much," pp. 12–34. Father Mathis was given to long speeches and homilies. Father Schidel (on page 33) remembered that before an *ad experimentum* Easter Vigil at Saint Mary's College in 1951, Father Mathis said, "I'll go out and say a few words of explanation and then we can start." The few words lasted forty-five minutes.

24. Francis Hayes, "Living Endowment," *Notre Dame Alumnus* VII, no. 3 (November 1928), pp. 67–68. The term "living endowment" had earlier been used by Father Burns (see chapter 9, page 219) to denote the savings to the university of not paying salaries to the Holy Cross religious.

25. Armstrong, *Onward to Victory*, pp. 265–339.

26. Armstrong, *Onward to Victory*, pp. 340–58, and Cavanaugh Oral History, pp. 253–65, UORL, UNDA.

27. Schoor, *100 Years*, pp. 137–38, and the *Notre Dame–Pittsburgh* program, October 5, 1946, p. 28.

28. Schoor, *100 Years*, p. 139; Steele, *Fighting Irish*, pp. 118–19; and *Scholastic*, Vol. LXXXVIII, No. 1 (September 20, 1946), p. 22.

29. Schoor, *100 Years*, pp. 140–41; Steele, *Fighting Irish*, p. 119; and *Scholastic*, Vol. LXXXVIII, No. 10 (December 6, 1946), p. 19.

30. Schoor, *100 Years*, pp. 141–43, and Steele, *Fighting Irish*, p. 120.

31. Schoor, *100 Years*, p. 143, and Bill Furlong, "The Year Notre Dame Had an NFL Franchise," in Katz, *Glory*, p. 73.

32. Furlong, "The Year," p. 74.

33. Fred Katz, in his introduction to Furlong, "The Year," p. 73.

34. Fitzgerald, "Frank Leahy," p. 105.

35. Furlong, "The Year," pp. 75–79, and Steele, *Fighting Irish*, p. 366. Lujack's backup, George Ratterman, went into the pros and played for the Buffalo Bills in the All-America Conference. The following quotation is from the *Observer*, Vol. XXXIV, No. 12 (September 6, 2000), pp. 21 and 24.

36. Quoted in Furlong, "The Year," p. 75.

37. Steele, *Fighting Irish*, pp. 329, 376, and 386, and Furlong, "The Year," pp. 75–76. The final quotation is from Furlong, p. 76.

38. Furlong, "The Year," pp. 76–77; Steele, *Fighting Irish*, pp. 337, 339, 354, and 368; and *Scholastic*, Vol. LXXXVIII, No. 6 (October 25, 1946), p. 33.

39. Schoor, *100 Years*, p. 143; Steele, *Fighting Irish*, pp. 346 and 391; and Furlong, "The Year," pp. 77–78.

40. Steele, *Fighting Irish*, pp. 120–23; Furlong, "The Year," pp. 79–82; and Schoor, *100 Years*, pp. 143–46 and 370.

41. Steele, *Fighting Irish*, pp. 124–28, and Schoor, *100 Years*, pp. 147–51.

42. Steele, *Fighting Irish*, pp. 128–31, and Ed Fitzgerald, "Bob Williams: One More in the Great Tradition," in Katz, *Glory*, pp. 129–51.

43. Steele, *Fighting Irish*, pp. 132–42.

44. Steele, *Fighting Irish*, pp. 142–47, and Schoor, *100 Years*, pp. 164–71.

45. *Scholastic*, Vol. XC, No. 23 (April 8, 1949), pp. 16–19; and Vol. XCV, No. 5 (October 23, 1953), p. 12.

46. *Scholastic*, Vol. XCIII, No. 10 (November 16, 1951), p. 17, and No. 26 (May 9, 1952), p. 23; and Vol. XCV, No. 1 (September 25, 1953), p. 17; Doug Hennes, *That Great Heart* (Edina, MN, 2014), pp. 133–49.

47. *Scholastic*, Vol. XCII, No. 10 (November 17, 1950), p. 20, and conversation of Father John J. Cavanaugh with the author.

48. *Scholastic*, Vol. XCV, No. 1 (September 25, 1953), p. 17.

49. *Alumnus*, Vol. XXX, No. 4 (August–September, 1952), p. 5.

50. *Scholastic*, Vol. XCI, No. 10 (December 2, 1949), p. 10; Temple, *O'Hara's Heirs*, pp. 41–42; Moore, *A Century of Law*, p. 139; and Klimek, *Zahms' Legacy*, p. 40. Science and engineering were combined under one council for the first few years, and the Law Advisory Council may not have been formally established until the year after Father Cavanaugh left office.

51. Moore, *A Century of Law*, pp. 85–87 and 107–8, and Father Hesburgh's eulogy at Dean O'Meara's funeral, *Notre Dame Report*, Vol. 12, No. 19 (June 24, 1983), p. 501.

52. The provincial superior made all of these assignments, of course, but almost certainly on the recommendation of the president.

53. *Dome* (yearbook) 1948, pp. 18–22; *Scholastic*, Vol. LXXIX, No. 9 (September 10, 1943), p. 3; Vol. LXXXI, No. 10 (May 26, 1944), p. 2; Vol. LXXXIII, No. 5 (December 5, 1944), p. 4; and Vol. XCI, No. 1 (September 23, 1949), p. 9.

Chapter 15.   The Early Presidency of Father Theodore M. Hesburgh

1. Hesburgh, *God, Country, Notre Dame*, pp. 1–12; Michael O'Brien, *Hesburgh: A Biography* (Washington, DC, 1998), pp. 5–19; and Walton Collins, "Growing Up Ted," special issue, *Notre Dame Magazine* (March 2015), pp. 8–9. Other studies are John Lungren, Jr., *Hesburgh of Notre Dame* (New York, 1987); Thomas Stritch, "A Short Biography of Theodore M. Hesburgh," in Charlotte Ames, *Theodore M. Hesburgh: A Bio-Bibliography* (New York, 1989), pp. 1–24; and Jill Boughton and Julie Walters, *God's Icebreaker* (Notre Dame, IN, 2012).

2. Hesburgh, *God, Country, Notre Dame*, p. 14.

3. Hesburgh, *God, Country, Notre Dame*, pp. 13–36; O'Brien, *Hesburgh*, pp. 19–28; and Collins, "Growing Up Ted," pp. 9–11.

4. Hesburgh, *God, Country, Notre Dame*, pp. 37–46; O'Brien, *Hesburgh*, pp. 28–35; Collins, "Growing Up Ted," p. 11; and Theodore M. Hesburgh, "The Relation of the Sacramental Characters of Baptism and Confirmation to the Lay Apostolate" (PhD diss., Catholic University of America, 1946). The dissertation was published as *The Theology of Catholic Action* by Ave Maria Press at Notre Dame in 1946. The following quotation is from pages 187–88.

5. Quoted in Collins, "Growing Up Ted," p. 11.

6. Hesburgh, *God, Country, Notre Dame*, pp. 46–53; O'Brien, *Hesburgh*, pp. 43–46; and Collins, "Growing Up Ted," pp. 11–12. The three textbooks were published by the University of Notre Dame Press: Cavanaugh's and Sheedy's in 1949, and Hesburgh's in 1950.

7. Hesburgh, *God, Country, Notre Dame*, pp. 54–56, and O'Brien, *Hesburgh*, pp. 46–48.

8. Hesburgh, *God, Country, Notre Dame*, pp. 57–59, and O'Brien, *Hesburgh*, pp. 48–51.

9. Hesburgh, *God, Country, Notre Dame*, p. 65.

10. As a student, the author heard him repeat this often.

11. Theodore M. Hesburgh, *Patterns For Education Growth* (Notre Dame, IN, 1958), pp. 23–32. The quotation is on pages 31–32. Also, Hesburgh, *God, Country, Notre Dame*, p. 64.

12. Hesburgh, *Patterns For Education Growth*, pp. 4–6.

13. Rev. Edmund P. Joyce, C.S.C., Personnel File, USPA. These appointments, of course, were made by the provincial superior but at the request of the president.

14. Personnel files of Rev. Philip Moore, C.S.C., Rev. James Norton, C.S.C., Rev. John H. Murphy, C.S.C., and Rev. Jerome Wilson, C.S.C., all in USPA.

15. *Alumnus* XXXI, no. 2 (March–April 1953), p. 14.

16. Moore, *A Century of Law*, pp. 109–16. The following quotation is from *Bulletin of Information: The College of Law*, 1953–1954, p. 15.

17. Hesburgh, *God, Country, Notre Dame*, p. 67. Dean McCarthy's comment, of course, was made at a time when Father Hesburgh was both president and religious superior, and as religious superior his term was limited to six years.

18. Temple, *O'Hara's Heirs*, pp. 39–48.

19. Hesburgh, *God, Country, Notre Dame*, p. 68.

20. Hesburgh, *God, Country, Notre Dame*, pp. 66–67, and *Alumnus* XXX, no. 5 (October 1952), p. 6.

21. Schoor, *100 Years*, pp. 166–71; Steele, *Fighting Irish*, pp. 142–47; Hesburgh, *God, Country, Notre Dame*, pp. 79–84; O'Brien, *Hesburgh*, p. 56; and *New York Times*, February 1, 1954, p. 1, cols. 6–7.

22. For a detailed discussion of the 1952 presidential election, see Barton Bernstein, "Election of 1952," in *History of American Presidential Elections, 1789–1968* VIII, ed. Arthur Schlesinger, Jr., and Fred Israel (New York, 1985), pp. 3,215–66.

23. *Chicago Tribune*, October 29, 1952, and Stevenson Faculty Support File, UDIS, 210/22 UNDA.

24. *Chicago Tribune*, October 29, 1952, and *South Bend Tribune*, October 30, 1952.

25. *South Bend Tribune*, October 30, 1952.

26. James Murphy to Hesburgh, November 21, 1952, Stevenson Faculty Support File, UDIS, 210/22, UNDA.

27. This view is summarized well by John A. Ryan and Francis J. Boland, C.S.C., *Catholic Principles of Politics* (New York, 1943), esp. pp. 308–21. See also Gleason, *Contending with Modernity*, pp. 274–82.

28. John Courtney Murray, S.J., "Current Theology: Freedom of Religion," *Theological Studies* VI (January 1, 1945), pp. 85–113; John Courtney Murray, S.J., "Contemporary Orientations of Catholic Thought on Church and State in the Light of History," *Theological Studies* X (January 1, 1949), pp. 177–234; John Courtney Murray, S.J., "The Problem of State Religion," *Theological Studies* XII (January 1, 1951), pp. 155–78; John Courtney Murray, S.J., "Leo XIII on Church and State: The General Structure of the Controversy," *Theological Studies* XIV (January 1, 1953), pp. 1–30; and John Courtney Murray, S.J., "Leo XIII: Separation of Church and State," *Theological Studies* XIV (January 1, 1953), pp. 145–214. On Father John Courtney Murray himself, see Thomas T. Love, *John Courtney Murray: Contemporary Church-State Theory* (New York, 1965), pp. 10–11, and Donald E. Pelotte, S.S.S., *John Courtney Murray: Theologian in Conflict* (New York, 1975), pp. 3–7.

29. Pelotte, *John Courtney Murray*, pp. 44–54, and John Courtney Murray, S.J., "On the Structure of the Church-State Problem," in *The Catholic Church in World Affairs*, ed. Waldemar Gurian and M. A. Fitzsimmons (Notre Dame, IN, 1954), pp. 11–32.

30. Hesburgh, *God, Country, Notre Dame*, pp. 223–27.

31. *Alumnus* XXXI, no. 1 (February 1953), p. 1.

32. *Alumnus* XXXII, no. 2 (March 1954), p. 1; *Alumnus* XXXIII, no. 2 (March 1955), p. 1; and Armstrong, *Onward to Victory*, p. 303.

33. *Alumnus* XXX, no. 5 (October 1952), p. 6; *Scholastic*, Vol. XCVI, no. 1 (October 1, 1954), pp. 6–7; and Vol. XCVII, No. 19 (March 23, 1956), p. 11.

34. *Scholastic*, Vol. XCVI, No. 1 (October 1, 1954), pp. 6–7 and 11; and *Alumnus* XXXII, no. 3 (May–June 1954), p. 2.

35. *Alumnus* XXXIII, no. 6 (November–December 1955), p. 5; *Scholastic*, Vol. XCVII, No. 2 (October 7, 1955), p. 13; *New York Times*, October 1, 1955, p. 39, col. 1; and Richard B. Morris and Jeffrey B. Morris, eds., *Encyclopedia of American History*, 7th ed. (New York, 1996), p. 960.

36. *Scholastic*, Vol. XCVI, No. 1 (October 1, 1954), p. 11; and Vol. XCVII, No. 7 (November 18, 1955), p. 14; *Alumnus* XXXII, no. 5 (November–December 1952), p. 11; and McCandless, "Endangered Domain," p. 73.

37. PNDP 10-Ke-1, Keenan-Stanford Halls, and PNDP 10-St-2, Stanford Hall, UNDA; *Alumnus* XXXV, no. 2 (February–March 1957), p. 11; *Alumnus* XXXV, no. 6 (October–November 1957), p. 3; *New York Times*, January 29, 1956, p. 57, col. 1; and *New York Times*, April 7, 1957, p. 122, col. 4.

38. *Alumnus* XXXV, no. 6 (October–November 1957), p. 3; and McCandless, "Endangered Domain," p. 73, for the quotation.

39. *Alumnus* XXXV, no. 2 (February–March 1957), pp. 2–3.

40. Moore, "Academic Development," p. 42, and Gleason, *Contending With Modernity*, pp. 250–56.

41. College of Arts and Letters *Bulletin*, 1956–1957, pp. 25–26. See also pages 56 and 57.

42. College of Arts and Letters *Bulletin*, 1956–1957, p. 27.

43. *Alumnus* XXXII, no. 5 (October 1954), p. 3, and Klimek, *Zahms' Legacy*, pp. 44–45.

44. *New York Times*, June 6, 1955, p. 48, col. 2; *Alumnus* XXXIV, no. 6 (November–December 1956), p. 12; and Hesburgh, *God, Country, Notre Dame*, p. 68. The quotation is from *Alumnus*.

45. Temple, *O'Hara's Heirs*, pp. 58, 61, 63, and 64. The quotations are from pages 63 and 64.

46. *College of Science Bulletin*, 1952–1953 and 1957–1958.

47. *Alumnus* XXXIII, no. 1 (January–February 1955), p. 3; *Alumnus* XXXIV, no. 6 (November–December 1956), p. 2; and box 259, folder 8, Meštrović Sculpture Studio, 1955–1996, UNDA. Hughes remained at Notre Dame until his death in 1967.

48. Pilkinton, *Washington Hall*, pp. 89–91, 179–87, 232–35, and 244–52.

49. Rev. Arthur Harvey, C.S.C., Papers, 2008/05, D-16, USPA; Pilkinton, *Washington Hall*, pp. 252–53 and 377; and *Scholastic*, Vol. XCVIII, No. 7 (November 9, 1956), pp. 14–15.

50. Nancy Fallon, "The Art of the Stage," *Notre Dame Magazine* 23, no. 3 (Autumn 1994), pp. 11–13; Pilkinton, *Washington Hall*, pp. 264–80; Stritch, *My Notre Dame*, pp. 130–31; and *Scholastic*, Vol. CVIII, No. 5 (October 28, 1996), pp. 14–15. The quotation is from Fallon, "Art of the Stage," p. 12.

51. *University of Notre Dame Faculty Manual*, 1954, esp. pp. 17–26 and 31–32.

52. Steele, *Fighting Irish*, pp. 148–66; Schoor, *100 Years*, pp. 178–99; Dick Schaap, "The Firing of Terry Brennan," in Katz, *Glory*, pp. 217–31; Hesburgh, *God, Country, Notre Dame*, p. 85; and O'Brien, *Hesburgh*, p. 69.

53. *Alumnus* XXXVII, no. 1 (March 1, 1959), pp. 16–19. The article in *Sports Illustrated* appeared in the January 5, 1959, issue.

54. Hesburgh, *God, Country, Notre Dame*, p. 104; O'Brien, *Hesburgh*, p. 65; and Gleason, *Contending with Modernity*, p. 217. The quotation is from O'Brien.

55. "Board of Visitors," United States Naval Academy, last modified March 16, 2020, https://www.usna.edu/PAO/Superintendent/bov.php.

56. Hesburgh, *God, Country, Notre Dame*, pp. 280–302.

57. Harvard Sitkoff, *The Struggle for Black Equality*, rev. ed. (New York, 1993), pp. 29–33; Mary Frances Berry, *And Justice for All* (New York, 2009), pp. 9–131; Hesburgh, *God, Country, Notre Dame*, pp. 190–91; and O'Brien, *Hesburgh*, pp. 71–73.

58. O'Brien, *Hesburgh*, p. 70, and Hesburgh, *God, Country, Notre Dame*, pp. 74 and 249–51.

Chapter 16.   The 1960s

1. See chapters 2, 3, and 4 of this present work, and see also Costin, *Priceless Spirit*, pp. 9–89.

2. The quotation is from *Alumnus* XXXVI, no. 4 (May–June 1958), p. 8.

3. In addition to chapters 2, 3, and 4 of this present work, see Sorin, *Chronicles*, pp. 88; Creek, *A Panorama*, p. 41; and *Alumnus* XXXVI, no. 4 (May–June 1958), p. 8.

4. PNDP 9002-13L, "Challenge: Clippings," UNDA; *New York Times*, January 26, 1958, p. 31, cols. 3–6, and September 25, 1960, p. 1, col. 1; *Scholastic* Vol. CII, No. 1

(September 30, 1960), p. 9; and Hesburgh, *God, Country, Notre Dame*, p. 68. The quotations are from the *Scholastic*.

5. PNDP 9002-13L, "Challenge 1960–1963," PNDP 9002-13L, "Challenge: Mailings and General Literature," PNDP 9002-13L, "A Challenge Met," UNDA; and *New York Times*, March 15, 1962, p. 19, col. 5, and March 27, 1962, p. 28, col. 8.

6. PNDP 9002-13L, "Challenge: Mailings and General Literature," UNDA; and *Scholastic*, Vol. CV, No. 21 (May 8, 1964), pp. 15–21.

7. PNDP 9002-13L, "A Challenge Met," UNDA.

8. PNDP 9002-13L, "A Challenge Met," UNDA.

9. PNDP 9002-15L, "Challenge II: Mailings and General Literature," and PNDP 9002-15L, "Challenge II: Another Challenge Met," UNDA.

10. PNDP 9002-15L, "Challenge II: Mailings and General Literature," PNDP 9002-15L, "Challenge II: Another Challenge Met," and PNDP 9002-17L, "SUMMA: Brochures," UNDA.

11. PNDP 9002-15L, "Challenge II: Newsletter," and PNDP 9002-15L, "Challenge II: Another Challenge Met," UNDA.

12. PNDP 9002-15L, "Challenge II: Another Challenge Met," UNDA.

13. PNDP 9002-15L, "Challenge II: Extending the Tradition of Great Teaching," and PNDP 9002-15L, "Challenge II: Another Challenge Met," UNDA; and *Alumnus* XLV, no. 2 (March–April 1967), p. 8.

14. The university had hoped to make another matching grant agreement with Ford, but the Ford Foundation had undergone a change in leadership and the Special Program in Education had been eliminated. See Richard Conklin, "Once Upon a Dime," *Notre Dame Magazine* 1, no. 4 (August 1972), p. 15.

15. *Scholastic*, Vol. CIX, No. 1 (September 22, 1967), p. 11; *Alumnus* XLV, no. 6 (November–December 1967), p. 10; and *Bulletin*, 1966–1967, p. 7.

16. Membership on these teams, of course, could change at times due to conflicts in each person's schedule.

17. PNDP 9002-17L, *SUMMAry*, and PNDP 9002-17L, "SUMMA: Kickoff Dinners," UNDA; and *Scholastic*, Vol. CIX, No. 1 (September 22, 1967), p. 11, and No. 13 (February 16, 1968), pp. 18–19 and 33; and Vol. CX, No. 15 (February 21, 1969), p. 18.

18. Conklin, "Once Upon a Dime," pp. 14–17.

19. ND Population Statistics, 1939–1992, PNDP 90-Pop-IL, UNDA; and *Alumnus* XLII, no. 4 (August–September 1964), p. 12.

20. PNDP 40–Ec–02, Ecumenical Institute for Theology (Tantur), UNDA; and Hennes, *That Great Heart*, pp. 201–10.

21. *New York Times*, December 8, 1964, p. 1, col. 2, and December 18, 1964, p. 1, cols. 2–4.

22. *Alumnus* XLIII, no. 2 (April 1965), pp. 6–7, and *New York Times*, December 19, 1964, p. 25, col. 1.

23. *Alumnus* XLIII, no. 2 (April 1965), pp. 6–7.

24. *Alumnus* XLIII, no. 2 (April 1965), pp. 2–4, and *New York Times*, December 27, 1964, p. 116, cols. 1–4.

25. *New York Times*, February 10, 1965, p. 1, col. 1.

26. *New York Times*, February 10, 1965, p. 1, col. 1.

27. PATH 3002-2, *Chicago American*, November 21, 1960, UNDA.

28. PATH 3002-2, *Chicago American*, November 23, 1960, UNDA; *Scholastic*, Vol. CII, No. 10 (December 9, 1960), p. 5; and Joel Connelly and Howard Dooley, *Hesburgh's Notre Dame* (New York, 1972), pp. 6–10.

29. Connelly and Dooley, *Hesburgh's Notre Dame*, pp. 42–43.

30. *Scholastic*, Vol. CIV, No. 13 (February 22, 1963), p. 7. For George Shuster, see Blantz, *George N. Shuster*.

31. *Scholastic*, Vol. CIV, No. 13 (February 22, 1963), pp. 7–8. The quotation is from page 8.

32. *Scholastic*, Vol. CIV, No. 14 (March 1, 1963), pp. 7–8. His comment on presidential absence was made in a conversation with the author.

33. *Voice*, Vol. I, No. 2 (March 28, 1963), pp. 1–2. The *Voice* was a student newspaper before the *Observer*.

34. Since the declaration does not seem to have been published or widely circulated, the author was not able to locate a copy. It was quoted and discussed in Joel Connelly and Howard Dooley's detailed study of student unrest in the 1960s, *Hesburgh's Notre Dame*, and the quotations are reprinted from that book, the present one from pages 51–52.

35. From Connelly and Dooley, *Hesburgh's Notre Dame*, pp. 52–53.

36. Connelly and Dooley, *Hesburgh's Notre Dame*, p. 53.

37. A copy of the letter is in PNDP 30-Pr-U1, "Protests," UNDA.

38. *Voice*, Vol. I, No. 1 (March 22, 1963); Vol. IV, No. 20 (February 10, 1966); Vol. V, No. 5 (October 13, 1966); Vol. V, No. 7 (October 27, 1966); PNDP 83-Vo-lo, "The Voice of N.D.," UNDA; and *Scholastic*, Vol. CVIII, No. 6 (November 4, 1966), pp. 20–21. On its demise, the *Voice* was succeeded by the *Observer*. See "50 Years of *The Observer*," *Observer*, Vol. LI, No. 45 (November 3, 2011), p. 1.

39. *Scholastic*, Vol. CVI, No. 5 (October 30, 1964), p. 17, and No. 12 (February 12, 1965), p. 5; Vol. CVII, No. 3 (October 8, 1965), p. 9, and No. 19 (April 1, 1966), p. 30; and Vol. CVIII, No. 11 (January 13, 1967), p. 5, and No. 17 (March 17, 1967), pp. 12–13.

40. *Scholastic*, Vol. CVI, Extra (September 18, 1964), p. 16; and Vol. CVII, No. 18 (March 18, 1966), p. 7; and Connelly and Dooley, *Hesburgh's Notre Dame*, pp. 101–4.

41. *Scholastic*, Vol. CVI, No. 18 (April 30, 1965), pp. 5 and 19; and Connelly and Dooley, *Hesburgh's Notre Dame*, pp. 108–12.

42. *Scholastic*, Vol. CVII, No. 1 (September 17, 1965), p. 9, and No. 6 (October 29, 1965), p. 13.

43. Schoor, *100 Years*, pp. 200–212; Steele, *Fighting Irish*, pp. 166–82; and *New York Times*, November 29, 1961, p. 48, col. 4. Hugh Devore's season was not a success, with two wins and seven losses and the Iowa game cancelled because of the death of President John Kennedy.

44. Schoor, *100 Years*, pp. 213–15; Steele, *Fighting Irish*, pp. 182–83; and Gary Cartwright, "Parseghian: 'I Have to Keep Moving,'" in Katz, *Glory*, pp. 281–87.

45. Schoor, *100 Years*, pp. 217–27; Steele, *Fighting Irish*, pp. 183–86; and Bill Furlong, "Waking Up the Echoes," in Katz, *Glory*, pp. 267–74. If the weather turned bad in the stadium during a game, the students occasionally chanted "Ara, stop the rain" or "Ara, stop the snow."

46. Schoor, *100 Years*, pp. 231–37; Steel, *Fighting Irish*, pp. 191–95; and "College Football: Babes in Wonderland," *Time*, October 28, 1966.

47. *New York Times*, November 20, 1966, sec. 5, pp. 1 and 3; Schoor, *100 Years*, pp. 237–40; and Steele, *Fighting Irish*, pp. 195–96.

48. Schoor, *100 Years*, pp. 241–50, and Steele, *Fighting Irish*, pp. 196–205.

49. *Scholastic*, Vol. CIX, No. 7 (November 10, 1967), p. 34. For unrest on Catholic campuses across the country, see Gleason, *Contending with Modernity*, pp. 305–17.

50. Quoted in Connelly and Dooley, *Hesburgh's Notre Dame*, p. 189.

51. *New York Times*, October 24, 1967, p. 45, col. 4.

52. *Scholastic*, Vol. CIX, No. 5 (October 27, 1967), p. 5.

53. *New York Times*, November 3, 1967, p. 42, col. 5; *Scholastic*, Vol. CIX, No. 6 (November 3, 1967), p. 7, and No. 7 (November 10, 1967), pp. 7 and 34.

54. *New York Times*, January 20, 1967, p. 34, cols. 1–2, and January 28, 1967, p. 56, col. 1; Hesburgh, *God, Country, Notre Dame*, pp. 170–73; and Alice Gallin, O.S.U., *Independence and a New Partnership in Catholic Higher Education* (Notre Dame, IN, 1996), pp. 52–55.

55. Hesburgh, *God, Country, Notre Dame*, pp. 173–76; and Gallin, *Independence*, pp. 55–65. The following quotation is from Gallin, p. 60.

56. *New York Times*, May 7, 1967, p. 82, cols. 4–6; Hesburgh, *God Country, Notre Dame*, 176–78; and Gallin, *Independence*, pp. 65–67.

57. See the earlier discussion of the incidents at the Catholic University of America and Saint John's College in this chapter, the discussion of Professor McMahon in chapter 13, and the discussion of Father Murray and the University of Notre Dame Press book in chapter 15.

58. For background on the "Land O'Lakes Statement," see Neil G. McCluskey, S.J., ed., *The Catholic University: A Modern Appraisal* (Notre Dame, IN, 1970), p. 107.

59. Alice Gallin, O.S.U., ed., *American Catholic Higher Education: Essential Documents, 1967–1990* (Notre Dame, IN, 1992), p. 7.

60. Gallin, *American Catholic Higher Education*, p. 7.

61. Gallin, *American Catholic Higher Education*, pp. 7–12.

62. PNDP 1010-1968, "Statement of Policy on Student Life by Board of Trustees, University of Notre Dame," PNDP 30-Pr-m1, "Protests-Miscellaneous/Various," UNDA; *Scholastic*, Vol. CX, No. 7 (November 8, 1968), pp. 7 and 21, and No. 14 (February 14, 1969), p. 20; and Connelly and Dooley, *Hesburgh's Notre Dame*, pp. 222–23, 229, and 264. The author was an early member of the Student Life Council.

63. Tara Hunt, "The Damnedest Experience We Ever Had," *Notre Dame Magazine* XLIV, no. 1 (Spring 2015), pp. 14–16, and Alfred Kelly and Winfred Harbison, *The American Constitution* (New York, 1970), pp. 1045–53.

64. *Observer*, Vol. III, No. 73 (February 5, 1969), p. 4; *Final Report of Student Life Council on the Student Union Academic Commission's Conference on Pornography and Censorship*, May 17, 1969, pp. 2–4, UDIC 204/28 1969, Pornography and Censorship Conference, UNDA; and "Law School Centennial," February 7–8, 1969, PNDP 1969, Chronological File, UNDA.

65. Hunt, "The Damnedest Experience," pp. 14–16; and *Observer*, Vol. III, No. 75 (February 7, 1969), pp. 2 and 4, and No. 76 (February 8, 1969), p. 1.

66. *Observer*, Vol. III, No. 133 (May 12, 1969), p. 1; *Final Report of Student Life Council on the Student Union Academic Commission's Conference on Pornography and Censorship*, May 17, 1969, pp. 19–59, UDIC 204/28, 1969 Pornography and Censorship Conference; the author's remembrance as a member of the Student Life Council Subcommittee; and the affidavit in UDIS 204/28 1969, "Pornography and Censorship Conference," UNDA.

67. Hesburgh, *God, Country, Notre Dame*, pp. 112–13.

68. Father Hesburgh's letter of February 17, 1969, PNDP 30-Pr-f2, "Fifteen Minute Rule 1969, UNDA. See also *New York Times*, February 18, 1969, p. 1, col. 7.

69. Father Hesburgh's letter, PNDP 20-Pr-f2, UNDA.

70. *New York Times*, February 25, 1969, p. 29, cols. 1–2, and March 1, 1969, p. 29, col. 1; O'Brien, *Hesburgh*, p. 109; Connelly and Dooley, *Hesburgh's Notre Dame*, pp. 242–43; and Father Hesburgh's letter to the vice president in Hesburgh, *God, Country, Notre Dame*, pp. 120–22.

71. O'Brien, *Hesburgh*, p. 109.

72. Connelly and Dooley, *Hesburgh's Notre Dame*, pp. 224–29.

73. *Observer*, Vol. IV, No. 46 (November 1, 1969), p. 1, and No. 47 (November 20, 1969), p. 1. See also "Defense of the Ten Accused Students involved in the Dow/CIA Demonstration of November 18, 1969," PNDP 30-Pr-V4, Protests-Dow/CIA, UNDA; "15 Minutes, 40 Years Later," *South Bend Tribune*, February 15, 2009; extended interview with one of the protesters from outside the university, Sister Joann Malone of Webster Groves, Missouri, in *Ave Maria* CXI, no. 4 (January 24, 1970), pp. 9–12; and *Scholastic*, Vol. CLXIII, No. 4 (November 14, 2019), p. 14.

Chapter 17. The 1970s

1. *Scholastic*, Vol. CXI, No. 3 (October 3, 1969), p. 30.

2. *Scholastic*, Vol. CXI, No. 7 (November 7, 1969), p. 4.

3. John A. O'Brien, *Road to Damascus* (New York, 1949), pp. 169–71; Willis Nutting, *The Free City* (Springfield, IL, 1967), pp. 136–44; and PNDP 30-Pr-N1, "Nutting for President/Free City Day," UNDA. The quotations are from PNDP 30-Pr-N1.

4. Nutting, *The Free City*, pp. 1–7, and PNDP 30-Pr-N1, "Nutting for President/ Free City Day," UNDA. The quotation is from Nutting, p. 7.

5. PNDP 30-Pr-fl, "Free University, 1968–1969," UNDA. For similar interests nationwide, see Gutek, *Education*, p. 310.

6. PNDP 30-Pr-N1, "Nutting for President/Free City Day, 1970," UNDA.

7. *New York Times*, July 14, 1970, p. 27, cols. 5–6; *Observer*, Vol. V, No. 1 (September 4, 1970), p. 1; O'Brien, *Hesburgh*, p. 141; and Connelly and Dooley, *Hesburgh's Notre Dame*, pp. 273–77. At the same time, Philip Faccenda was named vice president and general counsel, and the present author was named vice president of student affairs to replace Father Charles McCarragher, who had earlier resigned.

8. O'Brien, *Hesburgh*, pp. 71–73, and Hesburgh, *God, Country, Notre Dame*, pp. 190–92.

9. "Negroes at Notre Dame," *Ebony Magazine* (February 1950), pp. 20–24; chapter 13 of this present work; and "The 1940s and 1950s" (pp. 1–4), "Frazier L. Thompson" (pp. 5–10), and "Arthur C. McFarland" (p. 135), in David Krashna and Don Wycliff, eds., *Black Domers: Seventy Years at Notre Dame* (Notre Dame, IN, 2014).

10. *Observer*, Vol. IV, No. 13 (October 2, 1969), p. 1; "Arthur C. McFarland," in Krashna and Wycliff, *Black Domers*, p. 135; and Connelly and Dooley, *Hesburgh's Notre Dame*, p. 255.

11. *New York Times*, December 14, 1969, p. 61, col. 1; *Observer*, Vol. IV, No. 34 (November 3, 1969), p. 3, No. 109 (April 15, 1970), p. 1, No. 121 (May 4, 1970), p. 1, and No 130 (May 15, 1970), p. 1; and "Algernon Johnson 'Jay' Cooper" (p. 91), "Don Wycliff" (p. 124), "Francis X. Taylor" (p. 141), and "Ronald J. Irvine" (pp. 165–66), in Krashna and Wycliff, *Black Domers*.

12. *Observer*, Vol. IV, No. 93 (March 12, 1970), p. 1; and Vol. V, No. 91 (March 4, 1971), pp. 1–2; and "Percy A. Pierre" (p. 76), "Ronald A. Homer" (pp. 95–96), "Ronald J. Irvine" (p. 164), and "Gail Antoinette King" (p. 170), in Krashna and Wycliff, *Black Domers*.

13. The notes and recollections of the author, who was vice president of student affairs and a university trustee in the early 1970s. For an excellent study of the background of the movement into coeducation in the 1960s and 1970s, see Nancy Weiss Malkiel, *Keep the Damned Women Out* (Princeton, NJ, 2016), pp. 3–27.

14. Hesburgh, *God, Country, Notre Dame*, p. 182; *Observer*, Vol. III, No. 64 (January 7, 1969), p. 1; *New York Times*, March 17, 1968, p. 28, col. 8; and *Chicago Tribune*, December 24, 1968, p. 4. Three seminar papers written by Laura Navarre, Gregory Rodgers, and Megan Hannon on this Notre Dame–Saint Mary's topic were also helpful. All three papers are in the possession of the author.

15. *Scholastic*, Vol. CVI, No. 12 (February 12, 1965), p. 5; Vol. CVII, No. 3 (October 8, 1965), p. 9; Creek, *A Panorama*, p. 149; and *New York Times*, May 4, 1969, p. 66, cols. 4–8. The questionnaire is in PNDP 30-SA-02, ND-SMC Merger, Questionnaire re Cooperation, 1967, UNDA. See also *Scholastic*, Vol. CIX, No. 18 (April 14, 1967), pp. 12–13.

16. *Observer*, Vol. V, No. 13 (September 25, 1970), p. 1; and *Scholastic*, Vol. CVIII (CIX), No. 16 (March 10, 1967), p. 23, and No. 18 (April 14, 1967), p. 12.

17. *Observer*, Vol. III, No. 129 (May 6, 1969), p. 5, and No 131 (May 8, 1969), pp. 1 and 5; Vol. V, No. 97 (March 25, 1971), p. 1; and Vol. VI, No. 10 (September 23, 1971), p. 1; and Blantz, *George N. Shuster*, p. 338.

18. "Statement of Principles," May 2, 1969, PNDP 30-SA-02, ND-SMC Merger – Press Releases, etc., UNDA.

19. The report is in PNDP 30-SA-02, ND-SMC Merger – Press Releases, etc., UNDA.

20. Father Burtchaell's response of February 24, 1971, is in PNDP 30-SA-02, ND-SMC Merger-Press Releases, etc., UNDA.

21. *Observer*, Vol. V, No. 89 (March 2, 1971), p. 1.

22. *South Bend Tribune*, May 15, 1971, p. 1; and *Observer*, Vol. V, No. 97 (March 25, 1971), p. 1.

23. *South Bend Tribune*, November 30, 1971; *Observer*, Vol. VI, No. 29 (October 20, 1971), p. 1, No. 30 (October 21, 1971), p. 1, and No. 54 (December 1, 1971), p. 1.

24. *Observer*, Vol. VI, No. 54 (December 1, 1971), p. 1, No. 56 (December 3, 1971), p. 1, No. 57 (December 6, 1971), p. 1, No. 60 (January 20, 1972), p. 1, and No. 72 (February 7, 1972), p. 1; and *South Bend Tribune*, December 1, 2, and 8, 1971, January 13 and 19, 1972, and March 3, 1972.

25. Recollection of the author, who was the vice president of student affairs and a university trustee at the time. In fact, the majority of women, between 52.5 and 58.6 percent, did select the College of Arts and Letters in the first four years of coeducation. See *Report of the Committee to Evaluate Coeducation*, in *Notre Dame Report*, Vol. 6, No. 16 (May 6, 1977), p. 368.

26. *Observer*, Vol. VI, No. 70 (February 3, 1972), p. 1, No. 74 (February 9, 1972), p. 1, and No. 94 (March 7, 1972), p. 1.

27. *Observer*, Vol. VII, No. 2 (September 6, 1972), p. 1; and Ann Therese Darin Palmer, ed., *Thanking Father Ted* (Kansas City, MO, 2007), pp. 20–24 and 207–35.

28. *Student Manual*, 1969–1970, pp. 11 and 21–24; PNDP 30-Pr-V5, Protests – Vietnam and General Student Unrest, 1970, UNDA; Samuel E. Morison, *The Founding of Harvard College* (Cambridge, MA, 1935), p. 232; *Scholastic*, Vol. CVIII, No. 20 (April 28, 1967), p. 12; and Vol. CIX, No. 19 (April 21, 1967), p. 8.

29. *Observer*, Vol. V, No. 27 (October 16, 1970), p. 1, No. 42 (November 6, 1970), p. 1, No. 46 (November 12, 1970), p. 1, and No. 60 (January 20, 1971), p. 1.

30. *Observer*, Vol. V, No. 64 (January 26, 1971), p. 1.

31. Of the plethora of books on the Vietnam War, see Gary R. Hess, *Vietnam and the United States* (Boston, 1990), pp. 85–95.

32. Vaughn Davis Bornet, *The Presidency of Lyndon B. Johnson* (Lawrence, KS, 1983), p. 87; and *Scholastic*, Vol. CVII, No. 4 (October 15, 1965), pp. 11 and 38, and No. 5 (October 22, 1965), pp. 20–21.

33. PNDP 30-Pr-V1, Protests – Vietnam and General Student Unrest; 1965–1967, UNDA; *Scholastic*, Vol. CVII, No. 13 (February 11, 1966), pp. 18, 19, and 35; and Vol. CVIII, No. 4 (October 21, 1966), p. 26, and No. 17 (March 17, 1967), pp. 22–23. These last two citations are listed incorrectly as volume CIX in the journal itself.

34. *Observer*, Vol. I, No. 1 (February 9, 1967), p. 1; Vol. III, No. 95 (March 7, 1969), p. 1; and *South Bend Tribune*, May 8, 1968.

35. Hesburgh, *God, Country, Notre Dame*, pp. 123–24, and *Observer*, Vol. III, No. 94 (March 6, 1969), p. 1.

36. *Observer*, Vol. III, No. 107 (March 24, 1969), p. 1; *New York Times*, August 24, 1969, p. 60, cols. 4–5; *Bulletin of Information: Arts and Letters*, 1972–1973, p. 152; *Bulletin*

of Information: Arts and Letters, 1973–1975, p. 105; and Hesburgh, *God, Country, Notre Dame*, pp. 124–26.

37. PNDP 30-Pr-V3, Protests – Vietnam and General Student Unrest, 1969, UNDA; *This Day in History*, October 15, 1969; *Observer*, Vol. IV, No. 17 (October 8, 1969), p. 1, and No. 21 (October 14, 1969), p. 1; Bill Clinton, *My Life* (New York, 2005), pp. 161–62; and Nigel Hamilton, *Bill Clinton: An American Journey* (New York, 2003), pp. 206–8.

38. *Observer*, Vol. IV, No. 23 (October 16, 1969), pp. 1, 2, 4, and 9. The one woman, a Saint Mary's student, assisted in tearing up the draft cards: Schlereth, *University of Notre Dame*, p. 219.

39. *Observer*, Vol. IV, No. 24 (October 17, 1969), p. 8. Father Hesburgh's quotation is in the *Observer*, Vol. IV, No. 20 (October 13, 1969), p. 1.

40. Hess, *Vietnam*, pp. 119–23, and *New York Times*, May 6, 1970, p. 1, col. 5.

41. PNDP 30-Pr-V5, Protests-Vietnam-Student Strike, May 1970, UNDA; *Observer*, Vol. IV, No. 122 (May 5, 1970), p. 1; and O'Brien, *Hesburgh*, pp. 118–19.

42. *Observer*, Vol. IV, No. 122 (May 5, 1970), p. 1.

43. *Observer*, Vol. IV, No. 122 (May 5, 1970), p. 1.

44. *Observer*, Vol. IV, No. 122 (May 5, 1970), pp. 1 and 6, and No. 123 (May 6, 1970), p. 1. Thursday, May 7, was also the Feast of the Ascension, a Holy Day of Obligation, and no classes had originally been scheduled for that day.

45. *Observer*, Vol. IV, No. 124 (May 7, 1970), p. 1, and No. 125 (May 8, 1970), p. 1.

46. Minutes of Academic Council Meeting, May 11, 1970, PNDP 3100, UNDA; *Observer*, Vol. IV, No. 127 (May 12, 1970), p. 1; and O'Brien, *Hesburgh*, pp. 120–21. In the confusion of the time, no clear record seems to remain of how many students actually took advantage of the options. A letter from Charles McCollester of the Office of Institutional Studies to associate dean of of the College of Arts and Letters Devere Plunkett, dated September 3, 1970 (UCAS 3/77, UNDA), suggests a figure of 10 percent for Arts and Letters classes, although the figure was certainly much higher in individual classes.

47. *Observer*, Vol. IV, No. 122 (May 5, 1970), p. 1.

48. *Observer*, Vol. IV, No. 126 (May 11, 1970), p. 1, and No. 128 (May 13, 1970), p. 1; and O'Brien, *Hesburgh*, p. 120.

49. *Observer*, Vol. IV, No. 19 (October 10, 1969), p. 2, and No. 25 (October 20, 1969), p. 6.

50. *Observer*, Vol. VI, No. 83 (February 22, 1972), p. 1, and No. 87 (February 26, 1972), p. 1.

51. Recollection of the author as vice president of student affairs. For a much later review of that election by one of the defeated candidates, see Gary Caruso in the *Observer*, Vol. L, No. 108 (March 18, 2016), p. 6.

52. Recollections of the author as vice president of student affairs.

53. Richard Quebedeaux, *The New Charismatics II* (New York, 1983), pp. 18–21; and Kevin and Dorothy Ranaghan, *Catholic Pentecostals Today* (South Bend, IN, 1983), pp. 7–14 and 68–82. The quotation is from Kevin and Dorothy Ranaghan, p. 14.

54. Kevin and Dorothy Ranaghan, *Catholic Pentecostals Today*, pp. 19–20, and Quebedeaux, *New Charismatics II*, pp. 72–75.

55. Kevin and Dorothy Ranaghan, *Catholic Pentecostals Today*, pp. 22–23, and Patrick J. Couch, "The Rise and Fall of the Catholic Charismatic Renewal at the University of Notre Dame, 1967–1971" (senior seminar paper, University of Notre Dame, 2016), in the possession of the author.

56. *Scholastic*, Vol. CIX, No. 18 (April 14, 1967), pp. 18–20; and Vol. CXIII, No. 10 (March 10, 1972), p. 15; and Kevin and Dorothy Ranaghan, *Catholic Pentecostals Today*, pp. 23–26.

57. Kevin and Dorothy Ranaghan, *Catholic Pentecostals Today*, p. 30; Quebedeaux, *New Charismatics II*, pp. 78–79; and *Notre Dame Magazine* 2, no. 4 (August 1973), pp. 6–7.

58. PNDP 30–Cu–01, Cushwa Center for the Study of American Catholicism, UNDA.

59. Steele, *Fighting Irish*, pp. 206–9, and Schoor, *100 Years*, pp. 250–54.

60. Steele, *Fighting Irish*, pp. 209–15, and Schoor, *100 Years*, pp. 255–61.

61. Steele, *Fighting Irish*, pp. 215–19, and Schoor, *100 Years*, pp. 261–66.

62. Steele, *Fighting Irish*, pp. 219–22, and Schoor, *100 Years*, pp. 266–70.

63. Schoor, *100 Years*, pp. 271–75; Dan Devine, *Simply Devine: Memoirs of a Hall of Fame Coach* (Champaign, IL, 2000), pp. 9–119; and *New York Times*, May 10, 2002, sec. C, p. 13, col. 1.

64. Steele, *Fighting Irish*, pp. 222–25; Schoor, *100 Years*, pp. 275–78; and Devine, *Simply Devine*, pp. 123–28.

65. Steele, *Fighting Irish*, pp. 225–27; Schoor, *100 Years*, pp. 280–83; and Devine, *Simply Devine*, pp. 129–32.

66. Steele, *Fighting Irish*, pp. 228–32; Schoor, *100 Years*, pp. 285–96; and Devine, *Simply Devine*, pp. 132–38.

67. Steele, *Fighting Irish*, pp. 232–37; Schoor, *100 Years*, pp. 297–302; and Devine, *Simply Devine*, pp. 141–48.

68. Steele, *Fighting Irish*, pp. 237–43; Schoor, *100 Years*, pp. 303–11; and Devine, *Simply Devine*, pp. 148–61.

69. He acquired the name "Digger" because his father was an undertaker.

70. Neely, *Hooping It Up*, pp. 106–25 and 330–33.

71. Neely, *Hooping It Up*, pp. 126–70 and 333–43.

72. Neely, *Hooping It Up*, pp. 171–202 and 343–49.

73. *Notre Dame Basketball Guide*, 1991–1992, p. 202, PATH, UNDA.

74. Neely, *Hooping It Up*, pp. 203–7 and 349–51, and Digger Phelps, *Tales from the Notre Dame Locker Room* (New York, 2015), pp. 10–29. Shumate sat out his freshman year, recovering from a blood clot.

75. Neely, *Hooping It Up*, pp. 207–11, and Phelps, *Tales*, pp. 30–47.

76. Neely, *Hooping It Up*, pp. 214–68; *Notre Dame Basketball Guide*, 1991–1992, pp. 153–55; and Phelps, *Tales*, pp. 123–33. The quotation is from Neely, p. 251.

77. Written to Phelps in 1996 and quoted in Phelps, *Tales*, p. 9.

78. Phelps, *Tales*, pp. 55–103, and *Notre Dame Basketball Guide*, 1991–1992, p. 160.

79. Robert Schmuhl, *Fifty Years with Father Hesburgh: On and Off the Record* (Notre Dame, IN, 2016), pp. 26–27.

80. *Observer*, Vol. III, No. 24 (October 15, 1968), p. 2.

81. *Observer*, Vol. X, No. 21 (October 1, 1975), p. 1.

82. *Observer*, Vol. VI, No. 15 (September 30, 1971), p. 1.

83. A mutual friend in conversation with the author.

84. *Observer*, Vol. VI, No. 95 (March 8, 1972), p. 1, and No. 104 (April 6, 1972), p. 1; and Vol. VIII, No. 49 (November 16, 1973), p. 3, and No. 67 (January 31, 1974), p. 1.

85. *Observer*, Vol. V, No. 70 (February 3, 1971), p. 1; Vol. IX, No. 75 (February 6, 1975), p. 1; Vol. X, No 59 (December 2, 1975), p. 1, No. 61 (December 4, 1975), p. 1, and No. 68 (January 21, 1976), p. 1.

86. *Observer*, Vol. VI, No. 101 (March 16, 1972), p. 1; and Vol. VIII, No. 70 (February 1, 1974), p. 1. The students had also asked for membership on departmental Appointments and Promotions Committees but Father Burtchaell had rejected this, noting that promotions involved matters outside the competence of students. *Observer*, Vol. V, No. 70 (February 3, 1971), p. 1.

87. *Observer*, Vol. X, No. 125 (April 28, 1976), p. 1; and Vol. XI, No. 29 (October 8, 1976), p. 1, No. 58 (December 3, 1976), p. 1, and No. 124 (May 3, 1977), p. 1.

88. *Observer*, Vol. VI, No. 84 (February 23, 1972), p. 1; and Vol. VII, No. 33 (October 24, 1972), p. 1.

89. *Notre Dame Report*, Vol. 1, No. 11 (February 15, 1972), pp. 179–80.

90. *Notre Dame Report*, Vol. 6, No. 16 (May 6, 1977), pp. 395–96.

91. PNDP 90-Pop-IL, ND Population Statistics, etc., UNDA; *Notre Dame Report*, Vol. 2, No. 13 (March 16, 1973), pp. 274–87; and Vol. 7, No. 4 (October 28, 1977), pp. 107–25.

92. PNDP 2100-1, Endowed Professorships at the University of Notre Dame, UNDA; *Notre Dame Report*, Vol. 4, No. 5 (November 15, 1974), p. 113; and Vol. 5, No. 6 (November 28, 1975), p. 147. In the 1950s there were unfunded (honorary) chairs and so-called "living chairs" in which part of a faculty member's salary would be paid from an annual gift: UNDP 9997-Cha, Archives Research re Pre-Named, Endowed, and Living Chairs and Professorships, UNDA.

93. *Notre Dame Report*, Vol. 1, No. 11 (February 15, 1972), pp. 175–76; Vol. 6, No. 7 (December 17, 1976), pp. 204–5; Vol. 7, No. 16 (May 5, 1978), p. 379; and *Observer*, Vol. VIII, No. 86 (February 25, 1974), p. 1; Vol. IX, No. 5 (September 4, 1974), p. 1; and Vol. X, No. 48 (November 7, 1975), p. 1.

94. The report is most accessible in *Notre Dame Magazine* 2, no. 6 (December 1973), pp. 8–41. This material is on page 10. In addition to Father Burtchaell and the two mentioned, the other members were Howard Bathon, arts and letters senior; Fr. David Burrell, C.S.C., associate professor of theology and philosophy; Dr. James Daschbach, associate professor of mechanical engineering; Dr. James Frick, vice president of public relations and development; Dr. Yusaku Furuhashi, professor of marketing; Dr. Robert Gordon, vice president of advanced studies; Fr. Ernan McMullin, professor of philosophy; Dr. O. Timothy O'Meara, professor of mathematics; Frank Palopoli, graduate student in government; Dr. Thomas Shaffer, dean of the Law School; and Dr. Marshall Smelser, professor of history. For the reaction of female rectors, see the *Observer*, Vol. VII, No. 22 (October 10, 1972), p. 1.

95. *COUP Report*, p. 13.

96. *COUP Report*, p. 13.

97. *COUP Report*, pp. 15–17.

98. *COUP Report*, pp. 19–21.

99. *COUP Report*, p. 23.

100. *COUP Report*, p. 25.

101. *COUP Report*, pp. 28–29.

102. *COUP Report*, pp. 31–33. The quotations are on page 33. The graduate enrollment figures do not include law and MBA students since their earning potential made their financial need less urgent.

103. *COUP Report*, p. 35.

104. *COUP Report*, p. 36.

105. *COUP Report*, pp. 36–37.

106. *COUP Report*, p. 38.

107. *COUP Report*, p. 39.

108. *COUP Report*, p. 40.

109. The report is most accessible in *Notre Dame Report*, Vol. 4, No. 5 (November 15, 1974), pp. 130–42. The quotations are from pages 135–39 and 131.

110. *Academic Manual*, article II, section 1.

111. *Notre Dame Report*, Vol. 5, No. 8 (December 26, 1975), p. 215; Vol. 6, No. 7 (December 17, 1976), pp. 187 and 189; Vol. 7, No. 1 (September 16, 1977), p. 1; and Minutes of the Board of Trustees' Meeting of November 12, 1976, UNDA.

112. *Notre Dame Report*, Vol. 7, No. 1 (September 16, 1977), p. 1.

113. *Faculty Senate Journal*, February 6, 1974, in *Notre Dame Report*, Vol. 3, No. 12 (March 15, 1974), p. 263.

114. For criticisms of Father Burtchaell's lack of consultation, see the *Observer*, Vol. VI, No. 101 (March 16, 1972) and No. 116 (April 25, 1972), and Vol. XI, No. 81 (February 16, 1977); for discussions of possible unionization, see Vol. VII, No. 68 (January 29, 1973), Vol. IX, No. 66 (January 24, 1974), and Vol. XI, No. 103 (March 29, 1977). The quotations are from the *Observer*, Vol. XII, No. 7 (September 7, 1977).

115. *Notre Dame Report*, Vol. 7, No. 1 (September 16, 1977), p. 25.

Chapter 18.   The 1980s

1. *Notre Dame Report*, Vol. 7, No. 5 (November 18, 1977), p. 151.

2. *Notre Dame Report*, Vol. 7, No. 4 (October 28, 1978), p. 104, and No. 5 (November 18, 1977), pp. 151–52.

3. UDIS 130/02, UDIS 175/25-26, and PNDPOI-m-3, Timothy O'Meara, UNDA; *Scholastic*, Vol. CXX, No. 1 (September 8, 1978), p. 7; and *Observer*, Vol. XIII, No. 1 (August 26, 1978), p. 4, and No. 2 (August 30, 1978), p. 1. The quotation is from the *Scholastic*.

4. *Observer*, Vol. XIII, No. 31 (October 10, 1978), p. 1; and *Notre Dame Report*, Vol. 8, No. 6 (December 1, 1978), pp. 174–76.

5. *Bulletin*, 1937–1938, p. 351; *Bulletin of the College of Arts and Letters*, 1956–1957, p. 8; and *General Bulletin*, 1957–1958, p. 87.

6. *Faculty Handbook*, 1976–1977, p. 28.

7. *Observer*, Vol. XIII, No. 115 (April 10, 1979), pp. 1, 5, and 9, and No. 124 (April 30, 1979), p. 1; and Vol. XIV, No. 9 (September 7, 1979), p. 1. See also *Observer*, Vol. XI, No. 90 (March 1, 1979), p. 1; and Vol. XII, No. 82 (February 14, 1979), pp. 1 and 11.

8. *Observer*, Vol. XIII, No. 61 (December 6, 1978), p. 1; Vol. XIV, No. 73 (January 29, 1980), p. 1, and No. 83 (February 12, 1980), pp. 1 and 5; and Vol. XV, No. 91 (February 13, 1981), p. 1, and No. 105 (March 5, 1981), p. 1.

9. *Observer*, Vol. XVI, No. 1 (August 22, 1981), p. 1.

10. *Observer*, Vol. XV, No. 105 (March 5, 1981), p. 1.

11. *Notre Dame Report*, Vol. 11, No. 7 (December 11, 1981), pp. 204–5.

12. The university faced other lawsuits also. The publication *Go Irish* sued because it was denied credentials other publications had; two other professors claimed they had been denied promotion because of age and gender (and religion in one case); a Saint Mary's student sued because she was sexually assaulted along the road from the Grotto to Saint Mary's. See the *Observer*, Vol. XVII, No. 24 (September 28, 1982), p. 1, and No. 125 (April 22, 1983), p. 1; Vol. XIX, No. 8 (September 5, 1984), p. 1; and Vol. XX, No. 46 (November 5, 1985), p. 1.

13. *Notre Dame Report*, Vol. 10, No. 18 (June 12, 1981), pp. 502–3.

14. *Notre Dame Report*, Vol. 11, No. 5 (November 13, 1981), p. 127.

15. *Notre Dame Report*, Vol. 11, No. 5 (November 13, 1981), p. 129. Father Michael McCafferty of the Law School faculty was also a possible future candidate.

16. *Observer*, Vol. XVI, No. 39 (October 13, 1981), p. 1, and No. 44 (October 27, 1981), p. 1.

17. *Notre Dame Report*, Vol. 12, No. 8 (December 24, 1982), pp. 255–57. The quotation is on page 256.

18. *Notre Dame Report*, Vol. 12, No. 8 (December 24, 1982), pp. 257–66. See also *Notre Dame Report*, Vol. 10, No. 14 (April 10, 1981), p. 411; and Vol. 11, No. 1 (September 11, 1981), p. 7.

19. *Notre Dame Report*, Vol. 12, No. 8 (December 24, 1982), pp. 266–71. The first two quotations are from page 266 and the third from page 269.

20. *Notre Dame Report*, Vol. 12, No. 8 (December 24, 1982), pp. 271–76.

21. *Notre Dame Report*, Vol. 12, No. 8 (December 24, 1982), p. 277.

22. *Notre Dame Report*, Vol. 12, No. 8 (December 24, 1982), p. 278.

23. *Notre Dame Report*, Vol. 8, No. 13 (March 16, 1979), p. 282, and No. 20 (July 27, 1979), p. 432; Vol. 9, No. 16 (May 2, 1980), p. 345; Vol. 11, No. 13 (March 19, 1982), p. 344; Vol. 13, No. 5 (November 18, 1983), p. 159; Vol. 14, No. 5 (November 30, 1984), p. 217; and Vol. 16, No. 3 (October 3, 1986), p. 33, and No. 14 (April 3, 1987), p. 252.

24. *Fact Book*, 1988–1989, Table 7.1, UNDA. If part-time professors and lecturers are included, the numbers increase to 811 in 1980 and 1046 in 1988: PNDP 90-Pop-IL, ND Population Statistics, UNDA. The *Fact Book* of 1987–1988 was the first the university published, and the *Fact Book* of 1988–1989 contains information of the complete 1980s.

25. *Fact Book*, 1988–1989, Table 7.1, and *Bulletins* 1977–1978 and 1987–1988. Figures in the *Bulletins* can include visiting and emeriti professors, some probably not teaching full-time.

26. See chapter 17, page 473, and *Notre Dame Report*, Vol. 7, No. 8 (December 30, 1977), p. 204.

27. *Notre Dame Report*, Vol. 9, No. 6 (November 30, 1979), p. 183; and Vol. 14, No. 4 (November 16, 1984), p. 215.

28. *Notre Dame Report*, Vol. 14, No. 5 (November 30, 1984), p. 218.

29. *Notre Dame Report*, Vol. 7, No. 19 (June 23, 1978), p. 455; Vol. 8, No. 19 (June 29, 1979), p. 411; Vol. 9, No. 19 (June 27, 1980), p. 419; Vol. 10, No. 19 (June 26, 1980), p. 521; Vol. 11, No. 19 (June 25, 1982), p. 512; and Vol. 12, No. 20 (July 29, 1983), p. 513.

30. Mention of these and similar complaints appear in many *Faculty Senate Journals* published in the *Notre Dame Report* during these years.

31. *Notre Dame Report*, Vol. 12, No. 13 (March 18, 1983), p. 369.

32. *Notre Dame Report*, Vol. 14, No. 3 (October 19, 1984), pp. 138–40. The quotation is from page 138.

33. *Notre Dame Report*, Vol. 14, No. 3 (October 19, 1984), p. 134.

34. *Notre Dame Report*, Vol. 14, No. 3 (October 19, 1984), pp. 135–38.

35. *Notre Dame Report*, Vol. 14, No.19 (July 5, 1985), p. 623.

36. *Notre Dame Report*, Vol. 15, No. 5 (November 15, 1985), p. 116; and *Observer*, Vol. XX, No. 44 (November 1–2, 1985), p. 1. The quotations are from the *Observer*.

37. *Notre Dame Report*, Vol. 15, No. 16 (May 2, 1986), pp. 295–306; and *Observer*, Vol. XX, No. 114 (March 18, 1986), pp. 1 and 4. The quotations are on page 1.

38. *Notre Dame Report*, Vol. 16, No. 5 (November 14, 1986), pp. 108–10, and No. 9 (January 16, 1987), pp. 171–74; and *Observer*, Vol. XXI, No. 136 (May 4, 1987), pp. 1 and 7. The quotation is on page 7.

39. PNDP 30-In-6, Institute for International Peace Studies, UNDA; *Notre Dame Report*, Vol. 15, No. 9 (January 17, 1986), p. 197; and *Observer*, Vol. XX, No. 69 (December 13, 1985), p. 1, and No. 83 (February 4, 1986), p. 6.

40. PNDP 10-He-9, Theodore M. Hesburgh Center for International Peace Studies, UNDA; *Observer*, Vol. XXI, No. 126 (April 20, 1988), pp. 1 and 6; and Hesburgh, *God, Country, Notre Dame*, pp. 307–8. The quotation is from page 308.

41. *Observer*, Vol. XXI, No. 72 (January 19, 1987), pp. 1 and 4, and No. 131 (April 27, 1987), pp. 1 and 5; and *Notre Dame Report*, Vol. 16, No. 17 (May 16, 1987), p. 322. The quotations are from the *Observer*, No. 72 (January 19, 1987), pages 1 and 4.

42. *Observer*, Vol. XIX, No. 15 (September 14, 1984), pp. 1 and 6.

43. Mario Cuomo, "The Confession of a Public Man," *Notre Dame Magazine*, Vol. 13, No. 4 (Autumn 1984), p. 21.

44. Cuomo, "Confession," p. 22.

45. Cuomo, "Confession," p. 22.

46. Cuomo, "Confession," p. 25.

47. Cuomo, "Confession," pp. 23 and 25–26.

48. The first two quotations are from Cuomo, "Confession," page 27, and the second two from Cuomo, page 28.

49. *Notre Dame Magazine*, Vol. 13, No. 4 (Autumn 1984), p. 23.

50. *Observer*, Vol. XIX, No. 23 (September 25, 1984), pp. 1 and 3.

51. Reprinted in *Observer*, Vol. XIX, No. 27 (October 1, 1984), p. 6.

52. *Observer*, Vol. XIV, No. 40 (October 30, 1979), p. 1, No. 94 (February 27, 1980), pp. 1 and 7, and No. 118 (April 14, 1980), p. 2; Vol. XVI, No. 59 (November 16, 1981), p. 7, No. 106 (March 1, 1982), p. 3, No. 113 (March 10, 1982), p. 4, No. 125 (April 5, 1982), p. 1, No.127 (April 7, 1982), p. 1, No. 132 (April 20, 1982), p. 1, and No. 134 (April 22, 1982), p. 1; Vol. XVIII, No. 34 (October 12, 1983), p. 1, and No. 124 (April 9, 1984), p. 1; and Vol. XX, No. 28 (October 2, 1985), p. 1, and No. 48 (November 7, 1985), p. 1. For the mock conventions, see *Observer*, Vol. XIV, No. 74 (January 30, 1980), p. 3; Vol. XVIII, No. 122 (April 5, 1984), p. 1; and Vol. XXI, No. 117 (April 7, 1988), p. 7.

53. *Observer*, Vol. XV, No. 98 (February 24, 1981), p. 1.

54. *Fact Book*, 1988–1989, Table 3.1. The freshman class of 1980 numbered 1,258 men and 434 women, and the class of 1988 numbered 1,139 men and 468 women: Table 3.3.

55. *Fact Book*, 1988–1989, Tables 3.2, 3.5, 3.6, and 3.8.

56. *Observer*, Vol. XVII, No. 15 (September 16, 1983), p. 1; Vol. XIX, No. 34 (October 9, 1984), p. 3, and No. 79 (January 24, 1985), p. 1; and Vol. XXI, No. 1 (August 23, 1986), p. 1, and No. 84 (February 4, 1987), p. 1. The quotations are from Vol. XIX, No. 34 (October 9, 1984), p. 3.

57. *Observer*, Vol. XV, No. 90 (February 12, 1981), p. 1; and Vol. XVI, No. 99 (February 18, 1982), p. 1, No. 100 (February 19, 1982), p. 1, No. 108 (March 3, 1982), p. 1, and No. 109 (March 4, 1982), p. 2. For an excellent background of the boycott, see Tehila Sasson, "Milking the Third World? Humanitarianism, Capitalism, and the Moral Economy of the Nestlé Boycott," *American Historical Review* 121, no. 4 (October 2016), pp. 1,196–224.

58. *Observer*, Vol. XV, No. 90 (February 12, 1981), p. 1; Vol. XVII, No. 93 (February 9, 1983), p. 1; and Vol. XX, No. 101 (February 27, 1986), p. 1. The quotations are from Vol. XV, No. 90 (February 12, 1981), p. 1, and Vol. XX, No. 101 (February 27, 1986), p. 1.

59. Minutes of Board of Trustees Meetings of October 13, 1978, and May 9, 1986, UBTS, 1967–1990, UNDA; *Observer*, Vol. XIX, No. 99 (February 21, 1985), p. 1, and No. 129 (April 18, 1985), p. 4; and Vol. XX, No. 36 (October 14, 1985), p. 1, No. 41 (October 29, 1985), p. 1, No. 96 (February 20, 1986), p. 1, No. 123 (April 10, 1986), p. 1, No. 124 (April 11, 1986), p. 1, and No. 140 (May 16, 1986), p. 1. The quotations are from Vol. XIX, No. 99 (February 21, 1985), p. 1, and Vol. XX, No. 41 (October 29, 1985), p. 1.

60. *Observer*, Vol. XIV, No. 91 (February 22, 1980), p. 1; Vol. XV, No. 32 (October 3, 1980), p. 1, and No. 102 (March 2, 1981), p. 1; Vol. XVII, No. 94 (February 10, 1983), p. 1; Vol. XVIII, No. 98 (February 23, 1984), p. 4; and Vol. XIX, No. 88 (February 6, 1985), p. 6. It may be significant that the festival does not rate page one in the student newspaper in later years.

61. Annual An Tostal programs are preserved in PNDP, An Tostal, 1980s, UNDA. The present description is from the 1986 program, but each year is quite similar. See also *Observer*, Vol. XX, No. 128 (April 21, 1986), p. 5.

62. *Observer*, Vol. XVIII, No. 28 (October 4, 1983), p. 1, No. 35 (October 13, 1983), p. 1, and No. 42 (November 1, 1983), p. 4.

63. *Observer*, Vol. IV, No. 117 (April 27, 1970), p. 1, and No. 118 (April 28, 1970), pp. 1 and 4; Vol. XV, No. 9 (September 4, 1980), p. 1; and Vol. XVIII, No. 14 (September 15, 1983), p. 1. The quotation is from Vol. XVIII, No. 14 (September 15, 1983).

64. Peter Balestracci, "The Drinking Irish: The History of the Alcohol Policy and Its Development at the University of Notre Dame" (senior seminar paper, University of Notre Dame, 2010), in possession of the author.

65. *Observer*, Vol. XV, No. 61 (November 20, 1980), p. 1; Vol. XVI, No. 13 (September 10, 1981), p. 1; and *Notre Dame Report*, Vol. 12, No. 15 (April 22, 1983), p. 409. The quotations are from the *Notre Dame Report*.

66. *Notre Dame Report*, Vol. 13, No. 16 (May 18, 1984), pp. 435–42; and *Observer*, Vol. XVIII, No. 105 (March 5, 1984), p. 1, and No. 112 (March 14, 1984), p. 1. The quotation is from the *Notre Dame Report*, page 439.

67. *Observer*, Vol. XVIII, No. 130 (April 17, 1984), pp. 1, 4, and 5, No. 131 (April 18, 1984), p. 1, No. 132 (April 19, 1984), p. 1, No. 136 (April 30, 1984), p. 1, and No. 141 (May 7, 1984), p. 1; and Vol. XIX, No. 76 (January 21, 1985), p. 1. The quotations are from Vol. XVIII, Nos. 131 (April 18, 1984) and 132 (April 19, 1984).

68. *Observer*, Vol. XX, No. 60 (November 27, 1985), p. 1. See also Steele, *Fighting Irish*, pp. 244–60, and Schoor, *100 Years*, pp. 312–18 and 382–84.

69. *Observer*, Vol. XX, No. 64 (December 6, 1985), p. 9.

70. *Observer*, Vol. XX, No. 68 (December 12, 1985), p. 9.

71. *Observer*, Vol. XX, No. 61 (December 3, 1985), p. 1; and Schoor, *100 Years*, pp. 317–19.

72. Schoor, *100 Years*, pp. 320–31, and Steele, *Fighting Irish*, pp. 260–67.

73. Steele, *Fighting Irish*, pp. 267–72, and Lou Holtz, *The Fighting Spirit: A Championship Season at Notre Dame*, with John Heisler (New York, 1989), pp. 91–378.

74. Steele, *Fighting Irish*, pp. 272–75.

75. *Observer*, Vol. XVII, No. 124 (April 7, 1983), p. 1, and No. 141 (May 13, 1983), p. 6.

76. *Province Review*, December 2007, pp. 12–18; *Scholastic*, Vol. XXIII, No. 3 (September 21, 1889), p. 46, and No. 35 (May 10, 1890), p. 562; and *Observer*, Vol. XXIII, No. 139 (May 18, 1990), p. 5.

77. PNDP 10-Ec-3 Folder – Eck Pavilion/Indoor Tennis Center – 1987, UNDA.

78. "History," Snite Museum of Art, University of Notre Dame, https://sniteart museum.nd.edu/about-us/history.

79. *Notre Dame Report*, Vol. 12, No. 2 (September 24, 1982) p. 39; and *Observer*, Vol. XV, No. 1 (August 25, 1980), p. 4, and No. 88 (February 10, 1981), p. 3.

80. *Notre Dame Report*, Vol. 9, No. 8 (December 28, 1979), p. 197; and *Observer*, Vol. XV, No. 1 (August 25, 1980), p. 4, No. 55 (November 12, 1980), p. 1, No. 70

(January 15, 1981), p. 3, and No. 88 (February 10, 1981), p. 3. For criticisms of the architecture of the Father Hesburgh years, see McCandless, "Endangered Domain," pp. 73–94.

81. *Notre Dame Report*, Vol. 13, No. 5 (November 18, 1983), p. 160; and *Observer*, Vol. XVII, No. 22 (September 25, 1982), p. 3; Vol. XVIII, No. 130 (April 18, 1984), pp. 1 and 3; and Vol. XIX, No. 16 (September 17, 1984), pp. 8 and 9.

82. *Notre Dame Report*, Vol. 12, No. 9 (January 21, 1983), p. 300; Vol. 15, No. 5 (November 15, 1985), p. 115; and *Observer*, Vol. XVIII, No. 4 (September 1, 1983), p. 1.

83. *Observer*, Vol. XVIII, No. 26 (September 30, 1983), pp. 1 and 5.

84. *Notre Dame Report*, Vol. 13, No. 10 (February 3, 1984), p. 311.

85. *Observer*, Vol. XV, No. 1 (August 25, 1980), pp. 1 and 5, No. 42 (October 16, 1980), pp. 1 and 4, and No. 79 (January 28, 1981), p. 1; and Vol. XVI, No. 9 (September 4, 1981), pp. 1 and 8–9.

86. *Notre Dame Report*, Vol. 11, No. 15 (April 23, 1982), p. 409; *Observer*, Vol. XVII, No. 74 (January 13, 1983), pp. 1 and 4, and No. 129 (April 14, 1983), p. 1; and Rev. Don McNeill, C.S.C., and Margaret Pfeil, eds., *Act Justly, Love Mercifully, and Walk Humbly with Your God* (Kansas City, MO, 2016), esp. chaps. 1, 2, 3, 4, and 7.

87. *Notre Dame Report*, Vol. 15, No. 5 (November 15, 1985), p. 116; and *Observer*, Vol. XV, No. 1 (August 25, 1980), p. 1; Vol. XVI, No. 21 (September 21, 1981), p. 1; Vol. XX, No. 38 (October 16, 1985), pp. 1 and 3; and Vol. XXI, No. 34 (October 13, 1986), p. 1, No. 38 (October 17–18, 1986), pp. 1 and 5, and No. 64 (December 9, 1986), pp. 1 and 4. The first quotation is from Vol. XX, No. 38 (October 16, 1985), page 3, and the second from Vol. XXI, No. 34 (October 13, 1986), page 1.

88. *Observer*, Vol. XV, No. 23 (September 22, 1980), p. 1; Vol. XX, No. 22 (September 24, 1985), pp. 1 and 5, and No. 28 (October 2, 1985), p. 3.

89. O'Connell, *Sorin*, dedication page. See also "The Hesburgh Legend," the *New York Times* tribute, May 22, 1987, sec. A, p. 30, cols. 1–2.

90. Dean Manion of the Law School had been replaced earlier but Father Hesburgh, as executive vice president, had had a hand in it.

91. "America's Best Colleges," *U.S. News*, 1983–2007.

Chapter 19.   A President Called "Monk"

1. Edward A. Malloy, C.S.C., *Monk's Tale: The Pilgrimage Begins, 1941–1975* (Notre Dame, IN, 2009), pp. 1–36.

2. Malloy, *The Pilgrimage Begins*, pp. 39–56.

3. Malloy, *The Pilgrimage Begins*, pp. 57–68.

4. The team won twenty-seven straight the following year, and that streak of fifty-five consecutive victories was a record at the time. Thompson and Hoover were eventually drafted into the National Basketball Association, and Leftwich would have been had he not ruined his knee in an auto accident.

5. Malloy, *The Pilgrimage Begins*, pp. 57–86.

6. Malloy, *The Pilgrimage Begins*, pp. 87–106.

7. Malloy, *The Pilgrimage Begins*, pp. 99–150.

8. Malloy, *The Pilgrimage Begins*, pp. 151–252.

9. Malloy, *Monk's Tale: Way Stations on the Journey* (Notre Dame, IN, 2011), pp. 1–130.

10. Hesburgh, *God, Country, Notre Dame*, pp. 60–61.

11. *Observer*, Vol. XXI, No. 23 (September 24, 1987), p. 1

12. *Observer*, Vol. XXI, No. 23 (September 24, 1987), pp. 1, 3, and 5.

13. *Notre Dame Report*, Vol. 17, No. 4 (October 31, 1987), pp. 113–14.

14. Letter of Father Malloy to Notre Dame Community, April 1988, in the *Notre Dame Report*, special issue, Vol. 17 (April 8, 1988), n.p. (prior to p. 1) and p. 2 of first report.

15. The report is published in the *Notre Dame Report*, special issue, Vol. 17 (April 8, 1988). See esp. pp. 2–4 and 45–51.

16. The task force report is published in the *Notre Dame Report*, special issue, Vol. 17 (April 8, 1988). Pages are not numbered, but see especially the sections on "Alcohol Policies of American Colleges and Universities: A Selective Comparison," "Programmatic and Policy Recommendations," and "Minority Recommendations."

17. *Notre Dame Report*, special issue, Vol. 17 (April 8, 1988). The quotation is on page 2, and the recommendations are on pages 3–15.

18. *Notre Dame Report*, special issue, Vol. 17 (April 8, 1988). The quotation is on page 2 and the recommendations are on pages 6–46.

19. *Notre Dame Report*, Vol. 18, No. 2 (September 16, 1988), p. 27; and Malloy, *Monk's Tale, The Presidential Years, 1987–2005* (Notre Dame, IN, 2016), pp. 71–72.

20. *Fact Book*, 1988–1989, PNDP 1050, UNDA; and *Notre Dame Report*, Vol. 19, No. 1 (September 1, 1989), pp. 10–14.

21. For these thematic years, the author profited greatly from an excellent seminar paper by Patrick Overdorf, "The First Term of Father Monk Malloy and the Thematic Year System" (senior seminar paper, University of Notre Dame, 2005), in possession of the author. The quotation is from *Scholastic*, Vol. CXXX, No. 4 (September 22, 1988), p. 11.

22. *Scholastic*, Vol. CXXX, No. 3 (September 15, 1988), pp. 9, 10, and 20.

23. Malloy, *The Presidential Years*, pp. 85–87, and *Scholastic*, Vol. CXXXI, No. 1 (September 21, 1989), p. 17.

24. *Scholastic*, Vol. CXXXI, No. 1 (September 21, 1989), p. 16.

25. *Scholastic*, Vol. CXXXI, No. 1 (September 21, 1989), pp. 16, 17, and 18; *Observer*, Vol. XXIII, No. 9 (September 7, 1989), p. 7, and No. 10 (September 8, 1989), p. 1; and *Notre Dame Report*, Vol. 19, No. 18 (June 8, 1990), pp. 387–88. Mr. Cosby's honorary degree was revoked by the university in April 2018 when he was convicted of three counts of sexual assault. *Observer*, Vol. LII, No. 122 (April 27, 2018), p. 1.

26. Malloy, *The Presidential Years*, pp. 108–9; and *Notre Dame Report*, Vol. 20, No. 5 (November 2, 1990), pp. 140–41, and No. 18 (June 14, 1991), pp. 396–99.

27. *Scholastic*, Vol. CXXXII, No. 1 (September 13, 1990), pp. 10–12, No. 15 (February 21, 1991), pp. 6–7, No. 22 (April 19, 1991), pp. 19–20, and No. 23 (April 25, 1991), pp. 16–17; and *Notre Dame Report*, Vol. 21, No. 2 (September 13, 1991), pp. 38–40.

28. Malloy, *The Presidential Years*, pp. 128–29; *Notre Dame Report*, Vol. 21, No. 18 (June 12, 1992), pp. 451–54; and *Scholastic*, Vol. CXXXIII, No. 3 (September 12, 1991), pp. 9–11 and 14.

29. *Notre Dame Report*, Vol. 17, No. 19 (July 8, 1988), p. 427.

30. *Notre Dame Report*, Vol. 18, No. 17 (May 12, 1989), p. 229; Vol. 19, No. 18 (June 8, 1990), p. 375; Vol. 20, No. 14 (April 5, 1991), p. 327; and Vol. 21, No. 19 (July 10, 1992), p. 481.

31. *Notre Dame Report*, Vol. 17, No. 10 (January 29, 1988), pp. 259–60, and No. 15 (April 15, 1988), pp. 350–51.

32. *Observer*, Vol. XXIII, No. 32 (October 10, 1989), p. 1.

33. *Observer*, Vol. XXIII, No. 114 (March 29, 1990), p. 3.

34. *Observer*, Vol. XXIII, No. 73 (January 23, 1990), p. 1.

35. *Observer*, Vol. XXIV, No. 5 (August 30, 1991), p. 1.

36. *Observer*, Vol. XXI, No. 68 (January 14, 1988), p. 1; and Vol. XXIII, No. 49 (November 9, 1990), p. 1.

37. *Observer*, Vol. XXII, No. 110 (April 3, 1989), p. 3.

38. *Observer*, Vol. XXIII, No. 6 (September 4, 1989), p. 1.

39. *Observer*, Vol. XXII, No. 63 (December 5, 1988), p. 1.

40. *Observer*, Vol. XXII, No. 109 (March 31, 1989), pp. 1 and 8.

41. *Notre Dame Report*, Vol. 19, No. 5 (November 3, 1989), pp. 130–32. The senate meeting was on April 13, 1989.

42. *Notre Dame Report*, Vol. 19, No. 5 (November 3, 1989), pp. 133 and 138, No. 6 (November 17, 1989), p. 168, No. 10 (January 26, 1990), p. 241, No. 12 (February 23, 1990), p. 267, and No. 18 (June 8, 1990), pp. 402–4.

43. *Notre Dame Report*, Vol. 20, No. 8 (December 14, 1990), p. 214; and Vol. 21, No. 5 (November 1, 1991), pp. 150–52.

44. *Notre Dame Report*, Vol. 21, No. 17 (May 15, 1992), pp. 412–13, and No. 19 (July 10, 1992), pp. 492–94; and *Observer*, Vol. XXIV, No. 123 (April 2, 1992), p. 1, and No. 127 (April 8, 1992), p. 1.

45. *New York Times*, December 3, 1991, sec. A, p. 20, col. 5; *National Catholic Reporter*, December 6, 1991; *Observer*, Vol. XXIV, No. 64 (December 4, 1991), p. 1, and No. 69 (December 10, 1991), p. 1; *Common Sense*, December 1991; and *South Bend Tribune*, May 4, 2003.

46. *Observer*, Vol. XXI, No. 40 (October 28, 1987), p. 1.

47. *Notre Dame Report*, Vol. 17, No. 8 (December 18, 1987), p. 229; Vol. 18, No. 9 (January 13, 1989), p. 179; and Vol. 20, No. 9 (January 18, 1991), p. 224; and *Observer*, Vol. XXI, No. 96 (February 23, 1988), p. 1; and Vol. XXIII, No. 70 (December 13, 1990), p. 1.

48. *Observer*, Vol. XXIII, No. 79 (January 25, 1991), p. 1, No. 80 (January 28, 1991), p. 1, No. 81 (January 29, 1991), p. 1, No. 82 (January 30, 1991), p. 1, No. 113 (March 21, 1991), p. 1, and No. 130 (April 18, 1991), p. 6; and "Azikiwe T. Chandler" in Krashna and Wycliff, *Black Domers*, pp. 333–40.

49. *Notre Dame Report*, Vol. 21, No. 1 (August 30, 1991), p. 16.

50. *Observer*, Vol. XXIII, No. 131 (April 19, 1991), p. 1.

51. *Observer*, Vol. XXIII, No. 130 (April 18, 1991), pp. 1 and 4.

52. *Observer*, Vol. XXIII, No. 133 (April 23, 1991), pp. 1 and 5.

53. *Observer*, Vol. XXIII, No. 133 (April 23, 1991), p. 1, No. 134 (April 24, 1991), p. 1, and No. 139 (May 1, 1991), p. 1. There was also a protest against the Gulf War around this time but it was short-lived. See *Observer*, Vol. XIII, No. 72 (January 16, 1991).

54. *Notre Dame Report*, Vol. 22, No. 7 (December 4, 1992), p. 196.

55. *Observer*, Vol. XXV, No. 1 (August 22, 1992), p. 1.

56. *Observer*, Vol. XXIII, No. 82 (February 5, 1990), p. 3.

57. *Observer*, Vol. XXIV, No. 18 (September 18, 1991), p. 1.

58. *Observer*, Vol. XXI, No. 72 (January 20, 1988), p. 16, and No. 79 (January 29, 1988), p. 16; and Vol. XXIV, No. 130 (April 13, 1992), p. 20, and No. 131 (April 14, 1992), p. 16.

59. *Observer*, Vol. XXII, No. 9 (September 4, 1987), p. 1.

60. "SYR" was short for "Screw Your Roommate" and was originally a dance where a student's roommate arranged a date for him or her, but eventually it meant any all-hall or semiformal dance.

61. *Observer*, Vol. XXII, No. 2 (August 24, 1988), p. 1.

62. *Observer*, Vol. XXII, No. 5 (August 29, 1988), p. 1.

63. *Observer*, Vol. XXII, No. 6 (August 30, 1988), p. 1, and No. 55 (November 16, 1988), p. 1.

64. *du Lac*, 1991–1993, pp. 31–37.

65. *Observer*, Vol. XXI, No. 93 (February 18, 1998), p. 1.

66. *Observer*, Vol. XXI, No. 136 (May 4, 1987), p. 1.

67. *Notre Dame Report*, Vol. 17, No. 2 (September 25, 1987), pp. 77–80.

68. *Notre Dame Report*, Vol. 22, No. 18 (June 11, 1993), pp. 451–59.

69. PNDP 10-Kn-2, Marion Burk Knott Hall, and PNDP 10-Si-1, Siegfried Hall, UNDA.

70. *Observer*, Vol. XXI, No. 99 (February 26, 1988), pp. 1 and 4; and Vol. XXII, No. 14 (September 9–11, 1988), p. 1.

71. *Observer*, Vol. XXIII, No. 49 (November 10, 1989), p. 1; and Vol. XXIC, No. 75 (January 17, 1992), p. 1.

72. *Observer*, Vol. XXIII, No. 53 (November 16, 1989), p. 1, No. 54 (November 17, 1989), p. 1, No. 57 (November 28, 1989), p. 1, No. 66 (December 11, 1989), p. 1, and No. 111 (March 26, 1990), p. 1.

73. UDIS 79/15, Band Building, UNDA; and *Notre Dame Report*, Vol. 18, No. 16 (April 28, 1989), p. 281.

74. The Navy unit included the Marines contingent.

75. PNDP 10-Pa-2, Pasquerilla Center, UNDA; *Notre Dame Report*, Vol. 16, No. 18 (June 19, 1987), p. 336; and *Observer*, Vol. XXIII, No. 26 (October 1, 1990), p. 1. Also in 1990, the Mason Support Services Building, for campus maintenance, was constructed north of the main campus near the Notre Dame Federal Credit Union and the future new laundry.

76. *Observer*, Vol. XXX, No. 5 (September 1, 1989), p. 1; and *Notre Dame Report*, Vol. 18, No. 20 (August 4, 1989), p. 383.

77. PNDP 10-He 9, Hesburgh Center for International Studies, UNDA; and *Notre Dame Report*, Vol. 17, No. 17 (May 13, 1988), p. 379; and Vol. 21, No. 3 (September 27, 1991), p. 47.

78. PNDP 10-De-2, DeBartolo Classroom Building, UNDA; and *Notre Dame Report*, Vol. 18, No. 18 (June 9, 1989), p. 313.

79. *South Bend Tribune*, January 24, 1992, and May 24, 1994; Malloy, *The Presidential Years*, pp. 141–44; *Observer*, Vol. XXIX, No. 80 (January 24, 1992), p. 1, No. 81 (January 27, 1992), p. 1, and No. 82 (January 28, 1992), p. 1; and the deeply moving *What Though the Odds: Haley Scott's Journey of Faith and Triumph* by Haley Scott DeMaria with Bob Schaller, foreword by Lou Holtz (Kearney, NE, 2008).

Chapter 20.   The 1990s

1. *Colloquy for the Year 2000*, special edition, *Notre Dame Report*, Vol. 22 (1992–1993), p. 2.

2. This and the following quotations are from *Colloquy*, p. 3.

3. *Colloquy*, p. 4.

4. *Colloquy*, p. 2.

5. *Colloquy*, pp. 5–10.

6. *Colloquy*, pp. 10–12.

7. *Colloquy*, pp. 13–14. That last concern was met by the expansion of the stadium in 1995–1999.

8. *Colloquy*, pp. 14–15.

9. *Colloquy*, pp. 15–17.

10. *Colloquy*, pp. 18–19.

11. UDIS 269/15 Rudy, UNDA; Malloy, *The Presidential Years*, pp. 150–51; *South Bend Tribune*, December 13, 1992; and *Michiana Now*, October 1993.

12. UDIS 269/17 Rudy, UNDA; *South Bend Tribune*, October 26, 1992, December 13, 1992, and October 7, 1993; *Observer*, Vol. XXV, No. 59 (November 20, 1992), pp. 12–13; and Vol. XXVI, No. 28 (October 6, 1993), p. 7; and Press Release of Lyn Leone, Attorney-at-Law, October 4, 1993, in UDIS 269/15 Rudy, UNDA. Holy Cross Junior College was founded in 1966. The college changed its name on January 19, 1990, to Holy Cross College.

13. Karen Harris in *Michiana Now*, October 1993.

14. *Notre Dame 2001 Football* (guide), pp. 267 and 358; Steele, *Fighting Irish*, pp. 293–301; and University of Notre Dame Department of Athletics, "#049, College Gameday," 125 Moments, Notre Dame Football 125, 1887–2012, https://125.nd.edu/moments/college-gameday/.

15. *Notre Dame 2001 Football* (guide), pp. 267–68 and 358; and *Observer*, Vol. XXXI, No. 35 (October 10, 1997), p. 1, and No. 38 (October 15, 1997), p. 1.

16. *South Bend Tribune*, February 26 and 27, 1997, July 28, 1998, and October 3, 1998; and *Observer*, Vol. XXX, No. 65 (December 6, 1996), p. 20; and Vol. XXXII, No. 2 (August 1998), p. 1.

17. *South Bend Tribune*, March 6, 1998, p. 1, March 8, 1998, p. D1, and March 10, 1998, p. C1; and *Observer*, Vol. XXXI, No. 108 (March 18, 1998), p. 1, No. 118 (April 1, 1998), p. 20, and No. 125 (April 15, 1998), p. 1.

18. *South Bend Tribune*, May 27, 1998, p. C1, May 28, 1998, p. C1, August 7, 1998, p. 1, and September 29, 1998, p. D1; and *Observer*, Vol. XXXII, No. 2 (August 25, 1998), p. 1, No. 25 (September 29, 1998), p. 1, No. 29 (October 1, 1998), p. 1, and No. 111 (March 25, 1999), p. 1; and Vol. XXXIII, No. 4 (September 27, 1999), p. 1, and No. 65 (January 19, 2000), p. 1.

19. *Notre Dame 2001–2002 Men's Basketball Guide*, pp. 163–65 and 183–85. See also Tim Frank, "Monty Williams," in *Strong of Heart*, 2010, pp. 77–79, PATH 112-Str, UNDA.

20. *Notre Dame 2001–2002 Women's Basketball*, pp. 151–55 and 170.

21. *Notre Dame Fencing*, 2001–2002, pp. 40 and 58–59; and Jeremy D. Bonfiglio, *A Notre Dame Man: The Mike DeCicco Story* (Notre Dame, IN, 2013), pp. 35–58.

22. *Notre Dame Women's Soccer*, 2001, pp. 66–72 and 80–82.

23. *Notre Dame Men's Soccer*, 2001, pp. 58 and 68–69.

24. *Notre Dame Baseball*, 2001, pp. 102–7 and 136–40.

25. *Notre Dame Softball*, 2001, pp. 56–64 and 66–68.

26. *Notre Dame Men's Lacrosse*, 2000, pp. 56–57; *Notre Dame Women's Lacrosse*, 2000, pp. 24 and 36; *Notre Dame Men's Swimming and Diving*, 2001–2002, p. 40; *Notre Dame Women's Swimming and Diving*, 2001–2002, pp. 42 and 54; *Notre Dame 2001–2002 Men's Golf*, pp. 45–47; *Notre Dame 2001–2002 Women's Golf*, p. 32; *Notre Dame 2000–2001 Men's Tennis*, p. 34; *Notre Dame 2001–2002 Women's Tennis*, pp. 43–45; and *Notre Dame 2000–2001 Cross Country/Track and Field*, pp. 69–91.

27. Bonfiglio, *A Notre Dame Man*, pp. xiv–xvi, 1–5, and 67.

28. *University of Notre Dame Fact Sheet*, 1991–1992 and 2000–2001, PNDP 1051, Fact Sheets, UNDA; *University of Notre Dame Bulletin of Information, Undergraduate Programs*, 1990–1991 and 1999–2000, and *The Commencement Exercises*, 1990 and 2000, PNDP 1300-1990 and 1300-2000, UNDA.

29. Hugh Davis Graham and Nancy Diamond, *The Rise of American Research Universities: Elites and Challengers in the Postwar Era* (Baltimore, 1997), pp. 183–97. For *U.S. News* rankings, see iceman1, "US News Top 25 for 1991–2009," August 21, 2008, College Confidential, http://talk.collegeconfidential.com/dartmouth-college/555606-us-news -top-25-for-1999-2009.html.

30. *The Commencement Exercises*, 1990 to 2000, PNDP 1300-2000, UNDA.

31. Since 1969, all third-year students of architecture have studied in Rome.

32. Stamper, "Between Two Centuries, pp. 1–23; *Notre Dame Report*, Vol. 23, No. 9 (January 21, 1994), p. 199; and Vol. 24, No. 5 (November 1, 1996), p. 125; and Klimek, *Zahms' Legacy*, pp. 19–20, 49–50, and 77–78.

33. University of Notre Dame International Study Program, Dublin, Ireland, UDIS 253/10, UNDA.

34. University of Notre Dame International Study Program, Dublin, Ireland, UDIS 253/10, UNDA. This folder contains numerous pertinent clippings, especially from the *Chronicle of Higher Education*, December 15, 1993, p. A8, and December 12, 1997, p. 12; *South Bend Tribune*, August 22, 1993; and *Irish Times*, March 17, 1997. Also see *Notre Dame Report*, Vol. 27, No. 6 (November 14, 1997), p. 159.

35. "The Erasmus Institute," UDIS 244/1 Erasmus Institute, UNDA.

36. Press releases, newspaper clippings, and other pertinent materials are preserved in UDIS 244/1, UNDA. See especially *South Bend Tribune*, November 28, 1997, and *National Catholic Register*, December 14–20, 1997.

37. *South Bend Tribune*, September 1, 1964, materials in UDIS 96/22 Jerusalem Center, UNDA; and Hennes, *That Great Heart*, pp. 201–10.

38. *Observer*, Vol. XX, No. 12 (September 10, 1985), p. 5.

39. Notre Dame Press Releases of November 11, 1986, January 25, 1989, November 6, 1990, and June 23, 2008, in UDIS 253/11 International Studies—Israel, UNDA; and *Observer*, Vol. XXVII, No. 130 (April 24, 1996), p. 1.

40. *Our Sunday Visitor*, September 10, 1995.

41. *Our Sunday Visitor*, September 10, 1995.

42. *Our Sunday Visitor*, September 10, 1995.

43. Press Releases in UDIS 229/28—230/01 Alliance for Catholic Education, vol. I, UNDA; *South Bend Tribune*, July 6, 1995.

44. *National Catholic Reporter*, March 31, 1995, vol. I, UNDA.

45. *Alliance for Catholic Education Annual Report*, 2000, UDIS 229/28—230/01 ACE, UNDA.

46. "ACE: Success Beyond Statistics," UDIS 229/28-230/01 ACE, vol. II, UNDA.

47. "Take a look at the faces of ACE," UDIS 229/28-230/01 ACE, vol. II, UNDA.

48. The committee reports and the final draft of Father Malloy's *Colloquy for the Year 2000* are published as a special edition in the *Notre Dame Report*, Vol. 22 (1992–1993).

49. *Notre Dame Report*, Vol. 22, No. 16 (April 30, 1993), pp. 390–404. The quotation is on page 403.

50. *Notre Dame Report*, Vol. 23, No. 3 (October 1, 1993), pp. 30–32.

51. *National Catholic Reporter*, January 21, 1994, p. 21.

52. *Notre Dame Report*, Vol. 23, No. 17 (March 13, 1994), pp. 373–74, No. 20 (September 29, 1994), p. 479; and Vol. 24, No. 6 (November 18, 1994), p. 247.

53. *Notre Dame Report*, Vol. 23, No. 20 (September 29, 1994), pp. 478–86.

54. *Notre Dame Report*, Vol. 24, No. 18 (June 16, 1995), p. 564. The ordinances concerned the apostolic constitution *Ex Corde Ecclesiae*, which will be discussed in the following chapter.

55. The *Faculty Handbook* at the time made no mention of how the associate provost was to be elected by the board of trustees but, after this controversy, the handbook of 1995 required that the provost consult with the Provost's Advisory Committee and report the results of that consultation to the president for his recommendation to the board. (*Faculty Handbook*, 1995, pp. 12–13.)

56. *Notre Dame Report*, Vol. 23, No. 18 (January 10, 1994), p. 391; and Vol. 24, No. 7 (December 2, 1994), p. 274, and No. 11 (February 17, 1995), p. 377.

57. *Notre Dame Report*, Vol. 24, No. 13 (March 24, 1995), pp. 424–28.

58. *Notre Dame Report*, Vol. 26, No. 6 (November 15, 1996), pp. 191–93.

59. *Statutes*, Section V, and *Notre Dame Report*, Vol. 26, No. 9 (January 17, 1997), pp. 245–54.

60. *Chronicle of Higher Education*, February 7, 1997. The *Observer*, Vol. XXX, No. 85 (February 6, 1997), p. 3, lists all the signers. See also *Notre Dame Report*, Vol. 26, No. 9 (January 17, 1997), pp. 260–74.

61. *Notre Dame Report*, Vol. 26, No. 11 (February 14, 1997), pp. 307–12. The quotation is from page 312.

62. *Observer*, Vol. XXVI, No. 76 (January 31, 1995), p. 1.

63. *Observer*, Vol. XXVI, No 81 (February 7, 1995), p. 1, No. 85 (February 13, 1995), p. 1, and No. 91 (February 21, 1995), p. 1. The quotations are from February 21, 1995.

64. *Observer*, Vol. XXVI, No. 100 (June 3, 1995), pp. 6 and 7.

65. *Observer*, Vol. XXVII, No. 100 (February 29, 1996), pp. 16–17.

66. *Observer*, Vol. XXVII, No. 117 (April 2, 1996), insert.

67. *Observer*, Vol. XXVII, No. 118 (April 3, 1996), p. 3, and No. 119 (April 4, 1996), p. 9; and *South Bend Tribune*, October 15, 1996.

68. *Observer*, Vol. XXXI, No. 5 (August 29, 1997), p. 15.

69. *Observer*, Vol. XXXI, No. 5 (August 29, 1997), p. 15.

70. *Observer*, Vol. XXXI, No. 109 (March 19, 1998), p. 1, and *South Bend Tribune*, March 21, 1998.

71. *Observer*, Vol. XXXI, No. 113 (March 25, 1998), p. 1.

72. *Observer*, Vol. XXXI, No. 113 (March 25, 1998), p. 1.

73. *Observer*, Vol. XXXI, No. 121 (April 6, 1998), p. 1.

74. *Notre Dame Report*, Vol. 27, No. 18 (June 12, 1998), pp. 417 and 423.

75. *Observer*, Vol. XXXII, No. 54 (November 18, 1998), p. 1.

76. *Observer*, Vol. XXXII, No. 84 (February 8, 1999), p. 1.

77. UDIS 310/7-8 and 248/7-8, Freshman Attitude Survey, vols. 1 and 2, UNDA; and *The American Freshman National Norms for Fall 2000*, American Council on Education, University of California, Los Angeles, 2000.

78. *Observer*, Vol. XXV, No. 50 (November 15, 1993), pp. 1 and 3; Vol. XXVI, No. 48 (November 9, 1994), p. 1, and No. 49 (November 10, 1994), p. 1.

79. DeMaria, *What Though the Odds*, pp. 194–98, and Matthew Storin, "Haley Scott," in *Strong of Heart*, 2011, pp. 59–61, PATH 112-Str, UNDA.

80. *Observer*, Vol. XXXIV, No. 8 (August 31, 2000), p. 11, and No. 9 (September 1, 2000), pp. 1, 14–15; and Vol. XXV, No. 24 (September 24, 1992), p. 1; *South Bend Tribune*, August 23, 2000, and September 13, 2003; and Julia Hail Flory, "Molly Kinder: From the Irish Guard to a World of God," *Strong of Heart*, 2012, pp. 46–49, PATH 112-Str, UNDA.

81. Karla Peterson, "Missing Limbs Makes for Extra Motivation," *San Diego Union-Tribune*, April 20, 2012; *South Bend Tribune*, May 30, 2013; and *Observer*, Vol. XXV, No. 120 (April 2, 1993), p. 1. The quotation is from the *Observer* article.

82. PNDP 10-Ec-1, Eck Baseball Stadium, UNDA.

83. "Early Childhood Development Center," PNDP 30-Ch-7 Child Care/ECDC, UNDA.

84. PNDP 10-Ke-2 Marilyn M. Keough Hall, 10-Mc-1 McGlinn Hall, 10-On-1 O'Neill Hall, and 10-We-1 Welsh Family Hall, UNDA.

85. PNDP 10-Bu-1, Business Administration College Building, UNDA.

86. *South Bend Tribune*, September 8, 1997, and PNDP 10-Un-2, Beichner Community Center, UNDA. The quotation is in the press release of September 23, 2003, in PNDP above.

87. PNDP 10-Ec-2, Eck Center, UNDA.

88. PND 10-Go-1, Warren Golf Course, UNDA, especially the press release of April 19, 2000; and *South Bend Tribune*, April 20, 1997.

89. *Notre Dame Report*, Vol. 23, No. 18 (June 10, 1994), p. 391; *Observer*, Vol. XXXI, No. 17 (September 9, 1997), p. 1; and Reifsteck, *Two Million Bricks*, pp. 260–63. The quotation is in Reifsteck, p. 261.

90. *Observer*, Vol. XXVI, No. 133 (May 3, 1995), p. 1.

91. *Observer*, Vol. XXVII, No. 37 (October 10, 1995), p. 1, No. 61 (November 21, 1995), p. 1, and No. 77 (January 29, 1996), p. 1. The quotation is from No. 37 (October 10, 1995).

92. PNDP 10-Ad-7, Administration Building: Restoration and Renovation, UNDA; *South Bend Tribune*, October 4, 1998; and *Observer*, Vol. XXXIII, No. 1 (August 21, 1999), p. 1. In a national survey of bathrooms by the Best of USA organization, the renovated building was ranked number 1 and praised for its solid oak stall doors, classic chrome sinks, and shiny brass fixtures. (Father Sorin's four-month construction, of course, did not include the east and west wings.)

93. *Observer*, Vol. XXXIII, No. 64 (December 7, 1999), p. 1, and No. 65 (January 19, 2000), p. 3.

94. *Notre Dame Report*, Vol. 28, No. 10 (February 5, 1999), p. 285.

95. *Notre Dame Report*, Vol. 28, No. 10 (February 5, 1999), pp. 280–93; and *Observer*, Vol. XXXII, No. 65 (December 9, 1998), p. 1, and No. 70 (February 1, 1999), p. 1.

96. *Observer*, Vol. XXXII, No. 80 (February 2, 1999), p. 1.

97. *Notre Dame Report*, Vol. 28, No. 11 (February 19, 1999), pp. 301–3. The quotation is from page 303.

Chapter 21.   Entering the New Millennium

1. The Land O'Lakes Statement can be found in Gallin, *American Catholic Higher Education*, pp. 7–12. The quotation is from section 6.

2. Gallin, *American Catholic Higher Education*, pp. 87–124. The quotation is from part one, section I, article 2.

3. Code of Canon Law, Canons 808 and 812.

4. *Ex Corde Ecclesiae* is reprinted in Gallin, *American Catholic Higher Education*, pp. 413–37. For detailed background material, see pages 189–283. See also Malloy, *Way Stations on the Journey*, pp. 209–31; and Philip Gleason, "The American Background of *Ex Corde Ecclesiae*," in Joseph M. O'Keefe, S.J., ed., *Catholic Education at the Turn of the New Century* (New York, 1997), pp. 79–97.

5. Malloy, *Way Stations on the Journey*, pp. 232–53.

6. Catholic Church. National Conference of Catholic Bishops, *The Application of* Ex Corde Ecclesiae *for the United States* (Washington, DC, 2000), part one, sec. 7, "Catholic Identity."

7. Catholic Church, *Application*, part two, art. 2, "The Nature of a Catholic University," par. 2.

8. Catholic Church, *Application*, part one, sec. 2, "The Ecclesiological Concept of Communion," par. 2.

9. Catholic Church, *Application*, part two, art. 6, "The Pastoral Care," pars. 1 and 2.

10. Catholic Church, *Application*, part two, art. 4, "The University Community," secs. 3a and 4a.

11. Catholic Church, *Application*, part two, art. 4, "The University Community," sec. 4e, esp. sec. 4e, iv, 1, 2, and 3.

12. Malloy, *Way Stations on the Journey*, p. 253. See also Malloy, *The Presidential Years*, pp. 291–96.

13. *Observer*, Vol. XXXV, No. 12 (September 12, 2001), pp. 1, 2, 3, 6, 11, 12, and 13; and Malloy, *The Presidential Years*, pp. 309–15.

14. *Observer*, Vol. XXXV, No. 13 (September 13, 2001), p. 3, No. 14 (September 14, 2001), p. 1, No. 22 (September 26, 2001) p. 1, and No. 27 (October 3, 2001), p. 1.

15. *Observer*, Vol. XXXVIII, No. 101 (March 1, 2004), pp. 1 and 4.

16. *Observer*, Vol. XXXVIII, No. 101 (March 1, 2004), pp. 1, 3, and 4, and No. 102 (March 2, 2004), pp. 1 and 4.

17. *Observer*, Vol. XXXVII, No. 22 (September 25, 2002), p. 1, and No. 68 (December 5, 2002), p. 1.

18. *Observer*, Vol. XXXIX, No. 47 (November 5, 2004), p. 1, and No. 132 (April 26, 2005), p. 1; and minutes of the Academic Council meeting of April 20, 2005, "The University of Notre Dame, The Academic Council, Meeting of April 20, 2005," Office of the Provost, University of Notre Dame, https://provost.nd.edu/assets/59631/ac4_20_05.pdf.

19. *Notre Dame Report*, Vol. XXIX, No. 5 (January 7, 2001), pp. 279–80.

20. Journal of the Faculty Senate, May 9, 2000, and September 6, 2000, on the website of the Faculty Senate, Office of the Provost, University of Notre Dame, faculty-senate.nd.edu/meetings; and *Observer*, Vol. XXXIII, No. 131 (May 3, 2000), p. 1.

21. *Observer*, Vol. XXXIV, No. 116 (April 4, 2001), p. 1; and Vol. XXXV, No. 47 (November 8, 2001), p. 1, and No. 81 (February 6, 2002), p. 1; and *Faculty Handbook*, 2002–2003, pp. 31–32. See also Malloy, *The Presidential Years*, pp. 44–48 and 139–41.

22. *Observer*, Vol. XXXVII, No. 87 (February 4, 2003), p. 1; and *Bulletin of Information*, 2009–2010, pp. 62–63.

23. *Observer*, Vol. XXXVIII, No. 41 (October 29, 2003), p. 1.

24. PNDP 10-Ra-2, Raclin-Carmichael Hall, and UDIS 253/26 IU Medical School, UNDA; *Observer*, Vol. XXXVIII, No. 94 (February 19, 2004), p. 1; and *Bulletin of Information, Graduate Programs*, 2005–2006, pp. 33–34. The hall was named for its benefactor, Ernestine Morris Raclin, a prominent South Bend business executive, philanthropist, and Notre Dame trustee, and her late husband, O. C. "Mike" Carmichael, a civic leader and former president of Converse College.

25. *Observer*, Vol. XXXVIII, No. 67 (December 10, 2003), p. 1.

26. *Observer*, Vol. XXXIV, No. 46 (November 1, 2000), p. 1; Vol. XXXVII, No. 45 (October 29, 2002), p. 1, and No. 46 (October 30, 2002), p. 1.

27. *Observer*, Vol. XXXIII, No. 96 (March 2, 2000), p. 3; and Vol. XXXVIII, No. 104 (March 4, 2004), p. 4.

28. James D. Wetherbee "Biographical Data" document, Lyndon B. Johnson Space Center, NASA, January 2007, https://www.nasa.gov/sites/default/files/atoms/files/wetherbee_james.pdf.

29. *Observer*, Vol. XXXVII, No. 62 (November 21, 2002), p. 3.

30. *Observer*, Vol. XXXVII, No. 63 (November 22, 2002), p. 1; Vol. XXXIX, No. 27 (September 29, 2004), p. 1, and No. 106 (March 16, 2005), p. 1. The quotation is from issue number 27 (September 29, 2004).

31. *South Bend Tribune*, August 25, 2004, p. 10, August 28, 2004, p. 1, September 3, 2004, p. 4, September 5, 2004, p. 10, September 10, 2004, p. B3, December 15, 2004, p. 1, and August 31, 2005, p. B3; *Observer*, Vol. XXXIX, No. 2 (August 25, 2004), p. 1, No. 4 (August 27, 2004), p. 1, and No. 6 (August 31, 2004), p. 1; and Minutes of Academic Council Meeting of September 1, 2004, in *Notre Dame Report*, Vol. XXXIV, No. 6 (November 12, 2004), pp. 227–29.

32. *Notre Dame Report*, Vol. XXIX, No. 12 (March 10, 2000), p. 316; and Vol. XXX, No. 18 (June 30, 2000), p. 363; *South Bend Tribune*, May 6, 2000, p. A1; *Notre Dame Basketball Guide*, 2005–2006, pp. 142 and 177; Malloy, *The Presidential Years*, pp. 265–67; and *Observer*, Vol. XXXIII, No. 70 (January 26, 2000), p. 1; and Vol. XXXIV, No. 69 (January 19, 2001), p. 1. Father Beauchamp went on to become the very successful president of the University of Portland.

33. *Observer*, Vol. XXXV, No. 60 (December 3, 2001), p. 1, and *Notre Dame Football, 2005, Media Guide*, pp. 140–43. To his credit, Coach Davie's players had an impressively high graduation rate, and he generously assisted one dismissed player in transferring to another school. This incident received some notoriety because the student had also been banned from ever returning to the campus but the school to which he transferred played at Notre Dame three years later. He played halfback and discussion was rife about whether he would return, even with a disguised number. Apparently he did not, at least not to the field. *South Bend Tribune*, February 17, 1998, p. B1, October 11, 2001, p. B1, and October 12, 2001, p. B1.

34. *South Bend Tribune*, December 15, 2001, pp. A1, A4, and A5, and December 17, 2001, p. B1; and Malloy, *The Presidential Years*, pp. 329–31.

35. *Observer*, Vol. XXXV, No. 67 (January 16, 2002), p. 1; Vol. XXXIX, No. 61 (December 1, 2004), p. 1; and *Notre Dame 2006 Football Media Guide*, p. 144.

36. *Notre Dame Men's Basketball*, 2005–2006, pp. 44–47, 142–43, and 153, PATH, UNDA.

37. *Notre Dame Women's Basketball*, 2001–2002, pp. 64–67 and 167–70, and *Notre Dame Women's Basketball*, 2005–2006, pp. 150–51, PATH, UNDA.

38. *Notre Dame Fencing*, 2006–2007, pp. 54–57, PATH, UNDA.

39. *Notre Dame Women's Soccer*, 2006, pp. 99–104, PATH, UNDA.

40. *Observer*, Vol. XXXIV, No. 89 (February 16, 2001), p. 1; and Vol. XXXV, No. 79 (February 4, 2002), p. 1, and No. 90 (February 15, 2002), p. 1.

41. UDIS 234/04 Bengal Bouts, UNDA; *Observer*, Vol. XXXV, No. 100 (March 1, 2002), p. 1; and Vol. XXXVII, No. 91 (February 10, 2003), p. 1, and No. 99 (February 20, 2003), p. 1; and *South Bend Tribune*, February 24, 2003.

42. *Observer*, Vol. XXXIII, No. 75 (February 3, 2000), p. 1; and Vol. XXXVIII, No. 100 (February 21, 2003), p. 1. The quotation is from issue number 75 (February 3, 2000), p. 4.

43. *Observer*, Vol. XXXVII, No. 8 (September 6, 2002), p. 1, and No. 26 (October 2, 2002), p. 1; and Vol. XXXVIII, No. 6 (September 2, 2003), p. 1.

44. *Observer*, Vol. XXXV, No. 106 (March 19, 2002), p. 1; and Jodi S. Cohen, "Family Turns Tragedy into a Field of Dreams," Notre Dame News, Office of Public Affairs and Communications, University of Notre Dame, July 17, 2006, https://news.nd.edu/news/family-turns-tragedy-into-a-field-of-dreams/.

45. *Observer*, Vol. XXXVII, No. 73 (January 15, 2003), p. 1, No. 94 (February 13, 2003), p. 1, and No. 95 (February 14, 2003), p. 1. On the occasion of a Mass in Fisher Hall for Sharon's safety on January 16, 2003, an altercation took place in a parking lot between Father Timothy Scully, executive vice president and resident of Fisher Hall, and two news reporters who had parked in reserved spaces. Father Scully later apologized for his part, his apology was accepted, no charges were filed, and a board of trustees committee determined that the incident would not cost Father Scully his position. However, Father Scully did resign as executive vice president at the next meeting of the board of trustees and Father Malloy assumed the executive vice president's duties until John Affleck-Graves was named to the position the following year. *South Bend Tribune*, January 21, 2003, p. A1, January 23, 2003, p. A1, February 11, 2003, p. D3, and May 25, 2003, p. A1; and Malloy, *The Presidential Years*, pp. 350–55.

46. *Observer*, Vol. XXXVIII, No. 90 (February 13, 2004), pp. 1 and 4.

47. *Observer*, Vol. XXXVIII, No. 88 (February 11, 2004), p. 1.

48. *Observer*, Vol. XXXIX, No. 89 (February 11, 2005), pp. 1 and 8, and No. 90 (February 14, 2005), p. 1. The quotation is in issue number 89 (February 11, 2005), page 8.

49. *Observer*, Vol. XXXVIII, No. 129 (April 21, 2004), pp. 1 and 8. The quotation is on page 8.

50. *Observer*, Vol. XXXV, No. 106 (March 19, 2002), p. 1.

51. *Observer*, Vol. XXXV, No. 107 (March 20, 2002), p. 1.

52. *Observer*, Vol. XXXV, No. 107 (March 20, 2002), p. 1 and letters to the editor on p. 11, No. 108 (March 21, 2002), p. 1, No. 109 (March 22, 2002), p. 1 and op-ed articles on pp. 12–13, and No. 111 (March 26, 2002), p. 1.

53. *Observer*, Vol. XXXV, No. 120 (April 10, 2002), pp. 1 and 4, and No. 125 (April 16, 2002), p. 1.

54. *Observer*, Vol. XXXVII, No. 92 (February 11, 2003), p. 1.

55. *Observer*, Vol. XXXIV, No. 22 (September 20, 2000), pp. 1 and 4, and No. 38 (October 12, 2000), p. 1; and Vol. XXXV, No. 25 (October 1, 2001), p. 1, and No. 119 (April 11, 2002), p. 1.

56. PNDP 10-Co-4, Coleman-Morse Building, UNDA.

57. PNDP 10-Ma-1, Malloy Hall, UNDA.

58. PNDP 10-Le-3, Legends of Notre Dame, UNDA; and *Observer*, Vol. XVI, No. 87 (February 2, 1983), p. 3; and Vol. XXXVIII, No. 4 (August 29, 2003), pp. 1 and 4.

59. PNDP 10-De-3, DeBartolo Center for the Performing Arts, UNDA.

60. *ND Works* II, No. 9 (January 18, 2005), p. 4.

61. PNDP 10-Po-3, Post Office, UNDA; and *South Bend Tribune*, January 9, 2005.

62. *Observer*, Vol. XXXIX, No. 105 (March 15, 2005), p. 1, and No. 120 (April 8, 2005), p. 1.

63. PNDP 10-Jo-1, Jordan Hall of Science, UNDA.

64. PNDP 10-Sa-4, St. Liam Hall, UNDA.

65. Malloy, *The Presidential Years*, p. 369, and *Observer*, Vol. XXXVIII, No. 131 (April 23, 2004), p. 1. The quotation is from the *Observer*.

66. Malloy, *The Presidential Years*, p. 384.

67. *South Bend Tribune*, December 1, 2004, p. A1, and December 12, 2004, p. A1; *New York Times*, December 2, 3, 9, 12, 14, and 19, 2004; and Malloy, *The Presidential Years*, pp. 396–97.

68. Rudolph, *American College*, pp. 47 and 219.

69. Fr. John I. Jenkins, "Fr. John I. Jenkins Inaugural Address," Notre Dame News, Office of Public Affairs and Communications, University of Notre Dame, September 22, 2005, https://news.nd.edu/news/fr-john-i-jenkins-inaugural-address.

BIBLIOGRAPHY

ARCHIVAL MATERIALS

UNDA – University of Notre Dame Archives

UACO – Academic Council Records
CPLE – Auguste Lemonnier Papers
UBTS – Board of Trustees (Post–1967) Records
CCIJ – Congregation of Holy Cross. Indiana Province Records
CSCG – Congregation of Holy Cross Records
ULDG – Early Notre Dame Student, Class, and Financial Recordbooks
CSOR – Edward Sorin Papers
UFMM – Faculty Meeting Records / Council of Professors
CEDW – James Farnham Edwards Papers
COBR – John A. O'Brien Papers
CJWC – John W. Cavanaugh Papers
UDIS – Notre Dame: Department of Information Services Records
PATH – Notre Dame Athletics Collection
UNDR – Notre Dame Miscellaneous University Records
UPWC – Notre Dame President 1905–1919: J. W. Cavanaugh
UPWL – Notre Dame President 1922–1928: Rev. Matthew J. Walsh
UPCO – Notre Dame President 1928–1934: Rev. Charles O'Donnell
UPHO – Notre Dame President 1940–1946: J. Hugh O'Donnell
PNDP – Notre Dame Printed and Reference Material
CNDS – Notre Dame Student Collection
UORL – Oral Histories Collection
UPGE – President Burns: General Education Board (Rockefeller Foundation)
CEWI – Thomas Ewing Family Papers

USPA – United States Province of Priests and Brothers Provincial Archives

Congregation of Holy Cross Personnel Files
Materia Generale
Provincial Council Meeting Records

Holy Cross Sisters Archives, Saint Mary's, Notre Dame

Mother Angela Gillespie Collection
Mother Augusta Anderson Collection

NARA – National Archives and Records Administration (Washington, DC, and Chicago)

Records of the Michigan Superintendency of Indian Affairs

Saint Joseph County Archives and Records

Saint Joseph County Court Order Books

BOOKS

Ahern, Patrick. *The Life of John J. Keane*. Milwaukee, 1955.
Alvic, J. F., S.J. *La Congrégation de la Providence de Ruillé-sur-Loir*. Tours, 1923.
Ames, Charlotte. *Theodore M. Hesburgh: A Bio-Bibliography*. New York, 1989.
Armstrong, James E. *Onward to Victory*. Notre Dame, IN, 1973.
Austen, Roger. *Genteel Pagan*. Amherst, MA, 1991.
Ayo, Rev. Nicholas, C.S.C., Micheal Crowe, and Julia Marvin, eds. *Notre Dame's Program of Liberal Studies: The First Fifty Years*. Notre Dame, IN, 2000.
The Band of the Fighting Irish, Memory Book. Vol. I. Notre Dame, IN, 2002.
Barrosse, Thomas. *Moreau: Portrait of a Founder*. Notre Dame, IN, 1969.
Beechloss, Michael. *Kennedy and Roosevelt*. New York, 1980.
Beirne, Brother Kilian, C.S.C. *From Sea to Shining Sea: The Holy Cross Brothers in the United States*. Valatie, NY, 1996.
Berg, A. Scott. *Lindbergh*. New York, 1998.
———. *Wilson*. New York, 2013.
Bernstein, Barton. "Election of 1952." In *History of American Presidential Elections, 1789–1968*, Vol. VIII, edited by Arthur Schlesinger, Jr., and Fred Israel. New York, 1985.
Bernstein, Mark. *Football: The Ivy League Origins of an American Obsession*. Philadelphia, 2001.
Berry, Mary Frances. *And Justice for All*. New York, 2009.
Billington, Ray Allen. *The Protestant Crusade, 1800–1860*. New York, 1952.
Birch, James Gardner. *They Flew Proud*. Nappanee, IN, 2007.

Blantz, Rev. Thomas, C.S.C. *George N. Shuster: On The Side of Truth*. Notre Dame, IN, 1993.

Bonfiglio, Jeremy D. *A Notre Dame Man: The Mike DeCicco Story*. Notre Dame, IN, 2013.

Bornet, Vaughn Davis. *The Presidency of Lyndon B. Johnson*. Lawrence, KS, 1983.

Boughton, Jill, and Julie Walters. *God's Icebreaker*. Notre Dame, IN, 2012.

Brosnahan, Sister M. Eleanore, C.S.C. *On the King's Highway*. New York, 1931.

Brown, Sister Mary Borromeo, PhD. *History of the Sisters of Providence of Saint Mary-of-the-Woods*. Vol. I. New York, 1949.

Burns, Robert E. *Being Catholic, Being American*. Vol. 1, *The Notre Dame Story, 1842–1934*. Notre Dame, IN, 1999. Vol. II, *The Notre Dame Story, 1934–1952*. Notre Dame, IN, 2000.

Burrell, Rev. David B., C.S.C. *When Faith and Reason Meet: The Legacy of John Zahm, CSC*. Notre Dame, IN, 2012.

Byrnes, Joseph F. *Catholic and French Forever*. University Park, PA, 2005.

Cartwright, Gary. "Parseghian: I Have to Keep Moving." In Katz, *The Glory of Notre Dame*, 281–91.

Catholic Church. National Conference of Catholic Bishops. *The Application of* Ex Corde Ecclesiae *for the United States*. Washington, DC, 2000.

A Catholic Program for World Peace. Published by the Catholic Association for International Peace (CAIP). Washington, DC, n.d.

Catta, Canon Etienne, and Tony Catta. *Basil Anthony Mary Moreau*. 2 vols. Translated by Edward L. Heston, C.S.C. Milwaukee, 1955.

Catta, Tony. *Father Dujarié*. Translated by Edward L. Heston, C.S.C. Milwaukee, 1960.

Cavanaugh, Rev. John W., C.S.C., *Daniel E. Hudson, C.S.C., A Memoir*. Notre Dame, IN, 1934.

———. *The Priests of Holy Cross*. Notre Dame, IN, 1905.

Chadwin, Mark Lincoln. *The Warhawks*. New York, 1968.

Chalmers, David. *Hooded Americanism*. New York, 1965.

Chelland, Patrick. *One for the Gipper*. Chicago, 1973.

Clasby, Everett. *The Potawatomi Indians in Southwestern Michigan*. Dowagiac, MI, 1966.

Clifton, James A. *The Pokagons, 1683–1983*. Landam, MD, 1984.

Clinton, Bill. *My Life*. New York, 2005.

Cole, Wayne. *America First*. Madison, WI, 1953.

Connelly, Joel, and Howard Dooley. *Hesburgh's Notre Dame*. New York, 1972.

Connelly, Rev. James T., C.S.C. *Basile Moreau and the Congregation of Holy Cross*. Portland, OR, 2007.

Connolly, Owen. *The French Revolution and Napoleonic Era*. 2nd ed. New York, 1991.

Conyngham, David Power. *Soldiers of the Cross, the Authoritative Text: The Heroism of Catholic Chaplains and Sisters in the American Civil War*. Edited by David J. Endres and William B. Kurtz. Notre Dame, IN, 2019.

Cooper, Jackie. *Please Don't Shoot My Dog*. New York, 1981.

Corby, Rev. William, C.S.C. *Memoirs of a Chaplain Life*. New York, 1992.

Corson, Dorothy. *A Cave of Candles*. Nappanee, IN, 2000.

Costin, Sister M. Georgia, C.S.C. *Priceless Spirit: A History of the Sisters of the Holy Cross, 1814–1893*. Notre Dame, IN, 1994.

Creek, Sister Mary Immaculate, C.S.C. *A Panorama, 1844–1977: Saint Mary's College, Notre Dame, Indiana*. Notre Dame, IN, 1977.

Cullen, Franklin, C.S.C. *Holy Cross on the Gold Dust Trail*. Notre Dame, IN, 1989.

Curran, Robert Emmett. *A History of Georgetown University*. Vol. I. Washington, DC, 2010.

Dansette, Adrien. *Religious History of Modern France*. Vol. I. New York, 1961.

Dawson, John W. *Logical Dilemmas: The Life and Work of Kurt Gödel*. Wellesley, MA, 1997.

DeMaria, Haley Scott. *What Though the Odds: Haley Scott's Journey of Faith and Triumph*. With Bob Schaller. Foreword by Lou Holtz. Kearney, NE, 2008.

Devine, Dan. *Simply Devine: Memoirs of a Hall of Fame Coach*. Champaign, IL, 2000.

Devine, Jane A., ed. *100 Years of Architecture at Notre Dame*. Notre Dame, IN, 1999.

Doyle, William. *The Oxford History of the French Revolution*. 2nd ed. New York, 2002.

Edmunds, R. David. *The Potawatomis: Keepers of the Fire*. Norman, OK, 1978.

Egan, Maurice Francis. *Recollections of a Happy Life*. New York, 1924.

Ellis, John Tracy. *The Formative Years of the Catholic University of America*. Washington, DC, 1946.

Esarey, Logan. *History of Indiana from its Exploration to 1922*. Vol. II. Dayton, OH, 1923.

Evan, John Whitney. *The Newman Movement*. Notre Dame, IN, 1980.

Faherty, William, S.J. *Better the Dream: St. Louis University and Community*. St. Louis, MO, 1968.

Faulkner, Harold U. *Politics, Reform and Expansion, 1890–1900*. New York, 1959.

Ferrell, Robert H., ed. *FDR's Quiet Confidant: The Autobiography of Frank C. Walker*. Niwot, CO, 1997.

Fitzgerald, Ed. "Bob Williams: One More in the Great Tradition." In Katz, *The Glory of Notre Dame*, 129–51.

———. "Frank Leahy: The Enigma." In Katz, *The Glory of Notre Dame*, 83–109.

Furet, Francois. *Revolutionary France, 1770–1880*. Cambridge, MA, 1988.

Furlong, Bill. "Waking Up the Echoes." In Katz, *The Glory of Notre Dame*, 267–74.

———. "The Year Notre Dame Had an NFL Franchise." In Katz, *The Glory of Notre Dame*, 73–82.

Gagnon, Cappy, *Notre Dame Baseball Greats*. Chicago, 2004.

Gallin, Alice, O.S.U., ed. *American Catholic Higher Education: Essential Documents, 1967–1990*. Notre Dame, IN, 1992.

———. *Independence and a New Partnership in Catholic Higher Education*. Notre Dame, IN, 1996.

Ganss, George E., S.J., *The Jesuit Tradition and Saint Louis University*. St. Louis, MO, 1969.

Garraty, John A., and Mark C. Carnes, eds. *American National Biography*. 24 vols. New York, 1999.

Gibson, Ralph. *A Social History of French Catholicism, 1789–1914*. London and New York, 1989.

Gleason, Maureen, and Katharina Blackstead, eds. *What Is Written Remains*. Notre Dame, IN, 1994.

Gleason, Philip. *Contending with Modernity*. New York, 1995.

Graham, Hugh Davis, and Nancy Diamond. *The Rise of American Research Universities: Elites and Challengers in the Postwar Era*. Baltimore, 1997.

Grant, Chet. *Before Rockne at Notre Dame*. Notre Dame, IN, 1968.

A Guide to the University of Notre Dame and the Academy of St. Mary of the Immaculate Conception. Philadelphia, 1865.

Gurian, Waldemar, and M. A. Fitzsimmons, eds. *The Catholic Church in World Affairs*. Notre Dame, IN, 1954.

Gutek, Gerald L. *Education in the United States*. Englewood Cliffs, NJ, 1986.

Hamilton, Nigel. *Bill Clinton: An American Journey*. New York, 2003.

Hanratty, Kelly, ed. *Badin Hall, 1897–1997*. Notre Dame, IN, 1997.

Hellenthal, Barbara J., Thomas J. Schlereth, and Robert P. McIntosh. *Trees, Shrubs, and Vines on the University of Notre Dame Campus*. Notre Dame, IN, 1993.

Hennes, Doug. *That Great Heart*. Edina, MN, 2014.

Hesburgh, Theodore M., C.S.C., *God, Country, Notre Dame*. New York, 1990.

———. *Patterns For Education Growth*. Notre Dame, IN, 1958.

Hess, Gary R. *Vietnam and the United States*. Boston, 1990.

Holtz, Lou. *The Fighting Spirit: A Championship Season at Notre Dame*. With John Heisler. New York, 1989.

Hope, Rev. Arthur, C.S.C. *Notre Dame: One Hundred Years*. Notre Dame, IN, 1943. Rev. ed. Notre Dame, IN, 1948.

Howard, Timothy. *A Brief History of the University of Notre Dame du Lac, Indiana, From 1842 to 1892*. Chicago, 1895.

———. *A History of St. Joseph County*. 2 vols. Chicago, 1907.

Katz, Fred. *The Glory of Notre Dame: 22 Great Stories on Fighting Irish Football from the Pages of Sport Magazine*. N.p., 1971.

Kelly, Alfred, and Winfred Harbison. *The American Constitution*. New York, 1970.

Kennedy, David. *Freedom from Fear*. New York, 1999.

Kennedy, Robert J. *Michael Mathis: American Liturgical Pioneer*. Washington, DC, 1987.

Kertesz, Stephen. *Between Russia and the West: Hungary and the Illusions of Peacemaking, 1945–47*. Notre Dame, IN, 1984.

Kervick, Francis. *Architecture at Notre Dame*. Notre Dame, IN, n.d.

King, Rev. James B., C.S.C. *Holy Cross and Christian Education*. Notre Dame, IN, 2015.

Klawitter, George, ed. *Adapted to the Lake: Letters by the Brother Founders of Notre Dame, 1841–1849*. New York, 1993.

———. *After Holy Cross, Only Notre Dame: The Life of Brother Gatian (Urbain Monsimer)*. Lincoln, NE, 2003.

———, ed. *The Poems of Charles O'Donnell, C.S.C.* New York, 2010.

Klimek, Anne. *The Zahms' Legacy: Engineering at Notre Dame, 1873–1993*. Notre Dame, IN, 1993.

Kohl, Lawrence Frederick. *Memoirs of Chaplain Life*. New York, 2001.

Kosoff, David. *Joseph P. Kennedy*. Englewood Cliffs, NJ, 1974.

Krashna, David, and Don Wycliff, eds. *Black Domers: Seventy Years at Notre Dame*. Notre Dame, IN, 2014.

Krieger, Alan D. "Notre Dame Library Collections of the Nineteenth Century: The Legacy of the Fire of 1879." In Gleason and Blackstead, *What Is Written Remains*, 4–20.

Kselman, Thomas. *Conscience and Conversion: Religious Liberty in Post-Revolutionary France.* New Haven, CT, 2018.

Kuzniewski, Anthony J., S.J. *Thy Honored Name: A History of the College of the Holy Cross*. Washington, DC, 1999.

Lahey, Rev. Thomas A., C.S.C. *Colonel Hoynes of Notre Dame*. Notre Dame, IN, 1948.

Lefebvre, Jim. *Coach for a Nation*. Minneapolis, 2013.

———. *Loyal Sons: The Story of the Four Horsemen and Notre Dame Football's 1924 Champions*. Minneapolis, 2008.

Lemarie, Rev. Charles, C.S.C. *De La Mayenne a l'Indiana: le Pere Edouard Sorin (1814–1893)*. Angers, 1978.

Leuchtenburg, William E. *The Perils of Prosperity*. Chicago, 1958.

Logan, Sister Eugenia, S.P. *History of the Sisters of Providence of Saint Mary-of-the-Woods*. Vol. II. Terre Haute, IN, 1978.

Love, Thomas T. *John Courtney Murray: Contemporary Church-State Theory*. New York, 1965.

Lungren, John, Jr. *Hesburgh of Notre Dame*. New York, 1987.

Lyons, Joseph A. *Silver Jubilee of the University of Notre Dame, June 23, 1869*. Chicago, 1869.

MacEoin, Gary. *Basil Moreau: Founder of Holy Cross*. Notre Dame, IN, 2007.

Maggio, Frank. *Notre Dame and the Game that Changed Football*. New York, 2007.

Maher, Sister Mary Denis. *To Bind Up the Wounds*. New York, 1998.

Malkiel, Nancy Weiss. *Keep the Damned Women Out*. Princeton, NJ, 2016.

Malloy, Rev. Edward A., C.S.C. *Monk's Tale: The Pilgrimage Begins, 1941–1975*. Notre Dame, IN, 2009.

———. *Monk's Tale, The Presidential Years, 1987–2005*. Notre Dame, IN, 2016.

———. *Monk's Tale: Way Stations on the Journey*. Notre Dame, IN, 2011.

Marcus, Sheldon. *Father Coughlin*. Boston, MA, 1973.

Massa, Rev. Mark S., S.J. *Anti-Catholicism in America*. New York, 2003.

McAllister, Anna. *Ellen Ewing: Wife of General Sherman*. New York, 1936.

———. *Flame in the Wilderness*. Notre Dame, IN, 1944.

McAvoy, Rev. Thomas T., C.S.C. *Father O'Hara of Notre Dame*. Notre Dame, IN, 1967.

———. *The History of the Catholic Church in the South Bend Area*. South Bend, IN, 1953.

McCluskey, Rev. Neil G., S.J., ed. *The Catholic University: A Modern Appraisal*. Notre Dame, IN, 1970.

McLynn, Frank. *Napoleon: A Biography*. New York, 1997.

McMahon, Francis. *A Catholic Looks at the World*. New York, 1945.

McNamara, Rev. William, C.S.C. *The Catholic Church on the Northern Indiana Frontier, 1789–1844*. Washington, DC, 1931.

McNeill, Rev. Don, C.S.C., and Margaret Pfeil, eds. *Act Justly, Love Mercifully, and Walk Humbly with Your God*. Kansas City, MO, 2016.

McPherson, James. *Battle Cry of Freedom*. New York, 1988.

Miller, Robert J. *Both Prayed to the Same God*. Lanham, MD, 2007.

Miscamble, Rev. Wilson D., C.S.C. *American Priest*. New York, 2019.

———. *Go Forth and Do Good*. Notre Dame, IN, 2003.

Moore, Rev. Philip S., C.S.C. *A Century of Law*. Notre Dame, IN, 1969.

Moreau, Basile Antoine Marie. *Circular Letters of the Very Reverend Basil Anthony Mary Moreau*. 2 vols. Translation by Edward L. Heston, C.S.C. Notre Dame, IN, 1943.

———. *Excerpts from "Christian Education."* Translated by Brother Edmund Hunt, C.S.C. N.p., n.d.

Morin, Brother Garnier. *From France to Notre Dame*. Notre Dame, IN, 1952.

Morris, Richard B., and Jeffrey B. Morris, eds. *Encyclopedia of American History*. 7th ed. New York, 1996.

Morison, Samuel E. *The Founding of Harvard College*. Cambridge, MA, 1935.

Murray, John Courtney, S.J. "On the Structure of the Church-State Problem." In Gurian and Fitzsimmons, *The Catholic Church in World Affairs*, 11–32.

Neely, Tim. *Hooping It Up: The Complete History of Notre Dame Basketball*. Notre Dame, IN, 1985.

Nichols, Thomas Low. *Forty Years of American Life, 1821–1861*. New York, 1937.

Nutting, Willis. *The Free City*. Springfield, IL, 1967.

O'Brien, John A. *Road to Damascus*. New York, 1949.

O'Brien, Michael. *Hesburgh: A Biography*. Washington, DC, 1998.

O'Connell, Marvin R. *Edward Sorin*. Notre Dame, IN, 2000.

O'Dwyer, Brother Ephrem, C.S.C. *Curé of Ruillé*. Notre Dame, IN, 1941.

O'Keefe, Rev. Joseph M., S.J., ed. *Catholic Education at the Turn of the New Century*. New York, 1997.

Palmer, Ann Therese Darin, ed. *Thanking Father Ted*. Kansas City, MO, 2007.

Pelotte, Rev. Donald E., S.S.S. *John Courtney Murray: Theologian in Conflict*. New York, 1975.

Phelps, Digger. *Tales from the Notre Dame Locker Room*. New York, 2015.

Phillips, C. S. *The Church in France, 1789–1848*. London, 1929.

Pilkinton, Mark. *Washington Hall at Notre Dame*. Notre Dame, IN, 2011.

Quebedeaux, Richard. *The New Charismatics II*. New York, 1983.

Ranaghan, Kevin, and Dorothy Ranaghan. *Catholic Pentecostals Today*. South Bend, IN, 1983.

Reifsteck, William E. *Two Million Bricks in 160 Days*. Notre Dame, IN, 2012.

Remini, Robert. *Andrew Jackson and the Course of American Freedom, 1822–1832*. Vol. II. New York, 1981.

Robinson, Ray. *Rockne of Notre Dame*. New York, 1999.

Rudolph, Frederick. *The American College and University: A History*. Athens, GA, 1962.

Ryan, Rev. John A., and Rev. Francis J. Boland, C.S.C. *Catholic Principles of Politics*. New York, 1943.

Sayre, Kenneth M. *Adventures in Philosophy at Notre Dame*. Notre Dame, IN, 2014.

Schaap, Dick. "The Firing of Terry Brennan." In Katz, *The Glory of Notre Dame*, 217–31.

Schama, Simon. *Citizens: A Chronicle of the French Revolution*. New York, 1989.

Schauinger, J. Herman. *Stephen T. Badin: Priest in the Wilderness*. Milwaukee, 1956.

Schlereth, Thomas J. *A Dome of Learning: The University of Notre Dame's Main Building*. Notre Dame, IN, 1991.

———. *A Spire of Faith: The University of Notre Dame's Sacred Heart Church*. Notre Dame, IN, 1991.

———. *The University of Notre Dame: A Portrait of Its History and Campus*. Notre Dame, IN, 1976.

Schmidt, James M. *Notre Dame and the Civil War: Marching Onward to Victory*. Charleston, SC, 2010.

Schmuhl, Robert. *Fifty Years with Father Hesburgh: On and Off the Record*. Notre Dame, IN, 2016.

Schneider, James G. *The Navy V-12 Program*. Boston, 1987.

Schom, Alan. *Napoleon Bonaparte: A Life*. New York, 1997.

Schoor, Gene. *100 Years of Notre Dame Football*. New York, 1988.

Schroth, Raymond A., S.J. *Fordham: A History and Memoir*. Chicago, 2002.

Sitkoff, Harvard. *The Struggle for Black Equality*. Rev. ed. New York, 1993.

Sorin, Rev. Edward, C.S.C. *The Chronicles of Notre Dame du Lac*. Translated by John M. Toohey, C.S.C., and edited by James T. Connelly, C.S.C. Notre Dame, IN, 1992.

———. *Circular Letters of the Very Rev. Edward Sorin*. Vol. I. Notre Dame, IN, 1885. Vol. II. Notre Dame, IN, 1894.

Sperber, Murray. *Shake Down the Thunder*. Bloomington, IN, 2002.

Stamper, John W. "Between Two Centuries: A History of the School, 1898–1998." In Devine, *100 Years of Architecture at Notre Dame*, 1–23.

Steele, Michael R. *The Fighting Irish Football Encyclopedia*. Champaign, IL, 1996.

A Story of Fifty Years: From the Annals of the Congregation of the Sisters of the Holy Cross, 1855–1905. Notre Dame, IN, n.d.

Stritch, Thomas. *My Notre Dame*. Notre Dame, IN, 1991.

———. "A Short Biography of Theodore M. Hesburgh." In Ames, *Theodore M. Hesburgh*, 1–24.

Sullivan, Richard. *Notre Dame: Reminiscences of an Era*. Notre Dame, IN, 1961.

Temple, Kerry. *O'Hara's Heirs: Business Education at Notre Dame, 1921–1991*. Notre Dame, IN, 1992.

Thompson, Kenneth W. *Diplomacy and Values*. Lanham, MD, 1984.

Tucker, Todd. *Notre Dame vs. The Klan*. Chicago, 2004.

Vanier, Rev. Phileas, C.S.C. *Le Chanoine Dujarie*. Montreal, 1948.

Veneziani, Charles. *Frauds of the University of Notre Dame*. Chicago, 1901.

———. *A Plea for the Higher Education of Catholic Young Men of America: With an Exposure of the Frauds of the University of Notre Dame, Ind.* Chicago, 1900.

Wade, Wyn Craig. *The Fiery Cross*. New York, 1987.

Wallace, Anthony F. C. *The Long Bitter Trail: Andrew Jackson and the Indians*. New York, 1993.

Waring, George J. *United States Catholic Chaplains in the World War*. New York, 1924.

Warshauer, Matthew. *Andrew Jackson in Context*. New York, 2009.

Weber, Ralph E. *Notre Dame's John Zahm*. Notre Dame, IN, 1961.

Whalen, Richard. *The Founding Father*. New York, 1964.

Wheeler, Kenneth H. *Cultivating Regionalism: Higher Education and the Making of the Midwest*. Dekalb, IL, 2011.

White, Joseph M. *Worthy of the Gospel of Christ*. Fort Wayne, IN, 2007.

Willard, Shirley, and Susan Campbell. *Potawatomi Trail of Death: 1838 Removal from Indiana to Kansas*. Fulton County Historical Society, 2003.

Wukovits, John, F. *Soldiers of a Different Cloth*. Notre Dame, IN, 2018.

Zahm, Rev. John, C.S.C., *Bible, Science, and Faith*. Baltimore, MD, 1894.

———. *Evolution and Dogma*. Chicago, 1896.

———. *Sound and Music*. Chicago, 1892.

———. *Women in Science*. New York, 1913.

ARTICLES

"America's Best Colleges." *U.S. News & World Report*, 1983–2007.

Blantz, Rev. Thomas E., C.S.C. "The Founding of the Notre Dame Archives." *American Catholic Studies Newsletter* 32, no. 1 (Spring 2005): 1 and 7–10.

———. "James Gillespie Blaine, His Family, and 'Romanism.'" *The Catholic Historical Review* XCIV (October 2008): 695–716.

Brauer, Richard. "Emil Artin." *Bulletin of the American Mathematical Society* 73, no. 1 (January 1967): 27–43.

Buechner, Cecilia Bain. "The Pokagons." *Indiana Historical Society Publications* 10, no. 5 (Indianapolis, IN, 1933): 298–99.

Carroll, Patrick J., C.S.C. "Mind in Action." *Ave Maria* LXIII (January 1946): 82.

Cassey, Marion T. "The Minims of Notre Dame: Underpinnings of Sorin's University, 1842–1929." *American Catholic Studies* 127, no. 1 (Spring 2016): 45–72.

Collins, Walton. "Growing Up Ted." Special issue, *Notre Dame Magazine* (March 2015): 8–9.

Colloquy for the Year 2000. Special edition, *Notre Dame Report* 22 (1992–1993).

Conklin, Richard. "Once Upon a Dime." *Notre Dame Magazine* I, no. 4 (August 1972): 15.

Cuomo, Mario. "The Confession of a Public Man." *Notre Dame Magazine* 13, no. 4 (Autumn 1984): 21.

Doll, Rev. James, C.S.C. "The History of Graduate Training for Holy Cross Priests." *Educational Conference Bulletin of the Priests of Holy Cross* XXV (December 1957): 24–42.

Donovan, Raymond. "Notre Dame's Contributions in World War II." *Illinois v. Notre Dame* program (September 29, 1945): 21.

Fabun, Sean. "Catholic Chaplains in the Civil War." *The Catholic Historical Review* XCIX, no. 4 (October 2013): 682–97.

Fallon, Nancy. "The Art of the Stage." *Notre Dame Magazine* 23, no. 3 (Autumn 1994): 11–13.

Filchak, Kenneth E. "In Homage to Our Founder: A Brief Biography of Reverend Julius Aloysius Nieuwland, C.S.C." *American Midland Naturalist* 161, no. 2 (April 2009): 178–88.

Fosmoe, Margaret. "1947 Saw First Black Notre Dame Grads." *South Bend Tribune*, February 26, 2009.

Gale, Robert L. "Charles Warren Stoddard." In Garraty and Carnes, *American National Biography*. Vol. 20, 815–16.

Gollar, C. Walter. "Early Protestant-Catholic Relations in Southern Indiana and the 1842 Case of Roman Weinzaepfel." *Indiana Magazine of History* 95 (September 1999): 233–54.

Gurian, Waldemar. "The Catholic Publicist." *Review of Politics* XVII, no. 1 (January 1955): 5–18.

Hayes, Francis. "Living Endowment." *Notre Dame Alumnus* VII, no. 3 (November 1928): 67–68.

"The Hesburgh Legend." *New York Times*, May 22, 1987: sec. A, p. 30, cols. 1–2.

Hunt, Tara. "The Damnedest Experience We Ever Had." *Notre Dame Magazine* XLIV, no. 1 (Spring 2015): 14–16.

Kass, Seymour. "Karl Menger." *Notices of the American Mathematical Society* 43, no. 5 (May 1996): 558–61.

LaFleur, Pete. "Irish Trailblazers." http:www.und.com/ot-60bca-champions-blazers-html.

Letter of William Francis. *Chicago Tribune*, May 18, 1879.

Markowski, Kimberly. "Maurice Francis Egan." In Garraty and Carnes, *American National Biography*. Vol. 7, 344–45.

Marten, Jenny. "Jake Kline's Impact on Irish Baseball Spanned a Lifetime." *Observer* XXVI, no. 100 (March 1, 1994): 14.

———. "A Tradition is Born: Irish Baseball in the Early Years." *Observer* XXVI, no. 99 (February 28, 1994): 14.

McAvoy, Rev. Thomas T., C.S.C. "The Ave Maria after 100 Years." *Ave Maria* 101, no. 18 (May 1, 1965): 6–9, 21.

———. "Father Badin Comes to Notre Dame." *Indiana Magazine of History* XXIX (1933): 7–16.

———. "Manuscript Collections Among American Catholics." *The Catholic Historical Review* XXXVII (October 1951): 281–95.

———. "Notre Dame 1919–1922: The Burns Revolution." *The Review of Politics* 25, no. 4 (October 1963): 438.

———. "The War Letters of Father Peter Paul Cooney of the Congregation of the Holy Cross." *The Records of the American Catholic Historical Society of Philadelphia* XLIV (1933): 47–69, 151–69, and 220–37.

Murray, John Courtney, S.J. "Contemporary Orientations of Catholic Thought on Church and State in the Light of History." *Theological Studies* X (January 1, 1949): 177–234.

———. "Current Theology: Freedom of Religion." *Theological Studies* VI (January 1, 1945): 85–113.

———. "Leo XIII: Separation of Church and State." *Theological Studies* XIV (January 1, 1953): 145–214.

———. "Leo XIII on Church and State: The General Structure of the Controversy." *Theological Studies* XIV (January 1, 1953): 1–30.

———. "The Problem of State Religion." *Theological Studies* XII (January 1, 1951): 155–78.

Pare, George. "The St. Joseph Mission." *The Mississippi Valley Historical Review* XVII (June 1930 to March 1931): 24–54.

Peterson, Karla. "Missing Limbs Make for Extra Motivation." *San Diego Union-Tribune,* April 20, 2012.

Powers, John. "The Charm President." *Notre Dame Magazine* (Spring 1992): 14.

"The Purpose of the V-12 Program." *Scholastic* LXXXII, no.1 (July 7, 1994): 15 and 27.

Rauch, R. W. "Notre Dame's New Coat of Arms." *Notre Dame Alumnus* IX, no. 6 (February 1931): 195.

Sasson, Tehila. "Milking the Third World? Humanitarianism, Capitalism, and the Moral Economy of the Nestlé Boycott." *American Historical Review* 121, no. 4 (October 2016): 1,196–224.

Schidel, Rev. George, C.S.C. "Never Too Much: In Memoriam: Rev. Michael Ambrose Mathis, C.S.C. (1885–1960)." *Yearbook of Liturgical Studies* 3 (Notre Dame, IN, 1962): 1–11.

Schroth, Raymond A., S.J. "Death and Resurrection: The Suppression of the Jesuits in North America." *American Catholic Studies* 128, no. 1 (Spring 2017): 51–66.

Shuster, George. "Have We Any Scholars?" *America* XXXIII (August 15, 1925): 418.

———. "Insulated Catholics." *The Commonweal* II (August 19, 1925): 338.

Stuart, Benjamin F. "The Deportation of Menominee and His Tribe of the Pottawattomie Indians." *Indiana Magazine of History* XVIII (1922): 257–58.

Temple, Kerry. "The Day Notre Dame Burned." *South Bend Tribune,* April 22, 1979, Michiana section, 3–6.

Thompson, W. K. "The Naval Officer Training Program." *Journal of Educational Sociology* 16, no. 9, Our Changing Armed Forces (May 1943): 557–61.

Trahey, Rev. James J., C.S.C. "Dujarie Hall." *Scholastic* XXXIX (March 31, 1906): 399–400.

Vilensky, Joel. "Dew of Death." *Washingtonian* (March 2003): 97–99.

Wall, Barbara Mann. "Grace under Pressure: The Nursing Sisters of the Holy Cross, 1861–1865." *Nursing History Review* I (1993): 71–87.

Walsh, James J., MD, PhD. "Dr. Austin O'Malley." *The Catholic World* CXXXV, no. 806 (May 1932): 157–65.

Whitten, David O. "The Depression of 1893." EH.Net Encyclopedia, ed. Robert Whaples. August 14, 2001. https://eh.net/encyclopedia/the-depression-of-1893.

UNPUBLISHED MATERIALS (*INDICATES IN POSSESSION OF AUTHOR)

*Andrassy, A. J. "The History of Notre Dame Track and Field." Senior seminar paper, University of Notre Dame, 2005.

Arthur, David Joseph. "The University of Notre Dame, 1919–1933: An Administrative History." PhD diss., University of Michigan, 1973.

*Balestracci, Peter. "The Drinking Irish: The History of the Alcohol Policy and Its Development at the University of Notre Dame." Senior seminar paper, University of Notre Dame, 2010.

Callahan, Sister M. Ruberta, C.S.C. "The Educational Contributions of Reverend John William Cavanaugh, C.S.C." MA thesis, University of Notre Dame, 1942.

Cavanaugh, John W., C.S.C. "Notes on Early History of Notre Dame." University of Notre Dame Archives. http://archives.nd.edu/research/texts/notes.htm.

*Conroy, Mary. "For God, Country, Notre Dame: A Look Into War Efforts on Campus During WWII." Senior seminar paper, University of Notre Dame, 2008.

*Couch, Patrick J. "The Rise and Fall of the Catholic Charismatic Renewal at the University of Notre Dame, 1967–1971." Senior seminar paper, University of Notre Dame, 2016.

"Dr. A. F. Zahm, As Pioneer in Aeronautics." Unpublished manuscript, University of Notre Dame Hesburgh Library, 1942.

*Feltault, Jaimie. "God, Country, Notre Dame: The Navy on Campus during World War II." Senior seminar paper, University of Notre Dame, 2005.

*Hannon, Megan. "The Early Years of Coeducation at the University of Notre Dame." Senior seminar paper, University of Notre Dame, 2008.

Hesburgh, Rev. Theodore, C.S.C. "The Relation of the Sacramental Characters of Baptism and Confirmation to the Lay Apostolate." PhD diss., Catholic University of America, 1946.

"History of the University Seal." Office of the Registrar, University of Notre Dame, 2012.

Hope, Rev. Arthur, C.S.C. "Life of John W. Cavanaugh, C.S.C." University of Notre Dame Archives and United States Province of Priests and Brothers Provincial Archives.

*Hovde, Matthew. "The History of the Old College." Senior seminar paper, University of Notre Dame, 2010.

Jones, Rev. Thomas Patrick, C.S.C. "The Development of the Office of Prefect of Religion at the University of Notre Dame from 1842 to 1952." PhD diss., Catholic University of America, 1960.

*Kadon, Karl. "The Navy at Notre Dame During the Second Word War." Senior seminar paper, University of Notre Dame, 2007.

Kearney, Anna Rose. "James A. Burns, C.S.C., Educator." PhD diss., University of Notre Dame, 1975.

Kehoe, Rev. Joseph, C.S.C. "Holy Cross Military Chaplains in World War II." Paper delivered at Holy Cross History Conference, 1995.

———. "The Legacy of Father Andrew Morrissey, C.S.C." Paper delivered at Holy Cross History Conference, 1987.

*Kleiber, Thomas. "An Honor of a Permanent Character: The U.S. Navy and the University of Notre Dame in WWII." Senior seminar paper, University of Notre Dame, 2014.

*Kuhls, Garret. "Fr. Peter Paul Cooney, C.S.C., Civil War Chaplain." Senior seminar paper, University of Notre Dame, 2008.

Kunkle, Edward B. "Father John W. Cavanaugh." Unpublished student essay, University of Notre Dame Hesburgh Library, 1941.

*Lawlor, Catherine. "The Life and Times of Vetville." Senior seminar paper, University of Notre Dame, 2005.

*Mauro, Philip. "Early Military Training at Notre Dame: As Seen Through Student Publications." Senior seminar paper, University of Notre Dame, 2007.

McCandless, Kenneth William. "The Endangered Domain: A Review and Analysis of Campus Planning and Design at the University of Notre Dame." MA thesis, University of Notre Dame, 1974.

Moore, Philip S., C.S.C. "Academic Development: University of Notre Dame Past, Present and Future." Privately published, 1960.

*Mulflur, John. "Notre Dame's War Effort During World War II." Senior seminar paper, University of Notre Dame, 2003.

*Nah, Baraem. "The Transformation of the University of Notre Dame During WWII into a Cog of the War Machine." Senior seminar paper, University of Notre Dame, 2010.

*Navarre, Laura. "The Story of the Co-Exchange Program, Coeducation, and the Events Leading up to the Failed Merger between the University of Notre Dame and Saint Mary's College between 1965 and 1972." Senior seminar paper, University of Notre Dame, 2007.

Newberry, Brother James, C.S.C. "Brother Charles Borromeo Harding, 1838–1922: American Architect." Paper delivered at Holy Cross History Conference, Holy Cross College, Notre Dame, IN, 2010.

*O'Connell, Rev. Marvin. "The Magnificent Six." Convocation address, Holy Cross College, Notre Dame, IN, March 7, 2002.

*Overdorf, Patrick. "The First Term of Father Monk Malloy and the Thematic Year System." Senior seminar paper, University of Notre Dame, 2005.

*Pratt, Dorothy O. "Notre Dame and the Civil War Draft: Fact or Fiction." Graduate seminar paper, University of Notre Dame, 1995.

*Rodgers, Gregory. "Saint Mary's College and the Unification Talks." Senior seminar paper, University of Notre Dame, 2008.

Secunda, W. Benjamin. "In the Shadow of the Eagle's Wings: The Effects of Removal on the Unremoved Potawatomis." PhD diss., University of Notre Dame, 2008.

Stabrowski, Brother Donald, C.S.C. "Brickmaking at Notre Dame." Paper delivered at the Holy Cross History Conference, 1991.

*Stibili, Rev. E. C. "Refugee Professors at Notre Dame, 1930–1960." Graduate seminar paper, University of Notre Dame, 1970.

Tambola, Sister Damien, O.S.B. "James F. Edwards, Pioneer Archivist of Catholic Church History in America." MA thesis, University of Notre Dame, 1958.

Wack, John T. "The University of Notre Dame du Lac: Foundation, 1842–1857." PhD diss., University of Notre Dame, 1967.

*Walter, Rev. Joseph L., C.S.C. *History of Premedical Studies at Notre Dame.* Privately printed at the University of Notre Dame.

Weber, Ralph E. "The Life of Reverend John A. Zahm, C.S.C., American Catholic Apologist and Educator." PhD diss., University of Notre Dame, 1956.

INDEX

apprentices, 45, 46, 56, 68, 69, 79, 186

Archconfraternity of the Blessed Virgin Mary, 99

Archconfraternity of the Sacred and Immaculate Heart of Mary, 53

Architecture: Department of, 260, 410, 413, 513; program in, 161, 222, 223, 260, 560; School of, 559–60, 585, 603–4

Aristide, Jean-Bertrand, 590

Arnett, Trevor, 220

Arnett, William, 182

Arnzen, Bob, 465

Arthur D. Little, Inc., 505

Arthur Vining Davis Foundations, 563

Artin, Emil, 305–6, 309, 482

Associated Alumni of the University of Notre Dame. *See* Alumni Association

associate provost position, 566, 688n55

Association of American Law Schools, 218, 219

Astin, Sean, 552, 553

Athletic and Convocation Center, 410, 513, 518

athletics: administrative control of, 297, 592; benefits of, 551; bicycling, 168; Big Ten Conference, 579; boating, 171; boxing, 595; costs of, 551; critical view of, 175; facilities, 513, 514, 577; fencing, 556–57; golf, 558; intercollegiate games, 169–70; lacrosse, 558; men's wrestling, 540; national championship trophies, 556–57; popularity of, 268, 490; regulations of, 170; scandals, 592; soccer, 557, 594; softball, 557–58; swimming, 558; tennis, 558; track and field, 170, 300; women in, 540, 594–95. *See also* baseball; basketball; football

Atkinson, Ti-Grace, 450

Atomic Energy Commission, 407

Augusta, Mother (Ann Amanda Anderson), 156, 157

Augustine, Brother, 34, 35

Ave Maria (journal), 93–94, 101, 404

Baasen, Michael, 105

Bach, Ferdinand, 30, 612n37

Bach, Joe, 247

bachelor of arts degree, 49, 70, 73, 95, 107, 259

Bachelor Program: reform of, 109

Badin, Stephen, 5, 27, 30, 182–84

"Badin Bog," 153–54, 390

Badin Hall, 154, 186, 198, 216, 264–65, 266, 292, 293, 336, 390

Baldinger, Lawrence, 395

band rehearsal building. *See* Ricci Band Rehearsal Hall

Baroux, Louis, 42, 46, 57–58

Barry, Joseph, 342

Bartell, Ernest, 454, 487–88, 521

Bartholomew, Paul, 309

baseball, 169, 298, 299, 557

Basil, Brother (Timothy O'Neil), 30, 47

Basilica of San Lorenzo, 331

Basin, John (bishop of Vincennes), 615n18

basketball: coaches, 269, 465, 556, 593, 594; establishment of, 271; games, 269, 270, 465; longest non-baskets in NCAA history, 467; men's team, 556, 682n4; national competitions, 466–67, 594; star players, 269–70, 465–66; "The Era of Austin Carr," 465–66; women's team, 556, 594

Bathon, Howard, 676n94

Batteast, Jacqueline, 594

Battista, F. P., 102

Baxter, Michael, 567

Beard, Ralph, 465

Beattie, Judith Anne, 516

Beatty, Ned, 552

Beaubien, Louis, 37

Beaubien family, 38, 65

Beauchamp, E. William, 488, 509, 524, 526, 577, 592

Becker, Joseph, 395

Beeler, Meghan, 548

Beichner, Paul E., 575–76

Belles-Lettres Program, 123–24

Belloc, Hilaire, 294

Benedict XV (pope), 213

benefactors, 97, 291–92, 351, 360, 361, 369, 389, 405, 560–61, 563, 576, 589

Bengalese, The (magazine), 359

Benitz, William, 161

Bennett, Elmer, 556

Benson, Robert Hugh, 205

tific Course, 95, 259; service in the Civil
War, 82–83; teaching responsibilities of,
97, 109, 127, 176

Carroll, Charles, 140

Carroll, John (bishop of Baltimore), 5, 19, 27,
140

Carroll, Thomas, 155, 157

Carroll Hall, 136

Carter, Jimmy, 530

Cartier, Warren, 220

Cartier Field, 250, 251, 288, 290, 406, 654n8

Casablanca Conference (1943), 331

Casper, Dave, 462

Castner, Paul, 243, 245

Catholic Association for International Peace,
328

Catholic Charismatic movement, 459–61

Catholic Church in France: Concordat of 1801,
9–10, 14; confiscation of property of, 3–4;
"Constitutional" priests and bishops, 8, 9,
13; French Revolution and, 3–5, 7; government support of, 12; land ownership, 3; in
Napoleonic era, 5; oath-taking by priests
and bishops of, 4, 5, 7–9; during post-
revolution years, 5–6; public services of, 3

Catholic Church in the United States, 43, 61,
506

Catholic education system, 215, 261–63, 562,
581–82, 603, 645n37, 645n43

Catholic faith: attitude to abortion, 498;
modern challenges of, 497–98; problem of
slavery and, 499; public morality of, 499

Catholic Total Abstinence Society, 145

Catholic University of America, 145, 152, 428,
559

Catlett, Sid, 465, 466, 467

Catta, Tony, 608n35

Cavalli, Louis, 38

Cavanaugh, Francis "Frank", 343, 348, 377,
383

Cavanaugh, John J.: administrative duties of,
330, 332, 347, 350, 373, 377, 378, 523;
background of, 348, 370; construction
projects of, 368–70; education of, 348–49,
370; football coach search, 343; fundraising efforts, 360–61, 389, 400; Law

School reform, 371–72; modernization of
the university, 350; reliance on advisory
council, 370–71; reorganization of the university's higher administration, 372, 377;
revision of undergraduate curriculum,
355–57; secretary of Father John W.
Cavanaugh, 349

Cavanaugh, John W.: administrative duties of,
177, 178, 184; attitude to Irish culture,
201–3, 204; background of, 174–76;
building dedicated to, 316; changes in
academic programs, 195–98; construction
projects of, 198–99; criticism of King
Henry VIII, 203; editor of the *Ave Maria*,
176, 177, 178; education of, 174–75; Ernest
Morris and, 369; Father Zahm and, 174,
176; health concerns, 213–14; and medical
program, 210–11; ordination of, 176; personality of, 177, 178; political views of,
205; on practice of religion, 181–82; as
prefect in Sorin Hall, 175, 176; presidency
of, 173, 174, 177–79, 182, 184–86, 213;
public speeches and addresses of, 180–81,
183, 202–3, 205, 225, 271; re-entombment of Father Badin, 182–84; reputation
of, 123, 172; resignation of, 213; and SATC
program, 206–7; scholarly vision of,
190–91; search for grants for the university,
217; Seumas MacManus and, 202; as superior of Holy Cross Seminary, 177, 639n7;
support of alumni, 186–87; teaching
responsibilities of, 176, 177–78; telegram
to president Wilson, 204; trips to New
York, 217, 218; view of college sports,
175–76; vision of education, 179–80, 181

Cavanaugh, Joseph, 377

Cavanaugh, Michael, 348

Cavanaugh, Patrick, 174

Cavanaugh (née Keegan), Mary Ann, 348

Cavanaugh Hall, 316, 368

Cavelli, Louis, 56

Cekanski, Kathleen, 449

Celestine, Brother, 127, 129

Celier, Paul, 16

Centenary Fund Drive, 360

Center for Continuing Education, 410, 489, 518

editor of *Ave Maria*, 94; education of, 67; personality of, 67; religious vows, 67; service in the Civil War, 84; translations of, 76; travel to France, 67; visit to grotto of Massabielle in Lourdes, 154

Gillespie, Neal, 49, 67, 94, 97, 101, 105, 113

Gilligan, John J., 491

Gillis, James, 311

Gilman, Sid, 426

Gilmour, Richard (bishop of Cleveland), 143

Gilson, Étienne, 310

Ginsberg, Allen, 434

Gipp, George: background of, 236; baptism of, 272, 648n28; baseball scholarship at Notre Dame, 236, 299; commemoration of, 280; concerns about behavior of, 239; fame of, 256; football career of, 235, 236–40, 243, 269, 271, 272; funeral of, 241; illness and death of, 240–41, 250; injuries of, 237; in popular culture, 551; tributes to, 241–42

Girac, Maximilian, 47

Gladieux, Bob, 427

Gleason, Philip, 567

Gödel, Kurt, 305

Goeddeke, George, 427

Goldbrunner, Joseph, 360

Goldwater, Barry, 413

golf course, 268–69

Golic, Bob, 463

Good Shepherd Monastery, 17

Good Woman of Setzuan, The (play), 530

Gordon, Helmut, 353–54

Gordon, Robert, 524, 676n94

Gorski, Eugene, 396

Gott, W. T., 210

Gouesse, François, 33, 38, 47, 50, 52, 55, 61

Goulet, Denis, 491

Grace, W. R., 276

Grace Hall, 483, 518, 543, 574

grade inflation, 585

graduate studies: admission and graduation requirements, 261; doctoral and master's programs, 346; enrollment, 373; establishment of, 346; fellowships, 496; reorganization of, 346–47; stipend, 476; during World War II, 346

Graham, Hugh Davis: *The Rise of American Research Universities*, 559

Graham, Otto, 270, 344

Grande, Peter, 424

Grange, Red, 239

Granger, Alexis: academic career of, 146; administrative duties of, 53, 99, 103, 106; background of, 53; Bengal mission, 60; death of, 145, 146, 175; design of Sacred Heart Church, 135; reputation among students, 54; support of religious societies, 99–100

Grant, Ulysses (general), 82, 84

Graves, David, 556

Gray, William "Dolly," 236

Great Books program, 356–57

Great Depression, 285, 287, 297, 302, 315

Green, Jerome, 160–61, 162, 260, 604

Greenberg, Henry Clay, 415

Gregori, Luigi, 113–14, 125, 126, 137, 513, 544, 578

Gregory, Dick, 397, 442

Gregory, Ron, 300, 442

Gregory XVI (pope), 499

Griese, Bob, 426

Griffith, A. A., 102

Griffith, Ruth Marie, 567

Grigg, Larry, 367

Grotto at Notre Dame, 154, 155, 157, 283, 516–17

Grotto of Lourdes, 154, 155

Grow, Liz, 558

Groza, Alex, 465

Grubb, Jen, 557

Guglielmi, Ralph, 367, 398

Gurian, Waldemar, 303–4, 306, 354

Guth, Eugene, 306–7, 308, 309

Gutiérrez, Gustavo, 599

gymnasium, 158–59, 168, 171, 267

Haakon VII (king of Norway), 255

Haas, Arthur, 306, 307, 308, 309

Haggar Fitness Center, 513

Haggar Hall, 589

Haggerty, Pat, 240, 648n28

Halas, George, 238, 245, 345

Halas, Walter, 245, 269, 298, 299

Haley, Art, 384

Hall of Commerce, 292–93

Hammes, Romy, 390

Hammes Bookstore, 518, 576

Hammes-Mowbray Hall, 600

Haney, Ericka, 594

Hanratty, Terry, 426, 427, 428

Harding, Brother Charles Borromeo, 103, 117, 130, 134, 135, 153

Harper, Jesse: at Alma College, 230; background of, 229; coaching career of, 230–32, 234–35, 242, 269, 298–99, 301; as director of athletics, 297; education of, 229

Harrison, Benjamin, 131

Hart, Leon, 362, 363, 364, 366, 367, 427

Hartke, Gilbert, 396

Hartney, Sister M. Gerald, 447

Harvey, Arthur, 396–97

Hatch, Nathan, 497, 546

Hauerwas, Stanley, 567

Hawkins, Tom, 465

Hayden, James Ryan, 217

Hayes, Francis, 288, 360

Hayes, Helen, 502

Hayes, Sara, 558

Hayes, Woody, 425

Hayes-Healy Center, 410, 518, 578

Healy, Robert, 81

Heap, Joe, 367

Heck, Andy, 512

Heffelfinger, William "Pudge," 226

Hefner, Christie, 502, 503

Hefner, Hugh, 428, 502

Heilman, Aaron, 557

Heisman, John, 226

Helen Branch Family Foundation, 563

Helen Kellogg Institute for International Studies, 488, 547

Hellriegel, Martin, 360

Hennepin, Louis, 26

Henry VIII (king of England), 203

Herbert, George, 286

Hering, Frank, 170, 228, 298

Hermens, Ferdinand, 304, 354

Hesburgh, Theodore M.: academic priorities of, 382, 389, 399; on access to abortion, 501–2; achievements of, 517, 518; administrative posts of, 487, 665n17; administrative style of, 377–78, 380–82, 384, 394–96, 441, 442–43, 481; appearance in *Rudy*, 552; appointed president, 378, 401–2, 405, 487–88, 523; attitude to the Jesuits, 388; background of, 374; chair of the Faculty Board in Control of Athletics, 377–78; Coach Brennan and, 398–99; construction projects of, 377, 378, 389–92, 518; correspondence of, 436–37; creation of the Office of the Provost, 468, 480; criticism of, 417–19, 437, 439; disagreements with Coach Leahy, 377–78; on divestment from South Africa, 506; doctoral dissertation of, 375–76; faculty appointments, 392; on Father Burtchaell, 479–80; Father Murray's controversy and, 388–89; fifteen-minute rule, 436, 439; fundraising campaigns of, 389, 405–6, 408, 411, 496; on the future of Notre Dame, 483–84; *God and the World of Man*, 377; *John Goldfarb, Please Come Home* controversy and, 413–14; language skills of, 375; lawsuits against the university and, 484–85; national and international commitments of, 341, 400–401, 417, 439, 442, 561; opposition to the Vietnam War, 454, 455–56; program in nonviolence, 453–54; on purpose of government, 387; reflections on Representative Henry Hyde's address, 501–2; reputation of, 378, 402, 417, 604; response to statement favoring election of Adlai Stevenson, 386–87; restructure of university governance, 431; retirement of, 517; on Sisters of the Holy Cross, 405; speeches and sermons of, 379–80, 457, 483; spiritual development of, 374; student affairs and, 433, 518; theological studies of, 374–75; trip to Europe of, 375; Vetville chaplaincy, 351; vice presidency of, 371, 372, 378, 381–82; vision of Catholic education, 378–79, 430–31, 582; visits to Vatican, 413; volunteer work of, 375; "Winter of Discontent" letter, 420–22

137; Golden Dome of, 136–37, 544, 601; illumination of, 138; interior decorations of, 137–38, 139; Law Department in, 133; lending library in, 198; murals of, 137–38, 139, 578; renovations of, 125, 136, 577–79; science courses in, 127; statue of the Blessed Mother, 136

Mainieri, Paul, 557

Makeba, Miriam, 529

Mäkinen, Anne, 557

Malcolm X (El-Hajj Malik El-Shabazz), 430

Malloy, Edward "Monk": academic changes implemented by, 531, 588–89; on academic honor code, 542; accomplishments of, 602–3; administrative duties of, 488, 522, 523–24, 581, 693n45; background of, 519; basketball skills of, 520–21; *Colloquy for the Year 2000* report, 549–50; commitment to cultural diversity, 536–37, 539; construction projects of, 543, 574–75, 600–601; dissertation of, 522; education of, 519–20, 521, 522; faculty recruitment policy, 565, 566–67, 568; Faculty Senate and, 534, 535, 536, 587–88; Father Burtchaell controversy and, 536; financial decisions of, 531; goals and priorities of, 551; inauguration as president, 523–24; love for reading, 520; Mass in the aftermath of 9/11 attack, 584; meeting with leaders of SUFR, 538–39; on mission of faculty committee, 494; nickname of, 520; on nondiscrimination clause, 572; ordination of, 522; presidential terms, 517, 547, 549, 588, 602; priesthood of, 521–22; speeches of, 523; student affairs, 548, 598; task force reports, 524, 528; thematic years inaugurated by, 528; "The Spirit of Inclusion at Notre Dame" statement, 570–71; tributes to, 602; trip to Mexico, 521; views of Catholic education, 582; vision of Notre Dame University, 580

Mandel, Howie, 530

Manion, Clarence, 252, 371, 382

Manthei, Holly, 557

Manual Labor School: academic strength of, 107; apprentices of, 69; building of, 46, 56, 93, 153–54; closure of, 186, 198, 287, 405; curriculum of, 68–69, 211; entrance fee, 69; establishment of, 68; fire of 1849, 73

Maravich, Pete, 466

Marconi, Guglielmo, 301

Mardi Gras celebration, 506

Marie Antoinette (queen of France), 3

Marie P. DeBartolo Center for the Performing Arts. *See* DeBartolo Performing Arts Center

Marilyn Keough Hall, 575, 576

Marin-Sola, Francisco, 209

Maritain, Jacques, 307, 308, 310

Marivault, Theophilus Jerome, 33, 38, 42, 55

Marquette, Jacques, 26

Married Student Housing complex, 352

Marsden, George, 567

Marshall, Thomas, 205

Martin, Jim, 361, 364

Martin, Ray, 467

Martinelli, Sebastiano, 162

Mary of Bethlehem, Sister (Marie Desneux), 33

Mary of Calvary, Sister (Marie Robineau), 33

Mary of Carmel, Sister, 63

Mary of Providence, Sister, 45

Mary of Saint Angela, Sister. *See* Gillespie, Eliza

Mary of St. Aloysius Gonzaga, Sister, 64

Mary of St. Anastasia, Sister, 64

Mary of the Compassion, Mother, 184

Mary of the Heart of Jesus, Sister (Marie Savary), 33

Masekela, Hugh, 529

Mason, Thomas, 524

Mason Support Services Building, 685n75

Mass. *See* Holy Mass

master of business administration (MBA) program, 409, 575

master's degree programs, 223, 261, 357, 358, 496, 546, 560, 563

Mathematics: Department of, 309

Mathile Family Foundation, 563

Mathis, Michael, 177, 359, 663n23

Mayhew, Louis, 446

Mayo, Charles, 315

Mayo, William, 315

Mays, Willie, 299
Mazzoli, Romano, 502
McBrien, Richard, 491, 497, 500
McCandless, Kenneth, 657n71
McCarragher, Charles, 417, 419, 672n7
McCarthy, Charles, 453
McCarthy, Eugene, 438, 453, 454
McCarthy, James, 310, 383, 394, 665n17
McCarthy, Joseph, 385, 519
McCauley, "Easy" Ed, 465
McCollester, Charles, 674n46
McCormack, James, 79
McCormack, John, 296, 300
McCormick, Richard, 491
McCue, Martin, 129, 222
McGarry, Moses, 146
McGee, Coy, 362
McGinn, John, 208
McGlinn, Terrence, 574
McGlinn Hall, 543, 575, 576
McGovern, George, 454
McGowan, Raymond, 310
McGraw, Muffet, 556, 594
McGuire, Francis, 411
MCJ Foundation, 563
McKeever, Ed, 345
McKenna, Andrew, 580
McKenzie, John, 409
McMahon, Francis: attitude toward Commu-
    nist Russia, 331, 332; background of,
    327–28; controversial remarks of, 331–32;
    debate with Father O'Brien, 324–32; letter
    to Irish Prime Minister, 329; meeting with
    Father O'Donnell, 330–31; on moral obli-
    gation of humanity, 328; on Nazi
    propaganda, 329–30; relocation to
    Chicago, 332; reputation of, 309, 432;
    resignation of, 332; *The Rights of Man*,
    328; view of Lend-Lease, 331
McManus, William (bishop of Fort Wayne–
    South Bend), 506
McMaster, James A., 140
McMullin, Ernan, 599, 676n94
McNeill, Don, 516
McNutt, Paul, 314
Meagher, Thomas Francis, 83

Mechanical Engineering Program, 129
medical education center, 589
Medicine: Department of, 210, 211
Medieval Institute, 357–58, 384, 406, 407
Meehan, Jackie, 467
Meignan, Guillaume (archbishop of Tours), 21
Meli, Giovanni, 136
Mello, Jim, 361
Mendoza College of Business, 603
Menger, Karl, 304–5, 308, 309
Menominee (Potawatomi chief), 28
Mercantile Department, 123
Mercier, Cardinal Désiré, 206
Merton, Thomas, 357, 457
Meštrović, Ivan, 391, 396
Meštrović Studio Gallery, 513, 518
Metallurgy: Department of, 308
Metzger, Bert, 251, 252
Meyer, Albert (cardinal of Chicago), 407
Meyer, Ray, 270
Meynell, Alice, 286
Michael Browning Family Cinema, 600
Michalak, Chris, 557
Michel, Dom Virgil, 360
Milani, Kenneth, 509
military training programs, 171–72, 205, 206–7
Miller, Creighton, 244, 344, 345
Miller, Don, 243–44, 246, 247
Miller, Edgar "Rip," 247, 248, 298
Miller, Frederick, 251, 272
Miller, Gerry, 243–44
Miller, Harry "Red," 243
Miller, Jay, 465
Miller, Joaquin, 124
Miller, Liz, 557
Miller, Ray, 209, 243
Miller, Tom, 244
Miller, Walter, 243–44
Miller, William E., 413
Millner, Wayne, 318
Mills, Rupe, 269
Mills, Tommy, 298–99
Miltner, Charles, 223
Minim Department: classes, 70, 93, 135, 166;
    enrollment, 68, 69, 79, 166, 258, 308,
    613n44; exhibitions, 172; faculty of, 69,

74, 135; location of, 133, 134; private park, 168; societies for, 99; student residence, 116, 135, 136; termination of, 287, 405; Washington Cadets (Sorin Cadets), 80, 171, 172, 190

Mining Engineering: Department of, 195

Missionaries' Retirement Home, 93

Mitchell, Clement, 220

Mohrmann, Christine, 360

Moir, Johnny, 270

Moley, Raymond, 314

Mollevaut, Gabriel Étienne Joseph, 15

Moloney, William, 184

Montalembert, Comte de (Charles Forbes René), 140

Montana, Frank, 410, 413

Montana, Joe, 463–64

Montoya, Alex, 573–74

Monty, Tim, 427

Moore, Joe, 554–55

Moore, Philip, 308, 346, 353, 357, 381

Moran, T. A., 102

Moreau, Basil Anthony: Algerian mission of, 17, 19; background of, 13–14; baptism of, 13; Circular Letters of, 17, 76; controversy over acquisition of St. Mary's College in Kentucky and, 54–55; educational mission of, 15, 16–19; Father Sorin and, 21, 24, 31, 40–41, 56, 76; founder of the Congregation of Holy Cross, 2, 74, 156; Fundamental Pact of, 16; governance of religious groups, 13, 15–16; Indian mission and, 59–60; North American tour, 75–76, 88; ordination of, 14; organization of auxiliary priests, 21; praise of knowledge, 18–19; resignation from the post of superior general, 90; retreat at the Sulpician Solitude, 14–15; superior of religious groups, 15, 16–17; theological opinions of, 15; treatise on teaching, 76; trips to Rome, 75

Moreau, Mary Basil, 74

Moreau Seminary, 392

Morgan, Beth, 556

Morris, Ernest, 361, 369

Morris Inn, 369–70, 377

Morrison, James, 228

Morrissey, Andrew: academic vision of, 159, 162–63, 172; administrative duties of, 133, 150, 172, 176; attitude to intercollegiate sports, 170; background of, 149; blessing of the statue of Father Corby, 189; building named after, 265–66; Charles Veneziani and, 162–64; construction of grotto, 157–58; controversial views of, 151–52; education of, 150; emigration to America, 149–50; Father Zahm and, 151–52, 215–16; financial matters, 150–51, 152–53; John Cushing and, 293; letters from Father O'Donnell, 644n22; liturgical services, 190; personality of, 150, 179; resignation of, 173, 174

Morrissey Hall, 265–66, 293, 336, 368

Morse, James, 599

Morse, Leah Rae, 599

Morse, Marston, 308, 401, 482

Morse, Samuel F. B., 43

Morton, Oliver, 83

Mother Angela. See Gillespie, Eliza

Mottais, André, 12, 15

Moynihan, Daniel Patrick, 530

Mulcaire, Sister Aloysius, 135, 193–94, 195, 287

Mulcaire, Michael, 254, 289, 297, 300, 349, 390

Mulholland, St. Clair, 83, 188

Mullins, "Moon" Larry, 251, 254

Mundelein, George (cardinal of Chicago), 199, 314

Munn, Clarence "Biggie," 462

Murdock, Samuel, 220

Murphy, Christopher, III, 411

Murphy, John Hoey, 372, 381–82

Murphy, Pat, 557

Murphy, Troy, 556, 592, 594

Murray, Edmund, 342

Murray, Jim, 468

Murray, John Courtney, 387–88, 428, 432, 561

Murray, John "Red," 299

Murray, Meghan, 558

Murray, Samuel Aloysius, 188

Murray, William, 206, 207

Museum and Cabinet of Natural Sciences, 115–16

Shumate, John, 466

Shuster, George: administrative duties of, 222, 408, 411; background of, 262; as some students' choice for university president, 417, 418, 440; criticism of Catholic education, 261–63, 280, 283, 332; "Have We Any Scholars?," 262

Siegfried Hall, 543, 544, 575

Siek, Jeremy, 557

Siemon, Kelley, 594

Silver, James: *Mississippi: The Closed Society*, 409

Simon, Yves, 307, 309

Simons, Joseph, 423, 424

Sinnott, Tom, 467

Sisters of Nazareth, 24

Sisters of Providence, 10–11, 13, 30, 36, 37, 275, 403–4, 608n35

Sisters of the Good Shepherd, 15

Sisters of the Holy Cross, 33, 36–37, 83–85, 156, 403–5

Sisters of the Sacred Heart, 22–23

Sitko, Emil, 361, 364, 366

Slager, Rick, 463

Smelser, Marshall, 676n94

Smith, Alfred E., 296, 313

Smith, Bubba, 427

Smith, Thomas Gordon, 560

Smurfit, Michael, 561

Snite, Fred B., 513

Snite, Frederick, Jr., 513

Snite Museum of Art, 513, 518

Snow, Jack, 426, 427

Sobieraj, Michal, 594

Sobrero, Kate, 557

Social Science Building, 369

Society for the Propagation of the Faith, 38, 55, 60

Society of Holy Angels, 53, 54, 618n60

Society of the Divine Word, 533

Society of the Holy Childhood, 99

Sociology: Department of, 409

Sodality of Our Lady of the Sacred Heart, 100

Sodality of the Holy Angels, 99

Soleta, Chester, 411

Sorin, Edward: administrative duties of, 37; American patriotism of, 43–44, 61, 62; approach to students' discipline, 51–52;

attendance at alumni meeting, 105; attitude to Irish, 111, 201; background and education of, 20–21; baptism of, 1; Bengal question and, 60–61; brickmaking business of, 77; Brother Gatian and, 55; building of grotto, 155; California Gold Rush and, 58–59; career of, 1–2; on Civil War, 78; correspondence with Father Moreau, 31, 40–41, 76; criticism of, 51, 76; curate in Parcé-sur-Sarthe, 21; description of Notre Dame du Lac, 40–41; description of Saint Peter's Mission, 24; design of Sacred Heart Church, 135; educational mission of, 25, 34, 68; Eliza Gillespie and, 67–68; emigration to America, 1, 19, 22–24, 144; establishment of novitiates, 36, 156; establishment of the university, 1, 26, 30–32; Father Colovin and, 111–12; Father Corby and, 122; Father Gouesse and, 61; Father Moreau and, 21; Father Walsh and, 121–22; financial matters, 41–42, 56–57, 614n58, 622n38, 633n48; funeral of, 147–48; Golden Jubilee as a priest, 141–45, 175; governance of the Holy Cross community, 37; illness and death of, 145, 146–48, 175; interest in music, 97; interest in theatrical performance, 396; land title of, 185, 612n37; Last Will and Testament of, 42; leadership abilities of, 21; legacy of, 148; letter to President Lincoln, 85; ministerial responsibilities of, 37; opinion about students, 57; plan for expansion of college, 138; political affairs of, 85–86; portrait of, 113; Potawatomi Indians and, 43; property dispute with Mr. Rush, 64, 65; public service of, 61–62, 68, 88; purchase of new carillon for Notre Dame, 102; reconstruction of the Main Building dome and, 136–37; religious vows of, 16, 21, 56; resignation as president, 90; retreat of, 45; sermon dedicated to, 143–45; statue of, 182, 188; sympathy to Indians, 42; tension with the faculty, 51–52; tribute to, 2; trips to Europe, 92, 102, 103, 113, 147; views of vocations, 25; withdrawal from the Congregation, 88

students (*cont.*)
507–8; religious life of, 45, 52–54, 99–100, 166, 276, 277, 279, 282–83, 459–61; social and political activism of, 430, 444, 454, 458, 484, 504–6; stipends, 476; surveys data, 281–83, 572; from wealthy families, 49; during World War II, 334. *See also* African American students
Students' Army Training Corps (SATC), 206–7, 238
Students United for Respect (SUFR), 537–39
study abroad program. *See* foreign study program
Stuhldreher, Harry, 243, 247, 248, 251, 273, 298
sub-college programs, 151
Suddarth, Shannon, 558
Suenens, Leon (cardinal of Belgium), 461
Sullivan, Gene, 466
Sullivan, Joe, 318
Sullivan, Leon, 505
Sullivan Principles, 505
"SUMMA: Notre Dame's Greatest Challenge," 411–12
summer session, 212–13
"Surrender at Notre Dame," 399
Sweeney, Robert, 361
Sweet, Daimon, 556
Swistowicz, Mike, 364
Symposium on Political and Social Philosophy, 308
Szafran, Joanne, 449
Szczesniak, Boleslaw, 353

Taft, William Howard, 162
Tallyrand, Charles-Maurice de (bishop of Autun), 4
Tancredi, Melissa, 594
Tantur: Ecumenical Institute for Advanced Theological Studies, 413, 561–62, 590
Task Force on Marriage, Family, and Other Life Commitments, 524–25
Task Force on Residentiality, 527–28
Task Force on the Quality of Teaching in a Research University, 527
Task Force on Whole Health and the Use and Abuse of Alcohol, 525–27, 541
Tax Reform Act (1969), 474

Taylor, Aaron, 553
Taylor, James, 81
Taylor, Lili, 552
Taylor, Zachary, 80
Teacher-Course Evaluations (TCEs), 470–71
television. *See* WNDU radio and television building
Terlep, George, 346
Terrell, Pat, 512
Terrence J. McGlinn Building, 575
theater program and performances, 47, 126, 172, 396, 397
Theismann, Joe, 461
thematic years, 528–30
Theodore M. Hesburgh Center for International Studies, 496, 546
Theology: Department of, 409
Thespian Society, 72, 99
Thomas, Chris, 594
Thomas, Ivo, 409
Thompson, Francis, 191
Thompson, Frazier, 339, 442
Thompson, John, 520, 682n4
Thoreau, Henry David, 140
Thorlakson, Katie, 594
Thorpe, Jim, 235, 243
Tianjin Foreign Language Institute, 533
Tisserant, Cardinal Eugene, 407
Tong, L. G., 102
Townsend, Mike, 462, 466
Townsend, Willie, 466
Toynbee, Arnold, 395
Trafton, George, 239
Trilling, Lionel, 422
Tripucka, Frank, 365, 366
Tripucka, Kelly, 467
Trojan Women, The (play), 530
True, Herb, 460
tuition, 35, 90–91, 118, 212, 287, 492, 530–31; land or livestock in lieu of, 37, 38, 614n58
Tull, Charles, 451
Tumpane, John, 396
Turner, Robert, 395
Turnitin.com (plagiarism detection service), 586
Twain, Mark, 124
Two Penny Gazette, The, 98
Tyson, David, 488, 509, 524, 527, 541

underground tunnels, 294
Unitas, Johnny, 427, 428
United States: 1952 national presidential election, 385–86; anti-Catholic attitudes in, 43, 246, 275; conservative trend in, 503; isolationism of, 324, 328; missionaries in, 2
United States Naval Academy Board of Visitors, 400
University Athletic Club of New York, 227
university charter, 38–39
University Committee for Afro-American Students, 443
University Committee on the Responsible Use of Alcohol, 508–9
university fire department, 117–18
University of Notre Dame Archives, 108, 139–40, 199
University of Notre Dame Foundation. *See* Notre Dame Foundation
University Village, 575
UPS Foundation, 563
urban riots, 430
USS *Maine* (ship), 189, 190

Vagina Monologues, The (play), 596
Van Dyke, Henry, 162
van Fraassen, Bas, 599
VanWolvlear, John, 483
Veneziani, Charles, 162, 163–64, 165
Versailles, Treaty of, 326, 327
Vessels, Billy, 367
Vetville Herald, 351
Vetville housing, 351–52, 406
Veuillot, Louis, 6, 140
Vidal, Eugene, 235
Vidal, Gore, 235
"Vienna Circle," 305
Vietnam War: invasion of Cambodia, 455–56; loss of popular support, 453; National Moratorium Day events, 454–55; Operation Rolling Thunder, 451; protests, 454–55, 456–57, 458; *Scholastic* article on, 452; student and faculty attitude toward, 451–54; Tet Offensive, 452, 453; withdrawal of troops, 455
Vincennes diocese, 24
Vincent, Brother (John Pieau), 21, 23, 25, 34, 35

Vincent J. Naimoli Building, 575
Vitry, Ermin, 360
Voice (student newspaper), 422–23
Voisin, Michel, 61
Vurpillat, Francis, 219, 222, 260

Wabash College, 229, 230, 231, 234, 247
Wadsworth, Mike, 592
Wagner, Honus, 299
Waldman, Bernard, 341, 604
Waldrum, Randy, 557
Walker, Doak, 366
Walker, Frank, 309, 313
Walker, Herschel, 464
Walker, John, 81
Wallace, Francis, 247
Wallace, Lew, 85
Walsh, Adam, 247, 298, 317
Walsh, Bill, 365
Walsh, Earl, 343
Walsh, James J., 205
Walsh, John, 406, 411
Walsh, Matthew: administrative duties of, 224, 251, 257, 258, 261, 263–67, 284, 287; background of, 191, 257, 258; changes in academic programs, 159; chaplaincy of, 257; construction projects of, 251, 264–66, 267–68; directives about Ku Klux Klan, 272–73, 274; education of, 152, 191, 257; as "Father Cavanaugh boy," 177; Father Hope and, 641n52; focus on student life, 263–64, 266, 282–83; fundraising campaigns, 221; ordination of, 257; participation in World War I, 208–9; speeches and addresses of, 274–75; support of athletics, 242, 245–46, 251, 288–89
Walsh, Sara, 557
Walsh, Thomas E.: background of, 121; departure from Notre Dame, 149; establishment of Laetare Medal, 141; faculty appointment by, 124–25; illness and death of, 145–46, 175; on Main Building's mural, 137; presidency of, 121, 122–23; speeches of, 205; teaching responsibilities of, 121; trip to Europe, 133
Walshe, Peter, 506
Walsh Hall, 46, 185, 264

Thomas E. Blantz, C.S.C.,

is professor emeritus of history at the University of Notre Dame.
He is the author of *George N. Shuster: On the Side of Truth* (1993) and
A Priest in Public Service: Francis J. Haas and the New Deal (1982),
both published by the University of Notre Dame Press.